March 22–24, 2017
Scottsdale, AZ, USA

I0028940

**Association for
Computing Machinery**

Advancing Computing as a Science & Profession

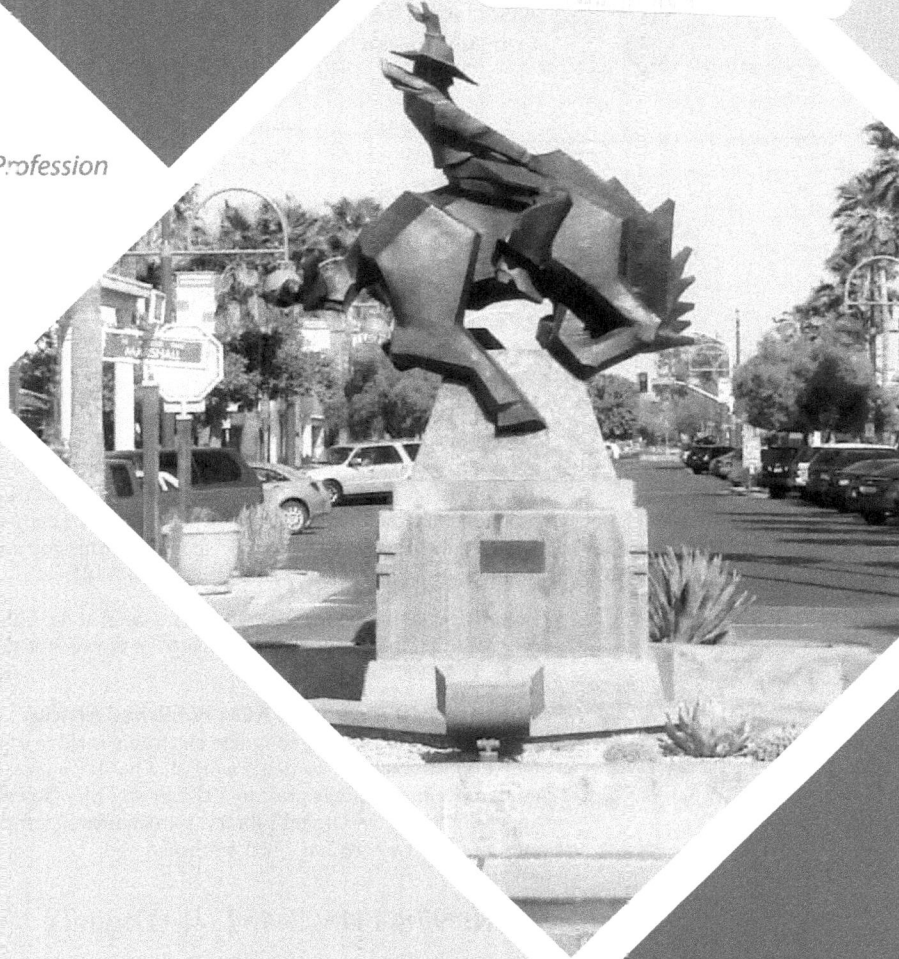

CODASPY'17

Proceedings of the Seventh ACM
**Conference on Data and Application Security
and Privacy**

Sponsored by:
ACM SIGSAC

Supported by:
**Allstate, Samsung, PayPal,
Center for Cybersecurity and Digital Forensics,
and Arizona State University**

Association for
Computing Machinery

Advancing Computing as a Science & Profession

The Association for Computing Machinery
2 Penn Plaza, Suite 701
New York, New York 10121-0701

ISBN: 978-1-4503-4523-1 (Digital)

ISBN: 978-1-4503-5451-6 (Print)

Additional copies may be ordered prepaid from:

ACM Order Department
PO Box 30777
New York, NY 10087-0777, USA

Phone: 1-800-342-6626 (USA and Canada)
+1-212-626-0500 (Global)
Fax: +1-212-944-1318
E-mail: acmhelp@acm.org
Hours of Operation: 8:30 am – 4:30 pm ET

Printed in the USA

Foreword

It is our great pleasure to welcome you to the seventh edition of the *ACM Conference on Data and Application Security and Privacy (CODASPY 2017)*, which follows the successful six editions held in February/March 2011-2016. This conference series has been founded to foster novel and exciting research in this arena and to help generate new directions for further research and development The initial concept was established by the two co-founders, Elisa Bertino and Ravi Sandhu, and sharpened by subsequent discussions with a number of fellow cyber security researchers. Their enthusiastic encouragement persuaded the co-founders to move ahead with the always daunting task of creating a high-quality conference.

Data and applications that manipulate data are crucial assets in today's information age. With the increasing drive towards availability of data and services anytime and anywhere, security and privacy risks have increased. Vast amounts of privacy-sensitive data are being collected today by organizations for a variety of reasons. Unauthorized disclosure, modification, usage or denial of access to these data and corresponding services may result in high human and financial costs. New applications such as social networking and social computing provide value by aggregating input from numerous individual users and the mobile devices they carry. The emerging area of Internet of Things also poses serious privacy and security challenges. To achieve efficiency and effectiveness in traditional domains such as healthcare, there is a drive to make these records electronic and highly available. The need for organizations to share information effectively is underscored by rapid innovations in the business world that require close collaboration across traditional boundaries. Security and privacy in these and other arenas can be meaningfully achieved only in context of the application domain. Data and applications security and privacy has rapidly expanded as a research field with many important challenges to be addressed.

In response to the call for papers of CODASPY 2017 a total of 134 papers were submitted from Africa, Asia, Australia, Europe, North America, and South America. The program committee selected 21 full-length research papers (16% acceptance rate). These papers cover a variety of topics, including data privacy in several distinct settings (cloud data, multi-party data aggregation), forensics, applications, and access control and security of smart appliances and mobile devices. The program committee also selected 10 short papers for presentation. The program includes a poster paper session presenting exciting work in progress, as well as a panel session led by Adam Doupé on "Trustworthy Data Science". The program is complemented by keynote speeches by Kang G. Shin and S. Raj Rajagopalan. This year's edition also features three workshops: the International Workshop on Security and Privacy Analytics, the ACM International Workshop on Security in Software Defined Networks & Network Function Virtualization, and the ACM Workshop on Attribute-Based Access Control.

The organization of a conference like CODASPY requires the collaboration of many individuals. First of all, we would like to thank the authors for submitting to the conference and the keynote speakers for graciously accepting our invitation. We express our gratitude to the program committee members and external reviewers for their efforts in reviewing the papers, engaging in active online discussion during the selection process and providing valuable feedback to authors. We also would like to thank Adam Lee (workshop chair), Jaehong Park (poster chair) and the committee of the poster track, Adam Doupé (panel chair), Hongxin Hu and Martín Ochoa (proceedings co-chairs), Ram Krishnan (web and publicity chair), and Ziming Zhao (local chair).

Finally, we thank our sponsor, ACM SIGSAC, and our generous corporate supporters, Arizona State University, Center for Cybersecurity and Digital Forensics, Allstate, Samsung, and PayPal.

We hope that you will find this program interesting and thought-provoking and that the *CODASPY 2017* will provide you with a valuable opportunity to share ideas with other researchers and practitioners from institutions around the world. Also, we hope you all enjoy your visit to Arizona!

Gabriel Ghinita, *University of Massachusetts Boston, USA*
Alexander Pretschner, *Technische Universität München, Germany*
CODASPY'17 Program Co-Chairs

Gail-Joon Ahn, *Arizona State University, USA*
CODASPY'17 General Chair

Table of Contents

Session 4: Privacy II

Session Chair: Ram Krishnan *(University of Texas at San Antonio)*

Session 5: Reception and Poster Session

Session Chair: Jaehong Park *(The University of Alabama in Huntsville)*

Keynote II

Session Chair: Gabriel Ghinita *(University of Massachusetts Boston)*

Session 6: Protection Against Malware and Static Analysis

Session Chair: Alexandros Kapravelos *(North Carolina State University)*

CODASPY 2017 Conference Organization

General Chair: Gail-Joon Ahn, Arizona State University, USA

Program Co-Chairs: Alexander Pretschner, Technische Universität München, Germany
Gabriel Ghinita, University of Massachusetts Boston, USA

Poster Chair: Jaehong Park, The University of Alabama in Huntsville, USA

Workshop Chair: Adam J. Lee, University of Pittsburgh, USA

Panel Chair: Adam Doupé, Arizona State University, USA

Publicity and Web Chair: Ram Krishnan, University of Texas at San Antonio, USA

Local Chair: Ziming Zhao, Arizona State University, USA

Proceedings Co-Chairs: Martín Ochoa, Singapore University of Technology and Design, Singapore
Hongxin Hu, Clemson University, USA

Local Arrangement Committee: Kristina Nelson, Arizona State University, USA
Aimee Hill, Arizona State University , USA
Carla McNeil-Baxter, Arizona State University, USA
Melissa Pagnozzi, Arizona State University, USA

Program Committee: Gail-Joon Ahn, Arizona State University, USA
Elisa Bertino, Purdue University, USA
Barbara Carminati, University of Insubria, Italy
Naranker Dulay, Imperial College London, UK
Manuel Egele, Boston University, USA
Elena Ferrari, University of Insubria, Italy
Philip W. L. Fong, University of Calgary, Canada
Debin Gao, Singapore Management University, Singapore
Gabriel Ghinita, University of Massachusetts, Boston
Hannes Hartenstein, KIT
Martin Johns, SAP Research, Germany
James Joshi, University of Pittsburgh, USA
Murat Kantarcioglu, University of Texas at Dallas, USA
Alexandros Kapravelos, North Carolina State University, USA
Guenter Karjoth, Lucerne University of Applied Sciences & Arts

Program Committee
(continued):

Florian Kelbert, Imperial College London, UK

Ram Krishnan, University of Texas at San Antonio, USA

Yves Le Traon, University of Luxembourg, Luxembourg

Adam J. Lee, University of Pittsburgh, USA

Qi Li, Tsinghua University, China

Peng Liu, The Pennsylvania State University, USA

Fabio Martinelli, IIT-CNR, Italy

Nick Nikiforakis, Stony Brook University, USA

Martín Ochoa, Singapore University of Technology and Design, Singapore

Jaehong Park, University of Alabama in Huntsville, USA

Alexander Pretschner, Technische Universität München, Germany

Indrajit Ray, Colorado State University, USA

Vassil Roussev, University of New Orleans, USA

Ravi Sandhu, University of Texas at San Antonio, USA

Anna Squicciarini, The Pennsylvania State University, USA

Hassan Takabi, University of North Texas, USA

Mahesh Tripunitara, University of Waterloo, Canada

Danfeng Yao, Virginia Tech, USA

Roland Yap, National University of Singapore, Singapore

Ting Yu, Qatar Computing Research Institute, Qatar

Chuan Yue, Colorado School of Mines, USA

Junyuan Zeng, Samsung Research America, USA

Poster Committee:

Mohamed Shehab, University of North Carolina at Charlotte, USA

Seung-Hyun Seo, Korea University, Republic of Korea

Hongxin Hu, Clemson University, USA

Dang Nguyen, Amazon, USA

Yazan Boshmaf, Qatar Computing Research Institute, Qatar

Yuan Cheng, California State University, Sacramento, USA

Additional reviewers:

Aisha Ali Gombe	Lei Jin
Alexander Afanasyev	Leila Bahri
Anand Mudgerikar	Leila Karimi
Andrea Saracino	Lianshan Sun
Aref Asvadishirehjini	Mike Mabey
Artsiom Yautsiukhin	Min Suk Kang
Behnaz Hassanshahi	Mina Sheikhalishahi
Carlos Rubio Medrano	Mingshen Sun
Ceren Abay	Nuray Baltaci Akhuseyinoglu
Changda Wang	Oyindamola Oluwatimi
Chao Li	Panagiotis Ilia
Dieudonne Mukamba	Pierre-Louis Aublin
Diptendu Kar	Pietro Colombo
Divesh Aggarwal	Rui Zhao
Erik Trickel	Runhua Xu
Faezeh Kalantari	Shagufta Mehnaz
Fahad Shaon	Subhojeet Mukherjee
Fang-Yu Rao	Syed Hussain
Faris Kokulu	Wonkyu Han
Francesco Mercaldo	Xingliang Yuan
Golden Richard	Yasmeen Alufaisan
Gregory Duck	Yeganeh Safaeisemnani
Haehyun Cho	Yinzhi Cao
Hong Hu	Yueqiang Cheng
Ibrahim Lazrig	Zhen Ling
Irfan Ahmed	Zhenkai Liang
Jia Xu	Zhibo Sun

CODASPY 2017 Sponsor & Supporters

Sponsor:

Supporters:

Research Issues and Approaches for Connected and Automated Vehicles

Kang G. Shin
The University of Michigan – Ann Arbor
Kgshin@umich.edu

ABSTRACT

Driverless and/or environment-friendly cars have recently received a great deal of attention from media and almost all industry and government sectors due mainly to their great potential impacts on safety, economy, and environments. In particular, enabling vehicles to communicate with one another via wireless devices holds the potential to automate vehicles while dramatically improving safety, reducing congestion, and conserving energy.

To move toward realization of this potential, we have been conducting research into various issues, including:

- Automation of vehicle sensing and control;
- Vehicle safety and passenger comfort;
- Securing information communication and computation;
- Developing environment-friendly solutions.

In this talk, I will discuss various issues and approaches related to security of connected and automated vehicles.

CCS Concepts

•General and reference → *Surveys and overview;*
•Embedded and cyber-physical systems;
•Security and privacy → *Network security; System security*

Author Keywords

Connected and/or automated cars; security of in-vehicle networks; intrusion detection

BIOGRAPHY

Kang G. Shin is the Kevin & Nancy O'Connor Professor of Computer Science, University of Michigan. His current research focuses on timeliness, reliability, security, and privacy of mobile or real-time and cyber-physical systems.

He has supervised the completion of 78 PhDs, and authored/coauthored more than 850 technical articles, one a textbook and more than 30 patents or invention disclosures, and received numerous best paper awards, including the Best Paper Awards from the 2011 ACM MobiCom, the 2003 IEEE Communications Society William R. Bennett Prize Paper Award and the 1987 Outstanding IEEE Transactions of Automatic Control Paper Award. He has also received several institutional awards, including the Research Excellence Award in 1989, Distinguished Faculty Achievement Award in 2001, and Stephen Attwood Award in 2004 from The University of Michigan (the highest honor bestowed to Michigan Engineering faculty); 2003 IEEE RTC Technical Achievement Award; and 2006 Ho-Am Prize in Engineering (the highest honor bestowed to Korean-origin engineers).

CODASPY'17, March 22–24, 2017, Scottsdale, AZ, USA.
ACM ISBN 978-1-4503-4523-1/17/03.
DOI: http://dx.doi.org/10.1145/3029806.3029846

Ghostbuster: A Fine-grained Approach for Anomaly Detection in File System Accesses

Shagufta Mehnaz
Dept. of Computer Science
Purdue University, West Lafayette, IN, USA
smehnaz@purdue.edu

Elisa Bertino
Dept. of Computer Science
Purdue University, West Lafayette, IN, USA
bertino@purdue.edu

ABSTRACT

Protecting sensitive data against malicious or compromised insiders is a challenging problem. Access control mechanisms are not always able to prevent authorized users from misusing or stealing sensitive data as insiders often have access permissions to the data. Also, security vulnerabilities and phishing attacks make it possible for external malicious parties to compromise identity credentials of users who have access to the data. Therefore, solutions for protection from insider threat require combining access control mechanisms and other security techniques, such as encryption, with techniques for detecting anomalies in data accesses. In this paper, we propose a novel approach to create fine-grained profiles of the users' normal file access behaviors. Our approach is based on the key observation that even if a user's access to a file seems legitimate, only a fine-grained analysis of the access (size of access, timestamp, etc.) can help understanding the original intention of the user. We exploit the users' file access information at block level and develop a feature-extraction method to model the users' normal file access patterns (user profiles). Such profiles are then used in the detection phase for identifying anomalous file system accesses. Finally, through performance evaluations we demonstrate that our approach has an accuracy of 93.64% in detecting anomalies and incurs an overhead of only 2%.

Keywords

Insider attacks; Anomaly detection; File system access

1. INTRODUCTION

Data stored in a file system can be compromised in various ways– by employees with malicious motivations inside an organization or by outsiders. An example of such insider attacks is the breach [1] at Sony Pictures Entertainment where at least one of the six attackers was a former system administrator with extensive technical background and knowledge of Sony's internal systems.

Organizations usually implement a combination of different techniques to protect data from unauthorized access.

CODASPY'17, March 22-24, 2017, Scottsdale, AZ, USA

© 2017 ACM. ISBN 978-1-4503-4523-1/17/03. . . $15.00

DOI: http://dx.doi.org/10.1145/3029806.3029809

The main such techniques are user authentication and access control [2, 3]. Authentication is a process by which a system verifies the identity of a user. Access control determines whether an authenticated user has permission to access a particular resource. However, such security solutions are unable to protect data against malicious or compromised insiders [4]. Insiders generally have prior knowledge about the organization's internal procedures, location of sensitive files and weaknesses in systems' security. Hence, insider attacks pose serious threats to organizations with critical or sensitive information and thus have been investigated extensively [4, 5, 6, 7, 8].

As attempts to steal data by malicious or compromised insiders are often characterized by unusual access patterns [9, 10], anomaly detection for data accesses can be a useful technique that well complements other security techniques, such as authentication, access control, and encryption. Anomaly detection (AD) techniques have been proposed for relational databases [11, 12, 13, 14] and networked systems [15, 16, 17]. However, as in many applications data is not managed by a database management system, it is critical that data access anomaly detection techniques be also developed for file systems. Initial approaches to detect anomalies in file system usage leverage different file system features, e.g., file system hierarchy [18], file name, working directory and parent directory [19]. Some techniques [20] use a file system in userspace (FUSE) to capture run-time operations. Approaches have also been developed that focus on file system integrity [21, 22]. A significant common limitation of these approaches is that they are unable to support fine-grained monitoring of accesses to the files. For example, consider the case of an employee that for his daily tasks accesses only 20% of the records in a file and therefore has a read permission on this file. Now, if the employee all of a sudden accesses 100% records of the file, such access is certainly anomalous with respect to his daily task. Even though there could be legitimate reasons for this access, it is critical that such an anomalous access be flagged.

In this paper we propose an effective and practical approach, dubbed as *Ghostbuster*, to detect anomalous accesses to the file system by creating fine-grained user profiles. Our proposed approach comprises of two phases: the *Profile Creation (PC)* phase and the *Anomaly Detection (AD)* phase. In the first phase, we collect detailed information about the file accesses resulting from a user's normal file system activities and create the user profile by using a combination of techniques including data mining. The profiles are later used in the second phase to monitor the file system usage and to raise alerts upon identifying anomalous activities.

The development of an access AD technique for file systems is challenging. In contrast to database AD techniques where SQL queries provide a structure to learn normal access patterns [11, 12], lack of semantic information about accesses in the case of file systems makes the task of profile construction complex. Moreover, the profile of a user's normal behavior must be accurate. A large number of false positives, i.e., non-anomalous accesses classified as anomalous may slow down the entire system and disrupt the users' normal activities. On the other hand, a large number of false negatives, i.e., undetected anomalous accesses undermine the security protection. This trade-off between performance and security is a major challenge [23] in creating effective profiles. Moreover, an AD technique must add minimal overhead to the data access times. To address the performance issue, we extract a minimal set of interesting features from the users' block level file access information in the PC phase. As a next step, we use these features to build the user profiles in a fine-grained manner. Later in the AD phase we define and utilize a set of distance functions to measure the difference between a user's profile (i.e., expected behavior) and his file accesses (i.e., observed behavior) at runtime. In the performance evaluation section, we show that our approach is able to identify anomalous access size, anomalous frequency of access, and anomalous access patterns on the whole. We use a Linux OS kernel module named $blktrace$ [24] to extract the file accesses at block level.

We list our contributions in the following:

- Our first contribution is the proposed block level access anomaly detection mechanism, which to the best of our knowledge is the first to model users' file access patterns at such a fine granularity.

- The second contribution is a set of efficient algorithms that (1) extract interesting features from the users' block level access information, (2) build effective and practical user profiles, and (3) identify anomalous accesses at runtime.

- As the third contribution, we present a taxonomy of anomalous file accesses and compare the accuracy of our approach with that of other existing approaches based on this taxonomy.

- The fourth contribution is an extensive evaluation of our fine-grained AD mechanism for file systems. We have collected data from a real organizations' file repository. The evaluation demonstrates that our approach achieves an accuracy of 98.64% in detecting anomalies while incurring an overhead of 2%.

The rest of the paper is organized as follows. Section 2 presents an overview of blktrace and other useful notions. Section 3 discusses the features of interest for profile creation and introduces a formal representation of user profiles. Section 4 presents a taxonomy of anomalous file accesses and provides a high-level comparison between our approach and other existing approaches. Section 5 and 6 present the PC and AD phases, respectively. We evaluate the performance of our approach in Section 7. Section 8 discusses the related work and Section 9 outlines conclusions and future work.

2. PRELIMINARIES

In this section we provide an overview of blktrace and other notions that are used throughout the paper.

2.1 Blktrace Overview

We use the blktrace utility implemented in the Linux kernel to trace block layer I/O operations where each block level access to a file is represented as an *event*. Another utility, *blkparse*, formats the events from the blktrace data. Blktrace has a very low overhead (2%) and can be configured to report a specific set of events, e.g. only read operations. An example of such an event from blktrace output is the following:

| 8,0 | 0 | 427 | 8.06743 | 57768 | I | R | 1729336 | +32 | [gedit] |

427	sequence number of the event
8.06743	timestamp of the event
R	read operation ('W' represents write)
1729336	starting sector number for the read operation
+ 32	32 sectors (or, 4 blocks) are read including sector 1729336 (1 sector = 512 bytes, 1 block = 4096 bytes)

Table 1: Blktrace event components

Table 1 provides a brief idea of the highlighted event components that we use in user profiling.

2.2 Event Sequence and Episodes

Blktrace generates a sequence of events while collecting block level access information from the OS kernel. The events in the sequence are ordered, i.e., the timestamps and sequence numbers that are associated with the events are strictly increasing. Let $E = \{e_1, e_2, \ldots, e_n\}$ be a sequence of n events. An event consists of several attributes. For simplicity, we use only three attributes in this example: en (event name); sr (sequence number of the event); and ts (timestamp of the event) which, for instance, represents the ith event as $e_i = (en_i, sr_i, ts_i)$. Since the events are ordered, $sr_i \leq sr_{i+1}$, and $ts_i < ts_{i+1}$ for $i = 1, 2, \ldots, n-1$. Figure 1 shows an event sequence, E, that consists of $n = 15$ events.

In order to find patterns in a sequence of events we use the notion of episode [25], i.e., set of events that occur together but not necessarily in a consecutive manner. Hence, the episodes that occur frequently represent patterns of an event sequence. If the order among the events of an episode is total, the episode is a *serial* episode; otherwise, it is a *parallel* episode. In the above example, event d occurs after event b twice and thus the two events form a serial episode $\alpha = \{b, d\}$. The occurrences are: $\{(b, 1, 1), (d, 2, 2)\}$ and $\{(b, 8, 11), (d, 10, 13)\}$. A parallel episode can be $\beta = \{c, f\}$ with occurrences: $\{(c, 4, 5), (f, 6, 7)\}$ and $\{(f, 13, 19), (c, 14, 21)\}$ where there is no constraint on the relative order of the events.

Episode α is a subepisode of a serial episode γ if the events in episode α form a *subsequence* of events in γ. For example, $\gamma = \{a, b, c, d\}$, and $\alpha = \{a, b, d\}$. Similarly, episode α is a subepisode of a parallel episode γ if the events in episode α form a *subset* of events in γ. For example, $\gamma = \{a, b, c, d\}$, and $\alpha = \{d, b, c\}$. We represent this relation as $\alpha \sqsubseteq \gamma$.

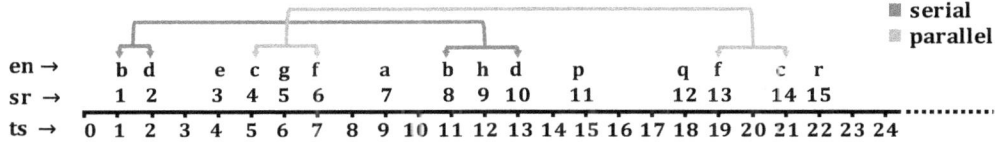

en →	b	d		e	c	g	f		a		b	h	d		p			q	f		c	r		

serial
parallel

| sr → | 1 | 2 | | 3 | 4 | 5 | 6 | | 7 | | 8 | 9 | 10 | | 11 | | | 12 | 13 | | 14 | 15 |

ts → 0 1 2 3 4 5 6 7 8 9 10 11 12 13 14 15 16 17 18 19 20 21 22 23 24

Figure 1: Event sequence E

3. PROFILE COMPONENTS

This section first presents a discussion about the features extracted from blktrace events and then introduces a formal representation of user profiles.

3.1 Features of Interest

- **User**: This feature represents the identity of the user originating a particular blktrace event, i.e., the id of the user reading (writing) from (into) a file.

- **File name**: A series of translations– sector to block, block to inode and inode to file name reveals this feature. This is used as the id of the file.

- **Type of access**: A blktrace event can either be a read ('R'), or a write ('W') operation.

- **Access size**: The number of blocks that are accessed in one blktrace event is represented by this feature.

- **Segment of file**: This feature identifies the relative position of the blocks that are accessed from a file. While profiling at file level only answers whether a user normally reads from a file, our approach leverages this segment information along with the 'access size' feature to precisely identify the portion of the file that a user normally reads. For example, if a file consists of 10 blocks and only the first block is read, we represent this feature as [0,0.1].

- **Timestamp**: The timestamp feature enables us to identify the temporal properties of accesses, e.g., temporal frequency of a file's access, temporal correlation between two files' accesses, etc.

- **Sequence number**: The sequence number feature provides us with the spatial properties of accesses, e.g., spatial frequency of a file's access, spatial correlation between two files' accesses, etc.

3.2 Profile Representation

1) Block level access: This profile component stores the maximum, average, and standard deviation of the size of accesses to each file by the user (in the unit of blocks), and a bit to denote whether the blocks accessed from the file are located in random segments. For a file $\mathbf{f} \in \mathbf{F}$ where $\mathbf{F}$ denotes the set of all files, we compute user $\mathbf{u}$'s block level access information as $B_{\mathbf{f}} = \{sz_{max}, sz_{avg}, sz_{sc}, R = 0/1\}$ and store it in the user $\mathbf{u}$'s profile. Finally, the profile component is denoted as $\mathcal{B} = \langle B_1, B_2, \ldots, B_{|\mathbf{F}|} \rangle$ where $|\mathbf{F}|$ is the cardinality of set $\mathbf{F}$.

2) Frequency of file access: This component accumulates the frequency of accesses to each file by the user. The temporal and spatial access frequencies of a file $\mathbf{f}$ are stored as $fr_{\mathbf{f}}^t$ and $fr_{\mathbf{f}}^s$, respectively. These frequencies are combined as $fr_{\mathbf{f}}$ to represent the profile component $\mathcal{F} = \langle fr_1, fr_2, \ldots, fr_{|\mathbf{F}|} \rangle$.

3) Cluster of accesses: The set of files that are frequently accessed together (represent a unit of task) by the user are considered as an access cluster. Episodes that are frequent in the blktrace event sequence identify these clusters. We store each such frequent episode ε as $C_{\varepsilon} = \{\varepsilon, cf, S/P\}$ where cf denotes cluster frequency, and S/P determines whether the episode is serial or parallel. Therefore, the access clusters for a user are stored as a vector $\mathcal{C} = \langle C_{\varepsilon 1}, C_{\varepsilon 2}, \ldots, C_{\varepsilon m} \rangle$ where m is the number of frequent episodes identified for the user.

Combining the above components, we represent a user profile as $\mathcal{P} = \langle \mathcal{B}, \mathcal{F}, \mathcal{C} \rangle$.

4. A TAXONOMY OF ANOMALOUS FILE ACCESSES

In this section, we present a taxonomy of anomalous file access cases and give a high-level comparison among our approach and other existing approaches based on the taxonomy. Table 2 summarizes different cases of anomalous file accesses and how different approaches respond to such anomalies. The columns *DC-1*, *DC-2*, and *DC-3* indicate the detection capability of access control mechanisms, a file level profiling approach (e.g., [18]) and our approach, respectively.

Case 1: Anomalous File Access w/o Permission. This case illustrates a masquerade attack where the attacker tries to read from a file to which the legitimate user does not have read permission. A masquerader who broke into the system with a legitimate user's credential but without the knowledge of file permissions may raise this kind of anomalies. This anomaly can be detected by all mechanisms in comparison.

Case 2: Anomalous Access Clusters. This case represents another masquerade attack where the attacker has enough intelligence about the file access permissions and thus does not try to access files to which the legitimate user does not have permissions. However, the accesses by the attacker do not comply with the learned access clusters. An outsider who has somehow gained a legitimate user's credential but does not have knowledge about the specific tasks of this compromised user raises this type of anomaly. While access control mechanisms fail to detect such anomalies, the approach by Gates et. al. [18] as well as our approach can detect such anomalies since both approaches learn access clusters from past history.

Case 3: Anomalous Frequency of Access Clusters. An insider with higher privilege or knowledge about the system's security vulnerabilities can masquerade as another user. This attacker also possesses knowledge about the compromised user's specific tasks, i.e., valid access clusters. However, while looking for sensitive data, the attacker repeats some set of access clusters (because he has background knowledge that the data he is searching for can be collected through this set of tasks). Such behavior by the attacker raises anomalous frequencies for the repeated access clusters and is identified by only our approach among the others in comparison.

Anomaly Cases		Attack Model	DC-1	DC-2	DC-3
Case 1:	Anomalous File Access w/o Permission	Masquerade Attack	✓	✓	✓
Case 2:	Anomalous Access Clusters	Masquerade Attack	×	✓	✓
Case 3:	Anomalous Frequency of Access Clusters	Masquerade & Insider Attacks	×	×	✓
Case 4:	Anomalous Size of File Access	Insider & Data Harvesting Attacks	×	×	✓
Case 5:	Anomalous Segment of File Access	Insider & Data Harvesting Attacks	×	×	✓
Case 6:	Anomalous Frequency of File Access	Insider & Data Harvesting Attacks	×	×	✓

Table 2: Taxonomy of anomalous file accesses and a comparison of detection capability among access control mechanism (DC-1), a file level profiling approach, e.g., [18](DC-2), and our fine-grained profiling approach (DC-3)

Case 4: Anomalous Size of File Accesses. An insider logged into his own account can access more blocks than normal from a file and thus gather larger amount of data from a sensitive file while complying with access clusters and their normal frequency. As shown in Table 2, identifying this data harvesting attack is impossible without a fine-grained approach and our approach is the only one able to detect such anomalous accesses.

Case 5: Anomalous Segment of File Accesses. An insider complying even with normal access size may harvest data by reading different segments of the file. Our fine-grained AD technique is able to detect such random accesses while the other methods fail.

Case 6: Anomalous Frequency of File Accesses. An insider complying even with normal access size may harvest data by reading the file with an elevated frequency. Again, our fine-grained AD technique detects such anomalous case while the other methods fail.

5. PROFILE CREATION PHASE (PC)

Our PC phase consists of a set of software modules (Figure 2). The blktrace tool traces block layer I/O operations from the kernel space during the user's normal file access activities. In the following we discuss the modules in detail.

5.1 Feature Extraction (FE)

The FE module transforms the output from the blktrace tool into an event sequence E. This module represents an event $e \in E$ as (uid, fname, atype, sz, sg, ts, sr), where uid is the id of the user, fname is the name of the file, atype is access type, sz is the size of access, sg is the segment of the file accessed, ts and sr are the timestamp and sequence number of the event, respectively. A sequence of n events is thus represented as $E=\{e_1, e_2, \ldots, e_n\}$.

Algorithm 1 Discovering access clusters $\mathcal{C}$

1: **Input:** E, L_{ts}, L_{sr}, $minSp$
2: **Output:** $\mathcal{C}$
3: $m \leftarrow 0$
4: $Cand_1 \leftarrow$ set of distinct events
5: **while** $Cand_{m+1} \neq \emptyset$
6:     $Freq_{m+1} \leftarrow findFreq(E, Cand_{m+1}, L_{ts}, L_{sr}, minSp)$
7:     $m \leftarrow m + 1$
8:     $Cand_{m+1} \leftarrow genCand(Freq_m)$
9: $\mathcal{C} \leftarrow Freq_1 \cup Freq_2 \cup \ldots \cup Freq_m$
10: **return** $\mathcal{C}$

5.2 Block Level Profiling (BLP)

This module utilizes the uid, fname, sz, and sg features. In order to profile the accesses at block level, the BLP module implements a mapping from each user **u** to each file **f** and stores all of **u**'s accesses to **f** in the map. Then it computes the values of sz_{max}, sz_{avg}, and sz_{sd} from the map entries. Furthermore, the BLP module compares the sg features of such access events. If e_1 and e_2 are two events representing accesses to file **f**, BLP identifies whether sg_1 and sg_2 overlap or these segments represent random portions of the file. This analysis is useful, for example, in identifying that a user accesses the latest blocks of a file. If the accessed segments are random, R is set to 1; otherwise set to 0. The value of $B_{\mathbf{f}} = \{sz_{max}, sz_{avg}, sz_{sd}, R = 0/1\}$ is finally stored in the profile of user **u**.

5.3 Frequency Profiling (FP)

The FP module utilizes the uid, fname, ts, and sr features. Two parameters– time interval, TI, and sequence interval, SI, are used in order to compute the temporal frequency ($fr_{\mathbf{f}}^t$) and spatial frequency ($fr_{\mathbf{f}}^s$), respectively. Here we explain how we compute $fr_{\mathbf{f}}^t$ for a file **f**. Since the access frequency of a file can vary widely over time, we store the frequencies in different granularity levels- hourly ($TI =$ one hour), daily ($TI =$ one day), weekly ($TI =$ one week), and monthly ($TI =$ one month). For example, if a file is accessed a number of times per hour, its frequency is stored in all granularity levels. However, if a file is accessed twice a week its frequency is stored only in weekly and monthly granularity.

5.4 Access Cluster Profiling (ACP)

The ACP module uses two parameters, L_{ts} and L_{sr}, to denote the maximum time and sequence number differences between two events in order for these events to be considered as related to each other. For example, while determining the occurrence of an event sequence $\{a, b, c\}$, the constraints $ts_c - ts_a < L_{ts}$ and $sr_c - sr_a < L_{sr}$ must be satisfied. These parameters are set to discard uninteresting episodes while searching for the frequent ones. Another parameter, $minSp$, sets the minimum frequency required for an episode to be classified as frequent. The steps for computing profile component $\mathcal{C}$ are presented in Algorithm 1. It is an iterative procedure where in each iteration frequent episodes of progressively larger size are obtained. At the first iteration, all the distinct events are considered as candidates ($Cand_1$). Once the set of frequent episodes of size m, i.e.

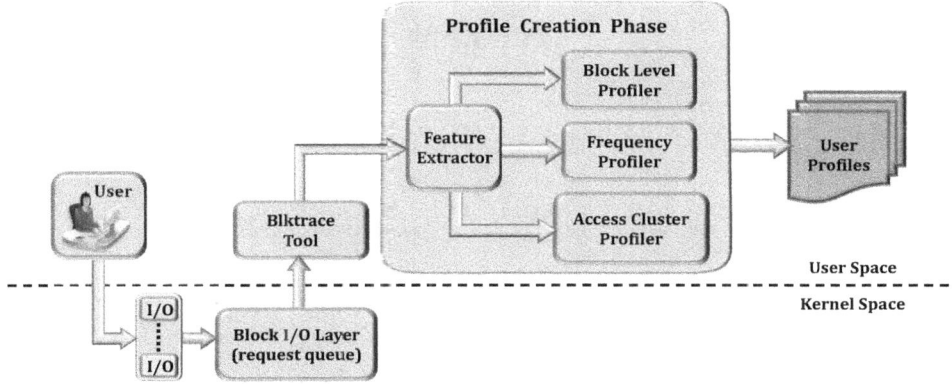

Figure 2: Profile Creation (PC) phase architecture

$Freq_m$, is computed from $Cand_m$ (using `findFreq`), the set of candidates for larger frequent episodes, i.e. $Cand_{m+1}$, is obtained from this $Freq_m$ (using `genCand`). The main idea is an Apriori [26] property as given in the following:

LEMMA 1. *Let γ and α be episodes s.t. $\alpha \sqsubseteq \gamma$. If γ is frequent, α is also frequent.*

According to this lemma, to generate candidate episodes of size $m + 1$, we consider only the ones for which all of its subepisodes of size m are frequent. In this way, we discard a number of infrequent episodes and avoid computing their frequency. In what follows, we explain the `findFreq` and `genCand` functions.

Algorithm 2 Finding frequent episodes (`findFreq`)

1: **Input**: E, $Cand_i$, L_{ts}, L_{sr}, $minSp$
2: **Output**: $Freq_i$
3: $Freq_i \leftarrow \emptyset$
4: for each candidate episode $\varepsilon \in Cand_i$
5:    $waits(\varepsilon[1]) \leftarrow waits(\varepsilon[1]) \cup (\varepsilon, 1, 0, 0)$ /*initialize $waits$ list*/
6:    $\varepsilon.freq \leftarrow 0$ /* set frequency to 0 for all candidates */
7: for each event $e \in E$
8:    for each cluster automaton $A_\varepsilon = (\varepsilon, j, ts_f, sr_f) \in waits(e)$
9:      if $ts_f = 0$ & $sr_f = 0$ /* automaton at the first state */
10:       $ts_f \leftarrow e.ts$ /* update first event timestamp */
11:       $sr_f \leftarrow e.sr$ /* update first event sequence number */
12:      $waits(e) \leftarrow waits(e) - A_\varepsilon$ /* remove the automaton from $waits(e)$ list */
13:      if $j = L$ & $e.ts - ts_f \leq L_{ts}$ & $e.sr - sr_f \leq L_{sr}$
14:       $j \leftarrow 1$ /* reached final state of automaton, reset to first state */
15:       $\varepsilon.freq \leftarrow \varepsilon.freq + 1$ /* increment frequency */
16:      else if $e.ts - ts_f \leq L_{ts}$ & $e.sr - sr_f \leq L_{sr}$
17:       $j \leftarrow j + 1$ /* move to the next state */
18:      else
19:       $j \leftarrow 1$ /* e is outside of L_{ts} or L_{sr} range, reset to first state */
20:      $waits(\varepsilon[j]) \leftarrow waits(\varepsilon[j]) \cup A_\varepsilon$ /* add A_ε to a new $waits$ list */
21: for each candidate episode $\varepsilon \in Cand_i$
22:    if $\varepsilon.freq \geq minSp$
23:      $Freq_i \leftarrow Freq_i \cup \varepsilon$
24: return $Freq_i$

Frequency Computation (`findFreq`): Although there are different definitions of frequency [25, 27], we consider a definition that is based on non-overlapping occurrences as this is the most practical in the context of file access. Two occurrences of an episode α, i.e., α_1 and α_2 are non-overlapping, if no event contained in α_1 appears among events contained in α_2 and vice versa. Let α be a serial episode $\{a, b, c\}$, and let $\alpha_1 = \{(a, sr_{a1}, ts_{a1}), (b, sr_{b1}, ts_{b1}), (c, sr_{c1}, ts_{c1})\}$ and $\alpha_2 = \{(a, sr_{a2}, ts_{a2}), (b, sr_{b2}, ts_{b2}), (c, sr_{c2}, ts_{c2})\}$ be two of its occurrences. We say that α_1 and α_2 are non-overlapping if for all events $x \in \alpha$, $sr_{x1} < sr_{a2}$ and $ts_{x1} < ts_{a2}$, or, for all events $x \in \alpha$, $sr_{x2} < sr_{a1}$ and $ts_{x2} < ts_{a1}$. For the following event sequence–

$$E = \{(b, 1, 2), (d, 2, 5), (a, 3, 6), (c, 4, 7), (f, 5, 10),$$
$$(c, 6, 12), (d, 7, 13), (c, 8, 14), (a, 9, 16), (f, 10, 20)\}$$

there are more than one overlapping occurrence of episode $\alpha = \{b, d, c\}$, e.g., $\{(b, 1, 2), (d, 2, 5), (c, 4, 7)\}$, and $\{(b, 1, 2), (d, 7, 13), (c, 8, 15)\}$. However, there can be only one non-overlapping occurrence, e.g., $\{(b, 1, 2), (d, 2, 5), (c, 4, 7)\}$ in E and choosing any of the other occurrences violates the given definition of frequency.

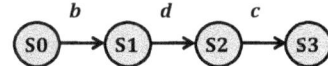

Figure 3: Finite state automata A_ε for $\varepsilon = \{b, d, c\}$

Frequency computation for serial episodes: We use finite state automata to recognize episodes in the event sequence. For example, to recognize the episode $\varepsilon = \{b, d, c\}$, an automaton A_ε transits to states $S1$, $S2$, and $S3$ after observing the events b, d, and c, respectively, as shown in Figure 3. Algorithm 2 shows the steps to count the frequency of serial episodes. It takes the event sequence E, the set of candidate episodes of length i, i.e. $Cand_i$, L_{ts}, L_{sr}, and $minSp$ as the input, and returns $Freq_i \subseteq Cand_i$ as frequent ones. Since we use finite state automata, counting the frequencies of all candidate episodes requires only one pass of the event sequence. Moreover, there is only one automaton for each candidate at a time. We use a $waits()$ list such that all automata waiting for an event e to transit to their next states are placed in the $waits(e)$ list. Therefore, upon scanning an event e from the given event sequence E, the automata waiting for this particular e event proceed to their next states. The automaton for candidate episode ε intending to transit to its jth state is represented as $A_\varepsilon = (\varepsilon, j, ts_f, sr_f)$, where ts_f and sr_f are the timestamp and sequence number of the first event in the automaton, respectively. An automaton

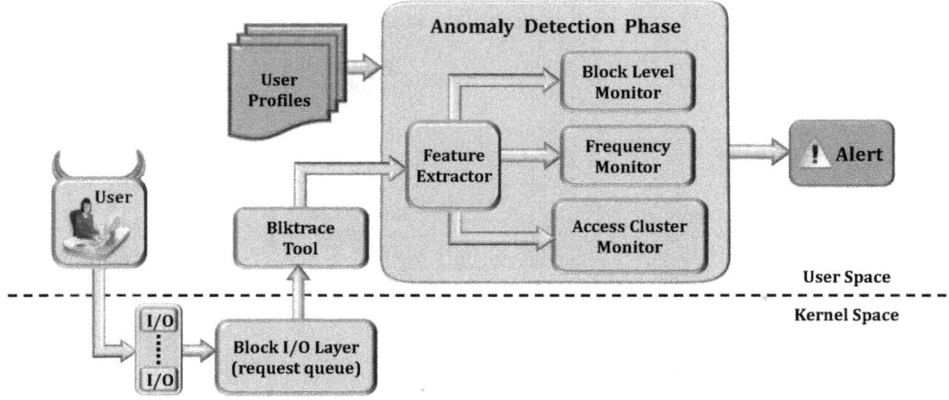

Figure 4: Anomaly Detection (AD) phase architecture

$A_\varepsilon = (\varepsilon, j, ts_f, sr_f) \in waits(e)$ means that the automaton for episode ε will transit to its jth state if it observes the event $e = (fname_e, atype_e, sg_e, sz_e, ts_e, sr_e)$ in the events' sequence for which $ts_e - ts_f \le L_{ts}$ and $sr_e - sr_f \le L_{sr}$.

Frequency computation for parallel episodes: A similar algorithm is used that we do not present in this paper for space constraint.

Algorithm 3 Candidate generation (`genCand`)

1: **Input:** $Freq_m$
2: **Output:** $Cand_{m+1}$
3: $Cand_{m+1} \leftarrow \emptyset$
4: $S_m \leftarrow sort(Freq_m)$
5: **for** each episode $s_{mi} \in S_m$
6:     **for** each episode $s_{mj} \in S_m$ where $j \ge i$
7:         **if** $S_m.msg[i] = S_m.msg[j]$
8:             **for** $k = 1$ to m
9:                 $\zeta[k] \leftarrow s_{mi}[k]$ /* generate new candidate */
10:              $\zeta[m+1] \leftarrow s_{mj}[k]$
11:             **for** each $\alpha \sqsubset \zeta$ where $|\alpha| = m$
12:                 **if** $\alpha \notin Freq_m$ /* if any α is not frequent */
13:                     **goto** 6 /* ζ is also not frequent, start over */
14:         $Cand_{m+1} \leftarrow Cand_{m+1} \cup \zeta$
15: **return** $Cand_{m+1}$

Candidate Generation (`genCand`): Algorithm 3 shows the procedure for generating candidates for parallel episodes. Since the order of events is not important for parallel episodes, events in each episode $\varepsilon \in Freq_m$ are sorted by their $fname$ lexicographically and are then stored in S_m. For example, episode $\varepsilon = \{d, a, f\}$ is sorted as $\{a, d, f\}$. The episodes in S_m are also sorted lexicographically for efficiency purpose. For instance, an episode $\{a, d, e\}$ appears before the episode $\{a, d, f\}$ in S_m. The ith episode in the collection of episodes of length m is denoted as $S_m[i]$. Note that, if episodes $S_m[i]$ and $S_m[j]$ have first l events in common, then all episodes $S_m[k]$, where $i < k < j$, also contain these l events. However, if episodes $S_m[i]$ and $S_m[j]$ share the first $m-1$ events, the only difference between the episodes is the mth event and we denote the group of such episodes with maximal similarity as msg. For each episode $S_m[i]$, we store its msg's first episode index in $S_m.msg[i]$. Hence, the msg array efficiently points to the first episode in the maximal similarity group while generating candidates of size $m+1$.

A simple modification of this algorithm generates candidates for serial episodes. For space constraint, we omit the algorithm for serial episodes in this paper.

6. ANOMALY DETECTION PHASE (AD)

The *Feature Extractor (FE)* module performs the same set of tasks as in the *PC* phase. Also, the *User Profiles* output from the *PC* phase are considered as input to this *AD* phase. The other three modules (see Figure 4) share a parameter W_{AF} for each user to weigh his anomalous actions. As soon as this parameter exceeds a threshold $minAnom$, the user's behavior is classified as anomalous. Depending on the user's file access activities, the modules raise different anomaly flags and thus update the value of this W_{AF} parameter. **Note that, the user's normal operations are not hindered until W_{AF} exceeds $minAnom$. Only after W_{AF} exceeds $minAnom$, a user is prevented from accessing the requested content.**

6.1 Block Level Monitoring *(BLM)*

The *BLM* module monitors whether the size of an access to a file in the *AD* phase is larger than sz_{max}, or significantly distant from the range $[sz_{avg} + \delta_1 * sz_{sd}, sz_{avg} - \delta_1 * sz_{sd}]$ where δ_1 is a positive real number. In these cases, this module raises flags of anomaly types AF_1 and AF_2, respectively. The amount of effect an anomaly flag, e.g., AF_1 has on W_{AF} is determined by a distance function. For example, if the sz attribute of an event is larger than sz_{max}, the distance is measured as $dist(AF_1) = (sz - sz_{max})$. Furthermore, if the value of R is 0 in the user profile, and if the user accesses random segments of the file, another anomaly type AF_3 is flagged.

6.2 Frequency Monitoring *(FM)*

This module identifies anomalous frequencies, either temporal or spatial, that exceeds the stored normal frequencies by a threshold $\delta_2 * fr_f$. Hence, the *FM* module raises anomaly type AF_4 and stores the frequency anomalous events with detail information for further analysis.

6.3 Access Cluster Monitoring *(ACM)*

The *ACM* module keeps finite state automata for the access clusters identified in Section 5.4. Only the superepisodes are considered for efficiency purpose. For example, if $\{a, b, c, d\}$ is a frequent episode, only one automata is used to monitor this episode and its subepisodes. Assume that the user attempts to read a file **f** in the *AD* phase. If the user does not have permission to read that file, anomaly type AF_5 is raised. Otherwise, we exploit the fact that if this access by the user is legitimate according to the user profile,

8

there should be at least one automaton to accept the blk-trace event resulted by this read operation and to transit to its next state. Otherwise, the ACM module flags this access as anomalous and an anomaly type AF_6 is raised. Note that there can be more than one automaton waiting for a single event in which case all of these automata transit to their next states upon the occurrence of that particular event. Anomalous frequencies of access clusters are also monitored and flagged as anomaly type AF_7.

Anomaly Cases	Anomaly Flags	Module (AD phase)
Case 1	AF_5	ACM
Case 2	AF_6	ACM
Case 3	AF_7	ACM
Case 4	AF_1, AF_2	BLM
Case 5	AF_3	BLM
Case 6	AF_4	FM

Table 3: Mapping between the anomaly cases and anomaly flags

Table 3 shows the mapping between the anomaly cases from Section 4 and the anomaly flags raised by the modules in the AD phase.

7. PERFORMANCE EVALUATION

In this section, we explain our experiment setup, present the evaluation metrics and the performance of our AD mechanism for different anomaly cases along with a comparison with the other existing approaches.

7.1 Experiment Setup

In order to setup the experiment environment, we collect blktrace data from accesses to a Wikipedia file repository for a duration of two months. A large directory containing 560 files is considered as the target directory. The blktrace data represents accesses to the files by 77 users with unique user IDs. Blktrace events that represent accesses outside the target directory are filtered out before profile creation. We use the data from the first four weeks as training data for profile creation in the PC phase whereas the data from the next four weeks is used as test data in the AD phase. The histogram in Figure 5(a) reports for different ranges of blk-trace events the number of users making accesses within each range whereas Figure 5(b) reports such number for different ranges of distinct file accesses. Each file access generates 6 blktrace events in average. The average number of blktrace

events resulting from a user's file accesses is $\sim 15K$ and each user accesses ~ 135 distinct files in average.

The accuracy of the user profiles depends on several parameters used in the PC phase, i.e., L_{ts}, L_{sr}, and $minSp$. During the experiment we vary these parameters to learn the users' normal file system activities effectively. According to the background knowledge about the users' tasks with the file system, each task takes 15-20 minutes in average. Figure 5(c) shows how the accuracy of discovered access clusters varies for different L_{ts} values. For instance, if L_{ts} is set to 1 working day (i.e., 8 hours, or 480 minutes), the algorithm interprets many irrelevant file accesses as relevant and thus results in a significant number of false positives in discovering access clusters. Conversely, setting L_{ts} to 1 minute fails to identify correlations in accesses, i.e., incurs high false negative rates and thus results in poor accuracy. Note that, these values of L_{ts} have been experimented only for demonstration purpose and setting such values to L_{ts} are not practical. Hence, in our experiments we set $L_{ts} = 20$ minutes, $L_{sr} = 10$ and use a variable $minSp$ for candidates of different lengths.

In order to evaluate how our approach performs in the presence of some malicious or compromised insiders, we generate 4 sets of test data, namely TS(I-IV). In TS-I, the data collected in weeks 5-8 remains unchanged. In TS-II, only 3% of TS-I is modified to include anomalous blktrace events which represent a smart attacker. In TS-III, 25% of TS-I is modified to represent a medium attacker scenario. Finally, we randomly access the target directory to generate test set TS-IV that represents a non expert attacker. In Section 7.3, we design three different attack scenarios that incorporate anomaly cases 1-3, 4-5, and 6, respectively, and evaluate the performance of our AD mechanism for these attack scenarios.

Our experiments have been performed on an Intel(R) Core (TM) i7-3770 CPU machine with two cores of speed 3.40 GHz each, using Ubuntu-14.04 operating system and 8GB of memory.

7.2 Evaluation Metrics

Considering TP as true positive, TN as true negative, FP as false positive, and FN as false negative, we analyze the performance of our approach using the following metrics:

- False positive rate (FPR) $= \frac{FP}{(FP+TN)}$

- False negative rate (FNR) $= \frac{FN}{(FN+TP)}$

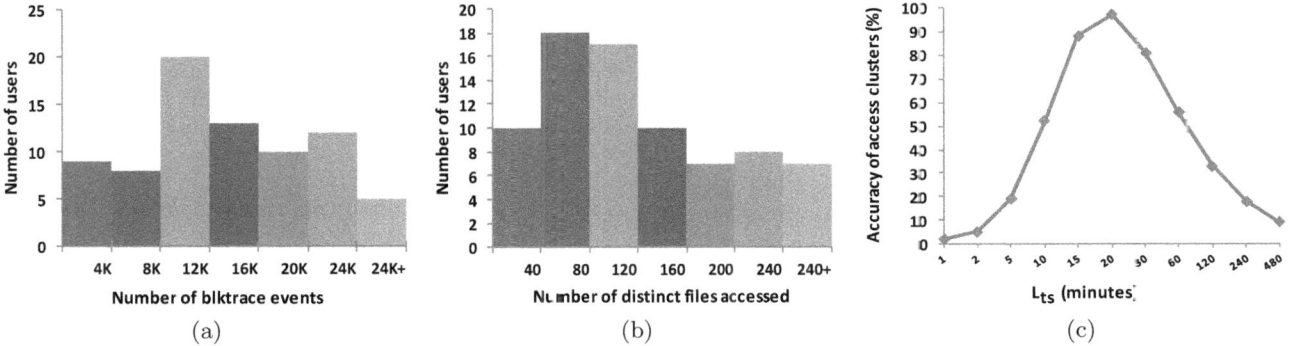

Figure 5: Different ranges of (a) blktrace events, and (b) distinct file accesses by the users, (c) Accuracy of access clusters

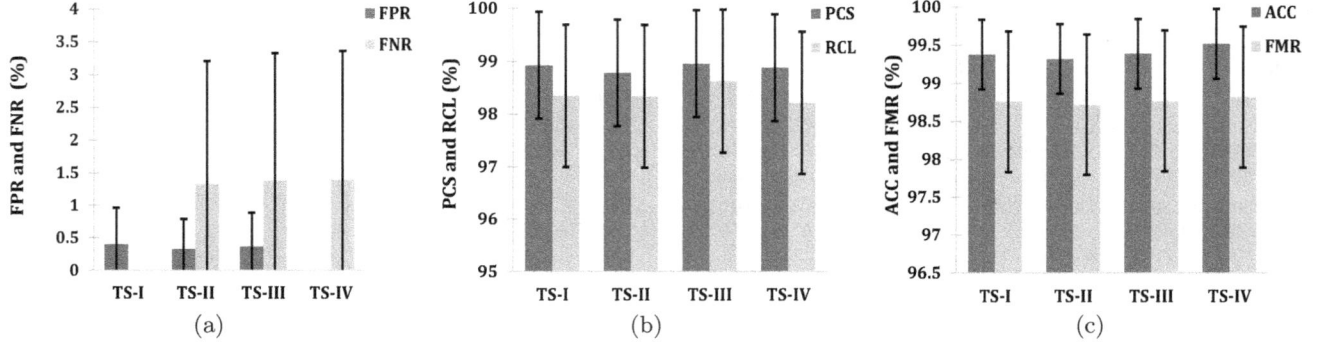

Figure 6: ACM module: mean (a) FPR and FNR, (b) PCS and RCL, (c) ACC and FMR values with confidence interval of standard deviation

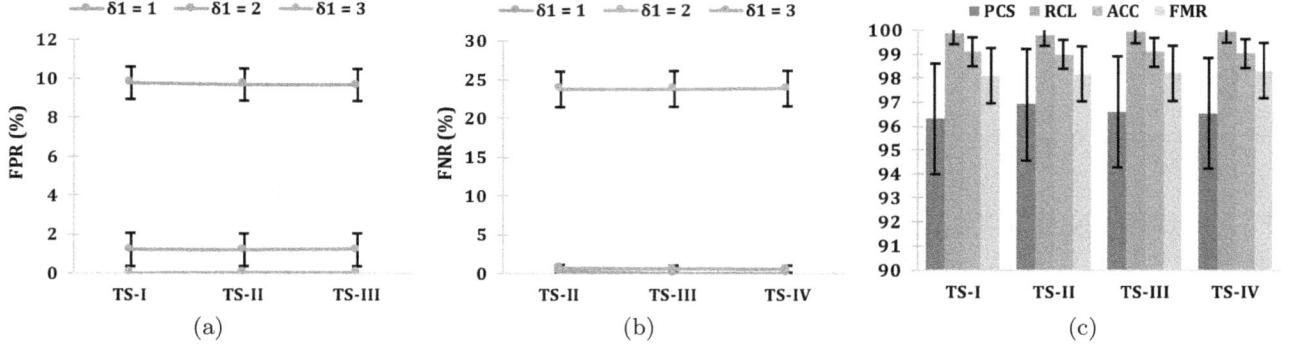

Figure 7: BLM module: mean (a) FPR, and (b) FNR for different δ_1, (c) PCS, RCL, ACC, and FMR for $\delta_1 = 2$ with confidence interval of standard deviation

- Precision (PCS) = $\frac{TP}{(TP+FP)}$

- Recall (RCL) = $\frac{TP}{(TP+FN)}$

- Accuracy (ACC) = $\frac{(TP+TN)}{(TP+TN+FP+FN)}$

- F-measure (FMR) = $\frac{2TP}{(2TP+FP+FN)}$

7.3 Experiment Results

7.3.1 Detecting Anomaly Cases 1-3 (Masquerade and Insider Attacks)

The modifications in TS(II-IV) include blktrace events that represent accesses to files to which the user has no permission, consecutive accesses to files having zero or negligible correlation, and abnormal frequency of some sets of tasks.

Figure 6(a) shows the *FPR* and *FNR* of the *ACM* module for test sets TS(I-III) and TS(II-IV), respectively. Since TS-IV is generated randomly, all the accesses in this set are considered anomalous and therefore, we do not evaluate *FPR* for this test set. Similarly, since TS-I is directly taken from the user's accesses, we do not evaluate *FNR* for this test set. The negligible *FPR* values for all test sets demonstrate the effectiveness of the *ACP* module in discovering the access clusters. In very few cases, the automata for the access clusters reject a normal file access which results in a false positive. The *FNR* is slightly higher than the *FPR* for

all test sets. The reason is that when a file is accessed, it requires acceptance by only one automaton to be considered as normal. However, there is a large number of automata in the *ACM* module that may accept the access. If the access is originally anomalous, the automata accepting this access eventually fail to reach their final states and identify the access as anomalous. However, in few cases, due to the complexity of users' interactions with the file system, the *ACM* module considers anomalous accesses as normal and results in false negatives. The average *FPR* and *FNR* values incurred by the *ACM* module are 0.36% and 1.37%, respectively. Note that the *FPR* and *FNR* values do not differ significantly for different test sets. The reason is that our AD approach analyzes each file access individually. Therefore, our AD approach is independent of different percentages of anomalous accesses. Figure 6(b) shows the *PCS* and *RCL* for the *ACM* module with average values of 98.95% and 98.62%, respectively, for all test sets TS(I-IV). Figure 6(c) shows *ACC* and *FMR* with average values of 99.38% and 98.77%, respectively.

7.3.2 Detecting Anomaly Cases 4-5 (Insider and Data Harvesting Attacks)

The test sets TS(II-IV) for these anomaly cases include blktrace events that represent abnormal access sizes, and abnormal access segments but comply with file permissions, access clusters and access cluster frequencies.

Figures 7(a) and 7(b) show the *FPR* and *FNR* of the

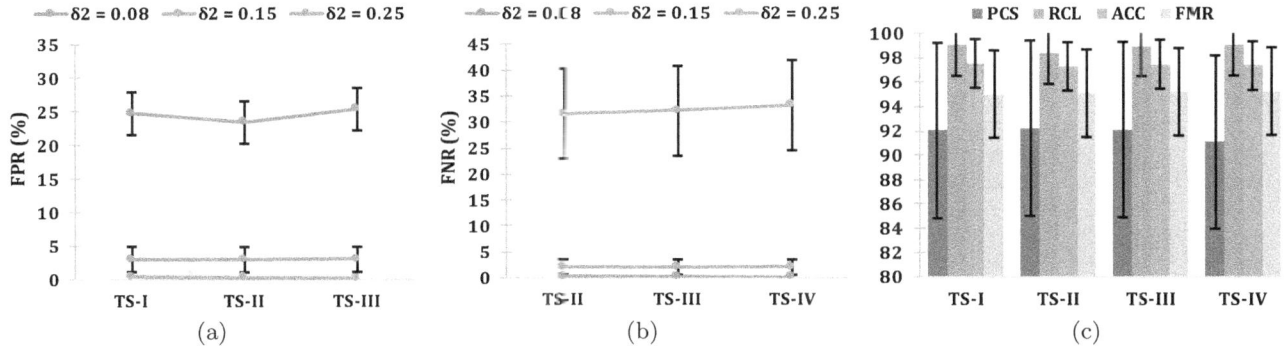

Figure 8: FM module: mean (a) FPR, and (b) FNR for different δ_2, (c) PCS, RCL, ACC, and FMR for $\delta_2 = 0.15$ with confidence interval of standard deviation

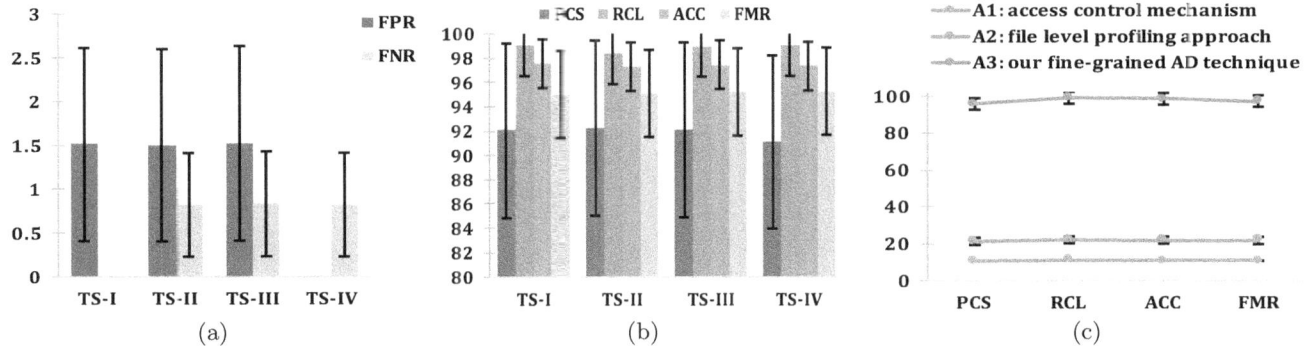

Figure 9: Combined (a) FPR, FNR, (b) PCS, RCL, ACC, FMR of our approach, (c) Comparison with access control mechanism and a file level AD technique

BLM module, respectively. For each test set we vary the δ_1 parameter with values 1, 2 and 3. The experiment shows that setting δ_1 to 1 incurs a high FPR of 9.66% in average as this value reduces the acceptable access size range to $[sz_{avg} + sz_{sd}, sz_{avg} - sz_{sd}]$. On the other hand, a value of δ_1 equal to 3 accepts a wide range of access sizes and results into 23.81% FNR. Therefore, we choose δ_1 to be equal to 2 which reduces both the FPR and FNR to 1.19% and 0.11%, respectively. Since the BLM module analyzes each access at block level, it has a slightly higher FPR. However, this module is able to detect a wide range of attacks including intelligent insiders who have knowledge about normal access patterns and thus results in a negligible FNR. The FNR in TS-IV is attributed to the random accesses that comply with the average access sizes in the profile. However, since we consider all the accesses in this test set as anomalous, the accesses that comply with the user profile result in false negatives. Figure 7(c) shows the PCS, RCL, ACC, and FMR of the BLM module for all test sets TS(I-IV) with average values of 96.5%, 99.89%, 99.08%, and 98.2%, respectively. Note that we set $\delta_1 = 2$ while computing these metrics.

7.3.3 Detecting Anomaly Case 6 (Insider and Data Harvesting Attacks)

For this anomaly case, the test sets TS(II-IV) include blk-trace events that represent abnormal access frequencies but comply with file permissions, access clusters and their frequencies, access sizes and segments.

The performance of the FM module is demonstrated in Figure 8. Figures 8(a) and 8(b) show the FPR and FNR, respectively. We evaluate this module by selecting different values for δ_2, i.e., 0.08, 0.15, and 0.25. As the value of δ_2 increases, this module increases the range of acceptable frequencies which results in a decrease of the FPR. The reason is that some of the files that are accessed with higher frequency than the frequency saved in the profile are not considered as anomalous. Conversely, the value of the FNR decreases for lower values of δ_2. However, setting $\delta_2 = 0.15$ results in the FPR and FNR to be 3.02% and 1.2%, respectively. The results for the FNR for TS-IV is due to the fact that some of the randomly accessed files in this test set have frequencies similar to the ones saved in the profile. Again, since we consider all the accesses in this test set to be anomalous, the files with expected frequency attribute to the false negatives. Figure 8(c) shows the PCS, RCL, ACC, and FMR of the FM module for all test sets TS(I-IV) that have average values of 92.09%, 98.97%, 97.47%, and 95.2%, respectively. Note that we set $\delta_2 = 0.15$ while computing these metrics.

7.4 Comparison with Existing Approaches

For comparison purpose, we combine the three attack scenarios from Section 7.3 where 1/3 of the anomalous accesses include anomaly cases 1-3; 1/3 include anomaly cases 4-5; and the remaining 1/3 include anomaly case 6. In Figure 9(a), we present the combined FPR and FNR with average values of 1.53% and 0.83%, respectively. Figure 9(b) represents the combined *PCS*, *RCL*, *ACC*, and *FMR* values with the average values of 95.88%, 99.17%, 98.64%, and 97.39%, respectively. Figure 9(c) reports a comparison among access control mechanism, a file level profiling approach (e.g., [18]) and our fine-grained AD technique for the combination of the attack scenarios above (denoted by *A1*, *A2*, and *A3*, respectively). The figure shows the *PCS*, *RCL*, *ACC*, and *FMR* values of the approaches in comparison. For example, the accuracy of these approaches are 98.64%, 21.92%, and 10.82%, respectively. The reason is that a file level profiling approach can detect only the anomaly cases 1 and 2 while an access control mechanism is able to detect only the anomaly case 1. From the evaluation, it is evident that an access control mechanism or a file level AD mechanism or even a combination of these two is inadequate to detect many anomalous accesses to file systems. Therefore, it is necessary that an approach be deployed to monitor file system activities in a fine-grained manner.

7.5 Overhead

Our AD mechanism operates as a passive component and, therefore, **does not disrupt normal file system activities of the users**. A separate host running our AD mechanism takes care of the computational cost of building user profiles and monitoring file system accesses at runtime. The only additional load that is added to the user's machine is the overhead of running the blktrace tool. However, blktrace has a very low overhead of only 2% [28].

The space requirement for computing and saving the user profiles depends on the duration of tracing blktrace events while collecting the training data, and also on the file system usage by the users. In our experiments, we observe the space requirement for a single user profile to be practical, i.e., less than 1 megabyte in average.

8. RELATED WORK

Most existing AD methodologies have been designed for relational databases [11, 12, 13, 14] and networked systems [15, 16, 17]. Nyalkalkar et al. [29] present a comparison of two network-based anomaly detection methods. Buschkes et al. [30] propose an anomaly detection technique based on profiling mobile users. Baracaldo et al. [31] extends the role-based access control (RBAC) model with a risk assessment process, and the trust the system has on its users. Görnitz et al. [32] devise a learning methodology for anomaly detection that requires less labeled data while achieving higher accuracy. Some research [33, 34] propose to build temporal user profiles in terms of multiple time granularities.

Bowen et al. [35] use believable decoys to detect malicious insiders and propose an automated decoy injection method [36]. In order to detect information theft by insiders Gates et al. [18] use the file system hierarchy for extracting information regarding the relevance of a resource with respect to the users. Due to the dependency on the file system hierarchy this approach cannot handle the case of dynamic file systems where files can be moved from one directory to another. Stolfo et al. [19] extract some file system features, e.g., file name, working directory and parent directory to detect abnormal accesses to the file system and therefore has similar limitations as Gates et al. [18]. On the contrary, our approach does not depend on the file system hierarchy and thus can be used for dynamic file systems.

Senator et al. [37] monitor user activity and combine different structural and semantic information to detect anomalies based on suspected scenarios of malicious insider behavior. Ray et al. [38] propose a framework that uses an attack tree to identify malicious activities from authorized insiders. Claycomb et al. [39] proposes an approach to monitor various systems across an enterprise in order to detect malicious insider activity by using directory virtualization. Huang et al. [20] use an unsupervised approach for detecting application's anomalous run-time operations. This approach collects the file access information of applications to create a baseline profile which is then used to score the file access requests at runtime. Camiña et al. [40] propose a task-based masquerader detector that avoids monitoring every single file system object. Compared to these approaches that work at a higher-level of abstraction, our approach leverages low-level access information (at block level) to detect a broader set of anomalies.

Moreover, some of the previous research work focus on file system integrity [21, 22] rather than confidentiality. I^3FS [22] is an on-access integrity checking file system that compares the checksums of files in real-time using cryptographic checksums to detect unauthorized modifications to files. These approaches are complementary to ours since their focus is on file system integrity.

9. CONCLUSION AND FUTURE WORK

In this paper, we have proposed a technique to create fine-grained profiles of file system users and to use these profiles for detecting anomalous accesses to file systems. We consider that these anomalous accesses are due to the abuse of data by an insider or by an external attacker who can gain access to the files by exploiting the vulnerabilities of the software or by stealing credentials using different techniques, e.g., man-in-the-middle attack, key-logging, phishing, and so on. However, we learn the normal access patterns of the users by utilizing the block level access information from the OS kernel space and detect such malicious accesses with an accuracy of 98.64%.

We notice that our AD system can be easily integrated with anomaly response system [41] that automatically takes actions when an anomaly is detected, based also on contextual parameters. Examples of actions include: blocking access to the file, disconnecting the user, raising an alarm to a system administrator. We believe that effectively and efficiently managing detected anomalies is important for real-world deployment of AD techniques.

In order to prevent a malicious security administrator from abusing the profiles, we consider multiple administrators with separation of duty policy [42]. Notice that our AD mechanism can also be used to monitor accesses by system administrators to the files storing the profiles. Furthermore, an insider or even an external attacker can get access to the profiles in some cases by breaking the security properties which may undermine the AD techniques. However, profiles can be secured by using available security techniques, such as isolating them on secure storage and monitoring accesses to the files storing the user profiles.

Though collusion attacks are not popular among insiders, such attacks may allow each of the insiders to remain under the anomaly threshold but to steal information from the file systems. Identifying these attacks is challenging and thus is left as future work.

Acknowledgment

The work reported in this paper has been partially supported by the Schlumberger Foundation under Faculty For The Future (FFTF) Fellowship and the Purdue PLM Center.

10. REFERENCES

[1] Security breach at sony– here's what you need to know. *http://www.forbes.com/sites/josephsteinberg/2014/12/11/massive-security-breach-at-sony-heres-what-you-need -to-know/*, December 2014.

[2] Ravi S. Sandhu, Edward J. Coyne, Hal L. Feinstein, and Charles E. Youman. Role-based access control models. *Computer*, 29(2):38–47, February 1996.

[3] J. Park and R. Sandhu. Originator control in usage control. In *Proceedings of the 3rd International Workshop on Policies for Distributed Systems and Networks (POLICY'02)*, POLICY '02, pages 60–. Washington, DC, USA, 2002. IEEE Computer Society.

[4] Elisa Bertino. *Data Protection from Insider Threats*. Synthesis Lectures on Data Management. Morgan & Claypool Publishers, San Rafael, 2012.

[5] Elisa Bertino and Gabriel Ghinita. Towards mechanisms for detection and prevention of data exfiltration by insiders: Keynote talk paper. In *Proceedings of the 6th ACM Symposium on Information, Computer and Communications Security*, ASIACCS '11, pages 10–19, New York, NY, USA, 2011. ACM.

[6] Cybersecurity watch survey: How bad is the insider threat? Technical report, Carnegie Mellon University, 2012. http://resources.sei.cmu.edu/asset_files/Presentation/2013_017_101_57766.pdf.

[7] Carly Huth and Robin Ruefle. Components and considerations in building an insider threat program. Technical report, Carnegie Mellon University, 2013. http://resources.sei.cmu.edu/asset_files/Webinar/2013_018_101_69083.pdf.

[8] Matthew Collins, Dawn M. Cappelli, Tom Caron, Randall F. Trzeciak, and Andrew P. Moore. Spotlight on: Programmers as malicious insiders (updated and revised). Technical report, Carnegie Mellon University, 2013. http://resources.sei.cmu.edu/asset_files/WhitePaper/2013_019_001_85232.pdf.

[9] David Mundie Andrew P. Moore, Michael Hanley. A pattern for increased monitoring for intellectual property theft by departing insiders. Technical report, Carnegie Mellon University, 2012. http://www.sei.cmu.edu/reports/12tr008.pdf.

[10] Andrew P. Moore, Matthew L. Collins, David A. Mundie, Robin M. Ruefle, and David M. McIntire. Pattern-based design of insider threat programs Technical report, Carnegie Mellon University, 2014. http://resources.sei.cmu.edu/asset_files/technicalnote/2014_004_001_427430.pdf.

[11] Ashish Kamra, Evimaria Terzi, and Elisa Bertino. Detecting anomalous access patterns in relational databases. *The VLDB Journal*, 17(5):1063–1077, August 2008.

[12] Syed Rafiul Hussain, Asmaa M. Sallam, and Elisa Bertino. Detanom: Detecting anomalous database transactions by insiders. In *Proceedings of the 5th ACM Conference on Data and Application Security and Privacy*, CODASPY '15, pages 25–35, New York, NY, USA, 2015. ACM.

[13] E. Bertino, A Kamra, and James P. Early. Profiling database application to detect sql injection attacks. In *IEEE International Performance, Computing, and Communications Conference, IPCCC 2007*, pages 449–458, April 2007.

[14] Sunu Mathew, Michalis Petropoulos, Hung Q. Ngo, and Shambhu Upadhyaya. A data-centric approach to insider attack detection in database systems. In *Proceedings of the 13th International Conference on Recent Advances in Intrusion Detection*, RAID'10, pages 382–401, Berlin, Heidelberg, 2010. Springer-Verlag.

[15] P. Garcia-Teodoro, J. Diaz-Verdejo, G. Macia-Fernandez, and E. Vazquez. Anomaly-based network intrusion detection: Techniques, systems and challenges. *Computers & Security*, pages 18 – 28, 2009.

[16] Matthew V. Mahoney and Philip K. Chan. Learning nonstationary models of normal network traffic for detecting novel attacks. In *Proceedings of the Eighth ACM SIGKDD International Conference on Knowledge Discovery and Data Mining*, KDD '02, pages 376–385, New York, NY, USA, 2002. ACM.

[17] M. Thottan and Chuanyi Ji. Anomaly detection in ip networks. *Signal Processing, IEEE Transactions on*, 51(8):2191–2204, Aug 2003.

[18] Christopher Gates, Ninghui Li, Zenglin Xu, SureshN. Chari, Ian Molloy, and Youngja Park. Detecting insider information theft using features from file access logs. In *Computer Security - ESORICS 2014*, volume 8713 of *Lecture Notes in Computer Science*, pages 383–400. Springer International Publishing, 2014.

[19] SalvatoreJ. Stolfo, Shlomo Hershkop, LinhH. Bui, Ryan Ferster, and Ke Wang. Anomaly detection in computer security and an application to file system accesses. In Mohand-Said Hacid, NeilV. Murray, ZbigniewW. RaÅŻ, and Shusaku Tsumoto, editors, *Foundations of Intelligent Systems*, volume 3488 of *Lecture Notes in Computer Science*, pages 14–28. Springer Berlin Heidelberg, 2005.

[20] Liang Huang and Kenny Wong. Anomaly detection by monitoring filesystem activities. In *Proceedings of the 2011 IEEE 19th International Conference on Program Comprehension*, ICPC '11, pages 221–222. Washington, DC, USA, 2011. IEEE Computer Society.

[21] *ZFS End-to-End Data Integrity*. https://blogs.oracle.com/bonwick/entry/zfs_end_to_end_data.

[22] Swapnil Patil, Anand Kashyap, Gopalan Sivathanu, and Erez Zadok. Fs: An in-kernel integrity checker and intrusion detection file system. In *Proceedings of the 18th USENIX Conference on System Administration*, LISA '04, pages 67–78, Berkeley, CA, USA, 2004. USENIX Association.

[23] Brendan Juba, Christopher Musco, Fan Long, Stelios Sidiroglou-douskos, and Martin Rinard. Principled

sampling for anomaly detection. In *Proceedings of the Network and Distributed System Security Symposium*, 2015.

[24] *Blktrace*. http://linux.die.net/man/8/blktrace/.

[25] Heikki Mannila, Hannu Toivonen, and A. Inkeri Verkamo. Discovery of frequent episodes in event sequences. *Data Min. Knowl. Discov.*, 1(3):259–289, January 1997.

[26] Rakesh Agrawal and Ramakrishnan Srikant. Fast algorithms for mining association rules in large databases. In *Proceedings of the 20th International Conference on Very Large Data Bases*, VLDB '94, pages 487–499, San Francisco, CA, USA, 1994. Morgan Kaufmann Publishers Inc.

[27] Srivatsan Laxman, P. S. Sastry, and K. P. Unnikrishnan. A fast algorithm for finding frequent episodes in event streams. In *Proceedings of the 13th ACM SIGKDD International Conference on Knowledge Discovery and Data Mining*, KDD '07, pages 410–419, New York, NY, USA, 2007. ACM.

[28] *Block I/O Layer Tracing using blktrace*. http://smackerelofopinion.blogspot.com/2009/10/block-io-layer-tracing-using-blktrace.html.

[29] Kaustubh Nyalkalkar, Sushant Sinha, Michael Bailey, and Farnam Jahanian. A comparative study of two network-based anomaly detection methods, 2011.

[30] R. Buschkes, D. Kesdogan, and P. Reichl. How to increase security in mobile networks by anomaly detection. In *Computer Security Applications Conference, 1998. Proceedings. 14th Annual*, pages 3–12, Dec 1998.

[31] Nathalie Baracaldo and James Joshi. A trust-and-risk aware rbac framework: Tackling insider threat. In *Proceedings of the 17th ACM Symposium on Access Control Models and Technologies*, SACMAT '12, pages 167–176, New York, NY, USA, 2012. ACM.

[32] Nico Görnitz, Marius Kloft, Konrad Rieck, and Ulf Brefeld. Toward supervised anomaly detection. *J. Artif. Int. Res.*, 46(1):235–262, January 2013.

[33] Yingjiu Li, Ningning Wu, Sean Wang, and Sushil Jajodia. Enhancing profiles for anomaly detection using time granularities. *J. Comput. Secur.*, 10(1-2):137–157, July 2002.

[34] Shagufta Mehnaz and Elisa Bertino. Building robust temporal user profiles for anomaly detection in file system accesses. In *Proceedings of the Fourteenth IEEE International Conference on Privacy, Security and Trust (PST)*, 2016.

[35] Brian M. Bowen, Shlomo Hershkop, Angelos D. Keromytis, and Salvatore J. Stolfo. *Baiting Inside Attackers Using Decoy Documents*, pages 51–70. Springer Berlin Heidelberg, Berlin, Heidelberg, 2009.

[36] Brian M. Bowen, Vasileios P. Kemerlis, Pratap Prabhu, Angelos D. Keromytis, and Salvatore J. Stolfo. Automating the injection of believable decoys to detect snooping. In *Proceedings of the Third ACM Conference on Wireless Network Security*, WiSec '10, pages 81–86, New York, NY, USA, 2010. ACM.

[37] Ted E. Senator, Henry G. Goldberg, Alex Memory, William T. Young, Brad Rees, Robert Pierce, Daniel Huang, Matthew Reardon, David A. Bader, Edmond Chow, Irfan Essa, Joshua Jones, Vinay Bettadapura, Duen Horng Chau, Oded Green, Oguz Kaya, Anita Zakrzewska, Erica Briscoe, Rudolph IV L. Mappus, Robert McColl, Lora Weiss, Thomas G. Dietterich, Alan Fern, Weng-Keen Wong, Shubhomoy Das, Andrew Emmott, Jed Irvine, Jay-Yoon Lee, Danai Koutra, Christos Faloutsos, Daniel Corkill, Lisa Friedland, Amanda Gentzel, and David Jensen. Detecting insider threats in a real corporate database of computer usage activity. In *Proceedings of the 19th ACM SIGKDD International Conference on Knowledge Discovery and Data Mining*, KDD '13, pages 1393–1401, New York, NY, USA, 2013. ACM.

[38] Indrajit Ray and Nayot Poolsapassit. Using attack trees to identify malicious attacks from authorized insiders. In *Proceedings of the 10th European Conference on Research in Computer Security*, ESORICS'05, pages 231–246, Berlin, Heidelberg, 2005. Springer-Verlag.

[39] William Claycomb, Dongwan Shin, and Gail-Joon Ahn. Enhancing directory virtualization to detect insider activity. *Security and Communication Networks*, 5(8):873–886, 2012.

[40] J. Benito Camiña, Jorge Rodríguez, and Raúl Monroy. *Towards a Masquerade Detection System Based on User's Tasks*, pages 447–465. Springer International Publishing, Cham, 2014.

[41] A. Kamra and E. Bertino. Design and implementation of an intrusion response system for relational databases. *IEEE Transactions on Knowledge and Data Engineering*, 23(6):875–888, June 2011.

[42] Richard Simon and Mary Ellen Zurko. Separation of duty in role-based environments. In *Proceedings of the 10th IEEE Workshop on Computer Security Foundations*, CSFW '97, pages 183–, Washington, DC, USA, 1997. IEEE Computer Society.

Mining Attributed Graphs for Threat Intelligence

Hugo Gascon
Technische Universität
Braunschweig

Bernd Grobauer
Siemens AG

Thomas Schreck
Siemens AG

Lukas Rist
Symantec Corporation

Daniel Arp
Technische Universität
Braunschweig

Konrad Rieck
Technische Universität
Braunschweig

ABSTRACT

Understanding and fending off attack campaigns against organizations, companies and individuals, has become a global struggle.
As today's threat actors become more determined and organized,
isolated efforts to detect and reveal threats are no longer effective.
Although challenging, this situation can be significantly changed
if information about security incidents is collected, shared and analyzed across organizations. To this end, different exchange data
formats such as STIX, CyBOX, or IODEF have been recently proposed and numerous CERTs are adopting these *threat intelligence*
standards to share tactical and technical threat insights. However,
managing, analyzing and correlating the vast amount of data available from different sources to identify relevant attack patterns still
remains an open problem.

In this paper we present MANTIS, a platform for threat intelligence that enables the unified analysis of different standards and the
correlation of threat data trough a novel type-agnostic similarity algorithm based on attributed graphs. Its unified representation allows
the security analyst to discover similar and related threats by linking patterns shared between seemingly unrelated attack campaigns
through queries of different complexity. We evaluate the performance of MANTIS as an information retrieval system for threat
intelligence in different experiments. In an evaluation with over
14,000 CyBOX objects, the platform enables retrieving relevant
threat reports with a mean average precision of 80%, given only a
single object from an incident, such as a file or an HTTP request.
We further illustrate the performance of this analysis in two case
studies with the attack campaigns *Stuxnet* and *Regin*.

Keywords

Threat Intelligence; Advanced Persistent Threat; Graph Mining;
Information Retrieval

CODASPY '17, March 22–24, 2017, Scottsdale, AZ, USA.

© 2017 Copyright held by the owner/author(s). Publication rights licensed to ACM.
ISBN 978-1-4503-4523-1/17/03. . . $15.00

DOI: http://dx.doi.org/10.1145/3029806.3029811

1. INTRODUCTION

Targeted attacks pose a serious threat to the security of individuals,
companies and organizations. In contrast to regular malware aiming
at widespread infections, these campaigns are tailored to maximize
the impact in the systems and networks of their victims. In many
occasions, such campaigns are conducted by experienced and even
government-sponsored actors that are specialized in industrial espionage and invest considerable resources in the preparation of their
attacks. For example, according to the eye-opening investigation of
the security company Mandiant, a group of attackers code-named
"APT1" successfully infiltrated 141 companies over a period of 7
years and obtained access to several terabytes of company data [24].
The group was believed to include several developers and operators,
likely with the support of a nation-state actor. Since then, reports
about newly disclosed operations tailored against companies, governments and individuals have become increasingly common in the
media [e.g. 32, 36, 37].

Unfortunately, the detection and analysis of attack campaigns is a
daunting task: First, due to the focused operation of the campaigns,
only few traces of the attackers are available for forensic investigation. Second, the employed malware often makes use of novel
exploits and infiltration techniques. As a consequence, conventional
security defenses such as intrusion detection systems and anti-virus
scanners fail frequently to spot these type of threats. Specially
because detection patterns become available only with significant
delay, if at all. It has become evident then, that isolated efforts to
detect attack campaigns within companies and organizations are
mostly ineffective against organized threat actors.

As a remedy, security research has recently started to explore
means for collecting, sharing and analyzing threat information
across organizations—evidence-based knowledge referred to as
threat intelligence [e.g., 3, 11, 18, 27]. As part of this process,
different exchange formats have been proposed to provide a standardized way for describing security incidents, forensic traces and
observations related to attack campaigns. Examples of these formats
are STIX [1], IODEF [9] and OpenIOC [23], which are gradually
adopted by national and enterprise CERTs in combination with
commercial and open source databases for storing knowledge about
ongoing attacks such as *Alien Vault's Open Threat Exchange* [28]
or the *Collective Intelligence Framework* [6].

However, collecting and sharing information alone is not sufficient for mitigating the threat of attack campaigns. Although such
threat intelligence platforms enable searching for indicators of compromise that exactly match a query, the actual crux is to correlate
the vast amount of available data and pinpoint similar characteristics
of novel campaigns that can help eliminating existing infections as
well as craft detection patterns more efficiently.

In this paper, we present MANTIS, an analysis platform that enables the aggregation and correlation of threat data into a unified representation based on attributed graphs. In particular, the platform is able to merge information from different exchange formats, solving the problem of analysing data contained in heterogeneous or overlapping standards. Furthermore, different threat objects that are typically analysed independently are correlated through a data type-agnostic representation. Such an approach allows unveiling high-level relations not visible within individual threat reports and linking unconventional patterns shared between seemingly unrelated attack campaigns.

At the core of our platform lies a novel graph-based similarity algorithm that allows discovering similarities between threat data objects at different levels of granularity. This analysis allows a security analyst to search the attributed graphs for threats related to individual observations—similar in spirit to a search engine. For example, given an object from a security incident, such as a suspicious file or an HTTP request, the platform can identify related nodes in the graphs and traverse them to the corresponding threat reports, ultimately returning information about the underlying attack campaign. In addition, MANTIS supports authoring reports for new incidents that can be used for searching and correlating existing information, as well as extending existing threat data with new insights.

We evaluate the utility of MANTIS as an information retrieval system for threat intelligence in a quantitative and qualitative fashion. To this end, we make use of a large data set of malware observed in the wild and collected by a security vendor at the end-point systems of different companies and organizations. We base our evaluation on the threat reports created during the analysis of such samples.

As a result, we show how given an object from a security incident, our platform is able to retrieve associated data to the corresponding malware with a mean average precision of 80% in a set of 14,000 standardized threat objects. This means that 4 out of 5 results returned to the security analyst are relevant to her query. We

further illustrate the performance of this analysis in two case studies based on threat intelligence from highly targeted attack campaigns: *Stuxnet*, the well-known joint endeavour of several west nations to sabotage Iran's nuclear program and *Regin*, a sophisticated espionage tool allegedly sponsored by a state-nation and distributed worldwide to selected individuals and organizations.

To the best of our knowledge, MANTIS is the first practical solution for performing similarity-based analysis of multi-format and structured data for threat intelligence. While the platform requires the interplay with other techniques for stopping attack campaigns, the analysis and query capabilities alone already provide a valuable tool for assessing the impact of security incidents. MANTIS is available as an open-source project and is currently used at a large CERT for managing threat data in day-to-day business.

In summary, we make the following contributions:

- *Unified representation of threat intelligence reports.* We present an open-source platform for threat intelligence that merges different standard exchange formats and provides a unified representation of threat reports as attributed graphs.

- *Similarity analysis of threats.* We introduce a similarity algorithm for attributed graphs that enables uncovering relations between threats at different levels of granularity.

- *Information retrieval for threat intelligence.* By incorporating the similarity analysis into our platform, we devise an information retrieval system that is capable of retrieving related reports given individual observations from security incidents.

The rest of the paper is organized as follows: we introduce the concept of threat intelligence and its standards in Section 2. We then proceed to present our system for analysis and retrieval of threat data in Section 3. We evaluate its effectiveness with real-world threat data in Section 5 and discuss its limitations in Section 6. Related work is discussed in Section 7 and Section 8 concludes the paper.

```
<stix:STIX_Package (...) id="package-37e">                              1
  <stix:STIX_Header>                                                    2
    <stix:Title>APT1</stix:Title>                                       3
    <stix:Description>                                                  4
      This package contains the IOCs referenced                         5
      in Appendix G of the APT1 report.                                 6
    </stix:Description>                                                 7
  </stix:STIX_Header>                                                   8
  <stix:Observables>                                                    9
    <cybox:Observable id="Observable-9ba">                            10
      <cybox:Object id="URI-9ba">                                     11
        <cybox:Properties type="URL">                                 12
          <URIObj:Value condition="contains">                         13
            /mci.jpg                                                   14
          </URIObj:Value>                                             15
        </cybox:Properties>                                           16
      </cybox:Object>                                                 17
    </cybox:Observable>                                               18
    <cybox:Observable id="Observable-2b2">                            19
      <cybox:Object id="File-2b2">                                    20
        <cybox:Properties type="File">                                21
          <FileObj:Name>gdocs.exe</FileObj:Name>                      22
          <FileObj:Extension>exe</FileObj:Extension>                  23
          <FileObj:Size>261822</FileObj:Size>                         24
          <FileObj:Attributed_List>                                   25
            <cybox:Object condition="contains">                       26
              v1.0 No Doubt to Hack You, Writed                       27
              by UglyGorilla, 06/29/2007                              28
            </cybox:Object>                                           29
          </FileObj:Attributed_List>                                  30
        </cybox:Properties>                                           31
      </cybox:Object>                                                 32
    </cybox:Observable>                                               33
  </stix:Observables>                                                 34
```

```
<stix:Indicators>                                                    35
  <stix:Indicator id="Indicator-a42">                                36
    <indicator:Title>                                                37
      MANITSME                                                       38
    </indicator:Title>                                               39
    <indicator:Description>                                          40
      This family of malware will beacon out at                      41
      random intervals to the remote attacker.                       42
      The attacker can run programs, execute                         43
      arbitrary commands, and easily upload and                      44
      download files.                                                45
    </indicator:Description>                                         46
    <indicator:Type>Backdoor</indicator:Type>                       47
    <indicator:Observable id="Observable-a42">                      48
      <cybox:Observable_Composition operator="OR">                  49
        <cybox:Observable idref="Observable-9ba">                   50
        </cybox:Observable>                                         51
        <cybox:Observable idref="Observable-2b2">                   52
        </cybox:Observable>                                         53
      </cybox:Observable_Composition>                               54
    </indicator:Observable>                                         55
    <indicator:Related_Campaigns>                                   56
      <indicator:Related_Campaign>                                  57
        <stixCommon:Campaign idref="Campaign-a58"/>                 58
      </indicator:Related_Campaign>                                 59
    </indicator:Related_Campaigns>                                  60
  </stix:Indicator>                                                 61
  ...                                                               62
  ...                                                               63
  ...                                                               64
  ...                                                               65
  ...                                                               66
</stix:Indicators>                                                   67
</stix:STIX_Package>                                                68
```

Figure 1: Exemplary STIX package for the "APT1" report by Mandiant [24]. Note that several identifiers and XML elements have been simplified for presentation.

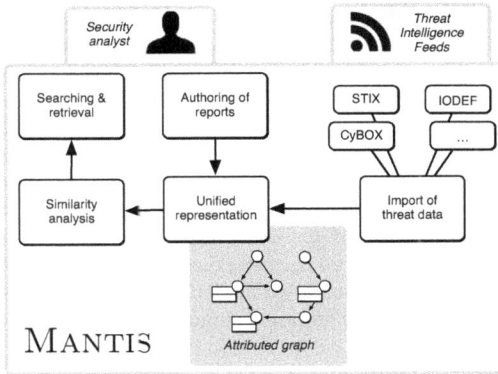

Figure 2: Schematic overview of the MANTIS architecture.

2. THREAT INTELLIGENCE

Companies and organizations dealing with security-sensitive data usually employ different security measures for protecting their infrastructure, including systematically monitoring network and host events. While this monitored data can be searched for security incidents on a regular basis, appropriate detection and search patterns are only available for known threats, leaving infrastructure vulnerable to novel and unknown attack campaigns. This situation, however, can be significantly changed if information about incidents, is collected, shared and analyzed across organizations. Although this approach may not be sufficient for spotting extremely focused attacks, it enables hunting down threat actors that re-use or gradually evolve their techniques and strategies.

However, information regarding security incidents, related observations, and threat actors is very heterogeneous and difficult to transmit without a lack of context. In order to overcome this problem, different standard formats have been recently proposed to provide a structured representation of threat data that can be easily shared and processed. These standardised but diverse threat insights constitutes what has been known as *threat intelligence*. Examples of these standards are *IODEF*, developed by members of the IETF [9], *OpenIOC*, implemented by Mandiant in many of its products [23], and *STIX* with its associated family of formats, like *CyBOX* or *MAEC* [1]. In particular, the *STIX* standard is currently leading the adoption by national and enterprise CERTs. In the following, we briefly cover its design as an illustrative example of the structured representations implemented by all of the mentioned threat intelligence standards.

The STIX standard comprises a family of XML schemes whose development is driven by the security community under supervision of the MITRE Corporation. The individual STIX formats and constructs allow to describe numerous types of threat information in a structured way and for different use cases. For example, observations related to threats can be described as *Observables*, ranging from registry keys and file names to network addresses and strings in URLs. These Observables can be combined with logical operators to form *Indicators* that reflect and describe concrete threats. Other constructs include representations for *Incidents*, *Courses of Action*, *Attack Campaigns* and *Threat Actors*. A detailed description of the different constructs is provided in the STIX specification [1].

As an example, let us consider the STIX package shown in Figure 1 which covers a tiny and simplified fragment of the indicators for the "APT1" campaign. This campaign was uncovered in February 2013 and comprised a series of targeted attacks against several companies and organizations [24]. Some common constructs of the STIX standard can be seen in the example: An Observable

matching the content of a URI (line 10–18), another Observable corresponding to a particular file (line 19–33), and an Indicator combining the two (line 36–61) that describes the malware family and references the underlying attack campaign. Note that although not included here, the original report in OpenIOC format covers over 3,000 Observables and 40 different Indicators for the attack campaign.

The use of threat intelligence standards allows to share and process a large amount of complex and enriched threat data in a standard and machine readable format. This has encouraged some companies with a large distributed infrastructure and a global view of the threat landscape to aggregate feeds that are made available to smaller organizations. However, the information received through these sources is highly heterogeneous and still needs to be put into context by the analyst. In our work, we aim at making this analysis much more efficient by providing a platform that integrates different standards into a unified representation and allows for exploring and searching structured threat data for relevant information.

3. THE MANTIS FRAMEWORK

As a first step for analyzing and understanding attack campaigns, we present MANTIS, an analysis platform for storing, authoring and managing threat data. The platform implements support for several common threat intelligence standards, including STIX and OpenIOC, two of the standards with the largest adoption in the security community. To support this adoption and encourage further research, MANTIS is available as an open-source project[1] and readily applicable for experimenting with threat data at organizations and CERTs and the implementation of new importers for additional standards.

To provide a flexible and platform-independent design, MANTIS is structured as a set of *Django* applications. Figure 2 shows a schematic view of its architecture. In the typical use case, the security analyst documents the findings of an investigation using the authoring interface, while at the same time accesses related information about already documented threats through the retrieval interface. Both interfaces provide different views for managing the creation and the collaborative maintenance of threat reports. Additionally, the platform supports receiving data feeds in different formats from other tools, organizations and security companies. The data contained in these feeds is jointly stored with authored reports and thereby enables an analyst to document her findings in the context of already known threats and attack campaigns.

3.1 Unified Data Model

To provide a joint view on the threat data collected, MANTIS expresses the different XML standards as directed graphs and links together constructs describing the same type of information.

Table 1: Example of flattened facts for an Observable.

Id	Fact term (key)	Fact value
f_1	Properties/File_Name	gdocs.exe
f_2	Properties/File_Extension	exe
f_3	Properties/Size_In_Bytes	261822
f_4	Properties/File_Attributed_List/Object@cond...	Contains
f_5	Properties/File_Attributed_List/Object	v1.0 No Doub...

As a result, related data describing campaigns at different levels, such as generic attack strategies and concrete malicious payloads, are merged into a single view and can be accessed by simply traversing the edges of the graphs.

---

[1]MANTIS— https://github.com/siemens/django-mantis

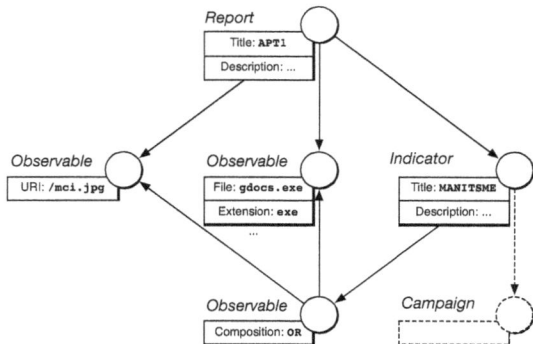

Figure 3: Attributed graph for STIX package in Figure 1.

Formally, we define this directed graph as a tuple $G = (V, E, L)$, where each node $v \in V$ symbolizes a standard construct from an original XML document. Two nodes $v, u \in V$ are connected by a directed edge $(v, u) \in E$, if the construct corresponding to u is either contained or referenced by the construct represented by v. Moreover, we attach a list of facts $l \in L$ to each node. This enables us to store unstructured data in the graph, assigning a set of attributes to each node. Each list $l \in L$ has the form $l = (f_1, f_2, \ldots, f_n)$ where a fact f_i results from flattening the inner structure of a standard construct into facts of key-value pairs.

As an example of this unified representation, Figure 3 depicts the attributed graph that abstracts the relations between objects and data in the STIX report from Figure 1, including the two Observables, their composition and the corresponding Indicator. Note how several substructures have been flattened into facts, such as the title of the report or the URI pattern.

In addition Table 1 shows the complete list of flattened facts for the Observable at the center of Figure 3. Note that the flattening is conducted recursively and the fact terms are built using a hierarchical structure. This generic representation within the nodes of the graph will let us compare effectively different threat reports and traverse between objects even if their are of different type, such as from an observed URI pattern to the corresponding attack campaign.

Each fact value in the platform is stored exactly once and referenced from any object containing the fact. This de-duplication saves storage space and, more importantly, enables an efficient calculation of correlation based on fact equality. Thus, the analyst can retrieve all nodes related to particular facts with a single query, for example to get a listing of all executable files with a size of 261,822 bytes. However, while equality-based searches already provide a powerful instrument for mining the collected threat data, it is obvious that more complex relations cannot be uncovered by focusing on exact fact matching alone. In the following, we introduce our analysis method, which as part of MANTIS allows the analyst to perform similarity-based queries on top of its unified graph data model.

4. SIMILARITY ANALYSIS

When working with threat intelligence, a security analyst investigating an incident begins by documenting any suspicious findings. Then, the analyst wonders if such an event has been observed in the past and, specially if relevant documentation about the incident already exists.

However, obtaining an answer to this question is far from trivial. Threat reports can be large and heterogeneous and contain data that, without being identical, are linked to related events. For example, consider the case of several Observables containing HTTP requests of similar URLs. While being slightly different in the URI or host

name, such objects may be associated to the same threat actor and thus should be retrievable to help investigating the new incident.

As a consequence, the analyst requires a method that can identify and retrieve similar objects regardless of their structure, size or content given a query object. Thus, we strive for a similarity-based search that is capable of identifying similar facts, nodes and subgraphs on top of the unified representation of MANTIS. In particular, we implement our approach in two steps: First, we draw on our unified representation and devise a method that enables non-exact matching based on *fingerprints* computed using the *simhash* algorithm (Section 4.1). Second, we implement a retrieval system to efficiently identify all fingerprints similar to a given query (Section 4.2).

4.1 Simhash Fingerprinting

To measure the similarity between arbitrary objects in our representation, we make use of the bag-of-words concept from the information retrieval field [30]. In its original form, this model is intended for text documents in order to obtain a numerical vector representation based on the words or phrases they contain. However, threat data is heterogeneous and may range from simple file names to code fragments and textual descriptions. Therefore, we employ *byte n-grams* to characterize the content of an object [8, 40]. This means that a fact f is represented by all byte strings of length n contained in the fact value. Similarly, a node v is characterized by all n-grams contained in its associated facts l and a subgraph rooted at a node u is represented by the n-grams of all nodes reachable from u.

While the extracted n-grams provide a versatile and generic representation of the underlying content, they are not suitable for an efficient analysis, as they require variable-size storage and cannot be compared in constant time. For example, if new data introduced into the platform contained previously unseen n-grams, the existing vector representation of the bag-of-n-grams model should be recomputed for all objects to accommodate the new n-grams. As a remedy, we employ the *simhash* algorithm introduced by Charikar [5], an approximation technique that maps an arbitrary set of objects to a fixed-bit fingerprint.

The simhash algorithm ensures that although each object is represented by a hash of its n-grams, similar objects have similar fingerprints. More specifically, the design of the algorithm guarantees that the Hamming distance [15] of fingerprints computed from similar objects is small. This property allow us to articulate the problem of finding a similar construct in MANTIS given an input query and its fingerprint F as the problem of finding those fingerprints that differ from F in at most b bits.

The algorithm proceeds as follows: First, each object is hashed to an m-bit value. Second, the bits at each position i in the hash values are counted, where a 1-bit is interpreted as +1 and 0-bit as -1. Finally, the resulting m count values are converted into an m-bit fingerprint by setting all positive counts to 1 and all negative counts to 0. In our setting we apply the simhash algorithm to compute m-bit fingerprints for the sets of n-grams associated with facts, nodes and subgraphs, where we set $n = 3$ and $m = 64$. Accordingly, the fingerprint F_f of a fact f is computed by

$$F_f = \text{simhash}(N(f))$$

where N is the set of n-grams contained in the fact value. Similarly, we compute the fingerprint F_v of a node v as

$$F_v = \text{simhash}\left(\bigcup_{f \in l(v)} N(f)\right)$$

where $l(v)$ is the list of facts associated with v, and arrive at the fingerprint F_g of a subgraph rooted at a node u by

$$F_g = \text{simhash}\Big(\bigcup_{v \in r(u)} \bigcup_{f \in l(v)} N(f) \Big)$$

where the auxiliary function $r(u)$ returns all nodes reachable from u. Figure 4 shows a complete example of this computation for a fact containing the value `/mci.jpg`.

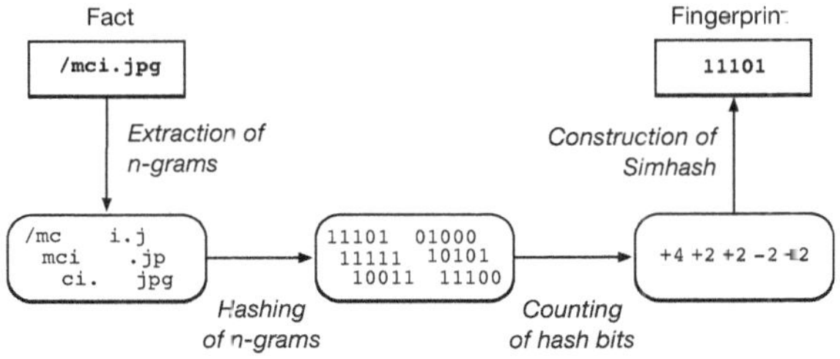

Figure 4: Computation of the simhash fingerprint of a fact.

The value is first represented by a set of 3-grams and then mapped to a set of 5-bit hash values. These values are finally aggregated to form the fingerprint $F_f = 11101$.

Note that n-grams are agnostic to the type of each fact, what results in determining similarity at a lexical level. This means that, in the same way as a search engine works, our method is not limited to measuring the similarity between constructs of the same type (e.g. two IP addresses), but between all possible types. This comparison enables to find relations in cases where standards are incorrectly filled or the types of data are unknown. For instance, a construct including a fact that describes the name of a file can be matched to a report including a description where this file is mentioned.

4.2 Hamming Distance-based Queries

When an large number of threat reports is loaded into the system the number of constructs that need to be analyzed can rapidly increase. For this reason, computing the Hamming distance between the query fingerprint and all queries in the platform can be computationally expensive.

As a remedy and to avoid precomputing the distance between all existing fingerprints at a maximum of b bits we follow the strategy proposed by Manku et al. [25]. In their approach, an index contains a series of *buckets* where each *bucket* has associated an integer p and a permutation of bits π. Each *bucket* is filled by first applying its permutation to all existing fingerprint and then sorting the resulting set of permuted fingerprints. Given a query fingerprint F and an integer b, we identify all permuted fingerprints in each *bucket* whose top p bits match the top p bits of $\pi(F)$. From these fingerprints, the ones that differ at most k bits from $\pi(F)$ are retrieved as result. Such approach can be completed in $O(p)$ and does not required the computation of a large distance matrix of fingerprints. For discussion on the optimal number of *buckets* and other implementation details, we refer the reader to the original description of the indexing approach introduced by Manku et al. [25].

For our particular application, we build three indexes: one for the fingerprints of individual facts, a second one for the fingerprints of nodes (i.e. individual constructs with their own semantics in the threat intelligence standard) and a third one for the fingerprints of subgraphs rooted at the different nodes. When a new report is imported into the system we first represent its data as an attributed graph. Then, we compute the fingerprints of its facts and constructs and add them to the corresponding index. When the analyst queries the system, the fingerprint of the query is computed and depending

of its type, the results obtained from the corresponding index are retrieved. Moreover, retrieval results are sorted according to their Hamming distance and therefore their predicted relevance. This means that even in case that a query returns a large list of results, the analyst can rapidly identify the most relevant entries and keep conducting a focused investigation. In the following, we proceed to evaluate the efficacy of our approach using real-world threat data.

5. EVALUATION

In this section we evaluate our method for similarity-based searches through a quantitative and qualitative analysis. In particular, we first explore the performance of the system responses when every object and fact value is used as the input query introduced by the analyst. Second, we evaluate the results provided by the system in two specific scenarios. These involve threat data from the targeted and, therefore, more elusive *Stuxnet* and *Regin* attack campaigns.

5.1 Data Set

We consider for our evaluation a dataset of STIX packages automatically generated from malware samples collected in the wild by a security vendor in June 2015 at the end-point systems of different companies and organizations. The samples cover a wide range of malicious activity, including common botnets, backdoors and attack campaigns. Each sample is analyzed in a sandbox environment, where the results of the underlying static and dynamic analysis are automatically converted to CyBOX objects and grouped in STIX packages.

Table 2: Raw dataset indexed by MANTIS.

Standard	Construct	Size
STIX	STIX Package	2,621
STIX	Observable	7,282
STIX	Indicator	2,764
CybOX	Observable	255,941
CybOX	DNSQueryObject	2,583
CybOX	FileObject	12,334
CybOX	ProcessObject	17,914
CybOX	SemaphoreObject	244
CybOX	WinMutexObject	18,513
CybOX	WinRegistryObject	186,990
CybOX	WinThreadObject	22,347

Based on results provided by VirusTotal [39], we assign a label to each STIX package according to the hash of the analysed binary. As the names assigned to different malware families by AV vendors vary, we use a majority voting strategy and select those reports with a consensus of more than 5 vendors. The resulting 2,621 STIX reports are then loaded into MANTIS for analysis. Table 2 contains a summary of the constructs present in the original data.

Moreover, we take into considerations certain characteristics of the data that are relevant for the analysis: First, we exclude all objects and facts that are unsuitable for a similarity search, such as local timestamps, identifiers and hash sums, reducing the size of the attributed graphs to 14,987 individual nodes. Note that although these types of objects are not included to evaluate the algorithm, they are still in the system and are thus, searchable. Second, if several objects in one or several STIX reports contain the same value, the importer stores this value only once in MANTIS. As a result, nodes in the unified representation contain only references to their values, saving storage space if a certain value occurs more than once. The de-duplication performed by our platform, results in a total of 46,015 unique facts being stored in the system for similarity analysis.

5.2 Quantitative Evaluation

From the perspective of the security analyst, our platform resembles the operation of an information retrieval system: an analyst enters a query and retrieves a list of relevant nodes from the attributed graphs. So in essence, MANTIS functions like a search engine and its performance will be as good as the relevance of the results retrieved. Accordingly, in order to evaluate its performance qualitatively we make use of a metric that is widely employed to assess the performance of search algorithms: the *mean average precision* (MAP) [26]. The MAP averages the precision of a retrieval system over a set of queries Q for different numbers k of retrieved results. Formally, it is defined as

$$\text{MAP}(Q) = \frac{1}{|Q|} \sum_{j=1}^{|Q|} \frac{1}{m_j} \sum_{k=1}^{m_j} \text{Precision}(R_{jk}),$$

where Q is the set of queries, m_j the number of relevant nodes to the query $q_j \in Q$ and R_{jk} the top retrieved nodes for the query q_j up to the k-th relevant node. Moreover, we consider a node to be relevant, if it is associated with the same AV label as the object used as the query. For a single query, the average precision is the mean of the precision values obtained for the set of top k documents. This average value is then averaged over all possible queries [26], in our case all available facts, nodes or subgraphs.

To understand the intuition behind this metric we consider again the example of a search engine. The performance of a query is better when more relevant results are returned on the first page of the search engine, that is, we get a high precision value for the top k results [26]. Furthermore, the MAP score can be interpreted as the percentage of relevant objects in the returned results. For example, a MAP of 75% implies that 3 out of 4 returned results are relevant to the query.

We compute the MAP for our analysis platform MANTIS by considering all facts, all nodes or all subgraphs reachable from a node as queries to the system. To gain further insights into the similarity analysis, we repeat the queries with different number of retrieved objects k and different numbers of bits to match between the fingerprints. The results of this experiment are presented in Figure 5, where the MAP is plotted for the different experimental setups. We note that the quality of the returned results depends on the complexity of the query. If subgraphs are used as query, MANTIS is able to achieve a MAP value of 80%, such that 4 out of 5 returned results are relevant and constitute similar threats. If the analyst enters only a node or a fact as query, the MAP decreases. However, even when entering only single facts, our platform attains a MAP of at least 50%, thus providing retrieval results where every second result matters. Moreover, our platform reaches a good MAP already at 15 retrieved items (Figure 5b) which is a reasonable amount of information to display on the first results page of the search interface.

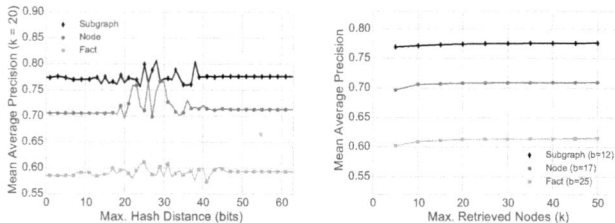

(a) MAP vs. maximum Hamming distance between fingerprints.

(b) MAP vs. maximum number of retrieved results.

Figure 5: Mean average precision (MAP) for queries of different complexity.

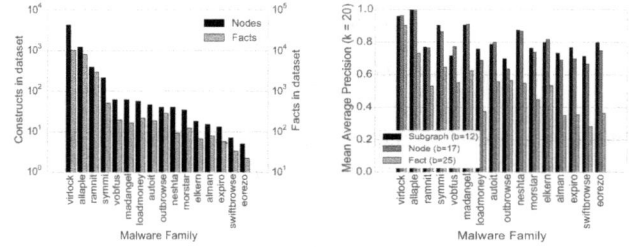

(a) Total number of constructs and facts per family.

(b) MAP for each family with best b and $k = 20$.

Figure 6: Data distribution and mean average precision per malware family.

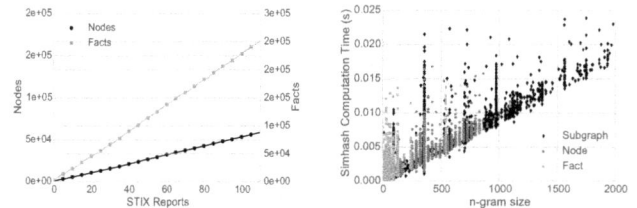

(a) Number of constructs and facts created per number of STIX reports imported in MANTIS.

(b) Computation Time of the Simhash Fingerprint vs. the number of *n-grams* in the object.

Figure 7: Scalability measurements respect to data size and fingerprint computation time.

As our dataset comprises a wide range of malware samples, we study how the diversity in the data affects the performance. Some samples, for instance, originate from small attack campaigns, while others are part of more common botnet and phishing activity. We evaluate then the results returned by the system when the queries belong to individual malware families. Figure 6a shows the amount of nodes and facts in each of the families. Note the logarithmic scale, that indicates a skewed distribution of samples per type of malware. Nonetheless and as shown in Figure 6b, the unbalance distribution has only a limited effect on the performance of our approach. Individual facts are retrieved with a MAP above 50% for most of the malware families, that is, every second returned result corresponds to the same malware family as the query. This is a remarkable result given that only individual facts, such as file names or URLs, are used to query the system.

Finally, scalability is another concern when designing an information retrieval system that is intended to accommodate large amounts of data. Figure 7a shows the evolution of the number of nodes and facts that need to be stored in the system per number of STIX reports imported. In both cases, a linear relation exist. As a result, we can expect our fingerprint indexes to also grow linearly with the number of imported reports. Moreover, every time the analyst introduces an individual fact or several facts as part of a construct, the fingerprint for each of them needs to be computed. As mentioned in Section 4.2, finding matching fingerprints for a query fingerprint F can be completed in $O(p)$, but the time computation of the fingerprint for the query object is directly related to its size. Figure 7b shows how even for large subgraphs with more than 2000 n-grams, the simhash fingerprint can be computed in less than 20 milliseconds with a linear dependency to the number of n-grams.

5.3 Qualitative Evaluation

To evaluate our approach qualitatively, we consider a small set of STIX packages from the *Stuxnet* and *Regin* attack campaigns. Such highly targeted APTs are characterized by disparate indicators of compromise and are typically very elusive to identify. Stuxnet, for instance, which was initially discovered in 2010, is a sophisticated malware developed by west state-nations in order to sabotage the nuclear program of Iran. After remaining undetected for some time, its uncontrolled propagation through several attack vectors led to the identification of different variants in systems worldwide [22, 34]. The Regin trojan, on the other hand, is an advanced espionage tool that was used to surveil several companies and government entities including the European Council. Due to its stealth techniques, different variants of the malware remained unnoticed for several years until their discovery in 2011 [19, 35].

Thus, we evaluate the performance of our method when the analyst tries to retrieve such indicators from among more generic threat data. After loading a set of 31 and 10 STIX reports of the *Stuxnet* and *Regin* campaigns, respectively, we measure the mean average precision of the results when objects from these campaigns are used as queries. Additionally, we compare our method with the performance of searches based on exact fact matchings, as this type of retrieval strategy is the default approach used in threat intelligence engines and standard databases.

Table 3 shows the number of APT reports and objects loaded into the system in relation to the total number of objects present in the platform. Thus, in Figure 8, each column indicates the MAP over all queries when similarity is measured through a specific type of object hash. The objects from the *Stuxnet* APT are retrieved with a MAP over 85% for subgraph-, node- and fact-based queries, while in the case of the Regin APT, fact-based queries allow to retrieve correct results with a MAP of 79%. Unlike in the previous case, the complexity of larger queries like subgraphs and nodes, do not compensate in average for the small numbers of objects present in the database, making simpler fact queries more effective. Furthermore and as shown by the baseline performance, queries based on the similarity of objects in attributed graphs offer a more effective alternative than generic searches based on exact matchings of facts.

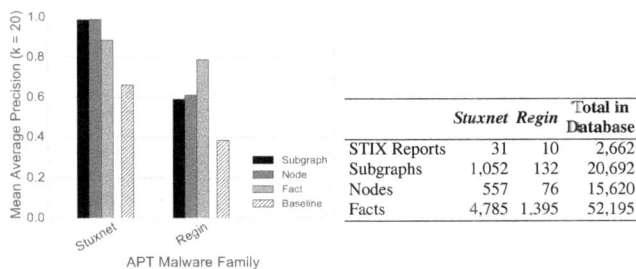

	Stuxnet	Regin	Total in Database
STIX Reports	31	10	2,662
Subgraphs	1,052	132	20,692
Nodes	557	76	15,620
Facts	4,785	1,395	52,195

Figure 8 & Table 3: MAP for query objects of APT families and comparison with baseline performance of standard search engines based on exact strings matching. Raw APT dataset indexed by MANTIS.

6. LIMITATIONS

The previous evaluation demonstrates the efficacy of MANTIS and our method to provide relevant similarity-based results for threat data queries. However, there exist certain limitations.

First, search results are always bounded to the data present in the system when a query is issued so an object cannot be retrieved if it has not been imported. Although an inherent limitation of every threat intelligence platform, this can be a disadvantage if an actor executes a highly targeted attack. In such a situation, it is likely that the attack will not be documented and become part of a repository or feed of threat data. For such events where no correlation is possible, reactive solutions like intrusion detection or behavioral analysis can be more effective to prevent and thwart the attack. Second, as other systems that aim at analyzing threat data,

MANTIS is also subject to possible evasion attacks. For instance, an actor targeting an organization could use several types of attacks as part of a unique but large campaign. If such attacks are chosen to be different enough, it is possible that the events can not be linked to each other through our similarity analysis, even if each one of them is well documented. Finally, our method compares n-grams and therefore determines similarity at a lexical level. This can lead to false positives when unrelated objects share certain n-grams. Yet, as described in Section 4.1, this type of feature representation enables to correlate heterogeneous data even when the standard is used incorrectly or the type of the data is unknown like, for example, in the case of binary strings that are part of indicators of compromise.

7. RELATED WORK

The body of work addressing threat intelligence issues has seen a surge in recent years thanks to the development of new sharing formats. Interestingly however, almost no previous work has been concerned with unifying and comparing the data described through different standards, as we do in this paper. Yet, some active and relevant areas exist that explore related research questions:

Threat intelligence. As discussed by Barnum [1], the community effort to design and extend the STIX format constitutes the most relevant and recent work to define a language that can add context and represent threat information in a structured and holistic way. Being this a recent development, current academic research is yet trying to understand the ecosystem of threat intelligence data by creating taxonomies and models [3]. Most researchers recognize the benefits of these technologies but their focus still lies on the design and implementation of efficient sharing systems [20, 31, 33] and the privacy implications resulting from distributing sensitive security data across heterogeneous organizations [10, 15]. Moreover, practitioners acknowledge the potential improvements for situational awareness [11, 27] that comes from the sharing, storage and analysis of threat data but also the difficulty to ensure consistent interpretation without the need of the analyst. Kampanakis [18], for example, presents an analysis of all the standards under current development and points to the underestimated challenge of data collection and automatic analysis. This is the exactly the field of operation of MANTIS. Most approaches in this direction stem from non-academic initiatives and are being developed both by the security community and by vendors like Microsoft [13], which holds large amounts of security data from its customers. For instance, the open-source framework CRITS [7] presents some resemblance to MANTIS. In particular, bucket lists and relationships can be assigned to top level objects in order to identify campaigns and attributions. However, these assignments need to be done manually by the analyst whereas finding such correlations and matchings automatically is precisely the main goal of our method. Finally, Woods et al. [41] have recently proposed a system to infer similarity relationships and functional clusters of indicators using information about reporting patterns. Although close to our work in its goal and methodology, their approach relies on data not based on standardized open formats.

Information retrieval for security. Tangential to our research is the field of information retrieval which covers a huge body of previous research and work. For brevity, we herein consider only previous research which like ours, makes use of information retrieval and data mining techniques for solving security problems. In particular, there exist several authors that deal with the question of how to efficiently detect and analyze new malware variants which have been submitted to application stores or analysis platforms by analyzing the output reports of their dynamic and static analysis [e.g., 2, 4, 14, 17]. For example, Graziano et al. [14] make use of ssdeep fuzzy hashes and code-based features to cluster malware binaries and identify new families. Although this approach also tries to identify similar strains of malware their scope is limited to types of malware, where our broader view allow us to pinpoint disconnected elements from the same campaign. Closer to our method is the work introduced in [12], which also aims at finding similarities between graphs, in this case, call graphs extracted from malware samples. Our method, however, differs in that we are not inspecting simple instances of malware, but instead model a global picture of the reported threat data. Another line of security research that has combined information retrieval techniques and analysis of structured data focuses on the identification of similar segments in code of large software projects [21, 29, 38]. In particular, Uddin et al. [38] demonstrate that the simhash algorithm can help detecting similar code regions. While different in scope to our method, their approach also proves the effectiveness of Charikar's algorithm as the basis to implement techniques that can identify similar entities in large repositories of data.

8. CONCLUSION

In this paper we present MANTIS, a system that enables the authoring, collection and, most importantly, the analysis and correlation of threat intelligence data. To the best of our knowledge, MANTIS is the first open-source platform to provide a unified representation of threat data constructs from different standards that allows for assessing the similarity between heterogeneous reports at different levels of granularity regardless of their content, size or structure. The security analyst can initiate a search for similar constructs to a related incident with a query that goes from a simple string to a full report describing a multi-faceted attack.

We evaluate the performance of MANTIS in a series of experiments where given a security incident with a malware family, the similarity search integrated in MANTIS allows to retrieve related objects with a mean average precision of over 80%. That is, 4 out of 5 returned results correspond to the same malware family as the query. Finally and based on data from the attack and espionage campaigns *Stuxnet* and *Regin*, we show how MANTIS can be effectively used to assist the security analyst in the investigation of highly targeted security incidents.

References

[1] S. Barnum. Standardizing cyber threat intelligence information with the structured threat information expression (STIX). Technical report, MITRE Corporation, 2014.

[2] U. Bayer, P. M. Comparetti, C. Hlauschek, C. Kruegel, and E. Kirda. Scalable, behavior-based malware clustering. In *Proc. of Network and Distributed System Security Symposium (NDSS)*, 2009.

[3] E. W. Burger, M. D. Goodman, P. Kampanakis, and K. A. Zhu. Taxonomy model for cyber threat intelligence information exchange technologies. In *Proceedings of the 2014 ACM Workshop on Information Sharing & Collaborative Security*, pages 51–60. ACM, 2014.

[4] S. Chakradeo, B. Reaves, P. Traynor, and W. Enck. Mast: Triage for market-scale mobile malware analysis. In *Proc. of ACM Conference on Security and Privacy in Wireless and Mobile Networks (WISEC)*, 2013.

[5] M. S. Charikar. Similarity estimation techniques from rounding algorithms. In *Proceedings of the thiry-fourth annual ACM symposium on Theory of computing*, pages 380–388. ACM, 2002.

[6] CIF. Collective intelligence framework. http://csirtgadgets.org/collective-intelligence-framework, visited August, 2016.

[7] CRITS. Collaborative research into threats. http://crits.github.io, visited July, 2016.

[8] M. Damashek. Gauging similarity with n-grams: Language-independent categorization of text. *Science*, 267(5199):843–848, 1995.

[9] R. Danyliw, J. Meijer, and Y. Demchenko. The incident object description exchange format (IODEF). Technical report, IETF RFC 5070, 2007.

[10] G. Fisk, C. Ardi, N. Pickett, J. Heidemann, M. Fisk, and C. Papadopoulos. Privacy principles for sharing cyber security data. In *Proceedings of the IEEE International Workshop on Privacy Engineering*, May 2015.

[11] P. Fonash. Using automated cyber threat exchange to turn the tide against ddos. http://rsaconference.com, 2014.

[12] H. Gascon, F. Yamaguchi, D. Arp, and K. Rieck. Structural detection of android malware using embedded call graphs. In *Proceedings of the 2013 ACM workshop on Artificial intelligence and security*, pages 45–54. ACM, 2013.

[13] C. Goodwin, J. P. Nicholas, J. Bryant, K. Ciglic, A. Kleiner, C. Kutterer, A. Massagli, A. Mckay, P. Mckitrick, J. Neutze, T. Storch, and K. Sullivan. A framework for cybersecurity information sharing and risk reduction. Technical report, Microsoft Corporation, 2015.

[14] M. Graziano, D. Canali, L. Bilge, A. Lanzi, and D. Balzarotti. Needles in a haystack: Mining information from public dynamic analysis sandboxes for malware intelligence. In *USENIX*, 2015.

[15] R. W. Hamming. Error-detecting and error-correcting codes. *Bell System Technical Journal*, 29(2):147–160, 1950.

[16] J. L. Hernandez-Ardieta, J. E. Tapiador, and G. Suarez-Tangil. Information sharing models for cooperative cyber defence. In *Cyber Conflict (CyCon), 2013 5th International Conference on*, pages 1–28. IEEE, 2013.

[17] J. Jang, D. Brumley, and S. Venkataraman. Bitshred: feature hashing malware for scalable triage and semantic analysis. In *Proc. of ACM Conference on Computer and Communications Security (CCS)*, pages 309–320, 2011.

[18] P. Kampanakis. Security automation and threat information-sharing options. *Security & Privacy, IEEE*, 12(5):42–51, 2014.

[19] Kaspersky. The Regin Platform: Nation-State Ownage of GSM Networks. Kaspersky Lab, November 2014.

[20] M. Korczynski, A. Hamieh, J. H. Huh, H. Holm, S. R. Rajagopalan, and N. H. Fefferman. DIAMoND: Distributed intrusion/anomaly monitoring for nonparametric detection. In *Proceedings the 24th International Conference on Computer Communications and Networks*, pages 1–8, 2015.

[21] J. Krinke. Identifying similar code with program dependence graphs. In *Proceedings of the Eighth Working Conference on Reverse Engineering (WCRE'01)*, 2001.

[22] R. Langner. Stuxnet: Dissecting a cyberwarfare weapon. *IEEE Security and Privacy*, 9(3), May 2011.

[23] Mandiant. Sophisticated indicators for the modern threat landscape: An introduction to OpenIOC. Technical report, Mandiant Whitepaper, 2013.

[24] Mandiant. APT1: Exposing one of China's cyber espionage units. Technical report, Mandiant Intelligence Center, 2013.

[25] G. S. Manku, A. Jain, and A. Das Sarma. Detecting near-duplicates for web crawling. In *Proceedings of the 16th international conference on World Wide Web*, pages 141–150. ACM, 2007.

[26] C. D. Manning, P. Raghavan, H. Schütze, et al. *Introduction to information retrieval*, volume 1. Cambridge university press Cambridge, 2008.

[27] M. Orlando. Threat intelligence is dead. long live threat intelligence! http://rsaconference.com, 2015.

[28] OTX. Open threat exchange. https://www.alienvault.com/open-threat-exchange, visited August, 2016.

[29] A. Sæbjørnsen, J. Willcock, T. Panas, D. Quinlan, and Z. Su. Detecting code clones in binary executables. In *Proceedings of the Eighteenth International Symposium on Software Testing and Analysis*, 2009.

[30] G. Salton, A. Wong, and C. Yang. A vector space model for automatic indexing. *Communications of the ACM*, 18(11):613–620, 1975.

[31] O. Serrano, L. Dandurand, and S. Brown. On the design of a cyber security data sharing system. In *Proceedings of the ACM Workshop on Information Sharing & Collaborative Security*, pages 61–69. ACM, 2014.

[32] Spamfighter/Der Spiegel. Top german official infected by regin malware. http://www.spamfighter.com/News-19917-Top-German-Official-Infected-by-Regin-Malware.htm, visited August, 2016.

[33] J. Steinberger, A. Sperotto, M. Golling, and H. Baier. How to exchange security events? overview and evaluation of formats and protocols. In *Integrated Network Management (IM), 2015 IFIP/IEEE International Symposium on*, pages 261–269. IEEE, 2015.

[34] Symantec. Stuxnet 0.5: The Missing Link. Symantec Security Response, February 2013.

[35] Symantec. Regin: Top-tier espionage tool enables stealthy surveillance. Symantec Security Response, August 2015.

[36] The Guardian. Uk company's spyware used against bahrain activist. https://www.theguardian.com/world/2013/may/12/uk-company-spyware-bahrain-claim, visited August, 2016.

[37] The New York Times. Computer systems used by clinton campaign are said to be hacked, apparently by russians. http://www.nytimes.com/2016/07/30/us/politics/clinton-campaign-hacked-russians.html, visited August, 2016.

[38] M. S. Uddin, C. K. Roy, K. A. Schneider, and A. Hindle. On the effectiveness of simhash for detecting near-miss clones in large scale software systems. In *WCRE*, 2011.

[39] VirusTotal. https://www.virustotal.com/.

[40] K. Wang, J. Parekh, and S. Stolfo. Anagram: A content anomaly detector resistant to mimicry attack. In *Recent Adances in Intrusion Detection (RAID)*, pages 226–248, 2006.

[41] B. Woods, S. Perl, and B. Lindauer. Data mining for efficient collaborative information discovery categories and subject descriptors. In *Proceedings of the 2nd ACM Workshop on Information Sharing and Collaborative Security*. ACM, 2015.

Decompression Quines and Anti-Viruses

Margaux Canet
Inria
Univ. Grenoble Alpes

Amrit Kumar
Inria
Univ. Grenoble Alpes

Cédric Lauradoux
Inria

Mary-Andréa
Rakotomanga
Inria
Univ. Grenoble Alpes

Reihaneh Safavi-Naini
University of Calgary

ABSTRACT

Data compression is ubiquitous to any information and communication system. It often reduces resources required to store and transmit data. However, the efficiency of compression algorithms also makes them an obvious target for hackers to mount denial-of-service attacks. In this work, we consider *decompression quines*, a specific class of compressed files that decompress to themselves. We analyze all the known decompression quines by studying their structures, and their impact on anti-viruses. Our analysis reveals that most of the anti-viruses do not have a suitable architecture in place to detect decompression quines. Even worse, some of them are vulnerable to denial-of-service attacks exploiting quines. Motivated by our findings, we study several *quine detectors* and propose a new one that exploits the fact that quines and non-quine files do not share the same underlying structure. Our evaluation against different datasets shows that the detector incurs no performance overhead at the expense of a low false positive rate.

Keywords

Compression; Quines; Anti-viruses; Denial-of-Service

1. INTRODUCTION

In a world of digital storage and transmission, the density of information within a piece of data is crucial to any information and communication system. To this end, data compression is a useful tool since it effectively reduces resources required to store and transmit data. The popularity of data compression can be easily judged from a W3C 2016 report which states that 68% of websites on the Internet support compression [18] and hence are capable of sending compressed data over the network.

Use of any effective compression algorithm however also comes with the attached security risks. The so-called *de-*compression bombs also known as the *zip of death* exploit the efficiency of compression algorithms to mount denial-of-service (DoS) attacks. They often target web servers and anti-viruses. Unfortunately, despite the fact that these threats have been known for years, some security products still remain vulnerable [9, 13].

The common definition of a decompression bomb found in the NIST guide [10] or the textbook [11] considers a small innocuous compressed file that decompresses to a gigantic file. A typical example of a decompression bomb is `42.zip`[1] ($\approx$ 42 Kilobytes) that expands to 4.5 Petabytes. When a software attempts to naively decompress such a file, it consumes all the available memory and eventually crashes.

Decompression bombs are not restricted to the previous definition. In fact, they can be far more dangerous. The previous definition is often associated to bombs that decompress to a finite number of files. It is also possible to design bombs that decompress to an infinite number of files. The idea is to target software packages which decompress files recursively in order to recover all the data. In this case, an adversary can submit the bomb to force the software into running an infinite decompression loop. Such bombs can be characterized as a compressed file that decompresses to itself. We call this particular kind of bomb a *decompression quine*. This designation respects the original definition of quines found in Thompson's seminal paper [17]. It is worth noting that a decompression quine can also be viewed as a fixed point of the decompression function.

In this work, we present a comprehensive analysis of the known decompression quines for the DEFLATE [5] algorithm. DEFLATE is currently implemented in several popular compression routines such as `gzip`, `zlib` and `zip` among others. Based on our study of the existing quines, we generalize the idea presented in [2] to create new ones. The generalization allows us to produce an arbitrary quine inexpensively. Additionally, it renders the obvious signature-based detection impossible. We further conduct experiments with several anti-viruses and incident response frameworks and observe that some of them implement a detector which requires several decompressions to identify a quine. To this end, we also propose a new detection scheme for quines. The underlying objective is to design a faster detector than the ad-hoc ones.

We propose a *statistical detector*, where the core idea is to parse compressed files to recover the internal block structure

CODASPY'17 March 22–24, 2017, Scottsdale, AZ, USA
© 2017 ACM. ISBN 978-1-4503-4523-1/17/03. . . $15.00
DOI: http://dx.doi.org/10.1145/3029806.3029818

---

[1]https://www.unforgettable.dk/

of DEFLATE. We also test the performance of our detector against a corpus of compressed files. The results show that the statistical detector is systematically more efficient than the ad-hoc detectors that include a fixed-point detector and a detector based on bounded recursion. The efficiency of our detector comes at the expense of a low false positive rate.

2. RELATED WORK

The first strike of decompression bombs occurred in the 90's with the goal of mounting a DoS attack against Fi-doNet systems [12]. Since then, several different types of decompression bombs have been designed to attack differ-ent services. Decompression bombs can be broadly classified into four types: *single (large) file bombs*, *nested bombs*, *self-reproducing bombs* (decompression quines) and *bogus bombs*.

The basic single file bomb exploits the efficiency of com-pression algorithms: a large file is compressed into a very small file. The website https://bomb.codes provides several examples of such bombs for the most popular compression formats. These compressed files are designed to crash soft-ware applications by consuming all the available memory.

Nested bombs are a composition of single file bombs. They are obtained by using archivers such as zip or tar. An example of a nested bomb is 42.zip. The file has a nested level of 6. Each level other than the last one consists of 16 zipped files. The files at the last level have a size of 4.2 GB.

Self-reproducing bombs or decompression quines are the focus of our work. A (decompression) quine is a compressed file that decompresses to itself. The threat posed by a quine during decompression is that it may force the software ap-plication to fall into an infinite loop and thus create a DoS exploit. The first decompression quine was provided by Cox [2]. The existence of a decompression quine also means that it is possible to find two different compressed files that decompress to the same file: r.gz decompresses to r.gz and so does r.gz.gz. The work by Cox [2] is the starting point of our study and it is analyzed in depth in the next section.

Finally, bogus bombs target errors and bugs in the imple-mentation of the decompression algorithm. In 2005, Chris Evans handcrafted a special bzip2 file (http://scary.beasts.org/misc/bomb.bz2) that causes an infinite loop in the de-compression algorithm of bzip2.

AERAsec Network Services and Security has published the first survey [15] on the threat of decompression bombs. It targets anti-viruses, web browsers and office suites using compressed binary files, compressed HTML and image files (such as PNG). Forensic tools are also an obvious target of decompression bombs. bulk_extractor due to Garfinkel [7] is one of the few tools hardened against this threat. In 2014, Koret [9] repeated the tests of AERAsec on anti-viruses. The author observed that despite the long history of decompres-sion bombs, some anti-viruses were still vulnerable. Pelle-grino *et al.* have discovered in [14] new vulnerabilities re-lated to compression/decompression in HTTP, XMPP and IMAP protocols (server side). More recently at BlackHat 2016, Cara [13] has extended the results of [15] to the most pop-ular image formats and compression formats supported by web browsers.

The countermeasures often mentioned in [9, 13, 14, 15] to thwart decompression bombs is to set two limits. The first limit is on the size of the decompressed file. It protects against single file bombs. The second is to limit the number of times a file can be decompressed. It protects against nested bombs and self-reproducing bombs. These two limits have been used in ARBOMB, the first decompression bomb detector [3].

All the related work on the impact of decompression bombs mainly focus on single file bombs and nested bombs. They however do acknowledge the existence of self-reproducing compressed files by citing the work of Cox [2]. Our goal is to study quines on software applications that allow recursive decompression. This leads to the obvious choice of testing against anti-viruses since they are designed to scan files and directories recursively.

3. DEFLATE QUINES

DEFLATE [5] is a lossless compression algorithm imple-mented in several popular compression routines including gzip, zlib and zip. We note that while, the term INFLATE has been used in the literature to refer to the associated decompression algorithm, in popular use though, the term DEFLATE often subsumes both compression and decompres-sion algorithms. We also abide by the usage of the term DEFLATE to take both denotations.

In this section, we first present an overview of DEFLATE and then in the sequel, we present decompression quines based on DEFLATE.

3.1 Deflate Compression

DEFLATE is based on the LZ77 compression algorithm [19] and the Huffman coding [8]. In fact, LZ77 is the core com-pression algorithm, the output of which is further compressed using Huffman coding.

The idea underpinning LZ77 compression is to find se-quences of data that are repeated. This is implemented in practice by maintaining a record of the previously seen data. To this end, a sliding window is employed. When-ever a next sequence of bytes is identical to one that can be found in the sliding window, the sequence is replaced by a pointer where it can be found in the window. The pointer is of the form <distance,length>. The distance value measures how far back into the window the sequence starts, while length counts the number of bytes for which the sequence is identical. Replacing a long sequence of bytes by a pointer effectively compresses the data sequence.

The DEFLATE specification states that the length value is drawn from [3, 258] while the value for distance is drawn from [1, 32768]. With these parameters, the window size is the maximum distance value, *i.e.*, 32,768 bytes.

Once, the data is compressed using LZ77, the output is coded using Huffman encoding [8]. Two different variants of Huffman coding are available in DEFLATE: static and dy-namic (briefly discussed below).

Compressed data in DEFLATE are grouped into blocks. There are three types of blocks depending upon the kind of compression applied to the data included into it:

- **Uncompressed blocks (STORED)**. Such a block is com-posed of a 2-byte field which contains the number of data bytes in the block. Another adjacent 2-byte field stores the one's complement of the previous field used to validate the length. This is followed by the uncom-pressed data. We note that no compression whatsoever (not even LZ77) is applied on the data. Uncompressed blocks are limited to 65,535 bytes.

- **Compressed blocks with a static Huffman code** (STATIC). The code is defined using several fixed tables. It is to note that the Huffman coded data is pre-compressed using LZ77.

- **Compressed blocks with a dynamic Huffman code** (DYNAMIC). The file is parsed during runtime to create a frequency table of symbols. The data is then encoded with this specific table. The block first contains this table that is needed for decompression, which is followed by the compressed data and finally the literal 256 encoded using the table to mark the end of the block. Again, the data in these blocks are pre-compressed using LZ77.

Each block starts with a 3-bit header. The bits are read from right to left (Big endian encoding). When the first bit of the header is set to one, it indicates that this is the last block of the file. The last two bits of the header are used to specify the block type: uncompressed block (00), static Huffman compressed (01) or dynamic Huffman compressed (10). The compression algorithm terminates a block when it determines that starting a new block would be useful, or when the block size fills up the compression block buffer. The DEFLATE algorithm has been implemented in different compression routines such as gzip and zip. Each routine implements its own algorithm to determine which block type needs to be used.

3.2 Quines

A *quine* (native to programming languages) is defined as a self-reproducing program, *i.e.*, when executed, the program should generate an output that is identical to its source code. To some extent, a compressed file can also be seen as a program which outputs a result, *i.e.*, the corresponding decompressed file. Hence, a quine for a decompression algorithm is a compressed file which decompresses to itself.

In fact, there is a subtle difference between a regular program and a compressed file. It stems from the fact that the source code of a regular program can be a simple text file, while a compressed file most certainly has a well defined header and a footer (See Appendix A for different file format specifications). The header and footer are required for the file to be correctly interpreted during decompression. For a compressed file, let us use H to denote the header and F for the footer. Using these notations, the actual source code in the context of a decompression quine is the compressed data that lies between H and F.

We note that a quine must generate the same header and the same footer upon decompression. However, when decompression is applied on a quine, the header and the footer part are eventually removed and only the code part gets decompressed (or in other words gets executed). As a consequence, for a decompression quine to be valid, the code part must generate itself and in addition it should also generate the header and the footer.

3.2.1 The LZ77 Language

The reason behind the existence of a quine is that the underlying compression algorithm can be viewed as a pseudo language with a small set of instructions. In fact, the task of constructing a quine essentially reduces to the task of identifying the underlying language. In this section, we present the LZ77 language due to Cox [2]. The language forms the

core of any known quines based on DEFLATE. The language has two instructions:

- literal(n) followed by n bytes: write these n bytes as the output. For instance, literal(3)foo → foo.

- repeat(d,n) which represents a <distance,length> pointer: copy the n bytes found d bytes backward from the current position of the output to the output. For instance, if the output at a given instant is: incant abracad, then repeat(7,4) → incant abracadabra.

In the rest of this section, we use the notation **Ln** for literal(n), **Rd,n** for repeat(d,n) and **Rn** for repeat(n,n). The operator **L0** is also used but gives no output. It should be apparent that LZ77 compression indeed builds upon the afore-described instructions. In fact, an **Ln** instruction represents a non-compressed data, while an **Rn/Rd,n** instruction represents a compressed data. The values d, n correspond to the <distance,length> pointers of the LZ77 compression.

The language can be used to write the code part of a DEFLATE generated compressed file and for that matter an LZ77 quine. Once, the desired code part is found, a suitable header and footer pair can be manually plugged into the file. We note that the language completely ignores the Huffman encoding that is applied atop LZ77 compression, hence it cannot exactly be considered as a well constructed DEFLATE compressed file. As a matter of fact, constructing a deflate quine essentially boils down to constructing a LZ77 quine. This is because, once an LZ77 quine is found, the data can then be easily grouped into blocks and appropriate Huffman coding can be applied. Hence, in the rest of the discussion we neither consider the block structure of DEFLATE nor the Huffman coding.

EXAMPLE 1. *We now present a simple example to illustrate the basic idea to generate a quine in this language. It is given in Table 1. The example presents a code that generates itself without the header and the footer. After the execution of the first instruction, the output lags behind the code by one instruction (since the execution of $L0$ yields nothing). After executing the second instruction, this lag increases to two instructions. The lag remains unchanged after the third instruction. The fourth instruction reduces the lag back to one. The interesting core of this self-producing code is the instruction number five, $L4\ R4,3\ L4\ R4,3\ L4$, which is in fact a palindrome. The palindrome property of the instruction allows it to recurse back to a previously appeared instruction of the output. It is evident that any Ln instruction increases the lag while any Rd,n decreases it.*

In the following section, we present a complete construction for a known quine which includes the necessary header and footer.

3.2.2 Known Quines

Currently, we know six quines for compressed files which use DEFLATE:

1. droste.zip[2]: a zip quine,

2. r.gz: a gzip quine proposed by Russ Cox [2]. It uses the same general construction as r.tar.gz and r.zip,

---

[2]https://alf.nu/ZipQuine

25

Table 1: A simple example of a quine code. Both the instructions **Ln** and **Rd,n** require 1 byte. In bold, the arguments of the **Ln** instruction. Note that the columns Code and Code Output have the same byte sequence.

Comment	Code	Code Output
1. `print nothing`	L0	
2. `print 4 bytes L0 L4 L0 L4`	L4 **L0 L4 L0 L4**	L0 L4 L0 L4
3. `print nothing`	L0	
4. `go 4 bytes back in the output and repeat the next 3 bytes`	R4,3	L0 L4 L0
5. `print 4 bytes R4,3 L4 R4,3 L4`	L4 **R4,3 L4 R4,3 L4**	R4,3 L4 R4,3 L4
6. `go 4 bytes back in the output and repeat the next 3 bytes`	R4,3	R4,3 L4 R4,3

Table 2: Quine construction for `rec_fix.gz`. H is a header of length 18 bytes, F a footer of length 8 bytes and **FP** are free bytes of length 4. **Ln** is encoded using 5 bytes while **Rd,n** using 3 bytes. In bold, the arguments of the **Ln** instruction.

Comment	Code	Code Output
1. `print 23 bytes H (18 bytes) L23 (5 bytes)`	L23 **H L23**	H L23
2. `go 23 bytes back in the output and repeat the next 15 bytes`	R23,15	H[1..15]
3. `print 16 bytes H[16..18] (3 bytes) L23 (5 bytes) R23,15 (3 bytes) L16 (5 bytes)`	L16 **H[16..18] L23 R23,15 L16**	H[16..18] L23 R23,15 L16
4. `repeat the 16 previous bytes of the output`	R16	H[16..18] L23 R23,15 L16
5. `print 16 bytes R16 (3 bytes) L16 (5 bytes) R16 (3 bytes) L16 (5 bytes)`	L16 **R16 L16 R16 L16**	R16 L16 R16 L16
6. `repeat the 16 previous bytes`	R16	R16 L16 R16 L16
7. `print 16 bytes FP (4 bytes) R12 (3 bytes) 00 (1 byte) F (8 bytes)`	L16 **FP R12 00 F**	FP R12 00 F
8. `repeat the 12 previous bytes`	R12	R12 00 F
9. `add extra padding`	00 (Padding)	

3. `r.tar.gz`: a tarball quine proposed by Russ Cox. It has the same construction as `r.gz` and `r.zip`,

4. `r.zip`: a zip quine proposed by Russ Cox. It has the same construction as `r.gz` and `r.tar.gz`,

5. `rec_fix.gz`: a **gzip** quine proposed by Mahaly Barasz (as a part of comments given on [2]). It contains free bytes which can take any value and yet remain a quine,

6. `rec_tst.gz`: a gzip quine very similar to `r.gz`, with `rec_tst.gz` in the filename option to replace **recursive** as in `r.gz`. It also comes from the comments given on [2].

We note that there exist some quine variants such as the file `rec_dup.gz` (see the comment section of [2]). The file is an "*ever expanding quine*" in the sense that the file upon decompression generates a `.gz` file twice the size of the original file. Hence, if a recursive decompression is applied on the initial file, at each recursion step, one obtains a file twice as large as the file at the previous recursion step.

In this section, we focus on the construction used in the quine `rec_fix.gz`. The construction of other quines essentially follows the same pattern. It assumes that the **Ln** instruction is coded using 5 bytes and the **Rd,n** instruction using 3 bytes. It is also assumed that we have a header H of 18 bytes and a footer F of 8 bytes. The header and footer size respect the `.gz` file format (details on the header and footer specifications can be found in Appendix A).

In order to present the code in a readable form, we further use the shorthand **H[i..j]** to collectively represent all the $(j - i + 1)$ bytes between the ith and the jth byte of the header H. The notation **FP** is used to denote the four free bytes available in `rec_fix.gz`. We recall that free bytes can take any value while maintaining the quine property. The quine construction is shown in Table 2.

One can easily verify that the output sequence is exactly the same as that of the content in the code except that the output additionally has the header H in the beginning and the footer F at the end. To understand how the construction works, one may notice that at the first instruction, the output lags behind the code by **H L23**. In the second instruction, the output is behind by the sequence **H[16..18] L23 R23,15**. The next two instructions allow the output to catch up on this delay. This is followed by a succession of **R16 L16** which reverses the situation with the code behind the output. At the end, we have the code and the output at the same point with the footer in addition (in the output). The padding is used to have enough bytes for the seventh instruction. Even, in this complete construction, the palindrome **L16 R16 L16 R16 L16** in the fifth instruction plays a crucial role.

3.2.3 A Generalization

The problem with the previous quine construction is the constraint that the header must be 18 bytes long. We propose in this section a natural generalization to this construction for a header of any arbitrary length.

First, we define p the length of the header H and k an integer such that $k = p - 3$. In fact, the header must be of a length greater than 3 bytes (due to the file format specification, see Appendix A for further detail), hence we have $p \geq 3$. The generalized quine construction is given in Table 3. As in the previous construction, the **Ln** instruction must be coded using 5 bytes, while, the **Rd,n** instruction using 3 bytes.

4. QUINES VERSUS ANTI-VIRUSES

All the quines presented in the previous section were tested on three online anti-virus aggregators (Virus Total, Jotti and VirScan), on two incident response frameworks (Mas-

Table 3: Construction for the generalization of rec_fix.gz. H is a header of length p bytes, F a footer of length 8 bytes and **FP** are free bytes of length 4. **Ln** is encoded using 5 bytes while **Rd,n** using 3 bytes. In bold, the arguments of the **Ln** instruction.

Comment	Code	Code Output
1. print p+5 bytes H (p bytes) L23 (5 bytes)	Lp+5 **H Lp+5**	H Lp+5
2. go p+5 bytes back in the output and repeat the next k bytes	Rp+5,k	H[1..k]
3. print 16 bytes H[k+1..p] (3 bytes) Lp+5 (p+5 bytes) Rp+5,k (3 bytes) L16 (5 bytes)	L16 **H[k+1..p] Lp+5 Rp+5,k L16**	H[k+1..p] Lp+5 Rp+5,k L16
4. repeat the 16 previous bytes of the output	R16	H[k+1..p] Lp+5 Rp+5,k L16
5. print 16 bytes R16 (3 bytes) L16 (5 bytes) R16 (3 bytes) L16 (5 bytes)	L16 **R16 L16 R16 L16**	R16 L16 R16 L16
6. repeat the 16 previous bytes	R16	R16 L16 R16 L16
7. print 16 bytes FP (4 bytes) R12 (3 bytes) 00 (1 byte) F (8 bytes)	L16 **FP R12 00 F**	FP R12 00 F
8. repeat the 12 previous bytes	R12	R12 00 F
9. add extra padding	00 (Padding)	

tiff v0.7.1 and Viper v0.12.9) and on several anti-viruses (see Table 4 and Table 5). The tests were conducted in August 2016.

Online anti-virus aggregators allow a user to submit files to be checked by several anti-viruses. Our goal was to determine if quines were detected by anti-viruses and if yes, identify the method employed.

VirusTotal (www.virustotal.com) is operated by Google and it aggregates 54 anti-viruses. It is by far the most popular online anti-virus aggregator. Jotti (virusscan.jotti.org) and VirScan (www.virscan.org) aggregate 19 and 39 anti-viruses respectively. The information on the different anti-viruses including their version are available for VirScan. It is important to note that aggregators may use a common anti-virus but not necessarily the same version. This may eventually produce inconsistent behavior across the aggregators for the same anti-virus.

The result of the submission of the quine to the aggregators and incident response frameworks is given in Table 4. We first observe that quines are detected only by a few anti-viruses. Let us first start with the **zip** quine droste.zip. This quine is detected as a decompression bomb by **Sophos**, **ESET** in VirusTotal and Jotti. **Qihoo 360** also detects it in Jotti and VirScan. The second quine tested was **r.zip**. It is only detected by **Sophos** in Jotti only and not by **ESET** and **Qihoo 360**. **Sophos** being used by all the aggregators, we observe an inconsistent behavior which might be caused by the different setups or versions of the anti-virus.

At this step of our analysis, we may conclude that **Qihoo 360** and **ESET** employ a signature-based detection. These anti-viruses maintain a list of signatures of known bombs and check whether a given file has a signature that belongs to the list. **Zoner** (for VirusTotal) and **F-Secure** (for Jotti) are not able to provide an analysis for both files (53 answers out of 54 for VirusTotal and 18 out of 19 for Jotti). It means that they can be a potential victim of a decompression quine.

In the second step of our analysis, we look at **gzip** quines. Most of the time, all the gzip quines are declared as safe. **Sophos** in Jotti is the only anti-virus that identifies all **gzip** quines except **r.tar.gz**. A possible explanation behind why **Sophos** misses **r.tar.gz** could be that the **tar** archive format is not well supported by most anti-viruses. Otherwise, **Sophos** detects decompression quines in a consistent way. To understand how it works, we took a safe file and compressed it several times. We submitted the resulting compressed

Table 4: Quine detection by anti-virus aggregators and incident response frameworks. x/y means that x out of y anti-viruses detected the file as a quine. ✓ for detecting the file as a quine, while ✗ for not doing so. ∞ implies that the tool ran an infinite recursion loop.

Quine	Agregators and Frameworks				
	VirusTotal	Jotti	VirScan	Mastiff	Viper
droste.zip	3/53	2/18	1/39	∞	✗
r.zip	0/53	1/18	0/39	∞	✗
rec_tst.gz	0/54	1/19	0/39	✗	✗
rec_fix.gz	0/54	1/19	0/39	✗	✗
r.tar.gz	0/54	0/19	0/39	✗	✗
r.gz	0/54	1/19	0/39	✗	✓

file to Jotti. It appears that after compressing the file 6 times, **Sophos** declared it to be a decompression bomb. We can safely assume that the decompression bomb detector in **Sophos** is similar to the Python code provided in Code 1.

Code 1: Quine detector with a recursion bound.

```python
#!/usr/bin/python

import sys
import zlib

magic_nb="\x1f\x8b\x08"
MAX=6

def uncompress(data,depth):
    if data.startswith(magic_nb) and depth<MAX:
        original=zlib.decompress(data,zlib.
            MAX_WBITS|16)
        uncompress(original,depth+1)
    else:
        if depth>=MAX:
            print "Quine"
            sys.exit()
        else:
            return data

with open(sys.argv[1]) as f:
    data=f.read()
    uncompress(data,0)
    f.close()
```

We also analyzed a malware analysis tool named yextend[3] that is based on YARA[4] — a pattern matching tool to analyze malware files. yextend employs a detector identical to Code 1 to identify decompression bombs. The default recursion bound is set to 42 but can be tuned by the end user. It is pertinent to note that YARA is also used by VirusTotal.

Table 4 also provides the result on incident response frameworks. It appears that Mastiff recursively decompresses zip files (but not gzip files). droste.zip and r.zip are both decompressed infinitely many times by Mastiff. The only positive detection obtained was by Viper for r.gz.

We have also directly studied the behavior of 12 anti-viruses on a computer running Microsoft Windows 10 (see Table 5 for the list).

Table 5: Impact of quines on several anti-viruses running on Microsoft Windows 10. ✗ denotes that the tool could not detect the quine, while ∞ denotes that the tool most probably ran into an infinite recursion.

Anti-viruses	Version	Six quines tested
Ad-Aware	11.12.945.9202	✗
Avast	12.2.2276	✗
Avira	15.0.18.354	✗
AVG	16.101.7752	✗
Baidu	5.4.3.147185	✗
ClamWin	0.99.1	✗
Comodo	8.4.0.5068	✗
FortiClient	5.00233	✗
Panda	16.1.3	∞
Smadav	10.8	✗
Trend Micro	10.0.1150	✗
Windows Defender	1.225.361.0	✗

The results remain very similar to those observed on anti-virus aggregators: quines are largely undetected. The only notable result is that during the analysis of each quine on Panda, the anti-virus always indicated a scanned file of around 2000 bytes (but often different at each run) before a complete crash of the software.

In conclusion, quines are largely undetected by most anti-viruses. Several of them including the framework Mastiff, anti-viruses Panda, Zoner (from VirusTotal) and F-Secure are still vulnerable to quines. Sophos has the most rational method to detect quines while Qihoo 360 and ESET only employ signatures of known quines as a detection tool.

5. QUINE DETECTORS

As seen in the previous section, anti-viruses in general do not have a suitable architecture in place to detect quines. The limited few which do detect quines either employ a signature based technique or recursively decompress with a pre-defined or configurable bound on the depth. Our quine generalization of Table 3 clearly defeats any signature based detector. A naive recursive decompression with bounded depth is however inefficient as it requires several calls to the decompression routine. Moreover, it also entails false positives. In this section, we study several ad-hoc detectors and propose a new one.

5.1 Employing Memoization

Dynamic programming techniques and particularly memoization can improve the efficiency of a recursive decompression detector. In fact, memoization can avoid requiring to decompress multiple times the same file. The idea is to memoize the hash of a compressed file and whenever a new file needs to be decompressed, its hash is first checked in the memo table (which also stores a pointer to the decompressed file). If the hash has been previously seen, the extra decompression can be avoided by replicating the previously decompressed data.

Memoization is ideal for nested bombs such as 42.zip. This technique has indeed been employed in practice (see [7] for a use case). It can also reduce the number of decompressions to detect a quine in Code 1. However, it increases (depending on the implementation) the memory cost or the CPU cost for non-quine files without any additional benefit (the extra computation are unlikely to be reused). Furthermore, since memoization is based on identifying identical piece of compressed data, it can easily be made useless by creating bombs where internal files differ by a byte.

Since hashing is the core primitive of a memoization based detector, we compare the efficiency of decompression and hashing. Our implementation is in Python and it uses gzip as the compression routine and SHA-256 as the hash function. The tests were performed on a 64-bit processor laptop computer powered by an Intel Core i7-4600U CPU at 2.10GHz with 4MB cache, 8GB RAM and running Linux 3.13.0-36-generic. We employ the same machine throughout this paper.

We conduct tests on three datasets. Our first dataset includes two standard lossless data compression corpora namely, *Silesia* [4] and *Canterbury* [1]. These corpora provide datasets of files that cover the typical data types used in practice and hence are useful to test compression algorithms. The Canterbury corpus is an old corpus dating back to 1997. The corpus contains 11 files of sizes less than 1 MB. The more recent Silesia corpus on the other hand contains larger files, between 5 MB to 49 MB. A summary of the contents of these corpora is given in Appendix C. The dataset also includes some other files available on the Canterbury corpus webpage[5]. In total, the first dataset contains 44 files. The second dataset is a set of 1071 files filled with random bytes. Files in the dataset have increasing sizes starting from 1KB to 50MB. The third dataset contains the same number of files having the same sizes, but are filled with 0x00. In order to compare the efficiency of hashing and decompression, we first compress the files in each dataset using gzip, and measure the time required to decompress the output; the time to hash the compressed file and the time required to hash the decompressed file.

In Fig. 1, we plot the time to hash the compressed file and the time to hash the decompressed file as a percentage of the time required for decompression. We observe that 13% of the files from the first dataset require more time to hash the uncompressed file than decompression. Hashing a compressed file is relatively cheaper yet entails a considerable percentage of the decompression time. In fact, around 34% of the uncompressed files require a hashing time which is over 25% of the decompression time. As for the second dataset, all uncompressed files starting from 13 KB require

---

[3]https://github.com/BayshoreNetworks/yextend
[4]http://virustotal.github.io/yara/
[5]http://corpus.canterbury.ac.nz

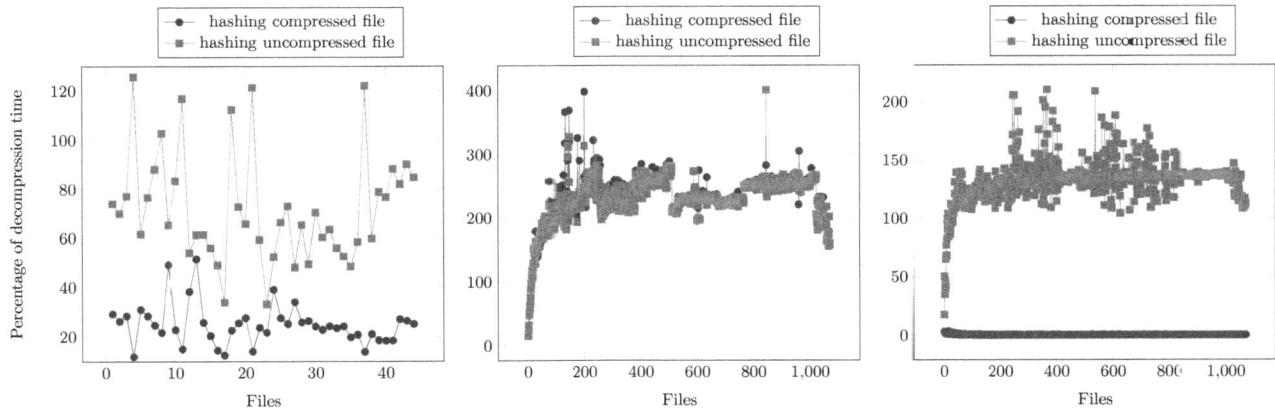

(a) Files from compression corpora.   (b) Files filled with random bytes.   (c) Files filled with zero bytes.

Figure 1: Comparison of time required to decompress a file, time to compute the hash of a compressed file and the time to compute the hash of a decompressed file. The files in all the three figures are sorted in the increasing order of the size. The reported data is the average over 1000 runs.

more time to hash than the time required to decompress the file. Similarly, all compressed files starting from 11 KB require more time to hash than the time required to decompress the file. As for the third dataset, we observe that all uncompressed files starting from 15 KB require more time to hash than the time required to decompress the file. Hashing compressed files however requires a negligible percentage of the decompression time.

These experiments clearly demonstrate that hashing often incurs a considerable cost compared to decompression. Hence, any detector should carefully use hashing to avoid introducing any overhead. In the next sections, we study two detectors specific to quine detection: *fixed-point detector* and *statistical detector*.

5.2 Fixed-point Detector

The first obvious decompression quine detector consists in checking whether a given compressed file is a fixed point of the decompression function. This requires decompressing the file and checking for equality between the compressed file and the decompressed file. Clearly, a fixed-point detector entails no false positives. A Python code for this detector is given in Code 2. It basically decompresses the file and then checks if the compressed and the decompressed files have the same size. If the files have the same size, it computes their SHA-256 digests to check the equality of their contents.

Code 2: The fixed-point detector

```
#!/usr/bin/python

import sys
import gzip
import hashlib

with open(sys.argv[1],'rb') as f:
    compress=f.read()
with gzip.open(sys.argv[1],'rb') as g:
    uncompress=g.read()
if len(compress)==len(uncompress):
    dc=hashlib.sha256(compress).digest()
    du=hashlib.sha256(uncompress).digest()
    if dc==du:
        print "Quine"
    else:
        print "Safe"
else:
    print "Safe"
```

We note that the step in Code 2 that consists in comparing the file sizes is critical for the performance of the detector. In fact, due to the efficiency of the compression algorithm, the decompressed file can be several order larger than the compressed one. For instance, in case of gzip, the compression ratio can be as high as 1032:1. Therefore, the computation of the SHA-256 digest of the decompressed file can be very costly. The a priori comparison of the file sizes eliminates costly digest computations for compressed files which are not quines.

The detector is very simple and performs well on most of the files it may encounter. However, there exists a class of compressed files for which it is rather inefficient. It is a class of large files for which the compressed and decompressed files are of the same size. In this case, the computation of the SHA-256 digests is unfortunately costly. Such files can be easily generated in practice by taking an arbitrarily large non-compressed file say example.txt. The file is then compressed to obtain example.gz. Let us assume that the size of example.gz is smaller than that of example.txt by k bytes. One can then change the field FNAME that stores the uncompressed filename in example.gz to add the remaining k bytes (see Appendix A for further details on the FNAME field). It is to note that such a file remains a valid .gz file. We followed this strategy to generate a 10 GB file. Hashing the compressed and the uncompressed files took around 1m40s using the bash sha256sum utility. Clearly, the time spent by the detector can be made arbitrarily large by choosing the initial file of suitable size.

We also note that the fixed-point detector is not capable of detecting quine variants such as rec_dup.gz — a file that recursively doubles its size upon decompression.

In the next section, we study another detector that does

not require a hash function and takes a decision based on the ratio of the number of different block types (`stored`, `static` and `dynamic`). It is also capable of detecting quine variants such as `rec_dup.gz`.

5.3 Statistical Detector

We propose a new detector which assumes that a legitimate compression software cannot produce a quine. In case of a quine the block structure (the type of the block — stored, static or dynamic, and their order) is manually chosen by a human, while, compression algorithms apply their own heuristics to decide on the blocks.

In order to illustrate the idea, let us consider the case of the quine `rec_fix.gz`. The file has a size of 130 bytes. If we compress it using either `gzip 1.2.4` or `zlib 1.2.8`, we obtain a compressed file with a single `static` block. However, `rec_fix.gz` itself is composed of 8 blocks as shown in Fig. 2, where, `stored` (uncompressed) and `static` blocks alternate. Moreover, there are no dynamic blocks. The block structure of other quines is left to Appendix B.

Figure 2: Structure of `rec_fix.gz`. The black blocks represent the header and the footer of the `.gz` file. The gray blocks correspond to `stored` (uncompressed) blocks and the light gray are compressed with the static Huffman table (`static` blocks).

To exploit the difference between the output of a legitimate compression algorithm and the manual design of quines, we directly analyze their block structure and study the statistics of block types. We use the following notation to denote the number of different block types:

- U : number of uncompressed blocks;
- S : number of static Huffman blocks;
- D : number of dynamic Huffman blocks;
- T : the total number of blocks (*i.e.*, $T = U + S + D$).

In order to study the block structure of compressed files, we use an instrumented version of the `gzip` compression routine. The instrumented version is obtained by modifying the source code such that the decompression routine jumps to the start of each block, and decodes the block type from the block header. It is to note that the instrumented code does not need to write the decompressed data to the disk. All modifications are limited to the `inflate.c` file available in the `gzip` source code package (version 1.2.4) for Linux. A similar instrumented library was obtained from the `zlib` library for Linux (version 1.2.8).

Using our instrumented `gzip` routine, we obtain the number of each block type in all the existing quines. Table 6 summarizes our findings. It is worth noticing that dynamic blocks are quite rare. Table 6, also shows the different ratios for quines, namely U/T, S/T and D/T. As for U/T, results vary from 0.5 to 0.66 for all files except one, `droste.zip`. In a similar vein, all files except `r.zip` have a S/T ratio larger than 0.35, while all files except `droste.zip` have a D/T ratio of 0. Clearly, these ratios are less homogeneous for `.zip` files, since they also perform archiving and hence the headers are much more complex than `.gz` files.

We hence propose a statistical detector that consists in using the instrumented code to compute the ratios and reporting a compressed file as potentially dangerous if it yields

Table 6: Block structures of quines.

Quine	U	S	D	T	U/T	S/T	D/T
`droste.zip`	27	75	1	102	0.26	0.73	0.01
`r.zip`	12	6	0	18	0.67	0.33	0
`rec_fix.gz`	4	4	0	8	0.5	0.5	0
`rec_tst.gz`	11	6	0	17	0.64	0.36	0
`r.gz`	11	6	0	17	0.64	0.36	0
`r.tar.gz`	13	7	0	20	0.65	0.35	0
`rec_dup.gz`	6	5	0	20	0.55	0.45	0

a U/T ratio larger than or equal to 0.5, or an S/T ratio larger than or equal to 0.35. The detector comes with the eventual possibility of having false positives.

In the rest of this section, we evaluate our statistical detector for false positives. To this end, we conduct experiments to study the block structure of safe files. In order to have a set of safe files, we have built a dataset of 3655 files from gnu.org. It includes the source code of the different versions of 338 software packages. We also include the data compression corpora Silesia and Canterbury.

All the safe files and the files in the corpora were first compressed using `gzip v1.2.4` with default parameters and then their block structure was determined using the instrumented version of the `gzip` source code. Fig. 3 provides the statistics on the block types for these files. The first three plots Fig. 3a, Fig. 3b and Fig. 3c present results on the 3655 files harvested from gnu.org, while the last three plots Fig. 3d, Fig. 3e and Fig. 3f present combined results for the Canterbury and Silesia corpora.

We observe that only three files from the GNU dataset (Fig. 3a, Fig. 3b and Fig. 3c) have a U/T ratio larger than 0.5. One of these files has a U/T ratio as high as 0.64, the same as that of `rec_tst.gz` and `r.gz`. Moreover, 89% of the files from the GNU dataset have a U/T ratio of 0. This shows that the `gzip` compression routine rarely includes an uncompressed block. As for the S/T ratio, only one file surpasses the quine bound of 0.35. This file yields an S/T ratio of 0.5. Again, 99.7% of the files do not contain any `static` block. As for D/T, all files have a ratio larger than 0.37. Hence, the overall false positive rate for this dataset is $4/3655 = 0.001$.

We observe even better results with Canterbury and Silesia corpora (Fig. 3d, Fig. 3e and Fig. 3f). Only one file out of a total of 23 has a non-zero U/T ratio of 0.0006 (yet much smaller than the quine bound of 0.5). As for S/T, all files yield a ratio of 0. And all files except one have a D/T ratio of 1; the file has a D/T ratio of 0.999. These results show that all the files from the corpora except one generate a single dynamic block that contains all the compressed data. Hence, the overall false positive rate is 0.

The experiments with the datasets show that the detector is quite efficient in terms of false positives. In the following section, we present a limitation that creates a potential to influence the false positive rate of the detector.

5.3.1 Limitation

The DEFLATE specification [5] allows a compression routine implementing the algorithm to choose a heuristic to decide on the block structure. That is, each compression routine may decide on 1) when to create a new block 2) the type of block to create. Clearly, compressing using different heuristics may produce different statistics on the blocks.

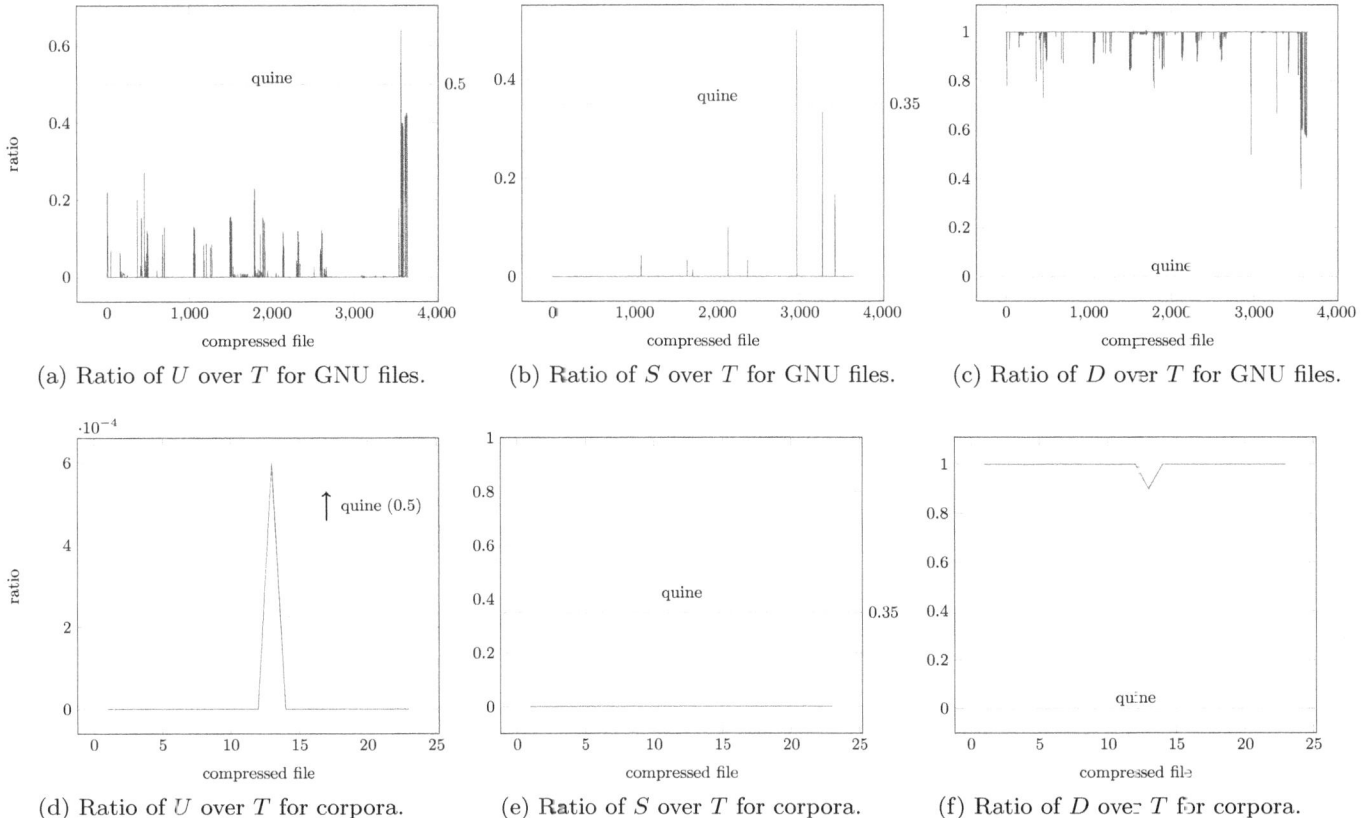

(a) Ratio of U over T for GNU files. (b) Ratio of S over T for GNU files. (c) Ratio of D over T for GNU files.

(d) Ratio of U over T for corpora. (e) Ratio of S over T for corpora. (f) Ratio of D over T for corpora.

Figure 3: Distribution of blocks for safe files. The first three plots present results on the 3655 files harvested from gnu.org, while the last three plots present combined results for the Canterbury and Silesia corpora.

Hence, it is possible to come up with a heuristic that may influence the false positive rate of our detector. For instance, one may apply a heuristic to increase the number of uncompressed blocks such that the ratio U/T surpasses the quine bound of 0.5. However, such a heuristic is clearly irrational.

In order to study this limitation, we compare the impact of the heuristics used in zlib and gzip. We also study the impact of modifying certain compression parameters in gzip and zlib on the statistics of blocks. To this end, we note that zlib provides a parameter memLevel that specifies how much memory should be allocated for the internal compression state. The parameter partly determines when a new block is created and which type of block is created. The parameter takes values between 1 and 9. With memLevel=1, the algorithm uses minimum memory but is slow and yields the smallest compression ratio; memLevel=9 uses maximum memory for optimal speed. The default value is 8. The value of memLevel can be set to a desired value using the MAX_MEM_LEVEL macro defined in the source code. gzip also provides a similar parameter as a command line option.

Fig. 4 and Fig. 5 present the result of modifying the memLevel parameter in zlib and gzip respectively. The first observation being that the two compression routines do not produce the same distribution of block types. We also observe that in both the cases, the increase in the value of memLevel, systematically decreases the ratios U/T and S/T, while increasing the ratio D/T. Since the increase in the value of memLevel leads to higher compression ratios, more and more blocks with dynamic Huffman coding are created. A comparison of the two figures shows that for memLevel=1 and memLevel=2, a zlib compressed file yields an S/T ratio which is higher than the quine bound of 0.35. However, for these values of memLevel, the gzip compressed file has ratios much within the quine bound.

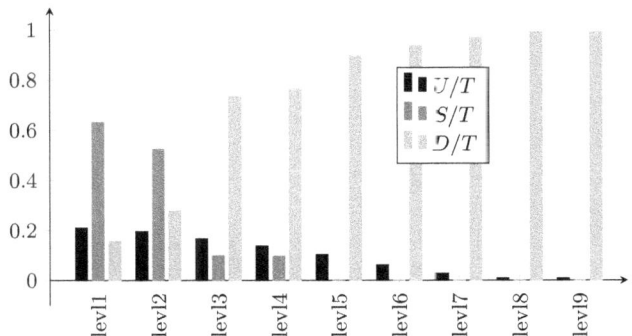

Figure 4: Results on the mozilla file from the Silesia corpus. The file was compressed using zlib with different values of memLevel.

These results show that it is possible to choose a specific parameter setting to skew the distribution of blocks. However, it would generally yield bad compression ratios.

31

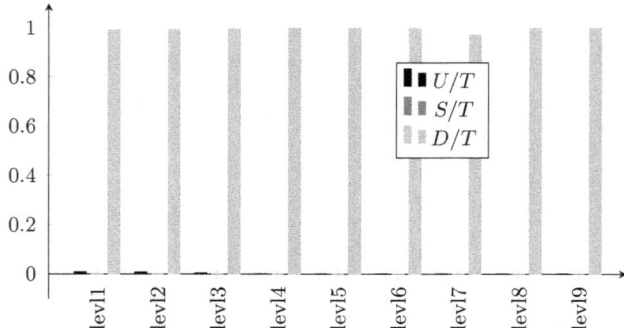

Figure 5: Results on the mozilla file from the Silesia corpus. The file was compressed using gzip with different values of memLevel. All U/T and S/T ratios are very close to 0.

5.3.2 Performance Comparison

In this section, we study the performance of three detectors: recursive decompression with bounded depth, fixed-point detector and statistical detector. The detectors use the gunzip decompression routine. The hash function implementation in the fixed-point detector comes from the bash sha256sum utility. In the rest of this section, we report the time required by the detectors on quines and safe files from the Silesia corpus (since it is the most recent one). The reported time is the average over 1000 runs.

In Table 7, we present the result on two quines. The detector based on recursive decompression with bounded depth is tested against three values for the bound: 2, 6 and 42. The first value corresponds to the base test, while the other two correspond to values currently used in Sophos and yextend respectively. Clearly, the detection time increases with the bound and the size of the quine. This is essentially due to the cost of the underlying decompression algorithm. We also observe that the statistical detector performs better than the fixed-point detector for both the quines. There are two reasons to explain this phenomenon: 1) Since the files under scrutiny are quines, the fixed-point detector needs to compute the SHA-256 digest of the compressed and uncompressed files. The statistical detector on the other hand does not require any hashing. 2) Since the fixed-point detector needs to compute the hash, it has to write the decompressed data. Writing decompressed files to the disk is an overhead that is clearly absent in our statistical detector. Comparing the results on the recursive detector with bounded depth and the statistical detector, we observe that even for the bound 2, the statistical detector performs better than the recursive decompression. This is again due to the fact that the recursive decompression writes the decompressed data while the statistical detector does not.

Table 7: Results on two quines. Recursive decompression is tested for three bounds: 2, 6 and 42.

File (size)	fixed-pt.	recursive			stat.
		2	6	42	
rec_fix.gz (130B)	5.2	5.3	11.6	65.6	4.7
r.gz (250B)	5.3	6.3	13.0	72.3	3.8

Table 8 presents the results on the detectors for safe files from the Silesia corpus. For safe files, the recursive decompression is able to detect the file as safe after the first de-

compression. The fixed-point detector needs to write the decompressed file and compute the size of the compressed and decompressed files. Again, since the statistical detector does not require writing the decompressed file, it performs the best among the three detectors. We observe that the statistical detector on an average required only 55% of the time required by the fixed-point detector and only 57% of that required by the detector based on bounded recursion.

Table 8: Results on files from the Silesia corpus.

File (size)	Time (ms)		
	fixed-point	recursive	statistical
xml (676K)	52.8	38.0	30.8
reymont (1.8M)	134.1	58.2	45.1
ooffice (3.0M)	108.2	70.1	59.7
nci (3.1M)	367.7	221.1	131.3
mr (3.6M)	158.7	121.1	76.0
osdb (3.6M)	100.8	124.8	74.6
dickens (3.7M)	106.8	151.8	82.1
sao (5.1M)	111.7	126.8	66.8
samba (5.3M)	309.2	407.3	117.6
x-ray (5.8M)	109.4	202.4	94.2
webster (12M)	527.6	606.7	257.8
mozilla (19M)	800.0	825.5	354.4

In conclusion, our statistical detector performs the best among all the detectors on both the quines and safe files.

6. CONCLUSION

In this paper, we showed that DEFLATE has an underlying pseudo-language that is sufficiently rich to produce quines. Moreover, the DELFATE specification gives several degrees of freedom such as the possibility to insert any arbitrary filename and create any block type of choice at any stage of compression among many others. Quines clearly exploit these liberties. Hence, it is much needed to redesign a new unified specification that reduces the attack surface available in DEFLATE.

Our tests with several anti-viruses and incident response frameworks show that most of them lack adequate architecture to efficiently detect quines. In face with this, we studied two ad-hoc detectors: the recursive decompression with bounded depth and the fixed-point detector. We also proposed a new statistical detector. Recursive detector is inefficient since it requires several calls to the decompression routine. Moreover, it has false positives as any archive file which has a larger number of compressed files that the hard-coded bound will be declared as unsafe. For some anti-viruses the bound is as low as 6. The fixed-point detector has no false positives and is more efficient on quines than the recursion based detector. However it performs poorly on a certain class of files. We have shown that such files are very easy to construct due to the flexible nature of the DELFATE specification. The proposed statistical detector is the most efficient of all but entails false positives. Again to the DEFLATE specification, it is possible to somewhat influence the false positive rate. However, tests with several datasets show that the false positive rate is very low.

7. ACKNOWLEDGMENTS

This research was partially supported by the Labex PERSYVAL-LAB (ANR-11-LABX-0025-01) funded by the French program Investissement d'avenir.

8. REFERENCES

[1] R. Arnold and T. C. Bell. A Corpus for the Evaluation of Lossless Compression Algorithms. In *Proceedings of the 7th Data Compression Conference (DCC '97)*, pages 201–210, 1997.

[2] R. Cox. Zip Files All The Way Down , March 2010. http://research.swtch.com/zip.

[3] P. L. Daniels. Arbomb, 2002. http://www.pldaniels.com/arbomb/.

[4] S. Deorowicz. Silesia Compression Corpus. http://sun.aei.polsl.pl/~sdeor/index.php?page=silesia.

[5] P. Deutsch. DEFLATE Compressed Data Format Specification version 1.3. RFC 1951 (Informational), May 1996.

[6] P. Deutsch. GZIP File Format Specification Version 4.3. RFC 1952 (Informational), May 1996.

[7] S. L. Garfinkel. Digital media triage with bulk data analysis and bulk_extractor. *Computers & Security*, 32:56–72, 2013.

[8] D. A. Huffman. A Method for the Construction of Minimum-Redundancy Codes. *Proceedings of the IRE*, 40(9):1098–1101, 1952.

[9] Joxlean Koret. Breaking Anti-Virus Software. In *Symposium on Security for Asia Network - Syscan 2014*, Singapore, Singapore, April 2014.

[10] K. Kent, S. Chevalier, T. Grance, and H. Dang. Guide to Integrating Forensic Techniques into Incident Response. Technical Report 800-68, NIST, 2006.

[11] J. Koret and E. Bachaalany. *The Antivirus Hacker's Handbook*. Wiley, 2015.

[12] K. Lansing. *Fidonet: A Study of Computer Networking*. Texas Tech University, 1991.

[13] Marie Cara. I Came to Drop Bombs: Auditing the Compression Algorithm Weapons Cache. In *Blackhat USA 2016*, Las Vegas, NV, USA, July–August 2016.

[14] G. Pellegrino, D. Balzarotti, S. Winter, and N. Suri. In the Compression Hornet's Nest: A Security Study of Data Compression in Network Services. In *24th USENIX Security Symposium*, pages 801–816, Washington, D.C., USA, 2015. USENIX Association.

[15] Peter Bieringer. Decompression bomb vulnerabilities. Technical report, AERAsec Network Services and Security GmbH, 2004. http://www.aerasec.de/security/advisories/decompression-bomb-vulnerability.html.

[16] PKWARE Inc. APPNOTE.TXT - .ZIP File Format Specification, 2014. version 6.3.4.

[17] K. Thompson. Reflections on Trusting Trust. *Commun. ACM*, 27(8):761–763, 1984.

[18] Usage of Compression for websites, July 2016. https://w3techs.com/technologies/details/ce-compression/all/all.

[19] J. Ziv and A. Lempel. A universal algorithm for sequential data compression. *IEEE Transactions on information theory*, 23(3):337–343, 1977.

APPENDIX

A. FILE FORMAT SPECIFICATIONS

The DEFLATE algorithm is implemented in three popular compression routines, namely, **gzip**, **zlib** and **zip**. The first two compression routines are very similar, while, **zip**, apart from being a compression routine is also an archiver, *i.e.*, it aggregates a collection of files and directories by storing them into a single container. In this appendix we present the file format specification for each of these routines.

GZIP: A **gzip** compressed file as specified in RFC 1952 [6] is composed of three mandatory parts and an optional part (see Fig. 6a). The mandatory parts include a header followed by the compressed data and a footer. The header is collectively 10 bytes long and stores the **gzip** magic number (two bytes for **MAGIC NUMBER 0x1F8B**), a 1-byte field to identify the compression method used (**CM**)[6], another 1-byte field for a flag meant to activate options (**FLG**), a 4-byte field for the unix time at which the file was last modified (**MTIME**), a one byte field for extra flags (**XFLG**) that is set depending on the compression method and finally the last byte reserved to indicate the operating system (**OS**). Depending on whether some of the bits of **FLG** are set or not, there can be an optional part which consists of three additional fields: **XLEN** gives the length of the optional field, **FNAME** is the filename and **FCOMMENT** is the file comment. **FNAME** and **FCOMMENT** terminate with a **0x00** byte. The optional part is followed by the actual compressed data blocks (**COMPRESSED BLOCKS**). A **gzip** file ends with a mandatory footer composed of a 4-byte cyclic redundancy code (**CRC32**) and the size of the uncompressed file modulo 2^{32} (**FSIZE**).

ZLIB: A **zlib** compressed file [5] has the same format as that of a **gzip** compressed file, except that the magic number is different (**0x789C**) and that the **CRC32** checksum is replaced by **ADLER32** which trades reliability for speed.

ZIP: In the description provided here, we do not take into account the archiving ability of **zip**. In other words, we assume that only a single file is zipped. The **zip** file format as specified in [16] is shown in Fig. 6b. Under the stated restriction, a **zip** compressed file is identified by a **MAGIC NUMBER**, *aka* a *file header signature* which is a 4-byte field (**0x04034b50**). It is followed by five 2-byte fields, namely, a field that identifies the version needed to extract the data (**VS**), a flag to store options (**FLG**), a field to identify the compression method used (**CM**)[7], a field to indicate the last modification time of the file (**MTIME**) and another to indicate the last modification date of the file (**MDATE**). This is followed by three 4-byte fields, namely, a CRC32 checksum to check file integrity (**CRC32**), a field to store the compressed file size (**CS**) and another to store the uncompressed file size (**UCS**). These size-related fields are followed by two 2-byte fields. The first stores the filename length (**FNLN**), while the other stores the length of the extra field (such as a file comment) (**XFL**). Then, there are two fields of variable length to store the filename and the extra field name (**XFLNAME**). This is followed by the actual compressed data (**COMPRESSED BLOCKS**). Finally, depending upon the bits of **FLG**, the file may have three 4-byte fields, namely, **CRC32**, **CS2** — a repetition of the compressed file size **CS** and **UCS2** — a repetition of the uncompressed file size **UCS**.

---

[6] Apart from the DEFLATE compression, other methods such as LZH and **pack** (a deprecated compression algorithm based on Huffman coding) are also supported.

[7] zip also implements LZMA, IBM LZ77, BZIP2.

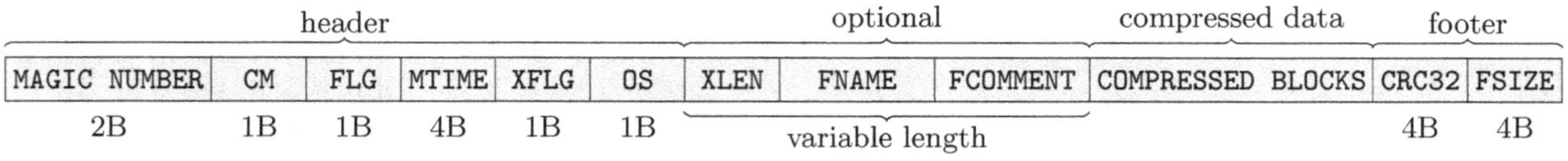

Figure 6

header						optional		compressed data	footer	
MAGIC NUMBER	CM	FLG	MTIME	XFLG	OS	XLEN	FNAME	FCOMMENT	COMPRESSED BLOCKS	CRC32	FSIZE
2B	1B	1B	4B	1B	1B	variable length			4B	4B

(a) A `gzip` compressed file.

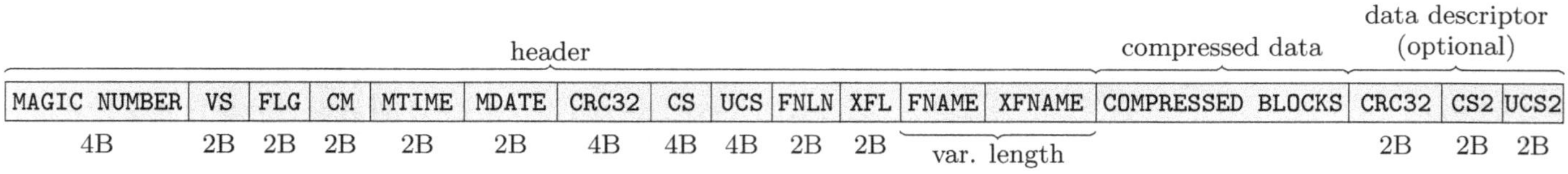

header												compressed data	data descriptor (optional)		
MAGIC NUMBER	VS	FLG	CM	MTIME	MDATE	CRC32	CS	UCS	FNLN	XFL	FNAME	XFNAME	COMPRESSED BLOCKS	CRC32	CS2	UCS2
4B	2B	2B	2B	2B	2B	4B	4B	4B	2B	2B	var. length			2B	2B	2B

(b) A `zip` compressed file.

Figure 6: File format of a `gzip` and `zip` compressed file.

(a) `rec_tst.gz`.

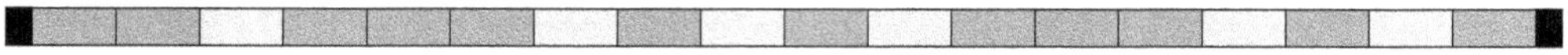

(b) `r.gzip`.

(c) `r.gz`.

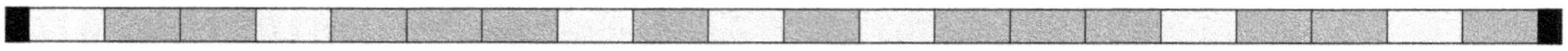

(d) `r.tar.gz`.

Figure 7: Block structure for different quines. The gray blocks correspond to uncompressed (`stored`) blocks and the light gray are compressed with the static Huffman table (`static` blocks).

Table 9: Canterbury corpus.

Filename	Description	Type	Filesize (KB)
alice29.txt	Alice in Wonderland	English text	148
asyoulik.txt	Shakespeare's play	English text	122
cp.html	sample HTML	HTML	24
fields.c	sample C source	C	10
grammar.lsp	list	LISP source	3
kennedy.xls	sample Excel	Excel spreadsheet	1005
lcet10.txt	technical writing	text	416
plrabn12.txt	poem	text	470
pt5	fax	CCITT	501
sum	SPARC	SPARC executable	37
xargs.1	GNU man page	man	4

Table 10: Silesia corpus.

Filename	Description	Type	Filesize (MB)
dickens	collected works of Charles Dickens	English text	9.7
mozilla	tarred executable of Mozilla 1.0	exe	48.8
mr	medical magnetic resonance image	picture	9.5
nci	chemical database	database	32
ooffice	dll from Open Office.org 1.01	exe	5.9
osdb	database in MySQL format from Open Source Database Benchmark	database	9.6
reymont	text of the book Chłopi by Władysław Reymont	Polish pdf	6.32
samba	tarred source code of Samba 2-2.3	src	20.6
sao	SAO star catalog	binary	6.9
webster	Webster Unabridged Dictionary (1913)	html	39.5
xml	XML files	html	5
x-ray	X-ray image	image	8

B. BLOCK STRUCTURE OF KNOWN QUINES

Fig. 7a, Fig. 7b, Fig. 7c, Fig. 7d, present the block structure for `rec_tst.gz`, `r.gzip`, `r.gz` and `r.tar.gz` respectively.

C. COMPRESSION CORPORA

We present details on the Canterbury and Silesia compression corpora in Table 9 and Table 10 respectively.

Statistical Security Incident Forensics against Data Falsification in Smart Grid Advanced Metering Infrastructure

Shameek Bhattacharjee[1], Aditya Thakur[2], Simone Silvestri[1], and Sajal K. Das[1]
{shameek, astvd3, silvestris, sdas}@mst.edu
[1]Department of Computer Science, [2]Department of Electrical Engineering
Missouri University of Science and Technology, Rolla, MO, USA

ABSTRACT

Compromised smart meters reporting false power consumption data in Advanced Metering Infrastructure (AMI) may have drastic consequences on a smart grid's operations Most existing works only deal with electricity theft from customers. However, several other types of data falsification attacks are possible, when meters are compromised by *organized rivals*. In this paper, we first propose a taxonomy of possible data falsification strategies such as *additive, deductive, camouflage and conflict*, in AMI micro-grids. Then, we devise a statistical anomaly detection technique to identify the incidence of proposed attack types, by studying their impact on the observed data. Subsequently, a trust model based on Kullback-Leibler divergence is proposed to identify compromised smart meters for additive and deductive attacks. The resultant detection rates and false alarms are minimized through a robust aggregate measure that is calculated based on the detected attack type and successfully discriminating legitimate changes from malicious ones. For conflict and camouflage attacks, a generalized linear model and Weibull function based kernel trick is used over the trust score to facilitate more accurate classification. Using real data sets collected from AMI, we investigate several trade-offs that occur between attacker's revenue and costs, as well as the margin of false data and fraction of compromised nodes. Experimental results show that our model has a high true positive detection rate, while the average false alarm rate is just 8%, for most practical attack strategies, without depending on the expensive hardware based monitoring.

Keywords

Statistical Anomaly Detection; Security Incident Forensics; Trust Models; Data Falsification; Information Theory; Supervised Learning; Smart Grid; Advanced Metering Infrastructure; Relative Entropy

CODASPY'17, March 22-24, 2017, Scottsdale, AZ, USA

© 2017 ACM. ISBN 978-1-4503-4523-1/17/03...$15.00

DOI: http://dx.doi.org/10.1145/3029806.3029833

1. INTRODUCTION

Advanced Metering Infrastructure (AMI) is one of the elementary units of the smart grid technology, which collects data on loads and consumer's power consumption [10], from Smart Meters installed on the customer site (see Fig. 1). Such data play a pivotal role in several critical tasks such as automated billing, demand response, load forecast and management [10].

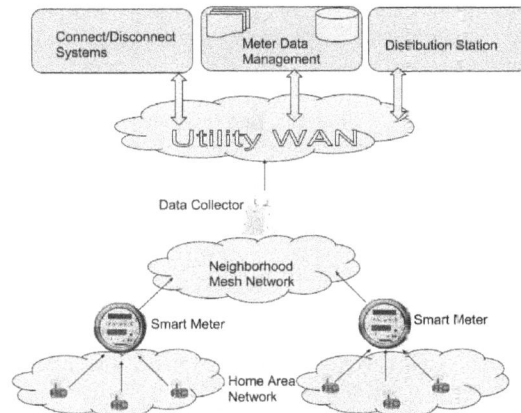

Figure 1: Architecture of AMI

Apart from automated billing, (already in use), strategic decisions are expected to be taken by future smart grids, based on the power consumption data. For example, these data will have implications on tasks such as daily and critical peak shifts [22]. When the consumption increases beyond a certain critical limit, emergency peaker plants' are currently used by most utilities for additional power generation to meet the demand. However, such peaker plants are extremely carbon as well as cost intensive. In the modern grid, the utility will also have the option for automated demand response where utilities pay customers to shut certain appliances temporarily (peak shifting) to obviate the need for additional generation [21]. In general, an accurate short or long term data on loads and consumption will aid in accurate demand response, load forecast and planned generation in the future smart grid. Hence, the integrity of the data generated from the AMI is of utmost importance.

Defense against falsification of power consumption data from AMIs, has largely focused on *electricity theft* [3, 7, 9, 17], where individual customers are primary adversaries who report lower than actual usage for lesser bills. Since isolated smart meters belonging to rogue customers reduce the value of power consumption, we term such adversarial strategy as a *Deductive* mode of data falsification.

However, it has been widely acknowledged that given the cyber and interconnected nature of AMI, it could potentially be the target of powerful and organized adversaries such as rival nation states, utility insiders [20], organized cyber criminals and business competitors [4]. Such adversaries can compromise *several smart meters* and then *spoof* false power consumption data [7] from smart meters. Powerful and organized adversaries are more equipped to crack/leak cryptographic secrets, have a higher attack budget, and possess the ability to simultaneously attack other elements of the grid (e.g., audit logs, transformers meters) in order to avoid easy consistency checks on false data. Existing research does not focus on defense against such adversaries and is only restricted to attacks from isolated adversaries.

Additionally, the goals of these organized adversaries are not just restricted to monetary benefits on the customer side that result from electricity theft. As a recent real example, in Puerto Rico [20] a manufacturer and a utility insider colluded to install a large number of tampered smart meters that reported higher than actual power consumption. We term such an attack as *Additive* mode of data falsification. Conversely, an additive attack launched by a rival utility on its competing company's meters may induce loss of business confidence by the customers of the victim company, due to higher bills as reported in [19]. A class action lawsuit filed against a victim utility was reported in this case. If the utility participates in demand response, then utility may lose revenue from additive attacks for undue compensation payed to customers for induced peak shifts. Indirectly, additive attacks can be triggered when a load altering attack *(LAA)* [11] occurs on the individual appliances of a Home Area Network (HAN), thus increasing the net consumption sensed by the smart meter. It may also be noted that rival nations, businesses, or organized cyber criminals may orchestrate large scale deductive attacks to cripple the utility companies through revenue losses. Additive and deductive attacks are termed as 'simple' attack types.

Furthermore, we argue the possibility of mixed attack types on the smart meter data. For example, a balancing additive and deductive attack with the same margin of falsification of either type, could evade mean aggregate demand check/forecast models. We term such a strategy as a *Camouflage* attack, which may be motivated for generating lesser bills to one set of customers at the expense of the other set. Such attacks may stay undetected, without raising any suspicion because the total inflow and outflow of power measured at the transformer meters, and the total demand and reported usage remain unchanged. The attacker in such a case need not attack other elements in the grid (for e.g. transformer meters) to prevent easy consistency checks. In general, random additive and deductive attacks may simultaneously coexist in the same AMI network, when launched by different adversaries with conflicting goals. We term such a scenario as a *Conflict attack*, which is a mixed attack type with unequal margins of falsification for each underlying simple attack type. Existing literature cannot handle all of the above data falsification strategies.

In this paper, we first introduce a taxonomy of possible data falsification attacks launched by organized adversaries. Then we study the statistical properties of the distribution of power consumption data and analyze the effects of various data falsification attacks types on the parameters of the power consumption data. With the help of the observed statistical effects, *a security incident forensics criterion* is proposed that indicates the presence and the type of attack while discriminating effect of attacks from legitimate changes. Subsequently, we propose a light weight Kullback-Leibler divergence based trust model that identifies compromised meters with a high detection rate, by exploiting knowledge of the statistical impact caused by each attack type, cyclostationarity of overall power consumption patterns, and factoring in for any legitimate change in the consumption patterns.

We use a generalized linear model (GLM) and Weibull function based kernel trick to extend our trust model, for robust classification of compromised nodes based on the computed trust values with least missed detections and false alarms, even for stealthy camouflage and conflict attacks. We also perform a cost benefit and sensitivity analysis for both of our attack and defense models. Specifically, we computationally study tradeoffs, such as *breakeven time* (i.e., the time required for attacker's revenue to equal its cost of attack) and *breakdown point* (i.e., the attack strategy for which the defense mechanism is no longer able to distinguish the compromised meters from honest ones). Experimental results show that our detection technique is able to identify compromised meters with higher detection rates while incurring lower false positives, than most existing works, under rational attack strategies that may be employed by adversaries. We perform extensive sensitivity analysis to show the limits of our model.

To the best of our knowledge, our proposed work is the first effort to establish trustworthiness in AMI against multiple attacks types and organized rivals. Secondly, ours is the first work that focus on data falsification strategies other than electricity theft, which can be devised by organized adversaries rather than rogue customers. Unlike most existing works, our approach works without meter specific storage and maintenance of fine grained consumption data from each meter to obviate important privacy concerns [26]. Our proposed method is also light weight compared to the classical bad data detection mechanisms. Since our method does not require installation of additional hardware as in the state based monitoring, it is more cost effective.

2. RELATED WORK

Existing work on AMI data falsification can be broadly categorized into *classical bad data detection*, and *state based detection*. Both categories focus only on the electricity theft. Classical bad data detection uses techniques such as Support Vector Machine (SVM), Neural Networks and Auto Regressive Moving Average (ARMA) models. In contrast, state based detection includes sensor based monitoring, mean aggregate outlier inspections and transformer state estimation.

Classical bad data detection schemes such as Multi-class SVM and Neural Networks are used in [3, 15] for offline and retrospective identification of rogue customers stealing electricity by reporting lower usage. Such techniques contain a series of seven steps for identifying abnormal customers. The obvious disadvantage of these approaches are that they are highly computation expensive, deal with long term retrospective identification, and do not consider organized adversaries or their attack strategies, and require full and fine grained profiling of each smart meter. A comparative analysis of classical bad data detection schemes is provided in [2] which concludes that while these schemes require full profiling of each customers' energy consumption (thus cannot protect their privacy), the detection rate of most of these schemes is approximately 60%-70%. Moreover, only two schemes provide a quantitative false positive rate.

Finally, ARMA based models [9] profile each customer's time series data separately to increase accuracy, using ARMA-GLR detector. However, in most practical cases, the consumption cannot be accurately modeled as an ARMA process [3], resulting in the detection rate of only about 62%. Additionally, several privacy threats [10, 26] are associated with such approaches since they require customer specific monitoring and maintainance of fine or coarse grained consumption data.

State based detection techniques like sensor based monitoring [5, 8], transformer state monitors [1] require additional hardware deployed at various points across the AMI and distribution network for identifying anomalies. However, most of them do not identify the compromised meters. Additional hardware requirement makes such approaches costly [2]. Some works (e.g., [8]) combines the audit logs for physical and cyber events in the meter to check for consistency in the data reported. But these approaches are nullified when the meters are compromised by external adversary who are intelligent enough to change the audit logs. Furthermore, cyber connected sensors/monitors are also similarly vulnerable to cyber attacks.

Mean aggregate based outlier approaches used in state based detection [15, 17] have the advantage that they do need not store and maintain fine grained meter specific trends on power consumption. In [17], an arithmetic mean aggregate approach is proposed; but the number of rogue meters is small compared to the population, hence the aggregate mean values are not affected enough. They also do not discriminate between legitimate and malicious changes in the mean consumption, thus incurring a high false positive rate of around 30%, and consider only electricity theft. Legitimate changes in consumption may occur due to weather and other contextual factors. Approaches focusing on only arithmetic mean aggregates and median have difficulty to discriminate malicious changes from legitimate ones when the margin of false data or the fraction of compromised nodes is higher. Thus, such approaches suffer from high false positive rates or lower detection rates. Additionally, such methods will also fail to identify camouflage and conflict attacks as discussed earlier. In [3], a false positive rate of 28% is reported although the detection rate is high.

Finally, cryptographic approaches [6, 16] may fail to provide any help as organized adversaries may be able to crack the cryptographic secrets. Moreover, given the latency critical nature of functions like demand response and management [23], advanced cryptographic defense is impractical due to additional overhead [14]. This further exacerbates the vulnerability of the AMI data falsification.

Given the above limitations, we believe there is a dire need for trustworthy computing approaches based on the anomaly detection in the data reported by each meter. This motivates us to propose a novel scheme that provides security forensics to identify various falsification attacks and a trust model based on aggregate data monitoring to identify compromised meters. Hence, our work significantly advances this field of research.

3. SYSTEM MODEL

We consider a collection of N smart meters reporting power consumption data to a Data Collector (DC) periodically and independently. The i-th smart meter, s^i, records an actual power consumption data $P_t^i(act)$ at the end of each time slot t. The reported power consumption $P_t^i(rep)$ is equal to $P_t^i(act)$ if s^i is not compromised. However, $P_t^i(rep) \neq P_t^i(act)$, if s^i is compromised by an adversary. We model $P_t^i(act)$ as the realizations of a random variable P^i. The Data Collector piggybacks data from each smart meter and sends it to the billing utility. The total power reported at a time by all N meters is sent to a transformer meter.

To characterize the distribution of P^i from the i-th smart meter, we conducted preliminary investigations on real power consumption data sets [25], of 200 houses from 16 different microgrids. Each home consists of one smart meter. We observed that for each house or meter, the power consumption can be approximated as a log normal distribution. We also observed that all such log normal distributions are *clustered close* to each other; that is, the variance between them is not arbitrarily large. Fig. 2(a) summarizes the results.

We approximate the aggregate of the individual log normals using a mixture distribution, which is also lognormal as evident from Fig. 2(a). We denote P_{mix} as the random variable (r.v.) of such aggregate approximate mixture distribution.

For mathematical tractability and visual intuitiveness, we transform P_{mix} on a natural logarithm scale to obtain an approximate *normally distributed* r.v. denoted as p_{mix}. Results of this approximate normal mixture p_{mix}, for different months in the recent past is depicted in Fig. 2(b). Note that both P_{mix} and p_{mix}, *do not reveal* any consumption pattern for each specific meter, but only a general trend on the consumption.

We also denote $p_t^i(act) = ln(P_t^i(act))$, as the effective power consumption report recorded at each meter s^i on a log scale at any time slot t. Note that, for certain other data sets (like a wider area monitoring), with more than one consumption clusters, as in [15], our approach can be applied to each such cluster independently. The proposed trust model calculates and updates trust of each smart meter at the end of each month. We assume a window size of T slots per month based on how t is slotted. To prove the generality, we repeated the experiments for a different AMI data set [3], and reported similar observations like Figs. 2(a) and 2(b) as shown in Appendix B.

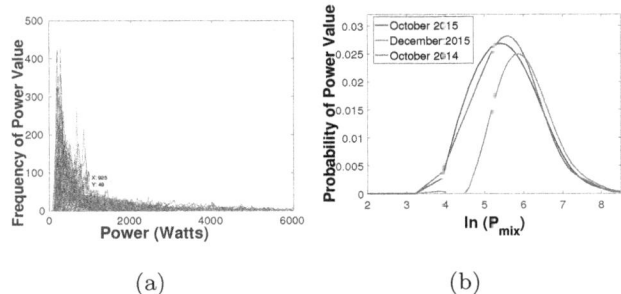

(a)   (b)

Figure 2: Power Consumption Behavior: (a) Actual (b) Normal Mixture

3.1 Threat Model

We consider the following assumptions in our threat model.

3.1.1 Types of Adversary

We assume that the organized adversary belongs to either rival nation states, business competitors, utility insiders or cyber criminals, possessing the ability to compromise several smart meters by bypassing cryptography.

False power consumption data from a meter can be achieved in the following ways: (a) manipulation of inputs to the meter, (b) in rest at the meter, and (c) in-flight from the meter. The adversary then launches data falsification from multiple such compromised smart meters concurrently. A compromised meter in this context means either the input, content, or output coming from one specific meter is compromised.

We assume rational attackers who may have a long or short term damage objective. *Long term damage* requires evading detection for the maximum possible time, while still benefiting from attacks. The adversary may accept to face some initial loss in the hope of evading detection and accruing incremental benefits over time. Examples of long term adversarial objectives include monetary gains in terms of electricity pricing and belief manipulation of learning demand forecast models. A *short term damage*, on the other hand, requires inflicting the maximum damage in a short time, before getting detected. Examples of short term objectives include an attacker aiming to, gain quick revenue or masquerade a false high demand response. Due to the contrasting requirements on these two objectives, adversarial decisions such as fraction of compromised nodes ρ_{mal} and the margin of false data are dependent on the nature of time deadlines associated with such objectives.

Unlike existing works [3], we assume organized adversaries to be intelligent enough to also tamper with transformer meters and other portions of the grid, to escape easy consistency checks on false data. We also assume that the smart meters report the consumed power to a data concentrator on every time slot (hourly). Compromised Meters spoof false data on all time slots, however, the attack margin Δ (explained below) may be more in peak periods than non-peak periods, to exploit the time dependent pricing of electricity.

3.1.2 Taxonomy of AMI Data Falsification

We define the manner in which the actual power consumption data $P_t^i(act)$ of each meter s^i is modified as the *mode* of data falsification. We identify the following modes:

Additive: The adversary reports $P_t^i(rep) = P_t^i(act) + \Delta_t$, where $\delta_{min} \leq \Delta_t \leq \delta_{max}$. This mode can lead to loss of business confidence from customers due to higher bills and masquerade a critical peak leading to remote disconnect of customer appliances, thereby causing utilities to pay undue incentives.

Deductive: The adversary reports $P_t^i(rep) = P_t^i(act) - \Delta_t$, where $\delta_{min} \leq \Delta_t \leq \delta_{max}$. This mode can lead to loss of revenue for power utility companies.

Camouflage: The adversary divides the compromised meters into two teams equal in number, which simultaneously adopt an additive and deductive mode, respectively. This mode can favor smart meter of one power utility at the expense of others, and has less impact on the strategic decisions in the grid. It cannot be detected by simple mean comparison approaches, because no suspicion is raised due to negligible change in the total reported power consumption.

Conflict: It is a scenario where additive and deductive attacks coexist simultaneously, but are not necessarily balanced. Such a scenario represents random attacks possible if there are more than one uncoordinated adversarial teams.

3.1.3 Margin of Falsified Data

The value Δ_t is generated randomly within an interval $[\delta_{min}, \delta_{max}]$, for $\delta_{min}, \delta_{max} > 0$, and accordingly added to or deducted from the actual power consumption. Note that, arbitrarily high δ_{max} may facilitate intuitively easy detection, while very low δ_{max} hardly accrues any revenue. The average value of Δ_t is represented as Δ_{avg}.

Apart from the type of attack, the attacker chooses a value of Δ_{avg} in the interval $[\delta_{min}, \delta_{max}]$ as part of its attack strategy. Δ_{avg} may be high or low depending on the amount of damage it wants to inflict, and the short or long time horizon of the attack. All units of Δ_{avg} values discussed throughout the paper is in Watts.

Since the distribution of power consumption is unimodal, the attacker refrains from any strategy that would make the resultant distribution, multi modal. In that sense, a uniformly distributed random noise injected into the actual smart meter data does not change the overall shape of the distribution but only effects its parameters. Such variants of uniform distribution over time is adopted from [3].

From the defender's perspective, we define the *breakdown point* $BDP = (\Delta_{avg}, \rho_{mal})$, as a combination of Δ_{avg} and ρ_{mal} values for which the proposed defense model is no longer able to identify between compromised and honest nodes.

3.1.4 Attacker Budget

We assume that organized adversaries compromise a certain number M_{max} of the N smart meters based on the *attack budget*. The fraction of compromised nodes is $\rho_{mal} = \frac{M_{max}}{N}$. Hence, ρ_{mal} can be high when N is small.

We assume a fixed cost C_{attack} is required to compromise a smart meter. We refer to the budget as the *total cost TC* of the attack, such that $TC = C_{attack} \times M_{max}$. We term the attacker's revenue as RR over an attack period of D days in terms monetary gain in the electricity bills.

We define T_{BE} as the *breakeven time*, that is the time required for the revenue accrued from attacks to match the total cost TC. The tradeoffs that impact T_{BE} and BDP is studied in Section 6.

In certain implementations, a transformer meter checks the total inflow of power versus total outflow. If δ_{avg} is high, then a smart adversary can may compromise the corresponding transformer meter, to avoid easy suspicion. Only simple attack types like additive and deductive would require the adversary compromising the transformer meter, given that in camouflage and conflict attacks, the total reported power consumption is not affected significantly.

3.1.5 A Concrete Example

Suppose in an AMI facility of $N = 100$ smart meters, $M_{max} = 20$ implying $\rho_{mal} = 0.2$. The actual aggregate power consumption distribution has a mean and a standard deviation of $\mu_A = 2000$ units and $\sigma_A = 100$ units, respectively. If the amount of additive error to be introduced in the final mean is $\Lambda = 500$ units, the Δ_{avg} for each malicious node is given by $\Delta_{avg} = \frac{\Lambda * N}{M_{max}} = 2500$. Since false noise values are generated uniformly at random in the range $(\delta_{min}, \delta_{max})$, $\Delta_{avg} = \frac{\delta_{min} + \delta_{max}}{2}$. Therefore in this example, if $\delta_{min} = 128$, as the minimum false value to be considered as attack, then $\delta_{max} = 4782$. Here δ_{max} and Δ_{avg} are a rather high value, which may easily be detected, given the nature of power consumption. However, if $\rho_{mal} = 0.4$, then to achieve the same $\Lambda = 500$, it is sufficient to have $\delta_{max} = 2372$ and $\Delta_{avg} = 1250$, which are more believable values.

The above proves that with higher ρ_{mal}, the adversary can afford to decrease the margin of false data to avoid getting intuitively and easily detected. Although the cost increases with higher ρ_{mal}, the adversary may reduce the chance of detection, and look to recover the initial cost in the long term. This is however not an option for adversaries with short term objectives. In this case, the attack revenue/payoff and the cost have to breakeven within a short time deadline. This implies very high ρ_{mal} and low Δ_{avg} do not lead to a practical attack strategy, since low Δ_{avg} accrues slow attack revenue per unit time. In the experimental results, we study the trade-offs between Δ_{avg} and ρ_{mal}.

4. STATISTICAL EFFECTS OF VARIOUS ATTACKS ON AMI DATA

In this section, we study how different data falsification strategies affect the attacked mixture distribution from the actual (authentic) mixture distribution from real data gathered from 215 smart meters from a solar Village [25]. In particular, we show effects of various attack types, on the Arithmetic Mean (AM), Geometric Mean(GM) and Harmonic Mean (HM). The mathematical definitions of the different means are $AM_t = \frac{\sum_{i=1}^{N} x_t^i}{N}$, $GM_t = (\prod_{i=1}^{N} x_t^i)^{\frac{1}{N}}$, $HM_t = \frac{N}{\sum_{i=1}^{N} \frac{1}{x_t^i}}$.

Based on the simultaneous changes between the various means, a security forensics criterion is provided to unravel the type of data falsification attack. This criterion that is based on the absolute difference (denoted by AD) between AM and HM of the observed mixture distribution, can also help to distinguish between a legitimate change and malicious change. Subsequently, a robust mean μ_R is derived exploiting the contrasting robustness of AM, GM, HM measures to various types of attacks.

All trends on power consumption use p^i values on an ln scale. For comparison between legitimate and attacked data, the reference authentic distribution is called historical distribution denoted by p_{mix}^{his}. The attacked distribution is called the observed distribution denoted by p_{mix}^{obs}.

4.1 Investigative Comparison under Various Attacks

4.1.1 Authentic Data on Different Years

Fig. 3(a) shows the actual mixture distribution for two different years (2014 and 2015) for the month of September. We can observe, that the difference between the distributions is not large. In fact, the mean, and higher moments are very similar. This is attributed to similar coarse grained usage patterns given the weather in a particular month at the same location. Hence, power consumption at a microgrid is cyclostationary in the wide sense. The AM for 2014 and 2015 are 7.053 and 7.07 respectively. The HM for the same are 6.680 and 6.675 respectively.

However, sometimes it may happen that the same month in two different years experience varying weather conditions at certain locations. For example, winter 2015 was much warmer than winter 2014 in certain geographical locations in USA. For example in this data set, AM is 6.88 and 6.58, while the HM are 6.52 and 6.23 respectively. Such a difference is shown in Fig. 3(b). Hence, we conclude that comparison of a meter's data with the parameters of observed (current) mixture distribution (p_{mix}^{obs}) is equally important, as is the comparison with the historical values of power consumption.

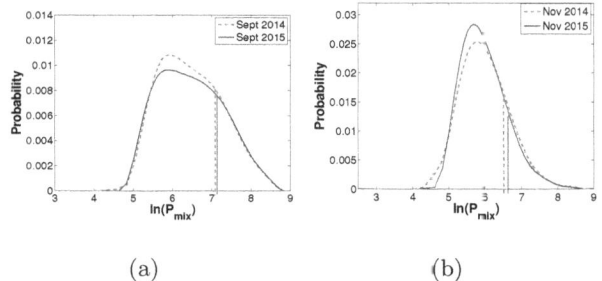

(a) (b)

Figure 3: Legitimate Data Comparison: (a) September (b) November

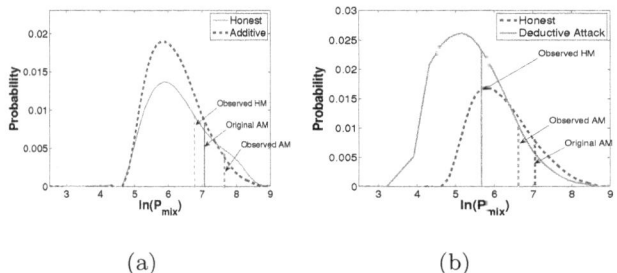

(a) (b)

Figure 4: Comparison: (a) Honest vs. Additive (b) Honest vs. Deductive

4.1.2 Authentic Data vs. Additive Attack

Fig. 4(a) shows the comparison between honest data set p_{mix}^{his} and the same data set polluted with additive falsification, with $\Delta_{avg} = 800$ and $\rho_{mal} = 0.40$ for the month of October. Due to higher than actual power consumption reported, the observed AM is highly shifted from the original AM. Hence, when using the observed mixture distribution for anomaly detection, the observed AM is biased towards the additive false data. We observe instead that the *harmonic mean* (HM) of the observed mixture, although shifted, is closer to the original AM. Hence false readings will be located farther away from the observed HM. Hence HM is a more robust aggregate in unraveling positive outliers. Another key observation is that the absolute difference between HM and AM, given by $AD = |AM - HM|$ is higher in the attacked data set than the legitimate data set. Geometric mean (GM) is an intermediate value, but slightly closer to the AM value as compared to HM.

4.1.3 Authentic Data vs. Deductive Attack

Figure 4(b) shows the results for the case of deductive attacks where $\Delta_{avg} = 500$ and $\rho_{mal} = 0.40$ for October. Intuitively, the observed mixture distribution, shifts to the left, due to reporting of lower than actual consumption. As a result, the observed AM is lower than the actual AM. Nonetheless, the observed HM is even lesser than observed AM since $HM \leq AM$ is always true. Hence for deductive attacks, the observed AM is more robust than HM. However, AD still increases.

Note that, the maximum possible bias introduced in the observed AM under deductive attacks is less than that of additive attacks, because the feasible margin of deductive false data is bounded by zero, because $P_t^i(rep) \geq 0$.

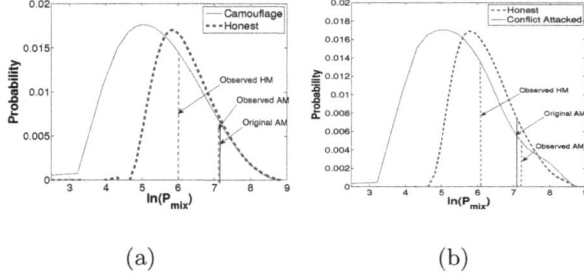

(a)   (b)

Figure 5: Comparison: (a) Honest vs. Camouflage (b) Honest vs. Conflict

4.1.4 Authentic Data vs. Camouflage Attack

Fig. 5(a) shows the effect of camouflage attacks where $\Delta_{avg} = 960$ and $\rho_{mal} = 0.40$. There is a negligible change in the AM. However, we observe that there is a shift in the HM of the observed mixture, thereby causing the resultant AD to increase.

4.1.5 Authentic Data vs. Conflict Attack

Fig. 5(b) shows the effect of conflict attacks where Δ_{avg} is 700 and 500 for additive and deductive attacks, respectively, with $\rho_{mal} = 0.40$. There is a little change in the AM. However, we observe a shift in the HM of the observed mixture. Hence, AD increases.

4.2 Security Incident Forensics

Based on the observations from comparison between authentic versus attacked data distributions, we identified a security incident forensics criteria, based on AD and the simultaneous change/bias in the observed AM, HM, and GM that indicate presence and type of data falsification (security incident). Based on this knowledge, we calculate a robust aggregate μ_R, which is less biased than the otherwise observed arithmetic mean values.

4.2.1 Detecting the Anomaly from Legitimate Change

We study how each attack type impacts various statistical parameters and identify a criterion (see Eqn. 1) that reveals the presence and the type of attack launched. From our statistical study, we found that $AD = |AM - HM|$ could be an effective indicator for anomalies.

Fig. 6 shows the comparison of instantaneous values of AD between historical (2014) and current non-attacked distribution (2015) for different years. It can be verified that under no attacks, the average value of AD is about 0.45 for both years, although contextual factors may have caused AM, GM and HM to readily change over time. The lowest AD^{min} and highest AD^{max} values of AD for two years are between 0.35 and 0.55 Hence, AD is almost stable for legitimate data sets, and we call this range AD^{norm}

In contrast, from Fig. 7, it is easy to conclude that for all attacks scenarios, the AD^{obs} is larger than AD^{norm} range. This figure clearly shows that when additive, deductive, camouflage, and conflict attack samples were introduced in the current data set, starting from the 250th day of 2015, AD has increased for each attack type.

$$AD^{obs} : \begin{cases} \in AD^{norm} & \text{No Falsification ;} \\ > AD^{norm} & \text{Falsification Occurred;} \end{cases} \quad (1)$$

Table 1: Effects of Different Attacks on AD

Parameter	Actual	Add	Deduct	Camo	Conf
AM	7.053	7.68	6.67	7.04	7.26
GM	6.860	7.35	6.29	6.65	6.79
HM	6.680	6.92	5.88	6.02	6.11
AD = |AM-HM|	0.373	0.76	0.79	1.02	1.15

From the above, we conclude that an authentic change in the observed distribution may cause the mean consumption to increase or decrease but AD^{obs} remains the same as compared to the historical range of values $AD^{norm} = [AD^{min}, AD^{max}]$. An additive attack causes the mean consumption to increase but also causes AD^{obs} to increase compared to historical values. This way a legitimate versus a malicious change can be distinguished. A deductive attack causes the mean consumption to decrease and causes AD^{obs} to increase from the historical range. Similarly, camouflage and conflict attacks do not have much change in the mean consumption but causes a large increase in the AD^{obs} from the normal. In this way, it is possible to detect which type of data falsification has been launched.

Table 2: Concluding the Security Incident Type

AD	AM	HM	GM	Conclusion
Increased	Increased	Increased	Increased	Additive
Increased	Decreased	Decreased	Decreased	Deductive
Increased	Same	Decreased	Decreased	Camouflage
Increased	Any	Any	Any	Conflict
Same	Don't Care	Don't Care	Don't Care	No Attack

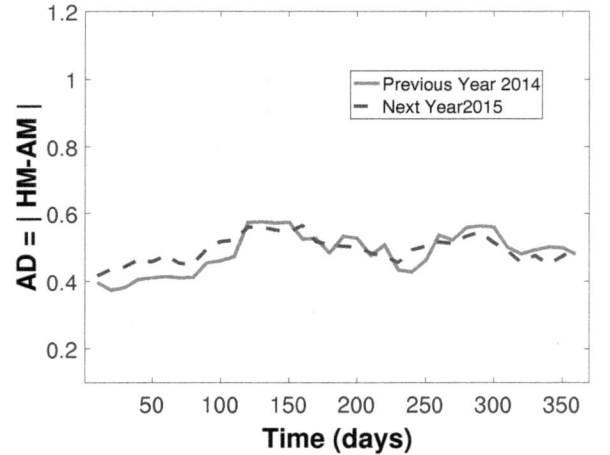

Figure 6: AD under No Attacks

4.2.2 A Robust Mean for Different Attacks

The manner and extent to which different observed mean aggregates like HM, GM and AM get biased by different attacks is unique. We exploit this property for the calculation of robust mean. Additionally, the magnitude of the bias depends on Δ_{avg} and/or ρ_{mal}. Hence, an adjusted robust mean helps to get an approximate value closer to the original mean. Note that, the highest possible Δ_{avg} is lesser in deductive attacks than additive ones, because the feasible margin of deductive false data is bounded by zero. As the margins of false data or compromised fraction increases, the observed means get biased from the actual mean.

From the statistical observations, we conclude that HM is more robust than AM to the effect of additive attacks, due to slower increase in HM as opposed to AM. However, this is

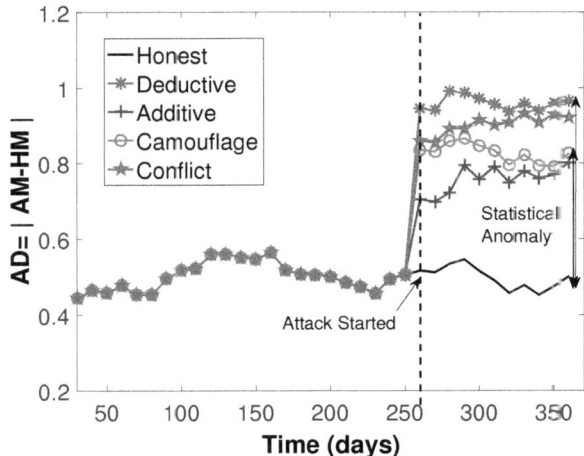

Figure 7: AD in Observed Data: Various Attacks

not the case for deductive attacks because of $HM \leq GM \leq AM$, causing HM to be even lesser than the already biased AM. But, $GM + AD$ is more robust than AM for deductive attacks, and results show that it is a good approximation to the actual mean. From the example in Table 2, it can be verified that for deductive attack, the robust mean $\mu_R = 6.29 + 0.79 = 7.08$ is closer to the actual mean 7.05. For camouflage attacks, AM is the most robust and hence μ_R is set as the AM. For conflict attacks, GM is an intermediate robust choice as it shows a relative stability to both partially positive and negative outliers.

Table 3: Robust Aggregate guided by Incident Type

Security Incident	Choice of Aggregate μ_R
Additive	HM
Deductive	GM+AD
Camouflage	AM
Conflict	GM
No Attack	AM

5. AN ENTROPY BASED TRUST MODEL

We pursue a light weight supervised learning approach for defending against data falsification from compromised smart meters. A prior historical data set is considered as the authentic distribution of power consumption. From the historical data set, a *true proximity distribution* denoted as X_i for each smart meter is generated based on its reported consumption's proximity to the arithmetic mean of the authentic data set. Since the authentic historical data set is attack-free, the measure of mean is arithmetic mean (AM), denoted by μ.

Then an observed data set is considered with data from spurious meters. We define μ_R as the robust mean of the observed distribution calculated as discussed in Section 4 based on the occurred security incident. The *current proximity distribution* Y_i of each smart meter s^i is calculated based on the proximity of its reported consumptions to μ_R. In contrast, to the historical distribution, when an attack is present, we set μ_R according to Table 3.

If the true distribution is very different from the current distribution, it is an indication that this meter is *unusually* far from the aggregate. This difference is measured as *Kullback-Leibler divergence* (also called KL Distance) which measures the *relative entropy* between the two distributions. The higher the divergence between the two distributions, the

more the indication of anomalous behavior. The trust of a meter is calculated at the end of the window (in days). The total number of observations (T) over the window depends on how time is slotted.

5.1 True and Current Proximity Distributions

We introduce a binary random variable $X_i = \{0, 1\}$ for each meter s^i, for $i = 1, \ldots, N$, which acts as a historical reference distribution. If the historical data reported $p_t^i(rep)$ at time t from meter s^i falls within one standard deviation of μ_t, then $X_i = 1$, else 0. Formally,

$$X_i(t) = \begin{cases} 1 & \text{if } p_t^i(rep) \in \{\mu_t \pm \sigma_t\}; \\ 0 & \text{otherwise} \end{cases} \quad (2)$$

where $X_i(t)$ follows a Bernoulli distribution with parameter r, that is the probability of $X_i = 1$ is r, and the probability of $X_i = 0$ is $1 - r$.

Suppose, $S(X)$ be the variable that denotes the number of successes, that is $S(X_i) = \sum_{t=1}^{T} X_i(t)$. Let $S(X) = k$ be the observed value of the variable.

Similarly, we have a binary random variable Y_i for the current distribution of each smart meter, such that the probability of $Y = 1$ is q and the probability of $Y = 0$ is $1 - q$. In this case, the number of successes is denoted by a variable $R(Y_i) = \sum_{t=1}^{T} Y_i(t)$. Let l be the observed value of $R(Y)$. If an anomaly has been detected through monitoring the HM, AM and AD, then μ_{R_t} is assigned accordingly, and the corresponding standard deviation σ_{R_t} is calculated. In absence of attacks, $\mu_{R_t} = \mu_t$. Thus,

$$Y_i(t) = \begin{cases} 1 & \text{if } p_t^i(rep) \in \{\mu_{R_t} \pm \sigma_{R_t}\}; \\ 0 & \text{otherwise} \end{cases} \quad (3)$$

Intuitively, in absence of attacks the distribution of Y should be very close to X. On the contrary, the two distributions should show a difference when an attack is present.

5.2 Estimating Parameters of True and Current Proximity Distributions

Next we need to estimate the parameters r and q for corresponding distributions X_i and Y_i. An obvious estimate is the minimum variance unbiased estimate (frequentist), which is the sum of all successes divided by the total number of observations T. However, this approach may cause $r = 0, q = 0$, or $r = 1, q = 1$, for which the relative entropy (see Eqn. 9) is undefined. Moreover, frequentist probability unbiased estimator makes sense only if there is a large set of observations [13]. However, since our trust model works on a shorter horizon of time (typically on a few days or monthly basis), such approaches are improper. Hence, we need to accommodate a Bayesian approach for estimation of r and q, so it is theoretically sound and mathematically tractable. Since the following is true for all meter's s^i, we drop the suffix i from the notational simplicity.

First, we estimate the parameter r. We prove that the estimated probability $r = \frac{k+1}{T+2}$, where k is the realization of the total number of successes observed. Thus $S(X) = k$ follows a binomial distribution with parameter r.

Hence, the probability of observing exactly k successes out T times, given the probability of success of each trial was r, is given by,

$$P(S(X) = k|r) = \binom{T}{k} r^k (1-r)^{T-k} \qquad (4)$$

The Bayesian posterior estimate of r, based on prior T observations by Bayes theorem, is given as:

$$P(X(T+1) = 1|S(X) = k) = \frac{P(X(T+1)), S(X) = k}{P(S(X) = k)} \qquad (5)$$

The denominator is the marginal probability of $P(S(X) = k)$ marginalized over all possible outcomes of r. Hence,

$$P(S(X)) = \int_0^1 \binom{T}{k} r^k (1-r)^{T-k} f(r) dr \qquad (6)$$

Assuming conditional independence between $S(X)$, r and $X_i(t+1)$ of the prior and likelihood can be solved as:

$$P(X_i(T+1)), S(X) = k) \Rightarrow$$

$$= \int_0^1 P(X(T+1) = 1|r) P(S(X) = k|r) dr \qquad (7)$$

Since there is no prior information on r, we assume a non-informative prior such that $f(r) = 1$, for the above Eqn (6) and Eqn. (7). Plugging in Eqn. (6) and Eqn. (7) to Eqn. (5), it can be shown that:

$$P(X_i(T+1) = 1|S(X) = k) = \frac{k+1}{T+2} = r \qquad (8)$$

Hence, $r = \frac{k+1}{T+2}$. Similarly, $q = \frac{l+1}{T+2}$.
It can be verified that $r, q \neq 0, 1$. Hence, the logarithms of distributions X and Y in terms of r and q are always defined and exist as evident from Eqn (9).

5.3 Kullback-Leibler Divergence based Trust Model

We adopt the *Kullback Leibler divergence* to measure the difference between the historical distribution X_i and the observed distribution Y_i for a smart meter. It may be noted that X_i and Y_i are not consumption patterns but a trend on proximity to the aggregate. Subsequently, the KL distance is transformed into a trust value between zero and one. The trust values are fed to a generalized linear model based logit link function for linearly separable trust values that facilitate classification between compromised and honest meters through a single threshold.

The KL distance between two distributions X and Y for a smart meter s^i, is given by:

$$D_i(X_i || Y_i) = (1-r) \times ln\left(\frac{1-r}{1-q}\right) + p \times ln\left(\frac{r}{q}\right) \qquad (9)$$

The $D_i(X||Y)$ is a positive real value. The final trust value of a smart meter s^i, is given by:

$$Q_i = \frac{1}{1 + \sqrt{D_i(X||Y)}} \qquad 0 \leq Q_i \leq 1 \qquad (10)$$

Any classification problem such as identifying compromised meters from honest ones, require a threshold for separation. In order to ensure the efficiency of our method, our

goal is to ensure that the compromised and honest meters form two clearly linearly separable clusters in terms of their trust values. However, for certain attacks, especially camouflage and conflict attacks, the distributions may not be sufficiently far from each other to ensure linear separation through a threshold.

To address this problem, we introduce a *kernelized trust metric* that maps the trust values into a higher dimension. We use a light weight two step kernel mapping function. The first step is the use of a generalized linear model (GLM) predictor (logit link function) where Q^i is mapped into $W^i \in \mathbb{R}$ as follows.

$$W^i = log_2\left(\frac{Q^i}{1 - Q^i}\right) \qquad (11)$$

The second step is a Weibull scaling function converting W^i into the final kernelized trust metric $KT^i \in [-1, +1]$:

$$KT^i = \begin{cases} 1 - e^{-|W^i|} & \text{if } W^i > 0; \\ -(1 - e^{-|W^i|}) & \text{if } W^i < 0; \\ 0 & \text{if } W^i = 0 \end{cases} \qquad (12)$$

Eqn. (11), is a logit link function used in logistic regression for binary classification problems. Since, our problem is to classify malicious from honest, the corresponding link function for such response variables is a logit function.

Remark on privacy concerns: Note that, our defense model does not require the storage and maintainance of actual power consumption trends of each individual house. Rather, we only store the information of X_i, thus less privacy intrusive. So, by policy the individual $P_t^i(rep)$ need not be used and may be discarded. In particular, the data collector only knows the historical mixture distribution p_{mix} and the historical private parameter r of each house. The q parameter is the current private parameter of each house. The challenge is resolved by depending on p_{mix}^{his} rather than the individual p_i distribution. Since r and q are compared for KL divergence, both comparison to history and comparison with current mixture distribution is achieved in a privacy preserved manner.

6. PERFORMANCE EVALUATION

The data set from three residential micro-grids of $N = 215$ houses, was obtained from PeCan Street Project [25], containing hourly power consumption data from a solar village near Austin, Texas. We studied some results of anomaly detection and trust model for various attacks. To display the performance of the defense models, a 30 day data from 2014 was used as a training data set. The training data set is used to derive a threshold (through K-means clustering) that linearly separates between honest and compromised labels based on their trust score. A data set for a 30 day period in 2015 is used as a testing data set.

The malicious data sets were generated from the real data samples that were fed into a simulated AMI micro-grid, and ρ_{mal} and Δ_{avg} were carefully chosen to avoid overfitting or underfitting. In the compromised testing data set, the resulting distributions of each smart meter is modeled as the distribution Y. The KL distance is calculated for each smart meter, and subsequently their trust values are plotted. Then, the threshold obtained from training is applied

6.1 Training Set

We use a training data set from 36 houses and use power consumption reported in 2014 for a month. We label some meters as compromised and alter their reported values and plot the corresponding trust values. We use these experiments to calculate a threshold that can linearly separate between compromised and non-compromised nodes. We use a logistic regression classifier to find the optimal linearly separable classifier. We choose $\rho_{mal} = 0.4$, and $\Delta_{avg} = 1024W$ which are intermediate values to prevent overfitting or underfitting. The results of training for various attack strategies are shown in Figs. 8(a) and 8(b).

Figure 9(a) shows the training sets for camouflage attacks with kernelized trust metrics bounded between $[-1, +1]$, for $\delta_{avg} = 960W$ and $\rho_{mal} = 0.45$. The kernel mapping function yield a clear separation between honest and compromised labels even for stealthy camouflage attacks. We derive the threshold as 0.155. Fig. 9(b) shows the training results for conflict attacks where Δ_{avg} is 900 and 600 for additive and deductive attacking meters respectively and $\rho_{mal} = 0.45$.

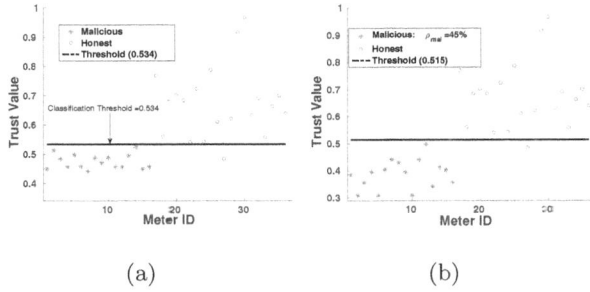

(a) (b)

Figure 8: Training Data: (a) Additive; (b) Deductive

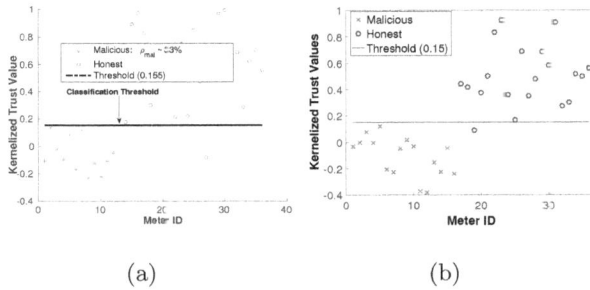

(a) (b)

Figure 9: Training Data: (a) Camouflage; (b) Conflict

6.2 Performance with Testing Set

We use the data set from 2015 as testing set. We set $\rho_{mal} = 0.4$ and $\Delta_{avg} = 768W$. More results with different $\rho_{mal} = \{0.2, 0.3\}$ are presented in Appendix A to prove the scalability. The results for additive and deductive attacks are shown in Figs. 10(a) and 10(b). They exhibit a clear separation between honest and compromised nodes with a false alarm rate of 8.3% in the additive case, and 9.3% in the deductive case. The missed detection rate is 0% for all attack modes, and no compromised meter remains undetected.

Figure 11(a) shows the results for the testing set for $\delta_{avg} = 880W$, demonstrating a clear difference between honest and compromised nodes. The false alarm rate in this case is 11.6%.

For conflict attacks, about 48% of the total meters are compromised, with additive attack of $\delta_{avg} = 1300W$, while the deductive attacks with $\delta_{avg} = 900W$. This is a case which considers random attacks from unorganized rivals.

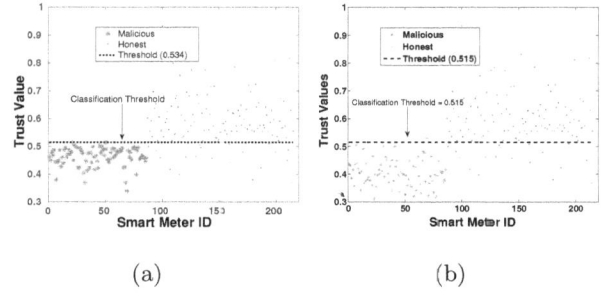

(a) (b)

Figure 10: Testing Data: (a) Additive; (b) Deductive

From Fig. 11(b), we show that our approach works with a high detection rate of 98% and the false alarm rate is about 7%. All the testing results, show improvement from most existing works in [2].

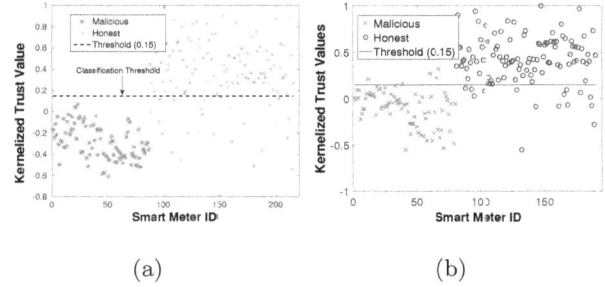

(a) (b)

Figure 11: Testing Sets: (a) Camouflage; (b) Conflict

6.3 Trust Values over Time

Figs. 12(a) and 12(b) show the trust value comparison between an honest meter and a compromised meter over time. Fig. 12(a), shows trust values calculated every 30 days while Fig. 12(b) shows them for every 10 days. The first 90 days are attack free, and hence trust values are above the threshold. After the 90th day, the attack starts, and a decrease in the trust of compromised meter is clear while the honest meter's trust is unaffected.

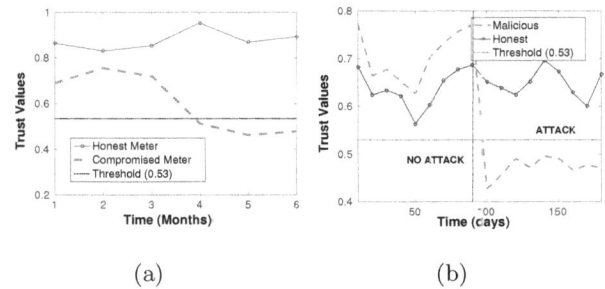

(a) (b)

Figure 12: Trust Propagation Over Time: (a) Every 30 days; (b) Every 10 days

6.4 Breakdown and Breakeven Point Analysis

We model the attacker revenue RR over an attack period of D days in terms monetary gain in the electricity bills as:

$$RR = \frac{\Delta_{avg} \times M_{max} \times \eta \times D \times E}{1000} \quad (13)$$

where Δ_{avg} is the average attack margin, η is the number of reports a day, and E is the per unit (KW-Hour) cost of electricity in dollars.

Recall that the *breakdown point* occurs for some Δ_{avg} and ρ_{mal} such that the proposed model is no longer able to distinguish between compromised and honest nodes because the average trust values of compromised meters are higher than honest ones. We study the existence of such breakdown points, the feasibility of the adversary achieving the breakdown point and associated cost benefit analysis. This analysis can be used by the insider attackers to accordingly design their attack strategy to evade detection.

The breakdown point could be achieved with very high or low margin Δ_{avg} given ρ_{mal}. Very low margins make short term attacks impossible and very large margins make attacks very obvious. Therefore, low margins make sense for long term attacks, but require either a large ρ_{mal} or a long time duration to be effective.

Figure 13 shows different breakdown points for ρ_{mal} values 0.10, 0.25, 0.4 and 0.6 for additive attacks over various Δ_{avg} values. Two break down points exist only for $\rho_{mal} = 0.6$, which suggest that to evade detection with lower margin of false data, the adversary has to compromise a large number of nodes, thus increasing its cost. For lower ρ_{mal}, the attacker cannot evade detection, unless Δ is very small, which in turn rules out short term attacks and increases breakeven time (T_{BE}) significantly.

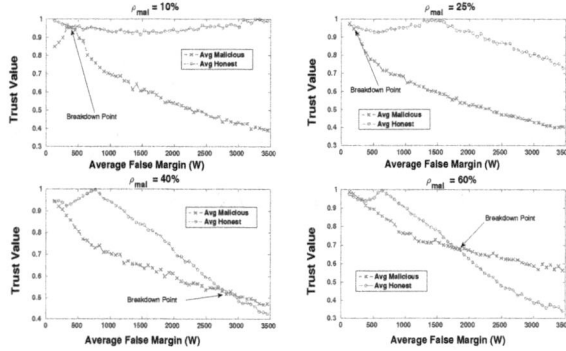

Figure 13: Sensitivity Analysis over Δ_{avg}: Additive

The breakdown points for deductive and camouflage attacks for different ρ_{mal} values are shown in Figs. 14 and 15.

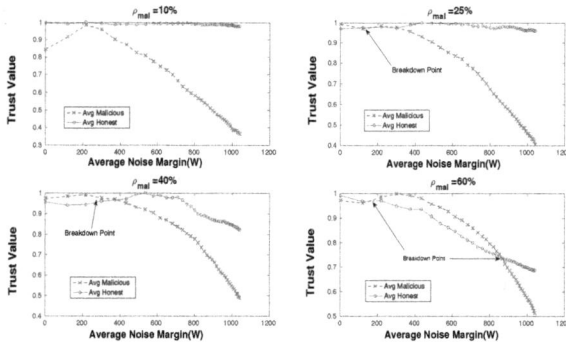

Figure 14: Sensitivity Analysis over Δ_{avg}: Deductive

Table 4 numerically shows that for a very low margin $\Delta_{avg} = 256W$ and $\rho_{mal} = 0.5$, the adversary needs 22 months to recover its initial investment and start to gain profit. This acts as deterrent to implement such a strategy although it may evade detection.

Another aspect shown in the plots and Table 4 is that the breakdown point and attack evasion could be achieved with

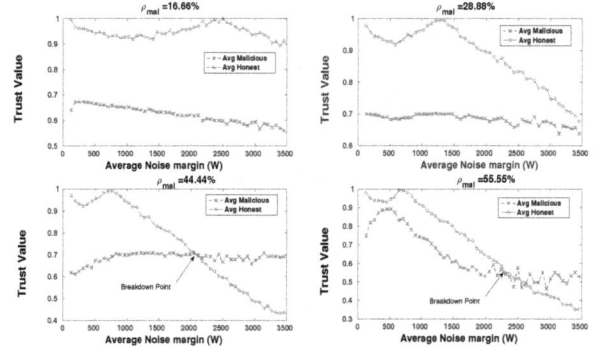

Figure 15: Sensitivity Analysis over Δ_{avg}: Camouflage

higher $\rho_{mal} \geq 0.42$ and a simultaneous higher margin Δ_{avg} of false data. However, our model ensures the breakdown happens only at very high levels of Δ_{avg}. This is intuitively detectable, since the power consumption has a thinner tail, and most of the power consumptions are below $2500W$.

In Table 4 we also observe that when $\Delta_{avg} = 3328W$ and $\Delta_{avg} = 3072W$, the breakdown point is achieved at lower cost of $\rho_{mal} = 0.42$, and breakeven duration is also significantly smaller. The problem for the adversary is the very high margin and fraction of compromised meters, which makes it easily detectable and cost inefficient. This observation shows that although our defense model has breakdown points, most of these correspond to strategies which are hardly convenient for the adversary.

Table 4: Breakdown and Breakeven analysis

Δ_{avg}	ρ_{mal}	TC	RR	T_{BE}
256	0.5	9000	398.13	22
512	0.69	12500	1105.9	11
768	0.80	14500	1924.3	7.53
1024	0.86	15500	2742.6	5.6
1280	0.72	13000	2875.3	4.52
1536	0.61	11000	2919.6	3.76
1792	0.58	10500	3251.4	3.22
2048	0.53	9500	3361.9	2.82
2304	0.50	9000	3583.1	2.5
2560	0.47	8500	3760.1	2.26
2816	0.44	8000	3892.8	2.05
3072	0.42	7500	3981.6	1.88
3328	0.42	7500	4313.0	1.73

7. CONCLUSION

In this paper we presented a taxonomy of various data falsification strategies in AMI micro-grids, as may be devised by powerful and organized adversaries such as rival nation states, business competitors, etc. rather than individual selfish customers only. We proposed statistical anomaly detection and forensics technique to identify presence of various attacks and a trust model based on Kullback-Leibler divergence to identify the compromised smart meters. Our analysis on real data sets shows that both the margin of false data and the fraction of compromised nodes play a key role in understanding the limits of a distributed detection scheme. We also studied some strategies that could be employed by attackers to escape detection and the cost benefit analysis of such strategies.

Acknowledgment: The work is partially supported by the NSF grants under award numbers CNS-1545037, CNS-1545050 and DGE-1433659.

8. REFERENCES

[1] S.-C. Huang, Y.-L. Lo, and C.-N. Lu, "Non-technical loss detection using state estimation and analysis of variance", *IEEE Trans. on Power Systems*, 28(3):2959-2966, Aug. 2013.

[2] R. Jiang , R. Lu, Y. Wang, J. Luo, C. Shen, and X. Shen, "Energy-Theft detection issues for advanced metering infrastructure in smart grids", *Tsinghua Science and Technology*, 19(2):105-120, April 2014.

[3] P. Jokar, N. Arianpoo, and V. Leung, "Electricity theft detection in AMI using customers' consumption patterns", *IEEE Trans. on Smart Grid*, 7(1):216-226, Jan. 2016.

[4] T. Koppel, "Lights Out: A Cyberattack, A Nation Unprepared, Surviving the Aftermath", *Crown Publishers, New York*, 2015.

[5] C.-H. Lo and N. Ansari, "CONSUMER: A novel hybrid intrusion detection system for distribution networks in smart grid", *IEEE Trans. on Emerging Topics in Computing*, 1(1):33-44, 2013.

[6] R. Lu, X. Liang, X. Li, X. Lin, and X. Shen, "EPPA: An efficient and privacy-preserving aggregation scheme for secure smart grid communications," *IEEE Trans. on Parallel and Distributed Systems* 23(9):1621-1631, Sept. 2012.

[7] S. McLaughlin, D. Podkuiko, and P. McDaniel, "Energy theft in the advanced metering infrastructure", *Proc. of Critical Information Infrastructures Security*, Springer-Verlag, pp. 176-187, Sept. 2009.

[8] S. McLaughlin, B. Holbert, S. Zonouz, and R. Berthier, "AMIDS: A multi-sensor energy theft detection framework for advanced metering infrastructures", *IEEE SmartGridComm*, pp. 354-359, Nov. 2012.

[9] D. Mashima and A. Alvaro, "Evaluating electricity theft detectors in smart grid networks", *Springer Intl. Workshop on Recent Advances in Intrusion Detection*, pp. 210-229, Sept. 2012.

[10] R. Mohassel, A. Fung, F. Mohammadi, and K. Raahemifar, "A survey on advanced metering infrastructure", *Elsevier Journal of Electrical Power & Energy Systems*, 63:473-484, Dec. 2014.

[11] A. Rad and A.L. Garcia, "Distributed internet-based load altering attacks against smart power grids", *IEEE Trans. on Smart Grids*, 2(4):667-674, Dec. 2011.

[12] R. Sevlian and R. Rajagopal, "Value of aggregation in smart grids", *IEEE SmartGridComm*, pp. 714-719, Oct. 2013.

[13] Y.L. Sun, W. Yu, Z. Han, K.J. Ray Liu, "Information Theoretic Framework of Trust Model and Evaluation for Ad Hoc Networks", *IEEE Journal on Sel. Areas in Communications*, 24(2):305-317, Feb. 2006.

[14] W. Wang and Z. Lu, "Cyber security in smart grid: Survey and challenges", *Computer Networks*, 57(5):1344-1371, Apr. 2013.

[15] E. Werley, S. Angelos, O. Saavedra, O. Cortes, and A. Souza, "Detection and identification of abnormalities in customer consumptions in power distribution systems", *IEEE Trans. on Power Delivery*, 26(4):2436-2442, Oct. 2011.

[16] J. Xia and Y. Wang, "Secure key distribution for the smart grid", *IEEE Trans. on Smart Grid*, 3(3):1437-1443, Sept. 2012.

[17] W. Yu, D. Griffith, L. Ge, S. Bhattarai and N. Golmie, "An integrated detection system against false data injection attacks in the Smart Grid, *Security and Commun. Networks*, 8(2):91-109, Jan. 2015.

[18] https://skyvisionsolutions.files.wordpress.com/2014/08/utility-smart-meters-invade-privacy-22-aug-2014.pdf

[19] http://www.nytimes.com/2009/12/14/us/14meters.html?ref=energy-environment&_r=0

[20] https://www.maximintegrated.com/content/dam/files/design/technical-documents/white-papers/smart-grid-security-recent-history-demonstrates.pdf

[21] https://energy-solution.com/2015/01/29/enabling-automated-demand-response-pge-dras/

[22] https://www.smartgrid.gov/files/The_Smart_Grid_Promise_DemandSide_Management_201003.pdf

[23] http://blog.comverge.com/intelligent-energy-management/does-ami-have-what-it-takes-for-demand-response/

[24] https://www.whitehouse.gov/sites/default/files/microsites/ostp/nstc-smart-grid-june2011.pdf

[25] https://www.smartgrid.gov/project/pecan_street_project_inc_energy_internet_demonstration.html

[26] https://skyvisionsolutions.files.wordpress.com/2014/08/utility-smart-meters-invade-privacy-22-aug-2014.pdf

[27] http://energy.gov/sites/prod/files/oeprod/DocumentsandMedia/14-AMI_System_Security_Requirements_updated.pdf

APPENDIX

A. TESTING SETS: LOWER FRACTION OF COMPROMISED NODES

Figs. 16(a) and 16(b) prove that our approach works for testing sets with ρ_{mal} values that very different from the training sets.

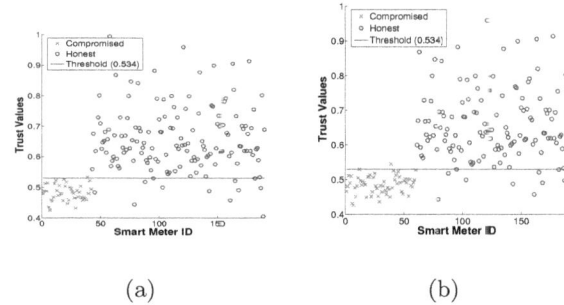

(a)   (b)

Figure 16: Testing Set for Additive: (a) $\rho_{mal} = 20\%$ **(b)** $\rho_{mal} = 30\%$

B. POWER CONSUMPTION DATA: DIFFERENT REGION

To prove that the nature of power consumption studied is generic, we show in Figs. 17(a) and 17(b) that the nature of power consumption is also similar for a different AMI data set as used in [3].

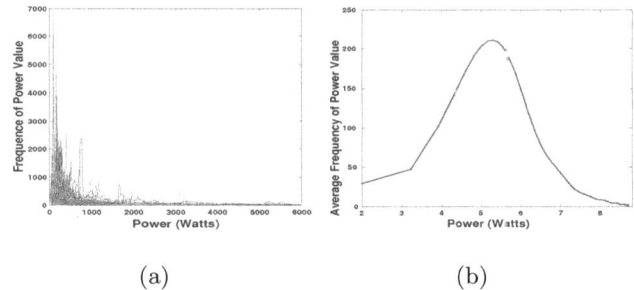

(a)   (b)

Figure 17: Power Consumption Behavior: Different Data Set

Canonical Completeness in Lattice-Based Languages for Attribute-Based Access Control

Jason Crampton
Royal Holloway University of London
Egham, TW20 0EX, United Kingdom
jason.crampton@rhul.ac.uk

Conrad Williams
Royal Holloway University of London
Egham, TW20 0EX, United Kingdom
conrad.williams.2010@live.rhul.ac.uk

ABSTRACT

The study of canonically complete attribute-based access control (ABAC) languages is relatively new. A canonically complete language is useful as it is functionally complete and provides a "normal form" for policies. However, previous work on canonically complete ABAC languages requires that the set of authorization decisions is totally ordered, which does not accurately reflect the intuition behind the use of the allow, deny and not-applicable decisions in access control. A number of recent ABAC languages use a fourth value and the set of authorization decisions is partially ordered. In this paper, we show how canonical completeness in multi-valued logics can be extended to the case where the set of truth values forms a lattice. This enables us to investigate the canonical completeness of logics having a partially ordered set of truth values, such as Belnap logic, and show that ABAC languages based on Belnap logic, such as PBel, are not canonically complete. We then construct a canonically complete four-valued logic using connections between the generators of the symmetric group (defined over the set of decisions) and unary operators in a canonically suitable logic. Finally, we propose a new authorization language $\mathrm{PTaCL}_4^{\leqslant}$, an extension of PTaCL, which incorporates a lattice-ordered decision set and is canonically complete. We then discuss how the advantages of $\mathrm{PTaCL}_4^{\leqslant}$ can be leveraged within the framework of XACML.

Keywords

XACML; PTaCL; decision operators; combining algorithms; functional completeness; canonical completeness

1. INTRODUCTION

Access control is one of the most important security services in multi-user computer systems, providing a mechanism for constraining the interaction between (authenticated) users and protected resources. Generally, access control is implemented by an authorization service, which includes an *authorization decision function* for deciding

CODASPY'17, March 22-24, 2017, Scottsdale, AZ, USA

© 2017 ACM. ISBN 978-1-4503-4523-1/17/03. . . $15.00

DOI: http://dx.doi.org/10.1145/3029806.3029808

whether a user request to access a resource (an "access request") should be permitted or not. In its simplest form an authorization decision function either returns an allow or deny decision.

Most implementations of access control use *authorization policies*, where a user request to access a resource is evaluated with respect to a policy that defines which requests are authorized. Many recent languages for the specification of authorization policies are designed for "open", distributed systems (rather than the more traditional "closed", centralized systems in which the set of users was assumed to be known in advance). Such languages do not necessarily rely on user identities to specify policies; instead, policies are defined in terms of other user and resource attributes. The most widely used attribute-based access control (ABAC) language is XACML [14, 17]. However, XACML suffers from poorly defined and counterintuitive semantics [10, 15], and is inconsistent in its articulation of policy evaluation. PTaCL is a more formal language for specifying authorization policies [6], providing a concise syntax for policy targets and precise semantics for policy evaluation.

Crampton and Williams [7] recently introduced the notion of *canonical completeness* for ABAC languages, showing that XACML and PTaCL are not canonically complete and developing a variant of PTaCL that is canonically complete. These results apply to languages that support three decision values, which are assumed to be totally ordered. However, there are certain situations where it is useful to have four decisions available, and some languages, such as PBel [4], BelLog [18] and Rumpole [12], use four decisions, which are partially ordered.

In this paper, we extend existing results to languages that support four decision values, which need not be totally ordered. We show that PBel [4], perhaps the best-known four-valued ABAC language, is not canonically complete. We then develop a canonically complete ABAC language, based on PTaCL syntax and semantics. The language is abstract, but its operators could be implemented as combining algorithms in XACML, thereby leveraging the features that XACML provides for specifying attribute-based requests and targets, the evaluation of targets with respect to requests, and the storage and evaluation of policies.

In Section 2 we discuss background material and related work, which provides us with the primary motivation for this paper: to develop a canonically complete 4-valued logic to support a tree-structured authorization language. The main contributions of this work are:

- to extend Jobe's work on canonical completeness in multi-valued logics to the case where the set of truth values forms a lattice (Section 3.2);

- to establish that existing 4-valued logics are not canonically complete (Section 3.3);

- to construct a canonically complete 4-valued logic (Section 4);

- to construct a 4-valued, canonically complete authorization language for ABAC (Section 5).

We conclude the paper with a summary of our contributions and a discussion of future work.

2. BACKGROUND AND RELATED WORK

In this section, we summarize background material and related work, including tree-structured ABAC languages, canonical completeness, and four-valued languages for ABAC, thereby providing motivation for the work in the remainder of the paper.

2.1 Completeness in Multi-valued Logics

Let V be a set of truth values. The set of formulae $\Phi(L)$ that can be written in a (multi-valued) propositional logic $L = (V, \mathsf{Ops})$ is defined by V and the set of operators Ops. For brevity, we will write L when V and Ops are obvious from context.

Let V be a totally ordered set of m truth values, $\{0, \ldots, m-1\}$, with $0 < 1 < \cdots < m-1$. Then we say $L = (V, \mathsf{Ops})$ is *canonically suitable* if and only if there exist two formulas $\phi_{\max}$ and $\phi_{\min}$ of arity 2 in $\Phi(L)$ such that $\phi_{\max}(x, y)$ returns $\max\{x, y\}$ and $\phi_{\min}(x, y)$ returns $\min\{x, y\}$. We will usually write $\phi_{\max}$ and $\phi_{\min}$ using the infix operators $\curlyvee$ and $\curlywedge$ respectively.

EXAMPLE 1. *Standard propositional logic with truth values 0 and 1, and operators $\vee$ and $\neg$, representing disjunction and negation, respectively, is canonically suitable: $\phi_{\max}(x, y)$ is simply $x \vee y$, while $\phi_{\min}(x, y)$ is $\neg(\neg x \vee \neg y)$ (that is, conjunction).*

A function $f : V^n \to V$ is completely specified by a truth table containing n columns and m^n rows. However, not every truth table can be represented by a formula in a given logic $L = (V, \mathsf{Ops})$. L is said to be *functionally complete* if for every function $f : V^n \to V$, there is a formula $\phi \in \Phi(L)$ of arity n whose evaluation corresponds to the truth table. In Section 2.2, we explain why we may regard a tree-structured authorization language as a logic defined by a set of decisions and the set of policy-combining operators. In this sense, XACML is not functionally complete [7], while PTaCL [6] and PBel are [4].

A *selection operator* $S^j_{(a_1, \ldots, a_n)}$ is an n-ary operator defined as follows:

$$S^j_{(a_1, \ldots, a_n)}(x_1, \ldots, x_n) = \begin{cases} j & \text{if } (x_1, \ldots, x_n) = (a_1, \ldots, a_n), \\ 0 & \text{otherwise.} \end{cases}$$

We will write $\mathbf{a}$ to denote the tuple $(a_1, \ldots, a_n) \in V^n$ when no confusion can occur. Note that $S^0_{\mathbf{a}}$ is the same for all $\mathbf{a} \in V^n$, and $S^0_{\mathbf{a}}(\mathbf{x}) = 0$ for all $\mathbf{x} \in V^n$. Illustrative examples of binary selection operators (for a 4-valued logic) are shown in Figure 1.

$S^1_{(0,2)}$	0 1 2 3
0	0 0 1 0
1	0 0 0 0
2	0 0 0 0
3	0 0 0 0

$S^2_{(1,1)}$	0 1 2 3
0	0 0 0 0
1	0 2 0 0
2	0 0 0 0
3	0 0 0 0

$S^3_{(3,0)}$	0 1 2 3
0	0 0 0 0
1	0 0 0 0
2	0 0 0 0
3	3 0 0 0

Figure 1: Selection operators $S^1_{(0,2)}$, $S^2_{(1,1)}$ and $S^3_{(3,0)}$

Selection operators play a central role in the development of canonically complete logics because an arbitrary function $f : V^n \to V$ can be expressed in terms of selection operators. Consider, for example, the function

$$f(x, y) = \begin{cases} 1 & \text{if } x = 0, \, y = 2, \\ 2 & \text{if } x = y = 1, \\ 3 & \text{if } x = 3, \, y = 0, \\ 0 & \text{otherwise.} \end{cases}$$

Then it is easy to confirm that

$$f(x, y) \equiv S^1_{(0,2)}(x, y) \curlyvee S^2_{(1,1)}(x, y) \curlyvee S^3_{(3,0)}(x, y).$$

Moreover, $S^c_{(a,b)}(x, y) \equiv S^c_a(x) \curlywedge S^c_b(y)$ for any $a, b, c, x, y \in V$. Thus,

$$f(x, y) \equiv (S^1_0(x) \curlywedge S^1_2(y)) \curlyvee (S^2_1(x) \curlywedge S^2_1(y)) \curlyvee (S^3_3(x) \curlywedge S^3_0(y))$$

In other words, we can express f as the "disjunction" ($\curlyvee$) of "conjunctions" ($\curlywedge$) of unary selection operators.

More generally, given the truth table of function $f : V^n \to V$, we can write down an equivalent function in terms of selection operators. Specifically, let

$$A = \{\mathbf{a} \in V^n : f(\mathbf{a}) > 0\};$$

then, for all $\mathbf{x} \in V^n$,

$$f(\mathbf{x}) = \bigcurlyvee_{\mathbf{a} \in A} S^{f(\mathbf{x})}_{\mathbf{a}}(\mathbf{x}).$$

Jobe established a number of results connecting the functional completeness of a logic with the unary selection operators, summarized in the following theorem.

THEOREM 1 (JOBE [9, THEOREMS 1, 2; LEMMA 1]).
A logic L is functionally complete if and only if each unary selection operator is equivalent to some formula in L.

The *normal form* of formula ϕ in a canonically suitable logic is a formula ϕ' that has the same truth table as ϕ and has the following properties:

- the only binary operators it contains are $\curlyvee$ and $\curlywedge$;

- no binary operator is included in the scope of a unary operator;

- no instance of $\curlyvee$ occurs in the scope of the $\curlywedge$ operator.

In other words, given a canonically suitable logic L containing unary operators $\sharp_1, \ldots, \sharp_\ell$, a formula in normal form has the form

$$\bigcurlyvee_{i=1}^{r} \bigcurlywedge_{j=1}^{s} \sharp_{i,j} x_{i,j}$$

where $\natural_{i,j}$ is a unary operator defined by composing the unary operators in $\natural_1, \ldots, \natural_\ell$. In the usual 2-valued propositional logic with a single unary operator (negation) this corresponds to disjunctive normal form.

A canonically suitable logic is *canonically complete* if every unary selection operator can be expressed in normal form. It is known that there are canonically suitable 3-valued logics that are: (i) not functionally complete [5, 11]; (ii) functionally complete but not canonically complete [9, Theorem 4]; and (iii) canonically complete (and hence functionally complete) [9, Theorem 6].

Jobe defined a canonically complete 3-valued logic [9]. The operators and the construction of the unary selection operators using these operators are given in Appendix A. The expression for f above could be expressed in normal form, providing we could find suitable unary operators for a 4-valued logic. In Section 4.3 we explain how to produce a suitable set of unary operators for an m-valued logic.

2.2 Tree-structured Languages for ABAC

Let D be a set of *authorization decisions*. Typically, we assume D contains the values 0, 1 and $\perp$ representing "deny", "allow" and "not-applicable", respectively. We call 0 and 1 *conclusive* decisions. Let $\oplus$ be an associative binary operator defined on D and $-$ be a unary operator defined on D. Then

- an *atomic policy* is a pair (t, d), where d is a decision in D and t is a *target predicate*;

- an atomic policy is a *policy*;

- if p and p' are policies, then $(t, p \oplus p')$ and $(t, -p)$ are policies.

We will write p to denote the policy (true, p).

The first stage in policy evaluation for a request q is to determine whether a policy is "applicable" to q or not. Every (well-formed) request q, allows us to assign a truth value to the target t. Specifically, t may evaluate to true, in which case the associated policy is *applicable*; otherwise the policy is *not applicable*.[1] Then, writing $\nu_q(t)$ to denote the truth value assigned to t by q and $\delta_q(p)$ to denote the decision assigned to policy p for request q, we define:

$$\delta_q(t, p) = \begin{cases} \delta_q(p) & \text{if } \nu_q(t) = 1, \\ \perp & \text{otherwise;} \end{cases}$$

$$\delta_q(d) = d;$$

$$\delta_q(-p) = -\delta_q(p);$$

$$\delta_q(p \oplus p') = \delta_q(p) \oplus \delta_q(p').$$

It is easy to see that we may represent a policy as a tree. Hence, we describe policy languages of this nature as *tree-structured*. The first stage in policy evaluation corresponds to labeling the nodes of tree applicable or not applicable. We then compute a decision for non-leaf nodes in the tree by combining the decisions assigned to their respective children. Figure 2 shows the tree for the policy

$$(t_6, (t_4, -(t_3, ((t_1, 1) \oplus_1 (t_2, 0)))) \oplus_2 (t_5, 0))$$

---

[1]The evaluation of requests is not relevant to the exposition of this paper. XACML provides a means of specifying requests and targets and an evaluation architecture for determining whether a target is applicable or not.

and the evaluation of that policy for a request q such that $\nu_q(t_i) = \mathsf{true}$ for all i except $i = 2$.

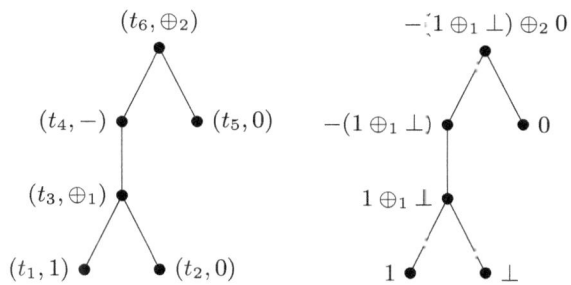

Figure 2: A policy tree and its evaluation

There are several tree-structured ABAC languages in the literature, including the OASIS standard XACML, PBel and PTaCL [17, 6, 4].[2] These languages differ to some extent in the choices of D and the set of operators that are used. XACML, for example, defines several rule- and policy-combining algorithms (which may be regarded as binary operators), but no unary operators.[3] PBel and PTaCL prefer to define a rather small set of operators: PTaCL defines a single binary operator and two unary operators, whereas PBel defines two binary operators and a single unary operator. XACML and PTaCL use a three-valued decision set comprising 0, 1 and $\perp$, to which PBel adds $\top$, which represents "conflict".

The main difference between existing languages, however, is the extent to which they are complete in the senses defined in Section 2.1 [7]. We summarize these differences in Table 1, where CS, FC and CC denote canonically suitable, functionally complete and canonically complete, respectively. In Section 3.3, we prove that PBel is canonically suitable but not canonically complete.

Language	Decisions	Unary Ops	Binary Ops
XACML	$\{0, 1, \perp\}$	0	12
PTaCL	$\{0, 1, \perp\}$	2	1
PTaCL(E)	$\{0, 1, \perp\}$	2	1
PBel	$\{0, 1, \perp, \top\}$	1	2

Language	CS?	FC?	CC?
XACML	No	No	No
PTaCL	Yes	Yes	No
PTaCL(E)	Yes	Yes	Yes
PBel	?	Yes	?

Table 1: Properties of ABAC languages

2.3 The Value of Canonical Completeness

One of the main difficulties with using a tree-structured language is writing the desired policy using the operators

---

[2]A number of policy algebras have also been defined, which have some similarities with tree-structured languages. The semantics of a policy are defined in terms of sets of authorized and denied requests [3, 19, 15, 16], and policy operators are defined in terms of set operations such as intersection and union.

[3]An XACML rule is equivalent to an atomic policy.

provided by the language. In particular, if it is not possible to express a policy using a single target and decision, the policy author must engineer the desired policy by combining sub-policies using the set of operators specified in the given language. This is a non-trivial task, in general. Moreover, in XACML it may be impossible to write the desired policy due to its functional incompleteness. Thus, a policy author may be forced to write a policy that approximates the desired policy, which may lead to unintended or undesirable decisions for certain requests.

An alternative approach, supported by XACML, is to define custom combining algorithms. However, there is no guarantee that the addition of a new combining algorithm will make XACML functionally complete. Thus, more and more custom algorithms may be required over time. This, in turn, will make the design decisions faced by policy authors ever more complicated, thereby increasing the chances of errors and misconfigurations.

In other words, we believe it is preferable to define a small number of operators having unambiguous semantics and providing functional completeness. A functionally complete ABAC language, such as PTaCL, can be used to construct any conceivable policy using the operators provided by the language. However, policy authors still face the challenge of finding the correct way to combine sub-policies using those operators to construct the desired policy.

For example, PTaCL defines three policy operators $\wedge_p$, $\neg$ and $\sim$. To express XACML's deny- and permit-overrides in PTaCL requires significant effort. For convenience, we introduce the operator $\vee_p$:

$$d \vee_p d' \stackrel{\text{def}}{=} \neg((\neg d) \wedge_p (\neg d')).$$

It is then possible to show that

$$d \text{ po } d' \equiv (d \vee_p (\sim d')) \wedge_p ((\sim d) \vee_p d'), \text{ and}$$
$$d \text{ do } d' \equiv \neg((\neg d) \text{ po } (\neg d')).$$

The operators po and do are equivalent to the permit- and allow-overrides policy-combining algorithms in XACML. As can be seen, the definitions of these operators in terms of the PTaCL operators are complex, and, more generally, it is a non-trivial task to derive such formulae.

Disjunctive normal form in propositional logic makes it trivial to write down a logical formula, using only conjunction, disjunction and negation, that is equivalent to an arbitrary Boolean function expressed in the form of a truth table. Similarly, a canonically complete ABAC language, such as PTaCL(E) [7], makes it possible to write down a policy in normal form from its decision table. In this paper, we show that there exist 4-valued canonically complete logics in which the set of truth values forms a lattice. We discuss why and how this can simplify policy generation in Section 5.2.

In addition, policies in normal form may be more efficient to evaluate. Given a formula in a 3-valued logic expressed in normal form, any literal that evaluates to 0 causes the entire clause to evaluate to 0, while any clause evaluating to 1 means the entire formula evaluates to 1. In short, the time required for policy evaluation may be reduced in many cases. (This is similar to the way in which algorithms such as first-applicable in XACML work: once an applicable policy is found policy evaluation terminates, even if there are additional policies that could be evaluated.)

2.4 The Value of a Fourth Decision

The XACML 2.0 standard includes a fourth authorization decision "indeterminate" [14]. This is used to indicate errors have occurred during policy evaluation, meaning that a decision could not be reached. The XACML 3.0 standard extends the definition of the indeterminate decision to indicate decisions that might have been reached, had evaluation been possible [17]. However, the indeterminate decision is used in XACML 3.0 for more than reporting errors. It is also used as a decision in the "only-one-applicable" combining algorithm, which returns indeterminate if two or more sub-policies are applicable.

More generally, a conflict decision is used in PBel (and languages such as Rumpole and BelLog) to indicate that two sub-policies return different conclusive decisions. PBel is functionally complete. In the remainder of this paper, we show that PBel is not canonically complete and then develop a canonically complete 4-valued ABAC language.

3. LATTICE-BASED MULTI-VALUED LOGICS

We first recall the definition of a lattice. Suppose $(X, \leqslant)$ is a partially ordered set. Then for a subset Y of X, we say u is an *upper bound* of Y if $y \leqslant u$ for all $y \in Y$. We say u' is a *least upper bound* or *supremum* of Y if $u' \leqslant u$ for all upper bounds u of Y. Note that a least upper bound of Y (if it exists) is unique. We define *greatest lower bound* or *infimum* in an analogous way. A lattice $(X, \leqslant)$ is a partially ordered set such that for all $x, y \in X$ there exists a least upper bound of x and y, denoted $\sup \{x, y\}$, and a greatest lower bound of x and y, denoted by $\inf \{x, y\}$. The least upper bound of x and y is written as $x \vee y$ (the "join" of x and y) and the greatest lower bound is written as $x \wedge y$ (the "meet" of x and y). If $(X, \leqslant)$ is a finite lattice, as we will assume henceforth, then $(X, \leqslant)$ has a maximum element (that is, a unique maximal element) and a minimum element.

In the remainder of this section we (i) describe Belnap logic [2], a well-known 4-valued lattice-based logic; (ii) extend the definitions of canonical suitability, selection operators and canonical completeness to lattices; and (iii) show that Belnap logic and PBel are not canonically complete.

3.1 Belnap Logic

Belnap logic was developed with the intention of defining ways to handle inconsistent and incomplete information in a formal manner. It uses the truth values 0, 1, $\perp$, and $\top$, representing "false", "true", "lack of information" and "too much information", respectively. In the remainder of this paper, we will denote the four valued decision set $\{\perp, 0, 1, \top\}$ by **4**.

The truth values 0, 1, $\perp$ and $\top$ have an intuitive interpretation in the context of access control: 0 and 1 are interpreted as the standard "deny" and "allow" decisions, $\perp$ is interpreted as "not-applicable" and $\top$ represents a conflict of decisions. PBel is a 4-valued tree-structured ABAC language [4] based on Belnap logic.

The set of truth values in Belnap logic admits two orderings: a truth ordering $\leqslant_t$ and a knowledge ordering $\leqslant_k$. In the truth ordering, 0 is the minimum element and 1 is the maximum element, while $\perp$ and $\top$ are incomparable indeterminate values. In the knowledge ordering, $\perp$ is the minimum element, $\top$ is the maximum element while 0 and 1 are incomparable. Both $(4, \leqslant_t)$ and $(4, \leqslant_k)$ are lattices, forming the interlaced bilattice illustrated in Figure 3.

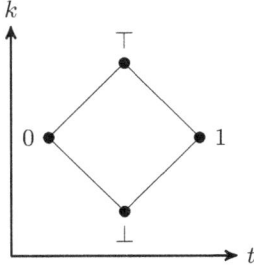

Figure 3: The 4 truth values in Belnap logic

We write the meet and join in $(4, \leqslant_t)$ as $\wedge_b$ and $\vee_b$, respectively; and the meet and join in $(4, \leqslant_k)$ as $\otimes_b$ and $\oplus_b$, respectively. (We use the subscript b to differentiate the Belnap operators from the PTaCL operators $\wedge_p$ and $\vee_p$.)

We may interpret values in V as operators of arity 0 (that is, constants). Then it is known that $L(4, \{\neg, \wedge_b, \vee_b, \otimes_b, \oplus_b, \supset_b, \bot, 0, 1, \top\})$ is functionally complete [1, Theorem 12] and that $\{\neg, \oplus_b, \supset_b, \bot\}$ is a minimal functionally complete set of operators [1, Proposition 17]. The truth tables for the binary operators $\wedge_b$, $\vee_b$, $\otimes_b$, $\oplus_b$ and $\supset_b$ are shown in Figure 11 (in Appendix B). The unary operator $\neg$ has the effect of switching the values 0 and 1, leaving $\bot$ and $\top$ fixed; in other words, it acts like "classical" negation.

3.2 Canonical Completeness

Jobe's definition of canonical suitability for multi-valued logics assumes a total ordering on the set of truth values. Given that Belnap logic [1], on which PBel is based, is a 4-valued logic in which the set of truth values forms a lattice, we seek to extend the definition of canonical suitability to lattice-based logics.

Let L be a logic associated with a lattice $(V, \leqslant)$ of truth values. Then L is *canonically suitable* if and only if there exist in L two formulas $\phi_{\max}$ and $\phi_{\min}$ of arity 2 such that $\phi_{\max}(x, y)$ returns $\sup\{x, y\}$ and $\phi_{\min}(x, y)$ returns $\inf\{x, y\}$. If a logic is canonically suitable, we will write $\phi_{\max}(x, y)$ and $\phi_{\min}(x, y)$ using infix binary operators as $x \curlyvee y$ and $x \curlywedge y$, respectively.

REMARK 1. *The existence of* $\sup\{x, y\}$ *and* $\inf\{x, y\}$ *is guaranteed in a lattice; this is not true in general for partially ordered sets. And for a totally ordered (finite) set,* $\sup\{x, y\} = \max\{x, y\}$ *and* $\inf\{x, y\} = \min\{x, y\}$, *so our definitions are compatible with those of Jobe's for totally ordered sets of truth values.*

We now extend the definition of selection operators to a lattice-based logic. Let L be a logic associated with a lattice $(V, \leqslant)$ of truth values, with minimum truth value $\underline{v}$. Then, for $\mathbf{a} \in V^n$, the n-ary *selection operator* $S_{\mathbf{a}}^j$ is defined as follows:

$$S_{\mathbf{a}}^j(\mathbf{x}) = \begin{cases} j & \text{if } \mathbf{x} = \mathbf{a}, \\ \underline{v} & \text{otherwise.} \end{cases}$$

Note $S_{\mathbf{a}}^{\underline{v}}(x) = \underline{v}$ for all $\mathbf{a}, \mathbf{x} \in V^n$.

The definitions for normal form and canonically completeness for lattice-based logics are identical to total-ordered logics. Nevertheless, we reiterate the definitions here in the interests of clarity. The *normal form* of formula ϕ in a canonically suitable logic is a formula ϕ' that has the same truth table as ϕ and has the following properties:

- the only binary operators it contains are $\curlyvee$ and $\curlywedge$;
- no binary operator is included in the scope of a unary operator;
- no instance of $\curlyvee$ occurs in the scope of the $\curlywedge$ operator.

A canonically suitable logic is *canonically complete* if every unary selection operator can be expressed in normal form.

3.3 Completeness of Belnap Logic and PBel

Having extended the definitions of canonical suitability, selection operators and canonical completeness to lattices, we now investigate how these concepts can be applied to Belnap logic [2]. The meet and join operators of the two lattices $(4, \leqslant_t)$ and $(4, \leqslant_k)$ defined in Belnap logic are different. Canonical suitability for a 4-valued logic, defined as it is in terms of the ordering on the set of truth values, will thus depend on the ordering we choose on 4. Consequently, the $\curlywedge$ and $\curlyvee$ operators, along with the selection operators, will differ depending on the lattice that we choose.

In Section 5, we will argue in more detail for the use of a lattice-based ordering on 4 to support a tree-structured ABAC language. For now, we state that we will use knowledge-ordered lattice $(4, \leqslant_k)$.[4] The intuition is that the minimum value in this lattice is $\bot$ (rather than 0 in $(4, \leqslant_t)$) and that this value should be the default value for a policy (being returned when the policy is not applicable to a request). In the interests of brevity, we will henceforth write 4_k, rather than $(4, \leqslant_k)$.

It follows from the functional completeness of $\{\neg, \oplus_b, \supset_b, \bot\}$ that $L(4_k, \{\neg, \oplus_b, \supset_b, \bot\})$ is canonically suitable. A similar argument applies to $\{\neg, \wedge_b, \supset_b, \bot, \top\}$, the set of operators used in PBel.

As $\bot$ is the minimum truth value in the lattice 4_k, the n-ary selection operator $S_{\mathbf{a}}^j$ for 4_k is defined by the following function:

$$S_{\mathbf{a}}^j(\mathbf{x}) = \begin{cases} j & \text{if } \mathbf{x} = \mathbf{a}, \\ \bot & \text{otherwise.} \end{cases}$$

Examples of selection operators are shown in Figure 4.

x	S_0^0	$S_1^\top$		$S_{(1,\top)}^0$	$\bot$	0	1	$\top$
$\bot$	$\bot$	$\bot$		$\bot$	$\bot$	$\bot$	$\bot$	$\bot$
0	0	$\bot$		0	$\bot$	$\bot$	$\bot$	$\bot$
1	$\bot$	$\top$		1	$\bot$	$\bot$	$\bot$	0
$\top$	$\bot$	$\bot$		$\top$	$\bot$	$\bot$	$\bot$	$\bot$

Figure 4: Examples of selection operators in a logic based on 4_k

Functional completeness also implies all unary selection operators can be expressed as formulas in the logics

---

[4] It is worth noting that results analogous to those presented in this paper can be obtained for the truth ordering. Results for a total ordering on 4 can be derived using existing methods [7, 9].

$L(\mathbf{4}_k, \{\neg, \oplus_b, \supset_b, \bot\})$ and $L(\mathbf{4}_k, \{\neg, \wedge_b, \supset_b, \bot, \top\})$. However, we have the following result, from which it follows that neither of these logics is canonically complete.

PROPOSITION 1. $L(\mathbf{4}_k, \{\neg, \wedge_b, \vee_b, \otimes_b, \oplus_b, \supset_b, \bot, 0, 1, \top\})$ is not canonically complete.

PROOF. It is impossible to represent all unary selection operators in normal form. The statement follows from the following observations: (i) Belnap logic defines one unary operator $\neg$; (ii) the only binary operators that may be used in normal form are $\oplus_b$ (λ) and $\otimes_b$ ($\curlyvee$); and (iii) for any operator $\oplus \in \{\neg, \otimes_b, \oplus_b\}$ we have $\bot \oplus \bot = \bot$. Thus it is impossible to construct a unary operator of the form $S_\bot^d$ for any $d \neq \bot$. $\square$

COROLLARY 1. *PBel is not a canonically complete authorization language.*

PROOF. PBel uses the set of operators $\{\neg, \wedge_b, \supset_b, \bot, \top\}$, which is a subset of $\{\neg, \wedge_b, \vee_b, \otimes_b, \oplus_b, \supset_b, \bot, 0, 1, \top\}$. Thus, by Proposition 1, this is not a canonically complete set of operators, so $L(\mathbf{4}_k, \{\neg, \wedge_b, \supset_b, \bot, \top\})$ is not canonically complete either. Hence, we may conclude that PBel is not a canonically complete authorization language. $\square$

4. A CANONICALLY COMPLETE 4-VALUED LOGIC

In the proof of Proposition 1, we were unable to construct all unary selection operators using operators from the set $\{\neg, \otimes_b, \oplus_b\}$, because there is no operator in which $\bot \oplus \bot \neq \bot$. This suggests that we will require at least one additional unary operator $-$, say, such that $-\bot \neq \bot$. Accordingly, we start with the unary operator, sometimes called "conflation" [8], such that

$$-\bot = \top, \quad -\top = \bot, \quad -0 = 0, \text{ and } -1 = 1.$$

Conflation is analogous to negation $\neg$, but inverts knowledge values rather than truth values. In addition to $-$, we include the operator $\otimes_b$ in our set of operators, since this is the join operator for $\mathbf{4}_k$.

PROPOSITION 2. $L(\mathbf{4}_k, \{-, \otimes_b\})$ is canonically suitable.

Informally, the proof follows from the fact that $-$ and $\otimes_b$ have exactly the same effect on $\mathbf{4}_k$ as $\neg$ and $\wedge_b$ have on $(\mathbf{4}, \leqslant_t)$. More formally, the following equivalence holds [1]:

$$d \oplus_b d' \equiv -(-d \otimes_b -d').$$

The decision table establishing this equivalence is given in Figure 12 (in Appendix C). Hence, we conclude that the set of operators $\{-, \otimes_b\}$ is canonically suitable, since λ corresponds to $\otimes_b$ and $\curlyvee$ corresponds to $\oplus_b$.

PROPOSITION 3. $L(\mathbf{4}_k, \{-, \otimes_b\})$ is not functionally complete.

PROOF. The proof follows from the following observations: (i) for the operators $-$ and $\otimes_b$, $-(0) = 0$ and $0 \otimes_b 0 = 0$; and (ii) any operator $\circ$ which is a combination of $-$ and $\otimes_b$, we have $0 \circ 0 = 0$. Thus it is impossible to construct an operator in which $0 \circ 0 \neq 0$. $\square$

To summarize: $L(\mathbf{4}_k, \{\neg, \wedge_b, \vee_b, \otimes_b, \oplus_b, \supset_b, \bot, 0, 1, \top\})$ is not canonically complete and $L(\mathbf{4}_k, \{-, \otimes_b\})$ is not functionally complete. We now investigate what additional operators should be defined to construct a set of operators which is canonically complete (and hence functionally complete).

Given that we cannot use any operators besides $\curlyvee$ and λ in normal form, we focus on defining additional unary operators on $\mathbf{4}_k$. An important observation at this point is that any permutation (that is, a bijection) $\pi : \mathbf{4} \to \mathbf{4}$ defines a unary operator on $\mathbf{4}$. Accordingly, we now explore the connections between the group of permutations on $\mathbf{4}$ and unary operators on $\mathbf{4}$.

4.1 The Symmetric Group and Unary Operators

The *symmetric group* $(S_X, \circ)$ on a finite set of $|X|$ symbols is the group whose elements are all permutations of the elements in X, and whose group operation $\circ$ is function composition. In other words, given two permutations π_1 and π_2, $\pi_1 \circ \pi_2$ is a permutation such that

$$(\pi_1 \circ \pi_2)(x) \stackrel{\text{def}}{=} \pi_1(\pi_2(x)).$$

We write π^k to denote the permutation obtained by composing π with itself k times.

A *transposition* is a permutation which exchanges two elements and keeps all others fixed. Given two elements a and b in X, the permutation

$$\pi(x) = \begin{cases} b & \text{if } x = a, \\ a & \text{if } x = b, \\ x & \text{otherwise,} \end{cases}$$

is a transposition, which we denote by $(a\,b)$. A *cycle* of *length* $k \geqslant 2$ is a permutation π for which there exists an element x in X such that $x, \pi(x), \pi^2(x), \ldots, \pi^k(x) = x$ are the only elements changed by π. Given a, b and c in X, for example, the permutation

$$\pi(x) = \begin{cases} b & \text{if } x = a, \\ c & \text{if } x = b, \\ a & \text{if } x = c, \\ x & \text{otherwise,} \end{cases}$$

is a cycle of length 3, which we denote by $(a\,b\,c)$. (Cycles of length two are transpositions.) The symmetric group S_X is *generated* by its cycles. That is, every permutation may be represented as the composition of some combination of cycles.

In fact, stronger results are known. We first introduce some notation. Let $X = \{x_1, \ldots, x_n\}$ and let S_n denote the symmetric group on the set of elements $\{1, \ldots, n\}$. Then $(S_X, \circ)$ is trivially isomorphic to $(S_n, \circ)$ (via the mapping $x_i \mapsto i$).

THEOREM 2. *For $n \geqslant 2$, S_n is generated by the transpositions $(1\,2), (1\,3), \ldots, (1\,n)$.*

THEOREM 3. *For $1 \leqslant a < b \leqslant n$, the transposition $(a\,b)$ and the cycle $(1\,2\ldots n)$ generate S_n if and only if the greatest common divisor of $b - a$ and n equals 1.*

In other words, it is possible to find a generating set comprising only transpositions, and it is possible to find a generating set containing only two elements.

4.2 New Unary Operators

We now define three unary operators $\sim_0, \sim_1$ and $\sim_\top$, which swap the value of $\bot$ and the truth value in the operator's subscript. The truth tables for these operators are shown in Figure 5. Note that $\sim_\top$ is identical to the conflation operator $-$. However, in the interests of continuity and consistency we will use the $\sim_\top$ notation in the remainder of this section.

d	$\sim_0 d$	$\sim_1 d$	$\sim_\top d$
$\bot$	0	1	$\top$
0	$\bot$	0	0
1	1	$\bot$	1
$\top$	$\top$	$\top$	$\bot$

Figure 5: $\sim_0, \sim_1$ and $\sim_\top$

Notice that $\sim_0, \sim_1$ and $\sim_\top$ permute the elements of 4 and correspond to the transpositions $(\bot\, 0), (\bot\, 1)$ and $(\bot\, \top)$, respectively. Thus we have the following elementary result.

PROPOSITION 4. *Any permutation on 4 can be expressed using only operators from the set $\{\sim_0, \sim_1, \sim_\top\}$.*

PROOF. The operators $\sim_0, \sim_1$ and $\sim_\top$ are the transpositions $(\bot\, 0), (\bot\, 1)$ and $(\bot\, \top)$ respectively. By Theorem 2, these operators generate all the permutations in S_4. $\square$

LEMMA 1. *It is possible to express any function $\phi : 4 \to 4$ as a formula in $L(4_k, \{\sim_0, \sim_1, \sim_\top, \otimes_b, \oplus_b\})$.*

PROOF. For convenience, we represent the function $\phi : 4 \to 4$ as the tuple

$$(\phi(\bot), \phi(0), \phi(1), \phi(\top)) = (a, b, c, d).$$

Then, given $x, y, z \in 4$, we define the function

$$\phi_x^y(z) = \begin{cases} x & \text{if } z = y, \\ \bot & \text{otherwise.} \end{cases}$$

Thus, for example, $\phi_a^\bot = (a, \bot, \bot, \bot)$. Then it is easy to see that for all $x \in 4$

$$\phi(x) = \phi_a^\bot(x) \oplus_b \phi_b^0(x) \oplus_b \phi_c^1(x) \oplus_b \phi_d^\top(x).$$

That is $\phi = \phi_a^\bot \oplus_b \phi_b^0 \oplus_b \phi_c^1 \oplus_b \phi_d^\top$.

Thus, it remains to show that we can represent $\phi_a^\bot$, ϕ_b^0, ϕ_c^1 and $\phi_d^\top$ as formulas using the operators in $\{\sim_0, \sim_1, \sim_\top, \otimes_b, \oplus_b\}$. First consider the permutations $\phi_{a,0}$, $\phi_{a,1}$ and $\phi_{a,\top}$, represented by the tuples $(a, \bot, b_1, c_1)$, $(a, b_2, \bot, c_2)$ and $(a, b_3, c_3, \bot)$, respectively.[5] Since $\phi_{a,0}, \phi_{a,1}$ and $\phi_{a,\top}$ are permutations, we know they can be written as some combination of the unary operators. Moreover,

$$\phi_a^\bot \equiv \phi_{a,0} \otimes_b \phi_{a,1} \otimes_b \phi_{a,\top}$$

Clearly, we can construct ϕ_b^0, ϕ_c^1 and $\phi_d^\top$ in a similar fashion. The result now follows. $\square$

The decision tables showing the construction of $\phi_a^\bot$ (column 5) and ϕ (column 10) are shown in Figure 6.

---

[5] Note that the specific values of b_i and c_i are not important: it suffices that each of $\phi_{a,0}, \phi_{a,1}$ and $\phi_{a,\top}$ are permutations; once b_i is chosen such that $b_i \notin \{a, \bot\}$, then c_i is fixed.

THEOREM 4. $L(4_k, \{\sim_0, \sim_1, \sim_\top, \otimes_b, \oplus_b\})$ *is functionally and canonically complete.*

PROOF. By Lemma 1, it is possible to express any function $\phi : 4 \to 4$ as a formula using operators from the set $\{\sim_0, \sim_1, \sim_\top, \otimes_b, \oplus_b\}$. In particular, all unary selection operators can be expressed in this way. Hence by Theorem 1, the set of operators $\{\sim_0, \sim_1, \sim_\top, \otimes_b, \ominus_b\}$ is functionally complete.

Moreover, all formulae constructed in the proof of Lemma 1 contain only the binary operators $\oplus_b(\Upsilon)$ and $\otimes_b(\lambda)$, and unary operators defined as compositions of $\sim_0, \sim_1$ and $\sim_\top$. Thus, by definition, the unary selection operators are in normal form. $\square$

COROLLARY 2. $L(4_k, \{\sim_0, \sim_1, \sim_\top, \otimes_b\})$ *is functionally and canonically complete.*

PROOF. The conflation operator $-$ and $\sim_\top$ are identical. Hence

$$d \oplus_b d' \equiv -(- d \otimes_b - d') \equiv \sim_\top(\sim_\top d \otimes_b \sim_\top d').$$

Therefore, the set of operators is canonically suitable, and, by Theorem 4, it is functionally and canonically complete (since we can construct $\oplus_b$). $\square$

COROLLARY 3. *Let $\diamond$ be the unary operator corresponding to the permutation given by the cycle $(\bot\, 0\, 1\, \top)$. Then $L(4_k, \{\sim_\top, \diamond, \otimes_b\})$ is functionally and canonically complete.*

PROOF. By Theorem 3, $\sim_\top$ and $\diamond$ generate all permutations in S_4. The remainder of the proof follows immediately from Lemma 1 and Theorem 4. $\square$

It is important to note that we could choose any transposition $(a\, b)$, such that $\gcd(b - a, n) = 1$. We specifically selected the transposition $(\bot\, \top)$, as this has the effect of reversing the minimum and maximum knowledge values. Another choice for this transposition is one which swaps 0 and 1, specifically the transposition $(0\, 1)$. This transposition is the truth negation operator $\neg$, which in the context of access control is a useful operator, since it swaps allow and deny decisions.

4.3 Unary Operators for Totally Ordered Logics

Having shown the construction for a canonically complete 4-valued logic, in which the set of logical values forms a lattice, we briefly return to totally ordered logics. We construct a totally ordered, canonically complete m-valued logic (thus extending the work of Jobe, who only showed how to construct a canonically complete 3-valued logic).

Let V be a totally ordered set of m truth values, $\{1, \ldots, m\}$, with $1 < \cdots < m$. We define two unary operators $\dagger$ and $\diamond$, which are the transposition $(1\, m)$ and the cycle $(1\, 2 \ldots m)$, respectively. In addition, we define one binary operator $\wedge_t$, where $x \wedge_t y = \max\{x, y\}$.

PROPOSITION 5. *Any permutation on V can be expressed using only operators from the set $\{\dagger, \diamond\}$.*

PROOF. The operator $\dagger$ is the transposition $(1\, m)$ and the operator $\diamond$ is the cycle $(1\, 2 \ldots m)$. By Theorem 3, these operators generate all the permutations in S_V. $\square$

PROPOSITION 6. $L(V, \{\dagger, \diamond, \wedge_t\})$ *is canonically suitable.*

53

x	$\phi_{a,0}$	$\phi_{a,1}$	$\phi_{a,\top}$	$\phi_{a,0} \otimes_b \phi_{a,1} \otimes_b \phi_{a,\top}$	$\phi_a^\perp$	ϕ_b^0	ϕ_c^1	$\phi_d^\top$	$\phi_a^\perp \oplus_b \phi_b^0 \oplus_b \phi_c^1 \oplus_b \phi_d^\perp$
$\perp$	a	a	a	a	a	$\perp$	$\perp$	$\perp$	a
0	$\perp$	b_2	b_3	$\perp$	$\perp$	b	$\perp$	$\perp$	b
1	b_1	$\perp$	c_3	$\perp$	$\perp$	$\perp$	c	$\perp$	c
$\top$	c_1	c_2	$\perp$	$\perp$	$\perp$	$\perp$	$\perp$	d	d

Figure 6: Expressing $\phi : 4 \to 4$ using operators in $\{\sim_0, \sim_1, \sim_\top, \otimes_b, \oplus_b\}$

PROOF. Clearly $x \curlywedge y \equiv x \wedge_t y$, it remains to show the operator $\curlyvee$ can be expressed in L. By Proposition 5 we can express any permutation of V in terms of $\dagger$ and $\diamond$. In particular, we can express the permutation f, where $f(i) = m - i + 1$, which swaps the values 1 and m, 2 and $m - 1$, and so on. We denote the unary operator which realizes this permutation by $\updownarrow$. Then $x \curlyvee y \equiv x \vee_t y \equiv \updownarrow(\updownarrow x \wedge_t \updownarrow y)$. $\square$

THEOREM 5. $L(V, \{\dagger, \diamond, \wedge_t\}$ is functionally and canonically complete.

We omit the proof, as it proceeds in an analogous manner to those for Lemma 1 and Theorem 4. It is interesting to note that we have constructed a canonically complete m-valued logic which uses only two unary operators. This is somewhat unexpected; intuition would suggest that $m - 1$ unary operators are required for a canonically complete m-valued logic.

5. A CANONICALLY COMPLETE 4-VALUED ABAC LANGUAGE

Having identified a canonically complete set of operators for Belnap logic, we now investigate how this set of operators can be used in an ABAC language, and consider the advantages in doing so. Crampton and Williams [7] showed the operators in PTaCL can be replaced with an alternative set of operators, taken from Jobe's logic E, to obtain a canonically complete 3-valued ABAC language. In the remainder of this section, we describe a 4-valued lattice-ordered version of PTaCL, based on the lattice 4_k, which we denote by $\text{PTaCL}_4^\leqslant$.

5.1 The Decision Set

We first reiterate there is value in having an ABAC language for which policy evaluation can return a fourth value $\top$. Such a value is used in both XACML and PBel, although its use in XACML is somewhat ad hoc and confusing since it can be used to indicate (a) an error in policy evaluation, or (b) a decision that arises for a particular operator during normal policy evaluation.

We will use this fourth value to denote that (normal) policy evaluation has led to conflicting decisions (and we do not wish to use deny-overrides or similar operators to resolve the conflict at this point in the evaluation). (We explain how we handle indeterminacy arising from errors in policy evaluation in Section 5.3.) Two specific operators, "only-one-applicable" (ooa) and "unanimity" (un) could make use of $\top$: the ooa operator returns the value of the applicable sub-policy if there is only one such policy, and $\top$ otherwise; whereas the un operator returns $\top$ if the sub-policies return different decisions, and the common decision otherwise. The decision tables for these operators are shown in Figure 7.

ooa	$\perp$	0	1	$\top$
$\perp$	$\perp$	0	1	$\top$
0	0	$\top$	$\top$	$\top$
1	1	$\top$	$\top$	$\top$
$\top$	$\top$	$\top$	$\top$	$\top$

un	$\perp$	0	1	$\top$
$\perp$	$\perp$	$\top$	$\top$	$\top$
0	$\top$	0	$\top$	$\top$
1	$\top$	$\top$	1	$\top$
$\top$	$\top$	$\top$	$\top$	$\top$

Figure 7: Operators using $\top$

In establishing canonical completeness for PTaCL(E), Crampton and Williams assumed a total order on the set of decisions ($0 < \perp < 1$). This ordering does not really reflect the intuition behind the use of 0, 1 and $\perp$ in ABAC languages. In the context of access control, 0 and 1 are incomparable conclusive decisions, and $\perp$ and $\top$ are decisions that reflect the inability to reach a conclusive decision either because a policy or its sub-policies are inapplicable ($\perp$) or because a policy's sub-policies return conclusive decisions that are incompatible in some sense ($\top$). Moreover, we can subsequently resolve $\perp$ and $\top$ to one of two (incomparable) conclusive decisions using unary operators such as "deny-by-default" and "allow-by-default". (The truth-based ordering on 4 does not correspond nearly so well to the above intuitions.)

5.2 Operators and Policies

We define the set of operators for $\text{PTaCL}_4^\leqslant$ to be $\{\sim_\top, \diamond, \otimes_b\}$, which we established is canonically complete in Corollary 3. Recall that $\sim_\top$ is equivalent to conflation $-$; we will use the simpler notation $-$ in the remainder of this section. An atomic policy has the form (t, d), where t is a target and $d \in \{0, 1\}$. (There is no reason for an atomic policy to return $\top$ – which signifies a conflict has taken place – in an atomic policy.) Then we have the following policy semantics.

$$\delta_q(t, p) = \begin{cases} \delta_q(p) & \text{if } \nu_q(t) = 1, \\ \perp & \text{otherwise;} \end{cases}$$

$$\delta_q(d) = d;$$
$$\delta_q(-p) = -\delta_q(p); \quad \delta_q(\diamond p) = \diamond \delta_q(p);$$
$$\delta_q(p \otimes_b p') = \delta_q(p) \otimes_b \delta_q(p').$$

We now show how to represent the operator only-one-applicable (ooa) in normal form. (Recall that it is possible to represent this operator as a formula in PBel; however, it is non-trivial to derive such a formula.) Using the truth table in Figure 7 and by definition of the selection operators and Υ, we have $x \, \mathsf{coa} \, y$ is equivalent to

$$S^\perp_{(\perp,\perp)}(x,y) \; \Upsilon \; S^0_{(\perp,0)}(x,y) \; \Upsilon \; S^1_{(\perp,1)}(x,y) \; \Upsilon \; S^\top_{(\perp,\top)}(x,y) \; \Upsilon$$
$$S^0_{(0,\perp)}(x,y) \; \Upsilon \; S^\top_{(0,0)}(x,y) \; \Upsilon \; S^\top_{(0,1)}(x,y) \; \Upsilon \; S^\top_{(0,\top)}(x,y) \; \Upsilon$$
$$S^1_{(1,\perp)}(x,y) \; \Upsilon \; S^\top_{(1,0)}(x,y) \; \Upsilon \; S^\top_{(1,1)}(x,y) \; \Upsilon \; S^\top_{(1,\top)}(x,y) \; \Upsilon$$
$$S^\top_{(\top,\perp)}(x,y) \; \Upsilon \; S^\top_{(\top,0)}(x,y) \; \Upsilon \; S^\top_{(\top,1)}(x,y) \; \Upsilon \; S^\top_{(\top,\top)}(x,y).$$

Moreover, $S^z_{(x,y)} = S^z_x \curlywedge S^z_y$ and S^z_x is a function $\phi : 4 \to 4$, which can be represented as a composition of unary operators. Hence, we can derive a formula in normal form for ooa.

Functional completeness implies we can write any binary operator (such as XACML's deny-overrides policy-combining algorithm) as a formula in $L(4_k, \{-, \diamond, \otimes_\mathsf{b}\}$, and hence we can use any operator we wish in $\mathrm{PTaCL}_4^{\leqslant}$ policies. However, canonical completeness and the decision set $(4, \leqslant_k)$ allows for a completely different approach to constructing ABAC policies. Suppose a policy administrator has identified three sub-policies p_1, p_2 and p_3 and wishes to define an overall policy p in terms of the decisions obtained by evaluating these sub-policies. Then the policy administrator can tabulate the desired decision for all relevant combinations of decisions for the sub-policies, as shown in the table below. The default decision is to return $\perp$, indicating that p is "silent" for other combinations.

p_1	p_2	p_3	p
$\perp$	0	0	0
0	0	0	0
1	0	0	$\top$
1	1	0	1
1	1	1	1

Then, treating p as a function of its sub-policies, we have

$$p \equiv \; S^0_{(\perp,0,0)} \; \Upsilon \; S^0_{(0,0,0)} \; \Upsilon \; S^\top_{(1,0,0)} \; \Upsilon \; S^1_{(1,1,0)} \; \Upsilon \; S^1_{(1,1,1)}.$$

The construction of p as a "disjunction" (Υ) of selection operators ensures that the correct value is returned for each combination of values (in much the same as disjunctive normal form may be used to represent the rows in a truth table). Note that if p_1, p_2 and p_3 evaluate to a tuple of values other than one of the rows in the table, each of the selection operators will return $\perp$ and thus p will evaluate to $\perp$. Each operator of the form $S^d_{(a,b,c)}$ can be represented as the "conjunction" ($\curlywedge$) of unary selection operators (specifically $S^d_a \curlywedge S^d_b \curlywedge S^d_c$).

Of course, one would not usually construct the normal form by hand, as we have done above. Indeed, we have developed an algorithm which takes an arbitrary policy expressed as a decision table as input, and outputs the equivalent normal form expressed in terms of the operators $\{-, \diamond, \otimes_\mathsf{b}\}$. In order to develop this algorithm, we also derived expressions for the unary selection operators in terms of the operators $\{-, \diamond, \otimes_\mathsf{b}\}$. (In Lemma 1 we only showed that such expressions exist.) Our implementation of the algorithm, comprising just less than 150 lines of Python code, shows the ease with which construction of policies can be both automated and simplified, utilizing the numerous advantages that have been discussed throughout this paper.[6]

---

[6]Code and test results available at goo.gl/0TM0RD.

5.3 Indeterminacy

XACML uses the indeterminate value in two distinct ways:

1. as a decision returned (during normal evaluation) by the "only-one-applicable" policy-combining algorithm; and

2. as a decision returned when some (unexpected) error has occurred in policy evaluation has occurred.

In the second case, the indeterminate value is used to represent alternative outcomes of policy evaluation (had the error not occurred). We believe that the two situations described are quite distinct and require different policy semantics. However, the semantics of indeterminacy in XACML are confused because (i) the indeterminate value is used in two different ways, as described above, and (ii) there is no clear and uniform way of establishing the values returned by the combining algorithms when an indeterminate value is encountered.

We have seen how $\top$ may be used to represent decisions for operators such as ooa and un. We handle errors in target evaluation (and thus indeterminacy) using sets of possible decisions [5, 6, 10]. (This approach was adopted in a rather ad hoc fashion in XACML 3.0, using an extended version of the indeterminate decision.) Informally, when target evaluation fails, denoted by $\nu_q(t) = ?$, PTaCL assumes that either $\nu_q(t) = 1$ or $\nu_q(t) = 0$ could have been returned, and returns the union of the (sets of) decisions that would have been returned in both cases. The formal semantics for policy evaluation in $\mathrm{PTaCL}_4^{\leqslant}$ in the presence of indeterminacy are defined in Figure 8.

$$\delta_q(t,p) = \begin{cases} \delta_q(p) & \text{if } \nu_q(t) = 1, \\ \{\perp\} & \text{if } \nu_q(t) = 0, \\ \{\perp\} \cup \delta_q(p) & \text{if } \nu_q(t) = ?, \end{cases}$$
$$\delta_q(d) = \{d\} \, ;$$
$$\delta_q(-p) = \{-d : d \in \delta_q(p)\} \, ;$$
$$\delta_q(\diamond p) = \{\diamond d : d \in \delta_q(p)\} \, ;$$
$$\delta_q(p_1 \otimes_\mathsf{b} p_2) = \{d_1 \otimes_\mathsf{b} d_2 : d_i \in \delta_q(p_i)\} \, .$$

Figure 8: Semantics for $\mathrm{PTaCL}_4^{\leqslant}$ with indeterminacy

The semantics for the operators $\{-, \diamond, \otimes_\mathsf{b}\}$ operate on sets, rather than single decisions, in the natural way. A straightforward induction on the number of operators in a policy establishes that the decision set returned by these extended semantics will be a singleton if no target evaluation errors occur; moreover, that decision will be the same as that returned by the standard semantics.

5.4 Leveraging the XACML Architecture

XACML is a well-known, standardized language, and many of the components and features of XACML are well-defined. However, it has been shown that the rule- and policy-combining algorithms defined in the XACML standard suffer from some shortcomings [10], notably inconsistencies between the rule- and policy-combining algorithms. PTaCL, on which $\mathrm{PTaCL}_4^{\leqslant}$ is based, is a tree-structured ABAC language that is explicitly designed to use the same general policy structure and evaluation methods as XACML. However, PTaCL differs substantially from XACML in terms of policy combination operators and semantics.

Thus, we suggest that $PTaCL_4^{\leqslant}$ operators could replace the rule- and policy-combining algorithms of XACML, while those parts of the language and architecture that seem to function well may be retained. Specifically, we use the XACML architecture to: (i) specify requests; (ii) specify targets; (iii) decide whether a policy target is applicable to a given request; and (iv) use the policy decision point to evaluate policies. In addition, we would retain the enforcement architecture of XACML, in terms of the policy decision, policy enforcement and policy administration points, and the relationships between them.

We believe it would be relatively easy to modify the XACML PDP to

- handle four decisions, extending the current set of values ("allow", "deny" and "not-applicable") to include "conflict";

- implement the policy operators $\{-, \diamond, \otimes_b\}$ as custom combining algorithms; and

- work with decision sets, in order to handle indeterminacy in a uniform manner.

For illustrative purposes, Appendix D specifies the modified decision set and pseudocode for the operator $\otimes_b$ in the format used by the XACML standard.

The main difference to end-users would be in the simplicity of policy authoring. Using standard XACML, policy authors must decide which rule- and policy-combining algorithms should be used to develop a policy or policy set that is equivalent to the desired policy. This is error-prone and it may not even be possible to express the desired policy using only the XACML combining algorithms. Using XACML with the policy-combining mechanisms of $PTaCL_4^{\leqslant}$, we can present an entirely different interface for policy authoring to the end-user. The policy author would first specify the atomic policies (XACML rules), then combine atomic policies using decision tables to obtain more complex policies (as illustrated in Section 5.2). Those policies can be further combined by specifying additional decision tables. At each stage a back-end policy compiler can be used to convert those policies into policy sets (using $PTaCL_4^{\leqslant}$ operators) that can be evaluated by the XACML engine.

6. CONCLUDING REMARKS

Attribute-based access control is of increasing importance, due to the increasing use of open, distributed, interconnected and dynamic systems. The introduction of *canonically complete* ABAC languages [7] provides the ability to express any desired policy in a normal form, which allows for the possibility of specifying policies in the form of a decision table and then automatically compiling them into the language.

In this paper, we make important contributions to the understanding of canonical completeness in multi-valued logics and thus in ABAC languages. First, we extend Jobe's work on canonical completeness to multi-valued logics to the case where the set of truth values forms a lattice. We show that the Belnap set of operators [2] (and thus any subset

thereof) is not canonically complete, hence any ABAC language based on these operators cannot be canonically complete. In particular, PBel [4], probably the most well known 4-valued ABAC language, is not canonically complete. We introduce a new four-valued logic $L(\mathbf{4}_k, \{-, \diamond, \otimes_b\})$ which is canonically complete, without having to explicitly construct the unary selection operators in normal form (unlike Jobe [9] and Crampton and Williams [7]). By identifying the connection between the generators of the symmetric group and the unary operators of logics, we have developed a simple and generic method for identifying a set of unary operators that will guarantee the functional and canonical completeness of an m-valued lattice-based logic. We also showed that there is a set of operators containing only three connectives which is functionally complete for Belnap logic, in contrast to the set of size four identified by Arieli and Avron [1].

Second, we show in $PTaCL_4^{\leqslant}$ how the canonically complete set of operators $\{-, \diamond, \otimes_b\}$ can be used in an ABAC language, and present the advantages of doing so. In particular, we are no longer forced to use a totally ordered set of three decisions to obtain canonical completeness (as in the case in PTaCL(E)). Moreover, the overall design of PTaCL and hence $PTaCL_4^{\leqslant}$ is compatible with the overall structure of XACML policies. We discuss how the XACML decision set and rule-combining algorithms can be modified to support $PTaCL_4^{\leqslant}$. Doing so enables us to retain the rich framework provided by XACML for ABAC (in terms of its languages for representing targets and requests) and its enforcement architecture (in terms of the policy enforcement, policy decision and policy administration points). Thus, we are able to propose an enhanced XACML framework within which any desired policy may be expressed. Moreover, the canonical completeness of $PTaCL_4^{\leqslant}$, means that the desired policy may be represented in simple terms by a policy author (in the form of a decision table) and automatically compiled into a PDP-readable equivalent policy.

Our work paves the way for a considerable amount of future work. In particular, we intend to develop a modified XACML PDP that implements the $PTaCL_4^{\leqslant}$ operators. We also hope to develop a policy authoring interface in which users can simply state what decision a policy should return for particular combinations of decisions from sub-policies. This would enable us to evaluate the usability of such an interface and compare the accuracy with which policy authors can generate policies using standard XACML combining algorithms compared with the methods that $PTaCL_4^{\leqslant}$ can support.

On the more technical side, we would like to revisit the notion of *monotonicity* [6] in targets and how this affects policy evaluation in ABAC languages. The definition of monotonicity is dependent on the ordering chosen for the decision set and existing work on monotonicity assumes the use of a totally ordered 3-valued set (comprising 0, $\perp$ and 1). So it will be interesting to consider how the use of a 4-valued lattice-ordered decision set affects monotonicity. We also intend to investigate methods of *policy compression*, analogous to the minimization of Boolean functions [13], where we take the canonical form of a policy (generated from a decision table) and rewrite it in such a way as to minimize the number of terms in the policy.

7. REFERENCES

[1] ARIELI, O., AND AVRON, A. The value of the four-values. *Artif. Intell. 102*, 1 (1998), 97–141.

[2] BELNAP JR, N. D. A useful four-valued logic. In *Modern uses of multiple-valued logic*. Springer, 1977, pp. 5–37.

[3] BONATTI, P. A., DI VIMERCATI, S. D. C., AND SAMARATI, P. An algebra for composing access control policies. *ACM Trans. Inf. Syst. Secur. 5*, 1 (2002), 1–35.

[4] BRUNS, G., AND HUTH, M. Access control via Belnap logic: Intuitive, expressive, and analyzable policy composition. *ACM Trans. Inf. Syst. Secur. 14*, 1 (2011), 9.

[5] CRAMPTON, J., AND HUTH, M. An authorization framework resilient to policy evaluation failures. In *Computer Security - ESORICS 2010, 15th European Symposium on Research in Computer Security, Athens, Greece, September 20-22, 2010. Proceedings* (2010), D. Gritzalis, B. Preneel, and M. Theoharidou, Eds., vol. 6345 of *Lecture Notes in Computer Science*, Springer, pp. 472–487.

[6] CRAMPTON, J., AND MORISSET, C. PTaCL: A language for attribute-based access control in open systems. In *Principles of Security and Trust - First International Conference, POST 2012, Proceedings*, P. Degano and J. D. Guttman, Eds., vol. 7215 of *Lecture Notes in Computer Science*. Springer, 2012, pp. 390–409.

[7] CRAMPTON, J., AND WILLIAMS, C. On completeness in languages for attribute-based access control. In *Proceedings of the 21st ACM on Symposium on Access Control Models and Technologies, SACMAT 2016, Shanghai, China, June 5-8, 2016* (2016), X. S. Wang, L. Bauer, and F. Kerschbaum, Eds., ACM, pp. 149–160.

[8] FITTING, M. Bilattices and the semantics of logic programming. *J. Log. Program. 11*, 1&2 (1991), 91–116.

[9] JOBE, W. H. Functional completeness and canonical forms in many-valued logics. *The Journal of Symbolic Logic 27*, 04 (1962), 409–422.

[10] LI, N., WANG, Q., QARDAJI, W. H., BERTINO, E., RAO, P., LOBO, J., AND LIN, D. Access control policy combining: theory meets practice. In *SACMAT 2009, 14th ACM Symposium on Access Control Models and Technologies, Proceedings* (2009), pp. 135–144.

[11] ŁUKASIEWICZ, J. Philosophische Bemerkungen zu mehrwertigen Systemen des Aussagekalküls. *Comptes rendus des séances de la Société des Sciences et des Lettres de Varsovie Classe III*, vol. 23 (1930), 55–57.

[12] MARINOVIC, S., DULAY, N., AND SLOMAN, M. Rumpole: An introspective break-glass access control language. *ACM Trans. Inf. Syst. Secur. 17*, 1 (2014), 2:1–2:32.

[13] MCCLUSKEY, E. J. Minimization of boolean functions. *Bell System Technical Journal 35*, 6 (1956), 1417–1444.

[14] MOSES, T. eXtensible Access Control Markup Language (XACML) Version 2.0 OASIS Standard, 2005. http://docs.oasis-open.org/xacml/2.0/access-control-xacml-2.0-core-spec-os.pdf.

[15] NI, Q., BERTINO, E., AND LOBO, J. D-algebra for composing access control policy decisions. In *Proceedings of the 2009 ACM Symposium on Information, Computer and Communications Security, ASIACCS 2009, Sydney, Australia, March 10-12, 2009* (2009), W. Li, W. Susilo, U. K. Tupakula, R. Safavi-Naini, and V. Varadharajan, Eds., ACM, pp. 298–309.

[16] RAO, P., LIN, D., BERTINO, E., LI, N., AND LOBO, J. An algebra for fine-grained integration of XACML policies. In *SACMAT 2009, 14th ACM Symposium on Access Control Models and Technologies, Stresa, Italy, June 3-5, 2009, Proceedings* (2009), pp. 63–72.

[17] RISSANEN, E. eXtensible Access Control Markup Language (XACML) Version 3.0 OASIS Standard, 2012. http://docs.oasis-open.org/xacml/3.0/xacml-3.0-core-os-en.html.

[18] TSANKOV, P., MARINOVIC, S., DASHTI, M. T., AND BASIN, D. A. Decentralized composite access control. In *POST* (2014), vol. 8414 of *Lecture Notes in Computer Science*, Springer, pp. 245–264.

[19] WIJESEKERA, D., AND JAJODIA, S. A propositional policy algebra for access control. *ACM Trans. Inf. Syst. Secur. 6*, 2 (2003), 286–325.

APPENDIX

A. JOBE'S CANONICALLY COMPLETE 3-VALUED LOGIC

Consider the 3-valued logic J [9], whose operators $\wedge_e, \sim_1$ and $\sim_2$ are defined in Figure 9.

x	$\sim_1 x$	$\sim_2 x$		$\wedge_e$	0	1	2
0	1	2		0	0	0	0
1	0	1		1	0	1	1
2	2	0		2	0	1	2

Figure 9: The operators in Jobe's logic

It is easy to establish that

$$x \curlywedge y \equiv x \wedge_e y \quad \text{and} \quad x \curlyvee y \equiv \sim_2(\sim_2(x) \wedge_e \sim_2(y)).$$

Thus J is canonically suitable [9, Theorem 6]. The normal-form formulas for the unary selection operators are shown in Figure 10. (Note that S_i^0 is the same for all i.) Thus J is functionally and canonically complete [9, Theorem 7]. Hence, it is possible to construct a canonically complete 3-valued logic using the operators $\{\wedge_e, \sim_0, \sim_1\}$.

$S_i^0(x)$	$x \wedge_e \sim_1(x) \wedge_e \sim_2(x)$
$S_0^1(x)$	$\sim_1(x) \wedge_e \sim_2 \sim_1(x)$
$S_1^1(x)$	$x \wedge_e \sim_2(x)$
$S_2^1(x)$	$\sim_1 \sim_2(x) \wedge_e \sim_2 \sim_1 \sim_2(x)$
$S_0^2(x)$	$\sim_2(x) \wedge_e \sim_1 \sim_2(x)$
$S_1^2(x)$	$\sim_2 \sim_1(x) \wedge_e \sim_2 \sim_1 \sim_2(x)$
$S_2^2(x)$	$x \wedge_e \sim_1(x)$

Figure 10: Normal forms for the unary selection operators

B. OPERATORS IN BELNAP LOGIC

$\wedge_b$	0	$\bot$	$\top$	1
0	0	0	0	0
$\bot$	0	$\bot$	0	$\bot$
$\top$	0	0	$\top$	$\top$
1	0	$\bot$	$\top$	1

(a) $\wedge_b$

$\vee_b$	0	$\bot$	$\top$	1
0	0	$\bot$	$\top$	1
$\bot$	$\bot$	$\bot$	1	1
$\top$	$\top$	1	$\top$	1
1	1	1	1	1

(b) $\vee_b$

$\otimes_b$	$\bot$	0	1	$\top$
$\bot$	$\bot$	$\bot$	$\bot$	$\bot$
0	$\bot$	0	$\bot$	0
1	$\bot$	$\bot$	1	1
$\top$	$\bot$	0	1	$\top$

(c) $\otimes_b$

$\oplus_b$	$\bot$	0	1	$\top$
$\bot$	$\bot$	0	1	$\top$
0	0	0	$\top$	$\top$
1	1	$\top$	1	$\top$
$\top$	$\top$	$\top$	$\top$	$\top$

(d) $\oplus_b$

$\supset_b$	0	$\bot$	$\top$	1
0	1	1	1	1
$\bot$	1	1	1	1
$\top$	0	$\bot$	$\top$	1
1	0	$\bot$	$\top$	1

(e) $\supset_b$

d	$\neg d$
0	1
$\bot$	$\bot$
$\top$	$\top$
1	0

(f) $\neg$

Figure 11: Operators in Belnap logic

C. PROOF OF PROPOSITION 2

The decision table in Figure 12 establishes the equivalence of $x \oplus_b y$ and $-(x \otimes_b -y)$, which proves that $L((4, \leqslant_k), \{-, \otimes_b\})$ is a canonically suitable logic (Proposition 2).

d	d'	$-d$	$-d'$	$-d \otimes_b -d'$	$-(-d \otimes_b -d')$	$d \oplus_b d'$
$\bot$	$\bot$	$\top$	$\top$	$\top$	$\bot$	$\bot$
$\bot$	0	$\top$	0	0	0	0
$\bot$	1	$\top$	1	1	1	1
$\bot$	$\top$	$\top$	$\bot$	$\bot$	$\top$	$\top$
0	$\bot$	0	$\top$	0	0	0
0	0	0	0	0	0	0
0	1	0	1	$\bot$	$\top$	$\top$
0	$\top$	0	$\bot$	$\bot$	$\top$	$\top$
1	$\bot$	1	$\top$	1	1	1
1	0	1	0	$\bot$	$\top$	$\top$
1	1	1	1	1	1	1
1	$\top$	1	$\bot$	$\bot$	$\top$	$\top$
$\top$	$\bot$	$\bot$	$\top$	$\bot$	$\top$	$\top$
$\top$	0	$\bot$	0	$\bot$	$\top$	$\top$
$\top$	1	$\bot$	1	$\bot$	$\top$	$\top$
$\top$	$\top$	$\bot$	$\bot$	$\bot$	$\top$	$\top$

Figure 12: Encoding $\oplus_b$ using $-$ and $\otimes_b$

D. ENCODING PTACL DECISIONS AND OPERATORS

In Figures 13 and 14 we illustrate how $\text{PTaCL}_4^{\leqslant}$ extensions could be incorporated in XACML by encoding the $\text{PTaCL}_4^{\leqslant}$ decisions and $\otimes_b$ operator using the syntax of the XACML standard.

```
<xs:element name=''Decision''
            type=''xacml:DecisionType''/>
<xs:simpleType name=''DecisionType''>
 <xs:restriction base=''xs:string''>
   <xs:enumeration value=''Permit''/>
   <xs:enumeration value=''Deny''/>
   <xs:enumeration value=''Conflict''/>
   <xs:enumeration value=''NotApplicable''/>
 </xs:restriction>
</xs:simpleType>
```

Figure 13: The $\text{PTaCL}_4^{\leqslant}$ decision set in XACML syntax

```
Decision ptaclCombiningAlgorithm(Node[] children)
{
 Boolean atLeastOneDeny  = false;
 Boolean atLeastOnePermit = false;
 for( i=0 ; i < lengthOf(children) ; i++ )
 {
   Decision decision = children[i].evaluate();
   if (decision == NotApplicable)
   { return NotApplicable;  }
   if (decision == Permit)
   {
     atLeastOnePermit = true;
     continue;
   }
   if (decision == Deny)
   {
     atLeastOneDeny = true;
     continue;
   }
   if (decision == Conflict)
   { continue;  }
 }
 if (atLeastOneDeny && atLeastOnePermit)
 { return NotApplicable;  }
 if (atLeastOneDeny)
 { return Deny;  }
 if (atLeastOnePermit)
 { return Permit;  }
 return Conflict;
}
```

Figure 14: The $\text{PTaCL}_4^{\leqslant}$ operator $\otimes_b$ encoded as an XACML combining algorithm

Classifying and Comparing Attribute-Based and Relationship-Based Access Control

Tahmina Ahmed
Univ. of Texas at San Antonio
qfk367@my.utsa.edu

Ravi Sandhu
Univ. of Texas at San Antonio
ravi.sandhu@utsa.edu

Jaehong Park
Univ. of Alabama in Huntsville
jae.park@uah.edu

ABSTRACT

Attribute-based access control (ABAC) expresses authorization policy via attributes while relationship-based access control (ReBAC) does so via relationships. While ABAC concepts have been around for a long time, ReBAC is relatively recent emerging with its essential application in online social networks. Even as ABAC and ReBAC continue to evolve, there are conflicting claims in the literature regarding their comparison. It has been argued that ABAC can subsume ReBAC since attributes can encode relationships. Conversely there are claims that the multilevel (or indirect) relations of ReBAC bring fundamentally new capabilities. So far there is no rigorous comparative study of ABAC vis a vis ReBAC.

This paper presents a comparative analysis of ABAC and ReBAC, and shows how various ReBAC features can be realized with different types of ABAC. We first identify several attribute types such as entity/non-entity and structured attributes that significantly influence ABAC or ReBAC expressiveness. We then develop a family of ReBAC models and a separate family of ABAC models based on the identified attribute types, with the goal of comparing the expressive power of these two model families. Further, we identify different dynamics of the models that are crucial for model comparison. We also consider different solutions for representing multilevel relationships with attributes. Finally, the ABAC and ReBAC model families are compared in terms of relative expressiveness and performance implications

Keywords

Access Control; ABAC; ReBAC; Attribute; Relationship

1. INTRODUCTION & MOTIVATION

The concept of using attributes for access control has been around for many years, e.g., the X.500 standard [16] was an early effort for managing object information with attributes. Attribute-based access control (ABAC) is considered one of the most generalized forms of access control

CODASPY'17, March 22-24, 2017, Scottsdale, AZ, USA

© 2017 ACM. ISBN 978-1-4503-4523-1/17/03...$15.00

DOI: http://dx.doi.org/10.1145/3029806.3029828

as it can capture the salient features of discretionary access control (DAC), mandatory access control (MAC) and role-based access control (RBAC) using appropriate attributes such as access control lists, security labels and roles respectively [35], and bring in additional elements such as location and time. ABAC enables more precise access control as it can consider a higher number of discrete inputs into an access control decision [33]. Different ABAC models with rich policy languages and sophisticated features have been proposed [34, 35, 36, 40, 48, 51].

Meanwhile, in recent years, various online social network (OSN) applications such as Facebook, Twitter and LinkedIn have become widely used. In OSNs, authorization for users' access to specific content is typically based on the interpersonal relationships between the accessing user and content owner. OSN ReBAC models mostly use user-to-user relationships [12, 15, 21, 22, 29, 30] while user-to-resource and resource-to-resource relationships have also been considered in some cases [13, 20]. Several access control models have been proposed for OSN ReBAC considering both single and multiple relationship types for authorization policy specification [13, 20, 21, 29]. Subsequently, additional models have been proposed to extend and generalize these OSN ReBAC models so that they can be applicable to computing systems beyond OSNs [7, 24, 28, 43].

ABAC has been around for a long time and can be viewed as a generalization, unification and extension of earlier access control concepts including discretionary, mandatory and role-based access control. ReBAC is relatively recent, with its initial motivation stemming from its essential application in online social networks but now generally regarded as having broader applicability. Both have considerable applications in industry, and are anticipated to continue being important for the foreseeable future.

From an ABAC perspective it is often claimed that attributes can express relationships [51], and indeed this is trivial for direct relationships such as a friend relation between two users [24]. However, the use of indirect relations, also called multilevel or composite relations, is fundamental to ReBAC [12, 24]; a familiar example being friend of friend. It is hard to see how ABAC can express long chains of relationships [24]. It has been suggested that ReBAC emerged to overcome this shortcoming of attributes [12].

Any attempt to compare ABAC and ReBAC is made additionally difficult by the fact that there are no consensus models for either one that are widely accepted. Rather both arenas exhibit a proliferation of models which are continuing to evolve as different aspects of each arena are explored.

In this paper we develop a rigorous comparison between ABAC and ReBAC. We do this by classifying ABAC and ReBAC models based on salient aspects that are relevant to their comparison. The main purpose of these classifications is to enable comparison. The classifications are not intended to be a complete characterization of ABAC models or ReBAC models. They are only a partial classification but sufficient to draw out the essential relationships between ABAC and ReBAC.

The rest of the paper is organized as follows. Section 2 provides appropriate background on ABAC and ReBAC for our purpose. Section 3 presents attribute types, characteristics, definitions and some assumptions on attributes. Sections 4 and 5 provide the classification of ReBAC and ABAC models respectively with structural variations and dynamics, giving us a family of ReBAC models and a separate family of ABAC models. Section 6 identifies two solutions for expressing multilevel relations with attributes. Section 7 compares the models in the ABAC and ReBAC families. Section 8 concludes the paper.

2. BACKGROUND

This section provides an overview of ABAC and ReBAC models, relevant to our purpose.

2.1 ReBAC Models

As OSNs have gained popularity, several ReBAC models have been introduced to capture various authorization policies. More recently, researchers have proposed extended ReBAC models applicable to other computing systems beyond OSNs. In this subsection, we review these two types of ReBAC models.

2.1.1 ReBAC for Online Social Networks

Fong et al. [29] presented a Facebook-like access control model, featuring four types of policies that cover four different aspects of access in OSNs. The four policies include user search, traversal of the social graph, communication between users and normal access to objects owned by users. The policy vocabulary supports expressing some topology-based properties, such as k common friends and k clique. The model uses single relationship types between users.

Carminati et al. [15] proposed an access control model which considers type, depth and trust metrics of user-to-user relationship between accessing user and target user. It also considers multiple types of relationships between users. In [13], Carminati et al. proposed a model which utilizes semantic web technology. This model considers multiple type relationships between users and resources.

Cheng et al. [21] proposed a user-to-user relationship based access control model with a regular expression-based policy specification language. Social graph of UURAC contains user-to-user relationships only. The connection between resources and users are referred to as controlling user (e.g., owner, tagged user). URRAC model [20] extends UURAC to include user-to-resource and resource-to-resource relations. In both models, multiple types of relationships are supported, and policy language can specify relationship path patterns between accessing user and target resource or user.

Subsequently Cheng et al. [22] defined an attribute-aware ReBAC model to express the contextual nature of relationships and users. The authors have extended their UURAC model to incorporate node attributes and relationship attributes. They further introduced the concept of a graph attribute such as count which is associated with the relationship graph other than with a particular node or edge.

Bennett et al. [9] proposed a ReBAC model that considers multiple types of relationships between users and demonstrates how conflicts and potential misconfigurations can be automatically detected using the Alloy Analyzer [1]. Pang et al. [39] proposed an access control scheme for OSN where they have taken hybrid logic approach to use public information along with relationships.

2.1.2 ReBAC Beyond Online Social Environment

Fong et al. [28] proposed a formal ReBAC model intending to widen the application of ReBAC beyond social computing. The model considers multiple relationship types between users with directional relationships and access contexts, and uses a modal logic language for policy specification. The connection between users and resources is maintained through a system function called 'resource owner.' Fong et al. [30] extended the policy language of [28] and characterized its expressiveness. Subsequently they defined hybrid logic for ReBAC which can express complex relationship requirements [12].

Crampton et al. [24] proposed the RPPM model that can be applied to general computing system. The model considers users, resources and other logical and physical entities (i.e., files, folders, organizations, etc.) as nodes of a labeled relationship graph. Policies are defined using path conditions. The model allows multiple types of relationship between different entities. The model uses a two-stage decision process: it first computes the path between requester and the requested resource and tries to find matches from a list of policies, and then it determines whether those policies are authorized. Rizvi et al. [43] demonstrated an implementation of RPPM model in an open-source medical record system. Subsequently they extended their model to be interoperable with RBAC [42]. Recently Crampton et al. [26] proposed a framework for inter-operating multiple ReBAC model instances by initiating request in one system to target resource in a second system.

Most ReBAC models consider user-to-user and possibly user-to-resource relationships. Very few of consider resource-to-resource relationships. Models that consider resource-to-resource relationships typically do so through users. Recently Ahmed et al. [7] proposed a ReBAC model which considers object-to-object relationships without intervening users, and demonstrated an implementation of the model in the OpenStack's [3] object storage, Swift [6].

All the models reviewed so far are operational models. Recently a number of ReBAC administrative models have also been proposed for general purpose ReBAC [19, 25, 49] which consider graph dynamics such as adding/deleting nodes (entities) and or edges (relationships). In particular, [19] introduces the concept of dependent edge in ReBAC and considering dependencies during edge deletion.

2.2 ABAC Models

ABAC has been studied for a long time and many different formal models have been proposed [34, 35, 36, 40, 48, 51]. Several of these are application specific or limited to a specific domain. ABAC for web services [51] proposed an ABAC model for web service authorization, while [48] defined an ABAC model for semantic web technology. UCON [40] was proposed to capture authorization continuity and attribute mutability. [36] defines an ABAC model for service oriented architecture considering requester's privacy preference. $ABAC_\alpha$ [35] is proposed to configure DAC, MAC and RBAC, while $ABAC_\beta$ [34] extends $ABAC_\alpha$ to incorporate different RBAC extensions. NIST ABAC [33] provides a detail explanation of ABAC concepts and considerations for deployment of enterprise ABAC capabilities. XACML [2] proposes a standardized mechanism to specify ABAC authorization policy, request and policy evaluation. Attribute-based encryption is supports fine-grained sharing of encrypted data [11, 17, 37, 38, 41, 44].

3. ATTRIBUTES

In our comparison and classification for ReBAC and ABAC models, attributes play an important role. In this section we identify and discuss various types of attributes based on several different criteria. Some of these attribute types are crucial for ABAC and ReBAC comparison as their existence in a model strongly influences its expressiveness and performance. Others are not quite significant for our comparison purpose. In the next two sections, we use these attribute types to classify ReBAC and ABAC models to facilitate comparison between them.

3.1 Attribute Types

In this subsection we present several attribute types classified using five different criteria. Specifically the criteria are based on (1) how attribute value(s) are structured, (2) what the attribute scope is, (3) boundedness of attribute range, (4) attribute association and (5) attribute mutability.

Depending upon the type of attribute value, there can be three types of attributes.

- **Atomic-valued or Single-valued Attribute:** If an attribute has at most one value associated with it at any one point in time, it is called atomic-valued or single-valued [4, 35] attribute. For example, gender attribute can have only a single value at a given time.

- **Set-valued or Multi-valued Attribute:** If an attribute can have more than one value associated with it at any one point in time, it is called set-valued or multi-valued attribute. For example, a person can have more than one phone number [4, 35].

- **Structured Attribute**: A structured attribute has a number of single or multi-valued sub-attributes [5]. For example, a Person-Info attribute can have sub-attributes of name, age and phoneNumber.

Depending upon the scope of the attribute, attributes can be either Entity Attribute or Non-entity Attribute.

- **Entity Attribute:** An entity is a thing which can be distinctly identified. A specific person, company an object or event is an example of entity [18]. Entity attribute takes an entity as input and returns another entity, a set of entities, or a structured tuple containing at least one entity. For example, an attribute value of parent of a person, owner of an object or friend of a person is another person (entity).

- **Non-entity Attribute:** Attributes whose range is not defined on the set of entities in the system are

called non-entity attributes. For example, user's age or gender does not include another entity as its value. The concept of non-entity attribute depends upon what is defined as entities in the system. For example, suppose roles or organizations are entities in a system, and the range of attributes "assigned-roles" and "worksAt" are a set of roles and a set of organizations, respectively. In that case both attributes are entity attributes. If roles and organizations are not defined as entities in the system, these are non-entity attributes.

Depending upon whether the range of an attribute is bounded or not, attributes can be either finite domain attribute or infinite domain attribute.

- **Finite Domain Attribute:** Range of this attribute type is a finite set of attribute value (e.g., gender, role).

- **Infinite Domain Attribute:** Range of this attribute type is a countably infinite set of attribute values (e.g, time). Entity attributes where new entities can be created without bound are infinite domain attributes.

Considering the association of an attribute we can have two types of attributes [33, 34, 51]

- **Contextual or Environmental Attribute**: These attributes are independent and not associated with any specific users, subjects, objects or entities in the system. They are global and managed by the system and associated with system. For example, *current-time* is system-wide information and not associated with a specific entity [34]. Other examples include system status, network security level, and so on [33, 51].

- **Meta Attribute**: Meta attributes are attributes of an attribute. Unlike regular attributes that are associated with entities, meta attributes are associated with other attributes. For example a user is associated with a role and the role is associated with a task. Here, the role is an attribute, and the task is a meta attribute [34].

Considering the mutability of attributes there are two types of attribute [40].

- **Mutable Attribute:** Mutable attributes are changed as a consequence or side effect of users' access or activity.

- **Immutable Attribute:** Immutable attributes can be changed only by direct administrative activity of a user or administrator.

The notions of entity/non-entity, finite/infinite domain, atomic-valued/set-valued/structured attributes are important for ReBAC-ABAC comparison as they are key attribute types that will strongly influence expressibility of relationships between entities or configurability of relationship graph.

Unlike these key attribute types, contextual/environmental attribute is a special type of attribute, not related to entities. Meta attribute defines relationship between attributes. Mutability is special feature specified in usage control for consumable authorization. These type of attributes are not relevant to ReBAC-ABAC comparisons with respect to expressiveness or performance. In the next two subsections, we will further discuss the definitions of these key attribute types and some assumptions for the rest of the paper.

3.2 Attribute Definitions for ReBAC and ABAC Comparison

For our ReBAC and ABAC comparison, we consider entity and non-entity, finite and infinite domain, atomic-valued, set-valued and structured attributes. In this subsection, we define these key attribute types (except for single-valued, multi-valued and structured attributes which have been adequately defined above).

DEFINITION 1. *Entity Attribute: An attribute att_i is an entity attribute if*

i. *range of att_i is a set of entities (i.e. $att_i: E_j \rightarrow E_k$),*

ii. *range of att_i is a powerset of entities (i.e. $att_i: E_j \rightarrow 2^{E_k}$), or*

iii. *att_i is a structured attribute with at least one sub-attribute being an entity attribute.*

For example, if user is defined as an entity in the system and best-friend is an atomic or set-valued attribute on user then best-friend is an entity attribute. At a specific time each entity set is fixed but can change over time if the system allows entity changes (i.e., creation or deletion of entities.). If att_i is a structured attribute and at least one sub-attribute of att_i is an entity attribute then att_i is also an entity attribute. For example let's say 'roleInfo(roles,assignedby)' is a structured attribute which has 'roles' and 'assignedby' as sub-attributes. Here 'roles' is non-entity attribute whose range is set of roles however 'assignedby' is an entity attribute whose range is set of users. So 'roleInfo' is an entity attribute.

DEFINITION 2. *Non-Entity Attribute: An attribute att_i is a non-entity attribute if it is not an entity attribute.*

Examples are phoneNumber and age. Note that if att_i is a structured attribute then every sub-attribute of att_i must be a non-entity attribute for att_i to be a non-entity attribute.

DEFINITION 3. *Finite Domain Attribute: An attribute domain is finite if the range of the attribute doesn't grow over time.*

For example, 'gender' is a finite domain attribute. Also, 'roles' and 'security clearance' are finite domain attributes if the system does not allow new roles or security clearances to be added over time.

DEFINITION 4. *Infinite Domain Attribute: An attribute domain is infinite if the range of the attribute grows over time.*

For example, in an OSN, if a new user can be created so he or she can be a friend of other users, the friend attribute is an infinite domain attribute as the range of friend is changed over time.

Finally, we introduce the familiar concept of attribute function composition [8, 31].

DEFINITION 5. *Attribute Function Composition: Nesting two or more attribute functions to form a single new function is known as attribute function composition. The composition of two attribute functions $f : X \rightarrow Y$ and $g : Y \rightarrow Z$ yields a function which maps $x \in X$ to $g(f(x)) \in Z$. Composition is denoted as $g \circ f$, where g is a function whose domain includes the range (or codomain) of f. We write $(g \circ f)(x)=g(f(x))$.*

A function $h(x) = f_n(......f_2(f_1(x))....)$ which is the composition of n functions (same or different), say f_1 to f_n, is also said to be a composite function. Intuitively, composing two or more functions is a chaining process in which the output of the first function becomes the input of the second one, and the output of the $(k-1)^{th}$ function becomes the input of the kth function.

3.3 Assumptions

For ease of our comparison, all the ReBAC and ABAC models considered in this paper comply with the following assumptions.

1. *All non-entity attributes are finite domain.* Attributes such as role, department, title, gender, etc., typically admit only a small number of finite values by their intrinsic nature. Attributes such as location can be ever finer grained, so in principle could be regarded as infinite domain but a large finite domain should be adequate. Time being modeled as a finite domain has similar issue. For our purpose a finite domain assumption is reasonable.

2. *Each entity has a countably infinite set for all possible entities of that type.* For example if users, subjects and objects are the only entities defined in a particular system then the countably infinite sets for users, subjects and objects are $\mathcal{U}$, $\mathcal{S}$ and $\mathcal{O}$. The existing set of users, subjects and objects at any moment are U, S, O respectively where U, S, O are finite sets, and $U \subset \mathcal{U}$, $S \subset \mathcal{S}$ and $O \subset \mathcal{O}$.

3. *Identity of an entity is not reusable.* If an entity gets deleted, its identity cannot be used for another entity that is created after the deletion.

4. *All entity attribute functions are partial functions defined on existing entities only.* For example let $\mathcal{U}$ is the countably infinite set of all possible users, and U the finite set of current users ($U \subset \mathcal{U}$). An entity attribute function $f : U \rightarrow Y$ is defined only for elements of U and is undefined for elements in $\mathcal{U}$-U. We understand $f : U \rightarrow Y$ for an entity set U to mean that U will change with time but is finite at any moment. Note that if the system allows creation of entities then the entity attributes have infinite or unbounded domain. If the system doesn't allow any entity creation or deletion then the entity attributes form a finite domain.

5. *For attribute function composition inner attribute functions should always be entity attributes.* We require that a non-entity attribute can only occur as the outermost function in a composition. So for a composition $f_n(......f_2 (f_1(x))....)$, for $1 \leq i \leq$ n-1, f_i must be an entity attribute function, while f_n can be either entity or non-entity attribute.

6. For any set valued attribute function f defined on set X, we understand $f(X) = \bigcup_{x_i \in X} f(x_i)$. So an attribute function composition friend(friend("Alice")) means: $\bigcup_{u_i \in friend("Alice")} friend(u_i)$

7. We understand that structured attribute is a multivalued tuple of atomic and or set-valued attributes. So it is more expressive than atomic or set valued attributes.

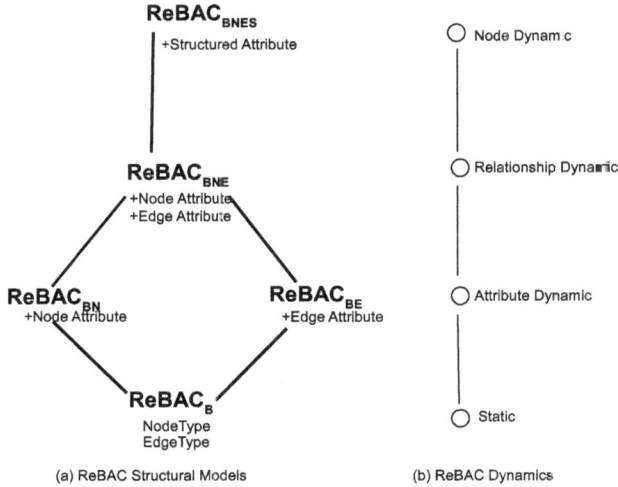

Figure 1: *ReBAC Framework*

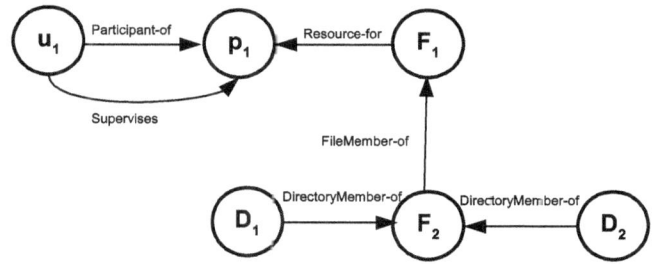

Figure 2: *An Example of a Relationship Graph Expressible in ReBAC$_B$ [24]*

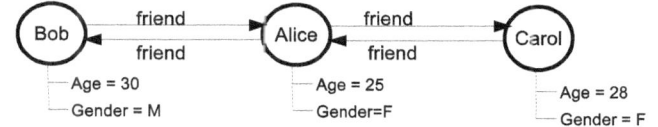

Figure 3: *An Example of Node Attributes in Relationship Graph Expressible in ReBAC$_{BN}$*

Structured attribute can express atomic or set-valued attribute by having a single sub-attribute.

4. ReBAC CLASSIFICATION

In this section we develop a ReBAC framework including a family of structural models. The framework is illustrated in Figure 1 and consists of two components. Specifically, Figure 1(a) shows a family of structural models while Figure 1(b) shows the different types of dynamics found in ReBAC models.

The goal of this framework is to build a classification of ReBAC models that facilitates comparison with ABAC models. While there are many sophisticated proposals on ReBAC policy expression mechanisms such as incoming versus outgoing policy, policy individualization, modal/hybrid/first order/propositional logic based policies, this framework does not focus on policy specification. Rather it is independent of policy languages and focusses on structural and dynamic aspects of ReBAC.

Figure 1(a) depicts ReBAC models with increasing capabilities as we go upwards in this hierarchy. In ReBAC, entities are represented as nodes in a relationship graph, and relations as entity to entity edges. We use the terms "node" and "entity" as synonyms, and likewise for the terms "edge" and "relation". The base model ReBAC$_B$ allows for multiple node types (e.g., user, resource project, organization, group, etc.) and multiple directed or undirected edge types (e.g., friend, coworker, spouse, parent, etc.) Figure 2 shows an example relationship graph [24] expressible in ReBAC$_B$. Most of the relationship graphs permitted in existing ReBAC models, including [20, 21, 24, 28, 29], can be expressed with the capabilities of ReBAC$_B$.

ReBAC$_{BN}$ adds node attributes to ReBAC$_B$. Node attributes enable consideration of entity attributes along with relationships in authorization policies. For example, in a professional social network we may have a policy that an employee of an organization o_1 can connect to a recruiter of organization o_2 only if the recruiter is not already connected to any employees of o_1. In this case, the organization attribute of users (nodes) needs to be considered along with professional relationships. Another example is an online dating site where a single male user wants to connect a single female who has less than 4th degree connection with him through only his female friends and is at least two years younger than him. Here we need to consider gender, age and relationship depth along with relationships Such attribute-aware ReBAC is discussed in greater detail in [22]. Figure 3 shows an example relationship graph with node attributes.

ReBAC$_{BE}$ extends ReBAC$_B$ with edge attributes. For example, some ReBAC models use trust value of relationships to show the connection strength between users [14, 15]. In general, when a ReBAC authorization policy needs to consider some properties of relationships beyond relationship types, the relationship graph needs edge attributes to store and express those criteria, such as proposed in [22]. Figure 4 provides an example of edge attributes in relationship graph. Here "Bob" is assigned to supervise "Project$_1$" and "assignedBy" is an edge attribute for relationship type "supervises" which specifies who has assigned "Bob" as supervisor. Similarly "tenant$_1$" has "tenantTrust" relationship with "tenant$_2$" and here "trustValue" specifies the strength of how much "tenant$_2$" trusts "tenant$_1$".

ReBAC$_{BNE}$ brings together the two separately motivated extensions of ReBAC$_{BN}$ and ReBAC$_{BE}$, such as in [22]. Following common practice, node and edge attributes in these models are atomic or set-valued attributes.

Recently Cheng et al. [19] proposed a ReBAC administrative model where they introduced the concept of dependent edge in relationship graph. A dependent edge example of MT-RBAC [19] is shown in Figure 5. Here user u owned by tenant x (with relationship type UO) can be "assigned to" a role r (with relation type UA) which is "owned by" tenant y (with relationship type RO) only if tenant y trusts tenant x (with relationship type TT). This particular tenant-trust relationship needs to be considered during role assignment or any time the trust-relationship between x and y changes. If the tenant's trust relationship is revoked at some point of time, the role assignment needs to be revoked as well. In order to configure this scenario using attributes, we need to store a paired set of the role values and the required trust relationship. This additional information allows the

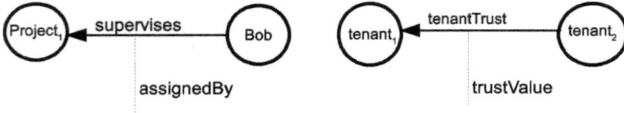

Figure 4: *An Example of Edge Attributes in Relationship Graph Expressible in* $ReBAC_{BE}$

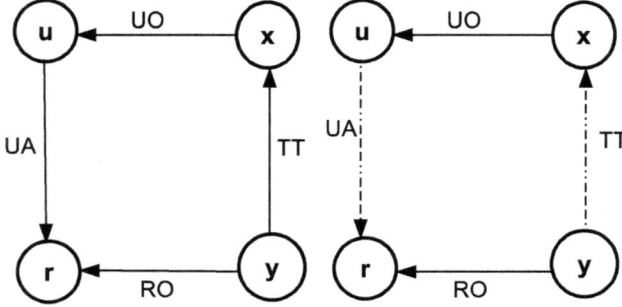

Figure 5: *Example of Dependent Edge Expressible in* $ReBAC_{BNES}$ [19]

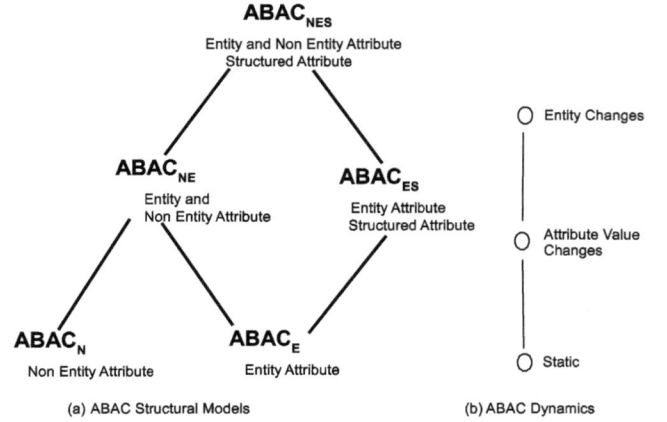

Figure 6: *ABAC Framework*

model to consider cascading revocation [10, 27, 32] of dependent edges. This edge dependency in a graph cannot be captured using edge types or atomic or set valued edge attributes. To be precise, we will need structured attributes which can store multiple relevant attributes as a single attribute in a certain structure. For the above scenario, the structured attribute can store information of those edges that are required to create another edge. For instance, "dependsOn" attribute of relationship type UA can store a tuple of three sub-attributes: (sourceNode, targetNode, relationshipType), hence, (y,x,TT) for the example above. Consider another example where "securityLabel" is an object attribute. If a graph needs to store the information who has assigned a particular "securityLabel" to an object, we can use a structured attribute where sub-attributes are (label, assignedBy). If relationship graph only considers atomic-/set-valued attributes it won't be able to store this information. Our final model $ReBAC_{BNES}$ considers structured attributes for both nodes and edges. This completes our discussion of Figure 1(a).

Considering the changes or dynamism in ReBAC there are 4 dynamics shown in Figure 1(b). The dynamics are as follows.

- **Static:** In a static ReBAC model, attribute values, nodes and edges of the graph remain unchanged. A static graph is used for access only. Actions such as add or delete relationship between two entities (add or delete edges in the relationship graph), add or delete entities (add or delete nodes in relationship graph are not allowed) and change of attribute values are not allowed.

- **Attribute Dynamic**: ReBAC that allows changes of node attribute and edge attribute values are attribute dynamic ReBAC. For example, consider Hobby is a node attribute of users in a social network. Suppose Hobby("Alice")={gardening, painting}. Recently "Alice" gets interested to do "knitting" and wants to change her hobby in the social network site. If the sys-

tem allows her to update her hobby as Hobby("Alice") = {gardening, painting, knitting} then it is an attribute dynamic ReBAC.

- **Relationship Dynamic**: ReBAC that allows changes of relationships between entities (add or delete edges in the relationship graph) is called relationship dynamic. Examples include establishing a new relationship between two entities, or deleting an existing relationship between two entities. We consider relationship dynamic includes attribute dynamic for the ReBAC models which have edge attributes, as adding new relationship needs to assign attribute values of that edge.

- **Node Dynamic**: ReBAC that allows changes of entities is called as node dynamic ReBAC. Some examples are creating or deleting a user or resource in a relationship graph. Here we consider node creation implies possible relationship establishment and attribute value assignments when ReBAC models have attributes for nodes and or edges. Hence, node dynamic includes attribute dynamic (for some cases) and relationship dynamic.

Each ReBAC dynamic can be combined with any of the ReBAC structural models excluding ReBAC$_B$. ReBAC$_B$ can only have static, relationship dynamic and node dynamic. However ReBAC$_B$ cannot have attribute dynamic as it doesn't have any attributes. Thus, attribute dynamism is irrelevant for ReBAC$_B$.

5. ABAC CLASSIFICATION

In this section, we develop a set of structural models for ABAC with capabilities to configure the ReBAC models defined in Section 4. We define the ABAC models by considering attribute types that are necessary to capture relationships and relationship graphs as shown in Figure 6(a). Specifically, we consider entity/non-entity, finite/infinite domain, and atomic-valued/set-valued/structured attributes. As shown in Figure 6(b), we also identify the dynamics of ABAC models. While this is not the most general framework for ABAC, it facilitates comparative analysis of relative expressiveness of ABAC and ReBAC.

Figure 6(a) depicts ABAC models with increasing capabilities as we go upwards in this hierarchy. $ABAC_N$ considers non-entity attribute only. According to our assumption 5 in Section 3, non-entity attribute cannot configure relationship composition, hence $ABAC_N$ is incomparable to $ReBAC_B$. $ABAC_N$ can only have attributes such as name, gender, location etc.

$ABAC_E$ considers entity attributes only and can configure $ReBAC_B$ model which has multiple relationship types and multiple entity types. Most of the ReBAC models fall under this category [20, 21, 24, 28, 29]. For example, consider the system graph in Figure 2 [24]. To configure it with $ABAC_E$ we need the following.

- entity types = {user, project, file, directory}

- user attributes = {Participant-of, Supervises},
  file attributes ={Resource-for, FileMember-of},
  project attributes = {},
  directory attributes ={DirectoryMember-of}.

$ABAC_{NE}$ considers both entity and non-entity attributes which is similar to considering node attributes along with multiple relationship types and multiple entity types as in $ReBAC_{BN}$. For example, in Figure 2, suppose the user has attributes {name, gender, age} and files have attributes {securityLabel, size}. Using $ABAC_{NE}$, we can configure these node attributes with non-entity attributes.

$ABAC_{ES}$ considers structured entity attributes which can configure relationships and edge attributes of relationship graph. Figure 4 shows some simple edge attributes in relationship graphs. To configure the relationship graph "Bob supervises Project$_1$" in ABAC, we need to have entity attribute "supervises" for user so we can express supervises (Bob)= {"Project$_1$"}. In addition, to express the edge attribute "assignedBy", we will need a structured attribute of user "assignedBy", so we can express assignedBy(Bob) = ("Project$_1$","supervises", "Alice"). Here the sub-attributes for "assignedBy" are (targetNode, relationshipType, assignedByUser). The same is true for the tenantTrust relationship between tenant$_1$ and tenant$_2$. Here we can configure the trustValue with structured attribute trustValue (tenant$_2$) = ("tenant$_1$", 'tenantTrust', 0.5). Consider the example in Figure 5 where the edge (u, r, UA) is dependent on edge (y, x, TT) and this dependency can be represented using a structured attribute for edge. To configure this structured edge attribute in ABAC, we need to have dependentEdge(u) = ("r","UA", {(y,x,TT)}). $ABAC_{ES}$ is comparable to $ReBAC_{BE}$.

$ABAC_{NES}$ considers entity and non-entity structured attributes which can configure relationships, node attributes and edge attributes. $ABAC_{NES}$ is comparable to $ReBAC_{BNES}$. This completes our discussion of Figure 6(a).

There are three types of ABAC in terms of possible changes in ABAC Models which we call ABAC dynamics. Figure 6(b) shows the dynamics as follows.

- **Static ABAC**: Nothing gets changed. In this type of ABAC, everything is static. Change of attribute values (i.e., assigning new values to attributes) or change of entities (i.e., adding or deleting entities) are not allowed.

- **Attribute Value Changes**: This ABAC allows changes of attribute values (assigning new values to attributes).

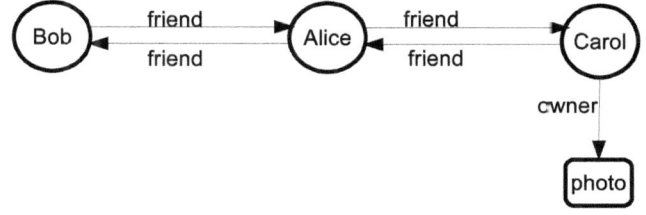

Figure 7: *A Simple Relationship Graph for Example 1*

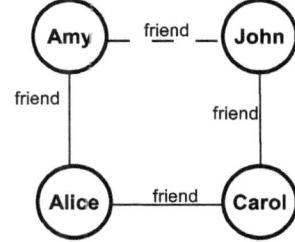

Figure 8: *A Simple Relationship Graph for Example 2*

- **Entity Changes**: This ABAC allows new entity creation and/or deletion. We understand that entity changes also includes attribute value changes as it needs assigning new values to attributes.

Each ABAC models shown in the Figure 6(a) can be combined with any dynamics shown in Figure 6(b).

6. EXPRESSING MULTILEVEL RELATIONSHIPS WITH ATTRIBUTES

Entity attributes can directly configure one level relationship such as parent, spouse, owner. Only entity attribute is allowed for attribute function composition. ReBAC is all about expressing authorization policy with multilevel or composite relationship (friend ∘ friend, friend ∘ parent etc.). In this subsection, we propose two methods of composite relationship expression using attributes.

1. **Attribute Composition or Chaining:** Attribute chaining is attribute function composition as defined in Section 3. Traditional ABAC uses direct attribute value of a user to specify policy. While attribute chaining approach allows to specify a policy through composition of attribute function. This approach requires runtime computation for relationship composition just like ReBAC.

2. **Composite Attribute:** In this approach, all possible or required paths of a relationship graph are captured as attributes. When an update occurs in the relationship graph, this approach needs to update attributes of directly and indirectly related entities. Here the term possible and required is used in the sense that the maximum possible depth of a graph depends upon its size while required depth means the limited depth required to specify authorization policy.

We discuss both concepts with some examples below.

65

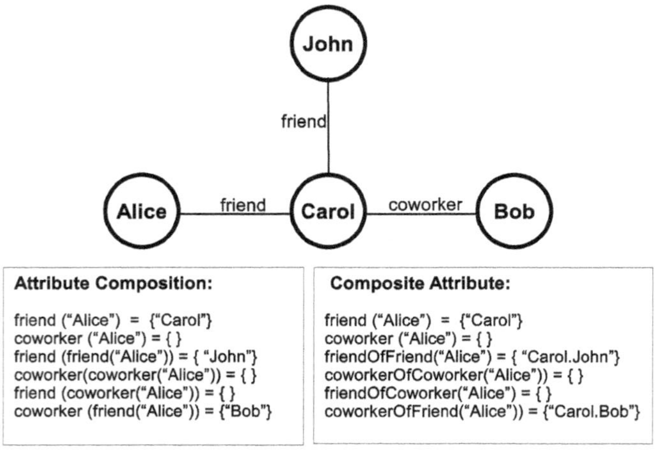

Figure 9: *Example of Attribute Composition and Composite Attribute in a Simple Relationship Graph (Example 3)*

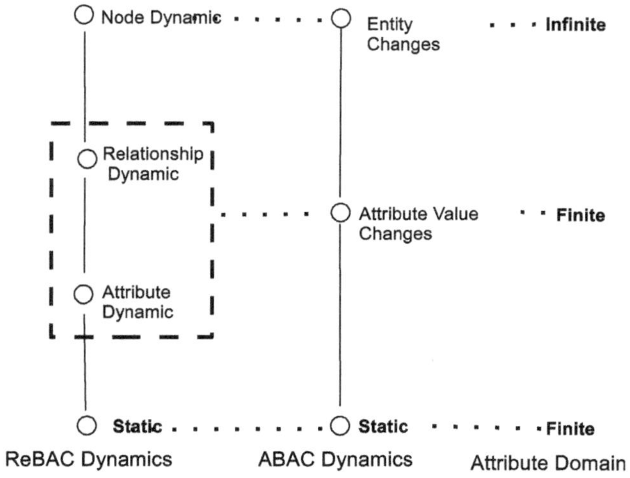

Figure 10: *Comparison Between ReBAC and ABAC with respect to Dynamics and Attribute Domain*

Example 1: Consider the relationship graph in Figure 7. Let's assume the policy for photo access allows only owner or owner's friend can access them.

Attribute Composition or Chaining : To configure this scenario with attribute composition approach, each user should have two entity attributes "friend" and "owner" and the authorization policy would check whether a particular user is in owner("photo") or friend(owner("photo")). According to this policy "Carol" and "Alice" can access "photo", but "Bob" cannot.

Composite Attribute: In this approach, to express the relationship graph and policy, ABAC should have user attributes, "friend" and "friendOfFriend", as well as object (photo) attributes, "owner", "friendOfOwner" and "friendOfFriendOfOwner". Here, "friendOfFriend", "friendOfOwner" and "friendOfFriendOfOwner" are composite attributes. The authorization policy would check whether a particular user is in owner("photo") or friendOfOwner("photo").

Here, owner("photo") = {"Carol"}, friendOfOwner("photo") = {"Alice"}, friendOfFriendOfOwner("photo") = {"Bob"}, fri-endOfFriend("Bob") = {"Carol"}, friendOfFriend("Carol") = { "Bob"}. If "friend" relationship between "Alice" and "Bob" is removed, it is necessary to update friend("Bob"), friend ("Alice") and friendOfFriend("Bob"). This action also requires indirect updates on friendOfFriend("Carol") and friend-OfFriendOfOwner("photo").

Example 2: Consider Figure 8 where "Alice" has friend "Carol" and "Amy". "Amy" and "Carol" both have a common friend "John". So "John" is Alice's friend ◦ friend through "Carol" and "Amy". Removing the relationship between "Amy" and "John" shouldn't remove "John" from "Alice"'s friendOfFriend list. This means, instead of simply storing friendOfFriend("Alice") = {"John"}, we need to store friend-OfFriend("Alice") = { "Amy.John", "Carol.John"}. Storing such path information as an attribute value would ensure availability of accurate attribute values. As demonstrated in this example, it is often not sufficient to store only the end user information as an attribute value in case composite attributes are used.

Example 3: Consider another example with the simple relationship graph shown in Figure 9.

Attribute Composition or Chaining: In this approach we need to have two entity attributes for users, "friend" and

"coworker". To express a policy that verifies a composite relationship such as friend ◦ friend, coworker ◦ friend or friend ◦ coworker, we can use attribute composition such as friend(friend("Alice"))= {"John"}, coworker(friend("Alice")) = {Bob}, friend(coworker("Bob")) = {"John"}.

Composite Attribute: In this approach, we need to have "friend", "coworker", "friendOfFriend", "friendOfCoworker", "coworkerOfFriend" as attributes, so we can express relationship paths that might be found in policies without chaining attributes. This approach has maximum depth limit in expressing relationship based policy dependent on the attribute configuration. Every entity attributes defined in this approach should have a fixed relationship depth. For example "friend" and "coworker" express one level relationships while "friendOfFriend", "friendOfCoworker" and "coworkerOfFriend" express two level relationships.

7. COMPARISON: ABAC vs. ReBAC

In this section we compare ReBAC with ABAC, using the classifications of Sections 4 and 5. We conduct a conceptual comparison using two metrics: i) dynamics and ii) structural models. As the goal of this paper is to provide high level comparison, we do not provide any formally defined models or policy specifications. In order to use the formal framework of [50] to compare expressive power it is necessary to give detailed formal specifications of access control models. This limits comparison results to the very specific models that have been fully specified. We rather seek an intuitive but rigorous and insightful comparison between structurally comparable models.

In this work, we assume only entity attributes can configure relationships and non-entity attributes are finite domain attributes. We have shown that multilevel relationships can be configured with either attribute composition or with composite attributes. ReBAC node attributes can be configured using ABAC atomic or set-valued, and entity or non-entity attributes. ReBAC edge attributes can be configured using ABAC structured attributes of entities. From ReBAC point of view, if ABAC has only non-entity attributes, it means ReBAC graph structure has disconnected nodes with node attributes only. If ABAC has the capability to define en-

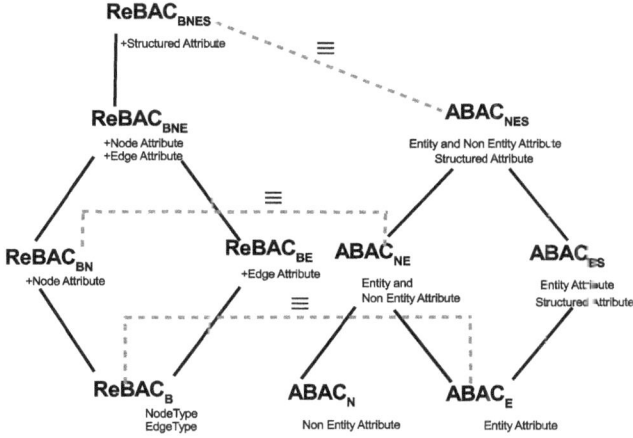

Figure 11: *Equivalence of ReBAC and ABAC Structural Classification*

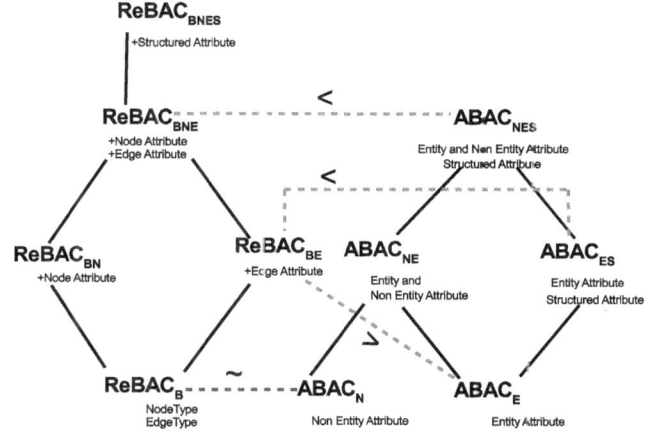

Figure 12: *Non-Equivalence of ReBAC and ABAC Structural Classification*

tity attributes, it can be configured to express relationships. Structured entity attributes can be configured as atomic or set-valued edge attributes or structured node attributes in relationship graph.

7.1 Comparison on Dynamics

Figure 10 shows a three-way alignment of ReBAC and ABAC dynamics with finite/infinite attribute domains. We understand this alignment to mean the following. The statement that $ABAC_X$ is equivalent to $ReBAC_Y$ is to be interpreted as given below.

- Static and finite attribute domain $ABAC_X$ is equivalent to static $ReBAC_Y$.

- $ABAC_X$ that allows change of attribute values with finite domain attribute is equivalent to relationship dynamic (which includes attribute dynamic where it is applicable) $ReBAC_Y$.

- $ABAC_X$ that allows entity changes and infinite domain entity attribute is equivalent to node dynamic $ReBAC_Y$.

This alignment and interpretation allows us to avoid explicit consideration of all combinations of dynamics and models, which would be overwhelming. It does impose an obligation to consider all three levels of dynamics from Figure 10 in making equivalence claims.

We also have the following general result.

THEOREM 1. *Finite domain ABAC cannot configure ReBAC that changes entities in the relationship graph (i.e., node dynamic ReBAC).*

PROOF. (Sketch) Entity changes in ReBAC entail creating new entities in the system and deleting existing ones. In order to configure any kind of ReBAC we need entity attributes in ABAC. Changes of entity from ReBAC requires changing the range of entity attribute for ABAC to potentially unbounded size. A finite domain ABAC cannot have attributes that changes its range over time in this manner. □

7.2 Comparable Structural Models for ReBAC and ABAC

In this sub-section we compare the ReBAC and ABAC structural models from Figures 1(a) and 6(a) respectively. Figure 11 shows the equivalence of different ABAC and ReBAC models (with blue dotted lines) Figure 12 shows the non-equivalence of different ABAC and ReBAC models (purple dotted line shows one model is incomparable with another while green dotted line shows one model is more expressive than another).

THEOREM 2. $ABAC_N$ *is incomparable to* $ReBAC_B$

PROOF. (Sketch) $ABAC_N$ has only non-entity attributes which cannot configure relations as discussed earlier. □

THEOREM 3. $ABAC_E$ *and* $ReBAC_B$ *are equivalent in expressive power.*

PROOF. (Sketch) To prove this we need to show

- $ABAC_E$ can configure $ReBAC_B$

- $ReBAC_B$ can configure $ABAC_E$

For the former, $ABAC_E$ has entity attributes which can configure relationships via the techniques discussed in Section 6. For the latter, $ABAC_E$ can be expressed as $ReBAC_B$ where the entity attributes are relationship types, entities are nodes in the graph and which allows only one level relationship expression in authorization policy. □

COROLLARY 1. $ABAC_N$ *is incomparable to* $ABAC_E$

PROOF. (Sketch) Theorem 2 proves that $ABAC_N$ is incomparable to $ReBAC_B$ and Theorem 3 proves that $ABAC_E$ and $ReBAC_B$ are equivalent in expressive power. The corollary follows. □

THEOREM 4. $ABAC_{NE}$ *and* $ReBAC_{BN}$ *have equivalent expressive power*

PROOF. (Sketch) With entity attribute $ABAC_{NE}$ can configure relationships of $ReBAC_{BN}$ and with non-entity attribute $ABAC_{NE}$ can configure non-entity node attribute of $ReBAC_{BN}$. So $ABAC_{NE}$ can configure $ReBAC_{BN}$. Conversely $ReBAC_{BN}$ can express entity attribute as relationships and non-entity attribute as node attribute in the relationship graph. So $ReBAC_{BN}$ can configure $ABAC_{NE}$. □

THEOREM 5. *ABAC$_E$ is less expressive than ReBAC$_{BE}$*

PROOF. (Sketch) Entity attribute of ABAC$_E$ can be configured with relationship of ReBAC$_{BE}$. So ReBAC$_{BE}$ can configure ABAC$_E$. On the other hand we have seen in Section 5 that structured attributes are required to configure edge attributes in ABAC. For example consider Figure 4 where "tenantTrust" has "trustValue" as edge attribute. Without structured entity attribute, ABAC$_E$ cannot configure this example of ReBAC$_{BE}$. □

THEOREM 6. *ABAC$_{ES}$ is more expressive than ReBAC$_{BE}$*

PROOF. (Sketch) By definition ABAC$_{ES}$ has structured entity attribute while ReBAC$_{BE}$ does not have structured attributes. We have seen in section 5 with structured valued entity attribute ABAC$_{ES}$ can configure relationships, nodes and atomic or set-valued edge attribute of ReBAC$_{BE}$. So ABAC$_{ES}$ can configure ReBAC$_{BE}$. On the other hand ReBAC$_{BE}$ cannot configure more than one level structured entity attribute because it can have only atomic or set valued edge attribute. A 2-level structured entity attribute means at least one subattribute is also a structured attribute. So ReBAC$_{BE}$ cannot configure ABAC$_{ES}$. □

THEOREM 7. *ABAC$_{NES}$ is more expressive than ReBAC$_{BNE}$*

PROOF. (Sketch) Essentially similar proof as the previous theorem. □

THEOREM 8. *ABAC$_{NES}$ and ReBAC$_{BNES}$ have same expressive power*

PROOF. (Sketch) ABAC$_{NES}$ has structured entity and non-entity attributes while ReBAC$_{BNES}$ has labeled relationship graph (multiple type of relationships) with multiple types of nodes (entities) and structured node and edge attributes. Section 5 has shown that ABAC$_{NES}$ can configure relationships, nodes and structured attributes for nodes and edges. So ABAC$_{NES}$ can configure ReBAC$_{BNES}$. On the other hand ReBAC$_{BNES}$ can configure entities with nodes, structured entity and non-entity attributes with structured entity and non-entity node attributes respectively. So ReBAC$_{BNES}$ can configure ABAC$_{NES}$. This proves that ABAC$_{NES}$ and ReBAC$_{BNES}$ have same expressive power. □

7.3 Performance Comparison

So far we have considered the theoretical expressive power equivalence between ABAC and ReBAC. There are clearly some differences between them in terms of performance. ReBAC does runtime computation of authorization. Even if relationship graph is static and nothing changes, ReBAC still needs to repeat the same computation. To eliminate this massive redundant computation load researchers have considered caching of relationship paths [23]. In Section 6 we proposed two solutions for multilevel relationship expression in ABAC, viz., attribute composition and composite attributes. Attribute composition is similar to ReBAC in expressing policy, while composite attribute is more like caching of path information. Attribute composition has polynomial complexity for authorization policy and constant complexity for update, on the other hand composite attribute has constant complexity in policy authorization and polynomial time complexity on update to maintain relationship changes.

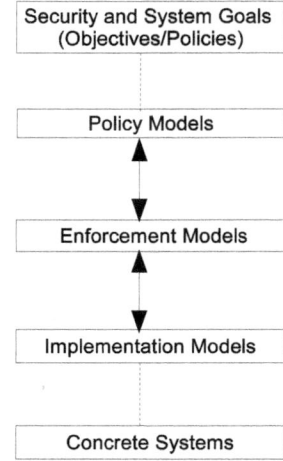

Figure 13: *PEI Framework [46]*

Performance also depends upon the characteristics of the system. A number of variances regarding system characteristics such as relationship dynamics, node dynamics and density of relationships between nodes (entities) affect performance. For meaningful performance comparison we need to formally define specific comparable models considering both approach, do their implementation and configure the system for different dynamics (attribute dynamics, node dynamics, relationship dynamics and density dynamics) variances.

7.4 Choices Of Models

Attribute composition or ReBAC approach puts the load on runtime computation, while caching or composite attribute may need significant update load. If relationship graph changes frequently, the caching or composite attribute approach needs to have excessive updates to keep the path information up-to-date.

The choice of models depends on node dynamics, relationship dynamics and the density of relationships between nodes (entities) in the system. If the relationship density of a system is high, adding or deleting a largely connected node will affect quite a large number of relationships in the system. For a static system or a system with non-entity attribute change, regardless of whether the graph is dense or sparse composite attribute is the best approach for relationship expression. If the system has huge node dynamics and relationship dynamics and relationship density is also high attribute composition would be the best solution. If the system is in the middle between these two extremes then we can think of an hybrid approach where both attribute composition and composite attribute are used in the same model. For example to achieve p level relationship composition we can use m level composite attribute and n level attribute composition where $p = n \times m$. To specify it more clearly we can say that a composite attribute with 4 level relationship expression capability such as ffff(u) or an attribute composition with 4 level relationship expression capability such as f(f(f(f(u)))) can be expressed with a composite attribute of 2 level relationship expression capability using 2 level attribute composition ff(ff(u)). This means ffff(u) = f(f(f(f(u)))) = ff(ff(u)).

Application context for security has the well established 3 layers (Policy P, Enforcement E and implementation I or PEI) [45, 46, 47], as shown in Figure 13. Policy level P is all about expressibility, modularity and convenience to express policy and independent of implementation detail. From expressibility point of view both the approaches are equal as we have already shown the equivalence of policy expression at the P layer. E layer is responsible for enforcement architecture wherein performance would come into consideration. Depending on the dynamics characteristics we conjecture that some hybrid combination of ABAC with attribute composition and composite attribute would be optimal for most situations.

8. CONCLUSION

In this paper we have provided an intuitive but rigorous comparative study of ABAC and ReBAC, and shown how various ReBAC features can be expressed with different types of ABAC. Our results indicate that the relationship between ABAC and ReBAC is subtle and variable depending on the precise flavor of these two access control approaches in any given model. At the same time we are able to make some general statements about this comparison. Additional work on comparing expressive power may yield additional insights. More significantly we believe metrics beyond theoretical equivalence need to be brought into consideration to better understand the relative advantages and disadvantages of these two approaches. Performance is one such metrics but others such as maintainability, robustness, and agility, also need to be studied.

Acknowledgements

This research is partially supported by NSF Grants CNS-1111925, CNS-1423481, CNS-1538418, and DoD ARL Grant W911NF-15-1-0518.

References

[1] Alloy language and tool. http://alloy.mit.edu/alloy/. Accessed 09/2016.

[2] OASIS, Extensible access control markup language (XACML), v2.0 (2005).

[3] Openstack. http://www.openstack.org/software/mitaka. Accessed 09/2016.

[4] Singlevalue multivalue. https://msdn.microsoft.com/en-us/library/aa746488(v=vs.85).aspx. Accessed 09/2016.

[5] Structured attribute. https://docops.ca.com/ca-identity-manager/12-6-5/en/configuring/user-console-design/configuring-profile-tabs-and-screens/field-styles/structured-attribute-display. Accessed 09/2016.

[6] Swift. http://docs.openstack.org/developer/swift/. Accessed 09/2016.

[7] T. Ahmed, F. Patwa, and R. Sandhu. Object-to-object relationship based access control: model and multi-cloud demonstration. In *IEEE Conference on Information Reuse and Integration (IRI)*. IEEE, 2016.

[8] M. Barr and C. Wells. Category theory for computing science. In *Prentice Hall*, page 6, 1998.

[9] P. Bennett, I. Ray, and R. France. Analysis of a relationship based access control model. In *Proceedings of the Eighth International C* Conference on Computer Science & Software Engineering*, pages 1–8. ACM, 2015.

[10] E. Bertino, P. Samarati, and S. Jajodia. An extended authorization model for relational databases. *IEEE Transactions on Knowledge and Data Engineering*, 9(1):85–101, 1997.

[11] J. Bethencourt, A. Sahai, and B. Waters. Ciphertext-policy attribute-based encryption. In *2007 IEEE symposium on security and privacy (SP'07)*, pages 321–334. IEEE, 2007.

[12] G. Bruns, P. W. Fong, I. Siahaan, and M. Huth. Relationship-based access control: its expression and enforcement through hybrid logic. In *ACM CODASPY*, pages 117–124, 2012.

[13] B. Carminati, E. Ferrari, R. Heatherly, M. Kantarcioglu, and B. Thuraisingham. A semantic web based framework for social network access control. In *Proceedings of the 14th ACM Symposium on Access Control Models and Technologies*, SACMAT '09, pages 177–186, New York, NY, USA, 2009. ACM.

[14] B. Carminati, E. Ferrari, and A. Perego. Rule-based access control for social networks. In *OTM Confederated International Conferences: On the Move to Meaningful Internet Systems*, pages 1734–1744. Springer, 2006.

[15] B. Carminati, E. Ferrari, and A. Perego. Enforcing access control in web-based social networks. *ACM Transactions on Information and System Security (TISSEC)*, 13(1):6, 2009.

[16] D. Chadwick. *Understanding X.500: The Directory*. Chapman & Hall, Ltd., London, UK, 1994.

[17] M. Chase. Multi-authority attribute based encryption. In *Theory of Cryptography Conference* pages 515–534. Springer, 2007.

[18] P. P.-S. Chen. The entity-relationship model toward a unified view of data. *ACM Transactions on Database Systems (TODS)*, 1(1):9–36, 1976.

[19] Y. Cheng, K. Bijon, and R. Sandhu. Extended ReBAC administrative models with cascading revocation and provenance support. In *Proceedings of the 21st ACM on Symposium on Access Control Models and Technologies*, pages 161–170. ACM, 2016.

[20] Y. Cheng, J. Park, and R. Sandhu. Relationship-based access control for online social networks: Beyond user-to-user relationships. In *International Conference on Privacy, Security, Risk and Trust (PASSAT)*, pages 646–655. IEEE, 2012.

[21] Y. Cheng, J. Park, and R. Sandhu. A user-to-user relationship-based access control model for online social networks. In *Data and applications security and privacy XXVI*, pages 8–24. Springer, 2012

[22] Y. Cheng, J. Park, and R. Sandhu. Attribute-aware relationship-based access control for online social networks. In *IFIP Annual Conference on Data and Applications Security and Privacy*, pages 292–306. Springer, 2014.

[23] J. Crampton and J. Sellwood. Caching and auditing in the RPPM model. In *International Workshop on Security and Trust Management*, pages 49–64. Springer, 2014.

[24] J. Crampton and J. Sellwood. Path conditions and principal matching: a new approach to access control. In *Proceedings of the 19th ACM symposium on Access control models and technologies*, pages 187–198. ACM, 2014.

[25] J. Crampton and J. Sellwood. ARPPM: Administra-

tion in the RPPM model. In *Proceedings of the Sixth ACM Conference on Data and Application Security and Privacy*, pages 219–230. ACM, 2016.

[26] J. Crampton and J. Sellwood. Inter-ReBAC: inter-operation of relationship-based access control model instances. In *IFIP Annual Conference on Data and Applications Security and Privacy*, pages 96–105. Springer, 2016.

[27] R. Fagin. On an authorization mechanism. *ACM Transactions on Database Systems (TODS)*, 3(3):310–319, 1978.

[28] P. W. Fong. Relationship-based access control: protection model and policy language. In *Proceedings of the first ACM conference on Data and application security and privacy*, pages 191–202. ACM, 2011.

[29] P. W. Fong, M. Anwar, and Z. Zhao. A privacy preservation model for facebook-style social network systems. In *Computer Security–ESORICS 2009*, pages 303–320. Springer, 2009.

[30] P. W. Fong and I. Siahaan. Relationship-based access control policies and their policy languages. In *Proceedings of the 16th ACM symposium on Access control models and technologies*, pages 51–60. ACM, 2011.

[31] J. Gallier. Discrete mathematics. In *PWS Publishing*, page 118. Springer, 2011.

[32] P. P. Griffiths and B. W. Wade. An authorization mechanism for a relational database system. *ACM Transactions on Database Systems (TODS)*, 1(3):242–255, 1976.

[33] V. C. Hu, D. Ferrariolo, R. Kuhn, A. Schnitzer, K. Sandlin, R. Miller, and S. Karen. Guide to attribute based access control (ABAC) definitions and considerations. In *NIST Special Publication 800-162*, SIN '13, 2014.

[34] X. Jin. *Attribute-Based Access Control Models and Implementation in Cloud Infrastructure as a Service*. PhD thesis, UTSA, 2014.

[35] X. Jin, R. Krishnan, and R. Sandhu. A unified attribute-based access control model covering DAC, MAC and RBAC. In *IFIP Annual Conference on Data and Applications Security and Privacy*, pages 41–55. Springer, 2012.

[36] J. Kolter, R. Schillinger, and G. Pernul. A privacy-enhanced attribute-based access control system. In *IFIP Annual Conference on Data and Applications Security and Privacy*, pages 129–143. Springer, 2007.

[37] M. Li, S. Yu, Y. Zheng, K. Ren, and W. Lou. Scalable and secure sharing of personal health records in cloud computing using attribute-based encryption. volume 24, pages 131–143. IEEE, 2013.

[38] R. Ostrovsky, A. Sahai, and B. Waters. Attribute-based encryption with non-monotonic access structures. In *Proceedings of the 14th ACM conference on Computer and communications security*, pages 195–203. ACM, 2007.

[39] J. Pang and Y. Zhang. A new access control scheme for facebook-style social networks. *Computers & Security*, 54:44–59, 2015.

[40] J. Park and R. Sandhu. The UCONabc usage control model. *ACM Trans. Inf. Syst. Secur.*, 2004.

[41] B. Qin, H. Deng, Q. Wu, J. Domingo-Ferrer, D. Naccache, and Y. Zhou. Flexible attribute-based encryption applicable to secure e-healthcare records. volume 14, pages 499–511. Springer, 2015.

[42] S. Z. R. Rizvi and P. W. Fong. Interoperability of relationship-and role-based access control. In *Proceedings of the Sixth ACM Conference on Data and Application Security and Privacy*, pages 231–242. ACM, 2016.

[43] S. Z. R. Rizvi, P. W. Fong, J. Crampton, and J. Sellwood. Relationship-based access control for an open-source medical records system. In *Proceedings of the 20th ACM Symposium on Access Control Models and Technologies*, pages 113–124. ACM, 2015.

[44] A. Sahai and B. Waters. Fuzzy identity-based encryption. In *Annual International Conference on the Theory and Applications of Cryptographic Techniques*, pages 457–473. Springer, 2005.

[45] R. Sandhu. Engineering authority and trust in cyberspace: The om-am and rbac way. In *Proceedings of the fifth ACM workshop on Role-based access control*, pages 111–119. ACM, 2000.

[46] R. Sandhu. The PEI framework for application-centric security. In *Security and Communication Networks (IWSCN), 2009 Proceedings of the 1st International Workshop on*, pages 1–6. IEEE, 2009.

[47] R. Sandhu, K. Ranganathan, and X. Zhang. Secure information sharing enabled by trusted computing and PEI models. In *Proceedings of the 2006 ACM Symposium on Information, computer and communications security*, pages 2–12. ACM, 2006.

[48] H. Shen. A semantic-aware attribute-based access control model for web services. In *International Conference on Algorithms and Architectures for Parallel Processing*, pages 693–703. Springer, 2009.

[49] S. D. Stoller. An administrative model for relationship-based access control. In *Data and Applications Security and Privacy XXIX*, pages 53–68. Springer, 2015.

[50] M. V. Tripunitara and N. Li. A theory for comparing the expressive power of access control models1. volume 15, pages 231–272. IOS Press, 2007.

[51] E. Yuan and J. Tong. Attributed based access control (ABAC) for web services. In *Proceedings of the IEEE International Conference on Web Services*, ICWS '05, pages 561–569, Washington, DC, USA, 2005. IEEE Computer Society.

SAMPAC: Socially-Aware collaborative Multi-Party Access Control

Panagiotis Ilia
FORTH
Heraklion, Greece
pilia@ics.forth.gr

Barbara Carminati
University of Insubria
Varese, Italy
barbara.carminati@uninsubria.it

Elena Ferrari
University of Insubria
Varese, Italy
elena.ferrari@uninsubria.it

Paraskevi Fragopoulou
FORTH
Heraklion, Greece
fragopou@ics.forth.gr

Sotiris Ioannidis
FORTH
Heraklion, Greece
sotiris@ics.forth.gr

ABSTRACT

According to the current design of content sharing services, such as Online Social Networks (OSNs), typically (i) the service provider has unrestricted access to the uploaded resources and (ii) only the user uploading the resource is allowed to define access control permissions over it. This results in a lack of control from other users that are associated, in some way, with that resource. To cope with these issues, in this paper, we propose a privacy-preserving system that allows users to upload their resources encrypted and we design a collaborative multi-party access control model allowing all the users related to a resource to participate in the specification of the access control policy. Our model employs a threshold-based secret sharing scheme, and by exploiting users' social relationships, sets the trusted friends of the associated users responsible to partially enforce the collective policy. Through replication of the secret shares and delegation of the access control enforcement role, our model ensures that resources are timely available when requested. Finally, our experiments demonstrate that the performance overhead of our model is minimal and that it does not significantly affect user experience.

1. INTRODUCTION

The popularity of content sharing services and Online Social Networks (OSNs) has increased dramatically during the last years. This increasing number of participants, and the volume and nature of the data available online, raises alarm regarding user privacy, especially after Snowden's recent revelation of large-scale surveillance programs [21].

In general, users can preserve their privacy by controlling the way resources are distributed in the network through the available privacy settings. However, despite the efforts by service providers and the research community to design effective access control mechanisms, users typically have limited control on resources published by others. The current mechanisms consider the uploader of a resource as *owner*, but not the users related to that resource as *co-owners*. This results in a lack of control from those users that are associated, in some way, with that resource. A notable example is that of photo management in Facebook as users are able to avoid being tagged in a photo [1], in order to prevent it from being accessible through their profile, but they cannot state how this photo has to be shared in the network.

Typically, the users associated with a resource are exposed to the access control decision of the data owner (i.e., the uploader), which may not be privacy sensitive. Several studies (e.g., [3, 13, 18, 20, 22]) demonstrated that a large number of users are slightly concerned about privacy, that they are possibly not aware of the implications that stem from disclosing sensitive information, and even that their privacy settings do not always reflect their privacy concerns, which emphasizes the problem of relying entirely on the data owner for controlling access to collective resources. To deal with this problem, several works (e.g., [7, 14, 26, 28]) propose approaches for collective privacy management and for solving privacy conflicts in multi-user environments. However, these approaches either fully rely on the service provider to solve the conflicts and enforce the access control policy, or they assume that the data owner and the associated users play in an honest way, that is, without the intention to enforce their own preferences over those of the other associated users.

Importantly, the existing approaches for collective privacy management consider service providers as fully trusted and allow them full access on user data. However, in reality, a service provider having access on user data can easily analyze them, collect information regarding users and even infer information that has not been previously published online. Furthermore, in some cases, user personal information and data can possibly end up to third parties, such as advertisers and cloud storage services. For example, Instagram utilizes Amazon storage and CDN infrastructure for storing and distributing user photos [2]. Thus, it is a realistic threat model to consider a service provider as *honest but curious*.

In this sense, several works in the literature present ap-

CODASPY'17, March 22 - 24, 2017, Scottsdale, AZ, USA

© 2017 Copyright held by the owner/author(s). Publication rights licensed to ACM.
ISBN 978-1-4503-4523-1/17/03...$15.00

DOI: http://dx.doi.org/10.1145/3029806.3029834

proaches that prevent service providers from accessing user data, by encrypting or moving the data to the cloud (e.g., [6, 9, 24, 29]). Also, multiple works propose decentralized architectures (e.g., [5, 8, 11, 17]) for allowing users to avoid centralized control. But, even if these approaches can protect users from service providers, they do not allow collective privacy management, as they do not take into account the privacy concerns of all the users associated with a resource.

In general, user privacy can be effectively protected if users are able to determine and control who can access their data. Thus, we consider that the following should be met:

i The access control policy of a collective resource should reflect the privacy preferences of all the users associated with that resource. None of the users should be able to enforce its own preferences over those of the other users.

ii Users should be able to protect their data from being accessed by the service provider and third parties. This can be typically achieved by allowing users to encrypt their data before uploading it online.

In order to protect user privacy, in this paper, we design a collaborative multi-party access control model that allows all the users related to a resource to participate on the specification of the access control policy, by setting their own rules. In particular, to cope with the limitations of previous works, we assume a threat model where the data owner is *honest*, but it might not be privacy sensitive. That is, the data owner might not maliciously intent to violate the privacy concerns of the associated users (i.e., *co-owners*), but violations could possibly occur due to his/her privacy insensitivity. Furthermore, we assume that co-owners might have the intention, and possibly try, to enforce their own preferences over those of the other associated users.[1]

For protecting user data from being accessed and processed by the service provider and third parties, we design a cryptography-based solution, according to which, resources have to be encrypted before being uploaded online.[2] In this sense, the provider is considered *honest but curious*, by the means that it will correctly perform the protocol, such as storing and providing the resources when requested, but it will probably try to infer user information from the managed resources. Thus, even if the provider is *trusted*, we avoid involving it in the process of access control enforcement, as this may allow him to infer user information, such as resource co-ownerships, users privacy preferences, and any other information that stem from the type and metadata of each resource, even if those resources are encrypted.

The encryption scheme proposed in this paper is defined such that each key used to encrypt a resource is protected by a *secret*, which in turn is generated by exploiting a (k,n)-threshold secret sharing scheme [25]. This allows us to associate a set of n *shares* to each secret. To deploy collaborative access control enforcement for a given resource o, we distribute the shares generated from the secret to the *co-owners*

---

[1]We do not consider cases of arbitrarily malicious users/co-owners that exhibit entirely non-conventional behavior (e.g., using secondary channels to illegitimately disclose non-encrypted data or encryption keys).

[2]The proposed model exploits users social relationships for enabling collaborative multi-party access control. Although the model is generic and suitable for online resources of any type, in this paper we give emphasis on its employment in the context of OSNs.

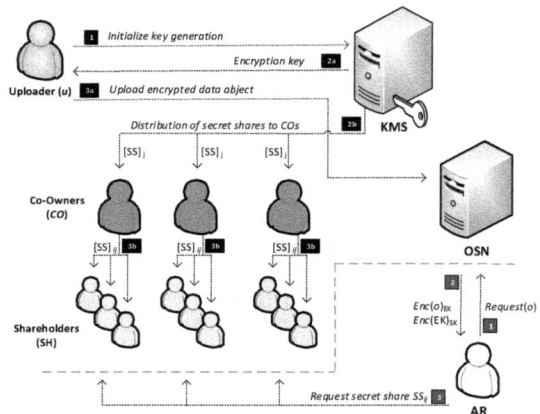

Figure 1: Overview of the proposed mechanism.

of o. The shares are then further selectively distributed by co-owners to their trusted contacts (called *shareholders*).

For accessing a resource, a requester needs to contact different shareholders for collecting a number of shares needed for reconstructing the secret (i.e., greater than a threshold k), and retrieving the encryption key. To make a shareholder able to determine whether to release or not the received share to a requester, each shareholder receives from the co-owner a *share provision rule* (SPR) that states the co-owner's preferences in the distribution of its share. If a requester succeeds in retrieving the needed number of shares to reconstruct the secret, it means that at least a threshold number of shareholders have positively evaluated the access control rules stated by the corresponding co-owners. In this way, users do not need to rely on the service provider for enforcing access control, as their *trusted* contacts are being set responsible for enforcing the collective policy.

2. OVERVIEW OF THE MECHANISM

In this work we consider the uploader of a data object o as *data owner* (DO) and the users associated with that object as *stakeholders* (STs). Both the data owner and stakeholders are considered *co-owners* (COs) of o and should collaborate to determine how the object is released in the network. Furthermore, for protecting co-owners privacy from the service provider and third parties we consider that data objects should be encrypted before being uploaded online.

In order to enable collective privacy management, we design a mechanism that allows all the co-owners of the data object o to specify their access control preferences for o. An overview of the basic mechanism is presented in Figure 1.

At first, we assume the existence of a *trusted* Key Management Service (KMS) that allows the co-owners to collaboratively generate a pair of keys: an *encryption* and a *secret* key. The encryption key is then used by the data owner for encrypting the object before uploading it online. The secret key, which is used for protecting the encryption key, is generated by exploiting a (k,n)-threshold secret sharing scheme. The shares generated from the secret key are selectively distributed to a set of trusted contacts of the co-owners, which are thus being set responsible to enforce access control.

It is relevant to note that the way the shares are generated and distributed to shareholders impacts the resource's sharing strategy. In general, as it will be discussed in Section 3, our system supports two different strategies, namely the *common pool* and the *layered* strategy. These two strategies have different characteristics and thus, each strategy is considered more suitable for particular types of data objects.

Furthermore, as presented in Figure 1, a user that wishes to access a data object o has to retrieve the encrypted object from the service provider and then contact the shareholders of o for retrieving the required number of secret shares, for reconstructing the secret and decrypting the encryption key.

Two important components of the proposed system are the Key Management Service (KMS) and the content sharing service (e.g., OSN). The role of the KMS, which is considered as a *trusted* service, is to support co-owners on specifying the sensitivity of the object and generating the encryption and secret keys, while ensuring that the privacy preferences of all the co-owners are taken into consideration. The data objects are not being revealed to the KMS, but only some metadata, such as their type and sensitivity. Importantly, the KMS is an independent service and should not be managed by the content sharing service provider. The role of the KMS can be played by trusted entities, such as reputable companies, universities, internet authorities etc.

Moreover, as already stated, the proposed model does not allow service providers to access user data, as data objects are uploaded in an encrypted form. The main roles of the service provider, which has knowledge of users relationships and the underlying social graph, is to provide information regarding relationships (in the form of *relationship certificates*) when requested, to store and provide the encrypted objects, and to provide information about the objects' shareholders. In general, we assume that users will create a private/public key pair during their registration, and that they will sign a "*relationship certificate*" during the establishment of each new relationship. These public keys and relationships will be stored by the service provider, in order to be retrievable by other users. Even if naturally the role of the service provider is assumed to be played by online social networks, our model can allow any entity that has relationship information and a users social graph, to be considered as a service provider.

Also, even though the KMS is considered *trusted*, we decided to only utilize it for supporting co-owners on specifying the sensitivity and creating the keys/shares, and not for any other core functionality (e.g., access control enforcement). The main reason behind this decision, which influenced our design, is that we wish a more generic scheme that is not highly dependent on the KMS or the service provider.

At this point, it is important to clarify that in this work we do not try to negatively impact the current design and use of the existing social-based services (content sharing services, online social networks etc.) but rather, to propose an alternative; a generic, privacy preserving system. According to our secure-by-design system architecture, users are not simply the "clients" of the service, but they actively contribute on achieving a high level of privacy, which after all, benefits their contacts, other users, and eventually the community.

2.1 Basic access control model

As already stated, in order to enforce collaborative access control we adopt a (k, n)-threshold secret sharing scheme. According to our system design a set of shares n, that is derived from the secret, is distributed to a set of the co-owners

contacts. A requester AR can access an object only if he/she can reconstruct the secret, by collecting a number of shares greater than k. The number of shares needed to obtain the secret as well as who are the shareholders (that is, those users that receive and manage the shares) is determined by considering the requirements of all the co-owners.

More precisely, each co-owner specifies its set of *selection rules*, by which it chooses a subset of its direct contacts as shareholders. More formally, the selection rules defined by a user u are specified following the paradigm of relationship-based access control (ReBAC) [10, 12], which is emerging in the context of information sharing in OSNs. According to this model, each social relationship is characterized by: (i) a relationship type $type \in RT$, where RT is the set of types supported by the service provider; (ii) a trust value $t\_val \in [0, 1]$, denoting the strength of the relationship. A selection rule is defined as: $\langle u; [(type, t\_val)] \rangle$, where $type \in RT$ and $t\_val \in [0, 1]$, stating that a node to be considered as shareholder by u has to be one of its direct contact with a relationship of type $type$, with minimum trust t_val.

Furthermore, as already stated, objects should be uploaded in an encrypted format. At this purpose, we assume the existence of a *trusted* Key Management Service (KMS) that allows co-owners to collaborate for creating the encryption and secret keys. In order to encrypt a resource, each co-owner CO_j submits to the KMS two random values (EK_j, SK_j) that are used for generating two symmetric keys: the encryption key (EK) and the secret key (SK), as it will be discussed in detail Section 4.2. The encryption key is distributed to all the co-owners and it is used by the uploader for encrypting o. With this key each co-owner is able to verify that the uploaded object has been encrypted properly. In contrast, SK is not distributed to the co-owners, but it is used by the KMS for encrypting EK, i.e., $Enc(EK)_{SK}$,[3] which will be uploaded online by the data owner along with the encrypted object. Moreover, the KMS creates a set of shares (SS) from the secret SK, which are distributed to the co-owners of the object, such that each co-owner receives a unique subset of them to be transmitted to its shareholders.

The way the shares are generated and distributed to shareholders is defined according to the *Access Control Strategy* (ACS) of the object. The proposed system supports two different strategies, namely the *common pool* and the *layered* strategy, which will be discussed in detail in Section 3. The KMS determines which is the most appropriate strategy to be followed for each object, with regards to the characteristics of the object. In general, the best strategy for o is determined by considering the *sensitivity level S* and the type OT of the object, and also, the total number of its co-owners. The *sensitivity level* of a data object is a value introduced to measure the relevance and importance of a given object for its co-owners. We recognize that this is very subjective, as each co-owner might have different preferred *sensitivity levels* for an object. As such, all the co-owners have to participate in the collaborative definition of S by submitting to the KMS their preferred sensitivity levels. Then, S is chosen as the maximum between the average value computed on the sensitivity levels argued by the co-owners (S_{CO}) and the value submitted by the data owner (S_{DO}).

According to both strategies, each co-owner delegates its shares to its trusted shareholders (SHs). Each shareholder

---

[3]Hereafter, we denote with $Enc(M)_K$ the encryption of message M with the key K.

along with a share also receives a *share provision rule* (SPR) that specifies the way shareholders should enforce o's policy, by outlining the requirements that should be satisfied by a requester AR for successfully collecting the delegated shares. Similarly to *selection rules*, SPRs are specified according to the ReBAC paradigm, as $\langle u; [(type, t\_val, dist)] \rangle$, posing conditions on *type*, the trust value (i.e., greater than t_val) and the distance (i.e., less than $dist$) of the relationships that must exist between the requesting user AR and the co-owners of the requested object.[4] An example SPR that is specified and delegated by *Alice* to her shareholders is given by $\langle Alice, [(co\text{-}workers, \star, 2)] \rangle$. Also, more generic rules, such as $\langle co\text{-}owner, [(family, \star, 1)] \rangle$ which allows every co-owner's family members to receive the share, or even complex composite rules, can be supported.

A requester AR who wishes to access o, requests the object to the service provider, which provides the encrypted object $Enc(o)_{EK}$, the protected encryption key $Enc(EK)_{SK}$ and a list that contains the identifiers of o's shareholders. Then, AR contacts the shareholders for requesting each individual share. In order to obtain a share, the requester has to prove that he/she has relationships that satisfy the constraints specified by co-owners' SPRs. At this purpose, the requester can retrieve from the service provider the set of *relationship certificates* that prove the existence of relationships that satisfy SPRs, and provide them to shareholders for validation. This design, in a sense, makes it easier for a well-connected requester, which has multiple indirect relationship connections with the co-owners, to find a path that satisfies the constraints of SPRs.

3. ACCESS CONTROL STRATEGIES

The proposed system can support two different access control strategies; the *common pool* and the *layered* strategy. The strategy followed for an object o determines the processes needed by a requester for being granted access to o.

3.1 Common pool approach

According to this approach, the Key Management Service employs a (k, n)-threshold secret sharing scheme to generate a number of non-distinguishable shares from the secret. These shares are distributed to the co-owners of the object *(i)* uniformly, or almost uniformly, or *(ii)* according to each co-owner's weight, denoted as δ. The process followed for the creation of shares ensures that the number of shares provided to each co-owner does not exceed the number of its shareholders. As such, the number of the created shares depends on the number of co-owners and the number of their contacts that can be selected as shareholders, according to co-owners' selection rules. At first , each co-owner CO_j determines the number of its contacts that satisfy its selection rules, say β_j, and informs the KMS. Then, for a given object o that has to be distributed according to the common

pool approach and under the uniform distribution, the KMS selects a number λ, such that $\lambda \le \beta_j$, and generates a set of $n = \lambda \times |CO|$ shares, and distributes a subset of λ shares to each co-owner. If the selection rule of a given co-owner CO_j is so strict that the corresponding β_j value decreases too much the number λ, the KMS chooses λ to satisfy most of the other co-owners and generates λ shares for them. Then it sends exactly β_j shares to CO_j (where, $\beta_j < \lambda$). Similarly, for the non-uniform distribution the total number of shares is $n = \lambda \times |CO|$, with the difference that the number of shares for each single co-owner CO_j depends on its relevance, that is, $n_j = \delta_j \times n$, where $n_j < k \le \beta_j$. After receiving the shares, each co-owner distributes them to its shareholders along with the corresponding share provision rule SPR. In the case where the number of received shares (n_j) is smaller than the number of a co-owner's potential shareholders (β_j), the co-owner is able to distribute the same share to multiple shareholders in order to achieve replication of its shares and thus, to increase the availability of shares in the system.

Another relevant parameter defined in the common pool approach is the value of the threshold k, denoting the number of shares required for key reconstruction. Here, the idea is to bind the value of k to the *sensitivity level* of the object. Therefore, the number of shares k required for key reconstruction is proportional to the object's sensitivity level S, with regards to the total number of shares n, such that: $k \leftarrow \lceil S \times n \rceil$, where $n = \lambda \times |CO| - \sum_{j=1}^{|CO|} (\lambda - \beta_j)$ if $\beta_j < \lambda$.

3.2 Layered approach

This access control strategy has been designed to give more control to co-owners. The basic idea behind this strategy is to have two-layers of shares, which we refer to as *master shares* and *subshares*, respectively. The master shares MSs are defined according to a (k, n)-threshold secret sharing scheme such that n master shares, where $n = |CO|$, are directly derived from the secret, and each co-owner receives just a single master share. The threshold k (called *top-layer threshold*), which represents the number of master shares needed to reconstruct the secret, is set to $k \leftarrow \lceil S \times n \rceil$, $n = |CO|$, where $S \in (0, 1]$ is the sensitivity level associated with the object to which the secret corresponds.

The second layer of shares, i.e., *subshares*, are generated directly by each co-owner. Again, each co-owner exploits a (k, n)-threshold secret sharing scheme in order to derive the *subshares* from the received master share, and distributes them to its shareholders. The number of subshares for each co-owner and the corresponding *sub-threshold* μ_j, are defined exclusively by the particular co-owner that holds the specific master from which the subshares are derived.[5]

In the *layered* approach, the requester AR contacts the shareholders of a particular CO and tries to collect enough subshares for reconstructing this co-owner's master. Then, the requester contacts the shareholders of another co-owner to collect its subshares, for reconstructing another master. AR is able to reconstruct the secret, only if he has managed to reconstruct enough master shares, according to the top-

---

[4]In general, an indirect relationship of type t between two users is defined as a path of relationship of type t connecting them. In this case, the distance is measured as the number of hops in the path, whereas the trust value is seen as the result of aggregation of all the trust values associated with each single traversed relationship. Literature proposes several algorithms for trust computation on indirect relationships. In this paper, for simplicity, we compute the overall trust as the average of the trust values that are associated with edges in the connecting path.

[5]In general, we consider that the number of subshares created by a co-owner depends on the number of its shareholders, according to its selection rules. Also, the sub-threshold can be defined according to the CO's preferred sensitivity level S_j. However, the system does not restrict COs from choosing different parameters for the creation of subshares.

layer threshold k. This implies that AR has to be authorized by at least k co-owners for being allowed to access o.

3.3 Selection of the best ACS

The shares created according to the *common pool* approach contribute equally on the policy enforcement. This property bears the *common pool* more simple than the *layered* approach, as it requires low effort by the requester for collecting the shares and reconstructing the secret. Also, it allows us to support hierarchy, by distributing the shares non-uniformly to the co-owners. In this case, the shares are distributed according to the weight δ_j of each co-owner CO_j and thus, particular co-owners (e.g., the uploader), can be given more influence on the access control decision for o.

On the other hand, it can be argued that the *layered* approach can preserve *fairness*, as master shares are equally weighted and thus, k-out-of-n co-owners should agree for approving access to the object. Also, this approach allows co-owners to have extended control on the object, as each co-owner is responsible for the specification of its preferred number of *subshares* and the corresponding *sub-threshold*.

In general, the KMS determines the best strategy for an object o by considering the *sensitivity level* S and type OT of o, and the total number of its co-owners. For instance, objects of type 'document' can be better handled by the *common pool* which can support hierarchies, while 'photo' objects are better handled by the *layered* approach. Furthermore, the layered approach is most suitable for objects having a large number of shares (i.e., large number of co-owners, high sensitivity level) as it exhibits lower performance overhead than the common pool approach.

4. DETAILED SYSTEM DESIGN

In the previous sections we presented an overview of the proposed system and the basic access control model. According to this basic design, some shares and objects may not be always timely available when requested, as users (co-owners and shareholders) may not be online during the object's upload and request time. In such a case, the requester may has to wait for some particular shareholders to become available, which can delay access to the object. In this section, we revise and extend our basic design in order to ensure that the great majority of shares will be timely available when requested. In particular, in this section we present in detail our revised design and the processes followed for uploading an object and distributing the shares to shareholders, and for collecting the shares and accessing the object.

4.1 Increasing availability

According to the basic system design, during the object's upload phase each co-owner specifies its preferred sensitivity level S_j for the object, the number of its contacts qualified for being chosen as shareholders β_j, according to its selection rules, and two values that will be used by the KMS for generating the keys. Also, as previously stated, the co-owners receive the shares created by the KMS and distribute them to their shareholders. For accessing an object, the requester contacts the shareholders of the object for proving that he satisfies the SPRs, in order to collect the shares. This design has two availability issues: (i) some co-owners of the object may not be online during the object's upload phase to specify their preferred values and to distribute the shares, and

(ii) some shareholders may not be online during the object's accessing time, when a requester tries to collect the shares.

In order to overcome co-owners' availability issues, we assume that each user is allowed to provide to the KMS a set of predefined sensitivity levels and sets of its shareholders' identifiers, which have been chosen according to the *selection rules*. If a co-owner is unavailable during the upload phase of a new object, the KMS determines whether this object can be associated with this co-owner's predefined sensitivity levels and sets of shareholders. Then, the KMS generates the shares normally and distributes the shares of the unavailable co-owner directly to its predefined shareholders. This process is further described in Algorithm 1 (lines 15, 39).

Furthermore, in order to overcome the issues regarding the availability of shares, we allow share replication and further delegation of the access control enforcement to co-owners' indirect contacts (i.e., shareholders' trusted contacts). More precisely, as previously stated, each co-owner specifies with its selection rules the number of its potential shareholders β_j and the KMS creates λ shares for each co-owner. Therefore, by specifically choosing λ and β_j values, such that $\lambda \ll \beta_j$, the model allows co-owners to provide each share to multiple shareholders, for achieving replication of the shares.

Additionally, according to the revised model, we consider that the co-owners of an object can allow their shareholders to further delegate access control enforcement to their trusted contacts. In order to allow this delegation, the co-owners set a special flag in the *share provision rule* specifying that the share can be further delegated. That is, a shareholder before becoming unavailable is able to set it's own trusted contacts responsible for managing the share, in order to preserve the availability of the share in the system. A requirement for this delegation is that the *selection rules* of the shareholder should be at least as strict as the *share provision rule* of the co-owner. In the case of further delegation, a shareholder includes its selected contacts' identifiers in the list containing the object's shareholders, which is stored by the service provider for being provided to the requesters. Also, when a shareholder becomes again available, it can choose to revoke its previously granted delegations by removing its contacts' identifiers from the list.

4.2 Object upload phase

In the following we describe in detail the process followed by the KMS and the co-owners during the object's upload phase. This process is initiated by the data owner who identifies and submits to the KMS the stakeholders' identifiers, as presented in Algorithm 1. Recall that we assume an *honest* but possibly privacy insensitive data owner, which does not maliciously intent to violate co-owners' privacy. Therefore, the data owner does not intentionally avoid specifying co-owners' identifiers for preventing them from contributing to the specification of the access control policy.

At the very first time, each co-owner initializes its access control settings to specify its preferred sensitivity levels and its selection and share provision rules. Then, for every new object to be uploaded, the following steps take place.

4.2.1 Generation of keys and shares

The process followed by the KMS for generating the keys and shares is presented in Algorithm 1. Initially, the KMS receives by the uploader u the object's identifier and type (ID_o, OT_o), the identifiers of the stakeholders (ID_{ST}), as

Algorithm 1 Process followed by the KMS during the object's upload phase.

1: **Inputs:**
$$ID_o, OT, [ID_{ST}], S_u, \beta_u, EK_u, SK_u$$
2: **Initialize:**
$$S_{CO}, S_{DO} \leftarrow S_u, \ EK \leftarrow EK_u, \ SK \leftarrow SK_u$$
$$N \leftarrow size[ID_{ST}], \ N_{CO} \leftarrow N + 1$$
3: **procedure** DETERMINESTRATEGY(OT, S, N_{CO})
4:     **if** $N_{CO} \geq 6 \ or \ S_o \geq 0.8$ **then**
5:         Return *layered*
6:     **else**   Return *common pool*
7:     **end if**
8: **end procedure**
9: **Process:**
10: **for** $j = 1$ to N **do**
11:     $ID_o \rightarrowtail ST_j$
12:     **if** ST_j *is online* **then**
13:         $S_j, EK_j, SK_j, \beta_j \leftarrow ST_j$
14:         $EK \leftarrow EK \oplus EK_j, \ SK \leftarrow SK \oplus SK_j$
15:     **else** $S_j, \beta_j, [ID_{SH}]_j \Leftarrow predefined$
16:     **end if**
17:     $S_{CO} \leftarrow S_{CO} + S_j$
18: **end for**
19: $S_{CO} \leftarrow S_{CO}/N_{CO}, \ S_o \leftarrow max(S_{DO}, S_{CO})$
20: $Enc(EK)_{SK} \leftarrow Encrypt(EK)_{SK}$
21: $ACS \Leftarrow$ DETERMINESTRATEGY(OT, S, N_{CO})
22: $n, k \Leftarrow (ACS, S, N_{CO})$
23: $[SS] \leftarrow ShareCreation(SK, n, k)$
24: **if** $ACS \Rightarrow layered$ **then**
25:     $n_j \leftarrow 1$
26: **else if** $ACS \Rightarrow common\ pool$ **then**
27:     **if** $n = \lambda \times N_{CO}$ **then**
28:         $n_j \leftarrow \lambda$
29:     **else** $n_j \leftarrow min(\lambda, \beta_j)$
30:     **end if**
31: **end if**
32: **for** $j = 1$ to N_{CO} **do**
33:     $att \Leftarrow Sign(ID_{CO_j}, ID_o)$
34:     **if** CO_j *is online* **then**
35:         $att, S_o, ACS, \rightarrowtail CO_j$
36:         $[SS]_j, n, EK, Enc(EK)_{SK}, \rightarrowtail CO_j$
37:     **else if** $ACS \Rightarrow common\ pool$ **then**
38:         **for** $i = 1$ to $size[ID_{SH}]_j$ **do**
39:             $SS_i, ID_o, ID_{ST} \rightarrowtail SH_i$
40:         **end for**
41:         $[ID_{SH}]_j, ID_{ST_j} \rightarrowtail u$
42:     **else** *Store CO's values*
43:     **end if**
44: **end for**

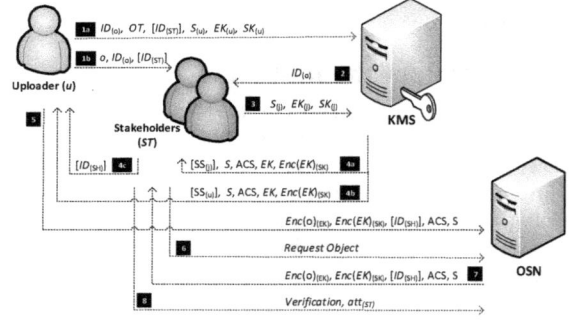

Figure 2: Dataflow between the users, the KMS and the provider for generating the keys and uploading the object.

KMS checks the predefined values of the stakeholders, those defined during the initialization phase. Then, the KMS uses the submitted sensitivity levels (and the predefined ones) to determine the sensitivity S_o of the object (lines 17, 19).

After that, the KMS encrypts the obtained EK with SK, determines the most suitable access control strategy (ACS) for the object and estimates the number of shares to be created (lines 20-22). A simplified example of the procedure followed for choosing the strategy is given in lines 3-8, where the strategy is selected according to the object's sensitivity and number of co-owners. Then, the KMS employs a secret sharing scheme to generate a number of shares from SK.

After the creation of the shares, the KMS determines the number of shares that correspond to each co-owner on the basis of the selected ACS. In the case of the layered approach only a single share is provided to each co-owner. On the other hand, in the case of the common pool, the KMS determines if the shares should be distributed uniformly to all the co-owners, by considering the number of their contacts that are qualifiable for receiving a share (β_j), and distributes them accordingly. In the case of a non-available co-owner, the KMS sends the co-owner's shares directly to its predefined shareholders, and the list of shareholders' identifiers to the uploader (lines 38, 39, 41). It is noted that each one of the predefined shareholders already holds a predefined SPR, delegated by the co-owner during the initialization.

Furthermore, the KMS provides an attestation (att) to each co-owner to confirm "co-ownership" of the object, as it will be discussed later. Additionally to the shares and the attestation, other information such as the object's sensitivity, the total number of shares, the followed strategy and the encryption key (also, $Enc(EK)_{SK}$) are provided to the co-owners by the KMS (lines 35, 36).

4.2.2 Distribution of secret shares

As previously presented, the co-owners that are available during the object's upload phase receive a number of shares, and some other information about the object, by the KMS. Upon receiving the shares, each co-owner employs Algorithm 2 for disseminating them to its trusted shareholders.

In the case of the common pool approach, a co-owner specifies a *share provision rule* SPR for each one of its shares,

well as, the uploader's sensitivity level S_u, number β_u of the contacts satisfying its selection rules (needed for the common pool approach), and two random values (EK_u, SK_u). Then, the KMS sends ID_o to the users whose ID is in the list of stakeholders (line 11) for requesting their participation and waits for their response, which also contains a sensitivity level S_j, a value β_j and two random numbers EK_j and SK_j. The KMS uses the submitted random values for generating EK and SK.[6] If a stakeholder is not available, the

---

[6]Specifically, it combines co-owners' random values, by applying the XOR bitwise operation (Algorithm 1, line 14).

Note that according to this approach the *freshness* of keys can be guaranteed even by a single co-owner that submits *fresh*, non-previously used, values EK_j and SK_j.

Algorithm 2 Distribution of secret shares of each co-owner to its shareholders.

```
 1: Inputs:
        [SS]_i, [ID_CO], n, S, ACS
 2: Initialize:
        n_i ← size[SS]_i, N_CO ← size[CO]
 3: if ACS ⇒ common pool then
 4:     for j = 1 to N_{SS_i} do
 5:         SPR_{ij} ← SpecifyRule(SS_{ij}, [CO])
 6:         SS_{ij}, SPR_{ij}, ⇝ SH_j
 7:     end for
 8: end if
 9: if ACS ⇒ layered & n_i = 1 then
10:     MS_i ⇐: SS_i
11:     N_{SH_i}, μ_i ← DetermineN_SH(S, S_i)
12:     [SSS]_i ← ShareCreation(MS_i, N_SH, μ_i)
13:     for j = 1 to N_{SH_i} do
14:         SPR_{ij} ← SpecifyRule(SSS_{ij}, [CO])
15:         SSS_{ij}, SPR_{ij}, ⇝ SH_j
16:     end for
17: end if
18: if μ_i ≠ ⊥ then
19:     [SH_i], μ_i ⇝ u
20: else [SH_i] ⇝ u
21: end if
```

and delegates the SPR along with the share to a shareholder (lines 4-6). In the case of the layered approach, we consider the single share received by each co-owner as a master share (MS). In this case, a co-owner has to employ secret sharing for creating a number of subshares from the received master (in Algorithm 2 we refer to subshares as SSS). Thus, each co-owner has to determine the number of its subshares N_{SH_i} and the sub-threshold $μ_i$ required for reconstructing its master (line 11). The number of subshares actually depends on the *selection rules* of the particular co-owner, that is, on the number of its contacts selected as shareholders. Furthermore, the sub-threshold $μ_i$ of each co-owner is determined according to its preferred sensitivity level S_i, which may be higher than the object's sensitivity S, such that $μ_i ← \lceil S_i × N_{SH_i} \rceil$. After specifying N_{SH_i} and $μ_i$, each co-owner employs secret sharing for generating its subshares, specifies a SPR for each subshare similarly to the case of the common pool approach, and disseminates a subshare and the corresponding rule to a shareholder (lines 14, 15).

Finally, independently of the followed strategy, each co-owner sends to the uploader a list of its shareholders' identifiers. In the case of the layered approach each co-owner also provides information regarding its sub-threshold $μ_i$. Then, a list of all the shareholders of the object (and information regarding ACS, S, $μ_i$, etc.,) is provided to the service provider by the uploader, for allowing requesters to locate and collect the shares.[7]

4.2.3 Encrypting and uploading the object

As already described in Algorithm 1, after the generation of the keys and shares, the KMS provides to each co-owner a subset of the shares, information about the access control

[7] It is noted that the proposed mechanism does not reveal the identity of co-owners to the service provider, as neither their identifier is provided, nor any interaction between them and the service provider takes place.

strategy and the sensitivity of the object, and the encryption key EK and $Enc(EK)_{SK}$. After receiving the encryption key, independently of the followed strategy, the data owner (i.e., *uploader*) encrypts the object with EK and uploads both the encrypted object $Enc(o)_{EK}$ and the encrypted key $Enc(EK)_{SK}$ online. Additionally to the encrypted object, the data owner uploads a list containing the identifiers of all the shareholders of the object, the access control strategy (also contains co-owners' sub-thresholds in the case of the layered approach), and the sensitivity of the object.

The list of shareholders' identifiers is constructed by the data owner by considering the identifiers of each co-owner's shareholders, provided by the co-owners and the KMS. As described in Algorithm 1, when a co-owner is unavailable the KMS distributes the shares directly to the co-owner's predefined shareholders and provides the list of their identifiers to the data owner. If a co-owner is available during the object's upload phase, it receives its shares by the KMS, distributes them according to Algorithm 2 to its trusted shareholders and then, provides a list of their identifiers to the data owner.

The list of shareholders' identifiers is provided by the service provider to a requester, along with the requested object, for allowing the requester to locate and collect the shares. Moreover, when the direct shareholders of a co-owner are allowed to delegate access control enforcement, as described in Section 4.1, they update the object's list of identifiers hosted by the service provider, for including their trusted contacts, or for revoking delegations they previously granted.

It is noted that this mechanism allows the co-owner to verify the correctness of the uploaded object, by checking if the object has been properly encrypted, with the correct key before being uploaded by the data owner. Similarly, they can verify the correctness of the strategy, sensitivity and list of shareholders. As presented in Figure 2, the co-owners can retrieve the object from the service provider, similarly to a typical requester. In the case of an improper, maliciously uploaded object, the co-owners can request removal or replacement. In this case, they present the attestation of the KMS to prove that they actually are co-owners of the object.

4.3 Object request

Contrarily to the upload phase, which requires some involvement of the end users for uploading the data object and specifying their rules, the processes employed by shareholders and the requester can be handled transparently, without requiring human intervention. The process followed by the requester can completely run in the background, and the object will be presented only after successful key reconstruction and decryption of the object. Also, the shareholders can validate the *share provision rules* in an automatic way (e.g., browser plugin), as these rules follow the ReBAC model.

The process followed by the requester for collecting the shares and accessing the object is presented in Algorithm 3. Initially, the requester asks the service provider for a specific object o, and the service provider sends the encrypted object $Enc(o)_{EK}$ and the encryption key EK (which is encrypted with the secret). It also provides information regarding the object's strategy (e.g. sensitivity, threshold, sub-thresholds) and the list of its shareholders' identifiers (lines 11-13).

In the case of the common pool approach, the requester starts contacting the shareholders whose identifiers are in the list, for requesting the shares. This process is terminated when the number of collected shares reaches the threshold

Algorithm 3 Process followed by the requester for accessing the data object o.

```
 1: procedure SHARECOLLECT($SH_j$)
 2:     $ID_{AR}, Req(SS_j) \twoheadrightarrow SH_j$
 3:     $Req(Verify(ID_{AR}, nonce)) \twoheadleftarrow SH_j$
 4:     $Req(R) := SPR_{(CO)} \twoheadleftarrow SH_j$
 5:     if $\exists R : SPR_{(CO)} \to True$ then
 6:         $Sgn(ID_{AR}, nonce)_{K_{AR}}, Sgn(R)_{K_{CO_i}} \twoheadrightarrow SH_j$
 7:         $SS_j \twoheadleftarrow SH_j$
 8:     end if
 9: end procedure
10: Process:
11: $Req(o) \twoheadrightarrow OSN$
12: $Enc(o)_{EK}, Enc(EK)_{SK} \twoheadleftarrow OSN$
13: $[SH], ACS(S, k, [\mu_i]) \twoheadleftarrow OSN$
14: if $ACS \Rightarrow common\ pool$ then
15:     $[SS] \leftarrow \perp, j \in [SH]$
16:     while $([SS] < k)\ \&\ (N \leq [SH])$ do
17:         $[SS] \xleftarrow{SS_j} $ SHARECOLLECT($SH_j$)
18:         $j \leftarrow j+1, N \leftarrow N+1$
19:     end while
20:     if $[SS] \geq k$ then
21:         $SK \leftarrow KeyReconstruction([SS])$
22:     end if
23: end if
24: if $ACS \Rightarrow layered$ then
25:     $[MS] \leftarrow \perp, i \in [CO]$
26:     while $([MS] < k)\ \&\ (N_i \leq [CO])$ do
27:         while $([SS]_i < \mu_i)\&(n_j \leq [SH]_i)$ do
28:             $[SS]_i \xleftarrow{SS_{ij}} $ SHARECOLLECT($SH_j$)
29:             $j \leftarrow j+1, n_j \leftarrow n_j+1$
30:         end while
31:         if $[SS]_i \geq \mu_i$ then
32:             $MS_i \leftarrow KeyReconstruction([SS]_i)$
33:         end if
34:         $i \leftarrow i+1, N_i \leftarrow N_i+1$
35:     end while
36:     if $[MS] \geq k$ then
37:         $SK \leftarrow KeyReconstruction([MS])$
38:     end if
39: end if
40: if $SK := True$ then
41:     $EK \leftarrow Decrypt(EK)_{SK}, o \leftarrow Decrypt(o)_{EK}$
42: end if
```

k, or after all the shareholders have been contacted. If this process is successful, the requester uses the collected shares for reconstructing the secret (line 21).

The SHARECOLLECT(SH) procedure, which is employed by the requester for contacting each shareholder, triggers a simple authentication and authorization protocol. According to this, the requester has to prove its identity by signing ID_{AR} and a given *nonce*. This can be verified with the requester's public key, which can be retrieved from the service if it is not known. Also, the shareholder asks the requester to provide its relationships that satisfy the co-owner's SPR that corresponds to the particular share (line 4). The requester checks if such relationships exist, and if this is the case, it submits the relationships to the shareholder. Then, the shareholder verifies the identity of the requester and the validity of the relationships, and provides the share.

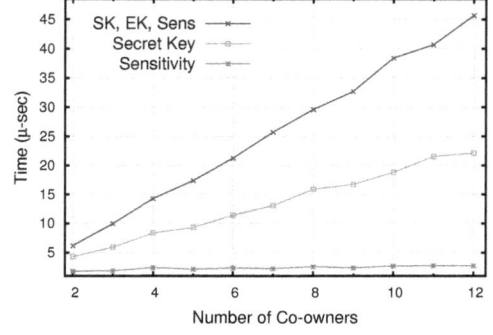

Figure 3: Time spent by the KMS for computing the keys and the sensitivity values

In the case of the layered approach, the requester needs to selectively collect subshares of particular shareholders, for reconstructing a sufficient number of master shares. Thus, the requester has to keep track of the reconstructed masters, with respect to the top-layer threshold k and accordingly, to target those shareholder that manage subshares needed for reconstructing a specific master (lines 25-39). In general, the requester categorizes shareholders into groups, according to which co-owner each shareholder serves, and starts contacting them in a manner that resembles the common pool approach at a group level. After the requester succeeds in reconstructing the first master, it tries to collect subshares of another co-owner, and this process is repeated until a sufficient number of masters are reconstructed. The process is terminated when the number of masters reaches the threshold k, or after all the shareholders needed for each master, according to the sub-thresholds μ_i, have been contacted.

5. PERFORMANCE EVALUATION

In general, it is noted that it is very difficult to evaluate the proposed approach in practice, with a large scale experimental deployment, as it is almost impossible to employ a number of users and their friends, that can reflect the characteristics of OSN population, by the means of their number of contacts, users' location distribution, online time patterns etc. For this reason, we decided to independently assess the performance of the core modules of the mechanism, that can affect user experience in the sense of incurred latency.

All the experiments have been conducted on commodity hardware (Intel i7-4702MQ, 2.2GHz), as our intention is to address the impact of the mechanism on a typical user.

In general, the conducted experiments refer to the main functionalities of our mechanism: (i) object upload and (ii) object request. For the upload phase, we measure the time required by the KMS for generating EK and SK, for calculating the sensitivity S and for generating the shares. Also, we estimate the time required for the data owner to encrypt the object. On the other hand, we assess the performance of the object's accessing phase by addressing the time spent by a requester to reconstruct the secret and decrypt the object. Here, we give more emphasis on the accessing phase, as this is actually the overhead that affects the end users.

Key Generation. We run this experiment multiple times to measure the average time spent by the KMS for generating EK and SK, and calculating the sensitivity. We also

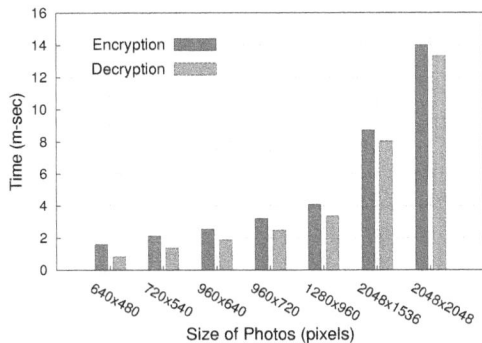

Figure 4: Time spent for encrypting and decrypting photos of different sizes.

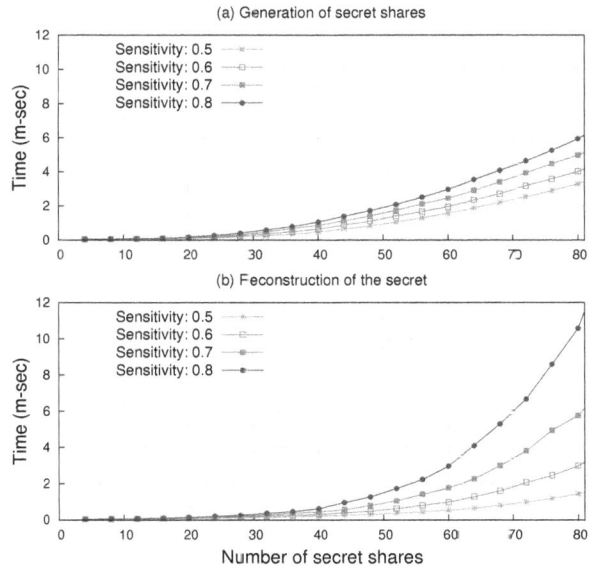

Figure 5: Time overhead for (a) generating a number of secret shares and (b) reconstructing the secret from a sufficient number of shares, with regards to object's sensitivity level.

examine how the number of co-owners affects the process, as all the co-owners contribute by submitting their preferred values. As depicted in Figure 3, the time spent for calculating the sensitivity and generating the keys linearly depends on the number of co-owners, but it is in the order of microseconds, which can be considered as negligible.

Encryption scheme. We implemented an encryption module that uses the AES-256 algorithm for encrypting and decrypting the data objects. We assess the performance of this module for estimating the overhead imposed to the uploader and the requester during o's uploading and accessing phase respectively. We invoke the encryption module multiple times, for encrypting and decrypting photos of different sizes (number of pixels). Specifically, we categorize different photos according to their size, as shown in Figure 4, encrypt and decrypt 500 photos of each category, and measure the time spent for each operation. We observe that most of the photos hosted in current services have dimensions of 960×720 pixels (mostly due to restrictions by the services), but since photos of a larger size, such as 2048×1536, have started becoming popular lately, we examine both categories as well. Our experiments demonstrate that it takes less than 4ms for encrypting or decrypting photos of the former category, and less than 9ms for those of the latter category.

Secret Sharing Scheme. In this experiment we assess the creation of secret shares by the KMS, and the reconstruction of the secret by the requester. We initially use 300 different 256-bit keys (generated by the KMS) to create a number of shares from each one of them, and measure the average time overhead. For all the 300 iterations we keep the total number of created shares and the sensitivity (e.g., threshold) constant. Then, we repeat this process multiple times, for different total number of shares each time, while keeping the sensitivity constant. Specifically, we generate from 4 to 80 shares, with the sensitivity being at 0.5. Then, we repeat this process for sensitivity values equal to 0.6, 0.7 and 0.8.

For assessing the process of reconstructing the secret we use the shares created in the previous experiment. Essentially, the reconstruction process is repeated multiple times, for reconstructing each one of the secret keys that have been used in the previous experiment. Also, it should be noted that in this experiment we reconstruct the secret by combining exactly k-out-of-n shares. The overhead for creating the shares and for reconstructing the key is shown in Figure 5.

The results of these two experiments indicate that both the total number of created shares and the sensitivity value

affect the performance of share creation and key reconstruction. The overhead for key reconstruction is lower than that of share creation, for a small number of created shares (e.g. 50). On the other hand, as the number of shares and the sensitivity increases, the overhead of the reconstruction grows in a faster rate, comparably to the share creation process.

Our results indicate that the time required for creating 50 shares, or reconstructing the secret, does not exceed 2ms. Thus, we consider that the common pool approach is more suitable for objects co-owned by a small number of users. On the other hand, it seems that the layered approach is more effective for objects that belong to a large number of co-owners or having high sensitivity, as the scheme is employed multiple times (for each co-owner's shares), but only a small number of shares is used each time.

These experiments demonstrate that the overhead for creating the shares, reconstructing the secret, and encrypting and decrypting the objects is minimal and that it does not actually affect the user experience. The main issues that can affect user experience are related to the availability of shareholders in the system. We consider that the enhancements proposed in Section 4.1, which allow replication of the shares and further delegation of the access control enforcement to shareholders' trusted contacts, can effectively overcome or at least, minimize the availability issues in the system.

6. SECURITY ANALYSIS

In general, we consider the Key Management Service fully trusted for computing the sensitivity and keys, and for generating and distributing the shares, as discussed in Section 2. **Service provider:** We consider the service provider as *honest but curious*, in the sense that it follows the protocol correctly, but possibly tries to infer user information from the managed resources. For this reason, our model requires that all the resources are being uploaded encrypted and that the metadata uploaded along with each resource do not reveal any information regarding the identity of co-owners. Also, the proposed model ensures that the provider does not perform any functionality related to access control, which could possibly reveal information regarding the co-owners and their privacy preferences. The only case where the co-owners have to reveal their identity to the service provider, is to prove co-ownership of a particular object, for requesting its replacement after detecting malicious behavior by the uploader (e.g., non-properly encrypted object).

Co-owners: As introduced in Section 1, many users are slightly concerned about privacy. In such a case, we do not consider the privacy insensitive users (i.e., data owner, stakeholders) as malicious, as they do not have the intention to impose damage to other users, and actually, their behavior does not deviate from the expected one.[8] This applies even for users having the intention to enforce their policy over those of other users, as soon as these users follow the protocol *honestly*. The proposed mechanism prevents the cases of unintentional privacy leakage as all the co-owners contribute on the specification of the object's sensitivity, which ensures that the concerns of all the associated users are taken into account. Also, the selection of trusted shareholders and the distribution of shares, as well as the guarantee that a single user cannot control a large number of shares with regards to the threshold, ensures that multiple co-owners should authorize a requester for accessing the object.

A stricter threat model can consider the existence of *arbitrarily malicious* users that collude for allowing a requester to access an object he/she is not authorized to. These users exhibit behavior that does not match the expected and allowed one. In this case our model cannot eliminate all the possible threats, but we establish mechanisms to prevent, identify and easily recover from such incidents. According to this strict threat model, a malicious data owner can possibly upload a non-properly encrypted object or provide incorrect information to the service provider for making the object inaccessible to requesters related to other co-owners (e.g., incorrect ID_{SH}). The co-owners can identify such malicious behavior of the data owner by requesting the object from the service provider, similarly to a typical requester. As a result the co-owners can request removal or replacement of the object. However, this functionality can possibly allow malicious co-owners, or even users that pretend to be the co-owners, to replace a proper object. Our model mitigates this by requiring the majority of co-owners to consent, and also to provide the signed attestations by the KMS.

Shareholders The shareholders are selected by co-owners' *selection rules* according to the trust value of the existing relationships among the co-owner and its contacts. This ensures that the selected shareholders are trusted by the co-owners to properly validate SPR. Also, in the case of access control enforcement delegation, the co-owners actually specify the minimum requirements on the selection rules of their contacts that delegate the process, as the selection rules have to be stricter than SPR. Thus, it is expected that

the shareholders behave correctly. However, in the following we examine the case of malicious shareholders that provide the shares without validating the share provision rules.

Common pool. According to this approach, a requester needs to collect k shares for being able to reconstruct the secret. In the case where the requester's relationships satisfy the rules of α shareholders (where $\alpha < k$), the requester is able to reconstruct the secret if there exist k-α malicious shareholders that provide the shares without validating $SPRs$. Thus, for objects with high sensitivity and strict $SPRs$, a large number of malicious shareholders is needed for allowing unauthorized access. We emphasize that we consider this as very rare, as shareholders are not selected randomly, or thoughtlessly, but according to relationship trust values.

Layered approach. In this approach $k \times (\mu_i - \alpha_i)$ malicious shareholders should collude to allow unauthorized access to the object. We consider it as stricter than the common pool, as malicious shareholders need to be selected by multiple co-owners, for allowing reconstruction of k master shares.

A final comment is due the fact that legitimate users can detect malicious behavior of other users. As such, the proposed system can prevent users from acting maliciously, as the detection of such behavior can result to some sort of punishment. As an example, the share provision rules consider the trust value of the user's relationships. Thus, when a malicious user is detected, the users affected by its actions can possibly revoke an existing relationship or reduce the level of the relationship trust. Thus, in reality, illegitimate behavior by a user can result to limited access to resources.

7. RELATED WORK

Multiple works (e.g, [10, 19, 27]) propose rule-based mechanisms for controlling access to resources in OSNs. In [19], the authors investigate whether organizational tags can be used for access control. According to this work, the users are able to annotate their photos with descriptive tags and to specify access control rules based on these tags. Squicciarini et al. [27] proposes an adaptive mechanism for classifying photos according to their content, and for predicting acceptable policies based on user's previous access control rules. Carminati et al. [10] propose a model that considers the type, trust and distance of user relationships for access control purposes. However, these approaches do not allow other associated users to contribute on access control.

An approach that utilizes threshold-based secret sharing is presented in [4]. This work considers that a set of shares are created and distributed to the contacts of the data owner. However, this work does not consider the users associated with the resource as co-owners, and does not allow them to take part in the specification and enforcement of the policy. Moreover, the work presented in [30] investigates the use of a secret sharing scheme in the context of Decentralized Online Social Networks. In order to minimize collusive attacks they exploit relationships among the secret owner, delegate candidates, and their friends. The proposed mechanism serves the purpose of allowing users to back their private keys up reliably, but not to control access to collective resources.

A number of works (e.g. [7, 16, 26, 28]) identify cases of conflicting user interests and highlight the lack of control from the associated users. Besmer et al. [7] designs a mechanism that allows the users tagged in a photo to send a request to the uploader for restricting a particular users from accessing the photo. However, it remains entirely on

---

[8]We do not consider a co-owner having loose *selection* and *share provision rules* as malicious, as this behavior is allowed by the model. Most likely this particular co-owner has set a low sensitivity level S_j for the object, and these rules reflect its perspective on the importance of the object. In the same sense, the co-owners that set high sensitivity level S_j are allowed to specify strict rules for the shares they control.

the data owner to fulfill the requests of the associated users. Also, [28] proposes a multi-party policy enforcement model that requires an agreement between the owner and the associated users for granting someone access to a resource. This mechanism is very strict, as it actually results to co-owners mutual friends. Also, the mechanism can be possibly overruled by an associated user that has the intention to restrict all the other users from accessing the resource. Similarly, the mechanism presented in [26] allows user collaboration but it does not prevent a small group of users from enforcing their own privacy preferences over those of the majority.

The approach proposed in [14, 15], which is close to our work, allows collective threshold-based access control. However, this approach except from allowing the service provider to access the data, it also allows the data owner to select the conflict resolution strategy that has to be followed in the case of a conflict among the policies specified by the associated users. Thus, the data owner can possibly overwrite the decisions of the associated users. Furthermore, [16] proposes a fine-grained access control mechanism that allows each user within a photo to decide which users are allowed to view the area of the photo that depicts its face. This approach solves privacy conflicts and prevents identification of the depicted users, but it considers the service provider as trusted and does not prevent it from accessing user data.

8. CONCLUSIONS

In this paper we propose a socially-aware privacy preserving system for protecting users' privacy from other users and the service provider. We design a collaborative multi-party access control model that allows all the users associated with a resource to participate on the specification of the access control policy. The proposed system prevents privacy leakage due to conflicting privacy settings and protects the users from other, less privacy sensitive users. According to this design, users do not need to rely on the service provider, as other trusted users are being set responsible for enforcing the policy. We plan to extend this work along several dimensions. First, we plan to complement our system with a global reputation mechanism to be used in conjunction with relationship trust values for defining the selection rules. Also, in this work we consider that relationships are stored by the provider for allowing requesters to discover indirect relationships. This allows a requester to become aware of the intermediate users in the path. Thus, we plan to extend our work with protocols that support privacy-preserving path discovery, such as those presented in [23] and [31]. Finally, we plan to investigate if other mechanisms, such as selective encryption, can be used to further enhance user privacy.

Acknowledgements

This work was supported by the FP7 project iSocial ITN, funded by the European Commission under Grant Agreement No. 316808, and by the SHARCS project, under Grant Agreement No. 644571. Any opinions, conclusions, or recommendations expressed herein are those of the authors, and do not necessarily reflect those of the European Commission.

9. REFERENCES

[1] Facebook Help Center - Tag Review. https://www.facebook.com/help/247746261926036/.

[2] What powers instagram: Hundreds of instances, dozens of technologies. http://instagram-engineering. tumblr.com/post/13649370142/ what-powers-instagram-hundreds-of-instances.

[3] A. Acquisti and R. Gross. Imagined communities: Awareness, information sharing, and privacy on the facebook. In *Proceedings of the 6th International Conference on Privacy Enhancing Technologies*, PET'06, pages 36–58, 2006.

[4] B. Ali, W. Villegas, and M. Maheswaran. A trust based approach for protecting user data in social networks. In *Proceedings of the 2007 Conference of the Center for Advanced Studies on Collaborative Research*, CASCON '07, pages 288–293, 2007.

[5] R. Baden, A. Bender, N. Spring, B. Bhattacharjee, and D. Starin. Persona: An online social network with user-defined privacy. In *Proceedings of the ACM SIGCOMM 2009 Conference on Data Communication*, SIGCOMM '09, 2009.

[6] F. Beato, I. Ion, S. Čapkun, B. Preneel, and M. Langheinrich. For some eyes only: Protecting online information sharing. In *Proceedings of the Third ACM Conference on Data and Application Security and Privacy*, CODASPY '13, 2013.

[7] A. Besmer and H. Richter Lipford. Moving beyond untagging: Photo privacy in a tagged world. In *Proceedings of the SIGCHI Conference on Human Factors in Computing Systems*, CHI '10, 2010.

[8] S. Buchegger, D. Schiöberg, L.-H. Vu, and A. Datta. Peerson: P2p social networking: Early experiences and insights. In *Proceedings of the Second ACM EuroSys Workshop on Social Network Systems*, SNS '09, 2009.

[9] B. Carminati, E. Ferrari, and J. Girardi. Trust and share: Trusted information sharing in online social networks. In *2012 IEEE 28th International Conference on Data Engineering*, pages 1281–1284, 2012.

[10] B. Carminati, E. Ferrari, and A. Perego. Rule-based access control for social networks. In *On the Move to Meaningful Internet Systems 2006: OTM 2006 Workshops*, pages 1734–1744, 2006.

[11] L. Cutillo, R. Molva, and T. Strufe. Safebook: A privacy-preserving online social network leveraging on real-life trust. *Communications Magazine, IEEE*, 47(12), 2009.

[12] P. W. Fong. Relationship-based access control: Protection model and policy language. In *Proceedings of the First ACM Conference on Data and Application Security and Privacy*, CODASPY '11, 2011.

[13] R. Gross and A. Acquisti. Information revelation and privacy in online social networks. In *Proceedings of the 2005 ACM Workshop on Privacy in the Electronic Society*, WPES '05, pages 71–80, 2005.

[14] H. Hu, G.-J. Ahn, and J. Jorgensen. Detecting and resolving privacy conflicts for collaborative data sharing in online social networks. In *Proceedings of the 27th Annual Computer Security Applications Conference*, ACSAC '11, 2011.

[15] H. Hu, G.-J. Ahn, and J. Jorgensen. Multiparty access control for online social networks: Model and mechanisms. *Knowledge and Data Engineering, IEEE Transactions on*, 25:1614–1627, 2013.

[16] P. Ilia, I. Polakis, E. Athanasopoulos, F. Maggi, and

S. Ioannidis. Face/off: Preventing privacy leakage from photos in social networks. In *Proceedings of the 22nd ACM SIGSAC Conference on Computer and Communications Security*, CCS '15, 2015.

[17] S. Jahid, S. Nilizadeh, P. Mittal, N. Borisov, and A. Kapadia. Decent: A decentralized architecture for enforcing privacy in online social networks. In *2012 IEEE International Conference on Pervasive Computing and Communications Workshops*, 2012.

[18] M. Johnson, S. Egelman, and S. M. Bellovin. Facebook and privacy: It's complicated. In *Proceedings of the Eighth Symposium on Usable Privacy and Security*, SOUPS '12, pages 9:1–9:15, 2012.

[19] P. Klemperer, Y. Liang, M. Mazurek, M. Sleeper, B. Ur, L. Bauer, L. F. Cranor, N. Gupta, and M. Reiter. Tag, you can see it!: Using tags for access control in photo sharing. In *Proceedings of the SIGCHI Conference on Human Factors in Computing Systems*, CHI '12, pages 377–386, 2012.

[20] B. Krishnamurthy and C. E. Wills. On the leakage of personally identifiable information via online social networks. In *Proceedings of the 2Nd ACM Workshop on Online Social Networks*, WOSN '09, 2009.

[21] S. Landau. Making sense from snowden: What's significant in the nsa surveillance revelations. *IEEE Security & Privacy*, 11(4):54–63, 2013.

[22] M. Madejski, M. Johnson, and S. Bellovin. A study of privacy settings errors in an online social network. In *Pervasive Computing and Communications Workshops (PERCOM Workshops), 2012 IEEE International Conference on*, pages 340–345, 2012.

[23] G. Mezzour, A. Perrig, V. D. Gligor, and P. Papadimitratos. Privacy-preserving relationship path discovery in social networks. In *Cryptology and Network Security, 8th International Conference, CANS*, pages 189–208, 2009.

[24] M. Ra, R. Govindan, and A. Ortega. P3: toward privacy-preserving photo sharing. In *Proceedings of the 10th USENIX Symposium on Networked Systems Design and Implementation*, NSDI '13, 2013.

[25] A. Shamir. How to share a secret. *Commun. ACM*, 22(11):612–613, 1979.

[26] A. C. Squicciarini, M. Shehab, and F. Paci. Collective privacy management in social networks. In *Proceedings of the 18th International Conference on World Wide Web*, WWW '09, 2009.

[27] A. C. Squicciarini, S. Sundareswaran, D. Lin, and J. Wede. A3p: Adaptive policy prediction for shared images over popular content sharing sites. In *Proceedings of the 22Nd ACM Conference on Hypertext and Hypermedia*, HT '11, 2011.

[28] K. Thomas, C. Grier, and D. M. Nicol. Unfriendly: Multi-party privacy risks in social networks. In *Proceedings of the 10th International Conference on Privacy Enhancing Technologies*, PETS'10, 2010.

[29] A. Tootoonchian, S. Saroiu, Y. Ganjali, and A. Wolman. Lockr: Better privacy for social networks. In *Proceedings of the 5th International Conference on Emerging Networking Experiments and Technologies*, CoNEXT '09, 2009.

[30] L. H. Vu, K. Aberer, S. Buchegger, and A. Datta. Enabling secure secret sharing in distributed online social networks. In *Computer Security Applications Conference, 2009. ACSAC '09. Annual*, pages 419–428, Dec 2009.

[31] M. Xue, B. Carminati, and E. Ferrari. P3d - privacy-preserving path discovery in decentralized online social networks. In *Computer Software and Applications Conference (COMPSAC), 2011 IEEE 35th Annual*, pages 48–57, 2011.

Privacy-Preserving HMM Forward Computation

Jan Henrik Ziegeldorf, Jan Metzke, Jan Rüth, Martin Henze, Klaus Wehrle
Communication and Distributed Systems (COMSYS), RWTH Aachen University, Germany
{ziegeldorf, metzke, rueth, henze, wehrle}@comsys.rwth-aachen.de

ABSTRACT

In many areas such as bioinformatics, pattern recognition, and signal processing, Hidden Markov Models (HMMs) have become an indispensable statistical tool. A fundamental building block for these applications is the Forward algorithm which computes the likelihood to observe a given sequence of emissions for a given HMM. The classical Forward algorithm requires that one party holds both the model and observation sequences. However, we observe for many emerging applications and services that the models and observation sequences are held by different parties who are not able to share their information due to applicable data protection legislation or due to concerns over intellectual property and privacy. This renders the application of HMMs infeasible. In this paper, we show how to resolve this evident conflict of interests using secure two-party computation. Concretely, we propose *Priward* which enables two mutually untrusting parties to compute the Forward algorithm securely, i.e., without requiring either party to share her sensitive inputs with the other or any third party. The evaluation of our implementation of *Priward* shows that our solution is efficient, accurate, and outperforms related works by a factor of 4 to 126. To highlight the applicability of our approach in real-world deployments, we combine *Priward* with the widely used HMMER biosequence analysis framework and show how to analyze real genome sequences in a privacy-preserving manner.

1. INTRODUCTION

Hidden Markov Models (HMMs) are used to model discrete stochastic processes whose internal state cannot be observed. They have become an indispensable statistical tool in many application areas, ranging from natural language processing and pattern recognition to bioinformatics or even finance and economics. An important algorithm associated with HMMs is the *Forward algorithm* which computes the probability that a given HMM generated a given sequence of observations. Forward computation is not only an integral part during training HMMs, but is also ubiquitously used in all application areas to score how well a given HMM explains the observed stochastic process. In bioinformatics, e.g., the Forward algorithm is applied to efficiently analyze the similarity of genome sequences [1].

Permission to make digital or hard copies of all or part of this work for personal or classroom use is granted without fee provided that copies are not made or distributed for profit or commercial advantage and that copies bear this notice and the full citation on the first page. Copyrights for components of this work owned by others than the author(s) must be honored. Abstracting with credit is permitted. To copy otherwise, or republish, to post on servers or to redistribute to lists, requires prior specific permission and/or a fee. Request permissions from permissions@acm.org.

CODASPY'17, March 22 - 24, 2017, Scottsdale, AZ, USA

© 2017 Copyright held by the owner/author(s). Publication rights licensed to ACM.
ISBN 978-1-4503-4523-1/17/03. . . $15.00

DOI: http://dx.doi.org/10.1145/3029806.3029816

Traditionally, both the HMM and the observation sequences are held by the same entity. However, we observe that a second scenario arises in which the HMM and the observation sequences are held by two parties that are unwilling or even forbidden to share this information with one another. For example, consider a service that offers HMM-based genetic disease testing. Clearly, it requires significant research efforts to build accurate disease models. To remain competitive, the service must hence protect its intellectual property. At the same time, users have valid security and privacy concerns which prevent them from sharing sensitive information such as their DNA or medical test results with untrusted services. We find similar examples in other application areas, e.g., biometric identification [39], location services [45], or speech processing [35].

This evident conflict of business interests, regulatory issues, and privacy concerns leads to the question whether two parties can compute the HMM Forward algorithm without either party learning the other's input? Secure multi-party computation [24] presents a promising answer. However, we face two difficult challenges in practice: performance and accuracy. Secure computations typically require large numbers of cryptographic and interactive operations that may well cause unreasonable overheads in real-world applications. Achieving accuracy is challenging as Forward computation entails computation over very small probabilities, which is known to cause problems even with plaintext floating point arithmetic [38].

Related work faces these challenges in different ways: [36] uses efficient blinding techniques together with a semi-trusted third party. The authors of [21, 35, 40] independently propose to compute in logspace using homomorphic encryption and oblivious lookup tables [21]. Techniques for secure floating point arithmetic are proposed in [4, 17]. Unfortunately, none of these approaches provides both sufficient accuracy and satisfiable performance in real-world use cases, hence leaving secure Forward computation an open problem.

In this paper, we propose *Priward* that allows two mutually untrusting parties to *efficiently* and *accurately* compute the Forward algorithm while remaining *oblivious* to each other's inputs. Our approach is based on a combination of additive secret sharing and garbled circuits that is secure against semi-honest adversaries. We carry out all computations in logspace using fixed-point precision which achieves sufficient accuracy and low runtimes for real-world problem instances. The following are our main contributions:

Problem Analysis: We first motivate the need for secure computation on HMMs and then compile a set of requirements from real-world use cases. Our rigorous analysis of related works reveals problems and pitfalls inherent to their design that need to be avoided in any secure computation on probabilities.

Secure HMM Forward Computation: We propose *Priward*, an efficient secure two-party computation protocol for the Forward algorithm. Thereby, we provide efficient and accurate techniques

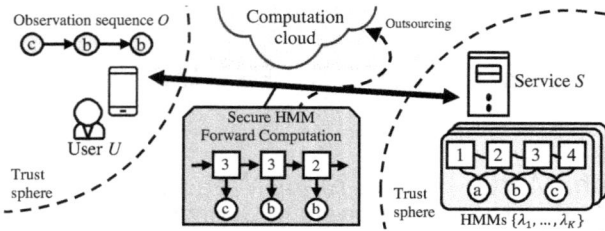

Figure 1: Our problem scenario: User $\mathcal{U}$ holds an observation sequence O, e.g., a genome string, while service $\mathcal{S}$ holds a database of HMMs $\{\lambda_1, ..., \lambda_K\}$, e.g., encoding certain diseases. Neither party wants to share her input with the other (trust spheres). *Priward* enables both parties to compute the Forward algorithm (gray box) in this setting while remaining oblivious to each other's inputs, and even to securely outsource computations to an untrusted cloud.

for computing in logspace that are relevant beyond the scope of this work. Our thorough evaluation shows that *Priward* is efficient and outperforms related work by a factor of 4 to 126. Additionally, our approach enables resource constrained devices that still cannot cope with the involved overheads to outsource computations (e.g., to an untrusted compute cloud) without loss of security.

Real-World Use Case: To showcase the applicability of *Priward*, we implement a secure version of the widely used HMMER biosequence analysis framework [1] and demonstrate privacy-preserving matchings against the Pfam protein families database [3]. Our results show that *Priward* achieves high accuracy and feasible overheads even on large real-world HMMs and long observation sequences.

This paper is structured as follows. Section 2 motivates the scenario, distils important requirements, and identifies limitations of previous proposals. We give a primer on secure computations and the cryptographic building blocks used in this paper in Section 3. Section 4 presents *Priward*, our approach to secure Forward computation. In Section 5, we present a general evaluation of *Priward* and show how to realize a real-world bioinformatics use case in a secure and privacy-preserving manner. Section 6 concludes this paper.

2. PROBLEM STATEMENT

Computations using HMMs have so far assumed that a single party holds all inputs, e.g., the model and observation sequences. We motivate an emerging problem scenario (Sect. 2.1) where the model and observation sequences are held by two different parties that do not trust each other. We proceed to establish concise requirements for Forward computation in this scenario based on real-world applications (Sect. 2.2) and finally analyze related work with regards to these requirements (Sect. 2.3). Our analysis identifies significant limitations among previous approaches that leave privacy-preserving HMM Forward computation an important and open problem.

2.1 Scenario

We consider two parties, a user $\mathcal{U}$ and a service $\mathcal{S}$ as illustrated in Figure 1. $\mathcal{U}$ holds an observation sequence O, while $\mathcal{S}$ holds a database of HMMs $\{\lambda_1, ..., \lambda_K\}$. Together, $\mathcal{U}$ and $\mathcal{S}$ want to compute $P(O|\lambda_i)$, i.e., the probability that a certain model has generated the observation sequence. This scenario is ubiquitous in different application areas of HMMs. In genetic disease testing, e.g., $\mathcal{S}$ has a database of HMMs representing specific diseases against which $\mathcal{U}$ wants to match relevant parts of her sequenced genome to determine susceptibility to certain diseases. In speech recognition [38], each of $\mathcal{S}$'s HMMs is trained to recognize single words or short phrases, while $\mathcal{U}$ supplies a sequence of spoken words to be transformed written text.

In traditional deployments, the desired results are computed with the Forward algorithm by one party which must obtain both inputs. However, in many emerging scenarios neither party is willing to share their inputs with the other or any third party, as indicated by the trust spheres in Figure 1. As a motivating example, consider that $\mathcal{S}$ offers a service and has invested significant research efforts to build high quality HMMs. Sharing the HMMs would give away the intellectual property that distinguishes $\mathcal{S}$ from other service providers [21]. On the other hand, $\mathcal{U}$ must carefully consider the privacy implications of sharing her personal data, especially for sensitive data such as DNA [7], voice recordings [35] or locations [45]. Finally, legal requirements may forbid to share models or observation sequences, e.g., HMMs might be trained on private patient data that must not be shared even in aggregated form.

In this paper, we thus pose the question how $\mathcal{U}$ and $\mathcal{S}$ can compute the desired results *obliviously*, i.e., without learning each other's inputs. Such a solution not only reconciles the evident conflict of business and privacy interests but enables new services that are hitherto prevented by applicable privacy legislation. Remaining oblivious to $\mathcal{U}'s$ sensitive inputs, the service provider $\mathcal{S}$ also does not have to fear the negative consequences of disclosure of customer data in case of attacks, database leaks, or seizure by governments.

2.2 Requirements

We survey how HMMs are used in real-world applications and distil a set of requirements for secure Forward computation.

Requirement 1 (Performance). Efficiency of Forward computation is of high importance in many real-world use cases. In speech processing, e.g., typically one five-state HMM is used to recognize a single word or utterance [38]. Thus, the performance of Forward computation directly determines the size of the vocabulary that, e.g., a voice command system can efficiently recognize. In contrast, profile HMMs used for sequence alignments in bioinformatics often have hundreds of states with observation sequences of equal lengths [3]. Although less time-sensitive than speech applications, Forward computation in bioinformatics must still be efficient to handle the involved large problem instances in adequate time. To ensure the applicability of secure Forward computation in its many diverse use cases, the first requirement is to minimize overheads w.r.t. the size and number of HMMs and observation sequences.

Requirement 2 (Outsourcing). The increasing number of *mobile* users, e.g., using speech-to-text services, poses additional challenges to secure Forward computation. Due to limitations on processing, bandwidth, or energy, mobile users may not be able to carry out computations themselves. It is thus highly desirable to allow outsourcing computations to more capable peers, e.g., to an untrusted computation cloud (cf. Fig. 1). To present a real alternative to constrained users, outsourcing must be both very efficient and uphold all security guarantees.

Requirement 3 (Accuracy). Ideally, a secure HMM Forward algorithm should compute results identical to those of a standard insecure implementation on plaintexts. However, most cryptographic protocols operate over integers and require heavy quantization to handle non-integers [15, 20] while those that operate over floats still introduce significant overheads [17]. Fortunately, inaccuracies may be tolerable to some degree in practice which allows us to strike a balance between performance and accuracy: In speech recognition, to recognize a word, we are only interested in the best guess, i.e., we compute only the arg max while the exact probabilities are less important. In sequence alignments, the goal is to separate matching from non-matching models, i.e., Forward scores are only compared against a certain threshold. Since the actual required accuracy of the numerical results depends on the actual use case, we only require that accuracy can be flexibly traded off against performance. This can often be achieved by adjusting the size of the HMMs or the length of the observation sequence. However, this usually requires expert knowledge and almost always involves expensive retraining of HMMs. We thus require a trade-off independent of the model and observation sequence that allows computation of either an accurate result when necessary or a quick approximation when sufficient.

Requirement 4 (Security). The capabilities of $\mathcal{U}$ and $\mathcal{S}$ to attack the computation are defined by the semi-honest model [23]: A *semi-honest* attacker correctly follows the protocol but may try to infer additional information from the protocol transcript. The semi-honest model has many applications and advantages: It allows for efficient protocols and protects against insider and outsider attacks when both parties are not actively cheating. This is reasonable to assume in our scenario since the user and service provider have a strong interest in executing the computation correctly. We further observe that data involved in typical HMM applications, e.g., in bioinformatics or speech, remains sensitive for longer periods of time. To sufficiently protect such data, we thus argue that all involved cryptographic primitives must be parameterized for long-term security, e.g., by choosing adequate key lengths as recommended in [8].

2.3 Analysis of Related Work

We discuss related work in chronological order and analyze the different approaches along our four requirements (cf. Table 1).

Smaragdis et al. [40] were first to consider privacy-preserving HMM computation in the context of speech recognition. Their approach is based on homomorphic encryption (HE) throughout. HE causes high performance overheads, especially for long-term security levels. Without an evaluation of performance overheads, it thus remains unclear whether their approach is practical. This is aggravated by the fact that many of their secure protocols e.g., the inner product, require plaintext knowledge of the inputs, which prevents outsourcing Forward computation to an untrusted computation cloud. A further concern is the numerical stability of the results: Forward computation involves real numbers while the crypto primitives of their approach operate over the integers. The authors neither explain how they represent probabilities as integers nor do they quantify the involved errors and how they propagate. Finally, missing discussions of security and the use of insecure primitives render the overall security of their approach doubtful.

Pathak et al. [34,35] adapt and improve the techniques from [40] to similar applications such as keyword recognition and speaker identification. Their approach, as well, makes heavy use of HE which is expensive and scales poorly to long-term security levels. This is confirmed by their evaluation results. As in the approach by Smaragdis et al. [40], outsourcing is not possible since some subprotocols require plaintext knowledge. Interestingly, Pathak et al. show that a fixed-point representation can indeed achieve reasonable accuracy on small HMMs when normalizing forward probabilities in each iteration. However, it remains questionable whether reasonable accuracy can also be achieved on larger HMMs and observation sequences. It is also left unclear whether the authors fixed the security issues found in [40].

Polat et al. [36] present a different approach based on additive blindings which promises high efficiency. However, their approach uses additive blinding over probabilities as if they were integers from a finite field which raises serious concerns over the numerical accuracy of the computed results. The authors provide only a limited evaluation of the performance of their subprotocols on random inputs and do not analyze the achieved accuracy. As in the previous approaches and for the same reasons, outsourcing is not possible. Furthermore, they rely on a third party to generate

Approach	R1	R2	R3	R4
Smaragdis et al. [40]	○	○	○	◑
Pathak et al. [34, 35]	○	○	◑	◑
Polat et al. [36]	●	○	○	◑
Franz et al. [20, 21]	◑	◑	●	●
Aliasgari / Kamm / Demmler et al. [5, 17, 28]	○	●	◑	●
Priward (this paper)	●	●	●	●

Table 1: Comparison against related work by the requirements, R1) performance, R2) outsourcing, R3) accuracy, R4) security. ●, ◑, and ○ mark completely, partly, or unfulfilled requirements.

correlated randomness for computing scalar products. If this third party colludes with either party, the other party's privacy is lost.

Franz et al. [20] propose a framework for secure computations on non-integer values in logarithmic representation which they apply to secure bioinformatics services [21]. Their approach is first to provide reasonable accuracy for computations on real-world HMMs and observation sequences. It uses lookup tables to compute the critical logsum operation that causes problems in the approaches by Smaragdis et al. [40] and Pathak et al. [34,35]. The size of the lookup tables constitutes a trade-off between performance (smaller tables) and accuracy (larger tables). However, the size of the lookup tables grows exponentially in the bit-length of inputs, which makes their solution rather inefficient when very accurate results are required. As this approach frequently relies on HE primitives, it scales poorly to long-term security levels and cannot be fully outsourced.

Aliasgari et al. [4,5], **Kamm et al. [28]** and **Demmler et al. [17]** propose provably secure floating point primitives in the multi- and two-party setting that can be fully outsourced. The proposed primitives could be used to implement the classical Forward algorithm in a secure manner but none of these works presents a concrete implementation. This leaves unclear whether standard IEEE 754 floating point numbers achieve sufficient accuracy or whether additional measures are required to avoid underflows of the very small probabilities involved in Forward computation [38]. Furthermore, the performance comparison of the proposed primitives presented in [17] indicates significant overheads.

Summary. The results of our analysis show that no approach provides a satisfying solution to the problem of computing the Forward algorithm in the secure two-party setting. Notably, almost all previous solutions depend on HE primitives and are thus subject to much higher overheads for long-term security levels. We conclude that the efficient, accurate, and secure computation of the HMM Forward algorithm is still an open and important problem.

3. CRYPTOGRAPHIC BUILDING BLOCKS

We give a brief overview of three secure two-party computation (STC) techniques, i.e., oblivious transfer, garbled circuits, and additive secret sharing, which are important to understand our approach and its advantages over related work.

Oblivious Transfer. Oblivious Transfer (OT) is an important building block for STC. OT is a protocol executed between a sender and a receiver. In the scope of this work, sender and receiver are always the service $\mathcal{S}$ and the user $\mathcal{U}$, respectively. The intuitive goal of OT is to allow $\mathcal{U}$ to choose exactly one of many secrets held by $\mathcal{S}$ without $\mathcal{S}$ learning $\mathcal{U}$'s choice and $\mathcal{U}$ learning the other secrets held by $\mathcal{S}$. In the most basic case, 1-2-OT, $\mathcal{S}$ holds two secret bits s_0 and s_1 while $\mathcal{U}$ holds a choice bit r. Running the OT protocol, $\mathcal{U}$ obtains exactly s_r and learns nothing about s_{1-r}, while $\mathcal{S}$ learns nothing about the choice r. As a short notation, we write $s_r \leftarrow$ 1-2-OT$(r, (s_0, s_1))$. 1-2-OT can be generalized to 1-n-OT$_l$, where $\mathcal{S}$ holds n l-bit secrets and $\mathcal{U}$ learns exactly one secret without revealing her choice nor learning any of the other secrets. A batch of m parallel 1-n-OT$_l$ is denoted by 1-n-OT$_l^m$. We can efficiently instantiate 1-n-OT$_l^m$ by first reducing it to a batch of $m \cdot \log_2(n)$ runs of 1-2-OT$_l$ [32, 33] and then reducing this large number of long l-bit OTs to a small number of short t-bit *base OTs* [6, 27] (*OT Extension*), where t is the symmetric security parameter. The base OTs can be precomputed and their processing and communication overheads amortize quickly over a large number of OT Extensions.

Garbled Circuits. Yao's Garbled Circuits (GCs) [42] were the first generic STC protocol. It allows two parties $\mathcal{U}$ and $\mathcal{S}$ with private inputs x and y to evaluate a function $\mathcal{F}(x, y)$ without either party learning the other party's input. Yao's protocol runs in three rounds, i) garbling and transmitting the circuit, ii) garbling and transmitting the inputs, and iii) evaluating the GC and exchanging the results. First, the desired computation $\mathcal{F}(x, y)$ is represented as a Boolean circuit $\mathcal{F}_{Bool}(x, y)$ which is facilitated by specific compilers [17]. Party $\mathcal{S}$ then *garbles* the circuit by encrypting and permuting the truth table entries of each logic gate. $\mathcal{S}$ sends the GC $\tilde{\mathcal{F}}_{Bool}(\cdot)$ to $\mathcal{U}$. In the second step, $\mathcal{S}$ sends its own garbled input $\tilde{y}$ to $\mathcal{U}$, while $\mathcal{U}$ obtains her own garbled input $\tilde{x}$ from $\mathcal{S}$ via OT from $\mathcal{S}$. This ensures that $\mathcal{S}$ learns nothing about $\mathcal{U}$'s input x. Finally, $\mathcal{U}$ evaluates $\tilde{\mathcal{F}}_{Bool}(\tilde{x}, \tilde{y})$ by decrypting the GC gate by gate.

The processing and communication overheads of GCs are mainly determined by the circuit size. It is thus critical to construct *size-efficient* circuits. Circuit size is measured in the number of non-XOR gates, as XOR gates cause virtually no overhead due to the optimizations proposed in [30]. Different size-efficient circuit building blocks have been proposed in [29] and are partly used in this work.

Additive Secret Sharing. Additive secret sharing is an alternative STC technique [12, 18] that uses an *arithmetic* circuit representation, i.e., the desired functionality $\mathcal{F}(\cdot)$ is represented using addition and multiplication gates. An arithmetic circuit $\mathcal{F}_{arith}(\cdot)$ over the ring $\mathbb{Z}_{2^l}$, i.e., all operations are modulo 2^l, is evaluated securely as follows. Both parties first share their input among each other, e.g., party $\mathcal{U}$ holding an input x draws a uniformly random $r \in_U \mathbb{Z}_{2^l}$ and sends $x^{\mathcal{S}} = x - r$ to $\mathcal{S}$ and keeps $x^{\mathcal{U}} = r$ as her own share (and vice versa if $\mathcal{S}$ shares to $\mathcal{U}$). Note that $x^{\mathcal{U}} + x^{\mathcal{S}} = x$ mod 2^l, thus we call the two shares $x^{\mathcal{U}/\mathcal{S}}$ an additive sharing of x. We denote the operation of creating shares from a plaintext input x by $x^{\mathcal{U}/\mathcal{S}} \leftarrow \texttt{Share}(x)$. Having shared their inputs, $\mathcal{U}$ and $\mathcal{S}$ then evaluate the arithmetic circuit representing the desired functionality f using only these shares. Note that addition gates can be evaluated locally, since $\mathbb{Z}_{2^l}$ preserves the commutative nature of additions, i.e., we have $x + y \mod 2^l = (x^{\mathcal{U}} + x^{\mathcal{S}}) + (y^{\mathcal{U}} + y^{\mathcal{S}})$ mod $2^l = (x^{\mathcal{U}} + y^{\mathcal{U}}) + (x^{\mathcal{S}} + y^{\mathcal{S}}) \mod 2^l$. In contrast, multiplication gates require an interactive protocol between $\mathcal{U}$ and $\mathcal{S}$, which can be sped up using precomputed multiplication triples (MTs) [9, 18]. Eventually, $\mathcal{U}$ and $\mathcal{S}$ obtain shares $r^{\mathcal{U}}, r^{\mathcal{S}}$ of the final result r which they exchange and add to obtain $r = r^{\mathcal{U}} + r^{\mathcal{S}}$ mod 2^l. We denote this operation by $r \leftarrow \texttt{Recombine}(r^{\mathcal{U}/\mathcal{S}})$.

Processing and communication overheads of this STC technique are dominated by the effort to generate the required MTs, i.e., by the number of multiplications. Similarly, the round complexity is determined by the multiplicative depth of the arithmetic circuit. Efficient high-level building blocks have been proposed in [14, 15]. Note that arithmetic circuits can also be evaluated using homomorphic encryption as many related works propose (cf. Sect. 2.3). However, STC over additive shares is more efficient for many tasks [18].

Hybrid STC. GCs are rooted in Boolean logic and are thus very efficient for logical operations such as comparisons. In contrast, the additive sharing approach is more efficient for arithmetic operations, i.e., addition and multiplication. Therefore, it is reasonable to ask whether the two representations can be combined to build efficient

hybrid STCs. This idea was first rigorously followed by the *Tasty* framework [25] and recently improved by the *ABY* framework [18]. The basic idea of these approaches is to build efficient conversion protocols and execute required operations in the most efficient representation. A rigorous performance evaluation and different use cases are presented in [18]. The results show that hybrid protocols can significantly improve the efficiency of STCs.

4. SECURE HMM FORWARD ALGORITHM

We have observed scenarios and emerging use cases that make evident the need for a secure Forward algorithm that allows users and services to keep their sensitive or valuable inputs private, e.g., patient data or intellectual property. Our analysis of related work reveals different limitations which render previous approaches unsuitable for our problem scenario. Hence, to solve the open problem of secure HMM Forward computation, we now present *Priward* which achieves the desired balance of accuracy and performance, allows outsourcing, and provides adequate long-term security. *Priward* combines additive sharings and garbled circuits (cf. Sect. 3) with custom protocols to an efficient hybrid secure Forward computation protocol. In the following, we briefly introduce basic HMM theory and our notation then present the design rationale and a high-level overview of *Priward*. The required subprotocols are explained in detail afterward. Due to space constraints, the security discussions of all (sub-) protocols are given in Appendix A.

HMM Primer. HMMs are used to model stochastic processes whose internal state and corresponding transitions are hidden and only the process' output, i.e., its emissions, can be observed. An HMM is defined by $\lambda = (S, V, A, B, \pi)$ with i) hidden states $S = \{s_1, ..., s_N\}$, ii) emission alphabet $V = \{v_1, ..., v_M\}$, iii) state transition matrix $A \in \mathbb{R}^{N \times N}$ with $a_{ji} = P(s_i|s_j)$ the probability of moving from state s_j into state s_i, iv) emission matrix $B \in \mathbb{R}^{N \times M}$ with $b_i(v_j) := b_{ij} = P(v_j|s_i)$ the probability of emitting v_j in state s_i, and v) initial state distribution $\pi \in \mathbb{R}^N$ with $\pi_i = P(s_i)$ the probability of starting in state s_i. In our scenario, the HMM is held by the service $\mathcal{S}$ while $\mathcal{U}$ holds a sequence of observations made about the Markov process. An observation sequence $O = o_1...o_T \in V^{1 \times T}$ is simply a sequence of emission symbols $o_t \in V$ of length T, e.g., a sequence of utterances in a speech recognition application. One important problem is to compute how likely it is that a given HMM has generated a given observation sequence. This problem can be solved using the classical *HMM Forward algorithm* which is also an integral part of training HMMs. The Forward algorithm computes $P(O|\lambda)$, i.e., the probability of λ to have generated O, iteratively using dynamic programming:

i) *Initialization:* $\alpha_1(i) = \pi_i \cdot b_i(o_1)$, $\forall i$.
ii) *Recursion:* $\alpha_t(i) = \left(\sum_{j=1}^{N} \alpha_{t-1}(j) \cdot a_{ji} \right) \cdot b_i(o_t)$, $\forall t, i$.
iii) *Termination:* $P(O|\lambda) = \sum_{i=1}^{N} \alpha_T(i)$.

Note that the probabilities $\alpha_t(i)$ get progressively smaller which quickly causes underflows and introduces numerical instability in the computation [19, 38]. Rabiner [38] proposes to normalize the forward variables $\alpha_t(i)$ after each iteration to deal with this problem. As an alternative, Durbin et al. [19] propose to compute and store all values in logarithmic space. We refer to probabilities in logspace as *scores*, with $\log(P(O|\lambda))$ being the *Forward score*.

Design Rationale. In our requirements analysis (Sect. 2.2), we identified performance and accuracy of a secure Forward algorithm as two main challenges. Indeed, we found no approach in related work (Sect. 2.3) that provides a satisfiable solution to these challenges. Our approach to overcome these challenges is threefold: First, to achieve reasonable accuracy, we store all involved probabilities in logarithmic representation and with fixed-point precision

Input: $\mathcal{U}$ has $O \in V^{1 \times T}$, $\mathcal{S}$ has $\lambda = (S, V, A, B, \pi)$
Output: Forward score $\hat{P}(O|\lambda)$

Initialization: For $1 \le i \le N$

$\quad \mathcal{U} \Leftrightarrow \mathcal{S}: \quad \hat{b}_i(o_1)^{\mathcal{U}/\mathcal{S}} \leftarrow \texttt{Emission}(o_1, \hat{B}_i)$

$\quad \mathcal{U}, \mathcal{S}: \quad \hat{\alpha}_1(i)^{\mathcal{U}/\mathcal{S}} = \hat{b}_i(o_1)^{\mathcal{U}/\mathcal{S}} + \hat{\pi}_i^{\mathcal{U}/\mathcal{S}}$
$\qquad\qquad$ with $\hat{\pi}_i^{\mathcal{U}} = \texttt{Logzero}$ and $\hat{\pi}_i^{\mathcal{S}} = \hat{\pi}_i$

Recursion: For $2 \le t \le T, 1 \le i \le N$

$\quad \mathcal{U} \Leftrightarrow \mathcal{S}: \quad \hat{b}_i(o_t)^{\mathcal{U}/\mathcal{S}} \leftarrow \texttt{Emission}(o_t, \hat{B}_i)$

$\quad \mathcal{U}, \mathcal{S}: \quad X_t^{\mathcal{U}/\mathcal{S}} = (\hat{\alpha}_{t-1}(1) + \hat{a}_{1i}, ..., \hat{\alpha}_{t-1}(N) + \hat{a}_{Ni})^{\mathcal{U}/\mathcal{S}}$
$\qquad\qquad$ with $\hat{a}_{ji}^{\mathcal{U}} = \texttt{Logzero}$ and $\hat{a}_{ji}^{\mathcal{S}} = \hat{a}_{ji}$

$\quad \mathcal{U} \Leftrightarrow \mathcal{S}: \quad \hat{\alpha}'_t(i)^{\mathcal{U}/\mathcal{S}} \leftarrow \texttt{Logsum}(X_t^{\mathcal{U}/\mathcal{S}})$

$\quad \mathcal{U}, \mathcal{S}: \quad \hat{\alpha}_t(i)^{\mathcal{U}/\mathcal{S}} = \hat{\alpha}'_t(i)^{\mathcal{U}/\mathcal{S}} + \hat{b}_i(o_t)^{\mathcal{U}/\mathcal{S}}$

Termination:

$\quad \mathcal{U}, \mathcal{S}: \quad X_T^{\mathcal{U}, \mathcal{S}} = (\hat{\alpha}_T(1), ..., \hat{\alpha}_T(N))^{\mathcal{U}/\mathcal{S}}$

$\quad \mathcal{U} \Leftrightarrow \mathcal{S}: \quad \hat{P}(O|\lambda)^{\mathcal{U}/\mathcal{S}} \leftarrow \texttt{Logsum}(X_T^{\mathcal{U}/\mathcal{S}})$

$\quad \mathcal{U} \Leftrightarrow \mathcal{S}: \quad \hat{P}(O|\lambda) \leftarrow \texttt{Recombine}(\hat{P}(O|\lambda)^{\mathcal{U}/\mathcal{S}})$

Protocol 1: The secure `Forward` protocol: $\mathcal{U}$ holds an observation sequence O that she wants to match against the HMM λ held by $\mathcal{S}$. Using the secure `Emission` and `Logsum` primitives proposed in this work, both parties are able to compute the Forward score $\hat{P}(O|\lambda)$ securely, i.e., without either party revealing their sensitive input to the other. `Logzero` represents the special case $\log(0)$.

which allows us to avoid the use of expensive secure floating point primitives [5, 17]. Second, based on the ideas proposed in [37], we replace the critical logsum operation that caused prohibitive inaccuracies and high overheads in related works [21, 34, 35, 40] with a piece-wise linear approximation (PLA) that we compute efficiently using GCs. The granularity of the approximation directly yields a performance/accuracy trade-off. Third, we replace the expensive HE primitives of related work with additive secret sharing and oblivious transfer which is more efficient, scales to long-term security levels, and supports outsourcing computations from constrained devices to the cloud without compromising security and at almost no costs.

Notation. Our protocols use the following notation: Forward computation is carried out between the user $\mathcal{U}$ and the service $\mathcal{S}$. A single message sent by $\mathcal{U}$ to $\mathcal{S}$ is written as $\mathcal{U} \Rightarrow \mathcal{S}$ while $\mathcal{U} \Leftrightarrow \mathcal{S}$ denotes multiple messages and rounds of communication between the two parties. Values in our logspace representation (cf. Sect. 4.1) are denoted by $\hat{x} \in \mathbb{Z}$ and normal real-valued probabilities by $x \in \mathbb{R}^+$. `Logzero` $:= \log(0)$ represents the special case $x = 0$. Secure subprotocols are marked in verbatim and are realized using OT, GCs, and additive sharings. An additive secret sharing of $x \in \mathbb{Z}_{2^l}$ is denoted by $x^{\mathcal{U}/\mathcal{S}}$ where each party holds one share. $r^{\mathcal{U}/\mathcal{S}} = (expr(x_1, ..., x_n))^{\mathcal{U}/\mathcal{S}}$ denotes the evaluation of an arithmetic expression on the variables x_i of which at least one is additively shared such that the result r is shared between them as well. $\mathcal{GC}_C(\tilde{x}_1, .., \tilde{x}_n, \mathcal{P})$ denotes the secure evaluation of a Boolean circuit C on *garbled* inputs $\tilde{x}_1, .., \tilde{x}_n$ and a set $\mathcal{P}$ of cleartext inputs using Yao's GC protocol [42]. All computations on additive sharings and within GCs are carried out in $\mathbb{Z}_{2^l}$ if not stated otherwise.

Overview. *Priward* computes exactly the same initialization, recursion, and termination steps as the classical Forward algorithm. However, to enable both parties to keep their inputs private, we substitute those steps that require both parties' inputs with secure interactive protocols carried out by $\mathcal{U}$ and $\mathcal{S}$. On the highest level, we only need two secure protocols, `Emission` and `Logsum`, to build the secure Forward. `Emission` takes an observation held by $\mathcal{U}$ and the emission score matrix held by $\mathcal{S}$ and selects the corresponding emission score and shares it additively between the two

parties without either party learning the other's input. `Logsum` computes the sum of two logspace values that are given as additive shares and returns the result again in shared form such that neither party is able to learn anything from the shares. Intuitively, having subprotocols operate over additive shares allows us to easily compose them in a secure manner. Protocol 1 shows the details of our secure Forward algorithm realized with these two primitives. In the following, we explain how $\mathcal{U}$ and $\mathcal{S}$ compute each of the three phases (initialization, recursion, and termination) in more detail. We defer discussions on outsourcing to Sect. 4.4.

Initialization: At the start, $\mathcal{U}$ holds an observation sequence $O = o_1...o_T$ and $\mathcal{S}$ holds the HMM λ. The goal of initialization is to compute additive shares of $\hat{\alpha}_1(i) = \hat{\pi}_i + \hat{b}_i(o_1)$ for $i = 1...N$. To this end, $\mathcal{U}$ and $\mathcal{S}$ invoke our `Emission` primitive N times after which both parties obtain additive shares of the emission scores $\hat{b}_{i=1..N}(o_1)^{\mathcal{U}/\mathcal{S}}$. $\mathcal{S}$ then adds the prior state scores $\hat{\pi}_i$ and $\mathcal{U}$ adds `Logzero` to compute the desired sharing $\hat{\alpha}_1(i)^{\mathcal{U}/\mathcal{S}}$. We base `Emission` (cf. Sect. 4.2) on OT, as this is significantly more efficient than HE-based constructions suggested in related work.

Recursion: The goal of the recursion step is to compute additive shares of the forward variables $\hat{\alpha}_t(i)^{\mathcal{U}/\mathcal{S}}$ for $i = 1...N$ given the additive shares $\hat{\alpha}_{t-1}(j)^{\mathcal{U}/\mathcal{S}}$ from the previous iteration. As before, $\mathcal{U}$ and $\mathcal{S}$ first invoke `Emission` to additively share the emission scores $\hat{b}_i(o_t)^{\mathcal{U}/\mathcal{S}}$. Next, they use our secure `Logsum` primitive to compute additive shares of $\hat{\alpha}'_t(i) = \log(\sum_{j=1}^{N} \alpha_{t-1}(j) \cdot a_{ji})$. Unlike related work [34, 35, 40], we avoid to work on the actual probabilities $\alpha_{t-1}(j)$ and a_{ji} because this is liable to cause critical inaccuracies and overheads. Instead, we compute a piece-wise linear approximation in logspace as explained in detail in Section 4.3. The result of `Logsum` is again distributed as additive shares between $\mathcal{U}$ and $\mathcal{S}$ and they only need to locally add their shares of the emission scores $\hat{b}_i(o_t)^{\mathcal{U}/\mathcal{S}}$ to obtain the desired additive sharing $\hat{\alpha}_t(i)^{\mathcal{U}/\mathcal{S}}$.

Termination: Finally, in the termination step the forward variables $\alpha_T(i)$ are summed up. Since we compute in logspace and over additive shares, we need to employ the `Logsum` primitive again. As the final result, the two parties $\mathcal{U}$ and $\mathcal{S}$ each hold additive shares $\hat{P}(O|\lambda)^{\mathcal{U}/\mathcal{S}}$ of the Forward score. Depending on who should learn the result in the concrete use case, the parties exchange their shares to enable reconstruction of the Forward score $\hat{P}(O|\lambda)$.

In the following, we explain our number representation (Sect. 4.1), our secure `Emission` (Sect. 4.2) as well as `Logsum` primitive (Sect. 4.3), and how to outsource computations (Sect. 4.4).

4.1 Number Representation

One of the main challenges for (secure) Forward computation are the extremely small probabilities involved. To this end, Aliasgari et al. [4] argue that full floating point precision is required. Indeed, the numerical instabilities encountered in the approach by Polat et al. [36] (cf. Sect. 2.3) underline that the dynamic range of the occurring probabilities is indeed too large to compute with *fixed-point precision in probability space*. Unfortunately, even recent highly optimized secure floating point primitives still incur high overheads [4, 17] and are still too expensive for secure computations on HMMs. Hence, we decide to follow the alternative approach proposed by Durbin et al. [19] and carry out all computations *in logspace using a fixed-point representation* of any involved non-integers. As the results presented in [21, 35] indicate, this approach achieves sufficiently accurate results for real-world use cases.

Formally, we transform a probability $p \in [0, 1] \subset \mathbb{R}$ to a fixed-point logspace representation $\hat{p}' = \lceil 2^s \cdot \log(p) \rceil$ ($\lceil \cdot \rceil$ denoting the nearest integer) and map $\hat{p}'$ to the ring $\mathbb{Z}_{2^l}$ by computing $\hat{p}'$ mod 2^l, where l is the chosen bitlength and typically $l \in \{32, 64\}$.

Input: Additive sharing $x^{\mathcal{U}/\mathcal{S}}$ of $x \in \mathbb{Z}_{2^l}$
Output: Additive sharing $x'^{\mathcal{U}/\mathcal{S}}$ of $x' = \lceil x/2^s \rceil \in \mathbb{Z}_{2^{l-s}}$

$$
\begin{aligned}
\mathcal{U} \Rightarrow \mathcal{S}: \quad & x_r^{\mathcal{U}} = x^{\mathcal{U}} + r, \ r \in_R \mathbb{Z}_{2^{l+\kappa}} \\
\mathcal{U}: \quad & x'^{\mathcal{U}} = -(r \gg s) \mod 2^{l-s} \\
\mathcal{S}: \quad & x_r = x^{\mathcal{S}} + x_r^{\mathcal{U}} \\
& x'^{\mathcal{S}} = x_r \gg s \mod 2^{l-s}
\end{aligned}
$$

Protocol 2: The `Rescale` primitive adapted to additive sharings from [15]: $\mathcal{U}$ and $\mathcal{S}$ hold additive shares of $x \in \mathbb{Z}_{2^l}$. By recombining a blinded x_r they are able to securely compute additive shares of $\lfloor x/2^s \rfloor \in \mathbb{Z}_{2^{l-s}}$. Rescaling is required after each multiplication of two fixed-point values represented as integers scaled by 2^s.

Note that scaling and rounding to integers is required due to our cryptographic building blocks. We handle the case $p = 0$ by the special symbol `Logzero` which is practically represented by a sufficiently small number, e.g., -2^{l-1}. After transforming the inputs, any intermediate values and results are also expressed in fixed-point logspace representation. Hence, we must ensure that no value exceeds the bit-length l to avoid incorrectness due to over- and underflows. Note that the sum of two scaled values is again an integer that is scaled by the same factor. However, multiplication leads to an accumulation of the scaling factors, i.e., the product is scaled by 2^{2s}, which would quickly exceed the maximum bit-length l and hence cause errors. To avoid this, we scale the product down by the scaling factor 2^s before any subsequent additions or multiplications are performed.

On plaintext values, this rescaling is a simple matter of division and rounding. However, in our approach, all values are additively shared in $\mathbb{Z}_{2^l}$ which prevents straightforward division and we cannot recombine them for rescaling without violating our security requirements. Instead, we propose an efficient and secure protocol, `Rescale` (Protocol 2). We adapt this protocol from [15] and extend it to work over additive shares in the two-party setting. Our adapted protocol proceeds as follows. Note that all operations are performed in $\mathbb{Z}$, i.e., without modular arithmetic. Initially, $\mathcal{U}$ and $\mathcal{S}$ hold shares $x^{\mathcal{U}}$ respectively $x^{\mathcal{S}}$ of an intermediate value $x \in \mathbb{Z}_{2^l}$ which is scaled by 2^{2s}. First, $\mathcal{U}$ blinds her share $x^{\mathcal{U}}$ using a random number r of length $l + \kappa$ bit and sends it to $\mathcal{S}$. Then, $\mathcal{U}$ truncates the lower s bits of r (a right shift by s bit scales down by 2^s), and uses the negative result as her share $x'^{\mathcal{U}}$. $\mathcal{S}$ obtains the blinded input $x_r = x^{\mathcal{S}} + x_r^{\mathcal{U}}$, similarly truncates the lower s bits of x_r and uses the result as its share $x'^{\mathcal{S}}$. The resulting values $x'^{\mathcal{U}}, x'^{\mathcal{S}}$ share the desired downscaled value x' in $\mathbb{Z}_{2^{l-s}}$. Note that `Rescale` introduces a random error in the least significant bit of the rescaled value, i.e., $x' = \lfloor x/2^s \rfloor + u$ with $u \in_R \{0,1\}$. It is, however, significantly more efficient than the deterministic pendant proposed in [41] and our experiments show that this error can be tolerated.

4.2 Secure Emission Primitive

The `Emission` primitive (Protocol 3) is used during initialization and at the beginning of each recursion step. It obliviously selects the required emission score $\hat{b}_i(o_t)$ and then shares it additively between both parties so that they can compute securely with it. `Emission` proceeds in the following steps: At the start, the user $\mathcal{U}$ holds the observation o_t and the service $\mathcal{S}$ inputs the ith row of the HMM's emission matrix $\hat{B}$. To hide the real values, $\mathcal{S}$ first blinds the entire row $\hat{B}_i$ by adding the same random value $r_{\mathcal{S}}$ to each emission score $\hat{b}_i(v_j) \in \hat{B}_i$. Both parties then engage in 1-M-OT_l after which $\mathcal{U}$ obtains the blinded emission score $\hat{b}'_i(o_t)$ corresponding to her observation o_t. The use of OT guarantees that $\mathcal{U}$ learns only $\hat{b}'_i(o_t)$ and that $\mathcal{S}$ learns nothing about o_t. Note that $\hat{b}_i(o_t)^{\mathcal{U}/\mathcal{S}} = (\hat{b}'_i(o_t), -r_{\mathcal{S}})$ already is the desired additive sharing of the emission score $\hat{b}_i(o_t)$.

Input: $\mathcal{U}$ has $o_t \in V$, $\mathcal{S}$ has $\hat{B}_i = (\hat{b}_i(v_1), ..., \hat{b}_i(v_M))$
Output: Additive sharing $\hat{b}_i(o_t)^{\mathcal{U}/\mathcal{S}}$ of $\hat{b}_i(o_t)$

$$
\begin{aligned}
\mathcal{S}: \quad & \hat{B}'_i = (b_i(v_1) + r_{\mathcal{S}}, ..., b_i(v_M) + r_{\mathcal{S}}) \\
& \text{with } r_{\mathcal{S}} \in_R \mathbb{Z}_{2^l} \\
\mathcal{U} \Leftrightarrow \mathcal{S}: \quad & \hat{b}_i(o_t)^{\mathcal{U}} \leftarrow 1\text{-M-OT}_l(o_t, \hat{B}'_i) \\
\mathcal{S}: \quad & \hat{b}_i(o_t)^{\mathcal{S}} = -r_{\mathcal{S}}
\end{aligned}
$$

Protocol 3: The `Emission` primitive: $\mathcal{U}$ holds an observation o_t and $\mathcal{S}$ holds the emission scores $\hat{B} \in \mathbb{R}^{N \times M}$. $\mathcal{U}$ and $\mathcal{S}$ securely compute additive shares of $\hat{b}_i(o_t)$ using additive blindings and a single invocation of 1-M-OT_l.

During the Forward algorithm, `Emission` is invoked once for each state $s_i \in S$ in each time step $1 \leq t \leq T$, i.e., a total of $N \cdot T$ times. Since for time step t the choice o_t is the same for all $s_i \in S$, we reduce the N calls to 1-M-OT_l per time step t to one 1-M-OT_{Nl} which is more efficient. Additionally, we batch all remaining T calls to `Emission` together to further improve efficiency resulting in one call to 1-M-OT_{Nl}^T.

4.3 Secure Logsum Primitive

In the recursion step of the logspace Forward, we need to compute the logarithm over a sum, i.e., $\hat{z} = \log(\sum_{j=1}^N \alpha_{t-1}(j) a_{ji})$, where we know the summands $\alpha_{t-1}(j) a_{ji}$ only as values in logspace, i.e., $\hat{\alpha}_{t-1}(j) + \hat{a}_{ji}$. This operation is referred to as *logsum* and is ubiquitous not only in HMM computation but in signal processing and pattern classification in general [37]. A logsum over N logspace values is usually reduced to $N-1$ successive or tree-wise calls to

$$
\text{logsum}(\hat{x}, \hat{y}) = \hat{x} + \log(1 + \exp(\hat{y} - \hat{x})) \tag{1}
$$

with $\hat{x} \geq \hat{y}$ (w.l.o.g.) where the term $\log(1 + \exp(\hat{y} - \hat{x}))$ is either computed directly or looked up in a precomputed table.

To compute the Forward algorithm securely, we need a secure `Logsum` primitive which computes Equation 1 on shared inputs $\hat{x}^{\mathcal{U}/\mathcal{S}}, \hat{y}^{\mathcal{U}/\mathcal{S}}$ and returns the results as additive shares, denoted by

$$
\hat{z}^{\mathcal{U}/\mathcal{S}} \leftarrow \text{Logsum}(\hat{x}^{\mathcal{U}/\mathcal{S}}, \hat{y}^{\mathcal{U}/\mathcal{S}}) \tag{2}
$$

We briefly discuss approaches in related work to securely computing logsums and then explain our approach in detail. Equation 1 could be computed using the secure floating point primitives from [5, 17] or using homomorphic encryption and fixed-point precision with rescaling as proposed in [35, 40]. Franz et al. [21] compute Equation 2 based on HE and oblivious lookup tables which grow exponentially in the bit-lengths of the inputs. We deem these approaches too expensive for our use case and follow the alternative idea of Portelo et al. [37] to compute a *piecewise linear approximation* (PLA) of Equation 2. While Portelo et al. [37] propose a completely GC-based solution, we propose a hybrid solution that efficiently combines GCs with additive sharings and achieves better performance than previous secure logsum computations.

The details of `Logsum` are given in Protocol 4. In a precomputation step (that can happen at any time and needs to be computed only once), $\mathcal{S}$ computes the parameters for the PLA: $\mathcal{S}$ selects k intervals $[l_i, r_i]_{1 \leq i \leq k}$ and computes a linear regression $m_i x + n_i$ of $\log(1 + \exp(-x))$ with $x \in [l_i, r_i]$. In the first protocol step, $\mathcal{U}$ and $\mathcal{S}$ convert their additively shared inputs into garbled inputs by evaluating a garbled addition circuit [18]. Both parties then evaluate the first part of Portelo's circuit which obliviously computes $\max(\hat{x}, \hat{y})$ and $d = |\hat{x} - \hat{y}|$ and then obliviously selects parameters $(l_i, r_i, m_i, n_i) \in \mathcal{P}$ where $l_i \leq d < r_i$. Different to [37], we now convert back to additive shares using the OT-based subtraction protocol proposed in [18]. The arithmetic representation then allows us to compute the final result $m \cdot d + n$ over additive shares much more efficiently than using GCs as proposed by [37].

88

```
Input:   Two shared summmands $\hat{x}^{\mathcal{U}/\mathcal{S}}, \hat{y}^{\mathcal{U}/\mathcal{S}}$, PLA parameter $k \in \mathbb{N}$
Output:  Additive sharing $\hat{z}^{\mathcal{U}/\mathcal{S}}$ of $\hat{z} = \log(x + y)$
         $\mathcal{S}:$  Compute PLA $\mathcal{P} = \{(l_i, r_i, m_i, n_i)_{1 \leq i \leq k}\}$
    $\mathcal{U} \Leftrightarrow \mathcal{S}:$  $\tilde{x}, \tilde{y} \leftarrow \mathcal{GC}_{C_{Add}}(\hat{x}^{\mathcal{U}/\mathcal{S}}, \hat{y}^{\mathcal{U}/\mathcal{S}})$
    $\mathcal{U} \Leftrightarrow \mathcal{S}:$  $(\tilde{max}, \tilde{d}, \tilde{m}, \tilde{n}) \leftarrow \mathcal{GC}_{C_{Select}}(\tilde{x}, \tilde{y}, \mathcal{P})$
    $\mathcal{U} \Leftrightarrow \mathcal{S}:$  $(max, d, m, n)^{\mathcal{U}/\mathcal{S}} \leftarrow \mathcal{GC}_{C_{Sub}}(\tilde{max}, \tilde{d}, \tilde{m}, \tilde{n})$
    $\mathcal{U} \Leftrightarrow \mathcal{S}:$  $md^{\mathcal{U}/\mathcal{S}} \leftarrow \texttt{Rescale}((m \cdot d)^{\mathcal{U}/\mathcal{S}})$
       $\mathcal{U}, \mathcal{S}:$  $\hat{z}^{\mathcal{U}/\mathcal{S}} = (max + md + n)^{\mathcal{U}/\mathcal{S}}$
```

Protocol 4: The `Logsum` primitive: We adapt the idea from [37] to compute the logsum of two logspace values by a piecewise linear approximation. To improve efficiency, only the selection of the approximation parameters is done using GCs while arithmetic operations are performed over additive shares.

4.4 Outsourcing

We consider a scenario where the two parties $\mathcal{U}$ and $\mathcal{S}$ need to outsource computation of the Forward algorithm to two other peers $P_{\mathcal{U}}$ and $P_{\mathcal{S}}$ of their choice, e.g., due to processing or bandwidth constraints. This could be the case, e.g., for a mobile user $\mathcal{U}$ that communicates to a cloud service which has become a ubiquitous communication pattern, today. Though this example would require only one party to outsource computations, we show how *both* parties outsource computations for the sake of generality. A scenario where only one party outsources is then straightforward even simpler to realize. Note that the outsourcing step itself must be inexpensive such that it respects $\mathcal{U}'s$ and $\mathcal{S}'s$ resource constraints. However, outsourcing must not break security, i.e., $P_{\mathcal{U}}$ and $P_{\mathcal{S}}$ must remain oblivious of the inputs and outcome of the computation.

To outsource computations, $\mathcal{U}$ and $\mathcal{S}$ first need to execute our `Emission` primitive to compute $\hat{b}_i(o_t) \, \forall t, i$. `Emission` is the only part that cannot be outsourced because it requires the executing parties to know the observation sequence O and the model λ in clear. However, our evaluation (Sect. 5) shows that `Emission` is very efficient and can thus be computed even by resource constrained devices. $\mathcal{U}$ now sends her shares $\hat{b}_i(o_t)^{\mathcal{U}}$ to $P_{\mathcal{U}}$ and $\mathcal{S}$ sends $\hat{b}_i(o_t)^{\mathcal{S}}$ to $P_{\mathcal{S}}$. Additionally, $\mathcal{S}$ shares all transition scores $\hat{a}_{ij}, 1 \leq i, j \leq N$ and the prior state distribution $\hat{\pi}_i, 1 \leq i \leq N$ to $P_{\mathcal{U}}$ and $P_{\mathcal{S}}$ by invoking $\texttt{Share}(\cdot)$ on each item, individually. $P_{\mathcal{U}}$ and $P_{\mathcal{S}}$ then compute `Forward` (Protocol 1) on the given shares. Finally, $P_{\mathcal{U}}$ and $P_{\mathcal{S}}$ send their share of the final result to $\mathcal{U}$ and $\mathcal{S}$, respectively, who only have to compute one local addition to reconstruct $\hat{P}(O|\lambda)$. Note that $P_{\mathcal{U}}$ and $P_{\mathcal{S}}$ must not collude which is the standard assumption in the secure two-party setting and clearly reasonable in our scenario since $P_{\mathcal{U}}$ and $P_{\mathcal{S}}$ are chosen individually by $\mathcal{U}$ and $\mathcal{S}$.

5. EVALUATION

To thoroughly quantify and evaluate the performance and accuracy of our approach, we implemented a prototype of *Priward*. Note that security of *Priward* is discussed in Appendix A. We first perform synthetic benchmarks on fully connected HMMs to derive a thorough understanding of the performance and accuracy of *Priward* (Sect. 5.1). We then show the applicability of our approach in a real-world bioinformatics use case by integrating *Priward* into the well-established HMMER framework [1] (Sect. 5.2). In contrast to generic fully connected HMMs, the special architecture of the HMMs involved in this use case allows significant performance optimizations. Finally, we qualitatively compare the performance of our approach against related works (Sect. 5.3). Now, we provide further details on our implementation and experimental setup.

Implementation. We implement the *Priward* prototype in C++. `Emission` requires the $1\text{-}n\text{-}OT_l^m$ primitive which we implement as one invocation of $1\text{-}2\text{-}OT_l^{m \log_2(n)}$ according to [32, 33]. For

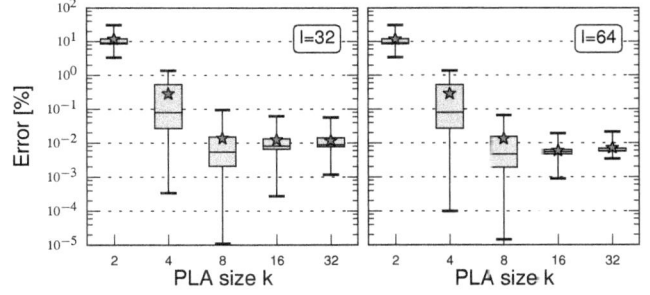

Figure 2: Relative error of `Forward` on matching and non-matching sequences: As we increase the number of approximation intervals k (x-axis) the accuracy increases. Increasing fixed-point precision from $l = 32$ (left) to $l = 64$ (right) shows less improvement but reduces the variance of the error.

$1\text{-}2\text{-}OT_l^m$ we employ the efficient OT Extensions described in [6]. `Logsum` requires building and evaluating GCs, for which we build upon the ABY two-party computation framework [18]. Besides the OT Extension and ABY framework, which are fully multithreaded, the rest of our implementation realizes only obvious optimizations, e.g., batching of the operations in the inner *for* loop of the Forward algorithm. Hence, further optimizations are possible, e.g., pipelining GC generation and evaluation as proposed in [26].

Experimental Setup. We perform all experiments between two standard desktop machines (Ubuntu 14.04 LTS, Intel i7-4770 @ 3.10 GHz, 16 GB RAM) that communicate over a Gigabit LAN. To offer long-term security according to NIST [8], we set the statistical security parameter to $\kappa = 80$ bits and the symmetric security level to $t = 128$ bits.

5.1 Generic HMMs

For the synthetic benchmarks, we create a dataset of ergodic (fully connected) HMMs and observation sequences to serve as inputs. Ergodic HMMs are the most general cases and also the most challenging in terms of performance and accuracy, as they require to take all other states into account as predecessors during the recursion steps of the Forward algorithm. Our dataset consists of random and circular HMMs as well as matching and non-matching observation sequences. Random HMMs and non-matching sequences are sampled completely at random, while for the circular HMMs, we sample state transitions and emission probabilities from a Gaussian distribution centered on the topologically next state leading to a roughly *circular* structure. With the intention to create good matches, we sample observation sequences for the circular HMMs as a noisy linear walk through the states of the HMM. Both sets of HMMs (random and circular) contain HMMs with a varying number of states $N = 10, 20, ..., 100$, emission alphabet sizes $M = 10^2, ..., 10^4$, and number of observations $T = 10, 20, ..., 100$. Our selection of parameters covers a wide range of actual use cases and choices made in related work [4, 34, 35, 38].

5.1.1 Accuracy

Our approach introduces numerical inaccuracies at two points, i) through the fixed-point representation of probabilities and probabilistic rescaling (cf. Sect. 4.1), and ii) through the approximation of logsum operations (cf. Sect. 4.3). In the following, we compare the results of our secure `Forward` against a reference implementation on plaintexts to show that our approach nevertheless computes accurate results. Our reference for accurate results is the widely-

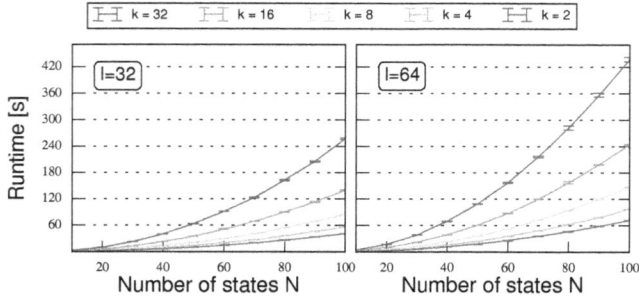

Figure 3: Runtime of `Forward` on HMMs with a different number of states N (x-axis) for different k (lines) and l (left and right plot): The runtime grows quadratically in N and linearly in k and l.

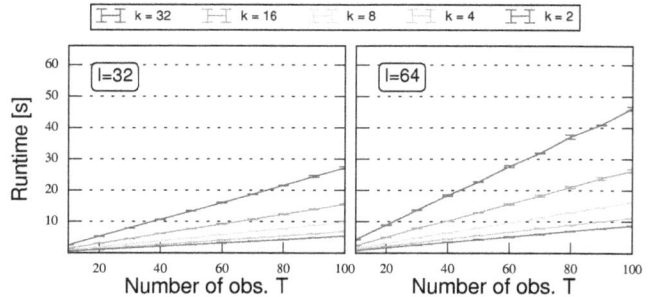

Figure 4: Runtime of `Forward` for HMMs with a different number of observations T (x-axis) for different choices of k (lines) and l (left and right plot): The runtime grows linearly in T, k and l.

used natural-language toolkit (NLTK) [2] which is implemented in double precision in Python.

Figure 2 plots the errors our approach introduces relative to the reference results obtained with NLTK. On the x-axis, we vary the number of approximation intervals $k = 2, 4, ..., 32$ in the piecewise linear approximation; left and right plots vary the bit-length $l = 32, 64$ used for the fixed-point logspace number representation. We show the second and third quartiles (boxes), the and max (whiskers) as well as the means (stars). As expected, the error decreases as we increase the accuracy of the PLA by increasing the number of approximation intervals k. While an approximation with only $k = 2$ intervals causes significant errors, the error decreases quickly for bigger values of k. Already, $k = 4$ achieves a mean error below 0.3 % for both $l = 32, 64$. For $k = 8$ even the maximum error (indicated by the whiskers) drops below 0.1 %. We observe that the average accuracy does not significantly improve beyond $k = 8$. This is due to the numerical errors introduced by the fixed-point number representation and rescaling protocol (cf. Sect. 4.1). Interestingly, using a higher bit-length of $l = 64$ shows only marginal improvements to the average accuracy. However, the variance of the error is reduced and outliers are less extreme.

In conclusion, our results confirm the expected: more approximation intervals k and higher fixed-point precision l improve the numerical accuracy of the results. Unfortunately, an increase in either parameter will also increase the size of the involved GCs which will incur a noticeable decrease in performance. We will put these numbers into perspective when discussing a real-world use case in Sect. 5.2. The performance results presented in the next subsection will allow us to strike a reasonable trade-off between accuracy and performance.

5.1.2 Runtime and Communication

We first analytically derive the critical parameters for *Priward*'s runtime and then thoroughly evaluate its performance. The runtime complexity $\mathcal{O}(TN^2)$ of the Forward algorithm is quadratic in the number of states N and linear in the number of observations T. In the secure `Forward` protocol, we additionally need to sahre all emission scores $\hat{b}_i(o_t)$ securely using `Emission` which scales in $\mathcal{O}(TMN)$ with M the size of the emission alphabet. Thus, N, T, and M are the critical parameters for which we have to analyze the runtime. All results are aggregated over 20 independent runs and plots show the mean values with corresponding standard deviation.

Number of States. Figure 3 plots the runtime of `Forward` on HMMs with $N = 10, 20, ..., 100$ states for different PLA sizes $k = 2, 4, ..., 32$ and bit-lengths $l = 32, 64$ with fixed $M = 1000$ and $T = 10$. As indicated by the overall complexity of the Forward algorithm, the runtime increases quadratically in the number

of states. Qualitatively, we observe the same growth for the communication overhead. Still, our approach is efficient and can evaluate a fully connected HMM with $N = 100$ states with a reasonable error smaller 1 % ($k = 4, l = 32$) in less than one minute requiring 1.59 GB for communication. As expected in the context of secure computations, the communication overhead is significant and may overtax especially mobile users. However, GCs are an active research area and all ongoing and future optimizations of garbling schemes [10,43] will also benefit our approach and reduce overheads further. Meanwhile, *Priward* can be outsourced to a computation cloud which can easily manage current communication overheads.

Increasing parameters k or l increases runtime and communication linearly. This is due to the fact that the runtime is dominated by the $(T-1)N(N-1) + (N-1)$ calls of the `Logsum` primitive whose core is a GC of size roughly linear in k and l. In total, the `Logsum` calls account for more than 99 % of the overall runtime and for more than 95 % of the total communication. The rest of the computational overhead is due to the `Emission` primitive, while the overhead of the operations on additive sharings are negligible. Since efficiently calculating secure `Logsum` is relevant beyond the scope of this work, e.g., for the secure computation of Gaussian Mixture Models [4,35], we provide a more elaborate evaluation of `Logsum` in Appendix B.

Length of the Observation Sequence. Figure 4 plots the runtime of `Forward` for $T = 10, 20, ..., 100$ observations and fixed $N = 10$ and $M = 1000$. Runtime and communication scale linearly in T as the number of required `Logsum` operations scales linearly in T. For example, processing $T = 10$ observations costs 0.65 s and 15.45 MB as opposed to 6.95 s and 167.05 MB for $T = 100$ observations. For the same reason as before, runtime and communication also scale roughly linearly in k and l.

Size of the Emission Alphabet. The alphabet size M only influences the performance of `Emission` which accounts for less than 1 % of the overall overhead of `Forward`. To provide greater detail, Figure 5 plots the runtime of the isolated `Emission` primitive. We choose different $T = 10, 20, ..., 100$ and $M = 10^2, 10^3, 10^4$ while fixing $N = 10$. Clearly, the runtime of `Emission` is linear in T which conforms with its complexity $\mathcal{O}(TMN)$. The communication overhead shows qualitatively the same growth. We increase M exponentially to show that, even for huge emission alphabets, `Emission` is very efficient. For example, less than 0.5 s and about 40.13 MB are required to securely share $T = 100$ emission scores over a huge alphabet of 10000 possible emissions. The ability to efficiently handle huge emission alphabets makes our `Emission` primitive a candidate for computing fast approximations of the emission scores for HMMs with continuous probability distributions such as Gaussian Mixture Models used in speech processing [35,38].

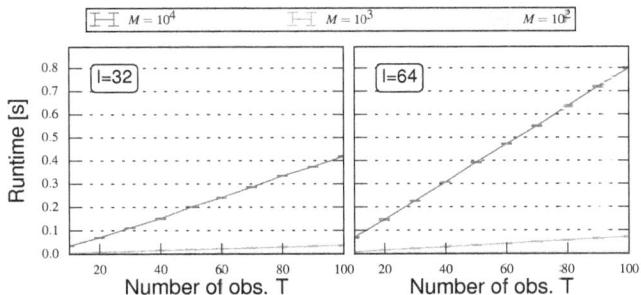

Figure 5: Runtime of `Emission` for a varying number of observations T (x-axis), alphabet sizes M (lines) with $l = 32$ (left) and $l = 64$ (right): Runtime grows linearly in T and M and causes only 1 % of the total runtime overhead of `Forward` (cf. Figs. 3 and 4).

Outsourcing. We briefly discuss the overheads imposed on either party $\mathcal{U}$ and $\mathcal{S}$ for outsourcing their computation to another peer. As explained in Section 4.4, the overheads consist in executing the batched `Emission` primitive as well as sending the resulting shares to the computation peers. The overheads for `Emission` are very low even for a large number of observations and huge emission alphabets, e.g., less than 0.5 s for 100 emissions out of an alphabet of 10000 possible observations (cf. Fig. 5). Distributing shares to the computation peers only requires tens of KB even for the larger considered models. The overhead is smaller for $\mathcal{U}$ than for $\mathcal{S}$ which has to share the whole HMM. This is desirable as in many cases only $\mathcal{U}$ will need to outsource computations (cf. Sect. 4.4). Hence, outsourcing is clearly feasible for most mobile devices nowadays.

5.2 Use Case: Secure Bioinformatics Services

Recent advances have made whole genome sequencing (WGS) fast, accurate, and affordable for the masses. It is widely expected that WGS will pave the way for innovative research and novel applications [16, 44]. As we can already observe, an industry will emerge that offers genomics-based services such as drug testing or diagnosis of diseases based on proprietary research [44]. To remain competitive, service providers will need to protect the mathematical models upon which their businesses are built. On the other hand, users of such services are required to contribute genomic data which is most sensitive information [7]. The approach presented in this paper allows preserving the service provider's intellectual property while offering strongest protection for users' genomic data.

To present a concrete use case, we consider the following genetic disease testing scenario: The service provider holds a set of HMMs that model specific diseases. The user holds an observation sequence, e.g., parts of her sequenced genome, that she wants to test against the service's database. Concretely, we use HMMs from the Pfam database [3], which contains 16 295 protein families that relate to, e.g., certain phenotypes and diseases. HMMER [1] is widely used tool in bioinformatics to query Pfam. Thus, we implemented *Priward* in the most recent version, HMMER 3.1. It is important to note that HMMER and Pfam are based on *profile HMMs*. Profile HMMs have a special architecture that allows only a certain subset of transitions which significantly speeds up the Forward computation. Since we adapt these optimizations which are specific to the HMMER framework and the profile HMM architecture, the results presented in the remainder of this section are not comparable to those presented in Sect. 5.1 which were obtained on fully connected HMMs. However, it becomes clear that our approach is flexible enough to capitalize on the optimization potential offered by certain reduced HMM architectures such as profile HMMs.

From Pfam [3], we choose the same models as [21], i.e., SH3_1 (Length $L = 48$), Ras ($L = 162$), BID ($L = 191$), and added one of the smallest model found in Pfam, Extensin_1 ($L = 10$), another midsize model, Ribosomal_S3_C ($L = 83$) as well as two of the largest models, IDO ($L = 408$) and 3HBOH ($L = 689$). The average length[1] of HMMs in Pfam is 175 and more than 98.5 % of the HMMs have a length smaller than 3HBOH, the largest model we consider. We use observation sequences of the same length as the HMM length ($T = L$) of two types: i) *matching* sequences where we use the seeds on which the respective models were trained and ii) *non-matching* sequences which we choose randomly from the seeds of other models. The considered profile HMMs are built over the amino acids alphabet which has $M = 20$ symbols.

5.2.1 Accuracy

Figure 6 plots the relative error *Priward* introduces in comparison to the real scores computed by the HMMER framework on plaintexts. We restricted the evaluation to $k = 2, 4, 8$ and $l = 32$ since these choices achieve the best trade-off between accuracy and performance according to the results presented in Sect. 5.1. Clearly, $k = 2$ leads to large errors that grow roughly linearly with the combined length of the model and observation sequence. For $k = 4, 8$ the error mostly drops below 1 % and now seems mostly model specific with little correlation to the length of model and observation sequence. Considering the use case, the more important question is whether our approach is accurate enough to distinguish matching from non-matching sequences. To answer this question, we classify sequences according to the *noise cutoffs* (NC) and *trusted cutoffs* (TC) specified for each model in the Pfam database: Anything below the NC can safely be considered a non-matching sequence and anything above the TC a match. For $k = 4, 8$, our approach is able to perfectly distinguish between matching and non-matching sequences. Notably, even for $k = 2$ our classification is perfectly accurate for all but the largest model, 3HBOH.

5.2.2 Runtime and Communication

Figure 7 plots the performance overhead for the chosen Pfam models. The x-axis denotes both length L of the model[1] and length T of the observation sequence. As before, the runtime is dominated by the overhead for `Logsum`. Since the Forward algorithm over profile HMMs as implemented in HMMER 3.1 requires $T(7L + 2)$ `Logsum` operations, the runtime grows linear in both T and L. Note that we increase both L and T in Figure 7, thus the growth is quadratic. While, the smaller models can be computed in the order of seconds (e.g., 0.82 s for Extensin_1, 13.43 s for SH3_1, and 37.46 s for Ribosomal_S3_C for $k = 2$), the larger models range in the order of minutes (e.g., 2.28 min for Ras, 3.15 min for BID, and 13.75 min for IDO, 38.5 min for 3HBOH for $k = 2$). Although runtimes in the latter cases are not unreasonable, they emphasize the necessity and benefit for mobile users to be able to securely outsource computations as offered by *Priward*.

Similar to the runtime, the communication overhead is dominated by the calls to `Logsum` and thus grows quadratically as well, e.g., from 10.68 MB for the smallest model (Extensin_1) to 47.19 GB for the largest considered model (3HBOH) with $k = 2$ and $l = 32$. Clearly, the communication overhead is significant and may result in additional runtime overheads when our approach is deployed in networks with less bandwidth or higher latency than assumed in our evaluation setup. However, these overheads are clearly manageable by outsourcing *Priward* to a computation cloud.

---

[1] L determines the number of *nodes* in a profile HMM and each node has three distinct states. Together with four special states, a profile HMM thus has a total of $N = 3L + 4$ states.

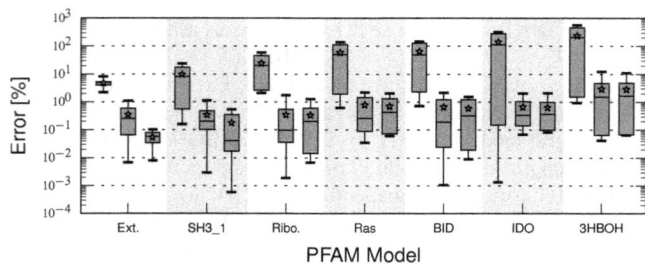

Figure 6: Relative error of `Forward` on different profile HMMs from Pfam [3] for $k = 2, 4, 8$: $k = 2$ (left bar per model) causes errors that increase linearly. For $k = 4, 8$ (middle and right bars) the accuracy increases significantly and classification of matching and non-matching sequences is 100 % correct.

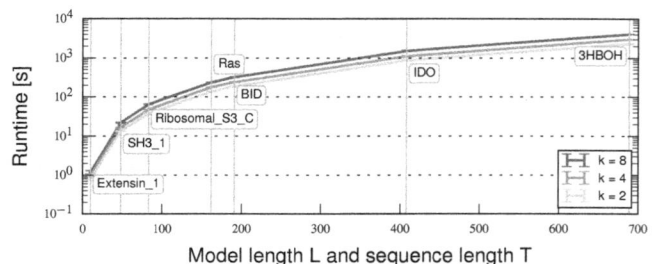

Figure 7: Runtime of `Forward` on profile HMMs from Pfam [3] with different length L on observation sequences of length $T = L$ (x-axis): Short models can be computed in the order of seconds while medium to large models are in the order of minutes. Growth is quadratic since T increases equally with L.

5.3 Comparison to Related Work

In Section 2.3, we have qualitatively discussed other approaches to secure Forward computation and summarized them in Table 1. In this section, we compare the performance of our approach quantitatively to these works by the reported performance numbers.

Pathak et al. [34, 35] report a runtime of 784.58 s for the evaluation of one HMM with $N = 5$ states on an observation sequence of length $T = 98$ on a 3.2 GHz CPU. For a fair comparison, we restricted *Priward* to run on one core at 3.1 GHz and set $k = 4$ and symmetric security to $t = 80$ bits which achieves comparable accuracy and security as in [34, 35]. In this setting, we measure the runtime of *Priward* at 6.21 s which is 126x faster.

Franz et al. [21] do not evaluate their approach on generic fully connected HMMs but concentrate on profile HMMs as in our use case (cf. Sect. 5.2). Unfortunately, we could not obtain their source code and a direct comparison with the results presented in Section 5.2 is unreasonable for different reasons: First, the Forward algorithm in HMMER 3.1 requires to compute an additional $T \cdot L + 1$ logsum operations compared to version 2.3.2 used in [21]. Switching to HMMER 2.3.2 would reduce the overheads of our approach by $\sim 14\%$. Second, Franz et al. do not implement any networking, yet we observe networking to cause non-negligible overheads even on the local loopback interface. Third, Franz et al. use legacy/short-term security while we use long-term security which causes additional overheads in comparison. Finally, the evaluation machines differ between a 2.1 GHz 8 core processor used in [21] and a 3.1 GHz 4 core processor machine used in our evaluation. The authors report runtimes of 33 s, 499 s, and 632 s on the Pfam models SH3_1, Ras, and BID, respectively. On the same models, we achieve a runtime of 16.95 s, 180.68 s, and 241.61 s, respectively. In a more comparable setting (communication over the loopback interface, short-term security, and HMMER 2.3.2 style Forward computation), the runtime decreases by roughly a factor of 2 to 8.15 s, 89.92 s, and 125.25 s improving over [21] by a factor of 4 to 5. However, we emphasize again that latter results were still obtained on different machines and are thus only a rough indicator.

Aliasgari et al. [4,5], **Kamm et al. [28]** and **Demmler et al. [17]** propose secure computation on floats which could be used to implement a secure Forward algorithm over probability space and using normalization [38] to avoid underflows. Then, only selection of the required emission probabilities is not straightforward, but can be realized through component-wise multiplication which is the fastest previous method proposed in [21]. To draw a concrete comparison, we estimate runtimes by counting the calls to the required primitives and weighting them according to the performance measurements presented in [17], for which we choose a high batch-

size of 1000 which yields very defensive estimates. In this setting, we estimate that Forward computation of $T = 100$ observations over an HMM with $N = 10$ states and an alphabet of $M = 100$ symbols would cost at least 251.82 s, 51.76 s, and 39.37 s using the primitives from [5], [28], and [17], respectively. In contrast, even when parameterized with $k = 8$ for high accuracy, our approach requires only 9.85 s which is approximately 25x, 5x, and 4x faster.

6. CONCLUSION

We presented *Priward*, which computes the HMM Forward algorithm in an efficient and privacy-preserving manner. At the core of our approach are efficient techniques to compute securely and accurately over non-integers in a fixed-point logspace representation, which are relevant beyond the scope of this work for a variety of privacy-preserving services [20, 35]. As a thorough evaluation shows, our novel and improved building blocks make *Priward* faster than previous works by factors of 4 to 126 while providing tuneable accuracy. Despite our significant improvements, secure computations on HMMs still involve overheads that may well overtax the resources of the protocol peers, e.g., drain the battery of a mobile user. To overcome such limitations, our approach allows outsourcing computations very efficiently and securely, e.g., to an untrusted computation cloud which remains oblivious of the inputs and results of the computation. As a concrete use case, we implement *Priward* in the widely used HMMER framework and demonstrate the feasibility of privacy-preserving bioinformatics services. Here, our approach improves upon the performance of related work by a factor of 4 to 5 while the accuracy of the computed results clearly satisfies the use case's requirements. To conclude, *Priward* provides the basis for a wide variety of privacy-preserving HMM-based services ranging from genomic testing over speech processing to localization and makes them affordable even for mobile users.

Acknowledgments

This work has been funded by the German Federal Ministry of Education and Research (ref. no. 16KIS0443). The responsibility for the content of this publication lies with the authors.

7. REFERENCES

[1] HMMER. http://hmmer.org/.
[2] Natural Language Toolkit. http://www.nltk.org/.
[3] Pfam Database, version 29.0. http://pfam.xfam.org/, 2015.
[4] M. Aliasgari and M. Blanton. Secure computation of Hidden Markov models. In *SECRYPT*, 2013.
[5] M. Aliasgari, et al. Secure Computation on Floating Point Numbers. In *NDSS*, 2013.

[6] G. Asharov, et al. More Efficient Oblivious Transfer and Extensions for Faster Secure Computation. In *ACM CCS*. ACM, 2013.

[7] E. Ayday, et al. The Chills and Thrills of Whole Genome Sequencing. *Computer*, 99(PrePrints):1, 2013.

[8] E. Barker, et al. Recommendation for Key Management - Part 1: General (Revised). In *NIST Special Publication 800-57*. NIST, 2007.

[9] D. Beaver. Efficient Multiparty Protocols Using Circuit Randomization. In *CRYPTO'91*. Springer, 1991.

[10] M. Bellare, et al. Efficient Garbling from a Fixed-Key Blockcipher. In *SP'13*. IEEE, 2013.

[11] M. Bellare, V. T. Hoang, and P. Rogaway. Foundations of garbled circuits. In *CCS'12*. ACM, 2012.

[12] M. Ben-Or, S. Goldwasser, and A. Wigderson. Completeness Theorems for Non-Cryptographic Fault-Tolerant Distributed Computation. In *STOC '88*. ACM, 1988.

[13] R. Canetti. Security and composition of multiparty cryptographic protocols. *Journal of CRYPTOLOGY*, 13(1):143–202, 2000.

[14] O. Catrina and S. De Hoogh. Improved Primitives for Secure Multiparty Integer Computation. In *SCN'10*. Springer, 2010.

[15] O. Catrina and A. Saxena. Secure Computation with Fixed-point Numbers. In *FC'10*. Springer, 2010.

[16] E. De Cristofaro, et al. Genodroid: Are Privacy-preserving Genomic Tests Ready for Prime Time? In *WPES'12*. ACM, 2012.

[17] D. Demmler, et al. Automated Synthesis of Optimized Circuits for Secure Computation. In *CCS'15*. ACM, 2015.

[18] D. Demmler, T. Schneider, and M. Zohner. ABY – A Framework for Efficient Mixed-Protocol Secure Two-Party Computation. In *NDSS'15*. The Internet Society, 2015.

[19] R. Durbin, et al. *Biological Sequence Analysis: Probabilistic Models of Proteins and Nucleic Acids*. Cambridge University Press, 1998.

[20] M. Franz, et al. Secure computations on non-integer values. In *WIFS'10*. IEEE, 2010.

[21] M. Franz, et al. Towards Secure Bioinformatics Services (Short Paper). In *FC'11*. Springer, 2011.

[22] N. Gilboa. Two party rsa key generation. In *Annual International Cryptology Conference*, pages 116–129. Springer, 1999.

[23] O. Goldreich. *Foundations of Cryptography: Volume 2 – Basic Applications*. Cambridge University Press, 2004.

[24] O. Goldreich, S. Micali, and A. Wigderson. How to Play ANY Mental Game. In *ACM STOC*, pages 218–229. ACM, 1987.

[25] W. Henecka, et al. TASTY: Tool for Automating Secure Two-party Computations. In *CCS'10*. ACM, 2010.

[26] Y. Huang, et al. Faster Secure Two-Party Computation Using Garbled Circuits. In *USENIX Security Symposium*, 2011.

[27] Y. Ishai, et al. Extending Oblivious Transfers Efficiently. In *CRYPTO'03*. Springer, 2003.

[28] L. Kamm and J. Willemson. Secure floating point arithmetic and private satellite collision analysis. *International Journal of Information Security*, 14(6):531–548, 2015.

[29] V. Kolesnikov, A.-R. Sadeghi, and T. Schneider. Improved Garbled Circuit Building Blocks and Applications to Auctions and Computing Minima. In *CANS'09*. Springer, 2009.

[30] V. Kolesnikov and T. Schneider. Improved Garbled Circuit: Free XOR Gates and Applications. In *ICALP '08*. Springer, 2008.

[31] B. Kreuter, A. Shelat, and C.-H. Shen. Billion-gate secure computation with malicious adversaries. In *USENIX Security*, 2012.

[32] M. Naor and B. Pinkas. Efficient Oblivious Transfer Protocols. In *SODA*, pages 448–457. SIAM, 2001.

[33] M. Naor and B. Pinkas. Computationally Secure Oblivious Transfer. *Journal of Cryptology*, 18(1):1–35, 2005.

[34] M. Pathak, et al. Privacy preserving probabilistic inference with Hidden Markov Models. In *ICASSP'11*. IEEE, 2011.

[35] M. A. Pathak, et al. Privacy-Preserving Speech Processing: Cryptographic and String-Matching Frameworks Show Promise. *IEEE Signal Processing Magazine*, 30(2):62–74, 2013.

[36] H. Polat, et al. Private predictions on hidden Markov models. *Artificial Intelligence Review*, 34(1):53–72, 2010.

[37] J. Portêlo, B. Raj, and I. Trancoso. Logsum Using Garbled Circuits. *PLoS ONE*, 10(3):1–16, 2015.

[38] L. R. Rabiner. A Tutorial on Hidden Markov Models and Selected Applications in Speech Recognition. *Proceedings of the IEEE*, 1989.

[39] A.-R. Sadeghi, T. Schneider, and I. Wehrenberg. Efficient privacy-preserving face recognition. In *ICISC*. Springer, 2009.

[40] P. Smaragdis and M. Shashanka. A Framework for Secure Speech Recognition. *TASLP*, 15(4), 2007.

[41] J. R. Troncoso-Pastoriza and F. Pérez-González. Efficient protocols for secure adaptive filtering. In *ICASSP'11*. IEEE, 2011.

[42] A. Yao. How to Generate and Exchange Secrets. In *IEEE SFCS*, 1986.

[43] S. Zahur, M. Rosulek, and D. Evans. Two Halves Make a Whole. In *EUROCRYPT*. Springer, 2015.

[44] P. J. Zettler, J. S. Sherkow, and H. T. Greely. 23andMe, the Food and Drug Administration, and the Future of Genetic Testing. *JAMA Internal Medicine*, 174(4):493–494, 2014.

[45] J. H. Ziegeldorf, et al. Poster: Privacy-preserving indoor localization. *WiSec'14*, 2014.

APPENDIX

A. SECURITY DISCUSSION

We now discuss the security of *Priward*. We assume the semi-honest adversary model (cf. Sect. 2.2). We first summarize security proofs of the building blocks that underly *Priward*. We then argue that our proposed protocols Rescale, Emission, Logsum, and Forward are secure based on modular sequential composition [13].

Security of the Building Blocks. We heavily rely on three well established secure computation techniques: OT, additive sharings, and GCs. First, Security of 1-n-OT has been proven in [32, 33] and the security of OT Extensions in [6,27]. Second, additive sharings over $\mathbb{Z}_{2^l}$ realize perfect blinding and thus essentially represent perfectly secure One-Time-Pad encryption. We perform additions and multiplications over additive sharings. Additions are local operations and thus irrelevant for security in the semi-honest model, while the security of the multiplication protocol directly follows from [18,22]. Finally, security of Garbled Circuits including recent optimizations has been rigorously addressed in [10, 11].

Security of Rescale. To argue security of Rescale (Sect. 4.1, Prot. 2), we show that neither party learns the value x that is rescaled. First, note that the shares $x^{\mathcal{U}}, x^{\mathcal{S}}$ are random and a single share conveys no information about x to either party. During the protocol, $\mathcal{U}$ blinds her share $x^{\mathcal{U}}$ by a $l + \kappa$ bit random number r and sends it to $\mathcal{S}$. $\mathcal{S}$ learns $x_r^{\mathcal{U}} + x^{\mathcal{S}} = x + r$. Blinding with a large random r over $\mathbb{Z}$ achieves statistical security towards $\mathcal{S}$ with security parameter κ. $\mathcal{U}$ receives no information from $\mathcal{S}$ and learns nothing about x.

Security of Emission. To show that our Emission primitive (Sect. 4.2, Prot. 3) is secure in the semi-honest model, we show that $\mathcal{U}$ does not learn anything about the emission scores $\hat{b}_i(v_j)$ held by $\mathcal{S}$ and $\mathcal{S}$ does not learn anything about $\mathcal{U}$'s observation o_t. In Step 1, $\mathcal{S}$ blinds the emission scores additively over $\mathbb{Z}_{2^l}$ with the random value $r_{\mathcal{S}} \in \mathbb{Z}_{2^l}$. From $\mathcal{U}'s$ perspective, the blinding represents a One-Time-Pad encryption which is perfectly secure. Since all emission scores are blinded by the same random value $r_{\mathcal{S}}$, we use 1-n-OT$_l^m$ to guarantee that $\mathcal{U}$ learns only exactly one blinded emission score in Step 2. $\mathcal{U}$ then arithmetically shares the value with $\mathcal{S}$, which does not leak information as the employed additive sharing uses perfect blinding over $\mathbb{Z}_{2^l}$. In the final step, $\mathcal{S}$ subtracts $r_{\mathcal{S}}$ from its share, which is a local operation and reveals no information. We conclude that Emission is secure.

Security of Logsum. To argue security of Logsum (Sect. 4.3, Prot. 4), we show that neither party learns anything about the summands $\hat{x}$ and $\hat{y}$ or the result $\hat{z}$. First note, that the summands $\hat{x}$ and $\hat{y}$ are given as additive shares and each party holds only a single share which does not reveal any information since shares appear completely random. Further, the PLA parameters k and $\mathcal{P}$ are completely independent of the inputs and thus reveal no information either. Steps 2, 3, and 4 are realized in one monolithic GC and involve i) input conversion, ii) the selection of approximation parameters, and iii) the conversion of outputs. We emphasize that we differentiate these three steps in our protocol description only for reasons of clarity but implement them in one single GC which yields better performance. Consisting of only one GC, security for these steps follows directly from the security of the GC building block. The output of these steps, i.e., $max^{\mathcal{U}/\mathcal{S}}$, $d^{\mathcal{U}/\mathcal{S}}$, $m^{\mathcal{U}/\mathcal{S}}$, and $n^{\mathcal{U}/\mathcal{S}}$, is additively shared over both parties which reveals no information to either party holding only a single share of each output since additive sharing implements perfect blinding over $\mathbb{Z}_{2^l}$. It is also important to note that the structure of the circuit is independent of all parameters except for the public parameter k, therefore leaking no sensitive information. Step 5 computes the product over additive shares using the secure protocols from [18, 22] and uses the secure Rescale on it. All outputs are again additively shared and reveal no information to either party. The last step involves an addition operation over additive shares which is executed locally and has no security implications in the semi-honest model. Finally, the output z is obtained by the two parties in shared form where a single share is indistinguishable from a random value and reveals no information. In summary, security of Logsum depends on the security of GCs and the Rescale protocol as well as the randomness of the additive sharings. As Rescale offers statistical security against a semi-honest $\mathcal{S}$, Logsum itself offers statistical security as well.

Security of Forward. To argue security of Forward (Sect. 4, Prot. 1), we show that $\mathcal{U}$ learns nothing about the HMM λ, i.e., $\mathcal{S}'s$ private input, and vice versa $\mathcal{S}$ learns nothing about the observations $o_1, ..., o_T$, i.e., $\mathcal{U}'s$ private input, except for what is implied in the final result $\hat{P}(O|\lambda)$. We argue that Forward is secure because the only interaction between $\mathcal{U}$ and $\mathcal{S}$ happens through the Emission and Logsum primitives. Since these primitives are secure and their output is received in the form of random additive sharings, their use reveals no information and neither does their composition according to the security of modular sequential compositions of semi-honest protocols [13]. All other steps are local operations that have no security implications in the semi-honest model. Finally, one or both parties learn the Forward score $\hat{P}(O|\lambda)$ by recombining their shares of the result, which is of course as intended.

Limitations. It is important to note that in our Forward design, $\mathcal{U}$ learns the dimensions of $\mathcal{S}'s$ HMM and, vice versa, $\mathcal{S}$ learns the length of $\mathcal{U}'s$ observation sequence. In this work and in most related works [4, 21, 40], such information is not considered sensitive. If desired, we can prevent leakage of this information by padding the HMM with dummy states and the observation sequence with predefined dummy symbols to a common predefined length. However, padding necessarily increases the size of the HMM and observation sequence and thus comes at the cost of performance and communication overheads. Finally, note that we develop protocols in the semi-honest model.

However, established techniques to make semi-honest computation robust against malicious behavior [31] can be applied to our approach when the problem scenario requires this.

B. EVALUATION OF THE SECURE LOG-SUM PRIMITIVE

Secure and accurate computation of logsum operations is challenging and has significant performance impacts in most previous works [21, 34, 35, 37]. Indeed, Logsum (Sect. 4.3, Prot. 4) clearly dominates the runtime of our approach. Since secure computation over non-integers is relevant beyond the scope of our work [15, 20], e.g., for securely evaluating Gaussian Mixture Models [35], we provide a detailed evaluation of the Logsum primitive in this section. All presented results are aggregated over 1000 runs and were obtained in the evaluation setup described in Section 5. The measured accuracy, runtime, and communication overheads for different choices of k and l are summarized in Table 2.

Accuracy. Logsum uses a piece-wise linear approximation with k intervals to compute the result. As expected, the error of the approximation decreases with increasing k. Increasing fixed-point precision by choosing $l = 64$ additionally improves accuracy, but only beyond $k = 8$. For the smaller values of k, the approximation error dominates the additional accuracy in the fixed-point representation. However, increasing k and l comes at the cost of runtime and communication overheads as analyzed in the following.

Runtime. We first measure runtime for *sequential* Logsum operations. The runtime grows linearly in k and l with 2.35 ms in our least accurate setup ($k = 2, l = 32$) to 23.52 ms in the most accurate setup ($k = 128, l = 64$). We now batch all m operations into one single invocation of Logsum and again report the average runtime of a single logsum operation. Sequential operation requires evaluation of m small GCs and requires $3 \cdot m$ rounds of communication, whereas batched operation corresponds to the evaluation of one very large GC in only three rounds of communication. Thus, batching achieves the best speed-up for small circuits (small k and l). For $l = 32$ and $k = 2$, we observe a speedup of 5.6x and still up to 4.13x for $l = 64, k = 2$. As expected, this decreases for bigger values of k, e.g., to 1.5x and 1.3x for $k = 128$ and $l = 32, 64$, respectively. We evaluated different batchsizes and observed no significant speedup beyond batches bigger than $m = 1000$. For both sequential and batched operation, we observe that to achieve a certain accuracy it is more efficient to increase k than to increase l.

Communication. Communication scales linearly in k and l and is in the order of tens to hundreds of kilobytes per run of Logsum. The dominating part is the transmission of two t bit keys per gate in the GC. Hence, communication overheads can be traded off against the security level t, e.g., switching to short term security $t = 80$ reduces communication by approximately 34 %. Also ongoing and future optimizations of the GC foundations [10, 43] will further reduce communication overheads.

Bit-length l	32							64						
PLA size k	2	4	8	16	32	64	128	2	4	8	16	32	64	128
Avg. abs. error	6.0e-2	4.4e-3	9.2e-4	5.3e-4	5.1e-4	5.4e-4	6.2e-4	6.0e-2	4.3e-3	7.7e-4	2.0e-4	5.5e-5	1.4e-5	2.7e-6
Runtime (seq.)	2.35	2.83	3.30	4.22	5.79	9.23	14.90	3.10	3.25	4.25	5.61	8.21	13.67	23.52
Runtime (batch)	0.42	0.59	0.89	1.49	2.70	5.10	9.98	0.75	1.00	1.52	2.61	4.66	8.88	17.74
Communication	0.02	0.02	0.03	0.05	0.08	0.15	0.28	0.03	0.04	0.05	0.08	0.14	0.26	0.49

Table 2: Evaluation of the secure Logsum primitive: The runtime [ms] and communication overhead [MB] increase and the approximation error decrease as the number of approximation intervals k and the bit-length l of the garbled circuits increase.

Share a pie? Privacy-Preserving Knowledge Base Export through Count-min Sketches

Daniele Ucci, Leonardo Aniello and Roberto Baldoni
Research Center of Cyber Intelligence and Information Security (CIS)
Department of Computer, Control, and Management Engineering 'Antonio Ruberti"
"La Sapienza" University of Rome, Italy
{ucci, aniello, baldoni}@dis.uniroma1.it

ABSTRACT

Knowledge base (KB) sharing among parties has been proven to be beneficial in several scenarios. However such sharing can arise considerable privacy concerns depending on the sensitivity of the information stored in each party's KB.

In this paper, we focus on the problem of exporting a (part of a) KB of a party towards a receiving one. We introduce a novel solution that enables parties to export data in a privacy-preserving fashion, based on a probabilistic data structure, namely the *count-min sketch*. With this data structure, KBs can be exported in the form of key-value stores and inserted into a set of count-min sketches, where keys can be sensitive and values are counters. Count-min sketches can be tuned to achieve a given key collision probability, which enables a party to deny having certain keys in its own KB, and thus to preserve its privacy. We also introduce a metric, the γ-*deniability* (novel for count-min sketches), to measure the privacy level obtainable with a count-min sketch. Furthermore, since the value associated to a key can expose to linkage attacks, noise can be added to a count-min sketch to ensure controlled error on retrieved values. Key collisions and noise alter the values contained in the exported KB, and can affect negatively the accuracy of a computation performed on the exported KB. We explore the tradeoff between privacy preservation and computation accuracy by experimental evaluations in two scenarios related to malware detection.

Keywords

Information sharing; knowledge base export; privacy metric; count-min sketches.

1. INTRODUCTION

Several well-known best practices show that setting up an information sharing environment, involving several parties, represents one of the main building blocks to face cyber attacks. This is why also policy makers are fostering the creation of organizations that share information within specific sectors or geographical regions (e.g., ISACs[1] and ISAOs[2]). A sharing environment includes organizations, policies and technical aspects. From the technical point of view, cyber information sharing basically allows a party to reason on a larger set of information to support its own defenses.

One of the main problems in handling information sharing environments is the different readiness of the parties. In general, distinct parties store different volumes of shareable added-value information. Indeed, there could be parties that, locally, collected huge amounts of data whose sharing can add value to others' defenses. On the other hand, there could be parties not owning relevant data to share. Collecting locally a quantity of added-value data, sufficiently big to support better defenses, can take very long (e.g., order of months). Having at disposal large amounts of data is the immediate advantage enabled by cyber information sharing, which is a key incentive for less-ready parties to join such an environment. On the long run, more-ready parties that initially shared their data will benefit from added-value information shared by other parties.

As an example, consider a malware detection system that needs to collect a huge amount of information from a monitored network before being able to accurately detect malicious samples (e.g., AMICO [26], Nazca [10], and [14]). During such bootstrapping period, an organization that deployed the system would be vulnerable to cyber attacks. More-ready parties using the same system could export (portions of) their KBs, providing to less-ready parties the information the malware detection system needs. However, exporting KBs may arise privacy issues when sensitive data are involved, indeed the receiving party may be malicious and take advantage from the shared information to the detriment of the exporting party.

In this paper, we address the following specific issue: exporting added-value information from one party to another one so that, while the privacy of the exporting party is preserved, the receiving one can immediately leverage this information to improve its defenses. Even though, in practice, exports can be periodically performed to exchange updated added-value information among the parties, in the paper we assume that the KB export is performed only once (see later in this section).

CODASPY'17, March 22-24, 2017, Scottsdale, AZ, USA
© 2017 ACM. ISBN 978-1-4503-4523-1/17/03. . . $15.00
DOI: http://dx.doi.org/10.1145/3029806.3029817

---

[1]Information Sharing and Analysis Center (ISAC), Presidential Decision Directive: https://fas.org/irp/offdocs/pdd/pdd-63.htm
[2]Information Sharing and Analysis Organizations (ISAO), Executive Order: https://www.whitehouse.gov/the-press-office/2015/02/13/executive-order-promoting-private-sector-cybersecurity-information-shari

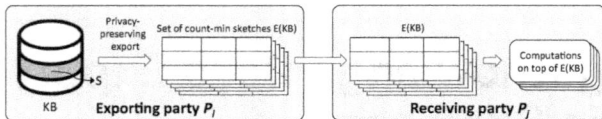

Figure 1: Privacy-preserving export, through a set of count-min sketches E(KB), of a KB portion (S, in gray) of a party P_i towards a possibly malicious receiving party P_j.

Aim of the paper. We introduce a novel solution for exporting KBs in a privacy-preserving fashion, based on a probabilistic data structure, namely the *count-min sketch*. This data structure allows to share KBs in the form of key-value stores, where the value associated to a key is a numeric counter. Keys can be generic strings, and their names are considered sensitive information (see Figure 1). We assume that the receiving party can be malicious and interested in breaching the privacy of the party exporting the KB. Once shared, a count-min sketch can be queried by KB's receiver to get the values associated to some keys chosen by the receiver itself. The receiver doesn't know what keys are stored in the count-min sketch, so it cannot enumerate all the key-value pairs that the owner shared. Furthermore, a count-min sketch can be tuned in such a way to have a certain key collision probability. From the owner's point of view, this means it can deny to a certain extent to have inserted a given key, which represents a statistically sound mean to preserve owner's privacy.

γ-deniability and linkage attacks. We introduce a novel metric to measure this extent, by taking inspiration from the work of Bianchi et al. [2] who applied a similar concept to bloom filters. This metric is called γ-deniability and represents the probability that any inserted key collides with some other keys (in the universe of keys known to the party exporting the KB) that have not been inserted, which in practice provides a statistical base to deny having inserted such key. We provide an analytical formula to calculate the γ-deniability of a count-min sketch configured in a certain way given the cardinalities of inserted keys and of the universe.

Likewise k-anonymity, γ-deniability is vulnerable to linkage attacks that can be used to discover what keys have been actually stored in a count-min sketch. Usually, the KB to export includes several attribute-value pairs for a given key, and a count-min sketch for each attribute is used, with all the values of this attribute for each key. For example, if we want to export a KB of physical traits (hair, eyes, height, etc...) of persons identified by their social security number (i.e., the key), then we can use a count-min sketch for each considered trait t, where for each person with social security number x and y as value of trait t, a pair $\langle x, y \rangle$ is put inside. If an attacker wanted to find out whether some key k has been really inserted in the shared KB, he would query with k all the given count-min sketches to obtain all the related attribute-value pairs. By combining obtained attribute-value pairs with some background knowledge about k, it would be possible to gain knowledge about the real key of the original KB to which these values refer to. With reference to the previous example about persons and traits, by combining the values of the traits stored in the count-min sketches for certain keys, it is possible to ob-

tain a physical profile of the persons that are included in the original KB. By "linking" these profiles with some background knowledge about physical profiles of known persons, it would be possible to infer whether any of these known persons is contained in the original KB. This would be especially true for persons having rarer profiles. Linkage attacks can be mitigated by adding noise to the values inserted in the count-min sketches, so that it becomes more difficult for an attacker to link the knowledge extracted from the shared KB with some external information.

If portions of the same KB are published in different releases, an attacker can potentially correlate them without needing any additional background knowledge. There exist attacks, namely *complementary release* and *temporal attacks*, which take advantage of possible linkages between different releases published in diverse times. Solutions to these types of attacks have already been proposed in [9]. In our case, complementary release attacks can be avoided by exporting, every time, keys that have no correlation among them. Temporal attacks can be prevented by always exporting releases containing keys stored in previous exports. This is why, in this paper, we don't specifically address this kind of attacks that leverage different exports over time of (part of) a same KB, rather we assume that the export is done only once.

The stricter are the privacy requirements of the owner, the higher should be the needed γ-deniability and the amount of noise in the exported KB. From the receiver's point of view, this affects the reliability of received KB, which in turn may impact its utility depending on the specific scenario and on what type of computation it has to execute on that KB. Deriving general results on the impact of γ-deniability and noise on computation soundness and accuracy is problematic because of the difficulty to generalize computations. We instead carried out experimental evaluations on two distinct scenarios to explore in practice this relationship.

Experimental scenarios. We present two scenarios, both related to malware detection. The first scenario concerns the malware detection algorithm implemented by AMICO system [26], which classifies samples using features based on sample download patterns. AMICO needs a large historical dataset of downloads for its bootstrap, which usually requires from one to three months to be collected. Sensitive keys in this case are information like visited websites and downloaded files. We implemented and evaluated an export of the AMICO KB based on count-min sketches, such that the receiving party can not infer which websites have ever visited the exporting party. The evaluation consisted in investigating the tradeoff between the γ-deniability of count-min sketches and the malware detection accuracy at the receiving side.

In the second scenario, a KB containing behavioral features of samples is exported, which enables an organization with such KB to execute local malware detection/analysis algorithms without having to actually execute the samples. The computation executed on the exported KB is the classification in malware/non-malware based on an already trained classifier. An attacker may extract further information on whether a certain malware m has been actually put in the shared KB by leveraging background knowledge regarding m's behavior. To cope with this kind of linkage attacks based on background knowledge, the KB's owner can add noise to the count-min sketches. The goal in this case was tuning count-min sketches to have a fixed γ-deniability and a variable amount of noise, and the evaluation consisted in showing in practice the tradeoff between the error in retrieved values and the malware detection accuracy.

Obtained results for the first scenario show that introducing deniability in the count-min sketches can impact the utility of exported KB, as higher deniability allows to export less data. When count-min sketches are queried with keys that have not been inserted, false positives can occur and mess the computation up. In this evaluation, false positive rate turned out to be independent from the required deniability. In the end, depending on the application scenario and in particular on what the KB has to be used for, the employment of count-min sketches, configured to ensure deniability guarantees, can be a viable option. The outcomes of the evaluations for the second scenario confirms the expected tradeoff between utility and privacy, as higher errors in retrieved values negatively affect the computation while complicating attacks based on background knowledge.

Paper Contributions and Organization. The main contributions of this paper are: (i) the definition of a deniability metric to measure the privacy level provided by a count-min sketch, (ii) a methodology to configure count-min sketches to obtain desired levels of deniability on keys and of noise on values, and (iii) an experimental evaluation in two scenarios showing how deniability and noise affect computation accuracy.

The rest of the paper is structured in this way. Section 2 introduces count-min sketches, how they work, and some basic properties that will be used later on. The definitions of deniability and noise for count-min sketches, together with the algorithms for configuring count-min sketches to obtain them, are presented in Section 3. Section 4 describes the two scenarios chosen for the evaluations. After a discussion on related work (Section 5) and on current limitations and open points (Section 6), conclusions and possible future work are presented in Section 7.

2. BACKGROUND

2.1 Count-min sketches

Count-min sketches are probabilistic data structures initially conceived for summarizing data streams [3].

A count-min sketch M contains key-value pairs of the universe set $\mathcal{U}$, where keys belong to the set $K_{\mathcal{U}}$ and values are in $\mathbb{R}_+ \cup \{0\}$. M is represented as a matrix of non-negative values, whose width w and depth d are defined by parameters ε and δ as follows:

$$w = \left\lceil \frac{e^3}{\varepsilon} \right\rceil \qquad d = \left\lceil \ln \frac{1}{\delta} \right\rceil \qquad (1)$$

Parameters ε and δ regulate the guarantees on the accuracy of the values retrieved from M, which will be detailed in Equation 4 right after having defined the semantics of count-min sketch operations. With $M[i,j]$ we refer to the value of M stored in the cell at row i and column j, where $i = 1, \dots, w$ and $j = 1, \dots, d$. At the beginning, each cell has value 0.

Additionally, d hash functions $h_1, \dots, h_d : K_{\mathcal{U}} \to \{1, \dots, w\}$ are chosen uniformly at random from a pairwise-independent

---

[3] e is the Euler's number.

family. Pairwise-independence, also known as strong universality [13], implies low collision probabilities among distinct hash functions, which means this property holds [27]:

$$\Pr[h_i(x) = h_i(y)] = \frac{1}{w} \qquad \forall i \in \{1, \dots, d\} \wedge \forall x, y \in K_{\mathcal{U}} \quad (2)$$

These hash functions are used to map any element of $K_{\mathcal{U}}$ to exactly d distinct cells of M, one for each row.

In this work we are interested in using the operations *point query* and *update* of count-min sketches. An *update* operation $U_M(k,v)$ updates the value associated to k in M by adding v to the values currently stored in all the cells where k is mapped to. It is defined as

$$M[i, h_i(k)] \leftarrow M[i, h_i(k)] + v \qquad \forall i \in \{1, \dots, d\} \quad (3)$$

Since collisions are possible, an update can alter cells where also other keys are mapped to. As these values are non-negative, the effect of collisions is to make some of stored values larger than they should, so the *point query* operation $Q_M(k)$ use the following approximation to retrieve the value v associated to k: $\widehat{v} = \min_{i \in \{1, \dots, d\}} M[i, h_i(k)]$

While count-min sketches have been originally conceived to keep and update counters, in this work we want to use them to export a KB in the form of key-value stores, so we are not actually interested in updating the values of already stored keys, rather we only need to store values once for each key we need to insert. Let S be the set of key-value pairs $\langle k, v \rangle$ to insert into a count-min sketch M. Once all the $n = |S|$ pairs have been inserted in M through as many update operations, we refer to M as $M(S)$. The value $\widehat{v}$ returned by a point query $Q_{M(S)}(k)$ provides the following guarantees:

$$\begin{cases} v \leq \widehat{v} \\ \widehat{v} \leq v + \epsilon \cdot \|S\|_1 \text{ with probability } (1 - \delta) \end{cases} \quad (4)$$

where $\|S\|_1 = \sum_{\langle k, v \rangle \in S} v$[4]. Thus, count-min sketches never underestimate real values and such estimation is bounded with probability $(1 - \delta)$ by $v + \epsilon \cdot \|S\|_1$.

By construction, count-min sketches have an implicit representation, meaning that, conversely to cleartext data, information contained in the sketch is readable only by issuing queries.

2.2 Hiding set of a count-min sketch

Let $K_S = \{k | \langle k, v \rangle \in S\}$ and $K_{\mathcal{U}} = \{k | \langle k, v \rangle \in \mathcal{U}\}$ be the sets of keys of the elements in S and $\mathcal{U}$, respectively. The hiding set for a count-min sketch $M(S)$ contains all the keys that have not been inserted in $M(S)$, but would result as inserted if $M(S)$ was queried on them.

DEFINITION 2.1. *A set $\mathcal{V}$ is called* hiding set *for a count-min sketch $M(S)$ if $\mathcal{V}$ contains all the elements $k_i \in K_{\mathcal{U}} \setminus K_S$ s.t. $Q_{M(S)}(k_i) > 0$ (i.e., k_i is a false positive).*

Given a count-min sketch $M(S)$ with width w, depth d, and n inserted keys out of u universe keys, the probability $\psi(w, d, n)$ that a query $Q_{M(S)}(k)$ would return a false positive can be computed by observing that a false positive occurs when all the cells where k is mapped to have a value greater than zero. The event that, in a given row, k hits an

---

[4] Since all inserted values are equal to or greater than 0, modulus can be omitted from the L_1 norm definition.

already covered cell is independent from and equiprobable to the event that this happens in any other row. In a single row, the probability that k gets mapped to one of the cells where any of the previously n keys have been mapped is $1 - \left(1 - \frac{1}{w}\right)^n$. The false positive probability can be computed as follows:

$$\psi(w, d, n) = \left(1 - \left(1 - \frac{1}{w}\right)^n\right)^d \qquad (5)$$

The cardinality v of the hiding set $\mathcal{V}$ is random variable N_v with binomial probability distribution

$$\Pr\left[N_v = v\right] = \binom{u - n}{v} \psi(w, d, n)^v \left(1 - \psi(w, d, n)\right)^{u-n-v} \qquad (6)$$

and mean value

$$E\left[N_u\right] = (u - n)\psi(w, d, n) \qquad (7)$$

3. PRIVACY PRESERVATION WITH COUNT-MIN SKETCHES

The basic idea of using count-min sketches to provide privacy guarantees lies in leveraging key collisions for (i) denying to have inserted a key by blaming a false positive (collisions with non-inserted keys), and for (ii) adding a controlled amount of error to retrieved values (collisions with inserted keys).

The first point shares similarities with the approaches based on *k-anonymity* [24]: a key is considered k-anonymous if it cannot be distinguished from at least other $k - 1$ keys because of collisions. Assuming that such property holds, an attacker who executes a point query $Q_{M(S)}(k)$, and obtains a value $v > 0$, cannot assert for sure that the key k has been inserted in $M(S)$. Indeed, who created the count-min sketch can attest that the cells of $M(S)$ where the key k is mapped are also mapped by some other keys in the universe set, so the value $v > 0$ returned by the point query for k cannot be used by someone else as a proof that k has been inserted in $M(S)$. Such uncertainty enables who creates count-min sketches to deny having inserted specific keys, and by consequence to deny having any information at all related to specific keys.

Likewise k-anonymity, this approach is weak against attacks exploiting background knowledge [24]: a value retrieved from a count-min sketch for a given key k (or more values retrieved from distinct count-min sketches for a same given key k) can be correlated with external information about k to infer whether k is known to who created the count-min sketch(es). This weakness can be addressed by resorting to *differential privacy* [5], which adds controlled amount of noise to stored values according to some distribution, usually Laplacian. Such noise has to be bound to limit the impact on the utility of the values retrieved. Differential privacy has been shown to be vulnerable to tracker style attacks [6, 22], indeed when an unlimited number of queries can be performed, which is exactly our case, the knowledge that the attacker can gain increases exponentially with the number of queries. We address this limitation by exploiting collisions among inserted keys to add controlled amount of noise. According to Equation 4, who creates the count-min sketch can control how much noise to add by properly

tuning its size. Actual collisions depend on what keys are inserted, which doesn't follow any known distribution and thus cannot be exploited by an attacker.

Setting count-min sketch dimensions is the mean to configure privacy preserving guarantees. In general, the wider and deeper the sketch, the less collisions are likely to occur, with both inserted and non-inserted keys. In this section we first define more formally system model and attacker model (Section 3.1), then we delve into how to properly dimension count-min sketches to have certain guarantees on the noise added to values (Section 3.2), and finally we introduce deniability metrics to measure privacy levels on exported keys (Section 3.3). We describe noise addition beforehand to introduce the iterative approach to tune count-min sketch width, which will be then used to better explain the simulation results obtained for the deniability metric.

3.1 System and Attacker Models

The owner O of a KB $\mathcal{U} = \{\langle k_i, v_i \rangle | i = 1, \ldots, u \wedge k_i = k_j \Rightarrow i = j\}$ creates a count-min sketch M with parameters ε and δ, having width w and depth d computed according to Equation 1. M is populated with a subset S of the universe set $\mathcal{U}$. Let $K_S = \{k_i | \langle k_i, v_i \rangle \in S\}$ be the set of the keys inserted into $M(S)$, with $|K_S| = n$. Let $V_S = \sum_{i=1}^{n} v_i$ be the sum of the values inserted into $M(S)$. Let $K_{\mathcal{U}} = \{k_i | \langle k_i, v_i \rangle \in \mathcal{U}\}$ be the set of keys in the universe set, with $|K_{\mathcal{U}}| = u$. We assume that each key of S and $\mathcal{U}$ is associated with exactly one value. Hence, their cardinalities coincide with the ones of their correspondent key sets (i.e. $|S| = |K_S| = n$ and $\mathcal{U} = |K_{\mathcal{U}}| = u$).

O shares $M(S)$ with a potential attacker A, who aims at obtaining information about the real content of $\mathcal{U}$ by executing on $M(S)$ as many queries she wants. In particular, A can read the values of any cell of $M(S)$, and knows all the hash functions $h_1, \ldots, h_d$, so she can derive what are the cells a given key is mapped to. A knows neither the elements in S nor its cardinality. O doesn't export over time different releases of M with A, rather O creates $M(S)$ once and sends it to A.

3.2 Noise Addition

Depending on the particular scenario, there can be different requirements on the amount of noise to add. The error is guaranteed with probability $1 - \delta$ to be within a fraction ε of V_S, according to Equation 4 and to the definition of V_S reported in Section 3.1. As the value of V_S may be very large, ε may need to be set very small to limit the error, which would imply to make the count-min sketch quite large (see Equation 1). Since calculating the L1 norm of V_S requires to iterate over all the n elements, computing the width in this way has $\mathcal{O}(n)$ time complexity.

If requirements specify to have guarantees on the error that are certain and not probabilistic, an alternative way can be taken to configure count-min sketch size, which however is much less time-efficient. Trivially, the real error on the values retrieved from a count-min sketch $M(S)$ can be computed by querying $M(S)$ with all the keys in K_S, and then comparing obtained results with the real values associated to these keys in S. Intuitively, by fixing the depth, the larger is the width the less collisions are likely to occur, and by consequence errors on retrieved values are lower (see Figure 2). Obviously, shrinking the width makes errors more probable. By proceeding iteratively, different widths

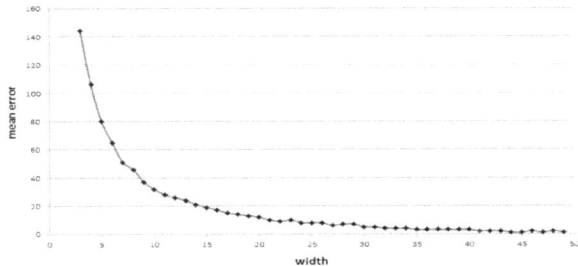

Figure 2: Mean error between real values and those retrieved from a count-min sketch, as its width varies. For each distinct value of the width, 100 simulations have been carried out by generating synthetic S with $n = 1000$. The depth was fixed to 5.

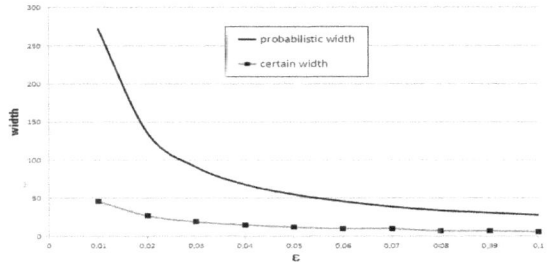

Figure 3: Comparison between the width computed using Equation 1 and the minimum width that provides the required guarantees on error upper bound, which depends on ε. For each distinct value of ε, 100 simulations have been carried out by generating synthetic S with $n = 1000$. The depth was fixed to 5.

can be tested to find the optimal one, which is the minimum width guaranteeing with certainty that any retrieved value has an error within a specific bound. For each test, the count-min sketch has to be populated with all the elements in S and then queried with all the keys in K_S, which costs $\mathcal{O}(n)$[5]. Contrary to what is shown in Figure 2, where each marker represents an average error over a large number of experiments with different sets S, for a specific set S there are no guarantees that the mean error decreases monotonically as the width increases, but it depends on the collisions among the keys. This is why it is necessary to start with a small width and then keep increasing it by one until the constraint on error upper bound is met. Using an asymptotic worst-case cost model, the number of different widths to test is $\mathcal{O}(n)$, which makes the overall approach have time complexity $\mathcal{O}(n^2)$.

We show through simulations how the two approaches differ for what concerns the width they compute. Figure 3 shows that the required width decreases for both as the constraint on the upper bound becomes weaker. Indeed, as ε increases, tolerated error is higher and less wide count-min sketches are needed. Moreover, it is clear that the width derived iteratively is always lower than the width computed with Equation 1, and the difference between the two grows as the constraint on error upper bound becomes stricter. As will be shown in Section 3.3, a lower width may be preferable because it allows higher deniability.

For what concerns the role of the depth in the iterative approach, it can be observed that a larger depth implies a lower collision probability among inserted elements, which allows to obtain the required certain error upper bound with a lower width. Figure 4 gives evidence of this aspect by showing the width required to have error 0 with certainty as the number of inserted elements varies with respect to the universe set cardinality, for different values of depth. In conclusion, adding controlled amount of noise to the values of a count-min sketch can be done in two ways: (i) *probabilistically*, by computing w and d according to Equation 1 which is faster ($\mathcal{O}(n)$) but likely to generate very wide count-min sketches, and (ii) *iteratively*, by explicitly finding the minimum width that satisfies the constraint on the error, which is time-consuming ($\mathcal{O}(n^2)$) but ensures lower width

[5]Since usually $n \gg d$, to keep notation as simple as possible we assume that both point query and update operations cost $\mathcal{O}(1)$, even though their actual time complexity is $C(d)$

3.3 Deniability

The basic idea behind the concept of *deniability* is providing probabilistic coverage for the cells where inserted elements are mapped, with elements that have not been inserted. If O created a count-min sketch where each element in K_S is mapped to cells that can be covered with elements in $\mathcal{K}_\mathcal{U} \setminus K_S$, then O would have solid arguments to deny having inserted any key $k \in K_S$. To define the concept of deniability and prove some probabilistic results, we take an approach very similar to the one used in [2], where the deniability is applied to bloom filters.

DEFINITION 3.1. *A key $k \in K_S$ inserted in a count-min sketch $M(S)$ is deniable if $\forall i = 1, \ldots, d$, there exist at least one key $z \in \mathcal{V}$ s.t. $h_i(k) = h_i(z)$.*

DEFINITION 3.2. *A count-min sketch $M(S)$ is γ-deniable if a randomly chosen key $k \in K_S$ is deniable with probability γ. In this case, $M(S)$ is said to have γ-deniability γ.*

It is important to note that this γ-deniability definition imposes that deniable keys have to be covered by keys in the hiding set, and not by other keys in S, otherwise the count-min sketch as a whole could not be deniable.

We provide an expression to compute the γ-deniability of a count-min sketch.

THEOREM 3.1. *The γ-deniability of a count-min sketch $M(S)$ having width u, depth d, $|S| = n$, and $|\mathcal{U}| = u$ can be computed exactly as*

$$\gamma(M(S)) = \left(\sum_{b=1}^{w} U_w(n;b) \sum_{v=0}^{u-n} \binom{u-n}{v} \left(\frac{b}{w} \right)^v \left(1 - \frac{b}{w} \right)^{u-n-v} \right.$$
$$\left. \sum_{r=0}^{b} U_b(v;r) \frac{r}{b} \right)^d$$

and can be approximated in closed form as

$$\gamma(M(S)) \approx \left(1 - \left(1 - \frac{1}{wp} \right)^{(u-n)p} \right)^d \qquad (8)$$

where $p = 1 - \left(1 - \frac{1}{w} \right)^n$

99

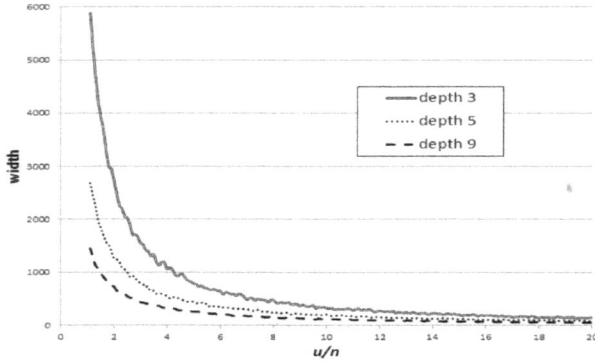

Figure 4: Comparison on how the width (computed with the iterative approach) changes by varying the ratio between the cardinality u of the universe set $\mathcal{U}$ (fixed to 1000 elements) and the cardinality n of the set S of inserted elements. The width has been computed iteratively to obtain 0 as certain error upper bound. Given a pair $\langle u/n, depth\rangle$, the value of the width reported in the graph has been computed as the average width over 100 experiments.

Proof. See Appendix A.

We carried out simulations to validate our model, where we compared the deniability obtained using Equation 8 with the real deniability of count-min sketches populated with synthetically generated elements. We fixed the cardinality u of the universe set to 1000 and varied the number n of inserted elements. We tuned the width w of count-min sketches so as to achieve 0 error using the iterative approach, the one which guarantees certainty on the error upper bound (see Section 3.2). For the depth d, we used values 3, 5, and 9. For each tuple $\langle u, n, w, d\rangle$ we ran 1000 experiments and took the average deniability. For each experiment we derived the actual deniability by counting how many keys out of the n inserted were deniable, according to Definition 3.1.

The results are reported in Figure 5. The average error between theoretic and real deniability is very small: 0.92% for depth 3, 0.57% for depth 5, and 0.36% for depth 9. In general, the deniability increases as the number of inserted elements is reduced, but the trend is not strictly monotonically increasing. Intuitively, the lower is n the greater is the cardinality of the candidate hiding set $K_{\mathcal{U}} \setminus K_S$, and thus there are more elements to choose from to deny any inserted element. The fact that the deniability grows with the depth actually depends on the width: a larger depth implies a lower collision probability among inserted elements, which allows to obtain certain 0 error upper bound with a lower width. In turn, a lower width guarantees more potential collisions with elements in $K_{\mathcal{U}} \setminus K_S$, which makes the deniability increase.

3.4 Count-min sketch tuning

We envision a scenario where a subset of a KB has to be exported, and count-min sketches have to be configured to provide guarantees on the maximum error of retrieved values and on the minimum deniability, and at the same time with the goal of maximizing the number of exported elements. We propose a heuristic to maximize n and compute w for

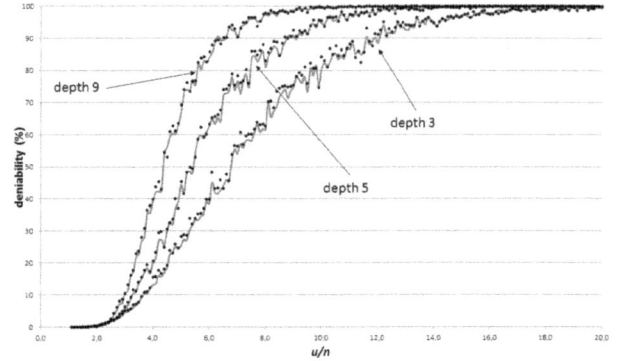

Figure 5: Comparison between the deniability computed with Equation 8 (gray lines) and the real deniability obtained through simulation (black markers), by varying the ratio between the cardinality u of the universe set $\mathcal{U}$ (fixed to 1000 elements) and the cardinality n of the set S of inserted elements.

each count-min sketch, such that

$$\begin{cases} \gamma\big(M(S)\big) \geq \gamma_{min} \\ \forall \langle k, v\rangle \in S, \quad |v - Q_M(k)| \leq err_{max} \end{cases} \quad (9)$$

The basic idea is to leverage the fact that the deniability almost grows as n is decreased, so an approximation of the optimum n can be obtained by performing a sort of binary search over n in the range $[0, u]$ to find the largest n satisfying the constraint on the γ-deniability. For each value of n to test, we compute the minimum w required to meet the requirement of the maximum allowed error on retrieved value. As the search goes on, we keep track of the best result got so far, which is the maximum n and correspondent w that are compliant with Equation 9. Once the search is over, the best result we found becomes the output of such heuristic. The time complexity is $\mathcal{O}(n^2 \log n)$.

We don't provide exact heuristics to choose the depth, rather we describe guidelines. A larger depth makes it easier to ensure the compliance with the conditions reported in Equation 9. On the other hand, the size of count-min sketches grows linearly with the depth. We leave as future work a more thorough investigation on the tuning of count-min sketch depth.

4. EXPERIMENTAL EVALUATION

This section describes experimental evaluations carried out in application scenarios related to malware detection, where machine learning techniques are used to classify samples in benign or malicious. Both scenarios need some form of KB to construct the feature vectors to be given as input to the classifiers, and obtaining such KB is time-consuming, so export turns out to be advantageous for who would like to begin using these malware detection techniques. For each scenario, we describe the content of such KB and why it takes time and effort to procure, how to export it through properly configured count-min sketches, and to what extent the γ-deniability and error upper bound properties affect the utility of the exported KB itself, measured by using the malware detection accuracy as main comparison metric.

4.1 Malware Detection based on Download Patterns

AMICO [26] is a system for malware detection which classifies samples using features on how they have been downloaded. Downloads are captured at the edge of the monitored network, and a random forest algorithm is used for the classification, trained on a set of labeled samples.

The features of interest include several information on the downloads occurred in the monitored network: past file downloads (i.e., how many clients downloaded a specific file), domain features (e.g., how many malware have been downloaded from a given domain), server IP features (e.g., how many benign files have come so far from some IP), URL features (number of files sharing a same URL and URL structure). This download history KB is required to properly create the feature vectors to be fed to the classifier, and a bootstrap period in the order of months is needed to collect enough statistics to start classifying samples [26]. Sharing such KB, along with the already trained classifier, can enable others to start using the malware detector without waiting months. While the classifier can be shared without incurring in privacy concerns, the KB can be shared using count-min sketches, by preparing a count-min sketch for each feature based on past download events. Each feature can be seen as key-value store. As an example the feature *domain_malware_downloads* can be seen as a set of pairs $\langle d, m \rangle$, each representing the fact that m malware have been downloaded from domain d. Since distinct count-min sketches represent different aspects of download history, they will have distinct key sets with distinct cardinalities, which in general are different from the number of downloads taken in account to populate the KB.

4.1.1 Count-min sketch configuration

Some count-min sketches have keys that can be considered sensitive. For example, the owner of the KB may have concerns in disclosing what domains have been visited by its network. In this scenario, we export different subsets of the whole KB according to different γ-deniability constraints (25%, 50%, 75%, 100%), and show how the classification is affected. A γ-deniability constraint means that all the count-min sketches have to have a deniability $\geq \gamma$. To show the impact of the deniability only, we configured the count-min sketches to have error upper bound equal to 0. Furthermore, we imposed the additional constraint that what we export has to be consistent with respect to the downloads: we populated all the count-min sketches with data coming from the same downloaded samples, to avoid that any two distinct count-min sketches would contain key-value pairs extracted from two different sets of downloads.

We fixed the depth to 11, according to empirical tests aimed at minimizing the dimension (width · depth) of count-min sketches. Figure 6 shows how the width varies for different γ-deniability constraints. Even though the width is reported for a limited number of count-min sketches only, the general trend is that the width decreases as the required deniability grows. A similar trend characterizes the number of exportable downloads: the higher the deniability the lower they are, as Table 1 highlights.

4.1.2 Detection accuracy

AMICO classifies a sample as benign or malicious on the base of a *malware score* output by the shared classifier, and

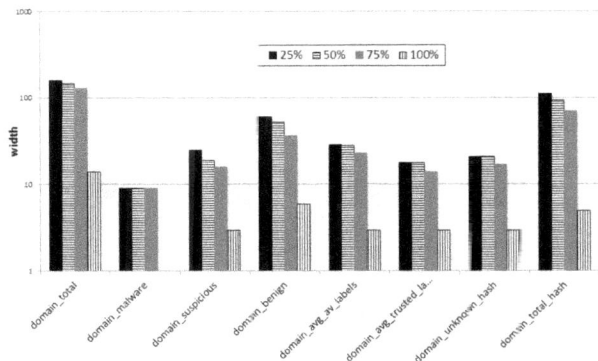

Figure 6: Comparison among widths of count-min sketches as the γ-deniability is varied. For space constraints, only a subset of the count-min sketches is reported here.

γ-deniability	exportable downloads
25%	1582
50%	1178
75%	961
100%	281

Table 1: Maximum number of exportable downloads for different constraints on γ-deniability.

using a given threshold such that if the score is above that threshold then the sample is classified as a malware. We first show the impact of the deniability on the detection accuracy, in terms of false positive and false negatives considering as ground truth the classification obtained by using the original KB. Figure 7 shows how increasing the size of the exported KB, that is loosing deniability constraint, does not necessarily imply a significant reduction of the false positive and false negative rates. Indeed the accuracy seems to remain almost the same as deniability is varied, in fact counterintuitively it seems that the highest deniability leads to the best accuracy.

To understand why this happens, we have to analyze the impact of the deniability on the malware score. Indeed, the classification accuracy is affected only when the malware score is perturbed in such a way that it crosses the given threshold. As can be observed in Figure 8, the average difference between the malware score obtained by using the exported KB, the score computed on the original KB, and the shared classifier is highest when the deniability is 100%, which is the expected result. Such a mismatch between the impact on the malware score (which corresponds to what expected) and the impact on the detection accuracy (which does not) seems to depend on the shared classifier employed in the evaluation. Indeed, it was trained with features computed over more than 15000 download events, while in our evaluations the features used to test the classifier derive from a download history including at most 1582 events (see Table 1). Such a difference in size is the likely reason why misclassifications occur, and seems to depend on the shared classifier and on the size of shared KB employed in the evaluation. It is to note that such issue regards sharing AMICO

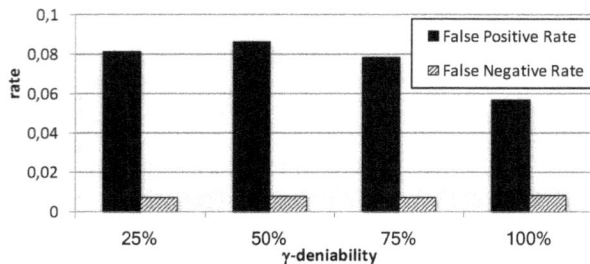

Figure 7: False positive/negative rates of AMICO classification using the exported KB to create feature vectors, for different γ-deniability constraints.

classifiers, and not sharing download events through count-min sketches, as proved by the results shown in Figure 8.

Another interesting aspect regards what happens when count-min sketches are queried with keys that had not been inserted: if the query returned a value witnessing the presence of such keys (i.e., a false positive for the single count-min sketch, not to be confused with the false positives of AMICO classification), then that value would be potentially harmful for whole classification. Figure 9 presents the average false positive rate of count-min sketches for each γ-deniability constraint. Although the reported values seem almost constant, there is a little (from 39% to 44%) increase when the deniability constraint is weakened. Such increase in the false positive rate is probably due to the fact that, as the amount of shared keys grows, the count-min sketches are more filled, and thus more likely to have a non-empty cell for each row for several keys that have not been actually inserted. This is in line with Equation 5, indeed false positive rate grows with n, and Section 6 reports some final considerations on this aspect.

4.2 Malware detection based on Behavior

In this scenario, we use the dataset provided by the 2nd Cybersecurity Data Mining Competition[6]. This dataset contains the logs of API/system calls invoked by malicious and benign samples, where each executable is uniquely identified by its MD5. The number of invocations for each API/system call can be used by a trained classifier to determine whether a sample is malicious or benign.

[6]Cybersecurity Data Mining Competition 2010:
h
d

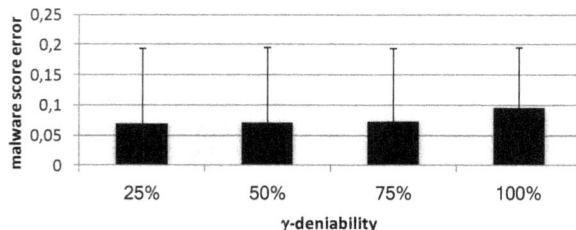

Figure 8: Mean difference (and bars representing standard deviation) between the malware score obtained by using the original KB and the one computed from sketches.

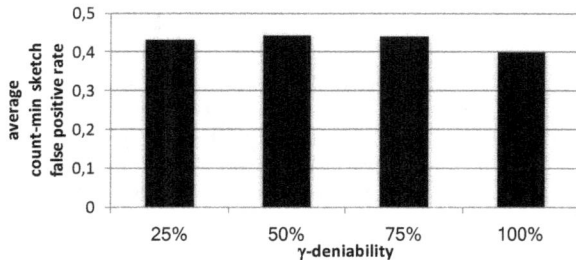

Figure 9: Average false positive rate of count-min sketches for different γ-deniability constraints. Sketches have been queried on keys associated to 100 distinct test download events.

The KB contains indeed all the information required to answer to questions like "how many time the API/system call c has been invoked by the sample having MD5 x?" for a possibly large number of distinct c and x. Collecting such a KB requires a lot of time to execute the dynamic analysis of samples for generating the counters of invocations. In turn, performing dynamic malware analysis necessitates of proper resources to setup the virtualization/emulation environments where samples can be executed, monitored, and traced. Sharing this kind of KB would enable others to test and evaluate their classifiers, based on API/sytem call invocation counters, without having to pay the effort in time and resources to run any dynamic analysis. Analogously to the previous scenario, both KB and trained classifier are exchanged between parties.

The KB can be exported through count-min sketches by using a sketch for each API/system call invoked by any sample included in the KB itself. For a count-min sketch related to API/system call c, a pair $\langle k, v \rangle$ represents the fact that the sample with MD5 k invoked c v times. Differently from the previous case, here all the count-min sketches have the same universe set for the keys, that is the set of MD5 signatures of analyzed samples.

4.2.1 Count-min sketch configuration

The owner of the KB may have concerns in sharing it because the fact that she has seen and analyzed a specific sample (identified univocally by its MD5) can be considered a sensitive information. For example, a party which has seen a sample known to be related to an APT, targeted at specific organizations or countries, may make suspicions arise on whether such party could be either one the target or involved in its development. While in the previous scenario we investigated the effect of the deniability on exported KB utility, here we are interested in deepening the role of noise. In this scenario, an attacker aiming at discovering whether the KB owner has seen a specific sample with MD5 x, could query the shared count-min sketches with key x to get API/system call counters, then compare them with the counters obtained by executing a dynamic analysis of the sample itself. The more the counters match, the more the attacker can be confident that the KB owner has x in its KB, regardless of the deniability guarantees provided by the way shared count-min sketches have been configured.

We configured the count-min sketches with 100%-deniability, inserting 378 MD5, and varied the err_{max} with values 0%, 5%, 10% and 20%. Universe cardinality has been computed taking into account the number of samples that a party could have analyzed. In order to have a lower bound on the universe cardinality, we have considered the number of samples received daily by VirusTotal[7], a free on-line analysis service of URLs and files. Also in this case, we fixed the depth to 11. Figure 10 presents the widths of a subset of the count-min sketches, for different constraints on error upper bound. As expected, in general, higher error upper bounds reduce the width, since indeed lower width leads to more collisions and thus more errors.

4.2.2 Detection accuracy

Similarly to what has been shown for the other scenario, here we present experimental results regarding how the amount of noise added to the values stored in the count-min sketches affects the detection accuracy of the shared classifier. As ground truth, we again use the classification provided with the classifier by creating the input feature vectors with the original values. Figure 11 reports the false negative rates obtained by varying err_{max}. As expected, the accuracy worsens as err_{max} grows, as the classification uses

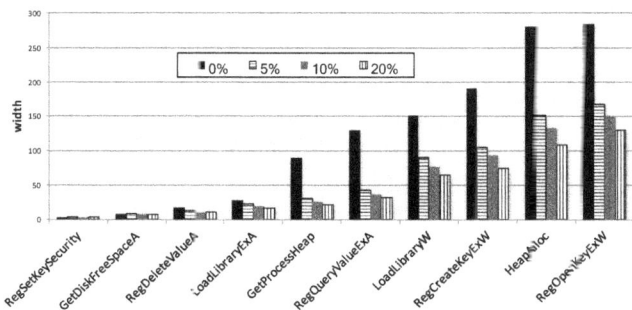

Figure 10: Comparison among the widths of count-min sketches as error upper bound varies. Due to space constraints, only a subset of APIs is reported.

5. RELATED WORK

Information sharing has already been proven to be promising in different fields [17, 23, 8, 25, 7, 11, 15]. Indeed, it allows to have larger KBs and, hence, perform more accurate statistical analyses and data mining tasks.

In [17], the Semantic Room abstraction is presented. It allows parties to share their data into a collaborative environment constituted by event-based platforms. The goal of a Semantic Room is to correlate coordinated Internet-based security threats and frauds. The privacy and the protection of possible sensitive data is demanded to the subscription of contracts, ruling requirements and service level specifications. Thus, the proposed abstraction assumes that its members are all trustworthy and prevent information leakage from the output diffused to Semantic Room members.

Shokri and Shmatikov [23] implement a system that allows multiple parties to jointly learn an accurate neural net-

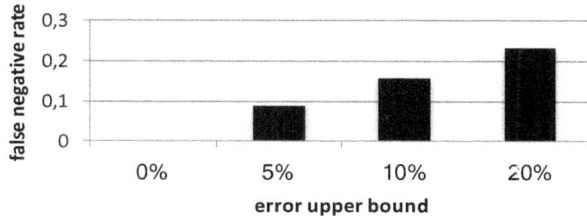

Figure 11: False negative rate for different error upper bounds. No false positive occurred.

work model without sharing their knowledge bases, formed by input datasets. Each party runs, in parallel and asynchronously, the stochastic gradient descent optimization method, training the model on its own dataset and, then, selectively shares small subsets of the trained models' key parameters. This enables parties to benefit from other participants' KBs, while preserving their own KB privacy.

Privacy-preservation becomes more and more important when parties own and need to share KBs related to Electronic Medical Record or Electronic Health Record (EMRs and EHRs, respectively). In the last decades, EMR/EHR systems have been largely deployed, disseminating data and preventing to store sensitive records in a unique KB [8]. From a statistical perspective, having a large centralized statistical database would allow to perform more accurate analyses and data mining tasks. On the other hand, EMRs/EHRs are highly distributed and, when these KBs are shared, patients' privacy needs to be preserved.

5.1 Privacy-preserving info sharing

Many models have been proposed to preserve the privacy of KBs. The most popular are k-anonymity and differential privacy. The first is vulnerable to many attacks [9], and solutions have been proposed for the majority of them, such as l-diversity [18] and t-closeness [16]. However, there not exists a real solution against the background knowledge attacks, which allow to re-identify records within an anonymized KB. A more recent attack, based on background knowledge, has threatened the anonymity of Netflix Prize[8] users [20]: taking advantage of very few information crawled from IMDb[9], Narayanan and Shmatikov have successfully de-anonymized the records of two users belonging to the Netflix Prize dataset. This proof of concept demonstrates how easy it is for an attacker to de-anonymize users by leveraging background knowledge, even when privacy-preserving mechanisms are put in place: the IDs of Netflix customers had been removed and noise was added to a very small portion of the total ratings. Whereas in the case of EMR/EHR systems the shared KB is a statical database, the aim of the Netflix was sharing a KB storing a large sparse dataset in order to let parties test their proposed collaborative filtering algorithms. This is very similar to the scenario where a company decides to share its own KB with other parties, allowing them to use their algorithms on its data. This is very common in privacy-preserving machine learning and data mining applications.

Differential privacy is another model for preserving privacy. Proposed by Dwork, it gives some guarantees on the

[7]VirusTotal: https://www.virustotal.com/en/statistics/

[8]Netflix Prize: http://www.netflixprize.com/
[9]Internet Movie Database: http://www.imdb.com

responses returned by arbitrary queries issued to a statistical database [5]. A database is differentially private if the attacker is not able to distinguish if a specific record is stored in it. As mentioned in Section 3, since Laplacian noise addition has been commonly used to implement differential privacy, this latter is vulnerable to tracker style attacks.

Other approaches rely on cryptographic protocols to share information in privacy-preserving fashion. Both [4] and [28] design and leverage secure protocols for sharing sensitive data. In [4], the authors focus on client-server interactions, in which the server shares the required minimum sensitive information. On the other hand, [28] addresses privacy concerns of sharing information in a collaborative environment. In both cases, the privacy leakage is non-zero.

5.2 Count-min sketches as privacy-preserving data structures

The idea of applying sketches to privacy-preserving computation is very recent. Similarly to our work, Balu and Furon leverage count sketches for adding a controlled amount of noise to matrix factorization tasks and providing differential privacy guarantees [1]. In [19], the authors design a cryptographic protocol in which count-min sketches, storing statistics of three different data sources, are encrypted. It is worth mentioning that the security of the proposed scheme depends on the protocol and sketches are only employed to reduce the network communication overhead. Conversely, Cormode [12] cites the work of Roughan and Zhang [21] that takes advantage of count-min sketches to run computations in privacy-preserving fashion. Nevertheless, the works on count-min sketches do not provide any guarantee about the privacy achieved, no privacy metric for count-min sketches has been designed or employed. One of the contributions of this article is also to propose a privacy metric for count-min sketches. The majority of the privacy metrics presented in Section 5.1 are not suitable for count-min sketches. Indeed, while the common differential privacy implementation is a noise addition technique, whose drawbacks have been extensively described in [22] and in the previous section, k-anonymity definition can be mapped to collisions within count-min sketches.

6. DISCUSSION

This section discusses some limitations and possible improvements with respect to the current state of this work.

Tuning the width. A relevant limitation is the $\mathcal{O}(n^2)$ time complexity of the procedure to configure the width of a count-min sketch to achieve a given guarantee on error upper bound (see Section 3.2), given the universe set cardinality u, the depth d of the count-min sketch, and the number n of elements to insert. The other procedure also is too time consuming, indeed it takes $\mathcal{O}(n)$ and, moreover, provides weaker guarantees on error upper bound, which depends on δ parameter. A direction to investigate could be devising a statistical model to provide probabilistic guarantees on error upper bound without having to iterate through all the n elements to insert. Rather, a mathematical expression based on u, d, w and n should allow to estimate the error on retrieved values. In this way it could be possible to directly derive the proper value for the width or, in the worst case, use some iterative method of numerical analysis to obtain a good approximation with $\mathcal{O}(\log n)$ time complexity.

Tuning the depth. How to configure the depth d of a count-min sketch is still an open point. Event though some practical guidelines are provided in Section 3.4, a more formal and neater way should be defined. A promising approach would consist in tuning together the width w and the depth d to achieve certain guarantees on error upper bound, and at the same time to minimize the product $w \cdot d$ to save on the memory required to store the count-min sketch. Some preliminary simulations show that this could be viable: by iterating incrementally through possible depths, and for each depth then increasing the width to find the one ensuring 0 error upper bound, it turned out that wd decreases up to some value $\hat{d}$, and then begins to increase.

False positive keys. The property of deniability enables the KB owner to deny having inserted a given key in a count-min sketch. An aspect that has not been investigated regards what guarantees could be possible to ensure with respect to the values returned by queries on keys that have not been inserted. In case of false positives, the utility of the exported KB could be affected relevantly. A desiderata could be including the count-min sketch false positive rate (defined by Equation 5) in the tuning process to achieve specific guarantees on what should happen when a query with a non inserted key occurs.

Stronger privacy guarantees. While the deniability requires that each cell of an inserted element should be covered by *at least one element* of the hiding set, stronger privacy properties could require each cell to be covered by *at least K elements* of the hiding set. This concept is defined as γ-K-*anonymity* and introduced by [2], where we mainly took inspiration from for the basic deniability property. An interesting addition to this work could be to translate also the concept of γ-K-anonymity to count-min sketches and extend the configuration procedure accordingly.

7. CONCLUSION

In this work we proposed to employ count-min sketches to export KBs in scenarios where privacy-preserving guarantees are required. We provided an analysis on the properties we can ensure on count-min sketches concerning the deniability of inserted keys (considered as sensitive information) and the error on retrieved values (considered as an information that could be leveraged for linkage attacks). We further presented a metric to measure the level of privacy that can be supplied, the γ-deniability, an adaptation of a metric used by [2] for bloom filters, and devised a probabilistic model proposing a procedure to tune count-min sketches, given specific goals on deniability and error upper bound. Such procedures have been applied to two scenarios related to malware detection, where count-min sketches can be used to export KBs in a privacy-preserving fashion: results mainly show the privacy/utility tradeoff that usually holds when data need to be altered to meet privacy requirements.

Acknowledgment

This work has been partially supported by a grant of the Italian Presidency of Ministry Council, by the Cybersecurity National Laboratory of CINI (Consorzio Interuniversitario Nazionale Informatica), and by Filierasicura project funded by Cisco Research and Leonardo SPA. We thank Roberto Perdisci for the helpful comments and references, provided during manuscript writing, and the anonymous reviewers for their careful reading and useful insights.

8. REFERENCES

[1] R. Balu and T. Furon. Differentially private matrix factorization using sketching techniques. *IMMSEC*, June 2016.

[2] G. Bianchi, L. Bracciale, and P. Loreti. Better than nothing privacy with bloom filters: To what extent? In J. Domingo-Ferrer and I. Tinnirello, editors, *Privacy in Statistical Databases*, volume 7556 of *Lecture Notes in Computer Science*, pages 348–363. Springer Berlin Heidelberg, 2012.

[3] G. Cormode and S. Muthukrishnan. Approximating data with the count-min sketch. *Software, IEEE*, 29(1):64–69, 2012.

[4] E. De Cristofaro, Y. Lu, and G. Tsudik. *Efficient Techniques for Privacy-Preserving Sharing of Sensitive Information*, pages 239–253. Springer Berlin Heidelberg, Berlin, Heidelberg, 2011.

[5] C. Dwork. Differential privacy. In *in ICALP*, pages 1–12. Springer, 2006.

[6] C. Dwork and A. Smith. Differential privacy for statistics: What we know and what we want to learn. *Journal of Privacy and Confidentiality*, 1(2):2, 2010.

[7] D. Gallego and G. Huecas. An empirical case of a context-aware mobile recommender system in a banking environment. In *MUSIC*, pages 13–20. IEEE, 2012.

[8] A. Gkoulalas-Divanis, G. Loukides, and J. Sun. Publishing data from electronic health records while preserving privacy: A survey of algorithms. *Journal of Biomedical Informatics*, 50:4–19, 2014.

[9] A. Hussien, N. Hamza, and H. Hefny. Attacks on anonymization-based privacy-preserving: A survey for data mining and data publishing. *Journal of Information Security*, 4:101–112, 2013.

[10] L. Invernizzi, S. Miskovic, R. Torres, C. Kruegel, S. Saha, G. Vigna, S.-J. Lee, and M. Mellia. Nazca: Detecting malware distribution in large-scale networks. In *NDSS*, volume 14, pages 23–26, 2014.

[11] A. J. P. Jeckmans, M. R. T. Beye, Z. Erkin, P. E Hartel, R. L. Lagendijk, and Q. Tang. Privacy in recommender systems. In *Social Media Retrieval*, Computer Communications and Networks, pages 263–281. Springer Verlag, London, January 2013.

[12] M. Kao, editor. *Encyclopedia of Algorithms*. Springer, 2015.

[13] O. Kaser and D. Lemire. Strongly universal string hashing is fast. *CoRR*, abs/1202.4961, 2012.

[14] M. Kruczkowski and E. N. Szynkiewicz. Support vector machine for malware analysis and classification. In *Proceedings of the 2014 IEEE/WIC/ACM International Joint Conferences on Web Intelligence (WI) and Intelligent Agent Technologies (IAT)-Volume 02*, pages 415–420. IEEE Computer Society, 2014.

[15] B. Li, J. Springer, G. Bebis, and M. H. Gunes. A survey of network flow applications. *Journal of Network and Computer Applications*, 36(2):567 – 581, 2013.

[16] N. Li, T. Li, and S. Venkatasubramanian. t-closeness: Privacy beyond k-anonymity and l-diversity. In *2007 IEEE 23rd International Conference on Data Engineering*, pages 106–115. IEEE, 2007.

[17] G. Lodi, L. Aniello, G. A. Di Luna, and R. Baldoni. An event-based platform for collaborative threats detection and monitoring. *Information Systems*, 39:175–195, 2014.

[18] A. Machanavajjhala, D. Kifer, J. Gehrke, and M. Venkitasubramaniam. l-diversity: Privacy beyond k-anonymity. *ACM Transactions on Knowledge Discovery from Data (TKDD)*, 1(1):3, 2007.

[19] L. Melis, G. Danezis, and E. D. Cristofaro. Efficient private statistics with succinct sketches. *CoRR*, abs/1508.06110, 2015.

[20] A. Narayanan and V. Shmatikov. How to break anonymity of the netflix prize dataset. *CoRR*, abs/cs/0610105, 2006.

[21] M. Roughan and Y. Zhang. Secure distributed data-mining and its application to large-scale network measurements. *SIGCOMM Comput. Commun. Rev.*, 36(1):7–14, Jan. 2006.

[22] R. Sarathy and K. Muralidhar. Some additional insights on applying differential privacy for numeric data. In J. Domingo-Ferrer and E. Magkos, editors, *Privacy in Statistical Databases*, volume 6344 of *Lecture Notes in Computer Science*, pages 210–219. Springer, 2010.

[23] R. Shokri and V. Shmatikov. Privacy-preserving deep learning. In *Proceedings of the 22nd ACM SIGSAC Conference on Computer and Communications Security*, pages 1310–1321. ACM, 2015.

[24] L. Sweeney. K-anonymity: A model for protecting privacy. *Int. J. Uncertain. Fuzziness Knowl.-Based Syst.*, 10(5):557–570, Oct. 2002.

[25] E. Toch, Y. Wang and L. F. Cranor. Personalization and privacy: A survey of privacy risks and remedies in personalization-based systems. *User Modeling and User-Adapted Interaction*, 22(1-2):203–220, Apr. 2012.

[26] P. Vadrevu, B. Rahbarinia, R. Perdisci, K. Li, and M. Antonakakis. Measuring and detecting malware downloads in live network traffic. In *Computer Security - ESORICS 2013*, pages 556–573. Springer Berlin Heidelberg, 2013.

[27] M. N. Wegman and J. Carter. New hash functions and their use in authentication and set equality. *Journal of Computer and System Sciences*, 22(3):265 – 279, 1981.

[28] N. Zhang and W. Zhao. Distributed privacy preserving information sharing. In *Proceedings of the 31st international conference on Very large data bases*, pages 889–900. VLDB Endowment, 2005.

APPENDIX

A. PROOF OF THEOREM (SKETCH)

According to Definition 3.1, a key k is deniable if, for each row $i \in \{1, \ldots, d\}$, $h_i(k) = h_i(z)$ for some $z \in K_\mathcal{U} \setminus K_S$. This event is independent and equiprobable for each row. Let q be the probability that this event occurs for a single row, then $\gamma(M(S)) = q^d$.

In order to prove Theorem 3.1, let consider a single row in which b is the number of cells (out of w) covered by keys in K_S, and r is the number of cells (out of b) covered by keys in the hiding set $\mathcal{V}$, with $r \leq b \leq w$. We have to restrict the cells covered by the hiding set to be a subset of the cells covered by K_S because we need to impose the occurrence of a collision. Given these definition, we have that $q = r/b$.

Both b and r are random variables following the probability distribution defined by Equation 10 (see Appendix B). Indeed, b is the number of non-empty cells, in a count-min sketch row with width w, after having inserted n elements. r is the number of cells, out of these b cells, where the elements of the hiding set are mapped, which can be seen as the number of non empty cells in a row with width b, after having inserted v elements. In turn, v is a random variable following a binomial distribution, but with a probability different from that used in Equation 6: rather than using the approximation given by the false positive probability, we can be more precise by conditioning the distribution to the knowledge that there are b non-empty cells, so we can use b/w. The exact formula reported in Theorem 3.1 can be derived by simply applying the law of total probability.

Equation 8 derives from the observation that the two probability distributions employed in this formula are both tightly centered around their mean [2]. The approximation consists in replacing r and b in q as follows

- $r \leftarrow b(1 - (1 - 1/b)^v)$
- $b \leftarrow w(1 - (1 - 1/w)^n)$
- $v \leftarrow (u - n)\frac{b}{w} = (u - n)(1 - (1 - 1/w)^n)$

B. PROBABILITY OF NON EMPTY CELLS

A result that is used in Appendix A regards the probability of having, in a row of a count-min sketch, a certain number of non empty cells after having inserted n elements.

LEMMA B.1. *Consider a row of a count-min sketch having width w where n elements with different keys have been inserted. Let U be the random variable representing the resulting number of non empty cells. The U has the following probability distribution:*

$$U_w(n, b) = \frac{\left\{ {n \atop b} \right\} \binom{w}{b} b!}{w^n}, \forall b \in \{1, \dots, w\} \qquad (10)$$

and mean value

$$E[U] = w \left(1 - \left(1 - \frac{1}{w}\right)^n\right) \qquad (11)$$

$\left\{ {n \atop b} \right\}$ is a Stirling number of the second kind, expressing the number of ways to partition a set of n elements into b non empty subsets, and is computed as

$$\left\{ {n \atop b} \right\} = \frac{1}{b!} \sum_{i=0}^{b-1} (-1)^i \binom{b}{i} (b - i)^n$$

Proof. See [2].

106

Efficient Commodity Matching for Privacy-Preserving Two-Party Bartering

Fabian Förg, Susanne Wetzel
Stevens Institute of Technology
Hoboken, NJ, USA
{ffoerg, swetzel}@stevens.edu

Ulrike Meyer
RWTH Aachen University
Aachen, Germany
meyer@itsec.rwth-aachen.de

ABSTRACT

Current bartering platforms place the burden of finding simultaneously executable quotes on their users. In addition, these bartering platforms do not keep quotes private. To address these shortcomings, this paper introduces a privacy-preserving bartering protocol secure in the semi-honest model. At its core, the novel bartering protocol uses a newly-developed bipartite matching protocol which determines simultaneously executable quotes in an efficient manner. While the new privacy-preserving bipartite matching protocol does not always yield the maximal set of simultaneously executable quotes, it keeps the parties' quotes private at all times. Moreover, our new privacy-preserving bipartite matching protocol is more efficient than existing solutions in that it only requires linear communication in the number of quotes the parties specify.

1. INTRODUCTION

In the past, bartering occurred predominantly one-to-one within local communities. Nowadays, online platforms such as *NATE* [20], *Read It Swap It* [22], *Craigslist* [6], and *TradeYa* [26] facilitate bartering beyond local communities. These bartering platforms typically allow their users to advertise their offered commodities and to indicate which demanded commodities they are willing to accept for an offer. This naturally leads to pairs of an offered and a demanded commodity which we refer to as quotes. If the offered commodity of a quote is equal to the demanded commodity of another user's quote and vice versa, we say that the quotes are compatible. As users commonly hold an offered commodity only at a single quantity (e.g., for books [22]), some quotes of a user may be competing in the sense that the offered or demanded commodities coincide. To facilitate an efficient exchange, it is desirable to determine as many simultaneously executable quotes as possible, i.e., to find a multitude of compatible quotes where the offered and demanded commodities are pairwise different. However, today's platforms generally require users to manually determine which

of their quotes are compatible with a quote from another user and force users to disclose their quotes.

To the best of our knowledge, the work from [7] is the only approach to date addressing privacy-preserving bartering for two parties that keeps quotes private and eliminates the need for a trusted third party. However, a shortcoming of the protocol from [7] is that as input it allows only one quote per party and the protocol is therefore restricted to a narrow use case. By combining [7] and [27] in a straightforward fashion, it is possible to build a bartering protocol which always yields a maximal set of simultaneously executable quotes but is inefficient in that its computation and communication complexities range from $\Omega(n_0 \cdot n_1)$ to $\mathcal{O}(\min(n_0, n_1) \cdot n_0 \cdot n_1)$ where n_0 and n_1 denote the number of quotes from the first party and second party, respectively.

It is in this context that this paper proposes a novel and efficient two-party bartering protocol that determines simultaneously executable quotes based on set intersection and bipartite matching. Our main contribution is a probabilistic privacy-preserving bipartite matching protocol whose computation and communication complexities are in $\mathcal{O}(\min(n_0, n_1))$. Unlike existing privacy-preserving bipartite matching protocols, our protocol does not yield a maximal matching in all cases, but allows us to keep compatible quotes as well as the quotes of both parties private. To the best of our knowledge, it is impossible to keep this information private using existing protocols. Our bartering protocol requires merely $\mathcal{O}((n_0 + n_1) \log(n_0 + n_1))$ computation and communication. We prove the security of our protocols in the semi-honest adversary model.

2. PRELIMINARIES

2.1 General Notations

Let $\mathbb{N} := \{1, 2, \dots\}$ denote the set of natural numbers. Then, $\mathbb{N}_i := \{1, 2, \dots, i\}$ for $i \in \mathbb{N}$. For $n \in \mathbb{N}$, Σ_n is the set of all permutations of $\mathbb{N}_n$. For a non-empty set S, $s \leftarrow_\$ S$ denotes that $s \in S$ is sampled uniformly at random from S. For $\ell \in \mathbb{N}$, $V := (V[\![1]\!], \dots, V[\![\ell]\!]) \in S^\ell$ denotes an ℓ-dimensional column vector with components $V[\![1]\!], \dots, V[\![\ell]\!] \in S$. For $n \in \mathbb{N}$ column vectors $V_i \in S^\ell$ $(i \in \mathbb{N}_n)$, we write $W := [V_1 \cdots V_n] \in S^{\ell \times n}$ to denote the $\ell \times n$ matrix with columns $V_1, \dots, V_n$ and $\ell \cdot n$ entries $V_i[\![j]\!] \in S$ $(j \in \mathbb{N}_\ell)$. Similarly, for matrices $W_1 \in S^{\ell \times n_1}$ and $W_2 \in S^{\ell \times n_2}$, $[W_1 \ W_2] \in S^{\ell \times (n_1 + n_2)}$ denotes the $\ell \times (n_1 + n_2)$ matrix formed by concatenating the columns of W_1 and W_2 $(\ell, n_1, n_2 \in \mathbb{N})$. For a plaintext $m \in \mathbb{P}$ and the corresponding ciphertext $E(m) \in \mathbb{C}$, we use the abbreviation $\overline{m} := E(m)$.

CODASPY '17, March 22–24, 2017, Scottsdale, AZ, USA.
© 2017 ACM. ISBN 978-1-4503-4523-1/17/03... $15.00
DOI: http://dx.doi.org/10.1145/3029806.3029831

We define $\mathbb{P}$, $\mathbb{C}$, and $\mathrm{E}(\cdot)$ for Paillier in Section 2.4. For vector $V' \in \mathbb{P}^{\ell}$ ($\ell \in \mathbb{N}$), $\overline{V'} \in \mathbb{C}^{\ell}$ is a component-wise encryption of V'. Analogously, for a matrix $W' \in \mathbb{P}^{\ell \times n}$ ($\ell, n \in \mathbb{N}$), $\overline{W'} \in \mathbb{C}^{\ell \times n}$ is an entry-wise encryption of W'. For a sequence of $n \in \mathbb{N}$ integers $x_1, \ldots, x_n \in \mathbb{Z}$, the prefix sum is the sequence $y_1, \ldots, y_n \in \mathbb{Z}$ with $y_i := \sum_{k=1}^{i} x_k$ for $i \in \mathbb{N}_n$. For $a, b \in \mathbb{Z}$ and $\star \in \{<, >, \leq, \geq, =\}$, $a \overset{?}{\star} b \in \{0, 1\}$ indicates whether $a \star b$ holds. The two parties participating in the protocols are denoted as P_0 and P_1.

2.2 Bipartite Matching

Following the definitions from [5], a *bipartite graph* $G := (A, B, M_0)$ is an undirected graph with nodes $A \cup B$ where $A \cap B = \emptyset$ and edges $M_0 \subseteq A \times B$. A *matching* in G is a subset of edges $M \subseteq M_0$ such that for all nodes $a \in A$ at most one edge of M is incident on a and for all nodes $b \in B$ at most one edge in M is incident on b. A node $a \in A$ (a node $b \in B$) is *matched*, if some edge in M is incident on a (on b). Otherwise, the node is *unmatched*. A *maximal matching* in G is a matching M such that for any edge $(a, b) \in M_0 \setminus M$, $M \cup \{(a, b)\}$ is not a matching. A *maximum matching* in G is a matching M such that for any matching M' it holds that $|M| \geq |M'|$.

2.3 Semantic Security

A formal treatment of semantic security is provided in [12]. The intuition behind semantic security is that adversaries should be unable to derive any partial information about the plaintext from the ciphertext [16]. There is an equivalent and much simpler definition of semantic security with regard to indistinguishable encryptions under a Chosen Plaintext Attack (CPA) [16]:

Definition 1. The $\mathrm{PubK}^{\mathrm{cpa}}_{\mathscr{A},(\mathrm{Gen},\mathrm{E},\mathrm{D})}(n)$ experiment consists of the of the following steps [16]:

1. Key generation algorithm Gen is run to obtain $(\mathrm{pk}, \mathrm{sk})$.
2. Adversary $\mathscr{A}$ is given pk as well as oracle access to encryption function $\mathrm{E}_{\mathrm{pk}}(\cdot)$. The adversary outputs a pair of messages m_0, m_1 of the same length. (These messages must be in the plaintext space associated with pk.)
3. A random bit $b \leftarrow \{0, 1\}$ is chosen, and then a ciphertext $\overline{m}_b \leftarrow \mathrm{E}_{\mathrm{pk}}(m_b)$ is computed and given to $\mathscr{A}$. We call $\overline{m}_b$ the challenge ciphertext.
4. $\mathscr{A}$ continues to have access to $\mathrm{E}_{\mathrm{pk}}(\cdot)$, and outputs a bit b'.
5. The output of the experiment is defined to be 1 if $b' = b$, and 0 otherwise.

Definition 2. A function f is *negligible* if for every polynomial $p(\cdot)$ there exists an n' such that for all integers $n > n'$ it holds that $f(n) < \frac{1}{p(n)}$. [16]

Definition 3. A public-key encryption scheme (Gen, E, D) has *indistinguishable encryptions under a chosen-plaintext attack* (or is *CPA secure*) if for all probabilistic polynomial-time adversaries $\mathscr{A}$, there exists a negligible function negl s.t. $\Pr\left(\mathrm{PubK}^{\mathrm{cpa}}_{\mathscr{A},(\mathrm{Gen},\mathrm{E},\mathrm{D})}(n) = 1\right) \leq \frac{1}{2} + \mathrm{negl}(n)$. [16]

2.4 Threshold Paillier

Our protocols require an additively homomorphic (2, 2) threshold cryptosystem that is semantically secure. As the threshold variant of the Paillier cryptosystem [21] from [8]

satisfies all of our requirements, we use it throughout this paper.

A (t, n) *threshold scheme* divides data d into n pieces $d_1, \ldots, d_n$ such that knowledge of any t or more d_i pieces allow the computation of d, whereas knowledge of any $t - 1$ or fewer d_i pieces leaves d undetermined [23].

We use the key generation, encryption, and decryption phases for the threshold cryptosystem by Fouque *et al.* [8].

Key Generation. Select a modulus $N = pq$ where p and q are strong primes and $p = 2p' + 1$ and $q = 2q' + 1$. Let security parameter κ denote the size of N in bits and set $N' := p'q'$. Pick $\beta \leftarrow_{\$} \mathbb{Z}_N^*$, $(a, b) \leftarrow_{\$} \mathbb{Z}^* \times \mathbb{Z}^*$ and set $g := (1 + N)^a \cdot b^N \mod N^2$. Share the private key $\beta N'$ among the two parties P_0 and P_1 using Shamir's $(2, 2)$ threshold scheme [23] such that party P_i ($i \in \{0, 1\}$) obtains share sk_i. The public key is $\mathrm{pk} := (g, N, \theta)$ where $\theta := L(g^{N'\beta}) = aN'\beta \mod N$ with $L(u) = \frac{u-1}{N}$.

Encryption. To encrypt plaintext $m \in \mathbb{P}$ in plaintext space $\mathbb{P} := \mathbb{Z}_N$, choose $r \leftarrow_{\$} \mathbb{Z}_N^*$, and compute $\mathrm{E}(m) := g^m r^N \mod N^2$. Ciphertext $\mathrm{E}(m)$ is in the ciphertext space $\mathbb{C} := \mathbb{Z}_{N^2}^*$.

Decryption. To decrypt $\overline{m} \in \mathbb{C}$, each party P_i ($i \in \{0, 1\}$) computes its decryption share $\breve{m}_i = \overline{m}^{2\Delta s_i} \mod N^2$ for $\Delta = 2$. The parties then jointly combine their shares to recover the corresponding plaintext m by computing $\mathrm{D}(\overline{m}) := L\left(\prod_{j \in \{0,1\}} \breve{m}_j^{2\mu_j} \mod N^2\right) \cdot \frac{1}{4\Delta^2 \theta} \mod N = m$ with $\mu_0 = 2 \cdot \Delta$ and $\mu_1 = -\Delta$. Protocol $\pi_{(2,2)\text{-Dec}}$ denotes the corresponding threshold decryption protocol.

Properties. The plaintext space $\mathbb{P}$ and the addition $+$ modulo N form the group $(\mathbb{P}, +)$, while the ciphertext space $\mathbb{C}$ and multiplication $\cdot$ modulo N^2 form the group $(\mathbb{C}, \cdot)$. For all $\overline{m}_1, \overline{m}_2 \in \mathbb{C}$, threshold Paillier enables *homomorphic addition* denoted as $\overline{m}_1 +_h \overline{m}_2 := \overline{m}_1 \cdot \overline{m}_2 \mod N^2$. As we have $\mathrm{D}(\overline{m}_1 +_h \overline{m}_2) = m_1 + m_2$, the group $(\mathbb{C}, +_h)$ is additive. Threshold Paillier allows for *re-randomizing* a ciphertext $\overline{m} \in \mathbb{C}$ by computing $\mathrm{Rnd}(\overline{m}) := \overline{m} +_h \mathrm{E}(0)$ where $\mathrm{E}(0)$ is a random encryption of 0 and thus $\mathrm{Rnd}(\overline{m})$ is a random encryption of m. For security reasons, it is typically necessary to re-randomize a ciphertext that results from one or more homomorphic additions. For $\overline{V} \in \mathbb{C}^{\ell}$ ($\ell \in \mathbb{N}$), $\mathrm{Rnd}(\overline{V})$ denotes a component-wise re-randomization of $\overline{V}$. Similarly, for $\overline{W} \in \mathbb{C}^{\ell \times n}$ ($\ell, n \in \mathbb{N}$), $\mathrm{Rnd}(\overline{W})$ denotes the entry-wise re-randomization of $\overline{W}$.

2.5 Security Model

In the following, we present the definitions necessary to describe the security model for our protocols. We consider a semi-honest adversary, i.e., the adversary controls a set of corrupted parties which follow the protocol but attempt to learn new information from their internal coin tosses and received messages. Furthermore, we assume that the adversary is computationally bounded and non-adaptive. The latter means that the corrupted parties are fixed throughout each protocol execution. Since we consider two parties, up to one party can be corrupted. We assume authentic communication channels which prevent tampering with exchanged messages but allow eavesdropping.

The next definition characterizes the information a party gathers during a protocol execution.

Definition 4. Let π be a two-party protocol for a functionality $\mathcal{F} : \{0, 1\}^* \times \{0, 1\}^* \to \{0, 1\}^* \times \{0, 1\}^*$ on inputs (x_0, x_1) where x_i ($i \in \{0, 1\}$) is the input of party P_i. Let $\mathring{r}_i$

denote the outcome of coin tosses on the random tape of P_i and let $m_{i,j}$ ($j \in \mathbb{N}_{n_i}$ with $n_i \in \mathbb{N}$) denote the jth message P_i received during an execution of π. The *view* of P_i during an execution of π is denoted as $\mathrm{VIEW}_i^\pi(x_0, x_1) := (x_i, \hat{r}_i, m_{i,1}, \ldots, m_{i,n_i})$. The *output* after an execution of π on inputs (x_0, x_1) is denoted as $\mathrm{OUTPUT}^\pi(x_0, x_1) := (\mathrm{OUTPUT}_0^\pi(x_0, x_1), \mathrm{OUTPUT}_1^\pi(x_0, x_1)))$ where $\mathrm{OUTPUT}_i^\pi(x_0, x_1)$ is the output of P_i. [11]

In the following, we define our adversary model. The underlying idea is that a party following the protocol specification is unable to learn anything from executing the protocol besides what it can deduce from its own input and its protocol output.

Definition 5. Let π be a two-party protocol for a functionality $\mathcal{F} : \{0,1\}^* \times \{0,1\}^* \to \{0,1\}^* \times \{0,1\}^*$ on inputs (x_0, x_1) where x_0 is the input of P_0 and x_1 is the input of P_1. Let $\mathcal{F}_i$ denote the output of party P_i where $i \in \{0,1\}$. Protocol π computes functionality $\mathcal{F}$ *securely in the semi-honest model* if two probabilistic polynomial-time algorithms $\mathcal{S}_0, \mathcal{S}_1$ exist such that for all $i \in \{0,1\}$, it holds that $\{\mathcal{S}_i(x_i, \mathcal{F}_i(x_0, x_1)), \mathcal{F}(x_0, x_1)\}_{x_0, x_1} \stackrel{c}{\equiv} \{\mathrm{VIEW}_i^\pi(x_0, x_1), \mathrm{OUTPUT}^\pi(x_0, x_1)\}_{x_0, x_1}$ where $\stackrel{c}{\equiv}$ denotes computational indistinguishability. [11]

Simulators $\mathcal{S}_0$ and $\mathcal{S}_1$ must run in polynomial-time in the security parameter of the underlying primitive. We assume that the security parameter is sufficiently large and omit the parameter in Definition 5 and the remainder of this paper.

Our security proofs utilize the *Sequential Composition Theorem* [3]. Assuming that a protocol π for functionality f is composed of a set of subprotocols $\rho_1, \ldots, \rho_m$ which securely implement functionalities $g_1, \ldots, g_m$, the theorem states that if a protocol π'—which replaces the subprotocol calls $\rho_1 \ldots, \rho_m$ of π by calls of a trusted third party computing $g_1 \ldots, g_m$—securely computes f, then π securely implements f. The calls of the trusted third party must happen sequentially rather than concurrently.

Throughout this paper, we write $(o_0, o_1) \leftarrow \mathcal{F}(x_0, x_1)$ to denote that on input x_i ($i \in \{0,1\}$) from party P_i, functionality $\mathcal{F}$ provides P_i with output o_i. In case both parties provide input x and both parties receive output o, we write $(o) \leftarrow \mathcal{F}(x)$. We use analogous notation for a protocol π.

3. INTUITION AND APPROACH

The goal of our bartering protocol is to determine a set of simultaneously executable quotes based on the quotes from P_0 and P_1 in a privacy-preserving manner. By viewing the offered and demanded commodities from P_0 as nodes in a graph where an offered and a demanded commodity is connected by an edge iff the commodities form a quote from P_0 for which a compatible quote from P_1 exists, we can reduce the problem of selecting simultaneously executable quotes to bipartite matching.[1] To obtain this graph, we need to first find the quotes from P_0 which are compatible with a quote from P_1. With P_0 and P_1 having a set of quotes, we are able to reduce this problem to the well-studied set intersection problem. Consequently, the components of our

---

[1] Note that in case the parties hold different numbers of quotes, lower complexities are achievable if the party with fewer quotes assumes the role of P_0.

privacy-preserving bartering protocol are privacy-preserving protocols for set intersection and bipartite matching.

Existing privacy-preserving set intersection protocols typically operate on integer elements. To make these protocols work with quotes, we encode each commodity and each quote as distinct integers. Specifically, the encoding of quotes is such that an encoded quote from P_0 is equal to an encoded quote from P_1 iff the quotes are compatible. Moreover, in bartering where the intersection corresponds to compatible quotes, the intersection is an intermediate result that must be kept private. To enable the further use of the intermediate result, we augment each quote with an encrypted indicator signifying quote compatibility. To implement set intersection, we choose the protocol by Huang *et al.* [13] as a basis owing to its efficiency. Furthermore, the generic design of the garbled circuit-based protocol allows us to adapt the protocol and implement it using threshold homomorphic encryption.

The main challenge for bipartite matching is to keep the compatible quotes and the quotes of both parties private at all times. In our approach, we leverage the fact that although P_0 must not learn which of its quotes are compatible, it naturally knows its own quotes. Thus, we strive to base our protocol on a suitable non-privacy-preserving matching algorithm. Candidates include the Hungarian algorithm or the flow network-based bipartite matching algorithm from [5]. However, to make these algorithms privacy-preserving, both parties would at least need to know the number of nodes (corresponding to the commodities from P_0), or the number of edges (corresponding to the compatible quotes), or both. As we must not disclose this information, to the best of our knowledge it is impossible to achieve our privacy requirements using these algorithms. To keep the information that these algorithms disclose by construction private, we base our approach on online bipartite matching. In online bipartite matching, the edges of the graph are revealed step-by-step rather than at once. The algorithm makes irreversible matching decisions when new edges are revealed. We use the online bipartite matching algorithm OBLIVIOUS by Mastin and Jaillet [18] as a starting point. OBLIVIOUS takes a bipartite graph $G = (A, B, M_0)$ as its input (edges are revealed iteratively per node $a \in A$) and outputs a matching in G. When the edges for a node $a \in A$ are revealed, the algorithm matches node a to a random node $b' \in \{b \in B \mid (a, b) \in M_0\}$, as long as b' is unmatched. If b' was matched before, OBLIVIOUS never matches node a.

OBLIVIOUS potentially leaks information about the edges to a party which learns the order in which the algorithm attempts to match the nodes $a \in A$. To illustrate this leakage, consider the bipartite graph $(\{a_1, a_2\}, \{b_1\}, \{(a_2, b_1)\})$ for which the output of OBLIVIOUS is $\{(a_2, b_1)\}$. If a party learns that OBLIVIOUS attempted to match a_1 before a_2, then the party can deduce that edge (a_1, b_1) does not exist. To overcome this issue, we derive the non-privacy-preserving matching algorithm PRUNE (Algorithm 1). PRUNE also allows us to leverage the fact that P_0 knows A and B but not the edges between them.

To implement PRUNE in a privacy-preserving fashion such that the compatible quotes are not disclosed to any party and the quotes from P_0 are kept private from P_1, both parties first obliviously shuffle the encrypted quotes from P_0. Then, they jointly decrypt the encrypted offered commodi-

Algorithm 1: PRUNE

Input: A bipartite graph $G = (A, B, M_0 \subseteq A \times B)$
Output: Matching M_2 in G

1   $M_1 := \emptyset$
2   **for** $a \in A$ **do**
3     $N_1(a) := \{b \in B \mid (a, b) \in M_0\}$
4   **if** $|N_1(a)| > 0$ **then**
5       $b \leftarrow_\$ N_1(a)$
6       $M_1 := M_1 \cup \{(a, b)\}$
7   $M_2 := \emptyset$
8   **for** $b \in B$ **do**
9     $N_2(b) := \{a \in A \mid (a, b) \in M_1\}$
10   **if** $|N_2(b)| > 0$ **then**
11      $a \leftarrow_\$ N_2(b)$
12      $M_2 := M_2 \cup \{(a, b)\}$
13 **return** M_2

---

ties such that only P_0 obtains the result. As both parties shuffle the quotes and only the offered commodities are decrypted (which P_0 already knows), P_0 will not learn the order among the quotes with the same offered commodity. For each distinct offered commodity, the parties obliviously select only the leftmost compatible quote by updating the encrypted quote compatibility indicators. In doing so, P_0 obliviously computes the prefix sum over the indicators of each offer-subsequence using homomorphic addition. For each quote, the parties then obliviously compute an indicator signifying whether both the corresponding prefix sum value is 1 and the corresponding quote compatibility indicator is 1. This idea of expressing the indicator condition using a prefix sum allows us to save communication, since P_0 can compute the prefix sums locally. As the quotes are shuffled, the parties select a random compatible quote for each distinct offered commodity. This procedure implements the first loop of PRUNE. We implement the second loop using the same idea. Finally, the parties obliviously filter the quotes w.r.t. the indicator to obtain the simultaneously executable quotes. To achieve low complexities for bipartite matching and the oblivious shuffling building block, we chose to implement our bartering protocol using threshold homomorphic encryption.

In the full version of this paper we show that PRUNE and OBLIVIOUS yield matchings of the same size (the matchings are potentially different), provided that both algorithms make the same random choices when they attempt to match a node $a \in A$. Consequently, we can apply the matching size analysis for OBLIVIOUS from [18] also to PRUNE.

4. BUILDING BLOCKS

This section discusses both existing building blocks and introduces novel building blocks used as part of our novel bartering protocol. We emphasize that if the input of a protocol is encrypted, then the parties are *not* required to know the corresponding plaintext. If the output of a protocol is encrypted, then a party will *not* learn the corresponding plaintext (unless the party can derive the plaintext from its input). In the following, all proofs are omitted and deferred to the full version of this paper.

4.1 Existing Building Blocks

Comparison. Functionality $\mathcal{F}_{\text{LT}}^{\text{CI-SO}}$ takes ciphertexts $\overline{m}_0$ and $\overline{m}_1 \in \mathbb{C}$ as its input and provides each party with an XOR-share of the bit $m_0 <^? m_1$.

Definition 6 ($\mathcal{F}_{\text{LT}}^{\text{CI-SO}}$: Less Than (LT) Comparison with Ciphertext Input (CI) and Shared Output (SO) [19]). Let P_0 and P_1 both hold encryptions $\overline{m}_0$ and $\overline{m}_1$ of $m_0, m_1 \in \mathbb{P}$ as their inputs. Then, functionality $\mathcal{F}_{\text{LT}}^{\text{CI-SO}}$ is given by $(b^{(0)}, b^{(1)}) \leftarrow \mathcal{F}_{\text{LT}}^{\text{CI-SO}}((\overline{m}_0, \overline{m}_1))$ with $b^{(0)} \leftarrow_\$ \{0, 1\}$ such that $b^{(1)} := b^{(0)} \oplus (m_0 <^? m_1)$.

Owing to the properties of XOR and $<^?$, $b^{(0)}$ and $b^{(1)}$ in Definition 6 are chosen such that we have $b^{(0)} \oplus b^{(1)} = 1 \Leftrightarrow m_0 < m_1$. To allow for the comparing of plaintexts, we assume that plaintexts are represented by their congruent integer in $\{0, 1, \ldots, |\mathbb{P}| - 1\}$. We refer to the variants of $\mathcal{F}_{\text{LT}}^{\text{CI-SO}}$ for Greater Than (GT), Less Than or Equal to (LTE), and Greater Than or Equal to (GTE) as $\mathcal{F}_{\text{GT}}^{\text{CI-SO}}$, $\mathcal{F}_{\text{LTE}}^{\text{CI-SO}}$, and $\mathcal{F}_{\text{GTE}}^{\text{CI-SO}}$, respectively. The definitions for $\mathcal{F}_{\text{GT}}^{\text{CI-SO}}$, $\mathcal{F}_{\text{LTE}}^{\text{CI-SO}}$, $\mathcal{F}_{\text{GTE}}^{\text{CI-SO}}$ follow from replacing $<^?$ by $>^?$, $\leq^?$, and $\geq^?$, respectively, in Definition 6.

A protocol implementing $\mathcal{F}_{\text{LT}}^{\text{CI-SO}}$ is introduced in [19] which extends the comparison protocol from [17] with shared output. Both protocols enforce an upper bound on the plaintexts corresponding to the encrypted inputs based on $(2, 2)$ threshold Paillier.

Oblivious Merge. The input of functionality $\mathcal{F}_{\text{O-Merge}}^{j^*, k^*}$ is an encrypted matrix with n columns such that the first k^* columns and the last $n - k^*$ columns are each in ascending order with respect to the plaintexts of the j^*th row. The functionality reorders the columns of the input matrix such that all columns of the re-randomized output matrix are in ascending order with respect to the plaintexts of the j^*th row.

Definition 7 ($\mathcal{F}_{\text{O-Merge}}^{j^*, k^*}$: Oblivious Merge). Let P_0 and P_1 hold $[\overline{V}_1 \cdots \overline{V}_n]$ with $\overline{V}_i \in \mathbb{C}^\ell$ ($i \in \mathbb{N}_n$) such that $V_1[\![j^*]\!] \leq \cdots \leq V_{k^*}[\![j^*]\!]$ and $V_{k^*+1}[\![j^*]\!] \leq \cdots \leq V_n[\![j^*]\!]$ where $k^* \in \mathbb{N}_{n-1}$ and $j^* \in \mathbb{N}_\ell$ are fixed. Then, functionality $\mathcal{F}_{\text{O-Merge}}^{j^*, k^*}$ is given by $(\text{Rnd}([\overline{V}_{\sigma(1)} \cdots \overline{V}_{\sigma(n)}])) \leftarrow \mathcal{F}_{\text{O-Merge}}^{j^*, k^*}([\overline{V}_1 \cdots \overline{V}_n])$ with $\sigma \in \Sigma_n$ such that $V_{\sigma(1)}[\![j^*]\!] \leq \cdots \leq V_{\sigma(n)}[\![j^*]\!]$.

Jónsson *et al.* [14] present a secret sharing-based protocol for $\mathcal{F}_{\text{O-Merge}}^{j^*, k^*}$ named odd-even-merge. Implementing the protocol from [14] using homomorphic encryption requires replacing the compare-exchange building block by the oblivious greater than swap protocol from [27].

Oblivious Shuffle. Given an encrypted matrix as its input, functionality $\mathcal{F}_{\text{O-Shuffle}}$ randomly shuffles the columns and re-randomizes all entries.

Definition 8 ($\mathcal{F}_{\text{O-Shuffle}}$: Oblivious Shuffle [27]). Let P_0 and P_1 hold $[\overline{V}_1 \cdots \overline{V}_n]$ with $\overline{V}_i \in \mathbb{C}^\ell$ ($i \in \mathbb{N}_n$). Then, functionality $\mathcal{F}_{\text{O-Shuffle}}$ is given by $(\text{Rnd}([\overline{V}_{\sigma(1)} \cdots \overline{V}_{\sigma(n)}])) \leftarrow \mathcal{F}_{\text{O-Shuffle}}([\overline{V}_1 \cdots \overline{V}_n])$ with $\sigma \leftarrow_\$ \Sigma_n$.

Oblivious Filtering. The input of functionality $\mathcal{F}_{\text{O-Filter}}^{j^*}$ is an encrypted matrix where the plaintexts corresponding to the entries in the j^*th row are either 0 or 1. The functionality determines a matrix which contains only the columns from the input matrix where the entry in the j^*th row is 1.

The resulting matrix does not include the j^*th row of the input matrix.

Definition 9 ($\mathcal{F}_{\text{O-Filter}}^{j^*}$: Oblivious Filtering). Let P_0 and P_1 hold $[\overline{V}_1 \cdots \overline{V}_n]$ with $\overline{V}_i \in \mathbb{C}^\ell$ and $V_i[\![j^*]\!] \in \{0,1\}$ ($i \in \mathbb{N}_n$) for a fixed $j^* \in \mathbb{N}_\ell$. Then, functionality $\mathcal{F}_{\text{O-Filter}}^{j^*}$ is given by $(\text{Rnd}([\overline{V}'_{\sigma(1)} \cdots \overline{V}'_{\sigma(n')}])) \leftarrow \mathcal{F}_{\text{O-Filter}}^{j^*}([\overline{V}_1 \cdots \overline{V}_n])$ with $n' := \#\{i \in \mathbb{N}_n \mid V_i[\![j^*]\!] = 1\}$, $\sigma \leftarrow_\$ \Sigma_{n'}$, and $\{\overline{V}'_1, \ldots, \overline{V}'_{n'}\} = \{(\overline{V}_i[\![1]\!], \ldots, \overline{V}_i[\![j^* - 1]\!], \overline{V}_i[\![j^* + 1]\!], \ldots, \overline{V}_i[\![\ell]\!]) \in \mathbb{C}^{\ell-1} \mid i \in \mathbb{N}_n \wedge V_i[\![j^*]\!] = 1\}$.

Protocols for $\mathcal{F}_{\text{O-Shuffle}}$ and $\mathcal{F}_{\text{O-Filter}}^{j^*}$ based on $(2, 2)$ threshold Paillier are presented by Wüller *et al.* in [27].

Shared Permutation. Functionality $\mathcal{F}_{\text{SP}}$ receives the same ciphertext pair from each party as its input. In addition, $\mathcal{F}_{\text{SP}}$ receives a share of a bit from each party as part of the input. If the bit is 0, $\mathcal{F}_{\text{SP}}$ outputs a re-randomization of the ciphertext pair. Otherwise, $\mathcal{F}_{\text{SP}}$ swaps and re-randomizes the components of the ciphertext pair and outputs the result.

Definition 10 ($\mathcal{F}_{\text{SP}}$: Shared Permutation (SP)). Let P_0 and P_1 hold $(\overline{m}_0, \overline{m}_1) \in \mathbb{C}^2$. In addition, let P_j ($j \in \{0, 1\}$) hold bit $b^{(j)} \in \{0, 1\}$ as its input. Then, functionality $\mathcal{F}_{\text{SP}}$ is given by $(\text{Rnd}((\overline{m}_b, \overline{m}_{1-b}))) \leftarrow \mathcal{F}_{\text{SP}}((\overline{m}_0, \overline{m}_1, b^{(0)}), (\overline{m}_0, \overline{m}_1, b^{(1)}))$ where $b := b^{(0)} \oplus b^{(1)}$.

In conjunction with a comparison protocol with shared output, shared permutation allows us to implement oblivious swapping [27] and oblivious predicate evaluations such as an equality test. It is possible to derive a protocol for $\mathcal{F}_{\text{SP}}$ from the main protocol in [7]: P_0 sends $\text{Rnd}((\overline{m}_0, \overline{m}_1))$ to P_1 iff $b^{(0)} =^? 0$. Otherwise, P_0 sends $\text{Rnd}((\overline{m}_1, \overline{m}_0))$. P_1 proceeds analogously based on the received ciphertexts as well as its bit $b^{(1)}$ and eventually transmits the result to P_0.

4.2 Novel Building Blocks

4.2.1 Oblivious Duplicate Marker

Functionality. $\mathcal{F}_{\text{O-Dup}}^{j^*}$ takes an encrypted matrix as its input where the plaintexts corresponding to the entries in the j^*th row are in ascending order and determines duplicates among these plaintexts. In doing so, it obliviously checks all adjacent entry-pairs for equality, thereby generating encrypted rows $l + 1$ and $l + 2$. For an entry in the j^*th row, the corresponding entries in rows $l + 1$ and $l + 2$ indicate a duplicate with the left and right j^*th row neighbor, respectively.

Definition 11 ($\mathcal{F}_{\text{O-Dup}}^{j^*}$: Oblivious Duplicate Marker). Let P_0 and P_1 hold $\overline{V} := [\overline{V}_1 \cdots \overline{V}_n] \in \mathbb{C}^{\ell \times n}$ such that for a fixed $j^* \in \mathbb{N}_\ell$, it holds that $V_1[\![j^*]\!] \leq \cdots \leq V_n[\![j^*]\!]$. Then, functionality $\mathcal{F}_{\text{O-Dup}}^{j^*}$ is given by $(\overline{V}') \leftarrow \mathcal{F}_{\text{O-Dup}}^{j^*}(\overline{V})$ with $\overline{V}' := [\overline{V}'_1 \cdots \overline{V}'_n] \in \mathbb{C}^{(\ell+2) \times n}$ such that $\overline{V}'_i[\![j]\!] := \overline{V}_i[\![j]\!]$ ($i \in \mathbb{N}_n, j \in \mathbb{N}_\ell$), $\overline{V}'_{i'}[\![\ell + 1]\!] := \bar{b}_{i'}^{(0,1)}$ ($i' \in \mathbb{N}_n \setminus \{1\}$), $\overline{V}'_{i''}[\![\ell + 2]\!] := \bar{b}_{i''+1}^{(0,1)}$ ($i'' \in \mathbb{N}_{n-1}$), and $(\overline{V}'_1[\![\ell + 1]\!], \overline{V}'_n[\![\ell + 2]\!]) := (\bar{b}_0, \bar{b}_0)$ where $\bar{b}_{i'}^{(0,1)} := \text{E}(V_{i'-1}[\![j^*]\!] =^? V_{i'}[\![j^*]\!])$ and $\bar{b}_0 := \text{E}(0)$.

Protocol. Implementing $\mathcal{F}_{\text{O-Dup}}^{j^*}$ requires an oblivious equality check for each pair of adjacent entries in the j^*th row of the input matrix. The oblivious equality check must yield

---

P_0: $[\overline{V}_1 \cdots \overline{V}_n] \in \mathbb{C}^{\ell \times n}$ P_1: $[\overline{V}_1 \cdots \overline{V}_n] \in \mathbb{C}^{\ell \times n}$

1. $(\bar{b}_0, \bar{b}_1) := (\text{E}(0), \text{E}(1))$

2. $\xrightarrow{\bar{b}_0, \bar{b}_1}$

3. **for** $i' \in \mathbb{N}_n \setminus \{1\}$
   $(b_{i',1}^{(0)}, b_{i',1}^{(1)}) \leftarrow \pi_{\text{LTE}}^{\text{CI-SO}}(\overline{V}_{i'-1}[\![j^*]\!], \overline{V}_{i'}[\![j^*]\!])$
   $(b_{i',2}^{(0)}, b_{i',2}^{(1)}) \leftarrow \pi_{\text{GTE}}^{\text{CI-SO}}(\overline{V}_{i'-1}[\![j^*]\!], \overline{V}_{i'}[\![j^*]\!])$
   $((\bar{b}_i''^{(0,1)}, \bar{b}_i'''^{(0,1)})) \leftarrow \pi_{\text{SP}}((\bar{b}_0, \bar{b}_1, b_{i',1}^{(0)}), (\bar{b}_0, \bar{b}_1, b_{i',1}^{(1)}))$
   $((\bar{b}_{i'}^{(0,1)}, \bar{b}'^{(0,1)}_{i'})) \leftarrow \pi_{\text{SP}}((\bar{b}_0, \bar{b}_{i'}''^{(0,1)}, b_{i',2}^{(0)}), (\bar{b}_0, \bar{b}_{i'}''^{(0,1)}, b_{i',2}^{(1)}))$
   end
   /* Each party locally builds the output: */
4. $\forall i \in \mathbb{N}_n \forall j \in \mathbb{N}_\ell, \overline{V}'_i[\![j]\!] := \overline{V}_i[\![j]\!]$
5. $\forall i' \in \mathbb{N}_n \setminus \{1\}, \overline{V}'_{i'}[\![\ell + 1]\!] := \bar{b}_{i'}^{(0,1)}$
6. $\forall i'' \in \mathbb{N}_{n-1}, \overline{V}'_{i''}[\![\ell + 2]\!] := \bar{b}_{i''+1}^{(0,1)}$
7. $(\overline{V}'_1[\![\ell + 1]\!], \overline{V}'_n[\![\ell + 2]\!]) := (\bar{b}_0, \bar{b}_0)$
8. **output** $[\overline{V}'_1 \cdots \overline{V}'_n]$

Protocol 1: $\pi_{\text{O-Dup}}^{j^*}$.

a ciphertext of the result to not leak intermediate results when used in bartering. The idea is to express equality as the conjunction of a $\leq^?$ and a $\geq^?$ comparison. Thus, the parties execute $\pi_{\text{LTE}}^{\text{CI-SO}}$ as well as $\pi_{\text{GTE}}^{\text{CI-SO}}$ and combine the shared outputs using π_{SP} to determine a ciphertext of the equality check.[2] In Steps 4 to 7, each party locally builds the output from these ciphertexts and the input.

Lemma 1. *Let P_0 and P_1 hold $[\overline{V}_1 \cdots \overline{V}_n] \in \mathbb{C}^{\ell \times n}$ such that for a fixed $j^* \in \mathbb{N}_\ell$, it holds that $V_1[\![j^*]\!] \leq \cdots \leq V_n[\![j^*]\!]$. Then, $\pi_{\text{O-Dup}}^{j^*}$ computes functionality $\mathcal{F}_{\text{O-Dup}}^{j^*}$ securely in the semi-honest model.*

Theorem 1. *If the subprotocols of $\pi_{\text{O-Dup}}^{j^*}$ are implemented as outlined above and composed as in $\pi_{\text{O-Dup}}^{j^*}$, then the communication and round complexities of $\pi_{\text{O-Dup}}^{j^*}$ are in $\mathcal{O}(n)$ and its computation complexity is in $\mathcal{O}(n \cdot \ell)$.*

4.2.2 Oblivious Prune

Functionality. Given $[\overline{V}_1 \cdots \overline{V}_n] \in \mathbb{C}^{\ell \times n}$ and $\{(V_i[\![j_1^*]\!], V_i[\![j_2^*]\!]) \mid i \in \mathbb{N}_n\}$ as the input, $\mathcal{F}_{\text{O-Prune}}^{j_1^*, j_2^*, j^*}$ updates $V_1[\![j^*]\!], \ldots, V_n[\![j^*]\!]$ such that $\{(V_i[\![j_1^*]\!], V_i[\![j_2^*]\!]) \mid i \in \mathbb{N}_n \wedge V'_i[\![j^*]\!] = 1\}$ is a matching in the bipartite graph $(\{V_i[\![j_1^*]\!] \mid i \in \mathbb{N}_n\}, \{V_i[\![j_2^*]\!] \mid i \in \mathbb{N}_n\}, \{(V_i[\![j_1^*]\!], V_i[\![j_2^*]\!]) \mid i \in \mathbb{N}_n \wedge V_i[\![j^*]\!] = 1\})$.

Definition 12 ($\mathcal{F}_{\text{O-Prune}}^{j_1^*, j_2^*, j^*}$: Oblivious Prune). Let $j_1^*, j_2^*, j^* \in \mathbb{N}_\ell$ be fixed and pairwise different. Let P_0 and P_1 hold $\overline{V} := [\overline{V}_1 \cdots \overline{V}_n] \in \mathbb{C}^{\ell \times n}$ such that $V_i[\![j^*]\!] \in \{0,1\}$ ($i \in \mathbb{N}_n$) and $G := (\{V_i[\![j_1^*]\!] \mid i \in \mathbb{N}_n\}, \{V_i[\![j_2^*]\!] \mid i \in \mathbb{N}_n\}, \{(V_i[\![j_1^*]\!], V_i[\![j_2^*]\!]) \mid i \in \mathbb{N}_n \wedge V_i[\![j^*]\!] = 1\})$ is a bipartite graph. Let P_0 additionally hold $V^{(j_1^*, j_2^*)} := \{(V_i[\![j_1^*]\!], V_i[\![j_2^*]\!]) \mid i \in \mathbb{N}_n\}$. Then, functionality $\mathcal{F}_{\text{O-Prune}}^{j_1^*, j_2^*, j^*}$ is given by $(\text{Rnd}([\overline{V}'_{\sigma(1)} \cdots \overline{V}'_{\sigma(n)}])) \leftarrow \mathcal{F}_{\text{O-Prune}}^{j_1^*, j_2^*, j^*}((\overline{V}, V^{(j_1^*, j_2^*)}), \overline{V})$ with $\sigma \leftarrow_\$ \Sigma_n$

---

[2] Our privacy-preserving equality test protocol supports (i) threshold Paillier, (ii) ciphertext input, and (iii) ciphertext output. Moreover, it is (iv) correct with non-negligible probability and (v) efficient in terms of complexity. Existing equality test protocols such as [25] do not exhibit all of these properties.

111

P_0: $[\overline{V}_1 \cdots \overline{V}_n] \in \mathbb{C}^{\ell \times n}$; P_1: $[\overline{V}_1 \cdots \overline{V}_n] \in \mathbb{C}^{\ell \times n}$
$\{(V_i[\![j_1^*]\!], V_i[\![j_2^*]\!]) \mid i \in \mathbb{N}_n\}$

---

1. $[\overline{V}_1' \cdots \overline{V}_n'] := [\overline{V}_1 \cdots \overline{V}_n]$ $[\overline{V}_1' \cdots \overline{V}_n'] := [\overline{V}_1 \cdots \overline{V}_n]$
   2a. **for** $b = 1$ **to** 2
       $([\overline{V}_{1,b} \cdots \overline{V}_{n,b}]) \leftarrow \pi_{\text{O-Shuffle}}([\overline{V}_1' \cdots \overline{V}_n'])$
   2b. **for** $i \in \mathbb{N}_n$
       $(v_i^{(j_b^*)}, \bot) \leftarrow \pi_{(2,2)\text{-Dec}}(\overline{V}_{i,b}[\![j_b^*]\!])$
       end
   2c. $(\bar{s}_{1,b}^{(j^*)}, \ldots, \bar{s}_{n,b}^{(j^*)}, \bar{b}_0, \bar{b}_1) := (\text{E}(0), \ldots, \text{E}(0), \text{E}(0), \text{E}(1))$
   2d. **for** $v^{(j_b^*)} \in \{v_1^{(j_b^*)}, \ldots, v_n^{(j_b^*)}\}$
       $\bar{s} := \text{E}(0)$
       $I := \{i \in \mathbb{N}_n \mid v_i^{(j_b^*)} = v^{(j_b^*)}\}$
       for $i \in I$ **from** $\min(I)$ **to** $\max(I)$
           $\bar{s}_{i,b}^{(j^*)} := \overline{V}_{i,b}[\![j^*]\!] +_h \bar{s}$
           $\bar{s} := \bar{s}_{i,b}^{(j^*)}$
       end
       end
   2e. $(\bar{s}_{1,b}'^{(j^*)}, \ldots, \bar{s}_{n,b}'^{(j^*)}) := \text{Rnd}((\bar{s}_{1,b}^{(j^*)}, \ldots, \bar{s}_{n,b}^{(j^*)}))$
       $\xrightarrow{\bar{s}_{1,b}'^{(j^*)}, \ldots, \bar{s}_{n,b}'^{(j^*)}, \bar{b}_0, \bar{b}_1}$ 2f.
   2g. **for** $i \in \mathbb{N}_n$
       $(\beta_{i,b}^{(0)}, \beta_{i,b}^{(1)}) \leftarrow \pi_{\text{GT}}^{\text{CI-SO}}((\bar{s}_{i,b}'^{(j^*)}, \bar{b}_1))$
       $((\overline{V}_{i,b}^{(j^*)}, \overline{V}_{i,b}'^{(j^*)})) \leftarrow \pi_{\text{SP}}((\overline{V}_{i,b}[\![j^*]\!], \bar{b}_0, \beta_{i,b}^{(0)}),$
       $\qquad\qquad\qquad\qquad (\overline{V}_{i,b}[\![j^*]\!], \bar{b}_0, \beta_{i,b}^{(1)}))$
   2h. $\overline{V}_{i,b}[\![j^*]\!] := \overline{V}_{i,b}^{(j^*)}$ $\overline{V}_{i,b}[\![j^*]\!] := \overline{V}_{i,b}'^{(j^*)}$
       end
   2i. $[\overline{V}_1' \cdots \overline{V}_n'] :=$ $[\overline{V}_1' \cdots \overline{V}_n'] :=$
       $[\overline{V}_{1,b} \cdots \overline{V}_{n,b}]$ $[\overline{V}_{1,b} \cdots \overline{V}_{n,b}]$
       end
   3. $([\overline{V}_1'' \cdots \overline{V}_n'']) \leftarrow \pi_{\text{O-Shuffle}}([\overline{V}_1' \cdots \overline{V}_n'])$
   4. **output** $[\overline{V}_1'' \cdots \overline{V}_n'']$ **output** $[\overline{V}_1'' \cdots \overline{V}_n'']$

Protocol 2: $\pi_{\text{O-Prune}}^{j_1^*, j_2^*, j^*}$.

and $\overline{V}_i' := (\overline{V}_i[\![1]\!], \ldots, \overline{V}_i[\![j^*-1]\!], \overline{V}_i[\![j^*]\!], \overline{V}_i[\![j^*+1]\!], \ldots, \overline{V}_i[\![\ell]\!])$ $(i \in \mathbb{N}_n)$ where $V_i'[\![j^*]\!] \in \{0,1\}$ such that $\{(V_i[\![j_1^*]\!], V_i[\![j_2^*]\!]) \mid i \in \mathbb{N}_n \wedge V_i'[\![j^*]\!] = 1\}$ is some matching in G.

Protocol. $\pi_{\text{O-Prune}}^{j_1^*, j_2^*, j^*}$ is a privacy-preserving implementation of PRUNE (Algorithm 1). In the bth iteration ($b \in \{1,2\}$) of the outer for-loop, which comprises Steps 2a to 2i of Protocol 2, the parties match each node in $\{V_i[\![j_b^*]\!] \mid i \in \mathbb{N}_n\}$ to a random node contained in $\{V_i[\![j_{2-b}^*]\!] \mid i \in \mathbb{N}_n\}$. In Steps 2c to 2e of Protocol 2, P_0 locally computes the encrypted prefix sums which the parties use in Steps 2g to 2i to obliviously update the indicators $V_1[\![j^*]\!], \ldots, V_n[\![j^*]\!]$.[3] In Step 3, the parties shuffle the columns to prevent the parties from deriving any information about the original edges if $\pi_{\text{O-Prune}}^{j_1^*, j_2^*, j^*}$ is used as a subprotocol and its output is decrypted.

Lemma 2. *Let* $j_1^*, j_2^*, j^* \in \mathbb{N}_\ell$ *be fixed and pairwise different. Let* P_0 *and* P_1 *hold* $\overline{V} := [\overline{V}_1 \cdots \overline{V}_n] \in \mathbb{C}^{\ell \times n}$ *such that* $V_i[\![j^*]\!] \in \{0,1\}$ $(i \in \mathbb{N}_n)$ *and* $(\{V_i[\![j_1^*]\!] \mid i \in \mathbb{N}_n\}, \{V_i[\![j_2^*]\!] \mid i \in \mathbb{N}_n\}, \{(V_i[\![j_1^*]\!], V_i[\![j_2^*]\!]) \mid i \in \mathbb{N}_n \wedge V_i[\![j^*]\!] = 1\})$ *is a bipartite*

---

[3] The set $\{v_1^{(j_b^*)}, \ldots, v_n^{(j_b^*)}\}$ from Step 2d potentially contains fewer than n elements. A computation complexity of $\mathcal{O}(n)$ in Step 2d can be achieved using a hash table that associates the indices I with each node $v^{(j_b^*)}$. Each party carries out Steps 2h and 2i locally, i.e., without communicating with the other party.

graph. Let P_0 *additionally hold* $V^{(j_1^*, j_2^*)} := \{(V_i[\![j_1^*]\!], V_i[\![j_2^*]\!]) \mid i \in \mathbb{N}_n\}$. *Then,* $\pi_{\text{O-Prune}}^{j_1^*, j_2^*, j^*}$ *computes functionality* $\mathcal{F}_{\text{O-Prune}}^{j_1^*, j_2^*, j^*}$ *securely in the semi-honest model.*

Theorem 2. *If the subprotocols of* $\pi_{\text{O-Prune}}^{j_1^*, j_2^*, j^*}$ *are implemented as outlined above and composed as in* $\pi_{\text{O-Prune}}^{j_1^*, j_2^*, j^*}$, *then the communication and computation complexities of* $\pi_{\text{O-Prune}}^{j_1^*, j_2^*, j^*}$ *are in* $\mathcal{O}(n \cdot \ell)$ *and its round complexity is in* $\mathcal{O}(n)$.[4]

5. BARTERING PROTOCOL

A *commodity* c is a good or a service from the *domain of commodities* $\mathscr{C} := \{c_1, \ldots, c_i, \ldots, c_k\}$. We encode commodity c_i using its unique index $i \in \mathbb{N}_k$. We assume that the domain of commodities $\mathscr{C}$ is public.

A *quote* $\gamma^{(j)}$ of P_j ($j \in \{0,1\}$) is a pair $\gamma^{(j)} = (c_o^{(j)}, c_d^{(j)})$ of an *offered commodity* $c_o^{(j)} \in \mathbb{N}_k$ and a *demanded commodity* $c_d^{(j)} \in \mathbb{N}_k$. Quote $\gamma^{(j)}$ expresses that P_j is willing to give $c_o^{(j)}$ in exchange for receiving $c_d^{(j)}$.

Quote $\gamma^{(j)} = (c_o^{(j)}, c_d^{(j)})$ ($j \in \{0,1\}$) and quote $\gamma^{(1-j)} = (c_o^{(1-j)}, c_d^{(1-j)})$ are *compatible* iff it holds that $(c_o^{(j)} = c_d^{(1-j)}) \wedge (c_d^{(j)} = c_o^{(1-j)})$. Otherwise, $\gamma^{(j)}$ and $\gamma^{(1-j)}$ are *incompatible*. The bijective functions $f_0 : \mathbb{N}_k^2 \to \mathbb{N}_{k^2}, (c_o, c_d) \mapsto (c_o-1) \cdot k + c_d$ used by P_0 and $f_1 : \mathbb{N}_k^2 \to \mathbb{N}_{k^2}, (c_o, c_d) \mapsto (c_d-1) \cdot k + c_o$ used by P_1 encode a quote as an integer, enabling us to check quote compatibility using an integer equality test.

The *set of quotes* from P_j is denoted as $\Gamma^{(j)} = \{(c_{o,1}^{(j)}, c_{d,1}^{(j)}), \ldots, (c_{o,n_j}^{(j)}, c_{d,n_j}^{(j)})\}$ where $\Gamma_o^{(j)} := \{c_{o,1}^{(j)}, \ldots, c_{o,n_j}^{(j)}\}$ ($\Gamma_d^{(j)} := \{c_{d,1}^{(j)}, \ldots, c_{d,n_j}^{(j)}\}$) is the set of offered (demanded) commodities associated with $\Gamma^{(j)}$.[5]

Given the sets of quotes $\Gamma^{(0)}$ and $\Gamma^{(1)}$, the *set of compatible quotes* $\Gamma_\cap^{(0,1)}$ from the perspective of P_0 is the set $\Gamma_\cap^{(0,1)} := \{(c_o^{(0)}, c_d^{(0)}) \in \Gamma^{(0)} \mid \exists (c_o^{(1)}, c_d^{(1)}) \in \Gamma^{(1)} : (c_o^{(0)} = c_d^{(1)}) \wedge (c_d^{(0)} = c_o^{(1)})\}$. Using f_0 and f_1, we can rewrite $\Gamma_\cap^{(0,1)}$ as $\Gamma_\cap^{(0,1)} = \{(c_o^{(0)}, c_d^{(0)}) \in \Gamma^{(0)} \mid \exists (c_o^{(1)}, c_d^{(1)}) \in \Gamma^{(1)} : f_0(c_o^{(0)}, c_d^{(0)}) = f_1(c_o^{(1)}, c_d^{(1)})\}$.

For the sets of quotes $\Gamma^{(0)}$ and $\Gamma^{(1)}$, a *set of simultaneously executable quotes* from the perspective of P_0 is a subset of compatible quotes $\Gamma_\|^{(0,1)} \subseteq \Gamma_\cap^{(0,1)}$ such that all offered commodities that are part of a quote in $\Gamma_\|^{(0,1)}$ are pairwise different and the same holds for all demanded commodities.

Given $\Gamma^{(0)}$ and $\Gamma^{(1)}$ as its input, $\mathcal{F}_{\text{BSEQ}}$ computes a set of simultaneously executable quotes $\Gamma_\|^{(0,1)}$.

Definition 13 ($\mathcal{F}_{\text{BSEQ}}$: Bartering with Simultaneously Executable Quotes (BSEQ)). Let P_j ($j \in \{0,1\}$) hold the set of quotes $\Gamma^{(j)}$ with $|\Gamma^{(j)}| = n_j$. Additionally, let P_j hold n_{1-j}. Then, functionality $\mathcal{F}_{\text{BSEQ}}$ is given by $(\Gamma_\|^{(0,1)}) \leftarrow \mathcal{F}_{\text{BSEQ}}(\Gamma^{(0)}, \Gamma^{(1)})$ where $\Gamma_\|^{(0,1)}$ is a set of simultaneously executable quotes from the perspective of P_0.

A protocol π_{BSEQ} implementing $\mathcal{F}_{\text{BSEQ}}$ is given in Protocol 3. As motivated in Section 3, the protocol has two main

---

[4] It is assumed that Step 2d of $\pi_{\text{O-Prune}}^{j_1^*, j_2^*, j^*}$ is implemented in $\mathcal{O}(n)$ time using, e.g., a hash table.
[5] Note that we assume that a party does not demand any commodity it offers, i.e., $\Gamma_o^{(j)} \cap \Gamma_d^{(j)} = \emptyset$ ($j \in \{0,1\}$).

$\boldsymbol{P_0}$: $\Gamma^{(0)} = \{(c_{o,1}^{(0)}, c_{d,1}^{(0)}),$ $\quad$ $\boldsymbol{P_1}$: $\Gamma^{(1)} = \{(c_{o,1}^{(1)}, c_{d,1}^{(1)}),$

$\dots, (c_{o,n_0}^{(0)}, c_{d,n_0}^{(0)})\}; n_1$ $\quad$ $\dots, (c_{o,n_1}^{(1)}, c_{d,n_1}^{(1)})\}; n_0$

---

1. Compute $\sigma_0 \in \Sigma_{n_0}$ s.t. $\quad$ Compute $\sigma_1 \in \Sigma_{n_1}$ s.t.

$f_0(c_{o,\sigma_0(1)}^{(0)}, c_{d,\sigma_0(1)}^{(0)}) < \cdots$ $\quad$ $f_1(c_{o,\sigma_1(1)}^{(1)}, c_{d,\sigma_1(1)}^{(1)}) < \cdots$

$< f_0(c_{o,\sigma_0(n_0)}^{(0)}, c_{d,\sigma_0(n_0)}^{(0)})$ $\quad$ $< f_1(c_{o,\sigma_1(n_1)}^{(1)}, c_{d,\sigma_1(n_1)}^{(1)})$

2. $\forall i \in \mathbb{N}_{n_0}$, set $\overline{U}_i^{(0)} :=$ $\quad$ $\forall i' \in \mathbb{N}_{n_1}$, set $\overline{U}_{i'}^{(1)} :=$

$(\mathrm{E}(c_{o,\sigma_0(i)}^{(0)}), \mathrm{E}(c_{d,\sigma_0(i)}^{(0)}),$ $\quad$ $(\mathrm{E}(c_{o,\sigma_1(i')}^{(1)}), \mathrm{E}(c_{d,\sigma_1(i')}^{(1)}),$

$\mathrm{E}(f_0(c_{o,\sigma_0(i)}^{(0)}, c_{d,\sigma_0(i)}^{(0)})), \mathrm{E}(1))$ $\quad$ $\mathrm{E}(f_1(c_{o,\sigma_1(i)}^{(1)}, c_{d,\sigma_1(i)}^{(1)})), \mathrm{E}(0))$

3. $\overline{U}^{(0)} := [\overline{U}_1^{(0)} \cdots \overline{U}_{n_0}^{(0)}]$
$\xleftarrow{\qquad\qquad\qquad\qquad\qquad}$
$\overline{U}^{(1)} := [\overline{U}_1^{(1)} \cdots \overline{U}_{n_1}^{(1)}]$
$\xrightarrow{\qquad\qquad\qquad\qquad\qquad}$

4. $(\overline{U}^{(0,1)}) \leftarrow \pi_{\text{O-Merge}}^{3,n_0}([\overline{U}^{(0)} \, \overline{U}^{(1)}])$

5. $(\overline{V}^{(0,1)}) \leftarrow \pi_{\text{O-Dup}}^3(\overline{U}^{(0,1)})$

6. $([\overline{V}_1^{(0)} \cdots \overline{V}_{n_0}^{(0)}]) \leftarrow \pi_{\text{O-Filter}}^4(\overline{V}^{(0,1)})$

7a. for $i \in n_0$

$(b_i^{(0)}, b_i^{(1)}) \leftarrow \pi_{\text{LT}}^{\text{CI-SO}}((\overline{V}_i^{(0)}[\![4]\!], \overline{V}_i^{(0)}[\![5]\!]))$

$((\overline{V}_{i,1}'^{(0)}, \overline{V}_{i,2}'^{(0)})) \leftarrow \pi_{\text{SP}}((\overline{V}_i^{(0)}[\![4]\!], \overline{V}_i^{(0)}[\![5]\!], b_i^{(0)}),$

$(\overline{V}_i^{(0)}[\![4]\!], \overline{V}_i^{(0)}[\![5]\!], b_i^{(1)}))$

7b. $\overline{V}_i'^{(0)} :=$ $\quad\quad$ $\overline{V}_i'^{(0)} :=$

$(\overline{V}_i^{(0)}[\![1]\!], \overline{V}_i^{(0)}[\![2]\!], \overline{V}_{i,1}'^{(0)})$ $\quad$ $(\overline{V}_i^{(0)}[\![1]\!], \overline{V}_i^{(0)}[\![2]\!], \overline{V}_{i,1}'^{(0)})$

end

8. $(\overline{W}) \leftarrow \pi_{\text{O-Prune}}^{1,2,3}([\overline{V}_1'^{(0)} \cdots \overline{V}_{n_0}'^{(0)}])$

9. $([\overline{W}_1' \cdots \overline{W}_w']) \leftarrow \pi_{\text{O-Filter}}^3(\overline{W})$

10. $S := \emptyset$ $\quad\quad\quad$ $S := \emptyset$

11a. for $i \in \mathbb{N}_w$

$(c_o^{(0)}) \leftarrow \pi_{(2,2)\text{-Dec}}(\overline{W}_i'[\![1]\!])$

$(c_d^{(0)}) \leftarrow \pi_{(2,2)\text{-Dec}}(\overline{W}_i'[\![2]\!])$

11b. $S := S \cup \{(c_o^{(0)}, c_d^{(0)})\}$ $\quad$ $S := S \cup \{(c_o^{(0)}, c_d^{(0)})\}$

end

12. **output** S $\quad\quad\quad$ **output** S

Protocol 3: π_{BSEQ}.

---

components: privacy-preserving set intersection for obliviously determining compatible quotes (Steps 1 to 7b) and privacy-preserving bipartite matching to select simultaneously executable quotes (Steps 8 to 12). The set intersection component starts with each party P_j ($j \in \{0, 1\}$) locally sorting its quotes with respect to the encoding function f_j. Each party then augments its quotes with a bit indicating the owner and encrypts the augmented quote. Next, the parties exchange their sorted and encrypted quotes and obliviously merge them as columns into a matrix such that the columns of this matrix are ordered according to the encodings. Then, the parties run $\pi_{\text{O-Dup}}$ to augment each column with two encrypted bits to indicate whether there is a duplicate in the left or right neighboring columns, respectively. Next, the parties use $\pi_{\text{O-Filter}}$ to remove all columns originating from P_1 based on the bit indicating the owner while keeping the columns from P_0. At the end of the set intersection component, the parties obliviously combine the two duplicate-indicators of each column to a single indicator corresponding to the compatibility of the respective quote from P_0 with a quote from P_1. Subsequently, the parties run $\pi_{\text{O-Prune}}$ to obliviously select a set of simultaneously executable quotes. Protocol $\pi_{\text{O-Filter}}$ allows the parties to keep the simultaneously executable quotes marked by $\tau_{\text{O-Prune}}$ and eliminate all other quotes. Finally, the parties jointly decrypt the encrypted quotes and output the result

Theorem 3. *Let P_j ($j \in \{0, 1\}$) hold the set of quotes $\Gamma^{(j)}$ with $|\Gamma^{(j)}| = n_j$. Additionally, let P_j hold n_{1-j}. Then, π_{BSEQ} computes functionality $\mathcal{F}_{BSEQ}$ securely in the semi-honest model.*

Theorem 4. *If the subprotocols of π_{BSEQ} are implemented as outlined above and composed as in π_{BSEQ}, then the communication, round, and computation complexities of π_{BSEQ} are in $\mathcal{O}((n_0 + n_1) \cdot \log(n_0 + n_1))$.*

6. RELATED WORK

In the context of privacy-preserving bartering, Förg *et al.* present a protocol for two parties supporting a single quote per party [7]. In contrast, our work supports multiple quotes per party. As is the case with π_{BSEQ}, the protocol from [7] keeps the commodities private at all times. In [7], a commodity is encoded as a $|\mathscr{C}|$-dimensional vector and quote compatibility is checked using a privacy-preserving scalar product protocol. Instead, we encode a commodity as its index in the domain of commodities which allows us to reduce the computation and communication complexity of the quote compatibility check from [7] by factor $|\mathscr{C}|$. While the protocol from [7] cannot determine simultaneously executable quotes, we can combine it with the conditional random selection protocol from [27] to achieve this goal. The idea is to form the Cartesian product of the quotes from P_0 and P_1 and then have the parties obliviously check each pair of quotes for compatibility using the scalar product approach from [7]. To randomly select one compatible pair of quotes, the parties utilize the conditional random protocol from [27]. The parties then decrypt the selected quote. The parties can subsequently remove all quotes which are not simultaneously executable anymore from their set of quotes and repeat the process until no more quotes can be added to the set of simultaneously executable quotes. When the parties repeat the protocol, they learn how many quotes the other parties removed in the prior iteration. To fix this leakage, each party can introduce dummy quotes that are never compatible with any quote from the other party. The resulting communication complexity ranges from $\Omega(n_0 \cdot n_1 \cdot |\mathscr{C}|)$ to $\mathcal{O}(\min(n_0, n_1) \cdot n_0 \cdot n_1 \cdot |\mathscr{C}|)$ depending on the number of simultaneously executable quotes found.[6] An advantage of the approach is that it adds quotes to the (initially empty) current set of simultaneously executable quotes in a greedy fashion, i.e., until no more quotes can be added to the set. Applying the analysis from [18], it follows that π_{BSEQ} still finds at least 63.2% of the simultaneously executable quotes on average that this approach would determine.

Aimeur *et al.* [1] as well as Frikken and Opyrchal [10] contribute further related work. Some differences of [1, 10] to the work by Förg *et al.* [7] as discussed in [7] also apply to our work. In particular, the work from [1] is centered around privacy issues in e-commerce such as price negotiation and tracking of customer product searches. Although the work from [1] also addresses the problem of keeping commodities private, Aimeur *et al.* [1] focus on the e-commerce scenario where a customer buys one product at a time from the merchant. In contrast, a prevalent issue in bartering is to find multiple executable trades at once. As pointed out in [7], the two-party protocols by Frikken and Opyrchal [10]

---

[6]The factor $|\mathscr{C}|$ can be eliminated by encoding each commodity using its index.

forces the parties to disclose their commodities to the other party. In contrast, our solution keeps commodities private from the beginning. Moreover, the work from [10] requires all parties to specify a valuation for all commodities. In practice, however, several bartering platforms enable their users to express their preferences in terms of quotes which is the setting we focus on.

As pointed out in [7], privacy-preserving matchmaking (e.g., [9, 13, 24, 28]) which addresses the problem of determining whether inputs match in a privacy-preserving fashion is related to privacy-preserving bartering. We answer the question from [7] whether matchmaking protocols can be used in bartering in the affirmative by determining compatible quotes based on the set intersection protocol from [13].

As shown above, determining simultaneously executable quotes can be phrased as a bipartite matching problem. To the best of our knowledge, to date there are only two privacy-preserving bipartite matching protocols [2, 4] which both determine a maximum matching. The protocol by Blanton and Saraph [2] obliviously computes the rank of an adjacency matrix to find a matching. The protocol utilizes garbled circuits and has a communication complexity of $\mathcal{O}(|V|^3 \log |V|)$ where V denotes the nodes in the graph (in the bartering context, V corresponds to the distinct commodities P_0 offers or demands). Chu and Chang [4] utilize homomorphic encryption and garbled circuits to build a matching protocol based on the Hungarian algorithm which operates on a cost matrix of size $|V|^2$ and has a computation complexity of $\mathcal{O}(|V|^4)$ (V denotes the nodes in the graph as before). The computation and communication complexities of our bipartite matching protocol $\pi_{\text{O-Prune}}$ are both in $\mathcal{O}(n_0)$ where n_0 denotes the number of quotes from P_0 (i.e., the graph has at most n_0 edges). As there is at most one edge between every offered and demanded commodity, we have $n_0 \in \mathcal{O}(|V|^2)$ and thus the computation and communication complexities are both bound by $\mathcal{O}(|V|^2)$. Although our matching protocol $\pi_{\text{O-Prune}}$ is more efficient than both maximum matching protocols, it does not always achieve a maximum matching. However, building the matrices for [2, 4] in the bartering context would require us to disclose at least how many distinct commodities some party specifies as part of its quotes or how many of these commodities belong to a compatible quote. As we have to keep this information private, to the best of our knowledge it is not possible to apply [2, 4] to our work.

Note that the work by Kannan *et al.* [15] is orthogonal to our work since the privacy notion in [15] is marginal differential privacy.

7. ACKNOWLEDGMENTS

In part, this work was supported by DFG Award ME 3704/4-1.

8. REFERENCES

[1] E. Aïmeur, G. Brassard, and F. S. Mani Onana. Blind Electronic Commerce. *Journal of Computer Security*, 14(6):535–559, 2006.

[2] M. Blanton and S. Saraph. Oblivious Maximum Bipartite Matching Size Algorithm with Applications to Secure Fingerprint Identification. In *ESORICS*, 2015.

[3] R. Canetti. Security and Composition of Multiparty Cryptographic Protocols. *Journal of Cryptology*, 13(1):143–202, Apr. 2000.

[4] W.-T. Chu and F.-C. Chang. A Privacy-Preserving Bipartite Graph Matching Framework for Multimedia Analysis and Retrieval. In *ICMR*, 2015.

[5] T. H. Cormen, C. E. Leiserson, R. L. Rivest, and C. Stein. *Introduction to Algorithms*. The MIT Press, 3rd edition, 2009.

[6] Craigslist. https://www.craigslist.org/.

[7] F. Förg, D. Mayer, S. Wetzel, S. Wüller, and U. Meyer. A Secure Two-Party Bartering Protocol Using Privacy-Preserving Interval Operations. In *PST*, 2014.

[8] P. Fouque, G. Poupard, and J. Stern. Sharing Decryption in the Context of Voting or Lotteries. In *FC*, 2001.

[9] M. J. Freedman, K. Nissim, and B. Pinkas. Efficient Private Matching and Set Intersection. In *EUROCRYPT*, 2004.

[10] K. Frikken and L. Opyrchal. PBS: Private Bartering Systems. In *FC*, 2008.

[11] O. Goldreich. *Foundations of Cryptography: Volume 2, Basic Applications*. Cambridge University Press, 1st edition, 2009.

[12] S. Goldwasser and S. Micali. Probabilistic Encryption. *Journal of Computer and System Sciences*, 28(2):270–299, 1984.

[13] Y. Huang, D. Evans, and J. Katz. Private Set Intersection: Are Garbled Circuits Better than Custom Protocols? In *NDSS*, 2012.

[14] K. V. Jónsson, G. Kreitz, and M. Uddin. Secure Multi-Party Sorting and Applications. In *ACNS*, 2011.

[15] S. Kannan, J. Morgenstern, R. Rogers, and A. Roth. Private Pareto Optimal Exchange. In *EC*, 2015.

[16] J. Katz and Y. Lindell. *Introduction to Modern Cryptography*. Chapman & Hall/CRC, 2007.

[17] F. Kerschbaum and O. Terzidis. Filtering for Private Collaborative Benchmarking. In *ETRICS*, 2006.

[18] A. Mastin and P. Jaillet. Greedy Online Bipartite Matching on Random Graphs. *arXiv.org*, cs.DS, 2013.

[19] D. A. Mayer. *Design and Implementation of Efficient Privacy-Preserving and Unbiased Reconciliation Protocols*. PhD thesis, Stevens Institute of Technology Hoboken, NJ, 2012.

[20] National Association of Trade Exchanges. http://www.natebarter.com/.

[21] P. Paillier. Public-Key Cryptosystems Based on Composite Degree Residuosity Classes. In *EUROCRYPT*, 1999.

[22] Read It Swap It. http://www.readitswapit.co.uk/.

[23] A. Shamir. How to Share a Secret. *Communications of the ACM*, 22(11):612–613, Nov. 1979.

[24] J. S. Shin and V. D. Gligor. A New Privacy-Enhanced Matchmaking Protocol. In *NDSS*, 2008.

[25] T. Toft. Sub-Linear, Secure Comparison with Two Non-Colluding Parties. In *PKC*, 2011.

[26] TradeYa! http://www.tradeya.com/.

[27] S. Wüller, U. Meyer, F. Förg, and S. Wetzel. Privacy-Preserving Conditional Random Selection. In *PST*, 2015.

[28] K. Zhang and R. Needham. A Private Matchmaking Protocol, 2001.

Achieving Differential Privacy in Secure Multiparty Data Aggregation Protocols on Star Networks

Vincent Bindschaedler[*]
University of Illinois at
Urbana-Champaign
bindsch2@illinois.edu

Shantanu Rane
Palo Alto Research Center
srane@parc.com

Alejandro Brito
Palo Alto Research Center
abrito@parc.com

Vanishree Rao
Palo Alto Research Center
vrao@parc.comt

Ersin Uzun
Palo Alto Research Center
euzun@parc.com

ABSTRACT

We consider the problem of privacy-preserving data aggregation in a star network topology, i.e., several untrusting participants connected to a single aggregator. We require that the participants do not discover each other's data, and the service provider remains oblivious to each participant's individual contribution. Furthermore, the final result is to be published in a differentially private manner, i.e., the result should not reveal the contribution of any single participant to a (possibly external) adversary who knows the contributions of all other participants. In other words, we require a secure multiparty computation protocol that also incorporates a differentially private mechanism.

Previous solutions have resorted to caveats such as postulating a trusted dealer to distribute keys to the participants, or introducing additional entities to withhold the decryption key from the aggregator, or relaxing the star topology by allowing pairwise communication amongst the participants. In this paper, we show how to obtain a noisy (differentially private) aggregation result using Shamir secret sharing and additively homomorphic encryption without these mitigating assumptions. More importantly, while we assume semi-honest participants, we allow the aggregator to be stronger than semi-honest, specifically in the sense that he can try to reduce the noise in the differentially private result.

To respect the differential privacy requirement, collusions of mutually untrusting entities need to be analyzed differently from traditional secure multiparty computation: It is not sufficient that such collusions do not reveal the data of honest participants; we must also ensure that the colluding entities cannot undermine differential privacy by reducing the amount of noise in the final result. Our protocols avoid this by requiring that no entity – neither the aggregator nor any participant – knows how much noise a participant contributes to the final result. We also ensure that if a cheating aggregator tries to influence the noise term in the differentially private output, he can be detected with overwhelming probability.

CODASPY'17, March 22-24, 2017, Scottsdale, AZ, USA
© 2017 ACM. ISBN 978-1-4503-4523-1/17/03... $15.00
DOI: http://dx.doi.org/10.1145/3029806.3029829

Keywords

secret sharing; homomorphic encryption; differential privacy

1. INTRODUCTION

Aggregate computations are the among the most basic and widely used primitives in today's networked environments. These computation usually involve a server (aggregator) computing aggregate measures, e.g., histograms, weighted summations, averages, etc., using data gathered from several devices (participants). In this work we are concerned with application scenarios in which participants and the aggregator form a star network, and the privacy of the participants must be protected. The need for privacy-preserving aggregate computations arises in several applications: telemetry from Internet-of-Things (IoT) devices, analytics on medical data furnished by wearables, smart grid power aggregation, histograms of websites visited by users of a particular browser, to name a few.

As participants in the internet economy, we generally allow our data to be used by service providers (aggregators), as a fair exchange for the services they provide. However there is a growing concern that our data may be used for purposes that we did not sanction. For example, smart meter readings can reveal a homeowner's life patterns, fitness apps may reveal private medical conditions, and browser activity and metadata reveal intimate details of a person's life and values. Furthermore, if the service provider is affected by a data breach, sensitive data belonging to unsuspecting individuals falls into the hands of an adversary.

Two kinds of privacy formulations may be used to express and resolve the above concerns. The first formulation, based on secure multiparty computation, is used to directly express which entities can communicate and how entities withhold knowledge of their data from other entities. In a star network, the main privacy constraint is that the data held by any individual participant should not be revealed to other participants, and also not to the aggregator. The aggregator should discover only the specified aggregate measure such as the summation or the probability distribution and nothing else. Additional constraints may be dictated by practical deployment. One such constraint, in a star network, is that the participants can communicate with the aggregator but may not be able to communicate with one another. A second constraint is that the participants cannot all be expected to remain online simultaneously while the protocol is being executed. Thus, an aggregation protocol must enable the aggregator to compute the correct result, while

[*]V. B. contributed to this work when he was an intern at PARC.

satisfying the privacy constraints and communication constraints, even when users dynamically join and leave.

The second formulation, based on differential privacy, is used to express how difficult it is for an adversary to observe the result of a computation, and make inferences about the protocol's participants. Suppose that the aggregator publishes the final result of the data aggregation protocol, e.g., the average power consumption, and makes it available to an analyst. Then, differential privacy quantifies the degree of confidence with which the analyst can claim that a particular participant, e.g., Alice, participated in the protocol. Seen another way, if the analyst repeated the protocol after Alice moved out of the neighborhood, he would discover Alice's power consumption, even if the protocol didn't directly reveal Alice's data to the analyst. A differentially private mechanism would modify the result, i.e., the average power consumption in a way that makes it hard for the analyst to discover Alice's power consumption. This is clearly a different notion of privacy compared to that encountered in secure multiparty computation. In this paper, we are concerned with situations where both kinds of privacy are desired.

2. OVERVIEW OF RELATED WORK

Addressing the privacy concerns related to multiparty computation is challenging predominantly because of the key management problem. Concretely, each participant should obfuscate its input so that all the obfuscated inputs can later be combined – for example, by means of a homomorphic cryptosystem – by the aggregator to reveal the aggregate function. However, this is not straightforward for the star network topology because each participant encrypts using its own unique key. Below, we present a short overview of attempts to solve this problem. For more details, we refer the reader to a comprehensive review by Erkin et al. [8]

Shi et al. considered an aggregation protocol that assumes a trusted dealer that distributes encryption keys to the participants, and ensures that the keys vanish when the aggregator combines the result in a prescribed way [4, 22]. A similar approach is followed by Bilogrevic et al., to compute means, variances and higher moments of distributions [3]. Rather than assuming a trusted dealer, Jawurek and Kerschbaum distribute the task of computation and the decryption between an untrusted aggregator and an untrusted key managing authority [11]. This is an efficient approach with a single public key homomorphic cryptosystem, that has only $O(m)$ overhead, where m is the number of participants. However, it introduces an extra participant, and introduces the risk of catastrophic privacy loss if the key managing authority colludes with the aggregator. Leontiadis et al. proposed a different solution that allows each participant to use a different encryption key, while distributing the knowledge of the overall decryption key between the aggregator and an extra entity called the collector [16]. Similar to the previous approach, their scheme forbids collusions between the aggregator and the collector.

Though additive secret sharing requires pairwise information exchange amongst the participants, this approach can still be considered in star networks, by allowing the participants to communicate via the aggregator. Specifically, Kursawe et al. employed public-key encryption to send encrypted shares of the participants' data (or keys) to a subset of participants (termed "leaders") via the aggregator [15]. The leaders add their own shares such that their effect vanishes upon combination, revealing only the sum of the participants' data. Garcia and Jacobs presented a protocol in which a participant homomorphically encrypts each share by using the public-key of each share's intended recipient, but only sends it to the aggregator [10]. The aggregator then homomorphically combines the encrypted shares, requests the decryption of partial summations from

each participant, and combines the partial sum to reveal the final sum, but nothing else. This approach has been generalized via the use of Shamir secret sharing [21], which provides fault tolerance in addition to collusion resistance [20]. In a strict star topology, all these approaches incur $O(m^2)$ ciphertext communication overhead at the aggregator.

We point to further efforts on this topic, which relax the strict star network topology in exchange for a gain in efficiency. Erkin and Tsudik allow the participants (smart meters) to communicate with one another, exchanging random values before each smart meter communicates with the aggregator [9]. This is a mode of secret sharing, in which the randomized values are chosen to vanish when the aggregator computes the sum. Ács and Castelluccia allow each participant to communicate with a small number of other participants [1]. These works show that by allowing a limited amount of communication amongst the participants, the ciphertext overhead of the protocol immediately becomes manageable, i.e., $O(m)$. On the other hand, if any participant leaves before the shares are combined, the final sum computed by the aggregator becomes error-prone. Though we do not have a proof, the above two papers suggest that a $O(m)$ ciphertext overhead may not be achievable, in general, for fault-tolerant aggregation with a star topology. Indeed, we are not aware of any protocol that achieves this. An improvement toward $O(m)$ overhead, has nevertheless, been attempted. Dividing the star-connected participants into a logical hierarchy composed of several "cohorts" of participants, it is possible to achieve a protocol complexity of $O(m^{1+\rho})$ [20]. By an appropriate choice of the cohort size, ρ can be made small.

Some of the schemes discussed above, have also proposed mechanisms to achieve differential privacy [1, 3, 4, 11, 22]. Recognizing that the aggregator has an incentive to obtain the most accurate aggregate value as possible, these studies have entrusted the task of noise addition to entities other than the aggregator. This is a departure from the differential privacy literature produced by the machine learning community, in which the database curator is trusted to add the correct amount of noise. For example, in Shi et al. [22], Chan et al. [4] and Bilogrevic et al. [3], the participants generate samples from the two-sided geometric distribution (a discrete version of the Laplace distribution), which add up to provide a differentially private summation of the participants' inputs. Similarly, in Acs and Castelluccia [1] the participants generate Gamma-distributed noise samples, which add up to a Laplace-distributed noise term at the aggregator.

Unfortunately, as we show later in the paper, this approach of having the participants add noise samples, is not sufficient to preserve differential privacy. In particular, we argue that collusions of semi-honest participants can subtract out their noise terms from the published result and reduce the differential privacy of honest participants. We present a protocol in which the participants and the aggregator must interact to determine the noise term. More importantly, our protocol is designed such that neither the participants nor the aggregator know the noise terms that have contributed to the differentially private output. Since the aggregator has an incentive to cause less noise to be added than necessary, we describe a protocol that can detect a cheating aggregator.

3. ADVERSARIAL MODEL

We consider a strict star topology, i.e., each participant can communicate only with the aggregator, and never with any other participants. Below, we explain several aspects of our adversarial model. To convey just the broad requirements, notation is kept at a minimum. Later on, following the description of our protocols, we will explain in detail how these requirements are satisfied.

Work	Approach	Network Topology	Correctness under Node Failures	Differential Privacy (DP)	Who knows the noise terms used for Differential Privacy?
Shi et al. [22], Bilogrevic et al. [3]	Differentially private aggregation with geometric distribution	Star network + trusted key dealer.	No	Yes	Each participant knows its own contribution.
Chan et al. [4],	Differentially private aggregation with fault tolerance	Star network + trusted key dealer.	Yes	Yes	Each participant knows its own contribution.
Joye and Libert [12]	Private aggregation with a large plaintext space using discrete logarithms	Star network + trusted key dealer.	No	No	N/A
Jawurek and Kerschbaum [11]	Practical scheme with a single additively homomorphic key-pair	Star network + key managing authority	Yes	Yes	Key managing authority knows the noise term in the final sum.
Leontiadis et al. [16]	Private Aggregation with Dynamic Group Management	Star network + untrusted "collector"	Yes	No	N/A
Erkin and Tsudik [9]	Efficient homomorphic aggregation with inter-participant communication	Fully connected network to share random values	No	No	N/A
Ács and Castelluccia [1]	Differentially private aggregation with additive secret sharing	Fully connected network to share secrets	Yes	Yes	Each participant knows its own contribution.
Kursawe et al. [15]	Private aggregation using additive secret sharing	Star network + L "leaders".	No	No	N/A
Garcia and Jacobs [10]	Additive secret sharing with homomorphic encryption	Star network	No	No	N/A
Rane et al. [20]	Shamir secret sharing and homomorphic encryption	Star network	Yes	No	N/A
This paper	Shamir secret sharing and homomorphic encryption, zero-knowledge proof to detect cheating aggregator	Star network	Yes	Yes	Neither participants nor aggregator know individual or final noise terms.

Table 1: Methods and Adversarial Models in the Privacy-preserving Aggregation Literature.

3.1 Participant & Aggregator Obliviousness

Consider that the participants' data elements d_i are collected in a vector denoted by $\mathbf{d}$. We require *Participant Obliviousness*, i.e., the input data, d_i, of a participant should not be revealed to the other participants. Further, we require *Aggregator Obliviousness*, which means that the aggregator discovers only the aggregate function being computed and nothing else about the inputs of individual participants. In our protocols, we first consider the simplest aggregate function, namely the sum of the participants' data. Later, we describe how to extend the summation protocols to the computation of other aggregate measures such as counts and histograms.

A typical assumption in studies of this kind is that the aggregator and all the participants are *semi-honest (honest but curious)*. For our purposes, a semi-honest entity is one which follows the rules of the protocol, but based on the information it sees during each step of the protocol, it can attempt to discover the data held by other entities. In particular, the participants and aggregator do not provide false or spurious inputs to the protocol. During privacy analysis, it then becomes necessary to consider the view of semi-honest participants, and collusions of semi-honest participants.

We remark that, many published works assume semi-honest entities but do not allow certain collusions. For example, in the scheme of Jawurek et al. [11] , the aggregator may not collude with a key authority. In the scheme of Leontiadis et al. [16], the aggregator may not collude with the collector. While these caveats are made in the interest of practical realizability, they present potentially serious concerns, because the forbidden collusion results in catastrophic privacy loss for all honest participants. Our goal, therefore,

is to design aggregation protocols that protect against privacy loss under collusions of all kinds. We go a step further than this by assuming that while the participants are semi-honest, the aggregator is "strictly stronger than semi-honest" in a particular sense, that we will clarify in Section 3.3.

3.2 Differential Privacy (DP)

Recent work on Differential Privacy [6] has shown that aggregator obliviousness is not enough when the aggregator (or an adversary that corrupts the aggregator) has side information about the participants. For example, if this side information consists of the sum of the inputs of $m - 1$ out of m participants, then running a privacy-preserving aggregation protocol with m participants trivially reveals the remaining participant's input. Therefore, to protect against attacks against adversaries armed with background information, we require a differentially private aggregation mechanism.

Let $\mathbf{d}'$ denote a vector that differs from $\mathbf{d}$ in only a single entry. This can be achieved by adding an element to $\mathbf{d}$, or removing a single element from $\mathbf{d}$, or by modifying the value of a single element in $\mathbf{d}$. In this case, $\mathbf{d}$ and $\mathbf{d}'$ are referred to as *adjacent* data sets. Then, (ϵ, δ)−Differential Privacy is defined as follows:

DEFINITION 1. (ϵ, δ)-*Differential Privacy* [7]: An algorithm or protocol or mechanism $\mathcal{M}$ is said to satisfy (ϵ, δ)-Differential Privacy if, for all adjacent data sets $\mathbf{d}$ and $\mathbf{d}'$, and for all sets $\mathcal{S} \subseteq Range(\mathcal{M})$,

$$P(\mathcal{M}(\mathbf{d}) \in \mathcal{S}) \leq e^\epsilon \cdot P(\mathcal{M}(\mathbf{d}') \in \mathcal{S}) + \delta$$

As a consequence of this definition, a differentially private protocol produces *nearly indistinguishable* outputs for adjacent data sets, thus preserving the privacy of the element that is different in $\mathbf{d}$ and $\mathbf{d}'$. The amount of indistinguishability is controlled by the parameters ϵ and δ with lower values implying greater privacy. Differential privacy can be achieved in many ways: One approach is *output perturbation*, which involves first computing a function of the data set and then adding noise to the function result. Another approach is *input perturbation*, which involves first adding noise to the data before evaluating the function result. In either case, a differentially private mechanism will ensure that the function value revealed to the aggregator at the end of the protocol, will contain some additive noise which will protect the participants against attackers equipped with background information. The amount of noise that needs to be added the final aggregate function f depends on the parameters ϵ, δ, and the "global sensitivity" of the function f, denoted by Δ and defined as

$$\Delta = \max_{\mathbf{d},\mathbf{d}'} \| f(\mathbf{d}) - f(\mathbf{d}') \|_1$$

for all adjacent data sets $\mathbf{d}$ and $\mathbf{d}'$.

For example, $(\epsilon, 0)$-Differential Privacy can be achieved by evaluating the function f and adding noise sampled from a Laplace distribution with scale parameter Δ/ϵ. Also, (ϵ, δ)-Differential Privacy can be achieved by evaluating the function f and adding noise sampled from a Gaussian distribution with zero mean and variance $\frac{\Delta}{\epsilon} \ln(1/\delta)$. Other mechanisms are possible in which the noise term is sampled from a different distribution, and is based on the "local sensitivity" rather than the "global sensitivity" [18]. In our scenario of computing aggregate functions on star networks, adding noise to a function value evaluated at the aggregator is not straightforward owing to the competing incentives of the participants and the aggregator which we now elaborate.

3.3 Secure Multiparty Differential Privacy

As we are interested in providing differential privacy to the participants, there are interesting adversarial scenarios that are not captured in pure secure multiparty computation or pure differentially private mechanisms. We now discuss these adversarial scenarios. Before that, we describe precisely the sense in which the aggregator is a more powerful adversary than a traditional semi-honest entity.

Aggregator can influence the noise term: The aggregator wants the revealed aggregate result to be as accurate as possible. Thus, he has an incentive to add a small amount of noise (even no noise at all), which would result in insufficient differential privacy for the participants. In most of the prior literature on differentially private machine learning, the database curator is the entity that adds noise to the data. We contend that when the curator (or analyst, or aggregator) himself has the incentive to obtain accurate measurements, he cannot be trusted to add the correct amount of noise to ensure differential privacy for the participants. In our model, the aggregator can try to influence (e.g., reduce) the level of noise that is added to the aggregate before it is published. By doing this, he can try to force a higher value of ϵ, thus resulting in lower differential privacy. In this respect, he is stronger than the semi-honest entity encountered in traditional secure multiparty computation[1].

Collusions of semi-honest participants: We assume that each participant is semi-honest. It may seem that the way to prevent the aggregator from influencing the noise term is to ask the participants, not the aggregator, to generate noise values for differential privacy. Since the participants are semi-honest, they do not present spurious data or wrongly distributed noise samples to the protocol. However, their curiosity has consequences beyond those normally observed in secure multiparty computation, where the goal of semi-honest

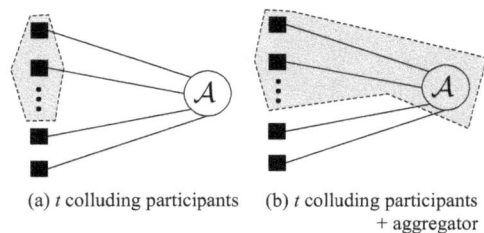

(a) t colluding participants (b) t colluding participants + aggregator

Figure 1: Our adversarial model permits a collusion between a subset of the semi-honest participants (a), or between a subset of the participants and a corrupted aggregator (b).

entities is to discover the data of honest entities. In our adversarial model, the goal of semi-honest entities is, additionally, to make *statistical* inferences about the honest entities that are more accurate than what the specified differential privacy parameter allows.

Consider, for example, the case in Fig. 1(a), in which the aggregator is following the protocol and t participants are honest, but all the remaining $m - t$ participants form a collusion. The colluding participants will now discover the noisy summation output by the aggregator, from which they can subtract their own inputs and their own noise contributions. This leaves the noisy contribution of the t honest participants, which may not guarantee sufficient differential privacy, i.e., a low enough value of ϵ. Thus, it is not sufficient to trust the semi-honest participants to generate noise values. Of course, the adversarial model also allows for the more serious collusion between a corrupted aggregator and a subset of the participants, as shown in Fig. 1(b).

In earlier work, e.g. [3, 22], the above situation is avoided by requiring that some fraction of the participants must remain honest, and that these honest participants must add enough noise to ensure differential privacy. Other earlier work, e.g. [20], does not consider differential privacy, hence a collusion of $m-1$ out of m participants trivially reveals the data of the remaining honest participant even if the aggregator remains honest. We claim that, with a differentially private aggregation protocol, it is possible to protect the lone honest participant even when all other participants collude (provided the aggregator stays honest). Intuitively, the way to achieve this is to have the participants generate noise samples, and make the aggregator blindly pick only a subset of those samples, unbeknownst to the participants. Our protocols will make this notion clear. In particular, we will ensure that an aggregator who tries to choose fewer than the prescribed number of noise samples is caught with overwhelming probability.

Our view is that the adversarial model described here is more realistic than a semi-honest model, and can protect participants in many real-world situations. For example, companies might want to *disaggregate* power usage data gathered from a neighborhood. Noising the power usage can provide some privacy against disaggregation. A ride-sharing service might want to extract ratings received by individual drivers, in order to penalize low scorers. Noising the scores provides some protection for drivers, encouraging them to participate.

---

1. We clarify that the aggregator is *not* as powerful as an "active" or "malicious" adversary in traditional secure multiparty computation. Such an adversary can arbitrarily deviate from the protocol. The corresponding defense mechanisms are significantly more complicated, and possibly impractical to implement.

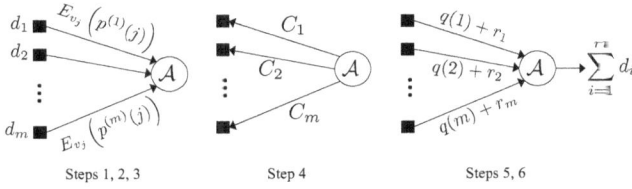

Figure 2: The protocol of Section 4 as described in [20]. Participants send homomorphically encrypted shares to the aggregator $\mathcal{A}$ to indirectly implement Shamir secret sharing in a star network.

4. SECRET SHARING FOR PRIVATE AGGREGATION

We first describe the basic protocol that is used to perform privacy-preserving aggregation in a star topology, without consideration of differential privacy. For this, we leverage existing work in the literature [20], and in subsequent sections, show how to achieve the desired level of differential privacy, even with an adversarial aggregator. As the steps for achieving differential privacy crucially depend on this basic protocol, we will describe it in some detail. In this section, assume that all entities, including the aggregator are semi-honest. Later on, when differentially private mechanisms are considered, we will make the aggregator more powerful, in the sense that he can influence the amount the noise added to the final result output by the protocol. At this point, we are still in the realm of traditional secure multiparty computation and there is no noise being added by any entity. Thus, nothing is lost by assuming a semi-honest aggregator, just for this section.

The protocol with m participants is based on Shamir Secret Sharing [21] and additively homomorphic encryption. The high-level idea is that each of the m participants generates a polynomial with secret coefficients whose constant coefficient is their input data. Each participant evaluates its polynomial at m distinct known points, encrypts the resulting values using the public keys of relevant participants, and sends them to the aggregator. The aggregator homomorphically combines the encrypted shares received from all participants, to obtain encrypted evaluations of a "sum" polynomial at those m points. Upon decrypting these evaluations, the aggregator performs polynomial interpolation to obtain the coefficients of the sum polynomial, evaluates the sum polynomial at $x = 0$ to discover the desired sum of inputs of all participants. A more precise description of the protocol follows below.

Inputs: Denote the aggregator by $\mathcal{A}$, and each participant by $\mathcal{P}_i$, $i = 1, 2, \ldots, m$. Let d_i be the input data held by each participant, such that d_i is a non-negative integer and $d_i < d_{\max}$. Associated with each $\mathcal{P}_i$ is the public-private key pair of a semantically secure additively homomorphic cryptosystem [5, 19]. Denoting the public key for $\mathcal{P}_i$ by v_i, the additive homomorphic property ensures that $E_{v_i}(a)E_{v_i}(b) = E_{v_i}(a + b)$. The semantic security property implies that a given plaintext maps to a different ciphertext at every encryption, thus providing protection against Chosen Plaintext Attacks (CPA).

Output: The aggregator discovers $\sum_{i=1}^{m} d_i$. The participants discover nothing else.

Protocol: Consider the following steps, also shown in Fig. 2:

1. The aggregator broadcasts a large prime number $\beta > md_{\max}$ to all participants.

2. Each participant, $\mathcal{P}_i, i = 1, 2, ..., m$ generates a polynomial

of degree $k < m$ given by:

$$p^{(i)}(x) = d_i + p_1^{(i)}x + p_2^{(i)}x^2 + \ldots + p_k^{(i)}x^k \mod \beta$$

where the coefficients $p_s^{(i)}$ where $s = 1, 2, .., k$, are chosen uniformly at random from the interval $[0, \beta)$. By construction, note also that $p^{(i)}(0) = d_i < \beta$, i.e., evaluating the polynomial at zero yields each participant's input data.

3. Each participant $\mathcal{P}_i$ evaluates the polynomial at m known, distinct points. Without loss of generality, let these points be the integers $j = 1, 2, \ldots, m$. Then, each $\mathcal{P}_i$ encrypts $p^{(i)}(j)$ using the public key v_j of the participants $\mathcal{P}_j, j = 1, 2, ..., m$, and sends the ciphertexts $E_{v_j}(p^{(i)}(j))$ to the aggregator, $\mathcal{A}$.

4. For each $i = 1, 2, \ldots, m$, the aggregator computes

$$E_{v_j}(r_j)\prod_{i=1}^{m} E_{v_j}(p^{(i)}(j)) = E_{v_j}\left(r_j + \sum_{i=1}^{m} p^{(i)}(j)\right)$$
$$= E_{v_j}(r_j + q(j)) = C_j$$

The aggregator then sends each $C_j, j = 1, 2, \ldots, m$ to participant $\mathcal{P}_j$ for decryption. Here, the constant r_j is chosen at random to hide the summation term from $\mathcal{P}_j$.

5. The participants $\mathcal{P}_j$ who are still online, decrypt the respective C_j and returns it to the aggregator. The aggregator subtracts r_j and obtains, for $j \subset \{1, 2, \ldots, m\}$, the values

$$q(j) = \sum_{i=1}^{m} p^{(i)}(j) \mod \beta$$

6. By construction, the above steps have enabled the aggregator to evaluate the polynomial,

$$q(x) = q_1 x + q_2 x^2 + \ldots + q_k x^k + \sum_{i=1}^{m} d_i \mod \beta$$

at some points in the set $\{1, 2, \ldots, m\}$. In order to recover the coefficients $q_1, q_2, \ldots, q_k$ and the desired summation, the aggregator needs the polynomial $q(x)$ to be evaluated at $k + 1$ or more points, i.e., the aggregator needs at least $k+1$ participants to be online. If this requirement is satisfied, the aggregator can perform polynomial interpolation to obtain $q_1, q_2, \ldots, q_k$, and recover the value of $q_0 = \sum_{i=1}^{m} d_i$, which is the quantity of interest.

Correctness: The use of additively homomorphic encryption with the appropriate participant's public keys distributes shares of the desired summation to the participants who are still online. Functionally, this is equivalent to distributing polynomial secret shares, and performing additions in the BGW protocol [2]. Alternatively, correctness follows from the realization that Shamir secret sharing is additively homomorphic modulo β.

Fault-Tolerance: The degree of the "sum" polynomial is $k < m$. Hence, the protocol is fault tolerant: The aggregator can compute the summation even when up to $m - k - 1$ participants go offline after Step 3, i.e., before polynomial interpolation is used to extract the final sum from the shares.

Privacy: First, consider privacy against individual semi-honest entities. Secret sharing ensures that no participant discovers the data held by an honest participant. Furthermore, the homomorphic cryptosystem ensures that the aggregator only discovers the coefficients

119

of the "sum" polynomial $q(x)$, but does not discover the coefficients of the component polynomials $p^{(i)}(x)$. The privacy guarantee against individual semi-honest participants is information-theoretic, while that against the aggregator is computational.

Next, consider privacy against collusions of semi-honest entities. An adversary that corrupts $m - 1$ out of m participants, can examine the published summation and discover the data of the remaining honest participant (We *can* protect the lone honest participant using a differentially private mechanism that we will describe in Section 5). Next, consider semi-honest coalitions that also contain the aggregator. In order to discover the data d_i of an honest participant $\mathcal{P}_i$, the coalition needs to access at least $k + 1$ decrypted polynomial secret shares $p^{(i)}(j)$ for $j \in \{1, 2, ..., m\}$ and perform polynomial interpolation. To achieve this, the coalition must comprise the aggregator and at least $k + 1$ other semi-honest participants. In other words, the protocol preserves privacy of an honest participant against coalitions consisting of the aggregator and up to k other participants.

Complexity: The ciphertext communication complexity of the protocol is $O(m^2)$ as determined by Step 3. Similarly, the ciphertext computation complexity is also $O(m^2)$ as determined by Step 4. Note that, the aggregator has to perform polynomial interpolation in Step 5. This can be accomplished using Lagrange interpolation, which has $O(m^2)$ complexity [13].

5. DIFFERENTIALLY PRIVATE AGGREGATION PROTOCOLS

Our approach is to make the participants and the aggregator generate and add noise to the aggregate function through interaction. This becomes challenging under the adversarial model described earlier. The aggregator has an incentive to add as little noise as possible. Furthermore, even if the aggregator is honest, it is very difficult to ensure differential privacy of a participant when all other participants are colluding. Our approach is to design protocols in which neither the aggregator nor any participant finds out the noise value that has been added to the final summation. In fact, we have a slightly stronger requirement: No single participant can discover how much noise she herself contributed to the final summation.

Broadly, the protocol has two phases: (1) Cheating-proof noise generation, and (2) Secure aggregation. In the first phase, the noise term is generated via interactions between the entities, in such a way that cheating attempts can be detected. The second phase executes the secure aggregation protocol of Section 4 such that the aggregated result will incorporate the noise term to guarantee differential privacy. We assume the following setup for all of the protocols (and sub-protocols) of this section.

Setup & Public Parameters: As before, denote the aggregator by $\mathcal{A}$, and each participant by $\mathcal{P}_i$, $i = 1, 2, \ldots, m$. The aggregator has a public-private key pair of a semantically secure additively homomorphic cryptosystem. The public key of the aggregator is denoted by v_A. The plaintext domain of the aggregator is $\mathbb{D}_A$. Let F, F_S denote noise distributions over $\mathbb{R}$. (For example, F is the Laplacian distribution with parameter $\frac{\Delta}{\epsilon}$, denoted by $\mathrm{Lap}(\Delta/\epsilon)$.)

Inputs: Each $\mathcal{P}_i$ has input data d_i. The aggregator has no inputs.

Output: The aggregator discovers $\sum_{i=1}^{m} d_i + \xi$, where $\xi \sim F$ is the noise term. The participants do not discover anything.

Protocol: Consider the following steps:

1. The participants and the aggregator jointly execute the cheating-proof noise generation protocol, to be described in Section 5.2.

Participant i obtains blinding term r_i. The aggregator obtains (from $\mathcal{P}_i$) a value $r_i + \xi_i$ for every participant, and computes the sum, $\sum_{i=1}^{m}(r_i + \xi_i)$.

2. The participants and the aggregator jointly execute the private aggregation protocol of Section 4, with every $\mathcal{P}_i$'s input set to $d_i - r_i$. The aggregator obtains the value $\sum_{i=1}^{m}(d_i - r_i)$ via interactions with the participants who are still online during Step 5 of the protocol in Section 4. It then calculates:

$$\sum_{i=1}^{m}(d_i - r_i) + \sum_{i=1}^{m}(r_i + \xi_i) = \sum_{i=1}^{m} d_i + \xi$$

which is the desired noised sum with $\xi = \sum_{i=1}^{m} \xi_i$.

In the subsections that follow, we describe the protocol in more detail. We first explain how the noise term needed for differential privacy can be computed by aggregating noise samples generated by the participants. Then, we describe the protocol to achieve differential privacy and analyze it with respect to correctness, fault-tolerance, and privacy under the threat model described in Section 3. [2]

5.1 Sampling Noise for Differential Privacy

There are several ways to sample noise in order to satisfy differential privacy. The popular Laplacian mechanism adds noise from the Laplace distribution, but other distributions (e.g., Gaussian) can be used as well [7]. In our setting, it is not sufficient to sample a single noise term from an appropriate distribution. Indeed, neither the participants nor the aggregator should find out the sampled noise value, and so no entity should perform the sampling on its own. Instead, we propose to sample the noise as the sum of several noise terms generated by the participants. Formally, we model the noise term ξ as a random variable $X \sim F$. The idea is to generate X as the sum of some i.i.d. random variables X_i.

Consider first the case where F is the Gaussian distribution. Write $S_n = \frac{1}{n}\sum_{i=1}^{n} X_i$, where X_i are i.i.d. random variables from some distribution F_S with finite variance σ^2. We know by the Central Limit Theorem (CLT) that $\sqrt{n}(S_n - E[S_n])$ converges in distribution to $\mathcal{N}(0, \sigma^2)$. This observation allows us to generate noise that approximately follows a Gaussian distribution with a given variance. Note that (ϵ, δ)-differential privacy can be achieved using Gaussian noise (see Section 3.2).

What if, instead, we want to achieve ϵ-differential privacy (i.e., $\delta = 0$)? This requires F to be a Laplace distribution, specifically $F = \mathrm{Lap}(\Delta/\epsilon)$. This can be accomplished using a similar idea for generating X by exploiting the infinite divisibility of the Laplace distribution [14]. Concretely, if X is a Laplace random variable with mean zero and scale parameter b, then for any $n \geq 1$, there exist i.i.d. random variables X_i such that $X = \sum_{i=1}^{n} X_i$. For example, this holds if $X_i = Y_{1,i} - Y_{2,i}$, where the random variables $Y_{1,i}, Y_{2,i}$ are distributed as $\mathrm{Gamma}(1/n, b)$.

More generally, we consider generating noise from any distribution F which can satisfy differential privacy, as long as we can sample $X \sim F$ by sampling i.i.d. X_i's for some distribution F_S such that $X = a_n \sum_{i=1}^{n} X_i$, for some constant a_n. It may also be

2. In addition to the adversarial actions described in Section 3, other deviations are possible. For example, a participant can be online but could refuse to provide the decryption key in Step 5 in the protocol of Section 4. In our construction, such deviations fall into the category of failures, from which recovery is possible owing to the fault tolerance provided by Shamir Secret Sharing. We also remark that the aggregator has no incentive to deviate in a way that would result in a failure to complete the protocol because that implies a failure to obtain the aggregate sum.

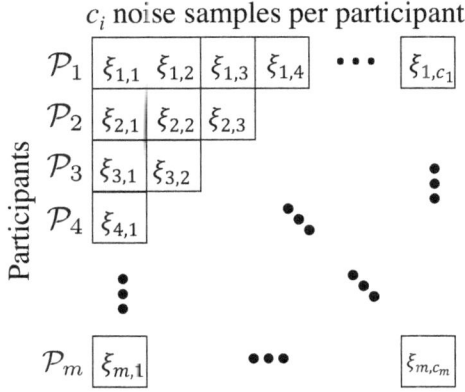

Figure 3: Every participant i generates c_i noise terms of the form $\xi_{i,j}$. The noise generation protocol ensures that, for the purpose of providing differential privacy, n out of these terms are aggregated into the final noise term ξ, without the participants discovering which n terms were included.

possible to exploit the geometric stability of the Laplace distribution, although we do not consider this explicitly here.

To deal with collusions, we will further set the parameters such that if only $n' < n$ terms are added to the sum, the noise is sufficient to ensure differential privacy. That is, if F_S is the distribution of the X_i's, we will choose the parameters such that $\sum_{i=1}^{n'} X_i = X \sim F$. This satisfies differential privacy since the final noise term will be $X + \hat{X}$, where $\hat{X}$ is a sum of up to $n - n'$ random variables distributed according to F_S independent of X. Clearly, if adding X is sufficient to satisfy differential privacy, then so is adding $X + \hat{X}$.

As discussed in the related work section, we are not the first to propose the idea of having participants generate noise samples that are eventually accumulated into a noise term from a desired distribution. The novel aspect of our treatment is, rather, in the adversarial incentives of the participants and the aggregator, and in the measures taken to detect such adversarial actions. These adversarial incentives, and detection measures are not considered in the prior art.

5.2 Noise Generation Phase

We present a double-blind noise addition protocol in which the participants generate noise components and the aggregator obliviously computes an overall noise term. This is achieved without the aggregator learning the noise term or being able to influence it (without being detected). To ensure that the aggregator does not cheat and influence the noise sampled, we use a lightweight verifiable computation subprotocol. In general, there are two challenges in such proofs of computation: (a) the proof must not reveal information (e.g., amount of noise), and (b) the protocol must be efficient. While the first concern could be addressed by using generic zero-knowledge proof techniques, the second concern (i.e., efficiency) remains. Therefore, we design a custom solution that exploits the structure and statistical properties of the computation. We first explain the protocol used to derive the overall noise term. The sub-protocol used to detect a cheating aggregator is explained immediately afterward in this section.

Setup: Let t, l be positive integers (security parameters). Let n be a positive integer ($n \geq m$), and F_S be a distribution such that $(\sum_{i=1}^n X_i) \sim F$, where $X_i \sim F_S$.

Inputs: The participants and the aggregator have no inputs.

Output: The aggregator obtains $\xi + r$, where ξ is a noise term distributed according to F. The participants have no output.

Protocol: Consider the following steps:

1. Each participant $\mathcal{P}_i$ chooses values $r_{i,j} \in \mathbb{D}_A$, and samples values $\xi_{i,j}$ from F_S, for $j = 1, 2, \ldots, t \cdot \lceil \frac{n}{m} \rceil$. This is depicted in Fig. 3.

2. For $i = 1, 2, \ldots, m$, the aggregator sets $c_i = t \cdot s_i$, where $s_i = \lfloor \frac{n}{m} \rfloor + \mathbb{1}_{\{i \leq n \pmod m\}}$. The aggregator then generates the binary sequence $b_{i,j} \in \{0, 1\}$, for $i = 1, 2, \ldots, m$, and $j = 1, 2, \ldots, c_i$, such that:

   - $\sum_{i,j} b_{i,j} = n$
   - $\sum_{t'=1}^{t} b_{i,t \cdot s + t'} = 1$, for $s = 0, 1, \ldots s_i - 1$:

   That is, the binary sequence $b_{i,j}$ has n ones (and $tn - n$ zeros), and for each i, $b_{i,j}$ consists of s_i sub-sequences each containing a single 1. An example of the binary sequence is depicted in Fig. 4. For $i = 1, 2, \ldots, m$, $\mathcal{A}$ sends $E_{v_A}(b_{i,j})$ to $\mathcal{P}_i$, for $j = 1, 2, \ldots, c_i$. In this step, a cheating aggregator can attempt to reduce the number of 1's in the selector vector of one or more participants. As we shall see, the fewer the number of 1's, the lower the amount of noise in the final computed aggregate. To detect such cheating, we require that the aggregator prove to every participant $\mathcal{P}_i$, that the above conditions on the $b_{i,j}$ are satisfied. However, the participants must not know the binary values $b_{i,j}$, so this proof should be carried out in zero knowledge. In Section 5.4, we describe an efficient method to accomplish this.

3. Each participant $\mathcal{P}_i$ computes for $j = 1, 2, \ldots, c_i$:

   $$e_{i,j} = E_{v_A}(b_{i,j})^{\xi_{i,j}} \cdot E_{v_A}(r_{i,j}) = E_{v_A}(b_{i,j}\xi_{i,j} + r_{i,j}).$$

   $\mathcal{P}_i$ then sends the values $e_{i,j}$ to the aggregator.

4. For $i = 1, 2, \ldots, m$, the aggregator computes $\prod_{j=1}^{c_i} e_{i,j} = E_{v_A}(\xi_i + r_i)$, where $\xi_i = \sum_{j:b_{i,j}=1} \xi_{i,j}$ and $r_i = \sum_{j=1}^{c_i} r_{i,j}$. Note that ξ_i is sum of only those $\xi_{i,j}$'s such that $b_{i,j} = 1$. $\mathcal{A}$ decrypts each term $\xi_i + r_i$ and computes its output as: $\sum_{i=1}^{m}(\xi_i + r_i) = \xi + r$.

Correctness: We show that the protocol correctly computes the sum $\xi + r$, where $\xi = \sum_{s=1}^{n} \xi_s$, and $r = \sum_{i=1}^{m} r_i$. Notice that, for j such that $b_{i,j} = 1$, participant i homomorphically computes the encryption of $\xi_{i,j} + r_{i,j}$. Thus, as there are n pairs (i,j) such that $b_{i,j} = 1$, the output that the aggregator computes is: $\sum_{(i,j):b_{i,j}=1} \xi_{i,j} + \sum_i (\sum_j r_{i,j})$. This quantity is $\sum_{s=1}^{n} \xi_s + r$, for some random r. The result follows by noting that each summand of $\sum_{s=1}^{n} \xi_s$ contains only one noise sample and is distributed according to F_S.

5.3 Secure Aggregation Phase

Once the noise term has been generated, the participants run the private aggregation protocol of Section 4 with the aggregator. Specifically, each online participant i sets his input to be $d_i - r_i$, where $r_i = \sum_j r_{i,j}$ generated in the first phase.

Correctness: This follows from the fact that

$$\sum_{i=1}^{m}(d_i - r_i) + \sum_{i=1}^{m}(r_i + \xi_i) = \sum_{i=1}^{n} d_i + \xi.$$

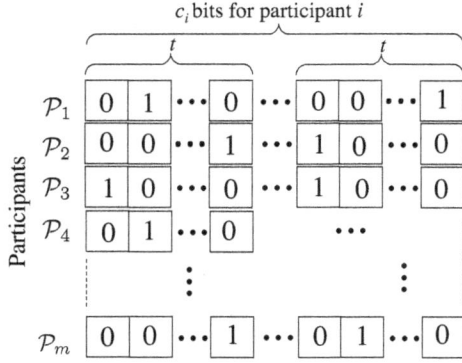

Figure 4: The aggregator generates a c_i-length selector vector for each participant i. The binary values, $b_{i,j}$, are encrypted and used to select which of the noise samples $\xi_{i,j}$ generated by the participants (See Fig. 3) will be added up to generate the final noise term ξ.

Fault-tolerance: We require that the participants send all their values $e_{i,j}$ (step 3 of the noise generation phase) and their evaluated polynomial points (step 3 of the private aggregation protocol of Section 4) in a single message (i.e., an atomic operation) to the aggregator. This ensures that, for each participant i, the aggregator gets all the $e_{i,j}$'s and the $E_{v_j}(p^{(i)}(j))$'s in one step. If he does not (e.g., if $\mathcal{P}_i$ fails) then participant i's values are ignored from the protocol. This is sufficient to ensure that fault-tolerance follows from the private aggregation protocol of Section 4. Indeed, if a participant $\mathcal{P}_i$ fails (or goes offline) before delivering its $e_{i,j}$'s and the $E_{v_j}(p^{(i)}(j))$'s, then none of r_i, ξ_i, or d_i will be included in the sum $\sum_j (d_j - r_j) + \sum_j (r_j + \xi_j) = \sum_j d_j + \xi$, which only includes the participants who are online until that step. If $\mathcal{P}_i$ fails after that step, then the blinded noise term $r_i + \xi_i$ will be known to the aggregator, and the fault-tolerance property of the private aggregation protocol ensures that his input (i.e., $d_i - r_i$) is included in the final result.

We emphasize that while $d_i - r_i$ is blinded (i.e., independent of d_i if r_i is not known), it cannot directly be sent to the aggregator. Indeed, given $r_i + \xi_i$ (obtained after the first phase) and $d_i - r_i$, the aggregator can compute $d_i + \xi_i$, but ξ_i is not enough noise (in general) to satisfy differential privacy. This is why the private aggregation protocol of Section 4 is used.

5.4 Detecting a Cheating Aggregator

As described above, the aggregator has no control over the noise terms generated by the participants. However, the aggregator generates the bit selector vector, i.e., the $b_{i,j}$'s. Thus the participants need to ensure that the $b_{i,j}$'s were correctly generated such that enough noise may be added. To do this, we use a protocol proposed by Stern [23], for proving in zero-knowledge that an encrypted vector includes only a single 1 and that the other elements are all 0s. We reproduce this protocol here for convenience.

Inputs: The prover $\mathcal{P}$ has a t bit vector $b_1, b_2, \ldots, b_t$, and an index $x \in \{1, 2, \ldots, t\}$ such that $b_x = 1$, but $b_{x'} = 0$, for $x' \neq x$. There is a public-private key pair of semantically secure additively homomorphic cryptosystem associated with $\mathcal{P}$. The public key is known to the verifier and is denoted by v_P. The verifier $\mathcal{V}$ has no inputs.

Output: The verifier determines that the prover's bit vector contains exactly $t - 1$ zeros and a single one, with probability $1 -$

$(4/5)^l$, for some positive integer l.

Protocol (from [23]):

1. $\mathcal{P}$ computes $E_{v_P}(b_i)$, for $i = 1, 2, \ldots, t$, and sends the results to $\mathcal{V}$.

2. $\mathcal{P}$ and $\mathcal{V}$ repeat l times the following steps:

   (a) $\mathcal{P}$ computes $e_0 = E_{v_P}(0)$ and $e_1 = E_{v_P}(1)$, and sends the results to $\mathcal{V}$

   (b) $\mathcal{V}$ picks $r \in_R \{1, 2, 3, 4, 5\}$.

   (c) If $r = 1$, then $\mathcal{V}$ asks $\mathcal{P}$ to reveal the plaintexts of e_0 and e_1.

   (d) Otherwise, $\mathcal{V}$ randomly partitions $\{1, 2, \ldots, t\}$ into (disjoint) subsets A and B, and calculates:
   - $e_a = \prod_{i \in A} E_{v_P}(b_i) = E_{v_P}(\sum_{i \in A} b_i)$, and
   - $e_b = \prod_{i \in B} E_{v_P}(b_i) = E_{v_P}(\sum_{i \in B} b_i)$.

   $\mathcal{V}$ then sends A and B to $\mathcal{P}$.

   (e) $\mathcal{P}$ proves that e_a and e_b represent ciphertexts of the same numbers as those of e_0 and e_1.

Using this protocol, we describe below, the sub-protocol to detect a cheating aggregator. As before, the steps in the protocol below are numbered according to the stage at which they occur in the protocol described in Section 5.2.

Inputs: There are no inputs.

Output: The participants determine if the aggregator is cheating.

(Sub)-Protocol:

2b Each participant $\mathcal{P}_i$ runs step 2 of the Stern protocol for $s = 0, 1, \ldots, s_i$ to verify that $E_{v_A}(b_{i, t \cdot s + t'})$, for $t' = 1, 2, \ldots, t$, is the encryption of $t - 1$ zeros, and 1 one. The participant plays the role of the verifier and the aggregator plays the role of the prover.

If $\mathcal{P}_i$ detects cheating from $\mathcal{A}$, it aborts and attempts to notify the other participants.

Security: Follows directly from [23]. Note that this protocol can also detect whether the aggregator has chosen non-binary values for any of the $b_{i,j}$'s.

5.5 Privacy Analysis

For non-colluding entities we evaluate the privacy against a single semi-honest participant and against the aggregator. For colluding entities, we evaluate privacy when semi-honest participants collude among themselves and when some participants collude with the cheating aggregator as shown in Fig. 1.

Privacy against a non-colluding semi-honest participant: Each $\mathcal{P}_i$ observes only semantically secure encryptions of the $b_{i,j}$'s. Because $\mathcal{P}_i$ does not know which of the $b_{i,j}$'s are encryptions of 1s, all he knows is that ξ_i will be one of the t^{s_i} possible combinations of the $\xi_{i,j}$. Any other participant $\mathcal{P}_{i'}$, $i' \neq i$ cannot discover the data $d_{i'}$ or the noise term $\xi_{i'}$.

Privacy against colluding semi-honest participants: Though the participants cannot directly communicate with each other, one can consider an attack in which a single entity compromises several participants (e.g., readings from several sensors are sent to a remote server engaging in industrial espionage). Once the protocol is completed, and the aggregator publishes the noisy summation, this entity can subtract the data d_i held by the participants in the colluding set. However, in the protocol of Section 5.2, none of the participants can tell which of their generated noise samples were aggregated into the final summation. This is because, the bits $b_{i,j}$ that determine which samples are chosen and which are discarded, are encrypted under the aggregator's key.

Let $\mathcal{S}$ be the colluding set and $\widetilde{\mathcal{S}}$ be the non-colluding set, where $|\mathcal{S} \bigcup \widetilde{\mathcal{S}}| = m$, and $|\mathcal{S} \bigcap \widetilde{\mathcal{S}}| = \phi$. Participants in $\mathcal{S}$ can recover:

$$\sum_{i=1}^{m}(d_i + \xi_i) - \sum_{j \in \mathcal{S}} d_j = \sum_{i \in \widetilde{\mathcal{S}}} d_i + \sum_{i=1}^{m} \xi_i$$

Thus, the colluders cannot cancel out their own noise samples from the published aggregate, so the term on the right hand side contains more noise than is needed to ensure differential privacy of the honest participants. For $1 \leq |\mathcal{S}| \leq m - 1$, the colluding participants cannot reduce the differential privacy of the honest participants.

Privacy against the aggregator: Since participants follow the protocol honestly, the noise added will be of the correct distribution F. The aggregator observes $\sum_i d_i - r_i$, and for every participant i, he observes the $e_{i,j}$'s. By itself, the summation $\sum_i d_i - r_i$ conveys no information about the participants' inputs d_i owing to the blinding terms r_i. Recall that whenever $b_{i,j} = 1$, $e_{i,j}$ is an encryption of $\xi_{i,j} + r_{i,j}$, which conveys no information about $\xi_{i,j}$, because $r_{i,j}$ is chosen uniformly at random within its domain. (In other words, $\xi_{i,j} + r_{i,j}$ is statistically independent of $\xi_{i,j}$). When $b_{i,j} = 0$, then $e_{i,j}$ is an encryption of $r_{i,j}$, and $\xi_{i,j}$ will not be included in ξ_i. Finally, from $\xi_i + r_i = \sum_{j:b_{i,j}=1} \xi_{i,j} + r_i$, and $\sum_i d_i - r_i$, the aggregator learns no information about d_i or ξ_i, other than what it can learn from $\sum_i d_i + \xi_i$. Thus, the aggregator learns neither the individual noise terms ξ_i, nor the amount of noise added, $\sum_i \xi_i$, nor the participant's private inputs d_i, nor their noise-free sum $\sum_i d_i$.

As we have argued in Section 5.4, the aggregator cannot convincingly cheat by preparing a bit vector $b_{i,j}$ which is not of the proper form. A cheating aggregator might also want to exclude some participants in an effort to learn more about the remaining participants inputs. To see why he cannot exclude too many participants, recall that he needs at least $k + 1$ out of m participants to obtain the summation, where k is the degree of the secret sharing polynomial.

Privacy against aggregator colluding with (some) participants: Unfortunately, the above favorable situation is lost if the aggregator is part of the colluding set. Suppose the aggregator colludes with some number k' of participants. Through such a coalition, the aggregator can subtract the noise generated by the colluding participants and also their private inputs. Thus, it is as if only $m - k'$ participants participated in the protocol, since the noise terms (and the inputs) of the honest participants are independent of those of the colluding participants. Further, by exploiting the fault tolerance, the aggregator can exclude up to $m - (k + 1)$ participants from the protocol and still get a noised sum over the inputs of the non-excluded participants. This means that, at least $k - 1 - k'$ honest participants will take part in the protocol. In principle, differential privacy can be guaranteed in this situation if the variance of the noise terms ξ_i contributed by those honest participants is large enough. E.g., if $k + 1 = \frac{2m}{3}$, and $k' = \frac{m}{3}$, then we need to choose the individual noise contributions such that the $k + 1 - k' = \frac{m}{3}$ honest (and non-failing) participants' noise terms add up to a sample from the distribution F. In practice, however, this defensive strategy is hard to implement because an honest participant does not know how many participants are colluding with the aggregator, and thus might not be able to choose his noise terms $\xi_{i,j}$ correctly.

Parameter Set	t	s	$t \cdot s$	l	p_{cheat}	t^s
Resource Bound	2	48	96	62	$\approx 2^{-20}$	2^{48}
High Security	2	80	160	125	$\approx 2^{-40}$	2^{80}

Table 2: Suggested security parameters. The probability p_{cheat} is the probability that the aggregator successfully fools a participant when running the cheating detection protocol. The quantity t^s is the number of possible noise terms.

Limitation: The star topology implies that honest participants can only communicate through (i.e., with the help of) the aggregator. Thus, a participant unfairly excluded from the protocol or one who detects the aggregator cheating is not guaranteed to be able to inform other participants. We remark that this is not a problem for this participant's privacy since he may simply abort the protocol thereby not revealing anything about his private input.

5.6 Choosing Security Parameters

We now discuss how to set the security parameters t, l, and n. In the noise generation protocol, $\mathcal{P}_i$ calculates c_i encrypted values. For simplicity, it is convenient to take $s = s_i$ to be fixed for all i, so that we have that $c_i = t \cdot s$ for all participants. In such cases, we have $s = \frac{n}{m}$, as n is a multiple of m. Naturally, the larger the values of t, l, and s, the higher the security. That said, both the communication and computation costs of each participant depend on these parameters. In fact, this cost is $O(t \cdot s \cdot l)$, where $O(t \cdot s)$ is the communication cost and computation cost for the $e_{i,j}$'s, and $O(l \cdot s \cdot t)$ is the cost of the protocol to detect a cheating aggregator.

Thus, parameter selection is a trade-off between the communication and computation costs and the level of security achieved. In terms of security, we want to maximize: (1) the probability of detecting a cheating aggregator, and (2) the number of possible final noise terms ξ_i for each participant given his noise components $\xi_{i,j}$. For (1) recall that the probability of detecting a cheating aggregator is $1 - (4/5)^l$ using the protocol of Section 5.4.[3] For (2) we want to ensure that the space of all possible final noise terms ξ_i produced by each participant given the components $\xi_{i,j}$ cannot feasibly be explored. (If a participant can explore a non-negligible fraction of that space, he gets information about the distribution of his noise term ξ_i.) Recall that there are t^s possible such combinations.

Table 2 shows two sets of parameters: one for resource-constrained devices which minimizes the communication and computation costs given an acceptable security level, and one providing a higher level of security but with increased communication and computation costs.

5.7 Implementation Considerations

Our noise adding technique (Section 5.1) consists in summing i.i.d. random variables. It is easier to work with integers, since the plaintext domain of additive homomorphic cryptosystems is typically the set of integers modulo some large positive integer. When the noise term is a real number, we can encode it into the plaintext domain using a fixed point representation. Concretely, we take

---

3. For the noise of a participant $\mathcal{P}_i$ to be eliminated or significantly reduced, the number of cheating attempts made by the aggregator must be comparable to the number of times the detection protocol is run, i.e., s. Otherwise, only a small fraction of the noise components $\xi_{i,j}$ will be affected. This, and the fact that the aggregator's cheating need only be detected once (as any failure leads to the protocol being aborted), implies that the *effective* probability that the aggregator fools participant i by cheating $s' \leq s$ times is the probability that the aggregator fools participant i all s' times. Therefore, we can drastically reduce the value of l (reducing the communication and computation costs) while keeping (almost) the same security.

a large positive integer exponent a. We then encode the number $x \in \mathbb{R}$ as the positive integer $x_a = \lfloor x \cdot 2^a \rfloor$. If the maximum allowable number of bits in the plaintext domain is b, then we must take $a < b$. This encodes exactly all numbers, x, whose decimal part can be fully represented in a digits or less, and allows us to represent numbers whose integer part is as large as 2^{b-a}. We can perform homomorphic additions as usual, provided all ciphertexts involved have had their plaintext encoded in the same fashion (with the same exponent a). To recover x after decryption, we simply divide the integer by 2^a and take the result as a real number.

Recall that multiplication of two numbers x and y can be performed with an additively homomorphic cryptosystem provided one number is encrypted, and the other number is available in plain text. Here, two cases arise in our protocols: Either the encrypted number (say x) is an integer and the plaintext number (say y) is a real number, or vice versa. Let v be a public key. Then, if x is a real number, we can simply perform $E_v(x_a)^y = E_v((xy)_a)$. On the other hand, if x is an integer and y is a real number, then given the ciphertext $E_v(x)$, we need to perform: $E_v(x)^{y_a} = E_v((xy)_a)$.

Due to the fixed point representation, not all real numbers can be exactly represented, but this is not a significant concern because the plaintext domain used in practice is quite large (e.g., 2^{1024} or even 2^{2048}) as it is related to the key size in bits. Another concern is that differential privacy might not be achieved due to the approximate nature of the noise sampled, but this is not the case. In fact, textbook floating point implementations are vulnerable to attacks as demonstrated by Mironov [17] while integer or fixed-point representations are not vulnerable to such attacks.

Negative integers can be represented by using the upper half of the plaintext domain: i.e., if the plaintext domain is $\{0, 1, \ldots, M-1\}$, then $-x$, for $1 \leq x \leq \lfloor \frac{M}{2} \rfloor$, is represented as the positive integer $M - x$. When decrypting or decoding we interpret a result as negative if it is greater than or equal $\lceil \frac{M}{2} \rceil$.

6. RELATED PROTOCOLS

The privacy-preserving summation protocol extends to other queries as we describe below. These extensions have also been considered in [20], but without regard for differential privacy as we do here.

Count queries: The aggregator wants to count the number of participants $\mathcal{P}_i$, whose data x_i falls in a set $\mathcal{P}$. The aggregator broadcasts $\mathcal{P}$, and each participant sets their input to the protocol as $d_i = 1$ if $x_i \in \mathcal{P}$, and $d_i = 0$ otherwise. The proposed protocol is then a count query on the set $\mathcal{P}$. To determine the distribution of the noise term for achieving differential privacy in the final count, note that the global sensitivity of the count query is $\Delta = 1$.

Histograms: The aggregator wants to compute a histogram based on data x_i held by the participants. It broadcasts a set of disjoint bins $\mathcal{B}_1, \mathcal{B}_2, \ldots, \mathcal{B}_h$ to the participants. Each participant $\mathcal{P}_i$ constructs a binary vector $\mathbf{d}_i \in \{0, 1\}^h$ where the jth element $d_{ij} = 1$ if $x_i \in \mathcal{B}_j$, otherwise $d_{ij} = 0$. Then the participants and the aggregator run a count query for each of the h bins, at the end of which the aggregator obtains the desired histogram without discovering the individual vectors $\mathbf{d}_i$. As a histogram is a generalization of a count query, the distribution of the noise term for achieving differential privacy in the aggregator's output histogram is again based on global sensitivity of a count query, i.e., $\Delta = 1$.

Linear combinations: For $i = 1, 2, \ldots, N$, the aggregator wants to run a classifier with non-negative weights $c_i < c_{\max}$ on the participants' inputs d_i to determine whether $\mathbf{c}^T \mathbf{d} \lessgtr b$. This is achieved by using a slightly modified version of the protocol in Section 4: In

Step 4, the aggregator computes the ciphertexts C_j using:

$$E_{v_j}(r_j) \prod_{i=1}^{m} E_{v_j}(p^{(i)}(j))^{c_i} = E_{v_j}\left(r_j + \sum_{i=1}^{m} c_i p^{(i)}(j)\right)$$

Consequently, in Step 5, the aggregator gets $q(j) = \sum_{i=1}^{m} c_i p^{(i)}(j)$ mod β. Here, the large prime number is chosen as $\beta > mc_{\max}d_{\max}$. Then, in Step 6, it evaluates the polynomial,

$$q(x) = q_1 x + q_2 x^2 + \ldots + q_k x^k + \sum_{i=1}^{m} c_i d_i \quad \mod \beta$$

at $k + 1$ or more points. While participant privacy is maintained as before, this process leaks more information than just the comparison $\mathbf{c}^T \mathbf{d} \lessgtr b$, as the aggregator discovers the value of $\mathbf{c}^T \mathbf{d}$.

One salient feature though, is that the aggregator does not need to reveal the classifier weights c_i to any of the participants. Multiple linear combinations (hence classifiers) can thus be realized, *without repeating the polynomial secret sharing step* in Section 4. This is an advantage over the prior art. Specifically, although the prior art could also be extended to compute linear combinations, in most cases ([1, 3, 4, 9, 12, 15, 16, 22]), the protocols have to reveal the weights c_i to the participants. Moreover, they have to repeat the secret sharing step whenever a new linear combination is computed.

In a differentially private realization, the classifier boundaries will be perturbed because of the noise term that is added to the inner product $\mathbf{c}^T \mathbf{d}$. The privacy/utility tradeoff is then based on the ϵ and δ values, and the classification error that occurs as a consequence of adding noise. Recall that, the distribution of the noise term ξ to be added to $\mathbf{c}^T \mathbf{d}$ is based on the global sensitivity of the linear combination, which is $\Delta = c_{\max}d_{\max}$. In this case, the aggregator has to multiply not just the perturbed data terms $d_i - r_i$, but also the perturbed noise terms $r_i + \xi_i$ of participant $\mathcal{P}_i$ with the constant c_i, to ensure that:

$$\sum_{i=1}^{m} c_i(d_i - r_i) + \sum_{i=1}^{m} c_i(r_i + \xi_i) = \sum_{i=1}^{m} c_i d_i + \xi$$

Note that, as the distribution of noise term ξ depends on $c_{\max}$, the aggregator must reveal $c_{\max}$ (but fortunately not the individual c_i's) to all participants, so that they can generate the appropriate candidate noise samples.

7. CONCLUDING REMARKS

We have considered privacy preserving aggregation in constrained scenarios where inter-participant communication is not realistically possible. We employed Shamir secret sharing within a star network to provide collusion resistance and fault tolerance. We developed protocols to add noise to the computed aggregate function, thereby ensuring differential privacy for the participants. The differential privacy requirement requires us to appreciate that collusions are capable of reducing privacy without necessarily discovering the honest participants' data.

To add the correct amount of noise, we make the participants generate several noise samples, with the aggregator deciding (obliviously) which of those samples are utilized in the differentially private mechanism. In this way, neither the cheating aggregator nor the semi-honest participants know which noise values are used to achieve differential privacy. This ensures that semi-honest colluding participants cannot reduce the differential privacy guarantees of honest participants. Our adversarial model allows the aggregator to influence (e.g., reduce) the noise term, so we describe a protocol to catch a cheating aggregator with overwhelming probability.

References

[1] G. Ács and C. Castelluccia. I have a DREAM! (differentially private smart metering). In *Information Hiding*, pages 118–132, 2011.

[2] M. Ben-Or, S. Goldwasser, and A. Wigderson. Completeness theorems for non-cryptographic fault-tolerant distributed computation. In *Proceedings of the twentieth annual ACM symposium on Theory of computing*, pages 1–10, 1988.

[3] I. Bilogrevic, J. Freudiger, E. De Cristofaro, and E. Uzun. What's the gist? privacy-preserving aggregation of user profiles. In *Computer Security-ESORICS 2014*, pages 128–145. 2014.

[4] T.-H. H. Chan, E. Shi, and D. Song. Privacy-preserving stream aggregation with fault tolerance. In *Financial Cryptography and Data Security*, pages 200–214. 2012.

[5] I. Damgård, M. Jurik, and J. Nielsen. A generalization of Paillier's public-key system with applications to electronic voting. *International Journal of Information Security*, 9(6):371–385, 2010.

[6] C. Dwork. Differential privacy: A survey of results. In *Theory and applications of models of computation*, pages 1–19. Springer, 2008.

[7] C. Dwork and A. Roth. The algorithmic foundations of differential privacy. *Theoretical Computer Science*, 9(3-4):211–407, 2013.

[8] Z. Erkin, J. R. Troncoso-Pastoriza, R. Lagendijk, and F. Perez-Gonzalez. Privacy-preserving data aggregation in smart metering systems: An overview. *Signal Processing Magazine, IEEE*, 30(2):75–86, 2013.

[9] Z. Erkin and G. Tsudik. Private computation of spatial and temporal power consumption with smart meters. In *Applied Cryptography and Network Security*, pages 561–577, 2012.

[10] F. Garcia and B. Jacobs. Privacy-friendly energy-metering via homomorphic encryption. In *Security and Trust Management*, pages 226–238. 2011.

[11] M. Jawurek and F. Kerschbaum. Fault-tolerant privacy-preserving statistics. In *Privacy Enhancing Technologies*, pages 221–238, 2012.

[12] M. Joye and B. Libert. A scalable scheme for privacy-preserving aggregation of time-series data. In *Financial Cryptography and Data Security*, pages 111–125. 2013.

[13] D. E. Knuth. Seminumerical Algorithms, The art of computer programming, Vol. 2, Section 4.6, 1981.

[14] S. Koltz, T. Kozubowski, and K. Podgorski. The laplace distribution and generalizations, 2001.

[15] K. Kursawe, G. Danezis, and M. Kohlweiss. Privacy-friendly aggregation for the smart-grid. In *Privacy Enhancing Technologies*, pages 175–191, 2011.

[16] I. Leontiadis, K. Elkhiyaoui, and R. Molva. Private and dynamic time-series data aggregation with trust relaxation. In *Cryptology and Network Security*, pages 305–320. Springer, 2014.

[17] I. Mironov. On significance of the least significant bits for differential privacy. In *Proceedings of the 2012 ACM conference on Computer and communications security*, pages 650–661. ACM, 2012.

[18] K. Nissim, S. Raskhodnikova, and A. Smith. Smooth sensitivity and sampling in private data analysis. In *Proceedings of the thirty-ninth annual ACM symposium on Theory of computing*, pages 75–84. ACM, 2007.

[19] P. Paillier. Public-key cryptosystems based on composite degree residuosity classes. In *Advances in cryptology, EUROCRYPT99*, pages 223–238, 1999.

[20] S. Rane, J. Freudiger, A. Brito, and E. Uzun. Privacy, efficiency and fault tolerance in aggregate computations on massive star networks. In *IEEE Workshop on Information Forensics and Security (WIFS 2015)*, Rome, Italy, November 2015.

[21] A. Shamir. How to share a secret. *Communications of the ACM*, 22(11):612–613, 1979.

[22] E. Shi, T.-H. H. Chan, E. Rieffel, R. Chow, and D. Song. Privacy-preserving aggregation of time-series data. In *NDSS*, volume 2, page 4, 2011.

[23] J. Stern. A new and efficient all-or-nothing disclosure of secrets protocol. In *Advances in Cryptology—ASIACRYPT'98*, pages 357–371. Springer, 1998.

"If You Can't Beat them, Join them": A Usability Approach to Interdependent Privacy in Cloud Apps

Hamza Harkous
EPFL, Switzerland
hamza.harkous@epfl.ch

Karl Aberer
EPFL, Switzerland
karl.aberer@epfl.ch

ABSTRACT

Cloud storage services, like Dropbox and Google Drive, have growing ecosystems of 3rd party apps that are designed to work with users' cloud files. Such apps often request full access to users' files, including files shared with collaborators. Hence, whenever a user grants access to a new vendor, she is inflicting a privacy loss on herself and on her collaborators too. Based on analyzing a real dataset of 183 Google Drive users and 131 third party apps, we discover that collaborators inflict a privacy loss which is at least 39% higher than what users themselves cause. We take a step toward minimizing this loss by introducing the concept of *History-based decisions*. Simply put, users are informed at decision time about the vendors which have been previously granted access to their data. Thus, they can reduce their privacy loss by not installing apps from new vendors whenever possible. Next, we realize this concept by introducing a new privacy indicator, which can be integrated within the cloud apps' authorization interface. Via a web experiment with 141 participants recruited from CrowdFlower, we show that our privacy indicator can significantly increase the user's likelihood of choosing the app that minimizes her privacy loss. Finally, we explore the network effect of History-based decisions via a simulation on top of large collaboration networks. We demonstrate that adopting such a decision-making process is capable of reducing the growth of user privacy loss by 40% in a Google Drive-based network and by 70% in an author collaboration network. This is despite the fact that we neither assume that users cooperate nor that they exhibit altruistic behavior. To our knowledge, our work is the first to provide quantifiable evidence of the privacy risk that collaborators pose in cloud apps. We are also the first to mitigate this problem via a usable privacy approach.

1. INTRODUCTION

The Rise of Cloud Apps:
The popularity of consumer cloud storage providers (CSPs) over the previous decade has been on a roll. Dropbox, Google Drive, and One Drive have each amassed hundreds of millions of users. In order to further appeal to their users, the CSPs have been transitioning from being pure *service providers* to becoming *app ecosystems*. Hence, they now offer APIs for developers to import and process users' files stored in the cloud. Consider, for example, a web app called PandaDoc,

CODASPY'17, March 22 - 24, 2017, Scottsdale, AZ, USA

© 2017 Copyright held by the owner/author(s). Publication rights licensed to ACM. ISBN 978-1-4503-4523-1/17/03...$15.00

DOI: http://dx.doi.org/10.1145/3029806.3029837

which allows creating, editing, and signing documents online. When a user uses PandaDoc from her laptop browser, she can import files stored in her Google Drive instead of her hard drive. Such a pattern is increasingly more prevalent with the growing number of 3rd Party Cloud apps (or 3PC apps) that are tightly integrated with cloud storage services. Dropbox alone claims that hundreds of thousands of apps have been integrated with its platform. Even in the enterprise setting, 3rd party cloud apps are on the rise. This is first because companies are officially adopting the likes of *Dropbox Business*, *OneDrive for Business*, and *Google Drive for Work*. Second, it is due to employees utilizing their personal cloud accounts to share company's files (a.k.a Shadow IT). Various reports from cloud application security providers state that organizations use from 10 to 20 times more cloud apps than their IT department thinks [4, 20].

Risks in 3rd Party Cloud Apps:
However, in our previous work, we have shown that 76% of the 3rd party Google Drive apps featured on Google Chrome Store request full access to users' Google Drive data [10]. Around 64% of these apps are *over-privileged*: they require more permissions than are needed for them to function. Accordingly, users are now faced with a new kind of privacy adversary: the 3rd party app vendors. With every app authorization decision that users make, they are trusting a new vendor with their data and increasing the potential attack surface. Elastica, the cloud application security provider, estimates that the average financial impact on a company as a result of a cloud-storage data breach is $13.85M, including remediation costs [3]. In 2015, the data breach at Anthem, a US insurance company, has reportedly cost more than $100M, with 80M unencrypted health records leaked. This was a result of an exfiltration exploit leveraging a popular public cloud storage application [4]. Even on the personal level, the risk extends from breaches exposing financial information and health records to unnoticeable, continuous profiling based on stored files.

Exposure through Collaboration:
An additional intricacy is that when users grant access to a 3rd party cloud app, they are not only sharing their personal data but also others' data. This is because cloud storage providers are inherently collaborative platforms where users share and cooperate on common files. Hence, protecting these files is not solely in the hands of the user. Skyhigh Networks, another provider of cloud security software, reports that 37.2% of documents (across 23 million users) are shared with at least one other user. In organizations, documents are shared, on average, with accounts from 849 external domains [21]. This further highlights what has been termed as the *interdependent privacy problem* [2], where the decisions of friends can affect the user's privacy and vice-versa. This concept was initially proposed in the context of social networking 3rd party apps, such as Facebook. However, while 1.92% of Facebook apps request friends' personal information,

this is much more pronounced in 3rd party cloud apps, where all apps accessing one's files get access to the part which is shared too. Moreover, unlike Facebook apps, due to the collaborative nature of cloud apps, the CSPs do not provide an option for users to control whether their collaborators' apps can get access to data they own.

Research Questions:
So far, the main approach to reducing the risk of 3PC apps has been focused on discovering over-privileged apps and deterring users from installing them [10]. Even then, a lot of users would still install such apps as they prioritize short-term utility over long-term risk aversion or due to the absence of alternatives. Furthermore, that approach relies on manually inspecting each app by experts and on applying a plethora of machine learning algorithms to visualize the various risks for users. These issues could present a hurdle towards a wide-scale deployment by CSPs. In this work, we address the wider problem of minimizing the risk of all 3PC apps, regardless of whether they are over-privileged or least-privileged. We are further driven by the rationale that users will inevitably continue to install apps to achieve various services. So instead of stopping them, we aim to lead them to select apps from vendors in a way that minimizes their privacy risk. We achieve this by leading users to take what we term as *History-based decisions*. Such decisions account for the vendors who previously obtained access to the user's data, whether directly (with her consent) or via her collaborators. Our strategy consists of introducing privacy indicators to the current permissions interfaces that help users minimize the number of vendors with access to their data. Our "usable privacy" approach is guided via a data-driven study and is evaluated via a data-driven simulation.

In essence, we tackle the following research questions:

- From a practical perspective, are the collaborators' decisions significant enough to be accounted for in users' app adoption decisions?
- Do users already account for entities with access to their data, and to what extent can the usage of privacy indicators lead to users taking History-based decisions?
- How significant is the effect of adopting these privacy indicators in the case of large user and team networks?

Contributions: Towards addressing these questions, we make the following contributions:

- In Section 3, we analyze a real-world dataset of Google Drive users, and we show that the median privacy loss that collaborators cause by installing apps can be much higher than that inflicted by the user's own app adoption decisions (39% higher with 5% of shared files and 523% higher with 60% of shared files). To our knowledge, this is the first usage of a real-world dataset to give a concrete evaluation of interdependent privacy in any ecosystem.
- Driven by the significant impact of collaborators, we design new privacy indicators for helping users mitigate the privacy risk via History-based decisions (Section 4). We assess these indicators via a web experiment with 141 users. We show that they significantly increase the likelihood that users choose the option with minimal privacy loss, even if not all of these users are motivated by privacy per se. To the best of our knowledge, this is also the first work to investigate a usable privacy approach to mitigating the problem of interdependent privacy. The few studies on this problem have mainly approached it from a theoretical perspective, such as developing game-theoretic or

economic models [2, 14] or from a behavioral perspective, such as studying the factors affecting real users' monetary valuation of others' privacy [15, 16].

- We explore the potential of History-based decisions by performing a simulation on two large user networks. We show that the network-effects of our approach result in curtailing the growth privacy loss by 70% in a synthetic Google Drive-based collaboration network and by 40% in a real author collaboration network (Section 5). In the extended version of this work [8], we also simulate the effect of such decisions in a teams' network. We demonstrate that teams can reduce the privacy loss by up to 40% by solely accounting for team members' decisions.

2. MODELS AND PRELIMINARIES

2.1 System Model

There are four main entities that interact in the third-party cloud app system:

1. a *user u* who uses that app for achieving a certain service
2. a *cloud storage provider (CSP)* hosting the user's *data*
3. a *data subject* to whom the files belong and whose privacy is being considered. We further define two levels of data subject granularity:
   - *individual-level granularity*: i.e., the user herself is interested in guarding her own data privacy,
   - *team-level granularity*: i.e., a group of users are interested in guarding the privacy of team-owned data (e.g., using an enterprise version of cloud storage services)
4. a *vendor v* that is responsible for programming and managing a 3rd Party Cloud app (or shortly a cloud app or a 3PC app). These vendors register their apps with the CSPs. The apps themselves are hosted on any website the vendors choose (i.e., not hosted by the CSP itself).

Each user has access to a set F_u of files stored at the CSP. A subset of these files is owned exclusively by the data subject while the other subset is composed of files that are each shared with at least one other *collaborator*. We denote the set of all collaborators of user u by $C(u)$. For simplicity reasons, we will assume throughout this work that the files of all data subjects, as well as the collaborators for each file, are all fixed from a reference step $t = 0$. Using the CSP's API, the vendor v can get access, at step $t \in \mathbb{N}$, to the subject's data upon *user authorization*, which consists of u accepting a list of *permissions*. We will alternatively refer to this as *app installation*, and we will assume that exactly one app is installed in each step t. Permissions are named differently across various providers, but, in general, we can categorize them into three categories:

- **per-file access**: where the user has to authorize the vendor for each file access individually. This is typically done via a file picker provided by the CSP itself.
- **full-access**: where the vendor gets access to all users' data. In the interface, this is worded, for instance, as "View the files in your Google Drive" or "access to the files and folders in your Dropbox".
- **per-type access**: where the vendor gets access to all files of a specific type. For example, Dropbox words it as "access to images in your Dropbox". Some platforms, like Google Drive, do not provide app developers with such fine-grained options.

The authorization can also give v access to files shared with the collaborators of u. Similarly, collaborators of u can install apps that expose files shared with u to new vendors. We denote the set of files of u accessible by vendor v at step t as $F_{u,v}(t)$[1].

2.2 User Model

A user is further assumed to be *self-interested*, i.e., only caring about optimizing the privacy of the data subject (a.k.a., privacy egoist), and *non-cooperative*, i.e., does not coordinate her decisions with others. We do not assume that the risks of installing each app are known to the users or calculated a priori. In fact, unlike other 3rd party app ecosystems, the risk of each cloud app cannot be automatically estimated based on techniques such as taint tracking [5] or code analysis [6] because the main app's functionality is typically implemented on the server side (which cannot be accessed by external entities). Such assumptions constitute the *worst case* in the scenarios we consider, and further privacy optimizations can be obtained by relaxing them.

We also assume that the mental model for privacy-concerned users matches the possible permission granularities they are given. Accordingly, privacy-concerned users can have one of the following privacy-goal granularities[2]:

- **per-type privacy goal**: where users aim to optimize their privacy independently for different file types. For example, in an ecosystem like Dropbox, where per-type access is an option, users might follow the separation-of-concerns principle. Hence, they might install photo-related apps from a set of vendors that is different from the set authorized for document processing.
- **all-files privacy goal**: where users aim to reduce the privacy risk for their entire set of files. This can be in the case of ecosystems which do not have the option of per-type access, like Google Drive. It can be also the case that a user of Dropbox has this goal in mind despite being presented with finer-grained app permissions.

2.3 Threat Model

We consider the 3rd party app vendors as the adversary (and not the CSP). The privacy indicator we introduce is best implemented by the CSP, which already has access to the users' and collaborators data. Alternatively, this can be a feature within Cloud Access Security Brokers (e.g. SkyHigh Networks, Netskope, etc.), which are already trusted by thousands of enterprises to protect their cloud data against other 3rd parties. Moreover, we consider the protection against over-privileged apps as an orthogonal problem, that we have considered in [10]. We rather focus on the interdependent privacy problem, which covers all vendors with full access and is an issue in least-privileged apps too.

2.4 Privacy Loss Metrics

In order to quantify the privacy loss that a user incurs with time, we introduce now the *Vendors File Coverage (VFC)* metric. Consider a user u and a set V of vendors at a certain time step. For notation simplicity, we will omit the time step henceforth. $VFC_u(V)$ is computed as the summation of the files' fractions shared with each of these vendors:

$$VFC_u(V) = \sum_{v \in V} \frac{|F_{u,v}|}{|F_u|} \quad (1)$$

Intuitively, $VFC_u(V)$ increases as vendors in V get access to more files of u. It has the range $[0, |V|]$.[3]

If we consider the set V_u of vendors explicitly authorized by user u, we can define the *Self-Vendors File Coverage* as:

$$Self\text{-}VFC_u = VFC_u(V_u) \quad (2)$$

Similarly, if we consider the set $V_{C(u)}$ of vendors authorized by the collaborators $C(u)$ of u, we can define the *Collaborators-Vendors File Coverage* as:

$$Collaborators\text{-}VFC_u = VFC_u(V_{C(u)}) \quad (3)$$

Finally, the *Aggregate VFC_u* for a user u is that due to all vendors authorized by u or its collaborators:

$$Aggregate\text{-}VFC_u = VFC_u(V_u \cup V_{C(u)}) \quad (4)$$

Throughout this work, we will use the terms *privacy loss* and *VFC* interchangeably. As will become evident in Section 4, this metric choice allows relaying a message that is simple enough for users to grasp, yet powerful enough to capture a significant part of the privacy loss. Obviously, one can resort to a deeper inspection of content or metadata sensitivity (as in [9]) had the purpose been finding the best privacy model in general. However, for instigating a behavioral change, telling users that a company has 30% of their files is more concrete than a black-box description informing them that the calculated loss is 30% and constitutes less information-overload than presenting them with detailed loss metrics.

3. COLLABORATORS' IMPACT

At this point, we are in a position to handle the first research question on the collaborators' impact on user's privacy loss. Hence, we want to test the following hypothesis:

H1: The collaborators' app adoption decisions have a significant impact on the user's privacy loss.

If this hypothesis is valid in practice, it provides a strong motivation for designing privacy notices that aid users in accounting for their collaborators' decisions, which is what we will study in Section 4. Towards that, we will be dissecting the privacy loss, quantified by *VFC*, that users incur in a realistic 3rd party cloud apps dataset.

3.1 The Case of Google Drive

To study the problem in a realistic context, we will be taking Google Drive as a case study in this work, given that it has one of the most popular 3rd party ecosystems. Nevertheless, the insights gained from our work are applicable to other cloud platforms as well. The main (content-related) Google Drive permissions that 3PC apps' vendors can request are presented Table 1, along with the Google-provided description for each. This short description is also presented to the user when installing an app (see Figure 1 for an example app). The user can click on the info button (i) next to each permission to read additional explanations in a popup. The user has to accept all permissions in order to utilize the app. These apps can be found on Google Chrome Web Store (and other Google stores), where users can rate and review them. In this work, we will focus on content-related permissions. Hence, as discussed in Section 2, we differentiate between two levels of access: (1) full access, which includes the DRIVE_READONLY and DRIVE permissions and (2) per-file access that includes the DRIVE_FILE permission.

---

[1] Although we do not consider file deletion in this work, we note that, in the worst case, the vendor can still have access to copies of files it saved before the user deleted them.

[2] Per-file access already achieves the least privilege possible.

[3] We do not normalize $VFC_u(V)$ it by $|V|$ as multiple vendors with access to all the user's files induce a higher privacy loss than one vendor with such access.

Permission	Short Name
View the **files** in your Google Drive.	DRIVE_READONLY
View and manage the **files** in your Google Drive.	DRIVE
View and manage Google Drive files that you have **opened or created with this app**.	DRIVE_FILE
View your Google Drive apps.	DRIVE_APPS_READONLY

Table 1: Requested permissions with the short reference name

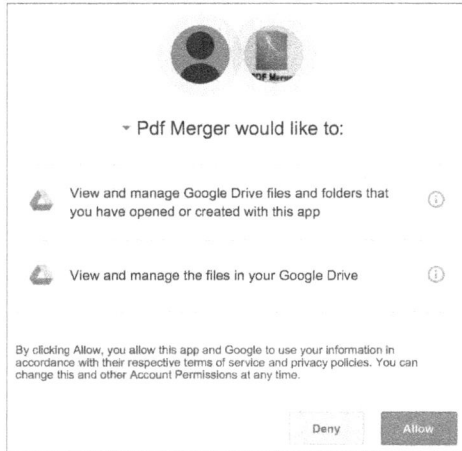

Figure 1: Current permissions interface of Google Drive

Google Drive does not offer the per-type permissions option.

3.2 Dataset

We benefit in this section from a dataset that we have collected in a previous work via the PrivySeal[4] service [10]. We build our analysis on it in order to evaluate the *VFC* of users in a realistic context. The dataset, henceforth referred to as the *PrivySeal Dataset*, was anonymized and contained metadata-only information. It included a subset of the files' metadata of 183 PrivySeal users in addition to the Google Drive apps installed by those users prior to authorizing PrivySeal's app (the DRIVE_APPS_READONLY permission was requested by PrivySeal). Each user had a minimum of $N_{files\_min} = 10$ files in total and at least $P_{min\_shared} = 5\%$ of files that are shared. The dataset specifically contained:
- list of user IDs (anonymized via a one-way hash function)
- IDs of files in each user's Google Drive
- list of anonymized collaborators' IDs for each file ID
- list of apps with full-access installed by each user
- the vendor of each app

In total, the number of users in addition to collaborators was 3422. Overall, these users had installed 131 distinct Google Drive apps from 99 distinct vendors. Figure 2 characterizes the PrivySeal Dataset. Particularly, it displays 4 distributions in this dataset, which realistically model the system under study:
- number of files per user, which follows a skewed distribution with a median of 67 files
- sharing pattern: percentage of shared files out of all user files, which also follows a skewed distribution with a median around 18%

- number of collaborators across all user files (a.k.a., the degree of the user node in the collaboration network): where 75% of the users had less than 23 collaborators
- number of vendors authorized per user: also follows a skewed distribution with a median of 1 vendor per user

3.3 Results

We computed the *Self-VFC*, the *Collaborators-VFC*, and the *Aggregate-VFC* (as defined in Section 2.4) for users in the PrivySeal Dataset [5]. As we did not have the actual number of apps for each collaborator in the dataset, we assigned to these collaborators a set of apps from a random user of the dataset. We show in Figure 3 how these metrics evolve as we gradually consider populations that collaborate more frequently. With $P_{min\_shared} = 5\%$, we had a median of 1.39 for *Collaborators-VFC*, which was 39% higher than a median of 1.00 for *Self-VFC*. The significance of the median difference is evidenced by the non-overlapping box-plot notches. This difference became much larger when we considered users that share more files. We had a 100% median difference at $P_{min\_shared} = 10\%$ and 523% median difference at $P_{min\_shared} = 60\%$. Such results indicate that:
- The collaborators' app adoption decisions contribute a core component to the user's privacy loss, thus confirming our hypothesis $H1$.
- The higher the number of collaborators is, the higher the magnitude of loss these collaborators can potentially inflict.

Both conclusions motivate the need for taking collaborators' decisions into account when designing privacy indicators for cloud apps, which is what we will embark on next.

4. USER STUDY

Up till now, we have confirmed that, if users want to minimize their privacy loss, they should not ignore the app installation decisions of collaborators. In this section, we tackle the next research question, where we investigate the potential of privacy indicators in leading users to minimize their exposure to 3PC app vendors. We show first our design methodology for the privacy indicators, and we follow that by a web experiment that investigates the efficacy of these indicators in realistic scenarios.

4.1 History-based Privacy Indicators

We call our proposed privacy indicators *"History-based Insights"* (HB Insights) as they allow users to account for the previous decisions taken by them or by their collaborators. We continue to consider Google Drive as a case study, and we show this indicator in the context of Google Drive apps' permissions in Figure 5. Compared to the current interface provided by Google (Figure 1), we added a new part to highlight the percentage of user files readily accessible by the vendor (computed based on $VFC_u(\{v\})$ for each vendor v). As we prove in Appendix B, selecting the vendor that already has the largest percentage of user files is the optimal strategy to minimize the privacy loss in our context. We denote this strategy as *"History-based decisions"*. Following the best practices in privacy indicators' design [17], our indicator was multilayered, with both textual and visual components. The wording of the main textual part was brief and general enough to hold for both the data percentage exposed by

[4] https://privyseal.epfl.ch

[5] To avoid double counting, we considered the vendors authorized by both the user and her collaborators in computing *Self-VFC* but not in computing *Collaborators-VFC*.

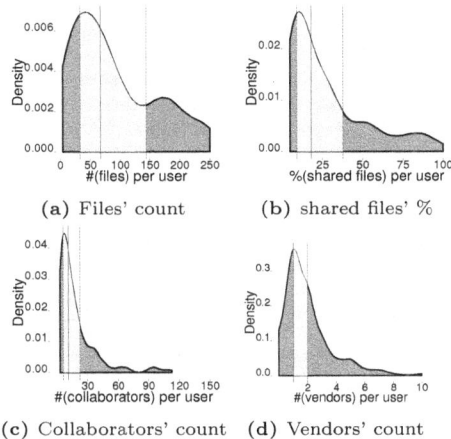

(a) Files' count **(b)** shared files' %

(c) Collaborators' count **(d)** Vendors' count

Figure 2: Density plots for various parameters, computed per user ($P_{shared\_min} = 5$). Median line is shown, and the light orange area represents the range between the 25% to 75% quantiles.

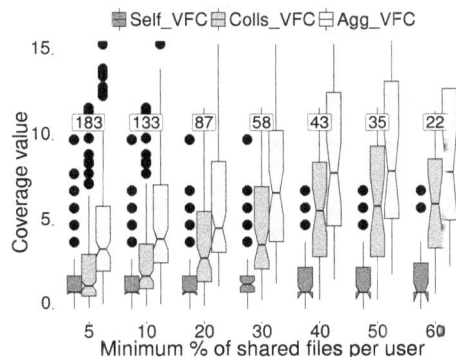

Figure 3: Evolution of metrics with populations that share more files ($N_{files\_min} = 10$, $N_{apps\_min} = 1$). The numeric labels denote the corresponding number of users in the dataset.

friends and that exposed by the user. We used a percentage value rather than a qualitative measure to facilitate making comparisons among apps based on this value. The visual part showed the percentage as a progress bar with a neutral violet color. The bottom textual part was added in a smaller font to provide further explanation for those interested. We used the term "company" in our interface instead of "vendor" as it is more commonly understood by the general audience.

4.2 Methodology

In order to evaluate the new permissions interface, we performed an online web experiment (rather than a lab study) as we were mainly motivated by obtaining a large sample of users that is also geographically and culturally diverse. The hypothesis we wanted to test is:

H2: Introducing the new privacy indicator significantly increases the probability that users take History-based decisions.

In addition, the study allowed us to build a realistic user decision model based on the choices taken by participants in different conditions. We will utilize this model in Section 5 to simulate the app choices in a large user network and to study the effect on the overall *VFC* in the network. We structured our study to have (1) an Introductory Survey, (2) a series of

Figure 4: Example app displayed in the list of apps

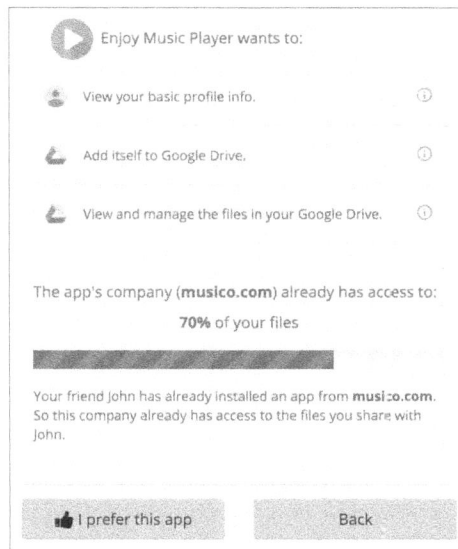

Figure 5: Proposed "History-based insights" interface

App Installation Tasks, and (3) a Concluding Survey[6].

User Recruitment: We recruited users via CrowdFlower's crowdsourcing platform. In our study, we restricted participation, via the platform's filtering system, to the highest quality contributors (Performance Level 3). We also geographically targeted countries where English is a main language as our interface was only in English. In order to further guarantee quality responses, each user was rewarded a small amount of $0.5 for merely completing the study and an additional amount of $1.25 that was manually bonused for those who did not enter irrelevant text in the free-text fields.

Instructions: Participants were first presented with introductory instructions that explained the context of the study (i.e., cloud storage services and 3rd party apps that can be connected to them). They were asked to only continue if they had good familiarity with cloud storage services (e.g., Google Drive, Dropbox, etc.). We did not explicitly require that participants have experience with 3rd party cloud apps. However, we educated them about such apps throughout the instructions, particularly showing them two examples of 3rd party apps in action (PandaDoc for signing documents and iLoveIMG for cropping photos). These apps were displayed via animated GIFs that play automatically and do not rely on the user clicking. We used limited deception by neither mentioning the focus of the study on participants' privacy nor giving hints about selecting apps based on the installation history. The advertised purpose was to "check how people make decisions when they install 3rd party apps."

Introductory Survey: After checking the instructions, users were presented with an introductory survey, where they first entered general demographic information. This

---

[6]presented in Appendix C

survey was also front-loaded with questions about cloud storage services (several of which required free-text input) in order to discourage users who had not used these services from continuing to the actual study.

4.3 Study Overview

Next, users could proceed to the study page. We used a split-plot design in the study. Participants were randomly assigned to one of two groups:

1. **Baseline Group (*BL*):** where the permissions interface used is that currently provided by Google Drive (Figure 1).
2. **History-based Group (*HB*):** where the *History-based Insights* permissions interface (Figure 5) is used.

In each group, the study consisted of 3 modules, which cover the main conditions that can occur when users desire to install a cloud app. On a high level, the modules investigate the following questions:

1. **Module 1:** are users likely to select apps from the same vendor they installed from before?
2. **Module 2:** are users likely to select apps from vendors that her collaborators have used before?
3. **Module 3:** do users consider the differences in access levels obtained by vendors that collaborators installed?

In all modules, whenever the user was asked to *choose* an app, she was presented with a list of 12 apps (Figure 4 shows an example app). Only two of these apps were relevant to the task purpose, and they were placed on top of the list (randomly positioned as first or second). With this setup, we wanted to mimic the realistic setup of app browsing while not squandering the user's effort on finding apps. All apps had the same full access permissions too (namely DRIVE permission). Unlike in Chrome Store, we removed elements such as ratings, user reviews, and screenshots and kept a minimal interface. This is all in order to reduce the distractions from factors outside the study. We refer the user to the work of Kelly et al., [11] who investigated the effects of those elements on users' decisions for Android apps.

In order to account for fatigue and learning effects, modules 1, 2, and 3 were presented in a random order for users. We piloted our experimental setup in two stages: with colleagues and with online users from the CrowdFlower community itself. For reviewing the online pilot testers work, we embedded a Javascript code for session recording in our study's web page, which allowed us to view the user's mouse and keyboard actions on our side.

Demographics: We had 157 users who completed the study. Based on manually reviewing the users' inputs, we removed 16 users who were inputting irrelevant free-text in the survey or in the study. We thus report the results of 141 users, 72 of which were in the *BL* group and 69 in the *HB* group. Of these participants, 66.4% were males and 33.6% were females. They were between 18 and 62 years old, with a median of 31. Moreover, 42.3% of the participants had worked or studied in IT before. Participants were mostly from India (37%), USA (35%), Britain (7%), Germany (7%), and Canada (7%).

4.4 Study Details and Results

We now move to the detailed description of the modules and the results obtained. These modules are summarized in Figure 9 of Appendix A, to which we refer henceforth. We also show sample screenshots from the online study in Figure 8 of Appendix A. The results are also presented in Table 2.

Module 1 (Self-History Scenario): tests whether the user is more likely to select an app from the same vendor she has just installed from before. In step (a), the user is made aware the she installed an app from a specific vendor v (Figure 8b). In step (b), she is asked to install[7] an app that satisfies the given purpose (Figure 8c) among a list of apps. Two of the listed apps were relevant, and one of them was from vendor v itself.

Despite the participants being informed one step earlier that they installed an app from "thetimetube.com", that didn't make a difference in the *BL* case: half of the users still chose the app from the new vendor "nitrosafe.org". In the absence of traditional signals that users follow for deciding on apps (reviews, ratings, permissions), participants apparently made decisions that cancelled out, making the two apps equally favored across participants. **The vast majority of users were not approaching the installation from the angle of keeping their data with fewer shareholders.** Based on their provided justifications, they rather looked for other cues, such as selecting the app that, in their opinion, has a more comprehensive description, a more professional logo, a better sounding name, or a more trustable URL. Still, 12 users have explicitly mentioned in their text input that they chose an app *because* it is from the same vendor they have dealt with earlier. Even then, neither of them has alluded to a privacy motivation behind the choice. These 12 participants mainly provided cross-app compatibility, interface familiarity, and satisfaction with the previous vendor as justifications. For example, one participant wrote: "*I favoured Malware Scanner due to the fact that the name 'thetimetube.com' was in the last app installed, and I tend to install apps from the same company due to cross-app compatibility usually found in apps by the same company.*" Interestingly, two users justified their installation of the app from the new vendor (nitrosafe.org) by writing that they had just installed an app from the same company before. This indicates that, **even when users try to account for previous decisions, they might find it difficult to remember the previous app vendors.** Given that our study had a short time span separating the current from the previous installation, we expect that such mistakes would be even more common in real scenarios when app installation instances are separated by longer time spans.

The *HB* group witnessed a much larger proportion of users who favored the option with less privacy loss. 72.2% of the participants selected the app from the "thetimetube.com" (the vendor which already has access). The difference of 22.8% compared to the *BL* group is statistically significant (Fisher's exact test, p-value = 0.005). Many of the participants who chose the app from "thetimetube.com" reported that they were motivated by the 100% access that the app already has. We counted around 40 such users (i. e., 57% of the *HB* group). Some of them went further and explicitly mentioned that their selection was motivated by giving data to fewer data owners (i. e., more privacy). For example, one user wrote: "*This company has access to all my files, so I would choose them as I don't want to have 2 companies with full access to my files*".

In a nutshell, we were able to verify our hypothesis in this scenario: **the new privacy indicator leads users to more frequently choose the app from a vendor they**

---

[7]Users were informed that this is a role-playing study, and no apps were actually installed.

already authorized. Furthermore, we have discovered that the *HB* Insights interface has indirectly made users think about various positive effects brought by using apps from the same vendor. This eventually lead them to make more privacy-preserving decisions.

Module 2.1 (Collaborator's App Scenario): tests the likelihood that the participant selects the same app that her collaborator had used. In step (a), the participant is made aware that she had shared all her photos with a friend f (Figure 8d). For more familiarity, we also added a picture for each of the two fictitious friends throughout the study. In step (b), the user is made aware that her friend f has installed an app a_0 (Figure 8e) from vendor v. She is asked to type the name of the app's vendor ("paste" option was disabled in the input field to further ensure the participant is aware of the vendor). In step (c), the user is asked to install an app with a certain purpose (similar to Figure 8c). One of the two matching apps is app a_0.

Similar to the previous module, the *BL* group witnessed an almost even split between "Online Player", installed previously by the friend, and "Enjoy Music Player", from a new vendor. We also noticed that 20 participants in this group justified their decision by mentioning that their friend has used the app. Still, neither of them alluded at privacy reasons in their justifications. Instead, the two most prevalent motivations were (1) considering the friend's use of the app as a *recommendation* or (2) achieving *compatibility* with their friends' app, which facilitates data sharing within the app itself. Quoting one user: "*This is the same app my friend is using so it should be quite compatible for us to both share.*"

In addition to having a significant 35.6% difference with the *HB* group, we noticed that 32 users mentioned the existing data access as a reason for choosing the app "Online Player". Also, 26 users referred to the fact that the friend has installed this app before (including those who mentioned both of the previous reasons). Unlike the *BL* group's justifications though, where the friend's recommendation and the app's compatibility prevailed, the privacy issue was explicitly brought up by at least 10 users. One participant put it as follows: "*Thanks to John, they have already access to 70% of my data. Sharing the last 30% isn't as bad as sharing 100% of my data with driveplayer.com.*"

Module 2.2 (Collaborator's Vendor Scenario): We proceed in steps (d) and (e) as in the previous scenario's steps (b) and (c), with the difference that a new app from v is included among the options in step (e) instead of the exact same app a_0. One interesting insight from this scenario is that **the line between the company and the app is blurred in the minds of several users** who used the two entities interchangeably. In fact, 3 users in the *BL* group and 7 participants in the *HB* group justified their choices by mentioning that their friend installed the *same app* before, which was not the case. For example, one user wrote: "*this app already has access to my files, and I don't want to install any new app.*"

Module 3 (Multiple Collaborators Scenario): Given collaborators f_{more} and f_{less}, where the user shares much more data with f_{more}, this scenario checks the likelihood of the participant authorizing an app that f_{more} has installed. In step (a), the participant is made aware that f_{more} has access to more data than f_{less} (Figure 8f). In steps (b) and (c), the participant is made familiar with the apps each of the friends installed (similar to Figure 8e). In step (d), the

Scenario	App Type	BL group (n=72)	HB group (n=69)	Δ	p-value
Self-History	VwA	50.0%	75.4%		
	NV	50.0%	24.6%	25.4%	0.003
Collaborator's app	VwA	52.8%	88.4%		
	NV	47.2%	11.6%	35.6%	< 0.001
Collaborator's vendor	VwA	58.3%	82.6%		
	NV	41.7%	17.4%	19.6%	0.002
Multiple collaborators	VwA	44.4%	82.6%		
	NV	55.6%	17.4%	38.2%	< 0.001

Table 2: App selection statistics in the study; VwA.: vendor with access; NV: new vendor. The comparisons in each experimental group were planned contrasts, and the p-values of difference between the percentages of users who selected each app type were computed using Fisher's exact test.

user is asked to select an app with a specific purpose. The two friends' apps are the only ones matching, and the choice is to be made between them (similar to Figure 8c).

In the *BL* group, we had 44.4% of the participants choosing the app installed by f_{more}. Still this percentage is relatively close to an equal split between the two apps. Out of this percentage, 13 users justified their choice by mentioning that they were encouraged to follow the choice of friend f_{more}. Even though they didn't mention privacy, the larger number of files shared with f_{more} was often used as a justification. For example, one participant wrote: "*This is the app that John already uses, and he has access to all of my files. The PDF Mergy app is used by Lisa, but she only has access to part of my files.*"

In the *HB* group, around 82.6% chose the app previously installed by the friend f_{more}, which is significantly more than those in the *BL* case (Fisher's exact test, p-value < 0.001). Looking at the justifications, around 37 users explicitly mentioned the higher access level that this app already possesses as a reason for their choice. Privacy was additionally mentioned by 8 of these users. Quoting one of them: "*PDF Mergy already has access to 70% of my files. Using PDF Files Merger would unnecessarily increase third party app access to my files.*" However, we still had 2 users who went for the app with less existing access, with one of them saying he favors the app that only "*had accessed 30% of files before installation*". What was interesting though is that **almost all users who mentioned friends were actually making a comparison between the two friends' existing access level**, regardless of their final choice.

4.5 Discussion and Limitations

Overall, we found out that, in the three modules, participants in the *HB* group were significantly more likely to install the app with less privacy loss (i.e., the app from the vendor with the largest share of the user's files) than those in the *BL* group. Despite showing the efficacy of History-based Insights, our study still has its limitations. In order to get a large, diverse sample size, we resorted to a web experiment based on role-playing with hypothetical data. It would be interesting to see how such results extrapolate to the case where users' own data is in question. Moreover, in our design, we have abstracted several factors (e.g., ratings and reviews), which have been previously studied in similar ecosystems [11], in order to focus on one factor. These factors might have diluted the effect of the privacy indicator. Still, we conjecture that, although the absolute values of our findings might not strictly apply, the differences between the two groups will still be practically significant. Furthermore, it is important to note that, although our experimental interface mentions the collaborators' name in the explanation under the progress bar, this does not have to be the case in actual deployments. We hypothesize that removing the name will not have a significant impact on the results as it was not highlighted in the interface. This allows the CSP to relay such information to the users without exposing sensitive data about particular collaborators. The CSP can resort to more sophisticated anonymization methodologies, such as showing a non-exact percentage that can be mapped to multiple collaborators. Exploring the impact of these techniques is left for a future work. Moreover, we note that this anonymization might not be needed at all in the enterprise settings, where apps installed by team members are supposed to be visible for the administrators. As we show in the extended version of this work [8], a significant reduction in privacy loss can be achieved without even accounting for decisions by users external to the team. Finally, the privacy indicator in our study has addressed two granularity levels: full and per-file access. However, the same indicator can be extrapolated to the case of per-type access. For example, the interface can say: "The app's company already has access to 70% of your *photos*" (instead of *files*).

5. LARGE NETWORKS' SIMULATIONS

In the previous section, we showed the significant change that our privacy indicator can effect through encouraging users to make History-based decisions. We will tackle the next research question, where we investigate the impact of adopting such privacy indicators on the privacy risk in realistic scenarios with large user networks. As we are not in the position of the CSP to study an actual implementation of the *HB* Insights interface over time, we will perform a simulation of potential users' installation behavior. We will base this on both the crowdsourced decision model inferred from the user study and on new collaboration networks that we construct.

5.1 Simulation Data

Collaboration Networks: For the purposes of this simulation, we constructed the following two networks[8]:

- **Inflated Google Drive Network**: We used the standard degree-driven approach for network topology generation to construct a larger Google Drive network based on the one in the *PrivySeal Dataset* of Section 3.2 [12]. Based on an input user degrees' distribution from that dataset, we particularly used the *Configuration Model* as described by Newman [13] and implemented by the library NetworkX [18] for inflating the graph. This model generates a random pseudograph (a graph with parallel edges and self-loops) by randomly assigning edges to match an input degree sequence. We removed the self-loops and parallel edges a posteriori from the generated graph. In the end, we had a collaboration graph with 18,000 users and 138,440 edges. This graph is, by construction, a connected graph, with an average node degree of 15.

- **Paper Collaboration Network**: In an effort to have a realistic, large collaboration network without resorting to graph inflation, we relied on the Microsoft Academic Graph, which consists of records of scientific papers along with the authors and their affiliations [19]. We used a snapshot

of 50,000 papers, and we constructed the collaboration graph based on it. We ended up with 41,000 collaborators and 199,980 edges. The graph itself is not a connected graph but is rather constructed of around 1700 connected components. The average node degree is 4. Our rationale is that this graph captures a realistic scenario of users collaborating on authoring documents, which is, in fact, an activity achieved via cloud services nowadays. Hence, it is fit for showing the efficacy of our privacy indicators.

Sharing and Installation Patterns: In order to closely model the user characteristics in Google Drive, we assigned to each user in the collaboration networks a file sharing distribution and a number of apps corresponding to a user with a matching degree in the PrivySeal Dataset.

Apps: As we wanted to perform the simulation with a much larger number of users than we had in the dataset described in Section 3.2, we also needed a larger collection of apps. Given that Google Chrome Store has only around 500 apps that are tagged by the "Works with Google Drive" tag, we decided to also include all Google Chrome Apps in the dataset (i.e., even those that do not have this tag). As far as the simulation is concerned, this step is justified since the only realistic information that we will rely on is the distribution of vendors per app. It is fair then to assume that this distribution does not differ significantly between the general category and the Google Drive category. Hence, we augmented the PrivySeal Dataset via apps from the Google Chrome Store to arrive at 1000 apps. In addition to the app's installation count and vendor name, we also collected the set of "*Related Apps*" that the store displays for each app. This is because, in our simulation, we will assume that users have the choice to choose the app itself or one of its related apps. Again, this is a fair assumption as these related apps are mostly the apps which deliver a close functionality to the app itself, and we will only rely on them to model the alternatives at each simulation step.

User Decision Models: For the purpose of this simulation, we define 3 user decision models:

- **Fully Aware Model (*FA*):** the user always makes the decision that minimizes the privacy loss of the data subject, taking into account all previous installation decisions by her or her collaborators.

- **Experimental History-based Model (*EHB*):** the user takes decisions similar to what a random user of the *HB* experimental group does. In specific, we model those users as taking a history-based decision with probability q and making a random app choice with probability $1 - q$. We set q based on the number of users who mentioned the app' existing access as a reason for their choice in each module of our study of Section 4. Based on Module 1's users' responses, we set $q = 0.57$ when the user encounters a vendor she previously authorized. Based on Module 2, we set $q = 0.70$ whenever the user has a collaborator who exposed her data to a single vendor. Based on Module 3, we set $q = 0.67$ for the cases where multiple collaborators have previously authorized different vendors.

- **Experimental Baseline Model (*EBL*):** the user takes decisions similar to what a random user of the *BL* experimental group does. As users in practice are rarely informed of what their friends have installed before, we do not integrate this knowledge into the model. Hence, we only account for the case of Module 1, where the user's previous decisions are concerned. Based on the fraction of users who

---

[8]In the extended version of this work, we construct and simulate a third network, representing users organized in teams [8].

mentioned the app's existing access as a motivation for their choice, we set the probability of taking history-based decision in this model as $q = 0.18$.

5.2 Simulation Details

We now move to the description of the simulation itself. We had three simulation groups, named after the three decision models: *FA* group, *EHB* group, and the *EBL* group. The simulation was run until the average number of apps installed across by users reached 30 apps[9]. On a high level, at each simulation step, the following actions are performed[10]:

- A user is selected from the collaboration network via a weighted random sampling based on the assigned installation frequencies. This accounts for the diversity of users' installation frequencies. An app a_0 is selected from the simulation apps' dataset via a weighted random sampling based on the actual app installations count in Google Chrome Store. That way, popular apps are installed more frequently (as is the case in practice).
- A user decision is simulated. The user is assumed to be choosing the app a_0 or one of its related apps. This choice is made depending on the user's decision model.
- Finally, the *Aggregate VFC$_u$* is computed for the user u and for her collaborators.

5.3 Simulation Results

To demonstrate the simulation results, we show three types of figures per collaboration network. On a high level, in Figures 6a and 7a, we show how the privacy loss (quantified using Aggregate-*VFC*) in each group evolves as users install more apps. In Figures 6b and 7b, we show ratios of the privacy loss in the two experimental groups *EHB* and *FA* with respect to the baseline *EBL* group. Finally, Figures 6c and 7c show the actual events contributing to the privacy loss growth, where we can specifically check the fraction of apps coming from new vendors, those coming from vendors previously authorized by the user, and those from vendors previously authorized by collaborators.

Based on these metrics we start by analyzing the results for the individuals' networks, where we observe the following:

Curtailed growth of privacy loss: From Figures 6a and 7a, we notice that the growth of the privacy loss is visibly curtailed in the cases of *EHB* and *FA* groups compared to the baseline *EBL* group. This significant divergence demonstrates the efficacy of our *HB* privacy indicators.

Impact of the network effect: Looking into the ratios in Figures 6b and 7b, we see that the privacy loss in the *EHB* group has dropped by 41% in the inflated network and by 28% in the authors-based network (both with respect to the baseline). In the *FA* group, where users always optimize their privacy, the privacy loss has dropped by 70% in the inflated network and by 40% in the authors-based network. This higher impact in the case of the inflated network is due to the fact that it is a connected graph, unlike the authors-based network, which is composed of smaller connected components. Nevertheless, we can state that, although our privacy indicators have a larger effect on highly connected networks, they are still significantly effective in less connected networks, like the authors-based dataset.

Importance of accounting for collaborators' decisions: To dive further into events that lead to the observed privacy loss patterns, we look into Figures 6c and 7c. First, we observe that users in the *EBL* group are mainly installing new apps from vendors that had no previous access to their data. This is reflected in the almost linear increase of privacy loss in Figures 6a and 7a. Second, we observe that, in the case of the inflated network, users have been frequently installing apps from vendors with existing access through their collaborators. In fact, as apparent in Figure 6c, this event outnumbers the event of installing from a new vendor. Third, the number of installations from collaborators' vendors is also significant in the case of the authors-based dataset. While it does not outnumber the installations from new vendors (due to the low-graph connectivity), this is still enough to lead to 28% and 40% decrease in the privacy loss. Finally, we note that, although the users are more frequently encountering vendors authorized by their collaborators than by themselves, the latter event is still significantly impacting the results. This is because users still incur an incremental privacy loss with vendors authorized by their collaborators while this loss is zero with vendors they have previously authorized. Accordingly, the obtained optimizations are a result of users' accounting for their own and for others' decisions.

In sum, our simulations provide further evidence of the efficacy of using History-based privacy indicators in a large network of collaborators. It is worth noting too that, although users in our study were following the *EHB* decision model, we believe that, in an actual deployment of such indicators, the model will move closer to the *FA* model. This is because users are more protective when their personal data is at risk than when they are put in a role playing scenario about fictitious data. Moreover, users in our study were exposed to this indicator for the first time. When users are educated more about this feature, they might be more likely to take advantage of it.

6. RELATED WORK

6.1 Interdependent Privacy

The problem of interdependent privacy has been tackled before in the context of social apps. The main approaches were high-level game-theoretic or economic modeling. In [2], the authors introduced the concept of interdependent privacy and modeled its impact via a game theoretic, (2-player, 1-app) model. The work by Pu and Grossklags [14] presented a more elaborate economic model that additionally accounts for the interplay among various social network parameters. They showed that app rankings do not accurately reflect the level of interdependent privacy harm the app can cause and that even rational users who consider their friends' well-being might adopt apps with invasive privacy practices. Evidently, these results do not apply in the cloud apps case, where *all* apps have the potential to inflict interdependent privacy harm. A later work by Pu and Grossklags [15] used a conjoint study approach to quantify the monetary value which individuals associate with their friends' personal data. They found that individuals place a significantly higher value on their own personal information than their friends' personal information. This further supports our assumption of self-interested users in this work. The same authors also built on a user survey in [16] to assess the factors affecting users' own privacy concerns as well as friends' privacy concerns

---

[9]Comparatively, mobile users have accessed 26.7 smartphone apps on average per month in the fourth quarter of 2014 [22].

[10]We refer the reader to the extended version for the detailed simulation algorithm [8].

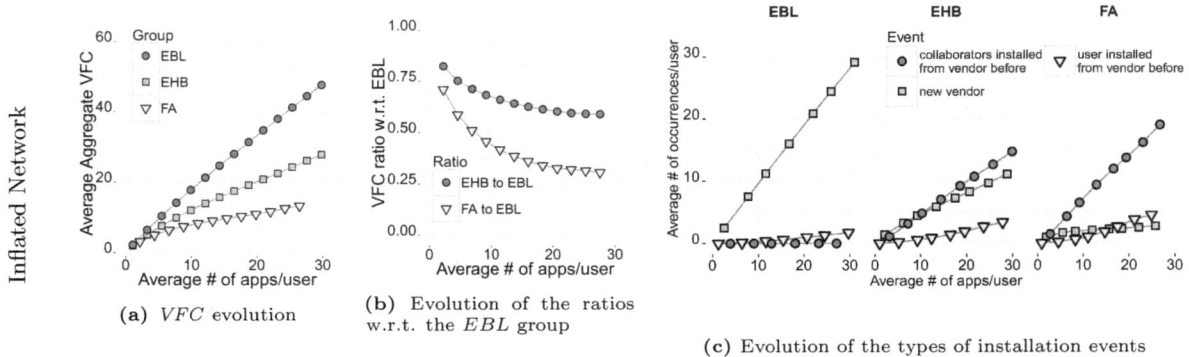

Figure 6: Simulation results in the inflated network

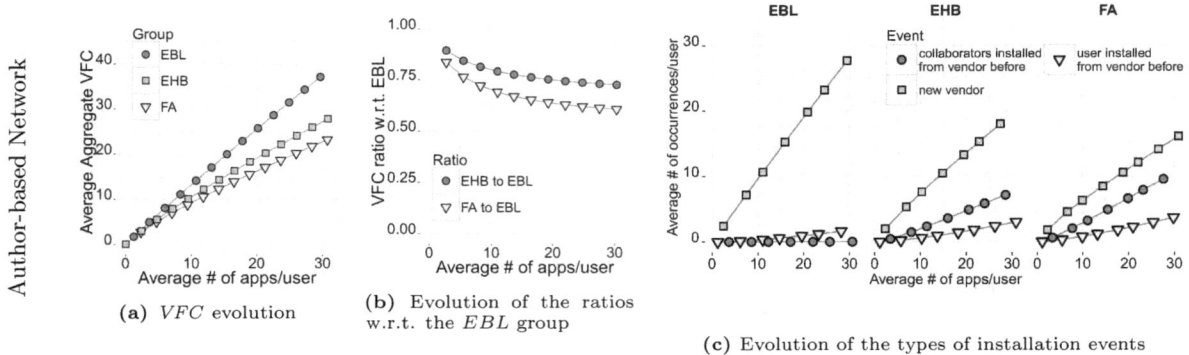

Figure 7: Simulation results in the author-based network

in the context of social app adoption. In particular, they found evidence of negative association between past privacy invasion experiences and the trust in 3rd party apps handling of their own data. They also found partial support for a positive effect of privacy knowledge on concerns for users' own privacy and their friends' privacy. In this work, we are focused on quantifying the interdependence of privacy in the context of cloud apps before addressing it from a usable privacy perspective, thus bridging the gap between the theoretical studies and the end-user needs.

6.2 Apps Privacy Indicators

Our previous work [10] was the first to study the privacy of 3rd party cloud apps and to expose that almost two thirds of those apps are over-privileged. In that work, we introduced a novel privacy indicator for deterring users from installing over-privileged apps by showing them Far-reaching insights that apps can needlessly infer from their data (e.g., top topics, faces, or locations of interest). In the context of Android apps, Kelly et al., showed that, by adding a set of privacy facts about an app, users will be more likely to choose apps with fewer permissions [11]. Harbach et al., tackled the same problem but presented users with random examples from their data (e.g., pictures, contacts, etc.) [7]. Almuhimedi et al. showed the effectiveness of privacy nudges, that regularly alert users about sensitive data collected by their apps, in encouraging users to review and adjust their permission [1]. All these works, however, tackle the problem of over-privileged apps and try to lead the user into either avoiding them or adjusting their permissions whenever possible. Our current work helps users improve their privacy

by reducing the vendors with access to their data, even if the functionality delivered by the vendor abides by the least-privilege principle. Hence, it complements these approaches and can be deployed alongside any of them.

7. CONCLUSION

The findings in this work are the first to concretely delineate the various aspects of interdependent privacy in 3PC apps. One of the major outcomes is that a user's collaborators can be much more detrimental to her privacy than her own decisions. Consequently, accounting for collaborators' decisions should be a key component of future privacy indicators in 3rd party cloud apps. We have shown the impact of History-based Insights as a privacy enhancing technology in this context, especially that, based on our user study, users are less likely to account for previous decisions on their own. Our privacy indicators would optimally be implemented by the CSPs themselves as they control the authorization interface and the application stores. The indicators can also be realized by third party privacy providers with access to users' data. Our approach can also be easily mapped to other ecosystems. In the mobile apps' scenario, it can enable users to reduce the number of vendors with access to her contacts. It can also be extended to the case where the goal is protection against 4th parties (e.g., ad providers and data brokers). There, the user can account for data previously held by a 4th party with which the app vendor cooperates. Finally, due to their usability and effectiveness, we envision History-based Insights as an important technique within the movement from static privacy indicators towards dynamic privacy assistants that lead users to data-driven privacy decisions.

References

[1] H. Almuhimedi, F. Schaub, N. Sadeh, I. Adjerid, A. Acquisti, J. Gluck, L. F. Cranor, and Y. Agarwal. Your location has been shared 5,398 times!: A field study on mobile app privacy nudging. In *Proceedings of the 33rd Annual ACM Conference on Human Factors in Computing Systems*, CHI '15, pages 787–796, New York, NY, USA, 2015. ACM.

[2] G. Biczók and P. H. Chia. Interdependent privacy: Let me share your data. In *Financial Cryptography and Data Security*, pages 338–353. Springer, 2013.

[3] Elastica Cloud Threat Labs. Q2 2015 Shadow Data Report. pages 1–14, 2015. https://www.elastica.net/q2-2015-shadow-data-report/.

[4] Elastica Cloud Threat Labs. 1H 2016 Shadow Data Report. 2016. https://www.elastica.net/1h-2016-shadow-data-report/.

[5] W. Enck, P. Gilbert, B.-G. Chun, L. P. Cox, J. Jung, P. McDaniel, and A. N. Sheth. Taintdroid: An information-flow tracking system for realtime privacy monitoring on smartphones. In *Proceedings of the 9th USENIX Conference on Operating Systems Design and Implementation*, OSDI'10, pages 1–6, Berkeley, CA, USA, 2010. USENIX Association.

[6] A. P. Felt, E. Chin, S. Hanna, D. Song, and D. Wagner. Android permissions demystified. In *Proceedings of the 18th ACM Conference on Computer and Communications Security*, CCS '11, pages 627–638, New York, NY, USA, 2011. ACM.

[7] M. Harbach, M. Hettig, S. Weber, and M. Smith. Using personal examples to improve risk communication for security & privacy decisions. In *Proceedings of the 32nd Annual ACM Conference on Human Factors in Computing Systems*, CHI '14, pages 2647–2656, New York, NY, USA, 2014. ACM.

[8] H. Harkous and K. Aberer. "If You Can't Beat them, Join them": A Usability Approach to Interdependent Privacy in Cloud Apps. Technical report, EPFL, January 2017. Extended Version, http://infoscience.epfl.ch/record/224430.

[9] H. Harkous, R. Rahman, and K. Aberer. C3p: Context-aware crowdsourced cloud privacy. In *International Symposium on Privacy Enhancing Technologies Symposium*, pages 102–122. Springer, 2014.

[10] H. Harkous, R. Rahman, B. Karlas, and K. Aberer. The Curious Case of the PDF Converter that Likes Mozart: Dissecting and Mitigating the Privacy Risk of Personal Cloud Apps. In *Proceedings on Privacy Enhancing Technologies (PoPETs)*, volume 2016, 2016.

[11] P. G. Kelley, L. F. Cranor, and N. Sadeh. Privacy as part of the app decision-making process. In *Proceedings of the SIGCHI Conference on Human Factors in Computing Systems*, CHI '13, pages 3393–3402, New York, NY, USA, 2013. ACM.

[12] M. Mihail and N. K. Vishnoi. On generating graphs with prescribed vertex degrees for complex network modeling. *Position Paper, Approx. and Randomized Algorithms for Communication Networks (ARACNE)*, 142, 2002.

[13] M. E. Newman. The structure and function of complex networks. *SIAM review*, 45(2):167–256, 2003.

[14] Y. Pu and J. Grossklags. An economic model and simulation results of app adoption decisions on networks with interdependent privacy consequences. In *Decision and Game Theory for Security*, pages 246–265. Springer, 2014.

[15] Y. Pu and J. Grosssklags. Using conjoint analysis to investigate the value of interdependent privacy in social app adoption scenarios. In *Proceedings of the International Conference on Information Systems, ICIS 2015*, 2015.

[16] Y. Pu and J. Grosssklags. Towards a model on the factors influencing social app users' valuation of interdependent privacy. *PoPETs*, 2016(2):61–81, 2016.

[17] F. Schaub, R. Balebako, A. L. Durity, and L. F. Cranor. A design space for effective privacy notices. In *Eleventh Symposium On Usable Privacy and Security (SOUPS 2015)*, pages 1–17, Ottawa, July 2015. USENIX Association.

[18] D. A. Schult and P. Swart. Exploring network structure, dynamics, and function using networkx. In *Proceedings of the 7th Python in Science Conferences (SciPy 2008)*, volume 2008, pages 11–16, 2008.

[19] A. Sinha, Z. Shen, Y. Song, H. Ma, D. Eide, B.-J. P. Hsu, and K. Wang. An overview of microsoft academic service (mas) and applications. In *Proceedings of the 24th International Conference on World Wide Web*, WWW '15 Companion, pages 243–246, New York, NY, USA, 2015. ACM.

[20] Skyhigh Networks. Cloud Report | Skyhigh Networks. https://www.skyhighnetworks.com/cloud-report/.

[21] Skyhigh Networks. Cloud Adoption and Risk Report. 2015. http://info.skyhighnetworks.com/rs/274-AUP-214/images/WP_Skyhigh_Cloud_Adoption_Risk_Report_Q4_2015.pdf.

[22] The Nielsen Company. So Many Apps, So Much More Time for Entertainment. http://www.nielsen.com/us/en/insights/news/2015/so-many-apps-so-much-more-time-for-entertainment.html.

Acknowledgments

We would like to thank Deniz Taneli and Nicolas Hubacher for their help in exploratory work that led to this project. The research leading to these results has received funding from the EU in the context of the project *CloudSpaces*: Open Service Platform for the Next Generation of Personal clouds (FP7-317555).

APPENDIX

A. USER STUDY MATERIAL

In Figure 9, we show the summary of the modules in the user study. Sample screenshots from these modules are shown in Figure 8. CrowdFlower presents the users with an optional satisfaction survey after completing the study, and 49 users took this survey. On average, the study received 4.2/5 for instructions clarity, 3.8/5 for questions' fairness, 3.8/5 for ease of job, 3.6/5 for pay sufficiency (before the bonus was rewarded). This ensures that participants' behavior has not been affected by either a lack of time to complete the task or the task design in general.

B. PROOF OF OPTIMAL USER STRATEGY

In this section, we complement Section 4.1 by providing a proof the optimal user strategy for minimizing the privacy risk, given our assumptions. We follow the notation introduced in Section 2. Let us consider that each 3PC app vendor has a probability p of exposing users' data. As we do not assume that users are provided with a per-vendor risk estimation utility, we set this probability to be the same for all vendors. In general, at a time t, a user u would have exposed his data to a set V of vendors, such that each vendor v has access to a fraction $f_{u,v}(t) = \frac{|F_{u,v}(t)|}{|F_u|}$ of the files. Without loss of generality, we will consider henceforth that the user has an all-files privacy goal (cf. Section 2.2). However, the same reasoning applies in the case of a per-type privacy goal. In that case, we simply replace "files" by "files of a specific type" (e.g. photos, documents). We will also be assuming that the users themselves are the data subjects (i.e., we consider individual-level subjects).

For a vendor v, we quantify the user's privacy risk magnitude as $p * f_{u,v}(t)$, i.e., the fraction of user files possessed by the vendor multiplied by the probability that the vendor exposes the user's files. This vendor could have obtained access due to app installations by the user herself or by her

- Take a breath.
- You will now play a role of someone who has a Google Drive account and has **already stored files** on it (like your images from your trips with the family, some official documents, music files, etc.).
- At some point, you'll be asked to choose some apps to connect to your Google Drive account. Although no apps will be actually installed, we ask you to think as if they were real apps and that this is a real Google Drive account.
- Once you install an app, assume **it is still installed throughout this experiment**.
  - For example, if the first tasks says: "you have installed an application from the company *pandadoc.com*", this application is still there when you go to the next task. So if the second task says: "who has access to your data?", the answer would be *"pandadoc.com company"*.
- Similarly, whenever you are informed that your friends have installed applications, consider that **these applications are still connected to their Google Drive throughout this experiment**.
- When this experiment ends and **you move to the next experiment, you will start from scratch** (i.e. with no apps installed).

(a) Instructions presented to users at the beginning of each module

As explained, we now start from scratch. Consider that this is the first app you will install. Please install any application from the company: **thetimetube.com**. (Only one such app exists, and you can click on the app to view its info.)

(b) Module 1; Task *a* : Vendor Familiarity

You now need an app that allows scanning your Google Drive files for viruses.
Two such apps exist below. Check them both by clicking on them. Then choose the one that you prefer to install.
Be prepared to give a reason for that choice.

(c) Module 1; Task *b*: App Selection

Google Drive allows you to share files with friends. You decided to share **all your photos** on Google Drive with your friend John. Up till now, who is the friend who has access to your data?

☐ John
☐ Lisa

(d) Module 2; Task *a*: Collaborator Awareness

Task:
Your friend John has installed an application called Photo Editor and has given its company access to all his files (including shared files). Write below the name of the company that owns this application. (You can click on the app to view its info.)

(e) Module 2; Task *b*: Vendor Familiarity

Assume that you have shared all your photos with John. Additionally, you have shared with Lisa some of your photos. Who has more files from you in their Google Drive?

☐ John
☐ Lisa

(f) Module 3; Task *a*: Collaborator Awareness

Figure 8: Screenshots from the user study

Figure 9: Summary of the experiment modules; a sample of the questions corresponding to each step are available in Figure 8.

collaborators. A user's privacy risk magnitude at time t can thus be defined as the sum of the risk magnitude across vendors in V: $\text{Risk}(t) = \sum_{v \in V} p * f_{u,v}(t)$.

When a user installs an app from a vendor $\hat{v}$ at time $t+1$, the vendor gets access to the whole set of user's files. Hence, the risk magnitude is increased by $p * (1 - f_{u,\hat{v}}(t))$. Given that p is constant, the risk magnitude can be minimized by choosing $\hat{v}$, such that $\hat{v} = \arg\max_v f_{u,v}(t)$ (which can also be written as $\hat{v} = \arg\max_v VFC_u(\{v\}, t)$). Hence, the optimal, greedy strategy to minimize the risk is to select the vendor that already has the largest fraction of user files. We call this strategy: "History-based decisions".

C. CONCLUDING SURVEY

At the end of the user study of Section 4, users were presented with a final set of questions. We asked them whether they would like to be notified when a friend installs an app that gets access to their shared files. Around 92% of users in the *BL* group and 90% of users in the *HB* group agreed. We further asked the participants whether they are fine with a collaborator being notified when they install applications that access files shared with that collaborator. The percentage of

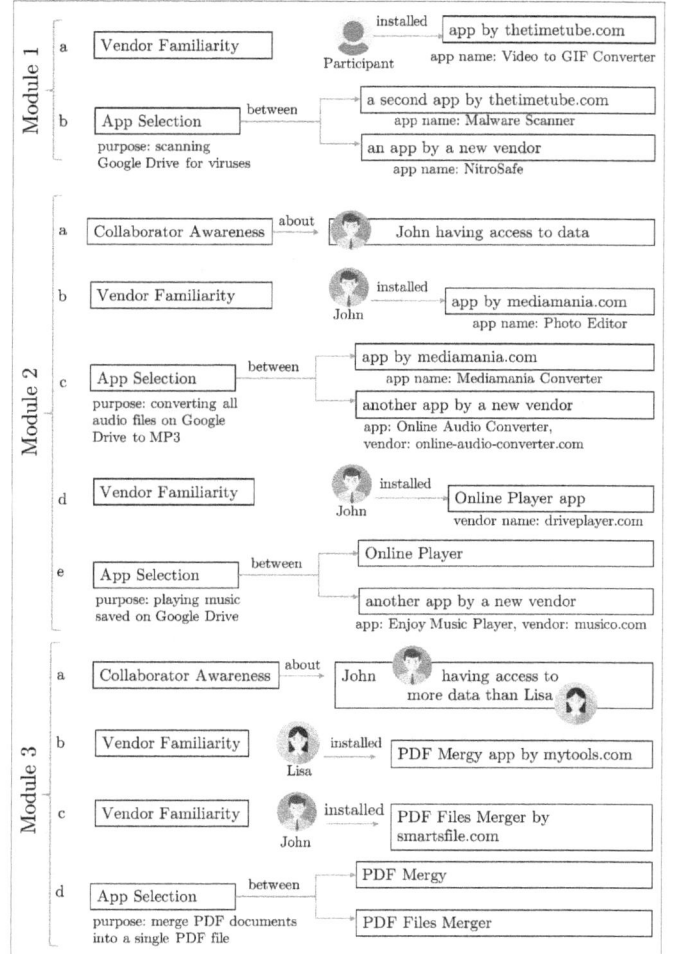

people who agreed dropped to 75% in the *BL* and 78% in the *HB* group. The difference between the answers to these two questions highlights that **only a minority of users is not willing to make the trade-off of contributing to the overall system.** Such users can be given the option to not use privacy indicators based on their friends' decisions. Next, users were asked the following question *"Assume you have installed an application called YouMusic from a company called Musicana and gave it access to all your files on Google Drive. Now you are considering installing an application called YouVideo from the same company. How do you think that this application will affect your privacy:"*. Only 11% of each group replied by *"negatively"*. The vast majority in both groups either perceived the avoidance of a new vendor as a positive outcome or considered that the privacy loss will remain the same. Interestingly, the users in the *BL* showed a similar reasoning in justifying their choices as the *HB* group although the latter were primed about these aspects via the privacy indicators. This indicates that **the privacy indicators actually match the first intuition for a large fraction of users.**

Sound and Static Analysis of Session Fixation Vulnerabilities in PHP Web Applications

Abdelouahab Amira
Research Center on Scientific
and Technical Information
CERIST, Algiers, Algeria
A.MIRA University, Bejaia,
Algeria
amira@mail.cerist.dz

Abdelraouf Ouadjaout
LIP6, University Pierre and
Marie Curie, Paris, France
abdelraouf.ouadjaout@lip6.fr

Abdelouahid Derhab
Center of Excellence in
Information Assurance
(CoEIA),
King Saud University, Riyadh,
Saudi Arabia
abderhab@ksu.edu.sa

Nadjib Badache
Research Center on Scientific
and Technical Information
CERIST, Algiers, Algeria
badache@mail.cerist.dz

ABSTRACT

Web applications use authentication mechanisms to provide user-friendly content to users. However, some dangerous techniques like session fixation attacks target these mechanisms, by making the legitimate user use a session identifier that is controlled by the attacker. In this way, he can then impersonate the legitimate user without the need to know his credentials. In this paper, we present SAWFIX, a PHP static analyzer that checks web applications for session fixation vulnerabilities. To the best of our knowledge, SAW-FIX is the first analyzer that checks exhaustively for this type of vulnerabilities, while the other methods only ensure partial correctness that is limited to a fraction of possible executions. SAWFIX is based on abstract interpretation, which is a theory for approximating the semantics of programs and allows designing static analyzers that are fully automatic and sound by construction. We implemented a prototype of our approach and tested it on several complex web applications. We obtained promising results in terms of detection accuracy and processing time, which reflects the efficiency of our system.

Keywords

Session fixation attacks; Web application security; Static program analysis; Abstract interpretation

1. INTRODUCTION

Nowadays, business activities and governments are relying more and more on web technology. The ease of implementation and deployment of web applications have made them ubiquitous and unavoidable, whether in e-commerce sites, in intranet/extranet applications or in Internet services. These applications are however increasingly targeted by malicious users. Indeed, a web application is accessible from anywhere on the network, which makes it easily exposed to the large panoply of existing security attacks.

Among the countermeasures that protect a web application from these threats, authentication is generally the first security shield considered during the design process. In the web paradigm, the authentication service relies on the concept of session management, which is principally based on SIDs (Session Identifiers). Session fixation attacks target these session management systems by tricking a legitimate user to use a SID controlled by a malicious user. This can be done either by providing a malicious URL that includes a SID to the victim, or by using other techniques such as XSS attacks.

To defend against this type of attacks, previous works [3, 4, 5] either detect the vulnerability by dynamically monitoring session values or protect the users by introducing additional SIDs that complement the already existing authentication mechanism. However, dynamic approaches are limited, in the sense that only certain attack scenarios are tested. On the other hand, more deployed SIDs add another layer of security but do not guarantee the attack prevention. The main common drawback of all these methods (like: IBM Security AppScan tool [1]) is that they do not check all the execution traces.

In this paper, we propose a new static analysis of web applications that verifies the immunity of the program against session fixation attacks. The novelty of our approach is twofold. First, the analysis is performed statically by operating directly on the source code of the application, which helps developers check their code base without requiring particular configuration of the runtime environment. Second, in contrast to other methods, it performs an exhaustive search of all possible executions. Indeed, our analysis is based on the theory of abstract interpretation [2] that provides a rigorous mathematical framework for analyzing efficiently the entire search space of program executions in finite time. The main benefit of this theory is that it provides sound verifi-

CODASPY'17 March 22-24, 2017, Scottsdale, AZ, USA

© 2017 Copyright held by the owner/author(s).

ACM ISBN 978-1-4503-4523-1/17/03.

DOI: http://dx.doi.org/10.1145/3029806.3029838

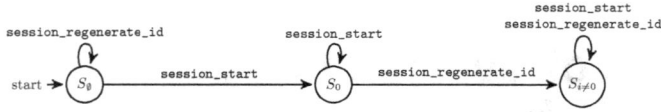

Figure 1: Session states and the effect of PHP session management functions.

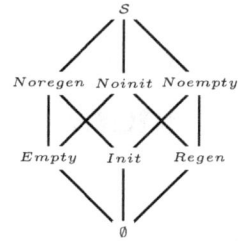

Figure 2: The lattice of abstract sessions.

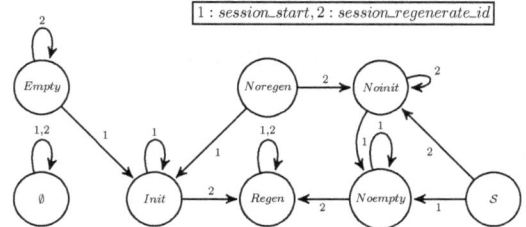

Figure 3: Abstract session values and the effect of PHP session management functions.

cation, which is guaranteed to find a vulnerability (in case one exists). It can also prove the absence of vulnerabilities, but might be subject to false alarms.

2. APPROACH DESCRIPTION

The basic idea of our approach is to detect the moment when the SID does not change after a successful authentication. Indeed, the attacker can control the legitimate user's initial SID. If this SID does not change after the authentication step, the attacker can use it to impersonate the user.

To track the occurrence of such situation statically, it is necessary to go through all execution paths that can be taken by the program. However, due to the undecidability of program verification, such precise enumeration can not be performed in finite time in general. To this end, the theory of abstract interpretation has been proposed in order to avoid the explosion of the size of the search space by abstracting away some of the details of the program semantics. In this section, we present a succinct description of the developed abstractions that are tailored to the verification of session fixation attacks in PHP web applications.

2.1 Abstraction of sessions

The first abstraction is related to the dynamic state of the session during execution. In PHP web application, the SID follows a specific workflow depicted in Figure 1. We can distinguish between three abstract session states that we denote by $\mathcal{S} = \{S_\emptyset, S_0, S_{i \neq 0}\}$. Initially, a web application is in the uninitialized state $S_\emptyset$. After that, the function *session_start* creates a new session or resumes the current one, which corresponds to the state S_0. Finally, the state $S_{i \neq 0}$ corresponds to the generation of a new SID during a session that has already been started.

This flow corresponds to the evolution of a single execution path. In abstract interpretation, we need to develop a computable abstraction of a set of executions in order to scale the analysis to possibly infinite search spaces. Consequently, we define our first abstraction $\mathcal{D}_{\mathcal{S}}^{\sharp}$ as the powerset lattice: $\langle \wp(\mathcal{S}), \subseteq, \cup, \emptyset, \mathcal{S} \rangle$

which corresponds to all possible combinations of the states of SIDs. In the sequel, we denote these abstract elements as $Empty = \{S_\emptyset\}$, $Init = \{S_0\}$, $Regen = \{S_{i \neq 0}\}$, $Noempty = Init \cup Regen$, $Noregen = Empty \cup Init$ and $Noinit = Empty \cup Regen$. In Figure 2, we show the corresponding Hass diagram. In addition, we need to abstract also the effect of PHP session management functions over the elements of $\mathcal{D}_{\mathcal{S}}^{\sharp}$, which is summarized in Figure 3.

2.2 Abstraction of classes

The second abstraction encapsulates the mappings between variables and classes. Indeed, we need to know for each variable of type object, the possible class whom it belongs to. So, when a method call is encountered, we can

decide which class methods code to analyze. Formally, we define the abstract class domain $\mathcal{D}_{\mathcal{C}}^{\sharp}$ as:

$$\langle \mathcal{V} \rightarrow \wp(\mathcal{C}), \dot{\subseteq}, \dot{\cup}, \lambda v. \emptyset, \lambda v. \mathcal{C} \rangle$$

where $\mathcal{V}$ represents the set of the program variables and $\mathcal{C}$ the set of classes. All lattice operators, such as order and join, are defined pointwise.

2.3 Put it all together

The final abstraction $\mathcal{D}^{\sharp} = \mathcal{D}_{\mathcal{S}}^{\sharp} \times \mathcal{D}_{\mathcal{C}}^{\sharp}$ is a simple product of the previous two domains. Two important facts should be noted about $\mathcal{D}^{\sharp}$. First, this domain is non-relational, which is due to the use of the cartesian product that removes the relation between session states and classes. Nevertheless, this level of abstraction is sufficient to successfully verify the web applications in our experiments.

Second, no information is preserved about the values of program variables. This implies that some spurious execution paths may be analyzed, for example when reaching conditional statements. Indeed, to ensure the soundness of the analysis, both branches of the if statement need to be analyzed even if in fact only one branch is taken by the program in a real execution. However, there exist many abstract domains dealing with this problem that can be easily integrated in our analysis.

In order to verify if the program is vulnerable to a session fixation attack, we check the session's abstract value at the authentication instruction: the elements *Empty*, *Regen* and *Noinit* reflect safe states. In this case, we are sure that the application is not vulnerable. The other values (except for $\emptyset$) are associated with dangerous states. So, the application may be vulnerable.

3. SYSTEM DESIGN

The general design of SAWFIX is given by figure 4. It is based on Phc[1], which is an open-source compiler for PHP.

---

[1] https://github.com/pbiggar/phc

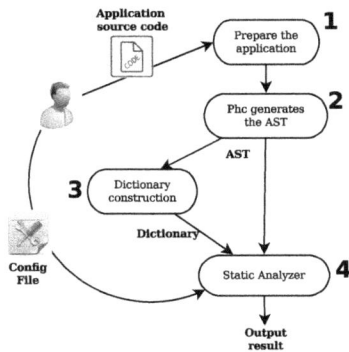

Figure 4: SAWFIX design.

It consists of four steps:

First, we prepare the application to be processed by Phc. This compiler permits the generation of an Abstract Syntax tree (AST) but does not support all of the PHP's functionalities, including dynamic inclusions and some inclusion functions. A dynamic inclusion is a case where the inclusion parameter contains a variable, for example, the command `include($basepath. "File.php")` receives a variable as a parameter. SAWFIX replaces the dynamic parts by static ones as follows: We start by obtaining the file names from the static portion of the inclusion. Then, we operate a recursive search on the application's sub-directories. Once the list of all the files is obtained, we merge their code to get a unique and a representative file. Finally, each instance of the dynamic parameter is replaced by the full path of the newly generated file. The two inclusion functions `include_once` and `require_once` are not supported by Phc. We replace them respectively by two functions: `include` and `require`. As this operation can generate loops in the application code, we move all the instances of these inclusions to the start of the entry web page.

In the second step, Phc is used to generate the AST of the prepared code.

In the third step, SAWFIX analyses the application's AST and builds what is called a function dictionary. The latter stores function (or method) names, the mapping of functions to the different classes, and for each map its physical address in the AST. By using the dictionary, SAWFIX can get the physical address of the code (function or method) in the AST without performing other operations.

In the last step, SAWFIX applies the approach described in Section 2 and analyses statically all the web application's AST. However, we want to know the session state on the lines that define a successful authentication (which are in the form of: `$_SESSION["logged_in"]= 'yes'`). To print the session state at a specific line of code. The user can either add the directive `__print__()` in the application's code or create a configuration file. The file must contain the name of the session's variable and its value (for example: `logged_in, yes`).

4. PRELIMINARY RESULTS

To demonstrate the efficiency of our system, we tested SAWFIX on multiple web applications of different complexities, ranging from 1K to 110K of lines of code. Some of these applications are vulnerable to session fixation attacks and our system successfully reported the vulnerabilities. The

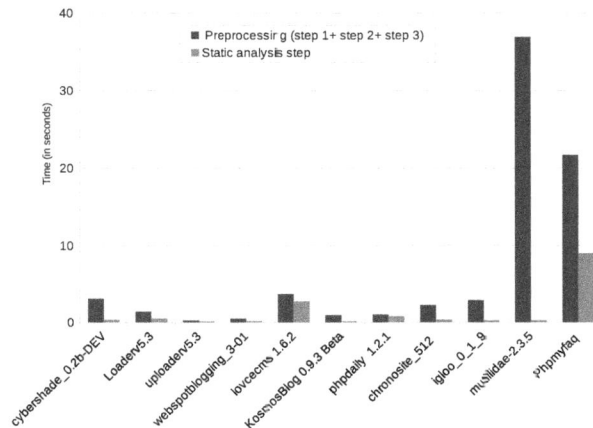

Figure 5: Processing time

processing time results are illustrated in Figure 5: the applications are shown in an ascending order with respect to the number of lines of codes. The obtained results show that SAWFIX can process an application (i.e., three preprocessing steps + static analysis step) in less than 40 seconds.

5. CONCLUSION AND FUTURE WORK

We presented a sound approach that checks for session fixation vulnerabilities in PHP based web applications. We also leveraged our approach and developed a static analyzer SAWFIX. We tested our prototype on a variety of complex web applications and obtained promising results in terms of detection accuracy and processing time. As future work, we plan to include variable tracking, inheritance and recursion into our analysis. It will also be interesting to test more large-scale open source web applications (up to 500K loc).

6. REFERENCES

[1] IBM Security AppScan. http: //www-03.ibm.com/software/products/en/appscan.

[2] P. Cousot and R. Cousot. Abstract interpretation: a unified lattice model for static analysis of programs by construction or approximation of fixpoints. In *Proc. 4th ACM symposium on Principles of programming languages*, pages 238–252. ACM, 1977.

[3] P. De Ryck, N. Nikiforakis, L. Desmet F. Piessens, and W. Joosen. Serene: self-reliant client-side protection against session fixation. In *Proc. 12th IFIP WG 6.1 international conference on Distributed Applications and Interoperable Systems*, DAIS'12, pages 59–72. Springer-Verlag, 2012.

[4] M. Johns, B. Braun, M. Schrank, and J. Posegga. Reliable protection against session fixation attacks. In *Proc. 2011 ACM Symposium on Applied Computing*, SAC '11, pages 1531–1537. ACM, 2011.

[5] Y. Takamatsu, Y. Kosuga, and K. Kono. Automated detection of session fixation vulnerabilities. In *Proc. 19th international conference on World wide web*, WWW '10, pages 1191–1192. ACM, 2010.

A New Bloom Filter Structure for Searchable Encryption Schemes

Chi Sing Chum
Computer Science Dept., Graduate Center
City Univ. of New York
365 5th Ave, New York, NY 10016 USA
cchum@gradcenter.cuny.edu

Xiaowen Zhang
Computer Science Dept., Graduate Center &
College of Staten Island, City Univ. of New York
2800 Victory Blvd, Staten Island, NY 10314 USA
xiaowen.zhang@csi.cuny.edu

ABSTRACT

We propose a new Bloom filter structure for searchable encryption schemes in which a large Bloom filter is treated as (replaced with) two smaller ones for the search index. False positive is one inherent drawback of Bloom filter. We formulate the false positive rates for one regular large Bloom filter, and then derive the false positive rate for the two smaller ones. With examples, we show how the new scheme cuts down the false positive rate and the size of Bloom filter to a balanced point that fulfills the user requirements and increases the efficiency of the structure.

Keywords

Searchable encryption; cryptographic hash function; Bloom filter; false positive rate;

1. INTRODUCTION

We are dealing with a large volume of data of different forms nowadays. As data grow exponentially, many companies start to store their data outside their premises in cloud storage provided by various cloud providers, e.g., Amazon, Google, etc. The advantages to use cloud storage mainly include shorter setup time, lower implementation cost "easier up/down scaling," cheaper ongoing cost (pay-as-you-go). However, as data are off the premises, security of the data is a big concern. Encrypting the data before sending to the cloud servers is a solution. But the next question would be how to search on these encrypted data effectively when the user wants to only retrieve a subset of the data without leaking any information to the server. Searchable encryption (SE) provides an answer.

Research on SE has been ongoing for over a decade; there have been many works done in the area [3, 9]. In particular, there are SE schemes that use Bloom filters, for example in [1, 5, 6, 7, 8]. Three entities are involved in SE: querier who queries the data, data owner who initially owns the data, and server who stores and processes the data. A querier issues a query to a server to directly search over encrypted stored

CODASPY'17 March 22-24, 2017, Scottsdale, AZ, USA

© 2017 Copyright held by the owner/author(s).

ACM ISBN 978-1-4503-4523-1/17/03.

DOI: http://dx.doi.org/10.1145/3029806.3029839

data. The query itself also is encrypted, and the server returns the encrypted version of matching results to the user. Searchable encryption scheme provides strong security and privacy guarantees. It does not leak any information to the server; other than returned matching results the querier does not get any information about the rest of the data stored on the server.

The rest of the paper is organized as follows. In Section 2, we describe how Bloom filter works; most importantly, we derive the false positive rate that closely depends on the size of Bloom filter, number of hash functions, and number of keywords stored in Bloom filter. In Section 3, we propose a new structure that splits a Bloom filter into two smaller ones. We use an example to illustrate that the proposed structure balances the Bloom filter size, false positive rate, and user requirements, and ultimately increases the efficiency of an SE. We conclude the paper in Section 4.

2. BLOOM FILTER

2.1 Background

A Bloom filter [2] is a dynamic data structure which can be used effectively to add elements into a set and test whether an element is in a given set. The Bloom filter B consists of a bit array of m bits which are denoted by $B[0], \ldots, B[m-1]$ and initially set to 0. The filter uses r independent uniformly distributed hash functions $h_1, \ldots, h_r$. The hash functions have hash length of s bits, $2^s = m$, and $h_i : \{0,1\}^* \to \{0,1\}^s$ for $i \in \{1, r\}$. Suppose we have a list of words $D = \{w_1, \ldots, w_l\}$ and want to set up a set for D using a Bloom filter. For each word $w_j \in D$, $j \in [1, \ldots, l]$, the array bits at the positions $h_1(w_j), \ldots, h_r(w_j)$ are set to 1. To see if a word w belongs to D, we check the bits at positions $h_1(w), \ldots, h_r(w)$. If all checked bits are 1's, then w is (possibly) contained in D. However, there is a small possibility of false positive. Even if all the bits corresponding to w are equal to 1, there is no guarantee that w is in D as these bits could be set to 1's by other words. That is, the bits at positions $h_1(w), \ldots, h_r(w)$ in B are 1's and w appears to be in D, but actually is not. But if any one of the checked bits is 0, then w is definitely not in D. It means that there is no false negative.

False positive is one drawback of Bloom filter. However, a Bloom filter does provide an effective tool for searching in searchable encryption. It does not store the word but only those bits corresponding to the hashes of the word are set to 1. This saves space and the server does not learn anything about the words stored in the filter. Adding words and testing any given word in a Bloom filter are efficient due to the fast calculation of the hash functions.

For each encrypted document, we create a Bloom filter to store (represent) all its keywords. Therefore, the Bloom filter acts as an index to the document. When the user supplies a keyword to the server, all the Bloom filters will be checked to see if the associated documents need to be selected. This avoids the time-consuming process to scan all the documents. We can even improve the security by storing the encrypted keywords in the Bloom filters and sending the encrypted keyword to the server for searching, like in [5].

2.2 False positive rate

Suppose we want to test if a word w is in the Bloom filter B, which stores l keywords $w_1, \ldots, w_l$ for the document D.

i) w is equal to one of w_j's $(1 \leq j \leq l)$. Then, we will get a "Yes" answer and that will be correct.

ii) w is not equal to any one of w_j's. Let $h_1(w) = x_1, \ldots, h_r(w) = x_r$. The probability that x_1th bit of B will not be set to 1 by h_1 on w_1 (assuming hash function h_i is uniformly distributed) is

$$Pr[h_1(w_1) \neq x_1] = \frac{m-1}{m} = 1 - \frac{1}{m}. \tag{1}$$

The probability that x_1th bit of B will not be set to 1 by all r hash functions (assuming all hash functions are independent) is

$$Pr[h_i(w_1) \neq x_1] = \left(1 - \frac{1}{m}\right)^r, 1 \leq i \leq r. \tag{2}$$

Since there are l words in B, the probability that x_1th bit of B will not be set to 1 by all r hash functions on l words:

$$Pr[h_i(w_j) \neq x_1] = \left(1 - \frac{1}{m}\right)^{rl}, 1 \leq i \leq r, 1 \leq j \leq l. \tag{3}$$

So, the probability that x_1th bit of B will be set to 1 by r hash functions on these l words is

$$1 - \left(1 - \frac{1}{m}\right)^{rl}. \tag{4}$$

Assuming that the probabilities of each bit $x_1, \ldots, x_r$ being set to 1 are independent, the probability that all the bits will be set to 1 by r hash functions on these l words (false positive rate) is

$$R = Pr[B[x_1] = 1, \ldots, B[x_r] = 1] = \left(1 - \left(1 - \frac{1}{m}\right)^{rl}\right)^r. \tag{5}$$

However, Bose et al [4] did a detailed analysis and showed that the false positive rate of a Bloom filter B is actually higher than the result stated in Equation (5). This is because from Equation (3) to Equation (5) we assume that all the bits being set to 1 are independent to each other. But this is not the case as collisions may occur.

3. NEWLY PROPOSED STRUCTURE

3.1 Description

The general idea of using a Bloom filter appears in the literature. However, there is no rigorous treatment about what the size of the filter should be. While it is obvious that increasing the size of the filter will decrease the false

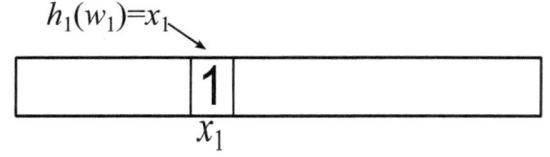

Figure 1: Bloom filter B of size $m = 2^s$.

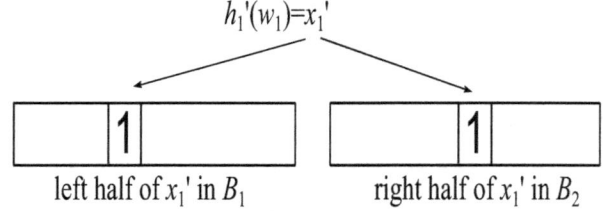

Figure 2: Bloom filters B_1 and B_2 of size $m' = 2^{s'}$ each.

positive rate, as shown in Equation (5), the relation is not discussed in details. It is through this motivation that we propose how to use/apply Bloom filters more effectively to cut down the false positive rate and the size of Bloom filters to a balance point which fulfills the user requirements.

Now suppose we replace these r hash functions h_i (here $1 \leq i \leq r$) with another set of r hash functions h_i' with the length of the hash equaling to $2 \times s'$ and the Bloom filter B with two Bloom filters B_1 and B_2 with size of $m' = 2^{s'}$ each. In essence, we treat one Bloom filter as two smaller Bloom filters.

The procedure remains the same with the exception that we set those bits in $B_1(B_2)$ that correspond to the left (right) halve of the hashes from h_i' to 1. Note that the length of x_i' now equals $2 \times s'$ in bits (see Figure 1 and Figure 2).

Following Equation (5), the false positive rate R'

$$R' = \left(1 - \left(1 - \frac{1}{m'}\right)^{rl}\right)^r \left(1 - \left(1 - \frac{1}{m'}\right)^{rl}\right)^r$$
$$= \left(1 - \left(1 - \frac{1}{m'}\right)^{rl}\right)^{2r}. \tag{6}$$

We need to find s' to fulfill the following condition:

$$2^{s'} + 2^{s'} = 2^{s'+1} < 2^s, \tag{7}$$

$$\left(1 - \left(1 - \frac{1}{2^{s'}}\right)^{rl}\right)^{2r} < \left(1 - \left(1 - \frac{1}{2^s}\right)^{rl}\right)^r. \tag{8}$$

Equations (7) and (8) demonstrate the reductions in space and false positive rate, respectively. If such s' exists, that means we can improve the efficiency of the original Bloom filter B by two smaller Bloom filters B_1 and B_2. If there exists a range of values for s', then it is up to the users to choose the one that balances both the space and false positive rate.

Table 1: Original Bloom filter B false positive rate R and space m.

s	R	m	$\log_{10}(m)$
30	8.67362E-15	1073741824	9.03089987

Table 2: New smaller Bloom filter false positive rate R' and space $2m'$

s'	R'	$2m'$	$\log_{10}(2m')$
15	8.62138E-11	65536	4.816479931
16	5.40466E-12	131072	5.117509926
17	3.38302E-13	262144	5.418539922
18	2.11598E-14	524288	5.719569918
19	1.32299E-15	1048576	6.020599913
20	8.27024E-17	2097152	6.321629909
21	5.16939E-18	4194304	6.622659905
22	3.23102E-19	8388608	6.9236899
23	2.01944E-20	16777216	7.224719896
24	1.26216E-21	33554432	7.525749892
25	7.88856E-23	67108864	7.826779887
26	4.93037E-24	134217728	8.127809883
27	3.08148E-25	268435456	8.428839879
28	1.92593E-26	536870912	8.729869874
29	1.20371E-27	1073741824	9.03089987

3.2 An example

Given an original Bloom filter B with $r = 2$ hash functions h_1 and h_2 of hash length $s = 30$. Let $l = 50$ be the number of keywords in B. Table 1 calculates the false positive rate $R = \left(1 - \left(1 - 1/2^{30}\right)^{100}\right)^2$ and the space $m = 2^s = 2^{30}$. Suppose we want to replace B with two smaller Bloom filters B_1 and B_2 with 2 hash functions h_1' and h_2' of hash length $2 \times s'$. We want to find out a range of s' such that there will be a reduction in both false positive rate and space. Table 2 calculates the false positive rates $R' = \left(1 - \left(1 - 1/2^{s'}\right)^{100}\right)^4$ and the space $2m' = 2^{s'-1}$.

Based on Equations (7) and (8), we are developing a method to effectively estimate the feasible range of s'. From Tables 1 and 2, hash lengths s' from 20 to 28 fulfill the requirements of the reductions in both false positive rate and space. The calculation of false positive rate is based on Equation (5). However, we can follow the idea mentioned in [4]. For the purpose of this paper, the exact calculation of the rate is not so important. Again, we assume there is no collision among l words in the Bloom filters B, E_1, and B_2. It means that rl bits are set to 1 in each Bloom filter.

4. CONCLUSIONS

We propose a technique to improve the efficiency of Bloom filters used for searchable encryption schemes.

A) Practical considerations: As we know the false positive rate will be reduced if we use a larger Bloom filter, or more hash functions. However, using a larger filter may not be efficient and difficult to implement. In the same way, using more hash functions may not be necessary, as they may degrade the performance.

We suggest using a cryptographic hash function for the following reasons:

1. By repeating the underlying compress function, it can take any message of arbitrary length.

2. Good performance due to collision, pre-image, and second pre-image resistance properties of a cryptographic hash function.

3. We can simply extract certain portions (for example, the first 30 bits), or combine portions of the hash value, as a new hash function.

B) Implementation of the automated system: After estimating a reasonable upper bound for the number of keywords and the acceptable false positive rate, we design a Bloom filter. Then we apply the above technique to subdivide the original Bloom filter B into smaller ones B_1 and B_2 for improvement. Based on the goals of the user, space vs. false positive rate, the optimum size of the smaller Bloom filters can thus be adjusted.

5. REFERENCES

[1] S. Bellovin and W. Cheswick. Privacy-enhanced searches using encrypted bloom filters. Technical Report CUCS-034-07, Dept. of Computer Science, Columbia Univ., Sept. 2007, 1–16.

[2] B. Bloom. Space/time trade-offs in hash coding with allowable errors. *Comm. of the ACM*, 13(7):422–426, 1970.

[3] C. Bosch, P. Hartel, W. Jonker, and A. Peter. A survey of provably secure searchable encryption. *ACM Comput. Surv.*, 47(2), 2014. Article 18.

[4] P. Bose, H. Guo, E. Kranakis, A. Maheshwari, and P. Morin. On the false-positive rate of bloom filters. Technical Report TR-07-07, School of Computer Science, Carleton University.

[5] E.-J. Goh. Secure indexes. Technical Report 2003/216, IACR ePrint Cryptography Archive, 2003.

[6] S. Pal, P. Sardana, and A. Sardana. Efficient search on encrypted data using bloom filter. In *Proc. of 2014 Int. Conf. on Computing for Sustainable Global Development (INDIACom)*, pages 412–416, 2014.

[7] V. Pappas, F. Krell, B. Vo, V. Kolesnikov, T. Malkin, S. Choi, W. George, A. Keromytis, and S. Bellovin. Blind seer: A scalable private dbms. In *Proc. of 2014 IEEE Symposium on Security and Privacy*, pages 359–374, 2014.

[8] M. Raykova, B. Vo, S. Bellovin, and T. Malkin. Secure anonymous database search. In *Proc. of 2009 CCSW, ACM*, pages 115–126, 2009.

[9] Q. Tang. Search in encrypted data: theoretical models and practical applications. Technical Report 2012/648, IACR ePrint Cryptography Archive, 2012.

Seamless and Secure Bluetooth LE Connection Migration

Syed Rafiul Hussain[1], Shagufta Mehnaz[1], Shahriar Nirjon[2], Elisa Bertino[1]
[1]Purdue University, [2] UNC Chapel Hill
hussain1@purdue.edu, smehnaz@purdue.edu, nirjon@cs.unc.edu, bertino@purdue.edu

ABSTRACT

At present, Bluetooth Low Energy (BLE) is dominantly used in commercially available Internet of Things (IoT) devices – such as smart watches, fitness trackers, and smart appliances. Compared to classic Bluetooth, BLE has been simplified in many ways that include its connection establishment, data exchange, and encryption processes. Unfortunately, this simplification comes at a cost. For example, only a star topology is supported in BLE environments and a peripheral (an IoT device) can communicate with only one gateway (e.g. a smartphone, or a BLE hub) at a set time. When a peripheral goes out of range, it loses connectivity to a gateway, and cannot connect and seamlessly communicate with another gateway without user interventions. In other words, BLE connections do not get automatically migrated or handed-off to another gateway. In this paper, we propose a system which brings seamless connectivity to BLE-capable mobile IoT devices in an environment that consists of a network of gateways. Our framework ensures that unmodified, commercial off-the-shelf BLE devices seamlessly and securely connect to a nearby gateway without any user intervention.

Keywords

BLE; IoT; Connection migration

1. INTRODUCTION

The Internet of Things (IoT) has entered the commercial market much faster than expected. The IoT industries predict that the total number of 'smart things' will be more than 30 billion by the year 2020. In a typical scenario, an IoT device connects to a gateway (e.g., a smartphone or a smart hub) over a low-power wireless network, and the gateway enables its access to the Internet. Because the connection process between an IoT device and a gateway requires active engagement of a user, *seamless connectivity of mobile IoT devices in a network of gateways* is still not happening. Ideally, an IoT device should be able to seamlessly communicate with a nearby gateway, without requiring an end-user to enter pins and passwords every time it moves near a different gateway in the same trusted network environment.

There are a number of wireless protocols such as Bluetooth LE (BLE), ZigBee, NFC, that have been used in different IoT communication scenarios. Among these, BLE is the most popular choice because of its simplicity, openness, and a promised battery life of

CODASPY'17 March 22-24, 2017, Scottsdale, AZ, USA

© 2017 Copyright held by the owner/author(s).

ACM ISBN 978-1-4503-4523-1/17/03.

DOI: http://dx.doi.org/10.1145/3029806.3029840

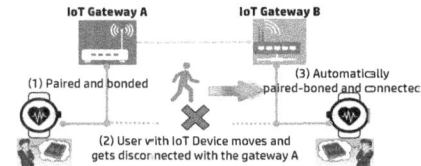

Figure 1: Seamless BLE connectivity architecture.

multiple years. The BLE protocol allows multiple devices ('peripherals') to attach themselves to a single gateway (the 'central'), but it restricts the mobility of the peripherals outside and into the range of a gateway. Moving the gateway along with a mobile IoT device seems like an option, but it is not always feasible as it causes disconnections of other IoT devices that are static or moving in a different direction from the gateway.

In order to ensure continuous BLE connectivity, Zachariah et al. [5] proposed an architecture where an IoT device may connect to multiple gateways located at different places. However, establishing a distinct connection with every gateway requires a peripheral to reset and broadcast advertising signals separately for all the gateways. Even if connections with multiple gateways is made possible by hacking [1], it comes at the cost of disconnecting the device from its previous gateway and then connecting to a new one. This incurs significant CPU, memory, energy, and bandwidth overhead in resource constrained IoT devices as even a single connection establishment requires advertisements, discovery, pairing and bonding [4], and several mutual agreements in different layers of BLE protocol stack. In addition, the process requires repeated manual interventions that disrupt the ongoing communication between a device and a remote service [2]. Because of these practical issues, we argue that an IoT device should be able to seamlessly communicate with different gateways [5] without requiring to create a separate connection with each of them.

In this paper, we propose a system which enables seamless BLE connection migration for mobile IoT devices in a network of BLE gateways. The contributions of this paper are the following:

- We propose a framework that ensures seamless communication between an unmodified, BLE-enabled mobile IoT device and a remote service in a network of BLE gateways, without requiring pairing-bonding and connections to individual gateways.

- We propose two approaches – *full stack cloning* and *partial stack cloning* for capturing a snapshot of connection states at the current gateway and then transferring and updating them at the next gateway during BLE connection migration.

- We propose a gateway selection mechanism for transferring the connection state to the most suitable gateway when an IoT device requires to migrate its connection.

2. USAGE SCENARIOS

- *In Hospitals:* Patients wearing BLE devices in hospitals can be localized and monitored using a network of gateways deployed at different locations in the hospital.

- *In Airports:* Upon arrival at the airport, passengers (and baggage) who are equipped with BLE beacons can voluntarily report their location and status to the deployed gateways from anywhere within the airport, and in return, they get personalized services and notifications.

- *In Theme Parks:* With the help of a BLE-enabled wristband on the child and static gateways deployed at different locations inside a theme park, parents can monitor and locate their missing kids via their mobile phone.

3. BLE BACKGROUND

Roles of BLE Device: A BLE device assumes either a *peripheral* or a *central* role. A peripheral, typically an IoT device such as a heart rate monitor, a blood pressure monitor, a smart lock, or a smart watch, comes with limited capabilities and contains advertisement information. A central device such as an access point, a personal computer, or a smartphone, scans for BLE advertisements, receives an advertisement, and initiates a connection.

Modes of Communication: Two modes of communication are available: *broadcast* and *connected* modes. The broadcast mode enables a peripheral to send data to any other device listening for transmissions. If two devices need to exchange data they can use the *connected* mode.

Pairing: In *connected* mode, if two devices want to exchange data securely, they perform a *pairing* process which results into a number of keys shared between the peripheral and the central.

Bonding: It is the process of storing the keys created during pairing for use in subsequent connections.

Privacy: BLE can use *Random Device Addressing* for privacy of connections and prevent 'tracking' based on the assumption that eavesdropping did not occur during pairing process.

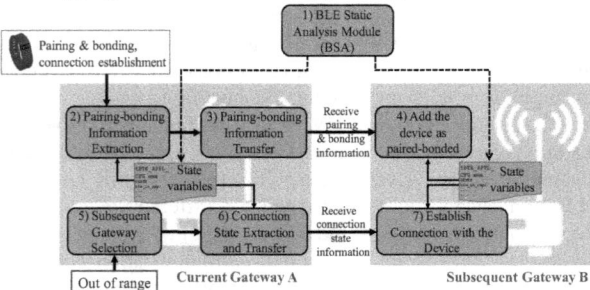

Figure 2: Workflow of connection migration

4. SYSTEM DESIGN

4.1 Threat model

We consider a strong threat model where only IoT gateways and IoT devices are parts of a trusted computing base. Also, we consider that the adversaries have capabilities of injecting unauthenticated packets, modifying legitimate packets, and sniffing messages.

4.2 Workflow

Figure 2 depicts the workflow of connection migration process.

Identify Connection State Information: In an off-line, one-time step, we analyze the BLE source code to identify the set of variables required for both pairing-bonding and connection information transfers. The *BLE Static Analysis (BSA)* module performs this static analysis on BLE source code and the identified set of variables (that are required for connection transfers) are stored in each of the gateways.

Extract Pairing-Bonding Information: A BLE central, serving as a gateway scans for peripheral devices that broadcast advertisement packets so that the central can connect with the peripherals

and receive the desired GATT services. We name the gateway to which the IoT device is currently connected as the *current* gateway. In order to ensure secure data transfer, the current gateway initiates pairing and bonding procedures as shown in Figure 3(a). After creating connection, the current gateway extracts the pairing-bonding related information.

We instrument the BLE source code to obtain the runtime values of the pairing-bonding variables for a connected IoT device (as shown in steps (2) in Figure 2). The current gateway stores the extracted information into memory and sends them to subsequent gateways. The runtime for this extraction module is distributed across different layers of BLE protocol stack.

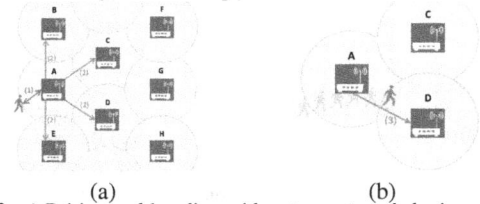

(a)   (b)

Figure 3: a) Pairing and bonding with gateway A and sharing of pairing-bonding information with gateways B, C, and D. (b) Subsequent gateway selection and connection transfer as the user with IoT device moves from gateway A to gateway D.

Disseminate Pairing-Bonding Information: The current gateway disseminates the pairing-bonding information to a set of gateways that are candidates for the subsequent gateway (the next gateway to which the IoT device may connect). This pairing-bonding information consists of both the bonded device's information as well as a subset of state variables. In Figure 3(a), the gateways that are in the vicinity of gateway A are the gateways B, C, D, and E. Therefore, the candidate gateways are B, C, D, and E but not the gateways F, G, or H.

Add as a Bonded Device: Upon reception of the pairing-bonding information, the candidate gateways B, C, D, and E store these information mapped with the Bluetooth device address of that IoT device so that whenever that device needs service from these gateways, they do not have to execute the pairing-bonding procedures. Note that the candidate gateways do not initiate connection at this stage since they do not have connection state information.

Subsequent Gateway Selection: If an IoT device moves during or after connection establishment, the current gateway or the IoT service providing cloud system is able to estimate the device's moving direction [3]. We leverage this mechanism and examines a device's locations at recent timestamps to infer the moving direction. Location information of IoT devices can also be obtained using existing indoor and outdoor localization techniques. Analyzing the movement direction and speed of the IoT devices, the current gateway or the service provider selects the subsequent gateway among the candidate gateways to whom the connection information will be transferred. As shown in Figure 3 (b), the current gateway A transfers connection information to the subsequent gateway D.

Extract and Transfer Connection State: The current gateway identifies the current state (or snapshot) of the connection and transfers the required state variables to the subsequent gateway so that the subsequent gateway can reconstruct the connection state with the same peripheral. The extraction of runtime values of connection state variables follows the same procedure as the extraction of pairing-bonding information.

Establish Connection with Subsequent Gateway: Upon reception of the connection state information, the subsequent gateway creates required objects related to connection, updates the connection state variables, and stores the connection information into gateway's non-volatile memory (NVRAM). As a result, the peripheral gets seamlessly connected to the subsequent gateway.

4.3 BLE Stack Cloning

Our system provides two modes for connection state extraction: *full stack cloning*, and *partial stack cloning*. Full stack cloning refers to cloning states of all the layers of Bluetooth stack starting from the application layer down to the link layer whereas partial stack cloning refers to the cloning of Bluetooth stack starting from the application layer down to the L2CAP layer.

4.4 Secure Connection Information Sharing

While sharing the pairing-bonding and connection information, the receiver gateways can be categorized into two groups: *trusted* and *untrusted* gateways.

Trusted Gateway: If the receiver gateways belong to the same cluster of gateways as the current gateway, the receiver gateways do not need to further authenticate themselves. They already share a secret group key with which they encrypt the data and then distribute the data in encrypted form securely. This secret group key can be shared between gateways through WiFi or 4G/LTE communication network and thus do not require any change in the existing Bluetooth protocol. An example of such data transfer is following:

$$Enc\_D \leftarrow E_{K_{grp}}(D||nonce), D||nonce \leftarrow D_{K_{grp}}(Enc\_D) \quad (1)$$

where D is the data to transfer, and K_{grp} is the symmetric group key. In Eqn. 1, the current gateway encrypts the data using K_{grp} and transfers Enc_D to the receiver gateway(s). A trusted receiver gateway has knowledge of K_{grp}, and thus decrypts Enc_D to D as shown in Eqn. 1.

Untrusted Gateway: If the subsequent gateway to which the BLE connection is going to be migrated is not already trusted, the current gateway needs to verify the public key certificate of the subsequent gateway. Upon certificate validation, the current gateway use the public key cryptography protocol as the following to share the bonding and connection information securely.

$$Enc\_D \leftarrow E_{PK_{rcv}}(D||nonce), D||nonce \leftarrow D_{SK_{rcv}}(Enc\_D) \quad (2)$$

where D is the data to transfer, and PK_{rcv} is the public key of the receiver gateway. In Eqn. 2, the current gateway encrypts the data using PK_{rcv} and transfers Enc_D to the receiver gateway. The receiver gateway has knowledge of the corresponding secret key, SK_{rcv}, and thus decrypts Enc_D to D as shown in Eqn. 2.

5. EVALUATION

Experimental Setup We use five Nexus 5 phones as gateways (i.e., BLE centrals), one Nexus 6 phone and one Alcatel Onetouch tablet as IoT devices. Nexus 5 phones have only the BLE central feature whereas Nexus 6 and Alcatel Onetouch tablet have both the BLE central and the BLE peripheral capabilities. We use the *nRF Connect* application downloaded from the Google Play store for BLE peripherals. For the gateways, we have developed a custom application. We use the heart rate monitoring service that periodically sends heart rate measurement in a single BLE packet of size 20-bytes every second. Each data point reported in the experiment is obtained by taking the average of at least five runs.

Migration Success Rate: We found every connection migration request successful when IoT devices are both static and moving at different speeds.

Extra bytes required for connection migration: In both *partial stack cloning* and *full stack cloning*, the current gateway sends a 512-bytes of blob containing the bonding related information to each of its neighbors. However, for *full stack cloning*, the current gateways sends a 2048-bytes of blob containing values of all the connection related variables to the next gateway.

Time required for adding a peripheral as a bonded device: To add the peripheral as a bonded device requires the IoT gateway needs to load the device information, e.g., device address, device type, address type, and keys from the main memory and then store

them into the gateway's NVRAM for using in future communications. Table 1 shows the mean time required by IoT gateways of different device types to load a peripheral.

Gateway	Loading Time (ms)	Storing Time (ms)	Total Time (ms)
Nexus 5	40.5	19.1	60.4
Nexus 6	36.7	17.4	54.1
Alcatel OneTouch	43.2	20.3	63.5

Table 1: Time required for adding a peripheral as a bonded device.

Time required for connection migration: Figure 4(a) shows the connection migration time increases with the increase of users speed as there are more packet losses associated with increased mobility of users. Also, the connection migration time for *partial stack cloning* is smaller than that of the *full stack cloning* because creating a new connection between the subsequent gateway and the IoT device does not require any cryptographic operation in case of *partial stack cloning*.

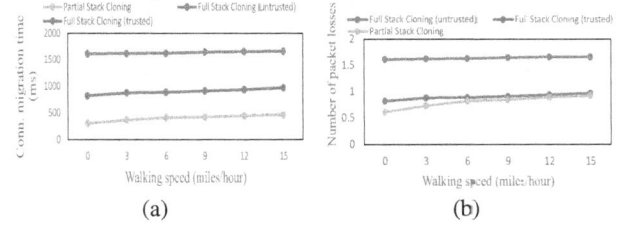

Figure 4: a) Time required for connection migration. (b) Number of packet losses when data packets are sent with 1 second time interval.

Packet loss: Fig. 4(b) shows the number of packet losses when BLE packets are sent from the IoT device to the gateway every after 1 second. *Full stack cloning* with untrusted gateway causes upto 2 packet losses which is about 2X of the other scenarios.

5.1 Security Analysis

Adversaries cannot inject or modify packets. Our system ensures that the gateways always perform secure communication with BLE devices through the long term keys established by pairing-bonding procedure. Thus maliciously injected or modified BLE packets by adversaries are always identified.

Adversaries cannot derive paring-bonding and connection information. The gateways use non-deterministic encryption to securely transfer the pairing-bonding information. Therefore, adversaries cannot derive the long term keys and the connection related values to impersonate a legitimate gateway.

6. CONCLUSION

In this paper, we focus on the problem of IoT devices being unable to connect to multiple gateways seamlessly and thus propose a framework that ensures seamless and secure communication between a mobile IoT device and a remote service in a network of BLE gateway environment.

7. REFERENCES

[1] W. Albazrqaoe, J. Huang, and G. Xing. Practical bluetooth traffic sniffing: Systems and privacy implications. In *MobiSys, 16*.

[2] P. A. Kodeswaran, R. Kokku, S. Sen, and M. Srivatsa. Idea: A system for efficient failure management in smart iot environments. In *MobiSys '16*.

[3] Y. Tao, C. Faloutsos, D. Papadias, and B. Liu. Prediction and indexing of moving objects with unknown motion patterns. In *SIGMOD '04*.

[4] J. L. Yan Michalevsky, Suman Nath. Mashable: Mobile applications of secret handshakes over bluetooth le. In *MobiCom*, 2016.

[5] T. Zachariah, N. Klugman, B. Campbell, J. Adkins, N. Jackson, and P. Dutta. The internet of things has a gateway problem. In *HotMobile '15*.

Differentially-Private Big Data Analytics for High-Speed Research Network Traffic Measurement

Oana-Georgiana
Niculaescu
UMass Boston
onic@cs.umb.edu

Mihai Maruseac
UMass Boston
mmarusea@cs.umb.edu

Gabriel Ghinita
UMass Boston
gabriel.ghinita@umb.edu

ABSTRACT

High-speed research networks (e.g., Internet2, Géant) represent the backbone of large-scale research projects that bring together stakeholders from academia, industry and government. Such projects have increasing demands on throughput (e.g., 100Gbps line rates), and require a high amount of configurability. Collecting and sharing traffic data for such networks can help in detecting hotspots, troubleshooting, and designing novel routing protocols. However, sharing network data directly introduces serious privacy breaches, as an adversary may be able to derive private details about individual users (e.g., personal preferences or activity patterns). Our objective is to sanitize high-speed research network data according to the de-facto standard of *differential privacy (DP)* thus supporting benefic applications of traffic measurement without compromising individuals' privacy. In this paper, we present an initial framework for computing DP-compliant big data analytics for high-speed research network data. Specifically, we focus on sharing data at flow-level granularity, and we describe our initial steps towards an environment that relies on Hadoop and HBase to support privacy-preserving NetFlow analytics.

1. INTRODUCTION

The last decade witnessed significant developments in the area of high-speed research networks. Such networks are characterized by high line rates (up to 100Gbps) and connect users from heterogeneous environments, such as academia, industry and government. The projects served by these networks have a diverse set of requirements with respect to quality of service, and often complex network configurations are needed. Existing network communication protocols need to be adapted or re-designed from scratch to cope with the increasing demands. To improve flexibility and configurability of operation, *software-defined networks (SDNs)* are becoming the technology of choice for the future. To better understand and monitor these networks, it is important to collect and share network measurement data, which can help both in improving network operations (e.g., detecting traffic hotspots, troubleshooting), as well as in network design (e.g., improving routing protocols, transport mechanisms, etc.). Due to the high bandwidth of research net-

CODASPY'17 March 22-24, 2017, Scottsdale, AZ, USA

© 2017 Copyright held by the owner/author(s).

ACM ISBN 978-1-4503-4523-1/17/03.

DOI: http://dx.doi.org/10.1145/3029806.3029841

Attribute	Description
IN_BYTES	count of incoming bytes in the flow
OUT_BYTES	count of outgoing bytes in the flow
IN_PKTS	count of incoming packets in the flow
OUT_PKTS	count of outgoing packets in the flow
PROTOCOL	IP layer protocol (1=ICMP, 6=TCP, etc)
IPV4_SRC_ADDR	IPV4 source address
IPV4_DST_ADDR	IPV4 destination address
L4_SRC_PORT	TCP or UDP (layer 4) source port
L4_DST_PORT	TCP or UDP (layer 4) destination port

Table 1: NetFlow v9 attributes used by our framework

works, such data are generated at high rates, and in high volumes, raising significant performance challenges to process them.

In addition, sharing such network data can introduce serious privacy breaches, as an adversary may be able to derive private details about individual users. For instance, traffic data may disclose the health status or political orientation of some users based on their visits to specific medical or news websites. One can also determine the activity patterns of individuals based on their access to e-mail, social media and other online services. Our objective is to sanitize high-speed research network data according to the de-facto standard of *differential privacy (DP)*. DP is a semantic model that prevents an adversary from learning whether data about a specific individual has been included or not in the release. This way, we can support the benefic applications of traffic measurement without compromising individual privacy. This objective has many challenges, due to the high rates and high volumes of traffic data.

In this paper, we present an initial framework for computing DP-compliant big data analytics for high-speed research networks. Specifically, we focus on sharing data at flow-level granularity, and we describe our initial steps towards a system that uses Hadoop and HBase to support privacy-preserving NetFlow analytics.

Section 2 introduces necessary background on the NetFlow protocol, big data tools and differential privacy. Section 3 presents the proposed framework for differentially-private processing of network flow data, as well as the main open research questions. We conclude with directions for future research in Section 4.

2. BACKGROUND

2.1 NetFlow Protocol. NetFlow is a network protocol for collecting IP traffic information developed by Cisco, and subsequently adopted by other manufacturers. A network flow is represented by a tuple with attributes such as: source and destination IP address, IP protocol, source and destination port numbers, type of service, timestamp, number of packets and bytes communicated, etc. A network flow models a logical end-to-end communication stream, which may comprise numerous individual packets, and thus is a compact but informative way of representing network traffic. We focus on the NetFlow version 9 specification, but we use only a subset of nine attributes out of the over 100 specified by NetFlow v9. Table 1 summarizes these attributes and their meaning.

2.2 Hadoop and HBase. High-speed research networks transfer very large amounts of data at high line rates, hence the amount of collected NetFlow data requires an environment that can provide large amounts of storage and efficient distributed processing. In our work, we make use of two prominent open-source big data tools, namely Apache Hadoop and HBase. Both Hadoop and HBase rely on the *Hadoop Distributed File System (HDFS)* environment [1]. HDFS provides a distributed file system that runs on two types of nodes: *NameNodes*, which store file system metadata, and *DataNodes*, which store the actual application data. The servers communicate with each other using the TCP protocol. To achieve reliability and high availability, HDFS replicates the data across several DataNodes, which also allows the processing of the data to be performed in distributed fashion.

On top of HDFS, Hadoop provides a framework for analyzing data using the MapReduce computation model [2]. A MapReduce program is composed of a *map* phase that performs filtering and sorting on the raw data, and a *reduce* phase that gathers the information from the map phase and performs a summarization operation (e.g., sum, max, etc.). In the map phase, data are partitioned into chunks processed by Map tasks in parallel on different nodes. Usually, each node works with local data (e.g., data stored on the HDFS system local to the node). This is an advantage as it reduces costly data transfers between different nodes. However, Hadoop does not provide any data indexing features, as it always performs a linear scan of the input. In our setting, we often access only a partition of the data (e.g., HTTP traffic, or net flows within a certain range). HBase is a column-oriented big data store that supports efficiently random access. In HBase, one unit of data is represented by a row, and every row has a *row key* that uniquely identifies it. Each column of an HBase table represents one attribute of the data. For example, in our case a column could be the source IP, another column the destination IP, etc. HBase allows different attributes to be grouped together in *column families*, so that queries that retrieve attributes in the same family run faster. In the distributed HDFS, column families are stored as contiguous blocks of data.

2.3 Differential privacy (DP) [3] guarantees that for any two *sibling* datasets $\mathcal{D}_1, \mathcal{D}_2$ that differ in a single net flow π, the probability of an adversary learning which of the two datasets was used to obtain a certain output $\mathcal{A}$ is bounded by $\left| \ln \frac{Pr[\mathcal{A}(\mathcal{D}_1)]}{Pr[\mathcal{A}(\mathcal{D}_2)]} \right| \leq \epsilon$, where parameter $\epsilon > 0$ represents the *privacy budget*. To achieve privacy for numerical queries, the Laplace mechanism adds to each query result noise randomly distributed according to a Laplace distribution with parameter $\lambda = S/\epsilon$ where S is the *sensitivity* of the query, i.e., the maximum change in the result of the query for any two sibling databases. An important property of differential privacy is *sequential composability* which guarantees that executing algorithm $\mathcal{A}_1$ with privacy budget ϵ_1 followed by algorithm $\mathcal{A}_2$ with budget ϵ_2 produces a differentially private algorithm with parameter $\epsilon_1 + \epsilon_2$. This allows composing algorithms which use the results of simpler queries to produce a more accurate result for a highly sensitive query/algorithm.

3. PROPOSED APPROACH

3.1 System Architecture. Our contribution consists of a framework to support differentially-private analytics for a NetFlow v9 big data repository. The system architecture is presented in Figure 1. The input flows are collected in NetFlow v9 format from de-

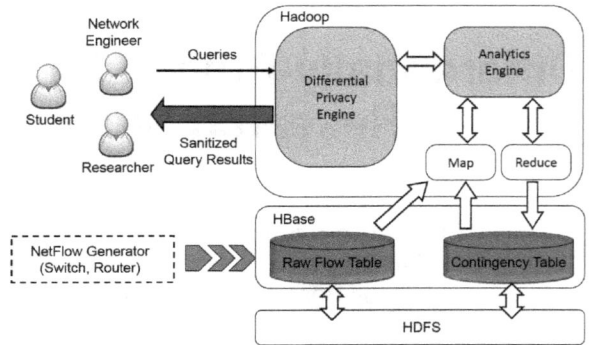

Figure 1: System Architecture

vices such as switches or routers. The flow data is pre-processed by retaining only the nine attributes from Table 1, and they are inserted in an HBase table of raw flows. The advantage of using HBase consists in the ability to perform random data access, as most user queries are interested in only a portion of the data (e.g., a certain time window, or data corresponding to a single protocol/service).

When users submit queries, the results are computed using a MapReduce job that accesses both the raw flow data, as well as the contingency tables that our system creates, and which will be described shortly. Both these tables contain sensitive data, so they are represented in red color. The analytics engine is responsible for performing the appropriate Map and Reduce phases, and may store additional results in the contingency table. Random noise is added to the results according to the DP model, and the noisy results are returned to the user.

3.2 Data Collection. We collect NetFlow data directly from network devices located at several Internet2 academic participants[1] (most manufacturers support NetFlow in their higher-end Layer 3 switches). Net flow metadata is generated in JSON format, which is delimited-text input. Each captured net flow contains numerous attributes, from which we select only a subset of interest (see Table 1 for the attributes we keep). Each flow record is generated after the session is closed, and is stored in the HBase repository. To enhance performance, before data insertion we convert numerical fields to integer types, which leads to a more compact representation (e.g., port 32768 can be represented as a two-byte integer, instead of a 5-byte string). We also convert IP addresses to binary format, which enhances operations such as flexible network mask computation. A sample of raw data format is illustrated in Table 2.

3.3 HBase Schema. The schema used to store flow data is very important, as it can have a significant impact on query performance. HBase stores data in sequence files, which contain key/value pairs. Our objective is to optimize the schema for rapid filtering using the row key and selection of attributes from specific column families. Most typical queries for the envisioned applications define a time range of interest, and require some statistic such as packet count or total bytes for flows between selected source and destination IPs. We devised the HBase schema in Table 3, where ts denotes the flow timestamp, BC and PC are byte and packet counts, respectively, and $md5$ is a hash over all flow attributes used to guarantee key uniqueness. The most important aspect in HBase schema design is the choice of row key. Our schema considers three types of row keys, corresponding to different types of queries. The general structure of our row keys comprises of several elements: (i) the time stamp at which the flow was generated, (ii) a type identifier (between 1 and 3) specifying how the row key must be interpreted, (iii) one attribute (sourceIP/destinationIP/port, based on the type value), and (iv) the $md5$ hash of the entire tuple.

---

[1]To preserve anonymity, we omit details about specific institutions.

Flow id	Source IP	Destination IP	Port	Protocol	Timestamp	Bytes Count	Packets Count
1	172.24.174.7	192.168.188.195	80	tcp	2016-02-24 19:18:28.0	1420	1
2	192.168.16.198	172.24.171.56	443	tcp	2016-02-24 19:18:28.0	104	1
3	172.24.171.250	172.24.171.255	138	udp	2016-02-24 19:18:28.0	229	1

Table 2: NetFlow data sample

The rationale for having three key types is to support efficiently distinct types of queries. Since most queries specify a time window, ts is a key prefix in all cases. Type 1 is designed for efficient processing of queries that ask for all flows originating at a given IP, whereas type 2 is relevant when the terminating end of a flow is specified in the query. Finally, type 3 is useful for queries that request statistics on specific service types (e.g., *http*, *ftp*, etc.). We also consider in the schema three different column families ($CF1$, $CF2$, $CF3$), which can drastically reduce the amount of data that needs to be scanned, based on the attributes requested by a query. The column families are a combination of the other attributes not included in the row key, and we also have a column family that combines the count information for bytes and packets.

3.4 Differentially-Private Queries. Querying big data repositories with differential privacy protection poses two challenges achieving good query performance, and maintaining data accuracy. According to the Laplace mechanism [3], the noise added to a query result is proportional to the sensitivity of the query set. In turn, sensitivity is proportional to the maximum number of queries that overlap a specific region of the attribute space. To maintain data accuracy, it is important to limit the amount of overlap. This can be achieved by deciding upon a *strategy query set* [3], and answering all future queries based on the results to the strategy set.

The focus of our work is to determine an appropriate set of queries that achieves low sensitivity, and based on which any query can be answered with fast performance and high accuracy. To achieve this goal, we build a number of *contingency tables*, which are the equivalent of the answers to the strategy queries. The contingency tables are multi-dimensional histograms, and each histogram bin contains the (noisy) answer to a statistical query. Below is a list of several typical queries that fit the strategy query profile:

```
Q1 : [Sum(BC) , (timerange = α) , ForEach srcIP]
Q2 : [Avg(PC) , (timerange = β) , ForEach destIP]
Q3 : [Sum(BC) , (timerange = γ) , ForEach port]
```

For instance, $Q1$ computes a histogram that contains for each IP the total number of bytes sent from that IP to all other destinations during the time period specified by $\alpha = [ts_{start}, ts_{end}]$. The result for $Q1$ can be determined using MapReduce on the raw flow table. Our framework creates a *Map* job for all those tuples that have the ts attribute contained within the range α, the key type 1 (because we want the row key to identify the source IP addresses) and the value of $srcIP$. The *Map* job will return all the matching tuples for that row key, and for each source IP there will be a count computed in the *Reduce* phase. Following the *Reduce* phase, all results will be stored in a contingency table inside HBase. According to the parallel composition property of differential privacy, the result for each distinct IP corresponds to a data partition that does not overlap with that of any other IP. However, the sequential composability property applies with respect to all other queries that specify the same IP in their predicates (e.g., $Q2$). One has to carefully quantify this overlap, which will determine the sensitivity value, and in turn the amount of noise that needs to be added to each bin

Each contingency table has its own specific structure, and we have to take in consideration what kind of direct queries would we need in order to return the users the result as fast as possible. The schema for the contingency table supporting queries $Q1 - Q3$ is illustrated in Table 4, where res denotes the resolution of the time slice supported (i.e., allow time ranges aligned at a multiple of minutes), qn denotes the query type (1-3), and q represents the query description, namely concatenated values of the attributes that are requested in the query. In the example of Table 4 all three queries have the res parameter as 15, which means that we will consider for our query all flows with a timestamp that is at most 15 minutes in the past from ts.

3.5 Research Challenges. There are several research challenges to be addressed within the proposed framework. One important aspect is choosing time granularities for strategy queries. One may allow reporting to be performed at hourly, daily and weekly intervals. According to sequential composition, doing so would triple sensitivity compared to having a single interval. In this case, one may choose to compute the results for weekly aggregation based on daily aggregation results, but in the general case, time intervals may be overlapping, rather than completely scoped, so sensitivity may need to be increased. Another important research challenge is privacy budget allocation. Instead of giving all granularities the same amount of budget, one can choose to use less budget for coarser granularities, where errors can be more easily absorbed.

Another important research question that may lead to gains in accuracy is considering hierarchies of attribute values. For instance, rather than considering all services independently, one can choose broader histogram bins, e.g, HTTP traffic may include ports 80, 443, 8080. This way, the histograms for ports become more coarse-grained, and the relative error will decrease. Of course, the trade-off is that one loses accuracy when individual ports are queried. A similar concept can be applied to the IP address space. One can choose bin granularity at the level of a class 'C' network for instance (netmask /24), or coarser granularity (e.g., /22), which may be still good enough to pinpoint cross-organization traffic.

4. CONCLUSION

In this paper, we proposed some initial steps towards efficient and accurate differentially-private analytics for high-speed research network measurement data. Our solution relies on Apache Hadoop and HBase big data tools. Query results are perturbed according to Laplace mechanism to achieve privacy. In future work, we plan to address the research challenges identified in Section 3.5.

5. REFERENCES

[1] R. Chansler, H. Kuang, S. Radia, K. Shvachko, and S. Srinivas. *The Architecture of Open Source Applications*, ISBN 978-1-257-63801-7. 2011.
[2] J. Dean and S. Ghemawat. Mapreduce: Simplified data processing on large clusters. In *Proceedings of the 6th Symposium on Operating Systems Design & Implementation*, pages 10–10, 2004.
[3] C. Dwork, F. McSherry, K. Nissim, and A. Smith. Calibrating noise to sensitivity in private data analysis. In *TCC*, pages 265–284, 2006.

Row Key	CF1	CF2	CF3
ts|1|srcIP|md5	destIP, port	destIP	BC,PC
ts|2|destIP|md5	srcIP, port	srcIP	BC,PC
ts|3|port|md5	srcIP	destIP	BC,PC

Table 3: HBase schema for raw flow tables

Row Key	CF4	CF5
ts|res|qn|q	noisyBC	noisyPC
ts|15|1|srcIP	noisyBC	noisyPC
ts|15|2|destIP	noisyBC	noisyPC
ts|15|3|port	noisyBC	noisyPC

Table 4: HBase schema for contingency tables

Comprehensive Method for Detecting Phishing Emails Using Correlation-based Analysis and User Participation

Rakesh Verma
University of Houston
4800 Calhoun Rd, Houston
Houston, TX 77004
rmverma@cs.uh.edu

Ayman El Aassal
ENSIAS
Avenue Mohamed Ben Abdellah Regragui
Rabat, Morocco
elaassal.ayman@gmail.com

ABSTRACT

Phishing email has become a popular solution among attackers to steal all kinds of data from people and easily breach organizations' security system. Hackers use multiple techniques and tricks to raise the chances of success of their attacks, like using information found on social networking websites to tailor their emails to the target's interests, or targeting employees of an organization who probably can't spot a phishing email or malicious websites and avoid sending emails to IT people or employees from Security department. In this paper we focus on analyzing the coherence of information contained in the different parts of the email: Header, Body, and URLs. After analyzing multiple phishing emails we discovered that there is always incoherence between these different parts. We created a comprehensive method which uses a set of rules that correlates the information collected from analyzing the header, body and URLs of the email and can even include the user in the detection process. We take into account that there is no such thing called perfection, so even if an email is classified as legitimate, our system will still send a warning to the user if the email is suspicious enough. This way even if a phishing email manages to escape our system, the user can still be protected.

Keywords

Phishing email; email format; Headers; Body; URL; Comprehensive method; Correlation

1. BRIEF PROBLEM DESCRIPTION

Phishing emails are one of the most dangerous forms of attacks used by attackers worldwide. It is considered an easy way to avoid multiple security layers and it is directed to the weakest link of the security chain, which is the end user. It takes on average 229 days to discover a breach [3]. The user receives an email with a link to a malicious website, or a malware embedded attachment, which is made by the attacker himself. The email is constructed in such a way as to appear as legitimate as possible, which raises the success probability of the attack. It has become easy now for attackers to mimic the email format of an organization or a company and they can either mass-mail it or be more selective. In the latter case it is called *spear phishing* and the email is tailored to each specific recipient, using personal information available in social networking websites (SNW), to appeal to his interests.

2. CONTRIBUTION AND HYPOTHESIS

2.1 Hypothesis

After analyzing a number of emails, we noticed that there always is some inconsistency between different parts of a phishing email. The most suspicious one is where an email is supposedly from a company asking the target to send personal information, and the sender is using a fake name and the email address is not from that company's domain. The better constructed a phishing email is, the more consistent it appears. The best phishing emails are hard to detect and tend to avoid detection measures, and smart attackers send these emails to people who are easy targets (e.g., non IT people). In the literature [16, 11, 14, 7, 9, 13, 15], nobody could detect 100% of phishing emails, this shows the limit of the current automatic detection systems. Hence, it is better to include the user either in the detection process, or at least by just sending him a warning to make him pay more attention [10, 5]. For this purpose, user training is necessary.

2.2 Contribution

We design a comprehensive method, which relies on a set of rules that determine if an email is a phish based on information extracted from all parts of the email. We correlate the information collected from the header, body and URLs contained in the email, and check if it make sense. We verify in our method, if the information extracted from the header relates to the information contained in the body and even the URLs (same company or same domain name for example). We also include the user in a simple and intuitive way, so that the user becomes an asset to the security process rather than being the weakest link. At the end of the detection process, the system sends the user a warning if the email is suspicious enough but was not classified as phish. This will count as a final countermeasure against the imperfection issue of the system, and at the same time sensitize the user and make him more aware of this threat

CODASPY'17 March 22-24, 2017, Scottsdale, AZ, USA

© 2017 Copyright held by the owner/author(s).

ACM ISBN 978-1-4503-4523-1/17/03.

DOI: http://dx.doi.org/10.1145/3029806.3029842

3. METHODOLOGY

3.1 Header analysis Algorithm

Algorithm 1 Header Analysis Algorithm

1: given an email *msg* (eml or txt format)
2: // Get the necessary information from the header.
3: *address* = email address in "From" field
4: *domain* = domain of email address in "From" field
5: *display* = displayed sender name in the "From" field
6: *message-ID* = right hand side of "Message-ID" field
7: *received1* = a list containing the "from" and "by" tokens in last "Received" field of email header
8: *received2* = a list containing the "from" and "by" tokens in the second last "Received" field of email header
9: *IPaddr1* = Ip address of sending host in last "Received" field of email header
10: *IPaddr2* = Ip address of sending host in the second last "Received" field of email header
11: *match* = initiated at 0 and incremented by one each time the Matching Algorithm returns 'Yes' in Line 22.
12: // analyze the header fields:
13: // Verify if the email passes the "DKIM" or "SPF" authentication
14: **if** $(dkim \parallel spf) = pass$ **then**
15:     $auth \leftarrow positive$
16: **else**
17:     $auth \leftarrow negative$
18: **if** $auth = positive$ **then**
19:     Body Analysis (Semantic and URL analysis)
20: **if** $auth = negative$ **then**
21: // Use reverse DNS Lookup to verify if the IP addresses in the "Received" field belong to the domain name of the claimed hosts.
22: //Call the Matching Algorithm on *domain, message-ID, received1* two by two.
23: // Decision is then based on the reverse DNS Lookup and the value of the variable *match*
24:     **if** $match = 0 \parallel [(IPaddr1 \notin Host$ **in** $received1)$ && $(IPaddr2 \notin Host$ **in** $received2)]$ **then**
25:       $email \leftarrow Phish$
26:     **if** $match = 1$ && $[(IPaddr1 \notin Host$ **in** $received1) \parallel (IPaddr2 \notin Host$ **in** $received2)]$ **then**
27:       $email \leftarrow Phish$
28:     **if** $(match = 2)$ && $(nameMatch = No)$ **then**
29:       $email \leftarrow Phish$
30:     **if** $(match = 3) \parallel (match = 2$ && $nameMatch = Yes)$ **then**
31:       Body Analysis (Semantic and URL analysis)
32:     **if** $URL\ Analysis$ **is** $Positive$ **then**
33:       $email \leftarrow Phish$
34:     **if** $URL\ Analysis$ **is** $Negative$ **then**
35:       **if** $Semantic\ Analysis$ **is** $Positive$ **then**
36:         Send recipient a warning
37: //If nameMatch=No then it is added to the warning.
38:       **else**
39:         $email \leftarrow Legit$

3.2 Matching Algorithm

DKIM: Domain-Keys Identified Mail is a mechanism that uses digital signature to authenticate multiple email header fields and the sender identity as well [8, 2].

Algorithm 2 Matching Algorithm

1: Given two header fields *head1* and *head2*
2: // Step1: extract domain names
3: $addr1 = head1$.split("@").lower()
4: $addr2 = head2$.split("@").lower()
5: // Step2: build list of bigrams for each address (bigrams are separated by ".")
6: // Step2.a: split the domain names using "."
7: $spltAddr1 = addr1$.split(.)
8: $spltAddr2 = addr2$.split(.)
9: // Step2.b: build the bigram list for each domain name
10:     $BigramtAddr1 = [spltAddr1[i:i+2]$ **for** i in range($len(spltAddr1$-1))]
11:     $BigramtAddr2 = [spltAddr2[i:i+2]$ **for** i in range($len(spltAddr2$-1))]
12: // Step3: Compare the two list of bigrams
13: // Step3.a: Define variables
14: $ratio = 0.0$
15: $threshold = 0.5$
16: // threshold can be modified to answer our expectations
17: // Step3.b: Comparison
18: **for** $bigram1$ **in** $BigramAddr1$ **do**
19:     **for** $bigram2$ **in** $BigramAddr2$ **do**
20:       $seqratio =$ Levenshtein.ratio($bigram1, bigram2$)
21:       **if** $seqratio > ratio$ **then**
22:         $ratio \leftarrow seqratio$
23: **if** $ratio >= threshold$ **then**
24:     $similar \leftarrow "Yes"$
25: **else**
26:     $similar \leftarrow "No"$
27: **return** $similar$

SPF: Sender Policy Framework enables to verify that the sending mail server is an authorized sender of the domain that appears in the "mail from" address [8].

The "From" header field shows the email address of the sender, and optionally the name of the sender. The "Received" header field contains two token: *from* which indicate the server sending the email as well as it's IP address; *by* that shows the machine receiving it and the protocol it's using. Each server that receives the emails add it's own "Received" header before transferring it.

URL Analysis: Verify if the URLs in the body of the email link to a malware or a phishing website.

Semantic Analysis: Analyze the body semantically to verify if it urges the recipient to either open an URL and fill in personal information or send that information by email to another address

In the Header Analysis Algorithm: In Line 29, URL Analysis is positive if the URL links to a malicious website or malware. In Line 34, Semantic Analysis is positive if the recipient is asked to send information and/or there is a sense of urgency in the text.

Note that our decision criteria are based on trial and error. Considering the randomness of the header fields' values in emails, we tried to choose thresholds that gave us the best compromise between true positives in phishing emails and true negative in legitimate emails. For the rest of the paper, the results we show are obtained by only the header analysis. In the Header Analysis Algorithm, instead of doing the body analysis, we will consider the email legitimate since it will have passed the rules set for the header.

4. PILOT EXPERIMENT

Dataset: We used 300 Legitimate emails: 100 from leaked DNC[1] and 200 from SpamAssassin's[12] easy ham. For phishing emails we used 400 emails in total; 100 collected from personal mailbox and 300 from Nazario's dataset[6]

Results: Phishing emails: 349 True positives, 51 False negatives. Legitimate emails: 164 True negatives, 136 False positives.

Analysis: 51 FNs phishing emails had similar and therefore consistent header fields. 136 FPs in legitimate emails were a result of inconsistent header values, and in most of them the IP addresses analyzed couldn't be resolved or were not matching the claimed hosts. This further proves the randomness of the content of header fields.

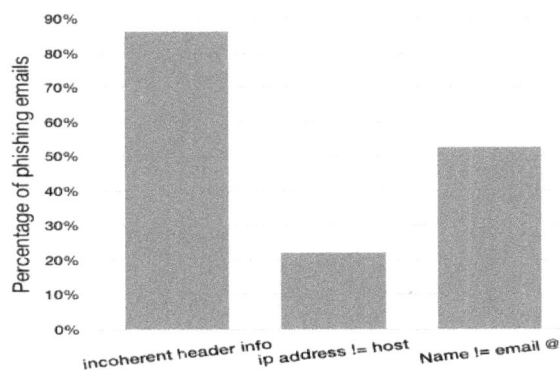

Figure 1: Percentage of phishing emails containing each factor

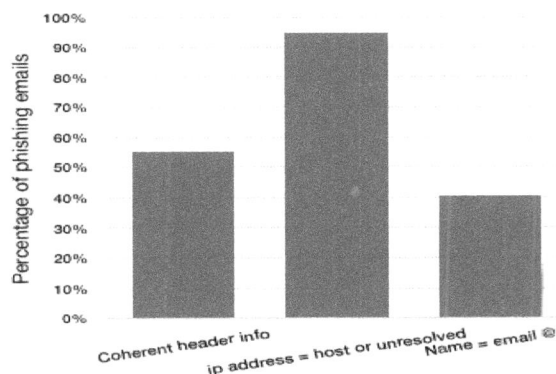

Figure 2: Percentage of legitimate emails containing each factor

5. CONCLUSION & FUTURE WORK

Header fields are an important source of information when it comes to emails. It is useful to analyze the header because we can correlate several pieces of information and verify their authenticity and coherence. However,header fields can not be trusted completely because they can be modified by the attacker and measures can be taken to avoid the authentication mechanisms (like changing the "whois" [4] information of the sending domain). This algorithm is meant to be the first step of the detection process. Higher detection rate and lower false positives may be obtained after implementing the body analysis method. The testing dataset is small but varied, and it gives a general idea about the randomness of the content of the header fields. Future work will be to incorporate into the system the body analysis, and then do a lab experiment. This will help us determine the best way to include the user in the detection process and the best kinds of notifications to use. User training programs must be considered, if we want to rely on user judgment in the detection process.

Acknowledgments

Research supported in part by NSF grants DUE 1241772, CNS 1319212 and DGE 1433817.

6. REFERENCES

[1] Dnc email database. https://wikileaks.org/dnc-emails/.

[2] Domainkeys identified mail (dkim) signatures, rfc4871. https://tools.ietf.org/pdf/rfc4871.pdf.

[3] Fireeye annual threat report 2014. http://investors.fireeye.com/releasedetail.cfm?releaseid=839454.

[4] Official icann whois search. https://whois.icann.org/en.

[5] D. D. Caputo, S. L. Pfleeger, J. D. Freeman, and M. E. Johnson. Going spear phishing/ exploring embedded training and awareness. volume 12, pages 28–38. IEEE, 2014.

[6] J. N. P. Corpus. http://monkey.org/jose/phishing/.

[7] H. Guo, B. Jin, and W. Qian. Analysis of email header for forensics purpose. In *Communication Systems and Network Technologies (CSNT), 2013 International Conference on*, pages 340–344. IEEE, 2013.

[8] A. Herzberg. Dns-based email sender authentication mechanisms: a critical review. volume 28, pages 731–742. Elsevier, 2009.

[9] M. C. Kotson and A. Schulz. Characterizing phishing threats with natural language processing. In *Communications and Network Security (CNS), 2015 IEEE Conference on*, pages 308–316. IEEE, 2015.

[10] A. Neupane, M. L. Rahman, N. Saxena, and L. Hirshfield. A multi-modal neuro-physiological study of phishing detection and malware warnings. In *ACM CCS*, 2015.

[11] F. Sanchez and Z. Duan. A sender-centric approach to detecting phishing emails. In *Cyber Security (CyberSecurity), 2012 International Conference on*, pages 32–39. IEEE, 2012.

[12] SpamAssassin. The apache spamassassin project. http://spamassassin.apache.org/.

[13] R. Verma, N. Shashidhar, and N. Hossain. Phishing email detection the natural language way. In *ESORICS*, 2012.

[14] R. M. Verma and K. Dyer. On the character of phishing urls- accurate and robust statistical learning classifiers. In *ACM CODASPY*, 2015.

[15] R. M. Verma and N. Hossain. Semantic feature selection for text with application to phishing email detection.

[16] R. M. Verma and N. Rai. Phish-idetector: Message-id based automatic phishing detection. In *SECRYPT, IEEE Xplore*, 2015.

Prioritized Analysis of Inter-App Communication Risks*

Fang Liu[1], Haipeng Cai[2], Gang Wang[1], Danfeng (Daphne) Yao[1],

Karim O. Elish[3], and Barbara G. Ryder[1]

[1]Department of Computer Science, Virginia Tech

[2]School of Electrical Engineering and Computer Science, Washington State University

[3]Department of Computer Science, Florida Polytechnic University

fbeyond@cs.vt.edu, hcai@eecs.wsu.edu, {gangwang,danfeng}@cs.vt.edu, kelish@flpoly.org, ryder@cs.vt.edu

ABSTRACT

Inter-Component Communication (ICC) enables useful interactions between mobile apps. However, misuse of ICC exposes users to serious threats such as intent hijacking/spoofing and app collusions, allowing malicious apps to access privileged user data via another app. Unfortunately, existing ICC analyses are largely incompetent in both accuracy and scale. This poster points out the need and technical challenges of prioritized analysis of inter-app ICC risks. We propose MR-Droid, a MapReduce-based computing framework for *accurate* and *scalable* inter-app ICC analysis in Android. MR-Droid extracts data-flow features between multiple communicating apps and the target apps to build a large-scale ICC graph. Our approach is to leverage the ICC graph to provide contexts for inter-app communications to produce precise alerts and prioritize risk assessments. This process requires large app-pair data, which is enabled by our MapReduce-based program analysis. Our initial extensive experiments on 11,996 apps from 24 app categories (13 million pairs) demonstrate the scalability of our approach.

1. Introduction

Inter-Component Communication (ICC) is an important mechanism for app-to-app communications on Android. It links the components of different apps via messaging objects (or *Intents*). While ICC contributes greatly to the development of rich third-party applications, this communication model has become a predominant security attack surface for Intent hijacking, Intent spoofing and app colusions. According to a recent report from McAfee Labs [1], app collusions are increasingly prevalent on mobile platforms.

To assess ICC vulnerabilities, various analytics methods have been proposed. However, most of them perform analysis for one *individual* app at a time, ignoring its feasible communication context with other apps. As the consequence,

they provide conservative risk estimations, producing a high number of (false) alarms [2, 3]. A more effective approach is inter-app analysis that consider ICCs across two or more apps. This allows researchers to gain empirical contexts on the actual communications between apps and produce more relevant alerts. However, existing solutions are largely limited in scale due to the high complexity of pair-wise components analyses. They were either applied to a much smaller set of apps (a few hundred only, versus a few thousand in single-app analyses), or a small set of inter-app links.

A recent study PRIMO reported ICC analyses of a large pool of apps [6]. Its goal is to approximate the likelihoods of ICC communications between app pairs through learning from training data. However, PRIMO is not designed for ICC risk analysis, thus it does not provide classification mechanisms for security. Moreover, PRIMO runs on a single workstation. Our evaluation shows that running PRIMO with 10K apps requires over 40GB memory even with highly compressed metadata. Using a single machine is not a practical solution to analyze market-wide apps with the space complexity being $O(N^2)$.

In this paper, we point out the need and technical challenges of prioritized analysis of inter-app ICC risks. We propose MR-Droid, a MapReduce-based parallel analytics system for *accurate* and *scalable* ICC risk detection. Our goal is to evaluate ICC risks based on an app's inter-connections with other real-world apps and efficiently identify high-risk pairs. Our intuition is that an ICC pair is of high-risk, not only because one of the apps is vulnerable, but more importantly it potentially communicates with other apps. To achieve this goal, we construct a large-scale *ICC graph*, where each node is an app component and the edge represents the corresponding inter-app ICCs[1]. To gauge the risk level of the ICC pairs (edge weight), our approach is to extract various features based on app flow analyses that indicate vulnerabilities. For instance, we can examine whether the ICC pair is used to pass sensitive data, or escalate permissions for another app. With the ICC graph, we can further *rank* the risk level of a given app by aggregating all its ICC edges with other apps.

To scale up the system, we implement MR-Droid with a set of new MapReduce algorithms atop the Hadoop framework for constructing the ICC graph. MapReduce has been used in various areas (e.g., data leak detection [5]). We independently exact ICC sources and sinks from each app, and

*This work has been supported in part by DARPA APAC FA8750-15-2-0076 and ARO YIP W911NF-14-1-0535.

[1]We use *ICC graph* to represent inter-app communications throughout the paper.

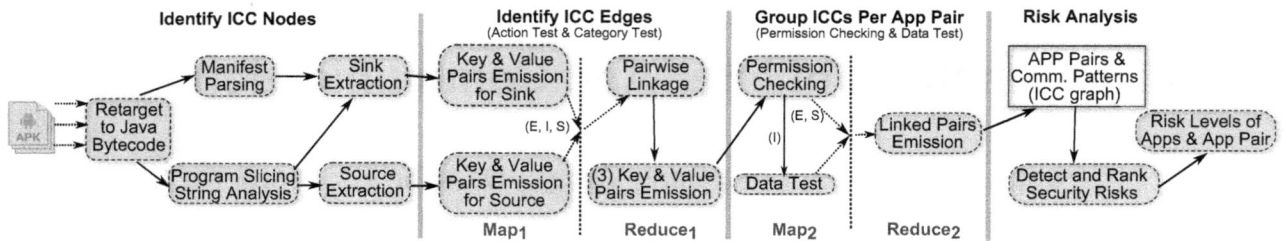

Figure 1: Our workflow for analyzing Android app pairs with MapReduce. The dashed vertical lines indicate redistribution processes in MapReduce. E, I, S represent explicit edge, implicit edge, and sharedUserId edge respectively.

jointly analyze those with matched source-sink pairs with MapReduce. The high-level parallelization from MapReduce allows us to analyze millions of app pairs within hours using commodity servers.

We evaluate ICC graph construction on a large set of 11,996 Android apps collected from 24 major Google Play categories (13 million ICC pairs). Our system is highly scalable. With 15 commodity servers, the entire process took less than 25 hours for an average of only 0.0012 seconds per app pair. More importantly, our runtime experiment shows the computation time grows near-linearly with respect to the number of apps.

2. Models and Methodology

In this section, we describe the threat model and computational goal of our work. Then we give an overview of our approach.

2.1 Threat Model

Our work focuses on security risks caused by inter-app communications realized through ICCs, covering three most important classes of inter-app ICC security risks.

- **Intent hijacking.** An Intent sent by an app via an implicit ICC may be intercepted (hijacked) by an unauthorized app. This threat scenario, referred to as Intent hijacking, can be categorized into three sub-classes according to the type of the sending component: broadcast theft, activity hijacking, and service hijacking, as introduced in [2].

- **Intent spoofing.** By sending Intents to exported components of a vulnerable app, an attacker can spoof the vulnerable (receiving) app to perform malicious actions. Intent spoofing can be classified into three sub-classes by the type of the receiving component: malicious broadcast injection, malicious activity launch, and malicious service launch [2].

- **Malware collusion.** Through inter-app ICCs, two or more apps may collude to perform malicious actions that none of the participating apps alone would be able to. Malware collusion can result in disguised data leak and system abuse.

2.2 Computational Goal

Our computational goal is two-fold.

1. Build a complete inter-app ICC graph and identify all communication app pairs for a set of apps to provide the communication context (i.e., the neighbor set) for each one.

2. Further perform neighbor-aware inter-app security analysis on top of the ICC graph and rank the apps and app pairs with respect to their risk levels.

The framework for building the ICC graph has to be able to process very large-scale real world apps efficiently. There is a potentially higher risk of missing true risk warnings if limited size of communication context are considered (e.g., a highly vulnerable app may be declared safe when only a few external apps are analyzed).

To rank the apps and app pairs with respect to their risk levels, one has to carefully represent the apps' communication context given the ICC graph. Different threat models may require different communication context for ranking.

2.3 Overview

As shown in Figure 1, our workflow involves two major phases: distributed ICC mapping for building ICC graph in large-scale and neighbor-based risk analysis to rank the apps according to their risk levels.

Distributed ICC mapping is implemented with MapReduce on top of Hadoop for scalability. It has three steps: step 1. IDENTIFY ICC NODES, 2. IDENTIFY ICC EDGES, and 3. GROUP ICCS PER APP PAIR.

1. In IDENTIFY ICC NODES, we extract the attributes of sources and sinks from apps. Sources are extracted from the attributes in outbound Intents. Sinks are extracted from the exported components in the manifest or from dynamic receivers created in the code.

2. IDENTIFY ICC EDGES is the first MapReduce job which identifies edges between communicating sources and sinks. The MapReduce job transforms the source and sinks into $\langle key, value \rangle$ pairs, which enable parallel edge finding.

3. GROUP ICCS PER APP PAIR is the second MapReduce job which performs the data test and permission checking, and identifies and groups edges belonging to the same pair.

In addition, we balance the workload among all the nodes in the MapReduce cluster for the best performance. Unbalanced workload highly impacts the performances because most of the nodes are idle while waiting for the nodes with the heavy workload. We address this problem by adding a tag before each key emitted by the Map function. The tag helps to divide the large amount of key-value pairs, which should be sent to one reducer, into m parts feeding m reducers.

Neighbor-based risk analysis is to utilize the ICC mapping results (ICC graph) from the previous phase to compute key ICC link features, and then uses the features to rank security risks for each app (for hijacking and spoofing attacks) and app pair (for collusion attacks). Different features may be used for different attack models.

- HIJACKING We assess the possibility of an intent to be hijacked be using the features with outbound links

160

(e.g., Number of outbound edges with data).

- SPOOFING We assess the possibility of component to be spoofed using the features with inbound links (e.g., Number of outbound edges with data).
- COLLUSION All communicating pairs are analyzed together to assess their collusion possibility. Both inbound and outbound features are involved for the assessment.

Given an app or app pair, our analysis first computes its risk with respect to individual features, and then aggregates them to obtain an overall risk value. The risk for an individual feature is ranked based on the feature value distribution of all apps/app pairs. An app's individual feature risk is higher, if the corresponding value is larger than other apps.

3. Evaluation

We implemented our system with native Hadoop MapReduce framework. The input is the ICC sources and sinks extracted from individual apps using IC3 [7]. We modified IC3 to accommodate the MapReduce paradigm. The Hadoop system is deployed on a 15-node cluster. Each node has two quad-core 2.8GHz Xeon processors and 8GB RAM.[2]

Datasets

For our evaluation, we apply our system to 11,996 most popular free apps from Google Play. We select the top 500 apps from each of the 24 major app categories (4 apps were unavailable due to bugs in program analysis). We downloaded the apps in December 2014 with an Android 4.2 client.

Risk Assessment

We apply our system to the collected app dataset. The resulting ICC graph contains 38,134,207 source nodes, 26,227,430 sink nodes and 75,123,502 edges. On the per-app level, there are in total 12,986,254 app pairs that have at least one ICC link. Each app averagely connects with 1185 external apps (9.9% of all apps). For non-connected app pairs, we can safely exclude them during the security analysis.

Our security analysis is focused on all potential security risks related to Intent hijacking, Intent spoofing and app collusion. We quantify and rank security risks into as categorical risk levels. In total, our system identified 150 high-risk apps, 1,021 medium and 10,825 low risk apps. We report the runtime performance of MR-Droid next. Our complete evaluation result will be reported in a full version soon.

Runtime of MR-Droid

We analyze the runtime performance of MR-Droid. Figure 2 depicts the time cost of our MapReduce pipeline (y axis) as the number of apps increases (x axis). Overall, the result shows that our approach is readily scalable for large-scale inter-app analysis. The running time of ICC node identification appears to dominate the total analysis cost, yet its growth is linear with the number of apps. In addition, given the sparse nature of the ICC graph (rarely does an app communicate to all apps), we manage to achieve near-linear complexity for edge identification and grouping ICCs. In total, it takes 25 hours to perform the complete analysis on 13 million ICC pairs for 12K apps. Currently, our cluster has 15 nodes. We anticipate that increasing the cluster size would further speed up the inter-app ICC analysis.

---

[2]The algorithms can also be implemented with Spark with faster in-memory processing. It will require much larger RAMs.

As a baseline comparison, we evaluated the performance of IccTA [4], a non-distributed inter-app ICC analysis system. IccTA needs to first combine two or more apps into one app and then perform ICC analytics. We evaluate IccTA with 57 randomly selected real world apps on a workstation (80GB RAM). It took IccTA over 200 hours to analyze all the apps. We estimate that processing 200 apps with IccTA would take about 18,000 hours, making it impractical for analyzing market-scale apps.

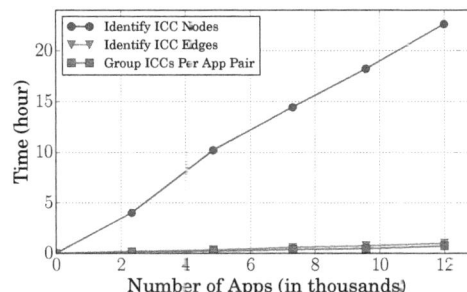

Figure 2: Analysis time of the three phases in our approach.

4. Conclusion and Future Work

In this paper, we pointed out the need and technical challenges of prioritized analysis of inter-app ICC risks. We presented the design and implementation of MR-Droid, a MapReduce pipeline for large-scale inter-app ICC risk analyses. By constructing ICC graphs with efficient parallelization, our system enables highly scalable inter-app security analysis for accurate risk prioritization.

Because of the lack of ground truth on the empirical data, we will further devote substantial future efforts to manually inspecting the apps for validation.

5. References

[1] Mcafee labs threats report. http://www.mcafee.com/us/resources/reports/rp-quarterly-threats-may-2016.pdf, 2016.

[2] E. Chin, A. P. Felt, K. Greenwood, and D. Wagner. Analyzing inter-application communication in Android. In *MobiSys*, 2011.

[3] K. O. Elish, D. D. Yao, and B. G. Ryder. On the need of precise Inter-App ICC classification for detecting Android malware collusions. In *MoST, IEEE S&P*, 2015.

[4] L. Li, A. Bartel, T. F. Bissyandé, J. Klein, Y. Le Traon, S. Arzt, S. Rasthofer, E. Bodden, D. Octeau, and P. Mcdaniel. IccTA: Detecting inter-component privacy leaks in Android apps. In *ICSE*, 2015.

[5] F. Liu, X. Shu, D. Yao, and A. R. Butt. Privacy-preserving scanning of big content for sensitive data exposure with mapreduce. In *CCDASPY*, 2015.

[6] D. Octeau, S. Jha, M. Dering, P. McDaniel, A. Bartel, L. Li, J. Klein, and Y. Le Traon. Combining static analysis with probabilistic models to enable market-scale Android inter-component analysis. In *POPL*, 2016.

[7] D. Octeau, D. Luchaup, M. Dering, S. Jha, and P. McDaniel. Composite constant propagation: Application to Android inter-component communication analysis. In *ICSE*, 2015.

The Authorization Policy Existence Problem

Pierre Bergé
LRI, Université Paris-Saclay
Bât 650, Rue Noetzlin
91190 Gif-sur-Yvette
France
pierre.berge@supelec.fr

Jason Crampton
Royal Holloway
University of London
Egham, TW20 9QY
United Kingdom
jason.crampton@rhul.ac.uk

Gregory Gutin
Royal Holloway
University of London
Egham, TW20 9QY
United Kingdom
gutin@cs.rhul.ac.uk

Rémi Watrigant
INRIA Sophia-Antipolis
2004 Route des Lucioles
06902 Sophia-Antipolis
France
remi.watrigant@inria.fr

ABSTRACT

Constraints such as separation-of-duty are widely used to specify requirements that supplement basic authorization policies. However, the existence of constraints (and authorization policies) may mean that a user is unable to fulfill her/his organizational duties because access to resources is denied. In short, there is a tension between the need to protect resources (using policies and constraints) and the availability of resources. Recent work on workflow satisfiability and resiliency in access control asks whether this tension compromises the ability of an organization to achieve its objectives. In this paper, we develop a new method of specifying constraints which subsumes much related work and allows a wider range of constraints to be specified. The use of such constraints leads naturally to a range of questions related to "policy existence", where a positive answer means that an organization's objectives can be realized. We provide an overview of our results establishing that some policy existence questions, notably for those instances that are restricted to user-independent constraints, are fixed-parameter tractable.

CCS Concepts

•Security and privacy → Access control; *Security requirements;* •Theory of computation → **Fixed parameter tractability;**

Keywords

access control; resiliency; satisfiability; computational complexity; fixed-parameter tractability

CODASPY'17, March 22-24, 2017, Scottsdale, AZ, USA
ACM 978-1-4503-4523-1/17/03.
http://dx.doi.org/10.1145/3029806.3029844

1. INTRODUCTION

Access control is a fundamental aspect of the security of any multi-user computing system, and is typically based on the specification and enforcement of an authorization policy. Such a policy identifies which interactions between users and resources are to be allowed by the system.

Over the last twenty years, access control requirements have become increasingly complex, leading to increasingly sophisticated authorization policies, often expressed in terms of constraints. A separation-of-duty constraint (also known as the "two-man rule" or "four-eyes policy") may, for example, require that no single user is authorized for some particularly sensitive group of resources. Such a constraint is typically used to prevent misuse of the system by a single user.

The use of authorization policies and constraints, by design, limits which users may access resources. Nevertheless, the ability to perform one's duties requires access to particular resources, and overly prescriptive policies and constraints may mean that some resources are inaccessible. In short, "tension" may exist between authorization policies and operational demands: too lax a policy may suit organizational demands but lead to security violations; whereas too restrictive a policy may compromise an organization's ability to meet its business objectives.

Recent work on workflow satisfiability and access control resiliency has recognized the importance of being able to identify whether or not security policies prevent an organization from achieving its objectives [1, 5, 6, 9, 11]. In this paper, we seek to generalize existing work in this area. Specifically, we introduce the AUTHORIZATION POLICY EXISTENCE PROBLEM (APEP). Informally, APEP seeks to find an authorization policy, subject to restrictions on individual authorizations (defined by a "base" authorization relation) and restrictions on collective authorizations (defined by a set of authorization constraints).

The framework within which APEP is defined admits a greater variety of constraints than is usually considered in either the standard access control literature [3, 7, 8, 10] or in workflow satisfiability [1, 4, 11]. In this paper we characterize the constraints of interest and extend the definition of user-independent constraints [4] to this framework. We conclude the paper by stating some results for the complexity of APEP when problem instances are characterized by the types of constraints that may be included.

2. THE AUTHORIZATION POLICY EXISTENCE PROBLEM

In this paper, we extend existing work on workflow satisfiability, constraints and resiliency, by defining a simple yet very expressive authorization framework. Roughly speaking, we specify a problem dealing with the existence of an appropriate authorization relation.

Given a set of users U and a set of resources R to which access should be restricted, we may define an *authorization relation* $A \subseteq U \times R$, where $(u, r) \in A$ if and only if u is authorized to access r. Given a resource r, we will write $A(r)$ to denote the set of users that are authorized to access resource r. More formally, $A(r) = \{u \in U : (u, r) \in A\}$. Similarly, for $u \in U$, we will write $A(u)$ to denote the set of resources that u is authorized to access, that is $A(u) = \{r \in R : (u, r) \in A\}$. We extend this notation to subsets of R and U in the natural way: for $R' \subseteq R$ and $U' \subseteq U$,

$$A(R') \stackrel{\text{def}}{=} \bigcup_{r \in R'} A(r) \quad \text{and} \quad A(U') \stackrel{\text{def}}{=} \bigcup_{u \in U'} A(u).$$

The AUTHORIZATION POLICY EXISTENCE PROBLEM is defined with reference to (i) a *base authorization relation* $A_{\text{Bse}} \subseteq U \times R$ such that $A_{\text{Bse}}(r) \neq \emptyset$ for each $r \in R$, and (ii) a set of *authorization constraints* C. Informally, A_{Bse} specifies restrictions on all valid authorization relations, while C specifies additional restrictions that any valid authorization relation must satisfy. We discuss constraints in more detail in Section 3.

Formally, given a base authorization relation A_{Bse} and a set of constraints C, we say an authorization relation $A \subseteq U \times R$ is

- *authorized* with respect to A_{Bse} if $A \subseteq A_{\text{Bse}}$;
- *complete* if $A(r) \neq \emptyset$ for every $r \in R$;
- *eligible* with respect to C if A satisfies c for all $c \in C$;
- *valid* with respect to A_{Bse} and C if A is authorized, complete and eligible.

Given A_{Bse} and C, the decision AUTHORIZATION POLICY EXISTENCE PROBLEM (APEP) asks whether there exists a valid authorization relation.

We assume that determining whether an authorization relation satisfies a constraint takes polynomial time. (This is a reasonable assumption for all constraints of relevance to access control.) Let n denote $|U|$, k denote $|R|$ and m denote $|C|$. Then a brute force approach to solving APEP (by simply examining every possible authorization relation) takes time $O^*(2^{nk})$. (The O^* notation ignores multiplicative polynomial terms.)

3. CONSTRAINTS

We first introduce constraints that generalize separation-of-duty and binding-of-duty constraints. They are defined in terms of pairs of resources r and r', and their satisfaction is defined by a relationship that must hold on $A(r)$ and $A(r')$.

1. $(r, r', \leftrightarrow, \exists)$ is satisfied if there exists $u \in U$ such that $u \in A(r)$ and $u \in A(r')$; that is, $A(r) \cap A(r') \neq \emptyset$.
2. $(r, r', \updownarrow, \exists)$ is satisfied if there exists $u \in U$ such that either (i) $u \in A(r)$ and $u \notin A(r')$ or (ii) $u \notin A(r)$ and $u \in A(r)$; that is, $A(r) \neq A(r')$.

3. $(r, r', \leftrightarrow, \forall)$ is satisfied if for all $u \in A(r) \cup A(r')$, $u \in A(r)$ if and only if $u \in A(r')$; that is, $A(r) = A(r')$.
4. $(r, r', \updownarrow, \forall)$ is satisfied if for all $u \in A(r) \cup A(r')$, either (i) $u \in A(r)$ and $u \notin A(r')$ or (ii) $u \notin A(r)$ and $u \in A(r')$; that is, $A(r) \cap A(r') = \emptyset$.

Constraints of the form $(r, r', \updownarrow, Q)$ correspond closely to the idea of separation-of-duty. Indeed, the satisfaction criterion for $(r, r', \updownarrow, \forall)$ is identical to that for a simple static separation-of-duty constraint. Similarly, constraints of the form $(r, r', \leftrightarrow, Q)$ correspond to the idea of binding-of-duty.

A constraint of the form $(r, r', \circ, \forall)$ is said to be *universal*, while a constraint of the form $(r, r', \circ, \exists)$ is said to be *existential*. Informally speaking, universal constraints are "stronger" than existential constraints: for any complete relation, the satisfaction of $(r, r', \sim, \forall)$ implies the satisfaction of $(r, r', \sim, \exists)$, but the converse does not hold.

3.1 Cardinality constraints

We may also define *cardinality constraints*, which come in two flavors. In the following, $\lhd$ is one of $=$, $<$, $>$, $\leqslant$ or $\geqslant$ and t is an integer greater than 0.

- A *global* (cardinality) constraint has the form $(\lhd, t)$. The constraint $(\lhd, t)$ is satisfied by relation A if for all $r \in R$, $|A(r)| \lhd t$.
- A *local* (cardinality) constraint has the form $(R', \lhd, t)$, where $R' \subseteq R$. The constraint $(R', \lhd, t)$ is satisfied by relation A if $|A(R')| \lhd t$.

Then, for example, the global constraint $(=, 1)$ requires a valid relation A to be a function (since the number of users assigned to each resource is precisely 1), while the local constraint $(\{r\}, \leqslant, t)$ is a cardinality constraint in the RBAC96 sense [10] (if resource r is interpreted as a role). Finally, the t-out-of-m static separation-of-duty constraint $\text{ssod}(\{r_1, \ldots, r_m\}, t)$, introduced by Li *et al.* [8], may be represented by the cardinality constraint $(\{r_1, \ldots, r_m\}, \geqslant, t)$.

3.2 User-independent constraints

User-independent (UI) constraints are important in the context of the WORKFLOW SATISFIABILITY PROBLEM (WSP) [4]. First, the class of UI constraints includes a very wide range of constraints, and almost all constraints that are of relevance to access control. Second, WSP is fixed-parameter tractable (FPT) if we restrict attention to UI constraints [4]. (WSP is not FPT if we allow arbitrarily complex constraints [11].) Informally, a constraint is UI in the context of workflow satisfiability if its satisfaction only depends on the relationships that exist between users assigned to steps in a workflow (and not on the specific identities of users) [4].

Let A be an authorization relation and $\sigma : U \to U$ a permutation of the user set (that is, σ is a bijection). Then, given an authorization relation $A \subseteq U \times R$, we write $\sigma(A) \subseteq U \times R$ to denote the relation $\{(\sigma(u), r) : (u, r) \in A\}$. A constraint c is *user-independent* if for every authorization relation A that satisfies c and every permutation $\sigma : U \to U$, $\sigma(A)$ satisfies c.

Elementary arguments may be used to show that constraints of the form $(r, r', \leftrightarrow, \exists)$ $(r, r', \leftrightarrow, \forall)$, $(r, r', \updownarrow, \exists)$ and $(r, r', \updownarrow, \forall)$ are UI. Equally, it is clear that global and local constraints, whose satisfaction is defined in terms of the cardinality of sets of the form $A(r)$, are UI, since a permutation will preserve the cardinality of such sets. In other words, all constraints we consider in this paper are UI.

3.3 Bounded UI constraints

We now define an important class of UI constraints that is useful for establishing positive results for variants of APEP. Given a base relation A_{Bse} and a constraint c, let A be valid with respect to A_{Bse} and c. We say A *requires* v if $\{(u, r) \in A : u \neq v\}$ is not valid. (Since A is valid, this means that $\{(u, r) \in A : u \neq v\}$ is either incomplete or does not satisfy c.) Then we define

$$\mathsf{core}(A : A_{\mathsf{Bse}}, c) \stackrel{\text{def}}{=} \{u \in U : A \text{ requires } u\}$$

to be the *core of A with respect to A_{Bse} and c*.

PROPOSITION 1. *Let $\mathcal{I} = (A_{\mathsf{Bse}}, C)$ be a satisfiable instance of* APEP *with a UI constraint $c \in C$. If A is a valid solution with respect to A_{Bse} and c then*

$$|\mathsf{core}(A : U \times R, c)| \geqslant |\mathsf{core}(A : A_{\mathsf{Bse}}, c)|$$

DEFINITION 2. *We say a UI constraint c is $f(k, n)$-bounded if $|\mathsf{core}(A : U \times R, c)| \leqslant f(k, n)$ for all A valid with respect to $U \times R$ and c.*

The definition of $f(k, n)$-bounded constraints and Proposition 1 impose an upper bound on the number of users we need to consider when constructing candidate solutions to an instance (A_{Bse}, C) of APEP.

Table 1 shows $f(k, n)$ for different types of constraints. Note that in all cases, $f(k, n)$ is independent of n. This is important as we are able to prove that APEP is FPT when all constraints are $f(k)$-bounded for some function f. The proofs of the above results, and those in Section 4, can be found in the extended version of this paper [2].

Constraint Type	Largest Core
$(r, r', \updownarrow, \forall), (r, r', \updownarrow, \exists)$	k
$(r, r', \leftrightarrow, \forall), (r, r', \leftrightarrow, \exists)$	$k - 1$
$(R', \leqslant, t)$	k
$(R', =, t), (R', \geqslant, t)$	$2 \max \{k, t\}$

Table 1: Upper bounds on the size of the core

4. COMPLEXITY RESULTS

It is straightforward to show that an instance of APEP containing only constraints of the form $(r, r', \updownarrow, Q)$, where $Q \in \{\exists, \forall\}$, and the constraint $(=, 1)$ is equivalent (in an appropriate complexity-theoretic sense) to an instance of WSP involving only separation-of-duty constraints. In short, APEP is at least as hard as WSP. An instance of WSP is parameterized by the number of workflow steps k, the number of users n, and the number of constraints c. It is known that WSP is fixed-parameter tractable (FPT) for UI constraints [4], where k is the small parameter. That is, informally, there exists an algorithm to solve the problem whose run-time is only exponential in k, which is generally an order of magnitude smaller than n in practice.

We have established the APEP is also FPT if we restrict our attention to particular types of constraints and the number of resources k is the small parameter (relative to the number of users n). Figure 1 summarizes our results for APEP, determined by constraint type. We write $(\circ, Q)$, where $Q \in \{\exists, \forall\}$ and $\circ \in \{\leftrightarrow, \updownarrow\}$, to denote that only constraints of the form $(r, r', \circ, Q)$ are permitted.

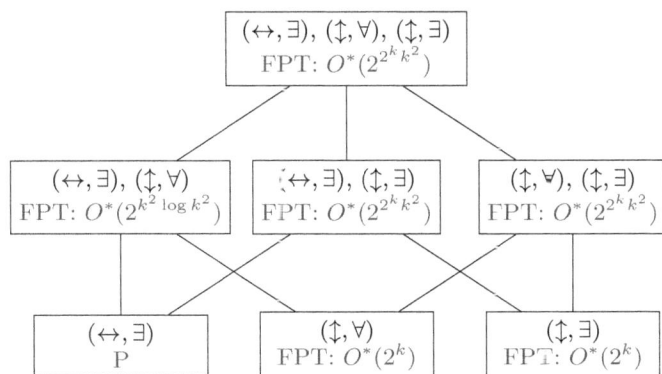

Figure 1: The complexity of variants of APEP

5. REFERENCES

[1] BASIN, D. A., BURRI, S. J., AND KARJOTH. G. Obstruction-free authorization enforcement: Aligning security and business objectives. *Journal of Computer Security 22*, 5 (2014), 661–698.

[2] BERGÉ, P., CRAMPTON, J., GUTIN, G., AND WATRIGANT, R. The authorization policy existence problem. *CoRR abs/1612.06191* (2016).

[3] BREWER, D. F. C., AND NASH, M. J. The Chinese wall security policy. In *Proceedings of the 1989 IEEE Symposium on Security and Privacy* (1989) pp. 206–214.

[4] COHEN, D., CRAMPTON, J., GAGARIN, A., GUTIN, G., AND JONES, M. Iterative plan construction for the workflow satisfiability problem. *J. Artif. Intell. Res. (JAIR) 51* (2014), 555–577.

[5] CRAMPTON, J., GUTIN, G., AND WATRIGANT, R. Resiliency policies in access control revisited. In *Proceedings of the 21st ACM on Symposium on Access Control Models and Technologies* (2016), ACM, pp. 101–111.

[6] CRAMPTON, J., GUTIN, G., AND YEO, A. On the parameterized complexity and kernelization of the workflow satisfiability problem. *ACM Trans. Inf. Syst. Secur. 16*, 1 (2013), 4.

[7] GLIGOR, V. D., GAVRILA, S. I., AND FERRAIOLO, D. F. On the formal definition of separation-of-duty policies and their composition. In *Security and Privacy - 1998 IEEE Symposium on Security and Privacy, Proceedings* (1998), IEEE Computer Society, pp. 172–183.

[8] LI, N., TRIPUNITARA, M. V., AND BIZRI, Z. On mutually exclusive roles and separation-of-duty. *ACM Trans. Inf. Syst. Secur. 10*, 2 (2007).

[9] LI, N., WANG, Q., AND TRIPUNITARA, M. V. Resiliency policies in access control. *ACM Trans. Inf. Syst. Secur. 12*, 4 (2009).

[10] SANDHU, R. S., COYNE, E. J., FEINSTEIN, H. L., AND YOUMAN, C. E. Role-based access control models. *IEEE Computer 29*, 2 (1996), 38–47.

[11] WANG, Q., AND LI, N. Satisfiability and resiliency in workflow authorization systems. *ACM Trans. Inf. Syst. Secur. 13*, 4 (2010), 40.

Towards Practical Privacy-Preserving Life Cycle Assessment Computations

Cetin Sahin, Brandon Kuczenski, Omer Egecioglu, Amr El Abbadi
University of California, Santa Barbara
{cetin, omer, amr}@cs.ucsb.edu, bkuczenski@bren.ucsb.edu

ABSTRACT

Life Cycle Assessment(LCA) is crucial for evaluating the ecological sustainability of a product or service, and the accurate evaluation of sustainability requires detailed and transparent information about industrial activities. However, such information is usually considered confidential and withheld from the public. In this paper, we present a study of privacy in the context of LCA. The main goal is to explore the privacy challenges in sustainability assessment considering the protection of trade secrets while increasing transparency of industrial activities. To overcome privacy concerns, we apply differential privacy to LCA computations considering the idiosyncratic features of LCA data. Our assessments on a specific real-life example show that it is possible to achieve privacy-preserving LCA computations without losing the utility of data completely.

1. INTRODUCTION

One of the greatest challenges facing society is to ensure that the industrial goods and services required by a growing population can be met sustainably and equitably. Industrial Ecology (IE) is the study of resource requirements and the social and ecological implications of industrial activities. One primary technique in IE is life cycle assessment (LCA), a standardized methodology for estimating the environmental implications of products or services 3].

Preparing an LCA requires access to a database of information about the inventory requirements and environmental emissions of industrial processes, called a life cycle inventory (LCI) database. Preparing an accurate and comprehensive LCI database is a tremendous task and the development and maintenance of these resources is an ongoing challenge. Because industrial processes are typically undertaken in a competitive economic context, the operators of these processes would like to prevent potential competitors from learning sensitive information about their activities. Inventory data about industrial processes is usually considered to be confidential, and therefore is often not available freely. This type

CODASPY'17 March 22-24, 2017, Scottsdale, AZ, USA

© 2017 Copyright held by the owner/author(s).

ACM ISBN 978-1-4503-4523-1/17/03.

DOI: http://dx.doi.org/10.1145/3029806.3029845

of information is nonetheless required to accurately assess environmental impact. Hence, the historical development of LCA has long been intimately bound to questions of confidentiality [4]. Despite its centrality to LCA, data privacy in the LCA domain has not been formally considered.

In this paper, we formulate the LCA computation in a way that introduces a privacy model, and consider possible threat models and attacks that could result in an adversary learning private data. Our goal is to provide the data security community with a real sense of the challenges faced by practitioners in the field of IE. We explore a particular problem in LCA and discuss the privacy issues and possible trade-offs between increase transparency by industrial companies and privacy protection of trade secrets that preserve competitive edge. The results of our attacks justify the concerns over publishing inventory data about industrial processes without any security provisions. To tackle this problem, we apply privacy techniques to LCA computations and illustrate their usage on a specific real life example. Our evaluations over a real life example highlight that it is possible to achieve privacy-preserving LCA publication without losing too much utility on the published data while ensuring privacy using differential privacy.

2. THE LCA AGGREGATION PROBLEM

LCA describes the delivery of a product or service as a network of industrial *unit processes*. Each unit process represents one form of industrial activity. Each edge in the network indicates a *flow* from one process to another, or between one process and the environment. Flows between a process and the environment are called *elementary* flows and may have environmental impacts. LCA studies distinguish between a *foreground model*, which represents the activities under scrutiny, and a *background model*, which represents the operations of the broader economy [8]. Private data are typically contained in the foreground model.

An *LCA aggregation study* can be described as three sequential matrix multiplications with respect to a background database B_x[5]. B_x is an $m \times n$ matrix that maps a set of n background processes to a set of m elementary flows. The foreground model is made up of a set of p foreground processes, each of which is defined by its dependencies on the n background processes. These are described in an $n \times p$ dependency matrix A_d, which comprises the study's private input data. Here w is a p-element weighting vector that specifies the relative significance of the different foreground processes. The first multiplication aggregates the foreground model into a weighted dependency vector a_p:

$$a_p = A_d \cdot w \qquad (1)$$

The dependency vector a_p is then applied to the background database to determine an emission vector b:

$$b = B_x \cdot a_p \qquad (2)$$

The vector b reports the aggregate amounts of different emissions released into the environment. The results of this computation are characterized with respect to a set of t environmental impact categories, represented by multiplication with a $t \times m$ characterization matrix E.

$$s = E \cdot b \qquad (3)$$

This multiplication results in a set of t impact scores s, which are the final results of the study.

The current practice in the IE community is to make the result of the study s publicly available, so that their product system can be compared to other competitive product systems. However, it is difficult to evaluate the significance of the elements of s without knowing something about b. For instance, an independent researcher making a critical evaluation of s may wish to know whether a given environmental emission's contribution in b was significant. Additionally, some research questions may require a practitioner to supply their own E matrix, which is not possible if b is not disclosed.

3. CONFIDENTIALITY & PRIVACY ISSUES

To verify the validity of practitioners' concerns about publishing b, we here investigate the possible information leakage from the publication of b. In other words, how much of a_p can be recovered when b is published, given that B_x is public?

3.1 Industrial Ecology Privacy Concerns

The operations of an LCA aggregation study are sequential matrix multiplications. If B_x is a nonsingular (invertible) matrix, there exists a unique inverse denoted by B_x^{-1}, i.e., $B_x \cdot B_x^{-1} = B_x^{-1} \cdot B_x = I$. Then, Equation 2 has a unique solution, $a_p = B_x^{-1} \cdot b$. This might be seen as a justification for the concern not to publish b along with impact scores, s. However, B_x in LCA is a singular matrix most of the time, which means it is not invertible and a_p cannot be solved directly from Equation 2. Is this enough to ensure privacy guarantees?

The answer to this question is unclear. The concept of Moore-Penrose pseudoinverse of matrices [6], generalizes the notion of a nonsingular (invertible) matrix and makes it applicable to singular matrices. This concept is useful when searching for an optimal approximation of a set of linear equation solutions like $A \cdot x = y$, where A is a known $m \times n$ matrix, y is a column vector with m components and x is an unknown column vector. This approach can be directly applied in the LCA study to reveal the secret a_p vector with some approximation.

3.2 Revealing Industry Secrets

The Moore-Penrose pseudoinverse [6] guarantees a unique solution to x when A has a full column rank. In the context of LCA, to the best of our knowledge, having a full column

rank in B_x is very rare, which leads to an infinite number of solutions for the linear system. One can claim that having an infinite number of solutions for x will create enough ambiguity and an adversary will not be able to distinguish which x is close to the original one. However, our empirical studies over a real LCA study disprove this and show that one can solve the linear system approximately close enough using the Moore-Penrose pseudoinverse. Therefore, we need to ensure the security of publication to prevent an adversary from recovering the solution even with the usage of Moore-Penrose inverse. In the context of privacy-preserving data publication, differential privacy is a canonical technique due to its strong privacy guarantees and capability to release useful aggregation information. Given that an LCA study is an aggregation problem, we propose differentially private LCA publications.

4. ACHIEVING LCA PRIVACY

Differential privacy provides a strong notion of privacy and is commonly used for statistical data publication [2]. It ensures that the removal or addition of a single record does not significantly affect the outcome of any analysis. Differential privacy can be achieved by the addition of random noise. The magnitude of the noise is chosen based on the sensitivity of a query function which considers the largest change in the output of the function with a change of a single record. Dwork [2] suggests using the Laplace mechanism to add noise to achieve differential privacy.

4.1 Differential Privacy for LCA Computation

Our goal is to perform differentially private LCA matrix multiplication in the form of Equation 2, where no adversary is able to recover a_p from the published b vector. Recall that B_x is a publicly known matrix. Each element in a_p represents a background process that is included in the production. The privacy goal is to make the publication such that either inclusion or exclusion of a specific background process has a negligible effect on the output, i.e., vector b. To achieve this goal, differential privacy might be applied by either perturbing the input or the output.

4.1.1 Input Perturbation

The initial approach to achieve differential privacy is to add noise to the input data itself. The straightforward approach is to generate a differentially private version of a_p, and then perform matrix factorization. In this case, the sensitivity of the publication considers the maximum change in all possible neighboring vectors.

Definition 1. Let $\mathbb{R}$ denote the set of real numbers. For $x_1, x_2 \in \mathbb{R}^d$, the sensitivity of the publication is:

$$\Delta f_1 = \max \| x_1 - x_2 \|_1 \qquad (4)$$

for all x_1, x_2 differing in at most one element in the vector.

Now, we can formally define our differentially private vector publication mechanism.

Proposition 1. The randomized mechanism M_K that outputs the following vector is ϵ-differentially private:

$$M_K(x) = x + k \qquad (5)$$

where k is a vector consisting of n independent samples drawn from the Laplace distribution function with a scale $\Delta f_1/\epsilon$, i. e., $Lap(\Delta f_1/\epsilon)$.

Recall that our motivation is to publish b, not a_p. Using M_K, it is possible to publish an ϵ-differentially private a_p. Now, this version of a_p can be used to compute b.

Proposition 2. *Given a public $A \in \mathbb{R}^{m \times n}$ and private $x \in \mathbb{R}^n$, the randomized mechanism M_{F_1} that performs the following operation ensures ϵ-differentially privacy for x.*

$$M_{F_1}(A, x) = A \cdot M_K(x) \qquad (6)$$

4.1.2 Output Perturbation

To achieve differential privacy by perturbing the output, the desired differentially private mechanism initially computes the function, and then adds noise to each element of the computed output to obtain differentially private publication.

Definition 2. *Let $\mathbb{R}$ denote the set of real numbers where $A \in \mathbb{R}^{m \times n}$ and $x \in \mathbb{R}^n$. A matrix multiplication function $f : \mathbb{R}^{m \times n} \times \mathbb{R}^n \to \mathbb{R}^m$ is defined by:*

$$f(A, x) = A \cdot x \qquad (7)$$

Definition 3. *For $x_1, x_2 \in \mathbb{R}^n$, $A_1, A_2 \in \mathbb{R}^{m \times n}$, the sensitivity of $f(A, x)$ is:*

$$\Delta f_2 = \max \| f(A_1, x_1) - f(A_2, x_2) \|_1 \qquad (8)$$

for all x_1, x_2 differing in at most one element.

In the proposition below, we define a differentially private matrix multiplication mechanism.

Proposition 3. *Given a matrix multiplication function $f(A, x)$, the randomized mechanism M_{F_2} that outputs the following vector is ϵ-differentially private:*

$$M_{F_2}(A, x) = f(A, x) + k \qquad (9)$$

where k is a vector consisting of m independent samples drawn from the Laplace distribution function with a scale $\Delta f_2 / \epsilon$, i.e., $Lap(\Delta f_2 / \epsilon)$.

Data dependent sensitivity: Although having a data independent sensitivity computation is a desired feature in differentially private publications, the sensitivity computations in our context are data dependent. In theory, the sensitivities, Δf_1 and Δf_2, are unbounded and can be infinity. Given this fact, differential privacy might be considered as an inappropriate methodology. However, this is not the case. LCA data has its own characteristics like sparsity, data distribution, which make differential privacy work in practice for the LCA computations. Due to lack of space, we skip the details. Please refer to the full version of the paper for detailed discussion and proofs [7].

5. EVALUATION OF PRIVACY-PRESERVING LCA COMPUTATION

We conducted experiments over a real LCA study for *distillers grain* using U.S. Life Cycle Inventory (USLCI) [1]. This study contains 39 background processes and 378 elementary flows. The distinctive property of this data set is the very broad range of numbers, i.e., from 10^{-15} to 10^3.

Attack against LCA publication: The attacker develops its attack by computing the Moore-Penrose pseudoinverse of B_x. The rank of B_x is 29 -not a full column rank-. This means the solution to the $B_x \cdot a_p = b$ linear system

is not unique, and there is an approximate solution. It is reasonable to assume that an expert in the field has enough background knowledge to estimate which processes are included in the computation pretty well. With such background knowledge, the adversary can recover almost 82.05% of a_p. This outlines the power of the pseudoinverse approach in the context of LCA domain. Publishing b without any privacy technique has severe security issues, which justifies the concerns over making b public in the LCA community.

Differentially Private LCA Computation: We perform differentially private LCA computations using the mechanisms introduced in Section 4.1. When $\epsilon = 1$, M_{F_1} publishes a perturbed b, whose 165 elements out of 378 (44%) are approximately close within the threshold of 10^{-10}, i.e., the absolute difference between the original and computed entries is less than 10^{-10}. This is a good sign of utility. In addition, an attacker cannot approximate any element of a_p within a threshold of 10^{-10}. M_{F_2} does not provide as good utility as M_{F_1} regarding individual emission analysis. However, it delivers better utility if the analysis contains aggregate computations. Similar to the case with M_{F_1}, the attacker is not able to approximate any entries in a_p. Our study explores a normalization technique to decrease the utility loss. The gathered results justify the effectiveness of such an optimization by providing better utility for both M_{F_1} and M_{F_2} without sacrificing privacy (refer to the full version of the paper for detailed results [7]).

6. CONCLUSION

In this paper, we presented a study to explore the privacy concerns over publicizing industrial activities in the form of LCA computations. Our empirical studies show that the application of privacy-preserving techniques is required to preserve the privacy of private data and differentially private LCA computations ensure strong privacy while revealing useful information for analysts.

ACKNOWLEDGMENT

This work is funded by an NSF grant CCF-1442966.

7. REFERENCES

[1] U.S. Life Cycle Inventory Database, 2012. National Renewable Energy Laboratory, 2012. Accessed March 11, 2016: https://www.lcacommons.gov/nrel/search.

[2] C. Dwork. Differential privacy. In *ICALP 2006 Proceedings, Part II*, pages 1–12. Springer Berlin Heidelberg, 2006.

[3] G. Finnveden, M. Z Hauschild, T. Ekvall, J. Guinée, R. Heijungs, S. Hellweg, A. Koehler, D. Pennington, and S. Suh. Recent developments in life cycle assessment. *Journal of Environmental Management*, 91(1):1–21, 2009.

[4] R. Frischknecht. Transparency in LCA-a heretical request? *Int J LCA*, 9(4):211–213, jul 2004.

[5] B. Kuczenski. Partial ordering of life cycle inventory databases. *The International Journal of Life Cycle Assessment*, 20(12):1673–1683, Oct 2015.

[6] E. H. Moore. On the reciprocal of the general algebraic matrix. *Bulletin of the American Mathematical Society*, 26:394–395, 1920.

[7] C. Sahin, B. Kuczenski, O. Egecioglu, and A. El Abbadi. Towards Practical Privacy-Preserving Life Cycle Assessment Computations. Technical report. January 2017. https://www.cs.ucsb.edu/research/tech-reports/2017-01.

[8] A.-M. Tillman. Significance of decision-making for LCA methodology. *Environ. Impact Assess. Rev.*, 20(1):113 – 123, 2000.

The Human Capital Model for Security Research New Insights into Technology Transition

S. Raj Rajagopalan
Honeywell
Phoenix, AZ, U.S.A.
Siva.Rajagopalan@Honeywell.com

ABSTRACT

As a security researcher, have you ever wondered how much of security research that is done and presented at research conferences is ever used by practitioners or is incorporated into products? Four years ago we formed a team with diverse backgrounds and embarked on a systematic study on the question of which technological solutions would security practitioners actually use if we built them. To carry this out program, we embedded our students who worked inside several Security Operation Centers (SOCs) both in universities and corporations, to learn how security solutions get used in reality. Previous efforts at improving the efficiency of SOCs have emphasized building tools for analysts or understanding the human and organizational factors involved, but they have not significantly changed the status quo – solutions are built or bought but seldom used. This was because these efforts did not view these solutions from multiple contextual perspectives of the local participants, the analysts and their managers. After some initial failures, we realized that this kind of study is beyond the reach of conventional Computer Science approaches, so we worked with a Professor in Socio-cultural Anthropology to get a fresh look at the problem and get a new set of tools to use in our research. In our 4-year project we have used Anthropological fieldwork methods to study SOCs and in the process uncovered inherent contradictions between the multiple objectives a SOC has to meet as an organization and the conflicts between the goals of the human participants. This discovery was guided by Activity Theory, a theory proposed by the famous social scientist Y. Engestrom [1], which provides a framework for analyzing such kinds of fieldwork data. We discovered that successful SOC innovations must continually resolve the extant conflicts to be effective in improving operational efficiency. Our analysis provides evidence of the importance of conflict resolution as a prerequisite for operations improvement, both process and technological. It also enabled us to understand the fundamental challenge in security research, namely, why some innovations work well in SOCs while others fail. It also helped us devise a potentially successful and repeatable mechanism for introducing new technologies to future SOCs.

In this talk, we will detail the important insights we gained in the course of this project so that the security research community may benefit from them and even incorporate these new tools. We will also present examples of the challenges faced by commercial manufacturers in designing security into their products and our ongoing work on using these insights to address these challenges in innovative ways that seem to fare better than previous attempts.

This is based partially on joint work with Professors Xinming Ou (Southern Florida University Computer Science Department), Michael Wesch (Kansas State University Department of Anthropology), and John McHugh (Dalhousie University and RedJack, Inc, Retired) as well as their graduate students, Sathya Chandran Sundaramurthy and Alexandru Bardas. •

CCS Concepts

•Security and privacy ~ Human and societal aspects of security and privacy • Security and privacy ~ Social aspects of security and privacy • Human-centered computing ~ Ethnographic studies • Applied computing ~ Ethnography •Applied computing ~ Psychology • General and reference ~ Metrics •Social and professional topics ~ Management of computing and information systems

Author Keywords

Security; SOC; practitioners; Anthropology; Activity Theory; field study

CODASPY'17, March 22–24, 2017, Scottsdale, AZ, USA.
ACM ISBN 978-1-4503-4523-1/17/03.
DOI: http://dx.doi.org/10.1145/3029806.3044200

BIOGRAPHY

S. Raj Rajagopalan is a Senior Principal Research Scientist at Honeywell Labs where he leads the Product cyber security research effort aimed at designed-in security for Honeywell's vast control system product portfolio. His research interests include all aspects of Computer Security, including Software Engineering techniques for training software development teams in security practices, especially in the context of product manufacture. In collaboration with Computer Science Prof. Simon Ou (University of South Florida) and Anthropology Professor Mike Wesch of Kansas State University, he has been involved in a five-year study of several Security Operations Centers across universities and corporations on why it is so hard to make security tools that actually get used. He also leads an initiative to enable more academic research to the areas of cyber security and personal privacy for modern buildings management systems. Dr. Rajagopalan has a PhD in Computer Science from Boston University, and a B.Tech. in Computer Science and Engineering from the Indian Institute of Technology at Mumbai.

REFERENCES

1. Y. Engestrom. Learning by Expanding: An Activity-Theoretical Approach to Developmental Research. Orienta-Konsultit Oy, 1987.

PT-CFI: Transparent Backward-Edge Control Flow Violation Detection Using Intel Processor Trace

Yufei Gu[†‡], Qingchuan Zhao[‡], Yinqian Zhang[*], Zhiqiang Lin[‡]
[†]Cloudera Inc, Palo Alto, California
[‡]Department of Computer Science, The University of Texas at Dallas
[*]Department of Computer Science and Engineering, The Ohio State University
firstname.lastname@utdallas.edu, yinqian@cse.ohic-state.edu

ABSTRACT

This paper presents PT-CFI, a new backward-edge control flow violation detection system based on a novel use of a recently introduced hardware feature called Intel Processor Trace (PT). Designed primarily for offline software debugging and performance analysis, PT offers the capability of tracing the entire control flow of a running program. In this paper, we explore the practicality of using PT for security applications, and propose to build a new control flow integrity (CFI) model that enforces a backward-edge CFI policy for native COTS binaries based on the traces from Intel PT. By exploring the intrinsic properties of PT with a system call based synchronization primitive and a deep inspection capability, we have addressed a number of technical challenges such as how to make sure the backward edge CFI policy is both sound and complete, how to make PT enforce our CFI policy, and how to balance the performance overhead. We have implemented PT-CFI and evaluated with a number of programs including SPEC2006 and HTTP daemons. Our experimental results show that PT-CFI can enforce a perfect backward-edge CFI with only small overhead for the protected program.

Keywords

Return oriented programming; Control flow integrity; Shadow stack; Intel PT

1. INTRODUCTION

Control flow hijacking has been one of the most severe cyber threats for over 40 years. When given an exploitable vulnerability such as a buffer overflow in a program that consumes untrusted input, an attacker can directly compromise the execution of the program and perform whatever malicious actions of his or her wishes. Over the past a few decades, we have witnessed numerous such attacks. Stack smashing [36], return-into-libc [52], return oriented programming (ROP) [42, 12] (and its variants such as BROP [5] and JIT-ROP [44]), jump-oriented programming (JOP) [7], and even call-oriented programming (e.g., COOP [39]) all belong to this category. It is likely that these attacks will continue to remain a major cyber threat for years to come.

CODASPY '17, March 22–24, 2017, Scottsdale, AZ, USA
© 2017 ACM. ISBN 978-1-4503-4523-1/17/03...$15.00
DOI: http://dx.doi.org/10.1145/3029806.3029830

Correspondingly, numerous defenses have been proposed to defend against control flow hijacking. Notable examples include stack canary [16] (which can defeat stack smashing), data execution prevention (DEP) [3] (which can defeat code injection), address space layout randomization (ASLR) [46] (which can make the hijack exploit code much harder to construct), and control flow integrity (CFI) [2] (which aims to ensure the integrity of control flow transfer always following legal program path). Canary, DEP, and ASLR are all practical defenses and they all have been adopted by industry in mainstream computing devices including even in the mobile platform. Therefore, simple stack smashing or code injection attack does not work anymore in modern computing platform, and the mainstream exploits have to use ROP or its variant (e.g., Q [41], return-to-signal [8], JIT-ROP [44], or BROP [5]). To really defeat these advanced attacks, it appears that CFI is the most promising technique since in theory it can fundamentally solve the control flow hijacking problem because all these attacks including ROP violate the intended program control flow. However, in practice CFI has not been widely adopted yet, at least in the case of protecting commercial-off-the-shelf (COTS) binaries.

CFI essentially is a program path-level access control model. For any access control mechanism to work, it needs a policy and an enforcement. The first CFI model by Abadi *et al.* [2] uses an inlined reference monitoring (IRM) [20] in the program code to enforce the CFI policy. Specifically, at each indirect control flow transfer point (*i.e.*, indirect `call`, indirect `jmp`, and `ret`), the CFI enforcement code inlined with the original program will check with a CFI policy to detect whether there is a violation. The security policy in the CFI is quite simple: the execution of any control-flow transfer should not diverge from its legitimate path. To construct the CFI policy, the traditional form of CFI builds a control-flow graph (CFG) from the protected program, from which to get all the legal target(s) of each indirect control transfer. Then at runtime, the inlined enforcement code will check the control flow target whether or not belongs to a set of white-listed ones. As such, CFI guarantees that the execution path of the program strictly follows an edge in its CFG.

Unfortunately, there are two main challenges that hinder the practicality of CFI. First and foremost, how to make sure the CFI policy is both sound and complete. Often times, the statically extracted CFG (either from program source code or binary) is an over-approximation of the legitimate control flows of the protected program. This is because precise static extraction of CFG requires accurate pointer analysis of each indirect call or jump to estimate its targeted "points-to" set. This type of analysis, however, is challenging due to the dynamic nature (e.g., computed `jmp` and `call` target) of low-level programming languages like C. Meanwhile, the same function may have multiple legitimate call sites, corresponding to multiple edges in the CFG. However, at runtime, only one of the edges should be allowed at any state of the execution. This issue cannot be addressed by CFI that relies on static code analysis alone; context-sensitive methods (*e.g.* using a shadow stack [2]) need to be used at runtime.

The second challenge that blocks the practicality of CFI is how to enforce its policy efficiently. When having program source code, one can use compilers to automatically insert an IRM at each indirect control flow transfer to enforce the policy. However, it becomes much more challenging when only given application binaries. While the first CFI model rewrites the protected binary for the enforcement, it requires the access of the corresponding debugging symbols. Without those debugging symbols, one has to solve both the binary disassembling and rewriting challenge. While dynamic binary instrumentation (DBI) does not face disassembling and rewriting issues since it rewrites the binary on-the-fly, it still faces other challenges such as the high performance overhead (as DBIs are usually slow).

Prior efforts on binary-level CFI have been striving to address these challenges. However, most studies fall short in addressing the first challenge. For instance, BinCFI [58], CCFIR [57] and BinCC [51] only enforce a coarse-grained CFI policy: indirect jumps or calls are restricted to a white-list of targets and function returns are constrained to call-preceded addresses. It has been shown, however, by follow-up studies that these coarse-grained CFI implementations can be bypassed by advanced ROP attacks [18]. Specifically the weak backward-edge policy—returning to only call-preceded targets—can be easily circumvented by ROP attacks with only call-preceded gadgets [11, 23]. A more recent work, TypeArmor [50], advances the state-of-the-art of the forward-edge policy for binary-level CFI by statically analyzing binary code to match callers and callees. But still, no backward-edge policy is provided. Shadow stacks [2, 19] match return addresses to their call sites, and hence offer strong backward-edge policy. However, shadow stacks are difficult to implement correctly when offering reliable security guarantee [12]. Moreover, existing implementations of shadow stacks mostly rely on binary rewriting, facing the second aforementioned challenges.

To overcome the limitations of binary rewriting or instrumentations, recent studies resort to existing CPU hardware features to assist CFI policy enforcement. For instance, last branch records (LBR) was exploited by many notable works such as kBouncer [37], ROPecker [15], CFIGuard [54], and PathArmer [49] to keep track of a short history (usually only upto 16 LBR entries) of indirect branches. The main issue of LBR-based solutions is that they are vulnerable to history-flushing attacks [40, 11], in which the malicious payload intentionally includes dummy branch instructions to flush LBR entries to hide suspicious indirect branches. Branch trace store (BTS), which in contrast to LBR records all prior indirect branches, was used by CFIMon [53], but it also comes along with higher performance overhead. As such, both LBR and BTS have limitations when used to enforce CFI policies, which therefore motivates us to seek alternative, more effective, approaches.

In this paper, we aim to fill this gap and propose PT-CFI, a practical backward-edge CFI that works for x86 COTS binaries by using a recent hardware feature, the Intel Processor Trace (PT). While Intel had offered prior hardware-based tracing features such as LBR and BTS, PT provides many compelling features. In particular, the path history recorded by LBR is limited to a few dozen instructions, and BTS has significant slowdown though it supports unlimited path history. Therefore, Intel recently introduced PT, which can log execution trace with extremely low performance impact (less than 5% performance overhead) and provide a complete control flow tracing with both cycle count and timestamp information.

However, PT is not designed for online security protection but rather for offline software debugging or performance analysis. As such, there are a number of technical challenges in order to make a practical backward-edge CFI. These challenges include how to derive the CFI policy based on the PT trace and the monitored binary, how to enforce the CFI policy, and how to make sure the control flow monitoring would not introduce large overhead. We have addressed these challenges by exploring the intrinsic properties inside PT with a system synchronization primitive and a deep inspection capability. We have implemented PT-CFI and evaluated with both the SPEC2006 CPUINT benchmark suite and Nginx HTTP daemon. Experimental results show that PT-CFI only introduces very small overhead for the protected binaries.

Contribution. The main contribution of this paper can be summarized as follows:

- We make the first attempt of exploring PT for real-time monitoring of control flow violation and propose PT-CFI, a new practical backward-edge CFI model for x86 COTS binaries.

- We devise a number of enabling techniques including system call based enforcement and synchronization which enforces the CFI policy at the entry point of selected system call, and a deep inspection primitive, which is invoked like exception handling when a CFI policy is incomplete.

- We have implemented PT-CFI, and applied it to detect ROP attacks, which overcomes several limitations of prior work such as Kbouncer and ROPecker. Meanwhile, the performance overhead of PT-CFI is quite small (around 20% on average for a set of tested SPEC2006 benchmarks).

2. BACKGROUND AND RELATED WORK

2.1 Control-Flow Hijacking and ROP

Memory corruptions are one of the most commonly exploited vulnerabilities in programs written in C/C++. By allowing unsanitized input to overwrite data or code in the victim program's memory space, these vulnerabilities enable a wide range of attacks, such as information leakage, arbitrary code execution and privileges escalation [45]. While non-control-data attacks [14, 24, 9, 43, 25] have been demonstrated in previous works (especially in recent years), control-flow hijacking still remains the most commonly used attack method. In control-flow hijacking attacks, control data that are used to direct the program's control flows are corrupted by the attacker. When these data (*e.g.*, return addresses, indirect jump targets) are loaded into the program counter the program's execution will be diverted from its designed target.

There are several instances of control flow hijacking attacks such as code injection [36], code-reuse [52], return-oriented programming (ROP) [42, 12], jump-oriented programming (JOP) [7], and the recently call-oriented programming (COP) [39]. Among them, ROP attacks are increasingly becoming the mainstream: they are more advantageous than code injection attacks, because they can defeat the widely used Data Execution Prevention (DEP) protection; ROP attacks are also resilient to defense against simple return-to-libc attacks because they can reuse library code without explicit function calls [42].

In ROP attacks, short sequences of code, dubbed *gadgets*, that already exist in the victim program are chained together and reused for purposes other than their designed logic. In conventional ROP attacks, these gadgets all end with `ret` instruction. Hence attackers can prepare a sequence of return addresses on the stack to "return"

Table 1: Binary-level control-flow integrity enforcement

	backward-edge policy	CFI enforcement
CFI [2] (2005)	shadow stack	binary rewriting
DROP [13] (2009)	heuristic	dynamic instrumentation
ROPDefender [19] (2011)	shadow stack	dynamic instrumentation
CFIMon [53] (2012)	call-proceded targets	critical function + async
MoCFI [17] (2012)	shadow stack	runtime hooking
CCFIR [57] (2013)	whitelist targets	binary rewriting
BinCFI [58] (2013)	call-proceded targets	dynamic instrumentation
kBouncer [37] (2013)	heuristic + call-proceded	critical function
ROPecker [15] (2014)	heuristic	non-exec page
CFIGuard [54] (2015)	whitelist targets	PMU interrupts
PathArmer [49] (2015)	call/return matching	dynamic instrumentation
BinCC [51] (2015)	bounds-check	static rewriting
O-CFI [32] (2015)	bounds-check	static rewriting
TypeArmer [50] (2016)	None	dynamic instrumentation

to these gadgets in orders that fulfill a specific functionality. Later work shown that indirect jumps or calls can also be used to construct "return" gadgets without `ret` instructions [12, 7].

2.2 Control-Flow Integrity

CFI is a widely studied technique to prevent control-flow hijacking attacks. It was first proposed by Abadi *et al.* [2] in 2005, which aims to enforce policies on the control-flow transfers of a program so that the execution of the program does not diverge from the legitimate path. The traditional form of CFI first constructs a control-flow graph (CFG) from a program and then checks the target of each indirect control flow transfer (*e.g.*, indirect jump, indirect call, and return) at runtime so that only a set of white-listed targets for each indirect control transfer is allowed. In this way, CFI guarantees that the execution of the program strictly follows an edge in its CFG. A CFI implementation can be either *fine-grained* or *coarse-grained*. In a fine-grained CFI, each indirect control transfer has its own set of target addresses that can be allowed to take at runtime. This is usually achieved through program analysis because the sets of targets are program-dependent. In contrast, a coarse-grained CFI partitions the indirect control transfers and their target addresses into several *equivalence classes* [35].

While many efforts have achieved fine-grained CFI via complex source code analysis, such as CFLocking [6], Forward-edge CFI [48], RockJIT [34], MCFI [33], CPI [27], CCFI [31], πCFI [35], *etc.*, fine-grained binary-level CFI remains a challenge. Table 1 summarizes prior research on binary-level control-flow integrity. Particularly, CFIMon [53], BinCFI [58], and kBouncer [37] only enforce a coarse-grained backward-edge policy: returns are only allowed to addresses preceded by a call-site. CCFIR [57] and CFI-Guard [54] enforce slightly finer-grained policy by allowing only a smaller set of white-listed return targets. BinCC [51] and O-CFI [32] restrict returns across a specified boundary, greatly reducing the usable gadgets. The strong backward-edge CFI policy is enforced by shadow stacks (implemented in the original CFI, ROPDefender [19], MoCFI [17] and PathArmer [49] through static binary rewriting or dynamic binary instrumentation), which strictly matches call/return pairs. In contrast to these prior efforts, PT-CFI aims to enforce a perfect backward-edge CFI policy by using shadow stacks, *without static binary rewriting or dynamic instrumentation*.

2.3 Hardware-Assisted ROP Detection

Besides our work, there has been a few studies exploring hardware-assisted approaches for ROP detection. Most notable results among them include CFIMon [53], kBouncer [37], ROPecker [15] and CFIGuard [54]. ROPecker, kBouncer and CFIGuard studied the

use of LBR that is available on Intel processors for ROP detection. Note that LBR provides a hardware mechanism to record the source address and target address of most recently used branches. These approaches statically scan the program binary to construct a database of ROP gadgets. Once the detection is triggered (the time of ROP check differs in these approaches), the most-recent branches are compared with the gadget database, and according to a specific security policy (*e.g.*, number of instructions in a gadget, consecutive gadget numbers detected in the LBR), the LBR data may indicate an ROP attack. Unfortunately, recent studies [40, 11] have shown that these LBR-based approaches are vulnerable to several attack methods. The most noteworthy attacks among them are LBR-flushing attacks, in which ROP code intentionally induce unimportant branches to fill the limited number of entries (usually less than 16) in LBR.

Most close to our work is CFIMon [53], which exploited Branch Trace Store (BTS) on Intel processors. Intel BTS is a processor component that provides program tracing mechanism to software layers, which captures all types of control flow information, including direct and indirect jump and call, and also function return. Both the source address and target address are stored in a specific memory region for batch processing. CFIMon is triggered to detect control flow violation when the memory buffer is full or sensitive functions are accessed. CFIMon detects control flow violation by monitoring if backward CFG edges return to a call-preceded target, and if indirect calls transfer control flows actually to the first instruction of a function. Indirect jumps are marked as suspicious if not seen before. But the policy to treat these suspicious indirect jumps is not clearly defined, leaving CFIMon potentially vulnerable to carefully crafted ROP attacks [53].

In addition to exploiting existing hardware features in commodity processors, some other works designed new hardware components to detect ROP attacks such as the one from Lee *et al.* [28] that implemented an FPGA-based ROP detection system for ARM devices that executes asynchronously with the protected program. Unlike our work, they do not maintain any synchronization between the monitoring program and monitored program, and therefore, ROP detection cannot effectively prevent the attacks from damaging the system. Moreover, their approach has a common issue as all other studies that detect ROP attack by developing new hardware components: while they all present interesting ideas, nevertheless, because they require additional hardware supports, the likelihood of real world adoption is low.

2.4 Intel Processor Trace

Intel Processor Trace (PT) is a new hardware feature for software program debugging and performance profiling, which is available in Intel Broadwell or later processors. It traces the control flow of software programs with minimum performance overhead that is sufficient low for PT to be used in production systems.

More specifically, the control flow information is collected by PT in *data packets* in real-time, which are then sent to memory buffers or other output methods for processing. While several types of PT packets are defined by Intel and collected at runtime, three types of packets are particularly useful in control flow tracing: Taken Not-Taken (TNT) packets, Target IP (TIP) packets, Flow Update Packets (FUP). The TNT packets collect taken and not-taken indication for conditional direct branches; the TIP packets collect target addresses for indirect calls, indirect jumps and returns; asynchronous events such as exceptions and interrupts will generate FUP packets together with TIPs. Unconditional direct branches are excluded from the PT packets. PT also compresses conditional branches and use only one bit to indicate branch taken or not-taken in TNT packets.

Intel PT supports filtering packets based on the Current Privilege Level (CPL) or CR3. Therefore, it is possible to trace all user-space programs or selectively trace only one program. Context switch can also be supported so that multiple programs can be traced sequentially. Moreover, the precise timing of each data packet are also optionally recorded. Therefore, with the knowledge of binary information, one can reconstruct the entire control flow of the original software program, together with the precise timing of each branch.

Given the capability of Intel PT in tracing program control flows, it is tempting to use PT for control-flow violation monitoring and detect ROP attacks. However, Intel has designed PT particularly to reduce overhead with the cost of increased decoding overhead, and unfortunately the decoding of the traces is several orders of magnitude slower than tracing. A typical use case defined by Intel is to execute a software program and capture the trace data asynchronously in memory regions that can be processed after the execution of the program. Therefore, our design of PT-CFI faces several technical challenges that we will elaborate in later sections.

Prior to ours, only a few work has explored the use of Intel PT in practical applications. Balakrishnan *et al.* [4] and Thalheim *et al.* [47] studied the use of Intel PT to implement fine-grained provenance systems. Kasikci *et al.* [26] developed a software failure diagnose system using PT. However, in all these existing work, PT packets are collected for offline analysis. Therefore, our study presents the first attempt of online uses of Intel PT technology.

Concurrent and independent to our work, most recently, there were two other efforts namely FlowGuard [29] and GRIFFIN [22] that also explored the use of PT for control flow integrity. At a high level, all of these works share similar insight of leveraging the PT packet traces for CFI enforcement, but differ at how to generate and enforce the CFI policy. Specifically, unlike PT-CFI in which only backward-edge CFI policy is enforced, FlowGuard and GRIFFIN also enforce a forward-edge CFI whose policy is acquired through either dynamic training or analysis of binary code as in PathArmer [49].

3. PT-CFI OVERVIEW

In this section, we present an overview of PT-CFI. We first describe a simplified running example in Section 3.1, which will be used throughout the paper to discuss various technical challenges we have to solve in Section 3.2. Then, we present our key insights of how to solve the challenges in Section 3.3. Next, we discuss our CFI policy in Section 3.4. Finally, we give an overview of PT-CFI in Section 3.5.

3.1 A Running Example

Figure 1(a) illustrates the source code of a very simple program, which accepts command line inputs and then executes one of the three functions accordingly: `foo`, `bar`, and `overflow`. Among them, `overflow` function contains a stack overflow, and an attacker can compromise this program to execute a shell for instance. We compile this program using `gcc` without canary protection. The partial binary code is illustrated in Figure 1(b).

We run this program with four different inputs: The first three just triggered the three different function pointers but the fourth one triggered the `overflow` along with a ROP payload to execute `/bin/sh`. The system call (syscall for short henceforth) traces for the first two were the same (both have 29 syscalls in total, and they both trigger a `write` syscall by function `printf`), as show in Figure 1(c). The third one has only 28 syscalls without the `write`

syscall compared to the first two, but the forth one triggered the unexpected `execve` syscall.

Note that PT is primarily designed for debugging and performance analysis. A typical use case of PT is the following: programmers compile the target program, and execute it atop a PT enabled platform. During the execution, the hardware will generate a large volume of PT packets, which is often stored in a log file for offline analysis. There are already available tools such as `perf` that is able to parse the PT packets and reconstruct the entire execution path history of a program based on the trace. While PT packets have already been compressed, usually it will still generate up to hundreds of megabytes of trace data per second per core. As an example, we also illustrate partially decoded PT packets in Figure 1(d). More specifically, we can notice that there are various types of PT packets, including:

- **Target IP (TIP) packets**: if a control flow transition is triggered by an *indirect* control flow transfer, the hardware will generate a TIP packet, which is particular useful for building our CFI model. Usually, a TIP packet contains a virtual address of the target or just an offset whose base address is shared by prior TIP packets. An instance of the TIP packet is TIP 0x4004d0, as illustrated in Figure 1(d), which is actually an indirect `jmp` to the starting address of _start. The next TIP packet TIP 0x4a6 is actually also a `jmp` target address, caused by the first instruction in the PLT entry of __libc_start_main. Note that direct call does not have a TIP packet. That is why there is no TIP pointing to the first instruction in the PLT entry of __libc_start_main.

- **Taken Not-Taken (TNT) packets**: if there is a conditional control flow transfer (i.e., all of the `jcc` instructions such as je/jne), then the hardware will generate a bit in a TNT packet and this bit represents taken or not-taken for that particular branch. A TNT packet can at most encode six TNT bits. There are also several TNT packets in Figure 1(d), such as TNT TTN (3) and TNT TNTNTN (6). Combined with the original binary code, TNT packets can be used to capture the exact execution path of a program. Since an attacker cannot alter the destination address of conditional branches, TNT packets are out of CFI interest. In addition, similar to `jcc`, unconditional direct branches (e.g., *direct* jmp/call) are excluded from the PT packets since they can be also directly recovered with program code.

- **Flow Update Packets (FUP)**: if there is an asynchronous event such as exceptions and interrupts, the hardware will generate a FUP packet together with TIPs. As an example, FUP 0x7f569383a1e0 means the control flow will transfer from instruction at 0x7f569383a1e0. Followed, there is also a TIP.PGD and TIP.PGE, which denotes Packet Generation Disable (PGD), and Packet Generation Enable (PGE). These two TIP sequences are usually from the interrupt handler execution. FUP packets are also out of our current CFI interest.

3.2 Technical Challenges

If we directly analyze the recorded PT packets offline without any additional effort, we can certainly use PT for control flow diagnosis or forensics since we can rebuild the entire control flow trace and any deviation from normal control flow will be detected. However, such an offline usage cannot be used for online CFI. Therefore, we have to solve a number of technical challenges including:

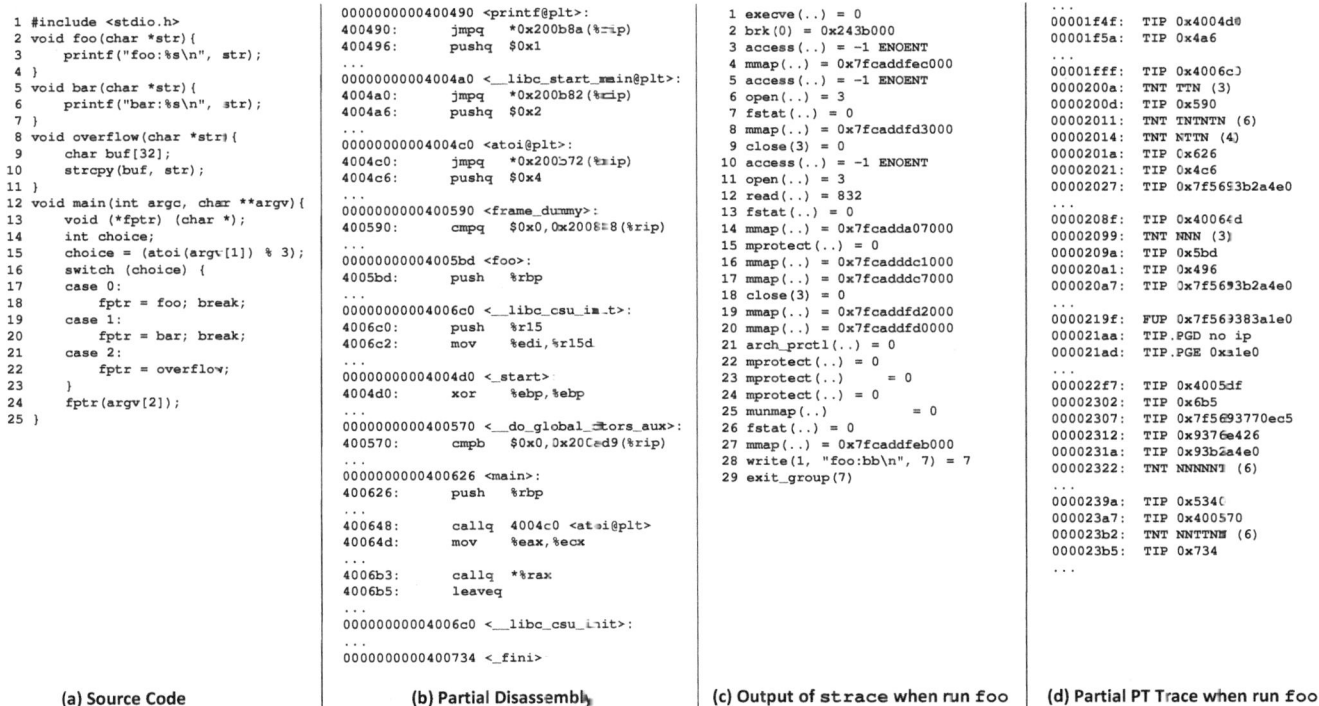

```
(a) Source Code

1  #include <stdio.h>
2  void foo(char *str){
3      printf("foo:%s\n", str);
4  }
5  void bar(char *str){
6      printf("bar:%s\n", str);
7  }
8  void overflow(char *str){
9      char buf[32];
10     strcpy(buf, str);
11 }
12 void main(int argc, char **argv){
13     void (*fptr) (char *);
14     int choice;
15     choice = (atoi(argv[1]) % 3);
16     switch (choice) {
17     case 0:
18         fptr = foo; break;
19     case 1:
20         fptr = bar; break;
21     case 2:
22         fptr = overflow;
23     }
24     fptr(argv[2]);
25 }
```

```
(b) Partial Disassembly

0000000000400490 <printf@plt>:
400490:    jmpq    *0x200b8a(%rip)
400496:    pushq   $0x1
...
00000000004004a0 <__libc_start_main@plt>:
4004a0:    jmpq    *0x200b82(%rip)
4004a6:    pushq   $0x2
...
00000000004004c0 <atoi@plt>:
4004c0:    jmpq    *0x200b72(%rip)
4004c6:    pushq   $0x4
...
0000000000400590 <frame_dummy>:
400590:    cmpq    $0x0,0x2008b8(%rip)
...
00000000004005bd <foo>:
4005bd:    push    %rbp
...
00000000004006c0 <__libc_csu_init>:
4006c0:    push    %r15
4006c2:    mov     %edi,%r15d
...
00000000004004d0 <_start>:
4004d0:    xor     %ebp,%ebp
...
0000000000400570 <__do_global_ctors_aux>:
400570:    cmpb    $0x0,0x20ced9(%rip)
...
0000000000400626 <main>:
400626:    push    %rbp
...
400648:    callq   4004c0 <atoi@plt>
40064d:    mov     %eax,%ecx
...
4006b3:    callq   *%rax
4006b5:    leaveq
...
00000000004006c0 <__libc_csu_init>:
...
0000000000400734 <_fini>
```

```
(c) Output of strace when run foo

1  execve(..) = 0
2  brk(0) = 0x243b000
3  access(..) = -1 ENOENT
4  mmap(..) = 0x7fcaddfec000
5  access(..) = -1 ENOENT
6  open(..) = 3
7  fstat(..) = 0
8  mmap(..) = 0x7fcaddfd3000
9  close(3) = 0
10 access(..) = -1 ENOENT
11 open(..) = 3
12 read(..) = 832
13 fstat(..) = 0
14 mmap(..) = 0x7fcadda07000
15 mprotect(..) = 0
16 mmap(..) = 0x7fcadddc1000
17 mmap(..) = 0x7fcadddc7000
18 close(3) = 0
19 mmap(..) = 0x7fcaddfd2000
20 mmap(..) = 0x7fcaddfd0000
21 arch_prctl(..) = 0
22 mprotect(..) = 0
23 mprotect(..) = 0
24 mprotect(..) = 0
25 munmap(..) = 0
26 fstat(..) = 0
27 mmap(..) = 0x7fcaddfeb000
28 write(1, "foo:bb\n", 7) = 7
29 exit_group(7)
```

```
(d) Partial PT Trace when run foo

...
00001f4f:   TIP 0x4004d0
00001f5a:   TIP 0x4a6
...
00001fff:   TIP 0x4006c0
0000200a:   TNT TTN (3)
0000200d:   TIP 0x590
00002011:   TNT TNTNTN (6)
00002014:   TNT NTTN (4)
0000201a:   TIP 0x626
00002021:   TIP 0x4c6
00002027:   TIP 0x7f5693b2a4e0
...
0000208f:   TIP 0x40064d
00002099:   TNT NNN (3)
0000209a:   TIP 0x5bd
000020a1:   TIP 0x496
000020a7:   TIP 0x7f5693b2a4e0
...
0000219f:   FUP 0x7f569383a1e0
000021aa:   TIP.PGD no ip
000021ad:   TIP.PGE 0xa1e0
...
000022f7:   TIP 0x4005df
00002302:   TIP 0x6b5
00002307:   TIP 0x7f5693770ec5
00002312:   TIP 0x9376e426
0000231a:   TIP 0x93b2a4e0
00002322:   TNT NNNNNT (6)
...
0000239a:   TIP 0x534c
000023a7:   TIP 0x400570
000023b2:   TNT NNTTNN (6)
000023b5:   TIP 0x734
...
```

Figure 1: A Running Example Used to Illustrate Our PT-CFI Approach.

- **How to define the CFI policy**. To design a CFI model, we have to first define the CFI policy and extract them from the program. However, what we have is merely the PT trace and also the binary code of the corresponding program we aim to protect. While we can build a run-time control flow graph based on PT traces and then compare with the CFG extracted from the static binary code, we may be able to form a CFI policy to detect most attacks. However, such an approach would be too slow. Meanwhile, statically we still do not know all of the legal target for indirect calls and indirect jumps, a grand challenge today for static binary code analysis (due to the need of the sophisticated point-to analysis).

- **How to enforce the CFI policy**. PT packets are directly generated by the underlying hardware in an asynchronized manner. However, the policy enforcement and program execution should be synchronized. Otherwise, a control flow hijack attack might have already caused damages before it is detected. While rewriting the binary code and insert our CFI enforcement code might work, we would like to avoid using any binary rewriting especially for x86 COTS binary (due to the disassembling and instruction relocating challenge), since we aim for a practical CFI.

- **How to minimize the overhead, and support thread-level tracing**. Performance is often a critical factor while designing CFI. For instance, one can easily design a CFI by using dynamic binary instrumentation (e.g., PIN [30]). However, such an approach often has high overhead. While PT packet generation has less than 5% overhead, PT packet consumption as well as our CFI enforcement must be designed in an efficient way. Meanwhile, Intel PT does not support per thread tracing in the hardware level, we have to enable such a feature in the software level, given the increasing popularity of multi-threading programs.

3.3 Key Insights

Having analyzed the internals of various PT packets and understood how software interacts with the PT hardware, we have obtained the following key insights to address the above challenges.

- **Using TIP sequence graph for the CFI policy**. Ideally, we should have used the entire PT trace to rebuild a complete CFG and compared with the statically extracted CFG from binary code for the policy. While purely static analysis of the binary code cannot resolve many indirect call and indirect jump edges, we can use the runtime traces to connect them. However, this is an expensive approach because parsing each PT packet to rebuild a dynamic CFG with the original binary code usually takes a large amount of time.

Fortunately, we notice that we can actually use a lightweight, TIP sequence graph to detect the anomalies. In particular, all indirect control flow transfers (call, ret, jmp) will trigger a corresponding TIP packet. Therefore, we can build a TIP sequence graph, and compare this graph with the legitimate TIP graph. As illustrated in Figure 2, the node of this graph is an indirect control flow transfer point, and the edge captures the transition between the two points. For instance, considering the first two sequences shown in Figure 1(d), namely TIP 0x4004d0 and TIP 0x4a6, the TIP sequence graph of these two nodes shown in Figure 2 captures the transition from _start to the PLT entry of __libc_start_main.

While we cannot build the legitimate TIP graph statically since we cannot resolve the corresponding destination addresses without any additional sophisticated point-to analysis, we can build it from the TIP trace since they exactly

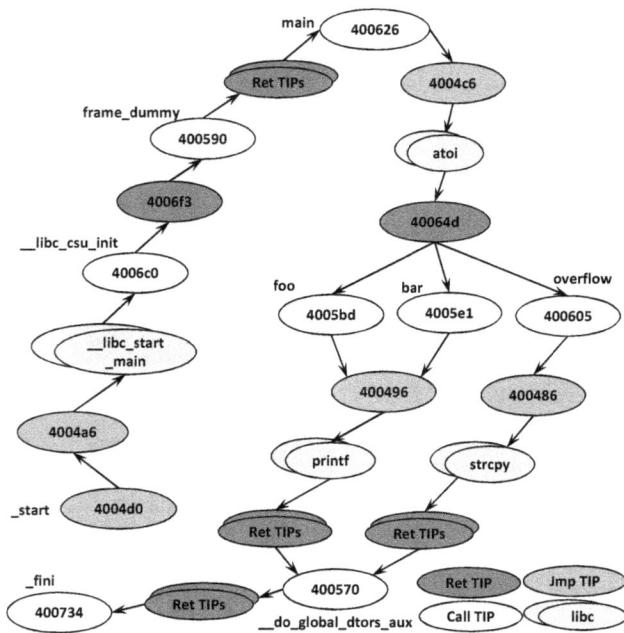

Figure 2: A Partial TIP Sequence Graph for Our Running Example.

capture the indirect control flow transitions. Then to really differentiate between legal and illegal control flow transfers (at least for the backward return edges), we can use a deep inspection technique discussed below. We will detail how we extract the CFI policy in Section 4.1.

- **Using syscall interposition for the enforcement.** Once we have defined the CFI policy, we must check it at runtime to ensure the software adhering the legitimate control flow path. The first CFI approach by Abadi *et al.* uses the binary rewriting (with debugging symbols) to enforce the policy. However, without debugging symbols, it is very hard to correctly rewrite a binary. Therefore, we would like to seek alternative approaches.

  Inspired by ROPecker and kBouncer, where they enforce the security policy at selected syscall execution point, we can also adopt such an approach. Specifically, while the PT packet generation is asynchronized, we can ask PT to stop at selected system call execution point, and the execution can continue only in the case that there is no violation of our CFI policy. It is true that an attacker might have already executed a number of gadgets before being detected, but they must invoke syscalls for any malicious actions. Therefore, it is a proved viable approach by using syscall interposition as shown in many of the prior efforts. Then, the rest challenge becomes how we synchronize the execution at the syscall execution point with our CFI policy checking. The detailed design of how we perform our enforcement is presented in Section 4.2.

- **Using deep inspection when needed.** If there is no malicious attack, the TIP graph extracted from the PT packet trace faithfully represents the legitimate control flow path. Only when an unknown TIP sequence occurs do we invoke the slow and expensive PT packet parsing to parse the runtime control flow transfer, and compare with our CFI policy

(discussed in Section 3.4) for the detection. At a high level, such a process works similarly to network packet inspection. Most of the time, we directly just parse the headers of most packet, and only when unknown packet arrives do we parse its content. Therefore, we call this slow PT parsing and CFI verification process *deep inspection*.

The purpose of designing this component is to speed up the performance of our CFI. As discussed earlier, one extreme case is to parse every PT packet to compute the dynamic CFG, and then inspect the binary code to check whether it conforms the legal control flow transfers. But this will render our system impractical because of its huge overhead. Our deep inspection solves this problem, and it only gets invoked when the CFI policy is incomplete. We will present in greater details of how we perform deep inspection also in Section 4.1.

- **Capturing context switch to enable thread level tracing.** PT is a hardware level feature tracing the CPU execution, and does not distinct any software level feature such as thread. Fortunately, a thread is a CPU scheduling unit, and we can uniquely associate the PT traces with a thread if we precisely capture the context switch event. Therefore, we instrument the `schedule` function of the OS kernel, and extract the value of CR3 and kernel stack pointer (`esp`) to resolve the thread context and associate it with the PT traces. Note that CR3 is process specific and PT only uses CR3 to differentiate the traces. By capturing the kernel `esp` under the same CR3, we resolve the thread context. Such an approach has been used in other contexts such as virtual machine introspection (e.g., [21, 56]).

3.4 Our CFI Policy

Nearly all control flow hijacking attack targets indirect control flow transfers that occur at instruction `call`, `jmp`, `ret`, because direct control flow transfers are hardened in the read-only binary code, which typically cannot be altered by attackers. The key idea of CFI is to build a CFG, and then at runtime verify whether an indirect control flow transfer follows an edge in the CFG. Based on the edge direction in the CFG, we can classify them into:

- **Backward Edge** where a control flow transfers back to a node in the CFG. Such an edge exists because of the `ret` instruction, which transfers control flow back to the next instruction right after a call-site. A large amount of modern exploits (e.g., ROP) target manipulating the backward edge by controlling the return addresses. The primary goal of PT-CFI is to design a perfect policy that captures various backward edge violation attacks.

  In PT-CFI, indeed we can have a precise policy to detect the illegal backward edge thanks to the design of PT as well as our deep inspection capability. In particular, as acknowledged by many prior works (e.g., [10, 50]), using a shadow stack can really stop various ROP attacks because fundamentally attackers have to redirect the return address to some other locations, which will inevitably make the executed return address mismatching with the legal one. Since PT provides a complete trace of all indirect control flow transfers, we are able to build a perfect shadow stack based on the TIP traces and examine with the original binary code to detect ROPs. That is why we call PT-CFI backward-edge CFI since it has a complete protection for all backward edges.

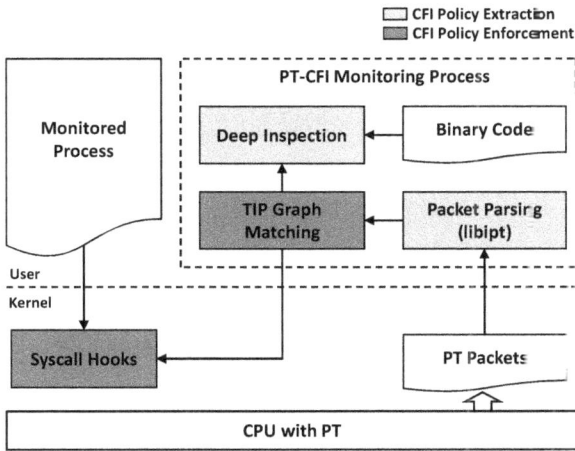

Figure 3: Architectural Overview of PT-CFI.

- **Forward Edge** where a control flow transfers to a new target. There are two types of forward edges: one is caused by indirect `call` and the other is caused by indirect `jmp`. One of the biggest challenges in any CFI is how to get the legal forward edges. This is because when an indirect call or jump occurs, e.g., `call eax`, statically it is hard to know what the value of `eax` should be, since it may require sophisticated point-to analysis but there is no sound and complete solution to this problem yet at binary code level. Therefore, CFI solutions often have to make approximations for forward edges. Unlike in backward-edge cases where we have a perfect CFI policy, we do not have a sound and complete solution to forward-edge yet. Therefore, we leave how to use PT for forward-edge CFI for future work. However, we also note that the two most recent works FlowGuard and GRIF-FIN have attempted to solve this problem via either training or sophisticated binary analysis.

3.5 Overview

An overview of our system is presented in Figure 3. The goal of PT-CFI is to detect control flow hijacking by enforcing a lightweight CFI model. Unlike the traditional CFI where inline reference monitoring is used, PT-CFI uses a separate dedicated monitoring process to detect any control flow violation of the monitored process.

There are four components of PT-CFI: When PT packets are generated for the monitored process, the first component *Packet Parsing* will parse each packet and generate the TIP sequences, which will be fed to our second component, *TIP Graph Matching*. If a stream of TIP sequences matches with the TIP graph, execution continues. Otherwise, it invokes our third component *Deep Inspection* to decode the packets and construct the shadow stack. If the decoded return addresses all are matched in the shadow stack, the new TIP sequence will be considered legal, and added to our TIP graph; Otherwise, it will inform the the last component *Syscall Hooking* to terminate the execution of the monitored process since there is a control flow violation.

Scope, Assumptions, and Threat Model. We focus on protecting x86 ELF binaries in Linux platform, and we assume they are not obfuscated since we need to disassemble the binary code to decide the TIP type. We do not assume perfect disassembling since our disassembler can leverage the runtime information such as the exercised code address to disassemble the code.

We design PT-CFI to detect various return-based control flow hijacks, and we assume the OS kernel and the CPU hardware are not compromised during the attacks. In particular, we primarily focus on ROP attacks against user-space applications from remote adversaries who, by manipulating the input to the vulnerable applications, aim to hijack the control flow of the target applications. Again, we do not attempt to address attacks that use JOP or COP since these attacks violate the forward-edge CFI policy whereas PT-CFI is designed as a backward-edge CFI solution.

4. DETAILED DESIGN

In this section, we present the detailed design of each component of PT-CFI. Based on how a typical CFI system works, we first present how we extract the CFI policies by our *Packet Parsing* and *Deep Inspection* in Section 4.1, and then describe how we enforce the CFI policy by our *TIP Graph Matching* and *Syscall Hooking* in Section 4.2.

4.1 CFI Policy Extraction

4.1.1 Packet Parsing

The goal of packet parsing is to parse various types of PT packet (e.g., TNT, TIP, PUF), to facilitate the construction of legal TIP graph (if it has not been created yet or incomplete) and meanwhile send the parsed TIP packet generated by each indirect call, jump, or return, to our *TIP Graph Matching* component.

TIP Graph (TIP-G) Construction. The detection of control flow violation in our PT-CFI is based on the TIP-G, which is defined $<N, E>$, where N denotes the set of nodes, each of which is indexed by each unique TIP packet, and E denotes a set of directed edges. There is an edge from A to B if and only if right after the execution of an indirect control flow transfer A, it will execute the indirect control flow transfer B. That is, the edge captures the sequential execution of two indirect control flow transfers.

N is further divided into three different types based on the three different types of indirect control flow transfers. Specifically, we have type N_{ret} if the TIP node is corresponding to a ret instruction, N_{call} if it is an indirect `call`, and N_{jmp} if it is an indirect jmp. There are several ways to build our TIP-G. An intuitive approach is to statically disassemble the binary code to first build a CFG, and then only keep those indirect control flow transfer nodes in the CFG, since statically we cannot resolve the target address but we can leverage the runtime values to connect the missing edges and nodes. While we can use this approach, we realize in fact we do not have to disassemble the code and instead we can directly use the traced TIP packet on the fly to build our TIP-G.

More specifically, the construction of TIP-G is quite simple, as illustrated in algorithm 1. Initially, the node of TIP-G will be just the first TIP packet (p_0), and the edge will be empty (line 2 and line 3). Whenever there is a new TIP packet p_i generated, we parse the type of p_i by a helper function GetTIPType, and the result could be N_{call}, N_{jmp}, and N_{ret} (line 6). Next, we insert p_i to the node of TIP-G if it has not been added yet (note that there will be only one instance of p_i in TIP-G). Meanwhile, we will also insert an edge $<p_{i-1}, p_i, t>$ with label t (which is acquired at line 6) from p_{i-1} to p_i if this edge has not been added before. The label of the edge indicates the three different indirect control flow transfers, which is important for PT-CFI to enforce the backward edges (essentially only the return control flow transfers). We keep iterating this process until all TIP packets have been processed (from line 5 to line 13). The resulting graph will be the desired TIP-G.

To build a complete TIP-G, we have two complementary ap-

Algorithm 1: TIP-G Construction

Input: TIP Packets: P $(p_i \in P)$
Result: The desired TIP Graph G
1 **begin**
2   G.node $\leftarrow p_0$;
3   G.edge $\leftarrow \emptyset$;
4      $i \leftarrow 1$;
5   **for** *each* $p_i \in P$ **do**
6          $t \leftarrow$ GetTIPType(p_i);
7   **if** $p_i \notin G.node$ **then**
8   G.node $\leftarrow G$.node $\cup$ p_i;
9   **end**
10   **if** $<p_{i-1}, p_i, t> \notin G.edge$ **then**
11   G.edge $\leftarrow G$.edge $\cup$ $<p_{i-1}, p_i, t>$;
12   **end**
13   **end**
14 **end**

---

proaches. One is to use *training*, and the other is to use the *deep inspection* discussed below. *Training* can be viewed as cached data, and when a cache misses we invoke the *deep inspection* for remediation. The reason why training works is because if we are running the protected software with all benign input, all p_i should be legitimate and we do not have to perform any deep inspection. Only when p_i is unknown (a new TIP node) or $<p_{i-1}, p_i, t>$ is unknown (a new edge), namely our CFI policy is incomplete, we invoke *deep inspection* to decide whether p_i or transition from p_{i-1} to p_i is legal or not.

It is important to note that there is no policy coverage issues in PT-CFI even though we use a training approach. This is because our *deep inspection* component can always return a policy to determine whether an indirect control flow transfer is legal or not. We can run PT-CFI without any training by invoking *deep inspection* every time when we observe a p_i or a transition from p_{i-1} to p_i to decide the security policy. However, such an approach will be extremely slow. Therefore, training is just to improve the performance. Meanwhile, training can be performed offline and TIP-G can be reused across different machines for the same software.

4.1.2 Deep Inspection

When our CFI policy is incomplete, our *Deep Inspection* component will be invoked to disassemble the corresponding binary code based on the runtime information and determine the type of the TIP packet and also whether it is legal or not. Specifically, we must parse the PT packet to determine the type of the TIP packet that causes the deep inspection; namely, whether it is N_{call} or N_{jmp}, or N_{ret}. Since PT trace is a sequence of various PT packets and there is no information of the type of p_i, unless we correlate the virtual address with the binary code. A rigorous way of deciding the type of p_i needs to disassemble and walk through the code based on the closest known virtual address in the PT packets. Note that hardware will generate an alignment PT packet that contains the virtual address of the executed program code. Based on this known virtual address, an offline analysis is able to reconstruct the program behavior and precisely know the type of the TIP packet.

Since a program often contains loops, an observed TIP sequences may be observed again. To avoid parsing the same set of sequences again, we use a caching mechanism to avoid the re-disassembling and re-walking of the binary code in order to identify the corresponding TIP type. Then, at runtime, only unknown TIP will trigger the deep inspection. According to the specific unknown TIP packet, we will take different actions. If it is an indirect call or an indirect jmp, we will add them to our TIP-G because we do not

have a perfect policy to precisely determine its legitimate target. If it is a return, we will build a shadow stack based on the PT traces. If the return address has matched the one in the shadow stack, this N_{ret} node and the corresponding edge will be added into our TIP-G. Otherwise, it is an attack, and our CFI enforcement will stop the execution of the monitored process.

4.2 CFI Policy Enforcement

Once a TIP-G is constructed (by the offline training and deep inspection), we can then use it to detect the control flow violations. The detection is done by our *TIP Graph Matching* component (which may also call our *Deep Inspection* discussed above). If it detects a real violation, it will inform our last component *Syscall Hooking* to terminate the execution of the monitored process.

4.2.1 TIP Graph Matching

When given a TIP packet p_j, the TIP-G matching becomes quite straightforward. Assume the CFI policy is complete, then at the given node n_i in TIP-G, there is only a set of allowed transition node; assume it is n_j, if p_j belongs to n_j, then there is no CFI violation. Otherwise, p_j is not known to TIP-G, and in this case, we will invoke our *Deep Inspection* component to decide whether p_j is a legal transfer. If not, an attack is detected. If it is not a CFI violation, p_j will be added to TIP-G.

In particular, to detect whether p_j violates CFI during the deep inspection, we use its type (recall all the edge has a type in our TIP-G). If it is N_{ret} for our aimed back-edge CFI enforcement, our deep inspection will check with the shadow stack built based on the PT traces. If the returning location is not the legal return address, it is an attack. Otherwise, this missing legal CFI transition will be added to TIP-G. If it is N_{call} or N_{jmp}, we do not have a precise policy and we will allow the execution by adding the missing node and edge in our TIP-G. That explains why PT-CFI will not detect any JOP or COP attacks as discussed in Section 3.

4.2.2 Syscall Hooking

Once we have detected there is a control flow violation, we must terminate the execution of the running process. To make PT-CFI get an control of the monitored process execution, we take a syscall interposition approach, which has been widely used by many other systems such as kBouncer and ROPecker. Basically, we selectively hook a number of security sensitive syscalls including `execve`, `write`, `mprotect`, `munmap`, `clone`, `fork`, `open`, `close` and `exit_group`. We introduce a lock at the entry point of these system calls. It will be only unlocked by our monitoring process to continue its execution, when there is no violation of CFI given the current parsed TIP packets. Otherwise, the monitored process will be terminated at the execution of these syscalls. Since syscall hooking is a standard approach, we omit its technical details here.

5. IMPLEMENTATION

We have implemented PT-CFI. We implemented the kernel component by using directly kernel code modification and kernel extensions, and implemented the rest component, especially *Packet Parsing* by borrowing a large amount of code from a user level program `perf`, the first and the industry strength tool for Intel PT.

More specifically, we use *Syscall Hooking* to create a sandboxed execution environment to the monitored program by hooking only a set of sensitive syscalls in the syscall table. Upon entering these syscalls, PT-CFI will consult with the user level component *TIP-G Matching* to ensure the backward-edge CFI of the monitored program. The monitored program will be paused on the sensitive syscall until there is no attack detected by our *TIP-G Matching*.

Program Name	$|N|$	$|E|$	#Syscall	PT Packet Size (MB)	Training Time (ms)
400.perlbench	3486	7294	160	1.27	3408.6
401.bzip2	483	677	77	210.94	1021.4
403.gcc	20233	71545	238	498.06	1115.8
429.mcf	456	642	357	158.5	1373.2
433.milc	1290	1920	6511	584.92	45.9
445.gobmk	1361	2740	365	10.22	62.5
456.hmmer	964	1662	88	20.64	1356.4
458.sjeng	960	1911	608	498.05	3009.2
462.libquantum	850	1323	96	9.48	33
464.h264ref	1696	2940	541	443.97	15464.2
470.lbm	640	850	711	54.87	1235.4
482.sphinx3	2823	4231	3168	468.07	1049.2
AVG	2936.84	8144.59	1076.67	246.59	2804

Table 2: Experimental Result with SPEC2006 CPUINT benchmark

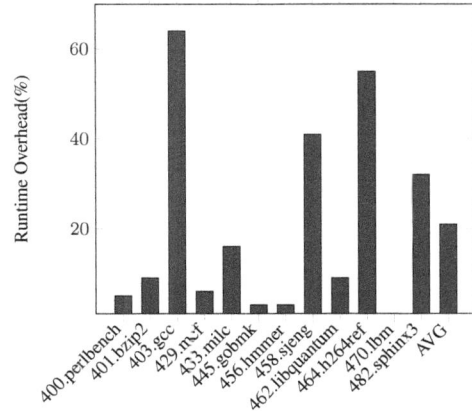

Figure 4: SPEC CPU2006 Benchmark Overhead

To control PT execution and parse PT packets at runtime, we extended `perf`, which is available since Linux kernel 4.3. Since PT is a system wide hardware level feature, we need to configure it to trace only user level program by setting the corresponding MSRs. To this end, we use the available `sys_perf_event_open` to initialize the PT hardware, and this syscall allows us to specify process ID and CPU Core number as well as other filtering for Intel PT hardware. To support thread level tracing, we catch both `CR3` and kernel `esp` by modifying the kernel `schedule` function, and associate the thread context with the PT traces.

Since PT packet parsing is a slow process, we use a thread pool to handle PT packets in parallel in order to improve the performance of the whole system. In addition, to better dispatcher threads, we bind the monitored program and our monitoring program to different cores and bind our working threads to the rest cores. For example, for an eight core computers, we bind the monitored program to core 0 and the monitoring program to core one and working threads from core two to seven. We use function `sched_setaffinity` to bind processes to a specific core and function `pthread_set affinity_np` to bind threads to cores.

During our *Deep Inspection*, PT-CFI needs to disassemble the binary code to determine the type of TIP packet, and check the shadow stack. To do that, PT-CFI first scans the decoder synchronization packet, usually a PSB at the beginning of the PT buffers, then it can find a TIP.PGE packet indicating the full starting instruction pointer (IP). With the full IP and PT packets, PT-CFI can follow the execution path to disassemble the binary code and tell the type of the TIP packet. For the shadow stack, it is incrementally built based on the traces from the beginning of the execution to the suspicious point. If the TIP packet is of return type, and if the shadow stack is not matched, then an attack is detected.

6. EVALUATION

In this section, we evaluate the effectiveness of PT-CFI for detecting the ROP attacks, and its efficiency in terms of runtime performance. Our testing platform is a desktop computer with an Intel i7-6700K Skylake 4.00 GHz CPU and 8G memory, running Ubuntu 14.04.1 LTS with Linux kernel 4.3.0.

6.1 Security Evaluation

By design, PT-CFI is able to detect all ROP attacks, thanks to our deep inspection and the shadow stack constructed from PT traces. To measure how PT-CFI really works in detecting the control flow violations, we use both a contrived attack against our running example in Figure 1 and a real attack against Nginx HTTP daemon (*i.e.*, Nginx-1.4.0) to evaluate the capability of PT-CFI in detecting the control flow violations. Such a security evaluation methodology has been used in many other ROP defenses such as ROPecker.

More specifically, to construct our attack payload, we leveraged a widely used ROP gadget searching and linking tool ROPgadget to analyze both the executable and linked libraries of these two programs. To make our gadget construction easier, we disabled the ASLR protection. We successfully constructed two ROP payloads and both spawned a shell without the protection from PT-CFI.

Then we applied PT-CFI to protect them. We first trained each of them: using the three benign inputs for our running example, and using 1000 requests with varied length generated from `attperf` [1] for the Nginx daemon, respectively. Then we injected the constructed attack payload to these two victim programs. As expected, both of them triggered our deep inspection, which took a 0.03 seconds for our running example, and 0.05 seconds for Nginx to report that a ROP attack is detected. The reason of why Nginx took sligtly more time is because more packets need to be used to disassemble the code and walk through the binary to build the shadow stack, which is a slow process. Also note that no false positive or false negatives occurred in these two security tests.

6.2 Performance Evaluation

To evaluate the performance overhead of our system, we tested with a set of SPEC2006 benchmark programs and the Nginx HTTP daemon.

SPEC2006 CPUINT. We used the 12 CPUINT benchmark programs from SPEC2006 in our evaluation. We compiled them with the default configuration by using gcc-4.8.4, then we executed and trained each of them with the default configured input to get their corresponding TIP-G. The detailed result for our training phase is presented in Table 2.

Specifically, it took a variety of amount time to train each of the benchmark, as reported in the last column in Table 2. To train the program, we run each SPEC CPUINT program with their default configured input. Some of them (*e.g.*, `464.h264ref`) took 15.46 seconds, and some of them (*e.g.*, `462.libquantum`) only costed 0.03 seconds. On average, it took 2.80 seconds to train each benchmark. During the training phase, we also observed 1076.67 syscalls on average (the 3rd column), and 2936.84 of nodes (2nd column) and 8144.59 edges (3rd column) in their TIP-G. The PT packet size is reported in the 4th column, and on average we col-

181

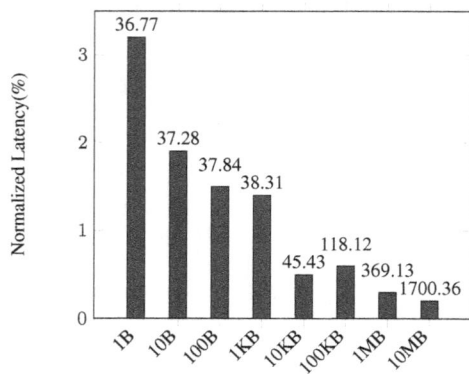

Figure 5: Nginx File Download Latency

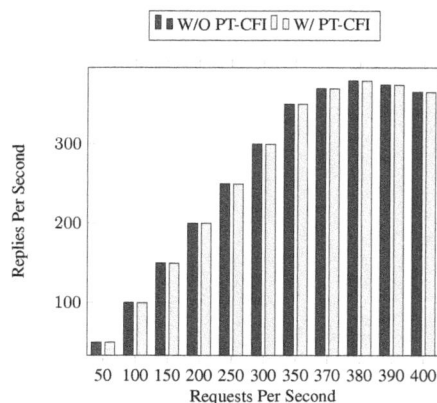

Figure 6: Nginx Throughput Impact

lected 246.58 MB traced PT packet during each run of these programs.

Next, we applied the obtained TIP-G for the CFI enforcement. We run these benchmarks again with their default input. The purpose of this experiment is to measure how slow our TIP-G matching is when used in real software. The performance overhead for this experiment is shown in Figure 4. While some programs such as gcc have high overhead (up to 65%), most of them has less than 10%. On average, it has 21% for these CPUINT benchmarks. The reason of why gcc has high overhead is that it has many more packets to process, and more nodes and edges in the TIP-G for the matching than that of others.

Network Daemon. While SPEC benchmark can provide an estimation of how slow our PT-CFI is for real software, in practice we believe PT-CFI will be mostly used to protect the network daemons. To understand the performance impact of our approach for network daemons, we again measured the latency and throughput of the HTTP daemon Nginx we tested in our security evaluation. To train Nginx, we used the same configuration as in our security evaluation by generating 1000 client request messages with httperf. During this training phase, we observed 391 nodes, and 1,213 edges in our TIP-G. To monitor the Nginx, we first get the PID of the worker process, then we attach PT-CFI to this process. Any threads spawned by this process will be monitored automatically thanks to our thread-tracing capability.

- **Latency**. To evaluate the latency of Nginx with PT-CFI, we use Apache HTTP server benchmarking tool (ab) to send 10,000 requests to Nginx to download different sizes of file, from one byte to 10M bytes. The normalized latency compared without PT-CFI protection is reported in Figure 5. We can see that for small size downloaded packets, the latency is slight larger than those bigger size ones, though they all appear to be quite negligible (less than 5%). Note that we also reported the absolute download time on top of each bar with unit milliseconds in this figure. For instance, when the request file is 1 byte, it took 36.77 milliseconds to download this file.

- **Throughput**. We also evaluate the file download throughput of Nginx. We use the tool httperf to generate different numbers of concurrent requests to access the same 300K-bytes file, then report the throughput of Nginx without and with PT-CFI in Figure 6. We can see that with different numbers of concurrent requests per seconds (x-axis), there

is negligible impact in the replies per seconds (y-axis) (almost the same height of bar in both cases). When the concurrent number of requests exceeds 380 (which appears to be the maximum number of requests Nginx can handle simultaneous), the throughput goes down as without PT-CFI protection.

Overall, we can observe for network daemons such as Nginx, our system does not have noticable performance impact against normal users (less than 5% latency and negligiable throughput impact).

7. DISCUSSION AND FUTURE WORK

While PT-CFI has made a first step of using Intel PT to build a practical CFI model, it is still not perfect and has a number of limitations. In this section, we examine these limitations and outline our future work.

First, PT-CFI has a clear policy for all ret based exploits. Unlike existing ROP defenses such as ROPecker that uses heuristics, PT-CFI can precisely detect all ROP instances due to our deep inspection. However, we currently do not have policies for all those forward-edges and we allow the monitored process continue the execution when encountering these call and jmp TIPs. As such, JOP or COP attacks are still possible.

Meanwhile, we have to note that there is no perfect solution to resolve the forward-edges at binary code level because the challenges from point-to analysis, though there are solutions at source code level such as the forward-edge CFI [48]. There could exist some approaches that use value-set analysis to approximate the possible indirect target, or use some loose security policy such as allowing the indirect call target always starts from the entry point of a function as in BinCFI, or use training as in FlowGuard [29], etc. We plan to investigate how to address these forward edge issues in one of our future works.

Finally, even though the performance overhead is small, it is higher than many other CFI implementations (e.g., [38, 55]). There are also a number of avenues to optimize the performance of PT-CFI, especially its deep inspection component. For instance, to differentiate the types of each TIP packet, we have to perform disassembling of the protected binary code whenever we encounter an unknown TIP. This disassembling process can be optimized by considering the history of the disassembling process, namely, if we have already disassembled some code, we do not have to disassemble it again. While we have already explored using the cache to optimize the re-disassembling, we have not systematically investigated the cache size factor yet. We plan to explore how to optimize PT-CFI further in our another future work.

8. CONCLUSION

We have presented PT-CFI, a new backward-edge CFI model based on a recently introduced Intel hardware feature—Processor Trace. Designed primarily for offline software debugging, PT offers the capability of tracing the entire control flow of a running program. In this paper, we have presented the design, implementation, and evaluation of using PT for security with a new practical CFI model for native COTS binaries based on the trace from PT. We have addressed a number of technical challenges such as making sure the control flow policy is complete, making PT enforce our CFI policy, and balancing the performance overhead, by exploring the intrinsic tracing property inside PT with a system synchronization primitive and a deep inspection capability. We have implemented PT-CFI and tested with both SPEC2006 and a popular network daemon. Experimental results show that PT-CFI only introduces small overhead for the monitored program with the capability of detecting all ROP attacks.

Acknowledgment

We thank the anonymous reviewers for their insightful comments. This research was supported in part by AFOSR under grant FA9550-14-1-0119 and FA9550-14-1-0173, NSF award 1453011. Any opinions, findings, conclusions, or recommendations expressed are those of the authors and not necessarily of the AFOSR and NSF.

9. REFERENCES

[1] Httperf, http://www.labs.hpe.com/research/linux/httperf/.

[2] M. Abadi, M. Budiu, U. Erlingsson, and J. Ligatti. Control-flow integrity. In *Proceedings of the 12th ACM Conference on Computer and Communications Security*, CCS '05, pages 340–353. ACM, 2005.

[3] S. Andersen and V. Abella. Data execution prevention. changes to functionality in microsoft windows xp service pack 2, part 3: Memory protection technologies, 2004.

[4] N. Balakrishnan, T. Bytheway, L. Carata, O. R. A. Chick, J. Snee, S. Akoush, R. Sohan, M. Seltzer, and A. Hopper. Recent advances in computer architecture: The opportunities and challenges for provenance. In *7th USENIX Workshop on the Theory and Practice of Provenance (TaPP 15)*, Edinburgh, Scotland, July 2015. USENIX Association.

[5] A. Bittau, A. Belay, A. Mashtizadeh, D. Mazieres, and D. Boneh. Hacking blind. In *Security and Privacy (SP), 2014 IEEE Symposium on*, pages 227–242. IEEE, 2014.

[6] T. Bletsch, X. Jiang, and V. Freeh. Mitigating code-reuse attacks with control-flow locking. In *Proceedings of the 27th Annual Computer Security Applications Conference*, ACSAC '11, pages 353–362. ACM, 2011.

[7] T. Bletsch, X. Jiang, V. W. Freeh, and Z. Liang. Jump-oriented programming: a new class of code-reuse attack. In *Proceedings of the 6th ACM Symposium on Information, Computer and Communications Security*, pages 30–40. ACM, 2011.

[8] E. Bosman and H. Bos. Framing signals — return to portable exploits. (working title, subject to change.). In *Security & Privacy (Oakland)*, San Jose, CA, USA, May 2014. IEEE.

[9] N. Carlini, A. Barresi, M. Payer, D. Wagner, and T. R. Gross. Control-flow bending: On the effectiveness of control-flow integrity. In *24th USENIX Security Symposium (USENIX Security 15)*, pages 161–176, Washington, D.C., Aug. 2015. USENIX Association.

[10] N. Carlini, A. Barresi, M. Payer, D. Wagner, and T. R. Gross. Control-flow bending: On the effectiveness of control-flow integrity. In *24th USENIX Security Symposium (USENIX Security 15)*, pages 161–176, 2015.

[11] N. Carlini and D. Wagner. ROP is still dangerous: Breaking modern defenses. In *Proceedings of the 23rd USENIX Conference on*

[12] S. Checkoway, L. Davi, A. Dmitrienko, A.-R. Sadeghi, H. Shacham, and M. Winandy. Return-oriented programming without returns. In *Proceedings of the 17th ACM Conference on Computer and Communications Security*, CCS '10, pages 559–572, New York, NY, USA, 2010. ACM.

[13] P. Chen, H. Xiao, X. Shen, X. Yin, B. Mao, and L. Xie. Drop: Detecting return-oriented programming malicious code. In *Proceedings of the 5th International Conference on Information Systems Security*, ICISS '09, pages 163–177, Berlin, Heidelberg, 2009. Springer-Verlag.

[14] S. Chen, J. Xu, E. C. Sezer, P. Gauriar, and R. K. Iyer. Non-control-data attacks are realistic threats. In *Proceedings of the 14th Conference on USENIX Security Symposium - Volume 14*. USENIX Association, 2005.

[15] Y. Cheng, Z. Zhou, M. Yu, X. Ding, and R. H. Deng. ROPecker: A generic and practical approach for defending against ROP attack. In *Proceedings of the 2014 Network and Distributed System Security Symposium*, NDSSâĂŹ14, 2014.

[16] C. Cowan, C. Pu, D. Maier, J. Walpole, P. Bakke, S. Beattie, A. Grier, P. Wagle, Q. Zhang, and H. Hinton. Stackguard: Automatic adaptive detection and prevention of buffer-overflow attacks. In *Usenix Security*, volume 98, pages 63–78, 1998.

[17] L. Davi, A. Dmitrienko, M. Egele, T. Fischer, T. Holz, R. Hund, S. Nürnberger, and A.-R. Sadeghi. MoCFI: A framework to mitigate control-flow attacks on smartphones. In *19th Annual Network & Distributed System Security Symposium (NDSS)*, Feb. 2012.

[18] L. Davi, A.-R. Sadeghi, D. Lehmann, and F. Monrose. Stitching the gadgets: On the ineffectiveness of coarse-grained control-flow integrity protection. In *Proceedings of the 23rd USENIX Conference on Security Symposium*, SEC'14, Berkeley, CA, USA, 2014. USENIX Association.

[19] L. Davi, A.-R. Sadeghi, and M. Winandy. Ropdefender: A detection tool to defend against return-oriented programming attacks. In *Proceedings of the 6th ACM Symposium on Information, Computer and Communications Security*, ASIACCS '11, pages 40–51. ACM, 2011.

[20] U. Erlingsson. *The Inlined Reference Monitor Approach to Security Policy Enforcement*. PhD thesis, Ithaca, NY, USA, 2004. AAI3114521.

[21] Y. Fu and Z. Lin. Exterior: Using a dual-vm based external shell for guest-os introspection, configuration, and recovery. In *Proceedings of the Ninth Annual International Conference on Virtual Execution Environments*, Houston, TX, March 2013.

[22] X. Ge, W. Cui, and T. Jaeger. Griffin: Guarding control flows using intel processor trace. In *Proceedings of the 22nd ACM International Conference on Architectural Support for Programming Languages and Operating Systems*, Apr. 2017.

[23] E. Göktaş, E. Athanasopoulos, M. Polychronakis, H. Bos, and G. Portokalidis. Size does matter: Why using gadget-chain length to prevent code-reuse attacks is hard. In *23rd USENIX Security Symposium*, pages 417–432, San Diego, CA, Aug. 2014. USENIX Association.

[24] H. Hu, Z. L. Chua, S. Adrian, P. Saxena, and Z. Liang. Automatic generation of data-oriented exploits. In *24th USENIX Security Symposium*, pages 177–192, Washington, D.C., Aug. 2015. USENIX Association.

[25] H. Hu, S. Shinde, S. Adrian, Z. L. Chua, P. Saxena, and Z. Liang. Data-oriented programming: On the expressiveness of non-control data attacks. In *2016 IEEE Symposium on Security and Privacy*. IEEE, 2016.

[26] B. Kasikci, B. Schubert, C. Pereira, G. Pokam, and G. Candea. Failure sketching: A technique for automated root cause diagnosis of in-production failures. In *Proceedings of the 25th Symposium on Operating Systems Principles*, SOSP '15, pages 344–360, New York, NY, USA, 2015. ACM.

[27] V. Kuznetsov, L. Szekeres, M. Payer, G. Candea, R. Sekar, and D. Song. Code-pointer integrity. In *11th USENIX Symposium on Operating Systems Design and Implementation*, pages 147–163, Broomfield, CO, Oct. 2014. USENIX Association.

[28] Y. Lee, I. Heo, D. Hwang, K. Kim, and Y. Paek. Towards a practical solution to detect code reuse attacks on arm mobile devices. In *Proceedings of the Fourth Workshop on Hardware and Architectural Support for Security and Privacy*, HASP '15. ACM, 2015.

[29] Y. Liu, P. Shi, X. Wang, H. Chen, B. Zang, and H. Guan. Transparent and efficient cfi enforcement with intel processor trace. In *The 23rd IEEE Symposium on High Performance Computer Architecture*, 2017.

[30] C.-K. Luk, R. Cohn, R. Muth, H. Patil, A. Klauser, G. Lowney, S. Wallace, V. J. Reddi, and K. Hazelwood. Pin: Building customized program analysis tools with dynamic instrumentation. In *Proceedings of the 2005 ACM SIGPLAN Conference on Programming Language Design and Implementation*, PLDI '05, pages 190–200, New York, NY, USA, 2005. ACM.

[31] A. J. Mashtizadeh, A. Bittau, D. Boneh, and D. Mazières. CCFI: Cryptographically enforced control flow integrity. In *Proceedings of the 22nd ACM SIGSAC Conference on Computer and Communications Security*, CCS '15, pages 941–951. ACM, 2015.

[32] V. Mohan, P. Larsen, S. Brunthaler, K. W. Hamlen, and M. Franz. Opaque control-flow integrity. In *Proceedings of the 2015 Network and Distributed System Security Symposium*, NDSSâĂŹ15, 2015.

[33] B. Niu and G. Tan. Modular control-flow integrity. In *Proceedings of the 35th ACM SIGPLAN Conference on Programming Language Design and Implementation*, PLDI '14, pages 577–587. ACM, 2014.

[34] B. Niu and G. Tan. Rockjit: Securing just-in-time compilation using modular control-flow integrity. In *Proceedings of the 2014 ACM SIGSAC Conference on Computer and Communications Security*, CCS '14, pages 1317–1328. ACM, 2014.

[35] B. Niu and G. Tan. Per-input control-flow integrity. In *Proceedings of the 22Nd ACM SIGSAC Conference on Computer and Communications Security*, CCS '15, pages 914–926. ACM, 2015.

[36] A. One. Smashing the stack for fun and profit. *Phrack magazine*, 7(49):14–16, 1996.

[37] V. Pappas, M. Polychronakis, and A. D. Keromytis. Transparent ROP exploit mitigation using indirect branch tracing. In *Proceedings of the 22Nd USENIX Conference on Security*, SEC'13, pages 447–462, Berkeley, CA, USA, 2013. USENIX Association.

[38] M. Payer, A. Barresi, and T. R. Gross. Fine-grained control-flow integrity through binary hardening. In *Detection of Intrusions and Malware, and Vulnerability Assessment*, pages 144–164. Springer, 2015.

[39] F. Schuster, T. Tendyck, C. Liebchen, L. Davi, A.-R. Sadeghi, and T. Holz. Counterfeit object-oriented programming: On the difficulty of preventing code reuse attacks in c++ applications. In *Security and Privacy (SP), 2015 IEEE Symposium on*, pages 745–762. IEEE, 2015.

[40] F. Schuster, T. Tendyck, J. Pewny, A. Maaß, M. Steegmanns, M. Contag, and T. Holz. Evaluating the effectiveness of current anti-ROP defenses. In *Proceedings of the 17th International Symposium on Research in Attacks, Intrusions and Defenses*. Springer International Publishing, 2014.

[41] E. J. Schwartz, T. Avgerinos, and D. Brumley. Q: Exploit hardening made easy. In *USENIX Security Symposium*, pages 25–41, 2011.

[42] H. Shacham. The geometry of innocent flesh on the bone: Return-into-libc without function calls (on the x86). In *Proceedings of CCS 2007*, pages 552–61. ACM Press, Oct. 2007.

[43] X. Shu, D. Yao, and N. Ramakrishnan. Unearthing stealthy program attacks buried in extremely long execution paths. In *Proceedings of the 22Nd ACM SIGSAC Conference on Computer and*

[44] K. Z. Snow, F. Monrose, L. Davi, A. Dmitrienko, C. Liebchen, and A.-R. Sadeghi. Just-in-time code reuse: On the effectiveness of fine-grained address space layout randomization. In *Security and Privacy (SP), 2013 IEEE Symposium on*, pages 574–588. IEEE, 2013.

[45] L. Szekeres, M. Payer, T. Wei, and D. Song. Sok: Eternal war in memory. In *Proceedings of the 2013 IEEE Symposium on Security and Privacy*, SP '13, pages 48–62. IEEE Computer Society, 2013.

[46] P. Team. Pax address space layout randomization (aslr). 2003.

[47] J. Thalheim, P. Bhatotia, and C. Fetzer. Inspector: A data provenance library for multithreaded programs, 2016. https://arxiv.org/abs/1605.00498.

[48] C. Tice, T. Roeder, P. Collingbourne, S. Checkoway, Ú. Erlingsson, L. Lozano, and G. Pike. Enforcing forward-edge control-flow integrity in gcc & llvm. In *23rd USENIX Security Symposium*, pages 941–955, San Diego, CA, Aug. 2014. USENIX Association.

[49] V. van der Veen, D. Andriesse, E. Göktaş, B. Gras, L. Sambuc, A. Slowinska, H. Bos, and C. Giuffrida. Practical context-sensitive CFI. In *Proceedings of the 22Nd ACM SIGSAC Conference on Computer and Communications Security*, CCS '15, pages 927–940. ACM, 2015.

[50] V. van der Veen, E. Goktas, M. Contag, A. Pawlowski, X. Chen, S. Rawat, H. Bos, T. Holz, E. Athanasopoulos, and C. Giuffrida. A tough call: Mitigating advanced code-reuse attacks at the binary level. In *Proceedings of the 37th IEEE Symposium on Security and Privacy (Oakland)*, San Jose, CA, USA, May 2016. IEEE.

[51] M. Wang, H. Yin, A. V. Bhaskar, P. Su, and D. Feng. Binary code continent: Finer-grained control flow integrity for stripped binaries. In *Proceedings of the 31st Annual Computer Security Applications Conference*, ACSAC 2015, pages 331–340. ACM, 2015.

[52] R. Wojtczuk. The advanced return-into-lib (c) exploits: Pax case study. *Phrack Magazine, Volume 0x0b, Issue 0x3a, Phile# 0x04 of 0x0e*, 2001.

[53] Y. Xia, Y. Liu, H. Chen, and B. Zang. CFIMon: Detecting violation of control flow integrity using performance counters. In *Proceedings of the 42nd Annual IEEE/IFIP International Conference on Dependable Systems and Networks*, DSN '12, Washington, DC, USA, 2012. IEEE Computer Society.

[54] P. Yuan, Q. Zeng, and X. Ding. Hardware-assisted fine-grained code-reuse attack detection. In *Proceedings of 18th International Symposium on Research in Attacks, Intrusions, and Defenses*, RAID'15. Springer International Publishing, 2015.

[55] B. Zeng, G. Tan, and Ú. Erlingsson. Strato: A retargetable framework for low-level inlined-reference monitors. In *Presented as part of the 22nd USENIX Security Symposium (USENIX Security 13)*, pages 369–382, Washington, D.C., 2013. USENIX.

[56] J. Zeng, Y. Fu, and Z. Lin. Automatic uncovering of tap points from kernel executions. In *Proceedings of the 19th International Symposium on Research in Attacks, Intrusions and Defenses (RAID'16)*, Paris, France, September 2016.

[57] C. Zhang, T. Wei, Z. Chen, L. Duan, L. Szekeres, S. McCamant, D. Song, and W. Zou. Practical control flow integrity and randomization for binary executables. In *2013 IEEE Symposium on Security and Privacy*, pages 559–573, May 2013.

[58] M. Zhang and R. Sekar. Control flow integrity for cots binaries. In *Proceedings of the 22nd USENIX Security Symposium*, pages 337–352. USENIX, 2013.

Detecting Patching of Executables without System Calls

Sebastian Banescu
Mohsen Ahmadvand
Alexander Pretschner
Technische Universität München, Germany
{banescu,ahmadvan,pretschn}@cs.tum.edu

Robert Shield
Chris Hamilton
Google Inc.
{robertshield,chrisha}@google.com

ABSTRACT

Popular software applications (e.g. web browsers) are targeted by malicious organizations which develop potentially unwanted programs (PUPs). If such a PUP executes on benign user devices, it is able to manipulate the process memory of popular applications, their locally stored resources or their environment in a profitable way for the attacker and in detriment to benign end-users. We describe the implementation of a tamper detection mechanism based on code self-checksumming, able to detect static and dynamic patching of executables, performed by PUPs or other attackers. As opposed to other works based on code self-checksumming, our approach can also checksum instructions which contain absolute addresses affected by relocation, without using calls to external libraries. We implemented this solution for the x86 ISA and evaluated the performance impact and effectiveness. The results indicate that the run-time overhead of self-checksumming grows proportionally with the level of protection, which can be specified as input to our implementation. We have applied our implementation on the Chromium web-browser and observed that the overhead is practically unobservable for the end-user.

CCS Concepts

•Security and privacy → Software security engineering;

Keywords

Software protection; Tamper detection; PUPs

1. INTRODUCTION

Code patching is performed for various reasons and by various stakeholders of a software application. Incremental updates are a typical example. Similarly, attackers patch the code of a software application either statically or during runtime, in order to change the program's behavior. Historically, this kind of attack was mainly aimed at cracking license checks in computer games, which was detrimental for

CODASPY'17, March 22 - 24, 2017, Scottsdale, AZ, USA

© 2017 Copyright held by the owner/author(s). Publication rights licensed to ACM.
ISBN 978-1-4503-4523-1/17/03. . . $15.00

DOI: http://dx.doi.org/10.1145/3029806.3029835

the profit of the game vendors. Starting from the late 2000s some organizations started to automate such code patching attacks targeting popular applications (e.g. web browsers) in order to change their behavior in a way that would bring financial gains to those organizations.

Such automated attacks fall into a category called *potentially unwanted programs* (PUPs). PUPs are often bundled together with (seemingly) useful software, which leads end-users into unknowingly installing them. Once installed, PUPs change a program's behavior by tampering with process memory, locally stored resources or the environment in which they run. For instance, they change the default search engine of a web-browser, aggressively display pop-up advertisements, track actions of end-users, cause an overall system slowdown and ask for fees to "fix performance."

Recent work on PUPs indicates that Google Safe Browsing generates over 60 million warnings related to PUPs per week, three times that of malware warnings [33]. Techniques employed by PUPs (e.g. code injection in the process memory, run-time memory patching, system call interposition) generally, do not raise any alarms in anti-virus software because they are also performed by non-malicious third party software including anti-virus software, accessibility and graphics driver tools [32]. Some anti-virus products are able to detect PUPs. However, the vendors of popular software applications (e.g. web browsers) cannot assume that such anti-virus software is present on all end-user systems. Therefore, developers of popular applications aim to incorporate lightweight software protection mechanisms inside of their own products, i.e. mechanisms that introduce a tolerable amount of overhead and are transparent for end-users.

This paper presents a mechanism that detects code patching attacks at runtime. The idea is based on software self-checking [5, 16] which can detect code tampering attacks, without communicating with a trusted server. The idea is to create a white-list containing checksums of pieces of code, which are invariant from one execution to another on any fixed OS version and at various states during execution. Integrity checks are interleaved with existing code and verify if invariants hold during execution. If these invariants do not hold, then process memory modification has been detected and a response action is executed. To prevent patching attacks on the code that performs the checksums itself, our integrity checks form a strongly connected network where multiple checks protect other checks.

We make the following contributions:

- Extending the state of the art on self-checking, we propose a way of checksumming instructions that contain absolute addresses, which may change each time the program is loaded into memory by the OS loader. Moreover, our idea does not employ system calls, which are susceptible to system call interposition attacks [12].

- We provide an open source implementation on top of the *Google Syzygy Transformation Toolchain* [14], which can be applied directly to binary executables.[1]
- We evaluate the effectiveness against attackers who are aware of the details of our protection mechanism and show that some attacks do not scale while others can be countered by obfuscating the code of checks.
- We evaluate the performance overhead that our mechanism has on multiple types of applications, including Chromium. We show that the overhead is acceptably small for applications that are not CPU intensive.

The rest of this paper is organized as follows. §2 presents related work. §3 describes the general design of our approach, while §4 presents its implementation for x86 Assembly language. §5 presents the evaluation of our implementation, and §6 concludes and gives directions for future work.

2. RELATED WORK

Software tamper protection consists of mechanisms that detect or prevent unauthorized modifications of software. One simple form of tamper protection is binary whitelisting [23] which checks the hash of a binary against a securely managed list. A second technique uses the currently executing code as a decryption key for code that is executed next [25]. This mechanism can be circumvented because the attacker can get all the correct keys and code by monitoring the executions of a non-patched program. Other tamper protection techniques are based on software self-checking [5, 16, 13], which have been successfully combined with self-modifying code. Unfortunately, self-modifying code as a defense mechanism requires memory pages which are both writable and executable, which enables remote code injection attacks [37].

Self-checksumming [5, 16] protects against tampering by adding code to an application. This code reads other parts of the code and compares their checksums to precomputed values. Junod et al. [21] have implemented a tamper protection mechanism based on the same self-checksumming techniques as our work. They do not include any details on how absolute addresses in code are handled, which is one of the main contributions of this paper.

Oblivious Hashing (OH) [6], computes a checksum over the dynamic state of an execution trace (e.g. code counters, memory values, branch conditions, etc.). This offers higher stealth than self-checking, because OH does not imply unusual execution patterns like self-checksumming does, i.e. a program reading its own code. However, OH has some shortcomings that makes it unusable for many applications, e.g. OH cannot handle branches based on program inputs.

Tamper protection via communication with trusted servers is employed in massive multiplayer online games (MMOGs) to detect cheating. Anti-cheat software such as PunkBuster [10], Valve Anti-Cheat (VAC) [35], Fides [22] and Warden [15] perform client-side computation, which are validated by a trusted server. Pioneer [30] and Conqueror [24] work similarly as anti-cheat software but target the protection of legacy systems. Jakobsson and Johansson [19] propose a similar

technique for detecting malware on mobile devices. Collberg et al. [8] propose tamper protection by pushing continuous updates from a trusted server to the client, which force the attacker to repeat reverse engineering and patching on each update. One disadvantage of these tamper protection techniques is their dependence on external trusted servers. This dependence may cause a denial-of-service to end-users of the protected software applications which are also meant to be used offline, in case Internet connectivity is unavailable. Our solution proposed operates locally, i.e., without dependence on a trusted server.

Tamper protection via *trusted computing* is usually enabled by trusted hardware. Intel has released a hardware based tamper resistance mechanism [1], known as *Software Guard eXtension* (SGX), which enables trusted computing. Morgan et al. [26] propose building a hypervisor to perform integrity checks at higher privilege levels than the attacker. Dewan et al. [9] also use a trusted hypervisor to protected the sensitive memory of programs. Feng et al. [11] propose performing randomly-timed stealthy measurements using Intel's Active Management Technology [17], which can be validated locally. These approaches provide high security guarantees. However, they require trusted hardware to be available and the installation of a hypervisor. Software developers of popular software (e.g. web browsers), generally do not want to restrict their user base by imposing such requirements.

Banescu et al. [2] as well as Blietz and Tyagi [4] propose tamper detection techniques based on runtime monitoring. The target program is transformed at compile time to report its control flow to a separate monitoring process, which verifies it according to a whitelist. The monitor can be protected using code hardening techniques because it is compact, e.g., by white-box cryptography [36] or control-flow obfuscation [29], without causing significant runtime overhead on the target program. However, this approach fails to detect code patches not violating control flow integrity, e.g. inline patching of sequential code. Moreover, this approach employs system calls, which are vulnerable to system call interposition attacks [12]. Our approach does not employ system calls and can detect inline patching of sequential code.

3. DESIGN

The idea behind software self-checking is to interleave *checkers* with the original code of an application. A checker is a piece of code which, firstly, reads a number of machine code bytes from different parts of the memory of the same process it is executing in. Checkers read continuous sequences of code bytes, so-called *blocks* of code, that we refer to as *checkees*. Secondly, the checker computes a *checksum* of those checkees, which we also refer to as *hash*. Thirdly, it compares the hash against a hard-coded *precomputed value* of the checkees. If the checksum matches the precomputed value, then normal execution continues, i.e., as in the original code. Otherwise, a *response function* is invoked. Typical response functions include halting execution (immediately or after a certain amount of time), degradation of output(s), logging the attack and/or restoring the patched code [20].

3.1 Checksumming Absolute Addresses

One challenge is checksumming absolute addresses which change dynamically each time the program is loaded in memory. This is illustrated in Figure 1, which shows x86 assembly code snippets (left column), their corresponding static ma-

[1]https://github.com/google/syzygy/tree/integrity

```
         x86 Assembly                  static code      dynamic code

1  call 0x00212348     ; FuncX.DLL1    1 e8 44 23 21 00  1 e8 44 23 c1 03
2  mov  edi, 0x00494344 ; FuncY.DLL2   2 bf 44 43 49 00  2 bf 44 43 f9 02
3  mov  [ebx+64h], eax                 3 89 43 40        3 89 43 40


4  call 0x003394560    ; FuncZ.DLL2    4 e8 5c 94 33 00  4 e8 5c 94 d3 02
5  push eax                            5 50              5 50
6  call 0x002593024    ; FuncV.DLL1    6 e8 20 93 25 00  6 e8 20 93 15 03
```

Figure 1: x86 Assembly vs. static and dynamic machine code.

chine code (middle column) and the machine code once it has been loaded in memory (right column). Note that the code does not fulfill any useful function and that similar problems occur for other CPU architectures, such as x64, ARM, MIPS, etc. The top snippet in Figure 1, starts with a call to the *FuncX* function from a dynamically loaded, shared library called *DLL1*. For ease of readability, we provide the function name in a comment following the absolute address of the function in the *call* instruction. The code snippet continues with moving the absolute address of the *FuncY* function from *DLL2* into the *edi* register, and one more *mov* instruction without any absolute references.

Statically, absolute addresses are constant, because they are the sum of a base address of a binary (which is zero before the program is loaded) and a constant offset (in that binary, e.g., a DLL), of the function being referenced. This means that the *precomputed* checksum value on the static code is fixed. However, at runtime absolute addresses change because executables are loaded at random base addresses, due to *address space layout randomization* (ASLR) [31], a software protection mechanism used against code injection attacks. ASLR loads binary executables and shared libraries at different memory locations if their preferred memory location is already occupied. For instance, Figure 1 shows that the underlined part of the absolute addresses (little-endian format) in the static and dynamic machine code are different. This is because after loading the code in memory, the base address of *DLL1* and *DLL2* are randomly assigned to 0x03200000, respectively 0x02100000. These base addresses get added to the offsets in the static code. Therefore, the checksum of the dynamic code from Figure 1, may be different every time the program is loaded in memory. The checksum computed at runtime then differs from the precomputed checksum, which (incorrectly) triggers the response function. This causes end-user annoyance and leads the software vendor to erroneously believe that code tampering has taken place.

3.2 Computing Invariant Checksums

A first approach to checksumming absolute addresses is to simply ignore all those machine code bytes which represent absolute addresses. This guarantees that any precomputed checksum will always be the same as the dynamically computed checksum. However, in order to compute such checksums at runtime, the checkers require information regarding the offsets of all bytes which represent absolute addresses. This increases the size of the checkers and lowers performance because these offsets need to be added to the code and used during checking. Moreover, it allows attackers to modify the ignored absolute addresses because they are skipped by self-checksumming.

We propose a different approach to checksumming absolute addresses based on the following two observations. Firstly, an *absolute address* a is the sum of the *base address* b of that PE

loaded in memory and a *relative offset* o inside that PE, i.e., $a = b + o$. b may change whenever the PE is started. In contrast, o is constant and, as we have seen the same in the static and the dynamic cases.

Secondly, we can eliminate variable base addresses if we subtract two absolute addresses with the same base. Let a' be another absolute address with the same base address as a but a different offset c', i.e. $a' = b + o'$. Then we eliminate the common base address by subtracting two absolute addresses: $a - a' = (b+o) - (b+o') = o - o'$, and $o - o'$ is invariant across multiple runs of the same program. If two checkees contain absolute addresses a and a', respectively, then the difference between the two checkees will be constant. We are hence interested in finding a byte array checksumming function H which maintains this invariant, $a - a' = o - o'$:

$$H(a) - H(a') = H(o) - H(o'). \qquad (1)$$

The left-hand side of Eq. 1 is computed while the protected program is running. The right-hand side can be precomputed from the static binary code, because the offsets in a PE do not change across different times that PE is loaded into memory by the OS. Therefore, we can hard-code $H(o) - H(o')$ as a precomputed checksum and use it at runtime.

Another solution for eliminating a variable base address from an absolute address is to somehow obtain the base address b of the dynamic libraries and subtract their values from the corresponding absolute address a, i.e. $H(a) - H(b) = H(o)$, which is constant. Obtaining base addresses can be done using system calls. However, attackers such as PUPs can easily detect and intercept ("hook") system calls via a technique called *system call interposition* (SCI) [12]. Using SCI a PUP can block or modify a system call such that it returns a different (incorrect) value.

Instead of using system calls, we propose statically inserting sequences of inconsequential instructions that reference the base address b of the binary or library, which is referenced by the absolute address $a = b + o$, whose base address needs to be canceled. Since the location of these inserted instructions is known, we can dynamically compute a hash of them, and know that they only contain one absolute reference, namely the base address b of the binary or library referenced by a. Hence, we can use this hash to eliminate the base address of a, i.e. $H(a) - H(b)$. However, this requires inserting additional code in the binary that we want to protect. Therefore, in order to reduce the amount of inserted instructions, we will only resort to inserting such instructions only when we cannot find a checkee containing an absolute address a' with the same base address as a, such that Eq. 1 cannot be applied.

3.3 Generalization

We can generalize this idea to the level of multiple instructions with references to multiple external dynamic libraries. To do this, the set of checkees associated with one checker is selected such that combining their checksums will cancel out all base addresses in absolute references according to the observation from Eq. 1. For example, the snippet of code (checkee) from the bottom of Figure 1 contains two instructions (lines 4 and 6) with absolute references to functions from the same DLLs[2] as the snippet (checkee) from the top of Figure 1.

---

[2]Technically speaking the absolute addresses from both snippets in Figure 1 are pointing to the so called *import address table* (IAT) in the data segment of the PE. The entries in the IAT actually contain absolute addresses to the ac-

This means that at runtime, the two *call* instructions from Figure 1, bottom, have the same base addresses as the first two instructions from Figure 1, top. If we denote the sequence of all dynamic code bytes of the checkees from Figure 1 as B_1 (top) and B_2 (bottom), then the value $H(B_1) - H(B_2)$ will be invariant across all application restarts.

This observation carries over to multiple blocks that call functions in DLLs with different base addresses multiple times. For instance, assume a PE with references to three DLLs having base addresses b_1, b_2, and b_3. Assume a (loaded) block B_3 referencing absolute addresses $b_1 + o_1$, $b_2 + o_2$, and $b_3 + o_3$; block B_4 referencing absolute addresses $b_2 + o_2$ and $b_2 + o_4$; and block B_5 referencing $b_1 + o_5$, $b_1 + o_6$, $b_3 + o_3$ and $b_3 + o_7$, for arbitrary constant offsets $o_1, \ldots, o_7$. Then we need to generate the linear combination $-2 * H(B_3) + H(B_4) + H(B_5)$, which is constant across multiple executions of the PE, because the base addresses cancel each other out.

More generally, let $\mathcal{B}$ be a set of blocks with $|\mathcal{B}| = n$, and a set of dynamically linked libraries (DLLs) $\mathcal{D}$ with $|\mathcal{D}| = d$. We can statically analyze how many times a block references functions from a DLL and store this information in matrix $Q \in \mathbb{N}^{n \times d}$. $Q(i, j)$ is the number of calls from block i to functions in DLL j. We will use the notation $Q(i)$ to denote the i-th row of Q. Let $B \in \mathbb{N}^d$ be the set of base addresses of the DLLs that are dynamically assigned at load time. $B(i)$ hence is the base address of DLL i. Remember that B cannot easily be obtained at runtime without using system calls (see §3.2). We now show how to exploit the idea of cancelling out base addresses with linear combinations.

3.3.1 Equation systems

Let $H_p \in \mathbb{Z}^n$ be the statically and $H_r \in \mathbb{Z}^n$ the dynamically computed checksums of each block, e.g., using function H that performs word addition modulo 2^N, where a word has N-bits. Because all base addresses are zero in the static code, we want to ensure $H_p(i) \equiv H_r(i) - \sum_{j=1}^d Q(i, j) * H(B(j))$ mod 2^N at runtime, for all $1 \leq i \leq n$, which we write as

$$H_p \equiv H_r - Q \cdot H(B) \mod 2^N \qquad (2)$$

when using matrix multiplication notation. The idea now is to compute linear combinations of checksums that add up to zero. Let $x \in \mathbb{Q}^n$ be the respective vector of coefficients. We want to find values for the components of $x \neq \mathbf{0}$ such that $\forall 1 \leq j \leq d : \sum_{i=1}^n Q(i, j) * x(i) = 0$, which we rewrite as

$$Q^T \cdot x = \mathbf{0}, \text{ or } x^T \cdot Q = \mathbf{0} \qquad (3)$$

where $\cdot^T$ denotes the transpose of a matrix. Multiplication of Eq. 2 with x^T then cancels out the base addresses:

$$x^T \cdot H_p \equiv x^T \cdot H_r - x^T \cdot Q \cdot H(B) \equiv x^T \cdot H_r \mod 2^N.$$

To perform integrity checks at runtime, we hence need to store only the non-zero values of the vector x satisfying Eq. 3 and the scalar $x^T \cdot H_p$.

Eq. 3 is a linear equation system for which it is easy to compute rational solutions (if they exist). However, for large numbers of blocks and rational coefficients, rounding errors are likely to materialize, and it is hard to predict their effects. It is therefore desirable to consider Eq. 3 as a linear Diophantine equation system and stipulate $x \in \mathbb{Z}^n$.

Linear Diophantine equation systems can effectively be solved using SMT solvers [3]. However, in our special case, effectiveness, scalability and efficiency quickly become concerns. Statically, the equation system may become too large to be handled by the SMT solver. The equation system need not have a non-zero solution, possibly not even a rational one. This can trivially be the case, for instance, if a DLL is called by exactly one block. Dynamically, if a frequently executed block needs to compute checksums of very many blocks, runtime performance becomes a concern.

3.3.2 Reducing large equation systems

Matrix Q is usually very sparse in practice. A first idea is thus to reduce Q to the dimension of its rank by computing the basis. However, this essentially is done by the SMT solver anyway, so we cannot expect too much effect here.

Because of the sparseness of Q, we can hope to compute a set of rather small submatrices for which we can solve the corresponding equation systems independently and in parallel. To do so, we choose subsets P of the rows of Q such that it is ensured that for each column of P, there are none or more than one non-zero elements. The interpretation is that we choose sets of blocks such that any DLL (column) is called either never (all elements zero) or by at least two blocks (at least two elements of this column are non-zero). By removing the all-zero columns we get a smaller equation system, and making sure that the sets P together cover all rows of Q, we have simplified the problem.

The algorithm takes as input a set of rows R of matrix Q and outputs a set of sets of rows $\{W_1, \ldots, W_k\} \subseteq 2^R$ such that (1) all rows of R are covered ($\bigcup_{i=1}^k W_i = R$) and (2) and for each set of rows (blocks) W_i and each column (DLL) d, d is either not called by any row in W_i, or there are rows $r_1 \neq r_2$ in W_i that both call d at least once. Each W_i is one independent equation system, usually much smaller than R.

The algorithm starts by initializing the counter of blocks of blocks (rows), $i = 0$ and consists of the following steps:

Step 0: Remove from R all rows that contain zeros only, all columns that contain zeros only, and all columns that contain exactly one non-zero element. The latter will be catered to by adding bogus calls to the respective DLL in a block that does not call any other DLL in §3.3.3.

Step 1: If $R = \emptyset$, stop. Otherwise, $W_i := \{r\}$ for a random row $r \in R$. W_i is the currently computed set of rows.

Step 2: Otherwise, if $R \neq \emptyset$, compute the *fitness* $\varphi(r', W_i)$ for each $r' \in R$ as described below. The row with the best fitness will be added to the current submatrix W_i. A fitness value of $-\infty$ indicates that the respective row does not help complete the equation system represented by W_i because there is no overlap with the DLLs called in W_i. Choose $r'' = \arg\max_{r' \in R}(\varphi(r', W_i))$ to be the row with the highest fitness.

Step 3: If $\varphi(r'', W_i) \neq -\infty$, let $W_i := W_i \cup \{r''\}$ and $R := R \setminus \{r''\}$ (because further blocks of the partition will usually not need to consider r''). If W_i now is such that every DLL is either called by no or by at least two rows, the current block of rows is ready. Let $i := i + 1$ and goto step 1. Otherwise goto step 2.

Step 4: Otherwise, if $\varphi(r'', W_i) = -\infty$, we need to resort to a row that has been picked before. Compute $\varphi(r', W_i)$ for all rows $r' \in \bigcup_{j<i} W_i$ that have already been picked earlier, and pick the best: $r''' = \arg\max_{r' \in \bigcup_{j<i} W_j}(\varphi(r', W_i))$.

Step 5: Because we have gotten rid of rows that make

---

tual function entry points in dynamic libraries loaded at different locations in memory. This level of indirection is similar for other executable formats.

equation systems inherently unsolvable in step 0, $\varphi(r''', W_i) \neq -\infty$ must hold. We let $W_i := W_i \cup \{r'''\}$ and $R := R \setminus \{r'''\}$. If W_i is now such that every DLL is either called by no or by at least two rows, we let $i := i + 1$ and goto step 1. Otherwise goto step 2.

Note that this schema gives priority to rows that have not been assigned to a previously computed W_j with $j < i$. It may hence well be, and sometimes is, the case that a perfectly fitting row in such a W_j would make the equation system represented by W_i solvable. The reason for this heuristic is runtime performance: With this approach, the number of fitness computations can greatly be decreased. Otherwise, n fitness computations need to be done for every pick of a candidate row to be included in any W_i which, for large numbers of blocks becomes a practical concern.

The **fitness** of a row r w.r.t. a set of rows W_i is computed as follows. Note that because r may have been chosen from W_i, it is possible that $r \in W_i$. Firstly, let $a = |\{j \in \mathcal{D} : r(j) = 0 \wedge \forall r' \in W_i \setminus \{r\} : r'(j) = 0\}|$ be the number of DLLs that are called neither by r nor by any row in $W_i \setminus \{r\}$. We do not really care about these, but the larger this number, the better. Secondly, let $b = |\{j \in \mathcal{D} : r(j) \neq 0 \wedge \forall r' \in W_i \setminus \{r\} : r'(j) = 0\}|$ be the number of DLLs that are called by r but by none of the rows in $W_i \setminus \{r\}$. These make the row r "inattractive" because we will need to find additional matching rows in further steps, which will potentially lead to large numbers of blocks that need to be hashed together. Thirdly, let $c = |\{j \in \mathcal{D} : r(j) \neq 0 \wedge \exists^{=1} r' \in W_i \setminus \{r\} : r'(j) \neq 0\}|$ count the number of DLLs in W_i that call a DLL that is also called by r and by one row in $W_i \setminus \{r\}$. These DLLs make the row r "attractive" because adding r to W_i reduces the number of DLLs for which no match has been found yet. Finally, if $c = 0$ let the fitness $\varphi(r, W_i) = -\infty$ and otherwise $\varphi(r, W_i) = \alpha \cdot a + \beta \cdot b + \gamma \cdot c$ for suitable parameters α, β, γ. Each W_i then gives rise to one equation system that can be solved in isolation. Note that the above computation amounts to a heuristic breakdown of R into smaller systems without any optimality guarantees.

In our performance experiments, we (somewhat arbitrarily) set $\alpha = 1, \beta = -2, \gamma = 4$ and varied the values of $n \in \{50, 100, 500, 1000\}$ and $d \in \{100, 200, 300, 400\}$. Due to lack of space, we present the results in Table 2 in the Appendix. Note that the time needed by our algorithm increases significantly as d increases, while the increase is not as significant as n increases. This is convenient, since most executables will have a high value for n, while d is much lower, e.g. in our Chromium experiments from §5.1.3, $n = 4749$ and $d = 277$.

3.3.3 No integer solutions

It may of course happen that the equation system, or one of the reduced systems, has no non-zero solution, not even a rational one. Let Q' consist of the m non-zero rows of one W_i as computed above. The problem then can be solved by artificially making the equation system $Q'^T \cdot x = 0^m$ underdetermined. To do so, we relax the requirement that the right hand side be 0 and rather leave that open: $Q'^T \cdot x = y$ for an undetermined vector $y \in \mathbb{Z}^m$ (that we construct below; its first $d - m + 1$ entries will be those of vector s below). If $m \leq d$, we simply juxtapose an upper diagonal matrix D of dimension $d \times (d - m + 1)$ to the right of Q'^T and add slack variables $s_1, \ldots, s_{d-m+1}$ to x, resulting in a vector x'. We can then solve $Q'^T D \cdot x' = 0$ which, by construction, is equivalent to solving $Q'^T \cdot x = (s_1, \ldots, s_{d-m+1}, 0, \ldots, 0)$. Because by

construction this system is underdetermined, it will have a non-zero integer solution.

Intuitively, the above construction of adding columns to Q'^T corresponds to adding rows to Q' which corresponds to adding bogus blocks to the program. These bogus blocks are never executed, because they are placed in dead branches of opaque predicates. However, statically they call the one DLL for which the entry in the respective row of Q'^T is 1.

3.4 Multiple Hash Functions

One attack on this self-checksumming mechanism is patching the code such that the checksum (addition module some number, denoted H_+) is preserved, as illustrated in Figure 2. The idea is to replace original code BB by malign code M and then replace other instructions by inconsequential instructions, such that the checksum of the modified code matches that of the original code. One such inconsequential instruction is `ADD x,x`. When choosing x such that $H_+(\texttt{ADD x,x}) + H_+(M) \equiv H_+(BB) \mod 2^N$, this tampering will not be detected by our algorithm. (Note that H_+ actually is applied to the machine code representation of `ADD x,x`.)

Because of the block structure of our schema, tampering must be performed in place, that is the malicious code M must be smaller than the benign code BB to be replaced.

To counter this attack, we may use a second checksumming function, other than H_+, which includes an operation over the individual machine code bytes. If we want to minimize the number of possible input bytes that result in the same checksum output, i.e. *checksum collisions* we can use a cryptographic hash function. However, computing such a function for every basic block would impose a higher runtime performance impact than using a lightweight checksumming or hashing function. One of the most lightweight checksumming functions is byte-wise XOR-ing (denoted $H_\oplus$). One can verify that byte-wise XOR-ing the machine code bytes before and after run-time memory patching (depicted in Figure 2) results in different checksums. Of course, using both $H_\oplus$ and H_+ together does not guarantee that there will be no collisions. However, it does reduce the probability of a collision.

Note that the above replacement attack as such is difficult (but not impossible) if M contains a call to some DLL. This invariably changes the hash values at runtime. However, the second hash function is necessary because PUPs may also tamper with other checkees and call exactly the same DLLs as M, hence "fixing" the hash value.

Regarding absolute addresses, $H_\oplus$ suffers from the same problems as H_+ described in §3.1. In fact, we are not aware of functions other than byte-wise addition which produce an

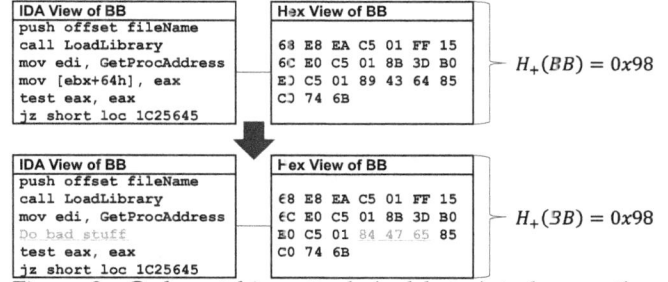

Figure 2: Code patching attack (red bytes) to bypass the checksum function H_+ (byte-wise addition modulo 256)

invariant checksum over all application restarts. Since x86 instructions are of variable length and are not aligned, at runtime we do not know where an absolute address begins in a sequence of machine code bytes. Therefore, given only the starting address and the size of a contiguous sequence of machine code bytes, one cannot know where the absolute addresses are without additional information or without performing disassembly on the fly, which would have a high performance impact. One could argue that such information is available in the *reloc* section of a PE. However, this would require the checksumming function (which must be lightweight), to look-up whether the current offset it is reading-from contains an absolute address. We consider this far too expensive to be performed before each byte that is read by the checksumming function. Our simple solution therefore is to ignore absolute addresses when using $H_\oplus$; they are checked by H_+ only. Absolute addresses are ignored by choosing the checkee blocks (statically, using the x86 Assembly), such that the instructions do not make any references to absolute addresses.

3.5 Cyclic Checks

We inject checks into blocks and want the checkers to be checked themselves. Which blocks check which other blocks is not discussed here; this can be done randomly or be the result of code execution frequency considerations. Let $CB_i = IC_i; BB_i$ be a checker i that combines the integrity check IC_i with the code of block BB_i. Assume that IC_i needs to check the checkee blocks $b(CB_i)$; the identification of these blocks is the result of the computation of a W_i above. Note $b(CB_i)$ may or may not contain CB_i.

Let $b_i = |b(CB_i)|$ be the number of blocks checked by IC_i. The code of IC_i consists of: (1) b_i addresses, sizes and co-efficients (computed by solving the equation system corresponding to W_i as constructed above and used as constant factors) of checkees, $CH_{i1}, \ldots, CH_{ib_i}$, each of which differs from the others, (2) one constant hash value for comparison of the aggregate hash values from all checkees,

$$KB_i = \sum_{CB_j \in b(CB_i)} c_{ij} * H(CB_j),$$

which is invariant across different runs of the system (which in turn is made sure by the above construction of linear Diophantine equations; the c_{ij} are the computed coefficients in vector x for the equation system corresponding to W_i); and (3) a pivot X_i, which is a placeholder for a value we need in order to account for cyclic dependencies. We hence have[3]

$$CB_i = CH_{i1}; \ldots; CH_{ib_i}; KB_i; X_i; BB_i.$$

The constant value of KB_i is determined by computing the linear combination of the hash values of the blocks as explained above; remember that the construction of the hash function is such that DLL base addresses are canceled out.

We now need to incorporate hash values for the integrity checks as well. The challenge is to check the integrity if there are cyclic dependencies between checkers, e.g. CB_1 checks CB_2 checks CB_3 checks CB_1. If the code of IC_is are not part of the checksummed bytes, then cyclic checks are not an issue. However, assume IC_is are subject to integrity checking *and* there are cyclic dependencies.

If $H(A; B) = H(A) + H(B)$, which is the case for the checksum functions we are using, we have

$$H(CB_i) = H(BB_i) + H(X_i) + H(KB_i) + \sum_{CB_j \in b(CB_i)} H(CH_{ij}).$$

$H(BB_i)$, $H(KB_i)$ and $\sum_{CB_j \in b(CB_i)} H(CH_{ij})$ are constants. Let G_i denote their sum. We then need to find integer solutions for all X_i such that $H(X_i) = G_i - H(CB_i)$, which is easy to solve if H is addition modulo some number.

4. IMPLEMENTATION

We have implemented the self-checking mechanism for the PE format and the x86 instruction set architecture (ISA). Because the x86 ISA has a variable length encoding where instructions can vary between one and fifteen bytes, byte-by-byte summation modulo 256 (denoted H_+) is the natural checksumming function candidate for satisfying Eq. 1. However, there is an issue with using H_+, which we discuss in §4.2.

4.1 Granularity of Checks

The impact on run-time performance is characterized by the frequency of the checks and the amount of data that is checked. We leave frequency considerations to future work. In terms of the amount of data, checksumming can be applied at various levels of granularity, e.g. memory segments, functions, basic blocks[4], tuples of instructions.

To precompute checksums H_p, we need the compiled and linked machine code. Therefore, we cannot perform the transformation of adding checks at source code level. We have implemented the self-checking transformation such that it is applicable post binary compilation and linking, which also minimizes the impact on the software development process. Because we want to apply our approach to Google Chromium, we use the Google Syzygy Transformation Toolchain as a binary instrumentation framework which is used to post process Chromium (but works for any PE). Among other things, Syzygy performs basic block optimizations via reordering, which improves the cold start times, executable layout and cache efficiency of the instrumented program [14].

Since Syzygy performs a mandatory basic block reordering, the coarsest level of granularity for our transformation is that of *basic blocks*. If we checksum a function composed of several basic blocks, Syzygy will likely reorder its basic blocks, possibly interleaving them with basic blocks of other functions. It is thus not guaranteed that all basic blocks of a function will be placed contiguously in the resulting binary.

4.2 Issues with Byte-by-Byte Addition

In deriving Eq. 1 we used the fact that the difference o between an absolute address a and a base address b is constant and we assumed that the difference between the byte-by-byte summation of these addresses will always be equal to the byte-by-byte summation of the offset o, i.e.,

$$H_+(a) - H_+(b) \equiv H_+(o) \mod 2^N \qquad (4)$$

where H_+ is addition modulo some number. This relation is always true for Microsoft Windows PEs that are smaller than 512 KBs because on 32-bit systems all base addresses are 16-bit aligned [27], which means that the base address will always have its least significant 16-bits equal to 0. However,

---

[3]This is slightly misleading because KB_i is a number; think of it as being subtracted from the sum of the hash values and compared to 0.

[4]A *basic block* is defined by a list of sequential instructions ending either with a jump or a return instruction. A basic block has branch-ins only onto its first instruction and branch-outs only from its last instruction.

for PEs larger than $2^{16} \times 8 = 512$ KBs, it could be the case that the base address b plus the offset o leads to a carry bit from one less significant byte to a more significant byte in the absolute address a. For example, consider $b = 0x02E00000$, $o = 0x00321234$, and $a = b + o = 0x03121234$. Relation (4) does not hold for these addresses: $H_+(a) = 03 + 12 + 12 + 34 = 5B$, $H_+(b) = 02 + E0 + 00 + 00 = E2$, and $H_+(o) = 00 + 32 + 12 + 34 = 78$; but $H_+(a) - H_+(b) \equiv H_+(o) + 1 \mod 2^N$. The reason is the bit that is carried from the 2nd byte of the absolute address to the most significant byte after adding the offset to the base address.

One intuitive solution would be to simply change the H_+ function such that it does not perform byte-by-byte addition, but word-by-word addition instead. This would solve the issue of the carry bit from one byte of the address to another. Unfortunately, this is not possible because instructions in x86 machine code have variable length, i.e. an instruction can have anywhere between 1 and 15 bytes in length. For example, the *call* instruction from Figure 1 is five bytes long, while the push instruction is one byte long. Therefore, if the H_+ function read one word (four bytes on a 32-bit system) at a time, it would be highly likely that the read words would contain the entire absolute addresses. Moreover, basic blocks have a size equal to a number of bytes divisible by four, which means that reading word-by-word could go outside the boundary of a basic block. Note, however, that word-by-word addition would work on an ISA with fixed width instructions (e.g. ARM, MIPS, etc.).

Another intuitive solution would be to partition the PE into 512 KB blocks and pick checkees and checkers only from within the same partition block, in order to be able to perform strict equality comparison. However, these partitions may not fall at function or basic block boundaries, plus the basic blocks are reordered by Syzygy after the checker to checkee associations are chosen (see §4.1).

Since the base address of a program is chosen randomly by ASLR, we cannot know the exact number of times this carry bit situation could occur. However we can statically compute how many absolute addresses a basic block contains and we can place an upper-bound on how many times this carry bit situation could occur across all possible program restarts (i.e. base addresses). Therefore, for binaries larger than 512 KBs we do not perform an equality comparison of the dynamically computed checksum d to the statically precomputed checksum s. Instead, we check that $|d - s|$ is below the number of absolute addresses in these basic blocks.

Approximately comparing the statically computed against the dynamically precomputed checksum weakens the protection mechanism. Assume an attacker patches a few instructions in protected basic blocks such that their new dynamically computed checksum is equal to d'. If $|d' - s| \leq |d - s|$, then this attack will not be detected by H_+. In §4.4 we add another checksumming function, which further raises the bar for such patching attacks along the lines of §3.4.

4.3 Processing Executable Files

Since a user may not want to protect all functions of an executable, our tool takes as additional input a list of function names to be protected. The tool first disassembles the executable and generates a graph of basic blocks. Second, the following sequence of assembly instructions—the checker—is inserted before each basic block in a function to be protected. These instructions can be obfuscated.

1. Save four values on the stack for each of the N checkees associated with the checker: (i) k_i the coefficients which will be multiplied by the checksum of the checkees, (ii) l_i the number of bytes of each checkee, (iii) a_i the starting address of each checkee and (iv) n_i the number of checkees of each checkee, which are needed for the following reason: each checkee is indicated by an absolute address with the base address equal to the base of the current executable, denoted b. Since the instructions of the checkee also include code that was inserted to perform checks on other checkees, we need to cancel out the absolute addresses of those checkees.

2. Call the checksumming function which reads the machine code bytes at the previously stored addresses on the stack. The checksumming function internally computes the byte-wise addition modulo 256, of the machine code bytes of each checkee. It also computes the *checksum of the base address* for the current binary (denoted $H_+(b)$)[5]. The linear combination of the checksums for all checkees (c_+), which will be the return value of the hash function is:

$$c_+ = \sum_{i=1}^{N} k_i \left(\left(\sum_{j=0}^{l_i - 1} \mathcal{M}[a_i + j] \right) - n_i H_+(b) \right) \mod 256,$$

where $\mathcal{M}$ denotes an array representing the process memory of the protected application. The intuition as to why absolute addresses are canceled out by this linear combination of checksums is given in §3.2.

3. Compare the value returned by the checksumming function (i.e. c_+) with a hard-coded pre-computed value.

4. Trigger the response functions if the values in the previous comparison are not equal, otherwise continue the normal execution of the original binary.

Thirdly, the basic blocks are reordered by Syzygy and laid out in the output executable. This reordering changes several relative and absolute addresses. In the final step, our tool hence patches the precomputed checksums (in-place) such that they will match the dynamically computed checksums.

4.4 Detecting Checksum Collisions

To detect patching attacks which result in checksum collisions we resort to using $H_\oplus$ only over consecutive instructions which do not contain absolute addresses (§3.4). We call them *chunks*. This checksumming function is used in addition to H_+ for basic blocks that contain absolute addresses. Note that we can use any checksum or hash function to hash such code chunks; we chose $H_\oplus$ because it has a low performance overhead. Technically, we consider chunks of code to be any maximum subset of consecutive instructions inside of a basic block that do not contain references to absolute addresses. For example, the basic block from Fig. 2 contains 2 chunks: the first consists of only the first instruction, and the second consists of the last 3 instructions.

For each of the M chunks associated with it, the checker saves the following values on the stack: (i) l_i the size in bytes of the chunk and (ii) a_i the starting address of the chunk. Let $c_\oplus$ denote the return value of the function:

$$c_\oplus = \sum_{i=1}^{M} \left(\bigoplus_{j=0}^{l_i - 1} \mathcal{M}[a_i + j] \right) \mod 256.$$

---

[5]This base address is known because (in the implementation of H_+) we inserted a *mov* instruction that copies the value of a reference to the base of this binary in an auxiliary register, which it then dynamically hashes.

The output of this $H_\oplus$ checksum function is combined with the result of the H_+ checksum function: $c_+ + c_\oplus \mod 256$. The resulting value is hard-coded in the protected PE and is compared against the checksum computed at runtime. If the comparison fails, the response function is called.

4.5 Response Functions

Response functions ideally are (1) *transparent*, i.e. not noticeable to the end-user. They must be effective against attacks and should be (2) *stealthy*, i.e. an attacker should not be able to identify and disable the response. We are not aware of response functions which are both transparent and stealthy. However, we did implement one transparent and one stealthy response function.

The transparent yet non-stealthy response function consists of sending a signal to a trusted server indicating a change in the process memory. This can only be achieved by using a system call that accesses the OS network interface.

The stealthier response function crashes the program after tampering is detected. Crashing could be implemented in a variety of ways, i.e. instead of comparing the precomputed hash to a hard-coded checksum, we can use the hash to compute a jump target or perform an operation with the stack pointer. This may not crash the program immediately, but eventually will lead to a crash with high probability.

4.6 Limitations

Currently we assign checkees randomly to checkers with the constraint that a linear combination of their hashes is invariant to application restarts. However, to reduce performance impact this random approach can be improved to always pick hot code as checkees and less hot code as checkers.

Due to the way in which self-checksumming works, it causes issues during debugging. Generally debuggers (e.g. the Microsoft Windows debugger, GDB) replace the first byte of a basic block with CC, which is the opcode for the *int 3* assembly instruction. This is the standard way for debuggers to gain control, from the application that is being debugged. After the debugger gains control it changes the CC value back to its original value. Therefore, if the application that is being debugged employs self-checksumming, then it could happen that a checker computes a checksum over a basic block where the debugger has changed the first byte to CC. This will lead to the wrong checksum value which will trigger the response function during debugging.

A solution to this issue is to use *hardware breakpoints* if the debugger supports them. These kinds of breakpoints do not cause the debugger to replace the first byte of a basic block with CC. The drawback to this solution is that the number of hardware breakpoints on the x86 architecture is limited to 4.

5. EVALUATION

5.1 Performance Evaluation

We evaluated the performance of our implementation over two categories of applications: (1) CPU-intensive applications such as an XML parser, which indicates the worst-case performance overhead due to a higher frequency of checksumming, and (2) GUI applications (that are less CPU-intensive) such as the Chromium browser, which involve continuous human-user interaction and indicate an average performance overhead for self-checksumming protection.

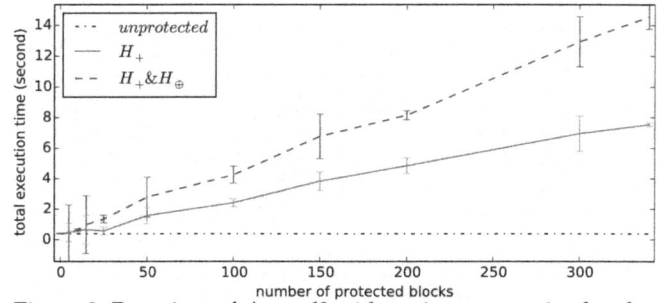

Figure 3: Run-time of *tinyxml2* with various protection levels.

5.1.1 XML Parser

We selected *tinyxml2* [34] from Github's trending repositories as the first candidate for our performance evaluation. It is an open source XML file parser library that reads an input file and constructs the corresponding Document Object Model (DOM). The library is written in C++ and consists of 4571 lines of code. The compiled binary consists of 340 basic blocks and occupies 136 KB of disk space.

To measure the overhead of our implementation, we selected ten random combinations of 5, 10, 15, 20, 50, 100, 150, 200, 300 and 340 basic blocks, and used them as input configurations for our tool. For each input configuration we generated two protected binaries: one where only the H_+ checksum was used, and one where both H_+ & $H_\oplus$ were used. This resulted in $10 \times 10 \times 2 = 200$ protected binaries.

These protected binaries were executed with the same input XML file set shipped with the library, which varies in size from 0 KB (empty test) up to 142 KB (dream.xml). We measured the total process run-time as the difference between the timestamp when the process terminated its execution and the time when execution was started. The total process run-time was measured 100 times for every application. The mean and standard deviation were computed across all applications that have the same number of protected functions, in order to weed out random influences on runtime performance. Figure 3 illustrates the evaluation results for protection with H_+ and with H_+ & $H_\oplus$. The baseline execution time of 0.4 seconds (y-axis) can be seen for zero protected blocks (x-axis). Using H_+ slows down execution about 20 times when all 340 blocks of the application are protected, while the slowdown induced by H_+ & $H_\oplus$ it about 35 times. This slowdown may be unacceptable in scenarios which require high-responsiveness or high-throughput. However, it may be acceptable in scenarios where behavior integrity of some software functions (e.g. license checks), is of utter importance.

5.1.2 Chromium

Chromium involves user interaction and therefore is not as CPU intensive as the XML parser. By measuring the total process run-time of versions of Chromium protected using different input configurations, we could not observe a slowdown compared to the unprotected version. Another reason for this low overhead is the multi-process and multi-threaded architecture of Chromium, where several processes depend on input values gathered via OS system calls (e.g. network communication) and are not controlled by the end-user inputs. Therefore, we measured the overhead incurred per protected function, i.e. the relative increase in run-time of a protected function w.r.t. its unprotected counterpart.

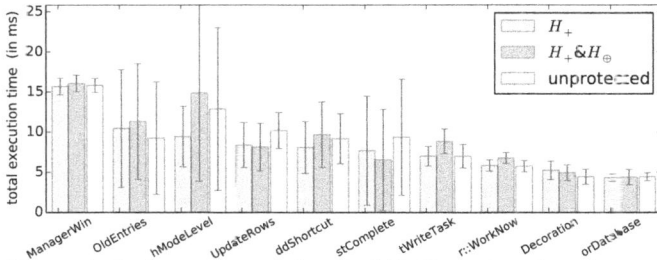

Figure 4: Performance overhead of 10 Chromium functions.

Protection	Mean	Std. Dev.	Median	Maximum
H_+	1.34	1.16	1.00	8.2
H_+ & $H_\oplus$	1.34	0.89	1.06	5.0

Table 1: Relative performance overhead in ms (protected function run-time divided by unprotected function run-time) of self-checksumming protection in Chromium.

One way of measuring the overhead per function is using a binary profiling tool such as *SyzyProf*, offered by the Syzygy toolchain. However, such tools also require instrumenting the application. Applying *SyzyProf* on an application transformed by our tool breaks the precomputed checksums due to the profiling instructions that *SyzyProf* adds to the code. Applying *SyzyProf* first and then transforming it using our tool solves this issue, however, it causes the profiling information collected by *SyzyProf* to be inaccurate, because code is inserted and reordered by our tool.

We therefore extract the profiling information from a protected version of Chromium via the browser itself using the chrome://profiler URL. Before the profile information is saved we let the browser run for 30 seconds. During this time it loads its homepage (i.e. https://www.google.com), then we search for the word "hello". After the search results are loaded we open the chrome://profiler. From the profile information we compute the average execution time per function by dividing the total execution time and the number of times a function was executed, for each of the protected functions. Similarly to the XML parser, we protect Chromium both with H_+ only and with both H_+ & $H_\oplus$.

We have protected 400 functions from Chromium, 73 of which were executed and consistently appearing in the profile information across 20 executions of Chromium. Looking at the names of the remaining functions, we realized that they are only called when performing other end-user actions, e.g. changing browser preferences, downloading files, etc., which we did not perform in our test runs. Table 1 shows the average overhead over these 73 functions protected with H_+ only and protected with H_+ & $H_\oplus$. The mean values are the same for both, however, the median is larger when both H_+ & $H_\oplus$ are used. Remarkably the maximum overhead was observed for a function protected with H_+. Figure 4 shows a bar chart with the average execution times and the standard deviation of 10 randomly chosen functions from Chromium protected with H_- only, protected with H_+ & $H_\oplus$ and unprotected. From the bar chart we can see that the impact of self-protection is relatively moderate. Also it seems that for some functions the performance impact of protection with H_+ is lower than with H_+ & $H_\oplus$. This is counter-intuitive, however, we are not certain that the inputs for these functions during different runs are the same, due to the previously

mentioned reason, i.e. Chromium performs several system calls, whose execution times vary depending on the OS state.

5.1.3 Protection Time and Protected Binary Size

The time required to protect an executable, i.e., to statically add the checking code, increases linearly with the number of basic blocks to be protected. For instance, protecting 400 functions with 4749 basic blocks from Chromium, takes around 27 minutes, out of which 14 minutes are used only by the Syzygy binary disassembler, which is performed before our protection mechanism is applied. On the other hand, protecting 5 functions with 49 basic blocks from Chromium, takes around 15 minutes, out of which 14 minutes are still required by the binary disassembler stage. Therefore, the disassembly stage is constant for a certain executable file, while our protection mechanism increases linearly with the number of protected basic blocks.

The size of the protected executable is increased w.r.t. the unprotected executable. Similarly to protection time, the size of the protected executable also increases linearly with the number of protected basic blocks. For each protected basic block the added integrity check code with H_+ is at least 82 bytes, when the added code is not obfuscated via *superdiversification* [18]. Note that this integrity check has two checkees and the size of the machine code that pushes the information on the stack for each checkee is 20 bytes per checkee. Adding also $H_\oplus$ also requires pushing the information for four chunks and some extra instructions to call the $H_\oplus$ hash function, save its result and combine it with the result of the H_+ hash function. The size of the machine code that pushes the information on the stack for each chunk is 15 bytes per chunk. Therefore, the total size of the resulting integrity check code is 163 bytes (unobfuscated) per basic block, when both H_+ & $H_\oplus$ are used.

5.2 Security Evaluation

One intuitive way of evaluating the security of our approach is to develop or use an existing PUP which tampers with the process memory of the application. However, we argue this is not a fair evaluation since such a browser hijacker would not be aware of the protection mechanism we are employing and would therefore be detected.

An alternative way of performing the security evaluation is to assume that the attacker is fully aware of all details of our protection mechanism and consider possible actions of such an attacker. The attack tree in Figure 5 on the next page shows possible attacks which an attacker may implement to bypass our protection mechanism. The root of the tree shows the goal of the attacker and each of the leaves are alternative ways to achieve this goal. The following subsections discuss each of the leaves of this attack tree.

5.2.1 Disable Checker of Targeted Code Bytes

Each basic block in a protected function is checked by at least one other basic block located in a different function. This causes cyclic dependencies between checks which are discussed in §3.5, resulting in a connected directed graph where each node is a basic block and each arc indicates the source node performing an integrity check over the destination node, illustrated in Figure 6a.

Additionally, each basic block in the protected executable also checks a number of chunks spread across different basic blocks, which adds another kind of directed arcs (showed

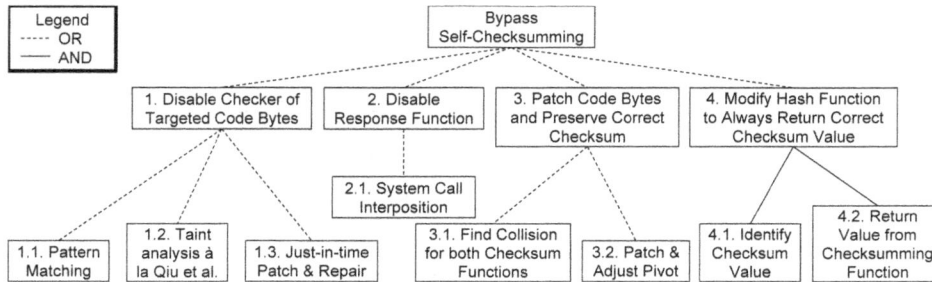

Figure 5: Attack tree for our self-checksumming tool.

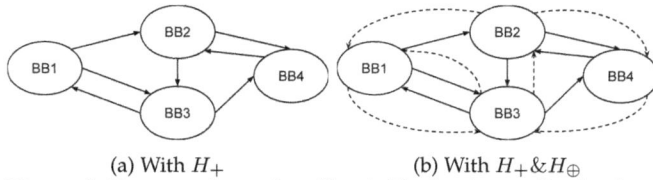

(a) With H_+ (b) With $H_+ \& H_\oplus$

Figure 6: Connected graphs of basic blocks, i.e. cyclic checks.

with dashed lines in Figure 6b) to the previously mentioned graph. Dashed lines also indicate that $H_\oplus$ is not computed over the entire destination basic block but only on a part of it (i.e. a chunk). This strongly connected graph forces the attacker to *identify and disable all checkers* before being able to patch any of the basic blocks in the executable.

The attacker could perform a pattern matching attack to identify all checkers inside a protected executable and disable them by replacing their code by NOP instructions. In order to avoid patterns in the integrity check code, we employed an obfuscation transformation known as *superdiversification* [18], i.e. replacing one sequence of instructions in a basic block by another sequence of instructions which is functionally equivalent. The drawback of employing this kind of obfuscation is that the size of the integrity checking code, which is added to each protected basic block, is increased 2-4 times relative to the current size of the code (see §5.1.3).

Another way of detecting and disabling checkers was presented by Qiu et al. [28]. They taint the code bytes of an executable and perform backward and then forward taint analysis to identify checker instructions, which use the (tainted) code as data for branch decisions. Together with the authors of [28], we employed their tool on an execution trace generated by a protected version of Chromium running for 1 minute. The tool executed on machine with 32GB of RAM and an Intel Xeon CPU with 2.0 GHz clock speed and was able to process 1% of the trace per day. We conclude that this attack is effective, however, it does not scale for applications which generate large execution traces.

The time interval (*detection interval*) between a patching attack and detection of the patch via our self-checksumming mechanism can vary greatly due to the random way in which checkers and checkees are picked, i.e. if a basic block executed rarely is checking another basic block which is patched, then the detection interval will be relatively large compared to the scenario where the basic block which is performing the check would be executed frequently. Checkers could be bypassed if the attacker patches the targeted code before it executes and reverts the patch after it executed and before any checksum is performed on it. We call this *just-in-time*

patch & repair. However, due to Chrome's multi-process and multi-threaded architecture it is highly unlikely that this attack could succeed reliably across a large number of end-users, due to the unpredictability of the OS scheduler [7]. In order to minimize the detection interval for more security sensitive code we propose using heuristics based on profiling information of the protected application. This way, security sensitive code would be checked by multiple integrity checks in frequently executing code. We leave this straightforward extension of our implementation for future work.

5.2.2 Disable Response Function

A process running under the same privileges as the target application process (which is the case for PUPs) can intercept all system calls and prevent the transparent response function from sending any information to a trusted server. This means that even if there were multiple response functions obfuscated and spread-out across the code of the PE, attacks such as system call hooking could still detect and stop such response functions.

An attacker would need to employ the techniques of §5.2.1 to identify the stealthy response function. A delayed crash is even harder to trace back to its root cause by an attacker.

5.2.3 Patch Code Bytes and Preserve Checksum

This attack was described in §§3.4 and 4.4. The idea is to patch a certain number of bytes in the machine code such that the checksum is preserved, as illustrated in Figure 2. To reduce collisions we added the $H_\oplus$ checksum function over chunks. This does not completely exclude the possibility of a collision, however, it decreases its likelihood.

Another attack is to modify bytes in the code even if the checksum is not preserved and then patch the pivot byte such that the checksum is corrected. This is detected by checking the chunk containing the pivot byte.

5.2.4 Modify Hash Function to Always Return Correct Checksum Value

An attacker who knows our self-checksumming implementation may attempt to modify the machine code of the checksumming function such that it always returns the correct checksum. This is possible by reading bytes starting from the return address of the checksumming function until a comparison instruction is first encountered (the check if the statically and dynamically computed hash values are identical). The attacker could then take the constant value from this instruction and return it from the checksumming function. We can raise the bar against this attack by employing superdiversification [18], i.e. use different types of instructions to compare the return value of the checksumming function with the precomputed checksum in different checkers.

194

6. CONCLUSIONS AND FUTURE WORK

We have presented the design, implementation and evaluation of a mechanism for software tamper detection via self-checksumming. The results indicate that for CPU-intensive applications, the run-time of an application having all functions protected may be 20 times as high as the unprotected application when using one checksumming function, and up to 35 times higher when using two checksumming functions. This kind of overhead may appear prohibitive for some applications. However, we note that an application developer may not necessarily want to protect *all* functions of an application, which significantly lowers the overhead. Moreover, the performance of a protected application depends on how frequently checks are executed. If checks are inserted inside frequently executing code such as deeply nested loops, then performance impact is higher than if checks are inserted in less frequently executed code.

For non CPU-intensive multi-process and multi-threaded applications such as GUI applications, the performance impact experienced by the end-user may be acceptable, which is the case in our Chrome case study.

Obfuscating the instructions of the inserted checks increases the security, but degrades the performance and increases the size of the protected binary. This makes application of self-checksumming practical for less CPU-intensive applications and in situations where only a subset security critical set of the functions of the PE are protected.

One possible direction of future work is protecting the information from data blocks. This feature would protect hard coded values such as URLs and pointers to functions in other libraries. Another direction of future work is using profiling information from the original (unprotected) PE, to create groups of basic blocks or functions according to their execution frequency. This would enable picking checkees as hotter code and checkers as less hot code. This feature would reduce the performance overhead of the protected binary.

7. REFERENCES

[1] I. Anati, S. Gueron, S. Johnson, and V. Scarlata. Innovative technology for cpu based attestation and sealing. In *Proceedings of the 2nd international workshop on hardware and architectural support for security and privacy*, volume 13, 2013.

[2] S. Banescu, A. Pretschner, D. Battré, S. Cazzulani, R. Shield, and G. Thompson. Software-based protection against changeware. In *Proceedings of the 5th ACM Conference on Data and Application Security and Privacy*, pages 231–242. ACM, 2015.

[3] C. W. Barrett, R. Sebastiani, S. A. Seshia, and C. Tinelli. Satisfiability modulo theories. *Handbook of satisfiability*, 185:825–885, 2009.

[4] B. Blietz and A. Tyagi. Software tamper resistance through dynamic program monitoring. *Lecture Notes in Computer Science (including subseries Lecture Notes in Artificial Intelligence and Lecture Notes in Bioinformatics)*, 3919 LNCS:146–163, 2006.

[5] H. Chang and M. J. Atallah. Protecting software code by guards. In *Security and privacy in digital rights management*, pages 160–175. Springer, 2001.

[6] Y. Chen, R. Venkatesan, M. Cary, R. Pang, S. Sinha, and M. H. Jakubowski. Oblivious hashing: A stealthy software integrity verification primitive. In *International Workshop on Information Hiding*, pages 400–414. Springer, 2002.

[7] A. Colesa, R. Tudoran, and S. Banescu. Software random number generation based on race conditions. In *Symbolic and Numeric Algorithms for Scientific Computing, 2008. SYNASC'08. 10th International Symposium on*, pages 439–444. IEEE, 2008.

[8] C. Collberg, S. Martin, J. Myers, and J. Nagra. Distributed application tamper detection via continuous software updates. In *Proceedings of the 28th Annual Computer Security Applications Conference*, pages 319–328. ACM, 2012.

[9] P. Dewan, D. Durham, H. Khosravi, M. Long, and G. Nagabhushan. A hypervisor-based system for protecting software runtime memory and persistent storage. In *Proceedings of the 2008 Spring simulation multiconference*, pages 828–835. Society for Computer Simulation International, 2008.

[10] Evenbalance. PunkBuster — Online Countermeasures, 2015. http://www.evenbalance.com/pbsetup.php, [Online; accessed 20-September-2016].

[11] W.-c. Feng, E. Kaiser, and T. Schluessler. Stealth measurements for cheat detection in on-line games. In *Proceedings of the 7th ACM SIGCOMM Workshop on Network and System Support for Games*, pages 15–20. ACM, 2008.

[12] T. Garfinkel et al. Traps and Pitfalls: Practical Problems in System Call Interposition Based Security Tools. In *NDSS*, volume 3, pages 163–176, 2003.

[13] J. T. Giffin, M. Christodorescu, and L. Kruger. Strengthening software self-checksumming via self-modifying code. In *Computer Security Applications Conference, 21st Annual*, pages 10–pp. IEEE, 2005.

[14] Google. Syzygy – profile guided, post-link executable reordering, 2013. https://github.com/google/syzygy/wiki/SyzygyDesign, [Online; accessed 12-September-2016].

[15] G. Hoglund. Hacking world of warcraft: An exercise in advanced rootkit design. *Black Hat*, 2006.

[16] B. Horne, L. Matheson, C. Sheehan, and R. E. Tarjan. Dynamic self-checking techniques for improved tamper resistance. In *Security and privacy in digital rights management*, pages 141–159. Springer, 2001.

[17] Intel. Intel Active Management Technology — Query, Restore, Upgrade, and Protect Devices Remotely, 2016. http://www.intel.com/content/www/us/en/architecture-and-technology/intel-active-management-technology.html, [Online; accessed 20-September-2016].

[18] M. Jacob, M. H. Jakubowski, P. Naldurg, C. W. N. Saw, and R. Venkatesan. The superdiversifier: Peephole individualization for software protection. In *International Workshop on Security*, pages 100–120. Springer, 2008.

[19] M. Jakobsson and K.-A. Johansson. Retroactive detection of malware with applications to mobile platforms. In *Proceedings of the 5th USENIX Conference on Hot Topics in Security*, HotSec'10, pages 1–13, Berkeley, CA, USA, 2010. USENIX Association.

[20] M. H. Jakubowski, C. W. N. Saw, and R. Venkatesan. Tamper-tolerant software: Modeling and implementation. In *International Workshop on Security*,

pages 125–139. Springer, 2009.

[21] P. Junod, J. Rinaldini, J. Wehrli, and J. Michielin. Obfuscator-LLVM: software protection for the masses. In *Proceedings of the 1st International Workshop on Software Protection*, pages 3–9. IEEE Press, 2015.

[22] E. Kaiser, W.-c. Feng, and T. Schluessler. Fides: Remote anomaly-based cheat detection using client emulation. In *Proceedings of the 16th ACM conference on Computer and communications security*, pages 269–279. ACM, 2009.

[23] S. Mansfield-Devine. The promise of whitelisting. *Network Security*, 2009(7):4–6, 2009.

[24] L. Martignoni, R. Paleari, and D. Bruschi. Conqueror: Tamper-proof code execution on legacy systems. *Lecture Notes in Computer Science (including subseries Lecture Notes in Artificial Intelligence and Lecture Notes in Bioinformatics)*, 6201 LNCS:21–40, 2010.

[25] W. Michiels and P. Gorissen. Mechanism for software tamper resistance: an application of white-box cryptography. In *Proceedings of the 2007 ACM workshop on Digital Rights Management*, pages 82–89. ACM, 2007.

[26] B. Morgan, E. Alata, V. Nicomette, M. Kaâniche, and G. Averlant. Design and implementation of a hardware assisted security architecture for software integrity monitoring. In *Dependable Computing (PRDC), 2015 IEEE 21st Pacific Rim International Symposium on*, pages 189–198. IEEE, 2015.

[27] M. Pietrek. Peering inside the PE: a tour of the win32 (R) portable executable file format. *Microsoft Systems Journal-US Edition*, pages 15–38, 1994.

[28] J. Qiu, B. Yadegari, B. Johannesmeyer, S. Debray, and X. Su. Identifying and understanding self-checksumming defenses in software. In *Proceedings of the 5th ACM Conference on Data and Application Security and Privacy*, pages 207–218. ACM, 2015.

[29] S. Schrittwieser, S. Katzenbeisser, J. Kinder, G. Merzdovnik, and E. Weippl. Protecting Software through Obfuscation: Can It Keep Pace with Progress in Code Analysis? *ACM Computing Surveys (CSUR)*, 49(1):4, 2016.

[30] A. Seshadri, M. Luk, E. Shi, A. Perrig, L. van Doorn, and P. Khosla. Pioneer: Verifying Code Integrity and Enforcing Untampered Code Execution on Legacy Systems. *ACM SIGOPS Operating Systems Review*, 2005.

[31] H. Shacham, M. Page, B. Pfaff, E.-J. Goh, N. Modadugu, and D. Boneh. On the effectiveness of address-space randomization. In *Proceedings of the 11th ACM conference on Computer and communications security*, pages 298–307. ACM, 2004.

[32] K. Thomas, E. Bursztein, C. Grier, G. Ho, N. Jagpal, A. Kapravelos, D. McCoy, A. Nappa, V. Paxson, P. Pearce, et al. Ad injection at scale: Assessing deceptive advertisement modifications. In *2015 IEEE Symposium on Security and Privacy*, pages 151–167. IEEE, 2015.

[33] K. Thomas, J. A. E. Crespo, R. Rasti, J.-M. Picod, C. Phillips, C. Sharp, F. Tirelo, A. Tofigh, M.-A. Courteau, L. Ballard, et al. Investigating Commercial Pay-Per-Install and the Distribution of Unwanted Software. In *USENIX Security Symposium*, 2016.

[34] L. Thomason. TinyXML2. https://github.com/leethomason/tinyxml2, 2016. [Online; accessed 20-September-2016].

[35] Valve. Valve Anti-Cheat System (VAC), 2015. https://support.steampowered.com/kb_article.php?p_faqid=370, [Online; accessed 20-September-2016].

[36] B. Wyseur. White-box cryptography. In *Encyclopedia of Cryptography and Security*, pages 1386–1387. Springer, 2011.

[37] Y. Younan, W. Joosen, and F. Piessens. Code Injection in C and C++ : A Survey of Vulnerabilities and Countermeasures. In *Technical report, KU Leuven*, 2004.

APPENDIX

Blocks vs. DLLs	100	200	300	400
50	0.394	0.481	0.676	1.240
100	0.580	1.105	1.317	1.086
500	3.045	223.579	6299.026	14894.043
1000	7.057	376.748	9023.435	21225.647

Table 2: Time (in seconds) needed by *equation system reduction algorithm* (presented in Section 3.3.2), to output the solution (including equation solving by the SMT solver), corresponding to randomly generated Q matrices having n blocks (indicated in the first column) and d DLLs (indicated in the first row). Note that the performance numbers may vary depending on the actual values inside of the Q matrix and the random seed used by the SMT solver.

Fault Attacks on Encrypted General Purpose Compute Platforms

Robert Buhren[3], Shay Gueron[1,2], Jan Nordholz[3], Jean-Pierre Seifert[4], Julian Vetter[3]
[1]shay@math.haifa.ac.il, University of Haifa, Israel
[2]Intel Corporation, Intel Development Center, Israel
[3]{robert, jnordholz, julian}@sec.t-labs.tu-berlin.de, TU Berlin, Germany
[4]jean-pierre.seifert@telekom.de, TU Berlin, Germany

ABSTRACT

Adversaries with physical access to a target platform can perform cold boot or DMA attacks to extract sensitive data from the RAM. To prevent such attacks, hardware vendors announced respective processor extensions. AMD's extension SME will provide means to encrypt the RAM to protect security-relevant assets that reside there. The encryption will protect the user's content against passive eavesdropping.

However, the level of protection it provides in scenarios that involve an adversary who cannot only read from RAM but also change content in RAM is less clear.

This paper addresses the open research question whether encryption alone is a dependable protection mechanism in practice when considering an active adversary. To this end, we first build a software based memory encryption solution on a desktop system which mimics AMD's SME. Subsequently, we demonstrate a proof-of-concept fault attack on this system, by which we are able to extract the private RSA key of a GnuPG user. Our work suggests that transparent memory encryption is not enough to prevent active attacks.

Keywords

Fault injection; main memory encryption

1. INTRODUCTION

Adversaries use cold boot attacks [13, 27] to steal data from main memory. Transparent encryption of the main memory (with a secret key that is not stored in RAM), leaves the adversary with only one snapshot of ciphertext, therefore providing perfect mitigation against it. Hardware vendors also acknowledged this threat, with AMD announcing new processor extensions to mitigate such a threat. AMD's SME (Secure Memory Encryption) [19] provides ways to encrypt parts of the RAM and leave the adversary only with ciphertext.

Although the above mechanism protects the privacy of the user's data, it is less clear whether such transparent encryption is enough against an active adversary. Looking

at previous work (e.g., [3, 6, 30]) reveals that a number of different hardware interfaces, e.g., Thunderbolt, Firewire, PCIe, PCMCIA and USB ports, can be used for attack purposes. Again the threat can be mitigated by adding integrity protection to the RAM. Unfortunately, adding integrity to the RAM is complex [11, 29] and requires dedicated storage on the RAM, for integrity tags, consuming an overhead of >20%.

Thus, the above discussion leads to the following question, which is the focus of this paper. Can transparent memory encryption protect the system from active attacks and obviate the need for expensive authentication? The presence of encryption limits the active adversary in a fundamental way, by blinding him in two ways. He does not know what data is being changed on the encrypted RAM, and he has no control on the resulting value when the modified RAM is decrypted. The security properties in our scenario cannot be proven, so the discussion is reduced to the question of the practicality of two-way blinded attacks. We address the problem here and show that the protection offered by transparent encryption against active adversaries is not guaranteed.

We make the following contributions: a) We designed a memory encryption scheme that replicates the functionality SME implements in hardware. Our prototype is embedded into the Linux kernel. b) We built a proof-of-concept fault attack on GnuPG [20]. With our attack we are able to reveal the private RSA key of a GnuPG user. We employed a mechanism based on LLC (Last Level Cache) probing to time our attack. We combine this information with a kernel page allocator prediction mechanism to inject a fault into the victim application's encrypted data in order to cause a predictable effect. c) We discuss the challenges that an adversary needs to overcome in order to extend our proof-of-concept attack to a real attack.

2. PRELIMINARIES & TECHNICAL BACKGROUND

This section describes some background that is crucial for understanding the rest of the paper without requiring the reader to be a priori familiar with these details.

The Boneh-DeMillo-Lipton fault attack on RSA-CRT.

We use the Boneh-DeMillo-Lipton fault attack [7], which can be applied to a device that computes RSA signatures using the CRT. The attack is based on obtaining two signatures of the same message m. The first one is correct, and denoted by s. The second one is faulty, and is obtained by injecting some corruption (to the computing apparatus),

CODASPY'17, March 22-24, 2017, Scottsdale, AZ, USA
© 2017 ACM. ISBN 978-1-4503-4523-1/17/03. . . $15.00
DOI: http://dx.doi.org/10.1145/3029806.3029836

that is *timed appropriately* so that the value of s_q is computed correctly, but s_p is corrupted to s'_p. The recombination yields the faulty signature s'. It satisfies (with very high likelihood) $q = gcd(s' - s, n)$, thus leading to factorizing n and hence to discovering the secret exponent d.

Cache architecture.

Modern x86 processors have multiple levels of caches. The LLC (Last Level Cache) is usually shared among all CPU cores on the chip. However Intel splits the LLC into several parts where each CPU core has a local part of the LLC and can access remote parts with an increased latency.

The cache is divided into so-called cache lines. On a x86-64 system, the typical size of a cache line is 64 Bytes. The x86-64 caches operate in a set-associative mode. All available slots are grouped into sets of a specific size. This number varies, depending on the processor and the size of the cache. Each memory chunk can be stored in all slots of one particular set.

The addressing of the cache is determined by various bits of the physical address. The lowest bits of each address denote the offset inside the cache line. The intermediate bits determine the set. The remaining high bits form the address tag, that has to be stored with each cache line for the later lookup. Additionally, when looking at the Sandy Bridge LLC, the high address bits are also taken into consideration for the calculation of the cache slice [15].

When looking at the set-associativity, it can be observed that, memory addresses with identical index bits compete on the available slots of one set. Hence, memory accesses may evict and replace other memory content from the caches.

3. ATTACK MODEL

In this paper we consider general purpose compute platforms (e.g. desktop computers or laptops) which are located in an untrusted environment. For such a scenario AMD's memory encryption provides an appealing option. SME is a general purpose mechanism to encrypt the RAM, which works on desktops, laptops and workstation systems.

We consider the following attack scenario. The adversary was able to install an unprivileged malware process on the system. He however does not have root privileges on the system. The adversary can also physically access the platform (e.g. plug in a USB stick or connect a firewire device). Of course, we suppose that the victim is aware of the valuable assets on his compute platform, and has therefore activated main memory encryption to protect specific processes. It is important to note that we do not assume any vulnerabilities in the underlying OS kernel. We also do not assume that the adversary and the victim necessarily share CPU cores.

In particular, this leads to the following assumptions: a) the memory is encrypted, i.e., the adversary does not know what values are encrypted; b) the memory accessing tools can retrieve only ciphertext, and the adversary has no access to the encryption keys; c) the adversary has the ability to modify memory locations using a physical device (as described in Section 1). Since he modifies only ciphertext, the modifications lead to some kind of unpredictable corruption of the plaintext.

4. SOFTWARE BASED MAIN MEMORY ENCRYPTION

We implemented a software based main memory encryption scheme to replicate the functionality of AMD's SME. It works transparently without any need to modify the running applications. We used AES as the block cipher and leveraged the dedicated hardware AES instructions (AES-NI).

4.1 Implementation

We wrote a kernel module that notifies the kernel on "protection worthy" applications, and extended the Linux kernel itself to perform the encryption. From the driver, we are able to enable/disable the encryption in general, and to notify the kernel about processes (identified by their process IDs) deserving encryption. The driver holds a protection list with PIDs, for which the memory pages should be encrypted when the process is currently not running.

Figure 1 illustrates the main encryption procedure. When the Linux OS decides to schedule a new process, it calls the function `schedule()`. In this function, the OS switches to the new process' memory context (`context_switch()` ①). We installed a hook in this function, to determine whether the last scheduled process belonged to our protection list. If so, we call `do_encmem` ② to encrypt all present (writable) 4 KBytes pages in place. After all the pages are encrypted, we return to the `context_switch()` method ③. Subsequently, normal execution is resumed, and the memory contents of our process has been encrypted ④. We also check whether the next process is in our protection list, and then decrypt all of its writable pages to make it ready for execution.

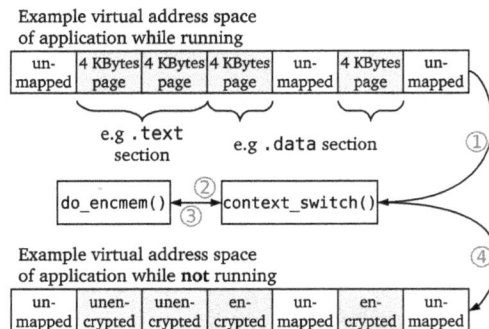

Figure 1: Main memory transparent encryption scheme. When the Linux kernel schedules a new process all present pages of our process are encrypted in place.

For simplicity, the encryption code and the necessary keys are stored in RAM, but it does not matter for our demonstration that only tests a fault injection. Other publications [9, 26] have already shown how to store cryptographic material outside of RAM and also perform cryptographic computation without leaking sensitive material to RAM. Our scheme could easily adopt such mechanisms. Still, it is important to note that our implementation does not provide a complete and secure solution by any means. Its sole purpose is to behave like a hardware scheme and provide a means to demonstrate our fault injection.

	Property	Software impl.	AMD SME
1	Unit of encryption	4096 Bytes	64 Bytes
2	DMA access to enc. memory possible	yes	yes
3	Memory authentication	no	no (?)
4	Encryption enforced by	Operating system	Memory controller

Table 1: Difference between AMD SME and our software prototype.

4.2 Software Implementation vs. AMD SME

Since AMD's processor extensions SME are not available on the market yet, we implemented the software based memory encryption as close as possible to the information AMD revealed thus far [2, 19]. The requirements for the fault attack to work can be broken down into four properties. In Tab. 1 we show what these properties are and to what extent our software implementation differs with respect to AMD SME. We now discuss whether or not this impacts the fault attack (with the indexing we refer to the properties as depicted in Tab. 1):

1 The *unit of encryption* determines the required precision of a fault attack and the size of the affected area. On decryption every bit in the affected plaintext block might be faulty. Whether this is an advantage or disadvantage for an attacker depends on the situation: sometimes the target of the injection may lie close to other vital data which an attacker would like to keep unscathed; at other times locating the target may be more difficult, so a reduced precision requirement would be beneficial.

The attack used in our paper is not affected by the block size, as we can reliably determine the location of the target prime with sufficient granularity. Furthermore it is irrelevant for the Boneh-DeMillo-Lipton fault attack how many bits are changed.

2 According to AMD's documentation *DMA read/write access to encrypted memory* is *possible*. This is of course a core requirement for the attack to work.

3 All documentation from AMD show that *memory authentication* is not applied, because authenticating the entire encrypted memory would cause a substantial storage overhead.

4 For our software implementation the *encryption* is *enforced by* the operating system, therefore a determined adversary with kernel-level access could disable the encryption. However, in this paper we only consider fault attacks on the encrypted memory itself, as our kernel-level implementation only serves as a vehicle to demonstrate unauthenticated memory encryption. We do not claim that our pure software implementation provides an equivalent security level to a hardware implementation inside the memory controller like AMD SME. Thus, this difference does not impact the attack mechanism.

5. ATTACKING GNUPG

Our attack combines the fault injection principle with traffic analysis based on cache side channels. It introduces

different ways to leverage this combination in order to attack cryptographic applications on a general purpose platform. To have a concise description, we kept our attack simple and describe only a proof-of-concept. We solve the practical problems in Section 6. To test our attack on a real application, we performed our fault attack on the RSA signing operation in GnuPG Version 1. As almost all commonly used email clients provide a way to integrate GnuPG into the application to sign and encrypt emails, we deemed this a reasonable target.

We first provide a short roadmap on the different components of the attack, because it integrates multiple mechanisms which have to be timed correctly in order for the attack to work. Fig. 2 gives an overview of each step of the attack. The details for every step of the attack are given in the following sections.

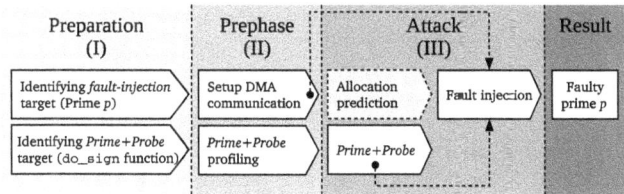

Figure 2: The three phases of our attack on GnuPG.

Preparation: fault injection target.

From Fig. 2-I can be obtained that the first step is to identify a potential fault injection target. GnuPG uses the CRT to speed up the exponentiation in RSA signatures (see Section 2). We run GnuPG 1.4.19 with the signature checking disabled[1]. An RSA key in GnuPG consists of six elements: n, e, d, p, q and q_{inv}, which are stored in a key file on disk. So for using the Boneh-DeMillo-Lipton we want to inject the fault into one of the primes p or q. The key file itself is protected with a passphrase (in this case, using 3DES). Before the signing operation commences, the user has to type in his password in order to unlock the key. Only then, the key elements are decrypted to main memory.

Preparation: Prime+Probe target.

In general *Prime+Probe* [23] monitors cache eviction. The adversary selects a number of addresses that fall into the same cache set as the one from the victim binary. In the *prime* phase the adversary fills the cache sets with his own garbage data. The adversary *idles* for a few cycles, and then *probes* in the last step. There, he measures the access time to the addresses that fall into that same cache set as the one from the victim binary. If the victim process executed at the specific address, it would have evicted some of the adversary's cache lines.

So for our attack we need to identify a feasible *Prime+Probe* target (Fig. 2-I). By inspecting the GnuPG binary we can determine an address in the executable section of the binary where the key is already present in main memory. In our case, this is the function `do_sign` in the file `g10/sign.c`. The virtual address of this function can be determined by

---

[1]The parameter `-no-sig-create-check` disables the signature checking.

inspecting the binary (e.g. by using `objdump`). By mapping the binary into our address space and again leveraging the `pagemap` we can determine the physical address of that function. Then, we have to determine where this physical address is stored in the LLC. Afterwards we have to determine a number of memory locations that, in terms of cache set and slice collide with the physical address of the `do_sign` function. With these information we can later carry out the *Prime+Probe* attack.

Prephase: setup DMA communication.

In the prephase of the attack we need to setup the DMA communication (Fig. 2-II) As described in Section 3 we defined that the adversary was able to spawn a process on the same host, but has also connected a remote DMA device (e.g. laptop). Now, in order to inject the fault at the right time the adversarial process has to notify the external DMA device about when to inject the fault. To do this, the adversarial process allocates a piece of memory and determines the physical address of the allocation using the `pagemap` (details are deferred to Section 6). The determined location is then sent to the external agent (who can then set his DMA device to this address location). Once negotiated, the adversarial process uses this memory location to notify the external DMA device when to inject the fault (by writing a specific pattern to this location)[2]. The adversary can of course also notify the external agent via network, but depending on the configuration of the system and the requirement for stealthiness of the attack this might be problematic.

Attack: Prime+Probe.

To successfully carry out the *Prime+Probe* attack we have to constantly calculate the mean access time over all twelve addresses. If this exceeds a certain threshold, we know that one of the addresses has been evicted from the cache, probably because the victim process has reached the *do_sign* function in its execution. The threshold value which needs to be exceeded is determined experimentally in a prephase of the attack (Fig. 2-II), details on exact values for our attacked platform are given in Section 7.

Attack: fault injection.

The actual attack starts by checking whether GnuPG was started, and then beginning to do the *Prime+Probe* (Fig. 2-III). When the attack process determines that GnuPG executes the `do_sign` function, we enforce a schedule call. GnuPG is then put in to the background, and its memory gets encrypted. This is of course just a vehicle because our software-based main memory encryption only works for processes in the background. In a real hardware implementation this would not be necessary. We then have to determine the location where to inject the fault. To do so we profiled GnuPG beforehand to determine the location of the key structure in memory (Fig. 2-III "Allocation prediction"). We predict the physical location of the key structure using a PFN leakage mechanism (again the details are described in Section 6). We then use the remote DMA to inject the fault (Fig. 2-III). For this purpose we extended the

---

[2]When using a DMA device to inject the fault, the RAM access is still performed by the memory controller through the root complex [30], therefore ECC (Error Correcting Code) is irrelevant.

Inception framework [24] to be able to read and write memory via a FireWire cable (limitations to this approach and countermeasures are discussed in Section 8). After the fault has been injected, we resume the execution of GnuPG. The kernel will decrypt all memory pages of GnuPG to make it runnable again, among them the one with the modified memory location. Once decrypted the value of p will be faulty. GnuPG will then create the faulty signature. Finally, we calculate q offline based on the obtained faulty signature (see Section 2).

6. REAL-WORLD CHALLENGES

In Section 5 we described a fault attack against GnuPG. In order to convert this proof of concept into a real world attack, the adversary faces four challenges:

1. Determine *Prime+Probe* target addresses.
2. Physical addresses of dynamic data structures.
3. Obtain two signatures of the same message.
4. Find suitable hardware interfaces.

We address these challenges in the following sections.

Determine Prime+Probe target addresses.

In general the adversary is looking into ways to obtain the translation of virtual to physical addresses for the use in his *Prime+Probe* attack, and also for the fault injection. Which addresses the adversary wants to obtain, is of course very specific to the attacked target. In our case, this is the `do_sign` function of GnuPG. Obtaining the virtual address of this function is quite easy (as shown in Section 5). The major Linux distributions only slowly adopt position independent binaries. For now we can safely rely on the virtual addresses we can obtain when inspecting the binary with, e.g. `objdump`.

The `/proc/<pid>/pagemap` file can be used to obtain a physical address. For every user-space page, the `pagemap` provides a 64 bit value, indexed by its virtual page number, which contains information regarding the presence of the page in RAM. Bit 63 determines whether the page is present in memory and bits 0 to 54 encode its page frame number. Under the assumption that the underlying memory is shared between adversary and victim, the adversary can just use `mmap` to map the GnuPG binary into his address space. Then he uses the `pagemap` to determine the physical address of the function.

Physical addresses of dynamic data structures.

The location of the key data structure (that includes p) is not only unknown, but also differs for every execution, because it is stored on a writable page (on the heap). To obtain the physical address of this dynamic data structure an adversary can again draw on the `pagemap` mechanism.

The adversary can trace a single execution run of GnuPG with the desired commandline parameters and concurrently monitor the pagemap for new page allocations. Mere syscall tracing is insufficient, as the adversary needs to know the actual physical memory footprint of the process, not the number and size of allocations. As Linux employs a lazy allocation strategy, page ranges which have been requested by `mmap` but not touched will not have physical backing at all. Whereas other areas that do not require explicit allocation (e.g. stack growth) may indeed cause the number of consumed physical pages to increase. Once the adversary has reached the point where p is copied into memory, the trace is complete.

In our case, we determined that p will be placed on the 10th allocated page. This knowledge still does not tell the adversary the exact physical address where the key will be located in a future run of GnuPG. However he can take advantage of the fact that the Linux kernel allocator tends to give out pages that where freed shortly before. So, most recently freed memory pages are given out first to processes. Thus the adversary can allocate a number of physical memory pages (i.e. allocate them and actually perform write operations to them), consult the `pagemap` to determine their physical addresses, and free the pages again. Since the Linux kernel will most likely give out these very same pages to GnuPG the adversary can predict which physical page will contain the key. Freeing the pages has of course to be timed correctly by the adversary so that no other program gets these pages. But this can easily be combined with the already running *Prime+Probe* attack.

Our observations also showed that if our prediction fails, i.e. the 10th page allocated to GnuPG did not match the 10th from last page freed beforehand, that no newly allocated page matched any freed page at all. Also the accuracy of the prediction astonishingly depends on the overall number of pages the adversary allocated before. The exact success probability of such an attack is presented in Section 7.

Obtaining two signatures of the same message.

There are several ways an adversary could obtain a signature for the same message twice. But first there is an obstacle the adversary has to overcome. Along with the message that should be signed GnuPG puts a Unix timestamp into the hash calculation. Fortunately for the adversary, the timestamp is only in second granularity. So, when the adversary is able to motivate the victim to create two signatures from the same message shortly one after the other he gets the desired double signature.

There are a number of scenarios the adversary could leverage. Any form of signed *auto-reply* message (e.g. *out-of-office* notifications) would work for the adversary. It is possible to configure all commonly used email clients (e.g. Outlook, Thunderbird, Apple Mail, etc.) to sign *auto-reply* messages with a defined key. The GnuPG options `-passphrase-file`, `-passphrase-fd` or `-passphrase` allow a user to provide the passphrase for the signing key either directly from the commandline, some file or from a file descriptor. It is questionable, from a security perspective, to store the passphrase for the key in a file, however, such scenarios exist.

Find suitable hardware interfaces.

In our attack we rely on the FireWire interface. One could argue that modern systems might not be equipped with a FireWire controller anymore. However, our attack can not only be performed through a native FireWire port, but also via ExpressCard/PCMCIA expansion ports or a Thunderbolt to FireWire adapter. It is likely that a system has at least one of the aforementioned interfaces.

7. ATTACK RESULTS

All experiments were conducted on a Lenovo Thinkpad

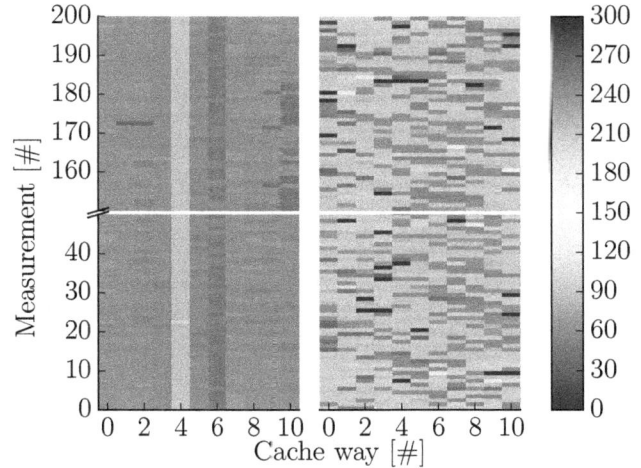

Figure 3: Cache way access times measured with `rtscp`.

T520 with an Intel Core i7-2670QM CPU and 4 GBytes of RAM. This platform uses the aforementioned hash function for LLC slice determination. The device is equipped with a FireWire interface, and we verified the above described memory modification capabilities. Software-wise we used Debian 8 "Jessie" with a Linux kernel version 4.0.

7.1 Prime+Probe results

For our attack we had to determine a threshold for the cache eviction in order to perform the *Prime+Probe* attack. All accesses were measured using the `rtscp` instruction[3]. We divided our measurements into two sets $\{A\}$ and $\{B\}$.

- Set $\{A\}$ was our baseline: we chose twelve set-colliding memory locations, accessed all of them to allocate them into the cache, and then immediately measured the access time for all twelve locations again.

- For set $\{B\}$, we chose twelve memory locations that fell into the same cache set and slice as the address we want to monitor. We accessed all of them once, then we executed one instruction from our victim application (GnuPG) at exactly that address, and finally measured the access time for our twelve lines again.

Cache ways.

First, we had to figure out if we are able to reliably measure variations in access times to addresses from the same cache set. Fig. 3 illustrates this experiment.

Set $\{A\}$ is represented by the left column. Our assumption was that the measured access time would be very low, because all twelve locations fit into the cache. Since no other application ran in between, all access requests would be served by the cache. In [22], Levinthal shows that when an access request to an address takes ~40 cycles, it indicates that it was served from the LLC. Indeed, all access times were in the range between 0 and 40 cycles.

---

[3] `rtscp` is a serializing call that prevents reordering around the call, and returns the number of executed processor cycles.

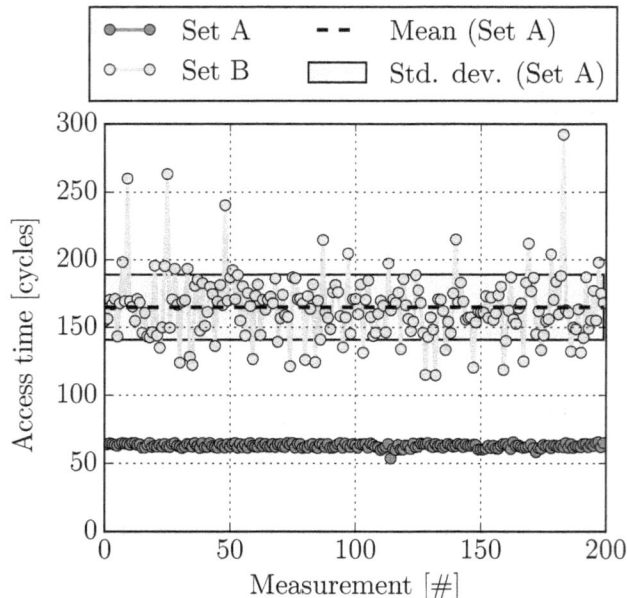

Figure 4: The mean access time over 200 measurements.

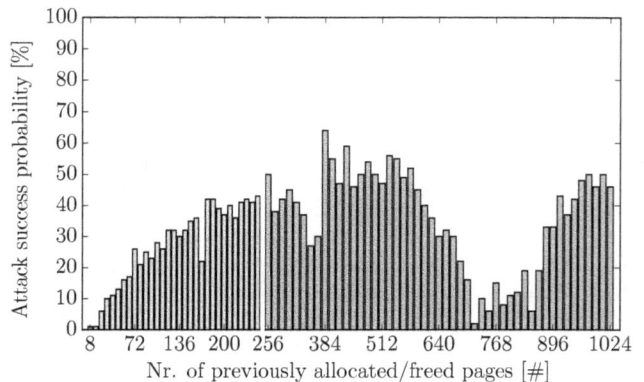

Figure 5: Attack success probability based on the previously allocated and freed memory pages.

Set $\{B\}$ is represented by the right column. Our assumption was that at least one of the addresses had to be evicted from the cache, because the cache only has twelve ways. Indeed, Fig. 3 supports this assumption. The processor had to load some addresses from main memory. We assume that more than one address was evicted from the cache, because our measurements were conducted from a separate application, so not only the victim code ran in between but also other kernel scheduling code, etc. In general we confirmed that we would be able to measure when the victim application executed its binary at a certain memory location.

LLC access.

So far, we confirmed that we could recognize cache eviction in terms of cache ways. To know when a certain application hit a certain address in the executable, we had to specify a reliable threshold. To this end, we calculated the mean value over all twelve access times for set $\{A\}$ and for set $\{B\}$. Fig. 4 illustrates the result, each showing the mean access times over all twelve addresses. Clearly, the mean access time is significantly higher when one of the addresses was accessed. Therefore, we were able to set the threshold to $delta\_mean = mean(\{A\}) \pm std(\{A\})$, corresponding to the yellow bar in Fig. 4. The noise we see in the figure is due to the fact that the victim's data can be partially cached in higher-level caches (leading to faster reads), and the variation in the L1 and L2 contents affects the cache probe time and induces measurement noise.

7.2 Page allocator prediction results

As already described in Section 6 it is necessary to find the physical address of the prime factor p. As it is allocated on the heap it is necessary to somehow predict the right physical address where p is located on. To predict the correct physical address we did the following experiment. First we annotated GnuPG to print the virtual and physical ad-

dress of the prime p. Then, in our adversarial process, we allocated a number of pages using mmap and calculated their respective physical address (using the pagemap). Afterwards we freed all these pages and let GnuPG run. We then compared if the physical address of the prime p was among our previously allocated and freed pages. We did this with a various number of allocations, ranging from only 8 allocations up to 1024. The result can be obtained from Fig. 5. The figure is split into two parts. The first green bars contain results in steps of 8, after 248 experiments we increased the number of allocations in every measurement run by 16. So the orange bars contain the results from 256 to 1024 in steps of 16. For every allocation step we performed 100 measurements.

What we observed is quite interesting. When the physical address of the prime was among the previously allocated/freed pages it was always on the same one (the 10th last page). It was entirely deterministic which of the previously allocated/freed pages would later contain the prime p. But as can be obtained from the figure only in a certain number of measurements the physical page of the prime was among the allocated/freed pages at all. Moreover, the overall success rate depended on the number of previously allocated/freed pages. We achieved a maximum success rate of $\sim$55-60% when allocating and freeing between 380 and 500 pages before executing GnuPG. This value is already surprisingly high, given that the window of uncertainty (the time between the release of the pages and GnuPG receiving a page for p) includes the creation of a process and thus a full address space. A determined attacker could employ the techniques used in this paper to release pages much closer to the critical allocation, thus further boosting his chances.

8. RELATED WORK

In the following section we present a number of topics which are relevant for this work.

Cache-based side channels.

Cache-based side channels have a long history [28]. In recent years, the focus has been shifted toward the LLC [12, 15, 32]. But these attacks are harder to carry out, because, e.g., Intel uses an undocumented hash function to distribute addresses to different segments of the LLC. Thus, initially, a lot of effort has been put into reverse engineering this hash function for different processor generations [15,25]. Based on these new findings, a number of attacks have been proposed. Yarom et al. [32] show how to extract the private encryption keys from a victim program in a single operating system and also over VM boundaries.

Mitigating cache-based side channels remains a challenging task. In [21], Kong et al. investigate several schemes to mitigate cache attacks. Also, modern Intel server CPUs provide a technology called CAT (Cache Allocation Technology) [17] to prevent traffic analysis by other processes or VMs through eavesdropping the LLC.

procfs.

The procfs provides user applications with useful information about the current system state. However, often these information can be used as a means to spy on other processes or resources in a system. Jana and Shmatikov [18] show how to exploit information provided by procfs to create detailed profiles of applications. They use memory consumption discrepancies of a browser to determine which website the user currently looks at. Zhou et al. [33] leverage, among other sources, the procfs and sysfs to gather detailed information about the user of an Android smartphone.

procfs is an important resources in Linux' system architecture. Many applications (e.g. `ps`, `netstat`) rely on information exported through procfs. Therefore disabling this filesystem is not an option. However, as already done with many other files in procfs the access to some security critical files should be limited to admin users. For the `pagemap` this already happened. Since Linux kernel version 4.2, when reading the file only returns valid data if the user holds an admin capability. The access to other security critical information that are exported through procfs, e.g., `kallsyms` were also limited in the past.

DMA.

In order to launch our fault attack we rely on DMA. A lot of attacks have been proposed to launch a DMA based attack using various interfaces [3,31]. In 2006 Boileau [6] showed the remote DMA capabilities of the Firewire bus. More recent attacks have been proposed by Sevinsky [30] in 2013. Sevinsky used the Thunderbolt interface to launch a DMA attack.

The obvious countermeasure to prevent DMA attacks is using an IOMMU [1,16]. However, when running a 32Bit Linux kernel the IOMMU (if present) never gets enabled. On 64Bit systems the Linux kernel makes use of the IOMMU to block remote DMA accesses. However, it is highly processor specific whether the system contains an IOMMU or not. If no IOMMU is present users are advised to disable the bus master capabilities of specific devices.

Fault attacks.

Fault attacks are a well-known concept in computer security. Initial work on fault attacks was done by Boneh et al. [7] in 1997. In this groundbreaking work they show that various cryptographic algorithms can be attacked using hardware fault injection. Since then, several fault attacks have been proposed. In 2003 Dusart et al. [10] describe a differential fault analysis attack on AES. They are able to break an AES128 key with around 10 faulty messages.

In the early work of Boneh et al. [7], the authors already propose the use of random padding[4] to protect against their attack (as suggested by Bellare and Rogaway [5]). Also cryptographic padding (e.g. OAEP [4]) was already discussed in [5,7] and would also prevent the fault attack to work.

Main memory encryption.

Henson et al. [14] provide a survey on memory encryption techniques. Other work on main memory encryption has been done by Chhabra et al [8]. They propose an encryption scheme for systems with NVMM (non-volatile main memory). The attack scenario is valid for mobile devices, where an adversary would be able to easily read out the RAM cells. In [26], Müller et al. propose an architecture called TRESOR. TRESOR makes cold boot attacks difficult, because instead of using RAM, it ensures that all encryption states as well as the secret key and any part of it are only stored in processor registers.

Memory authentication.

An integrity tree is the classical way to provide authentication to a larger amount of data. Elbaz et al. [11] provide an overview of several concepts for memory authentication. Among them are classical concepts like Merkle Trees. These are binary trees where each node holds a hash digest of its two children, and the lowest leaves hold digests of the protected data units. However, the overhead in storage (~20%) is infeasible when condering to encrypt the entire main memory.

Signature verification.

It is important to note that we did not exploit any vulnerability in GnuPG. In default operation mode, GnuPG verifies the generated signatures, and if an error is detected, it terminates with an error report without releasing the (faulty) signature. However, the command line parameter `-no-sig-create-check` exists, and made our attack possible. Fortunately, this parameter exists only in GnuPG version 1, and GnuPG version 2 removed the command line option completely. The OpenSSL library always verifies a signature before releasing it, and repeats the computation without using CRT in case an error is detected. There is no option to disable the check other than by modifying the source code, and this type of threat is not part of our attack model.

9. CONCLUSION

Threat scenarios that include an active adversary on a dynamic system require memory encryption for privacy, and memory authentication for integrity. The scenario became even more relevant due to the fact that hardware vendors now acknowledged this threat and therefore provide solutions. So the question addressed in this paper is the following. Is it reasonable (and to what extent), in order to save the high cost of dedicated authentication mechanisms, to rely on encryption to protect both privacy and integrity?

To answer this question, we showed the possibility of fault attacks on memory that is encrypted with no authentication. Of course, our attack is complex, and implementing it even as a proof-of-concept was a serious challenge. The complexity results from the protection that the encryption provides by itself.

---

[4]It is interesting that GnuPG version 1 is not using random padding.

Nevertheless, this work clearly illustrates that sophisticated attacks against the integrity of the memory cannot be dismissed, or at least cannot be ruled out. We therefore propose that memory encryption techniques should include integrity protection, despite the added complexity and performance costs.

10. ACKNOWLEDGMENTS

The second author is supported by the PQCRYPTO project, which is partially funded by the European Commission Horizon 2020 research Programme, grant #645622, by the Blavatnik Interdisciplinary Cyber Research Center (ICRC) at the Tel Aviv University, and by the ISRAEL SCIENCE FOUNDATION (grant No. 1018/16).

The fifth author is supported by the Helmholtz Research School on Security Technologies.

11. REFERENCES

[1] Advanced Micro Devices Inc. AMD I/O Virtualization Technology (IOMMU) Specification, February 2015.

[2] AMD. AMD64 Architecture Programmer's Manual Volume 2: System Programming, April 2016.

[3] M. Becher, M. Dornseif, and C. N. Klein. FireWire: all your memory are belong to us. *Proceedings of CanSecWest*, 2005.

[4] M. Bellare and P. Rogaway. Optimal asymmetric encryption. In *EUROCRYPT'94*, pages 92–111. Springer, 1994.

[5] M. Bellare and P. Rogaway. The exact security of digital signatures-How to sign with RSA and Rabin. In *EUROCRYPT'96*, pages 399–416. Springer, 1996.

[6] A. Boileau. Hit by a bus: Physical access attacks with Firewire. *Presentation, Ruxcon*, page 3, 2006.

[7] D. Boneh, R. A. DeMillo, and R. J. Lipton. On the importance of checking cryptographic protocols for faults. In *EUROCRYPT'97*, pages 37–51. Springer, 1997.

[8] S. Chhabra and D. Solihin. i-NVMM: A secure non-volatile main memory system with incremental encryption. In *38th ISCA*, pages 177–188, June 2011.

[9] P. Colp, J. Zhang, J. Gleeson, S. Suneja, E. de Lara, H. Raj, S. Saroiu, and A. Wolman. Protecting data on smartphones and tablets from memory attacks. In *ASPLOS*, pages 177–189. ACM, 2015.

[10] P. Dusart, G. Letourneux, and O. Vivolo. Differential fault analysis on aes. In *Applied Cryptography and Network Security*, pages 293–306. Springer, 2003.

[11] R. Elbaz, D. Champagne, C. Gebotys, R. B. Lee, N. Potlapally, and L. Torres. Hardware mechanisms for memory authentication: A survey of existing techniques and engines. In *Transactions on Computational Science IV*, pages 1–22. Springer, 2009.

[12] D. Gruss, R. Spreitzer, and S. Mangard. Cache template attacks: Automating attacks on inclusive last-level caches. In *24th USENIX Security*, pages 897–912, 2015.

[13] J. A. Halderman, S. D. Schoen, N. Heninger, W. Clarkson, W. Paul, J. A. Calandrino, A. J. Feldman, J. Appelbaum, and E. W. Felten. Lest we remember: cold-boot attacks on encryption keys. *Communications of the ACM*, 52(5):91–98, 2009.

[14] M. Henson and S. Taylor. Memory encryption: a survey of existing techniques. *ACM Computing Surveys (CSUR)*, 46(4):53, 2014.

[15] R. Hund, C. Willems, and T. Holz. Practical timing side channel attacks against kernel space ASLR. In *IEEE Security and Privacy*, pages 191–205, 2013.

[16] Intel Corporation. Intel Virtualization Technology for Directed I/O, October 2014.

[17] Intel Corporation. Improving Real-Time Performance by Utilizing Cache Allocation Technology Enhancing Performance via Allocation of the Processor's Cache. Whitepaper, April 2015.

[18] S. Jana and V. Shmatikov. Memento: Learning secrets from process footprints. In *IEEE Security and Privacy*, pages 143–157. IEEE, 2012.

[19] D. Kaplan, J. Powell, and T. Woller. White Paper AMD Memory Encryption, April 2016.

[20] W. Koch. The GNU Privacy Guard, January 2016. https://www.gnupg.org/.

[21] J. Kong, O. Aciicmez, J.-P. Seifert, and H. Zhou. Architecting against software cache-based side-channel attacks. *Computers, IEEE Transactions on*, 62(7):1276–1288, 2013.

[22] D. Levinthal. Performance analysis guide for intel core i7 processor and intel xeon 5500 processors. *Intel Performance Analysis Guide*, 30, 2009.

[23] F. Liu, Y. Yarom, Q. Ge, G. Heiser, and R. B. Lee. Last-level cache side-channel attacks are practical. In *IEEE Security and Privacy*, pages 605–622, 2015.

[24] C. Maartmann-Moe. Inception. http://www.breaknenter.org/projects/inception/, April 2016. Accessed: 2016-04-26.

[25] C. Maurice, N. Le Scouarnec, C. Neumann, O. Heen, and A. Francillon. Reverse engineering Intel last-level cache complex addressing using performance counters. In *Research in Attacks, Intrusions, and Defenses*, pages 48–65. Springer, 2015.

[26] T. Müller, F. C. Freiling, and A. Dewald. TRESOR Runs Encryption Securely Outside RAM. In *20th USENIX Security*, pages 17–17, 2011.

[27] T. Müller and M. Spreitzenbarth. Frost. In *Applied Cryptography and Network Security*, pages 373–388. Springer, 2013.

[28] D. A. Osvik, A. Shamir, and E. Tromer. Cache attacks and countermeasures: the case of AES. In *Topics in Cryptology–CT-RSA 2006*, pages 1–20. Springer, 2006.

[29] D. Owen Jr. *The feasibility of memory encryption and authentication*. 2013.

[30] R. Sevinsky. Funderbolt: Adventures in Thunderbolt DMA Attacks. *Black Hat USA*, 2013.

[31] R. Wojtczuk, J. Rutkowska, and A. Tereshkin. Xen 0wning trilogy. *Invisible Things Lab*, 2008.

[32] Y. Yarom and K. Falkner. Flush+reload: a high resolution, low noise, L3 cache side-channel attack. In *23rd USENIX Security*, pages 719–732, 2014.

[33] X. Zhou, S. Demetriou, D. He, M. Naveed, X. Pan, X. Wang, C. A. Gunter, and K. Nahrstedt. Identity, location, disease and more: Inferring your secrets from android public resources. In *2013 ACM CCS*, pages 1017–1028. ACM, 2013.

Analysis of Exception-Based Control Transfers

Babak Yadegari
University of Arizona
Tucson, AZ
babaky@cs.arizona.edu

Jon Stephens
University of Arizona
Tucson, AZ
stephensj2@cs.arizona.edu

Saumya Debray
University of Arizona
Tucson, AZ
debray@cs.arizona.edu

Abstract

Dynamic taint analysis and symbolic execution find many important applications in security-related program analyses. However, current techniques for such analyses do not take proper account of control transfers due to exceptions. As a result, they can fail to account for implicit flows arising from exception-based control transfers, leading to loss of precision and potential false negatives in analysis results. While the idea of using exceptions for obfuscating (unconditional) control transfers is well known, we are not aware of any prior work discussing the use of exceptions to implement conditional control transfers and implicit information flows. This paper demonstrates the problems that can arise in existing dynamic taint analysis and symbolic execution systems due to exception-based implicit information flows and proposes a generic architecture-agnostic solution for reasoning about the behavior of code using user-defined exception handlers. Experimental results from a prototype implementation indicate that the ideas described produce better results than current state-of-the-art systems.

Keywords

Binary Analysis; Dynamic Information Flow; Symbolic Execution

1. INTRODUCTION

Dynamic taint analysis and symbolic execution find numerous applications in privacy- and security-related program analyses. Dynamic taint analysis involves tracking certain data (the tainted values) through the execution of the program; symbolic execution generates path constraints that express the logic of the computation along an execution path. The two techniques can be combined to reason about how input values influence the execution path taken by the program, and thereby identify alternative inputs that can cause a different execution path to be taken. This approach has been applied to a wide variety of security and software testing applications, e.g., test case and exploit generation [7,8,14,24,46],

CODASPY '17, March 22–24, 2017, Scottsdale, AZ, USA.

© 2017 ACM. ISBN 978-1-4503-4523-1/17/03...$15.00

DOI: http://dx.doi.org/10.1145/3029806.3029826

vulnerability detection [9,10,16], and multi-path exploration during dynamic analysis of malware code [2,3,6,35,36].

Given the numerous security-related applications of dynamic taint analysis and symbolic execution, it is important to understand any potential shortcomings of current techniques and devise solutions to mitigate their weaknesses; a failure to do so can potentially lead to flawed conclusions about the software we analyze, e.g., leave application vulnerabilities unidentified or malware execution paths unexplored. Previous studies have discussed some of the limitations of dynamic taint analysis [13,44] and symbolic execution [48,56]. These works all involve "normal" executions where the execution path is (at least in principle) available for inspection. This paper focuses on a different kind of control flow construct, namely, exception-based control transfers where the execution path is not explicit and which can be significantly harder to analyze than conventional control transfers.

It turns out that exception-based control transfers—which are well-known as an obfuscation mechanism and have been widely used in malicious code—can be used to realize implicit information flows in ways that are not detected by any of the existing state-of-the-art dynamic analysis tools we tested including KLEE [7], S2E [16], FuzzBall [4] and angr [49]. The problem arises both for dynamic taint analysis and for symbolic execution. This is because currently, implicit information flow detection and symbolic execution techniques rely on information about the execution path and control flow of the program to reason about alternative execution paths. For instance, dynamic taint analysis approaches (e.g. [17,29]) use program's control flow graph (CFG) to determine whether a dataflow is implicit, i.e., occurs through a control transfer. Similarly in symbolic execution, the analysis relies on syntactic characteristics such as instruction opcodes to identify jump instructions and thereby determine branch conditions and path constraints.

On the other hand, operating systems provide powerful low-level mechanisms, namely, *exceptions*, that allow programs to deal with unexpected situations. These are hardware or software faults (e.g. memory access violation) that cause execution to be transferred to *exception handlers* that take appropriate action. The handlers may be custom routines implemented within an application or default handlers provided by the operating system, and the details of the exception-handling mechanism may depend on the underlying operating system, but at the end, they all have the common behavior of transferring the control of application to a handler that is responsible for handling the occurred exception or fault. The control flow behavior of a program can be obfuscated by using deliberately-induced exceptions to cause execution to be transferred to the handler code as part of the program's "normal" execution [31,40,57]. The simplest manifestation of this idea uses exceptions to implement unconditional jumps to the handler code; however, it is straightforward to extend this idea such that the exception is raised only under specific conditions, thereby realizing exception-based conditional control transfers.

Current techniques for dynamic taint analysis and symbolic execution only take into account normal control transfers and do not consider control transfers due to exceptions. This means that an attacker can exploit the exception mechanism to implement arbitrary control transfers and thereby realize implicit information flows that are not detected using existing analysis techniques. This represents a significant shortcoming of such analyses. Furthermore, fixing the problem is not straightforward because identifying the potential control transfer—i.e., the locations where exceptions can be raised and those where they may be handled—is not always straightforward. We have observed such information flows in existing exploit code. While symbolic execution has a number of challenges, such as path explosion, constraint solving, system calls etc., these have been previously discussed in the literature [11,45] and so are not pursued further here. This paper focuses on a different kind of challenge for symbolic execution that has not been previously studied in detail in the research literature.

This paper proposes a solution to excpetion-based control transers by taking into account the possiblity of a control transfer due to exceptions where the application code contains user-defined exception handlers. In particular, it makes the following contributions:

- It demonstrates the challenges that arise in current dynamic taint analysis and symbolic execution techniques when dealing with exception-based information flow.

- It proposes a generic architecture-agnostic solution for both dynamic taint analysis and symbolic execution to address the shortcomings and hence improves the accuracy and robustness of the analyses.

- It describes a prototype implementation that outperforms the state-of-the-art systems for symbolic execution and dynamic taint analysis if applied against real mal-intended code as well as sample test programs that use exception-based obfuscation techniques.

The remainder of the paper is organized as follows: section 2 discusses motivations and background on dynamic taint analysis and symbolic execution. Section 3 demonstrates the problem in more detail and discusses our ideas to solve this problem followed by our prototype implementation details in section 4. Our evaluation results are presented in section 5. Previous and related works discussed in section 6 and the paper concludes in section 7.

2. BACKGROUND AND MOTIVATING EXAMPLE

2.1 Signals

Signals (exceptions) serve to notify processes of an event or a software or hardware fault. There are two types of signals: *synchronous* and *asynchronous*. A synchronous signal typically results from an error in executing an instruction, e.g., "illegal instruction" (SIGILL) or "illegal memory access" (SIGSEGV). Asynchronous signals are delivered asynchronously and do not depend on the execution context, e.g., SIGSTOP, which stops execution of the receiving process, or SIGKILL, which terminates it. Modern operating systems provide APIs to user applications to overwrite default exception handler routines with their own code. When a signal is delivered to the process, control is transferred to the handler code. This gives the processes flexibility to provide their own routines to recover or clean up after unrecoverable faults. For instance, Windows uses a mechanism called *Structured Exception Handling (SEH)* and Linux uses *Signals*. Despite different implementation details, the high-level concepts are similar between different operating systems.

Synchronous signals are triggered in the course of execution of instructions if the hardware or the operating system is not able to successfully execute the instruction. Such errors are usually severe enough that the execution of the process that caused the fault can not be continued. This type of exceptions are common among different operating systems. Asynchronous signals, on the other hand, are specific to the Unix/Linux operating systems and can interrupt the execution of a process at any instruction. These signals are primarily used for synchronization purposes between different or parent/child processes. Since each category is fundamentally different from the other, we have different solutions for each of these types of events in the programs that are discussed in the rest of this section.

2.2 A Motivating Example

The mechanism allowing users to define their own signal handlers can be misused by attackers to obfuscate branch points in the code to confuse analysis. Figure 1 shows two sample programs using this technique to implicitly propagate sensitive data (Figure 1a), and to redirect the flow of execution on certain environments (Figure 1b).

2.2.1 Synchronous Signals

The code in 1(a) sets handlers for both SIGSEGV and SIGFPE signals where the former is raised by OS and sent to the process on memory access violations and the latter is raised in case of arithmetic errors such as divide by zero. After copying the sensitive data to secret value at line 13, the code intentionally dereferences a NULL pointer which raises a SIGSEGV and so transfers control to segv_handler. After the segv_handler function returns, the control transfers to the instruction that originally generated the fault and since the problem has not been fixed, the operating system raises another SIGSEGV signal and so on. This continues until variable c equals zero meaning that variable public is equal to secret at line 7. At this point, the division operation at line 8 generates an arithmetic fault (divide by zero) which then transfers the control to the fpe_handler. Doing so, the attacker is able to copy the secret value into another variable without any explicit or direct data flow or implicit flow since the control transfer edges are not part of the static CFG of the program.

2.2.2 Asynchronous Signals

Figure 1(b) shows a timing technique that is quite frequently used by malicious codes simply as a timeout mechanism. Figure 1(b) shows a variation of the technique where

```
1:   int public, secret;
2:   void fpe_handler(){
3:        /* public is equal
                to secret here! */
4:   }
5:   void segv_handler(){
6:        public++;
7:        int c = secret - public;
8:        c = c/c;
9:   }
10:  int main(){
11:       signal(SIGFPE,  fpe_handler);
12:       signal(SIGSEGV, segv_handler);
13:       secret  = get_secret();
14:       char *p = NULL
15:       *p++;
16:  }
```

(a) Using synchronous signals for implicit flow

```
     /* foo is a function pointer */
1:   foo = /* some malicious code */
2:   void alarm_handler(){
3:        foo = /* some benign code */
4:   }
5:   int main(){
6:        signal(SIGALRM, alarm_handler);
7:        alarm(1);
8:        for (int i=0; i < THRESHOLD; i+-){
                /* an empty loop that takes more than
                1 second in a hostile environment */
9:        }
10:       alarm(0);
11:       foo();
12:  }
```

(b) Using asynchronous signals to obfuscate control transfers

Figure 1: Branch obfuscation using signals

the signal mechanism can be used as an anti-analysis technique. The process sets a handler for SIGALRM signal at line
6 where the handler code changes the function pointer foo to
point to some malicious code. Line 7 registers a wake up call
being delivered to the process by the operating system in one
second. There is second call to alarm system call (line 11)
which clears pending alarm signals, if there is any, and does
not have any effect if the signal is already delivered. This
means if the code at lines $8-9$ is executed before the signal
arrives, i.e. in less than a second, the process continues and
the handler is never executed. Otherwise, the delivered signal
causes the exception handler to be called which changes the
behaviour of the code. An attacker can put a code in lines
$8-9$ that takes less than one second to execute on normal
hosts, and takes more than one second in an analysis environment or a "hostile" machine. This results in the malicious
part not being executed if the code is being monitored. This
behavior is similar to timing attacks used in malicious codes
to detect analysis environments and evade detection [32,42].
Similar to the code in Figure 1(a), there is no obvious control
flow edge in the code to guide the symbolic execution to
different execution paths. In fact, being able to automatically handle this case is even more subtle than the previous
example since the SIGALRM is raised asynchronously by the
operating system meaning that the *possible* control transfer
edge to alarm_handler function could be anywhere between
the two alarm system calls. Determining at what point in
the execution, the process will receive a signal depends on
many factors (with CPU cycles being the most important one)
making the problem non-trivially hard.

2.3 Dynamic Taint Analysis

Dynamic taint analysis involves tracking the flow of certain
marked (tainted) data throughout the program execution.
This analysis has numerous applications in different areas
such as in program debugging and software testing and application security. In the context of security, dynamic taint
analysis has led to many successful implementation of security tools that protect applications against a wide range
of attacks including buffer overruns [30,38], SQL injection
attacks [25,39] and formatted string attacks [38,41].

A potential problem for dynamic taint analysis is that
of *under-tainting* caused by not propagating taint through
control dependencies. Basically a tainted control transfer

results in different execution paths depending on the tainted
data which will lead to different data flow equations. To
address this problem, researches have tried to combine dynamic data flow analysis with static control flow graphs and
propagate taint along the control flow edges [17,29]. The
problem with these approaches is that a static CFG does not
capture possible dynamic execution paths that are caused by
unexpected events and errors. As showed earlier, this could
cause imprecision for the analysis that are sensitive to control
flow information, including dynamic taint analysis, and can
be used by attackers to evade currently used techniques.

2.4 Symbolic Execution

Symbolic execution consists of executing programs on symbolic variables rather than concrete data which represents
the program in terms of logical and arithmetic formulas.
Combined with dynamic taint analysis, symbolic execution
can represent program execution path with formulas and
constraints when the inputs to the program are marked as
symbolic. Using a SMT solver (e.g. [20,22]), one can solve the
path constraints to find alternative input values that cause
different paths to be executed. This turns out to be useful for
numerous security applications such as automatic vulnerability and exploit generation [7,14] and malware analysis [6,36].
However, vanilla symbolic execution relies on explicit control
flow constructs that might be obscured or obfuscated when
dealing with malicious codes as shown in Figure 1(b). Yadegari *et al.* [56] mentions some of the challenges of symbolic
execution when applied to obfuscated code. In this paper
we are showing some other obfuscation techniques that use
irregular control flow transfers and are already being used in
malicious or even legitimate programs causing problems for
symbolic execution.

3. ANALYZING EXECPTION BEHAVIOR

This section discusses our proposed solution to address
the analysis problems arising from exception-based control
transfers.

3.1 Synchronous Events

As discussed previously, to be able to detect implicit information flow propagation, dynamic taint analysis relies on the
static CFG of the program to propagate tainted data along
control transfer edges in the CFG. If a location (variable) x

is defined by an instruction J that is control dependent on a control transfer instruction I, then x inherits the taint marks of the variable(s) used by the control transfer instruction I; Schwartz *et al.* refer to this as *control-flow taint* [45]. Correct handling of control-flow taint requires a static CFG that reflects the possible control transfers of the program. A key problem in dealing with exception-based control transfers is that CFGs constructed using conventional techniques typically do not account for exception-based control transfers, potentially leading to under-tainting.

3.1.1 Control Flow Graph Augmentation

A natural approach to fixing the problem of missing control flow edges in the static CFG of the program would be to insert additional edges corresponding to exception-based control transfers. However, a naive solution that statically includes every possible exception-based control transfer edge, from any instruction or statement that can possibly raise an exception, can become so large and cluttered as to be unusable.

Our solution charts a middle ground where we augment a conventional static CFG with additional control transfer edges that are added at runtime as the program executes and more information is available. Additional control transfer edges are added from instructions that can potentially raise exceptions to the appropriate exception handlers, where the type of the exception (and thus the the corresponding handler) is determined at runtime. Given a program P and input $\bar{x}$, we do this as follows. Here, S is a mapping that maps different exceptions to (the address of) the handlers that have been registered for them.
1. Static analysis phase:
Construct the static CFG for P.
2. Dynamic analysis phase:

1. Initialize the exception-handler mapping S to $\emptyset$.

2. Execute P on the given input $\bar{x}$. For each instruction I of this execution, do:

   (a) If I is a call to register an exception handler H at address A_H for an exception e, update the exception-handler mapping S to map the exception e to A_H.

   (b) Otherwise: for each exception e for which a handler is known to exist in S, use symbolic execution to determine whether there exists an input that can cause instruction I to raise exception e. If there exists such an input, add a control flow edge from I to the handler $S[e]$.

Identifying whether an instruction raises an exception or not requires run-time information, such as virtual memory pages associated to the process, that are not available statically, so the static CFG needs to be modified or augmented at run-time to contain necessary control flow information that are not available otherwise.

Figure 2 shows this transformation on the CFG of the sample code in Figure 1(a). Figure 2(a) is the original CFG that is built using standard definition of control flow graph construction. It can be seen from the CFG that all three functions are isolated and there is no explicit control transfer edge between them, since there is not an explicit control flow statement. However, as shown in Figure 2(b), there

are control transfers between different functions at runtime. The reason is that functions `segv_handler` and `fpe_handler` are registered as signal handlers for `SIGSEGV` and `SIGFPE` signals respectively, causing the control being transferred to these functions on memory and arithmetic errors. The control flow edge from `main` to `segv_handler` is because of a `NULL` pointer dereference in the `*p++` statement in the `main` function and the control returns back to the same statement after it executes. Similarly, there is a control flow edge from the statement `c = c/c` in the segv_handler function to `fpe_handler` that is because of a divide by zero if variable `secret` is equal to `public` in `segv_handler` function. In fact, this logic implements a loop without any explicit control transfer statement where the code in function `segv_handler` is executed until the variable `secret` is copied to `public` and then exits to `fpe_handler` function.

After creating the augmented CFG, it needs to be analyzed to produce post-dominator information that is required for dynamic taint analysis. Basically, non-control flow instructions that have an outgoing edge to an exception handler can be treated as conditional jumps for the purpose of control dependence and post-dominator analyses. The following section discusses how to identify instructions that have a control flow edge to an exception handler.

3.1.2 Determining Control Flow Edges

As noted earlier, a challenge in identifying the possible control transfer edges from instructions to potential exception or signal handlers is that it requires specific runtime information that is not available statically. For synchronous signals, we use symbolic execution to determine the possibility of an exception during the course of an instruction's execution. This is done by constructing the path constraint along the execution path and sending appropriate queries to a SMT solver on instructions that can potentially raise exceptions. The idea is similar to those using symbolic execution for automatic fault detection [9] and exploit generation [7,14]. The following example describes the idea more clearly.

EXAMPLE 3.1. Consider the following code fragment:

1	$r_0 := \textbf{input}()$
2	$r_1 := r_0 - 10$
3	$r_2 := r_0 - 20$
4	$r_3 := r_1/r_1$
5	$\textbf{if } r_0 > 20:$
6	$\quad r_3 := r_2/r_2$

Instruction 1 gets an input value and copies it to the register r_0 and instructions 2 and 3 calculate $r_0 - 10$ and $r_0 - 20$ in r_1 and r_2 respectively. Instruction 4 performs a division operation which can raise an exception if the divisor (r_1) is zero. Knowing the symbolic expression for r_1, expression $r_1 == 0$ is satisfiable for inputs equal to 10, instruction 4 can raise an exception and, if there is a handler registered for divide-by-zero exception, a control flow edge should be added from instruction 4 to the the handler function. Similarly for instruction 6, inputs of 20 can cause an exception to be raised but since the path constraint mandates $r_0 > 20$ and so $r_2 > 0$, the formula $r_2 == 0$ is not satisfiable and the instruction is immune to divide-by-zero exceptions. ∎

In the symbolic execution engine we have implemented three major synchronous exceptions that are commonly used

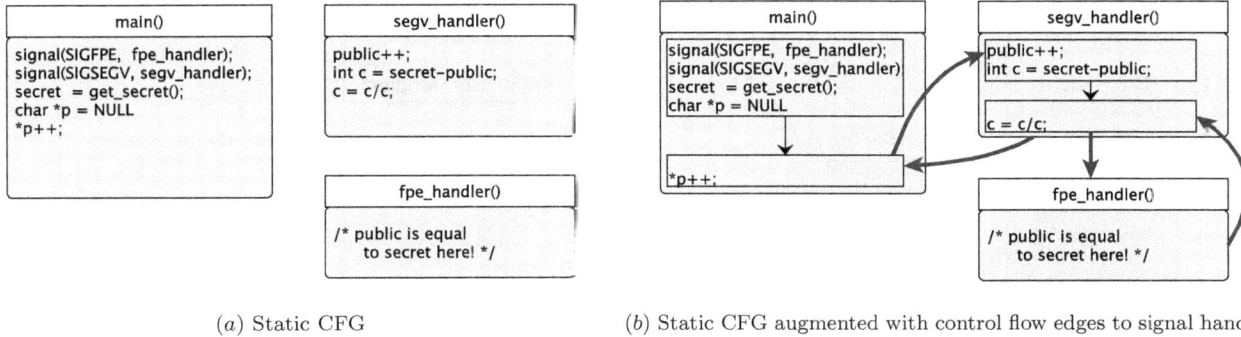

(a) Static CFG   (b) Static CFG augmented with control flow edges to signal handlers

Figure 2: Static and augmented static CFGs for the code in Figure 1(a)

to obfuscate normal control flow in malicious codes and/or in binary packer tools [21]. Our symbolic execution engine constructs appropriate constraints for synchronous exceptions that have a user exception handler registered for them. As mentioned earlier, we are interested in finding exceptions that are triggered based on some tainted or symbolic condition or value. For this purpose, the symbolic execution first checks whether a particular instruction has the desired characteristics, and then builds a formula to represent the exception and sends it to the SMT solver to check its satisfiability. A few of the most important exceptions and how they are handled by the symbolic execution engine are as follows:

- **SIGSEGV**: This exception is caused by memory access violations such as accessing a memory location that is not available to the process. For memory pointers that are tainted, the symbolic execution engine constructs a constraint that checks whether the symbolic pointer can point anywhere that is not a legal memory address at that point in the program. If the constraint is satisfiable, the constraint solver finds an input that will cause the pointer to point to an illegal address that if fed into the program and transfers control to the signal handler for **SIGSEGV**

- **SIGFPE**: This exception is raised in case of arithmetic errors such as divide by zero. In case of a divide instruction, the symbolic execution engine constructs a constraint that checks whether the dividend used in the instruction can be zero based on some inputs, if the dividend is symbolic. If such an input exists, it will report it to the user.

- **SIGILL**: This exception is raised when an instruction opcode is not recognizable by the **CPU**. If in the execution of the program, an instruction is being overwritten with a symbolic value [56], the symbolic execution engine constructs a constraint to check whether the opcode that is being written can be illegal based on some input.

Using symbolic execution to identify exception-based control transfers has two advantages. First, the analysis can find alternative inputs to trigger alternative execution paths in the code other than those paths existed because of normal control flow structure such as conditional jumps. One important application of this is in the analysis of malicious or obfuscated code that hide their control flow through exception-based control transfers. Secondly, the alternative paths that are

found can be used towards implicit information flow detection that otherwise was not possible to detect because of missing control transfer edges in the static CFG.

3.2 Asynchronous Events

Asynchronous signals are those that are not a direct result of the execution of an instruction, but rather are generated by some external sources and delivered to the process through the operating system (e.g. Figure 1(b)). Asynchronous signals are more challenging than synchronous ones to handle and can cause inaccuracies in both symbolic execution and dynamic taint analysis because the time an exception handled by the program receiving it may change the execution path and/or the data flow equations.

Similar to CFG augmentation for synchronous exceptions discussed in Section 3.1, we use the augmentation technique for unexpected control transfers caused by asynchronous signals. The only difference here is that since there is no fixed point in the code where the control diverges from the main execution thread, we need to analyze different possibilities and account for different situations. Of course the first non-trivial solution is to add a new control flow edge following every instruction in the main execution trace where there is a possibility of control divergence, but this imposes unnecessary computational complexity to the analysis.

To handle asynchronous signals, in general, we need to take into account the side effects of executing the handler code. Figure 3 tries to visualize this situation where as opposed to synchronous signals in which the control flow edge is at a fixed location (in the code), for asynchronous signals, control transfer points are determined by the possible locations that might be impacted by executing the handler function. As shown in Figure 3(a), variable X is defined globally where it can be accessed from both the main code and the signal handler. Suppose that the gray box in the main code is where a signal can be delivered to the process meaning that the control could be transferred to the signal handler at any point in the gray area. The variable X is accessed multiple times in the gray area, while the signal handler function modifies the variable X. Modification to X may have impact on the main code where X is used, i.e. points where there is an edge to the handler in Figure 3(b). Figure 3(b) shows the augmented CFG for the code and handler of Figure 3(a).

To handle asynchronous signals we are not necessarily proposing to use symbolic execution to identify alternative execution paths caused by signals. Although symbolic execu-

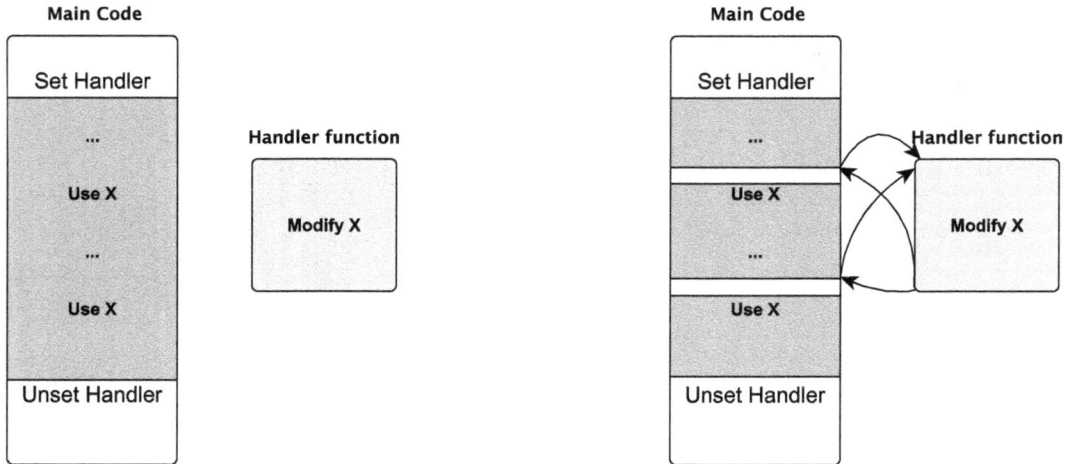

(a) Static CFG of the code. The grey box in the main code appears as a single basic block

(b) Augmented CFG for asynchronous signal handler

Figure 3: CFG Augmentation for asynchronous signal handler

tion can be helpful in some cases, such as when the argument to the `kill` function (that is used to send arbitrary signals to processes) is symbolic. This results in activation of different functions in the receiving process when there are different handlers registered for different signals, and symbolic execution can be used to help identifying those inputs that lead to different handlers being called in the execution. As mentioned earlier, asynchronous signals are generally generated externally which are then delivered to the process. However for an attacker to exploit these mechanisms provided by the OS, they need to arrange for the signals to be delivered to the process somehow, perhaps by forking multiple threads and have the threads to communicate with each other with signals and this arrangement that is necessary for an attack to succeed, makes the attack detectable and perhaps predictable.

The code example that are shown in this section for use `SIGALRM` signal as to show how to use asynchronous signals for control transfer purposes, however the idea that is discussed as a proposed solution is generalizable to the other types of asynchronous signals. Examples of other signals are those that are used for inter-process communications such as `SIGCHILD` that is raised when a forked child of a process dies or `SIGUSR1` that is left for user defined handlers.

3.3 Attack Model

As with other techniques that rely on symbolic execution and SMT solvers, our approach is limited by the theoretical boundaries of SMT solvers [48, 53]. An attacker can also add complexity to the code in order to add complexity to the path constraints. This can increase the processing time for the back-end SMT solver to check satisfiability of the path condition. A related attack is to use code that produces too much work for the analysis. For example by using opaque symbolic memory pointers (symbolic pointers that are not unsatisfiable), the analysis needs to send a lot of queries to the SMT solver which slows down the analysis [56]. In order to reduce the effects of these types of attacks, we have

incorporated a chaching mechanism built in to our prototype implementation that reduces the number of queries sent to the solver significantly, limitting the possibility of these types of attacks (see Sections and). However, note that in the context of identifying the possible exception-based control-flow behaviors of a program, the back-end SMT solver is used only for those exceptions for which exception handlers have been registered during execution and for those instructions that can give rise to such exceptions, not for all executed instructions.

4. IMPLEMENTATION

We have implemented a prototype system based on Intel PIN tool [34] which is a dynamic binary instrumentation tool. Our system works on the binary level and so we do not need access to the source code. The analysis is based on two main components: 1) dynamic taint analysis; and 2) symbolic execution. Our dynamic taint analysis engine takes the approach used in [55]. Our taint analysis uses bit-level granularity for taint taint propagation by using generic taint labels for inputs to the program. Our symbolic execution engine is a layer on top of the taint analysis engine which interfaces with STP [23] SMT library to solve symbolic expressions. We have implemented concolic testing that runs the input program with the given inputs and analyses the execution trace that is observed along the execution path. Both taint analysis and symbolic execution analyses are done on the X86 instruction set.

For dynamic taint analysis, we use `objdump` tool on Linux to produce disassembly and create CFG of the disassembled code. The post-dominator information then is extracted by analyzing the CFG which specifies post-dominators for conditional branches in the code. For signal handlers, however, we use PIN APIs to intercept user's registered signal handlers to analyze them. Our current implementation does not analyze the handler code statically because static analysis of binary code is hard in general and does not always guarantee correct results [33] due to code obfuscation or self-modification that are common among malware code. We instead take a dynamic approach where the handlers are intercepted at run-time and capture the implicit flow by marking those data flows that are tainted because of the exception-based control transfers. We realize that with this approach it is possible to miss some opportunities for symbolic execution, but the alternative assumption that we make here is quite realistic as we have observed in our evaluations with malicious codes.

To find specific user handlers that are registered by the user code, the tool intercepts the calls to `sigaction` and `signal` system calls that are used to register user handlers for given signals. Using the addresses of the signal handlers that are registered by the user, we are able to augment the static CFG and add explicit control flow edges whereever the symbolic execution engine finds a satisfiable input that would cause an instruction to raise a particular exception.

4.1 Symbolic Pointer Caching

A naive implementation of the ideas described above would query the SMT solver at every runtime memory reference. Since programs can have a large number of memory references, and the cost of querying an SMT solver can be quite large, this would result in unacceptably high runtime overheads. To mitigate this problem, we use a symbolic pointer caching mechanism that reuses the results of prior queries to the SMT solver where this is guaranteed to be sound, thereby reducing the number of queries to the solver.

In the x86 architecture, the most general form of an address computation involves two integer constants and two registers (the base and index registers) as follows:[1]

$$address = baseReg + scale \times indexReg + displacement.$$

We refer to this as an *address expression*. A pointer is marked as symbolic if, in its address expression, either the base register or index register is symbolic; the symbolic term of such a pointer is *baseReg* if the base register is symbolic and *scale × indexReg* if the index register is symbolic. All other terms can be considered as constant terms. If such a pointer is used to trigger a SIGSEGV, then at least one of the possible addresses that can be generated by the pointer must illegally reference a page in memory. Thus, by checking to see if a symbolic pointer can access an invalid page in memory it can be determined if the program will conditionally trigger a SIGSEGV. By taking advantage of the fact that an entire page will be marked as invalid, not just a particular memory location, we can cache and reuse results from previous queries sent to the solver.

Consider two pointers A and B. If the address expressions for A and B have the exact same symbolic and constant terms, then obviously they will access memory the exact same way. Thus we know that if it is possible for pointer A to illegally access a page in memory, then it must be possible for B to make an illegal access as well. Now let pointers A and B share the same symbolic terms, but not the same constant terms. Since the symbolic terms are the same, we know that for every memory location A can access, there must exist a corresponding memory location that B can access at some displacement d away, for some constant d. It is therefore possible that the displacement by d can cause B to access pages that A did not, meaning that we

can no longer reason about B from A. If, however, d is less than the size of a memory page (typically 4096 bytes) then B's corresponding access must either fall on the same page as A's, or on one of the adjacent pages. As a result, a third pointer C, which has the same symbolic terms as A and B but a displacement which places it between A and B, must only be able to access pages in memory that could be accessed by A or B. To that end, if both of them can only access memory pages legally, then C can only access pages legally. Likewise if both A and B can access a page illegally, then C must also be able illegally access a page. However, C cannot be reasoned about if A and B disagree since there would be an unknown boundary between A and B that determines C's state based on where it lies in relation to that boundary. With this information, a caching mechanism can be constructed. Whenever a symbolic pointer must be checked, we can construct and check a second symbolic pointer with the same symbolic terms and an offset less than a page. If the decisions from the solver for these two pointers agree, we can save the result for future reuse.

The cache has two parts: a storage mechanism capable of holding pointers whose solver decisions can be reused and; an invalidation mechanism to discard pointers whose symbolic terms have been changed. For the storage portion, we use a structure that maps a symbolic value to a list of entries whose pointers use that value. If the entries corresponding to a particular symbolic value need to be invalidated, the list corresponding to the value can simply be cleared. This means that to find a symbolic pointer, we have to check that all symbolic values used by the pointer can locate an entry in the cache. If an entry is not found, then that symbolic value must have been invalidated and any entries found are dirty. We use this structure because it makes invalidation, which occurs more frequently than searches, fast and easy.

To maintain the pointer validity requirements placed upon the cache, a strict set of rules is used to determine when to remove a pointer from the cache. If a symbolic pointer has an entry in the cache, the symbolic values it uses can only be modified by additions and subtractions of constants with no other symbolic operands. This guarantees that the symbolic terms of the pointer are the same when a cache entry is reused. If a symbolic value with entries in the cache is modified in any other way, all entries that use the value are removed from the cache. Additionally, if the program modifies the protection of any page in memory, the entire cache is flushed since it is not known which, if any, of the cache entries are affected.

To improve the performance of the cache, a few additional features are built in as well. The first is the ability to track symbolic operands if they are moved. Programs often temporarily store the operands needed for a pointer in registers, then once they have completed their memory access will either replace them or move them back to memory. We track the movement of the symbolic values to ensure that we can recognize when two symbolic pointers are the same without having to perform an expensive comparison between the constraints. A second optimization involves symbolic pointers in loops. Very often, the same symbolic pointer is used within a loop whose termination condition is based on a symbolic value. Since each iteration of the loop changes the path constraint to code in the loop body, a straightforward approach to cache management would invalidate cache entries that use the symbolic value, since any change to the path constraint

---

[1] The x86 architecture supports a number of other addressing modes that can be seen as special cases of that described here.

potentially implies a change to the symbolic value as well. This would cause a large number of cache misses within loop. However, a conditional can only further constrain a symbolic value and therefore a symbolic pointer. Thus, if a pointer can only make legal memory accesses, another pointer that can only access a subset of the same memory locations can also only access legal locations. If, on the other hand, a pointer can access an illegal location, it is possible that after being constrained the same pointer can only access legal locations. Therefore, the cache is only used for symbolic pointers that can only access valid memory regions and therefore cannot cause a SIGSEGV. Since the number of symbolic pointers that can access invalid memory regions are in the minority and many of them would be invalidated by a conditional anyway, this decision does not have a large impact on the hit rate of the cache.

5. EXPERIMENTAL EVALUATIONS

We evaluated our prototype tool against a variety of different test programs and malicious codes and we compared our results with current state-of-the-art available tools in both dynamic taint analysis and symbolic execution. The samples were all run on a Linux virtual machine running Ubuntu 14.04 which was given 8 processors and 8 GB of ram.

5.1 Dynamic Taint Analysis

For dynamic taint analysis we used two sets of programs for the evaluations:

- The first set consists of three sample test programs that use exception-based control transfers to obfuscate the branch points in the program. All three programs define exception handlers that will redirect the control, and have some input value that is used to conditionally trigger the exception. Additionally, all three samples propagate some tainted data in the handlers to resemble the idea of implicit information flow. These three programs are:

  1. *invalid-memory* uses user input to create a memory pointer that is a valid memory address if the input satisfies some conditions, otherwise an invalid pointer.

  2. *invalid-opcode* overwrites `nop` instructions in the code by an invalid opcode if the user input does not satisfy the conditions resulting in a `SIGILL` in the code.

  3. *divide-by-0* performs a division where the dividend is computed from input. The dividend is zero for inputs not satisfying the condition and non-zero otherwise.

- The second set consists of two exploit codes written in `C` that have behaviors similar to what is described in this paper. These are proof-of-concept exploits that are written for different vulnerabilities and are publicly available through web-sites such as http://www.exploit-db.com. The samples overwrite signal handlers for particular signals. The exploits are mentioned by their corresponding CVEs:

  1. *CVE-2004-1235* exploits a race condition in `load_elf_library` and `binfmt_aout` function calls that

exists in some Linux kernel versions, allowing an attacker to execute arbitrary code by manipulating the VMA descriptor. The exploit sets handler for `SIGALRM` signal and uses it to redirect control flow to propagate data.

  2. *CVE-2005-0736* exploits an integer overflow in `sys_epoll_wait` for some Linux kernels allowing an attacker to overwrite kernel memory with a large number of events. This sample also sets exception handlers for different signals that guide the execution in case of an unexpected event.

We found Dytan [17] the only dynamic taint analysis system that was available publicly and implements implicit taint propagation through control flow edges. For the test-cases that contained some form of implicit taint propagation through the signal handlers, we ran experiments with Dytan and our tool and the results are presented in Table 1. Dytan failed on all the test-cases while our tool was able to successfully identify the implicit flows caused by signal handlers, while the second exploit uses the handler to handle possible memory faults by setting variables that will eventually change the control flow of the code executed afterwards. We have identified these instances as implicit flow since the control flow caused by exceptions are implicitly used to set variables that consequently affect the flow of execution.

Programs	Dynamic Taint Analysis	
	Dytan	Our System
invalid-memory	✗	✓
invalid-opcode	✗	✓
divide-by-0	✗	✓
CVE-2004-1235	✗	✓
CVE-2005-0736	✗	✓

Table 1: Dynamic taint analysis results

5.2 Symbolic Execution

We evaluated our prototype against different malicious programs procured from `vxheaven`[2] and compared our results against current state-of-the-art symbolic execution tools.

To evaluate the symbolic execution engines, we started with a base set of the following Linux malware:

  1. *Caline* is a simple linux virus that infects ELF files resulting in a simple message being placed in the binary.

  2. *w00lien* that has various malicious capabilities, such as spawning a shell for remote connections, self-encryption and file infection.

  3. *lacrimae* is a malware mutation engine which reads in an ELF file and writes back a mutated version of the binary.

  4. *rapeme* is a RPM archive infector virus. It finds and infects an RPM file with a malicious payload and then recomposes the infected code into an RPM.

  5. *kaiowas11* is a proof-of-concept showing run-time binary encryption/decryption.

---

[2]http://www.vxheaven.org

For each of the malware sources, we selected a conditional or a set of conditionals in the malicious program that an analysis tool needed to explore in order to discover all of the behavior the malware could exhibit. The selected statements were typically conditionals important to the integrity of the malicious algorithm, or used for anti-analysis. For each sample, we then created two more samples by transforming the conditionals into an equivalent statement that instead branched using conditional exceptions by moving the code for true branch into the signal handler function registered for that particular signal. The first obfuscated sample uses an asynchronous conditional exception using `alarm` signal (similar to Example 1(b)) while the second sample uses illegal instruction exception (`SIGILL`). For samples using illegal instruction, the conditional code is transformed to a call to a buffer that contains illegal instructions, however the buffer is overwritten by `nop`s if the condition is evaluated to false. This results in the execution to continue the false branch in case the condition is not met, otherwise the control is transformed to the exception handler that contains the code for true branch.

In order to evaluate our ideas against state-of-the-art symbolic execution engines, we picked a handful of available symbolic execution engines and compared their results with ours. The symbolic execution engines that we used are KLEE [7], S2E [16], FuzzBall [4] and angr [49]. KLEE and S2E are automated test-case generation symbolic execution engines that maximize the code coverage, and FuzzBall and angr are symbolic execution frameworks. KLEE needs to have access to source code while the others work at the binary level. Test-cases were annotated to introduce symbolic variables for KLEE and S2E. FuzzBall and angr however accepts arguments which instructs the tool to mark inputs, memory locations or registers as symbolic at certain point in the execution.

The results are summarized in table 2. All of the tools were able to discover all of the targeted paths in the original unmodified programs. The number of paths (based on the conditional statements that we targeted for our obfuscation) is reported under the second column. The only error that we observed was that in the rapeme test, angr discovered 4 additional paths that were technically impossible to execute. Once the conditional exceptions were inserted, however, the state-of-the-art competition had difficulty discovering the alternative paths. The next 5 columns show the number of paths discovered by the tools in the test programs obfuscated using `ALARM` signal, and the remaining 5 columns show the same results for the test programs obfuscated using illegal instruction.

Only one of the state-of-the-art competition tools was able to successfully handle the asynchronous alarm signal. Neither angr nor KLEE supported calls to `alarm` with symbolic argument, so to allow these two engines to progress past the alarm call we had to hook the calls to alarm (and `sleep` for FuzzBall) and return the appropriate value. This allows them to explore the false path, but since neither of them know anything about the semantics of the alarm call in this case, they cannot properly explore all guarded paths. KLEE, on the other hand, has 3 different versions of `libc` that can be used to emulate the library functions. We tried running the samples on all versions of `libc` available, but none of them handled the alarm call so that the true path would be discovered. S2E was the only engine that handled the

asynchronous exception guard correctly. We believe that this is because S2E has access to code in the kernel and in user mode. With this, we believe it was able to observe how the alarm signal is triggered by the kernel and thereby could produce the correct results.

None of the other tools were able to handle the synchronous illegal instruction exception. KLEE only works on the C source code, and so it is unable to handle programs that modify their own binary like we did in this example. The other tools, on the other hand, do have the ability to handle self-modifying code. None of them, however, knew how to handle an illegal instruction. Rather, they all reported an error and exited the analysis. To overcome this, we had to use facilities built into the engines to `nop` an illegal instruction if one is encountered. This allowed execution to continue past the illegal instruction and always discover one path of the conditional statement. None of them, however, were about to reason about other instructions that could have been written into the buffer to cause alternative behavior. Our tool handles illegal instructions by keeping track of the instruction bytes that are modified using a symbolic value. When encountered with an illegal instruction, our tool constructs a symbolic expression involving the path constraint and asks the SMT solver if the expression can be solved so that the instruction can be a `nop`. If solvable, the results from the SMT solver can be used to determine the necessary input that could cause the alternative path to be taken.

5.3 Performance

5.3.1 Overhead

Table 3 shows the running time of each obfuscated sample versus the analysis time of our system and FuzzBall. All the times are in seconds and for our system, the analysis time includes both dynamic taint analysis and symbolic execution. The samples on the row numbered with 1 are obfuscated using `alarm` while the samples on row labeled with 2 are obfuscated using illegal instruction. To do a fair comparison, we have only compared our system to FuzzBall since it's behaviour is closest to that of our system. FuzzBall automatically discovers alternative execution paths if it finds any symbolic conditional statements in the code, but since it does not handle the obfuscated conditionals in our samples, it only analyzes the execution path based on the given input. This is similar to the behaviour of our tool since our tool does not automatically execute the alternative paths but reports any possible input value that would trigger them. As it can be seen from the table, the performance of our tool is generally better than FuzzBall and the overall analysis time remains in reasonable ranges.

5.3.2 Caching Improvements

To measure the efficacy of caching, we ran our tool on a modified version of Md5 from http://people.csail.mit.edu/rivest/Md5.c since it is both computation and memory intensive. We chose Md5 simply because our test cases do not cause a lot of interactions with the SMT solver. The original program was modified with a simple `SIGSEGV` handler and calls to force our prototype to generate many tainted pointers for some of the operations. We ran the program on three different input files as shown in Table 4. The first column in Table 4 shows the `CPU` time required to process the input file without analysis, while the second column shows the analysis

213

Programs	# of paths in original code	Number of discovered paths in obfuscated samples									
		Obfuscated using `alarm`					Obfuscated using illegal instruction				
		KLEE	FuzzBall	angr	S2E	Our System	KLEE	FuzzBall	angr	S2E	Our System
Caline	2	1	1	1	1	2	N/A	1	1	1	2
w00lien	2	1	1	1	2	2	N/A	1	1	1	2
lacrimae	2	1	1	1	2	2	N/A	1	1	1	2
rapeme	4	1	1	1	4	4	N/A	1	1	1	4
kaiowas11	2	1	1	1	2	2	N/A	1	1	1	2

Table 2: Symbolic execution results

	Programs	Execution times (s)		
		Original	FuzzBall	Our System
1	Caline	1.002	2.522	1.838
	w00lien	1.166	2.539	2.019
	lacrimae	1.000	2.588	2.174
	rapeme	2.048	18.763	4.909
	kaiowas11	1.001	5.392	1.791
2	Caline	0.002	4.151	1.014
	w00lien	0.093	4.336	0.831
	lacrimae	0.002	4.551	0.638
	rapeme	0.046	71.315	2.723
	kaiowas11	0.001	18.173	0.796

Table 3: Cost analysis of our prototype tool

time. Third column shows the time spent in the solver in seconds, and the rest of the columns show the number of queries that our tool encountered during the analysis, number of queries that were found in cache and the number of queries which needed to be sent to the solver. Under these workloads, cache hit rate is generally above 98% suggesting that the caching mechanism provides a lot of benefit when a pointer repeatedly accesses the same page(s) (e.g. in a loop). As the number of hits decreases, it can be seen that the time spent in the solver increases, so if there are a lot of misses in the cache, the solver will require a large portion of the runtime.

6. RELATED WORK

Many researchers have investigated symbolic code execution; see the survey by Schwartz et al. [45]. An important application of this approach is in analysis of malicious and/or obfuscated code [1,3,6,18,36,47,58,59]. However, these works generally do not explicitly address the challenges that arise in analyzing obfuscated code, which is especially prevalent in malware. Yadegari and Debray discuss approaches to symbolic analysis of obfuscated code [56], but this does not consider exception-based control transfers.

Our approach to find exception-based control transfers are similar to those used in existing systems such as KLEE, S2E or Mayhem. These systems use symbolic execution to guide the execution of the program under the analysis and find different combination of inputs that cause the program to crash [7,9] which then can be combined with other reasonings to automatically generate exploits [14]. This is different from our work that recognizes program faults as an obfuscation technique to obscure control flow transfers. [19] discusses the execution of enabled interrupts in analyzing firmware

code but their approach is limited to small binaries that are written in C and thus require source code. Their approach is not applicable to native large applications and easily results in state explosion.

The use of exceptions to obfuscate control flow is well known [40]. Malware have long used a simple instance of this approach to obfuscate direct unconditional jumps, by constructing and dereferencing a null pointer. In commonly encountered malware, this obfuscation is typically used to bypass ordinary anti-virus detectors rather than to propagate information through implicit flows. However, it is straightforward to modify this code to use exception-based control transfers to hinder dynamic taint propagation and symbolic execution.

A number of researchers have described security-related applications of dynamic taint analysis [26,27,29,38,54]. Clause et al [17], Schwartz et al. [45], Song et al. [52] and Nethercote et al. [37] discuss general frameworks for dynamic taint analysis, but do not address issues arising from implicit flows in obfuscated code, and exception-based control transfers in particular. The problems arising from dynamic taint analysis of code containing implicit information flows is discussed by Cavallarro et al. [12].

A number of researchers have looked into the problem of analysis of exception-handling behavior of programs. This work typically focuses on explicit exception-management mechanisms (throw-catch statements) at the source code level [5,15,28,43,50,51]. We are not aware of any work on reasoning about exception behavior at the binary level.

7. CONCLUSIONS

While dynamic taint analysis and symbolic execution have a number of important applications in security-related program analyses, existing techniques for these analyses have trouble dealing with many of the code obfuscations employed by malicious programs. A particular example of this is the use of exceptions to obfuscate control transfers. This paper discusses the problems that dynamic taint analysis and symbolic execution systems can encounter when analyzing programs containing implicit information flows arising from exception-based control transfers. We propose a generic solution for code where such exceptions are handled via user-defined exception handlers. Experimental results using a prototype implementation show that our approach yields better results than existing analysis techniques.

Acknowledgments

This research was supported in part by the National Science Foundation (NSF) under grants III-1318343, CNS-1318955, and CNS-1525820.

Workload	Normal Exec. Time (s)	Analysis Exec. Time (s)	Total Query Time (s)	No. Queries	Cache Hits	Cache Misses
4GB	0.065	157.633	3.346	268562	268496	66
1.5GB	0.023	54.420	2.808	90955	90889	66
75MB	0.004	6.624	2.646	4661	4595	66

Table 4: Caching performance of our prototype tool for different workloads on MD5

8. REFERENCES

[1] U. Bayer, P. Milani, C. Hlauschek, C. Kruegel, and E. Kirda. Scalable, behavior-based malware clustering. In *Proc. 16th Annual Network and Distributed System Security Symposium (NDSS 2009)*, Feb. 2009.

[2] U. Bayer, P. Milani Comparetti, C. Hlauscheck, C. Kruegel, and E. Kirda. Scalable, Behavior-Based Malware Clustering. In *16th Symposium on Network and Distributed System Security (NDSS)*, Feb. 2009.

[3] U. Bayer, A. Moser, C. Kruegel, and E. Kirda. Dynamic analysis of malicious code. *Journal in Computer Virology*, 2(1), Aug. 2006.

[4] Bitblaze. FuzzBALL: Vine-based Binary Symbolic Execution.

[5] M. Bravenboer and Y. Smaragdakis. Exception analysis and points-to analysis: better together. In *Proceedings of the eighteenth international symposium on Software testing and analysis*, pages 1–12. ACM, 2009.

[6] D. Brumley, C. Hartwig, Z. Liang, J. Newsome, D. X. Song, and H. Yin. Automatically identifying trigger-based behavior in malware. In *Botnet Detection: Countering the Largest Security Threat*, volume 36, pages 65–88, 2008.

[7] C. Cadar, D. Dunbar, and D. R. Engler. Klee: Unassisted and automatic generation of high-coverage tests for complex systems programs. In *OSDI*, volume 8, pages 209–224, 2008.

[8] C. Cadar and D. Engler. Execution generated test cases: How to make systems code crash itself. In *Model Checking Software*, pages 2–23. Springer, 2005.

[9] C. Cadar, V. Ganesh, P. M. Pawlowski, D. L. Dill, and D. R. Engler. Exe: automatically generating inputs of death. *ACM Transactions on Information and System Security (TISSEC)*, 12(2):10, 2008.

[10] C. Cadar, P. Godefroid, S. Khurshid, C. S. Păsăreanu, K. Sen, N. Tillmann, and W. Visser. Symbolic execution for software testing in practice: preliminary assessment. In *Proceedings of the 33rd International Conference on Software Engineering*, pages 1066–1071. ACM, 2011.

[11] C. Cadar and K. Sen. Symbolic execution for software testing: three decades later. *Communications of the ACM*, 56(2), 2013.

[12] L. Cavallaro, P. Saxena, and R. Sekar. Anti-taint-analysis: Practical evasion techniques against information flow based malware defense. *Stony Brook University, Stony Brook, New York*, 2007.

[13] L. Cavallaro, P. Saxena, and R. Sekar. On the limits of information flow techniques for malware analysis and containment. In *Detection of Intrusions and Malware, and Vulnerability Assessment*, pages 143–163. Springer, 2008.

[14] S. K. Cha, T Avgerinos, A. Rebert, and D. Brumley. Unleashing mayhem on binary code. In *IEEE Symposium on Security and Privacy*. IEEE, 2012.

[15] B.-M. Chang, J.-W. Jo, K. Yi, and K.-M. Choe. Interprocedural exception analysis for java. In *ACM Symposium on Applied Computing*, 2001.

[16] V. Chipounov, V. Kuznetsov, and G. Candea. S2e: A platform for in-vivo multi-path analysis of software systems. In *Proceedings of the 16th International Conference on Architectural Support for Programming Languages and Operating Systems (ASPLOS)*, Mar. 2011.

[17] J. Clause, W. Li, and A. Orso. Dytan: a generic dynamic taint analysis framework. In *Proceedings of the 2007 international symposium on Software testing and analysis*, pages 196–206. ACM, 2007.

[18] J. R. Crandall, G. Wassermann, D. A. S. de Oliveira, Z. Su, S. F. Wu, and F. T. Chong. Temporal search: detecting hidden malware timebombs with virtual machines. In *ASPLOS-XII: Proceedings of the 12th international conference on Architectural support for programming languages and operating systems*, pages 25–36, Oct. 2006.

[19] D. Davidson, B. Moench, T. Ristenpart, and S. Jha. Fie on firmware: Finding vulnerabilities in embedded systems using symbolic execution. In *Presented as part of the 22nd USENIX Security Symposium (USENIX Security 13)*, pages 463–478, 2013.

[20] L. De Moura and N. Bjørner. Z3: An efficient smt solver. In *Tools and Algorithms for the Construction and Analysis of Systems*, pages 337–340. Springer, 2008.

[21] P. Ferrie. Anti-unpacker tricks–part one. *Virus Bulletin*, 4, 2008.

[22] V. Ganesh and D. L. Dill. A decision procedure for bit-vectors and arrays. In *Computer Aided Verification*. Springer, 2007.

[23] V. Ganesh and T. Hansen. STP. https://github.com/stp/stp.

[24] P. Godefroid, N. Klarlund, and K. Sen. DART: directed automated random testing. In *Proceedings of the ACM SIGPLAN 2005 Conference on Programming Language Design and Implementation (PLDI)*. ACM, 2005.

[25] W. G. Halfond, A. Orso, and P. Manolios. Using positive tainting and syntax-aware evaluation to counter sql injection attacks. In *Proceedings of the 14th ACM SIGSOFT international symposium on Foundations of software engineering*, pages 175–185. ACM, 2006.

[26] C. Hauser, F. Tronel, L. Mé, and C. J. Fidge. Intrusion detection in distributed systems, an approach based on taint marking. In *Proc. 2013 IEEE International Conference on Communications (ICC)*, pages 1962–1967, 2013.

[27] C. Hauser, F. Tronel, J. F. Reid, and C. J. Fidge. A taint marking approach to confidentiality violation detection. In *Proc. 10th Australasian Information Security Conference (AISC 2012)*, Jan. 30 2012.

[28] J.-W. Jo and B.-M. Chang. Constructing control flow graph for java by decoupling exception flow from normal flow. In *Computational Science and Its Applications–ICCSA 2004*, pages 106–113. Springer, 2004.

[29] M. G. Kang, S. McCamant, P. Poosankam, and D. Song. Dta++: Dynamic taint analysis with targeted control-flow propagation. In *NDSS*, 2011.

[30] J. Kong, C. C. Zou, and H. Zhou. Improving software security via runtime instruction-level taint checking. In *Proceedings of the 1st workshop on Architectural and system support for improving software dependability*, pages 18–24. ACM, 2006.

[31] H. Lin, X. Zhang, M. Yong, and B. Wang. Branch obfuscation using binary code side effects. In *International Conference on Computer, Networks and Communication Engineering (ICCNCE 2013)*. Atlantis Press, 2013.

[32] M. Lindorfer, C. Kolbitsch, and P. M. Comparetti. Detecting environment-sensitive malware. In *Recent Advances in Intrusion Detection*, pages 338–357. Springer, 2011.

[33] C. Linn and S. Debray. Obfuscation of executable code to

improve resistance to static disassembly. In *Proceedings of the 10th ACM conference on Computer and communications security*, pages 290–299. ACM, 2003.

[34] C.-K. Luk, R. Cohn, R. Muth, H. Patil, A. Klauser, G. Lowney, S. Wallace, V. J. Reddi, and K. Hazelwood. Pin: Building customized program analysis tools with dynamic instrumentation. In *Proc. ACM Conference on Programming Language Design and Implementation (PLDI)*, 2005.

[35] A. Moser, C. Kruegel, and E. Kirda. Exploring multiple execution paths for malware analysis. In *Proc. IEEE Symposium on Security and Privacy*, pages 231–245, 2007.

[36] A. Moser, C. Kruegel, and E. Kirda. Exploring multiple execution paths for malware analysis. In *Security and Privacy, 2007. SP'07. IEEE Symposium on*, pages 231–245. IEEE, 2007.

[37] N. Nethercote and J. Seward. Valgrind: A framework for heavyweight dynamic binary instrumentation. In *Proc. ACM Conference on Programming Language Design and Implementation (PLDI)*, pages 89–100, June 2007.

[38] J. Newsome and D. Song. Dynamic taint analysis for automatic detection, analysis, and signature generation of exploits on commodity software. In *NDSS*, 2005.

[39] T. Pietraszek and C. V. Berghe. Defending against injection attacks through context-sensitive string evaluation. In *Recent Advances in Intrusion Detection*, pages 124–145. Springer, 2005.

[40] I. Popov, S. K. Debray, and G. R. Andrews. Binary obfuscation using signals. In *Proc. Usenix Security 2007*, pages 275–290, Aug. 2007.

[41] F. Qin, C. Wang, Z. Li, H.-s. Kim, Y. Zhou, and Y. Wu. Lift: A low-overhead practical information flow tracking system for detecting security attacks. In *Microarchitecture, 2006. MICRO-39. 39th Annual IEEE/ACM International Symposium on*, pages 135–148. IEEE, 2006.

[42] J. Qiu, B. Yadegari, B. Johannesmeyer, S. Debray, and X. Su. A framework for understanding dynamic anti-analysis defenses. In *Proceedings of the 4th Program Protection and Reverse Engineering Workshop*, page 2. ACM, 2014.

[43] M. P. Robillard and G. C. Murphy. Static analysis to support the evolution of exception structure in object-oriented systems. *ACM Transactions on Software Engineering and Methodology (TOSEM)*, 12(2):191–221, 2003.

[44] G. Sarwar, O. Mehani, R. Boreli, and M. A. Kaafar. On the effectiveness of dynamic taint analysis for protecting against private information leaks on android-based devices. In *SECRYPT*, pages 461–468, 2013.

[45] E. J. Schwartz, T. Avgerinos, and D. Brumley. All you ever wanted to know about dynamic taint analysis and forward symbolic execution (but might have been afraid to ask). In *IEEE Symposium on Security and Privacy*, 2010.

[46] K. Sen, D. Marinov, and G. Agha. Cute: a concolic unit testing engine for c. In *Proceedings of the 10th European Software Engineering Conference Held Jointly with 13th ACM SIGSOFT International Symposium on Foundations of Software Engineering*, pages 263–272, Sept. 2005.

[47] M. Sharif, A. Lanzi, J. Giffin, and W. Lee. Automatic reverse engineering of malware emulators. In *Proc. 2009 IEEE Symposium on Security and Privacy*, May 2009.

[48] M. I. Sharif, A. Lanzi, J. T. Giffin, and W. Lee. Impeding malware analysis using conditional code obfuscation. In *Proc. 15th Network and Distributed System Security Symposium (NDSS)*, Feb. 2008.

[49] Y. Shoshitaishvili, R. Wang, C. Hauser, C. Kruegel, and G. Vigna. Firmalice - automatic detection of authentication bypass vulnerabilities in binary firmware. 2015.

[50] S. Sinha and M. J. Harrold. Analysis of programs with exception-handling constructs. In *Software Maintenance, 1998. Proceedings., International Conference on*, pages 348–357. IEEE, 1998.

[51] S. Sinha and M. J. Harrold. Analysis and testing of programs with exception handling constructs. *IEEE Transactions on Software Engineering*, 26(9):849–871, 2000.

[52] D. Song, D. Brumley, H. Yin, J. Caballero, I. Jager, M. G. Kang, Z. Liang, J. Newsome, P. Poosankam, and P. Saxena. BitBlaze: A new approach to computer security via binary analysis. In *Proc. of the 4th International Conference on Information Systems Security*, Dec. 2008.

[53] Z. Wang, J. Ming, C. Jia, and D. Gao. Linear obfuscation to combat symbolic execution. In *Computer Security–ESORICS 2011*, pages 210–226. Springer, 2011.

[54] W. Xu, S. Bhatkar, and R. Sekar. Practical dynamic taint analysis for countering input validation attacks on web applications. Technical report, Technical Report SECLAB-05-04, Department of Computer Science, Stony Brook University, 2005.

[55] B. Yadegari and S. Debray. Bit-level taint analysis. In *International Working Conference on Source Code Analysis and Manipulation*. IEEE, 2014.

[56] B. Yadegari and S. Debray. Symbolic execution of obfuscated code. In *Proceedings of the 22Nd ACM SIGSAC Conference on Computer and Communications Security, ser. CCS*, volume 15, pages 732–744, 2015.

[57] X. Yao, J. Pang, Y. Zhang, Y. Yu, and J. Lu. A method and implementation of control flow obfuscation using SEH. In *Multimedia Information Networking and Security (MINES)*, pages 336–339. IEEE, 2012.

[58] H. Yin and D. Song. Analysis of trigger conditions and hidden behaviors. In *Automatic Malware Analysis*, SpringerBriefs in Computer Science, pages 59–67. 2013.

[59] H. Yin, D. Song, M. Egele, C. Kruegel, and E. Kirda. Panorama: Capturing system-wide information flow for malware detection and analysis. In *Proceedings of the 14th ACM Conference on Computer and Communications Security, CCS '07*, pages 116–127, 2007.

Panel: Trustworthy Data Science

Adam Doupé[*]
Arizona State University
doupe@asu.edu

ABSTRACT

Much of the research that our community publishes is based on data. However, an open question remains: are the results of data science trustworthy, and how can we increase our trust in data science? Accomplishing this goal is difficult, as we must trust the inputs, systems, and results of data science. This panel will discuss the current state of trustworthy data science, and explore possible technical, legal, and cultural solutions that can increase our trust in the input, systems, and results of data science.

CCS Concepts

•General and reference → General conference proceedings;

Keywords

Data Science; Panel; Trust

1. SUMMARY

Much of the research that we, as a community, publish is based on data. For this panel, we will call any research results based on data *data science*. An open question remains: are the results of data science trustworthy, and how can we increase our trust in data science? Accomplishing this goal is difficult, as we must trust the inputs, systems, and results of data.

Can we ensure that the input data sets that we are using are representative and unbiased, thus establishing trust in the inputs to our data science system? This problem is very difficult when we consider the large datasets that we work with, for instance the web, malware, or mobile applications. How can we ensure that the datasets that we use and base our research results on are unbiased and representative?

Many of our data science systems rely on machine learning to generate results, however recent work in adversarial machine learning has shown that machine learning classifiers can be evaded by manipulating the input data, and therefore the systems that we build can be untrustworthy. Can these systems be made resistant to an active adversary? What threat models are realistic and should be considered?

Finally, even if we fully trust the inputs and the systems, how can we trust the results of data science? Traditional academic disciplines rely on the scientific principle of reproducibility—however, this seems to be missing in our field, due to complex technical, legal, and cultural reasons. What are some techniques that we can use to share datasets and improve reproducibility of our results?

As more and more research is based on data, it is critical that we explore ways that we can increase the trust in our inputs, systems, and outputs of data science.

2. QUESTIONS TO CONSIDER

This panel will discuss the current state of trustworthy data science, and explore possible technical, legal, and cultural solutions that can increase our trust in the input, systems, and results of data science. Some broad questions that the panel will consider follows.

- How does the community view research that replicates other studies? Should we, as a community, encourage reproducible research and replication studies? If so, how can we actually achieve this goal?

- What prevents researchers from sharing data sets? What could be done to alleviate these problems? Are there technical research solutions that could prove useful?

- With many of our computing systems relying on machine learning algorithms, how much trust can we place in these systems? Can there be a trustworthy machine learning future, and if so how can we create that future?

- How does one know that a dataset is representative and unbiased? Are there techniques in collecting data that can improve the representativeness of the underlying population?

- How can we trust the output of research that is performed on datasets that the researchers are under legal obligations not to share (due to NDAs, privacy issues, etc.)?

---

[*]Panel Moderator.

CODASPY'17 March 22-24, 2017, Scottsdale, AZ, USA

© 2017 Copyright held by the owner/author(s).

ACM ISBN 978-1-4503-4523-1/17/03.

DOI: http://dx.doi.org/10.1145/3029806.3044199

Detecting ROP with Statistical Learning of Program Characteristics [*]

Mohamed Elsabagh
melsabag@gmu.edu

Daniel Barbará
dbarbara@gmu.edu

Dan Fleck
dfleck@gmu.edu

Angelos Stavrou
astavrou@gmu.edu

Department of Computer Science
George Mason University
Fairfax, VA 22030, USA

ABSTRACT

Return-Oriented Programming (ROP) has emerged as one of the most widely used techniques to exploit software vulnerabilities. Unfortunately, existing ROP protections suffer from a number of shortcomings: they require access to source code and compiler support, focus on specific types of gadgets, depend on accurate disassembly and construction of Control Flow Graphs, or use hardware-dependent (microarchitectural) characteristics. In this paper, we propose EigenROP, a novel system to detect ROP payloads based on unsupervised statistical learning of program characteristics. We study, for the first time, the feasibility and effectiveness of using *microarchitecture-independent* program characteristics — namely, memory locality, register traffic, and memory reuse distance — for detecting ROP. We propose a novel directional statistics based algorithm to identify deviations from the expected program characteristics during execution. EigenROP works transparently to the protected program, without requiring debug information, source code or disassembly. We implemented a dynamic instrumentation prototype of EigenROP using Intel Pin and measured it against in-the-wild ROP exploits and on payloads generated by the ROP compiler ROPC. Overall, EigenROP achieved significantly higher accuracy than prior anomaly-based solutions. It detected the execution of the ROP gadget chains with 81% accuracy, 80% true positive rate, only 0.8% false positive rate, and incurred comparable overhead to similar Pin-based solutions.

Keywords

Return Oriented Programming; Anomaly Detection; Program Characteristics; Directional Statistics .

---

[*]An extended version of this paper is available as a technical report at http://cs.gmu.edu/techreports/2017

CODASPY'17, March 22–24, 2017, Scottsdale, AZ, USA
© 2017 ACM. ISBN 978-1-4503-4523-1/17/03. . . $15.00
DOI: http://dx.doi.org/10.1145/3029806.3029812

1. INTRODUCTION

Since its introduction by Shacham in 2007 [19], Return-Oriented Programming (ROP) has become an increasingly popular technique for bypassing Data Execution Prevention (DEP) defenses on modern operating systems. DEP ensures that all writable memory pages of a program are non-executable, which prevents the execution of any input data, effectively mitigating all classic code injection attacks. In a ROP attack, on the other hand, the attacker does not inject new code. Instead, existing sequences of instructions in the process executable memory, called *gadgets*, are chained together to perform the intended computation. While the traditional Address Space Layout Randomization (ASLR) randomizes the location of most libraries and executables, ROP attacks can still bypass ASLR by finding a few code segments in statically known locations, or through brute-forcing and de-randomization by exploiting memory disclosure vulnerabilities.

Present ROP detection solutions aim at detecting ROP attacks at runtime, via means of signature-based or anomaly-based detection. Signature-based solutions detect ROP attacks by identifying static signatures (patterns) in the execution trace of programs. The most common method is to detect gadgets execution by enforcing predefined constraints over the program counter and the call stack, either through dynamic instrumentation [7, 12, 9] or by leveraging existing hardware branch tracing features [6]. These solutions incur very low overhead, but the employed signatures are often incomplete due to strong constraints on the ROP structure, allowing the defenses to be bypassed by attackers (e.g., [5]).

Anomaly-based detection, on the other hand, learns a baseline of normal (clean) behavior and detects attacks by measuring statistical deviations from the normal behavior. This approach has the significant advantage of being able to protect against a broad spectrum of attacks, including zero-day. Recent anomaly-based ROP defenses utilized hardware characteristics to detect attacks [14, 8, 15, 22]. They generally used two classes of characteristics: 1) architectural characteristics, which are dependent on the instruction set architecture (ISA), such as the number of load and store instructions retired. And, 2) microarchitectural characteristics, meaning characteristics that depend on the underlying microarchitecture configurations, such as branches misprediction rate and cache misses. These characteristics were typically measured by reading the hardware performance counters (HPC) of the underlying processor. However, a common pitfall is that characteristics measured using HPC may actually *hide* the underlying program behavior, making the HPC-based metrics appear similar for inherently different behaviors [10].

In this paper, we introduce EigenROP, a novel system for detecting ROP attacks. We study, for the first time, the feasibility and value of using microarchitecture-independent program characteristics for the detection of ROP attacks. We propose a new type of anomaly-based ROP detectors that leverages *microarchitecture-independent* program characteristics, including memory reuse distance, register traffic load, memory locality, among others, in addition to traditional hardware characteristics (see Section 4).

EigenROP employs a novel anomaly detection algorithm that builds on concepts from directional statistics (see Section 5). The fundamental idea is that strong relationships among the different program characteristics will appear as principal axes in some high-dimensional space. Since ROP executes against the control flow of the program, it is reasonable to assume that it causes some unexpected changes in the relationships between the program characteristics learned from benign runs. Such changes can be detected as statistically significant deviations in the directions of the axes in the high-dimensional space. We investigate if and to what extent ROP causes changes in program characteristics, and verify our hypothesis with extensive experiments using multiple in-the-wild ROP payloads and payloads generated by the ROPC ROP compiler.

We implemented a prototype of EigenROP on Linux, using the dynamic instrumentation framework Pin [13]. We conducted several experiments to quantify the accuracy of EigenROP, the effect of involved parameters and the incurred performance overhead (see Section 6). In our experiments, microarchitecture-independent characteristics resulted in 11% increase on average in detection accuracy, relative to using only microarchitectural characteristics. EigenROP achieved an overall accuracy of 81%, 80% true positive rate, and only 0.8% false positive rate. The incurred performance overhead decayed exponentially as the sampling interval increases, and faster than the deterioration in accuracy.

To summarize, we make the following contributions:
- We study the effectiveness of combining microarchitecture-independent program characteristics with typical hardware characteristics for the detection of ROP attacks.
- We propose a novel anomaly detection algorithm using directional statistics of program characteristics, embedded in high-dimensional space.
- We present EigenROP, a working prototype of our approach.
- We quantify the security effectiveness of EigenROP using in-the-wild ROP attacks against common Linux programs, as well as the accuracy-performance trade-off.

2. BACKGROUND

2.1 Return-Oriented Programming

Return Oriented Programming (ROP) enables attackers to execute arbitrary code *without* injecting new code into the victim process, by returning to arbitrary instruction sequences in the executable memory of the program.

A typical ROP attack operates as follows: first, the attacker overwrites the stack contents with addresses of the desired ROP gadgets. Once the ret instruction of the current routine is executed, the first return address of the current stack frame is used as a return target. Instruction sequences at that address will execute, till the next ret instruction. Upon execution of the ret instruction, control is transferred to the next gadget. This process repeats, jumping from one gadget to the next, till the gadget chain terminates.

It has been shown that ROP can perform Turing-Complete computations if the attacker can find sufficient gadgets to perform memory, arithmetic, logical operations and system calls [23]. Also, it is worth mentioning that ret-based ROP is not the only way to launch or chain attacks. We discuss in Section 7 how other variants of ROP are detected by EigenROP.

2.2 Microarchitecture-independent Characteristics

It has been shown that microarchitecture-independent characteristics have higher discrimination power between different inherent program behaviors, compared to architectural and microarchitectural characteristics [10]. Microarchitecture-independent characteristics are program characteristics that are unique to a given instruction set architecture (ISA) and a given compiler but are independent of a given microarchitecture. In other words, the characteristics are *invariant* of the underlying hardware cache size, pipeline size, branch predictors size and algorithm, number of cores and their configurations, and so on. In the context of ROP detection, several microarchitecture-independent characteristics can prove useful in discriminating between benign execution behavior and gadget execution, such as memory locality and reuse distance, and register traffic (see Section 4 for details). Note that while characteristics dependent on the ISA, i.e., architectural characteristics, can be regarded as a subset of microarchitecture-independent characteristics, we keep them distinct in this work as is the trend in prior program characterization work [10, 14, 22].

The main downside of solutions using microarchitecture-independent characteristics is that there is currently no kernel or hardware support to collect the characteristics. Therefore, our prototype implementation requires runtime instrumentation to measure the characteristics. However, the overhead decays over time as more efficient algorithms and tools are developed, as as hardware and kernel support becomes available [3].

In the following section, we outline the big picture of how EigenROP works.

3. OVERVIEW OF EigenROP

The key idea of EigenROP is to identify *anomalies* in program characteristics, due to the execution of ROP gadgets. In this context, it is difficult to precisely define what anomalies are since that depends on the characteristics of both the monitored program and the ROP. However, it is reasonable to assume that some unexpected change occurs in the relationships among the different program characteristics due to the execution of the ROP. By extracting and learning arbitrary relationships among the program characteristics, EigenROP detects ROP by looking for unexpected changes in the learned relationships.

Given our definition of anomaly, strong relationships among the measured program characteristics should appear as principal directions in some high-dimensional space. Such direc-

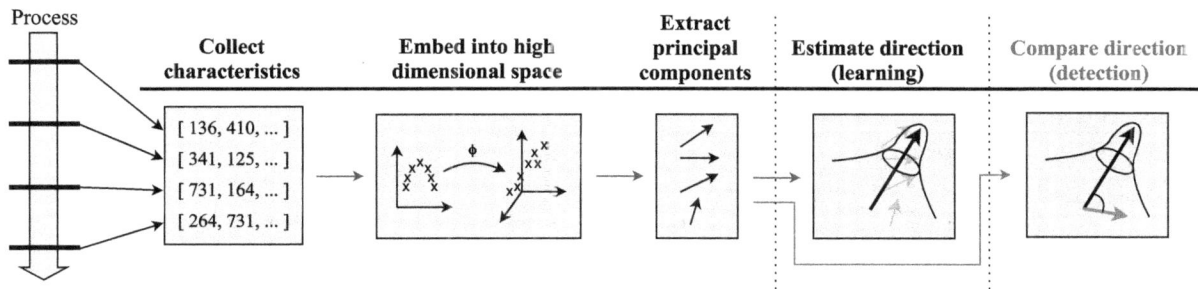

Figure 1: Workflow of EigenROP. It periodically interrupts the monitored process, measures the characteristics, embeds them into a high-dimensional space, extracts the principal directions in that space, and estimates a representative direction and density around the direction. In the detection phase, the principal directions of incoming measurements are test for significant deviation from the learned direction and density.

tions can be extracted using Kernel Principal Component Analysis (KPCA). More specifically, the principal component vectors of the measurements mapped into the high-dimensional space can be interpreted as the *relationships* among the program characteristics.

The general workflow of EigenROP is illustrated in Figure 1. First, the target program is loaded and executed. During execution, EigenROP takes a snapshot of the different program characteristics, every N instructions retired. Each snapshot is a $d-$dimensional vector of characteristics. The snapshots are pushed to a buffer that EigenROP iterates over using a sliding window.

In the learning phase, the target program is executed over benign inputs. For each window of measured characteristics, EigenROP maps the measurements into a high-dimensional space and extracts the principal components of the measurements in that space. EigenROP then estimates a representative *direction* from all the principal components, and estimates the density of the distances of all principal components around the representative direction. Recall, the idea here is that any strong relationships among the measured characteristics will appear as principal components in the high-dimensional space. In the detection phase, EigenROP computes the distances of the principal components of incoming measurements, in the high-dimensional space, to the representative direction. If the distance exceeds some threshold, then an alarm is raised.

In the following, we define the characteristics used by EigenROP and explain in detail how learning and detection work.

4. WHICH CHARACTERISTICS TO MEASURE?

To choose the most relevant characteristics for ROP detection, we conducted several experiments to collect clean and infected measurements from a variety of programs and exploits (see Section 6.2). We considered most of the characteristics used in previous program characterization work [10, 14, 22]. Then, we used the Fisher Score to quantify the discriminative power of each characteristic. The following is a brief description of the shortlisted categories of characteristics we measured. The letters between brackets denote the type of the characteristics: **A**rchitectural [A], **M**icroarchitecture-**I**ndependent [I], and **M**icroarchitectural [M]. We

emphasize that all the characteristics used in this work are computed in software.

- **Branch predictability [M].** Since ROP attacks disturb the normal control flow of execution, they may increase the number of mispredicted branches by the processor branch predictor.

- **Instruction mix [A].** This is a traditional architectural characteristic that measures the frequency of different classes of instructions (branch, call, stack, load and store, arithmetic, among others). Since ROP attacks depend on chaining blocks of instructions that load data from the hijacked program stack to registers, and for returning to the stack, they may exhibit different usage of `ret` and `call` instructions as well as stack `pop` and `push` instructions.

- **Memory locality [I].** Given a set of instructions, memory locality is the difference in the data addresses between subsequent memory accesses. Here, it is typical that a distinction is made between memory reads (loads) and writes (stores). Since ROP attacks depend on chaining gadgets from arbitrary memory locations, the attacks may exhibit low memory locality when compared to clean execution. The memory distance between subsequent reads and writes may indicate the execution of a ROP attack.

- **Register traffic [I].** Two useful register traffic characteristics can be measured: 1) the average number of register input operands to an instruction; and 2) the register reuse distance, i.e., the number of instructions between writing a register and reading it. ROP attacks load data from the hijacked stack to registers typically using pop instructions that take a single operand. Therefore, the number of instruction operands could be an indicator of the presence of a gadget chain. Additionally, the usage degree of the registers themselves could be different from that of clean execution.

- **Memory reuse [I].** This metric measures the number of unique cache blocks referenced between subsequent memory reads. For each memory read, the corresponding cache block is retrieved (assuming LRU cache). For each cache block, the number of unique cache blocks

Table 1: Top 15 characteristics sorted by discrimination power (highest to lowest). Chosen characteristics are marked with ⋆. All counts are for instructions (insns) retired.

Rank	Type	Name	Description
⋆ 1	A	INST_RET	# leave and ret insns.
⋆ 2	A	INST_CALL	# near call insns.
⋆ 3	I	MEM_REUSE	Memory reuse distance.
⋆ 4	A	INST_STACK	# pop and push insns.
⋆ 5	I	MEM_RDIST	Memory read distance.
6	A	INST_LOAD	# memory read insns.
⋆ 7	I	REG_OPS	Avg. # register operands.
⋆ 8	M	MISP_CBR	Mispredicted branches.
9	A	INST_ARITH	# arithmetic insns.
⋆ 10	M	MISP_RET	Mispredicted ret insns.
11	A	INST_STORE	# memory write insns.
⋆ 12	I	MEM_WDIST	Memory write distance.
⋆ 13	A	INST_NOP	# nop insns.
14	I	REG_REUSE	Register reuse distance.
15	I	ILP	Instruction level parallelism.

accessed since the last time it was referenced is determined. Since ROP attacks operate by using the stack for chaining the gadgets, and the gadgets are typically spread out across the memory of the program, they shall exhibit abnormal reuse of the same memory blocks when compared to clean execution.

Table 1 shows the top 15 characteristics, ranked by their Fisher scores. For each characteristic i, its Fisher Score is computed by:

$$ score_i = \frac{m^{(+)}\left(\bar{\mathbf{x}}_i^{(+)} - \bar{\mathbf{x}}_i\right)^2 + m^{(-)}\left(\bar{\mathbf{x}}_i^{(-)} - \bar{\mathbf{x}}_i\right)^2}{m^{(+)}s_i^{2(+)} + m^{(+)}s_i^{2(-)}}, \quad (1) $$

where $(+)$ and $(-)$ are the infected and clean classes of measurements, respectively; $\bar{\mathbf{x}}_i^{(y)}$ and $s_i^{2(y)}$ are the mean and variance of characteristic i in class $y \in \{+, -\}$, and $\bar{\mathbf{x}}_i$ is the overall mean of feature i over both the infected and clean measurements. The Fisher Score is a widely established feature filtering method that assigns higher scores to features that result in greater separation between the means of clean and infected samples. Note that we used infected and clean measurements here to quantify the discriminative power of the selected characteristics. The infected measurements are **not** used during the learning phase of EigenROP.

Since the Fisher Score ignores mutual information, some of the scored characteristics might be redundant. Therefore, we picked 10 features out of the top 15 as follows. First, we excluded Instruction Level Parallelism (a measure of how many instructions of a program can be executed in parallel) since it added significant performance overhead and is highly dependent on the type of application. For example, cryptography applications may exhibit low instruction level parallelism, while a scientific computation program may exhibit high parallelism. Similarly, we excluded INST_LOAD and INST_ARITH. Via experimentation, we found that REG_REUSE does not increase the accuracy of the model, so we excluded it as well.

5. LEARNING AND DETECTION

Given a sequence T of d-dimensional measurements, we divide T into n subsequences using a sliding window of width

m. Let us denote the resulting subsequences by:

$$ S^{(j)} = \begin{bmatrix} \mathbf{x}_1^{T(j)} \\ \mathbf{x}_2^{T(j)} \\ \vdots \\ \mathbf{x}_m^{T(j)} \end{bmatrix}, \quad (2) $$

for $j = 1 \dots n$. Note that each $\mathbf{x}_i^{(j)}$ is a vector of d measured characteristics.

Next, each $S^{(j)}$ is embedded (implicitly mapped) into a higher dimension space $\mathcal{H}$ with $\Phi : \mathbb{R}^d \to \mathcal{H}$, and the principal component vectors of $S^{(j)}$ in $\mathcal{H}$ are extracted. This is done using Kernel PCA [17], which solves the following eigenvalue problem:

$$ \lambda_i^{(j)} \mathbf{v}_i^{(j)} = K \mathbf{v}_i^{(j)}, \quad (3) $$

where $\lambda_i^{(j)}$ are the eigenvalues of K, $\mathbf{v}_i^{(j)}$ are the normalized eigenvectors of K, and K is the $m \times m$ kernel matrix $\left[k\left(\mathbf{x}_i^{(j)}, \mathbf{x}_l^{(j)}\right)\right]$ for $i = 1 \dots m; l = 1 \dots m$. Here, k is the kernel function, which we set to the Radial Basis Function (RBF) given by:

$$ k(\mathbf{x_1}, \mathbf{x_2}) = \Phi(\mathbf{x_1})\Phi(\mathbf{x_2})^T \quad (4) $$
$$ = \exp\left(-\gamma \|\mathbf{x_1} - \mathbf{x_2}\|^2\right), \quad (5) $$

where $\gamma = \frac{1}{d}$. We assume K is centered, i.e., $K = K - \mathbf{1}_m K - K \mathbf{1}_m + \mathbf{1}_m K \mathbf{1}_m$, where $\mathbf{1}_m$ is an $m \times m$ matrix for which each element takes the value $\frac{1}{m}$.

Using the eigenvalues and eigenvectors in $\mathcal{H}$, the *resultant* direction $\mathbf{v}^{(j)}$ of the data $S^{(j)}$, embedded in $\mathcal{H}$, is then computed by:

$$ \mathbf{v}^{(j)} = c \sum_{i=1}^{m} \lambda_i^{(i)} \mathbf{v}_i^{(j)}, \quad (6) $$

where c is a normalizing factor such that $\mathbf{v}^{(j)T}\mathbf{v}^{(j)} = 1$. This direction can be perceived as a representative direction of all the principal axes of $S^{(j)}$ in the kernel space $\mathcal{H}$.

We then compute the mean direction $\boldsymbol{\mu}$ of T by:

$$ \boldsymbol{\mu} = \frac{\sum_{j=1}^{n} \mathbf{v}^{(j)}}{\left\| \sum_{j=1}^{n} \mathbf{v}^{(j)} \right\|}. \quad (7) $$

The direction $\boldsymbol{\mu}$ is the representative direction for the entire trace of characteristics, where the extracted directions $\mathbf{v}^{(j)}$ distribute around $\boldsymbol{\mu}$. To handle multiple runs $\{T^{(i)}\}_{i=1}^k$, where each $T^{(i)}$ corresponds to a different run of the monitored program, we compute the family of sets of directions $\mathcal{V} = \{\{\mathbf{v}^{(j)}\}_{j=1}^{n^{(i)}}\}_{i=1}^k$, then compute $\boldsymbol{\mu}$ over $\mathcal{V}$.

Hence, the following similarity vector Z is constructed:

$$ Z = \begin{bmatrix} \mathbf{v}^{(1)T}\boldsymbol{\mu} \\ \mathbf{v}^{(2)T}\boldsymbol{\mu} \\ \vdots \\ \mathbf{v}^{(n)T}\boldsymbol{\mu} \end{bmatrix}, \quad (8) $$

where each row corresponds to the angular distance between each direction $\mathbf{v}^{(j)}$ and $\boldsymbol{\mu}$.

Next, a kernel density is estimated over Z using the standard normal kernel density estimator, given by:

$$ f_h(z) = \frac{1}{nh} \sum_{i=1}^{n} \mathsf{N}\left(\frac{z - z_i}{h}\right), \quad (9) $$

where h is the smoothing parameter (the bandwidth), $z_i \in Z$, and N is the standard normal function. In our implementation, we chose the value of h using grid search.

The resulting density is expected to be close to exponential since the directions extracted from clean measurements are expected to be concentrated (tightly distributed around $\boldsymbol{\mu}$), resulting in a skewed density with a peak around high similarity values. Therefore, we reduce the effect of skewness of f_h by applying the following logarithmic transform:

$$\hat{f}_h(z) = f_h(z) \log\left(f_h(z)\right), \qquad (10)$$

where the area under the curve of $\hat{f}_h(z)$ gives the entropy η of $\hat{f}_h$. This transforms the bulk of the density towards the peak, resulting in a shorter (easier to threshold) tail.

This concludes the learning phase. The following subsection explains the anomaly metric and the detection phase of EigenROP.

5.1 Anomaly Metric

Given an incoming subsequence of measurements $S'^{(j)}$, an anomaly is detected if the direction of $S'^{(j)}$, in the $\mathcal{H}$ space, is significantly different from the learned directions around $\boldsymbol{\mu}$. The decision r is computed by:

$$\mathbf{v}'^{(j)} \text{ from Eq. } (6) \qquad (11)$$

$$z'^{(j)} = \mathbf{v}'^{(j)T} \boldsymbol{\mu} \qquad (12)$$

$$\zeta = \int_{-1}^{z'^{(j)}} \hat{f}_h(z)\, dz \qquad (13)$$

$$r = \text{sgn}(\zeta - \theta\eta), \qquad (14)$$

where $\theta \in (0,1)$ is the detection threshold, which sets the fraction of the entropy that the model leaves out for detecting attacks. This concludes the detection phase.

5.2 Detection Time and Space Complexity

Computing the anomaly metric requires performing the KPCA computation (Eq. (3)) in $O(m^3)$ [17]. Computing the resultant vector (Eq. (6)) takes $\Theta(m^2)$. The distance in Eq. (12) is computed in $\Theta(m)$. Thus, it takes a total time of $O(m^3)$ to compute the anomaly metric. Our model requires space $m \cdot d$ for the incoming measurements window $S^{(j)}$, m for the representative direction $\boldsymbol{\mu}$, and c for the transformed density (Eq. (10)), where c is the number of points of the density. Thus, it takes a total space of $\Theta(md+c)$. Note that all terms in our prototype implementation of EigenROP are bounded: $d = 10$, $m \leq 10$ and $c \leq 1000$.

6. EVALUATION

We implemented EigenROP on top of MICA [11], a Pintool for collecting program characteristics. Pin [13] is a generic dynamic instrumentation framework with a rich API that Pintools use to specify own instrumentation code. Pintools are written in C/C++. We chose Pin since it achieves the best performance among various dynamic instrumentation platforms [13]. The EigenROP module is implemented in ~700 lines of Python, with the aid of the SciKit-Learn [2] machine learning toolkit.

We evaluate the security effectiveness, the added value of using microarchitecture-independent characteristics, and the tradeoff between runtime overhead and the detection accuracy of EigenROP. For security evaluation, we conducted several experiments using in-the-wild ROP attacks and attacks generated by the ROPC [1] compiler. For performance evaluation, we used the UnixBench systems benchmark. We ran our experiments on an Intel Core i7-487JHQ 2.5 GHZ machine with 4 GB of RAM, running 32-bit Linux Ubuntu 12.04, Intel Pin version 2.14, MICA version 0.40 and GCC version 4.6.3.

Table 2: Data set used in our experiments.

Program	Avg. Payload Length	# of Samples
cmp	800	80
cpio	650	210
diff	910	140
file	700	315
grep	631	150
hteditor	60	100
openssl	1021	195
php	400	265
sed	570	350
sort	712	110
stat	673	110
wget	813	90
	Total Samples:	2115

6.1 Dataset and Evaluation Procedure

We used two publicly available ROP exploits: OSVDB-ID:87289 and OSVDB-ID:72644, for the Linux Hex Editor (hteditor) version 2.0.20 and PHP version 5.3.6, respectively. We also used a number of exploits generated by the ROP gadgets finder and compiler ROPC [1], for common Linux programs (4 different exploits per program). Table 2 shows the programs used in our evaluation, the average payload length (the number of instructions) of each exploit, and the number of samples per program.

We collected clean samples for each target program by running the functionality tests that shipped with the program. In the case of hteditor, as it did not ship with functionality tests, we ran it on 100 random PDF files downloaded from the web. We collected infected samples following a similar approach to [6]: assume that the attacker had successfully compromised the target process, and inject code into the target process to load a given exploit payload into memory and execute it. The payload (gadgets) is executed by directly jumping to the beginning of the payload at random points during the execution of the process. Each payload execution was considered an infected (attack) sample.

For each program, we used 5-fold cross-validation: 4 clean folds for training, and 1 clean fold for testing along with infected samples. We used the same number of clean and infected samples in the testing fold. The mean of the resulting five TPRs and FPRs is then used in computing the Receiver Operating Characteristics (ROC) and its Area Under Curve (AUC). The higher the AUC, the higher the detection accuracy. The AUC reaches its best value at 1 and its worst at 0. We stress that labeled measurements were collected strictly for testing; EigenRCP uses only the clean measurements for training.

6.2 Detection Accuracy

EigenROP successfully detected the hteditor ROP exploit with sampling intervals up to 16k instructions retired and detected the PHP ROP with sampling intervals up to 32k. In both cases, EigenROP resulted in *zero* false positives. We emphasize that the focus here is on the detection of the ROP stage of the exploits, i.e., the execution of a gadget chain, rather than the execution of a shell code or a different process (both were shown to be easily detectable (e.g., [14]). Despite the very small ROP length (only ~60 instructions in the case of hteditor) when compared to the sampling window size, EigenROP still detected the deviation in the programs characteristics.

Figure 2 shows the overall ROC of all experiments, for a sampling interval of 16k instructions. EigenROP achieved an overall accuracy (AUC) of 81%. The best point of performance had 80% TPR and 0.8% FPR. This is significantly higher than the state-of-the-art microarchitectural defenses [22, 14], where the detection accuracy (AUC) ranged from ranged from 49% to 68%.

The breakdown of the detection accuracy for different sampling intervals is shown in Figure 3. As expected, the accuracy drops for very large sampling intervals, given the small number of instructions of the attacks. Out of all the programs, wget had the worst detection accuracy due to excessive use of signals, which exhibits poor locality and reuse (see Section 7 for discussion). The density estimate of wget was very heavy-tailed, which resulted in low discrimination between clean runs and attacks. On the other hand, openssl had the highest detection accuracy, as its characteristics had higher concentration around the mean direction. The bulk of the distribution of the AUC curves neared the best accuracy curve (the AUC was skewed towards the worst accuracy curve), indicating that the behavior of wget was possibly an outlier.

Figure 4 shows the difference in accuracy with and without the microarchitecture-independent characteristics. By including microarchitecture-independent characteristics, an increase of 9% to 15% in accuracy was achieved. This indicates that microarchitecture-independent characteristics contribute significantly to the detection performance of Eigen-ROP.

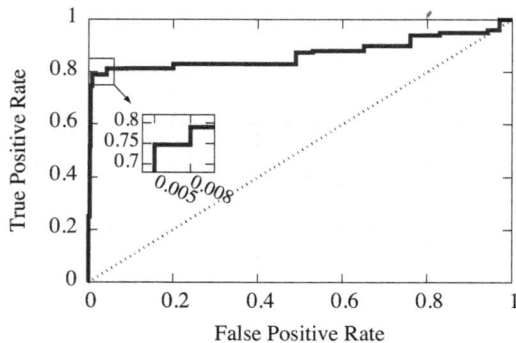

Figure 2: Overall ROC of EigenROP with 16k sampling interval. The AUC is 0.81.

6.3 Overhead-Accuracy Tradeoff

We quantified the overhead of EigenROP for different sampling intervals by measuring the overall percentage slowdown in execution of UnixBench. Figure 5 shows the overhead and accuracy tradeoff. The overhead incurred by Eigen-

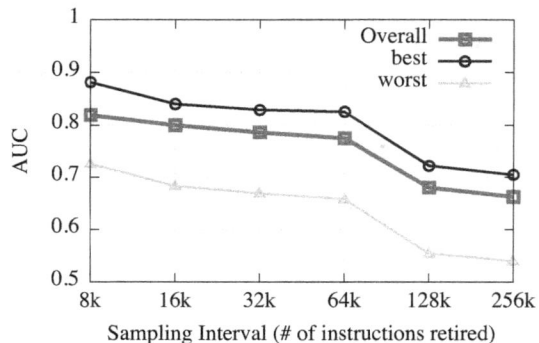

Figure 3: AUC for different sampling intervals. The higher the curve, the higher the accuracy.

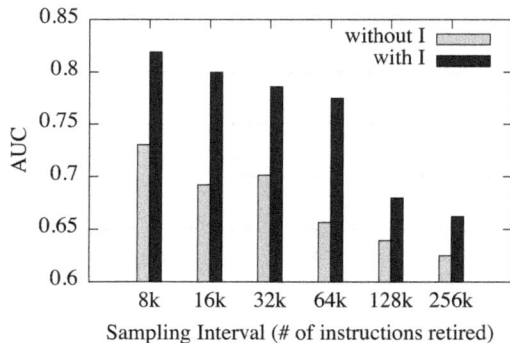

Figure 4: AUC for different sampling intervals, with and without the microarchitecture-independent characteristics.

ROP exponentially decreases as the sampling interval increases. We also observe that the reduction in overhead *outpaces* the decay in accuracy. The overhead incurred by MICA is approximately constant as MICA analyzes the individual instructions of target programs, and the total number of instructions of each execution is invariant of the sampling interval. Overall, the incurred runtime overhead is comparable to similar dynamic instrumentation and HPC-based defenses [7, 22]. Note that we did not perform any optimization attempts to reduce the overhead of EigenROP or MICA. Our work is orthogonal to how the program characteristics are collected. While we used MICA and Pin in our prototype implementation of EigenROP, they may not be the best tools for full build-out and full production. Finally, we emphasize that the memory and space overhead incurred by EigenROP are bounded and negligible (see Section 5.2).

7. DISCUSSION

7.1 False Positives and Negatives

The detection approach of EigenROP (and relevant HPC-based solutions [14, 8, 22]) is based on the hypothesis that programs exhibit characteristics that are relatively concentrated around some statistic – in our case, the mean direction. However, if a program exhibits behavior that has a large spread, it becomes harder to separate anomalies from

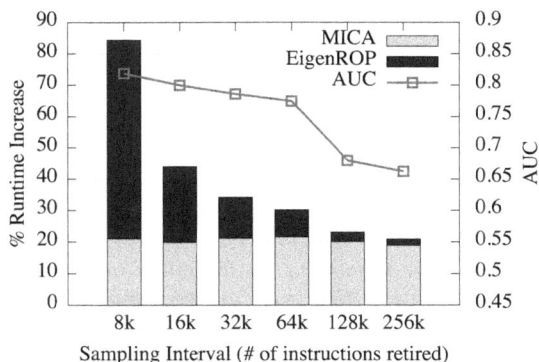

Figure 5: Overhead-accuracy tradeoff. The runtime overhead of MICA is measured relative to the overhead of Pin.

benign executions, resulting in a higher false positive rate (or a lower true positive rate).

From our experience with EigenROP, we observed that programs that use far jumps (e.g., `setjmp/longjmp`, `signal`) or extensively multiplex between data sources (e.g., using `select` for socket multiplexing) are more likely to suffer from false positives. The reason is that such programming constructs access far code and data, which inherently exhibits poor branch predictability, memory locality, and reuse. A possible workaround is to identify the entry and exit points of such code sites and build a separate model for the characteristics exhibited by those code sites. ROP chains missed by EigenROP were very short chains (<40 instructions) with small gadgets (2-4 instructions per gadget). This is mainly due to the relatively large sampling interval compared to the chain size. To handle such very short chains, EigenROP can be complemented by low-overhead solutions that target short gadgets and chains (e.g., kBouncer [15] and ROPecker [6]).

7.2 ROP Variants

In our evaluation of EigenROP, we used conventional ROP payloads that use return instructions to chain the gadgets. However, several variants of ROP were discovered by researchers. For example, in [4], Jump-Oriented Programming (JOP) was introduced where indirect jumps are employed to chain the gadgets rather than using return instructions. In [18], COOP was introduced where a loop in the program code that invokes attacker-controlled virtual function calls in C++ binaries is used to dispatch and chain the gadgets.

In EigenROP, we picked the characteristics that cover the behavior of all ROP variants (branches, calls and returns, memory locality and reuse, stack usage, and `nop` sleds) regardless of how the gadgets are chained. Also, it is easy and straightforward to include other relevant characteristics if need be, such as the number of indirect jump instructions retired. Overall, EigenROP has the advantage that the detection is robust against attack variations, since it captures the execution behavior of benign runs, and does not put strong assumptions on how the gadgets are chained at the ISA level.

7.3 Evasion and Mimicry Attacks

Three recent attack gadgets were presented [5] that bypass ROP defenses through evasion and mimicry: call-preceded gadgets, evasion gadgets, and history-flushing gadgets.

Call-preceded gadgets are violate a common key assumption made by defenses that depend on branch tracing [15, 6, 7, 12]: a sequence ending in `ret` must be legitimate if it was preceded by *any* `call`. Since EigenROP does not depend on branch tracing, it is not vulnerable to attacks based on call-preceded gadgets. Moreover, the return address will be mispredicted, regardless of the gadget type, unless the `call-ret` are strictly paired. Since EigenROP takes the misprediction rate of returns into account (see Section 4), call-preceded gadgets will result in abnormal mispredictions, potentially increasing the detection accuracy.

Evasion gadgets use long gadgets to evade ROP detectors that look for short gadgets within an executing gadget chain (e.g., [15, 6]). Such solutions put constraints on the chain length, with the main presumption being that short gadgets are likely part of an executing ROP. Evasion gadgets violate that assumption by using long enough gadgets to violate such constraints. Since EigenROP does not depend on the gadget chain length, rather on the execution characteristics of the gadgets, it is not vulnerable to attacks based on evasion gadgets.

History-flushing gadgets target defenses that only keep a limited history about execution (typically dependent on the available hardware buffer size where the history is recorded). History is flushed by utilizing innocuous gadgets to fill up the history. For example, kBouncer [15] uses the Last Branch Record (LBR), a hardware feature that records *only* the most recent 16 taken branches by the processor. Therefore, it can be evaded by a ROP chain that executes any 16 valid indirect jumps to fill the LBR with legitimate branches [5].

In our context, flushing the history means manipulating *all* affected characteristics by the ROP, such that they appear normal. The attacker would need to chain gadgets that exhibit similar characteristics to benign code, in addition to achieving the attack goal. While this is theoretically possible, we argue that it is hard to realize such attacks in practice. First, chaining more gadgets would require larger attacker-controlled memory space. Second, if the attacker includes benign code in the ROP to mimic normal behavior, the benign code would be required to either have no effect on the actual ROP execution or be undone by chaining, even more, gadgets. Third, and As noted in [5, 16], history flushing comes at the expense of significant slowdown (reported 20-times slowdown) in the execution of the ROP payload. Randomization-based defenses against evasion and mimicry (e.g., [24, 20]) can also be employed to further increase the attack cost.

8. RELATED WORK

Due to space constraints we briefly discuss only related anomaly-based solutions.

One of the first works on using hardware architectural characteristics of programs was the work of Malone et al. [14]. They showed that hardware performance counters (HPC) could be utilized to detect unauthorized software changes. The authors recorded HPC measurements of the original programs and used linear regression to detect if the program was modified at runtime. Demme et al. [8] ported the idea to Android, and proposed hardware modifications to detect malware using HPC measurements from good and malicious samples. Stewin et al. [21] proposed detecting DMA attacks by monitoring the number of transactions on the memory bus. In [22], Tang et al. combined microarchitectural characteristics with architectural characteristics to detect drive-by attacks. They assumed that attacks consist of three stages: ROP stage disables DEP, stage 1 downloads a malicious program, and stage 2 executes the malicious program. By training a one-class Support Vector Machine (oc-SVM) over the architectural and microarchitectural characteristics of benign samples, they showed that stage 1 of the attacks could be detected with high accuracy, while their model performed poorly on stage 2 of the attacks. This is because the oc-SVM is very sensitive to tuning parameters, and the chosen features did not have sufficient discrimination power to detect the execution of ROP chains. This is different from EigenROP since we solely focus on stage 2 of the attack.

9. CONCLUSION

We presented EigenROP, a novel anomaly-based ROP detector that utilizes program characteristics and directional statistics. To the best of our knowledge, we are the first to study the effectiveness of using microarchitecture-independent program characteristics versus typical architectural and microarchitectural characteristics, in the detection of ROP. We demonstrated the ability of EigenROP to detect both in-the-wild and pure ROP exploits, and discussed limitations and potential improvements. EigenROP is unsupervised, fully transparent, and does not require any side information about the protected programs.

While our work demonstrates that ROP payloads can be detected using simple program characteristics, there are still needed improvements concerning detection accuracy of very short chains and overhead reduction. Future hardware support can help on both fronts by enabling low-cost fine-grained monitoring. Despite that, EigenROP raises the bar for ROP attacks, and can easily run in-tandem with complementary ROP defenses.

Acknowledgments

We thank the anonymous reviewers for their comments. This material is based on work supported by the National Science Foundation (NSF) under grant no. SATC 1421747, and by the National Institute of Standards and Technology (NIST) under grant no. 60NANB16D285. Opinions, findings, conclusions, and recommendations expressed in this material are those of the authors and do not necessarily reflect the views of the NSF, NIST, or the US Government.

10. REFERENCES

[1] Ropc. https://github.com/pakt/ropc.

[2] Scikit. http://scikit-learn.org/stable/.

[3] Applications, tools and techniques on the road to exascale computing. In K. de Bosschere et al., editors, *Advances in Parallel Computing*, volume 22. 2012.

[4] T. Bletsch, X. Jiang, V. W. Freeh, and Z. Liang. Jump-oriented programming: a new class of code-reuse attack. In *6th ASIACCS*. ACM, 2011.

[5] N. Carlini and D. Wagner. Rop is still dangerous: Breaking modern defenses. In *USENIX Security*, 2014.

[6] Y. Cheng et al. Ropecker: A generic and practical approach for defending against rop attack. In *NDSS*, 2014.

[7] L. Davi, A.-R. Sadeghi, and M. Winandy. Ropdefender: A detection tool to defend against return-oriented programming attacks. In *6th ASIACCS*. ACM, 2011.

[8] J. Demme and others. On the feasibility of online malware detection with performance counters. *Computer Architecture News*, 41(3), 2013.

[9] I. Fratrić. Ropguard: Runtime prevention of return-oriented programming attacks, 2012.

[10] K. Hoste and L. Eeckhout. Comparing benchmarks using key microarch.-independent characteristics. In *Workload Characterization*. IEEE, 2006.

[11] K. Hoste and L. Eeckhout. Microarchitecture-independent workload characterization. *IEEE Micro*, 3, 2007.

[12] E. R. Jacobson and others. Detecting code reuse attacks with a model of conformant program execution. In *Engineering Secure Software and Systems*. Springer, 2014.

[13] C.-K. Luk et al. Building customized program analysis tools with dynamic instrumentation. In *PLDI*, 2005.

[14] C. Malone, M. Zahran, and R. Karri. Are hardware performance counters a cost effective way for integrity checking of programs. In *6th ACM workshop on Scalable Trusted Computing*, 2011.

[15] V. Pappas, M. Polychronakis, and A. D. Keromytis. Transparent rop exploit mitigation using indirect branch tracing. In *USENIX Security*, 2013.

[16] D. Pfaff et al. Learning how to prevent return-oriented programming efficiently. In *Engineering Secure Software and Systems*. Springer, 2015.

[17] B. Schölkopf, A. Smola, and K.-R. Müller. Kernel principal component analysis. In *Artificial Neural Networks - ICANN*, pages 583–588. Springer, 1997.

[18] F. Schuster et al. Counterfeit object-oriented programming: On the difficulty of preventing code reuse attacks in c++ applications. In *Security & Privacy*. IEEE, 2015.

[19] H. Shacham. The geometry of innocent flesh on the bone: Return-into-libc without function calls (on the x86). In *14th CCS*. ACM, 2007.

[20] C. Smutz and A. Stavrou. When a tree falls: Using diversity in ensemble classifiers to identify evasion in malware detectors. In *NDSS*, 2016.

[21] P. Stewin. A primitive for revealing stealthy peripheral-based attacks on the computing platformâĂŹs main memory. In *RAID*. Springer, 2013.

[22] A. Tang, S. Sethumadhavan, and S. J. Stolfo. Unsupervised anomaly-based malware detection using hardware features. In *RAID*. Springer, 2014.

[23] M. Tran et al. On the expressiveness of return-into-libc attacks. In *RAID*. Springer, 2011.

[24] K. Wang, J. J. Parekh, and S. J. Stolfo. Anagram: A content anomaly detector resistant to mimicry attack. In *RAID*. Springer, 2006.

Large-Scale Identification of Malicious Singleton Files

Bo Li
University of Michigan
bbbli@umich.edu

Chris Gates
Symantec Research Labs
Chris_Gates@symantec.com

Kevin Roundy
Symantec Research Labs
Kevin_Roundy@symantec.com

Yevgeniy Vorobeychik
Vanderbilt University
yevgeniy.vorobeychik@vanderbilt.edu

ABSTRACT

We study a dataset of billions of program binary files that appeared on 100 million computers over the course of 12 months, discovering that 94% of these files were present on a single machine. Though malware polymorphism is one cause for the large number of singleton files, additional factors also contribute to polymorphism, given that the ratio of benign to malicious singleton files is 80:1. The huge number of benign singletons makes it challenging to reliably identify the minority of malicious singletons. We present a large-scale study of the properties, characteristics, and distribution of benign and malicious singleton files. We leverage the insights from this study to build a classifier based purely on static features to identify 92% of the remaining malicious singletons at a 1.4% percent false positive rate, despite heavy use of obfuscation and packing techniques by most malicious singleton files that we make no attempt to de-obfuscate. Finally, we demonstrate robustness of our classifier to important classes of automated evasion attacks.

CCS Concepts

•Security and privacy → Software security engineering;

Keywords

Singleton files; malware detection; robust classifier

1. INTRODUCTION

Despite continual evolution in the attacks used by malicious actors, labeling software files as benign or malicious remains a key computer security task, with nearly 1 million malicious files being detected per day [29]. Some of the most reliable techniques label files by combining the context provided by multiple instances of the file. For example, Polonium judges a file based on the hygiene of the machines on which it appears [4], while Aesop labels a file by inferring its software-package relationships to known good or bad files,

based on file co-occurrence data [31]. These detection technologies are unable to protect customers from early instances of a file because they require the context from multiple instances to label malware reliably, only protecting customers from later instances of the file. Thus, the hardest instance of a malware file to label is its first, and regrettably, the first instance is also the last in most cases, as most malware samples appear on a single machine. In 2015 around 89% of all program binary files (such as executable files with .EXE and .DLL extensions on Windows computers) reported through Norton's Community Watch program existed on only one machine, a rate that has increased from 81% since 2012. To make matters worse, real-time protection must label files that have been seen only once even though they may eventually appear on many other machines, putting the effective percentage of unique files at any given time at 94%.

We present the first large-scale study of *singleton* files and identify novel techniques to label such files as benign or malicious based on their contents and context. We define a singleton file as any file that appears on exactly 1 machine. We consider two files to be distinct when a cryptographic hash taken over their contents (such as SHA-256) yields a different result, meaning that two files that differ by a single bit are considered distinct even though they may be functionally equivalent.

Due to the fact that malware is often polymorphic, many malicious files are among these singletons. However, singleton executable files do not trend towards being malicious; in fact the opposite is true: the ratio of benign to malicious singleton files is 80 to 1, resulting in a skewed dataset. This ratio gives low prevalence malware a large set of files to hide amongst and it makes effective classification models difficult to train, as most machine learning models require relatively balanced data sets for effective training. We study the root causes behind the large numbers of benign singleton files in Section 2.2 and study malicious singletons in Section 2.3. We study the properties of machines that are prolific sources of benign singleton files in Section 3.1. We filter obviously benign singletons by profiling the prominent categories of benign singleton files that appear on such systems (Section 3.2). We present the full machine learning pipeline and the features we use to classify these samples in Section 3.3. We present experimental results in Section 4.

Since the phenomenon of malicious singleton files was largely driven by the arms race between security vendors and malicious adversaries in the first place, it is important to analyze robustness of our model against evasion attacks, and we do so in Section 4.3. We form the interactions between and ad-

CODASPY'17, March 22-24, 2017, Scottsdale, AZ, USA
© 2017 ACM. ISBN 978-1-4503-4523-1/17/03. . . $15.00
DOI: http://dx.doi.org/10.1145/3029806.3029815

versary and our malware detection system as a Stackelberg game [34] and simulate evasion attacks on real singleton files to demonstrate that our proposed pipeline performs robustly against attacker interference.

In summary, we make the following contributions:

1. We provide the first detailed discussion of the role that benign polymorphism plays in making singleton file classification a challenging problem.

2. We identify root causes of benign polymorphism and leverage these to develop a method for filtering the most "obvious" benign files prior to applying malware classification methods.

3. We develop an algorithm that classifies 92% of malicious singletons as such, at a 1.4% false positive rate. We do so purely on the basis of static file properties, despite extensive obfuscation in most malware files, which we make no attempt to reverse.

4. We explore the adversarial robustness of multiple classification models to an important class of automated evasion/mimicry attacks, demonstrating the robustness of a performant set of features derived from static file properties.

2. SINGLETON FILES IN THE WILD

To address the paucity of information about singleton files, we study their causes, distribution patterns, and internal structure. We describe the predominant reasons for which software creators produce benign and malicious singleton files. For benign singletons, we identify the software packages that are the strongest predictors of the presence of benign singleton files on a machine. For malicious software, many singletons are produced from a relatively much smaller base of malware families. Thus, to better understand the nature of the polymorphism that is present in practice across a large body of singleton malware, we study the static properties of malicious singleton files across all malware families and within individual families.

2.1 Dataset Description

In the interest of performing a reproducible study, we perform the following study over data that is voluntarily contributed by members of the Norton Community Watch program, which consists of metadata about the binary files on their computers and an identifier of the machines on which they appear. Symantec shares a representative portion of this anonymized dataset with external researchers through its WINE program [10]. We use an extended window of time from 2012 through 2015 to generate high-level statistics about singleton data, and refer to this dataset as $D0$. We also use an 8-month window of data from 2014 for a more in depth analysis of the properties of singleton files and machines on which they appear, we call this $D1$. A portion of the files in $D1$ is labeled with high-confidence benign or malicious labels. We form dataset $D2$ by selecting a subset of the previous data that consists of labeled singleton files, and for which the file itself is available, allowing us to extract additional static features from the files that we describe in Section 3.3. The ground truth labels are generated by manually inspection and other high confident evidence. This dataset comprises 200,000 malicious and 16 million benign singleton files, and is the basis of the experimental evaluation of Section 4.

2.2 Benign Singleton Files

The abundance of benign singletons may be surprising given that there are not obvious benefits to distributing legitimate software as singleton files. Of course, some software is rare simply because it attracts few users, as in the case of software on a build machine that performs daily regression tests. However, there are also less obvious, but no less significant reasons behind the large numbers of singleton files, including the following:

1. The .NET Framework seeks to enable localized performance optimizations by distributing software in Microsoft Intermediate Language code so it can be compiled into native executable code by the .NET framework on the machine where it will execute, in a way that is specific to the machine's architecture. This is evident in practice, as .NET produces executables that are unique in most cases. Its widespread use makes it the largest driver of benign singleton files in our data.

2. Many classes of binary rewriting tools take a program binary file as input, producing a modified version as output, typically to insert additional functionality. For instance, tools such as Themida and Armadillo add resistance to tampering and reverse engineering, frequently to protect intellectual property and preserve revenue streams, as in the example of freemium games that require payment to unlock in-game features and virtual currency. Other examples of binary rewriting tools include the RunAsAdmin tool referenced in Table 1, which modifies executables so that administrative privileges are required to run them.

3. In many cases, software embeds product serial numbers or license keys in its files, resulting in a different hash-based identifier for otherwise identical files.

4. Singleton files can be generated by software that produces executable files in scenarios where other file formats are more typically used. For instance, Microsoft's Active Server Pages framework generates at least one DLL for every ASP webpage that references .NET code. Another example is ActiveCode's Building Information Modeling software that creates project files as executables rather than as data files. It is not uncommon for these frameworks to generate thousands of singleton binaries on a single machine.

5. Interrupted or partial downloads can result in files that appear to be singletons, even though they are really prefixes of a larger more complete file. If the entire file is available for inspection, this can be checked, but our dataset includes metadata for many files that have not been physically collected.

In Figure 1 we show the most common substring used in benign singleton filenames as extracted from dataset $D1$, many of which hint at the above factors. In particular, the most-observed filename pattern is "app-web-", which is seen in DLL files supporting web-pages created by ASP Web Applications. These files are often singletons because they are compiled from .NET code.

Using a subset of the data from dataset $D0$, we demonstrated in Figure 2 (a) that singleton files are not uniformly distributed across systems. The figure shows the number of machines that possess specific counts of singleton and non-singleton files. Figure 2 (b) is another way to view the same data, showing that almost 40% of machines have few or no singleton files and more than 94% of the systems have fewer than 100 singletons. Thus, the majority of singleton files

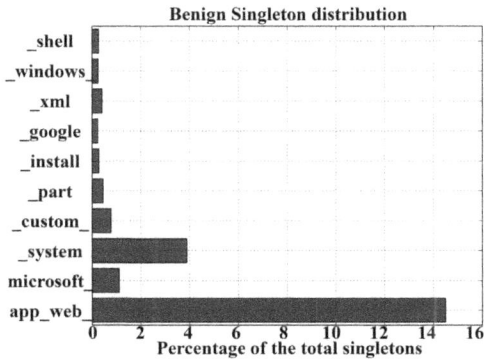

Figure 1: Percent of singleton files containing a specific substring.

come from the heavy tail of the distribution representing relatively few systems. Note that this data is from a specific period in time, and so machines with low numbers of non-singleton files indicate machines that experienced minimal changes/updates during the period when data was collected.

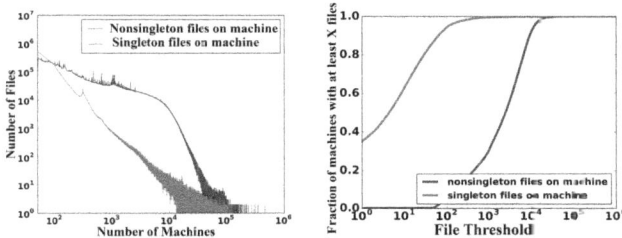

Figure 2: (a) Number of machines with a specific number of singleton/non-singleton files, (b) percent of machines that report more than X singleton and non-singleton files.

To help us work towards a solution that could identify benign singletons as such, we seek to better understand the machines on which they are most likely to exist. To identify software packages that could be responsible for the creation of singletons, we turn to the clustering approach proposed by Tamersoy et al. [31], which identifies software packages indirectly by clustering software files that are nearly always installed together on a machine, or not at all (see Section 3.1 for more details). Henceforth, we refer to these clusters as *software packages*. Once files are so clustered, we proceed by identifying the software packages that are most indicative of the presence of absence of singletons on a machine. Let S denote a specific software package (cluster). We identified a set of 10 million machines from $D1$, each of which contains at least 10 benign singleton files, which we denote by H (for *HasSingletons*). Likewise, we identified 10 million machines from $D1$ with no singleton files, which we denote by N, for *NoSingletons*. We identify the predictiveness of each software package S by counting its number of occurrences in each H and N, and use these counts to compute the odds ratios (OR) of a machine containing singletons given S, $OR(S) = H/N$. Intuitively, the higher $OR(S)$ is for a particular software package S, the more likely it is that this (benign) package generates many singletons. An $OR(S)$ ratio that is close to 1 is indicative of a software package that

is equally likely to appear on machines that do and do not contain singletons, and therefore probably does not generate singletons itself. On the other hand, an $OR(S)$ that is significantly lower than 1 indicates that machines on which S is installed are tightly controlled or special-use systems unlikely to contain singleton files.

Table 1 shows software packages that are strong predictors for the presence (or absence) of benign singletons on a machine. Software packages that correlate with increased numbers of singletons include compiler-related tools (Visual Studio, SoapSuds, SmartClient), tools that wrap or modify executables (RunAsAdmin, App-V), and software packages that include numerous signed singletons (Google Talk Plugin). Interestingly, there are also many software packages that correlate strongly with an absence of singletons on the system. These are indicative of tightly controlled or minimalist special-purpose systems.

Our ability to identify software packages that lead to presence/absence of many benign singleton files is a critical step towards developing a method for classifying malicious vs. benign singletons. In particular, as described in Section 3, it enables us to prune a large fraction of files as benign before applying machine learning methods, dramatically reducing the false positive rate.

2.3 Malicious Singleton Files

Malware files skew heavily towards low-prevalence files, and towards singleton files in particular. Using $D0$ we can see that this trend has increased in recent years: 75% of known malware files were singletons in 2012, and the rate increased to 86% by 2015. There are readily apparent reasons why malware files skew towards low-prevalence files, including the following:

1. Avoiding signature-based detection: Users typically want to prevent malware from running on their systems, and blocking a single high-prevalence file is much easier than blocking large numbers of distinct yet functionally equivalent files. Polymorphism is a widespread technique for producing many functionally equivalent program binaries, which aims to reduce the effectiveness of traditional Anti-Virus signatures over portions of the file.

2. Resistance to reverse engineering and tampering: Many malware authors pack, obfuscate or encrypt their binaries, often with the assistance of third-party tools that are inexpensive or free. Polymorphism is often a welcome byproduct of these techniques, though it is not necessarily the primary objective.

3. Malware attribution resistance: The ease with which malware authors can create many functionally equivalent malware files makes the problem of attributing a malicious file to its author much harder than it would be if the same file was used in all instances. For the same reason, polymorphism makes it difficult for security researchers to assess a malware family's reach. Modularity also allows for specific components to be used as needed, without unnecessarily exposing the binary to detection.

Despite the widespread availability and use of tools that can inexpensively apply polymorphism and obfuscation to malware binaries, the security industry has developed effective techniques to counter these. Much of the polymorphism seen in malware binaries is superficially applied by post-compilation binary obfuscation tools that "pack" the original contents of the malware file (by compressing or encrypting

Have singleton: Control set OR	Representative Filename	Software Name
13770:1	Appvux.dll	Microsoft App-V
11792:1	Soapsuds.ni.exe	SoapSuds Tool for XML Web Services
110501:2	Blpsmarthost.exe	SmartClient
36515:2	gtpo3d host.dll	Google Talk Plugin
13868:1	Runasadmin.exe	Microsoft RunAsAdmin Tool
8511:1	Microsoft.office.tools.ni.dll	Visual Studio
...	...	...
1:1702	Policy.exe	???
1:4392	vdiagentmonitor.exe	Citrix VDI-in-a-Box

Table 1: Software packages that are most predictive of presence/absense of benign singleton files. For succinctness, we represent each software package by its most prevalent filename.

the code), and add layers of additional obfuscation-related code [28]. There are some obfuscation tools that are far more complex than this, but most of them are used almost exclusively by either malicious or by benign software authors. Techniques used by the anti-virus industry to combat these obfuscations are discussed at the end of this section.

To provide additional insight into the nature of malware polymorphism, we study the use of polymorphism by 800 malware families that were observed in the wild in our $D1$ dataset. Overall, we found that 31% of these families are distributed exclusively as singletons, accounting for over 80% of all singleton malware files, while 60% of families rely exclusively on non-singletons. There is a subtle difference here, that by volume, the 60% of families account for many detections since they are higher prevalence, while the 80% of singletons account for a lower percent of all detections even though there are more of them, since they only occur on a single system.

To identify malware families that exhibit a high degree of polymorphism, we extracted about 200 static features from files belonging each malware family. Our features include most fields in the Portable Executable file header of Windows Executable files (such as file size, number of sections, etc.), as well as entropy statistics taken from individual binary sections, and information about dynamically linked external libraries and functions that are listed in the file's Import Table. For each malware family, we calculate variability scores as the average variance of our static features for the files belonging to that family. The families with the highest variability scores are:

- *Adware.Bookedspace*
- *Backdoor.Pcclient*
- *Spyware.EmailSpy*
- *Trojan.Usuge!gen3*
- *W32.Neshuta*
- *W32.Pilleuz*
- *W32.Svich*
- *W32.Tu1ik*

These malware families vary greatly in form, function, and scale, though they do share properties that help account for their high variance. In particular, all of these families are modular, infecting machines with multiple functionally different files that are of similar prevalence and have dramatically different characteristics. In all cases, there is at least an order of magnitude difference in file size between the largest and smallest binary. Furthermore, all samples apply binary packing techniques sporadically rather than in all instances.

Backdoor.Pcclient is a Remote Access Trojan and the lowest prevalence family that has high variance in the static features. Polymorphism is not evident in this family; its elevated variance is a reflection of a modular design, multiple releases of some of those modules, and large differences from one module to another. By contrast, *W32.Pilleuz* is a very prevalent worm family, but its Visual Basic executables achieve high variance through extensive obfuscation and highly variable file sizes, which add to the worm's modularity and occasional use of packing. *W32.Neshuta* is particularly interesting in that it infects all *.exe* and *.com* files on the machines that it compromises, resulting in many detected unique executables of differing sizes, in addition to its own modular and polymorphic code.

API Purpose	API Function
Anti-Analysis	$IsDebuggerPresent$
	$GetCommandLineW$
	$GetCurrentProcessId$
	$GetTickCount$
	$Sleep$
	$TerminateProcess$
Unpack Malware Payload	$GetProcAddress$
	$GetModuleHandleW$
	$GetModuleFileNameW$
Load/Modify Library Code	$CreateFileMappingA$
	$CreateFileMappingW$
	$MapViewOfFile$
	$SetFilePointer$
	$LockResource$
Propagation	$GetTempPathW$
	$CopyFileA$
	$CreateFileW$
	$WriteFile$

Table 2: Categories of Windows API functions that are disproportionately used by malware

The Windows API functions imported by malware files provide interesting insights into their behavior, and are useful as static features, because they are reasonably adversarially resistant. Though malware authors can easily add imports for API functions that they do not need, removing APIs is significantly harder, as these may be needed to compromise the system (e.g., CreateRemoteThread). The only inexpensive way in which a malware file can hide its use of API functions from static analysis is to use a binary packing tool so that its Import Table is not unpacked until runtime, when it is used to dynamically link to Windows API functions. However, this technique completely alters the file's static profile and introduces the static fingerprint of the obfuscation tool, offering an indication that the file is probably malicious. In addition, as discussed at the end of this section, these obfuscations can be reversed by anti-virus vendors.

Table 2 lists the API functions that are most disproportionately used by malware, categorized by the purpose for which malware authors typically use them. Many of these

APIs support analysis resistance, either by detecting an analysis environment, hiding behavior from analysis, or by actively resist against analysis. Most other APIs that are indicative of malware have to do with linking or loading to additional code at runtime, typically because the malware payload is packed, but also for more nefarious purposes, such as malicious code injection and propagation.

Anti-Virus Industry Response to Obfuscation:

The anti-virus industry has sought to adapt to malware's widespread use of obfuscation tools by applying static and dynamic techniques to largely reverse the packing process in a way that preserves many of the benefits of static analysis. In particular, these techniques allow malicious code to be extracted, along with the contents of the Import Address Table, which contains the addresses of functions imported from external dynamically linked libraries. Unpacking techniques include the "X-Ray" technique, which may be used to crack weak encryption schemes or recognize the use of a particular compression algorithm and reverse its effects [27]. Most unpacking techniques, however, have a dynamic component and can be broadly classified into emulators and secure sandboxes. Emulators do not allow malicious files to execute natively on the machine or to execute real system calls or Windows API calls, but provide a good approximation of a native environment nonetheless. They are frequently deployed on client machines so that any suspicious file can be emulated long enough to allow unpacking to occur, after which the program's malicious payload can be extracted from memory and the de-obfuscated code can be recovered and analyzed. Offline analysis of suspicious program binaries typically uses a near-native instrumented environment where the malware program can be executed and its dynamically unpacked malicious payload can be extracted [12]. Though there are more elaborate obfuscation schemes that can make executable files difficult to unpack with the aforementioned techniques, these are either not widely deployed (e.g., because they are custom-built for the malware family) or are used predominantly by benign or malicious software, but not both. Thus, effective benign vs. malicious determinations can be made even in these cases, because the obfuscation toolkits leave a recognizable fingerprint.

Though the effectiveness of the above de-obfuscation techniques is open to debate, in our methodology for this paper, we make the deliberate choice to use no de-obfuscation techniques at all in our attempts to classify singleton files. We demonstrate that malware classification based purely on static features can be successful, even in the face of extensive polymorphism, by good and bad files alike. The success we achieve demonstrates that the obfuscation techniques that are widely used by malware are themselves recognizable, and appreciably different from the kinds of polymorphism that are common in benign files. We expect that the classification accuracy of our methodology would improve when applied to files that have been de-obfuscated, given that other researchers have found this to be the case [13].

3. LEARNING TO IDENTIFY MALICIOUS SINGLETONS

Most prior efforts for identifying malicious files have either relied on the context in which multiple instances of the file appear (e.g., Polonium [4] and Aesop [31] systems) or

have relied exclusively on static or dynamic features derived from the file itself (e.g., MutantX-S [13]). The context that is available for a singleton file is necessarily limited, making the aforementioned context-dependent techniques not applicable. Making matters worse is the fact that the ratio of benign to malicious singleton files is nearly 80:1, which has the effect of multiplying the false positive rate of a malware detector by a factor of 80, and presents a significant class imbalance problem that makes effective classifier training difficult.

To address the lack of context for singleton files and the preponderance of benign singleton files, we leverage insights gleaned from our empirical observations about singleton files in the wild. In particular, as discussed in Section 2.2, a handful of software packages generate the lion's share of benign singletons, while other packages correlate with their absence. Furthermore, the toolchains that generate benign singletons in large numbers imbue them with distinctive static properties that make them easy to label with high confidence. We use these insights to develop a pipeline that filters benign singleton files with high confidence, yielding a more balanced dataset of suspicious files.

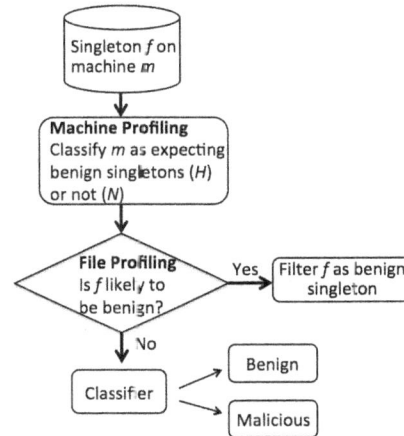

Figure 3: Pipeline of the singleton classification system.

Figure 3 presents a diagram of our pipeline. We take as input a pair (f, m), where f is a file and m is the machine on which it resides. The first step of the pipeline, which we call *machine profiling*, determines whether m is likely to host many benign singleton files. The second step is *file profiling*, in which we label obviously benign files, primarily from many-singleton machines, by determining that they closely match the benign files that are common on such systems. The final step, *classification*, uses a supervised classification algorithm (we explore the use of Support Vector Machines [30] and Recursive Neural Networks [21]) to render a final judgment on the remaining files. We proceed by describing each of our pipeline's components in detail.

3.1 Machine profiling

Machine profiling operationalizes the following insight gleaned from our empirical observations: since the distribution of benign singletons is highly non-uniform, singleton classification will benefit from identifying machines that are likely to host many benign singletons. As discussed in Section 2.2, the software packages present on a machine are highly predictive of the presence or absence of benign singletons.

The first challenge we face is that of automatically identifying software packages from telemetry about installations of individual program binary files. In mapping individual files to software packages, we wish to proceed in an automated way that is inclusive of rare software that is not available for public download. Our approach adopts the clustering portion of the Aesop system described by Tamersoy et al. [31], in which they leverage a dataset consisting of tuples of file and machine identifiers, each of which indicates the presence of file f on machine m. Specifically, let F be a set of (high-prevalence) files (in the training data). For each file $f \in F$, let $M(f)$ be the set of machines on which f appears. As Aesop did, we use locality sensitive hashing [11] to efficiently and approximately group files whose $M(f)$ sets display low Jaccard distance to one another. The Jaccard distance between two sets X and Y is defined as: $J(X,Y) = 1 - \frac{X \cap Y}{X \cup Y}$, and we define the distance between two files f and f' in terms of Jaccard distance as $d(f, f') = J(M(f), M(f'))$. We tune locality sensitive hashing to cluster files with high probability when the Jaccard distance between the files is less than 0.2, and to cluster them very rarely otherwise. We obtain a collection of clusters $\mathcal{C}$, such that each cluster $C \in \mathcal{C}$, serves as an approximation of a software package, since C represents a collection of files that are usually installed together on a machine or not at all.

We proceed by identifying the approximate software packages that are the best predictors for the presence of singleton files. We formulate this task as a machine learning problem. We define a feature vector for each machine m that encodes the set of software packages that exist on m. Specifically, given n clusters (software packages), we create a corresponding binary feature vector s_m of length n, where $s_{mj} = 1$ iff cluster j is present on machine m. Next, we append a label l_m to our feature vector such that we have $\{s_m, l_m\}$ for each machine, with feature vectors s_m corresponding to machines and labels $l_m \in \{H, N\}$ representing whether the associated machine *h*as benign singletons (label H) or has *n*o singletons (label N). With this dataset in hand, we are able to train a simple, interpretable classifier to predict l_m to good effect. Had we used individual files as predictors, we would have to choose a machine learning algorithm that behaves well in the presence of strongly correlated features, but software package identification dramatically reduces feature correlation. Thus, we select Naive Bayes as our classifier $g(s)$, which performs well and gives us significant insight into the software packages that are the best indicators of the presence or absence of benign singleton files, as reported in Table 1. Our classifier takes as input a feature vector s that represents the software packages on a given machine, and outputs a prediction as to whether or not the machine has benign singletons. To achieve a balanced dataset, we randomly selected 2,000,000 uninfected machines, half of which contain singletons and half of which do not.

3.2 File profiling

Given a classifier $g(m)$ that determines whether a machine m is expected to host benign many singletons, the next step in our pipeline—*file profiling*—uses this information to identify files that can be confidently labeled benign. The result is both a more balanced dataset that makes our pipeline's classifier easier to train, as well as a high-confidence labeling technique that reduces classifier's false positive rate. The main intuition behind our proposed file profiling method is that benign singleton files bear the marks of the specific benign software packages that generate them. Of course, different software generates singletons with dramatically different file structures and file-naming conventions. Consequently, we seek to identify prototypical benign singletons by clustering them based on their static properties, and filter benign files that closely match these prototypes. Since the information we have about the software installed on any given machine is typically incomplete, we filter benign files that closely match benign-file prototypes on all machines, but require much closer matches on machines where benign singletons are not expected. This point is operationalized below through the use of a less aggressive filtering threshold for machines m labeled as N (no benign singletons) than for machines labeled H (having benign singletons).

The full path, filename, and size of singleton files are the primary static attributes that we use in our file profiling study. We had little choice in this case because large collections of labeled benign singleton files that security companies share with external researchers are extremely hard to come by, and are limited in the telemetry they provide. In the interest of conducting a reproducible experiment, we limit ourselves to the metadata attributes provided for files in Dataset $D1$ (see Section 2.1) that Symantec shares with external researchers through its WINE program [10]. Though $D1$ gives us a representative dataset of singleton files, it also limits us to a small collection of metadata attributes about files, of which the path, filename, and size are the most useful attributes. In modest defense of the use of filename and path as a feature, though it is true that a malicious adversary can trivially modify the malware's filename (and the path, to a lesser extent), the malware author would frequently have to do so at the cost of losing the social engineering benefit of choosing a filename that entices the user to install the malware.

Due to the feature limitations of the file profiling step, we proceed by developing techniques to maximize the discriminative value of the path and filename. We seek to leverage the observation that a handful of root causes create a significant majority of benign singletons, and these origins are often strongly evident in the filename and path of benign singletons. Although malware files display significantly more diversity in their choice of filenames, these filenames typically bear the marks of social engineering, and their paths are frequently reflective of the vector by which they managed to install themselves on the machine, or are demonstrative of attempts to hide from scrutiny. Accordingly, we engineer features from filenames and paths to capture the naming conventions used by benign singletons. Given a file f, we divide its filename into words using chunking techniques. Specifically, we identify separate words within each file name that are demarcated by whitespace or punctuation, and separate words based on CamelCase capitalization transitions, and so on. Subsequently, we represent the filename and path components in a "bag of words" feature representation that is physically represented as a binary vector, where the existence of a word in the filename or path corresponds to a 1 in the associated feature, and a 0 indicates that the word is not a part of its name. In addition, we capture the relative frequencies of the words that appear in filenames by measuring the term frequency (TF) of each word. Term frequency is then used as a part of weighted Jaccard distance measure used to cluster files, as described below. More formally, let $T \subseteq \mathbb{R}^n$ represent the feature space of the singleton files, with n the number of features. Each singleton file f can be represented by a feature vector t, which is the dot product of a binary bag of words vector w and the normalized term frequency vector q corresponding to each word, $t = w \cdot q$, where t^j is the jth feature value. Note that we exclude words that appear extremely frequently, such as exe, dll, $setup$, as stop words, to prevent the feature vector t from becoming dominated by these. For any two files f_1 and f_2, the weighted Jaccard distance between them is then calculated as $J(f_1, f_2) = 1 - \frac{\sum_k \min(f_1^k, f_2^k)}{\sum_k \max(f_1^k, f_2^k)}$.

We use the weighted Jaccard distance to cluster benign singleton files in the training data using the scalable NN Descent algorithm [9] implemented on Spark [33], which efficiently approximates K-Nearest Neighbors and produces clusters C of of highly similar files.[1] We gain further efficiency and efficacy gains by choosing a bag of words representation over edit distance when making filename comparisons. This approach also has the benefit of producing an understandable model that identifies the most frequent filename patterns present in benign singleton files, such as those highlighted in Figure 1.

The final step in the file profiling process is to use the clusters derived above to filter benign files that align closely with the profile of benign singletons. To this end, for each benign singleton cluster $c \in C$, we compute the cluster mean $\bar{c} = \frac{1}{|c|} \sum_{t_j \in c} t_j$. For a given file f, we then find the cluster ; let c^* whose mean $\bar{c}$ is least distant from f, where distance is again measured based on weighted Jaccard distance: $J(\bar{c}, f)$. Then, if file f resides on a machine m that is expected to have singletons (that is, $g(m) = H$ as defined in Section 3.1), we filter it as benign iff $J(c^*, f) \leq \theta_H$; otherwise, it is filtered iff $J(c^*, f) \leq \theta_N$, where θ_H and θ_N are the corresponding filtering thresholds.

We select different θ values for the training and final versions of our pipeline. For training, our primary goal is to reduce the 80:1 benign to malicious class imbalance ratio so that we can train an effective classifier, whereas for testing, our goal is to achieve a high true positive rate while minimizing false positives. For purposes of creating a balanced training set, we select $\theta_N = 0.1$ and $\theta_H = 0.3$, which filters 91.8% of benign singletons, resulting in a more manageable 9:1 class imbalance ratio, at the cost of 7% of malware samples being thrown out of our training set. However this does not affect the performance of our model adversely, since during testing we can be less aggressive with the thresholds and pass more files to the classifier. In practice, we found values around $\theta_N = 0.07$ and $\theta_H = 0.13$ result in the best performance over the test data.

3.3 Malicious singleton detection

Having filtered out a large portion of predicted benign file instances, we are left with a residual data set of benign and malicious files that we classify using supervised-learning techniques. Though the filtering of benign files by the previous stages of our pipeline provide better class balance, we found that significant improvements in classification accu-

racy result when the residual data set is augmented by including 3 benign files that we sample randomly from each cluster C generated in the file profiling step. Doing so improves the classifier by adding additional benign files that are representative of the overall population of benign singleton files. We trained multiple classification algorithms with different strengths to determine which would be most effective at singleton classification.

Feature engineering is also key to the performance of our classifiers. Whereas machine and file profiling were designed for a backend system where a global view of the distribution of benign and malicious singleton files is available, here we design a classifier that we can deploy on client machines, based entirely on the static features of the file. Hence, we assume direct access to the files themselves and can build rich feature sets over the files, so long as they are not expensive to compute. This is in contrast to the telemetry used for machine and file profiling, for which network bandwidth constraints and privacy concerns limited the telemetry that could be collected. As mentioned in Section 2.3, we make no attempt to reverse the effects of obfuscation attempts employed by malware, finding that the use of the obfuscation techniques themselves provides strong discriminative power that helps us to disambiguate between benign and malicious singletons.

Features.

The features used by our learning algorithms to classify singleton program binary files fall into four categories.

1. The first category of features corresponds to features of file name and path. For these we used the same file name and path bag-of-words feature representation here as in the file profiling step of Section 3.2. To reduce the number of features included in our model, we applied a chi-squared feature selection to choose the most discriminative features [19].

2. The second category of features are derived from the header information of the executable file. We include all fields in the headers that are common to most windows executable files that exhibit some variability (some header fields never change). These header fields include the MS-DOS Stub, Signature, the COFF File Header, and the Optional Header (which is optional but nearly always present) [6].

3. We derive features from the Section Table found in the file's header, which describes each section of the binary, and also compute the entropy of each of the file's sections as features.

4. Our third category of features is derived from the external libraries that are dynamically linked to the program binary file. To determine which libraries the file links to, we create a feature for each of the most popular Windows library files (primarily Windows API libraries) that represents the number of functions imported from the library. We also create binary features for the individual functions in common Windows libraries that are most commonly used by malware. These take a value of 1 when the function is imported and 0 otherwise.

In all, category 1's bag of words features for filename and path consist of 300 features, while category 2, 3, and 4 features together comprise close to 1000 features.

---

[1] Note that this clustering of files is entirely distinct from the clustering of files in machine profiling, where non-singleton files are clustered based on machines that they appear on.

Classification.

We apply two learning models, a Recurrent Neural Network (RNN) [23] and a Support Vector Machine with a radial basis function as its kernel [3], and compare their performance and ability to withstand adversarial manipulation in Section 4. The RNN model is particularly suited for textual data, so we train it solely using file names and path information as features. Given the sequential properties of the file name text, RNNs aim to make use of the dependency relationship among characters to classify malicious vs benign singletons. The goal of the character-level learning model is to predict the next character in a sequence and thereby classify the entire sequence based on the character distribution. Here, given a training sequence of characters $(a_1, a_2, ..., a_m)$, the RNN model uses the sequence of its output vectors $(o_1, o_2, ..., o_m)$ to obtain a sequence of distributions $P(a_{k+1}|a_{\leq k}) = softmax(o_k)$, where the softmax distribution is defined by $P(softmax(o_k) = j) = exp(o_k^{(j)})/\sum_k exp(o_k^{(l)})$. The learning model's objective is to maximize the total log likelihood of the training sequence, which implies that the RNN learns a probability distribution over the character sequences used in a full path + filename.

For the SVM model, we apply the text chunking technique described in Section 3.2, and use the bag-of-words representation as described above, concatenated with static and API-based features, where relevant. While numerous other classification algorithms could be used here, our purpose of exploring RNN and SVM specifically is to contrast an approach specifically designed for text data (making use of filename and path information exclusively) with a general-purpose learning algorithm that is known to perform well in malware classification settings [16].

Putting Everything Together.

The high-level algorithm for the entire training pipeline is shown in Algorithm 1. The input to this algorithm is a

---

Algorithm 1 Train($\{S_{tr}, Z_{tr}, M_{tr}, Y_{tr}\}$):

1: $g = \text{machineProfiling}(\{S_{tr}, Z_{tr}, M_{tr}, Y_{tr}\})$
2: $(D, \theta_H, \theta_N, C) = \text{fileProfiling}(\{S_{tr}, Z_{tr}, M_{tr}, Y_{tr}\}, g)$
3: $h = \text{learnClassifier}(D)$
4: **return** $g, h, \theta_H, \theta_N, C$

---

collection of tuples
$\{s_i, z_i, m_i, y_i\} \in \{S, Z, M, Y\}$ describing file instances on machines, which are partitioned into training (tr) and testing (te) for the pipeline. Each file instance is represented by s_i, the 256-bit digest of a SHA-2 hash over its contents and the size z_i of the file in bytes. The machine is represented by a unique machine identifier m_i, and each instance of the file receives a label y_i, which designates a file as benign, malicious, or unknown. Machine profiling processes the file-instance data to identify singleton files (those for which only one instance exists) from more prevalent software that it groups into packages and uses to predict the presence or absence of singletons. The end result of training the pipeline includes the two classifiers: g classifies machines into H (has benign singletons) and N (no benign singletons), while h classifies files as malicious or benign, trained based on the selected representative data D. Additional by-products include, the clusters of benign files C and the thresholds θ_H

and θ_N that determine how aggressively files projected to be benign are filtered before the classifier h is applied.

Our test-time inputs include a set of singleton files that we withheld from training and our model parameters, and it returns simply whether or not to label f as benign or malicious. The specifics of the associated testing process, which use of our training pipeline, are given in Algorithm 2.

Algorithm 2 Predict($\{S_{te}, M_{te}\}, g, h, \theta_H, \theta_N, C$):

1: $l = g(M_{te})$: label the machine as H or N
2: $c^* = \arg\min_{c \in C} J(S_{te}, c)$ // find closest cluster center to S_{te}
3: **if** $J(S_{te}, c) \leq \theta_l$ **then**
4:    **return** B // "benign" if S_{te} is close to a benign cluster center
5: **end if**
6: **return** $h(S_{te})$ // otherwise, apply the classifier

---

4. EXPERIMENTAL EVALUATION

We conduct experiments on a large real-world dataset, dataset $D2$ as described in Section 2.1, to evaluate the proposed pipeline as well as analyze the robustness of learning system. As mentioned above, in implementing and deploying such a system in practice, we face a series of tradeoffs. The first is how much information about each file we should be collecting. On the one hand, more information will likely improve learning performance. On the other hand, collecting and analyzing data at such scale can become extremely expensive, both financially and computationally. Moreover, collection of detailed data about files on end-user machines can become a substantial privacy issue. For all of these reasons, very little information is traditionally collected about files on end-user systems, largely consisting of file name and an anonymized path, as well as file hashes and machines they reside on. For a subset of files, deeper information is available, including static features as well as API calls, as discussed above. However, these involve a significant cost: for example, extracting API calls requires static analysis. Our experiments are therefore designed to assess how much value these additional features have in classification, and whether or not it is truly worthwhile to be collecting them at the scale necessary for practical deployment. Since we are the first work to deal with the singleton malware detection problem, here we compare our proposed method with standard machine learning algorithms in various settings. Our evaluation applies Machine Profiling (MP), File Profiling (FP), an RNN based on only file name features, a SVM based on file name features, a SVM based on both file name and the static features (SVMS), and a SVM based on file name, static features, and API function features (SVMSF).

4.1 Baseline Evaluation

Our first efficacy study demonstrates the benefit provided by our machine learning pipeline as compared to two natural baselines. Our first baseline applies machine and file profiling, ranking all examples based on their similarity to benign files, and identifying the samples that are furthest from benign cluster centers as malicious. Our second baseline is our best-performing classifier trained over our entire feature set (SVMSF), but trained without the benefit of an initial machine/file profiling step, which reduces the ratio of benign to malicious files from an 80:1 ratio to a 9:1 ratio. This baseline is similar to prior work in malware classification based on static features [13]. As seen in Figure 4, our full pipeline demonstrates clear improvement over the two baselines, with a significantly higher AUC score. The spot on the curve with the maximal $F_{0.5}$ score achieves a 92.1% true positive rate at a 1.4% false positive rate, a dramatic improvement over applying FP or SVMSF on its own. Different locations on the ROC curve are achieved by selecting increasing values for θ_N and θ_H. The maximal $F_{0.5}$ score is achieved with $\theta_H = 0.13$ and $\theta_N = 0.07$.

Though uninformed downsampling of benign files may reasonably be suggested as an alternative means to reduce the class imbalance and achieve better classification results with SVMSF, our attempts to do so resulted in classifiers that perform worse than the SVMSF classifier of Figure 4. The reason for this is likely that downsampling decimates small clusters of benign files, resulting in a model that represents benign singletons only by its most massively populated clusters. Our pipeline can be thought of as providing an informed downsampling of benign files that reduces massively populated clusters of benign files to a few prototypes, allowing the SVM to train a model that represents the full gamut of benign singletons with the additional benefit of doing so over a more balanced dataset.

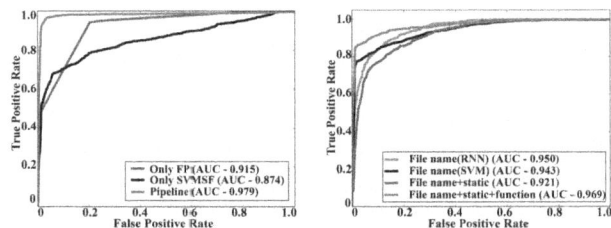

Figure 4: (a) ROC-curve comparison of the pipeline performance with the two baselines: no machine/file profiling, and only machine/file profiling. (b) Comparisons for models with different features without attacker.

4.2 Evaluating Performance of the Classification Step

To assess the relative importance of the three classes of features (text, static, and API) used by our model, we analyze the relative performance of just the last classification step of four models on the dataset produced by MP and FP filtering: 1) RNN (using text features only), 2) SVM (using text features only), 3) SVM with both text and static features, and 4) SVM with text, static, and API features.

To highlight the performance differences between these classifiers, we evaluate them over a test set of singletons from which obviously benign singletons have been pre-filtered by file profiling (for this reason this figure does not reflect the overall performance of our pipeline as reported in Figure 4). Our first observation is that RNN outperforms SVM when only textual features are used, which is not surprising, given that RNN's are particularly well suited to text data. Second, our model's performance drops when training over filename and anonymized path plus static features, which demonstrates the high discriminative value of the filename and anonymized path relative to features derived from header information in the executable. However, these static fea-

tures do offer value when we account for the potential for adversarial manipulation, as discussed in Section 4.3. Third, the value of features based on imported API functions is evident in the performance of the SVMSF model compared to all other models, particularly when we choose a threshold that limits the false positive rate, as security vendors are prone to do: The precision and recall scores that produce a maximal $F_{0.5}$ score for SVMSF are 83% recall at a 1% false positive rate, as compared to 76% recall at a 5% false positive rate for RNN, which is this model's closest competitor on an Area Under the Curve (AUC) basis. Note that the performance of the full pipeline is better than either of these classifiers alone (see Figure 4), because many of the benign files that are causing the FPs are labeled correctly using the machine and file profiling steps. Finally, our adversarial evaluation of these classifiers (Section 4.3) offers additional justification for incorporating static and imported function-based features into our model.

We evaluated the run-time required to train each step of our pipeline, including Machine Profiling (MP), File Profiling (FP), and the selected classifier, which is one of the following: RNN, SVM (based on only file name), SVMS, and SVMSF. The run-time of each step, when performed on a single powerful machine, is illustrated in Figure 5. Training Machine Profiling and File Profiling is fairly expensive, However, these two steps can be done offline, and updated incrementally as new data arrives. Training the SVM classifiers is inexpensive, whereas training the RNN takes on the order of three hours with GPU acceleration. Though we do not believe that this is a cause for concern, the inferior performance of the RNN as compared to SVMSF makes it less appealing for inclusion in the final version of our pipeline. We do not include test-time performance evaluation since the cost to test a single file is negligible for all stages of the pipeline.

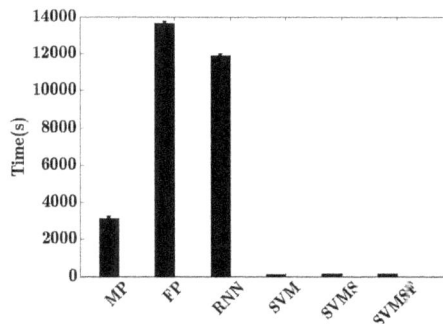

Figure 5: Comparisons of the runtime of different components within the pipeline.

4.3 Adversarial Evaluation

Though the evaluation of our classifiers, presented in Figure 4 (b) is fairly typical for a malware classification tool, it is not necessarily indicative of the long-term performance of a classifier once it has been massively deployed in the wild. In particular, what is missing is an evaluation of the ability of our classifier to withstand the inevitable attempts of malware authors to respond to its deployment by modifying their malicious singleton files to mimic benign file patterns in order to evade detection. Whereas researchers have traditionally discussed an algorithm's robustness to evasion based on subjective arguments about the strength or weakness of individual features, the now well-developed body of research on *adversarial machine learning* provides more rigorous methods for evaluating the adversarial robustness of a machine learning method [8, 20], and provides guidelines for developing more adversarially robust learning techniques [18, 32].

We proceed by providing an evaluation of our model's adversarial robustness. The adversarial resistance of a classifier evaluation presupposes a given classifier, h, that outputs for a given feature vector x, a label $h(x) \in \{-1, +1\}$, where in our case, -1 represents a benign prediction and $+1$ represents a malicious prediction. Given h, the adversary is modeled as aiming to minimize the cost of evasion,

$$x^* = \arg \min_{x' | h(x') = -1} c(x, x'),$$

where $c(x, x')$ is the cost of using a malicious instance x' in place of x to evade h (by ensuring that $h(x') = -1$, that is, that the malicious file will be classified as benign). The optimal evasion is represented by x^*. Because this model always results in a successful evasion, no matter its cost, we follow a more realistic model presented by Li and Vorobeychik [17], where the evasion only occurs when its cost is within a fixed adversarial budget B, thus: $c(x, x^*) \leq B$. Similarly, we mainly focus on the binary features here and prioritize the ones that have the most distinguished values for malicious and benign to modify, focusing the adversaries budget on the features that will be most useful for them to modify under the assumption that they known how to mimic benign software. In effect, we assume that the adversary will evade detection only if the gains from doing so outweigh the costs. The budget represents the percentage of the total number of features that the attacker is able to modify. A natural measure of the evasion cost $c(x, x')$ is the weighted l_1 distance between x and x': $c(x, x') = \sum_i a_i \|x_i - x_i'\|$. The choices of weights can be difficult to determine in a principled way, although some features will clearly be easier for an adversary to modify than others. We use $a_i = 1$ for all features i below as a starting point. As we will see, this already provides us with substantial evidence that a classifier using solely filename-based features is extremely exploitable by an adversary, without even accounting for the fact that such features are also easier to modify for malware authors than, say, the functions they import from the Windows API and other libraries.

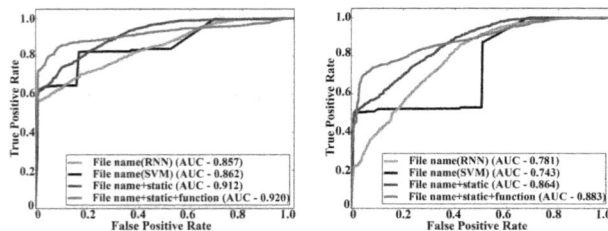

Figure 6: Comparisons for models with attacker budget as (a) 5 (b) 10.

We now perform a comparison of the same classifier and feature combinations presented in Section 4.2, but we now evaluate these classifiers using evasion attacks, as shown in Figures 6 (a) and (b) with budgets $B = 5\%$ and $B = 10\%$,

respectively. These figures highlight a significant trend: whereas the RNN's performance was previously rather close to that of the SVM with filename, static, and imported function features, the former has displays poor adversarial resistance, while the latter is far more robust. The RNN's AUC drops to 0.857 under pressure from a weaker attacker, and to 0.78 when pressured by a stronger one, whereas the AUC for the SVM with the largest feature set only drops to 0.92 under a smaller adversarial budget, and to 0.88 with a larger one). The SVM based only on filename features performed even worse than the RNN. Interestingly, while adding static features (and not imported function features) to the SVM degrades its adversary-free performance, the classifier performs considerably better than the RNN and SVM with filename features, in the presence of an adversary.

In summary, our experimental results point consistently to the use of a Support Vector Machine with features derived from the filename, path, static properties of the file, and imported functions, as the model that performs the best, even against an active adversary. Thus, the best version of our overall pipeline leverages this support vector machine as its classifier, achieving the overall performance results shown in Figure 4.

5. RELATED WORK

The problem of detecting malicious files has been studied extensively. Perdisci *et al.* have dealt with the static detection of malware files [25] and malware clustering using HTTP features [26]. Other malware detection systems have also been proposed [15, 7, 5]. Particularly relevant is work that is designed to deal with low-prevalence malware. This prior art includes work designed to reverse the effect of packing-based obfuscation tools by either statically decompressing or decrypting the malicious payload [27], or simply executing the program until it has unrolled its malicious payload into main memory [12]. At this point, traditional anti-virus signatures may be applied [22], and clustering may serve to identify new malicious samples based on their similarity to known malicious samples [13, 14]. By contrast, we make no effort to undo obfuscation attempts, which are frequently evidence of malicious intent. Whereas these researchers have focused on the causes behind low-prevalence malware, we augment this by providing the first detailed study of benign singleton files.

The importance of an adversarially robust approach to malicious singleton detection is evident, given that the high volume of singleton malware is largely the byproduct of adaptations to anti-virus technology [1, 17, 2]. Researchers have formalized the notion of evasion attacks on classifiers through game theoretic modeling and analysis [8, 24]. In one of the earliest such efforts, Dalve et al. [8] play out the first two steps of best response dynamics in this game. However, there has been a disconnect between the learner-attacker game models and real world dataset validation in these prior work. We bridge this gap by considering a very general adversarial learning framework based on an evaluation of a real, large-scale dataset.

6. CONCLUSIONS

We analyzed a large dataset to extract insights about the properties and distribution of singleton program binary files and their relationships to non-singleton software. We leverage the *context* in which singletons appear to filter benign files from our dataset, allowing us to train a model over a more balanced set of positive and negative examples. We build a classifier and feature set over the *static contents* of the file to effectively label benign and malicious singletons, in a way that is adversarial robust. Together, these components of our pipeline classify singletons much more effectively than either a context or a content-based approach can do on its own.

7. ACKNOWLEDGMENTS

This research was partially supported by the NSF (CNS-1238959, IIS-1526860), ONR (N00014-15- 1-2621), AFO (W911NF-16-1-0069), AFRL (FA8750-14-2-0180), Sandia National Laboratories, and Symantec Labs Graduate Research Fellowship.

8. REFERENCES

[1] BRÜCKNER, M., AND SCHEFFER, T. Nash equilibria of static prediction games. In *Advances in neural information processing systems* (2009), pp. 171–179.

[2] BRUCKNER, M., AND SCHEFFER, T. Stackelberg games for adversarial prediction problems. In *Proceedings of the 17th ACM SIGKDD international conference on Knowledge discovery and data mining* (2011), ACM, pp. 547–555.

[3] CHANG, C.-C., AND LIN, C.-J. LIBSVM: A library for support vector machines. *ACM Transactions on Intelligent Systems and Technology 2* (2011), 27:1–27:27.

[4] CHAU, D. H., NACHENBERG, C., WILHELM, J., WRIGHT, A., AND FALOUTSOS, C. Polonium: Tera-scale graph mining and inference for malware detection. In *SIAM International Conference on Data Mining* (2011), vol. 2.

[5] CHRISTODORESCU, M., JHA, S., SESHIA, S. A., SONG, D., AND BRYANT, R. E. Semantics-aware malware detection. In *Security and Privacy, 2005 IEEE Symposium on* (2005), IEEE, pp. 32–46.

[6] CORPORATION, M. Microsoft portable executable and common object file format specification. Revision 6.0.

[7] DAHL, G. E., STOKES, J. W., DENG, L., AND YU, D. Large-scale malware classification using random projections and neural networks. In *Acoustics, Speech and Signal Processing (ICASSP), 2013 IEEE International Conference on* (2013), IEEE, pp. 3422–3426.

[8] DALVI, N., DOMINGOS, P., SANGHAI, S., VERMA, D., ET AL. Adversarial classification. In *Proceedings of the tenth ACM SIGKDD international conference on Knowledge discovery and data mining* (2004), ACM, pp. 99–108.

[9] DONG, W., MOSES, C., AND LI, K. Efficient k-nearest neighbor graph construction for generic similarity measures. In *Proceedings of the 20th international conference on World wide web* (2011), ACM, pp. 577–586.

[10] DUMITRAS, T., AND SHOU, D. Toward a standard benchmark for computer security research: the worldwide intelligence network environment (wine). In *Proceedings of the First Workshop on Building Analysis Datasets and Gathering Experience Returns for Security (BADGERS)* (Salzburg, Austria, 2011).

[11] GIONIS, A., INDYK, P., AND MOTWANI, R. Similarity search in high dimensions via hashing. In *Proceedings of the 25th International Conference on Very Large Data Bases (VLDB)* (Edinburgh, Scotland, UK, 1999).

[12] GUO, F., FERRIE, P., AND CHIUEH, T. A study of the packer problem and its solutions. In *Symposium on Recent Advances in Intrusion Detection (RAID)* (Cambridge, MA, 2008), Springer Berlin / Heidelberg.

[13] HU, X., SHIN, K. G., BHATKAR, S., AND GRIFFIN, K. Mutantx-s: Scalable malware clustering based on static features. In *Presented as part of the 2013 USENIX Annual Technical Conference (USENIX ATC 13)* (San Jose, CA, 2013), USENIX, pp. 187–198.

[14] JANG, J., BRUMLEY, D., AND VENKATARAMAN, S. Bitshred: feature hashing malware for scalable triage and semantic analysis. In *Proceedings of the 18th ACM conference on Computer and communications security* (2011), ACM, pp. 309–320.

[15] KOLBITSCH, C., COMPARETTI, P. M., KRUEGEL, C., KIRDA, E., ZHOU, X.-Y., AND WANG, X. Effective and efficient malware detection at the end host. In *USENIX security symposium* (2009), pp. 351–366.

[16] KOLTER, J. Z., AND MALOOF, M. A. Learning to detect and classify malicious executables in the wild. *Journal of Machine Learning Research 7* (2006), 2721–2744.

[17] LI, B., AND VOROBEYCHIK, Y. Feature cross-substitution in adversarial classification. In *Advances in Neural Information Processing Systems* (2014), pp. 2087–2095.

[18] LI, B., AND YEVGENIY, V. Scalable optimization of randomized operational decisions in adversarial classification settings. In *Proc. International Conference on Artificial Intelligence and Statistics* (2015).

[19] LIU, H., AND SETIONO, R. Chi2: Feature selection and discretization of numeric attributes. In *Proceedings of 7th Intenational Conference on Tools with Artificial Intelligence (ICTAI)*, pp. 383–391.

[20] LOWD, D., AND MEEK, C. Adversarial learning. In *Proceedings of the eleventh ACM SIGKDD international conference on Knowledge discovery in data mining* (2005), ACM, pp. 641–647.

[21] LUKOŠEVIČIUS, M., AND JAEGER, H. Reservoir computing approaches to recurrent neural network training. *Computer Science Review 3, 3* (2009), 127–149.

[22] MARTIGNONI, L., CHRISTODORESCU, M., AND JHA, S. Omniunpack: Fast, generic, and safe unpacking of malware. In *Annual Computer Security Applications Conference (ACSAC)* (Miami Beach, FL, 2007).

[23] MIKOLOV, T., KOMBRINK, S., BURGET, L., CERNOCKY, J., AND KHUDANPUR, S. Extensions of recurrent neural network language model. In *IEEE International Conference on Acoustics, Speech and Signal Processing (ICASSP) (ICASSP)* (Prague, Czech Republic, 2011).

[24] PARAMESWARAN, M., RUI, H., AND SAYIN, S. A game theoretic model and empirical analysis of spammer strategies. In *Collaboration, Electronic Messaging, AntiAbuse and Spam Conf* (2010), vol. 7.

[25] PERDISCI, R., ARIU, D., AND GIACINTO, G. Scalable fine-grained behavioral clustering of http-based malware. *Computer Networks 57*, 2 (2013), 487–500.

[26] PERDISCI, R., LANZI, A., AND LEE, W. Mcboost: Boosting scalability in malware collection and analysis using statistical classification of executables. In *Computer Security Applications Conference, 2008. ACSAC 2008. Annual* (2008), IEEE, pp. 301–310.

[27] PERRIOT, F., AND FERRIE, P. Principles and practise of x-raying. In *Virus Bulletin Conference* (Chicago, IL, 2004).

[28] ROUNDY, K. A., AND MILLER, B. P. Binary-code obfuscations in prevalent packer tools. *ACM Computing Surveys (CSUR) 46*, 1 (2013).

[29] SECURITY, AND GROUP, R. Internet security threat report, 2015.

[30] SUYKENS, J. A., AND VANDEWALLE, J. Least squares support vector machine classifiers. *Neural processing letters 9*, 3 (1999), 293–300.

[31] TAMERSOY, A., ROUNDY, K., AND CHAU, D. H. Guilt by association: large scale malware detection by mining file-relation graphs. In *Proceedings of the 20th ACM SIGKDD international conference on Knowledge discovery and data mining* (2014), ACM, pp. 1524–1533.

[32] VOROBEYCHIK, Y., AND LI, B. Optimal randomized classification in adversarial settings. In *International Joint Conference on Autonomous Agents and Multiagent Systems* (2014), pp. 485–492.

[33] ZAHARIA, M., CHOWDHURY, M., FRANKLIN, M. J., SHENKER, S., AND STOICA, I. Spark: cluster computing with working sets. In *Proceedings of the 2nd USENIX conference on Hot topics in cloud computing* (2010), vol. 10, p. 10.

[34] ZHANG, J., AND ZHANG, Q. Stackelberg game for utility-based cooperative cognitiveradio networks. In *Proceedings of the tenth ACM international symposium on Mobile ad hoc networking and computing* (2009), ACM, pp. 23–32.

Scalable Function Call Graph-based Malware Classification

Mehadi Hassen
Florida Institute of Technology
150 W University Blvd
Melbourne, FL 32901, USA
mhassen2005@my.fit.edu

Philip K. Chan
Florida Institute of Technology
150 W University Blvd
Melbourne, FL 32901, USA
pkc@cs.fit.edu

ABSTRACT

In an attempt to preserve the structural information in malware binaries during feature extraction, function call graph-based features have been used in various research works in malware classification. However, the approach usually employed when performing classification on these graphs, is based on computing graph similarity using computationally intensive techniques. Due to this, much of the previous work in this area incurred large performance overhead and does not scale well.

In this paper, we propose a linear time function call graph (FCG) vector representation based on function clustering that has significant performance gains in addition to improved classification accuracy. We also show how this representation can enable using graph features together with other non-graph features.

Keywords

Malware Classification, Graph Classification

1. INTRODUCTION

Anti-malware vendors receive large numbers of files to be examined on a daily basis. For instance, Microsoft's real-time detection anti-malware products generate tens of millions of daily data points that need to be analyzed on a daily basis. The reason behind this huge influx of malware samples is that in an effort to avoid detection, malware authors constantly modify and/or obfuscate what would have been otherwise similar malware samples so that they look like many different files [3]. We refer to these similar samples as belonging to a single malware "family".

The large amount of malware makes it impossible to have human experts analyze all of these files. Hence, the use of machine learning based approaches can be very helpful in combating the malware epidemic.

One of the ways in which automated machine learning based techniques can be used is to group malware samples into groups and identify their respective families. Doing so

enables human analysts to focus their attention and analyze fewer representative samples from each family. Hence, machine learning methods for categorizing these samples into groups that contain similar malware samples are a necessity.

Various machine learning based approaches have been proposed in past research works. Many of these approaches rely on features extracted using static analysis of the malware samples. These features range from simple features, such as the ones based on strings found in malware binaries, to more complex features based on function call graph (FCG) representation of the malware binaries. FCG based features preserve the structural information in malware code in the form of functions and the caller-callee relation between them. Past research efforts that used FCG based features incurred performance overheads introduced as a result of evaluating the similarities between call graphs.

In this paper, we propose a malware classification method that groups malware samples into malware families. Our method is based on FCGs, but unlike past works, we overcome the performance overhead associated with the FCG based approach by using a novel technique to convert FCG representation into a vector representation. Our proposed approach has the following advantages:

- It is faster compared to previous works for FCG based malware classification.

- It has a higher classification accuracy compared to previous works.

- The graph feature vector, extracted from FCGs, can be easily combined with other non-graph features.

We will start by first reviewing related research works in Section 2. In Section 3, we will describe the details of our approach and implementation. And finally, we will evaluate our approach and compare its efficiency and effectiveness with previous research works in Section 4.

2. RELATED WORKS

Graph-based features have been used in many research works for malware clustering and classification. The main attraction of graph-based features is that they preserve information on how different parts of the malware code interact.

There are many types of graph information that can be extracted from malware samples: FCGs, control flow graphs and system-call dependency graphs. FCG is a directed graph representation of code where the vertices of the graph correspond to functions (procedures), and the edges represent

CODASPY'17, March 22-24, 2017, Scottsdale, AZ, USA
© 2017 ACM. ISBN 978-1-4503-4523-1/17/03... $15.00
DOI: http://dx.doi.org/10.1145/3029806.3029824

the caller-callee relation between the functions (vertices) [24]. FCGs are usually constructed from disassembled binary code using static analysis. Various research works [14, 17, 27, 19, 18] have used FCGs to extract features for malware classification, indexing and clustering.

When representing malware as FCGs, be it for classification, indexing or clustering, the fundamental question that needs to be addressed is that of measuring graph similarity. Graph edit distance (GED) is one such metric that is used in various domains for measuring the dissimilarity between two graphs by providing a measure which quantifies the minimum amount of edit operations that need to be performed to transform one graph into the other. The appealing aspects of this metric is its customizability (flexibility), which it provides in the form of vertex and edge related edit distance costs that can be defined to incorporate domain knowledge [23]. However, exact computation of GED has exponential time complexity in the number of vertices. Hence, approximations of the metric are used.

As mentioned earlier, one needs to define cost functions to be used for calculating GED. In [17, 19], the authors define GED in terms of three cost function: vertex insertion/deletion cost, edge cost, and vertex relabeling cost. In their approach, before computing GED, a filtering step is applied to remove most similar function pairs from the two graphs, based on the Jaccard Index of the function instruction frequency vector. Then a random bipartite graph mapping of the remaining vertices between the two graphs is constructed. Simulated annealing [26] is then applied to find a bipartite mapping to approximate graph edit distance. Finally, the approximated GED is used in [17] to perform malware clustering.

In [14], a malware database management system is implemented that indexes malware samples based on their FCG similarity using on approximate GED. Similar to previously discussed works, they also approximate GED by finding minimum cost bipartite graph mapping between the vertices of the two graphs. In their case, however, they used the Hungarian Algorithm to find this mapping. The Hungarian algorithm finds the minimum cost of a bipartite mapping based on an input cost matrix. This matrix specifies the cost of mapping a vertex (function) in one graph to a vertex in a second graph. In their implementation this cost is composed of Relabeling Cost, which accounts for the cost of matching functions, and Neighborhood Cost, which takes into consideration matches between the neighboring vertices as well. Because of the time complexity of the Hungarian algorithm, they filter out highly similar functions based on names for external functions, and based on the similarity of instruction mnemonic sequences for local functions.

There are other research works that do not use GED for measuring graph similarity. For example, [27] uses the normalized number of common edges between two graphs as a measure of similarity. The authors begin by first matching external functions based on their function names. Local functions are first matched based on their external function calls, and matching functions (vertices) are removed. The remaining functions are next matched based on their instruction opcode. Then, they match the still remaining functions based on whether the neighboring vertices are matched. Finally, the similarity metric is calculated as the number of common edges between the two graphs and normalized by the sum of number of edges in both graphs over two.

[11] is another example that used a different metric than GED to measure graph similarity. They approximate graph similarity via fixed point propagation. A fixed point between two graphs is defined as a two nodes (one each from graph) that can be determined to represent the same item in both graphs. Their algorithm starts from an initial fixed point and propagates to more fixed points by considering the neighboring nodes.

In [18], the authors use FCGs to extract new features to compute the similarity between two graphs. They start by extracting FCGs, where each function is represented in terms of size types of initial features. They proceed to learning a distance metric for each attribute type and an optimal vertex matching matrix that maximizes between-class distance while minimizing within-class distance. Finally, they train classifiers for each feature type and combine the results in an ensemble classifier.

In [12], the authors propose a way to map function call graphs (FCGs) to vector form inspired by linear-time graph kernel[13]. First, FGSs are extracted from android APK files. To label the graph vertices, instructions are grouped into 15 categories. A 15-bit vector is used to label the vertices, which indicates the presence or absence of these instructions. This label is further changed to the neighborhood hash[13], which is computed as bit-wise XOR of the vertices 15-bit vector and all of it's successors vertices. Finally, the neighborhood hash of the complete graph is obtained by calculating hashes for each node individually and replacing the original labels with the calculated hash values. The graphs are represented as multiset of these hash values. This work presents a way of representing these graphs as feature vectors such that the inner product between the two feature vectors is equal to the multi-set intersection of the two graphs.

The difference between [12] and our work arises primarily from the way we label the FCG. In our case, we label vertices by cluster-id of the function clusters. This allows us to represent functions in more detail because all instructions, as well as the sequence of the instructions, are encoded. It also allows us to control the granularity of this labeling by controlling the number of clusters. Secondly, our vector representation explicitly encodes graph edges, hence preserving more information.

System-call dependency is another type graph representation of a malware. A system-call graph is a graph representation where the vertices correspond to system calls made during the execution of the malware, and edges represent data-flow dependency between system calls, usually determined by dynamic taint analysis. In [20], the authors extract this graph from a malware sample using dynamic taint analysis and then convert it into a smaller graph where the vertices represent a group of system-calls that serve a similar purpose and the edges represent the dependency between these groups based on the dependency between individual system calls. Once this representation is extracted, they define different similarity metrics for detection and classification.

3. APPROACH

There are various ways to extract features through static analysis, for the purpose of classifying malware using machine learning. Previous research works have extracted features from printable strings in malware binaries [25, 16],

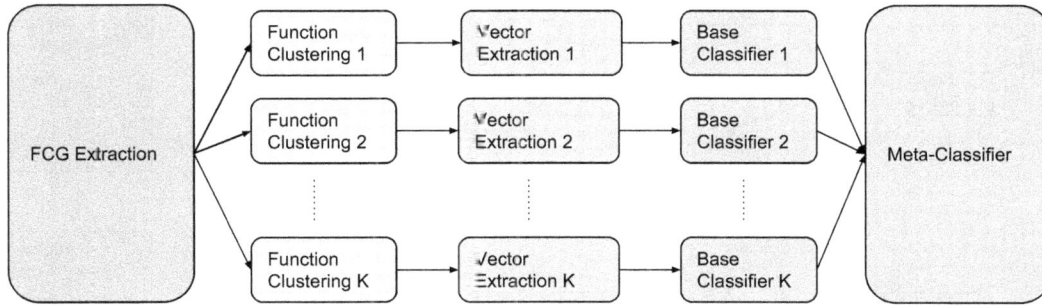

Figure 1: System overview with K pipelines

from the length of the functions in disassembled file [16], from instruction n-grams [15, 28, 21], FCGs [14, 17, 27, 19, 18], or a combination of different features [4].

In this paper we chose to focus on features generated from function call graphs (FCGs). The main reason for this is that FCGs better preserve structural information in binaries, for instance, compared to n-gram features. In addition to containing information about the malware code in the form of functions and their code, they also contain information about the interaction between the functions. The details of FCG extraction are discussed in Subsection 3.1.

One of the challenges with using FCG is that the names of the local functions (the functions written by the program author) are lost during compilation; hence, the vertices of FCG corresponding to these functions are unlabeled. This makes it difficult to compare two functions in different FCGs. Our solution to this problem is to cluster functions based on their instruction sequence and use these cluster-ids as labels for the functions. One of the concern we had about clustering functions was that we would lose some information as multiple functions get hashed to same cluster. Even thought this is true, our results show that classification accuracy is still very high. Function clustering is discussed in Subsection 3.2.

There are multiple ways of comparing the labeled FCGs, such as graph edit distance [17, 14], fixed point propagation [11], etc. In our approach, in addition to being able to efficiently compare FCGs, we also wanted to be able to have the capability for integrating non-graph features when needed. So unlike many past research efforts that classify FCGs, our approach first converts a FCG into a feature vector and then applies machine learning algorithms on these vectors, as discussed Subsection 3.3.

A high level view of our approach is shown in Figure 1. Our system starts by first extracting FCG representations from disassembled malware binaries. Once a FCG is extracted, the functions (which are the graph vertices) are clustered using Locality Sensitive Hashing(LSH) based on the function's instruction opcode sequence. The FCG vertices are then labeled using the cluster-ids. After labeling the FCG, our system extracts a vector representation from the call graph, which will serve as the feature vector of the malware sample.

During function clustering, some functions that are similar might be grouped into different clusters due to the randomized nature of LSH functions. To address this shortcoming, during function clustering, graph labeling and extraction of

vector representation is done K times. Each of these vector representations, extracted in parallel, are given as input to a separate classifier, which we refer to in Figure 1 as a base classifier. This is done both during training and test. The predictions of the base classifier are further used as input features for the meta-classifier. We will describe the functionality of each module in the following subsections.

3.1 FCG Extraction

There is much structural information that gets lost when features are extracted from a malware binary. For example, when extracting features, such as instruction n-gram, the organization of malware code into different functions, and the interactions between these functions is not captured in the extracted feature. So in an attempt to preserve the structural information, we use FCGs to represent malware binaries.

A FCG is a directed graph representation of code where the vertices of the graph correspond to functions and the directed edges represent the caller-callee relation between the functions (vertices) [24]. The vertices in this graph can represent local functions defined in the malware code or external functions imported from libraries.

As shown in Figure 1, the first module of our system takes disassembled malware binaries and extracts FCG representations. When extracting FCG, we label vertices of external functions with the function names. The original names of local functions are not preserved during compilation and eventually disassembly. Even if they were, these names may not represent well the instruction sequences that the function implements. Therefore, we leave the vertices corresponding to local functions unlabeled for now. Vertices representing local function also contain the instruction opcode sequence of that function. We represent the caller-callee relation between functions as directed, unweighted edges. After extracting FCG we pass this graph to the next module for clustering the local functions (vertices) and relabeling them with their cluster-id.

To help explain the different modules, we will use a toy example shown in Figure 2. In this example, we assume we have two disassembled binary files. These files are given as an input to the FCG Extraction module, which converts the two samples into a FCG representation. The first sample has FCG consisting of 4 functions: $UF11$, $UF12$, $UF13$ and $UF14$. The second sample has 3 functions $UF21$, $UF23$ and $UF24$. The function names, for the local function, at this point are arbitrary names. Hence, it is difficult to compare

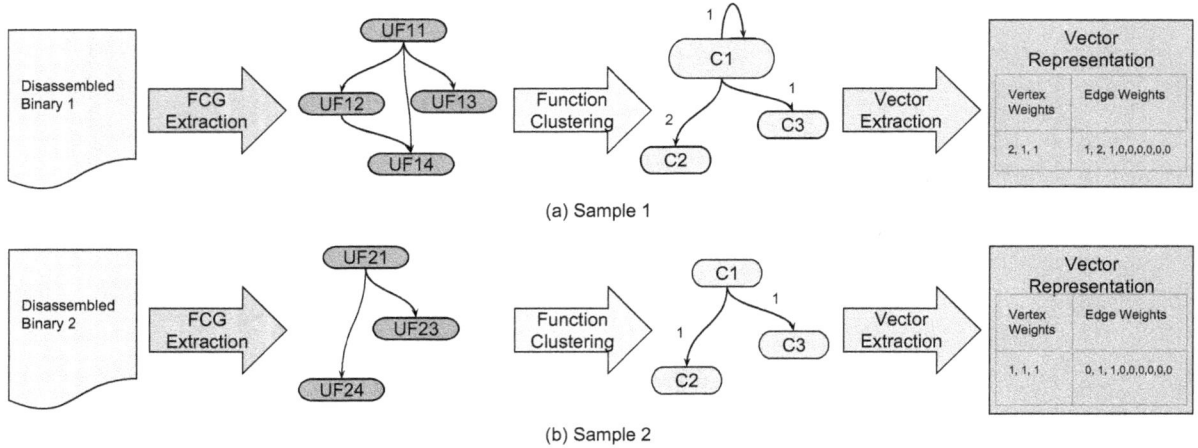

(a) Sample 1

(b) Sample 2

Figure 2: Example

3.2 Function Clustering

As discussed in the previous section, local functions in FCG are unlabeled. This makes comparing two FCGs very difficult. Our solution to this problem is to cluster the functions (vertices) of FCG and label them with a cluster-id. To perform clustering, we need to have a way of identifying similar functions. In [14], for instance, researchers use the instruction mnemonic sequence edit distance to calculate the similarity between functions which do not have similar names or CRC values of their mnemonic sequence. Even though edit distance might be a good measure of similarity, it has $O(n^2)$ time complexity in the number of instructions. In our work, we try to alleviate this bottleneck using Locality Sensitive Hashing(LSH) for computing an approximate edit distance between the instruction sequences of two functions.

The challenge here is that there are no locally sensitive family of hashes, that we know of, for approximating the edit distance. To address this, we explored the possibility of approximating edit distance with Jaccard Index. We evaluated the effectiveness of Jaccard Index in approximating edit distance by carrying out experiments where we computed the similarity between opcode sequences of functions using edit distance as well as Jaccard Index and computed the Pearson's correlation coefficient between the two. For Jaccard Index, we represent the functions as a set of unigram, bi-gram, or trig-ram opcode. Out of the three, Jaccard Index of uni-gram opcodes had the highest Pearson's correlation coefficient with edit distance at 0.957.

Using Jaccard Index to approximate edit distance, however, is still not fast enough. Fortunately, there is a family of locality sensitive hash functions, commonly known as Minhash [7], that can be used to approximate Jaccard Index, allowing us to efficiently approximate the similarity between functions.

Minhash is a LSH technique based on the idea that a hash of a set is the index of the first element under a random permutation. Then the probability that two sets will have the same index value of the first element is equal to the Jaccard similarity between the two sets. However, generating these permutations is computationally expensive. Hence, in practice, the random permutations are approximated by computing the Minhash of a set S as:

$$h(S) = \min_{\forall x \in S}((c_1 * x + c_2) \mod P) \quad (1)$$

where

- x is the index of an element in set S w.r.t. the super set of S;

- c_1 and c_2 are constants and chosen at random for each hash function;

- P is a prime much larger than the size of the universal set of all sets [22].

To improve the precision of the Minhash signature, L hash functions in Equation 1 are used together to generate a single Minhash signature by concatenating the values from the different hash functions. However, it is still possible to have false negatives (i.e. sets that are highly similar but declared to be not similar by Minhash). Multiple runs of Minhash can be used to address this [10].

Algorithm 1: Function Clustering

Input : G: Function call graph. Where functions are represented in terms of their instruction opcode sequence.
$[h_1, \ldots, h_L]$: L hash functions, in Equation 1, for generating Minhash signature.

Output: Function call graph labeled with function cluster ids

1 **foreach** *internal function v in* G.vertices **do**
2   signature ← minhashSignature(v.ngramOpcodeSequence, $[h_1, \ldots, h_L]$);
3   clusterId ← hash(signature);
4   v.label ← clusterId;
5 **return** G;

In our systems case, instead of using Minhash to directly calculate the similarity between functions, we use it to cluster functions (vertices) of the given graph. Unlike normal clustering where we would have needed to calculate the similarity between each pair of functions, using LSH we can simply hash the functions into buckets which represent clusters. Logically, we can consider this process as if we are clustering all functions of all FCGs. In reality, however, our use of LSH allows us to cluster the vertices in one FCG without the need to look at other FCGs in an efficient way.

The pseudo-code for our implementation is shown in Algorithm 1. For each vertex, we compute the cluster-id by first generating a Minhash signature for the n-gram opcode sequence. The function *minhashSignature*, in line 2, takes the n-gram opcode sequence and a list of hash functions, defined in Equation 1, as input and generates the Minhash signature. We represent this signature as an array of L hash values for the n-gram opcode sequence computed using the given L hash functions. Note that Minhash operates on set inputs rather than a sequence, as is the case in line 2, where the input to Minhash is an opcode n-gram sequence. One way to convert the n-gram sequence into a set representation is to have a universal set that contains all the n-grams observed in our training samples, and then the individual functions represented as subsets of this universal set. However, to speed up computation in our implementation we take the hash of an opcode n-gram and use this value as the index of the opcode n-gram when calculating the Minhash. The hash function used to compute the index value can be any hashing function with uniform value distribution and a large range of hash values to minimize collisions. In our case, we use murmurhash [5].

Next, these Minhash signatures are further hashed using an ordinary hash function to compute the cluster-id for that vertex (function) and this cluster-id value is used to label the vertex, as shown in lines 3-4. This secondary hashing also allows us to control the number of clusters.

During our implementations, we also experimented with the use of different hash functions for the secondary hash. As mentioned earlier, a hash function that uniformly distributes its keys across buckets is used. However, we thought it might make better sense to have hash collisions when the Minhash hash signatures closely match. So we experimented with using Simhash [9] as the secondary hash function. Our experiments, however, revealed that although using Simhash did improve the classification accuracy of a single base classifier, the hash function which uniformly distributes its keys achieves better accuracy on the overall meta-classifier. Therefore, we decided to use an ordinary hash function for the secondary hash.

At this point the FCGs, labeled by the cluster-ids, can be logically viewed as a graph where the vertices are clusters and the edges are calls made from functions in one cluster to a function in another cluster, or even in the same cluster. This logical representation is shown in Figure 2. However, in actual implementation we simply label the the vertices of input FCG with the cluster-ids.

In our running example in Figure 2, the FCGs extracted by the FCG Extraction module are given as input to the current module. In this module a Minhash signature is generated for each function in the input FCG, a cluster-id is determined using this signature and the function (vertex) is labeled by this id. In case of sample 1, we assume, functions

$UF11$ and $UF12$ are hashed to cluster $C1$, $UF13$ is hashed to cluster $C3$, and $UF14$ is hashed to cluster $C2$. In the case of sample 2, we assume functions $UF21$, $UF23$ and $UF24$ are hashed to clusters $C1$, $C3$ and $C2$, respectively.

The resulting graphs shown in Figure 2 are logical view of FCG after labeling. This view shows a graph where the vertices are clusters and the edges are calls made from functions in one cluster to a function in another cluster, or even the same cluster. Now the labeled graphs of sample 1 and 2 are much easier to compare.

3.3 Vector Extraction

In past research works, techniques used for computing graph similarity have been a source of performance bottleneck on FCG based malware classification. Not only were these a performance bottlenecks, but they also made it difficult to integrate non-graph features with graph features. Motivated by these two aspects, we proposed a vector representation of FCGs.

Algorithm 2: Creating Vector Representation

Input : G: Function call graph labeled with function cluster ids;

Output: Graph vector representation

1 Initialize vertexWeight with zero vector;
2 Initialize edgeWeight with zero vector;
3 **foreach** v *in* G.vertices **do**
4 | vertexWeight [v.label] $+= 1$;
5 **foreach** e *in* G.edges **do**
6 | index $\leftarrow$ EdgeIndex(e.source.label, e.target.label);
7 | edgeWeight [index] $+= 1$;
8 graphVector $\leftarrow$ concatenate vertexWeight with edgeWeight;
9 return graphVector;

We extract vector representation from a FCG labeled using the cluster-ids. This representation consists of two parts, vertex weight and edge weight. The vertex weight specifies the number of times a vertex with a given label (cluster-id) is found in a FCG, or in other words the number of vertices in each cluster for that FCG. The edge weight specifies the number of times an edge is found from a vertex in one cluster to a vertex of another cluster or a vertex within the same cluster.

As shown in Algorithm 2, we start by initializing *vertexWeight* and *edgeWeight* vectors to zero vectors. In lines 3-4, we iterate over all the vertices in the input graph and count the number of vertices labeled with each cluster-id. Next, in lines 5-7 we compute edge weights for the edges between cluster-ids (i.e., an edge from a vertex labeled with one cluster-id to a vertex labeled with another cluster-id) or within a cluster (i.e. an edge between two vertices labeled with the same cluster-id). To do so we iterate over each edge in the input graph and update the frequency of occurrence edges. In our implementation, we use the *EdgeIndex* function to perform a simple lookup for the index representing the edge type. Finally, we concatenate *vertexweight* and *edgeWeight* vectors to form one vector representing the input FCG.

As mentioned in the Section 3.1, vertices of the FCG corresponding to external functions are already labeled by the name of the external functions. While computing the vertex weight we can use a lookup table to map the external function names to index values in the vertex weight vector that correspond to that external function. This requires first identifying all external functions observed in training dataset samples and adds an additional processing. To avoid this, we simply use an arbitrary hash which uniformly distributes its keys to relabel the external functions with this value and use this to as the labels refereed in lines 4 and 6 in Algorithm 2. The same applies for the edge weights. Through our experiment we didn't notice significant decrease in classification accuracy as a result of this hashing. Therefore, we decided to use this approach to avoid processing overhead.

We acknowledge that our vector representation does not preserve every detail of a graph structure. For instance, it is possible to have slightly different graphs with the same vector representation. However, we believe that this can have its own advantage in the field of malware classification by making this representation less susceptible to obfuscation techniques that might change function calling patterns. That is because small variations in the graph structure might not get expressed in the vector representation as long as the edge and vertex frequencies are not changed. Hence, this representation becomes more resilient to changes such as re-ordering of function calls.

In our running example, in the case of sample 1 for instance, the labeled FCG contains two functions that are labeled $C1$, one $C2$, and one $C3$. The vector representation of the vertex weight part will be $2, 1, 1$. The second part represents edge weights. In sample 1, we have one edge $C1 - C1$, two $C1 - C2$ and one $C1 - C3$. The vector representation of the edge weight part will be $1, 2, 1, 0, 0, 0, 0, 0, 0$. The zeros in the edge weight show that there are no edges, for example, $C2 - C2$. The final vector representation will be a concatenation of these two vectors.

Once the vector representation of all instances is created, the next step is to train models for classification of the malware samples.

3.4 Base Classifiers

The function clusters generated as discussed in Section 3.2 has high precision but lower recall. That is, each cluster has similar functions, but some similar functions may be hashed into different clusters. Recall can be improved by repeating this clustering step. In our system, K repeated clustering steps are run independently and in parallel. For each run, a separate vector representation is computed. Then separate base classifiers are trained using the output of each run.

Each of our base classifier is a Random Forest classifier [6]. The inputs to a base classifier are the vector representations for the malware FCGs. As shown in Algorithm 3, the input dataset, which is a list of vector representations for the malware FCGs, is segmented into T parts (line 2). Then for each data segment, a classifier is trained on the remaining data segments and used to predict, in the form of a probability distribution of over all classes, for each sample in the segment (lines 3-7). This is used to reconstruct the data set in terms of the predictions of the based classifier.

3.5 Meta-Classifier

The meta-classifier combines the predictions of the individual base classifiers to output a final prediction. It first re-

---

Algorithm 3: Training base classifier and creating training data for meta-classifier

Input : D: Training set containing FCGs vector representation

Output: D_{new}: The training set represented in terms of class distributions.

1 Initialize D_{new} to empty list;
2 Segment D into T parts;
3 **for** $t = 1$ *to* T **do**
4   Train classifier C on $D - D_t$;
5   **foreach** *Sample* d *in* D_t **do**
6          $distribution_d \leftarrow$ C.predict(d);
7   Add $distribution_d$ to D_{new};

8 return D_{new};

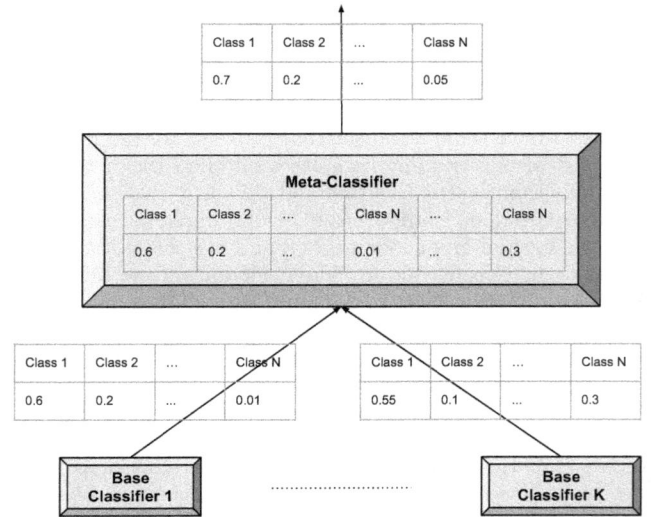

Figure 3: The meta-classifier

ceives the predictions for each data instance from the based classifiers. These predictions are in the form of probability distribution over the class labels. Then for each instance, these probability distributions are concatenated to form a single feature vector. In other words, the prediction from the base classifiers serve as an input feature to the meta-classifier. The meta-classifier is then trained on this vector. The output of the meta-classifier is a predicted class label for each data instance as illustrated in Figure 3.

3.6 Enhancements

For a meta-classifier to be effective, we need the base classifiers to be sufficiently different from each other [8]. In the case of our original design presented so far, the difference between the base classifiers comes as a result of the false negatives introduced by function clustering with LSH. Through our experiments, we were able to determine that the different runs of the Function clustering using a same number of Minhash functions(L) were not producing enough variation to take full advantage of ensembling. So to introduce more variation, we used different values for L in Function clustering for the K different runs.

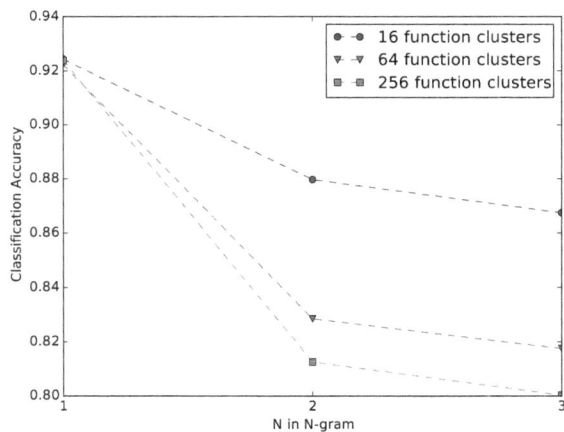

Figure 4: Effect of n-gram length on classification accuracy

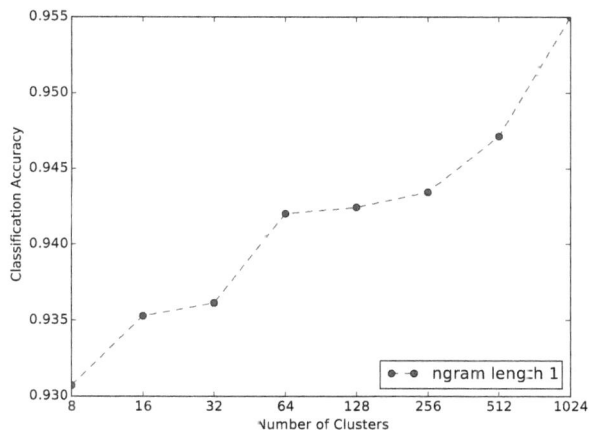

Figure 5: Effect of number of function clusters on classification accuracy

4. EXPERIMENTAL EVALUATION

4.1 Dataset

For the purpose of evaluating our proposed approach for classifying malware into families, we will be using the Microsoft Malware Classification Challenge (BIG 2015) dataset [3]. The original dataset consists of 10,867 labeled malware samples. Our disassembled file parser were able to properly parse 10,260 of the samples. Hence, we will be using these in the following evaluations. The class distribution of these samples are shown in Table 1.

To compare our work with Adagoi [12], we will use a secondary dataset consisting of 1,113 benign android apps and 1,200 malicious android apps. The malicious samples are from the Android Malware Genome Project [2]. A colleague at our university provided us with the benign samples, downloaded from the Google Play Store.

Table 1: Microsoft malware dataset class distribution

Malware Family Name	Number of Samples
Ramnit	1513
Lollipop	2470
Kelihos ver3	2936
Vundo	446
Simda	34
Tracur	294
Kelihos_ver1	387
Obfuscator.ACY	1168
Gatak	1012

4.2 Parameter Selection

The first two parameters of our algorithm that need to be configured experimentally are the length of instruction opcode n-grams, and the number of function (vertex) clusters. N-gram length determines how many instructions are used in each n-gram when representing local functions as sets of n-grams; in other words it determines the n in n-gram. Cluster number determines the number of buckets functions are hashed into.

Figure 4 shows the classification accuracy results when us-

ing uni-gram, in both the n-gram length and cluster number experiments, only a single base classifier was used. In the Figure 4, using uni-grams results in better accuracy than both bi-grams and trig-rams and that using bi-grams results in better accuracy than tri-gram. This result can be explained by going back to the distance function (we are trying approximate function similarity in our approach.) As discussed in Section 3.2, we are trying to approximate edit distance using Jaccard Index, which we in turn approximate using Minhash. When computing edit distance, the insertion and deletion operations work on uni-grams. So the longer the n-gram we use when approximating edit distance with Minhash, the less accurate our approximation.

When it comes to the number of function clusters, we expect the classification accuracy to increase as the number of function clusters increases. This expectation can be understood by considering the fact that by hashing function into smaller number of clusters, we increase the likelihood of dissimilar functions being hashed into the same cluster. Obviously, this in turn results in lower classification accuracy. The results in Figure 5 agree with our expectations. The experiments to determine the number of function clusters were carried out using uni-gram opcode sets to represent functions and clustering the functions (vertices) into the specified number of clusters before converting to vector representation.

The other parameters that need to be tuned experimentally are the number of base classifiers(K), and the number of Minhash functions used for computing the Minhash Signature (L). In our experiments, we evaluated various values of K. We observed that in the case the current evaluation dataset increasing the value of K above 6 didn't result in much improvement. As discussed in Section 3.6, using different values for L for the K different runs, results in more variation among the K base classifiers and results in better meta-classifier performance. In our experiments we evaluated a couple of L value combinations and picked the one that resulted in better performance.

4.3 Classification Accuracy Comparison

We evaluate our approaches accuracy by comparing it

with our implementation of Kinable et.al. [17, 19] work on FCG classification. In [17], they use an approximate GED to measure the similarity between FCGs. GED distance is approximated using Simulated Annealing (SA) to find a bipartite graph mapping between the vertices of the two graphs that minimizes the GED. Since this is a computationally intensive task, functions in the two graphs that have instruction edit distance greater than some threshold τ are filtered out before creating the bipartite graph mapping. Then the FCGs are clustered based on GED.

Since using SA to approximate GED was computationally intensive, we evaluated both our proposed method and our implementation of Kinable et.al. work on a smaller sub set of the dataset consisting of 1000 malware samples. In our implementation of Kinable et.al. research, we filtered out most similar functions between pairs of graphs by setting the filter threshold τ to 0.9 and then created bipartite mapping on the remaining functions (vertices). We cluster the malware samples using k-medoids and then assigned a class label to each cluster based on the majority class. Hence, we determined every element of a cluster whose class label is different from the majority class as being misclassified. Figure 6 shows the confusion matrix of classifying the thousand samples in this way.

Next we evaluated our approach on the same 1000-malware sample with 10-fold cross validation to predict the labels on the thousand samples. Our system is set-up using six base classifiers(i.e. $K = 6$), which means that there are six parallel pipelines consisting of the Function clustering, Call graph vector extraction, and Base classifier modules. In all the of Function clustering modules, we represented functions (vertices) with uni-gram opcode sequence and clustered them into 64 clusters. To make the base classifiers more decorrelated, the Minhash signatures are generated using varying number of hash functions (i.e. value of L in Algorithm 1). In first two of the six pipelines $L = 1$, in the next two $L = 3$ and in the last two $L = 5$.

As can be seen from the results in Figures 6 and 7, our approach clearly out performs the SA based method with an overall accuracy of 0.979 versus the 0.840 of the previous works on the smaller dataset. Our system has high accuracy for almost all of the malware families, apart from the malware family Simda. The reason behind the poor accuracy in the case of Simda is the very small number of training samples. In the entire evaluation dataset there are only 34 instances, and in the case of the sampler 1000 instance dataset used in this section there were only 4 samples.

Figure 8 shows the classification accuracy of our approach when applied on the entire dataset using a 10-fold cross validation. Again we see that our system gets near perfect classification accuracy for all families except Simda. Which is again due to the smaller number of training samples.

4.4 Speed Comparison

We will now empirically compare the speed of our approach with that of SA based approach. For our approach, we timed the execution in the components starting with Call Graph Extraction to Call graph Vector representation (inclusive). We excluded the time taken by the learning
algorithm. For the SA based approach we timed the process starting with Call Graph Extraction up to the GED com-putation between all pairs of malware samples,

using SA. Similarly here, we excluded the time taken by the learning algorithm.

Table 2: Speed comparison

Approach	Average Time (min)
All pair similarity SA and GED	2006
Graph Vector Representation	7

The results in Table 2 show these time measurements, averaged over three runs, on a smaller subset of the evaluation data set consisting of 1000 samples. As we expected, our approach is significantly faster than the SA based technique making FCG classification scalable. These experiments were carried out on a machine with 2.3 GHz quad code CPU with 8 GB memory.

Time Complexity Comparison: To compare the training time complexity of these two approaches we will only consider the feature extraction phase in both methods and exclude the machine learning algorithms.

For the Simulated Annealing based approach, we consider the time complexity of graph similarity computation and exclude the clustering part when looking at the time complexity. As shown in [19], the time complexity of running Simulated Annealing to approximate Graph Edit Distance between two graphs is $O(|V_{max}|^2 \cdot d_{max})$, where $|V_{max}|$ is the number of vertices of the largest graph, and d_{max} is the maximum value of degree for any node. For N graphs then $O(N^2)$ distance (similarity) computations are going to be required. Therefore, for N graphs the worst case time complexity becomes $O(N^2 \cdot |V_{max}|^2 \cdot d_{max})$.

In case of our system we consider time complexity of the Function clustering and Vector extraction modules. When we look at the Function clustering module, it is clear from Algorithm 1 that given an input graph $G = (V, E)$, it has time complexity of $O(|V|)$. For N graphs then the worst case time complexity becomes $O(N \cdot |V_{max}|)$, where $|V_{max}|$ is the number of vertices of the largest graph in the training dataset. For the Vector extraction module, we visit each vertex and each edge only once. Hence, the complexity of the module for a given input graph $G = (V, E)$ is $O(|V| + |E|)$. For N graphs then, the worst case time complexity becomes $O(N \cdot (|V_{max}| + |E_{max}|))$. Finally, the total worst case time complexity of the two modules together for N graphs is $O(N \cdot (|V_{max}| + |E_{max}|))$. So it can be clearly seen here that our approach compares favorably to the one based on Simulated Annealing.

4.5 Classifying benign and malware applications

In this section we will compare our approach with another closely related work, Adagoi [12]. We used the authors implementation of Adagoi [1], which performs classification between benign and malicious Android apps. To work with android apk files, we modified the implementation of the FCG Extraction module, in our system.

The evaluation was performed by randomly splinting the initial dataset to use 80% as training data and the remaining as test data. This was repeated 10 times, and the resulting average ROC curve is shown in Figure 9. As seen in the figure, our approach performs better than Adagoi. For instance, at 0.01 false positive rate, the area under the curve for our approach is 0.0099 where as for Adagoi it is 0.0092.

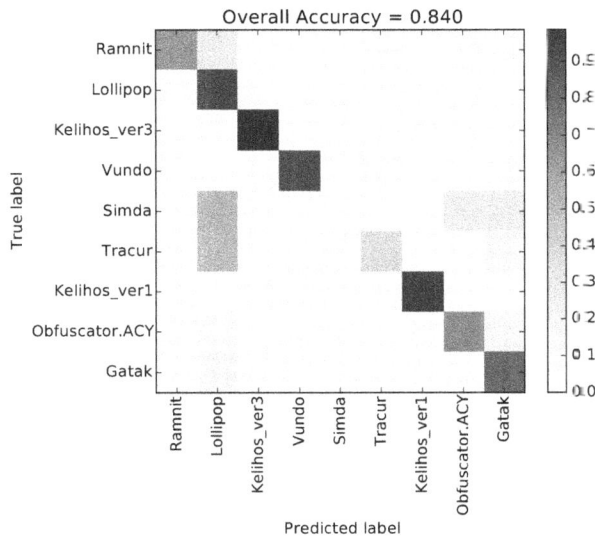

Figure 6: Confusion matrix for using Simulated Annealing on 1000-sample dataset

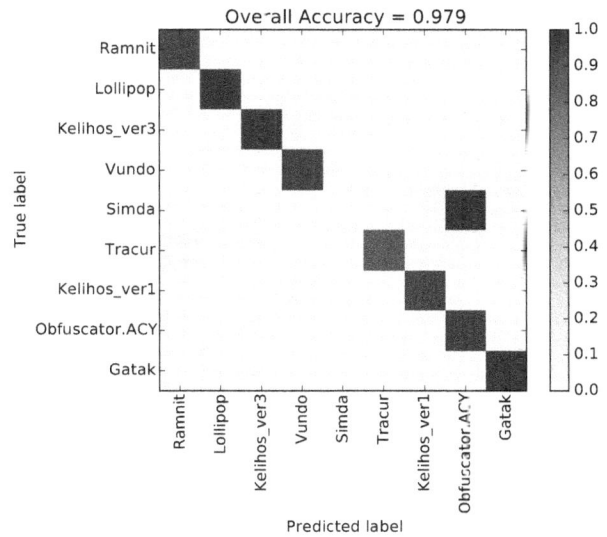

Figure 7: Confusion matrix using meta-classifier on 1000-sample dataset

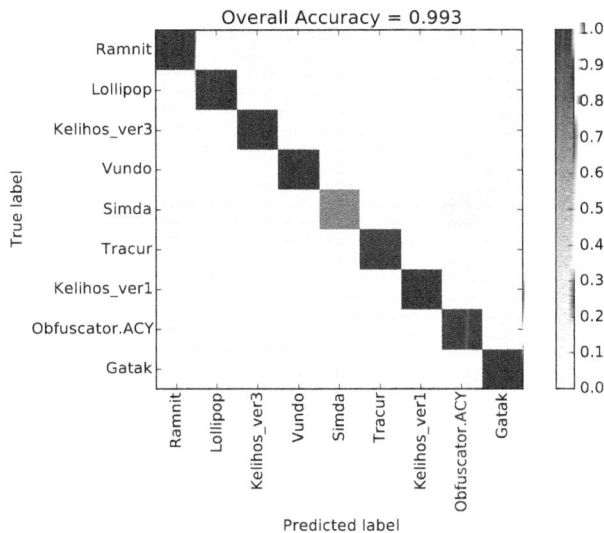

Figure 8: Confusion matrix using meta-classifier on entire dataset

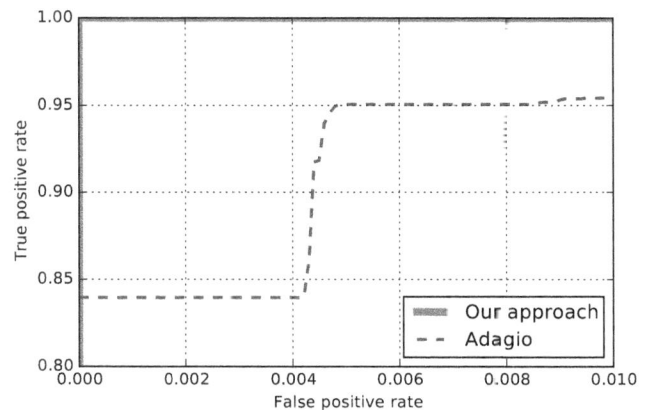

Figure 9: ROC curve

4.6 Combining with Non-graph Features

The former FCG based techniques, which relied solely on graph representation and on measuring graph similarity, were not easy to use together with other non-graph based features. Our proposed approach, on the other hand, extracts feature vectors from FCGs that can be easily used with other features by simply concatenating the feature vectors.

To demonstrate this, we use binary byte bi-gram frequency features. These features are extracted by computing the frequency of byte bi-grams in malware sample raw binary files. We take these feature vectors and concatenate a random subset of them with the graph vectors before passing them to the base classifiers. The reason for taking a random sub-set of these features is to help make the base classifiers more decorrelated.

Combining these features with the graph features, our overall classification accuracy slightly increased to 0.9933 from 0.993. This can be explained by the fact that both the graph and the n-gram frequency features are have overlaps in that they both are extracted based on the content of malware binary. As a future work we would like to examine combining our FCG features with the various features used in [4].

5. CONCLUSIONS

In this paper we presented a fast and effective malware classification system based on extracting feature vector from FCG representation. Our approach was able to address two bottlenecks in previous malware classification systems that were based on FCG features. First, we were able to speed up the process of measuring similarity between functions using

Minhash, an Locality Sensitive Hashing technique. Second, we avoided the major bottleneck of computing graph similarity by converting the graph representation into vector representation using function clustering based on the Minhash signatures of the functions.

6. REFERENCES

[1] Adagio. https://github.com/hgascon/adagio.
[2] Android malware genome project. http://www.malgenomeproject.org/.
[3] Microsoft malware classification challenge (big 2015). https://www.kaggle.com/c/malware-classification, 2015. [Online; accessed 27-April-2015].
[4] M. Ahmadi, D. Ulyanov, S. Semenov, M. Trofimov, and G. Giacinto. Novel feature extraction, selection and fusion for effective malware family classification. In *Proceedings of the Sixth ACM Conference on Data and Application Security and Privacy*, pages 183–194. ACM, 2016.
[5] A. Appleby. Murmurhash3. https://github.com/aappleby/smhasher, 2008.
[6] L. Breiman. Random forests. *Machine learning*, 45(1):5–32, 2001.
[7] A. Z. Broder. On the resemblance and containment of documents. In *Compression and Complexity of Sequences 1997. Proceedings*, pages 21–29. IEEE, 1997.
[8] P. Chan. *An Extensible Meta-Learning Approach for Scalable and Accurate Inductive Learning*. PhD thesis, Department of Computer Science, Columbia University, New York, NY, 1996.
[9] M. S. Charikar. Similarity estimation techniques from rounding algorithms. In *Proceedings of the thiry-fourth annual ACM symposium on Theory of computing*, pages 380–388. ACM, 2002.
[10] A. S. Das, M. Datar, A. Garg, and S. Rajaram. Google news personalization: scalable online collaborative filtering. In *Proceedings of the 16th international conference on World Wide Web*, pages 271–280. ACM, 2007.
[11] T. Dullien and R. Rolles. Graph-based comparison of executable objects (english version). *SSTIC*, 5:1–3, 2005.
[12] H. Gascon, F. Yamaguchi, D. Arp, and K. Rieck. Structural detection of android malware using embedded call graphs. In *Proceedings of the 2013 ACM workshop on Artificial intelligence and security*, pages 45–54. ACM, 2013.
[13] S. Hido and H. Kashima. A linear-time graph kernel. In *2009 Ninth IEEE International Conference on Data Mining*, pages 179–188. IEEE, 2009.
[14] X. Hu, T.-c. Chiueh, and K. G. Shin. Large-scale malware indexing using function-call graphs. In *Proceedings of the 16th ACM conference on Computer and communications security*, pages 611–620. ACM, 2009.
[15] X. Hu, K. G. Shin, S. Bhatkar, and K. Griffin. Mutantx-s: Scalable malware clustering based on static features. In *USENIX Annual Technical Conference*, pages 187–198, 2013.
[16] R. Islam, R. Tian, L. Batten, and S. Versteeg. Classification of malware based on string and function

feature selection. In *Cybercrime and Trustworthy Computing Workshop (CTC), 2010 Second*, pages 9–17. IEEE, 2010.
[17] J. Kinable and O. Kostakis. Malware classification based on call graph clustering. *Journal in computer virology*, 7(4):233–245, 2011.
[18] D. Kong and G. Yan. Discriminant malware distance learning on structural information for automated malware classification. In *Proceedings of the 19th ACM SIGKDD international conference on Knowledge discovery and data mining*, pages 1357–1365. ACM, 2013.
[19] O. Kostakis, J. Kinable, H. Mahmoudi, and K. Mustonen. Improved call graph comparison using simulated annealing. In *Proceedings of the 2011 ACM Symposium on Applied Computing*, pages 1516–1523. ACM, 2011.
[20] S. D. Nikolopoulos and I. Polenakis. A graph-based model for malware detection and classification using system-call groups. *Journal of Computer Virology and Hacking Techniques*, pages 1–18, 2016.
[21] S. Pai, F. Di Troia, C. A. Visaggio, T. H. Austin, and M. Stamp. Clustering for malware classification. *Journal of Computer Virology and Hacking Techniques*, pages 1–13, 2016.
[22] A. Rajaraman, J. D. Ullman, J. D. Ullman, and J. D. Ullman. *Mining of massive datasets*, volume 1. Cambridge University Press Cambridge, 2012.
[23] K. Riesen and H. Bunke. Approximate graph edit distance computation by means of bipartite graph matching. *Image and Vision computing*, 27(7):950–959, 2009.
[24] B. G. Ryder. Constructing the call graph of a program. *Software Engineering, IEEE Transactions on*, (3):216–226, 1979.
[25] M. G. Schultz, E. Eskin, E. Zadok, and S. J. Stolfo. Data mining methods for detection of new malicious executables. In *Security and Privacy, 2001. S&P 2001. Proceedings. 2001 IEEE Symposium on*, pages 38–49. IEEE, 2001.
[26] L. Xu and E. Oja. Improved simulated annealing, boltzmann machine, and attributed graph matching. In *Neural Networks*, pages 151–160. Springer, 1990.
[27] M. Xu, L. Wu, S. Qi, J. Xu, H. Zhang, Y. Ren, and N. Zheng. A similarity metric method of obfuscated malware using function-call graph. *Journal of Computer Virology and Hacking Techniques*, 9(1):35–47, 2013.
[28] G. Yan, N. Brown, and D. Kong. Exploring discriminatory features for automated malware classification. In *Detection of Intrusions and Malware, and Vulnerability Assessment*, pages 41–61. Springer, 2013.

All Your VMs are Disconnected: Attacking Hardware Virtualized Network

Zhe Zhou[1,3], Zhou Li[2], Kehuan Zhang[1,3]
Department of Information Engineering, Chinese University of Hong Kong[1]
ACM Member[2]
CUHK Shenzhen Research Institute[3]
{zz113, khzhang}@ie.cuhk.edu.hk[1], lzcarl@gmail.com[2]

ABSTRACT

Single Root I/O Virtualization (SRIOV) allows one physical device to be used by multiple virtual machines simultaneously without the mediation from the hypervisor. Such technique significantly decreases the overhead of I/O virtualization. But according to our latest findings, in the meantime, it introduces a high-risk security issue that enables an adversary-controlled VM to cut off the connectivity of the host machine, given the limited filtering capabilities provided by the SRIOV devices.

As showcase, we demonstrate two attacks against SRIOV NIC by exploiting a vulnerability in the standard network management protocol, OAM. The vulnerability surfaces because SRIOV NICs treat the packets passing through OAM as data-plane packets and allow untrusted VMs to send and receive these packets on behalf of the host. By examining several off-the-shelf SRIOV NICs and switches, we show such attack can easily turn off the network connection within a short period of time. In the end, we propose a defense mechanism which runs on the existing hardware and can be readily deployed.

Keywords

SRIOV; Virtualization; OAM

1. INTRODUCTION

Virtualization techniques are important to today's computing infrastructure like cloud. They enable hardware resources to be shared among different users through running heterogeneous virtual machines (VMs). They also provide secure computing environment to users based on the strong guarantees of isolation. In the beginning, virtualization suffered from significant runtime performance penalty. As one main cause, a lot of computation has to be taken in order to emulate the access to I/O devices, which becomes the major bottleneck. To address this issue, a suite of I/O virtualization techniques were proposed to reduce such unnecessary overhead.

CODASPY'17, March 22-24, 2017, Scottsdale, AZ, USA
© 2017 ACM. ISBN 978-1-4503-4523-1/17/03...$15.00
DOI: http://dx.doi.org/10.1145/3029806.3029810

The initial I/O virtualization design required the participation of the hypervisor who emulates I/O devices and acts as a bridge between VMs and I/O devices [27]. Such design is called para-virtualization and unnecessarily consumes a lot of extra computing resources due to the replication of numerous I/O operations. In recent years, a new technique, Single Root I/O Virtualization (SRIOV) was developed and is quickly gaining tractions. This technique can partition the hardware into multiple compartments and *directly* assign each compartment to a VM [11, 26, 31, 21]. As such, the hypervisor is removed from the I/O process path and most I/O operations cab achieve nearly bare-metal performance [20, 18, 15, 28]. According to VMware's recent research, the SRIOV passthrough mode NIC virtualization achieves 99.8% throughput of a native machine, while less than 50% for para-virtualization. In terms of latency, in average, SRIOV passthrough mode is only 13% higher than a native machine while the number is 107.7% for the para-virtualized mode [30].

Meanwhile, the security of SRIOV was studied since the very beginning. In principle, an SRIOV device should not be directly configured by a VM, as the VM can be easily controlled by an attacker. Therefore, the functions provided by the device are separated into two groups under control-plane and data-plane, and by assigning only data-plane functions to the VM. Control-plane functions are assigned to the hypervisor and all requests from the VM regarding configurations are firstly routed to the hypervisor for sanitization. Under this setting, the security requirements seem to be satisfied.

However, such design is problematic under today's complicated network environment when numerous network protocols have to be supported. In particular, we found one network protocol, Ethernet OAM (Operations, Administration, Maintenance), could cause severe disruption to the network environment if abused by the adversary. To launch the attack, the adversary controlling a VM simply needs to send **3 OAM packets** to a multicast address. Then, the port connected by the host will be closed, causing other VMs and the hypervisor residing on the same host all disconnected. This kind of attack could lead to much worse consequence when numerous VMs are controlled by attackers.

This vulnerability is a result of the combination of multiple factors. First, the switch can be configured to automatically turn off the port when receiving an error signal from the entity at the other end. This design is reasonable when the other end is a single host but questionable when multiple untrusted VMs run on the end host. Second, **the**

OAM packet is considered as a data-plane packet as there is no command in the packet content, which bypasses checks performed by the hypervisor. Though this issue is not limited to SRIOV devices, the design principle of the SRIOV (data transparent to hypervisor) **makes it very difficult to fix**. Third, the existing SRIOV networking devices have rather limited **hardware-based** filtering capabilities regarding the packets sent to multicast addresses.

To demonstrate the severity of this vulnerability, we showed a new attack against SRIOV NIC (Network Interface Card) by abusing a VM on the same host. We overcame several obstacles, including adding the VM's address into the recipient list of multicast packets and finishing the handshake process of OAM, and showed that it is possible to achieve the goal of disconnecting the host. We found that the attack can immediately take effect but recovering from the failure requires considerable manual efforts. Then, we developed a defense mechanism based on our observation that the legitimate VM does not need to initiate OAM conversations. The defense requires a small modification to the NIC driver to prevent VM from adding itself to the recipient list of OAM packet. As a result, the attack is thwarted since the adversary cannot finish the handshake process, a required step before sending valid OAM messages to the switch.

Next, we explored the possibilities of bypassing our basic defense and it turns out the adversary is able to completely skip the handshake process. By thoroughly evaluating the OAM protocol, we found that the possible values indicating the switch configuration are within limited range. In fact, learning the configuration can be done without going through the handshake process. By repeatedly sending OAM packets with possible configuration values, the attack could still succeed. As shown in our evaluation, the switch does not check the contents of the handshake packets, which enables attackers to freely set up OAM connections and launch the attack without receiving any packet. Considering its severity, we reported the issue to the switch manufacture. The manufacture confirmed the vulnerability and promised to fix it soon. In addition, as noted by the manufacture, **the relevant RFC standard does not require handshake validation** and we speculate the issue could exist in other switches as well.

At last, we explored the existing implementations of all entities involved and found that an unused field in OAM packets can be retrofitted to include a secret value that is hard to be guessed by the adversary. We proposed a mitigation approach that only requires small changes to the switch firmware and the test result showed that it is quite effective.

Contributions. The contributions of this work are summarized below:

- We discovered a vulnerability on SRIOV NIC in handling the OAM protocol and the multicast channel. Such vulnerability can result in a severe consequence where untrusted VM can cut off the physical machine's entire network connectivity.

- Based on this finding, we successfully launched attacks in a virtualized environment, leveraging a flaw of the switches shipped by a well-known manufacturer. In fact, the cause of the flaw comes from the rough specification by the RFC OAM standard.

- We proposed a method to defend against the attack without any modification to the physical layer of the

existing hardware. The method only requires modification to the switch firmwares and NIC drivers. We also set up a emulation environment to validate the defense method.

Roadmap. Section. 2 introduces two main technologies that are related to this work. Section. 3 describes how attacker can launch the attack. Section. 4 shows a simple defense that only modifies the NIC driver which is later turned out to be not enough. Section. 5 describes an updated attack method that can be used to counter the defense. Section. 6 analyzes the root reason of the vulnerability. Section. 7 includes a practical defense that can truly prevent attackers from launching this kind of attack. Section. 8 describes related works and Section. 9 concludes this paper.

2. BACKGROUND

Our study reveals a critical vulnerability underlying SRIOV devices when handling Ethernet OAM (Operations, Administration, Maintenance) packets. In this section, we briefly describe these two technologies.

2.1 SRIOV

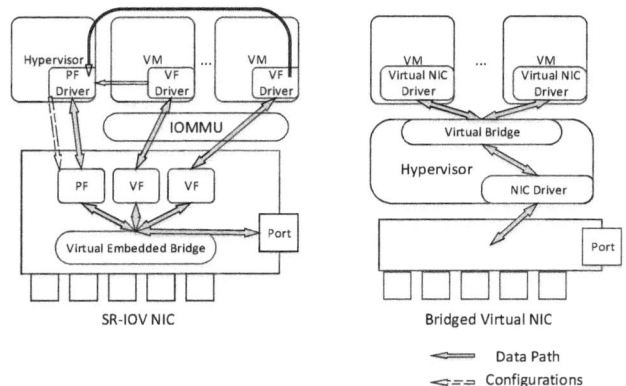

Figure 1: SRIOV NIC workflow.

Design. SRIOV was proposed by the PCI Special Interest Group (PCI-SIG) to allow a PCIe device to appear as multiple separate physical PCIe devices and be manipulated by VMs directly. Under the traditional I/O virtualization model, a hypervisor mediates all the flows between VMs and I/O devices. The flows have to be multiplexed before being forwarded to hardware. The right part of Figure 1 shows an example of the bridged Virtual NIC. In this setting, the hypervisor must virtualize software NICs (including interfaces and ring buffers) for an VM to access network and set up virtualized bridge to connect VM's virtualized NICs to the physical port. Extra CPU and memory resources are consumed by hypervisor to forward the packets to the correct destinations (software-based forwarding). The penalty exacerbates when a huge volume of data has to be processed, e.g., in 10G Ethernet network.

To the contrary, SRIOV directly assigns the logical accessing port of the hardware to VM and makes the whole processing flow *transparent* to hypervisor, achieving nearly bare-metal performance. The left part of Figure 1 illustrates the processing flow through SRIOV capable NIC [1]. Such NIC integrates an efficient hardware unit called *Virtual Embedded Bridge (VEB)* [17, 12, 13]. Flow forwarding is done by VEB and no extra performance penalty is incurred by hypervisor. To notice, VEB is not required by every SRIOV device. But in this NIC case, it is a must-have because an NIC has only one physical port and VEB enables the port sharing among different VMs.

To enable the access from the upper levels, SRIOV device offers *Physical Function (PF)* and *Virtual Function (VF)*. Each device is required to provide at least one PF and multiple VFs.

A PF is a fully featured PCIe function supported by a hardware driver, via which its owner can fully control the hardware device including configure its setting (control plane) as well as performing I/O operations (data plane).

A VF has only a subset of features of PCIe function and is supported by a driver different from PF's. It is only allowed to exchange data with hardware device (data-plane only). VF is designed to be invoked by VMs and a hardware unit IOMMU (Input output memory management unit) is built to map a VM to a specific VF.

Take SRIOV NIC as an example. The interface controller usually provides 63 VFs to serve up to 63 VMs simultaneously. NIC receives all the packets from VF, PF and devices outside of the machine, and then passes them to its VEB. VEB needs to route the packets to their destination, as a result it forwards them to either PF/VF of the same machine or sends them out to other machines through network cable.

Many devices nowadays are SRIOV capable, like storage controller, GPU and NIC. These devices have already been widely deployed by cloud service providers (e.g., Amazon EC2 HPC), enterprise data centers and high performance computers (HPC) [2, 3].

Security model. A major security requirement for SRIOV is to protect the hardware from being tampered by untrusted parties, i.e., VMs controlled by attackers, on the host machine. In the traditional I/O virtualization model, hypervisor is leveraged as the guard to apply filtering rules on the virtual bridge. For example, hypervisor can use **ebtables** to set rules for filtering packets from VM based on the protocol, source MAC address, or destination MAC address. In the SRIOV model, hypervisor is removed from the path, so, as a replacing security mechanism, SRIOV device separates its functionalities into data-plane and control-plane, and group them into PF and VF. Then, it delegates PFs to trusted party, usually hypervisor, and VFs to untrusted parties, usually VMs. If the owner of VF intends to change the hardware configuration, it has to issue a request to the owner of PF (i.e., hypervisor). If the request is approved, PF will be used by its owner to fulfill the requests.

Under this setting, adversary who controls VM can only exchange data through the hardware and configuring hardware is out of her reach. This security model appears to be sound but our attack (see Section 3 and Section 5) shows that such design is not perfect. The problem emerges due to the ill-conceived integration of old management protocol and new virtualized environment, and further complicates due to the lack of finer-grained filtering capabilities on SRIOV devices.

---

[1]We use the term SRIOV NIC afterwards for brevity.

2.2 Ethernet OAM

To help the network operator diagnose the network, IEEE 802 working group established IEEE 802.3ah (Ethernet in the First Mile, EFM) protocol which supports link layer Ethernet management (Ethernet OAM) and included it into the overall standard 802.3-2008. To date, Ethernet OAM was implemented by the majority of the network device vendors. The features required by OAM include link discovery and monitoring, remote fault detection and remote loopback [8]. Below, we describe the data format of OAM packet and the handshake process within the protocol.

OAM Data Packet. As defined by the EFM protocol family, OAM data packets are exchanged under basic 802.3 slow protocol frames, which are also called *OAMPDU (OAM Protocol Data Units)*. By default, OAMPDUs are transmitted at limited speed, which is up to 10 packets per second. Another restriction on OAMPDU is that it is designed to be **transmitted between two endpoints of a single link.** Even when the receiving endpoint does not support OAM, **OAMPDU cannot be relayed to other entities.** To communicate across links, support from higher-layer applications is required.

Length	Field	Value
6	Destination Address Slow Protocol Address	01-80-c2-00-00-02
6	Source MAC address	any
2	Type	88-09
1	Sub-type	0x03
2	Flags	any
1	Code	any
42-1496	Payload	any
4	Check Sum	any

Table 1: OAMPDU format.

Table 1 elaborates the format of OAMPDU. When the endhost attempts to send OAMPDUs, the destination can only be the device at the other end of the cable, e.g., switch. Therefore, the Rx (Receive) address is a constant value (first row in Table 1) and defined as a *multicast* address, while the Tx (Transmit) address can be any valid value (second row in Table 1). Such setting disables packet relays as required by OAM protocol. In addition, every packet of OAMPDU carries 15 bits of flags representing entity's real-time status, including the OAM connection status (4 bits, 2 bits for local status and the other 2 bits for remote status) and emergency link events (4 bits with each bit referring to **Link Fault**, **Dying Gasp**, **Critical Event** and **Link Loss**).

There are 3 types of OAMPDU defined by EFM: *information OAMPDU, event notification OAMPDU* and *loopback control OAMPDU*. Information OAMPDU is used to exchange information between OAM entities, including the process of handshaking and error reporting. In this work, we discovered the vulnerability of SRIOV device when handling information OAMPDU and we introduce its structure here (also illustrated in Figure 2).

For an information OAMPDU, the data field in the payload section contains one or more TLV (Type-length-value), which is the container for entity configurations. The TLV can be used to describe local entity, remote entity or be filled with customized information. Each Local/Remote TLV is 16 bytes long and composed of 9 fields.

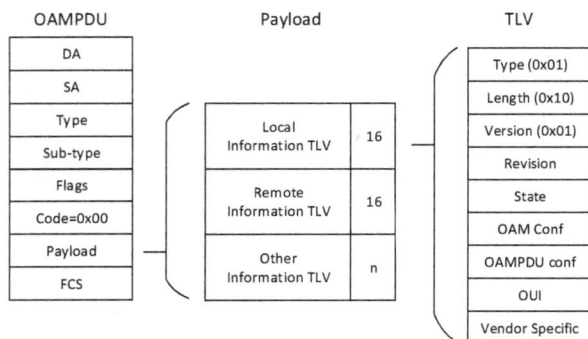

Figure 2: Information OAMPDU format.

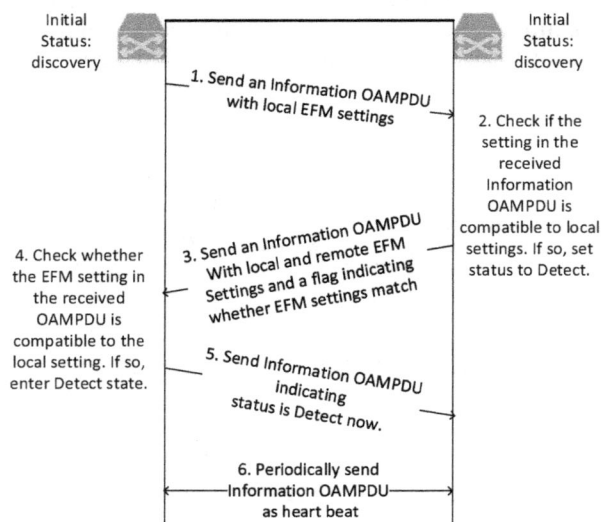

Figure 3: OAM handshake flow chart.

Handshake flow of information OAMPDU. Essentially, the handshake process has to be successfully completed before actual conversation of OAM. Figure 3 illustrates this process and the details are elaborated as follows:

1. In the beginning, the entities of the both ends set their status to `Discovery`. Then, either one of them in active mode continuously broadcasts its own configuration settings through OAMPDUs to indicate the intention of setting up connection. Only a local information TLV is contained in OAMPDU.

2. When the remote entity successfully receives the packet, it checks if the received configurations are compatible with its pre-defined format. If the check is passed, it replies to the sender with an Information OAMPDU that carries flags indicating that it is satisfied with the configuration and changes the connection status to `Detect`. The Information OAMPDU embeds both its own information TLV (in local TLV) and the received information (in remote TLV) into the payload.

3. After the responding OAMPDU reaches the sender, the embedded configuration information will be checked

as well in the same compatibility checking process. If compatibility requirement is fulfilled and the attached configuration of the remote entity conforms to that of the first packet issued by the sender, the sender's status will be switched to `Detect`, announcing that the connection is successfully set up. Following that, both entities will periodically send Information OAMPDUs as heart-beat signal.

All other OAM functionalities are enabled after the connection is set up, like link quality measurement. The most commonly used feature is error isolation, through which the remote entity turns the interface status to `Error Down` if the entity detects the link failure by itself or receives the error report sent through that interface. This feature is very helpful to accelerate the routing converge of the higher layers and avoid the problematic link being clogged by the network data. However, this feature could be turned into an attack vector if abused by the adversary, i.e., to disconnect other legitimate hosts sharing the same network, and our attack demonstrates this is feasible.

3. ATTACK

In this section, we elaborate how we leverage the OAM protocol to attack the SRIOV device and disconnect all VMs and the hypervisor linked to it. We first describe the adversary model and attacker's motivation. Then, we show the details of the attack and evaluate the attack effectiveness.

3.1 Adversary Model

We assume the adversary is targeting the network infrastructure of a cloud service, which could be either public cloud (like Amazon EC2) or private cloud deployed within an organization. Attacker's goal here is to disrupt the service operation. The computer of the cloud service runs multiple VMs connected to a switch. The NIC of the computer is SRIOV capable and the feature is already enabled. Each VM on the machine is assigned with an NIC VF to allow direct access to network consisting of a switch that supports OAM protocol. .

Comparing to controlling hypervisor or switch for the attack purpose, obtaining access to the VMs is a more attainable goal. In public cloud, the adversary could rent a VM and issue malfeasant configuration requests. In private cloud, attacker could exploit the vulnerability of a less protected VM and take the full control. As described later in Section 3, by just issuing carefully crafted OAMPDU from an attacker-controlled VM to SRIOV NIC of the host, all the network connections between the VMs and the hypervisor to the switch will be terminated, causing network failures hard to recover. Given that a cloud host-machine usually runs many VMs at the same time, the damage to the users or customers could be tremendous. Since SRIOV devices are widely deployed by cloud services and these devices are usually off-the-shelf, the number of cloud services under threat is potentially very large. In addition, our attack does not break the isolation mechanisms of VM-to-VM and VM-to-hypervisor, making prevention very difficult.

We also assume the administrator follows the security guidance of SRIOV, under which PF is controlled by benign hypervisor and VF is delegated to untrusted VMs. While the attacker could request hypervisor to adjust settings that are exposed to her, hypervisor can easily reject such illegal requests by enforcing the standard detection logic. In contrast, our attack only leverages VF to communicate with the host NIC and all the checks from the hypervisor are bypassed.

A recent work by Smolyar *et al.* has shown that SRIOV-capable NIC is vulnerable to DoS attack launched by VM [24]. By sending illegal flow control packets, the performance of the network is significantly dropped, e.g., 250% increase of network latency. Comparing to that attack, ours could cause much more severe consequence - disconnecting the entire network connections.

3.2 Attack Method

Attack Overview. Our attack exploits the error isolation feature provided by OAM protocol. As described in Section 2.2, an entity could send an information OAMPDU packet to the linked switch to indicate if there is a link fault. Receiving this signal, the switch could cut off the connection of the host machine. This feature is innocuous when the sender is a hypervisor: even if the hypervisor is controlled by attacker, sending this packet only disconnects itself. The attack cannot be easily launched if virtualization is realized through software bridges, because hypervisor can easily filter out OAM packets. However, damage could be caused when it is sent by an attacker-controlled VM, as all other VMs and their hypervisor sharing the same NIC would be disconnected while the hypervisor is agnostic.

While it is assumed that the sender reports only *after* detecting the link error, such assumption is not guaranteed. VM could *fake* a link fault message and there is no mechanism in place to check its authenticity. Though error reporting is supposed to be the responsibility of the hypervisor, we suspected VM could undertake this task as well. We tested such hypothesis by sending the OAMPDU packet through VM and discovered that VEB treats the packet as a normal multicast packet (data-plane packet) and forwards it to the remote switch. To complete the error reporting process, a handshake has to be completed ahead. Again, this is achievable by VM: VM can register its address as the destination address of the OAM protocol and receive all the OAMPDUs sent by the switch. Below, we elaborate how the attack can be launched.

Attack Implementation. Our attack takes two steps: the first step is to set up an OAM connection and the second step is to send the heart beat packet with the fault flag toggled.

Attacker could set up the OAM connection using *raw socket* and inject crafted packets that accord to the OAM handshaking format. By setting the destination address to a multicast address *01:80:C2:00:00:02* (see Section 2.2), the packet will be sent out by the NIC of the host and reach the switch. However, receiving the packet and completing the handshake process are not trivial for VM: by default, the responding packet is also sent to the same multicast address instead of the Tx address provided by the VM and then transmitted to the NICs of the linked hosts. It turns out the VEB of host NIC normally would refrain from forwarding multicast packet to VMs due to two performance concerns: 1)It consumes a lot of computations unnecessarily as not every VM needs multicast packet. 2) Handling those multicast packets not belonging to the VM costs the VM considerable resources.

Here, we let the VM configure *Multicast Table Array (MTA)* of the host NIC to receive the reply packets. For an Intel SRIOV NIC, when it receives a packet towards a multicast address, it will look up MTA which logs a list of destination addresses and forward the packet to the VMs whose addresses are enlisted. Though MTA has to be updated by the hypervisor and cannot be configured by VM directly, it turns out that VF driver of Intel SRIOV NIC provides API for a VM to ask hypervisor for updating MTA. By default, hypervisor will accept the request and fulfill it automatically without any actions from the administrator. In particular, the attacker could run `IP maddr add` command on the VM to append the address into MTA. After that, the malicious VM is able to receive OAMPDUs and complete the handshake process.

The latter step is rather straightforward. When the attacker wants to cut off the network of the physical machine, she only needs to set the link fault flag in the Information OAMPDU to 1, which represents "critical errors". The switch will shut down the corresponding connection once this OAMPDU is received.

3.3 Evaluation

To test the effectiveness of the attack, we set up a testbed consisting of a SRIOV capable server and an OAM capable switch. We created two VMs supervised by KVM hypervisor and all of them run Ubuntu 14.04.3 LTS OS. Table 2 shows the detailed information of the platform.

We assume one VM (VM_1) has been controlled by the attacker while the other is benign (VM_2). Both of them have been assigned with NIC VF. Meanwhile, VM_1, VM_2 and the host OS are all configured to use static IP addresses belonging to the same class-C IP subnet. The physical NIC port of the machine is connected to a HUAWEI S3328TP-EI switch that connects to a LAN with Internet access through another port. The OAM of the switch is turned on and the fault isolation is enabled, which means the switch will terminate all the connections for the port and turn the status of the port to `Error Down` if an error is received or perceived from the port.

As for the experiment result, after VM_1 set up OAM connection and sent an Information OAMPDU carrying a link fault flag, we found that the switch cut the connection as expected, immediately after the OAMPDU is received, in less than 1 second. Consequently, VM_2 can no longer access the Internet, together with the hypervisor. From the console of the switch, we observed that the status of the port was turned to `Error Down`, and all the services associated with the port were terminated. This result clearly proves our attack is effective and easy to carry out.

We also evaluated the difficulty for an technician to restore the network from such failures.

First, it turns out without the admin privilege, the switch cannot recover the network activities by itself. We detached the cable from the port and attached it to the port again after 30 seconds. The status of the port was not changed and the connection was still blocked. According to the configuration guide of the tested switch [1], traffic will not be resumed even if the faulty link recovers, because the error status of the interface is not reset.

Second, we also tested whether the administrator could use the network manager account to reset the connection. The link status came back to normal after we restarted the interface. However, the restarting process should be conducted carefully, as the guide warns network managers that

Table 2: Platform Information.

	Host	VM
CPU	Intel Xeon E5-2620 V3	Intel Xeon E5-2620 V3 (2 cores)
Memory	16G DDR4	8G
Mother board	ASUS Z10PE-D16	/
NIC	Dual Port Intel Ethernet Controller i350-AM2	Intel Ethernet Controller i350 VF
OS	Ubuntu 14.04.3 LTS	Ubuntu 14.04.3 LTS
NIC driver	igb 5.3.2	igbvf 2.3.5
Hypervisor	KVM + virt-manager	/

they should manually check link quality after switching back the traffic. Therefore, the network manager still has to manually examine the network status or even recover by herself, a very time-consuming task.

The consequence can be much more severe if the network manager configured *EFM Association* [1]. When the switch receives the Information OAMPDU with link fault, firstly it invokes Layer-2 operations (e.g., turn down the interface.) to the port according to the configurations. Besides, it may also trigger other modules or other EFM entities by broadcasting the error. The error broadcast could incur further damage to the network. For example, it could trigger *BFD (Bidirectional Forwarding Detection)* module to change the routing behavior of a upper layer router. It may also trigger another switch to shut down a port, etc. Such snowball effect would cause more machines to be disconnected.

4. BASIC DEFENSE SCHEME

To protect the cloud service from being disrupted by this attack, we propose a defense mechanism which can be easily implemented without any change to the hardware and network infrastructure. We believe the capabilities of the VM in configuring OAM should be controlled. In the meantime, all other communication channels from VMs should not be affected. Below, we elaborate our defense scheme and the evaluation result.

4.1 Method

Shutting down the OAM channel of a VM while ensuring other data communication channels run normally are in fact not easy. Hypervisor has no visibility and control over the data sent by VM, when VM accesses SRIOV NIC. One intuitive idea is to grant hypervisor the ability to block certain data flows between VM and SRIOV NIC, in particular through manipulating the functional registers provided by the NIC, which however requires hardware modification and cannot be readily deployed.

As described in Section 3.2, VM has to enlist the OAMPDU multicast address in MTA of SRIOV NIC to receive the response OAMPDU packet and this registration process has to go through hypervisor, therefore we could ask the hypervisor to supervise the process. In particular, we found NIC is responsible for writing a specific multicast address in MTA [4] and we implemented the checking routine as a module in NIC which blocks the registration request of OAMPDU multicast address.

Before describing the details of our mitigation, we first introduce the process on how address is registered in MTA to motivate our implementation choice.

The functionality of multicast filtering is implemented in NIC. Specifically, the *VM Offload Register (VMOLR)* in the

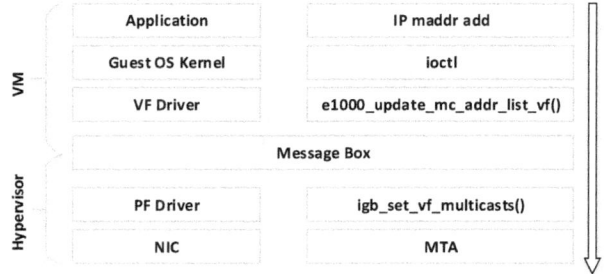

Figure 4: Multicast Addr Registration Call Graph.

NIC has a field *ROMPE* (the 25th bit) that can be used to enable or disable multicast forwarding (enabled by default). NIC will forward a multicast packet if the destination address of the packet is in the MTA when multicast forwarding is enabled. Therefore, VM has to write the multicast address ahead to MTA to let NIC forward those packets, which is accomplished by calling PF upon the request of VF invoked by VM.

Figure 4 shows the important functions invoked during multicast registration. On VM's side, command IP parses the request from user and invokes the relevant system calls based on the input parameters. When Linux kernel receives those calls, it checks the privilege of the invoking process and then forward the request to VF drivers' corresponding interface, i.e., function e1000_update_mc_ad dr_list_vf() of the igbvf driver, which is a linux base driver for Intel network connection[7]. The function computes the hash values for at most 30 input multicast addresses (the remaining ones will be discarded). Then this function composes a message using the least significant 12 bits of every hash value and sends the message to PF through the *mailbox system* which exchanges messages between VM and hypervisor. Mailbox system routes the message to the handler function igb_set_vf_multicasts() in the igb driver (PF driver) owned by the hypervisor. The PF function parses the message to get the hash values and stores them to the MTA for that VF. After that, the hypervisor replies ACK (if success) or NACK (if fail) to VF through the mail box. When these steps are completed, NIC forwards the multicast packets to VF if the destination address is in the VF's MTA.

Since the VM could be fully controlled by the adversary, we added a filtering module to the MTA updating functions in the PF driver code, i.e., within igb_set_vf_multicasts() (see Figure. 5) of the NIC, to prevent NIC from writing the OAM protocol address to the MTA for any VM. And all other parts of the driver are kept unchanged. In other words, a VM could still receive multicast packets from NIC except the ones related to OAM. Because the address will never appear in the MTA, forwarding unit in the NIC would not forward the OAMPDUs to VMs. As a result, VM can no longer set up the OAM connection with the switch to further launch the attack.

```
1 static int igb_set_vf_multicasts(...){
    /*get number of maddr from msg;*/
3   int n = ...;

5   /*get pointer of hash list from msg*/
    u16 *hash_list = ...;
7
    /*Add Filter Here*/
9   for(i = 0; i < n && i < 30; i++)
      if(hash_list[i] == hash(OAMAddr))
11      hash_list[i] = dummyAddrHash;
    /*End of the Filter*/
13  ......
    /*Sanitized hash_list is written*/
15  for (i = 0; i < n; i++)
      vf_data->vf_mc_hashes[i]=
17      hash_list[i];
    ......
19 }
```

Figure 5: Code illustration of the filter. Line 9 to 11 are added while other codes are kept unchanged.

4.2 Evaluation

We modified the PF driver to add our code blacklisting the OAMPDU multicast address and compiled the customized driver. Then, we updated the driver of NIC and relaunched our attack. As expected, the adversarial VM can no longer complete the handshake process with the switch because it cannot receive the replies from the switch, thwarting our attack. The performance cost is negligible to hypervisor and VMs, since the check only takes place during address registration process. However, as shown in the next section, this check can be bypassed by an improved version of our attack.

5. UPDATED ATTACK

In this section, we propose an updated version of the attack scheme which can circumvent the defense scheme proposed in Section 4. The regular OAM communication process requires the handshake step to be completed before using other OAM functionalities. While our last defense could prevent adversarial VM from receiving OAMPDU packets from the switch, it does not stop adversary sending out packet to the switch. As such, it is possible for the adversary to *guess* the right parameters of the outbound OAM-PDU packets to complete handshake process. Below, we elaborate the new attack scheme.

5.1 Attack without OAM replies

For a successful OAM handshake, VM needs to receive the TLV information returned from the switch. Without knowing that TLV, what the attacker can do is just to enumerate all the possible value and send the link fault signal with the guessed value to the switch. However, this is doable in rea-

sonable time as shown later. We assume the switch works in passive mode to constantly receive and process the packets from the adversary. Even if the switch works in active mode, it will be switched to passive mode when the counterpart of the channel is in active mode, which can be set by the adversarial VM. The attack works as follows:

1. First, the attacker sends an Information OAMPDU with its own configuration contained in the local information TLV, like the regular process.

2. When the switch receives this packet, it replies an Information OAMPDU with switch's configuration in local information TLV field and the attacker's configuration in remote information TLV field. Local Discovery status and Remote Discovery status of the OAMPDU are set to be `Satisfied` and `Discovery` respectively according to the EFM standard. The reply packet however cannot be received by the adversary this time when our basic defense is deployed.

3. The adversary has to respond to the switch with a valid OAMPDU to finish the handshake process. In particular, the adversary has to correctly fill Local Discovery status, Remote Discovery status, Local TLV and Remote TLV. The first three fields are easy to fill: the adversary can assign `Satisfied` to both Discovery status fields and set the same local TLV value of the first packet. For remote TLV, the attacker enumerates the possible configuration setting of the remote switch and fills the corresponding value.

4. The attacker sends the OAMPDU packet to switch using the above crafted values. If the connection is terminated, the attack is successful. Otherwise, the attacker should go back to step 1 for another round and try a new remote TLV at step 3.

One would worry that the attack is not practical as a huge number of TLV has to be enumerated and the attack would be discovered before succeeded. Interestingly, **the range of valid TLV is quite narrow**, making the guess attempts ends in short time. Figure 6 shows the format of a TLV which can represent either local configuration information or remote configuration information. Some of the fields can be fixed with constant value: `Remote Information` for the information type field, `0x10` (16 bits) for Information length field (the length of a TLV), `0x01` for OAM version and `0x0000` for Revision. The valid values for the remaining fields are described below.

- **State.** There are only 3 possible values for Parser Action (forwarding, looping back, discarding) and 2 values (0 or 1) for Mux.

- **OAM configuration.** This segment has 5 fields while each one is only 1-bit long, adding up to $2^5 = 32$ possible values in total.

- **Max OAMPDU Size.** Maximum OAMPDU size is often set to the default value 128.

- **Vendor Identifier.** Organizationally Unique Identifier is assigned per manufacturer. According to the

	7	6	5	4	3	2	1	0
Information Type	0x01 for Local Information, 0x02 for Remote Information							
Information Length	0x10							
OAM Version	0x01							
Revision	0							
State	Reserved					Mux	Parser Action	
OAM Configuration	Reserved			Vars	Events	LB	Unidir	Mode
OAMPDU Configuration	Reserved							
	Max OAMPDU Size							
Vendor Identifier	24 bits Organizational Unique Identifier							
	32 bits Vendor Specific Information							

Figure 6: Information OAMPDU TLV format

statistics from IDC [9], the top 5 Ethernet switch vendors have taken the lion's share of the market, as shown in Table 3. In other words, using 5 values corresponding to the top vendors is sufficient in most cases. Vendor Specific Information is often set to all 0 as we examined a large number of the switch documents of mainstream switches.

Vendor	Cisco	HP	Huawei	Juniper	Arista	Others
Revenue	3827	592	393	243	217	1190

Table 3: Market share of switch vendors ($M).

Hence, an attacker only needs to guess at most $3 * 2 * 32 * 5 = 960$ TLV values till finding the right TLV. As one optimization, the adversary could start from the most popular configurations, e.g., the top switch vendor identifier, to reach the correct answer more quickly.

Next, we compute the time required for trying the 960 possible TLV values. An end host can send at most 10 OAMPDU packets per second, while a switch replies 1 OAMPDU per second by default. Our attack requires 1 VM to send 3 OAMPDU packets and wait the switch to reply with 1 OAMPDU packet, so the attacker can try a TLV value in less than 1.5-second interval, assuming that the switch works at the default setting. In the end, an attacker can exhausts all possibilities in 24 minutes at most.

Under the real-world settings, the time overhead could be reduced to a much lower amount. Network managers tend to modify only several fields and keep others unchanged. Assuming that at most 2 bits among the 5 OAMPDU configuration bits are modified by the network manager, attacker needs to try $(C_5^2 + C_5^1 + C_5^0) * 5 = 80$ times maximally to find the right TLV, which means in average, the attacker only needs to guess 40 times, taking around 1 minute.

5.2 Evaluation

We tested the updated attack scheme on the same platform mentioned in Section 3.3. The basic defense described in Section 4 is deployed to prevent VMs from receiving OAMPDUs. We discussed with an experienced network adminis-trator and modified two configuration item of the switch to non-default values and kept other configurations unchanged to simulate the real-world settings.

Though based on the theoretical analysis, in average tens of guesses have to be made to pass the check from switch, surprisingly it took only one guess to succeed no matter what value we chose for the two configuration items. It turns out the root reason is that the switch does not compare the remote TLV within the received OAMPDU packet with its own configuration at all. We consider this is a severe vulnerability and have reported it to the product security team (PSIRT) of the vendor (Huawei). The team confirmed the vulnerability and committed to fix it in the later versions. The team also replied to us that **the switch does not check the TLV because the RFC standard does not specify the checking process**. Hence, they considered it a generic problem they plan to report to IETF. We foresee it would take a long time before the standard is mended, but even it happens, our attack is still viable as the attacker is able to guess the right configuration in short time.

The consequence is similar: the attacker can successfully disconnect the physical machine and the recovery process is also painful. The network manager must use her account to login the switch and reset the interface to wake the port up from `Error Down`.

6. LIMITATIONS OF SRIOV NIC

For the updated attack, leveraging hypervisor to terminate the handshake process between VM and switch is impossible as hypervisor is not on the data plane. The only countermeasure available is letting the NIC to inspect the outbound packets but unfortunately there is no way to easily implement the filtering mechanism. We read through the document of the I350 NIC we experimented with [6] and other documents of the advanced models (e.g., Intel 82599 10GbE NIC [5]). It turns out there is no programmable internal filter inside the NIC, or VEB more specifically, that we can use to switch packets between VMs and external LAN, handle broadcast or multicast packet forwarding.

The outbound packets could be controlled by the Tx switching to some extent. There are some filters like L2 filters and VLAN filters implemented in the original SRIOV NIC which redirect the packets to the virtual pool and decide which one should be sent out through a series of matching process. However, there is one exception of Tx packet filtering [2]: **multicast and broadcast packets are always sent to external LAN**. That means there is no way for an existing NIC to stop VMs from sending multicast or broadcast packets. Routing multicast packet to its destinations is implemented in MTA but MTA cannot be used for filtering. Intel does provide 3 outbound security mechanisms: MAC anti-spoofing, VLAN tag-validation and VLAN anti-spoofing. However, these mechanisms are all targeting spoofed and invalid Tx address which cannot be leveraged for defense, since the Tx address used for attack is valid. In fact, the SRIOV NIC design overlooked the special usage of multicast protocol and simplified the multicast forwarding procedure such that all ethernet control protocols based on multicast run mistakenly over the virtualized environment.

In addition, the OAM vulnerability not only impacts machines equipping SRIOV NIC, but also neighboring machines

---

[2]Rx switching does not have this exception.

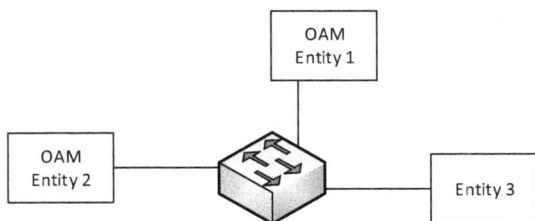

Figure 7: An incorrect network structure.

sharing the same network, when the network is configured incorrectly. We show one such network structure in Figure. 7, where 2 OAM entities (`Entity 1` and `Entity 2`) and an OAM incapable entity (`Entity 3`) are connected to an OAM incapable switch. As the switch cannot handle OAM packets, it will *always forward* them to other connected entities. In this case, when `Entity 1` reports link error, the link between `Entity 2` and the switch will be shut down because the OAMPDU is relayed to `Entity 2` who assumes the error is reported by the connected switch. Subsequently, the link between `Entity 3` and `Entity 2` will be cut off. As such, an attacker controlling one entity could force disconnections of other innocent entities. We tested this attack following the paradigm shown in Figure. 7 and found the attack always succeeded. To mitigate this issue, the network administrator should keep the devices consistent in OAM handling (on/off for all devices).

7. UPDATED DEFENSE

Filtering outbound multicast packets from VM on the NIC side is not a feasible defense solution due to the limited filtering capabilities provided by the current hardwares. As an alternative way, we look for the defense schemes on the switch side which aims to identify whether the OAMPDU is from VM. Below we describe a practical defense method and also discuss other solutions.

7.1 Defense through Distinguishing VMs

Our updated attack could succeed because the amount of valid TLV values in the inbound OAMPDU to NIC is too small. While the handshake process is designed to prevent a random entity from reporting error message through OAM, it is bypassed under this problematic implementation. Intuitively, we could fix this vulnerability through introducing more randomness into the OAMPDU.

Extending the OAM protocol to add an additional field bearing a random number could serve the defense purpose but might cause compatibility issues. Fortunately, we found the 32-bit Vendor Specific Information (VSI) field could be used (see last row of Figure 6). It is always set to all 0 and unused by switch. Therefore, we design the updated defense by filling a random number into this field as a secret in the outbound OAMPDU and checks if the same value is observed in the follow-up inbound OAMPDU. This modification occupies the VSI that is designed for vendor specific purpose. If a vendor has already occupied this field for its private functionalities, the private functionalities can be implemented in Organization Specific TLV that is also designed

for vendor specific purpose and has better extensibility resulted from a larger space.

Specifically, we could command switch to generate a random 32-bit number and fill it into the VSI field whenever sending reply OAMPDUs to the remote entity, as shown in Figure.8. A valid entity would see the random number and the response will automatically include the same number (in remote TLV) according to the EFM standard. For an adversary, since the handshake reply never reaches VM, she has to guess the number, which lies in a much larger range. On the side of switch, if VSI field of the inbound reply OAMPDU packet has an unmatched value, the packet is dropped.

We further analyze this scheme in three aspects below.

- **Effectiveness.** Attacker has to explore the configuration space of 2^{32} values to launch one successful attack. There is a 1.5-second interval between two attempts. As the result, it takes the attacker over 200 years in worst case (100 years in average for uniformly generated random number) to succeed. Without this defense, an attacker could succeed under a minute. Therefore, our defense substantially raises the bar for the attack.

- **Cost.** The only change to OAM protocol is adding a random number to OAMPDU, which requires modification to the switch firmware for random number generation and received value verification. The NIC vendors need to provide a patch to the driver and notify the customers to upgrade their NIC driver to deploy the basic defense scheme described in Section 4. The raised cost is moderate to them. For hypervisor and VMs, there is no extra cost.

- **Performance.** The penalty is incurred when exchanging OAM packets, while all other components are not impacted. Given that OAM is a slow protocol (0.1-second interval between communications at most), the increased time delay is very small comparing to the overall overhead.

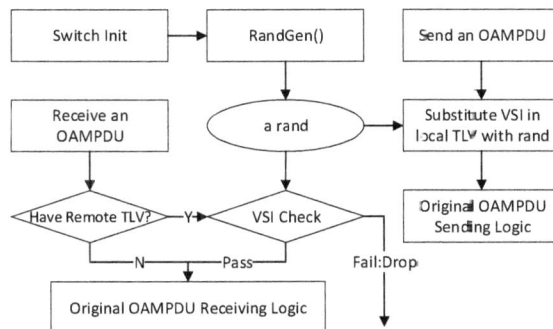

Figure 8: Flow chat of the defense scheme.

Evaluation. The ideal scenario for evaluating our new defense scheme is to modify the switch firmware and test under the same settings as Section 5.2. This is very difficult since we cannot get the source code from the switch vendor. As an alternative solution, we implemented an emulated switch that runs the modified OAM protocol using a PC (we call it switch PC) and connected the virtualized server to the switch PC. The virtualized server follows all the steps required by the OAM standard and the additional routines for randomness.

We let the VM to repeatedly guess the vendor specific information and send out OAMPDU to the switch PC. In the meantime, we check if any such packet can successfully arrive at the destination. After running the experiment for 24 hours, no OAMPDU packet sent from VM can be observed, suggesting our defense is effective.

7.2 Other Approaches

7.2.1 Checking MAC Address

If the switch could differentiate VMs and hypervisor, our attacks will be easily thwarted. The most straightforward way to achieve this goal is to examine the source MAC address of OAMPDU. Network manager could compile a whitelist of hypervisors' MAC addresses and integrate the list into the switch. When the switch receives an OAMPDU packet from an unlisted sender, it drops the packet. Because VMs cannot fake a source MAC address, OAMPDUs from VMs are always dropped.

The major advantage of this defense scheme is that it requires only changes to the receiving logic of the switch. The program logic to read the MAC address of the remote OAM entity has been built into the switch we tested (the MAC address of remote OAM entity is displayed in the management interface of the switch). So, switch vendors could just add a small piece of code to check if the address is in the whilelist. Besides, the scheme has negligible performance penalty because all changes are made in control plane and date plane is kept unchanged.

This scheme has a drawback that a lot of manual works have to be introduced when the network is quite dynamic. For instance, when a new network device is connected to the switch, manager must use her credential to login to the switch and add its MAC address to the whitelist.

7.2.2 Filtering by Hypervisor

We also consider filtering out the OAMPDUs by a software based switch instead of the NIC or physical switch. Smolyar et al. proposed a filtering technique to mitigate DoS attack in virtualized environment [24]. The main idea is to let one Ethernet controller forward all packets it received to the hypervisor by utilizing a software bridge. The bridge removes all the illegal packets and forwards the remaining packets to another Ethernet controller that is connected to the switch. We evaluated the feasibility of this defense here as well and concluded it is not practical for defending our attack.

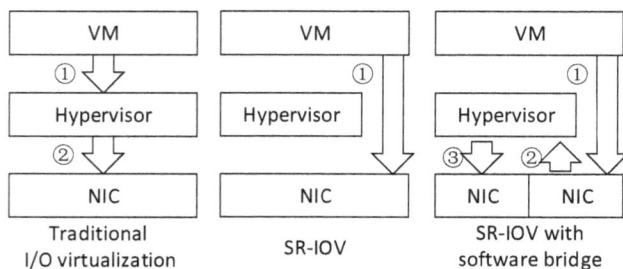

Figure 9: Comparison of the 3 other approaches.

This method seems to be effective against our attacks but it dims the benefits of high performance SRIOV NICs: transparent data path to hypervisors.

First, obviously, two Ethernet controllers (one for inbound and one for outbound) are required which means there is one Ethernet controller not available to the user.

More importantly, the performance penalty is also non-negligible, because all the communications on the data path need to go through hypervisor, which violates the fundamental goal of SRIOV. As shown in Figure. 9, for the SRIOV scheme, a packet sent by VM is transferred from VM's memory directly to NIC's buffer. For traditional I/O virtualization technique, the packet is copied from VM's memory to hypervisor's memory through a virtual NIC first, and then a software bridge in the hypervisor forwards it to physical NIC, which incurs 2 times I/O overhead compared to SRIOV scheme. For SRIOV with defense scheme from [24], packets are sent from VM to NIC and then copied back from NIC to hypervisor's memory for filtering and finally sent with another NIC, which incurs overall 3 times I/O overhead. Such heavy performance penalty makes the adoption questionable, because it is even worse than the traditional I/O virtualization.

7.2.3 Updating NIC Hardware

NIC vendors are able to update their next generation products to provide enough outbound filtering capabilities and open interfaces to hypervisor to defend this attack. This mitigation could resolve all the security issues discovered by us, but the cost could be considerable. In the meantime, the old models are still vulnerable.

8. RELATED WORKS

Network interface virtualization is a hot research area and the related techniques have been widely adopted by many organizations. Sheta et al. surveyed the widely used NIC virtualization techniques and evaluated them with different metrics [23]. Yassour et al. evaluated the SRIOV method for the network interface [31]. Dong et al. elaborated the SRIOV networking architecture in the Xen hypervisor [14].

The security problems of network interface virtualization are also studied. Recently, Richter et al. and Smolyar et al. proposed two different DoS attacks [22, 24] against virtualized network interface. Pek et al. discovered a series of attacks that can be launched under a direct device assignment settings [19], using an automatic tool to discover hardware-level vulnerabilities. Different from their works, our attacks can totally cut off the network connectivity of the machine, resulting in much worse consequences. Besides causing connectivity issues, SRIOV NIC can be exploited as a side channel for detecting co-located VMs in the cloud, as shown in [10].

The I/O virtualization technologies can be used to launch or defend against other attacks. Wojtczuk et al. showed a Message Signalled Interrupt(MSI) based attack on x86-64 machine, allowing a virtual machine to run privileged code in Xen environment [29]. Stewin et al. studied how malware can attack the host machine stealthily [25]. As an example, they implemented a key logger that attacks both Windows and Linux platforms. They used IOMMU to defend that kind of attacks. Still, attacker can modify the hardware-level data structure or configuration table to bypass the IOMMU isolation, as stated in [16].

9. CONCLUSION

We discovered a new vulnerability in SRIOV NIC. The root cause is that SR-IOV NIC does not provide sufficiently fine-grained outbound traffic filtering capability and the hypervisor is bypassed in SRIOV model. Exploiting such vulnerability, an attacker can fake OAM packets to break the connection between the host machine and the switch. As the result, the network connectivity of all VMs and hypervisor can be cut off.

The key to the successful attack is to handshake with the switch through SRIOV NIC. We show one attack scheme which asks help from MTA in the SRIOV NIC, and another which could even succeed without the help of MTA. The result suggests that both attacks are effective and practical.

In the end, we propose an effective defense scheme by using an implied challenge response. Since SRIOV devices are largely deployed only in recent years, we urge the community to thoroughly examine the attack surface against SRIOV devices and the vendors to actively fix the relevant security issues.

Acknowledgment

This work was supported in part by National Natural Science Foundation of China (NSFC) under Grant No. 61572415 and Hong Kong S.A.R. Research Grants Council (RGC) under Early Career Scheme No. 24207815.

10. REFERENCES

[1] Configuration guide - reliability. http://support.huawei.com/enterprise/docinforeader.action?contentId=DOC1000019450&partNo=10062.

[2] Enabling enhanced networking on linux instances in a vpc. http://docs.aws.amazon.com/AWSEC2/latest/UserGuide/enhanced-networking.html.

[3] How to: Enable single root i/o virtualization in exalogic elastic cloud. https://blogs.oracle.com/opscenter/entry/how_to_enable_single_root.

[4] Intel 82576 sr-iov driver: Companion guide. http://www.intel.com/content/www/us/en/embedded/products/networking/82576-sr-iov-driver-companion-guide.html.

[5] Intel 82599 10 gbe controller datasheet. http://www.intel.com/content/dam/www/public/us/en/documents/datasheets/82599-10-gbe-controller-datasheet.pdf.

[6] Intel ethernet controller i350: Datasheet. http://www.intel.com/content/www/us/en/embedded/products/networking/ethernet-controller-i350-datasheet.html.

[7] Intel linux based igb driver. http://www.intel.com/content/www/us/en/support/network-and-i-o/ethernet-products/000005767.html.

[8] Oam introduction from cisco. http://www.cisco.com/c/en/us/td/docs/ios/12_2sr/12_2sra/feature/guide/srethoam.html.

[9] Worldwide ethernet switch market and enterprise and service provider router market. http://www.idc.com/getdoc.jsp?containerId=prUS41061316.

[10] A. Bates, B. Mood, J. Pletcher, H. Pruse, M. Valafar, and K. Butler. Detecting co-residency with active traffic analysis techniques. In *Proceedings of the 2012 ACM Workshop on Cloud Computing Security Workshop*, CCSW '12, pages 1–12, New York NY, USA, 2012. ACM.

[11] M. Ben-Yehuda, J. Mason, J. Xenidis, O. Krieger, L. Van Doorn, J. Nakajima, A. Mallick, and E. Wahlig. Utilizing iommus for virtualization in linux and xen. In *OLSâĂŹ06: The 2006 Ottawa Linux Symposium*, pages 71–86. Citeseer, 2006.

[12] Y. Dong, X. Yang, J. Li, G. Liao, K. Tian, and H. Guan. High performance network virtualization with sr-iov. *Journal of Parallel and Distributed Computing*, 72(11):1471–1480, 2012.

[13] Y. Dong, X. Yang, X. Li, J. Li, K. Tian and H. Guan. High performance network virtualization with sr-iov. In *HPCA-16 2010 The Sixteenth International Symposium on High-Performance Computer Architecture*, pages 1–10, 2010.

[14] Y. Dong, Z. Yu, and G. Rose. Sr-iov networking in xen: Architecture, design and implementation. In *Workshop on I/O Virtualization*, 2008.

[15] A. Gordon, N. Amit, N. Har'El, M. Ben-Yehuda, A. Landau, A. Schuster, and D. Tsafrir. Eli bare-metal performance for i/o virtualization. *ACM SIGPLAN Notices*, 47(4):411–422, 2012.

[16] O. Isfort, K. Müller, D. Münch, and M. Paulitsch. Decreasing system availability on an avionic multicore processor using directly assigned pci express devices. In *European Workshop on System Security (EUROSEC2013)*. Czech Republic Prague, 2013.

[17] P. Kutch. Pci-sig sr-iov primer: An introduction to sr-iov technology. *Intel application note*, pages 321211–002, 2011.

[18] J. Liu. Evaluating standard-based self-virtualizing devices: A performance study on 10 gbe nics with sr-iov support. In *Parallel & Distributed Processing (IPDPS), 2010 IEEE International Symposium on*, pages 1–12. IEEE, 2010.

[19] G. Pék, A. Lanzi, A. Srivastava, D. Balzarotti, A. Francillon, and C. Neumann. On the feasibility of software attacks on commodity virtual machine monitors via direct device assignment. In *Proceedings of the 9th ACM symposium on Information, computer and communications security*, pages 305–316. ACM, 2014.

[20] H. Raj and K. Schwan. High performance and scalable i/o virtualization via self-virtualized devices. In *Proceedings of the 16th international symposium on High performance distributed computing*, pages 179–188. ACM, 2007.

[21] K. K. Ram, J. R. Santos, Y. Turner, A. L. Cox, and S. Rixner. Achieving 10 gb/s using safe and transparent network interface virtualization. In *Proceedings of the 2009 ACM SIGPLAN/SIGOPS international conference on Virtual execution environments*, pages 61–70. ACM, 2009.

[22] A. Richter, C. Herber, T. Wild, and A. Herkersdorf. Denial-of-service attacks on pci passthrough devices: Demonstrating the impact on network-and storage-i/o performance. *Journal of Systems Architecture*, 61(10):592–599, 2015.

[23] R. Shea and J. Liu. Network interface virtualization: challenges and solutions. *Network, IEEE*, 26(5):28–34, 2012.

[24] I. Smolyar, M. Ben-Yehuda, and D. Tsafrir. Securing self-virtualizing ethernet devices. In *Proceedings of the 24th USENIX Conference on Security Symposium*, pages 335–350. USENIX Association, 2015.

[25] P. Stewin and I. Bystrov. Understanding dma malware. In *Detection of Intrusions and Malware, and Vulnerability Assessment*, pages 21–41. Springer, 2013.

[26] J. L. V. U. J. Stoess and S. Götz. Unmodified device driver reuse and improved system dependability via virtual machines. In *Proceedings of the 6th conference on Symposium on Opearting Systems Design & Implementation*, 2004.

[27] J. Sugerman, G. Venkitachalam, and B.-H. Lim. Virtualizing i/o devices on vmware workstation's hosted virtual machine monitor. In *USENIX Annual Technical Conference, General Track*, pages 1–14, 2001.

[28] P. Willmann, J. Shafer, D. Carr, S. Rixner, A. L. Cox, and W. Zwaenepoel. Concurrent direct network access for virtual machine monitors. In *High Performance Computer Architecture, 2007. HPCA 2007. IEEE 13th International Symposium on*, pages 306–317. IEEE, 2007.

[29] R. Wojtczuk and J. Rutkowska. Following the white rabbit: Software attacks against intel vt-d technology. *ITL: http://invisiblethingslab.com/resources/2011/Software\%20Attacks\%20on\%20Intel\%20VT-d.pdf*, 2011.

[30] X. Xu and B. Davda. Srvm: Hypervisor support for live migration with passthrough sr-iov network devices. In *Proceedings of the12th ACM SIGPLAN/SIGOPS International Conference on Virtual Execution Environments*, pages 65–77. ACM, 2016.

[31] B.-A. Yassour, M. Ben-Yehuda, and O. Wasserman. Direct device assignment for untrusted fully-virtualized virtual machines. Technical report, Technical Report H-0263, IBM Research, 2008.

SGXIO: Generic Trusted I/O Path for Intel SGX

Samuel Weiser
Graz University of Technology, Austria
samuel.weiser@iaik.tugraz.at

Mario Werner
Graz University of Technology, Austria
mario.werner@iaik.tugraz.at

ABSTRACT

Application security traditionally strongly relies upon security of the underlying operating system. However, operating systems often fall victim to software attacks, compromising security of applications as well. To overcome this dependency, Intel SGX allows to protect application code against a subverted or malicious OS by running it in a hardware-protected enclave. However, SGX lacks support for generic trusted I/O paths to protect user input and output between enclaves and I/O devices.

This work presents SGXIO, a generic trusted path architecture for SGX, allowing user applications to run securely on top of an untrusted OS, while at the same time supporting trusted paths to generic I/O devices. To achieve this, SGXIO combines the benefits of SGX's easy programming model with traditional hypervisor-based trusted path architectures. Moreover, SGXIO can tweak insecure debug enclaves to behave like secure production enclaves. SGXIO surpasses traditional use cases in cloud computing and digital rights management and makes SGX technology usable for protecting user-centric, local applications against kernel-level keyloggers and likewise. It is compatible to unmodified operating systems and works on a modern commodity notebook out of the box. Hence, SGXIO is particularly promising for the broad x86 community to which SGX is readily available.

1. INTRODUCTION

Software vulnerabilities are still a predominant issue for application security. A major reason for this fact is code complexity, which makes traditional secure design paradigms like software verification or testing reach its limits. Hence, research focuses on securing sensitive code only and executing it in architecturally isolated containers, often referred to as enclaves. Since an enclave is protected against all non-enclave code, the whole OS stack can safely be considered untrusted.

Intel SGX [14] provides such enclaves in its latest x86 mainline CPUs. It targets high-performance cloud computing, where the cloud provider is entirely distrusted, as well

CODASPY'17, March 22 – 24, 2017, Scottsdale, AZ, USA

© 2017 Copyright held by the owner/author(s). Publication rights licensed to ACM.
ISBN 978-1-4503-4523-1/17/03...$15.00

DOI: http://dx.doi.org/10.1145/3029806.3029822

as Digital Rights Management (DRM). In order to protect not only enclave execution but also user I/O, one requires trusted paths between enclaves and I/O devices. Currently, SGX only works with proprietary trusted paths like Intel Protected Audio Video Path (PAVP), which rely on the Intel Management Engine (ME) [13,33]. However, proprietary trusted paths are hard to analyze regarding security. Moreover, they are not generic and address specific devices and scenarios only. Unfortunately, SGX lacks support for generic trusted paths.

Contributions. In this work we present the concept of SGXIO, which is, to our knowledge, the first generic trusted path architecture for SGX. SGXIO protects secure user applications as well as associated trusted paths against an untrusted OS. User applications benefit from SGX protection while trusted paths are established via a small and trusted hypervisor. To that end, we identify and solve several challenges in linking the security domains of SGX and the trusted hypervisor. This allows a remote party to attest not only enclave code but also the whole trusted path setup. Also, SGXIO allows human end users to verify trusted paths without requiring additional hardware. SGXIO improves upon existing generic trusted paths for x86 systems with an easier and more intuitive programming model. Furthermore, we show how SGXIO can tweak debug enclaves to behave like production enclaves. Therefore, the trusted hypervisor selectively disables enclave debug instructions. Finally, we give a novel zero-overhead, non-interactive key transport scheme for establishing a 128-bit symmetric key between two local SGX enclaves. The extended version of this paper can be found in [39].

The rest of this paper is structured as follows: Section 2 gives related work, followed by an overview of SGX in Section 3. Section 4 discusses the threat model and challenges. Section 5 presents our SGXIO architecture while Section 6 gives a thorough security analysis. Section 7 shows how SGXIO can apply the debug enclave tweak. It is followed by a conclusion in Section 8.

2. RELATED WORK

This section discusses prior work on isolated execution and trusted paths. Specifically, we compare to ARM TrustZone, which is ARM's counterpart to Intel SGX.

2.1 Isolated Execution

There exist various techniques for isolated execution, which range from pure hypervisor designs [7] over hardware-software co-designs [6,8,34] to pure hardware extensions [3,5,9,10,14,

29]. SGXIO uses Intel SGX [14], which, from a functional perspective, cumulates previous work in software isolation, attestation and transparent memory encryption.

The Trusted Platform Module (TPM) [36] is a security co-processor which does not directly offer software isolation on its own. However, it can be used in conjunction with Intel TXT [16] to set up an isolated execution environment [25].

2.2 Trusted Paths

There exist various attempts for integrating trusted paths directly into existing commodity OSes. However, they usually suffer from a bloated TCB, covering the whole OS [11,22, 24,37]. More sound trusted paths consider the OS untrusted. One can distinguish between generic trusted paths and specific trusted paths. Latter are limited to specific devices or scenarios.

Generic Trusted Paths. Zhou *et al.* establish a generic trusted path in a pure hypervisor-based design [42]. They show the first comprehensive approach on x86 systems, protecting a trusted path all the way from the application level down to the device level. They consider PCI device misconfiguration, DMA attacks as well as interrupt spoofing attacks. However, pure hypervisor-based designs come at a price. They strictly separate the untrusted stack from the trusted one. Hence, the hypervisor is in charge of managing all secure applications and all associated resources itself. This includes secure process and memory management with scheduling, verified launch and attestation. In contrast, SGXIO uses the comparably easy programming model of SGX enclaves, in which the untrusted OS is in charge of managing secure enclaves. Moreover, SGX provides verified launch and attestation out of the box.

Specific Trusted Paths. In [41] and [43], Zhou *et al.* discuss a trusted path to a single USB device. Yu *et al.* show how to apply the trusted path concept to GPU separation [40]. Filyanov *et al.* discuss a pure uni-directional trusted path [12]. However, their approach is limited to trusted input paths only and the OS is suspended during secure input. In contrast, SGXIO supports full parallelism between the untrusted OS and secure applications.

Others use dedicated I/O devices, which natively support encryption [31,32]. This allows applications to open a cryptographic channel to it, bypassing any untrusted software. However, this concept does not generalize to arbitrary I/O devices, especially legacy devices.

Many trusted paths build on proprietary hardware and software like Intel's Protected Audio Video Path (PAVP) as well as its successor, Intel Insider [21,33]. Both rely on Intel's proprietary Management Engine (ME), which hinders transparent security assessment. Hoekstra *et al.* outline integration of PAVP in SGX applications to achieve secure video conferencing and one-time password generation [13]. However, they do not come up with any trusted input path. In [33], Ruan describes a Protected Transaction Display (PTD) application, which uses PAVP to securely obtain a one-time PINs from the user.

2.3 ARM TrustZone

ARM TrustZone combines secure execution with trusted path support. A TrustZone compatible CPU provides a secure world mode, which is orthogonal to classical privilege levels. The secure world is isolated against the normal world and operates a whole trusted stack, including security kernel,

device drivers and applications. In addition, TrustZone is complemented by a set of hardware modules, which allow strong isolation of physical memory as well as peripherals. Also, device interrupts can be directly routed into the secure world. TrustZone can be combined with a System MMU, similar to an IOMMU, which can prevent DMA attacks. Thus, TrustZone not only allows isolated execution [35] but also generic trusted paths [23], which is a significant advantage over SGX. In contrast to SGX, TrustZone does not distinguish between different secure application processes in hardware. It requires a security kernel for secure process isolation, management, attestation and similar.

3. SOFTWARE GUARD EXTENSIONS

Intel Software Guard Extensions (SGX) define a new set of x86 instructions for enclaves [2,13–15,17,18,26]. User applications can host enclaves in their virtual address spaces. Any access into enclave memory is prohibited by the CPU, while enclaves can access their hosting application's memory for data exchange. In addition, SGX encrypts enclave memory when written to DRAM. The OS is entirely distrusted and is supervised by the CPU in all enclave management operations. The Trusted Computing Base (TCB) only consists of enclave code and the CPU itself.

SGX implements verified enclave launch. During enclave initialization the CPU hashes enclave memory into a protected register, called `MRENCLAVE`. Before running the enclave, the CPU verifies `MRENCLAVE` against a vendor-signed version. Hence, `MRENCLAVE` vouches for integrity of the enclave startup. Other parties can verify `MRENCLAVE` via local or remote attestation. Attestation is based on a report structure holding `MRENCLAVE`, which is cryptographically signed by the CPU. The report structure is able to hold additional user data, which can be used to authentically exchange information between enclaves to agree on an encryption key, for example. Moreover, SGX can derive per-enclave sealing keys from their `MRENCLAVE` values to allow encrypted storage of secrets [1].

SGX distinguishes between debug and production enclaves. Former can be accessed by the OS via SGX debug instructions while latter cannot. During enclave initialization, developers choose between debug and production mode. This choice yields different `MRENCLAVE` values for either option, making a debug enclave distinguishable from a production enclave.

SGX restricts enclave execution via a launch enclave, which is discussed controversially [4]. All production enclaves need to be licensed by Intel. Unlicensed enclaves can only be launched in debug mode [19].

4. THREAT MODEL AND CHALLENGES

SGXIO utilizes SGX as building block to provide isolated execution. However, the threat models of pure SGX and SGXIO differ. This section elaborates on the differences as well as the challenges arising from the combination of SGX with a trusted hypervisor.

4.1 Distinction

SGX enforces a minimal TCB, covering only the processor and enclave code. All other software components (e.g., OS, hypervisor) as well as the processor's physical environment is considered potentially malicious. Therefore, SGX not only considers logical attacks but also physical attacks. This threat model perfectly fits the requirements of secure cloud

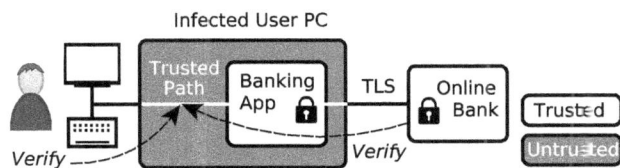

Figure 1: SGXIO enhances security of online banking via trusted paths.

computing in which a customer wants to protect enclaves against an untrusted cloud provider. Also, content providers can use SGX to enforce a DRM scheme on an untrusted consumer PC.

In a local setting, however, a user wants to benefit from SGX by protecting user-centric applications against a potentially compromised OS. Although user apps can be protected by SGX enclaves, the communication between user apps and the user via I/O peripherals cannot. A compromised OS can easily intercept and alter I/O communication. This local setting overcharges plain SGX as it somehow contradicts its threat model, which considers the physical environment, and therefore also the local user, a threat.

Currently, in order to achieve a trusted path with SGX, one has to rely on encrypted interfaces like PAVP. However, the prevalence of unencrypted I/O devices in todays computers and the lack of support to securely communicate with these devices demands other, more generic mechanisms.

SGXIO fixes this shortcoming by extending SGX with a generic trusted path, which protects user I/O against the OS. Additionally, SGXIO provides attestation mechanisms to verify that trusted paths are established and functional.

SGXIO supports user-centric applications like confidential document viewers, login prompts, password safes, secure conferencing and secure online banking. To take latter as example, with SGXIO an online bank cannot only communicate with the user via TLS but also with the end user via trusted paths between banking app and I/O devices, as depicted in Figure 1. This means that sensitive information like login credentials, the account balance, or the transaction amount can be protected even if other software running on the user's computer, including the OS, is infected by malware.

Having a trusted path has implications on the threat model of SGXIO. A physical attacker has direct access to I/O devices and can impersonate the user without subverting trusted paths. Thus, trusted paths can only protect against logical attacks but cannot provide physical security at all. The following section explains the threat model of SGXIO in detail.

4.2 Threat Model

In general, adversaries attempt to subvert a trusted path between a user app and an I/O device. They succeed when breaking the confidentiality or authenticity of a trusted path.

Logical attacks are the main concern of SGXIO. Attackers are assumed to have full control over the OS and know the whole software configuration, including all enclave code. This is a realistic scenario, addressing both local and remote attacks, which might yield kernel privileges to attackers. Attackers can therefore directly attack enclave interfaces visible

to the OS by running enclaves in a fake environment within the OS. Also, attackers can dynamically load and execute custom user apps and drivers and open other trusted path sessions. Moreover, attackers can tamper with the boot image of the trusted hypervisor, which SGXIO is based on.

Indirect attacks on a trusted path can be performed by misconfiguring devices under OS control to interfere with a trusted path, as outlined by Zhou et al. [42]. Also, malicious Direct Memory Access (DMA) requests could be issued and interrupts could be spoofed.

All code in the trusted computing base (e.g., secure user applications, secure I/O drivers and the trusted hypervisor) is assumed to be correct and not vulnerable to logical attacks. Using a formally verified hypervisor such as seL4 [20] supports this assumption.

Physical attacks are not considered in SGXIO, as already explained, since the user interacting with the system has to be trusted anyway. As with SGX, Denial-of-Service (DoS) and side channel attacks are out of scope for SGXIO.

Note that SGXIO requires a modern Intel platform with SGX support as well as support for TPM-based trusted boot. All hardware (CPU, chipset, peripherals) is expected to work correctly.

4.3 Challenges

SGXIO combines SGX with a trusted hypervisor to provide a generic trusted path. However, the hypervisor and SGX form two disjoint security domains with two different trust anchors, which are not designed to collaborate. Subsequently, connecting both domains is a non-trivial task.

This essentially breaks down to two major challenges which had to be solved: First, the security domains of the hypervisor and SGX enclaves have to be linked. More concretely, we need a way for SGX enclaves to check the presence and the authenticity of the hypervisor. We name this problem *hypervisor attestation*. Once the hypervisor is attested, it extends trust to any trusted path it establishes.

Second, the SGXIO architecture relies on multiple SGX enclaves, which are executed in different security contexts (trusted hypervisor vs. untrusted OS). However, SGX enclaves are unaware of their context, making them vulnerable to *enclave virtualization attacks*. SGXIO prevents such attacks via a careful interface design between both contexts.

5. SGXIO ARCHITECTURE

This section presents our SGXIO architecture and elaborates on its isolation guarantees. We discuss the design of secure user apps, secure I/O drivers as well as the hypervisor.

5.1 Architecture

SGXIO is composed of two parts: a trusted stack and a Virtual Machine (VM), as seen in Figure 2. The trusted stack contains a small security hypervisor, one or more secure I/O drivers, which we simply call *drivers*, as well as a Trusted Boot (TB) enclave. The VM hosts an untrusted commodity OS like Linux, which runs secure user applications, also abbreviated with *user apps*.

User apps want to communicate securely with the end user. They open an encrypted communication channel to a secure I/O driver to tunnel through the untrusted OS. The driver in turn requires secure communication with a generic user I/O device, which we term *user device*. To achieve this, the hypervisor exclusively binds user devices to the corresponding

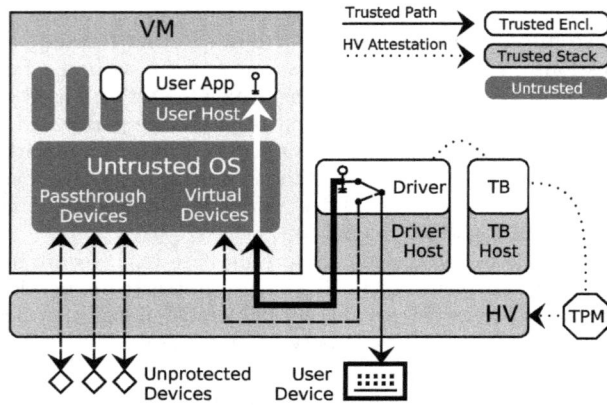

Figure 2: The trusted stack consists of a hypervisor (HV), a Trusted Boot (TB) enclave and one or more secure I/O drivers. The Virtual Machine (VM) operates an untrusted OS, hosting secure user apps. To establish a trusted path (solid line), the driver encrypts secret data (bold line) for a user app. The TB enclave allows drivers to attest the HV.

drivers. Note that any other device is directly assigned to the VM. I/O on those unprotected devices directly passes through the hypervisor without performance penalty. The trusted path names both, the encrypted user-app-to-driver communication and the exclusive driver-to-device binding. It is indicated with a solid line in Figure 2. Drivers use the TB enclave to get assured of correct trusted path setup by attesting the hypervisor, which is indicated by a dotted line.

5.2 Isolation Guarantees

SGXIO establishes a trusted path all the way from a user app to the user device. This requires isolation on several layers. First, all trusted stack memory needs to be isolated from the untrusted OS and Direct Memory Access (DMA). Second, the trusted path itself requires isolation from the OS. Third, the user device needs isolation from all other devices which are under control of the OS. This section outlines how SGXIO meets these isolation requirements.

Trusted Memory Isolation is a prerequisite for securely executing trusted code in an untrusted environment. This affects user apps as well as the trusted stack. To achieve memory isolation of the user app, it is executed within an enclave. SGX isolates all enclave memory from the untrusted OS. To achieve memory isolation for the trusted stack, the hypervisor confines the untrusted OS in a VM. Moreover, the hypervisor implements a strict memory partitioning by configuring the Memory Management Unit (MMU) appropriately. This prevents the OS from escaping the VM and tampering with the trusted stack.

Direct Memory Access (DMA) is a more subtle threat to memory isolation [42]. A DMA-capable device can directly access memory, bypassing any MMU protection and potentially violating integrity and confidentiality of trusted memory. SGX prevents DMA from accessing enclave memory, hence the user app is safe against DMA attacks [14]. Likewise, the trusted stack has to be protected against such attacks. Modern chipsets typically incorporate an I/O Memory Management Unit (IOMMU), also termed VT-d on Intel systems. The IOMMU restricts device DMA to specific por-

tions of RAM. By properly configuring the IOMMU, the hypervisor can protect the whole trusted stack against device DMA attacks.

Trusted Path Isolation. The trusted path has to be protected on two layers, namely the communication between user app and driver as well as the interaction between driver and user device. The user app communicates with the driver via the untrusted OS stack, hence encryption is necessary. The interaction between driver and user device is protected by the hypervisor. Therefore, the hypervisor establishes an exclusive binding between a driver and the corresponding user device. Moreover, the hypervisor mutually isolates all drivers. Thus, an attacker, loading arbitrary driver code at will, cannot interfere with trusted paths established by other drivers.

User Device Isolation. As outlined before, a malicious OS could misconfigure devices to interfere with the trusted path. In that way, OS-controlled PCI devices could be forced to overlap their MMIO region or I/O port range with those of the user device or issue forged interrupts on behalf of the user device. To protect against these attacks, Zhou et al. implement several policies in the hypervisor to detect and prevent malicious device configurations [42]. This effectively isolates user devices from other OS-controlled devices. Their approach is also applicable to SGXIO.

5.3 User App Design

Secure user apps process all sensitive data inside an enclave. Sensitive data leaves an enclave only in an encrypted form. For example, the user enclave can securely communicate with the driver enclave or a remote server via encrypted channels or store sensitive data offline using SGX sealing.

To set up an encrypted channel between enclaves, one needs to share an encryption key. Anati et al. propose Diffie-Hellman over SGX local attestation for this purpose [1,18]. However, local attestation inherently provides a much faster way of exchanging key material. We give a novel, lightweight key transport scheme, which comes with just a single unidirectional invocation of local attestation. We reuse the already pre-shared report key to derive random 128-bit encryption keys. The scheme works as follows: The user enclave generates a local attestation report over a random salt, targeted at the driver enclave. However, instead of delivering the actual report to the driver enclave, the user enclave keeps it private and uses the report's MAC as symmetric key. It then sends the salt and its identity to the driver enclave, which can recompute the MAC to obtain the same key. Details of this scheme are given in [39].

5.4 Driver Design

Drivers are hosted and protected by the hypervisor. Although hypervisor protection is sufficient to isolate drivers from the untrusted OS, actual driver logic is in addition executed in an enclave. This helps in setting up an encrypted communication channel with user apps, as previously described. Also, driver enclaves are subject to attestation, allowing identification via their `MRENCLAVE` values.

As shown in Figure 2, drivers can multiplex I/O data between user app and OS to account for trusted path setup and tear down, making SGXIO compatible to legacy OSes.

5.5 Hypervisor Design

The hypervisor enforces a bunch of isolation guarantees,

as previously outlined: First, it isolates all trusted stack memory. Second, it binds a user device exclusively to the corresponding driver and mutually isolates drivers. Thus achieves trusted path isolation. Third, it isolates user devices from malicious interference with other devices.

We recommend to use seL4 as hypervisor, as it directly supports isolation of trusted memory as well as user device binding via its capability system [28]. With seL4, isolation breaks down to a correct distribution of memory and device capabilities among the VM and the drivers.

seL4 makes heavy use of Intel's VT-x hardware virtualization to intercept illegitimate memory or device accesses. Thus, VT-x also helps in blocking device misconfiguration attacks [42] and achieving user device isolation. Furthermore, seL4 uses Intel VT-d, also referred to as IOMMU, to protect against DMA attacks from misconfigured devices. Moreover, seL4 is formally verified [20,27], which helps making strong claims about security of the trusted path.

6. DOMAIN BINDING AND ATTESTATION

Having explained our SGXIO architecture, this section elaborates on challenges which arise when binding the SGX domain with the trusted hypervisor domain. Specifically, this covers trusted boot and hypervisor attestation. We discuss how to protect hypervisor attestation against remote TPM attacks as well as enclave virtualization attacks. Having a domain binding in place allows remote attestation of trusted paths as well as user verification.

6.1 Challenges

SGXIO enables a remote party as well as a local user to verify security of trusted paths. In the first place, this requires a domain binding between SGX and the trusted hypervisor. In the second place, an appropriate user verification mechanism needs to be in place which is both secure and usable.

Domain Binding. In order to bind the SGX and the hypervisor domain, the hypervisor must level up to certain security guarantees SGX regarding isolated code execution. In SGX, all enclave memory is isolated from the rest. Moreover enclave loading is guarded by a verified launch mechanism, which can be attested to other parties. SGXIO rebuilds similar mechanisms for the hypervisor. Isolation of trusted memory has already been discussed in Section 5.2. Verified launch is implemented via *trusted boot* of the hypervisor with support for *hypervisor attestation*.

With trusted boot and hypervisor attestation in place, SGXIO can bind the SGX and the hypervisor domain. The binding needs to be bidirectional, allowing both the hypervisor and SGX enclaves to put trust in the other domain. One direction is easy: The hypervisor can extend trust to SGX by running enclaves in a safe, hypervisor-protected environment. These enclaves can in turn use local attestation to extend trust to any other enclaves in the system. However, the opposite direction is challenging: On the one hand, enclaves need confidence that the hypervisor is not compromised and binds user devices correctly to drivers. Effectively, this requires enclaves to invoke hypervisor attestation. SGXIO achieves this with assistance of the TB enclave. On the other hand, SGX is not designed to cooperate with a trusted hypervisor. Recall that SGX considers all non-enclave code untrusted. In fact, SGX explicitly prohibits use of any instruction inside an enclave that might be used to communicate with the hypervisor [17]. Even if hypervisor attestation succeeds, an enclave cannot easily learn whether it is legitimately executed by the hypervisor or virtualized by an attacker in a fake environment. This makes driver enclaves and the TB enclave vulnerable to virtualization attacks. SGXIO defends against such attacks by hiding hypervisor attestation from the untrusted OS.

User Verification. An end user wants to be able to verify if he is indeed communicating with the correct user app via a trusted path. This is non-trivial because the user cannot simply evaluate an cryptographic attestation report Instead, the user requires some form of notification whether a trusted path is present. This notification needs to be unforgeable to prevent the OS from faking it. Moreover, it needs to help the user distinguish different user apps, not least because an attacker might also run arbitrary user apps under his control.

6.2 Trusted Boot & Hypervisor Attestation

Trusted boot does not prohibit booting a compromised hypervisor but uncovers any such compromise. To achieve this, trusted boot makes use of a TPM to measure the whole boot process, starting from a trusted piece of firmware code up to the hypervisor image. Each boot stage measures the next one in a cryptographic log inside the TPM using the `extend` operation. All measurements are cumulated in a TPM Platform Configuration Register (PCR). The final PCR value reflects the whole boot process and is used to prove integrity of the hypervisor to other parties

Hypervisor Attestation allows enclaves to verify the trusted boot process in order to get assured of hypervisor's integrity. Since the hypervisor is responsible for loading drivers and doing trusted path setup, its attestation also vouches for security of all trusted paths.

To ease hypervisor attestation, SGXIO uses a Trusted Boot (TB) enclave which attests the hypervisor once. Afterwards, any driver enclave can query the TB enclave to get approval if hypervisor attestation succeeded, see Figure 3/I. The driver enclaves in turn can communicate the attestation result to user apps, which can finally implement a mechanism for remote parties or the end user to verify a trusted path.

To attest the hypervisor, the TB enclave needs to verify the PCR value, obtained during trusted boot. Therefore, the TB enclave requests a TPM `quote` [36], which contains a cryptographic signature over the PCR value alongside with a fresh nonce. This ensures not only integrity of the PCR value but also prevents replay attacks.

6.3 Attacks

The interaction between TB enclave and TPM is crucial for security of the hypervisor attestation scheme. One has to prevent remote TPM attacks as well as enclave virtualization attacks, which is outlined in the following.

6.3.1 Remote TPM attacks.

Naive hypervisor attestation is vulnerable to remote TPM attacks, also called cuckoo attacks [30], as shown in Figure 3/II. Here, the attacker compromises the hypervisor image, which yields a wrong PCR value during trusted boot. To avoid being detected by the TB enclave, the attacker generates a valid `quote` on an attacker-controlled remote TPM and feeds it into the TB enclave, which successfully approves the compromised hypervisor.

Defense. In order to stop cuckoo attacks, the TB enclave needs to identify the TPM it is talking to, *e.g.*, by means of

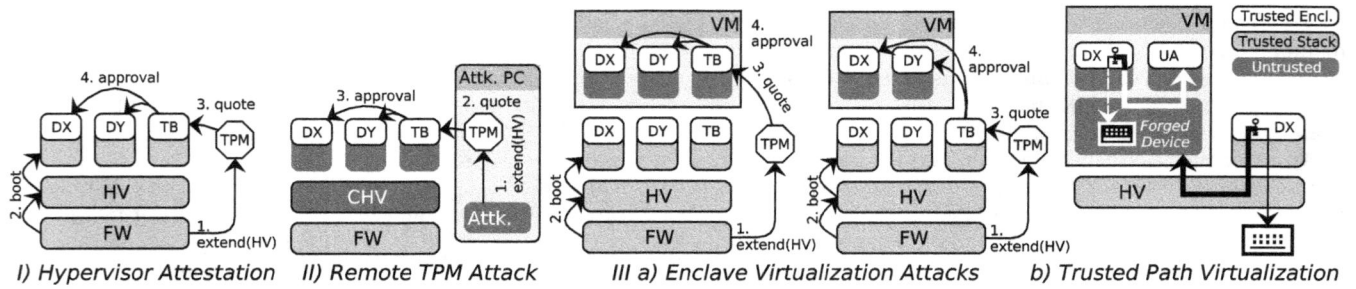

Figure 3: I) During trusted boot, Firmware (FW) measures the Hypervisor (HV) via a TPM. The TB enclave attests the HV via a TPM quote and approves other drivers (DX) and (DY). II) An attacker injects a remotely-generated quote to hide the presence of a Compromised HV (CHV). IIIa) An attacker diverts steps 3 or 4 to a virtualized environment. IIIb) This allows to virtualize a trusted path to a user app (UA).

the TPM's Attestation Identity Key (AIK) used for signing the quote. This allows the TB enclave to verify the origin of the quote. To make the AIK known to the TB enclave, one has to provision it, e.g., during initial system integration. The TB enclave stores the provisioned AIK by means of SGX sealing. Since sealing uses a CPU-specific encryption key, an attacker cannot trick the TB enclave to unseal an AIK not sealed by the same CPU. This effectively binds execution of the TB enclave to the TPM.

Provisioning of AIKs could be done by system integrators. One has to introduce proper measures to prevent attackers from provisioning arbitrary AIKs. For example, the TB enclave could encode a list of public keys of approved system integrators, which are allowed to provision AIKs.

6.3.2 Enclave Virtualization Attacks

In an enclave virtualization attack, the attacker does not compromise the actual trusted boot process. Rather, he virtualizes driver enclaves or even the TB enclave in a fake environment on the same computer, as depicted in Figure 3/IIIa. To make hypervisor attestation for the virtualized enclaves succeed, the attacker diverts the legitimate TPM quote or the TB enclave approval to the virtualized TB enclave or driver enclaves, respectively. As shown in Figure 3/IIIb, the attacker can now impersonate the user by rerouting user apps to a virtualized driver, reading driver's output and providing fake input. Note that the attacker did not change enclave code. Hence, SGX will generate the same MRENCLAVE value and thus the same derived cryptographic keys for both, legitimate and virtualized enclave instances. Neither the TB enclave nor the driver enclave or a user app can detect such virtualization. However, the attacker does not learn actual user input, which still arrives at the legitimate driver enclave.

Defense. The problem of enclave virtualization stems from the design of SGX which treats all enclaves equally, regardless of the security context they are executed in. As a defense, SGXIO restricts the communication interface between the hypervisor and the OS context. Therefore, the hypervisor hides the TPM as well as the TB enclave from the untrusted OS[1]. Only the legitimate TB enclave is given access to the TPM. Thus, the TB enclave might only succeed in hypervisor attestation if it has been legitimately launched by the hypervisor. Likewise, only legitimate driver enclaves are granted access to the legitimate TB enclave by the hypervisor. A driver enclave might only get approval if it can talk

---

[1]This breaks path 3 on the left side and path 4 on the right side of Figure 3/IIIa, respectively.

to the legitimate TB enclave, which implies that the driver enclave too has been legitimately launched by the hypervisor.

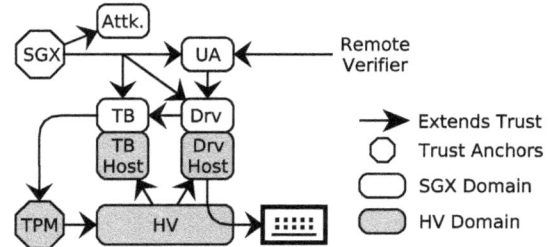

Figure 4: Trust hierarchy of SGXIO.

6.4 Remote Trusted Path Attestation

As already mentioned, hypervisor attestation vouches for security of trusted paths and serves as basis for remote attestation. This section describes the whole trust hierarchy involved in remote attestation, as shown in Figure 4.

SGXIO has two main hardware trust anchors, namely SGX and the TPM. SGX extends trust to all enclaves running on the system by means of verified launch. This also includes enclaves with attacker-controlled code (Attk.). It is up to a remote verifier and individual enclaves to build a trust hierarchy among "good" enclaves. To do this, trust is extended via SGX remote and local attestation, respectively. The entrusting party does not only verify validity of an SGX attestation report but also check for a correct MRENCLAVE value, which uniquely identifies an enclave codebase.

In a typical scenario, a remote verifier wants to establish a trusted path to a user. It therefore extends trust to a specific user app (UA) under its control, which in turn entrusts appropriate secure I/O drivers (Drv). Drivers extend trust to the TB enclave, which does hypervisor attestation as previously outlined. If hypervisor attestation succeeds, trust is implicitly extended to the TB host and all driver host processes together with all trusted paths to user devices. If at any point in the trust hierarchy attestation fails, the affected entities will terminate trusted path attestation.

6.5 User Verification

SGXIO allows a user to locally assess if he is talking with the correct user app via a trusted path. This does not require additional hardware such as an external handheld verification device [42] or similar. Instead, we stick to sharing a secret piece of information between user and user app, similar to [38].

For the sake of simplicity we discuss the common scenario of a trusted screen path and a trusted keyboard path. When the user starts the user app, the user app requests a trusted input path to the keyboard and a trusted output path to the screen from the corresponding drivers. If for any reason one or both trusted path setups fail, the user app terminates with an error. In the case of success, the user app displays the pre-shared secret information via the screen driver to the user. The user verifies this information to get assured of a valid trusted path setup for this user app. Since an attacker does not know the secret information, he cannot fake this notification. This approach requires provisioning secret information to a user app, which seals it for later usage. Provisioning could be done once at installation time in a safe environment, *e.g.*, with assistance of the hypervisor, or at any time via SGX's remote attestation feature.

7. TWEAKING DEBUG ENCLAVES

SGXIO makes heavy use of SGX enclaves. However, Intel's licensing scheme for production enclaves might be too costly for small business or even incompatible with the open-source idea. We show how to level up debug enclaves to behave like production enclaves in our threat model. This requires special handling of SGX remote attestation and sealing.

Recall that the only difference between debug and production enclaves is the presence of SGX debug instructions, which we aim to disable manually. The debug tweak leverages SGX's support for VT-x instruction interception. Via the so-called ENCLS-exiting bitmap the hypervisor can selectively intercept all SGX debug instructions which are ever executed from within a VM. By doing so, the only code which is able to debug enclaves is the trusted hypervisor itself. Hence, we have effectively turned all debug enclaves inside the VM into production equivalents.

Tweaked Cloud Enclaves. This tweak only applies to a setting similar to SGXIO, where a trusted hypervisor is present. In general, this is not the case for cloud scenarios where the cloud provider is untrusted and expected to subvert the hypervisor. In such cases, one has to opt for real production enclaves. Nevertheless, honest server administrators could use the tweak to obtain SGX protection without licensing. This would help in strongly isolating server code and reducing the TCB from the whole system down to the hypervisor and the enclave code.

Remote Attestation. With tweaked debug enclaves, remote attestation requires special care since a remote verifier cannot easily determine whether the debug tweak is correctly enabled or not. For example, an attacker could compromise the hypervisor and manipulate (debug) the TB enclave to issue wrong approvals. Next, the attacker could stealthily debug all enclaves on the system.

To do remote attestation with tweaked debug enclaves, one can run only the TB enclave in production mode and do remote attestation towards it. Once a remote party verified the TB enclave, it can be sure that the hypervisor correctly enforces the tweak for all debug enclaves in the system.

Sealing. Both, non-tweaked and tweaked debug enclaves share the same sealing keys. This is no problem unless an attacker manages to compromise the hypervisor and disables the tweak. Although hypervisor attestation would fail in that case, the attacker would be able to extract all sealing keys by simply debugging all enclaves. To prevent this, one can delegate sealing key derivation to the TB enclave. The

TB enclave, running in production mode, only derives actual sealing keys if hypervisor attestation succeeds.

8. CONCLUSION

We present SGXIO, the first SGX-based architecture to support generic trusted paths. Therefore, we augment SGX with a small and trusted hypervisor for setting up a generic trusted path, while SGX helps in protecting user apps from an untrusted OS. We solve the challenge of combining the security domains of SGX and the hypervisor. We do so by attesting the hypervisor with assistance of a TPM towards a special trusted boot enclave, which is bound to the local computer. With SGXIO, both a remote party and a local user can verify security of trusted paths.

Furthermore, we show how SGXIO can omit enclave licensing by making debug enclaves behave like production enclaves. To achieve this, the trusted hypervisor disables SGX debugging instructions for the whole untrusted VM.

SGXIO demonstrates that SGX is not limited to cloud computing and DRM scenarios. SGXIO addresses user-centric application security, making generic trusted paths available to SGX enclaves. This can greatly improve application security, protecting against kernel-level keyloggers and screenloggers, for example. SGXIO is compatible to unmodified legacy OSes and runs on off-the-shelf notebooks.

Acknowledgments

This work was partially supported by the TU Graz LEAD project "Dependable Internet of Things in Adverse Environments".

9. REFERENCES

[1] I. Anati, S. Gueron, S. Johnson, and V. Scarlata. Innovative technology for CPU based attestation and sealing. In *HASP'13*, volume 13, Aug. 2013.

[2] I. Anati, F. McKeen, S. Gueron, H. Huang, S. Johnson, R. Leslie-Hurd, H. Patil, C. V. Rozas, and H. Shafi. Intel Software Guard Extensions (Intel SGX), 2015. Tutorial Slides presented at ICSA 2015.

[3] ARM. TrustZone. http://www.arm.com/products/processors/technologies/trustzone/index.php. (accessed 2016-04-04).

[4] J. Beekman. Intel has full control over SGX. https://jbeekman.nl/blog/2015/10/intel-has-full-control-over-sgx/, Oct. 2015. (accessed 2016-03-03).

[5] R. Boivie and P. Williams. SecureBlue+–: CPU Support for Secure Executables. Research report, IBM, Apr. 2013. Reference no. RC25369.

[6] D. Champagne and R. B. Lee. Scalable architectural support for trusted software. In *HPCA'16*, pages 1–12, Jan. 2010.

[7] X. Chen, T. Garfinkel, E. C. Lewis, P. Subrahmanyam, C. A. Waldspurger, D. Boneh, J. Dwoskin, and D. R. Ports. Overshadow: A Virtualization-based Approach to Retrofitting Protection in Commodity Operating Systems. In *ASPLOS XIII*, pages 2–13. ACM, 2008.

[8] S. Chhabra, B. Rogers, Y. Solihin, and M. Prvulovic. SecureME: A Hardware-software Approach to Full System Security. In *ICS '11*, pages 108–119. ACM, 2011.

[9] V. Costan, I. A. Lebedev, and S. Devadas. Sanctum: Minimal Hardware Extensions for Strong Software Isolation. In *USENIX Security'16*, pages 857–874, Aug. 2016.

[10] D. Evtyushkin, J. Elwell, M. Ozsoy, D. Ponomarev, N. A. Ghazaleh, and R. Riley. Iso-X: A Flexible Architecture for Hardware-Managed Isolated Execution. In *MICRO'14*, pages 190–202, Dec. 2014.

[11] E. Fernandes, Q. A. Chen, G. Essl, J. A. Halderman, Z. M. Mao, and A. Prakash. TIVOs: Trusted Visual I/O Paths for Android. *University of Michigan CSE Technical Report CSE-TR-586-14*, 2014.

[12] A. Filyanov, J. M. McCune, A. R. Sadeghi, and M. Winandy. Uni-directional trusted path: Transaction confirmation on just one device. In *DSN'11*, pages 1–12, June 2011.

[13] M. Hoekstra, R. Lal, P. Pappachan, V. Phegade, and J. Del Cuvillo. Using Innovative Instructions to Create Trustworthy Software Solutions. In *HASP '13*. ACM, 2013.

[14] Intel Software Guard Extensions Programming Reference, Oct. 2014. Reference no. 329298-002US.

[15] Intel 64 and IA-32 Architectures Software Developer's Manual, Sept. 2015. Reference no. 325462-056US.

[16] Intel Trusted Execution Technology (Intel TXT), Software Development Guide, July 2015. Reference no. 315168-012.

[17] Intel Software Guard Extensions Developer Guide, 2016.

[18] Intel Software Guard Extensions Evaluation SDK for Windows OS. User's Guide, Jan. 2016. Revision 1.1.1.

[19] S. Johnson, D. Zimmerman, and B. Derek. Intel SGX: Debug, Production, Pre-release what's the difference? https://software.intel.com/en-us/blogs/2016/01/07/intel-sgx-debug-production-prelease-whats-the-difference, Jan. 2016. (accessed 2016-04-04).

[20] G. Klein, K. Elphinstone, G. Heiser, J. Andronick, D. Cock, P. Derrin, D. Elkaduwe, K. Engelhardt, R. Kolanski, M. Norrish, T. Sewell, H. Tuch, and S. Winwood. seL4: Formal Verification of an OS Kernel. In *SOSP '09*, pages 207–220. ACM, 2009.

[21] N. Knupffer. Intel Insider – What Is It? (Is it DRM? And yes it delivers top quality movies to your PC). https://blogs.intel.com/technology/2011/01/intel_insider_-_what_is_it_no/, Jan. 2011. (accessed 2016-04-04).

[22] M. Lange and S. Liebergeld. Crossover: Secure and Usable User Interface for Mobile Devices with Multiple Isolated OS Personalities. In *ACSAC '13*, pages 249–257. ACM, 2013.

[23] W. Li, M. Ma, J. Han, Y. Xia, B. Zang, C.-K. Chu, and T. Li. Building Trusted Path on Untrusted Device Drivers for Mobile Devices. In *APSys '14*, pages 8:1–8:7. ACM, 2014.

[24] D. Liu, E. Cuervo, V. Pistol, R. Scudellari, and L. P. Cox. ScreenPass: Secure Password Entry on Touchscreen Devices. In *MobiSys '13*, pages 291–304. ACM, 2013.

[25] J. M. McCune, B. J. Parno, A. Perrig, M. K. Reiter, and H. Isozaki. Flicker: An Execution Infrastructure for Tcb Minimization. In *Eurosys '08*, pages 315–328. ACM, 2008.

[26] F. McKeen, I. Alexandrovich, A. Berenzon, C. V. Rozas, H. Shafi, V. Shanbhogue, and U. R. Savagaonkar. Innovative instructions and software model for isolated execution. In *HASP'13*, page 10, 2013.

[27] T. Murray, D. Matichuk, M. Brassil, P. Gammie, T. Bourke, S. Seefried, C. Lewis, X. Gao, and G. Klein. seL4: From General Purpose to a Proof of Information Flow Enforcement. In *SP'13*, pages 415–429, May 2013.

[28] *seL4 Reference Manual, Version 3.0.0*. NICTA, Mar. 2016. https://wiki.sel4.systems/Documentation (2016/04/04).

[29] E. Owusu, J. Guajardo, J. McCune, J. Newsome, A. Perrig, and A. Vasudevan. OASIS: On Achieving a Sanctuary for Integrity and Secrecy on Untrusted Platforms. In *CCS '13*, pages 13–24. ACM, 2013.

[30] B. Parno. Bootstrapping Trust in a "Trusted" Platform. In *HotSec'08*, 2008.

[31] PCI Security Standards Council. Approved PIN Transaction Security Devices. https://www.pcisecuritystandards.org/assessors_and_solutions/pin_transaction_devices. (accessed 2016-04-04).

[32] J. M. M. A. Perrig and M. K. Reiter. Safe Passage for Passwords and Other Sensitive Data. In *NDSS'09*, 2009.

[33] X. Ruan. *Platform Embedded Security Technology Revealed. Safeguarding the Future of Computing with Intel Embedded Security and Management Engine*. ApressOpen, 2014.

[34] G. E. Suh, D. Clarke, B. Gassend, M. van Dijk, and S. Devadas. AEGIS: Architecture for Tamper-evident and Tamper-resistant Processing. In *ICS '03*, pages 160–171. ACM, 2003.

[35] H. Sun, K. Sun, Y. Wang, J. Jing, and H. Wang. TrustICE: Hardware-Assisted Isolated Computing Environments on Mobile Devices. In *DSN'15*, pages 367–378, June 2015.

[36] TCG. *Trusted Platform Module Library. Part 1: Architecture. Family 2.0*. Oct. 2014. Revision 01.16.

[37] T. Tong and D. Evans. Guardroid: A trusted path for password entry. *Mobile Security Technologies*, 2013.

[38] Verified by Visa. https://www.visaeurope.com/making-payments/verified-by-visa/. (accessed 2016-08-10).

[39] S. Weiser and M. Werner. SGXIO: Generic Trusted I/O Path for Intel SGX. *arXiv:1701.01061*, Jan. 2017.

[40] M. Yu, V. D. Gligor, and Z. Zhou. Trusted Display on Untrusted Commodity Platforms. In *CCS '15*, pages 989–1003. ACM, 2015.

[41] Z. Zhou. *On-Demand Isolated I/O for Security-Sensitive Applications on Commodity Platforms*. PhD thesis, Carnegie Mellon University, 2014.

[42] Z. Zhou, V. D. Gligor, J. Newsome, and J. M. McCune. Building Verifiable Trusted Path on Commodity x86 Computers. In *SP'12*, pages 616–630, May 2012.

[43] Z. Zhou, M. Yu, and V. D. Gligor. Dancing with Giants: Wimpy Kernels for On-Demand Isolated I/O. In *SP'14*, pages 308–323, May 2014.

A Study of Security Vulnerabilities on Docker Hub

Rui Shu, Xiaohui Gu and William Enck
North Carolina State University
Raleigh, North Carolina, USA
{rshu, xgu, whenck}@ncsu.edu

ABSTRACT

Docker containers have recently become a popular approach to provision multiple applications over shared physical hosts in a more lightweight fashion than traditional virtual machines. This popularity has led to the creation of the Docker Hub registry, which distributes a large number of official and community images. In this paper, we study the state of security vulnerabilities in Docker Hub images. We create a scalable Docker image vulnerability analysis (DIVA) framework that automatically discovers, downloads, and analyzes both official and community images on Docker Hub. Using our framework, we have studied 356,218 images and made the following findings: (1) both official and community images contain more than 180 vulnerabilities on average when considering all versions; (2) many images have not been updated for hundreds of days; and (3) vulnerabilities commonly propagate from parent images to child images. These findings demonstrate a strong need for more automated and systematic methods of applying security updates to Docker images and our current Docker image analysis framework provides a good foundation for such automatic security update.

Keywords

Docker Images; Security Vulnerabilities; Vulnerability Propagation

1. INTRODUCTION

The container abstraction has become a popular technique for running multiple application services on a single host. Similar to system virtualization, containers provide an isolated runtime environment and easy methods to package and deploy many instances of an application. However, in contrast to system virtualization, containerized applications on the same host share the host operating system kernel and services. Containers wrap system libraries, files, and code that are needed to support the target application. In doing

so, containers become significantly more lightweight than system virtualization, leading to its recent popularity.

Docker is one of the most widely used container-based technologies. Docker distributes applications (e.g., Apache, MySQL) in the form of *images*. Each image contains the target application software as well as its supporting libraries and configuration files. As a result, Docker images provide a convenient way to store and deliver applications. New images need not to start from scratch. Rather, a new image can extend existing images, creating a parent-child relationship between images. At the roots of these inheritance trees are a set of base (or root) images that provide bare-bones functionality for a specific platform (e.g., Ubuntu).

A community has been developed around the creation and sharing of Docker images. Docker Hub,[1] introduced in 2014, is a cloud registry service for sharing application images. Images are distributed using *repositories*, which allow versioned image development and maintenance. Repositories can branch off of other repositories. For example, a maintainer can create an image myimage:v1 in the myimage repository by building upon the ubuntu:16.04 image in ubuntu repository. After installing application softwares, the maintainer can tag the working image as myimage:v2. Later, after applying some security updates, the image can be tagged myimage:v3.

Docker Hub contains two types of public repositories: official and community. Official repositories contain public, certified images from vendors (e.g., Canonical, Oracle, Red Hat, and Docker). In contrast, community repositories can be created by any user or organization. At the time of writing, there were nearly 100 official repositories. While there is no list of community repositories, our study has identified about 100,000 public community repositories.

In January 2015, a Forrester survey [14] of enterprises indicated that security was a top concern when deciding whether to deploy containers. The survey found that of the various security concerns, the Vulnerabilities & Malware concern was the greatest. Therefore, we hypothesize that the complexity of software configuration in Docker Hub images, combined with a large number of images built by various parties, results in a significantly vulnerable landscape. This intuition leads us to the primary research question of this work: *what is the state of security vulnerabilities in Docker Hub images?*

In this paper, we provide an evaluation of security vulnerabilities in both official and community images that are

CODASPY'17, March 22-24, 2017, Scottsdale, AZ, USA
© 2017 ACM. ISBN 978-1-4503-4523-1/17/03...$15.00
DOI: http://dx.doi.org/10.1145/3029806.3029832

---

[1]https://hub.docker.com/

publicly available on Docker Hub. Particularly, we aim at answering three key research questions:

RQ1 What is the composition of security vulnerabilities in official and community images based on the number and severity of Common Vulnerabilities and Exposures (CVEs) [4]?

RQ2 How much time has lapsed since images were last updated by their repository maintainers?

RQ3 Does creating images based on other images on Docker Hub lead to the propagation of security vulnerabilities, and to what extent?

To answer those questions, we build a framework that automatically discovers, downloads, and analyzes Docker images. With this tool, we analyze over 300,000 image versions from over 85,000 unique image repositories. Our major findings include: (1) both official and community images contain more than 180 vulnerabilities on average when considering all versions, and more than 80% of both official and community images include at least one high severity vulnerability; (2) a large number of both community and official images have not been updated for hundreds of days, but the latest version of official images are better maintained; and (3) vulnerabilities commonly propagate from parent images to child images.

We make the following contributions:

- *We build a scalable Docker Image Vulnerability Analysis (DIVA) system that automatically discovers, downloads, and analyzes images from Docker Hub. We note that while Docker Hub is searchable, there is no prior enumeration of available community images. Our system supports parallel image analysis and extracts inter-image inheritance relationships among a large number ($> 300,000$) of image versions.*

- *To the best of our knowledge, we perform the first systematic study of public community images on Docker Hub. Our analysis demonstrates the significant need for more automated methods of applying security updates to Docker images.*

We are not the first to study vulnerabilities in Docker Hub images. Prior studies have focused on official images on Docker Hub. For example, BanyanOps [24] reported that over 30% of official images include software with high-priority security vulnerabilities. However, the study was limited to official images and a small random sampling of community images. Additionally, Docker Inc. has worked with the Center for Internet Security (CIS) to release a Docker Security Benchmark to recommend best security practices for deploying Docker [5]. In May 2016, Docker Inc. also announced Docker Security Scanning [20] service (formerly called "Project Nautilus") to analyze security risks in Docker images. However, this service is currently limited to official repositories and some private repositories on Docker Hub.

The remainder of this paper proceeds as follows. Section 2 describes DIVA system design. Section 3 describes experimental evaluations. Section 4 discusses our findings. Section 5 focuses on our future work discussion. Section 6 overviews related work. Section 7 concludes.

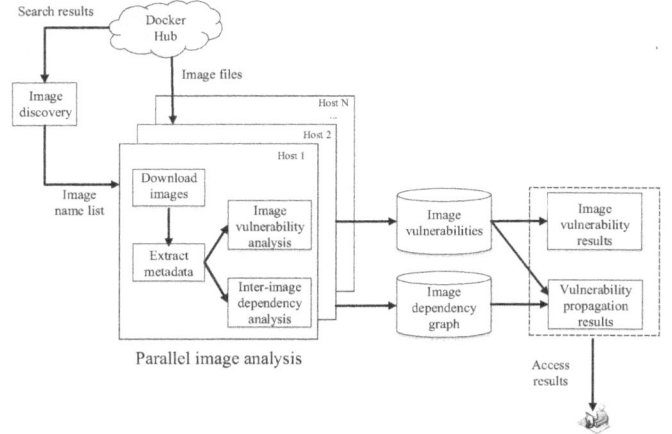

Figure 1: Docker Image Vulnerability Analysis (DIVA) System Framework.

2. DIVA SYSTEM DESIGN

In order to study the broader collection of community and official images on Docker Hub, we must overcome the following challenges:

C1 *There is no public list of community repositories or images on Docker Hub.* While Docker Hub lists around 100 official repositories, community images can only be discovered through keyword-based search.

C2 *The entire registry of Docker Hub images is too large to mirror locally.* While the exact number of images is unknown, our experiments indicate there are hundreds of thousands of images on Docker Hub, and the number continues to grow. The size of images ranges from hundreds of megabytes to several gigabytes. It is impractical to store all images locally before analysis. Thus, our system must support stream-based image analysis, that is, extracting needed information continuously as new images are loaded into the memory and old images are deleted to make space for the new images.

C3 *The number of images prohibits sequential processing.* Our initial experiments indicated an average downloading and processing time of two minutes per image. Therefore, hundreds of thousands of images require tens of months of analysis time. For this reason, our system must support parallel processing to complete the analysis of hundreds of thousands of images within reasonable amount of time.

Figure 1 depicts the architecture of our Docker Image Vulnerability Analysis (DIVA) framework. There are three main components: 1) *the image discovery module* generates random strings to search Docker Hub to identify image names and retrieves images from Docker Hub; 2) *the image vulnerability analysis module* extracts useful metadata and detects vulnerabilities in different images; and 3) *the inter-image dependency analysis* module identifies the inheritance relationships between images.

We now describe these components in detail.

Table 1: Data collected from Docker images.

Data field	Description
Image ID	A 256 bits long ID for each unique image
Image Name	An identifier for each image that follows certain name policy
Last Update Time	Exact date and time of last update to the images
Layer ID	Unique ID of each layer and the relationship between layers
Commands	The history of building the image

Table 2: Data collected from Clair.

Data field	Description
Timestamp	Exact time of analysis by Clair
Vulnerability ID	Unique CVE identifier to identify vulnerability
Severity Ranking	Severity of each vulnerability
Description of CVE	Description of each identified vulnerability
Associated Packages	Name and exact version of the package that associates with each vulnerability
Layer ID	Flag the specific image layer where the vulnerability resides

2.1 Image Discovery

Our first challenge (**C1**) is to discover Docker Hub repositories and their corresponding images.

Official images are built by using an automated system called bashbrew,[2] which is composed of a set of scripts to clone, build, tag and push official images into Docker Hub. We collect names of official images from the recipes which are available in the docker library in github [32].

There is no public list of community repositories or images on Docker Hub. Instead, Docker Hub provides a case-insensitive, keyword-based search interface to discover repositories [9]. Search strings match repository name, user name, and words in the image description. The search results include: (1) the repository name, (2) a description of the repository, (3) the community rating for the repository in the form of number of stars, (4) whether the repository is official or not, and (5) whether or not the repository is built automatically from github. Each search query to Docker Hub returns at most 25 results.

We discover repository names by creating a dictionary of search keyword strings. Similar to PlayDrone [38], we generate random strings with lengths between 1 and 20 characters[3]. Our resulting dictionary includes 5,000,000 unique strings. The name crawler queries Docker Hub for each string and records the matched repository names. Duplicated names are removed. As we report in Section 3, we discovered 99,843 unique repository names using this method.

Once the repository names are known, we must determine the images within the repositories. For each repository, we perform an additional search to Docker Hub to enumerate all of the tags (e.g., 16.10, latest, trusty). We then combine the repository name with the tag to create the list of image names. Using this method, we discovered 440,524 unique image names. However, between the time of image name discovery and image analysis, a number of repositories and images were not downloadable. We discuss this reduction further in Section 3. Note that our approach discovers both official and community images. We further separate our results into two lists: official image names and community image names based on their image name format (i.e., official image names follow a format of *repo-name:tag* while community image names follow the format of *hub-user/repo-name:tag*).

We note that a Web search engine such as Google could have also been used to discover Docker Hub repository names. For example, the Google search query: *site:hub.docker.com*

---

[2]https://github.com/docker-library/official-images≠bashbrew

[3]We limit our name string length to 20 because we observe that most of the image names include less than 20 characters. Our framework is generic, which can be configured with longer string length easily.

"short description" "full description" "official repository" returns a list of official image repository names. However, when using Google search to identify community image repositories, we were limited by the search results, identifying only a few hundred repositories.

2.2 Image Vulnerability Analysis

Once the image names are identified, we need to download the corresponding image files for analysis. Since it is impractical to download all the images from the Docker Hub to our local hosts, we need to adopt a stream-based parallel image analysis approach. Specifically, each host fetches a set of image names from the name list and downloads those images using the Docker daemon's `docker pull` command (e.g., *"docker pull hub-user/repo-name:tag"* for community images). Next, we perform the image analysis. Once the analysis completes for the image set, all of those images are deleted. We iterate the above process over sets of new images on each host. We can scale up the processing by performing the analysis on a large number of hosts concurrently. We also found that images from the same repository often share common layers and therefore the Docker daemon can avoid pulling a layer again if the layer already exists on the local host. This observation can lead to further speedup by always retrieving the images of the same repository together.

To analyze the security vulnerability of each image, we first extract metadata about each image, such as its name, IDs, and layer information. Specifically, for each downloaded image, we collect five data fields, shown in Table 1. Note that for the last update time, we use `docker inspect` to fetch the details of each docker image and store the results in an array. The creation time is the date of the latest `docker build`, therefore, we use this timestamp to denote the latest update to images.

We then leverage Clair [16] to detect vulnerabilities in each image. Clair is an open-source tool from CoreOS designed to identify known vulnerabilities in container images. Clair has been primarily used to scan images in CoreOS's private container registry, Quay.io, but it can also analyze Docker images.

We collect several types of vulnerability information using Clair, as shown in Table 2. Clair uses static analysis to extract: 1) the version of all installed software packages, and 2) the operating system metadata in each layer of an image. Clair identifies insecure packages by matching the metadata against the Common Vulnerabilities and Exposures (CVE) vulnerability database[4] and similar databases such as Ubuntu CVE Tracker [37], Debian Security Bug Tracker [18], Red Hat Security Data [34], etc. Note that Clair only identifies the presence of packages with known

Figure 2: A sample output of Clair for CVE-2016-2842 from image ruby:2.0.0-p594-onbuild.

vulnerabilities. It does not determine if those packages are actually used by container instances. Similarly, it does not detect dynamic behavior in running instances, e.g., installing vulnerable package versions at runtime.

Clair identifies the package versions based on the file system view that is observable at runtime. If the image is built from a Dockerfile, which specifies a set of instructions to produce a local image, Clair is executed on the resulting image. As discussed further in Section 2.3, Docker images are based on layers. Each layer stores copy-on-write information to produce a file system view. For example, we define the base layer to be a scratch image (used before Docker version 1.5.0 [28]) or created from a Dockerfile instruction (e.g., ADD). The layers above the base layer are the results of installing additional packages via installing commands or upgrading commands such as `apt-get install` or `apt-get upgrade`, or operations on existing files (e.g., add, modify, delete) in running containers. In addition, executing instructions specified in Dockerfiles (e.g., ADD, COPY) also creates new layers. Since Clair operates statically, it must process all the layers in one image to identify any vulnerable packages. However, it must take care not to report a vulnerable package in a lower layer if it is superseded by a patched version of the package in a higher layer. We experimentally confirmed that Clair does not report a vulnerable package in a lower layer when a higher layer upgrades the package. For example, we ran Clair on the ubuntu:14.04 image and observed that vim 2:7.4.052-1ubuntu3 is identified as a vulnerable package. We performed an `apt-get upgrade` to upgrade vim to version 2:7.4.052-1ubuntu3.1 and committed the result to a new image. When running Clair on the new image, the vulnerability for the upgraded vim package was no longer present and was not reported by Clair.

Figure 2 shows a sample output from Clair for CVE-2016-2842 from image ruby:2.0.0-p594-onbuild. For each CVE entry, Clair collects the unique CVE identifier with the vulnerability severity rating. In Clair version 1.0 (used for our study) the analysis outputs specific advice for security flaws. In most cases, Clair recommends upgrading specific packages to a more recent version. We also note that CVE identifiers are unique IDs for known security vulnerabilities (e.g., CVE-2016-1977). Red Hat Security Advisories (RHSA) uses a different format of identifier (e.g., RHSA-2016:0176), which must be mapped to CVE identifiers [34, 10]. When Clair identifies a package with a vulnerability, it outputs a URL for the corresponding CVE, along with the layer ID that contains the package.

Each CVE's severity is ranked by the National Vulnera-

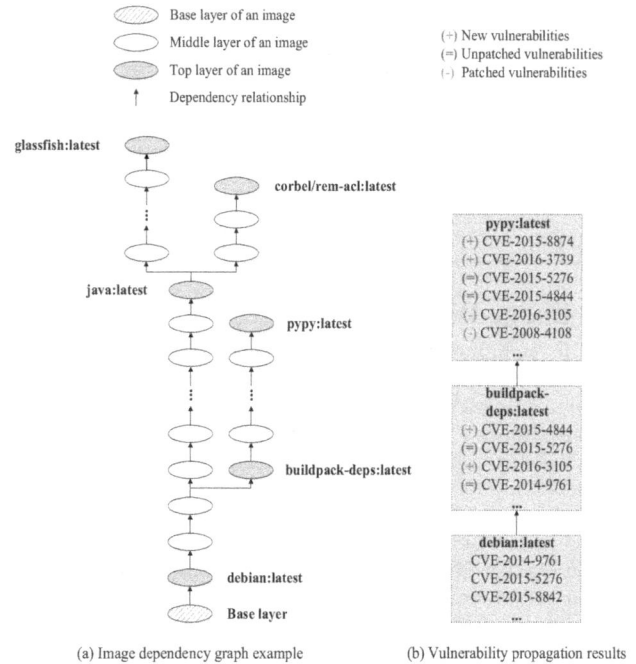

(a) Image dependency graph example (b) Vulnerability propagation results

Figure 3: Inter-image dependency analysis example.

bility Database (NVD) [6] using the Common Vulnerability Scoring System (CVSS) [8]. CVSS assigns a severity score based on a formula including exploitability and impact metrics. The NVD also provides a qualitative severity rating of "Low", "Medium" and "High" based on the CVSS score (Low: 0.0-3.9; Medium: 4.0-6.9; High: 7.0-10.0). We use these qualitative scores to report statistics in our study.

2.3 Inter-Image Dependency Analysis

Basing new images on existing images on Docker Hub minimizes effort. However, it also propagates any software vulnerability to the new image, if care is not taken apply security updates. In this section, we design an algorithm to investigate the dependency relationship between images, as well as identify vulnerability propagation patterns (**RQ3**).

Each Docker image is composed of a list of read-only layers. On a Docker host, each layer is stored as a tar file within a unique directory. Layers are stacked hierarchically, the order of which is specified in a JSON configuration file. The configuration file references a layer ID, which is unique throughout Docker Hub. Prior to Docker version 1.10, the layer ID was a randomly generated 256-bit UUID. However, for versions 1.10 and later, the layer ID is the SHA256 hash of the tar file content. Commonly, the first 12 hex characters are used as a short identifier for a layer. Note that our study uses Docker version 1.9.0, which was the stable version during our experiment. There are some differences between these two versions, e.g., the way how images are stored in the host; however, the changes would only require minor modification in the DIVA source code.

To study dependency relationships between images, we represent all layers in all images on Docker Hub using one *directed graph* $G = (V, E)$, where the set of vertices V represents the layer IDs, and the set of edges E represents relationships between layer IDs, as specified in the JSON configuration files of images. We call G the *image dependency graph*. In our representation, we label vertices with the set of image names that have the corresponding layer ID as the topmost layer. We represent G as an adjacency list. We maintain the lists of vertices and edges separately in order to label vertices when they are the topmost layer in an image.

To construct the image dependency graph, we process each image using three key steps: 1) updating the set of vertices V with newly discovered layer IDs, 2) updating the set of edges E with newly discovered edges based on the inter-layer relationships specified in the JSON configuration file (e.g., if the layer l_j is placed on top of the layer l_i in one image, we add an edge $l_i \rightarrow l_j$ in the image dependency graph), and 3) annotating a vertex corresponding to the topmost layer with the image name. Note that if an image only has one layer, no edges are added, but the vertex corresponding to that layer is annotated with the image name. Since multiple images may have the same topmost layer, the vertex annotation is a set. An example graph containing six Docker Hub images is shown in Figure 3 (a), which contains both official images (e.g., debian:latest) and community image (e.g., corbel/rem-acl:latest). In this example, these images share the same base layer.

We use the image dependency graph to determine the propagation of vulnerabilities between images on Docker Hub. To do this, we perform a depth-first search on G and compare the vulnerabilities of each image to its direct children. Let $\mathcal{V}(\cdot)$ be a function that returns the set of CVEs for an image, as reported by Clair (Section 2.2). We can then define the set of new vulnerabilities ($\mathcal{V}^+$), patched vulnerabilities ($\mathcal{V}^-$), and unpatched vulnerabilities ($\mathcal{V}^=$) for each pair of parent and child images (i_p, i_c) as follows:

$$\mathcal{V}^+(i_p, i_c) = \mathcal{V}(i_c) \setminus \mathcal{V}(i_p)$$
$$\mathcal{V}^-(i_p, i_c) = \mathcal{V}(i_p) \setminus \mathcal{V}(i_c)$$
$$\mathcal{V}^=(i_p, i_c) = \mathcal{V}(i_p) \cap \mathcal{V}(i_c)$$

Figure 3 (b) shows an the vulnerability propagation for the rightmost branch of the graph.

3. EXPERIMENT

To identify the names of community images, we generated 5,000,000 random strings. During the month of February 2016, we queried Docker Hub for each string. After removing duplicates, the search query process identified 89,843 different repository names, including all 98 official repositories. Querying Docker Hub for repository tags produced a list of 440,524 unique image names, composed of 436,722 community images and 3,802 official images.

We did not start to download and analyze images immediately after we generated the image name list. Instead, we randomly selected a sample of 20,000 images, downloaded and analyzed them to further test and improve our analysis framework between March and April. When we performed our image analysis in late April 2016, not all repositories and images were still available. We found that some repositories were purely deleted by users, and we also detected deletions of tags within repositories. Our final dataset consisted of 86,066 repositories, containing 356,218 images, including 3,802 images from the 98 official repositories.

We performed the image metadata extraction using our university's cloud computing infrastructure called the Vir-

tual Computing Lab (VCL) [7]. We reserved 100 virtual machines, each with 4GB memory and 40GB storage, and configured with Ubuntu version 14.04, Docker version 1.9.0, Clair version 1.0. We dedicated one processing node for the official images. The remaining 99 processing nodes were used to analyze community images. The list of community image was split up into 99 sublists, taking care to ensure that images within the same repository were on the same sublist and processed by the same host to avoid repeated downloading of the same layers shared among different images in the same repository.

As for image vulnerability detection, we ran Clair as a container instance on each virtual machine. The Clair instance uses a PostgreSQL container instance to periodically update local vulnerability database (e.g., Ubuntu vulnerabilities database, Debian vulnerabilities database and Red Hat vulnerabilities database). Both the Clair instance and the PostgreSQL instance kept running and waiting for analysis requests throughout the entire experiment. In the end, we aggregated the raw results from Clair for analysis.

4. RESULTS

We now return to our motivating research questions:

RQ1 What is the composition of security vulnerabilities in official and community images based on the number and severity of CVEs?

RQ2 How much time has lapsed since images were last updated by their repository maintainers?

RQ3 Does creating images based on other images on Docker Hub lead to the propagation of security vulnerabilities, and to what extent?

This section presents our experimental results.

4.1 Vulnerabilities per Image

The number of vulnerabilities per image characterizes the Docker Hub vulnerability landscape. Each Docker Hub repository is a collection of related images. Images refer to repository tags, which are commonly different versions of an application or a distribution. Since older, potentially more vulnerable, images may not ever be updated, it is useful to consider both the vulnerabilities per image, as well as the vulnerabilities in the latest version of that repository. To identify the latest image in a repository, we leverage the Docker Hub convention to use the tag ":latest" to indicate the latest version. The :latest tag is also automatically assigned if a maintainer does not specify any tag when creating a repository. However, if the user specifies any other tag but the :latest tag, the repository does not include the :latest tag, which is not included in our results about the latest versions. In our dataset, we found that 10,435 out of 85,968 community repositories and 5 out of 98 official repositories did not have a :latest tag.

Table 3 reports the number of vulnerabilities for all versions of images, as well as only the latest images. The table includes the mean, median, max, min, and standard deviation of vulnerabilities for the 352,416 community images and 3,802 official images that we analyzed. Interestingly, the number of vulnerabilities per community image does not significantly differ when considering all images verses latest images. In contrast, there is a significant difference between

Table 3: Number of Vulnerabilities per Image.

Image Type	Total Images	Number of Vulnerabilities				
		Mean	Median	Max	Min	Std. Dev.
Community	352,416	199	158	1,779	0	139
Community :latest	75,533	196	153	1,779	0	141
Official	3,802	185	127	791	0	145
Official :latest	93	76	76	392	0	59

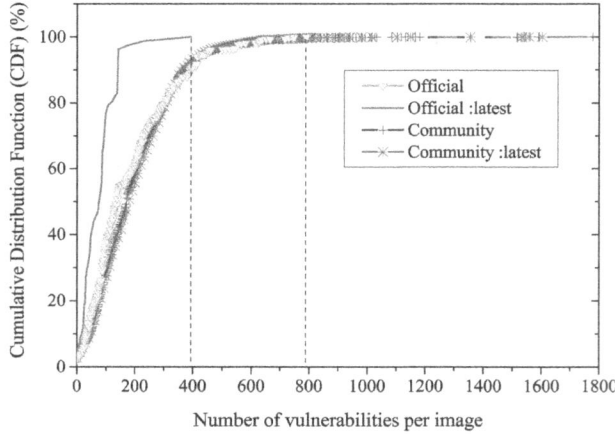

Figure 4: Cumulative distribution function (CDF) of the number of vulnerabilities per image.

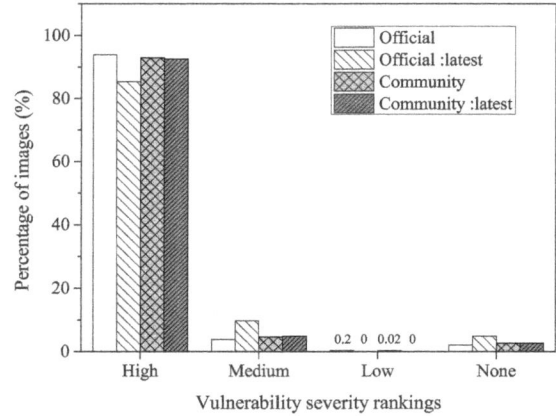

Figure 5: Distribution of images based on most severe vulnerability.

the two classes for official images. This phenomenon is likely the result of better maintenance for official images.

Figure 4 depicts the cumulative distribution function (CDF) for these same images classes. Note that the dashed vertical lines indicate the maximum number of vulnerabilities per image for that class. The CDF corroborates our take-aways from Table 3. The CDF also shows that both classes of community images track the CDF of the vulnerabilities in the class containing all official images. One possible explanation is that many community repositories are based off of old versions of official images, and the maintainers have not applied security updates to the latest image in the repository. We consider vulnerability propagation further in Section 4.5.

4.2 Vulnerability Severity

Clair provides five types of security rankings for vulnerabilities: "Negligible", "Low", "Medium", "High", "Critical". However, we chose to use the more standard NVD severity ranking: "Low", "Medium" and "High". To identify the severity of a vulnerability, we crawled the vulnerability type and CVSS score from the CVE Details database[4] for each CVE vulnerability. We then mapped the score to the NVD ranking based on their thresholds.

Figure 5 categorizes community and official images into four groups: high, medium, low and none. An image is placed in the group corresponding to the highest severity ranking of its most severe CVE. For example, if an image contains at least one "High" severity ranking CVE, it is placed in the "High" group.

This figure shows that even though the latest version of official repositories generally has less vulnerabilities, the vulnerabilities it contains generally include at least one that is high severity. Although it is difficult to determine whether

[4]http://www.cvedetails.com/

the packages with high severity vulnerabilities are used in running containers, they are still important to address. For example, they may be exploited by attacks that chain together multiple vulnerabilities.

4.3 Image Age

Many Docker Hub repositories are well maintained, whereas others remain unmaintained. Intuitively, an image that has not been updated in a long time is more likely to contain more vulnerabilities. Therefore, we seek to characterize the age of images at the time of analysis. We determine the age by subtracting the last update timestamp from the time of our analysis for that image. For example, we analyzed the clojure:lein-2.5.3-onbuild image on May 17, 2016 and its last update time was March 24, 2016. Therefore, its age is 54 days.

Figure 6 shows the CDF of the age of images at the time of analysis for the four classes of images. As depicted in the figure, for images of all versions, official images are somewhat similar to community images: about 70% of both types of images are updated in less than 400 days at the time of analysis. There is some difference in the percentage of very recently updated images: approximately 20% for all official images verses approximately 10% for all community images. In contrast, nearly 86% of the latest official images are recently updated. This result suggests that official images, particularly the latest official images, are much more frequently maintained on Docker Hub than community images. Finally, we note that the CDF of the latest community images nearly matches the CDF of all community images.

There are several possible explanations for the significant number of images that have not received updates for a long time. For example, some images may deliberately not be updated in order to reproduce bugs in specific experimental environments. Another explanation is that image maintain-

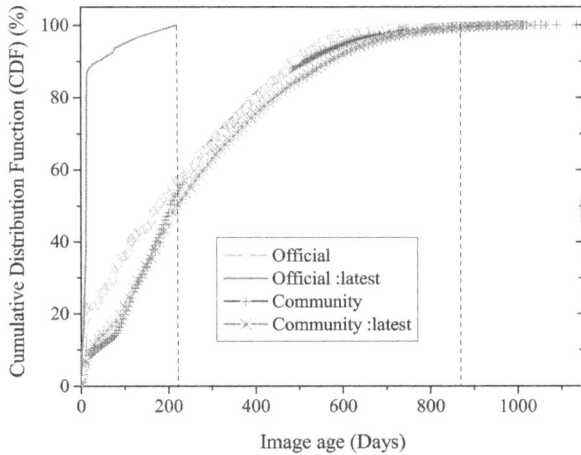

Figure 6: Cumulative distribution function (CDF) of percentage distribution of the age of images at the time of analysis.

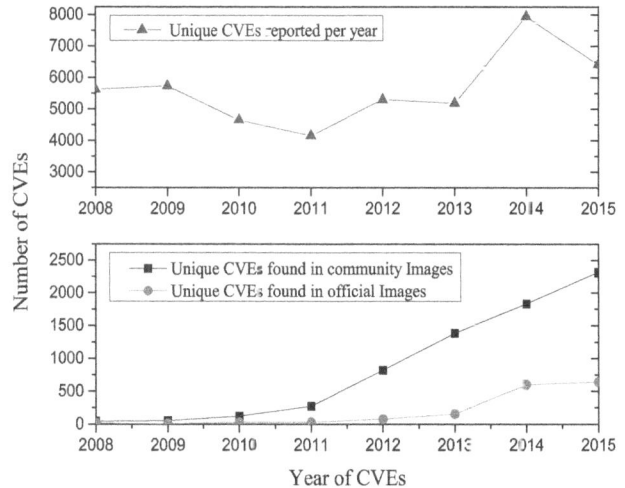

Figure 7: Comparison between CVEs discovered in CVE database and CVEs found in community images and official images from 2008 to 2015.

ers do not update images to ensure software compatibility. Finally, images not marked as :latest may be intentionally unmaintained to provide snapshots of runtime environments.

4.4 Vulnerability Composition

Thousands of new vulnerabilities are discovered each year. In this subsection we consider the composition of security vulnerabilities that exist in Docker Hub images. We first look at the composition of unique vulnerabilities. Next we consider the composition of vulnerability types. Finally, we report the packages contributing to the most vulnerabilities.

Number of Unique Vulnerabilities: Figure 7 compares the total number of CVE vulnerabilities discovered between 2008 to 2015 [1] to the corresponding CVEs that exist in our dataset of Docker Hub images. The figure shows that the number of CVEs per year remained approximately the same between 2008 and 2013, with a steep increase in 2014, and then a decrease in 2015. In contrast, the CVEs found in our dataset of images grows steadily. We found 6,845 unique CVE vulnerabilities in the set of all community images and 1,554 unique CVE vulnerabilities in the set of all official images from the year 2008 to 2015. Since our dataset reports vulnerabilities from the images state in 2016, this trend is to be expected, as some, but not all images are patched over time. However, Docker Hub was not published until 2014, and the existence of CVEs from prior years suggests that some images have included very old software packages.

Types of Vulnerabilities: The CVE Details database taxonmizes CVEs into several vulnerability types. Most of CVE vulnerabilities are associated with one or more vulnerability types. For example, CVE-2015-1781 [2], which is a buffer overflow vulnerability that can be exploited in DNS services and causes denial of service or arbitrary code execution, can fall into three types: denial of service, execute code, and overflow. However, some CVE vulnerabilities are not categorized with any type, e.g., CVE-2015-4000 [3] (a Logjam vulnerability that allows a man-in-the-middle attacker to downgrade the cipher suites used for TLS connections). Fur-

thermore, a small portion of the CVEs in our dataset belong to reserved CVE entries, which are not included in the CVE Details database. On the whole, we were able to categorize 5,116 of 6,845 unique CVEs for community images and 1,069 of 1,554 unique CVEs for official images.

Tables 4 and 5 show the prevalence of CVE types in the latest version of official and community images. We focus on the latest version, because these images are most likely to represent the most recent version offered by the maintainers. The tables report vulnerability type ranked by the number of images that contain at least one vulnerability of that type discovered in that year. For example, Table 4 shows that 66 of the 93 official images contains an overflow vulnerability from 2010 in its *latest* version. Specifically, this high prevalence of overflow vulnerabilities from 2010 is caused by 2 unique CVEs (i.e., CVE-2010-3192, CVE-2010-4051) found in 2 packages (i.e., eglibc, glibc). The most significant vulnerability was CVE-2010-4051, which was related to a "RE_DUP_MAX overflow", which can lead to denial of service. This vulnerability can be exploited in some applications, e.g., ProFTPD. Finally, comparing official images (Table 4) to community images (Table 5), we see that trends are fairly similar, but community images have more variety in vulnerabilities. One explanation is that the number of studied community images is much larger than the number of official images.

We also observe that a significant portion of the latest community images are impacted by vulnerabilities from 2012 and 2013. However, the latest official images are not. This phenomenon correlates with our previous finding for image age, since a large number of community images, even of the latest version, are not as well-maintained as official images. For example, CVEs from some previous years do not receive enough attention.

Most Vulnerable Packages: Finally, we investigate which packages most frequently cause Docker images to contain

Table 4: Vulnerability types ranked per year by the number of impacted `:latest` official images.

Vulnerability Type	Rank (Number of impacted images)						
	2015	2014	2013	2012	2011	2010	2009
Overflow	1 (78)	1 (75)	3 (14)	5 (5)	2 (2)	1 (66)	1 (14)
Denial of service	2 (77)	1 (75)	1 (56)	1 (44)	2 (2)	1 (66)	4 (1)
Obtain information	2 (77)	7 (6)	5 (12)	6 (0)	5 (0)	4 (30)	5 (0)
Bypass a restriction or similar	4 (57)	4 (40)	6 (1)	2 (28)	1 (3)	1 (66)	2 (2)
Execute code	5 (56)	1 (75)	2 (34)	3 (22)	5 (0)	6 (0)	2 (2)
Gain privileges	6 (33)	10 (0)	6 (1)	4 (15)	5 (0)	6 (0)	5 (0)
Memory corruption	7 (4)	6 (7)	4 (4)	6 (0)	4 (1)	6 (0)	5 (0)
Cross site scripting	8 (2)	8 (4)	6 (1)	6 (0)	5 (0)	6 (0)	5 (0)
Directory traversal	9 (1)	5 (8)	6 (1)	6 (0)	5 (0)	5 (13)	5 (0)
Http response splitting	10 (0)	9 (2)	10 (0)	6 (0)	5 (0)	6 (0)	5 (0)

Table 5: Vulnerability types ranked per year by the number of impacted `:latest` community images.

Vulnerability Type	Rank (Number of impacted images)						
	2015	2014	2013	2012	2011	2010	2009
Denial of service	1 (60k)	1 (60k)	1 (54k)	1 (39k)	1 (5k)	1 (30k)	3 (2k)
Overflow	2 (60k)	2 (59k)	3 (38k)	5 (6k)	4 (3k)	2 (26k)	1 (7k)
Obtain information	3 (59k)	7 (23k)	4 (36k)	6 (4k)	8 (174)	4 (17k)	7 (2)
Bypass a restriction or similar	4 (58k)	4 (49k)	5 (15k)	3 (20k)	3 (3k)	3 (26k)	5 (277)
Execute code	5 (58k)	3 (59k)	2 (47k)	2 (20k)	2 (3k)	6 (1k)	2 (2k)
Gain privilege	6 (52k)	9 (5k)	8 (942)	4 (11k)	7 (255)	7 (94)	9 (0)
Memory corruption	7 (31k)	5 (40k)	6 (5k)	7 (871)	5 (2k)	9 (6)	6 (10)
Cross site scripting	8 (7k)	10 (4k)	7 (980)	8 (198)	6 (387)	8 (88)	4 (486)
Directory traversal	9 (4k)	6 (35k)	11 (69)	10 (94)	10 (4)	5 (14k)	9 (0)
Cross site request forgery	10 (2k)	11 (276)	9 (644)	12 (54)	10 (4)	10 (0)	9 (0)
Http response splitting	11 (466)	8 (9k)	12 (0)	11 (67)	9 (58)	10 (0)	9 (0)
Sql injection	12 (16)	12 (42)	10 (218)	9 (158)	10 (4)	10 (0)	8 (1)

vulnerabilities. Recall from Section 2.2 that Clair reports the vulnerable package name. Table 6 shows the top-ten packages for both community images (all and latest) and official images (all and latest). Note that the statistics are calculated across all versions of the package. For official images, `glibc` is the most frequent offender, affecting over 80% images in both all versions and the latest version. The `glibc` package is also the most significant offender for community images. Another observation is that some packages (e.g., util-linux, shadow, perl, openssl, etc.) appear in each category. Therefore, it is possible that a small number of vulnerable packages cause a significant impact on Docker Hub. These packages could be targeted specifically to improve the security of the Docker Hub ecosystem.

4.5 Image Dependency Relationship

Our third research question seeks to understand the relationship between image dependencies and vulnerability propagation. Child images can be created from both official and community images. There are two general ways to build child images from parent images. First, if a user updates a running image that was downloaded from Docker Hub, that image can be committed as a new image. Second, a Docker Hub repository maintainer can specify a *FROM* instruction in the Dockerfile of a new image. This instruction specifies the base image, which Docker automatically downloads to the Docker host when building the new image from the Dockerfile. Both of the methods may lead to vulnerability propagation. We study this relationship from two perspectives: (1) the degree of propagation from parent image to child image, and (2) the factors that promote propagation.

RQ3.1: *To what degree do child images add, inherit, or remove vulnerabilities?* In Section 2.3 we described an algorithm of identifying the CVEs relationships between a parent and child image. Figure 8 shows the average number of new,

unpatched, and patched CVEs per edge between images in the dependency graph. Further, we distinguish between the types of inheritance: official to official, official to community, and community to community. The figure shows that child images inherit on average 80 or more vulnerabilities from their parents, regardless if the parent is official or community. Furthermore, child images frequently introduce new vulnerabilities. This is an interesting observation, because it suggests that when a child installs new software packages, the maintainer is not applying security updates (e.g., with `apt-get upgrade`). That said, Figure 8 does indicate the vulnerability propagation is slightly better for child images that are created from official images.

RQ3.2: *How does image popularity promote vulnerability propagation?* We answer this question in three stages. First, we identify the top most influential OS and non-OS base images, as determined by the number of descendant images. Tables 7 and 8 list the top 10 OS and non-OS base images along with the number of descendant images. Our results for top OS base images is consistent with an August 2015 study by CenturyLink [19]. Second, we look at the distribution of influential base images (Figure 9), we see that there are a relatively small number of very influential images. Finally, we correlate top ranked images with top vulnerable packages.

Tables 7 and 8 list the top vulnerable packages (from Table 6) for the top OS and non-OS base images. The tables show that many of the top vulnerable packages appear in the top influential base images. Thus, *it is highly likely that the root cause of pervasive vulnerabilities on Docker Hub is the result of propagation from a relatively small set of highly influential base images.* As such, future work should investigate methods of automatically pushing updates based on the dependency graph.

276

Table 6: Top ten packages causing images to contain vulnerabilities.

Rank	Package name (Percentage of impacted images)			
	Official	Official :latest	Community	Community :latest
1	glibc (89.81%)	glibc (81.31%)	glibc (84.24%)	glibc (84.82%)
2	util-linux (89.55%)	util-linux (81.91%)	openssl (78.32%)	openssl (78.51%)
3	shadow (89.55%)	shadow (81.91%)	util-linux (77.01%)	util-linux (77.24%)
4	perl (87.29%)	audit (77.66%)	shadow (77.01%)	shadow (77.24%)
5	apt (83.82%)	perl (73.40%)	perl (74.07%)	perl (73.05%)
6	openssl (83.79%)	tar (72.34%)	pam (70.92%)	pam (70.53%)
7	tar (83.58%)	apt (70.21%)	pcre3 (66.54%)	audit (67.10%)
8	openldap (76.85%)	openssl (67.02%)	audit (65.48%)	pcre3 (65.59%)
9	krb5 (76.06%)	systemd (67.02%)	krb5 (64.99%)	dpkg (64.36%)
10	audit (73.51%)	gcc (65.36%)	libidn (64.54%)	libidn (62.93%)

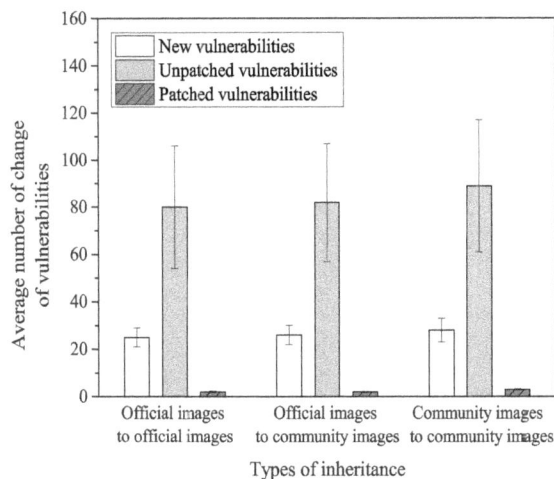

Figure 8: Statistics of the pattern of CVE propagation.

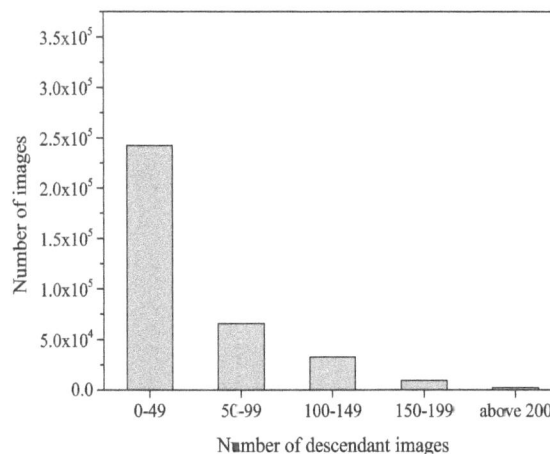

Figure 9: Distribution of the number of descendant images.

4.6 Summary

Our experimental study reveals a set of key findings about the security vulnerabilities of Docker Hub:

1. Both official and community images contain more than 180 vulnerabilities on average when considering all versions. Although the latest official images contain fewer vulnerabilities, the average number of vulnerabilities per image still reach more than 70. In contrast, the number of vulnerabilities contained in the latest community images shows little difference from that of all community images. In addition, more than 80% of both types of images have at least one high severity level vulnerability.

2. About 50% of both community and official images have not been updated in 200 days, and about 30% of images have not been updated in 400 days. There is some difference in the percentage of more frequently updated images (i.e., updated in 14 days) between official images and community images: approximately 20% for all official images verses approximately 10% for all community images. In contrast, nearly 36% of the latest official images have been updated in less than 14 days.

3. Child images bring in about 20 more new vulnerabilities on average, and they also inherit 80 vulnerabilities

on average from their parent images. The vulnerability propagation is slightly better when child images are created from official images. In addition, there are a relatively small number of influential base images, and we also find top vulnerable packages mostly appear in all top influential base images.

5. FUTURE WORK DISCUSSION

First, our current architecture depends on Clair to statically identify vulnerabilities from installed packages. One possible enhancement for our work is to dynamically scan independent packages that are being installed in the running containers. As a result, we can achieve most timely detection of vulnerabilities introduced by the package update to running docker containers.

Second, we hope to patch the running containers when a vulnerability is detected. One possible approach is to upgrade packages to secure version in running containers, e.g., with `apt-get upgrade`. However, creating containers from images and committing patched containers into images incur resource overhead (e.g., CPU, disk) to the hosts. Moreover, applications or containers might require rebooting after patching, which would incur undesirable unavailability for server applications (e.g., a production web server). Therefore, it is challenging to develop an effective and practical security patching solution, which is also part of our future work.

Table 7: Top ten referenced OS base images. (✓: A package is included in the image; ✗: A package is not included in the image. *: These vulnerable packages appear in Table 6 in both all versions and the latest version of official images.)

Rank	Image name	Number of descendant images	glibc	util-linux	shadow	perl	apt	openssl	tar	openldap	krb5	audit	systemd	gcc
			\multicolumn{12}{c}{Vulnerable packages (*)}											
1	ubuntu:trusty-20150528	11440	✓	✓	✓	✓	✗	✓	✗	✗	✗	✓	✗	✓
2	ubuntu:trusty-20151001	10820	✓	✓	✓	✓	✗	✓	✗	✗	✗	✓	✗	✗
3	ubuntu:trusty-20150630	8781	✓	✓	✓	✓	✗	✓	✗	✗	✗	✓	✗	✗
4	debian:8.3	6642	✓	✓	✓	✓	✓	✗	✓	✗	✗	✓	✓	✗
5	ubuntu:trusty-20151028	5862	✓	✓	✓	✓	✗	✓	✗	✗	✗	✓	✗	✗
6	ubuntu:trusty-20150730	4912	✓	✓	✓	✓	✗	✓	✗	✗	✗	✓	✗	✗
7	ubuntu:trusty-20160217	4755	✓	✓	✓	✓	✗	✓	✗	✗	✗	✓	✗	✗
9	ubuntu:trusty-20151218	4497	✓	✓	✓	✓	✗	✓	✗	✗	✗	✓	✗	✗
10	ubuntu:14.04.2	3328	✓	✓	✓	✓	✗	✓	✗	✗	✗	✓	✗	✓

Table 8: Top ten referenced non-OS base images. (✓: A package is included in the image; ✗: A package is not included in the image. *: These vulnerable packages appear in Table 6 in both all versions and the latest version of official images.)

Rank	Image name	Number of descendant images	glibc	util-linux	shadow	perl	apt	openssl	tar	openldap	krb5	audit	systemd	gcc
			\multicolumn{12}{c}{Vulnerable packages (*)}											
1	node:5.3	3935	✓	✓	✓	✓	✓	✓	✓	✓	✓	✓	✓	✓
2	ruby:2.2.4-alpine	3279	✓	✓	✓	✓	✓	✓	✓	✓	✓	✓	✓	✓
3	buildpack-deps: jessie-curl	3149	✓	✓	✓	✓	✓	✓	✓	✓	✓	✓	✓	✓
4	node:4.2.2-onbuild	2972	✓	✓	✓	✓	✓	✓	✓	✓	✓	✓	✓	✓
5	nginx:1.9.7	2887	✓	✓	✓	✓	✓	✓	✓	✗	✗	✓	✓	✓
6	golang:1.5.2-alpine	2749	✓	✓	✓	✓	✓	✓	✓	✓	✓	✓	✓	✓
7	node:5.2	2691	✓	✓	✓	✓	✓	✓	✓	✓	✓	✓	✓	✓
8	node:4.2.3-onbuild	2597	✓	✓	✓	✓	✓	✓	✓	✓	✓	✓	✓	✓
9	nginx:1.9	2551	✓	✓	✓	✓	✓	✓	✓	✗	✗	✓	✓	✓
10	node:5.1.1-onbuild	2544	✓	✓	✓	✓	✓	✓	✓	✓	✓	✓	✓	✓

Third, the size of Docker Hub community continues to grow at a rapid pace, and more vulnerabilities are being discovered in the meantime. We encourage the participation from image publishers, image users, and repository maintainers to improve the whole ecosystem. For instance, image publishers and maintainers could eliminate security vulnerability risks by utilizing vulnerability assessing tools during image pushing, sharing, and maintaining. Image users should check security threats before running an image downloaded from Docker Hub repositories.

6. RELATED WORK

Docker vulnerability assessment: The first area of related work includes recent efforts in auditing and assessing the security of Docker. For example, Docker's Benchmark for Security [5] assesses the deployment environment and suggests best practices. However, many suggestions are general best practices for Linux. In May 2016, Docker Inc. announced the Docker Security Scanning service [20], formerly known as "Project Nautilus", which provides automated security analysis, validation and continuous monitoring for binary images that hosted on Docker Hub. Images are scanned before every push to Docker Hub, and users are notified when vulnerabilities are discovered. Unfortunately, this service is currently only available to Docker Cloud private repository customers.

There are also several analysis approaches providing vulnerability detection. Banyan Collector [12] can facilitate analysis by launching image containers and running scripts inside them to collect specific information, e.g., installed packages. OpenSCAP Container Compliance [33] provides multiple tools to assist administrators and auditors with assessment, measurement and enforcement of security baselines. Container Compliance provides vulnerabilities assessment of running containers and images (e.g., Red Hat Docker containers) against Common Vulnerabilities and Exposures (CVE) vulnerability database. Twistlock [36] is a closed-source utility that performs heuristics and dynamic profiling at runtime to identify potential risks. Twistlock runs as a dedicated privileged container on each host and looks at the resources being consumed by a container application, including API processes that are spawned, as well as ports being opened. IBM's Vulnerability Advisor [27] is specific to images hosted on IBM's Bluemix cloud. It monitors images pushed to its registry by inspecting features such as packages, configurations, and opened ports. It then compares installed packages against known vulnerability databases for security issues. Vulnerability Advisor also provides guidance for basic security policies.

Our study is the first systematic study of security vulnerabilities in both official and community images on Docker Hub. Compared to previous vulnerability detection techniques, our scalable framework leverages static analysis that provided by Clair, which enables the analysis of a large number of images in a reasonable time. Our findings reveal not only the security vulnerabilities of each image, but also the propagation of vulnerabilities between images.

Virtual machine image security: The second category of related work includes efforts that study virtual machine images, which in many ways parallel Docker images. For example, Amazon's EC2 platform provides customers with a community repository of pre-built Amazon Machine Images (AMIs). If attackers inject malicious code into images and publish them in public repositories, other users who retrieve these images may be compromised [26, 39, 25, 23, 11, 21]. In other cases, confidential information may accidentally leak due to template image cloning [23]. Bugiel et al. [15] provided a systematic analysis of security and privacy in AMIs on Amazon EC2. Their framework extracts sensitive information that can be used as a backdoors in virtual machines created from vulnerable AMIs.

Public virtual machines images are commonly customizable by consumers. Therefore vulnerabilities may propagate that similar to our findings in Docker. Zhang et al. [40] analyzed the cost and effectiveness of exploiting popular vulnerabilities in IaaS Cloud, and then used game theory to model attacks and defenses. Arun Thomas et al. [35] discussed the problem of *virtual machine image sprawl* or *image sprawl* for short. Simply put, the problem is that since creating or cloning an image is easy, the number of images is continuously growing. As a result, the storage and maintainance will become complicated.

To protect VM images against leaking sensitive data by publishers or running malicious images, Mirage [39] provides a set of management approaches (e.g., image filters, virtual scanners) to remove confidential information or detect malicious images. Similarly, *Nuwa* [41] enables automated offline image patching to reduce security threats.

Finding unpatched code in OS distributions: There are also parallels to the propagation of vulnerable code propagating within software packages themselves. For example, ReDeBug [29] is a scalable syntax-based pattern matching approach for finding unpatched copies in OS-distribution scale code bases. Some other work about the detection of cloned code [17, 13, 22, 30, 31] have applied to security. These works have conceptual similarity to vulnerability extrapolation in images. Both copied code and the reusable Docker images can lead to vulnerability propagation.

7. CONCLUSION

Docker Hub provides a public registry for users to store and share containerized-applications. In this paper, we studied the state of security vulnerabilities in these images. We proposed a scalable Docker Image Vulnerability Analysis (DIVA) framework for automatically discovering, downloading, and analyzing vulnerabilities in images from Docker Hub. DIVA also assesses vulnerability propagation between images. We used DIVA to analyze over 300,000 images and found significant and pervasive vulnerabilities in Docker Hub images. We also found strong correlations between top influential images and top ranked vulnerable packages, which implies that the widespread image vulnerabilities are likely the result of propagation from a small number of influential images. These findings demonstrate a strong need for more automated and systematic methods of applying security updates to Docker images and we believe DIVA provides a good foundation to meet the need with its stream-based Docker image processing framework.

8. ACKNOWLEDGMENTS

This work is supported by the NSA Science of Security Lablet at North Carolina State University, under Contract # H98230-14-C-0139. Any opinions, conclusions or recommendations expressed in this article are those of the authors and do not necessarily reflect the views of the funding agencies. The authors would also like to thank Adwait Nadkarni, our shepherd Dr. Florian Kelbert, and the anonymous reviewers for their valuable feedback during the writing of this paper.

9. REFERENCES

[1] Browse vulnerabilities by date from CVE Details. http://www.cvedetails.com/browse-by-date.php/.

[2] CVE-2015-1781. http://www.cvedetails.com/cve/CVE-2015-1781/.

[3] CVE-2015-4000. http://www.cvedetails.com/cve/CVE-2015-4000/.

[4] CVE: Common Vulnerabilities and Exposures. https://cve.mitre.org/.

[5] Docker Bench for Security. https://github.com/docker/docker-bench-security.

[6] National Vulnerability Database. https://nvd.nist.gov/home.cfm.

[7] NCSU Virtual Computing Lab. https://vcl.ncsu.edu/.

[8] NVD Common Vulnerability Scoring System. https://nvd.nist.gov/cvss.cfm.

[9] Repositories on Docker Hub. https://docs.docker.com/docker-hub/repos/.

[10] RHSA to CVE and CPE mapping. https://www.redhat.com/security/data/metrics/rhsamapcpe.txt.

[11] M. Almorsy, J. Grundy, I. Müller, et al. An analysis of the cloud computing security problem. In *Proceedings of APSEC 2010 Cloud Workshop, Sydney, Australia, 30th Nov*, 2010.

[12] Banyan Collector. https://github.com/banyanops/collector.

[13] S. Bellon, R. Koschke, G. Antoniol, J. Krinke, and E. Merlo. Comparison and evaluation of clone detection tools. *IEEE Transactions on Software Engineering*, 33(9):577–591, 2007.

[14] A. Bettini. Vulnerability exploitation in Docker container environments. https://www.blackhat.com/docs/eu-15/materials/eu-15-Bettini-Vulnerability-Exploitation-In-Docker-Container-Environments-wp.pdf, 2015.

[15] S. Bugiel, S. Nürnberger, T. Pöppelmann, A.-R. Sadeghi, and T. Schneider. AmazonIA: When elasticity snaps back. In *Proceedings of the 18th ACM Conference on Computer and Communications Security*, CCS '11, pages 389–400, New York, NY, USA, 2011. ACM.

[16] CoreOS Clair. https://github.com/coreos/clair.

[17] Y. Dang, D. Zhang, S. Ge, C. Chu, Y. Qu, and T. Xie. Xiao: tuning code clones at hands of engineers in practice. In *Proceedings of the 28th Annual Computer Security Applications Conference*, pages 369–378. ACM, 2012.

[18] Debian Security Bug Tracker. https://security-tracker.debian.org/tracker.

[19] B. DeHamer. Docker Hub Top 10. https//www.ctl.io/developers/blog/post/docker-hub-top-10/, August 2015.

[20] Docker Security Scanning. https://docs.docker.com/docker-cloud/builds/image-scan/.

[21] D. A. Fernandes, L. F. Soares, J. V. Gomes, M. M. Freire, and P. R. Inácio. Security issues in cloud

environments: a survey. *International Journal of Information Security*, 13(2):113–170, 2014.

[22] M. Gabel, J. Yang, Y. Yu, M. Goldszmidt, and Z. Su. Scalable and systematic detection of buggy inconsistencies in source code. In *ACM Sigplan Notices*, volume 45, pages 175–190. ACM, 2010.

[23] B. Grobauer, T. Walloschek, and E. Stocker. Understanding cloud computing vulnerabilities. *IEEE Security & Privacy*, 9(2):50–57, 2011.

[24] J. Gummaraju, T. Desikan, and Y. Turner. Over 30% of official images in docker hub contain high priority security vulnerabilities. Technical report, BanyanOps, 2015.

[25] K. Hashizume, D. G. Rosado, E. Fernández-Medina, and E. B. Fernandez. An analysis of security issues for cloud computing. *Journal of Internet Services and Applications*, 4(1):1, 2013.

[26] K. Hashizume, N. Yoshioka, and E. B. Fernandez. Three misuse patterns for cloud computing. *Security engineering for Cloud Computing: approaches and Tools*, pages 36–53, 2012.

[27] IBM's Vulnerability Advisor. http://www-03.ibm.com/press/us/en/pressrelease/47165.wss.

[28] Is FROM scratch the root of all Docker Images? https://www.ctl.io/developers/blog/post/is-from-scratch-the-root-of-all-docker-images/.

[29] J. Jang, A. Agrawal, and D. Brumley. Redebug: finding unpatched code clones in entire os distributions. In *Security and Privacy (SP), 2012 IEEE Symposium on*, pages 48–62. IEEE, 2012.

[30] L. Jiang, G. Misherghi, Z. Su, and S. Glondu. Deckard: Scalable and accurate tree-based detection of code clones. In *Proceedings of the 29th international conference on Software Engineering*, pages 96–105. IEEE Computer Society, 2007.

[31] T. Kamiya, S. Kusumoto, and K. Inoue. Ccfinder: a multilinguistic token-based code clone detection system for large scale source code. *IEEE Transactions on Software Engineering*, 28(7):654–670, 2002.

[32] Library of official images. https://github.com/docker-library/official-images/tree/master/library/.

[33] OpenSCAP Container Compliance. https://github.com/OpenSCAP/container-compliance.

[34] Red Hat Security Data. https://www.redhat.com/security/data/metrics/.

[35] D. Reimer, A. Thomas, G. Ammons, T. Mummert, B. Alpern, and V. Bala. Opening black boxes: using semantic information to combat virtual machine image sprawl. In *Proceedings of the fourth ACM SIGPLAN/SIGOPS international conference on Virtual execution environments*, pages 111–120. ACM, 2008.

[36] Twistlock. https://www.twistlock.com/product/vulnerabilitymanagement/.

[37] Ubuntu CVE Tracker. https://launchpad.net/ubuntu-cve-tracker.

[38] N. Viennot, E. Garcia, and J. Nieh. A measurement study of google play. In *The 2014 ACM International Conference on Measurement and Modeling of Computer Systems*, SIGMETRICS '14, pages 221–233, New York, NY, USA, 2014. ACM.

[39] J. Wei, X. Zhang, G. Ammons, V. Bala, and P. Ning. Managing security of virtual machine images in a cloud environment. In *Proceedings of the 2009 ACM workshop on Cloud computing security*, pages 91–96. ACM, 2009.

[40] S. Zhang, X. Zhang, and X. Ou. After we knew it: Empirical study and modeling of cost-effectiveness of exploiting prevalent known vulnerabilities across iaas cloud. In *Proceedings of the 9th ACM Symposium on Information, Computer and Communications Security*, ASIA CCS '14, pages 317–328, New York, NY, USA, 2014. ACM.

[41] W. Zhou, P. Ning, X. Zhang, G. Ammons, R. Wang, and V. Bala. Always up-to-date: scalable offline patching of vm images in a compute cloud. In *Proceedings of the 26th Annual Computer Security Applications Conference*, pages 377–386. ACM, 2010.

Ripple: Reflection Analysis for Android Apps in Incomplete Information Environments

Yifei Zhang, Tian Tan, Yue Li and Jingling Xue
School of Computer Science and Engineering, UNSW Australia

ABSTRACT

Despite its widespread use in Android apps, reflection poses graving problems for static security analysis. Currently, string inference is applied to handle reflection, resulting in significantly missed security vulnerabilities. In this paper, we bring forward the ubiquity of incomplete information environments (IIEs) for Android apps, where some critical data-flows are missing during static analysis, and the need for resolving reflective calls under IIEs. We present RIPPLE, the first IIE-aware static reflection analysis for Android apps that resolves reflective calls more soundly than string inference. Validation with 17 popular Android apps from Google Play demonstrates the effectiveness of RIPPLE in discovering reflective targets with a low false positive rate. As a result, RIPPLE enables FlowDroid to find hundreds of sensitive data leakages that would otherwise be missed.

Keywords

Android; Reflection Analysis; Pointer Analysis

1. INTRODUCTION

Static analysis is a fundamental tool for detecting security threats in Android apps. However, reflection poses graving problems for static analysis. According to a recent study [19], malware authors can use reflection to hide malicious behaviors from detection by all the 10 commercial static analyzers tested. Similarly, academic static analyzers either ignore reflection [7, 17] or handle it partially [3], resulting in also significantly missed program behaviors.

In Android apps, reflection serves a number of purposes, including (1) plug-in and external library support, (2) hidden API method invocation, (3) access to private API methods and fields, and (4) backward compatibility. Indeed, reflection is widely used in both benign and malicious Android apps. For a sample of 202 top-chart free apps from Google Play that we analyzed on 15 April 2016, we found that 92.6% of these apps use reflection. Elsewhere, in a malware sam-

ple consisting of 6,141 Android apps from the VriusShare project [1], 48.13% of them also use reflection.

Reflection can introduce implicitly many caller-callee edges into the call graph of the program. If some targets at a reflective call are ignored, their corresponding caller-callee edges will not be discovered. As a result, possible security vulnerabilities in the invisible part of the program, such as Obad [26] and FakeInstaller [20], may go undetected.

Therefore, the objective of reflection analysis is to discover the targets at reflective calls (e.g., objects created, methods called and fields accessed). For Android apps, regular string inference is currently performed to discover the string constants used as class/method/field names at reflective calls [4, 6, 9]. This is inadequate for framework-based and event-driven Android apps. In practice, reflection analysis is usually performed together with many other analyses, including pointer analysis [8, 10, 11, 13, 22], inter-component communication (ICC) analysis [16, 17], callback analysis [3, 8, 27], and library summary generation [2, 5, 8]. Soundness, which demands over-approximation, is often sacrificed in order to achieve efficiency and precision tradeoffs. As a result, class/method/field names used at reflective calls may be non-constant (either non-null but statically unknown or simply null). Similarly, the receiver objects at reflectively method call sites (i.e., the objects pointed to by v in `Method.invoke(v,...)`) may be non-null with statically unknown types or simply null. All these can happen due to, for example, unsound library summaries, unmodeled Android services, code obfuscation, and unsound handling of hard-to-analyzed Android features such as ICC, callbacks and built-in containers. In this case, regular string inference, which keeps track of only constant strings, is ineffective, resulting in missed program behaviors.

In this paper, we bring forward the ubiquity of incomplete information environments (IIEs) for Android apps, where some critical data-flows are inevitably missing during static analysis. As discussed above, these include not only the case when class/method/field names are non-null but statically unknown, which is studied previously for Java programs [10, 11, 13, 22], but also the case when these string names are null, which is investigated for the first time for Android apps in this paper. We therefore emphasize the need for resolving reflective calls in Android apps under IIEs. To this end, we introduce RIPPLE, the first IIE-aware static reflection analysis for Android apps that can resolve reflective calls more soundly than string inference at a low false positive rate. We also demonstrate its effectiveness in improving the precision of an important security analysis.

CODASPY'17, March 22-24, 2017, Scottsdale, AZ, USA

© 2017 ACM. ISBN 978-1-4503-4523-1/17/03. . . $15.00

DOI: http://dx.doi.org/10.1145/3029806.3029814

For an extended version of this paper, we refer to [28]. In summary, this work makes the following contributions:

- We present (for the first time) an empirical study for IIEs in real-world Android apps, and examine some common sources of incomplete information, discuss their impact on reflection analysis, and motivate the need for developing an IIE-aware reflection analysis.

- We introduce RIPPLE, the first IIE-aware reflection analysis for Android apps, which performs type inference automatically (without requiring user annotations) and thus subsumes regular string inference.

- We have implemented RIPPLE in SOOT with RIPPLE working together with its pointer analysis, SPARK. We evaluate the soundness, precision, scalability and effectiveness of RIPPLE by using 17 popular real-world Android apps from Google Play. RIPPLE discovers 72 more (true) reflective targets than string inference in seconds at a low false positive rate of 21.9%. This translates into a total of 310 more sensitive data leakages detected by FLOWDROID [3].

2. IIES IN ANDROID APPS

There are two types of missing information under IIEs. In one case, the data flows needed for resolving reflective calls exist but are statically unknown. For example, class/method /field names used at reflective calls are non-null but unknown. We can resolve such reflective calls by performing type inference, as done for Java programs [10, 11, 22].

In the other case, the data flows needed for resolving reflective calls are completely missing, indicated by the presence of null. To understand this case, which has never been studied before, for Android apps, we have performed an empirical study on 45 Android apps, with 20 popular Android apps from Google Play and 25 malware samples from the VirusShare Project [1]. We discuss the four most common sources of incomplete information in IIEs: (1) undetermined intents, (2) behavior-unknown libraries, (3) unresolved built-in containers, and (4) unmodeled services. We delve into their bytecode to explain why regular string inference is inadequate, since it fails to enable FLOWDROID [3] to discover many data leaks from *sources* (API calls that inject sensitive information) to *sinks* (API calls that leak information). We also provide insights on why our IIE-aware RIPPLE can handle IIEs more effectively than string inference.

2.1 Undetermined Intents

ICC via intents is one of the most fundamental features in Android as it enables some components to process the data originating from other components. Thus, the components in an Android app function as building blocks for the entire system, enhancing intra- and inter-application code reuse.

In practice, some inter-component control- and data-flows cannot be captured by ICC analysis [16, 17]. If a data flow from an intent into a reflective call is missing, the reflection call cannot be fully resolved. The code snippet in Figure 1 taken from the game *Angry Birds* illustrates this problem.

In this app, the class name cName is obtained from an intent (line 4) and then used in a call to Class.forName() (line 5) to create a class metaobject clz. Then, an object of this class is created reflectively (line 6) and assigned to mmBase after a downcast to MMBaseActivity is performed. Finally, onCreate() is invoked on this object (line 7).

Android App Name: Angry Birds
```
1 public class MMActivity extends Activity {
2   protected void onCreate(Bundle savedInstanceState) {
3     Intent intent = getIntent();
4     String cName = intent.getStringExtra("class");
5     Class clz = Class.forName(cName);
6     MMBaseActivity mmBase = (MMBaseActivity)clz.newInstance();

7     mmBase.onCreate(savedInstanceState);
    ... } }
```

Figure 1: Undetermined intents. Here, --► denotes a missed data-flow and ⟶ the post-dominating-cast-based type inference used in Ripple.

To discover what cName is, we applied IC3, a state-of-the-art ICC analysis [17], but to no avail. Thus, the data-flow for cName, denoted by --►, is missing, rendering clz to be a null pointer. In this case, string inference is ineffective. As a result, the reflectively allocated object in line 6 and the subsequent call on this object in line 7 are ignored.

RIPPLE is aware of the incomplete information caused by this undetermined intent, which manifests itself in the form of cName = null. By taking advantage of the post-dominant cast MMBaseActivity for clz.newInstance() in line 6, RIPPLE infers that mmBase may point to five objects with their types ranging over MMBaseActivity and its four subtypes, which are all confirmed to be possible by manual code inspection. As a result, RIPPLE discovers 3,928 caller-callee edges in lines 5 – 7 (directly or indirectly), thereby enabling FLOWDROID [3] to detect 49 new sensitive data leaks that will be all missed by string inference in this part of the app that has been made analyzable by RIPPLE.

2.2 Behavior-Unknown Libraries

To accelerate the analysis of an application, the side effects of a library on the application are often summarized. Library summaries are either written manually [8] or generated automatically [2, 5]. However, both approaches are error-prone and often fail to model all the side-effects of a library for all possible analyses. DroidSafe [8] provides the Android Device Implementation (ADI) to model the Android API and runtime manually, with about 1.3 MLOC for Android 4.4.3. However, as the Android framework evolves with both new features and undocumented code added, how to keep this ADI in sync can be a daunting task.

Therefore, unsound library summaries are an important source of incomplete information in IIEs. The code snippet in Figure 2 taken from the app *Twist* illustrates this issue.

Android App Name: Twist
```
1 private static void writeToLog(UnityAdsDeviceLogEntry entry) {
2   String mName = entry.getLogLevel().getReceivingMethodName();
3   Method logMtd = Log.class.getMethod(mName,
                            String.class, String.class);
4   String tag = ...;
5   String msg = ...;                    Sensitive data
6   logMtd.invoke(null, tag, msg); } }

7 public class Log {
8   public static int i(String tag, String msg) {}
9   public static int d(String tag, String msg) {}  Sink
10  public static int w(String tag, String msg) {}  Calls
11  public static int e(String tag, String msg) {}
12  public static int v(String tag, String msg) {}
13  public static int wtf(String tag, String msg) {}
    ... }
```

Figure 2: Behavior-unknown libraries. --► marks the methods invoked at a reflective call, ⟶ denotes sensitive data-flow, and ● denotes tainted data.

This code snippet is used to log messages at different verbosity levels. In line 2, a method name mName is retrieved.

In line 3, its method metaobject `logMtd` is created. In line 6, this method, which is static, is invoked reflectively.

If we apply FLOWDROID [3] to detect data leaks in this app, by relying on string inference to perform reflection analysis, then the reflective call `logMtd.invoke()` in line 6 will be ignored. In FLOWDROID, the behaviors of maps are not summarized. However, `entry` was retrieved from a `HashMap` and then passed to `writeToLog`. Thus, `mName = null`, rendering string inference to be ineffective.

RIPPLE is aware of unsound library summaries and thus attempts to infer the target methods at `logMtd.invoke()`. Based on the facts that (1) these methods are static (since the receiver object is null), declared in or inherited by class `android.util.Log`, (2) each target method has two formal parameters, and (3) each parameter has a type that is either `String` or its supertype or its subtype, RIPPLE concludes that the six target methods, `i()`, `d()`, `w()`, `e()`, `v()` and `wtf()`, as shown in class `android.util.Log` may be potentially invoked. According to FLOWDROID, these six methods are all sinks for sensitive data contained in `msg`. Thus, resolving `logMtd.invoke()` causes 12 data leaks from two different sensitive data sources to be reported (as 2 sources × 6 sinks = 12 leaks). By manual code inspection, we found that the first four methods, `i()`, `d()`, `w()` and `e()`, shaded in class `android.util.Log` are true targets, implying that 8 data leaks will not be reported if string inference is used.

2.3 Unresolved Built-in Containers

Android apps can receive a variety of user inputs from, e.g., intents, databases, internet, GUI actions, and system events. These data are stored in different types of containers, such as `Bundle`, `SharedPreferences`, `ContentValues` and `JSONObject`, for different purposes. Unhandled user inputs represent an important source of incomplete information in IIEs. The code snippet in Figure 3 taken from a game named *Seven Knights* illustrates this problem.

```
Android App Name: Seven Knights
1 public static WXMediaMessage fromBundle(Bundle bundle) {
2   String cName = bundle.getString("_wxobject_identifier_');
3   Class clz = Class.forName(cName);
4   IMediaObject media = (IMediaObject) clz.newInstance();

5   media.unserialize(bundle); }
6 public class WXFileObject implements IMediaObject {
7   public void unserialize(Bundle bundle) {
8     Object s = bundle.getString('_wxfileobject_filePath');
  ... } }
```

Figure 3: Unresolved Bundles.

In this code snippet, different types of objects are created (line 4) to handle different types of media data according to their unique identifiers stored in a `Bundle` (line 2), which is constructed according to the types of media introduced by third-party apps. `IMediaObject` is an interface implemented by eight types (i.e., classes) of media, with only `WXFileObject` shown partially. Therefore, `cName` represents the name of one of these eight classes. In line 4, `media` points to a reflectively created object of the class identified by `cName`. In line 5, a call is made to `unserialize()` on the receiver object pointed to by `media` with `bundle` as its argument.

If we apply again FLOWDROID to detect data leaks in this app, by relying on string inference to resolve the reflective calls in the app, then `cName` will be null, since the behaviors of bundles are not modeled in FLOWDROID. As a result, the reflectively created object in line 4 and the subsequent call on this object in line 5 will be ignored.

By being IIE-aware, RIPPLE will infer the inputs retrieved from `bundle` to resolve the call to `clz.newInstance()` in line 4. By taking advantage of the post-dominant cast `IMediaObject` for this reflective call, RIPPLE deduces that `media` points to potentially eight objects with their types ranging over all the eight classes implementing `IMediaObject`, confirmed by manual code inspection. As a result, a total of 37 caller-callee edges, together with 16 sensitive data sources, which would otherwise be missed by string inference, are discovered in lines 3 – 5 directly or indirectly. Currently, these 16 sensitive data sources do not flow to any sinks but may do so in a future app release. The resulting leaks will be then detected by FLOWDROID, assisted by RIPPLE.

2.4 Unmodeled Services

The Android framework provides an abstraction of abundant services for a mobile device, such as obtaining the device status, making phone calls, and sending text messages, which are all related to critical program behaviors. These services are usually initialized during system startup and subsequently used by calling the factory methods in the Android framework with often reflective calls involved. Unsound modeling for Android's system-wide services can be an important source of incomplete information in IIEs. The code snippet in Figure 4 taken from a text message management app named *GO SMS Pro* illustrates this issue.

```
Android App Name: Go SMS Pro
1 public void getSubScriberId() {
2   Class clz = Class.forName("android.telephony.TelephonyManager");
3   Method getDefMtd = clz.getMethod("getDefault");
4   Object telephonyManager = getDefMtd.invoke(null);
5   Method getSubIdMtd = clz.getMethod("getSubScriberId");
6   String id = (String) getSubIdMtd.invoke(telephonyManager);
  ... }
```
Sink   Sensitive   Source call
         data

Figure 4: Unmodeled services.

In line 2, `clz` represents a class metaobject for `android.telephony.TelephonyManager`. In line 3, `getDefMtd` represents a method metaobject for a static method named `getDefault` in `clz`. In line 4, this method is invoked reflectively, with its returned object, an instance of `clz`, assigned to `telephonyManager`. In lines 5 – 6, a method metaobject, `getSubIdMtd`, for an instance method named `getSubScribeId` in `clz` is created and then invoked reflectively on the receiver object pointed to by `telephonyManager`.

In this code snippet, all the class and method names are string constants. Thus, regular string inference can resolve precisely the reflective targets at all the reflective calls shown. However, this still does not enable the target methods invoked in line 6 to be analyzed, because the `getDefault` method invoked in line 4 is part of the hidden API and thus not available for analysis. Thus, `telephonyManager` is null, causing the reflective call in line 6 to be skipped.

RIPPLE is aware of the existence of unmodeled services. By examining the class type in the `getSubIdMtd` metaobject, RIPPLE concludes that `telephonyManager` points to an object of type `android.telephony.TelephonyManager`. As a result, the reflective call in line 6 can be resolved, resulting in the target method `getSubscriberId` to be discovered. For this app, FLOWDROID is unscalable. Otherwise, the potential data link as shown will be detected automatically.

Finally, if the `getDefault` method is native with its method body unmodeled but available for analysis, then RIPPLE will be able to infer in line 4 that `telephonyManager` may point to an object of type `android.telephony.TelephonyManager`. As a result, the reflective call in line 6 can also be resolved.

3. METHODOLOGY

Figure 5 depicts an overview of RIPPLE, an IIE-aware reflection analysis introduced in this paper for Android apps. To handle IIEs effectively, RIPPLE resolves reflective calls in the presence of incomplete information about these calls, so that their induced caller-callee edges can be discovered.

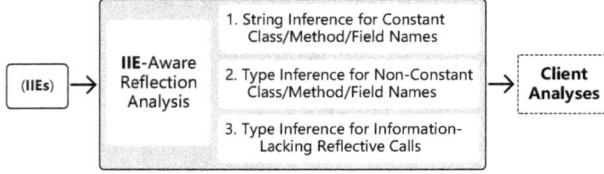

Figure 5: An overview of RIPPLE.

We have developed RIPPLE by leveraging recent advances on reflection analysis for Java [10, 11]. Conceptually, RIPPLE performs reflection analysis by distinguishing three cases:

- **Case 1. String Inference for Constant Strings.** If class/method/field names used at reflective calls are string constants, regular string inference is conducted.

- **Case 2. Type Inference for Unknown Strings.** If class/method/field names are non-constant but non-null strings, which may be read from configuration files or command lines, then type inference that was previously introduced for Java programs [10, 11, 13, 22] can be leveraged.

- **Case 3. Type Inference for Information-Missing Reflective Calls.** Again, type inference is performed to infer the missing information at reflective calls in the following three categories, as reviewed in Section 2:

  - **Null-Name.** Class, method or field names are null, as illustrated in Figure 1 (with `cName = null` for undetermined intents), Figure 2 (with `mName = null` for behavior-unknown libraries), and Figure 3 (with `cName = null` for unmodeled bundles). We will replace a null object by an unknown string and then go back to Case 2.

  - **Missing-RecvObj.** Given a call to `mtd.invoke(y,...)`, a target method pointed to by `mtd` does not have a corresponding receiver object pointed to by `y`, as illustrated in Figure 4 for the `getSubscriberId` method invoked in line 6, where `telephonyManager = null`. If we know the class type of the target method pointed to by `mtd`, its corresponding receiver object can be inferred.

  - **Missing-RetObj.** Given `x = mtd.invoke(...)`, a target method pointed to by `mtd` is available for analysis but its method body is unmodeled. This can happen to `telephonyManager = getDefMt.invoke(null)` in Figure 4, as discussed in Section 2, when the `getDefault` method is hypothetically assumed to be an unmodeled native method. In general, if we know the return type of the target method pointed to by `mtd`, then objects of this type or its subtypes are created and assigned to `x`.

To the best of our knowledge, RIPPLE is the first automated reflection analysis (without relying on user annotations) for handling Cases 2 and 3 and also the first for handling Cases 1 – 3 in a unified framework for Android apps.

In RIPPLE, reflection analysis is performed together with pointer analysis mutually recursively, as effectively one single analysis. Once the entire analysis for an app is over, its call graph is readily available (at the same time).

4. FORMALISM

We formalize RIPPLE as a form of reflection analysis, performed together with a flow- and context-insensitive pointer analysis. We restrict ourselves to a small core of the Java reflection API. For simplicity, we consider only instance methods as static methods are handled similarly.

4.1 Notations

Figure 6 gives the domains used in our formalism. The abstract heap objects are labeled by their allocation sites. $\mathbb{C}$ represents the set of class metaobjects and $\mathbb{M}$ the set of method metaobjects. The class type of a class or method metaobject is identified by its superscript and the signature of a method metaobject, which consists of the method name and descriptor (i.e., return type and parameter types), is identified by its subscript. In particular, u indicates an unknown class type or an unknown method signature (with some parts of the signature being statically unknown).

class type	$t, u \in \mathbb{T}$
variable	$v \in \mathbb{V}$
abstract heap object	$o_1^t, o_2^t, o_-, ... \in \mathbb{O}$
class metaobject	$c^t, c^u, c_-, ... \in \mathbb{C}$
method metaobject	$m_s^t, m_s^u, m_u^t, m_u^u, m_-, ... \in \mathbb{M} = \mathbb{T} \times \mathbb{S}$
method name	$n \in \mathbb{N}$
method parameter type	$p \in \mathbb{P} = \bigcup_{i=0}^{\infty} \mathbb{T}^i$
method signature	$s, u \in \mathbb{S} = \mathbb{T} \times \mathbb{N} \times \mathbb{P}$

Figure 6: Domains.

4.2 Pointer Analysis

Figure 7 gives a standard formulation of a flow- and context-insensitive Andersen's pointer analysis. $pts(v)$ represents the points-to set of a pointer v. An array object is analyzed with its elements collapsed to a single field, say, arr.

Figure 7: Rules for pointer analysis.

In a reflection-free program, only five types of statements exist. In [P-NEW], o_i^t uniquely identifies the abstract object created as an instance of t at this allocation site, labeled by i. [P-COPY], [P-LOAD] and [P-STORE] are self-explanatory.

In [P-CALL] (for non-reflective calls), the function $dispatch(o_i^t, m)$ is used to resolve the virtual dispatch of method m on the receiver object o_i^t to be m'. We assume that m' has a formal parameter m'_{this} for the receiver object and $m'_{p_0}, ..., m'_{p_{n-1}}$ for the remaining parameters, and a pseudo-variable m'_{ret} is used to hold the return value of m'.

$$\text{Class clz = Class.forName(cName)} \qquad [\text{C12-FORNAME}]$$

$$\frac{o^{String}_- \in pts(\text{cName}) \quad c^- = toClass(o^{String}_-)}{pts(\text{clz}) \supseteq \begin{cases} \{c^t\} & \text{if } c^- = c^t \\ \{c^u\} & \text{if } c^- = c^u \end{cases}}$$

$$\text{Method mtd = clz.getMethod(mName, \_)} \qquad [\text{C12-GETMTD}]$$

$$\frac{o^{String}_- \in pts(\text{mName}) \quad c^- \in pts(\text{clz}) \quad s \in toMtdSig(c^-, o^{String}_-)}{pts(\text{mtd}) \supseteq \begin{cases} \{m_s^t\} & \text{if } c^- = c^t \\ \{m_s^u\} & \text{if } c^- = c^u \end{cases}}$$

$$i : \text{x = (T) clz.newInstance()} \qquad [\text{C12-NEW}]$$

$$\frac{c^- \in pts(\text{clz})}{pts(\text{x}) \supseteq \begin{cases} \{o_i^t\} & \text{if } c^- = c^t \\ \{o_i^s \mid t <: T\} & \text{if } c^- = c^u \end{cases}}$$

$$\text{\_ = mtd.invoke(y, \_)} \qquad [\text{C12-INVTYPE}]$$

$$\frac{o_-^t \in pts(\text{y}) \quad m^u_- \in pts(\text{mtd})}{pts(\text{mtd}) \supseteq \{m^t_-\}}$$

$$\text{\_ = (T) mtd.invoke(\_, args)} \qquad [\text{C12-INVSIG}]$$

$$\frac{m_u^- \in pts(\text{mtd}) \quad t \ll: T \quad p \in toParasTys(\text{args})}{pts(\text{mtd}) \supseteq \{m_s^- \mid s.para = p \land s.ret = t\}}$$

Figure 8: Rules for Cases 1 and 2 in Figure 5.

4.3 Reflection Analysis: Cases 1 and 2

Figure 8 gives the rules for resolving reflective calls for Cases 1 and 2 in Figure 5 simultaneously. In Case 1, regular string inference for constant class and method names is applied. In Case 2, type inference for non-constant but non-null class and method names is applied. Recall that $<:$ denotes the standard subtyping relation.

[C12-FORNAME] handles a `Class.forName(cName)` call. For the auxiliary function $toClass : \mathbb{O} \to \mathbb{C}$, $toClass(o^{String}_-)$ takes a string object o^{String}_- and returns its corresponding class metaobject. If o^{String}_- is a constant, then $toClass(o) = c^t$, where t is the class type named by `cName`. Otherwise, $toClass(o^{String}_-) = c^u$, since `cName` is a non-constant but no-null string. The missing type u may be inferred later.

[C12-GETMTD] handles a `clz.getMethod(mName, ...)` call analogously. For the auxiliary function, $toMtdSig : \mathbb{C} \times \mathbb{O} \to \mathcal{P}(\mathbb{S})$, $toMtdSig(c^-, o^{String}_-)$ returns the set of method signatures for the methods declared in or inherited by the class c^- with their method name identified by `mName`. If $c^- = c^u$ but `mName` is a string constant, say, "**foo**", then **foo** is recorded: $toMtdSig(c^-, o^{String}_-) = \{(u, \mathtt{foo}, u)\}$. If `mName` is a non-constant but no-null string, then $toMtdSig(c^-, o^{String}_-) = \{(u)\}$. Therefore, this rule distinguishes two cases for every signature $s \in toMtdSig(c^-, o^{String}_-)$. If $c^- = c^t$ is a statically known type t, a method metaobject m_s^t is created. Otherwise, a method metaobject m_s^u is created. In both cases, the missing information may be inferred later.

[C12-NEW] handles reflective object allocation at a call to `x = (T) clz.newInstance()`, where T symbolizes an intra-procedurally post-dominating type cast for the call if it exists or `java.lang.Object` otherwise. If $c^- = c^t$ is a statically known type t, then `x = clz.newInstance()` degenerates into `x = new t()` and can thus be handled as in [P-NEW]. Otherwise, $c^- = c^u$. If T $\neq$ `java.lang.Object`, then u is inferred to be T or any of its subtypes.

There are two rules for handling reflective method invocation. To infer a target method invoked reflectively, we need to infer its class type, which is handled by [C12-INVTYPE], and its signature, which is handled by [C12-INVSIG].

[C12-INVTYPE] is simple. The class type of a method metaobject m^u is inferred to be m^t_- for every possible dynamic type t of every receiver object pointed to by y.

[C12-INVSIG] is more involved in handling (T) `mtd.invoke(_, args)`, where T is defined identically as in [C12-NEW]. This rule attempts to infer the missing information in the signature s of a method from its `args` and its possible return type. We write $s.para$ and $s.ret$ to identify its parameter types and return type, respectively. The typing relation $\ll:$ is defined by distinguishing two cases. First, $u \ll:$ `java.lang.Object`. Second, if t is not `java.lang.Object`, then $t' \ll: t$ holds if and only if $t' <: t$ or $t <: t'$ holds. Therefore, $s.ret$ is deduced from a post-dominating cast T (which is not `java.lang.Object`). As for $s.para$, we infer it intra-procedurally from `args`. For the auxiliary function $toParaTys : \bigcup_{i=0}^{\infty} \mathbb{V}^i \to \mathcal{P}(\mathbb{S})$, $toParaTys(\text{args})$ returns the set of parameter types of a target method invoked with its argument list `args`, computed intra-procedurally for efficiency reasons. If `args` is not defined locally, $toParaTys(\text{args}) = \varnothing$. Otherwise, let D_i be the set of declared types of all possible variables assigned to the i-th argument $args[i]$. Let $P_i = \{t' \mid t \in D_i \land (t' <: t \lor t <: t')\}$. Then, $toParaTys(\text{args}) = P_0 \times \cdots \times P_{n-1}$. With $s.para$ or $s.ret$ inferred for m_u^-, `mtd` is made to point to a new method metaobject m_s^-, where s contains the missing information in u deduced via inference.

4.4 Reflection Analysis: Case 3

Figure 9 gives the rules for resolving reflective calls for Case 3 in Figure 5. There are four rules for handling three categories of incomplete information, NULL-NAME, MISSING-RECVOBJ and MISSING-RETOBJ, as discussed in Section 3.

$$\text{Class clz = Class.forName(cName)} \qquad [\text{C3-FORNAME}]$$

$$\frac{pts(\text{cName}) = \varnothing}{pts(\text{clz}) \supseteq \{c^u\}}$$

$$\text{Method mtd = clz.getMethod(mName, \_)} \qquad [\text{C3-GETMTD}]$$

$$\frac{pts(\text{mName}) = \varnothing \quad c^- \in pts(\text{clz})}{pts(\text{mtd}) \supseteq \begin{cases} \{m_u^t\} & \text{if } c^- = c^t \\ \{m_u^u\} & \text{if } c^- = c^u \end{cases}}$$

$$i : \text{\_ = mtd.invoke(y, \_)} \qquad [\text{C3-INVRECV}]$$

$$\frac{t'' \in (\{t \mid m_-^t \in pts(\text{mtd})\} \setminus \{t' \mid o_-^t \in pts(\text{y}) \land t <: t'\}) \quad t'' \neq \text{java.lang.Object}}{pts(\text{y}) \supseteq \{o_i^{t'''} \mid t''' \ll: t''\}}$$

$$i : \text{x = mtd.invoke(\_, \_)} \qquad [\text{C3-INVRET}]$$

$$\frac{m_s^- \in pts(\text{mtd}) \quad s.ret = t \quad t' <: t \quad \forall o_-^{t'} \in pts(\text{x}) : t' \not<: t}{pts(\text{x}) \supseteq \{o^{t'}\}} \quad t \neq \text{java.lang.Object}$$

Figure 9: Rules for Case 3 in Figure 5.

[C3-FORNAME] and [C3-GETMTD] deal with NULL-NAME by treating null as a non-constant string and then resorting to [C12-NEW], [C12-INVTYPE] and [C12-INVSIG] to infer the missing information. [C3-FORNAME] handles a `Class.forName(cName)` call with `cName = null` identically as [C12-FORNAME] for handling a `Class.forName(cName)` call when `cName` is non-constant. [C3-GETMTD] handles a `clz.getMethod(mName, ...)` call with `mName = null` identically as [C12-GETMTD] for handling a `clz.getMethod(mName, ...)` call when `mName` is non-constant.

[C3-INVRECV] handles MISSING-RECVOBJ by inferring the missing receiver objects pointed to by `y` from the known class types of all possibly invokable target methods, except that `java.lang.Object` is excluded for precision reasons. This rule covers an important special case when $pts(y) = \varnothing$.

[C3-INVRET] handles MISSING-RETOBJ by inferring the missing objects returned from a target method that is unmodeled (with its body missing) but available for analysis from the return type $s.\texttt{ret}$ of its signature s. Objects of all possible subtypes of $s.\texttt{ret}$ are included in $pts(x)$, unless x already points to an object of one of these subtypes.

4.5 Transforming Reflective to Regualar Calls

Fig. 10 shows how to transform a reflective into a regular call, which will be analyzed by pointer analysis.

$$\frac{x = \text{mtd.invoke(y, args)} \qquad\qquad\qquad [\text{T-Inv}]}{\mathtt{m}_s^t \in pts(\text{mtd}) \quad m' \in MTD(\mathtt{m}_s^t) \quad o_i^t \in pts(\text{args})}$$
$$\frac{o_j^{t'} \in pts(o_i.arr) \quad t'' \text{ is declaring type of } m'_{p_k} \quad k \in [0, n-1] \quad t' <: t''}{\{o_j^{t'}\} \subseteq pts(\text{arg}_k) \quad x = y.m'(\text{arg}_0, ..., \text{arg}_{n-1})}$$

Figure 10: Rule for *Transformation*.

For the auxiliary function $MTD : \mathbb{M} \rightarrow \mathcal{P}(M)$, where M is the set of methods in the program, $MTD(m_s^t)$ is the standard lookup function for finding the methods in M according to a declaring class t and a signature s for a method metaobject, except that (1) the return type in s is also considered and (2) any u in s is treated as a wild card.

As discussed earlier, `args` points to a 1-D array of type `Object[]`, with its elements collapsed to a single field arr during the pointer analysis. Let $\text{arg}_0, ..., \text{arg}_{n-1}$ be the n freshly created arguments to be passed to each potential target method m' found by in $MTD(m_s^t)$. Let $m'_{p_0}, ..., m'_{p_{n-1}}$ be the n parameters (excluding *this*) of m', such that the declaring type of m'_{p_k} is t''. We include $o_j^{t'}$ to $pts(\text{arg}_k)$ only when $t' <: t''$ holds in order to filter out the objects that cannot be assigned to m'_{p_k}. Finally, the regular call obtained can be analyzed by [P-CALL] in Figure 7.

5. EVALUATION

We show that RIPPLE is more effective than string reference by addressing the four research questions:

- **RQ1.** Is RIPPLE capable of discovering more reflective targets, i.e., more sound than string inference?

- **RQ2.** Can RIPPLE achieve this with a good precision?

- **RQ3.** Does RIPPLE scale for real-world Android apps?

- **RQ4.** Is RIPPLE effective in enabling existing Android security analyses to detect security vulnerabilities?

To answer RQ1 – RQ3, we examine the reflective targets resolved by RIPPLE in Android apps. To answer RQ4, we investigate how RIPPLE enables FLOWDROID [3], a taint analysis for Android apps, to find more sensitive data leaks.

Real-World Android Apps. We examined the top-chart free apps from Google Play downloaded on 15 April 2016, which are the most popular apps in the official app store. A set of 17 apps is selected, such that they exhibit a wide range of incomplete information with null class and method names and are scalable under FLOWDROID within 2 hours.

State-of-the-Art Reflection Analysis. To resolve reflection for Android apps, there are only two existing static techniques, with both performing string inference, CHECKER [4, 6] and DROIDRA [9]. We cannot compare with CHECKER since its reflection analysis relies on user annotations. We cannot compare with DROIDRA either, since its latest opensource tool (released on 9 September 2016) is unstable [28]. Instead of comparing with CHECKER and DROIDRA directly, we compare RIPPLE with STRINF, which is a simplified RIPPLE that performs regular string inference in Case 1.

Implementation. We have implemented RIPPLE in SOOT, a static analysis framework for Android and Java programs. RIPPLE works with its SPARK, a flow- and context-insensitive pointer analysis, to resolve reflection and points-to information in a program. Based on the results of this joint analysis, the call graph of the program, on which many security analyses such as FLOWDROID operate, can be constructed.

Currently, RIPPLE handles a core part of the Java reflection API: `Class.forName()`, `Class.newInstance()`, `Method.invoke()`, and all four method-introspecting calls, `Method.getMethod()`, `Method.getDeclaredMethod()`, `Method.getMethods()`, and `Method.getDeclaredMethods()`.

Computing Platform. Our experiments are carried out on a Xeon E5-2650 2GHz machine with 64GB RAM running Ubuntu 14.04 LTS. The time measured for analyzing an app by a particular analysis is the average of 20 runs.

5.1 RQ1: More Soundness

Table 1 compares RIPPLE and STRINF in terms of the number of reflective targets discovered at all reflective calls to `Class.newInstance()` and `Method.invoke()`. For each of these two methods, only its calls reachable from the harness `main()` used during the analysis are included. We determine whether a target is true or not by manual code inspection.

By design, RIPPLE always finds every true target that STRINF does. In 11 out of the 17 apps, RIPPLE has successfully discovered more true targets than STRINF. This highlights the importance of making reflection analysis fully IIE-aware for Android apps, by handling not only Case 2 as for Java programs [10, 11, 13, 22] but also Case 3.

In the 17 apps, RIPPLE finds 64 and 168 but STRINF finds only 29 and 131 true targets for `Class.newInstance()` and `Method.invoke()`, respectively. Therefore, for both methods combined, RIPPLE finds 232 but STRINF finds only 160 true targets in total, yielding a net gain of 72 true targets and thus a 45% increase in soundness on reflection analysis.

Let us revisit Figure 1. For the call to `clz.newInstance()` in line 6, RIPPLE infers five reflectively created objects, which are all true targets configured to provide different forms of advertisement. A similar pattern appears also in the app named *Dumb Ways to Die*. Let us consider now Figure 3. For the call to `clz.newInstance()` in line 4, RIPPLE infers 8 reflectively created objects, which are all true targets used for handling eight different types of media according to user inputs. All these targets are missed by STRINF, which relies only on a simple string analysis for string constants.

5.2 RQ2: Precision

Table 1 reveals also the false positive rates for STRINF and RIPPLE. RIPPLE finds a total of 297 reflective targets with 232 true targets, representing a false positive rate of 21.9%. STRINF finds a total of 167 reflective targets with 160 true targets, representing a false positive rate of 4.2%.

Due to 72 more true targets discovered, as discussed in Section 5.1, RIPPLE is regarded to exhibit a satisfactory precision for Android apps. For many security analyses such as security vetting and malware detection, and even debugging, it is important to analyze reflection-related program behaviors even if doing so may cause some false warnings to be triggered. Consider the app in Figure 2. For the call to `logMtd.invoke(null, tag, msg)` in line 6, RIPPLE infers its target to be the six methods, `i()`, `d()`, `w()`, `e()`, `v()` and

App (Package Name)	STRINF								RIPPLE							
	Class.newInstance()				Method.invoke()				Class.newInstance				Method.invoke()			
	#Calls		#Targets		#Calls		#Targets		#Calls		#Targets		#Calls		#Targets	
	Reachable	Resolved	Resolved	True	Reachable	Resolved	Resolved	True	Reachable	Resolved	Resolved	True	Reachable	Resolved	Resolved	True
com.facebook.orca	0	0	0	0	7	0	0	0	0	0	0	0	7	1	7	7
com.netmarble.sknightsgb	2	0	0	0	11	4	8	4	2	2	26	11	11	4	8	4
com.productmadness.hovmobile	1	0	0	0	7	5	31	29	1	1	11	1	7	5	31	29
com.facebook.moments	0	0	0	0	5	0	0	0	0	0	0	0	5	1	7	7
me.msqrd.android	0	0	0	0	11	4	4	4	0	0	0	0	11	4	4	4
com.nordcurrent.canteenhd	3	0	0	0	16	5	6	5	4	3	27	10	20	5	6	5
com.ea.game.simcitymobile_row	0	0	0	0	6	2	2	2	0	0	0	0	6	2	2	2
com.imangi.templerun	0	0	0	0	7	1	1	1	0	0	0	0	7	1	1	1
com.rovio.angrybirds	3	1	1	1	10	3	3	3	3	2	6	6	14	8	13	11
com.sgn.pandapop.gp	0	0	0	0	13	3	3	3	0	0	0	0	13	3	3	3
com.gameloft.android.ANMP.GloftA8HM	1	1	16	16	9	0	0	0	1	1	16	16	9	0	0	0
com.appsorama.kleptocats	2	2	5	5	3	0	0	0	2	2	5	5	3	1	6	4
air.au.com.metro.DumbWaysToDie	1	0	0	0	18	8	34	34	1	1	5	5	21	11	37	37
com.ketchapp.twist	3	2	5	5	8	2	2	2	3	2	5	5	8	3	8	6
com.stupeflix.legend	4	2	2	2	1	0	0	0	4	3	13	5	1	0	0	0
com.maxgames.stickwarlegacy	1	0	0	0	2	1	1	1	1	0	0	0	2	2	7	5
air.com.tutotoons.app. animalhairsalon2jungle.free	0	0	0	0	14	7	43	43	0	0	0	0	14	7	43	43

wtf() in class Log, where the last two are false positives, enabling FLOWDROID to report 12 leaks via msg from two data sources, with 4 from v() and wtf() being false positives.

We can lift the precision of RIPPLE by improving the precision of its collaborating analyses, as disucssed in [28]

Table 2: Efficiency and effectiveness.

App Package Name	STRINF			RIPPLE		
	CG Edges	Analysis Time (s)	Total Leaks	CG Edges	Analysis Time (s)	Total Leaks
com.facebook.orca	5598	2.1	15	5605	2.2	15
com.netmarble.sknightsgb	12148	8.0	96	12779	8.?	**142**
com.productmadness.hovmobile	6278	3.1	44	6480	3.?	**48**
com.facebook.moments	6647	2.6	10	6654	2.?	10
me.msqrd.android	11064	4.8	25	11064	4.9	25
com.nordcurrent.canteenhd	16759	10	184	21625	12.8	**289**
com.ea.game.simcitymobile_row	8403	4.2	50	8403	4.1	50
com.imangi.templerun	10592	2.5	54	10592	2.3	54
com.rovio.angrybirds	13448	7.4	66	17384	10.2	**120**
com.sgn.pandapop.gp	10588	5.9	575	10590	5.9	575
com.gameloft.android. ANMP.GloftA8HM	16015	7.2	144	16016	6.6	144
com.appsorama.kleptocats	3707	2.8	39	3714	3.3	39
air.au.com.metro.DumbWaysToDie	10312	5.3	26	11679	5.9	**103**
com.ketchapp.twist	14144	8.7	97	14151	8.7	**109**
com.stupeflix.legend	8852	3.4	47	9066	3.5	47
com.maxgames.stickwarlegacy	3831	2.5	5	3844	2.4	**17**
air.com.tutotoons.app. animalhairsalon2jungle.free	12075	5.5	9	12075	5.7	9

5.3 RQ3: Scalability

Table 2 compares the analysis times of STRINF and RIPPLE. For all the 17 apps except canteenhd and angrybirds, RIPPLE finishes in under 10 secs. For all the 17 apps, STRINF and RIPPLE spend 86.0 and 93.4 seconds, respectively.

5.4 RQ4: Security Analysis

Table 2 also compares STRINF and RIPPLE in terms of their effectiveness for enabling FLOWDROID to find sensitive data leaks in Android apps. For each analysis, FLOWDROID calls it iteratively to build a harness for an app (by modeling more and more callbacks discovered) until a fixed-point is reached. FLOWDROID will then perform a flow- and context-sensitive taint analysis on the inter-procedural CFG, which is constructed based on the call graph (CG) that is computed for the app with respect to the final harness obtained.

For each app, RIPPLE's CG is a super-graph of STRINF's and RIPPLE's leak count is no smaller than STRINF's. For 10 out of the 17 apps, FLOWDROID reports the same number of leaks for each app under both analyses. For the remaining 7 apps, FLOWDROID reports 310 more leaks under RIPPLE than STRINF (highlighted by the numbers in bold in Table 2). RIPPLE's ability in finding more true reflective targets than STRINF, as shown in Table 1, has paid off.

Let us revisit two examples discussed in Section 2 to understand reflection-induced privacy violations. Consider Figure 1 first. Due to an undermined intent, cName = null. RIPPLE infers five reflectively created objects for Class. newInstance() in line 6 based on its post-dominant cast MMBaseActivity. As discussed in Section 2.1, all these five objects are true targets configured to provide different forms of advertisement, enabling FLOWDROID to detect 49 leaks that are missed by STRINF, on the methods called directly or indirectly on these objects. For this entire app, FLOWDROID finds 54 more leaks under RIPPLE than STRINF. A similar code pattern also appears in *Dumb Ways to Die* where FLOWDROID finds 77 more leaks under RIPPLE than STRINF.

Let us now consider Figure 2. RIPPLE infers that i(), d(), w(), e(), v() and wtf() in class Log, where the last two are false positives, are the potential targets invoked at logMtd.invoke(null, tag, msg) in line 6. Some sensitive data may be accidentally passed to msg and get written to log files, resulting in potential security vulnerabilities. Due to the six target methods discovered, FLOWDROID finds 12 data leaks ($= 2$ sources $\times$ 6 sinks) from two sensitive sources, of which 4 from v() and wtf() are false positives.

6. RELATED WORK

Android Apps. Ernst et al. [6] presented CHECKER, a dataflow analysis for Android apps with reflective calls handled later [4]. As for the reflection resolution approach used, CHECKER performs regular string inference as DROIDRA for constant class and method names but requires user annotations to handle non-constant class and method names. Li et al. [9] introduced DROIDRA, a string inference analysis for resolving reflection in Android apps. Rasthofer et al. [18] developed HARVESTER, an approach for automatically extracting runtime values, such as some class and method names, from Android apps. Zhauniarovich et al. [29] introduced STADYNA, a system that interleaves static and dynamic analysis in order to reveal the program behaviors caused by dynamic code update techniques, such as reflection.

Java Programs. There are several reflection analysis techniques for Java programs [10, 11, 13, 22]. Earlier, Livshits et al. [13] suggested to discover reflective targets by tracking the flow of string constants representing class/method/field names and infer reflective targets based on post-dominating type casts for Class.newInstance() calls if their class names are statically unknown strings. Recently, Li. et al. introduced ELF [10] and SOLAR [11] to apply sophisticated type inference to resolve reflective targets effectively. In particular, SOLAR is able to accurately identify where reflection is resolved unsoundly or imprecisely. In addition, it provides a mechanism to balance soundness, precision and scalability, representing a state-of-the-art solution for Java. A recent program slicing technique, called program tailoring [12], can also be leveraged to resolve reflection calls precisely. However, all the reflection analysis techniques proposed for Java cannot resolve a reflective call fully if the data-flows needed (e.g., class or method names) at the call are null.

Reflection analysis usually works together with pointer analysis to discover the targets at reflective calls. Many pointer analysis techniques for Java exist [14, 15, 21, 23–25].

7. CONCLUSION

In this paper, we introduce a reflection analysis for Android apps for discovering the behaviors of reflective calls, which can cause directly or indirectly security vulnerabilities. We advance the state-of-the-art reflection analysis for Android apps, by (1) bringing forward the ubiquity of IIEs for static analysis, (2) introducing RIPPLE, the first IIE-aware reflection analysis, and (3) demonstrating that RIPPLE can resolve reflection in real-world Android apps precisely and efficiently, and consequently, improve the effectiveness of downstream Android security analyses.

Acknowledgement

This research is supported by Australian Research Council grants, DP150102109 and DP170103956.

8. REFERENCES

[1] Virusshare project. http://virusshare.com/.
[2] S. Arzt and E. Bodden. Stubdroid: automatic inference of precise data-flow summaries for the Android framework. In *ICSE '16*, pages 725–735.
[3] S. Arzt, S. Rasthofer, C. Fritz, E. Bodden, A. Bartel, J. Klein, Y. Le Traon, D. Octeau, and P. McDaniel. Flowdroid: Precise context, flow, field, object-sensitive and lifecycle-aware taint analysis for Android apps. In *PLDI '14*, pages 259–269.
[4] P. Barros, R. Just, S. Millstein, P. Vines, W. Dietl, M. D. Ernst, et al. Static analysis of implicit control flow: Resolving Java reflection and Android intents. In *ASE '15*, pages 669–679.
[5] O. Bastani, S. Anand, and A. Aiken. Specification inference using context-free language reachability. In *POPL '15*, pages 553–566.
[6] M. D. Ernst, R. Just, S. Millstein, W. Dietl, S. Pernsteiner, F. Roesner, K. Koscher, P. B. Barros, R. Bhoraskar, S. Han, P. Vines, and E. X. Wu. Collaborative verification of information flow for a high-assurance app store. In *CCS '14*, pages 1092–1104.
[7] Y. Fratantonio, A. Bianchi, W. Robertson, E. Kirda, C. Kruegel, and G. Vigna. Triggerscope: Towards detecting logic bombs in Android applications. In *S&P '16*, pages 377–396.
[8] M. I. Gordon, D. Kim, J. H. Perkins, L. Gilham, N. Nguyen, and M. C. Rinard. Information flow analysis of Android applications in DroidSafe. In *NDSS '15*.

[9] L. Li, T. F. Bissyandé, D. Octeau, and J. Klein. DroidRA: taming reflection to support whole-program analysis of Android apps. In *ISSTA '16*, pages 318–329.
[10] Y. Li, T. Tan, Y. Sui, and J. Xue. Self-inferencing reflection resolution for Java. In *ECOOP '14*, pages 27–53.
[11] Y. Li, T. Tan, and J. Xue. Effective soundness-guided reflection analysis. In *SAS '15*, pages 162–180.
[12] Y. Li, T. Tan, Y. Zhang, and J. Xue. Program tailoring: slicing by sequential criteria. In *ECOOP '16*.
[13] B. Livshits, J. Whaley, and M. S. Lam. Reflection analysis for Java. In *APLAS '05*, pages 139–160.
[14] Y. Lu, L. Shang, X. Xie, and J. Xue. An incremental points-to analysis with CFL-reachability. CC '13, pages 61–81.
[15] A. Milanova, A. Rountev, and B. G. Ryder. Parameterized object sensitivity for points-to and side-effect analyses for Java. ISSTA '12, pages 1–11.
[16] D. Octeau, S. Jha, M. Dering, P. McDaniel, A. Bartel, L. Li, J. Klein, and Y. Le Traon. Combining static analysis with probabilistic models to enable market-scale Android inter-component analysis. In *POPL '16*, pages 469–484.
[17] D. Octeau, D. Luchaup, M. Dering, S. Jha, and P. McDaniel. Composite constant propagation: Application to Android inter-component communication analysis. In *ICSE '15*, pages 77–88.
[18] S. Rasthofer, S. Arzt, M. Miltenberger, and E. Bodden. Harvesting runtime values in Android applications that feature anti-analysis techniques. In *NDSS '16*.
[19] V. Rastogi, Y. Chen, and W. Enck. Appsplayground: Automatic security analysis of smartphone applications. In *CODASPY '13*.
[20] F. Ruiz. "fakeisntaller" leads the attack on Android phones. *McAfee Labs Website, Oct*, 2012.
[21] L. Shang, X. Xie, and J. Xue. On-demand dynamic summary-based points-to analysis. In *CGO '12*, pages 264–274.
[22] Y. Smaragdakis, G. Balatsouras, G. Kastrinis, and M. Bravenboer. More sound static handling of Java reflection. In *APLAS '15*, pages 485–503.
[23] Y. Smaragdakis, M. Bravenboer, and O. Lhoták. Pick your contexts well: understanding object-sensitivity. POPL, pages 17–30, 2011.
[24] M. Sridharan and R. Bodík. Refinement-based context-sensitive points-to analysis for Java. PLDI, pages 387–400, 2006.
[25] T. Tan, Y. Li, and J. Xue. Making k-object-sensitive pointer analysis more precise with still k-limiting. SAS '16, pages 489–510.
[26] E. Tinaztepe, D. Kurt, and A. Güleç. Android obad. *Technical Analysis Paper*, 2013.
[27] S. Yang, D. Yan, H. Wu, Y. Wang, and A. Rountev. Static control-flow analysis of user-driven callbacks in Android applications. In *ICSE '15*, pages 89–99.
[28] Y. Zhang, T. Tan, Y. Li, and J. Xue. Ripple: Reflection analysis for Android apps in incomplete information environments. *arXiv preprint arXiv:1612.05343*, 2016.
[29] Y. Zhauniarovich, M. Ahmad, O. Gadyatskaya, B. Crispo, and F. Massacci. Stadyna: addressing the problem of dynamic code updates in the security analysis of Android applications. In *CODASPY '15*, pages 37–48. ACM.

Detecting Mobile Application Spoofing Attacks by Leveraging User Visual Similarity Perception

Luka Malisa
Institute of Information
Security
ETH Zurich
malisal@inf.ethz.ch

Kari Kostiainen
Institute of Information
Security
ETH Zurich
kari.kostiainen@inf.ethz.ch

Srdjan Capkun
Institute of Information
Security
ETH Zurich
capkuns@inf.ethz.ch

ABSTRACT

Mobile application spoofing is an attack where a malicious mobile app mimics the visual appearance of another one. A common example of mobile application spoofing is a phishing attack where the adversary tricks the user into revealing her password to a malicious app that resembles the legitimate one. In this paper, we propose a novel spoofing detection approach, tailored to the protection of mobile app login screens, using screenshot extraction and visual similarity comparison. We use deception rate as a novel similarity metric for measuring how likely the user is to consider a potential spoofing app as one of the protected applications. We conducted a large-scale online study where participants evaluated spoofing samples of popular mobile app login screens, and used the study results to implement a detection system that accurately estimates deception rate. We show that efficient detection is possible with low overhead.

1. INTRODUCTION

Mobile application spoofing is an attack where a malicious mobile application mimics the visual appearance of another one. The goal of the adversary is to trick the user into believing that she is interacting with a genuine application while she interacts with one controlled by the adversary. If such an attack is successful, the integrity of what the user sees as well as the confidentiality of what she inputs into the system can be violated by the adversary. This includes login credentials, personal details that users typically provide to applications, as well as the decisions that they make based on the information provided by the applications.

A common example of mobile application spoofing is a phishing attack where the adversary tricks the user into revealing her password, or similar login credentials, to a malicious application that resembles the legitimate app. Several mobile application phishing attacks have been seen in the wild [19, 32, 37]. For example, a recent mobile banking spoofing application infected 350,000 Android devices and

caused significant financial losses [13]. More sophisticated attack vectors are described in recent research [4, 7, 12, 36].

The problem of spoofing has been studied extensively in the context of phishing websites [1, 2, 10, 15, 16]. Web applications run in browsers that provide visual cues, such as URL bars, SSL lock icons and security skins [9], that can help the user to authenticate the currently displayed website. Similar application identification cues are not available on modern mobile platforms, where a running application commonly controls the whole visible screen. The user can see a familiar user interface, but the interface could be drawn by a malicious spoofing application — the user is unable to authenticate the contents of the screen.

Security indicators for smartphone platforms have been proposed [11, 30], but their effectiveness relies on user alertness and they typically require either hardware modifications to the phone or a part of the screen to be made unavailable to the apps. Application-specific personalized indicators [21, 36] require no platform changes, but increase the application setup effort. Static code analysis can detect API call sequences that enable certain spoofing attacks [4]. However, code analysis is limited to known attack vectors and many spoofing attacks do not require any specific API calls, as they only draw on the screen.

We propose a novel spoofing detection approach that is tailored to the protection of mobile app *login screens* using visual similarity. Our system periodically grabs screenshots on the user's device and extracts visual features from them, with respect to *reference values* — the login screens of legitimate apps (on the same device) that our system protects. If a screenshot demonstrates high similarity to one of the reference values, we label the currently running app potentially malicious, and report it to the platform provider or warn the user. As our system examines screenshots, it is agnostic to the spoofing screen implementation, in contrast to approaches that examine screen similarity through code analysis. While straight-forward approaches based on visual similarity can detect simple cases of spoofing, where the attacker creates a perfect copy of the target app, or introduces other minor changes (e.g., changes the background color), our system can detect also more sophisticated spoofing.

In order to label spoofing apps accurately, our system needs to understand what kind of attacks are successful in reality, i.e., how much and what kind of visual similarity the two compared applications should have, so that the user would mistake the spoofing app as the legitimate one and fall for the attack. We capture this notion as a novel similarity metric called *deception rate*. For example, when deception rate is 20%, one fifth of the users are estimated to consider the spoofing app genuine and enter their login credentials into it. Deception rate is a conceptually different similarity metric from the ones previously proposed for similarity analysis of phishing websites. These works extract structural [3, 17, 26, 38, 39] as well as visual [8, 14, 22] similarity features and combine them into a similarity score that alone is not expressive, but enables comparison to known attack samples [17, 23]. While the previously proposed metrics essentially tell how similar the spoofing app is to one of the known attacks, our metric determines how likely the attack is to succeed. Deception rate can be seen as a risk measure and we consider it a powerful new way to address spoofing attacks, especially in cases where a large dataset of known attacks is not available.

Our system requires a good understanding of how users perceive and react to changes within mobile app user interfaces. Change perception has been studied extensively in general [24, 25, 31], but not in the context of mobile apps. We conducted a large-scale online study on mobile app similarity perception. We used a crowd sourcing platform to carry out a series of online surveys where approximately 5,400 study participants evaluated more than 34,000 spoofing screenshot samples. These samples included modified versions of Facebook, Skype and Twitter login screens where we changed visual features such as the color or the logo. For most of the experimented visual modifications we noticed a systematic user behavior: the more a visual property is changed, the less likely the users are to consider the app genuine.

We used the results of our user study to train our system using common supervised learning techniques. We also developed novel visual feature extraction and matching techniques. Our system shows robust screenshot processing and good deception rate accuracy (6–13% error margin), i.e., our system can precisely determine when an application is so similar to one of the protected login screens that the user is in risk of falling for spoofing. No previous visual similarity comparison scheme gives the same security property.

Additionally, we describe a novel collaborative detection model where multiple devices take part in screenshot extraction. We show that runtime detection is effective with very little system overhead (e.g., 1%). Our results can also be useful to other spoofing detection systems, as they give insight into how users perceive visual change.

To summarize, we make the following contributions:

- We propose a novel approach for detecting mobile application spoofing attacks using *visual similarity* and introduce *deception rate* as a novel similarity metric.

- We conducted a *large-scale user study* on perception of visual modifications in mobile application login screens.

- Leveraging our study results, we implemented a runtime *spoofing detection system* for Android.

- We developed novel *visual feature extraction* techniques.

The rest of this paper is organized as follows. In Section 2 we explain the problem of mobile application spoofing. Section 3 introduces our approach, Section 4 describes the user study, and in Section 5 we describe the spoofing detection system. We evaluate its performance and accuracy in Section 6 and discuss collaborative detection in Section 7. Section 8 reviews related work, and we conclude in Section 9.

2. PROBLEM STATEMENT

In mobile application spoofing, the goal of the adversary is to either violate the integrity of the information displayed to the user or the confidentiality of the user input. Application phishing is an example of a spoofing attack where the goal of the adversary is to steal confidential user data. The adversary tricks the user into disclosing her login credentials to a malicious app with a login screen resembling the legitimate one. A malicious stock market app that resembles a legitimate one, but shows fake market values, is an example of an attack where the adversary violates the integrity of the visual information displayed to the user and affects the user's future stock market decisions. Below we review different ways of implementing application spoofing attacks.

The simplest way to implement a spoofing attack is a repackaged or otherwise cloned application. To the user, the application appears identical to the target application, except for subtle visual cues such as a different developer name. Application repackaging has become a prevalent problem in the Android ecosystem, and the majority of Android malware is distributed using repackaging [6, 40].

In a more sophisticated variant of mobile application spoofing, the malicious app masquerades as a legitimate application, such as a game. The user starts the game and the malicious app continues running in the background from where it monitors the system state, such as the list of currently running applications. When the user starts the target application, the malicious application activates itself on the foreground and shows a spoofing screen that is similar, or exactly the same, to the one of the target app. On Android, background activation is possible with commonly used permissions and system APIs [4, 12]. Background attacks are difficult to notice for the user. While API call sequences that enable background attacks can be detected using code analysis [4], automated detection is complicated by the fact that the same APIs are frequently used by benign apps.

A malicious application can also present a button to share information via another app. Instead of forwarding the user to the suggested target app, the button triggers a spoofing screen within the same, malicious application [12]. Fake forwarding requires no specific permissions or API calls which makes such attack vectors difficult to discover using code analysis. Further spoofing attack vectors are discussed in [4].

Mobile application spoofing attacks are a recent mobile malware type and a large corpus of known spoofing apps is not yet available. However, serious attacks have already taken place. The Svpeng malware infected 350,000 Android devices and caused financial loss worth of nearly one million USD [13]. The malware presents a spoofed credit card entry dialog when the user starts the Google Play application and monitors startup of targeted mobile banking applications to mount spoofing attacks on their login screens. As spoofing detection using traditional code analysis techniques has inherent limitations and many spoofing attacks are virtually impossible for the users to notice, the exact extent of the problem remains largely unknown. Due to the already seen serious attacks, we believe it is useful to seek novel ways to address the problem of mobile application spoofing.

The problem of mobile application spoofing has many similarities to the one of web phishing. The majority of the existing web phishing detection schemes [3, 17, 26, 38, 39] train a detection system using a large dataset of known phishing websites. As a similar dataset is not available for mobile

Figure 1: Spoofing application example. The legitimate Netflix app and the Android.Fakeneflic malware [33]. The spoofed user interface includes subtle visual modifications.

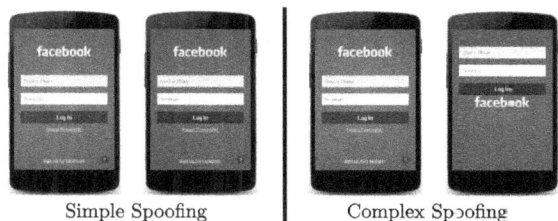

Figure 2: Examples of simple (changing background color) and more complex spoofing (repositioning elements).

apps, these approaches are not directly applicable to mobile app spoofing detection. We also argue that the specific nature of mobile applications benefits from a customized approach, and in the next section, we introduce a novel detection approach that is tailored to mobile app login screens. The focus of this work is on mobile app spoofing and web phishing is explicitly out of scope.

3. OUR APPROACH

In this section, we first describe the rationale behind our approach and introduce deception rate as a similarity metric. We then describe how this approach is instantiated into a case study on login screen spoofing detection. Finally, we describe our attacker model.

3.1 Visual Similarity and Deception Rate

The problem of application spoofing can be approached in multiple ways. Code analysis has been proposed to detect API call sequences that enable spoofing attacks [4]. However, code analysis is limited to known attack vectors and cannot address spoofing attacks that do not require specific API calls (e.g., fake forwarding). Another approach is to analyze the application code or website DOM trees to identify apps with *structural* user interface similarity [3,17,26,38,39]. A limitation of this approach is that the adversary can complicate code analysis, e.g., by constructing the user interface pixel by pixel. Third, the mobile platform can be enhanced with security indicators [11,30]. However, indicator verification imposes a cognitive load on the user and their deployment typically requires either part of the screen to be made unavailable to the applications or hardware modifications to the device. Application-specific personalized indicators [21,36] can be deployed without platform changes, but their configuration increases user effort during app setup.

In this paper, we focus on a different approach and study the detection of spoofing attacks based on their *visual similarity*. Previously, visual similarity analysis has been proposed for detection of phishing websites [14,35,38]. Designing an effective spoofing detection system based on visual similarity analysis is not an easy task, and we illustrate the challenges by providing two straw-man solutions.

The first straw-man solution is to look for mobile apps that have exactly the same visual appearance. To avoid such detection, the adversary can simply create a slightly modified version of the spoofing screen. For example, small changes in the login screen element positions are hard to notice and are unlikely to retain the user from entering her login credentials. Consequently, this approach would fail to catch many spoofing attacks. Such visually modified attacks are observed in the wild. For example, the An-

droid.Fakeneflic malware [33], discovered on Google's Android market, impersonated the legitimate Netflix application with minor visual modifications (Figure 1). Such attacks would not be detected by a simple comparison scheme that looks for an exact visual match. To summarize, we do not focus on detection of perfect copies, as such detection is easy to avoid, and spoofing apps seen in the wild often show minor visual differences. The adversary has an incentive to introduce enough visual change to evade simple detection, but not enough for users to become alarmed. The primary contribution of this paper is to explore this space; to determine how much change do users tolerate.

The second straw-man solution is to flag all applications that have high similarity to a reference application, with regards to a common image similarity metric. e.g. converting a screenshot to gray-scale, and scaling it down to a fixed size (64 × 64 pixels). Comparing such thumbnails by pixel difference is tolerant to many minor visual modifications. For example, screenshots with change of colors, or other minor pixel differences, would be deemed highly similar, and the metric would detect such spoofing attacks. However, the metric would fail on more complex examples (Figure 2), as it does not capture the visual properties that users consider relevant. As our user study shows (Section 4), many screens are perceived as similar by users, even though the screens are *very dissimilar* in terms of their pixel values. For example, many users mistook a pink Facebook screen with perturbed element positions as genuine. Such advanced spoofing would not be caught by the above simple metric — for robust detection more sophisticated techniques are needed.

In this paper we explore visual similarity as perceived by the users. We take a different approach and design a spoofing detection system that estimates how many users would fall for a spoofing attack. We use *deception rate* as a novel similarity metric that represents the estimated attack success rate. Given two screenshots, one of the examined app and one of the protected reference app, our system (Figure 3) estimates the percentage of users that would mistakenly identify the examined app as the reference app (deception rate). This estimation is done by leveraging results from a study on how users perceive visual similarity on mobile app user interfaces. The deception rate can be seen as a risk measure that allows our system to determine if the examined application should be flagged as a potential spoofing application. An example policy is to flag any application where the deception rate exceeds a threshold.

Deception rate is a conceptually different similarity metric from the ones previously proposed for similarity analysis of phishing websites. These works extract structural [3,17,26, 38,39] as well as visual [8,14,22] similarity features and combine them into a similarity score that alone is not expressive,

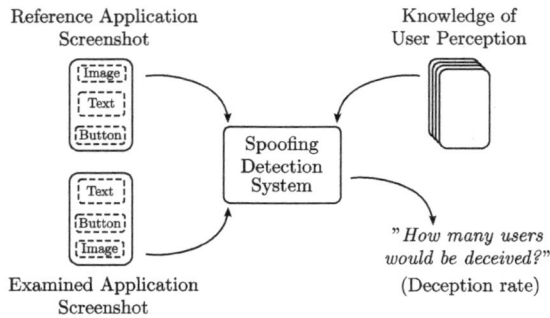

Figure 3: Approach overview. The spoofing detection system takes as inputs screenshots of a reference app and an examined app. Based on these screenshots and knowledge on mobile application user perception, the system estimates deception rate for the examined app.

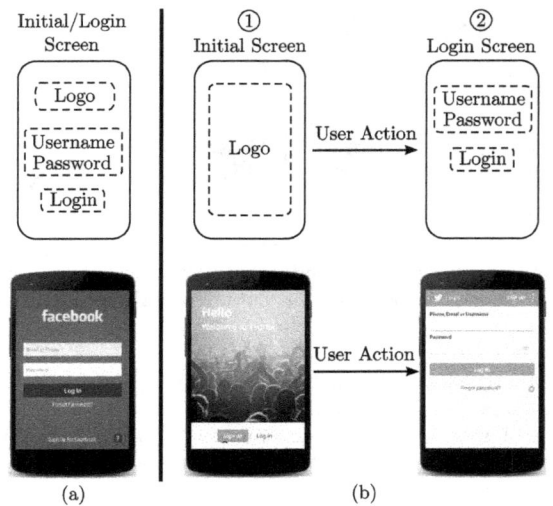

Figure 4: Model for mobile application login screens. The login screen has three main elements: logo, username and password input fields, and login button. The login functionality is either (a) standalone or (b) distributed.

but enables comparison to known attack samples [17, 23]. The extracted features can also be fed into a system that is trained using known malicious sites [14, 35, 38]. Such similarity metrics are interpreted with respect to known attacks, and may not be effective in detecting spoofing attacks with an appearance different from the ones previously seen.

Deception rate has different semantics, as it captures the *perceived similarity* of spoofing screens. For example, a mobile app login screen where elements have been reordered may have different visual features but, as our user study shows, is perceived similarly by many users. Deception rate estimates how many people would mistakenly identify the spoofing app as the genuine one (risk measure) and, contrary to previous similarity metrics, is applicable also in scenarios where a large dataset of known spoofing samples are not available. We emphasize that our system is complementary to existing approaches, and that realization of such a system requires good understanding of what type of mobile app interfaces users perceive as similar and what type of visual modifications users are likely to notice. This motivates our user study, the results of which we describe in Section 4.

3.2 Case Study: Login Screen Spoofing

We focus on spoofing attacks against mobile application login screens, as they are the most security-sensitive ones in many applications. We examined the login screens of 230 different apps and found that they all follow a similar structure. The login screen is a composition of three main elements: (1) the logo, (2) the username and password input fields, and (3) the login button. Furthermore, the login screen can have additional, visually less salient elements, such as a link to request a forgotten password or register a new account. Some mobile apps distribute these elements across two screens: the first (initial) screen contains the logo, or a similar visual identifier, as well as a button that leads to the login screen, where the rest of the main elements reside.

The common structure of mobile app login screens enables us to model them, and their simple designs provide a good opportunity to experiment on user perception. Mobile app login screens have fewer modification dimensions to explore, as compared to more complex user interfaces, such as websites. Throughout this work we use the login screen model illustrated in Figure 4 that captures both standalone and distributed logins screens. Out of the 230 apps we examined, 136 had a standalone login screen, while 94 had a distributed

one. All apps conformed to our model. We experiment on user perception with respect to this model, as the adversary has an incentive to create spoofing screens that resemble the legitimate login screen. Our study confirms this assumption.

3.3 Attacker Model

We assume a strong attacker capable of creating arbitrary spoofed login screens, including login screens that deviate from our model. We distinguish between two spoofing attack scenarios regarding user expectations and goals. In all the spoofing attacks listed in Section 2, the user's intent is to access the targeted application. This implies that the user expects to see a familiar user interface and has an incentive to log in. The adversary could also present a spoofing screen unexpectedly, when the user is not accessing the target application. In such cases, the user has no intent, nor similar incentive, to log in. We focus on the first case, as we consider such attacks more likely to succeed.

We assume an attacker that controls a malicious spoofing app running on the user smartphone. Besides the spoofing screen, the attacker-controlled app appears to the user as entirely benign (e.g., a game). The attacker can construct the spoofing screen statically (e.g., using Android manifest files) or dynamically (e.g., creating widgets at runtime). In both cases, the operating system is aware of the created element tree, a structure similar to DOM trees in websites. The attacker can draw the screen pixel by pixel, in which case the operating system sees only one element, a displayed picture. The attacker can also exploit the properties of human image perception. For example, the attacker can display half of the spoofed screen in one frame, and the other half in the subsequent frame. The human eye would average the input signal and perceive the complete spoofing screen.

4. CHANGE PERCEPTION USER STUDY

Visual perception has been studied extensively in general, and prior studies have shown that users are surprisingly poor at noticing changes in images that are shown in succession

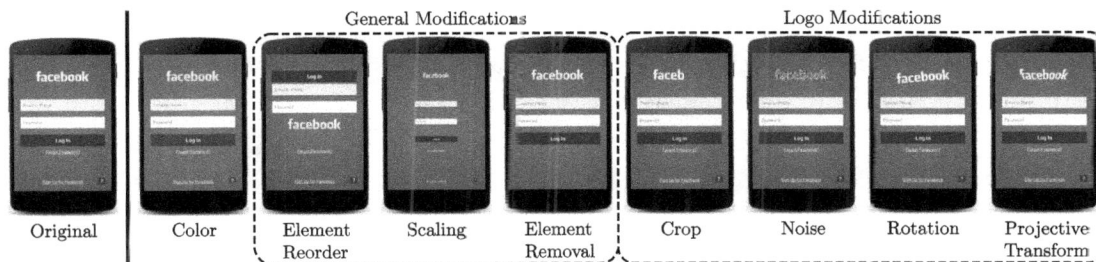

Figure 5: Examples of Facebook login screen spoofing samples. The original login screen is shown on the left. We show an example of each type of visual modification we performed: color, general modifications, and logo modifications.

(change blindness) [25,31]. While such studies give us an intuition on how users might notice, or fail to notice, different login screen modifications, the results are too generic to be directly applied to the spoofing detection system outlined above. User perception of visual change in mobile app user interfaces has not been studied thoroughly before.

We conducted a large-scale online study on the similarity perception of mobile app login screens. The purpose of this study was three-fold: we wanted to (1) understand the effect of different types of visual login screen modifications, (2) gather training data for the spoofing detection system, and (3) gain insights that could aid us in the design of our system. The study was performed as online surveys on the crowd-sourcing platform CrowdFlower. The platform allows creation of online jobs that human participants perform in return of a small payment. In each survey, the participants evaluated a single screenshot of a mobile app login screen by answering questions (see Appendix A).

We first performed an initial study, where we experimented with visual modifications on the Android Facebook application. We chose Facebook, as it is a widely used application. After that, we carried out follow-up studies where we tested similar visual modifications on Skype and Twitter apps, as well as combinations of visual changes. Below, we describe the Facebook study and summarize the results of the follow-up studies. We did not collect any private information about our study participants. The ethical board of our institution reviewed and approved our study.

4.1 Sample Generation

A *sample* is a screenshot image presented to a study participant for evaluation. We created eight datasets of Facebook login screens, and in each dataset we modified a single visual property. The purpose of these datasets was to evaluate how users perceive different types of visual changes as well as to provide training data for the spoofing detection system. Figure 5 illustrates each performed modification:

- *Color modification.* We modified the hue of the application login screen. The hue change affects the color of all elements on the login screen and the dataset contained samples representing uniform hue changes over the entire hue range.
- *General modifications.* We performed three general modifications on the login screen elements. (1) We reordered and (2) scaled down the size of the elements. We did not increase the size of the elements as the username and the password fields are typically full width of the screen. Furthermore, (3) we removed any extra elements from the login screen.

- *Logo modifications.* We performed four modifications on the logo: we (1) cropped the logo to different sizes, taking the rightmost part of the logo out, (2) added noise of different intensity, (3) rotated the logo both clockwise and counterclockwise, and (4) performed projective transformations on the logo.

We created synthetic spoofing samples as no extensive mobile spoofing app dataset is available. While the chosen modifications cover some known spoofing attacks (e.g., Figure 1), they are certainly not exhaustive, as the attacker can change the interface in many different ways, e.g., adding different background images, replace logo with text. The goal of our work is not to optimize the system for the detection of known attacks, but rather to create a system that is able to detect also previously unseen spoofing screens. The sample set could be extended in many ways, but a single user study cannot cover all possible modifications.

4.2 Recruitment and Tasks

We recruited test participants via a crowd sourcing platform. An example survey had a description *"How familiar are you with the Facebook Android application?"*. Each survey contained 12 to 16 question and, in total 2,910 unique participants evaluated 5,900 Facebook samples. We showed the study participant a sample login screen screenshot and asked the participant the following questions: *"Is this screen the Facebook login screen as you remember it?"* and *"If you would see this screen, would you login with your real Facebook password?"*. We provided *Yes* and *No* reply alternatives on both questions. Using the percentage of *Yes* answers, we compute *as-remembered rate* and *login rate* for each sample. Appendix A provides details on study procedure, statistics and participants demographics.

Through the chosen design of our user study, we purposefully primed the participants to expect to see a login screen of the studied apps. We simulate the setting in which the user wants to login, but is presented with a login screen that is different than the user remembers.

4.3 Results

We discarded survey responses where the participants did not indicate active usage of the Facebook app or gave an incorrect reply to the control question. After filtering, we had 5,376 completed surveys and, on the average, 91 user evaluations per screenshot sample.

Color modification. The color modification results are illustrated in Figure 6. We plot the observed login rate in green and the as-remembered rate in blue for each evaluated sample. The red bars indicate bootstrapped 95% con-

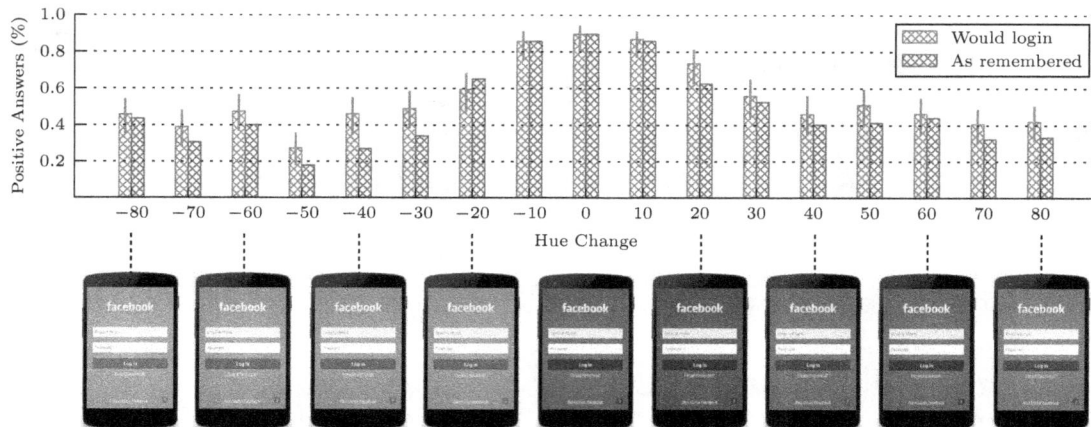

Figure 6: Color modification results. We illustrate the percentages of users that perceived a Facebook login screen sample with modified color as genuine (*as-remembered rate*) and would login to the application if such a screen is shown (*login rate*). Color has a significant effect on both rates.

fidence intervals. We performed a chi-square test of independence with a significance level of $p = 0.05$ to examine the relation between the login responses and the sample color. The relation between these variables was significant $(\chi^2(16, N = 1551) = 194.44), p < 0.001)$ and the study participants were less likely to log in to screens with high hue change. When the hue change is maximal, approximately 40% of the participants indicated that they would still log in. For several samples we noticed slightly higher login rate compared to as-remembered rate. This may imply that some users were willing to log in to an application, although it looked different from their recollection. We investigated reasons for this behavior from the survey questions and several participants replied that they noticed the color change, but considered the application genuine nonetheless. One participant commented: *"Probably Facebook decided to change their color."* However, our study was not designed to prove or reject such hypothesis.

General modifications. The general element modification results are shown in Figure 7. Both element reordering $(\chi^2(5, N = 546) = 15.84, p = 0.007)$ and scaling $(\chi^2(9, N = 916) = 245.56, p < 0.001)$ had an effect on the observed login rates. Samples with scaling 50% or less showed login rates close to the original, but participants were less likely to login to screens with high scaling. This could be due to users' habituation of seeing scaled user interfaces across different mobile device form factors (e.g., smartphone user interfaces scaled for tablets). One participant commented his reason to login: *"looks the same, just a little small."* When the elements were scaled more than 50%, the login rates decreased fast. At this point the elements became unreadably small. Removal of extra elements (forgotten password or new account link) had no effect on the login rate $(\chi^2(1, N = 180) = 0.0, p = 1.0)$.

Logo modifications. The logo modification results are shown in Figure 8. The relation between the login rate and the amount of crop was significant $(\chi^2(5, N = 540) = 83.75, p < 0.001)$. Interestingly, we noticed that the lowest login rate was observed at 40% crop. This implies that the users may find the login screen more trustworthy when the logo is fully missing compared to seeing a partial logo, but our study was not designed to prove such hypothesis.

The amount of noise in the logo had an effect on login rates $(\chi^2(4, N = 460) = 75.30, p < 0.001)$, as users were less likely to log in to screens with noise. Approximately half of the study participants answered that they would login even if the logo was unreadable due to noise. This result may imply habituation to software errors and one of the participants commented the noisy logo: *"I would think it is a problem from my phone resolution, not Facebook."* Participants were less likely to log in to screens with a rotated logo $(\chi^2(4, N = 462) = 57.25, p < 0.001)$ or a projected logo $(\chi^2(5, N = 542) = 102.45, p < 0.001)$.

Conclusions. The experimented eight visual modifications were perceived differently. While some modifications caused a predominantly systematic pattern (e.g., color), in others we did not notice a clear relation between the amount of the modification and the observed login rate (e.g., crop). One modification (extra element removal) caused no effect. We conclude that the system should be trained with samples that capture various types of visual modifications.

4.4 Follow-up Studies and Study Method

We performed similar studies for the Skype and Twitter apps. Skype results were comparable to those of Facebook. Twitter app has a distributed login screen and we noticed different patterns than in the previous two studies. We also evaluated combinations of two and three visual modifications. We collected 34,240 evaluations from 5,438 participants, and we used the data to train our detection system.

We measured login rates by asking study participants questions in contrast to observing participants under login operation. We chose this approach to allow large-scale data collection for thousands of sample evaluations. Participants in our study were allowed to evaluate multiple samples from different datasets which may have influenced the results.

5. SPOOFING DETECTION SYSTEM

Through our user study we gained insight into what kind of visual modifications users notice, and more importantly, fail to notice. In this section we design a spoofing detection system that leverages this knowledge. We instantiate the system for Android, while many parts of the system are applicable to other mobile platforms as well.

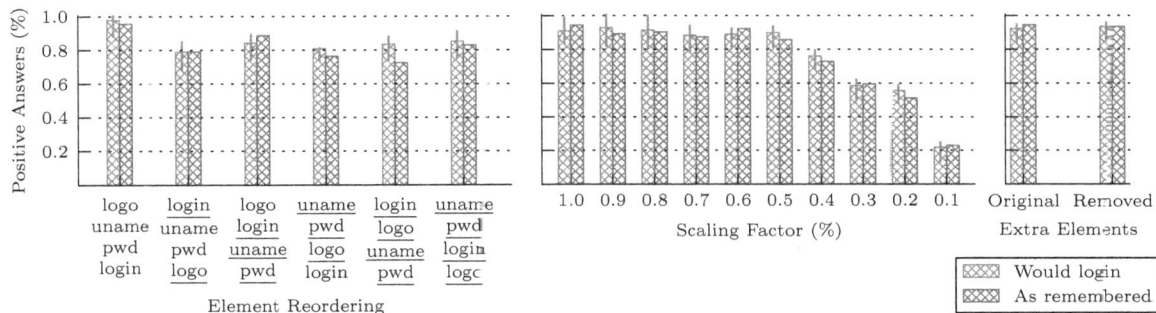

Figure 7: General modifications results. Percentages of users that perceived a Facebook login screen sample with general modifications as genuine and would login. Element reordering modification had a small but statistically significant effect, scaling caused a significant effect, and extra element removal showed no effect.

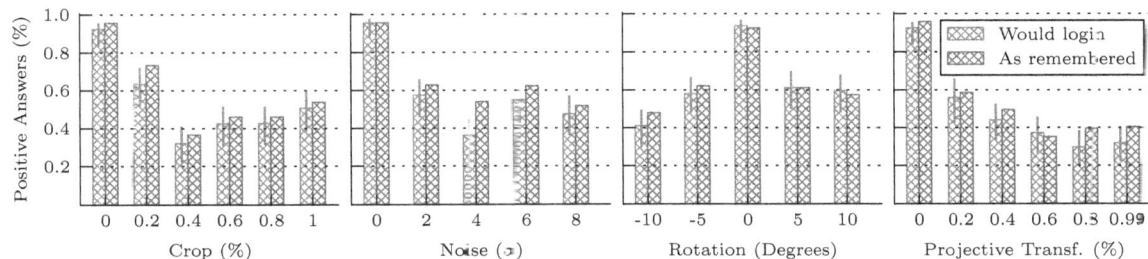

Figure 8: Logo modifications results. Percentages of users that perceived a Facebook login screen sample with logo modifications as genuine and would login to the application. All logo modifications caused a significant effect.

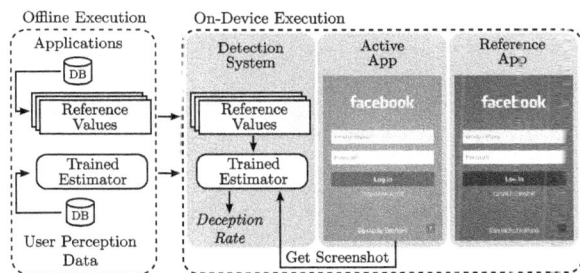

Figure 9: Detection system overview. The system preprocesses legitimate apps offline (e.g., at the marketplace) to obtain reference values, and trains an estimator. On the user's device, the system periodically extracts screenshots and estimates their deception rate.

5.1 System Overview

Our system is designed to protect *reference applications*, i.e., legitimate apps with login functionality. The goal of our system is to, given a screenshot, estimate how many users would mistake it for one of the known reference apps. The system (Figure 9) consists of two parts: a training and pre-processing component that runs on the market and a runtime detection system on users' phones. On the market, each reference app's login screen is detected, pre-processed, and a deception rate estimator is trained using the user perception data from our user study. The analyzed login screens serve as the *reference values* for the on-device detection.

On the device, the system periodically extracts a screenshot of the currently active app. We analyze screenshot extraction rates needed for effective detection in Section 7. Each extracted screenshot is analyzed using the estimator

with respect to the reference values of the protected apps. Both the trained estimator and the reference values are downloaded from the market (e.g., upon installing an app). The system outputs a deception rate for each analyzed screenshot, with respect to each protected app. The deception rates can be used to inform the market or warn the user.

The apps that should be protected (i.e., labeled as reference apps), can be determined in multiple ways: the user can choose the apps that require protection, the system can automatically select the most common spoofing targets (e.g., Facebook, Skype, Twitter), or all installed apps with login functionality can be protected. We focus on the approach where the protected apps are chosen by the user. A complete view of the system is illustrated in Figure 10, and we proceed by describing each system component

5.2 Reference Application Analysis

Our system protects reference apps from spoofing. To analyze an extracted screenshot with respect to a reference value, we first obtain the reference app login screen and identify its main elements (reference elements) according to our login screen model (Figure 4). We assume reference app developers that have no incentive to obfuscate their login screen implementations. On the contrary, developers can be encouraged to mark the part of the user interface (activity) that contains the login screen that should be protected. The reference app analysis is a one-time operation performed, e.g., at the marketplace on every app update, and its results distributed to the mobile devices. To find the activity that represents the login screen, we developed a tool that automatically explores a specified application and stores any found login screens. From the login screens, the tool detects and stores *reference elements* into a tree structure.

295

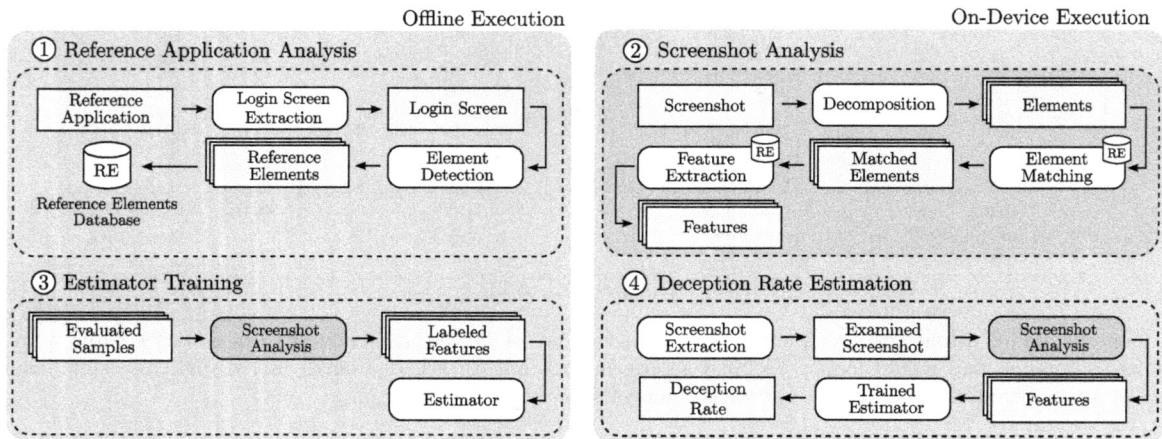

Figure 10: Detection system details. The system consist of four main components: reference app analysis, screenshot analysis, estimator training and deception rate estimation.

5.3 Screenshot Analysis

The goal of the screenshot analysis is to, given the screenshot of the examined application, as well as the reference elements, produce suitable features for deception rate estimation and estimator training. The screenshot analysis includes three operations: decomposition, element matching, and feature extraction, as shown in Figure 10.

Decomposition. Mobile application user interfaces commonly exhibit a clean and simple design, when compared to more complex ones, e.g., web sites. Such design simplicity enables us to efficiently split the screenshot into constituent elements. To identify element borders we perform a set of image processing steps, including edge-detection, dilation, closure and gradient.

Element matching. The next step is to match the detected elements to the reference elements. To find the element that is the closest match to the reference logo, we use the ORB feature extractor [27]. While SIFT extractors [18] have been successful in detecting logos in natural images [28], we found SIFT to be ill-suited for mobile app logos, especially in cases where only partial (cropped) logos were present. We compute ORB keypoints over the reference logo as well as the whole examined screenshot and we match the two sets. The element that matches with the most keypoints, and exceeds a minimum point density threshold, is declared as the logo. For the remaining elements, we perform template matching to every reference element (username field, password field, login button), on different scaling levels. Keypoint extraction is generally not effective, as the login screen elements are typically simple, and have few keypoints. After these steps, we have a mapping between the examined application elements and the reference elements.

Feature extraction. Once the elements are matched, we extract two common visual features (color and element scaling) and more detailed logo features, as users showed sensitivity to logo changes. The extracted features are relative, rather than absolute, as their values are computed with respect to the reference elements or entire reference screen. We explain our features below:

1. *Hue.* The difference between the average hue value of the examined screenshot and the reference screen.

2. *Element Scaling.* The ratio of minimum-area bounding boxes between all reference and examined elements, except the logo.

3. *Logo Rotation.* The difference between the angles of minimum-area bounding boxes of the examined and reference logos.

4. *Logo Scaling.* We perform template matching between the examined and reference logos at different scales and express the feature as the scale that produces the best match.

5. *Logo Crop.* We calculate the amount of logo crop as the ratio of logo bounding box areas.

6. *Logo Degradation.* As precise extraction of logo noise and projection is difficult, we approximate similar visual changes with a more generic feature that we call logo degradation. Template matching algorithms return the position and the minimum value of the employed similarity metric and we use the minimum value as the logo degradation feature.

In cases where no logo was identified in the matching phase, all logo features are set to null (except logo crop which is set to 100%). Our analysis is designed to extract features from screenshots that follow our login screen model. Many of these features (color change, scaling) are seen known in spoofing apps (Android.Fakeneflic).

5.4 Training and Deception Rate Estimation

The detection system is trained once, using the available user perception data from our user study, and subsequently used for all apps. We extract features from every sample of the study and augment the resulting feature vectors with the observed login rate. In feature extraction, as the reference value we use the unmodified login screen of the app that the sample represents. As deception rate (i.e., the percentage of users that would confuse the examined screenshot with the reference app) is a continuous variable, we estimate it using a regression model. Training can be performed offline for each reference app separately.

Deception rate estimation is performed on the device at detection system runtime. As shown in Figure 10, the extracted screenshot is first analyzed. The decomposition phase of the analysis is performed once, and the rest of the analysis steps are repeated for each reference app. The extracted features are used to run the trained estimator. The result of the estimation operation is a set of deception rates, one for each protected app. If any of the deception rates exceeds a threshold value, one or more possible spoofing apps have been found and their identities can be communicated to the application marketplace or the user can be warned.

5.5 Implementation

We implemented the reference application analysis tool as a modified Android emulator environment. Similar analysis can be implemented by instrumenting the reference application, but we modified the runtime environment to support the analysis of native applications as well. We implemented the remaining offline tools as various Python scripts using the OpenCV [5] library for image processing and scikit-learn for estimator training. The on-device detection system can be implemented in multiple ways, including a modification to the Android runtime or as a standalone application. For ease of deployment, we implemented the on-device components as a regular Android (Java) app using OpenCV.

6. EVALUATION

In this section, we evaluate the estimation accuracy and the runtime performance of the detection system. We provide more a detailed evaluation of the system's various components in Appendix B.

6.1 Estimation Accuracy

To evaluate the deception rate estimation accuracy, and to demonstrate the feasibility of this approach, we trained our detection system using the results of our user study (a deployed system would, of course, be trained with more data). Our total training data consists of 316 user-evaluated samples of visual modifications and each sample was evaluated either by 100 (single modification) or 50 (two and three modifications) unique users. From the training data, we omitted samples that express visual modifications that our current implementation is unable to extract (e.g., noise).

We experimented with several regression models of different complexities and trained two linear models (Lasso and linear regression), a decision tree, as well as two ensemble learning methods (gradient boosting, random forests). To compare our detection accuracy to straightforward approaches, we use four baseline models out of which the latter two utilize prior knowledge obtained from our user study:

- *B1 Linear.* The deception rate drops linearly with the amount of visual modification from 1 to 0.
- *B2 Constant.* The deception rate is always 0.75
- *B3 Linear.* The deception rate drops linearly with the amount of visual modification from 1 to 0.2. Login rates stayed predominantly above 20% in our study.
- *B4 Random.* The deception rate is a random number in the the most observed range in our study (0.3–0.5).

To estimate the deception rate, we extract features from the analyzed screenshot with respect to a reference app and we feed the feature vector to the trained regressor. The estimator outputs a deception rate that can be straightforwardly converted into a spoofing detection decision. We performed two types of model validation: leave-one-out and 10-fold cross-validation. We report the results in Figure 11

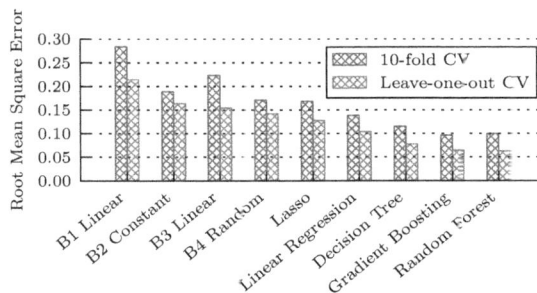

Figure 11: Deception rate accuracy. Evaluation of five regression and four baseline models (B1–B4) trained on the combined datasets of Facebook and Skype. The random forest regressor performs the best.

and we observe that the more complex models perform significantly better than our baseline models. The best model was random forest, with a root mean square (RMS) error of 6% and 9% for the leave-one-out and 10-fold cross validations respectively (95% of the estimated deception rates are expected to be within two RMS errors from their true values). The low RMS values show that a system trained on user perception data can accurately estimate deception rates for mobile application spoofing attacks.

The detection system should estimate deception rate accurately even for apps it did not encounter before To evaluate the estimation accuracy of attacks that target apps that were not present in the training data, we trained a random forest regressor using Facebook samples, and evaluated it on Skype samples, and vice-versa. We observed an RMS error of 13% in both cases. When samples from the spoofing target app are not part of the training dataset, the estimation accuracy decreases slightly. We conclude that our system is able to accurately estimate deception rate in the tested scenarios, even if the target app is not part of the training data. Our training set has limited size and with more extensive training data we expect even better accuracy.

To evaluate false negatives of our system, we estimated the deception rates of various screenshots that we extracted by crawling the user interfaces of randomly chosen mobile apps, with regards to the Facebook reference login screen. Due to the large difference between the login screens, as expected, all screenshots reported very low deception rates. We do not provide a ROC analysis, as it would require a significant dataset of spoofing apps. At the moment such dataset does not exist.

6.2 Performance Evaluation

We evaluated the performance of the on-device screenshot analysis and deception rate estimation. For the offline (marketplace) components we only evaluated accuracy, as those are fast and not time-critical operations. We measured the performance of our implementation on three devices: an older smartphone model (Samsung Galaxy S2) and two more recent devices (Nexus 5 and Nexus 6). Averaged over 100 runs, a single reference app comparison takes 183 ± 28 ms (Nexus 5), 261 ± 26 ms (Nexus 6) and 407 ± 69 ms (Galaxy S2). The process scales linearly with the number of protected apps: the decomposition of the extracted screenshots is performed once, and the remaining analysis steps are repeated for each reference value. Assuming five protected apps, the complete analysis takes 667 ms (Nexus 5).

We argue that the number of apps requiring protection would be low, as the majority of apps running on the phone are commonly not security-sensitive.

The detection system extracts and analyzes screenshots only when an untrusted (i.e., not whitelisted) app is active. For example, the platform provider can whitelist popular apps from trusted developers (Facebook, Twitter, Whatsapp). The detection system can also perform a less expensive *pre-filtering* operation to determine, and only proceed with the full analysis, if the examined screenshot vaguely resembles a login screen. We leave development of such pre-filtering mechanisms as future work.

The on-device performance primarily depends on the size of the analyzed screenshot. Modern smartphones have high screen resolutions (e.g., 1080×1920) and analyzing such large images is expensive and does not increase system accuracy. It is important to note that screenshot extraction time depends only on the output screenshot resolution and not on the physical screen resolution itself. For all our measurements we extracted screenshots of size 320×455 pixels as the resolution provides a good ratio of element detection accuracy and runtime performance. Our initial experiments show that the image resolution (and with it, execution time) can be decreased even further, and determining the optimal resolution we leave as future work.

7. ANALYSIS

Collaborative detection. Extracting screenshots frequently and analyzing each of them can be expensive. However, if multiple devices take part in detection, we can reduce the overhead on every device without sacrificing detection probability. This can be achieved with fewer devices sampling more often or more devices sampling less often. For example, the screenshot rate can be controlled based on the popularity of the currently running, unknown app. If an app is present on many devices (e.g., 50 or more), the detection system can safely reduce the screenshot rate to save system resources without sacrificing detection probability. If an application is installed in only a small number of devices (e.g., less than 10), the system can increase the screenshot rate for better detection probability. Such adjustments can be done so that, in total, no more than the pre-allocated amount of system resources are spent for spoofing detection.

We show that collaborative detection provides an efficient way to detect spoofing attacks in the majority of practical spoofing scenarios. For example, only 10 devices, each dedicating 1% of computation overhead, are needed to detect phishing attacks with a probability upwards of 95%. We provide a more detailed analysis in an extended version of this paper [20].

Detection avoidance. The adversary can try to avoid runtime detection by leveraging the human perception property of averaging images that change frequently (e.g., quickly and repeatedly alternate between showing the first and second halves of the spoofing screen). The user would perceive the complete login screen, but any acquired screenshot would cover only half of the spoofing screen. Such attacks can be addressed by extracting screenshots frequently and averaging them out, prior to analysis.

While the adversary has an incentive to create spoofing screens that resemble the original login screen, the adversary is not limited to these modifications. To test how well our system is able to estimate deception rate for previously unseen visual modifications and spoofing samples that differ from the login screen model, further tests are needed. This limitation is analogous to the previously proposed similarity detection schemes that compare website to known phishing samples – the training data cannot cover all phishing sites.

Our current implementation has difficulties in decomposing screenshots with background noise, and consequently the adversary could try to avoid detection by constructing noisy spoofing screens. Developers could be encouraged to create clean login screen layouts for improved spoofing protection. While we did not experiment with noisy backgrounds, our study shows that the more the adversary deviates from the legitimate screen, the less likely the attack is to succeeded.

The goal of this work was to demonstrate a new spoofing detection approach, and we recommend that a deployed system be trained with more samples including (a) more visual modifications and (b) more apps.

False positives. Many mobile apps use single sign-on functionality from popular services, such as Facebook. An unknown application with a legitimate single sign-on screen matching to one of the reference values would be flagged by our detection system. Flagged applications should be manually verified and in such cases found benign.

8. RELATED WORK

Spoofing detection systems. Static code analysis can be effective in detecting spoofing apps that leverage known attack vectors, such as ones that query running tasks and after that create a new activity [4]. Our approach is more agnostic to the attack implementation technique, but has a narrower focus: protection of login screens. We consider our work complementary to code analysis.

Many web phishing detection systems analyze a website DOM tree and compare its elements and structure to the reference site [3, 17, 26, 38, 39]. We assume an adversary that constructs spoofing apps in arbitrary ways (e.g., per pixel), and thus complicates structural code analysis.

Another approach is to consider the visual presentation of a spoofing application (or a website), and compare its similarity to a reference value [8, 14, 22]. Previous schemes typically derive a similarity score for a website and compare it to known malicious sites, while our metric determines how many users would confuse the application for another one.

Spoofing detection by users. Similar to web browsers, the mobile OS can be enhanced with security indicators. The OS can show the name of the running app in a dedicated part of the screen [4, 12, 30]. Such schemes require that parts of the mobile device screen are made unavailable to applications or need hardware changes to the device. A mobile app can also allow the user to configure a personalized security indicator (e.g., a personal image) that is shown by the app during each login [21].

Several studies, in the context of web sites, show that users tend to ignore the absence of security indicators [10, 29, 34]. A recent study shows that personalized security indicators can be more effective on mobile apps [21]. We are the first to study how likely the users are to notice spoofing attacks, where the malicious application resembles, but is not a perfect copy of, the legitimate application.

9. CONCLUSION

We have proposed a novel mobile app spoofing detection system that in collaborative fashion extracts screenshots periodically and analyzes their visual similarity with respect to protected login screens. We express the similarity in terms of a new metric called deception rate that represents the fraction of users that would confuse the examined screen for one of the protected login screens. We conducted an extensive online user study and trained our detection system using its results. Our system estimates deception rate with good accuracy (6-13% error) and low overhead (only 1%), and our system tells how likely the user is to fall for a potential attack. We consider this a powerful and interesting security property that no previous schemes provide. In addition to supporting a spoofing detection system, the results of our user study, on their own, provide insight into the perception and attentiveness of users during the login process.

10. REFERENCES

[1] Google safe browsing. http://googleonlinesecurity.blogspot.com/2012/06/safe-browsing-protecting-web-users-for.html.

[2] Spoofguard. http://crypto.stanford.edu/SpoofGuard/.

[3] S. Afroz and R. Greenstadt. Phishzoo: Detecting phishing websites by looking at them. In *Fifth IEEE International Conference on Semantic Computing (ICSC)*, 2011.

[4] A. Bianchi, J. Corbetta, L. Invernizzi, Y. Fratantonio, C. Kruegel, and G. Vigna. What the app is that? deception and countermeasures in the android user interface. In *Symposium on Security and Privacy (SP)*, 2015.

[5] G. Bradski. *Dr. Dobb's Journal of Software Tools*. 2000.

[6] K. Chen, P. Wang, Y. Lee, X. Wang, N. Zhang, H. Huang, W. Zou, and P. Liu. Finding unknown malice in 10 seconds: Mass vetting for new threats at the google-play scale. In *USENIX Security*, volume 15, 2015.

[7] Q. A. Chen, Z. Qian, and Z. M. Mao. Peeking into your app without actually seeing it: Ui state inference and novel android attacks. In *USENIX Security Symposium*, 2014.

[8] T.-C. Chen, S. Dick, and J. Miller. Detecting visually similar web pages: Application to phishing detection. *ACM Trans. Internet Technol.*, 10(2):1–38, 2010

[9] R. Dhamija and J. D. Tygar. The battle against phishing: Dynamic security skins. In *Symposium on Usable Privacy and Security (SOUPS)*, 2005.

[10] R. Dhamija, J. D. Tygar, and M. Hearst. Why phishing works. In *Conference on Human Factors in Computing Systems (CHI)*, 2006.

[11] A. P. Felt, M. Finifter, E. Chin, S. Hanna, and D. Wagner. A survey of mobile malware in the wild. In *Workshop on Security and Privacy in Smartphones and Mobile Devices (SPSM)*, 2011.

[12] A. P. Felt and D. Wagner. Phishing on mobile devices. In *Web 2.0 Security and Privacy Workshop (W2SP)*, 2011.

[13] Forbes. Alleged 'Nazi' Android FBI Ransomware Mastermind Arrested In Russia, April 2015. http://goo.gl/c91izV.

[14] A. Fu, L. Wenyin, and X. Deng. Detecting phishing web pages with visual similarity assessment based on earth mover's distance (EMD). *IEEE Transactions on Dependable and Secure Computing*, 3(4):301–311, 2006.

[15] J. Hong. The state of phishing attacks. *Communications of the ACM*, 55(1), 2012.

[16] International Secure Systems Lab. Antiphish, last access 2015. http://www.iseclab.org/projects/antiphish/.

[17] W. Liu, X. Deng, G. Huang, and A. Fu. An antiphishing strategy based on visual similarity assessment. *IEEE Internet Computing*, 10(2) March 2006.

[18] D. G. Lowe. Distinctive image features from scale-invariant keypoints. *International journal of computer vision*, 60(2), 2004.

[19] MacRumors. Masque attack vulnerability allows malicious third-party iOS apps to masquerade as legitimate apps. http://www.macrumors.com/2014/11/10/masque-attack-ios-vulnerability/.

[20] T. R. L. Malisa, K. Kostiainen, and S. Capkun. Detecting mobile application spoofing attacks by leveraging user visual similarity perception. Cryptology ePrint Archive, Report 2015/709, 2015. http://eprint.iacr.org/2015/709.

[21] C. Marforio, R. Jayaram Masti, C. Soriente, K. Kostiainen, and S. Capkun. Personalized Security Indicators to Detect Application Phishing Attacks in Mobile Platforms. *ArXiv e-prints*, Feb. 2015.

[22] M.-E. Maurer and D. Herzner. Using visual website similarity for phishing detection and reporting. In *Extended Abstracts on Human Factors in Computing Systems (CHI)*, 2012.

[23] E. Medvet, E. Kirda, and C. Kruegel. Visual-similarity-based phishing detection. In *International Conference on Security and Privacy in Communication Networks (SecureComm)*, 2008.

[24] W. Metzger. *Laws of Seeing*. The MIT Press, 2009.

[25] R. A. Rensink. Change detection. *Annual review of psychology*, 53(1), 2002.

[26] A. P. Rosiello, E. Kirda, C. Kruegel, and F. Ferrandi. A layout-similarity-based approach for detecting phishing pages. In *Conference on Security and Privacy in Communications Networks (SecureComm)*, 2007.

[27] E. Rublee, V. Rabaud, K. Konolige, and G. Bradski. Orb: An efficient alternative to sift or surf. In *International Conference on Computer Vision (ICCV)*, 2011.

[28] H. Sahbi, L. Ballan, G. Serra, and A. Del Bimbo. Context-dependent logo matching and recognition. *Image Processing, IEEE Transactions on*, 22(3), March 2013.

[29] S. E. Schechter, R. Dhamija, A. Ozment, and I. Fischer. The emperor's new security indicators. In *IEEE Symposium on Security and Privacy (SP)*, 2007.

[30] M. Selhorst, C. Stuble, F. Feldmann, and U. Gnaida. Towards a trusted mobile desktop. In *International Conference on Trust and Trustworthy Computing (TRUST)*, 2010.

[31] D. J. Simons and R. A. Rensink. Change blindness: past, present, and future. *TRENDS in Cognitive Sciences*, 9(1), 2005.

[32] Spider Labs. Focus stealing vulnerability in android. http://blog.spiderlabs.com/2011/08/twsl2011-008-focus-stealing-vulnerability-in-android.html.

[33] Symantec. Will Your Next TV Manual Ask You to Run a Scan Instead of Adjusting the Antenna?, April 2015. http://goo.gl/xh58UN.

[34] M. Wu, R. C. Miller, and S. L. Garfinkel. Do security toolbars actually prevent phishing attacks? In *Conference on Human Factors in Computing Systems (CHI)*, 2006.

[35] G. Xiang, J. Hong, C. P. Rose, and L. Cranor. Cantina+: A feature-rich machine learning framework for detecting phishing web sites. *ACM Transactions on Information and System Security (TISSEC)*, 14(2):21, 2011.

[36] Z. Xu and S. Zhu. Abusing notification services on smartphones for phishing and spamming. In *USENIX Workshop on Offensive Technologies (WOOT)*, 2012.

[37] J. Zhai and J. Su. The service you can't refuse: A secluded hijackrat. https://www.fireeye.com/blog/threat-research/2014/07/the-service-you-cant-refuse-a-secluded-hijackrat.html.

[38] H. Zhang, G. Liu, T. Chow, and W. Liu. Textual and visual content-based anti-phishing: A bayesian approach. *IEEE Transactions on Neural Networks*, 22(10), Oct 2011.

[39] Y. Zhang, J. I. Hong, and L. F. Cranor. Cantina: A content-based approach to detecting phishing web sites. In *International Conference on World Wide Web (WWW)*, 2007.

[40] W. Zhou, Y. Zhou, X. Jiang, and P. Ning. Detecting repackaged smartphone applications in third-party android marketplaces. In *Conference on Data and Application Security and Privacy (CODASPY)*, 2012.

APPENDIX
A. USER STUDY DETAILS

Participant recruitment. We recruited test participants by publishing survey jobs on the crowd sourcing platform. An example survey had a title *"Android Application Familiarity"* and the description of the survey was *"How familiar are you with the Facebook Android application?"*. We specified in the survey description that the participant should be an active user of the tested application, and we recruited 100 study participants for each sample, accepted participants globally, and required the participants to be at least 18 years old. The study participants were allowed to evaluate multiple samples from different datasets, but only one sample from each dataset. For example, a study participant could complete two surveys: one where we evaluated color modification samples and another regarding logo crop, but the same participant could not complete multiple surveys on color modification. In total 2,910 unique participants evaluated 5,900 Facebook samples. Statistics and participant demographics are listed in Table 1 and Table 2.

Study tasks. Each survey included 12 to 16 questions. We asked preliminary questions on participant demographics, tested application usage frequency, and a control question with a known correct answer. We showed the study participant a sample login screen screenshot and asked the

Unique study participants	2,910
Participants that completed multiple surveys	1,691
Screenshot samples	59
Total evaluations	5,900
Accepted evaluations after filtering	5,376
Average number of accepted evaluations per sample	91

Table 1: Statistics of the Facebook user study.

Age		Gender	
18-29	55.12%	Male	72.54%
30-39	29%	Female	27.45%
40-49	11.82%	**Education**	
50-59	3.33%	Primary school	2.06%
60 or above	0.72%	High school	34.57%
		Bachelor	63.36%

Table 2: Demographics of the Facebook user study.

participant the following questions: *"Is this screen (smart phone screenshot) the Facebook login screen as you remember it?"* and *"If you would see this screen, would you login with your real Facebook password?"*. We provided *Yes* and *No* reply alternatives on both questions. Using the percentage of *Yes* answers, we compute *as-remembered rate* and *login rate* for each sample. We also asked the participants to comment on their reason to log in, or retain from it.

B. DETECTION SYSTEM DETAILS

In this appendix we provide additional evaluation on how accurately the different components of the system perform.

B.1 Accuracy Evaluation

Reference Application Analysis Accuracy. We evaluated the accuracy of our reference app analysis tool (Section 5.2) on 1,270 apps, downloaded from Google Play and other marketplaces. The tool reported 572 potential login screens. Through manual verification, we found 230 login, 153 user registration, and 77 password change screens. The remaining 120 screens contained no login related functionality, and those we classify as false positives.

We manually verified 50 random apps from the set of 698 apps our tool reported as not having a potential login screen. We found 3 false negatives due to an implementation bug that was since fixed. We conclude that the tool can effectively find all login screens that require protection. The tool provides an over approximation, but a small number or false positives does not hamper security, as they only introduce additional reference values for similarity comparison. Moreover, developers have an incentive to help the reference login screen detection and they can explicitly mark which activity constitutes the login screen for even more accurate detection.

Decomposition Accuracy. To evaluate the accuracy of our algorithm, we decomposed 230 login screen screenshots. We manually verified the results and found that we detected all login screen elements correctly on 175 screens, 29 screens that correctly decomposed all but one element, and 9 screens with all but two correct decompositions. Our algorithm failed to decompose 18 screens.

Certain types of login screens are challenging for our approach. For example, the login screen of the Tumblr application contained a blurred natural image in the background, and our algorithm detected many erroneous elements. Our current implementation is optimized for clean login screens, as those are the pre-dominant login screen types. The majority (92%) of analyzed screenshots were visually simple and decomposed. We discuss noisy spoofing screens in Section 7.

300

Deep Android Malware Detection

Niall McLaughlin[*], Jesus Martinez del Rincon, BooJoong Kang, Suleiman Yerima,
Paul Miller, Sakir Sezer
Centre for Secure Information Technologies (CSIT)
Queen's University Belfast, UK

Yeganeh Safaei, Erik Trickel, Ziming Zhao, Adam Doupe, Gail Joon Ahn
Center for Cybersecurity and Digital Forensics
Arizona State University, USA

ABSTRACT

In this paper, we propose a novel android malware detection system that uses a deep convolutional neural network (CNN). Malware classification is performed based on static analysis of the raw opcode sequence from a disassembled program. Features indicative of malware are automatically learned by the network from the raw opcode sequence thus removing the need for hand-engineered malware features. The training pipeline of our proposed system is much simpler than existing n-gram based malware detection methods, as the network is trained end-to-end to jointly learn appropriate features and to perform classification, thus removing the need to explicitly enumerate millions of n-grams during training. The network design also allows the use of long n-gram like features, not computationally feasible with existing methods. Once trained, the network can be efficiently executed on a GPU, allowing a very large number of files to be scanned quickly.

CCS Concepts

•Security and privacy → Malware and its mitigation; *Software and application security;* •Computing methodologies → *Neural networks;*

Keywords

Malware Detection, Android, Deep Learning

1. INTRODUCTION

Malware detection is a growing problem, especially in mobile platforms. Given the proliferation of mobile devices and their associated app-stores, the volume of new applications is too large to manually examine each application for malicious behavior. Malware detection has traditionally been based on manually examining the behavior and/or de-compiled code

---

[*]Corresponding author: n.mclaughlin@qub.ac.uk

CODASPY'17, March 22 - 24, 2017, Scottsdale, AZ, USA

© 2017 Copyright held by the owner/author(s). Publication rights licensed to ACM.
ISBN 978-1-4503-4523-1/17/03. . . $15.00

DOI: http://dx.doi.org/10.1145/3029806.3029823

of known malware programs in order to design malware signatures by hand. This process does not easily scale to large numbers of applications, especially given the static nature of signature based malware detection, meaning that new malware can be designed to evade existing signatures. Consequently, there has recently been a large volume of work on automatic malware detection using ideas from machine learning. Various methods have been proposed based on examining the dynamic application behavior [13, 21], requested permissions [14, 16, 19] and the n-grams present in the application byte-code [7, 11, 10]. However many of these methods are reliant on expert analysis to design the discriminative features that are passed to the machine learning system used to make the final classification decision.

Recently, convolutional networks have been shown to perform well on a variety of tasks related to natural language processing [12, 26]. In this work we investigate the application of convolutional networks to malware detection by treating the disassembled byte-code of an application as a *text* to be analyzed. This approach has the advantage that features are automatically learned from raw data, and hence removes the need for malware signatures to be designed by hand. Our proposed malware detection method is computationally efficient as training and testing time is linearly proportional to the number of malware examples. The detection network can be run on a GPU, which is now a standard component of many mobile devices, meaning a large number of malware files can be scanned per-second. In addition, we expect that as more training data is provided the accuracy of malware detection will improve because neural networks have been shown to have a very high learning capacity, and hence can benefit from very large training-sets [20].

Our proposed malware detection method takes inspiration from existing n-gram based methods [7, 11, 10], but unlike existing methods there is no need to exhaustively enumerate a large number of n-grams during training. This is because the convolutional network can intrinsically learn to detect n-gram like signatures by learning to detect sequences of opcodes that are indicative of malware. In addition, our proposed method allows very long n-gram type signatures to be discovered, which would be impractical if explicit enumeration of all n-grams was required. The malware signatures found by the proposed method may be complementary to those discovered by hand as the automated system will have different strengths and biases from human analysts, therefore they could be valuable for use in conjunction with conventional malware signatures databases. Once our system has been trained, large numbers of files can be efficiently scanned using a GPU implementation, and given that new malware is constantly appearing, a useful feature of our proposed method is that it can be re-trained with new malware samples to adapt to the changing malware environment.

2. RELATED WORK

2.1 Malware Detection

Learning based approaches using hand-designed features have been applied extensively to both dynamic [18, 21] and static [23, 22, 25] malware detection. A variety of similar approaches to static malware detection have used manually derived features, such as API calls, intents, permissions and commands, with different classifiers such as support vector machine (SVM) [5], Naive Bayes, and k-Nearest Neighbor [19]. Malware detection approaches have also been proposed that use static features derived exclusively from the permissions requested by the application [14, 16].

In contrast with approaches using high-level hand-designed features, n-grams based malware detection uses sequences of low-level opcodes as features. The n-grams features can be used to train a classifier to distinguish between malware and benign software [10]. Perhaps surprisingly, even a 1-gram based feature, which is simply a histogram of the number of times each opcode is used, can distinguish malware from benign software [7]. The length of the n-gram used [10] and number of n-gram sequences used in classification [7] can both have an effect on the accuracy of the classifier. However increasing either parameter can massively increase the computational resources needed [7], which is clearly a disadvantage of standard n-gram based malware detection approaches. N-grams method also require feature selection to reduce the length of the feature-vector, which would otherwise be millions of elements long in the case of long n-grams. In this work we propose a method that allows very long n-grams features to be used, and allows an n-grams classifier to be trained in a much more efficient manner, based on neural networks.

2.2 Neural Networks

Recently, convolutional neural networks (CNNs) have shown state-of-the-art performance for object recognition in images [20] and natural language processing (NLP) [12]. In NLP, local patterns of symbols, known as n-grams, have been used as features for a variety of tasks [27]. It has recently been shown that if sufficient training data is available, very deep CNNs can outperform traditional NLP methods [26] across a range of text classification tasks. We postulate that static malware analysis has much in common with NLP as the analysis of the disassembled source code of a given program can be understood as a form of textual processing. Therefore, techniques such as CNNs have huge potential to be applied in the field of malware detection.

A variety of approaches to malware detection using other neural network architectures have been proposed. Several of the proposed methods are based on learning which sequences of operating system calls or API calls are indicative of malware [15, 9, 8] during dynamic analysis. The existing neural network based approaches to malware detection differ from our proposed method as they make use of a virtual machine to capture dynamic behavioural features [15, 9, 8]. This may prove problematic given that malware is often designed to detect when it is being run in a virtual environment in order to evade detection. Other existing neural network based malware detection methods use hand-designed features, which may not be the optimal way to detect malware [17]. We will attempt to address the limitations of existing neural network based malware detection methods, by using a novel static analysis method based on a CNN architecture that automatically learns an appropriate feature representation from raw data.

In this work we apply convolutional neural networks to the problem of malware detection. The CNN learns to detect patterns in the disassembled byte-code of applications that are indicative of malware. Our approach has several advantages over existing methods of malware detection, such as those based on high-level hand-designed features and those based on detection of n-grams. Scalability and performance are major drawbacks of existing n-gram based approaches, as the length of the feature vector grows rapidly when increasing the n-gram length. In contrast, our approach eliminates the need for counting and storing millions of n-grams during training and can learn longer n-grams than conventional methods used for malware detection. The improved efficiency makes it possible to use our proposed method with larger datasets, where the use of traditional methods would be intractable. Our whole system is jointly optimized to perform feature extraction and classification simultaneously by showing the system a large number of labeled samples. This removes the need for hand-designed features, as features are automatically learned during supervised network training, and removes the need for an ad-hoc pipeline consisting of feature-extraction, feature-selection and classification, as feature extraction and classification are optimized together. The existence of a fully end-to-end system also saves time when the system is presented with new malware to be recognized, as the network can easily be updated by simply increasing the size of the training-set, which may also improve its overall accuracy. Finally, the features discovered by our method may be different from, and complementary to, those discovered by manual analysis.

3. METHOD

In this work we propose a malware detection method that uses a convolutional network to process the raw Dalvik byte-code of an Android application. The overall structure of the malware detection network is shown in Fig. 2. In the following section we will first explain how an Android application is disassembled to give a sequence of raw Dalvik byte-codes, and then explain how this byte-code sequence is processed by the convolutional network.

3.1 Disassembly of Android Application

In our system, the preprocessing of an application consists of disassembling the application and extracting opcode sequences for static malware analysis, as shown in Fig.1. An Android application is an *apk* file, which is a compressed file containing the code files, the *AndroidManifest.xml* file, and the application resource files. A code file is a *dex* file that can be transformed into *smali* files, where each *smali* file represents a single class and contains the methods of such a class. Each method contains instructions and each instruction consists of a single opcode and multiple operands. We disassemble each application using *baksmali* [1] to obtain the *smali* files that contain the human-readable Dalvik bytecode of the application, then extracting the opcode sequence from each method, discarding the operands. As the result of the preprocessing we obtain all the opcode sequences from all the classes of the application. The opcode sequences from all classes are then concatenated to give a single sequence of opcodes representing whole application.

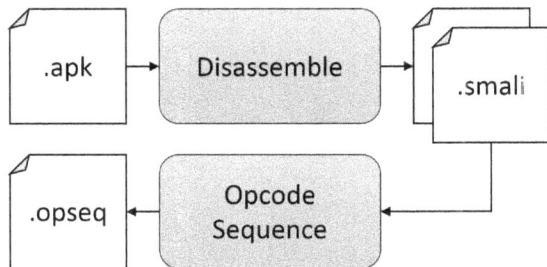

Figure 1: Work-flow of how an Android application is disassembled to produce an opcode sequence.

3.2 Network Architecture

3.2.1 Opcode Embedding Layer

Let $X = \{x_1...x_n\}$ be a sequence of opcode instructions encoded as one-hot vectors, where x_n is the one-hot vector for the n'th opcode in the sequence. To form a one-hot vector we associate each opcode with a number in the range 1 to D. In the case of Dalvik, where there are currently 218 defined opcodes, $D = 218$ [2]. The one-hot vector x_n is a vector of zeros, of length D, with a '1' in the position corresponding with the n'th opcode's integer mapping. Any operands associated with the opcodes were discarded during disassembly and preprocessing, meaning malware classification is based only on patterns in the sequence of opcodes.

Opcodes in X are projected into an embedding space by multiplying each one-hot vector by a weight matrix, $W_E \in \mathbb{R}^{D \times k}$, where k is the dimensionality of the embedding-space as follows

$$p_i = x_i W_E \qquad (1)$$

projection of all opcodes in X, the program is represented by a matrix, P, of size $n \times k$, where each row, p_i, corresponds to the representation of opcode x_i. The weights in W_E, and hence the representation for each opcode, are initialized randomly at first then updated by back-propagation during training along with the rest of the network's parameters.

The purpose of representing the program as a list of one-hot vectors then projecting into an embedding space, is that it allows the network to learn an appropriate representation for each opcode as a vector in a k-dimensional continuous vector space, $\mathbb{R}^k$ where relationships between opcodes can be represented. The embedding space may encode semantic information for example, during training the network may discover that certain opcodes have similar meanings or perform equivalent operations, and hence should be treated similarly by deeper network layers for classification purposes. This can be achieved by projecting those opcodes to nearby points in the embedding space, while very different opcodes will be projected to distant points. The number of dimensions used in the embedding space may influence the network's ability

to perform such semantic mapping, hence using more dimensions may, up to a point, give the network greater flexibility in learning the expected highly non-linear mapping from sequences of opcodes to classification decisions.

3.2.2 Convolutional Layers

In our proposed network we use one or more convolutional layers, numbered from 1 to L, where l refers to the l'th convolutional layer. The first convolutional layer receives the $n \times k$ program embedding matrix P as input, while deeper convolutional layers receive the output of the previous convolutional layer as input. Each convolutional layer has m_l filters, which are of size $s_1 \times k$ in the first layer, and of size $s_l \times m_{l-1}$ in deeper layers. This means filters in the first layer can potentially detect sequences of up to s_l opcodes. During the forward pass of an example through a convolutional layer, each of the m_l convolutional filters produces an activation map $a_{l,m}$ of size $n \times 1$, which can be stacked together to produce, a matrix, A_l, of size $n \times m_l$. Note that before applying the convolutional filters we zero-pad the start and end of the input by $s_l/2$ to ensure that the length of the output matrix from the convolutional layer is the same as the length of its input. The convolution of the first layer filters with program embedding matrix P can be denoted as follows

$$a_{l,m} = relu(Conv(P)_{W_{l,m}, b_{l,m}}) \qquad (2)$$

$$A_l = [a_{l,1} \mid a_{l,2} \mid ... \mid a_{l,m}] \qquad (3)$$

where $w_{l,m}$ and $b_{l,m}$ are the respective weight and bias parameters of the m'th convolutional filter of convolution layer l, where $Conv$ represents the mathematical operation of convolution of the filter with the input, and where the rectified linear activation function, $relu(x) = \max\{0, x\}$, is used. In deeper layers the convolution operation is similar, however we replace input matrix P in Eq. 2 by the output matrix from the previous convolutional layer, A_{l-1}. Given output matrix A_L from the final convolutional layer, max-pooling [27] is then used over the program length dimension as follows

$$f = [\max(a_{L,1}) \mid \max(a_{L,2}) \mid ... \mid \max(a_{L,m})] \qquad (4)$$

to give a vector f of length m_L, which contains the maximum activation of each convolutional filter over the program length. Using max-pooling over the length of the opcode sequence allows a program of arbitrarily length to be represented by a fixed-length feature vector. Moreover, selecting the maximum activation of each convolutional filter using max-pooling also focuses the attention of the classification layer on parts of the opcode sequence that are most relevant to the classification task.

3.2.3 Classification Layers

Finally, the resulting vector f is passed to a multi-layer perceptron (MLP), which consists of a full-connected hidden layer and a full-connected output layer. The purpose of the MLP is to output the probability that the current example is malware. The use of the MLP with hidden layer allows high-order relationships between the features extracted by the convolutional layer to be detected [6] and used for clas-

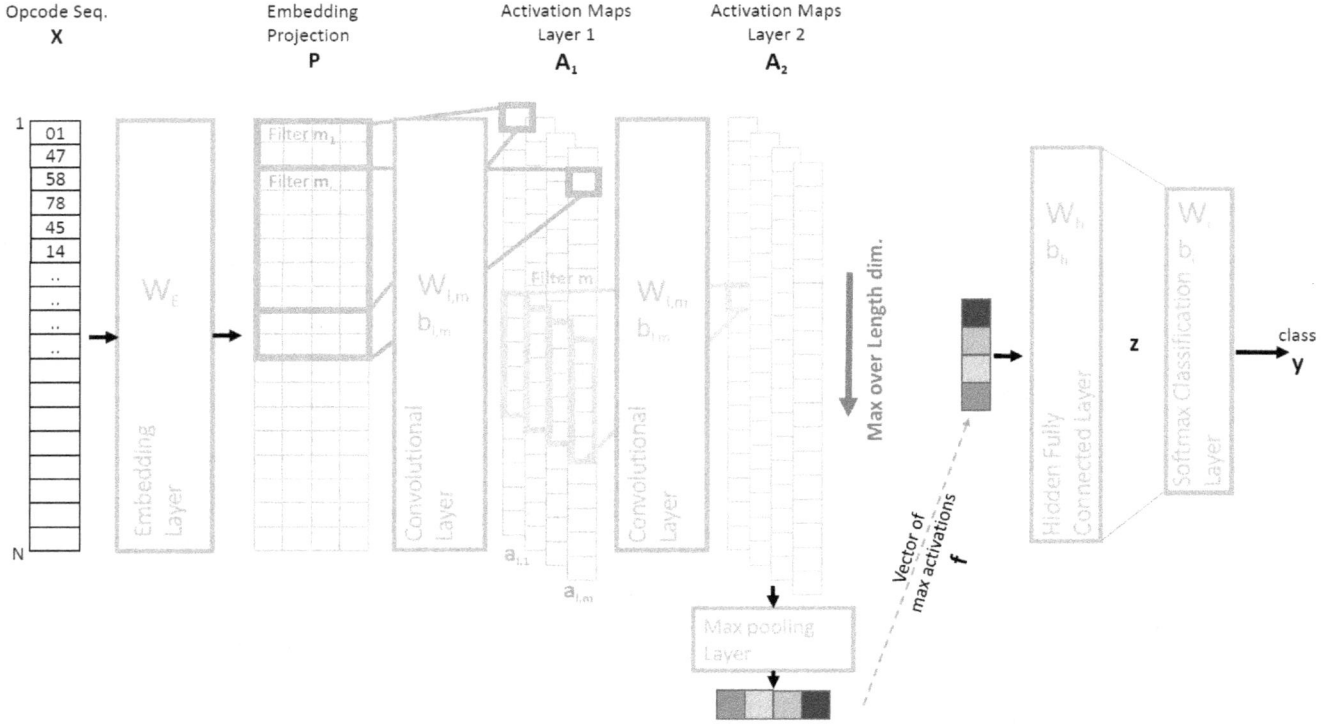

Figure 2: Malware Detection Network Architecture.

sification. We can write the hidden layer as follows

$$z = relu(W_h f + b_h) \qquad (5)$$

where W_h, b_h, are the parameters of the fully-connected hidden layer, and where the rectified linear activation function is used. Finally, the output, z, from the MLP is passed to a soft-max classifier function, which gives the probability that program X is malware, denoted as follows

$$p(y = i|z) = \frac{\exp(w_i^T z + b_i)}{\sum_{i'=1}^{I} \exp(w_{i'}^T z + b_{i'})} \qquad (6)$$

where w_i and b_i denote the parameters of the classifier for class $i \in I$, and the label y indicates whether the current sample is either malware or benign. The softmax classifier outputs the normalized probability of the current sample belonging to each class. As malware classification is a two class problem (benign/malware) i.e., $I = 2$ and z is a two element vector. Other applications such as the problem of malware family classification, could be targeted by increasing the number of classes, I, to be equal to the number of malware families to be classified.

3.3 Learning Process

Given the above definitions, the cost function to be minimized during training for a batch of b training samples, $\{X^{(1)} \dots X^{(b)}\}$, can be written as follows

$$C = -\frac{1}{b} \sum_{j=1}^{b} \sum_{i=1}^{I} 1\{y^{(j)} = i\} log\, p(y^{(j)} = i|z^{(j)}) \qquad (7)$$

where $z^{(j)}$ is the vector output after applying the neural network to example training example $X^{(j)}$, where $y^{(j)}$ is the

provided correct label for the example $X^{(j)}$, and where $1\{x\}$ is an indicator function that is 1 if its argument x is true and is 0 otherwise. The cost is dependent on both the parameters of the neural network, Θ, i.e. the weights and bias across all layers -W_E, $w_{l,m}$, $b_{l,m}$,W_h, b_h,w_i, and b_i - and on the current training sample. The objective during training is to update the network's parameters, which are initialized randomly before training begins, to reduce the cost. This update is performed stochastically by computing the gradient of the cost function with respect to the parameters, $\frac{\partial C}{\partial \Theta}$, given the current batch of samples, and using this gradient to update the parameters after every batch to reduce the cost as follows

$$\Theta^{(t+1)} = \Theta^{(t)} - \alpha \frac{\partial C}{\partial \Theta} \qquad (8)$$

where α is a small positive real number called the learning rate. During training the network is repeatedly presented with batches of training samples in randomized order until the parameters converge.

To deal with an imbalance in the number of training samples available for the malware and benign classes, the gradients used to update the network parameters are weighted depending on the label of the current training sample. This helps to reduce classifier bias towards predicting the more populous class. Let the number of malware samples in the training-set be M and number of benign samples in the training-set be B. Assuming there are more samples of benign software than malware, the weight for malware samples is $1 - M/(M + B)$ and the weight for benign samples is $M/(M + B)$ i.e. the gradients are weighted in inverse proportion to the number of samples for each class.

Note that a consideration when designing our proposed ar-

304

chitectures was to keep the number of parameters relatively low, in order to help prevent over-fitting given the relatively small number of training samples usually available. A typical deep network may have millions of parameters [20], while our malware detection network has only tens of thousands of parameters, which drastically reduces the need for large numbers of training samples.

4. RESULTS

In order to evaluate the performance of our approach a set of experiments was designed. The architecture used in all experiments had only a single convolutional layer. This architecture was used because the available datasets have a relatively small number of training samples which means that networks with large numbers of parameters could be prone to over-fitting. Convolutional networks with only a single convolutional layer have been shown to perform well on natural language text classification tasks [27]. In this architecture, the remaining hyperparameters, such as the dimension of the embedding space and the length and the number of convolutional filters, are set empirically using 10-fold cross validation on the validation-set of the small and large dataset. The resulting values are a 8-dimensional embedding space, 64 convolutional filters of length 8, and 16 neurons in the hidden fully connected layer.

Our experiments were carried out on three different datasets. The first dataset consists of malware from the Android Malware Genome project [28] and has been widely used [10, 11]. This dataset has a total of 2123 applications, of which 863 are benign and 1260 are malware from 49 different malware families. Labels are provided for the malware family of each sample. The benign samples in this dataset were collected from the Google play store and have been checked using virusTotal to ascertain that they were highly probable to be malware free. We refer to this dataset as the 'Small Dataset'.

The second dataset was provided by McAfee Labs (now Intel Security) and comes from the vendor's internal repository of Android malware. After discarding empty files or files that are less than 8 opcodes long, the dataset contains 2475 malware samples and 3627 benign samples. This dataset does not include malware family labels and may include malware and/or benign applications present in the small dataset. Hence to ensuring training hygiene i.e. to ensure we do not train on the testing-set, the network is trained and tested on each dataset separately without cross-contamination. We refer to this dataset as the 'Large Dataset'.

We also have an additional dataset provided by McAfee Labs containing approximately 18,000 android programs, and which was collected more recently than the first two datasets. This was used for testing the final system after setting the hyper-parameters using the smaller datasets. After discarding short files, the dataset contains 9268 benign files and 9902 malware files. We refer to this dataset as the 'V. Large Dataset'.

Each dataset was split into 90% for training and validation and the remaining 10% was held-out for testing. Care was taken to ensure that the ratio of positive to negative samples in the validation and testing sets was the same as in the dataset as a whole.

Results are reported using the mean of the classification accuracy, precision, recall and f-score. The key indicator of

performance is f-score, because the number of samples in the malware and benign classes is not equal. In this situation, classification accuracy is too influenced by the number of samples in each class. For example if the majority of samples were of class x, and the classifier simply reported x in all cases, the classification accuracy would be high, although the classifier would not be useful. However, given the same conditions, the f-score, which is based on the precision and recall, would be low.

Our neural network software was developed using the Torch scientific computing environment [4]. During training the network parameters were optimized using RMSProp [3] with a learning rate of 1e-2, for 10 epochs, using a mini-batch size of 16. The network weights were randomly initialized using the default Torch initialization. We used an Nvidia GTX 980 GPU for development of the network, and training the network to perform malware classification takes around 25 minutes on the large dataset (which contains approximately 6000 example programs). Once the network has been trained our implementation can classify approximately 3000 files per-second on the GPU.

4.1 Classification Accuracy

In this experiment, the network's performance is measured in terms of accuracy. The network was trained using the complete training and validation set, then tested on the held-out test-set that was not seen during hyper-parameter tuning. We compare the performance of our proposed system with our own implementation of an n-gram based malware detection method [10]. For both datasets we measured the performance of this system using 1, 2 and 3-gram features. The same training and testing samples were used for both systems in order to allow for direct comparison of their performance. The results for the small and large and v. large datasets are shown in Table 1. We have endeavored to select papers from the literature that use similar Android malware datasets to give as fair a comparison as possible.

In the small dataset our proposed method clearly achieves state-of-the-art performance, and is comparable to methods such as [10] and [23]. It achieves better performance than our baseline n-gram system with 1-gram features and near identical performance to the baseline with 2 and 3-gram features.

The large dataset is more challenging due to the greater variably of malware present. Our system achieves similar performance to the baseline n-gram system, while having far greater computational efficiency (See Section 4.2). Although other methods have achieved better performance on similar tests, they make use of additional outside information such as the application's requested permissions or API calls [25]. In contrast, our proposed method needs only the raw opcodes, which avoids the need for features manually designed by domain experts. Moreover, our proposed method has the advantage over existing methods of being very computational efficient, as it is capable of classifying approximately 3000 files per-second.

The results on the v. large dataset, which was obtained from the same source as the large dataset and hence likely shares similar characteristics, shows that our system's performance improves as more training data is provided. This phenomenon has been observed when training neural networks in other domains, where performance is highly correlated with the number of training samples. We expect that

Classification System	Feature Types	Benign	Malware	Acc.	Prec.	Recall	F-score
Ours (Small DS)	CNN applied to raw opcodes	863	1260	0.98	0.99	0.95	0.97
Ours (Large DS)	CNN applied to raw opcodes	3627	2475	0.80	0.72	0.85	0.78
Ours (V. Large DS)	CNN applied to raw opcodes	9268	9902	0.87	0.87	0.85	0.86
n-grams (Small DS)	opcode n-grams (n=1)	863	1260	0.95	0.95	0.95	0.95
	opcode n-grams (n=2)	863	1260	0.98	0.98	0.98	0.98
	opcode n-grams (n=3)	863	1260	0.98	0.98	0.98	0.98
n-grams (Large DS)	opcode n-grams (n=1)	3627	2475	0.80	0.81	0.80	0.80
	opcode n-grams (n=2)	3627	2475	0.81	0.83	0.82	0.82
	opcode n-grams (n=3)	3627	2475	0.82	0.83	0.82	0.82
DroidDetective [13]	Perms. combination	741	1260	0.96	0.89	0.96	0.92
Yerima [23]	API calls, Perms., intents, cmnds	1000	1000	0.91	0.94	0.91	0.92
Jerome [10]	opcode n-grams	1260	1246	-	-	-	0.98
Yerima [25] *	API calls, Perms., intents, cmnds	2925	3938	0.97	0.98	0.97	0.97
Yerima (2) [24]*	API calls, Perms., intents, cmnds.	2925	3938	0.96	0.96	0.96	0.96

Table 1: **Malware classification results for our system on both the small and large datasets compared with results from the literature. Results from the literature marked with a (*) use malware from the McAfee Labs dataset i.e. our large dataset, while all others use malware sampled from the Android Malware Genome project [28] dataset i.e. our small dataset**

these results can be further improved given greater quantities of training data, which will also allow more complex network architectures to be explored. Unfortunately comparisons with the baseline n-gram system on the v. large dataset were not possible due to computational cost associated with the n-gram method.

4.2 Computational Efficiency

In this experiment we compare the computational efficiency of our proposed malware classification system with our implementation of a conventional n-gram based malware classification system [10]. Note that when reporting the results we do not include the time take to disassemble the malware files as this is constant for both systems. The results in Table 2 are presented in terms of both the average time to reach a classification decision for a single malware file, and the corresponding average number of programs that can be classified per second.

System	Time per program (s)	Programs per second
Ours	0.000329	3039.8
1-gram	0.000569	1758.3
2-gram	0.010711	93.4
3-gram	0.172749	5.8

Table 2: **Comparing the time taken to reach a classification decision and number of programs that can be classified per second, for our proposed neural network system and a conventional n-gram based system.**

It can be seen from Table 2 that our system can produce a much higher number malware classification decisions per second than the n-gram based system. The n-gram based system also experiences exponential slow-down as the length of the n-gram features are increased. This severely limits the use of longer n-grams, which are necessary for improved classification accuracy. Our proposed system is not limited in the same way, and in fact, the features extracted by the first layer of the CNN can be thought of as n-grams where $n = 8$. Use of such features with a conventional n-gram based system would be much too computationally expensive. Our proposed neural network system is implemented on a desktop GPU, specifically an Nvidia GTX-980, however it could easily be moved to the GPU of a mobile device, allowing for fast and efficient malware classification of Android applications.

Finally, the memory usage required to execute the trained neural network is constant. Increasing the length or number of convolutional filters, or increasing the number of training examples linearly increases memory usage. Whereas with n-gram based systems, increasing the training-set size dramatically increases the number of unique n-grams and hence memory usage. For instance, with the small dataset there are 213 unique 1-grams, 1891 unique 2-grams, and 286471 unique 3-grams. This means our proposed neural network based system also more efficient in terms of memory usage during training.

4.3 Learning Curves

In this experiment we aim to understand the system's performance as a function of the quantity of training data, with the aim of predicting how its performance is likely to change if more training data were to be made available.

This experiment was performed on the V. Large dataset. As in previous experiments, the dataset is split into training and validation sets. Throughout the experiment the validation-set remains fixed. An artificially reduced size training-set is constructed by randomly sub-sampling from the complete set of training examples. The network is then trained from scratch on this reduced size training-set, and the system's performance measured on both the training and validation sets. This process is repeated for several different sizes of training-set, ranging from a small number of examples up to the complete set of all training-examples. The system's performance on the validation-set and training-set are then plotted as a function of the training-set size. Performance is recorded in terms of $1 - $ f-score, meaning that perfect performance would produce a value of zero.

In figure 3, we can see that when only a small number of training-examples are provided, training-set performance is perfect, while validation-set performance is very poor. This is to be expected as with such a small number of training-examples the system will over-fit to the training-set and the learned parameters will not generalize to the unseen validation-set. However, as more training-examples are provided the validation-set error decreases, showing that the system has learned to generalize from the training-set. We can predict from the learning curves in figure 3 that if more training-examples were to be provided, the validation-set error would continue to decrease.

These results suggest that our system benefits from larger quantities of training-data as expected with neural networks [20]. They also show that the poor performance on the 'Large Dataset', which was obtained from the same source as the 'V. Large dataset' and hence shares similar characteristics, is caused by lack of data. This is indicated by the gap between the validation and testing-set errors when only approximately 6000 training examples are provided.

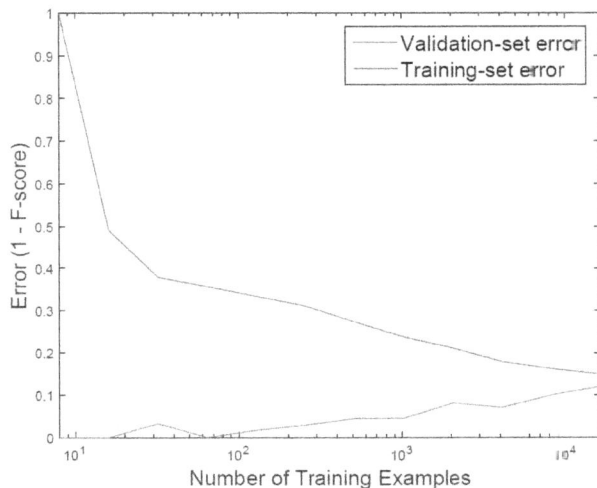

Figure 3: Learning curves for the Validation-set and Training-set as the number of training examples is varied. Note the log-scale on the x-axis.

4.4 Realistic Testing

In order to assess the potential of our proposed classification technique in realistic environments we apply our trained network to a completely new dataset. This allows us to demonstrate the real-world potential of our classification technique when applied to an unknown and realistic dataset at a bigger scale. The network used in this experiment was trained on the V. Large dataset, introduced in Section 4.

Our new dataset consists of 96,412 benign apps and 24,103 malware apps. The benign apps were randomly selected from the Google Play store, and were collected during July and August 2016. To represent a distinct set of malicious apps, we used another dataset containing known malware apps, including those from the Android Malware Genome project [28], but removing the ones overlapping with the training set of the network.

Approximately 1 TB of APKs were used in this experiment. The APKs were converted to opcode sequences using

a cloud architecture consisting of 29 machines running in parallel, in a process which took around 11 hours. Classification of the opcode sequences was performed using an Nvidia GTX 1080 GPU, and took an hour to complete.

Note that for this experiment we assume that all APKs in the Google Play dataset are benign, and all the APKs in the malicious dataset are malicious. Of course, this may be a naive assumption, as it is possible for malicious apps to exist on Google Play.

Cross validation testing was performed on our new dataset. In each cross validation fold approximately 24,000 malware applications and 24,000 benign application were used. Therefore, in order to present all applications to the network four-fold cross validation was used. The results of this experiment are reported in Table 3.

Classification System	Acc.	Prec.	Recall	F-score
Ours	0.69	0.67	0.74	0.71

Table 3: Malware classification results of our system tested on an independent dataset of benign and malware Android applications.

We can see from the results in Table 3 that although the f-score is lower than previous experiments, our system has the potential to work in realistic environments. This is because our new testing dataset is much larger than the one used for training the network and contains greater variability of applications. The results of this experiment show that the network has learned features with the ability to generalise to realistic data. In future work we hope to take advantage of our new dataset to explore more complex network architectures that can be learned given more training data.

5. CONCLUSIONS

In this paper we have presented a novel Android malware detection system based on deep neural networks. This innovative application of deep learning to the field of malware analysis has shown good performance and potential in comparison with other state-of-art techniques, and has been validated in four different Android malware datasets. Our system is capable of simultaneously learning to perform feature extraction and malware classification given only the raw opcode sequences of a large number of labeled malware samples. The main advantages of our system are that it removes the need for hand-engineered malware features, it is much more computationally efficient than existing n-gram based malware classification systems, and can be implemented to run on the GPU of mobile devices.

As future work, we would like to extend our methodology to both dynamic and static malware analysis in different platforms. Our proposed method is general enough that it could be applied to other types of malware analysis with only minor changes to the network architecture. For instance, the network could process sequences of instructions produced by dynamic analysis software. Similarly, by changing the disassembly preprocessing step the same network architecture could be applied to malware analysis on different platforms.

Another open problem for malware classification, which may allow networks with more parameters, and hence greater discriminative power, to be used, is data augmentation. Data augmentation is a way to artificially increase the size of the training-set, by slightly modifying existing training-examples.

The transformations used in data augmentation are usually chosen to simulate variations that occur in real world data, but which may not be extensively covered by the available training-set. We would like to investigate the design of data-augmentation schemes appropriate to malware detection.

6. ACKNOWLEDGEMENTS

This work was partially supported by the grants from Global Research Laboratory Project through National Research Foundation (NRF-2014K1A1A2043029) and the Center for Cybersecurity and Digital Forensics at Arizona State University. This work was also partially supported by Engineering and Physical Sciences Research Council (EPSRC) grant EP/N508664/1.

7. REFERENCES

[1] Baksmali. https://github.com/JesusFreke/smali. Accessed: 2015-02-15.

[2] Dalvik bytecode. https://source.android.com/devices/tech/dalvik/dalvik-bytecode.html. Accessed: 2015-02-01.

[3] RMSProp. www.cs.toronto.edu/~tijmen/csc321/slides/lecture_slides_lec6.pdf. Slide 29.

[4] Torch. http://torch.ch/.

[5] D. Arp, M. Spreitzenbarth, M. Hubner, H. Gascon, and K. Rieck. Drebin: Effective and explainable detection of android malware in your pocket. In *NDSS*, 2014.

[6] C. M. Bishop. *Neural networks for pattern recognition.* Oxford university press, 1995.

[7] G. Canfora, F. Mercaldo, and C. A. Visaggio. Mobile malware detection using op-code frequency histograms. In *Proc. of Int. Conf. on Security and Cryptography (SECRYPT)*, 2015.

[8] G. E. Dahl, J. W. Stokes, L. Deng, and D. Yu. Large-scale malware classification using random projections and neural networks. In *Acoustics, Speech and Signal Processing (ICASSP), 2013 IEEE Int. Conf. on*, pages 3422–3426, 2013.

[9] O. E. David and N. S. Netanyahu. Deepsign: Deep learning for automatic malware signature generation and classification. In *Neural Networks (IJCNN), 2015 Int. Joint Conf. on*, pages 1–8, 2015.

[10] Q. Jerome, K. Allix, R. State, and T. Engel. Using opcode-sequences to detect malicious android applications. In *Communications (ICC), 2014 IEEE Int. Conf. on*, pages 914–919, 2014.

[11] B. Kang, B. Kang, J. Kim, and E. G. Im. Android malware classification method: Dalvik bytecode frequency analysis. In *Proc. of the 2013 Research in Adaptive and Convergent Systems*, pages 349–350, 2013.

[12] Y. Kim. Convolutional neural networks for sentence classification. *arXiv preprint arXiv:1408.5882*, 2014.

[13] S. Liang and X. Du. Permission-combination-based scheme for android mobile malware detection. In *Communications (ICC), 2014 IEEE Int. Conf. on*, pages 2301–2306, 2014.

[14] X. Liu and J. Liu. A two-layered permission-based android malware detection scheme. In *Mobile Cloud Computing, Services and Engineering (MobileCloud), 2014 2nd IEEE Int. Conf. on*, pages 142–148, 2014.

[15] R. Pascanu, J. W. Stokes, H. Sanossian, M. Marinescu, and A. Thomas. Malware classification with recurrent networks. In *Acoustics, Speech and Signal Processing (ICASSP), 2015 IEEE Int. Conf. on*, pages 1916–1920, 2015.

[16] B. Sanz, I. Santos, C. Laorden, X. Ugarte-Pedrero, P. G. Bringas, and G. Álvarez. Puma: Permission usage to detect malware in android. In *Int. Joint Conf. CISIS´12-ICEUTE´12-SOCO´12*, pages 289–298, 2013.

[17] J. Saxe and K. Berlin. Deep neural network based malware detection using two dimensional binary program features. In *2015 10th International Conference on Malicious and Unwanted Software (MALWARE)*, pages 11–20, Oct 2015.

[18] A. Shabtai, U. Kanonov, Y. Elovici, C. Glezer, and Y. Weiss. " andromaly": a behavioral malware detection framework for android devices. *Journal of Intelligent Information Systems*, 38(1):161–190, 2012.

[19] A. Sharma and S. K. Dash. Mining api calls and permissions for android malware detection. In *Cryptology and Network Security*, pages 191–205. 2014.

[20] K. Simonyan and A. Zisserman. Very deep convolutional networks for large-scale image recognition. *arXiv preprint arXiv:1409.1556*, 2014.

[21] X. Su, M. C. Chuah, and G. Tan. Smartphone dual defense protection framework: Detecting malicious applications in android markets. In *Mobile Ad-hoc and Sensor Networks (MSN), 2012 Eighth Int. Conf. on*, pages 153–160, 2012.

[22] D.-J. Wu, C.-H. Mao, T.-E. Wei, H.-M. Lee, and K.-P. Wu. Droidmat: Android malware detection through manifest and api calls tracing. In *Information Security (Asia JCIS), 2012 7th Asia Joint Conf. on*, pages 62–69, 2012.

[23] S. Y. Yerima, S. Sezer, G. McWilliams, and I. Muttik. A new android malware detection approach using bayesian classification. In *Advanced Information Networking and Applications (AINA), 2013 IEEE 27th Int.l Conf. on*, pages 121–128, 2013.

[24] S. Y. Yerima, S. Sezer, and I. Muttik. Android malware detection: An eigenspace analysis approach. In *Science and Information Conference (SAI), 2015*, pages 1236–1242, 2015.

[25] S. Y. Yerima, S. Sezer, and I. Muttik. High accuracy android malware detection using ensemble learning. *Information Security, IET*, 9(6):313–320, 2015.

[26] X. Zhang, J. Zhao, and Y. LeCun. Character-level convolutional networks for text classification. In *Advances in Neural Information Processing Systems*, pages 649–657, 2015.

[27] Y. Zhang and B. Wallace. A sensitivity analysis of (and practitioners' guide to) convolutional neural networks for sentence classification. *arXiv preprint arXiv:1510.03820*, 2015.

[28] Y. Zhou and X. Jiang. Dissecting android malware: Characterization and evolution. In *Security and Privacy (SP), 2012 IEEE Symp. on*, pages 95–109, 2012.

DroidSieve: Fast and Accurate Classification of Obfuscated Android Malware

Guillermo Suarez-Tangil[1], Santanu Kumar Dash[1], Mansour Ahmadi[2],

Johannes Kinder[1], Giorgio Giacinto[2] and Lorenzo Cavallaro[1]

[1] Royal Holloway, University of London*

[2] University of Cagliari†

ABSTRACT

With more than two million applications, Android market-places require automatic and scalable methods to efficiently vet apps for the absence of malicious threats. Recent techniques have successfully relied on the extraction of lightweight syntactic features suitable for machine learning classification, but despite their promising results, the very nature of such features suggest they would unlikely—on their own—be suitable for detecting obfuscated Android malware. To address this challenge, we propose DroidSieve, an Android malware classifier based on static analysis that is fast, accurate, and resilient to obfuscation. For a given app, DroidSieve first decides whether the app is malicious and, if so, classifies it as belonging to a family of related malware. DroidSieve exploits obfuscation-invariant features and artifacts introduced by obfuscation mechanisms used in malware. At the same time, these purely static features are designed for processing at scale and can be extracted quickly. For malware detection, we achieve up to 99.82% accuracy with zero false positives; for family identification of obfuscated malware, we achieve 99.26% accuracy at a fraction of the computational cost of state-of-the-art techniques.

Keywords

Android Malware Detection, Malware Family Identification, Obfuscation, Native Code, Security, Machine Learning, Classification, Scalability

1 Introduction

The Android ecosystem continues to grow, and with close to two million apps published on marketplaces today, it is clear that fast and reliable mechanisms are required to detect

*{guillermo.suarez-tangil, santanu.dash, johannes.kinder, lorenzo.cavallaro}@rhul.ac.uk

†{mansour.ahmadi, giacinto}@diee.unica.it

and analyze potentially dangerous apps. The first problem we look at is *malware detection*: operators of app markets wish to automatically check submitted apps for malicious or potentially harmful code to protect users. The second problem we are interested in is *family identification*: an important step of forensic analysis of malicious apps is to differentiate families of related or derived malware [35]. For both detection and family identification, we strongly prefer light-weight and scalable methods to cope with the numbers of apps, both benign and malicious.

In general, static analysis techniques are computationally cheaper than emulation-based dynamic analysis; unfortunately, many static analysis techniques are easily thwarted by obfuscation, which is becoming increasingly common on Android [28]. Family identification in particular also suffers from the widespread code reuse in malware, which leads to different malware families sharing code and entire modules.

To address these challenges, we introduce DroidSieve, a system for malware classification whose features are derived from a fast and scalable, yet accurate and obfuscation-resilient static analysis of Android apps. DroidSieve relies on several features known to be characteristic of Android malware, including API calls [1, 38, 5], code structure [35], permissions [40], and the set of invoked components [5]. In addition, DroidSieve performs a novel deep inspection of the app to identify discriminating features missed by existing techniques, including native components, obfuscation artifacts, and features that are invariant under obfuscation. In particular, we make the following contributions to the state of the art:

- We introduce a novel set of features for static detection of Android malware that includes the use of embedded assets and native code; it is at the same time robust and computationally inexpensive. We evaluate its robustness on a set of over 100K benign and malicious Android apps. For detection, we achieve up to 99.82% accuracy with zero false positives. The same features allow family identification with an accuracy of 99.26%.

- We analyze the relative importance of our features and demonstrate that artifacts introduced by state-of-the-art obfuscation mechanisms provide high-quality features for reliable detection and family identification. Moreover, we show that there is a small set of features that perform consistently well regardless of whether they are derived from obfuscated or plain malware.

The rest of the paper is organized as follows: We first motivate our choice of features by briefly reviewing obfuscation techniques in Android malware (§2). We then describe our two main classes of features (§3) before presenting our experimental setup and results (§4). Finally, we review related work (§6) and conclude (§7).

2 Obfuscation in Android

We now briefly review the state of the art in Android obfuscation as it motivates our work. Thorough taxonomies of software obfuscations are available in the literature [10, 31].

String Obfuscation. Recent approaches to fingerprinting malware have made use of string-based features such as permissions and apps/package names [1, 5, 21]. Some strings, such as the declaration of application permissions, follow a strict syntax and must appear in the clear; other strings, such as names and identifiers, can be easily randomized or encrypted [9, 24].

Native Code. Native code is also frequently used to offload malicious functionality from the main Dalvik executable (DEX) to dynamically linked libraries or other executables (ELF files), which are then invoked at runtime.

Dynamic Code Loading. Native code and additional Dalvik bytecode can be loaded from a library included in the app's assets, from another app (collusion attack) or from a remote system after being retrieved at runtime. In our experiments, we found many examples of dynamic code loading, including cases where code was loaded from outside of the app. However, the mere presence of dynamic code loading is not malicious in itself, since many regular software frameworks employ this technique, which makes it even more attractive to malware writers.

Code Hiding. Malware authors often proactively hide malicious components to make the overall application look benign to cursory inspection [4]. For instance, the *GingerMaster* malware hides Bash scripts for its packaged root exploit under innocuous file names such as `install.png` and `gbfm.png` in its resources [33]. Other malicious apps go a step further and use a form of steganography, e.g., by hiding malicious code inside a valid image file [34]. The app loads the image through a seemingly benign action but uses a decoding algorithm to extract a malicious executable payload[1].

Finally, Android malware can also hide its malicious payload in an APK file hosted as a resource of the main app. When the app is executed, the user is lured into installing the hidden APK and the system then dynamically loads the hidden component. In the rest of the paper, we refer to these apps as *incognito apps*. In a related scenario, the *update attack*, the app just contains a component that downloads and executes a malicious payload from an external server. Such attacks are hard to detect and mitigate as the app misleads the user to grant the additional permissions while pretending to update itself [26].

The aforementioned methods for code hiding can easily be combined with encryption to further obfuscate the malicious payloads and decrypt them only at runtime [4]. While encryption makes it harder to assess the component statically,

its presence can be detected by measuring the entropy of the component. However, encryption is also commonly employed by benign apps, and during our experiments, we particularly found that many benign apps were using encrypted strings.

Reflection. Reflection is a commonly used feature in various Java frameworks, but it is also a notorious impediment to static analysis, since it may be infeasible to statically determine which code is executed at runtime. As a consequence, malware writers have long discovered reflection for obfuscating sensitive API calls and libraries [4]. In a recent large-scale study, Lindorfer et al. [22] showed that the general use of reflection among apps has increased significantly.

The state of obfuscation on Android has caught up with that on desktop systems, and there are already automatic frameworks available for obfuscating Android app components [9, 24, 28]. Hence, obfuscation now poses a serious challenge for static malware analysis on Android and has to be addressed to achieve robust malware classification.

3 Feature Engineering

We now introduce our proposed set of features for both malware detection and identification of malware families. Based on an analysis of existing malware (§3.1), we identify two major classes: *resource-centric* features are derived from resources used by the app (§3.2); *syntactic* features are derived from the code and metadata of the app (§3.3). A map relating classes of features is shown in Figure 1. We use both binary and continuous features. The presence or absence of a particular trait, such as a permission, is encoded as a binary feature; numeric properties, such as string lengths or opcode frequency, are encoded as continuous features.

3.1 Prevalence of Features

Robust classification requires a diverse set of features. Features such as API calls are highly relevant for classifying non-obfuscated malware but are susceptible to obfuscation. The presence of obfuscations may indicate malware, but it is not by itself sufficient to form judgment, since benign software can also use the same techniques for legitimate purposes. Therefore, we propose to employ a portfolio of features that covers both non-obfuscated and obfuscated malware.

As a first step towards selecting effective features, we measured the prevalence of a wide range of features that could be effective at identifying both obfuscated and non-obfuscated Android malware. We hypothesize that features centered around steganography, where the sample hides its malicious payload in its assets, or inconsistent nomenclature of components of an app by a careless malware developer are important features. To test our hypothesis, we run an assessment on a collection of over 100,000 benign and malicious samples from multiple sources. To put our findings in perspective, we also select some features from published works on Android malware identification.

For benign samples, we obtained a dataset of clean apps vetted by McAfee (McGW). For the malicious samples, we relied on two commonly used datasets: the Malgenome Project (MgMW) [41] and the Drebin dataset [5]. We further extended our dataset with the goodware (MvGW) and malware (MvMW) collected by Lindorfer et al. [21]. To measure feature prevalence in obfuscated malware, we also include the recent PRAGuard (PgMW) dataset [24]. The samples in PRAGuard were obtained by obfuscating the samples of the

---

[1]A recent example is *Android/TrojanDropper.Agent.EP* (*MD5:1f41ba0781d51751971ee705dfa307d2*), November 2015. b0n1.blogspot.co.uk/2015/11/android-malware-drops-banker-from-png.html

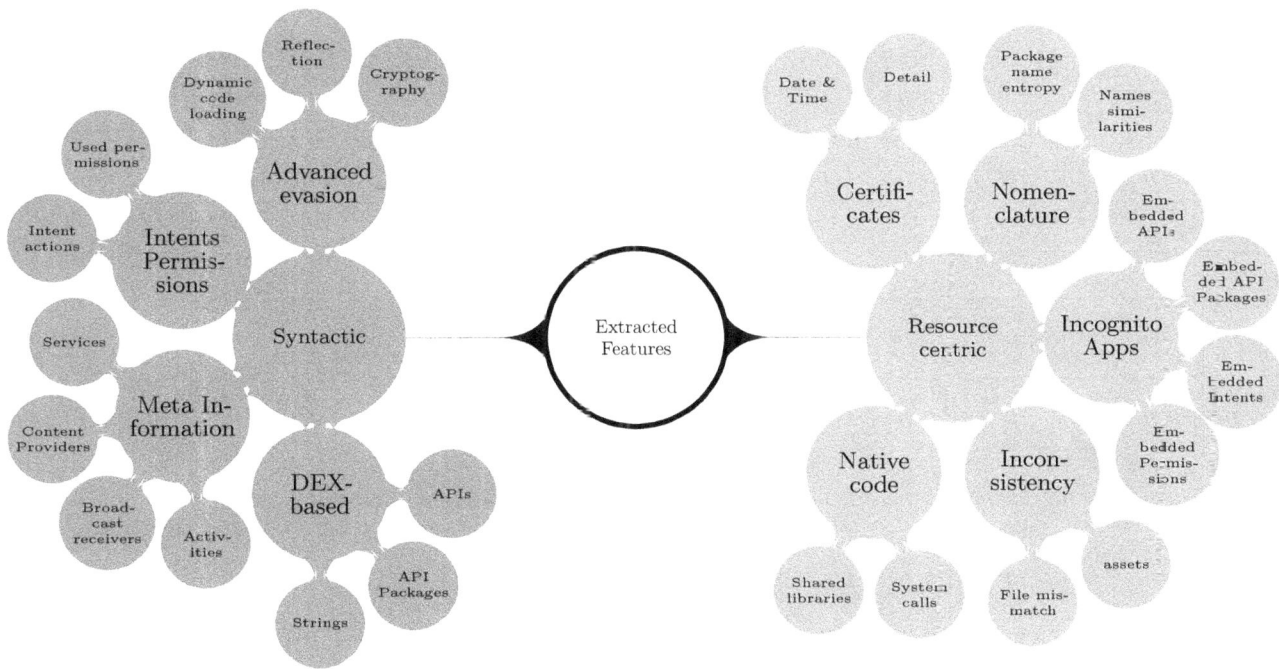

Figure 1: Non-exhaustive map of extracted features. The left side shows syntactic features derived from the source code of the app; the right side shows resource-centric features derived from the assets of the app.

MgMW dataset with techniques such as class and method renaming, reflection, and class encryption, among others.

Table 1 summarizes the results of our investigation. We can observe that most of the features are more prevalent in malware than in goodware. In particular, structural and logical inconsistencies are between 5% and 35% more prevalent in malware. In fact, the difference in prevalence of these features is comparable to well-understood features such as permissions, sensitive API calls, and those related to SMS messaging. Thus, inconsistencies are an important class of feature that have not been reported in the literature so far.

Our work also identifies obfuscated malware. In view of this, we also looked for prevalence of features that may hint at obfuscation in the form of reflection or the use of native code. In our study, McGW contained a prevalence higher than either MvGW and most of the malware datasets. This is because McGW is a more recent dataset with samples ranging from 2012 to 2016 and use advanced coding techniques while other datasets with the exception of PgMW are from 2012 and 2013. One may wonder the utility of including these features as a part of the classifier if they cannot be used to classify modern samples. A key assumption that we make here is that the classification model should evolve over time as pointed out recently in the literature [12]. Features that are relevant today will naturally become irrelevant in the future and it is the responsibility of malware analyst to purge obsolete features from the model while retraining. For our experiments, we retain these features as we test our features over a large timespan.

The PgMW dataset deserve special mention as it highlights how standard forms of obfuscation can confound the classification model. For the PgMW dataset, it can be seen that some features that are common in malware can be easily obfuscated. For example, methods that are crucial for the

detection of malicious activities, such as communications (*SMS*) or the access to sensitive information (*getSimSerial-Num.*), have been nearly eliminated in the obfuscated dataset. Therefore, relying on these features alone when dealing with obfuscation is detrimental to malware analysis and detection. These findings further reinforce our original suggestion of using a diverse portfolio of features for resilient classification.

3.2 Resource-centric Features

We propose a set of new features extracted from the app's resources stored in the APK. An excerpt of the resource-based features that we use can be seen in Table 1.

The two main guiding criteria that we use for building the set of resource-based features are *structural inconsistencies* and *logical inconsistencies*. Structural inconsistencies refer to the artifacts left behind after hiding a malicious component. Logical inconsistencies refer to the footprints typically left when repackaging a piece of malware as part of a benign app.

Certificates. We check whether the times at which the app was signed and at which the certificate was generated are similar. The intuition behind this feature is that automated repackaging tools modify existing apps and sign them using auto-generated ad-hoc certificates before distribution. Thus, if the date when the certificate was created is close to the date on which the app was signed, it can reveal the use of an automated tool for app repackaging. We mark apps where the time difference was below ten minutes. For each certificate, we also build features from the timezone and the common name's string length, which allows to identify similar certificates generates by repackaging tools.

Nomenclature. For each of the components in the app, we verify whether the correct package name is used as a prefix of the components in a package directory which is

Type	Capability	Goodware		Malware				Summary	
		McGW	MvGW	MgMW	Drebin	PgMW	MvMW	Goodware	Malware
Logical Inconsistencies	Main Activity	15.01%	8.85%	29.44%	18.71%	29.60%	8.23%	9.31%	13.13%
	Service	43.44%	4.60%	72.62%	54.17%	74.29%	35.34%	7.51%	44.18%
	Receiver	46.23%	13.57%	74.29%	56.06%	75.87%	36.60%	16.02%	45.66%
Structural Inconsistencies	APK File Match	1.77%	0.07%	24.21%	6.51%	24.13%	2.23%	0.20%	5.18%
	APK File Extension Mismatch	1.41%	0.02%	23.89%	6.28%	24.13%	2.22%	0.12%	5.10%
	Image File Extension Mismatch	3.69%	1.48%	19.92%	8.22%	18.17%	1.44%	1.65%	4.82%
Sensitive API	Package: SMS	5.63%	1.92%	20.79%	36.53%	0.00%	57.80%	2.20%	46.82%
	TelephonyManager.getSimSerialNum.	9.24%	4.69%	50.63%	24.06%	0.08%	14.22%	5.03%	16.34%
Permissions	READ_CONTACTS	22.93%	6.26%	36.27%	23.29%	38.8%	17.20%	7.52%	20.71%
	ACCESS_FINE_LOCATION	28.04%	16.40%	34.29%	30.04%	32.30%	15.53%	17.28%	21.38%
Obfuscation	Dynamic Code	32.22%	0.44%	19.60%	6.98%	0.00%	2.04%	2.83%	3.47%
	Reflection	74.08%	39.37%	67.62%	56.04%	99.21%	40.14%	41.97%	49.50%
	Native Code	49.61%	3.69%	54.13%	19.51%	0.16%	6.43%	7.14%	10.15%
	Native Code without ELF	8.10%	0.58%	1.67%	0.70%	0.00%	0.52%	1.14%	0.54%
Total Number of samples		8,041	99,037	1,260	5,560	1,260	10,581	107,078	17,401
Total Number of families		–	–	49	179	49	–	–	–

Table 1: Percentages of apps with given properties in the McAfee Goodware (McGW), Malgenome (MgMW), Drebin malware, PRAGuard's obfuscated Malgenome (PgMW), Marvin Goodware (MvGW) and malware (MvMW) dataset. Note that the summary shows the total number of apps after removing overlapping samples.

the usual practice in most apps. If there is a mismatch, we treat it as a potential case of tampering with the original contents of a benign app. Table 1 shows an overview of the percentage of samples that exhibit such a mismatch. For each of the package names, we also derive its length and its Shannon entropy, which help to identify automatically generated names.

Inconsistent Representations. We check whether the file extensions match the file contents (as identified by the file header or a magic number) to allow highlighting apps that try to hide shell scripts or ELF binaries as images or other resources. Table 1 shows that such inconsistencies are good indicators of malicious intent in some (e.g., Malgenome) but not all (e.g., Marvin) datasets, potentially owing to trends in malware writing and repackaging tools.

Incognito Apps. In some cases the payload of a malicious app is in an APK that is disguised among the assets of the *host* app. To capture this malicious payload, we recursively extract both syntactic and resource centric features for any *incognito* APK and DEX found within the app. We pigeonhole these features under a different category in order to separate these statistics from the ones related to the *host* app. For instance, *permission.INTERNET* counts the static number of accesses to the Internet, while *icg.permission.INTERNET* does the same for the incognito app.

Native Code. We also scan the assets of the app to identify any native ELF files. The files are parsed to extract features from the header and individual sections of the file. We extract the number of entries in the program header, the program header size, and the number and size of the section headers. From individual sections, we extract the flags of the section to understand if they are W (writable), A (allocatable), X (executable), M (mergeable), S (strings), etc. and use them as Boolean features. Within code sections, we also look for instructions invoking critical system calls such as `ioctl`, which is used for Android's inter-procedural and inter-component communication.

3.3 Syntactic Features

We present our syntactic features; several of these, such as API calls [1] and permissions [40], are already known to perform well with non-obfuscated malware. We don't claim novelty by including these features. Instead, we use them to build a classifier that is robust against both well-known and modern malware which tends to be increasingly obfuscated. To enrich the set of syntactic features, we propose some new features such as *explicit intents* and additional ones mined from the *meta-information*. These are discussed below. We reiterate here that a combination of diverse features is crucial for robust detection of both plain and obfuscated malware. This is corroborated in Section 4.2 where important features come from diverse categories, yet they all rank highly in relation to other features (see Figure 2 and 3).

DEX-based Features. We tag each method based on the libraries it invokes from the Android Framework (*method tag*). These tags represent the class of APIs used by the method and are encoded as binary features. We also scan the app for the presence string variables in DEX files containing keywords we obtained from reverse engineering malware from the Malgenome data set. For instance, `su` relates to executing code with super user privileges; `emulator` and `sdk` suggest that the app checks for the presence of an emulator.

Intents and Permissions. We parse the Manifest to identify all implicit intents that can be received from other apps. We also scan the code to identify any explicit intents, which are used to start services within the same app. The count of individual intents is used as a continuous feature for classification. We break down the set of intents into sub-categories for further granularity: (i) intents containing the keywords `android.net.*`, which are related to the connection manager; (ii) intents containing `com.android.vending.*` for billing transactions; (iii) intents that target framework components (`com.android.*`); (iv) all intent actions, beginning with `android.intent.action.*`; and (v), a catch-all category for the reminder intents. Finally, we also extract the set of permissions declared in the manifest of the app.

Meta-information. Apart from the specific type of permission used, we also count the number of Android framework permissions and custom third-party permissions used by the app. The number of times that a permission is used throughout the code is encoded as a feature. Similarly, we count the number of activities, broadcast receivers, content providers, services, and entry points of the app. Entry points are ways in which an app can be invoked or executed.

Evasion Techniques. We further look for techniques that are frequently used to confuse analysis systems, i.e., native code, cryptographic libraries, or reflection. For example, `Ldalvik/system/DexClassLoader` indicates dynamic code loading, `Ljava/lang/reflect/Method` is required for invoking a method through reflection, and any access to `Ljavax/crypto` is a sign for the use of cryptography. For native code invocations, we count the number of times the Dalvik opcode `0x100` is present in the bytecode, which corresponds to loading and executing native code.

4 Experiments and Results

We implemented our proposed feature set in DroidSieve, a system for static detection and family identification of Android malware. We begin our evaluation by describing our experimental setup and evaluation metrics (§4.1). We then address the following questions:

- **Feature Engineering (§4.2):** Which types of features are most effective for regular and obfuscated malware?

- **Classification of Standard Samples (§4.3):** How effective is DroidSieve in classifying non-obfuscated malware only, and how does it compare to other approaches that address the same problem?

- **Classification of Obfuscated Samples (§4.4):** How effective is DroidSieve in classifying obfuscated malware or a mix of non-obfuscated and obfuscated malware?

- **Computational Efficiency (§4.5):** Do the computational costs of using DroidSieve allow its application at scale?

4.1 Experimental Setup

We mean to evaluate the choice of our features for two distinct problems:

Evaluation Categories. We evaluate DroidSieve along two dimensions, the classification task and the type of dataset. The classification task is either (1) *malware detection* among a set of malicious and benign samples or (2) *family identification* among a set of samples known to be malicious. The type of dataset is either non-obfuscated, obfuscated, or mixed. We use the datasets introduced in §3.1 and combinations thereof; details are shown in Table 2a.

Choice of Learning Algorithm. We implemented both malware detection and family identification in DroidSieve using Extra Trees. As alternatives we considered one-vs-all Support Vector Machines (SVM), Random Forests, and eXtreme Gradient Boost (XGBoost). In the past, SVM and Random Forest have been successfully applied to malware detection [5, 32] and they have been shown to have better performance than others after comparing them to 180 classifiers on various datasets [15]. Ensemble tree-based classifiers perform well on many real world settings, however. For example, Extra Tree [18] and Gradient Tree Boosting [19] have

been achieving great performance in most of recent "Kaggle" competitions [2] on various domains, including malware classification[2] or spam detection[3].

We use feature selection to restrict the classifier to important discriminating features. A feature is selected when the importance score assigned to the feature by the classifier is higher than the mean of all the features' scores. For decision trees, this importance is computed from the mean decrease impurity (MDI) where a higher score implies a more important feature.

Evaluation Metrics. For evaluating the classification results, we use the detection rate (DR), the false positive rate (FPR), the accuracy (ACC), and the F_1-score (F1) which is the harmonic mean of the precision and recall as quality metrics. Detection rate is the correct number of predictions made over the set of malware, whereas accuracy reports the number of correct predictions made after considering both goodware and malware. We only use the detection rate for the case of malware detection and we report this metric together with the false positive rate, i.e., the number of goodware samples wrongly classified as malware divided by the total number of goodware samples in the dataset.

For assessing the performances of the proposed models, we use hold-out validation to avoid overfitting [14]; samples used to fit the model are different from the ones used to validate it. We retained one third of the samples for validation and trained the model on the remaining two thirds of the data. For each sample that was retained, we ensured that we trained on samples from the same category. For malware detection, a category for a sample indicates whether it is benign or malicious. For family identification, a category indicates the name of family. Consequently, we do not have a case of testing on samples from unseen families or categories; this would be an instance of zero-shot learning [25], a problem we consider out of scope for this paper. We did not use any form of re-sampling, such as cross-validation, to avoid biasing our results [27].

4.2 Ranking of Features

We now analyze the quality of our features, ranking them when used on unobfuscated and obfuscated datasets. We expect features that are easily obfuscated to decrease in importance, whereas features that are invariant under obfuscation should remain stable.

We pass the feature vectors for our samples to the *Extra Tree* algorithm and rank them by *mean decrease impurity* [23]. As decision trees split the dataset by considering one feature at a time, it is easy to measure how much *impurity* is introduced in the classification by choosing a particular feature. Note that these rankings are informative and do not dictate our choice of features in all sets of experiments in §4.3 and §4.4. For classification, DroidSieve uses automatic feature ranking and chooses the top features for the respective training set.

For malware detection, we passed all samples in McGW + MgMW and McGW + PgMW through the Extra Tree classifier. Figure 2a and Figure 2b depict the top 30 features for these cases, respectively. In the case of McGW + MgMW,

[2] http://blog.kaggle.com/2015/05/26/microsoft-malware-winners-interview-1st-place-no-to-overfitting/
[3] http://mlwave.com/winning-2-kaggle-in-class-competitions-on-spam/

313

ID	Dataset Name	Ground Truth	#samples
—	Drebin [5]	Malware	5,560
MgMW	MalGenome [41]	Malware	1,260
PgMW	PRAGuard * [24]	Malware	1,260
McGW	McAfee	Goodware	8,041
McMW	McAfee	Malware	13,289
MvGW	Marvin [21]	Goodware	99,037
MvMW	Marvin [21]	Malware	10,581

(a) Dataset sources

Set	Detection	Family Identification
1	{McAfee Goodware, Drebin}	Drebin
2	{McAfee Goodware, MalGenome}	MalGenome
3	{McAfee Goodware, PRAGuard*}	PRAGuard*
4	{Marvin Goodware, Marvin Malware}	–
5	{McAfee Goodware, McAfee Malware}	–
Hold-out Ratio: 67% Training – 33% Testing		

(b) Dataset combinations

Table 2: Overview of chosen datasets for malware detection and family identification. The set of experiments involving obfuscated samples is marked with an asterisk(*). The holdout ratio shows the percentage of samples retained for validation. For the case of Marvin and McAfee malware we retain the splitting given by the authors, otherwise we use a random split.

these 30 features account for the top 40% features, while in the case of McGW + PgMW these features account for the top 36% features. We repeated a similar experiment for the case of family identification and the top features for samples from MgMW and PgMW are presented in Figure 3a and Figure 3b, respectively. They denote the top 26% and the top 43% most important features for identifying Android malware families from MgMW and PgMW, respectively.

For both plain and obfuscated malware, it may be seen from Figures 2a and 2b that permissions (prepended with PER) play an important role in the detection process. Permissions are hard to obfuscate as scrambling them would break the Android programming model. Alongside permissions, novel syntactic features such as used-permissions (prepended with used.PER) also rank highly. These features derived after scanning the code to understand what permissions are being used and how often.

Apart from syntactic features, there are many resource-centric features which also rank highly. In particular, features derived from assets such as ELF files (prepended with elf) as well as intents, and API calls from incognito apps (prepended with icg) rank highly when detecting plain malware samples as shown in Figure 2a.

The high-ranked features for malware detection is similar for both plain and obfuscated apps. A noticeable difference in the case of obfuscated malware is that the top-ranked feature is Stat(cert_diff.1). which is derived from the certificate of the app. It checks whether the time difference between the date when the certificate was issued and time when the app was signed is within a day. A temporal proximity means that the app was signed during a time when the malware developer piggybacked the app with malicious code. This is a common practice which signals that the malware developer may be using automated tools to repackage the app.

The ranking of features for classifying malware into families for plain and obfuscated malware is shown in Figures 3a and 3b, respectively. The high-ranked features in both cases are similar to those observed in the case of classification except for two noticeable differences. Firstly, incognito features are not as important for classifying malware into families as they are for malware detection. This is understandable as incognito apps are a means to achieve a malicious action but they do not characterize what malicious action is carried out or how it is carried out. Secondly, we can see that features derived from the file type of the assets (prepended with file) and those related to logical inconsistencies (features such as Stat(PackageMismatchService) and Stat(PackageMismatchReceiver)) are highly ranked. This

could point to the fact that the app is repackaged using an attack vector that is specific to a given family.

4.3 Classification Results

In this section we evaluate the effectiveness of DroidSieve in classifying unobfuscated malware, to allow a comparison against approaches from the literature. To not put DroidSieve at a disadvantage, we therefore start with a feature set that includes all features, including those that are susceptible to obfuscation.

As datasets, We first evaluate on detection of malware samples where we use the dataset obtained by combining malicious samples from the Drebin dataset with the Goodware set as shown in Table 2b. Note that we only report results for the Drebin dataset here because it includes all MalGenome samples and is both larger and more recent.

Malware Detection. The table shows that in our best scenario we are able to identify if a given app is malicious or benign with accuracy of 99.64% for the case of Drebin, and 99.82% for MvGW. The breakdown of the accuracy shows a detection rate of 99.44% for Drebin, with 0.226% of false positives. Similarly, the detection rate for MvGW is 98.42% with only 0.008% of false positives. For the case of Drebin we obtained slightly higher detection rate with respect to MvGW. However, the false positive rate is better in the case of MvGW. In fact, in this case the number of goodware classified as malware is negligible (2 out of 25493). In most cases, the performance is improved with feature selection. It allows to drastically reduce the complexity of the feature space, e.g., from over 20,000 features to less than 1,000. This means that we are able to reduce redundant or irrelevant features and improve the performance of classification.

Family Identification. After detection, DroidSieve is also able to determine if the given malware belongs to a known family. Our experiments on the Drebin dataset show that Extra Trees achieve an accuracy of 97.68% when considering all 2,564 the features (see Table 2b). Interestingly, keeping the top 320 most informative features increases the accuracy to 98.12% while adding features that are not unimportant can hurt classification accuracy [29].

4.4 Obfuscation Evaluation

We now evaluate the effectiveness of our system against obfuscated malware and against a mix of obfuscated and unobfuscated malware, as it would be encountered in an actual deployment. In particular, we ran three sets of experiments for both malware detection and family identification.

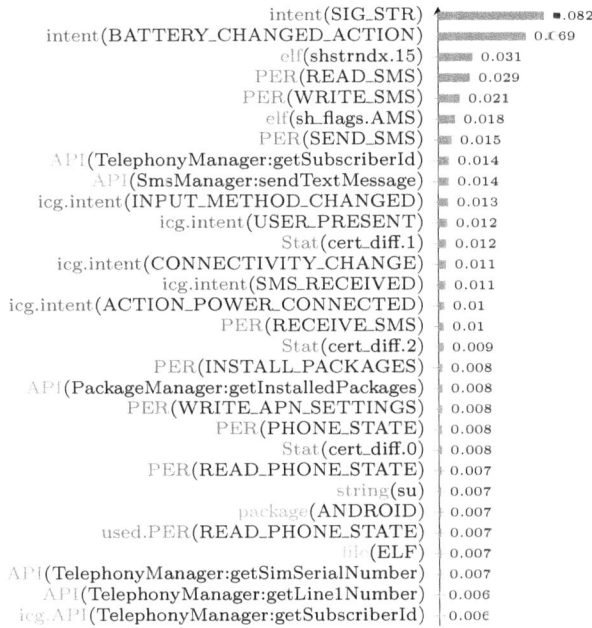

(a) Non-obfuscated malware.

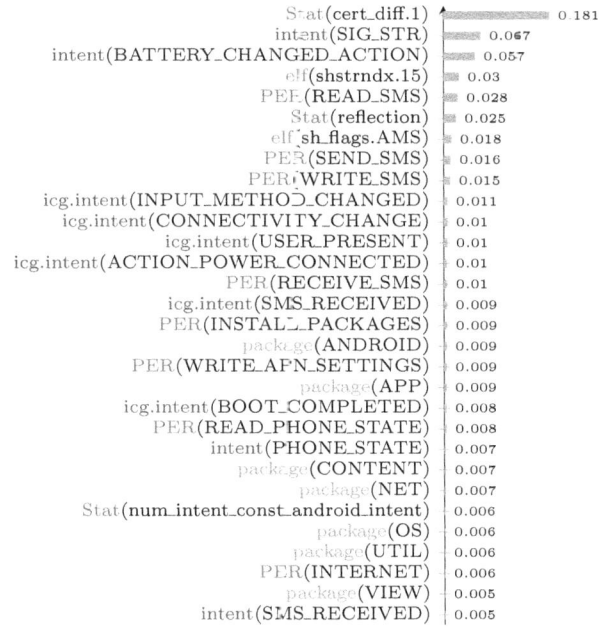

(b) Obfuscated malware.

Figure 2: Ranking of features for malware detection: Figure 2a shows importance of features by considering all features on MalGenome while Figure 2b shows importance of features for the MalGenome obfuscated (PRAGuard) dataset.

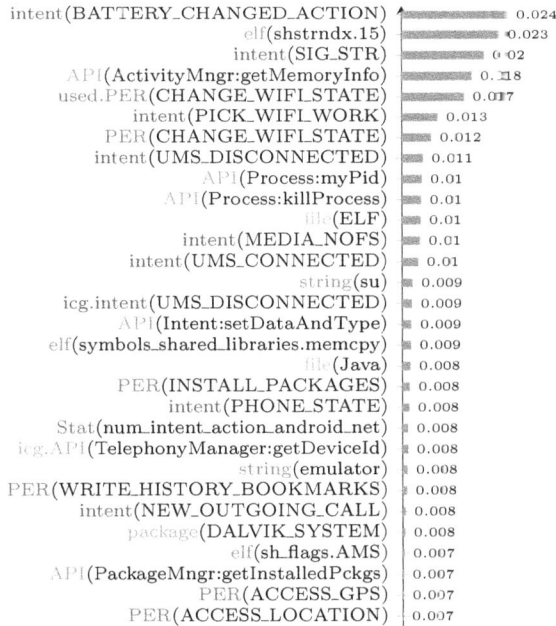

(a) Non-obfuscated malware.

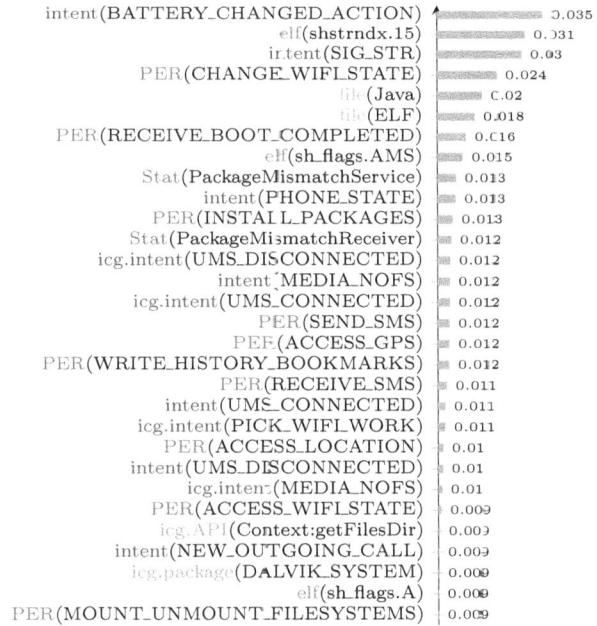

(b) Obfuscated malware.

Figure 3: Ranking of features for family identification.

The three cases are based on scenarios where the training and/or testing samples are obfuscated. Note that our original dataset consists of samples from the Goodware set and samples from the MalGenome project. For each malware sample, we obtain the corresponding obfuscated sample from the PRAGuard project.

Detection of Obfuscated Malware. Our training sets for malware detection are as follows:

Type	Classifier	#F	ACC(%)	F1(%)	DR(%)	FPR(%)
Malware Detection		**Drebin + McGW**				
	Extra Trees	22,584	**99.64**	**99.64**	**99.44**	**0.226**
	Extra Trees + FS	**859**	99.57	99.57	99.39	0.302
		MvGW + MvMW				
	Extra Trees	26,396	99.72	99.72	97.58	0.012
	Extra Trees + FS	**634**	**99.82**	**99.81**	**98.42**	**0.008**
Family Identification		**Drebin** (108 families)				
	Extra Trees	2,564	97.68	97.31	–	–
	Extra Trees + FS	**320**	**98.12**	**97.84**	–	–

Table 3: Results for detection and family classification on unobfuscated malware with and without Feature Selection (FS) for the Marvin, McAfee and Drebin datasets. #F stands for number of features, ACC for Accuracy, F1 for F_1-Score, DR for the detection rate, and FPR for False Positive Rate. Best scores for each setting are shown in bold. Although feature selection drastically reduces the number of features, it mostly outperforms the full-feature setting.

1. **McGW + MgMW**: We train on samples from the Goodware and MalGenome data sets only to show a baseline classification without obfuscation.

2. **McGW + PgMW**: We train on the obfuscated malware samples from PRAGuard and include the Goodware.

3. **McGW + MgMW + PgMW**: We train on both the original and obfuscated versions of the malware obtained from MalGenome and PRAGuard, respectively, together with the Goodware.

We chose our test cases for the trained model to highlight that the choice of our features performs consistently well regardless of whether we train on the obfuscated samples or on the original ones. In the first experiment on detecting malware, we retained 33% of samples from PgMW and McGW and trained with the rest. With the retained samples, we obtained accuracies of 100% for the McGW samples (0% false positives) and 99.02% for the PgMW samples. We repeated the experiment with the non-obfuscated set of samples (MgMW + McGW) and obtained similar accuracy values.

To further validate our features and trained models, we also tested on malware samples from a dataset that is different from the one used for training (i.e., 100% hold-out). First, we trained on all MgMW + McGW samples, and tested on PgMW samples. Then, we trained on all PgMW + McGW samples, and tested on MgMW samples. For these two experiments, our accuracy was 92.38% and 96.11% respectively. As a final experiment to validate our features for detection, we also performed a hold-out validation of the 33% of the dataset on all samples i.e. McGW + MgMW + PgMW and obtained an accuracy of 99.71%. A summary of our results for the detection task can be found in Table 4. These results show that our features are effective at distinguishing benign and malicious samples, a task made more difficult by many obfuscation techniques also having valid use cases in benign software (see Table 1).

To compare our performance with recent approaches, we use Drebin framework [5] to extract features from MgMW, McGW and PgMW datasets. We trained on all MgMW + McGW samples and tested on the obfuscated set of samples (i.e.: PgMW) using the same classification algorithm (Random Forest) used by DroidSieve. The detection rate obtained with Drebin's feature engineering is 0%. Note that our framework reported 92.38% on this experiment. We repeated the same experiment by training over the original set of malware

samples collected by Drebin and testing again on PgMW. The feature set of Drebin in this setting is of 101,055 features while ours is of 22,584. After applying feature selection, Drebin retained 13,602 while we retained 859 informative features. For this experiment, the features used by the Drebin framework reported a detection rate of 11% while our framework reported 100%. Among the most important features used by Drebin were different strings such as URLs which are a soft target for obfuscation. Contrarily, our framework retained several *logical inconsistencies* (e.g.: PackageMissmatchIntentConsts and PackageMissmatchService), other resource-centric features (e.g.: PackageNameEntropy), ELF features and other statistical features (such as the number of third party permissions found).

Identification of Obfuscated Families. We now demonstrate the effectiveness of our features for identifying the classes each malware sample belongs to. Our training sets for the identification of malware families are as follows:

1. **MgMW**: We train on samples from MalGenome only.

2. **PgMW**: We train on the obfuscated malware samples from PRAGuard.

3. **MgMW + PgMW**: We train on both the original and obfuscated versions of the malware obtained from MalGenome and PRAGuard respectively.

By following the same settings as in the previous experiments, for each dataset we retained 33% of the samples from each family, when that dataset was used for both training and testing. A summary of our results on family identification can also be found in Table 4. The accuracy after training on MgMW samples was 97.79% and the accuracy after training on PgMW was 99.26%. Additionally, we also applied 100% hold-out validation between MgMW and PgMW showing accuracies of 97.94% and 97.86% respectively. It is worth noting here that training on obfuscated malware enables our classifier to perform better. On the contrary, when obfuscated samples are not included in the training set, the resulting model is not able to prioritize all features needed to perform higher than 97.79%. Finally, we tested the trained models on a combination of both obfuscated and non-obfuscated samples (MgMW + PgMW) and obtained an overall accuracy of 99.15%.

Malware Detection				Family Identification		
	Test				Test	
Training	McGW	MgMW	*PgMW*	Training	MgMW	*PgMW*
MgMW + McGW	100.00	99.02	*92.38**	MgMW	97.79	*97.94**
PgMW + McGW	100.00	96.11*	*99.02*	*PgMW*	97.86*	*99.26*
MgMW + PgGW + McGW	**99.71**			MgMW + *PgMW*	**99.15**	

Table 4: Evaluation of classification on the *McAfee Goodware* (McGW), *Malgenome* (MgMW), and *PRAGuard* (Malgenome obfuscated–*PgMG*) dataset with feature filtering and using hold-out validation (*100% hold-out ratio, otherwise we use the hold-out ration described in Table 2b).

4.5 Efficiency

A main design point for DroidSieve was to allow computationally inexpensive feature extraction. Figure 4 shows the runtime for feature extraction on the Marvin dataset, which contains more than 100,000 samples. The median lies at just 2.53 seconds for processing one sample on a single core (Intel Xeon E5-2697 v3 @ 2.60GHz). The overall time for feature extraction on the Marvin dataset took less than 8 hours when executed in parallel on 40 cores.

Other approaches that have been proposed and shown effective for obfuscation-resilient Android malware detection are based on analyzing information flow [7, 16]. However, information flow analysis requires running times that are several orders of magnitude above those seen in DroidSieve's feature extraction. In particular, when attempting to process the 5,560 samples of the Drebin dataset with FlowDroid [6], we were only able to finish half the dataset within three days. Hence, we believe DroidSieve to be better suited for deployment of obfuscation-resilient detection at scale.

For the sake of simplicity, in this section we only report the runtime for feature extraction, we refer the reader to [12] additional details on the running times for training and testing the underlying classification algorithms. As expected, the time taken to process the test samples is negligible.

5 Limitations

The techniques proposed in this paper use lightweight code and resource parsing to build features. Our framework is not built on traditional program analysis techniques such as flow analysis or proofs of non-interference but on mining patterns for API invocations in individual apps. Additionally, we collect lightweight statistics on resources which are derived using simple heuristics which do not required involved program/resource analysis. Consequently, our analysis scales to a large number of apps without hitting performance bottlenecks such as those observed in flow analysis. Having said that, our techniques may not be robust against mimicry

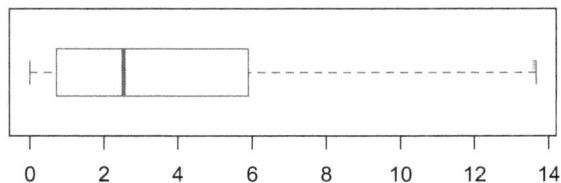

Figure 4: Frequency distribution of running times for feature extraction, in seconds. Most samples require less than six seconds to be analyzed.

attacks as the features that we mine can be contrived. For contemporary mobile malware, though, our features seem to work well. For more sophisticated attacks, it may be necessary to explore formal program analysis techniques.

Some of our features are built on the use of cryptography in the app. For building such features, we used a two-pronged approach. Firstly, we check the entropy of resources of the app and secondly, we parse the DEX files to identify any calls to the Java cryptography libraries. We expect the conjunction of these features to be indicative of packing and consequently, obfuscation. However, it is possible that the app uses its own libraries or a weaker encryption scheme that produces little observable difference in entropy. In such cases, we would only be relying on features from the DEX to identify uses of cryptography thus weakening our feature engineering.

The performance of the classifier might naturally degrade over time as malware becomes increasingly sophisticated. This phenomenon is commonly referred to as *concept drift*. Our system does not take into account concept drift and we do not provide any retraining strategies that would fortify the system against it. Having said that, dealing with concept drift is crucial in the face of obfuscation. While concept drift is well-known problem in machine learning, it is only recently that approaches have been proposed to provide retraining guidance for malware detection [12]. Whether these approaches can be adapted to detect concept drift in the presence of obfuscated malware remains unknown. In this paper, we argue that it is the responsibility of analyst to purge obsolete features from the model while retraining and incorporate novel features when needed.

There are a number of evasion techniques against machine learning that can potentially target the learning process and the models rather than feature extraction phase. These kind of threats are commonly known as adversarial machine learning attacks [20]. We can find a number of practical techniques to evaluate the robustness of classifiers under attack [8, 17]. Additional experiments would be needed to make a quantitative evaluation of our system in an adversarial environment.

6 Related Work

We now give an overview of the most relevant Android malware detection and classification techniques (see Table 5 for a summary).

Malware Detection. Several systems perform Android malware detection, i.e., perform binary classification [1, 5]. DroidAPIMiner [1] is a detection system based on features generated at API level. Drebin [5] is a lightweight detec-

Year	Method	Type Det	Type Class	Feature	# Malware	DR/FP(%)	ACC(%)	Time(s)	Environment
2014	Dendroid [35]	–	✓	CFG	1,247	–	94	–	
2014	DroidAPIMiner [1]	✓	–	API,PKG,PAR	3,987	99/2.2	–	15	Core i5,6G RAM
2014	DroidMiner [38]	✓	✓	CG,API	2,466	95.3/0.4	92	19.8	
2014	Drebin [5]	✓	–	PER,STR,API,INT	5,560	94.0/1.0	–	0.75	Core 2 Duo, 4G RAM
2014	DroidSIFT [39]	✓	✓	API-F	2,200	98.0/5.15	93	175.8	Xeon, 128G RAM
2014	DroidLegacy [13]	✓	✓	API	1,052	93.0/3.0	98	–	
2015	AppAudit [37]	✓	–	API-F	1,005	99.3/0.61	–	0.6	Core i7, 8G RAM
2015	MudFlow [7]	✓	–	API-F	10,552	90.1/18.7	–	–	
2015	Marvin [21]	✓	–	PER, INT, ST, PN	15,741	98.24/0.0	–	–	
2015	RevealDroid [16]	✓	✓	PER,API,API-F,INT,PKG	9,054	98.2/18.7	93	95.2	8-Core, 64G RAM
2016	DroidScribe [11]	–	✓	SYSC, BIND, FILE, NET	5,246	–	94	–	
2016	Madam [30]	✓	–	SYSC, API, PER, SMS, USR	2,800	96/0.2	–	–	
Ours	**DroidSieve**	✓	✓	*As described in §3*	16,141	**99.3/0.0**	**99**	2.5	40-Core Xeon, 378G RAM

API: Application Programming Interface, API-F: Information Flow between APIs, INT: Intents, CG: Call Graph, PER: Requested Permissions, CFG: Control Flow Graph, STR: Embedded strings, PKG: Package information of API, ST: Statistical features, PN: Package names, SYSC: System calls, BIND: Binder transactions, FILE: Filesystem Transactions, NET: Network Transactions, USR: User Activity, SMS: SMS Monitoring

Table 5: Static analysis techniques on Android malware. Results are reported based on the most representative setting. (Almost all of the systems have difficulty against reflection as they are mostly based on API). The performance time of different systems is subjected to specification of computing environments.

tion method that uses static analysis to gather the most important characteristics of Android applications such as permissions, API calls, and network addresses declared in clear text. It uses machine learning (Support Vector Machines) to detect whether a given sample is malicious or benign. DroidSIFT [39] builds contextual API dependency graphs that provide an abstracted view of the possible behaviors of malware and employs machine learning and graph similarity to detect malicious applications. MudFlow [7] and AppAudit [37], however, leverage the analysis of flows between APIs to detect malware.

The main weakness of semantics-based static analysis is that it generally shows poor performance against encryption, reflection, native code, and other cross-platform code such as HTML5. These drawbacks motivate dynamic analysis and hybrid approaches [21, 30]. Marvin [21] shows how the combination of static and dynamic analysis can improve the detection rate as well as reducing the number of false positives. It uses a number of statically extracted features and combines them with additional dynamically extracted features, overall more than 490,000. Moreover, it leverages machine learning to detect malware as well as providing a risk score associated with a given unknown sample. Madam [30] proposed a host-based malware detection system that analyzed features at four levels: kernel, application, user and package. It derived features such as system calls, sensitive API calls and SMS through dynamic analysis while complementing these with statically derived features such as permissions, the app's metadata and market information.

Malware Family Classification. In addition to malware detection systems, a number of methods have been proposed just for classification [35, 11] and others [38, 39] evaluated the features used by their detection system for classification. DroidLegacy [13] is a system using API signature similarity to detect and classify malware. Dendroid [35] proposed an approach based on text mining to automatically classify malware samples and analyze families based on the control flow structures found in them. Similarly, RevealDroid [16] aims at identifying Android malware families. Their approach uses information flow analysis and sensitive API flow

tracking built on top of two machine learning classifiers, i.e., C4.5 and 1NN. DroidScribe [11] used a purely dynamic approach to malware classification and classified malware into families by observing system calls, Android ICC through the Binder protocol and file/network transactions made by the app. To classify apps that could not be satisfactorily stimulated during dynamic analysis, DroidScribe built on a statistical evaluation framework of the underline machine learning approach [36] to properly trigger a set-based classification scheme that identified the top matching families for a malware sample, given a desired statistical confidence level.

Discussion. We summarize the most prominent static analysis approaches for Android malware analysis tailored to either detection or classification in Table 5. The column **Type** shows whether a system was mainly proposed for detection or classification. The **Feature** column shows the extracted attributes from malware. **# Malware** is the total number of malware considered for evaluation. **DR/FP** refers to the detection rate and false positive rate of a detection system, and **ACC** shows the accuracy of the system when it is applied for malware family classification. **Time** shows the average required time for analysis of every application.
Systems like DroidMiner, DroidAPIMiner and Drebin are mainly based on APIs, which are inherently vulnerable to reflection. API-flow based approaches like RevealDroid, AppAudit, MudFlow, and DroidSIFT are more precise and consider features related to the semantics of application, but they are still vulnerable to reflection. Furthermore, flow extraction is expensive unless done in the manner of AppAudit where efficiency is derived from incomplete flow coverage.

In contrast, our system is robust against obfuscation techniques like reflection and encryption while still being computationally efficient. Authors in [3] also evaluate their system against common types of obfuscation. However, we evaluate our system on a wide variety of datasets and combinations to avoid unreliable performance measurements. Specifically, we use more than 100,000 goodware apps and over 17,000 malware apps, while authors in [3] limit their evaluation to 207 goodware apps and 1,192 malware apps. Additionally, while past studies focus on a smaller set of behaviors, our method encompasses a larger set of characteristics and behaviors to distinguish goodware from malware and to identify Android malware families more effectively.

Finally, Roy et al. [29] discuss design choices for evaluating detection systems. Going forward, we plan on taking their important lessons into account. As of now, the focus in DroidSieve lies decidedly on comparing our novel feature engineering for potentially obfuscated malware against existing results in their published settings.

7 Conclusion

In this paper, we have presented a fast, scalable, and accurate system for Android malware detection and family identification based on lightweight static analysis. DroidSieve uses deep inspection of Android malware to build effective and robust features suitable for computational learning. This is key in scenarios where security analysts require intelligent instruments to automate detection and further analysis of Android malware.

We have introduced a novel set of characteristics and showed the importance of systematic feature engineering to achieve a diversified and large range of features that can adjust to different malware. Our findings show that static analysis for Android can succeed even when confronted with obfuscation techniques such as reflection, encryption and dynamically-loaded native code. While fundamental changes in characteristics of malware remain a largely open problem, we showed that DroidSieve remains resilient against state-of-the-art obfuscation techniques which can be used to quickly derive new and syntactically different malware variants.

Acknowledgments

This research has been partially supported by the UK EPSRC grant EP/L022710/1. We are equally thankful to the anonymous reviewers for their invaluable inputs, comments and suggestions to improve the paper. Moreover, we appreciate VirusTotal's collaboration for providing access to their private API so that we could query additional information about the malware.

8 References

[1] Y. Aafer, W. Du, and H. Yin. DroidAPIMiner: Mining API-level features for robust malware detection in Android. In *International Conference on Security and Privacy in Communication Networks (SecureComm)*. 2013.

[2] M. Ahmadi, D. Ulyanov, S. Semenov, M. Trofimov, and G. Giacinto. Novel feature extraction, selection and fusion for effective malware family classification. In *ACM Conference on Data and Application Security and Privacy (CODASPY)*, pages 183–194, 2016.

[3] A. Ali-Gombe, I. Ahmed, G. G. Richard III, and V. Roussev. Opseq: Android malware fingerprinting. In *Proceedings of the 5th Program Protection and Reverse Engineering Workshop*, page 7. ACM, 2015.

[4] A. Apvrille and R. Nigam. Obfuscation in android malware, and how to fight back. *Virus Bulletin*, pages 1–10, 2014.

[5] D. Arp, M. Spreitzenbarth, M. Hubner, H. Gascon, and K. Rieck. Drebin: Effective and explainable detection

[6] of Android malware in your pocket. In *Network and Distributed System Security Symposium (NDSS)*. 2014.

[6] S. Arzt, S. Rasthofer, C. Fritz, E. Bodden, A. Bartel, J. Klein, Y. Le Traon, D. Octeau, and P. McDaniel. Flowdroid: Precise context, flow, field, object-sensitive and lifecycle-aware taint analysis for android apps. In *35th ACM SIGPLAN Conference on Programming Language Design and Implementation (PLDI)*, pages 259–269, New York, NY, USA, 2014. ACM.

[7] V. Avdiienko, K. Kuznetsov, A. Gorla, A. Zeller, S. Arzt, S. Rasthofer, and E. Bodden. Mining apps for abnormal usage of sensitive data. In *37th International Conference on Software Engineering (ICSE)*, 2015.

[8] B. Biggio, G. Fumera, and F. Roli. Security evaluation of pattern classifiers under attack. *IEEE Transactions on Knowledge and Data Engineering*, 26(4):984–996, April 2014.

[9] Z. Cai and R. H. Yap. Inferring the detection logic and evaluating the effectiveness of android anti-virus apps. In *ACM Conference on Data and Application Security and Privacy (CODASPY)*, pages 172–182, 2016.

[10] C. Collberg, C. Thomborson, and D. Low. A taxonomy of obfuscating transformations. Technical Report TR148, Department of Computer Science, University of Auckland, 1997.

[11] S. K. Dash, G. Suarez-Tangil, S. Khan, K. Tam, M. Ahmadi, J. Kinder, and L. Cavallaro. Droidscribe: Classifying android malware based on runtime behavior. In *Mobile Security Technologies (MoST 2016)*, 2016.

[12] A. Deo, S. K. Dash, G. Suarez-Tangil, V. Vovk, and L. Cavallaro. Prescience: Probabilistic guidance on the retraining conundrum for malware detection. In *ACM Workshop on Artificial Intelligence and Security (AISec)*, 2016.

[13] L. Deshotels, V. Notani, and A. Lakhotia. DroidLegacy: Automated familial classification of Android malware. In *ACM SIGPLAN on Program Protection and Reverse Engineering Workshop (PPREW)*, 2014.

[14] T. Dietterich. Overfitting and undercomputing in machine learning. *ACM Computing Surveys (CSUR)*, 27(3):326–327, Sept. 1995.

[15] M. Fernández-Delgado, E. Cernadas, S. Barro, and D. Amorim. Do we need hundreds of classifiers to solve real world classification problems? *The Journal of Machine Learning Research (JMLR)*, 15(1):3133–3181, Jan. 2014.

[16] J. Garcia, M. Hammad, B. Pedrood, A. Bagheri-Khaligh, and S. Malek. Obfuscation-resilient, efficient, and accurate detection and family identification of android malware. Technical report, Dept. of Computer Science, George Mason University, 2015.

[17] J. Gardiner and S. Nagaraja. On the security of machine learning in malware c&c detection: A survey. *ACM Comput. Surv.*, 49(3):59:1–59:39, Dec. 2016.

[18] P. Geurts, D. Ernst, and L. Wehenkel. Extremely randomized trees. *Machine Learning*, 63(1):3–42, 2006.

[19] T. Hastie, R. Tibshirani, and J. Friedman. *The elements of statistical learning: data mining, inference, and prediction: with 200 full-color illustrations*. New York: Springer-Verlag, 2 edition, 2009.

[20] L. Huang, A. D. Joseph, B. Nelson, B. I. P. Rubinstein,

and J. D. Tygar. Adversarial machine learning. In *Proceedings of the 2016 ACM Workshop on Artificial Intelligence and Security*, AISec '11, pages 43–58. ACM, 2011.

[21] M. Lindorfer, M. Neugschwandtner, and C. Platzer. Marvin: Efficient and comprehensive mobile app classification through static and dynamic analysis. In *Proceedings of the 39th Annual International Computers, Software & Applications Conference (COMPSAC)*, volume 2, pages 422–433, July 2015.

[22] M. Lindorfer, M. Neugschwandtner, L. Weichselbaum, Y. Fratantonio, V. van der Veen, and C. Platzer. Andrubis-1,000,000 apps later: A view on current android malware behaviors. In *3rd International Workshop on Building Analysis Datasets and Gathering Experience Returns for Security (BADGERS)*, 2014.

[23] G. Louppe, L. Wehenkel, A. Sutera, and P. Geurts. Understanding variable importances in forests of randomized trees. In *Advances in Neural Information Processing Systems (NIPS)*, pages 431–439, 2013.

[24] D. Maiorca, D. Ariu, I. Corona, M. Aresu, and G. Giacinto. Stealth attacks: An extended insight into the obfuscation effects on android malware. *Computers & Security*, 51:16 – 31, 2015.

[25] M. Palatucci, D. Pomerleau, G. E. Hinton, and T. M. Mitchell. Zero-shot learning with semantic output codes. In *Advances in neural information processing systems (NIPS)*, pages 1410–1418, 2009.

[26] S. Poeplau, Y. Fratantonio, A. Bianchi, C. Kruegel, and G. Vigna. Execute This! Analyzing Unsafe and Malicious Dynamic Code Loading in Android Applications. In *Network and Distributed System Security Symposium (NDSS)*, San Diego, CA, Feb 2014.

[27] R. B. Rao, G. Fung, and R. Rosales. On the dangers of cross-validation. an experimental evaluation. In *SIAM International Conference on Data Mining (SDM)*, pages 588–596. SIAM, 2008.

[28] V. Rastogi, Y. Chen, and X. Jiang. Droidchameleon: Evaluating android anti-malware against transformation attacks. In *ACM SIGSAC Symposium on Information, Computer and Communications Security*, ASIA CCS '13, pages 329–334, New York, NY, USA, 2013. ACM.

[29] S. Roy, J. DeLoach, Y. Li, N. Herndon, D. Caragea, X. Ou, V. P. Ranganath, H. Li, and N. Guevara. Experimental study with real-world data for android app security analysis using machine learning. In *Proceedings of the 31st Annual Computer Security Applications Conference*, pages 81–90. ACM, 2015.

[30] A. Saracino, D. Sgandurra, G. Dini, and F. Martinelli. Madam: Effective and efficient behavior-based android malware detection and prevention. *IEEE Transactions on Dependable and Secure Computing*, PP(99):1–1, 2016.

[31] S. Schrittwieser, S. Katzenbeisser, J. Kinder, G. Merzdovnik, and E. Weippl. Protecting software through obfuscation: Can it keep pace with progress in code analysis? *ACM Computing Surveys*, 49(1), Apr. 2016.

[32] C. Smutz and A. Stavrou. Malicious pdf detection using metadata and structural features. In *28th Annual Computer Security Applications Conference (ACSAC)*,

pages 239–248, New York, NY, USA, 2012. ACM.

[33] G. Suarez-Tangil, J. Tapiador, F. Lombardi, and R. Di Pietro. Alterdroid: Differential fault analysis of obfuscated smartphone malware. 2016.

[34] G. Suarez-Tangil, J. E. Tapiador, and P. Peris-Lopez. Stegomalware: Playing hide and seek with malicious components in smartphone apps. In *10th International Conference on Information Security and Cryptology (Inscrypt)*, pages 496–515. Springer, December 2014.

[35] G. Suarez-Tangil, J. E. Tapiador, P. Peris-Lopez, and J. Blasco. Dendroid: A text mining approach to analyzing and classifying code structures in android malware families. *Expert Systems with Applications*, 41(1):1104–1117, 2014.

[36] R. J. Z. Wang, D. Papini, I. Nouretdinov, and L. Cavallaro. Misleading Metrics: On Evaluating Machine Learning for Malware with Confidence. Technical Report 2016-1, Royal Holloway, University of London, 2016.

[37] M. Xia, L. Gong, Y. Lyu, Z. Qi, and X. Liu. Effective real-time android application auditing. In *IEEE Symposium on Security and Privacy (SP)*, pages 899–914, May 2015.

[38] C. Yang, Z. Xu, G. Gu, V. Yegneswaran, and P. A. Porras. DroidMiner: Automated mining and characterization of fine-grained malicious behaviors in Android applications. In *European Symposium on Research in Computer Security (ESORICS)*. 2014.

[39] M. Zhang, Y. Duan, H. Yin, and Z. Zhao. Semantics-aware Android malware classification using weighted contextual API dependency graphs. In *ACM SIGSAC Computer and Communications Security (CCS)*, 2014.

[40] Y. Zhang, M. Yang, B. Xu, Z. Yang, G. Gu, P. Ning, X. S. Wang, and B. Zang. Vetting undesirable behaviors in Android apps with permission use analysis. In *ACM SIGSAC Computer and Communications Security (CCS)*, 2013.

[41] Y. Zhou and X. Jiang. Dissecting Android malware: Characterization and evolution. In *IEEE Symposium on Security and Privacy (SP)*, 2012.

Aegis: Automatic Enforcement of Security Policies in Workflow-driven Web Applications*

Luca Compagna
SAP Labs France
luca.compagna@sap.com

Daniel R. dos Santos
Fondazione Bruno Kessler
SAP Labs France
University of Trento
dossantos@fbk.eu

Serena Elisa Ponta
SAP Labs France
serena.ponta@sap.com

Silvio Ranise
Fondazione Bruno Kessler
ranise@fbk.eu

ABSTRACT

Organizations often expose business processes and services as web applications. Improper enforcement of security policies in these applications leads to business logic vulnerabilities that are hard to find and may have dramatic security implications. AEGIS is a tool to automatically synthesize run-time monitors to enforce control-flow and data-flow integrity, as well as authorization policies and constraints in web applications. The enforcement of these properties can mitigate attacks, e.g., authorization bypass and workflow violations, while allowing regulatory compliance in the form of, e.g., Separation of Duty. AEGIS is capable of guaranteeing business continuity while enforcing the security policies. We evaluate AEGIS on a set of real-world applications, assessing the enforcement of policies, mitigation of vulnerabilities, and performance overhead.

Keywords

Web Application; Policy Enforcement; Workflow Satisfiability

1. INTRODUCTION

Web applications are one of the preferred ways of exposing business processes and services to users. Many web applications implement workflows, i.e. there is a pre-defined sequence of tasks that must be performed by users to reach a goal [1]. If an application does not correctly enforce its workflows, attackers can exploit this vulnerability to subvert it. In an e-commerce application, for instance, users must *Select products, Checkout, Enter shipping information, Pay*, and *Confirm*. If the application does not verify that user actions follow this sequence, a user can, e.g., skip the payment step

---

*This work has been partly supported by the EU under grant 317387 SECENTIS (FP7-PEOPLE-2012-ITN).

and receive products without paying. Control-flow integrity, i.e. the enforcement of an application's workflow, has been used in web applications to prevent workflow attacks and others, e.g., forceful browsing and race conditions [3].

Data-flow integrity is also crucial and incorrect enforcement can lead to vulnerabilities where, e.g., a user can change the price of a product being purchased to pay less for it [20]. This kind of vulnerability is even more prominent in multi-party scenarios, where a user receives data from one party and must relay it to another party. Several vulnerabilities have been discovered in recent years due to improper enforcement of data-flow integrity [20, 12, 14].

Besides control- and data-flow integrity, access control is fundamental whenever users must access only data and functionalities that they are authorized to by a given policy. Access control vulnerabilities are common and hard to find [15]. Moreover, some web applications implement collaborative work, in which users work together to complete a workflow. Examples are Enterprise Resource Planning (ERP) software and e-health applications. In these applications, not only it is important to enforce authorization policies, but it may also be necessary to support authorization constraints, which impose more restrictions on what users can do at run-time. Examples of such constraints are Separation or Binding of Duty (SoD or BoD), requiring two different users (same user, respectively) to execute a pair of tasks. These constraints can be used to avoid errors and frauds in applications that must follow compliance rules. Nonetheless, none of the applications we experimented with provided support for an easy to use, declarative specification of constraints. Without declarative specifications and proper enforcement, authorization constraints have to be implemented as application code embedded into each task or translated to static assignments in the authorization policy. Both solutions are error-prone and can hardly scale.

Even with suitable specification and enforcement mechanisms, support for authorization policies and constraints may lead to situations where an application workflow cannot be completed because no user can execute an action without violating them, thereby hindering business continuity. Determining if such a situation can be avoided, i.e. if a workflow can be completed in the presence of a policy and constraints, is known as the Workflow Satisfiability Problem (WSP) [18]. The WSP has received much attention in the workflow security community, but, to the best of our knowledge, has never been considered in web applications. Transferring WSP solutions to the web domain is not trivial, since these solutions rely on workflow models and a workflow management system to handle the control-flow of tasks and to provide an interface for users to request task executions, elements which are frequently not available for web applications.

In this paper, we present AEGIS[1], a tool to synthesize run-time monitors for web applications that are capable of automatically (i) enforcing security policies composed of combinations of control- and data-flow integrity, authorization policies and constraints; and (ii) solving the run-time version of the WSP by granting or denying requests of users to perform tasks based on the satisfaction of the policy and constraints and the possibility to terminate the current workflow instance. AEGIS is based on [2], where a technique to synthesize run-time monitors that solve the WSP for security-sensitive workflows was presented. We extend [2] by supporting data integrity. To synthesize a monitor, AEGIS first infers, using process mining [17], workflow models of the target application from a set of HTTP traces representing user actions. Traces must be manually edited to contain only actions that should be controlled by the monitor. Inferred models are Petri nets [11] labeled with HTTP requests representing tasks and annotated with data-flow properties obtained by using a set of heuristics based on differential analysis (as in, e.g., [20, 14]).

The main contributions of this paper are the description and implementation of AEGIS, as well as an empirical evaluation on a set of relevant applications. The rest of this paper is organized as follows: Section 2 presents an overview using motivating examples; Section 3 details the three steps of the technique; Section 4 shows the implementation and evaluation of our work; and Section 5 concludes the paper.

2. OVERVIEW

AEGIS synthesizes run-time monitors for workflow-driven web applications, i.e. applications implementing business processes and customer services as workflows. Hereafter, *web application* is used as an abbreviation for *workflow-driven web application*, unless stated otherwise.

A monitor synthesized by AEGIS can enforce three security properties: authorization policies ($\mathcal{P}$), defining which users are entitled to perform which tasks; authorization constraints ($\mathcal{C}$), defining run-time restrictions on the execution of tasks, e.g., SoD; and control- and data-flow integrity ($\mathcal{I}$), specifying the authorized control-flow paths that the application must follow, as well as data invariants. Different web applications have different enforcement needs, which requires the synthesis of different configurations of monitors, depending on which properties are switched on or off. We identify each configuration as a tuple containing the active properties, e.g., $\langle\mathcal{P},\mathcal{C},\mathcal{I}\rangle$, $\langle\mathcal{P},\mathcal{I}\rangle$, $\langle\mathcal{C},\mathcal{I}\rangle$, $\langle\mathcal{I}\rangle$. Control- and data-flow integrity are in the same category because it is not realistic that an application needs to enforce one and not the other.

AEGIS takes as input sets of HTTP traces representing user actions executed while interacting with a target web application. It synthesizes an external monitor to be used by a proxy sitting between users and the application. Each set of input traces is produced by a user simulating real clients completing a workflow as foreseen by the application ("good traces"). The monitor only enforces those workflows given

---

[1] Aegis was the mythological shield carried by Athena.

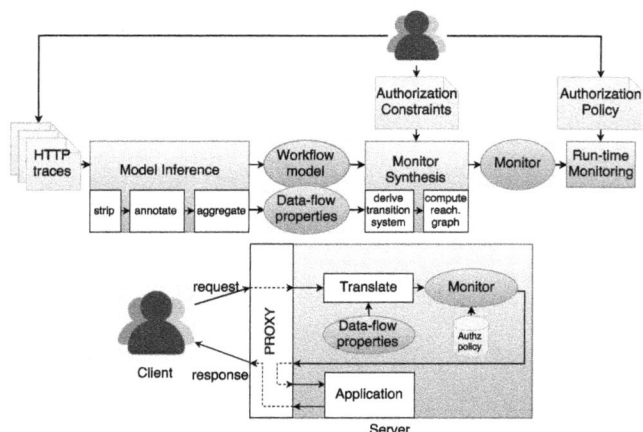

Figure 1: Overview of the technique

in input, having no impact on the rest of the application. Traces can be collected using test automation tools such as Selenium[2] or ZAP[3] and must be manually edited to contain only critical tasks. After trace collection, the whole technique is fully automated.

Figure 1 shows an overview of AEGIS. The top of the Figure shows the entire approach, where rectangles represent the three main steps, yellow notes are inputs, and ovals are generated artifacts. The bottom of the Figure details the internals of the *Run-time Monitoring* component. The three main steps are the following.

1. Model Inference. The set of *HTTP traces* is automatically *stripped* of all information except request and response URLs, headers, and bodies; each request and response is *annotated* with *data-flow properties* inferred by a set of heuristics; traces are *aggregated* into a file called event log; and a process mining tool takes the log as input to generate a Petri net *workflow model* whose transitions are labeled by the annotated requests.

2. Monitor Synthesis. Given a workflow model, the user specifies the *Authorization Constraints* to be enforced (if any) and whether an *Authorization Policy* will be provided at run-time. Control- and data-flow integrity are obtained automatically from the model and are always enforced. The workflow model is presented in a convenient BPMN [19] notation, and the specification of constraints is done graphically. A run-time monitor capable of enforcing the chosen properties is synthesized by translating the model to a symbolic *transition system* (the translation among BPMN, Petri nets, and transition systems is automatic [2]) and computing a *reachability graph* that represents all possible valid executions of the workflow by symbolic users, allowing us to support different authorization policies at run-time. The *Monitor* is a set of queries derived from the graph.

3. Run-time Monitoring. A reverse *proxy* is instantiated with the synthesized monitor and a concrete authorization policy (when provided by the user). It sits between users and the application, filters *requests* and *translates* them to the monitor. The monitor enforces the properties defined in step 2, granting a request if the control-flow is respected, the data-flow invariants hold ($\mathcal{I}$), the user issuing the request is

---

[2] http://www.seleniumhq.org/
[3] https://goo.gl/XvxKd1

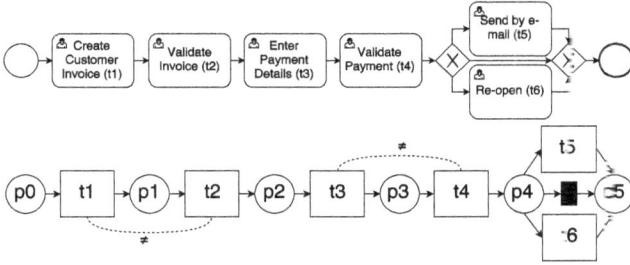

Figure 2: Customer invoice process in BPMN (top) and as a Petri net (bottom)

authorized by the policy ($\mathcal{P}$), the authorization constraints are not violated ($\mathcal{C}$) and the current instance execution can still terminate. The proxy, based on the response from the monitor, may forward requests to the application or drop them to prevent the violation of some property.

A single application may implement several workflows. Steps 1 and 2 are performed for each workflow to be monitored, generating one monitor per workflow. Step 3 uses all the synthesized monitors and queries the correct one depending on the incoming request. Requests not related to any monitored workflow go directly to the application, without triggering a monitor query.

Below, we present two motivating examples that illustrate the configurations $\langle \mathcal{P}, \mathcal{C}, \mathcal{I} \rangle$, $\langle \mathcal{C}, \mathcal{I} \rangle$ (first example) and $\langle \mathcal{I} \rangle$ (second example).

2.1 Example 1 - Enforcing constraints

Dolibarr[4] is an open-source ERP web application that implements a business process similar to the one shown at the top of Figure 2 (in BPMN) to manage customer invoices.

The process contains 6 tasks (depicted by rounded boxes). Tasks $t1$ to $t4$ must be performed in sequence (as indicated by the solid arrows), while either $t5$, $t6$ or neither are performed last (as indicated by the diamond-shaped gateway). Dolibarr implements each of the tasks shown in Figure 2. An authorization policy, control-flow, and possible data-flow invariants are implemented in an ad-hoc way, whose correctness is hard to verify, which may lead to vulnerabilities. The authorization policy provided by the application has a granularity of permissions that does not match the user-task assignment we support (there is no specific permission to, e.g., re-open an invoice). Authorization constraints are not supported. As a result, it is not trivial to prevent a malicious user from creating and validating a customer invoice (SoD between $t1$ and $t2$) or inserting and validating a payment (SoD between $t3$ and $t4$), which would allow him to, e.g., close invoices with an incorrect payment.

A user who wants to securely deploy this application can use AEGIS to generate a $\langle \mathcal{P}, \mathcal{C}, \mathcal{I} \rangle$ monitor to enforce control-flow integrity, ensuring that all the steps in the customer invoice process are performed in the correct order; an authorization policy, ensuring that only authorized users can execute each task; and the SoD constraints described above, to avoid frauds. If the user prefers to leave authorization enforcement to the application, a $\langle \mathcal{C}, \mathcal{I} \rangle$ monitor could be generated to only add support for constraints and integrity.

---
[4]http://www.dolibarr.org/

To generate a monitor for the invoicing process, without impacting other parts of the application, the user starts by collecting traces simulating users performing the process. Some HTTP traces representing these executions are (for the sake of readability, we show only simplified URLs, but headers and body are also part of the traces):

$\tau_1 = $ {/invoice?action=create&value=10&prod=abc, /invoice/validate?id=1, /invoice/pay/create?id=1&value=10, /invoice/pay/validate?id=1},

$\tau_2 = $ {/invoice?action=create&value=20&prod=def, /invoice/validate?id=2, /invoice/pay/create?id=2&value=20, /invoice/pay/validate?id=2, POST /invoice/send BODY id=2},

$\tau_3 = $ {/invoice?action=create&value=30&prod=ghi&prod2=jkl, /invoice/validate?id=3, /invoice/pay/create?id=3&value=30, /invoice/pay/validate?id=3, /invoice/reopen?id=3}.

Each trace τ_i represents one possible execution of the invoicing process and each request represents one task. The first four requests in each trace are essentially the same, but with different parameter values (e.g., **id** is 1 in τ_1, 2 in τ_2, and 3 in τ_3). They represent tasks $t1$, $t2$, $t3$, and $t4$. τ_1 is an example of the branch where only the first four tasks are executed, while $t5$ is executed after $t4$ in τ_2, and $t6$ is executed after $t4$ in τ_3. The traces are automatically analyzed to extract data-flow properties, annotated and aggregated into an event log, sent to a process mining tool and the resulting Petri net labeled with a task-to-URL map (**Step 1**). Figure 2 shows, at the bottom, the Petri net obtained from the process mining tool (ignore for a moment the dashed lines). The tasks in the net are labeled as t_i, with the following task-to-URL map:

t_1 : /invoice?action=create&value=<<I>>&prod=<<DC>>,

t_2 : /invoice/validate?id=<<IID>>,

t_3 : /invoice/pay/create?id=<<IID>>&value=<<I>>,

t_4 : /invoice/pay/validate?id=<<IID>>,

t_5 : POST /invoice/send BODY id=<<IID>>,

t_6 : /invoice/reopen?id=<<IID>>

Data-flow properties are represented by annotations on the URLs. The <<IID>> (instance identifier) annotation is applied to the elements used to bind all the requests to the same instance of a workflow, in this case the **id** parameter. The <<I>> (invariant) annotation is applied to values that should not change during the workflow, in this example the **value** of the invoice in t_1 should be the same as the **value** of the payment in t_2. The <<DC>> ("don't care") annotation is applied to parameters that should be present in the request to help identify it as a unique action, but whose values are irrelevant. The parameter **prod2**, which is present in the request of $t1$ only in τ_3, is dropped in the task-to-URL map because it is considered optional, i.e. a trace may represent an invoice with one or more products, so only the first **prod** parameter needs to be present.

The user then specifies the constraints that must be enforced, shown as dashed lines labeled by $\neq$ (abbreviating a SoD constraint) in Figure 2. The model is used to synthesize a monitor (**Step 2**), which is composed of a set of SQL queries encoding the fact that to perform a task t, all the predecessor tasks (according to the control-flow of the model) must have been executed, there must be an authorized user u who has not performed any conflicting tasks, and there must be other users capable of executing the remaining tasks without violating the policy and the constraints.

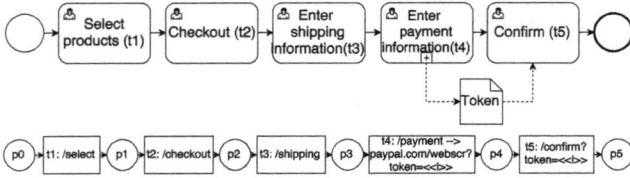

Figure 3: Checkout process in BPMN (top) and as a Petri net (bottom)

At run-time (**Step 3**), in the $\langle \mathcal{P}, \mathcal{C}, \mathcal{I} \rangle$ configuration, a policy is specified as a task-user assignment, e.g., $TA = \{(u1, t1), (u1, t2), (u2, t2), (u3, t3), (u4, t3), (u4, t4), (u5, t5), (u6, t6)\}$, where $(u, t) \in TA$ means that u is authorized to execute t. The assignment is stored in the database, and a reverse proxy is instantiated with the synthesized monitor. The proxy is capable of receiving a request such as `GET /invoice/validate?id=5` with the header `Cookie: sid=abcd1234` and identifying that it refers to task $t2$ of instance 5 of the invoicing process being performed by user $u2$ (whose cookie `sid` has been stored during login). It then queries the monitor and, assuming that $u1$ has previously executed $t1$ and $t2$ has not yet been executed, the SQL query is satisfied and the request is granted. On the other hand, a request can be blocked in several cases, such as if $u3$ tries to execute $t2$ ($(u3, t2) \notin TA$), if $u1$ tries to execute $t2$ (SoD), if any user tries to execute $t3$ before $t2$, or if any user issues a request for $t3$ with a `value` different from the one sent for $t1$.

To solve the WSP, regardless of the execution history, any request of $u4$ to execute $t3$ should be blocked. Granting that request would mean that the only user authorized to execute $t4$ has already executed $t3$, while both tasks are in SoD. Therefore, any execution where $u4$ performs $t3$ would either not terminate or terminate with the violation of some constraint or policy. This tension between business compliance and business continuity should be resolved and the synthesized monitor avoids it by blocking requests that lead to undesired situations.

2.2 Example 2 - Mitigating vulnerabilities

TomatoCart[5] is a popular e-commerce application that implements the checkout process depicted on the top of Figure 3. It is composed of 5 tasks executed in sequence, where $t4$ is a sub-process that can be implemented in different ways, but must produce a data object representing a token issued by a trusted third party, that is read in $t5$.

This is an example of a multi-party web application [14], which implements the payment step by using a third-party such as PayPal. An execution of this workflow, using PayPal Express Checkout, involves three actors: a client C, a service provider SP implementing TomatoCart and a trusted third party TTP implementing the payment provider. The execution starts with the client browsing the SP, selecting some product ($t1$), requesting checkout ($t2$), and entering shipping information ($t3$). The SP then contacts the TTP and receives a token identifying the transaction (not shown in the workflow). The user is redirected to the TTP with the token ($t4$), completes the payment (again not shown in the Figure), and is redirected back to the SP passing the token, which is verified to complete the transaction ($t5$).

_____
[5] http://www.tomatocart.com/

In version 1.1.7, TomatoCart had a vulnerability that allowed users to replay a token in $t5$ of a new transaction and shop for free [14]. This vulnerability was manually fixed in a later release of the application, but AEGIS could have been used to mitigate it until a patch was available (or until the patch could be applied, which is not always trivial). To mitigate the replay vulnerability, we can generate a monitor in the configuration $\langle \mathcal{I} \rangle$, enforcing control-flow integrity and the data invariant that the token received in $t4$ is the same one sent in $t5$. An authorization policy and authorization constraints are not specified since every user can execute the steps in the checkout process and all steps are executed by the same user. Details of the communication between SP and TTP and between C and TTP are not shown in the workflow because the monitor only needs to enforce that no user can replace the token that has been sent to him/her. Although AEGIS ignores some messages, many vulnerabilities in multi-party web applications can be mitigated this way [20].

To generate the monitor, we repeat the steps presented for Example 1. Below, there are some traces of the execution of the checkout process, again simplified for readability. Now the traces involve three parties, thus each request must be identified with its host.

$\tau_1 = \{$`shop.com/select, shop.com/checkout, shop.com/shipping,`
　　　`shop.com/payment -> paypal.com/webscr?token=abcd1234,`
　　　　　`shop.com/confirm?token=abcd1234`$\}$,

$\tau_2 = \{$`shop.com/select, shop.com/checkout, shop.com/shipping,`
　　　`shop.com/payment -> paypal.com/webscr?token=efgh5678,`
　　　　　`shop.com/confirm?token=efgh5678`$\}$.

Figure 3 shows the Petri net obtained for the checkout process, labeled directly with the URL of each task (where `->` represents a redirect). The invariant annotation `<<I>>` is applied to the `token` received from PayPal, specifying that its value must be the same in `/payment` and `/confirm`.

A monitor is synthesized as before, however with neither authorization policy nor constraints. Workflow instances can be identified by the user identifier, since each user has only one checkout process at any given time. At run-time, whenever a user tries to replay a token, the monitor blocks this request because the token sent in $t5$ is different from the one received in $t4$. If the user tries to bypass the monitor by skipping step $t4$ and sending the token directly in $t5$, the monitor blocks the request because of a control-flow violation.

3. DETAILS

An HTTP trace (or a web session) is a sequence $S = \{(u_1 : r_1, s_1), (u_2 : r_2, s_2), ..., (u_n : r_n, s_n)\}$ of pairs of web requests r_i issued by users u_i (which may or may not be all distinct) and responses s_i. Each web request or response is defined as $r_i = (headers, body)$ and the information we derive from a request is a tuple $(method, url, P)$, where $method \in \{$GET, POST$\}$, url is the requested URL, and P is a set of parameters of the form (k, v), which can be in the URL (in GET requests), the body (in POST requests) or in the headers (e.g., cookies or _Location_ in redirects). Data values passed as, e.g., JSON can be flattened to the same representation. The parameters in P represent the data values later annotated with data-flow properties.

A workflow $W(T, U)$ is a set of tasks ($t \in T$) endowed by execution constraints involving users ($u \in U$). A web application is composed of a set of workflows $\Psi = \{W_1(T_1, U_1), ..., W_n(T_n, U_n)\}$. We take as input sets of web sessions $WS_i = \{S_1, S_2, ..., S_n\}$ and infer from each WS_i a workflow $W_i(T_i, U_i)$, using an off-the-shelf process mining algorithm, and a set of data property labels L_i, using heuristics. We also take as input, optionally, sets of authorization constraints C_i. We then use a monitor synthesis procedure $\mathcal{MS}(W_i, L_i, C_i)$ that returns a monitor M_i. M_i is capable of answering requests of the form "can user u perform task t?"—encoded as $can\_do(u,t)$— with True iff the control-flow in W_i and the data-flow in L_i are respected, no authorization constraint in C_i is violated, the requesting user u is authorized by an authorization policy TA (specified at run-time), and the workflow can be executed until the end.

At run-time, a reverse proxy receives an incoming request $u : r$ and based on the information taken from it, tries to translate it into a query of the form $can\_do(u, t)$, for $u \in U_i$ and $t \in T_i$ of workflow $W_i(T_i, U_i)$, which can be answered by M_i. Attacks on the application at the level of web requests characterized as follows [10]: a request forgery is an extra request not foreseen in a workflow ($\{r_1, r_2, ..., r_{forged}, ..., r_n\}$); a workflow bypass is a missing request ($\{r_1, r_2, ..., r_{i-1}, r_{i+1}, ..., r_n\}$); a workflow violation is an attempt to either repeat a unique request ($\{r_1, r_2, ..., r_i, ..., r_i, .., r_n\}$) or execute a request out of order ($\{r_1, r_2, ..., r_{i+1}, ..., r_i, ..., r_n\}$); and authorization violations happen when a request is issued by a user who is not entitled to do so by the policy or when, for two tasks t_1 and t_2 in SoD, a user who previously issued a request r_1 to execute t_1, issues a new request r_2 to execute t_2. The monitor can mitigate these attacks because they do not comply with the expected workflow (naturally, they are only mitigated in the parts of the application covered by the inferred model).

3.1 Step 1 - Model inference

The goal of Step 1 is not to produce an accurate model of the whole application, but workflow models containing only security-relevant actions. These are the requests related to workflow tasks, whose execution should be controlled by the monitor. The definition of what is relevant varies from application to application, but besides the usual noise in HTTP traces (e.g., loading images and other resources), any request that leaves the application state unchanged should be filtered out. Such requests are called navigation events, as opposed to system-interaction events [13]. Not every system-interaction event should be controlled by the monitor (this should be decided by the user). However, discarding navigation events is crucial to keep the inferred models to a reasonable size and to eliminate imprecision due to variations in the process when executed by different users. We assume that this treatment of the input traces is done before AEGIS is invoked. It can be done manually, but there are automated techniques to detect state changing requests [6, 13]. Such techniques are usually embedded in crawlers to obtain a model of the entire application. Applying just state-change detection to traces of a single workflow may have sub-optimal results (this evaluation is left to future work).

Since some URLs in an application can take different parameters and different values for these parameters, while still representing the same action, and since we apply differential analysis to identify data-flow properties, we need at least two different traces as input, each containing a possible value for each of the parameters (including their presence and absence). The input traces should also represent all the possible execution paths of the process (control-flow). The

number of input traces required for a precise model depends on the number of control-flow branches in the workflow being analyzed, as well as the diversity of the traces. Related works use, e.g., four traces as input [20] or traces with specific requirements for each of the parties in the process [14]. At least two login traces with distinct users must also be present, so that cookies defining the user session identifier and parameters representing user names can be mined, to map requests to concrete users at run-time. From the set of HTTP traces, we extract three artifacts: a workflow model, a task-to-URL map, and a set of data properties.

Workflow model and map. A workflow model is automatically obtained from a process mining tool. There are many well-known process mining algorithms and a simple example is the α-algorithm [17]. It mines workflow nets by recording all the events in a log and detecting relations between them, such as sequence, exclusive, and parallel executions. In the traces used in Example 1, it is possible to see that $t1$ always precedes $t2$ and $t2$ never precedes $t1$, so the algorithm infers a causal dependency between them and adds a place connecting transitions $t1$ and $t2$ in the output net (place $p1$ in Figure 2). It is also possible to see that $t4$ precedes $t5$, $t4$ precedes $t6$, and $t5$ and $t6$ never happen in the same trace, thus the algorithm creates a place after $t4$ that branches the execution ($p4$ in Figure 2). Since the input traces contain only relevant URLs and each unique URL becomes a transition after process mining, the task-to-URL map is trivial to obtain.

Data-flow properties. We use five annotations, namely *constant, don't care, invariant, instance identifier,* and *user identifier*, which are used for three goals. *Constants* and *don't cares* are used to restrict and generalize, respectively, the input traces by fixing or hiding given values that are used to match incoming requests at run-time. A *user identifier* is used to detect the user issuing a request and an *instance identifier* to detect the workflow instance that the request is related to, since several instances of the same workflow may be running at the same time and they may have different execution histories. *Invariants* indicate values that should not be modified during a workflow instance execution.

Data-flow properties are obtained by using differential analysis, i.e. comparing the differences in the data values between traces, as is done in related work (e.g., [20, 14]). For each trace, the analysis compares the values of all parameters in each request in relation to (i) the same parameter in other requests of the same trace, (ii) the same parameter in other traces, (iii) other parameters in the same trace, and (iv) other parameter in other traces. AEGIS does not apply syntactic annotation (as, e.g., [14]) to identify the data type of each parameter, and does not try to discover possible values or intervals for data elements, because it does not enforce particular values that were seen in the traces (except for *constants*). Below, we describe the differential analysis used to identify each kind of data-flow property.

Let WS be the set of traces τ_i used for analysis, each τ_i be composed of requests r_j and responses s_j, and each request or response have a set P of parameters (k, v) Considering the same request r_j in every trace $\tau \in WS$, if a parameter (k, v) appears in only a strict subset $\tau' \subset \tau$ of the traces, it is considered optional and ignored, i.e. dropped from the URL in the labeling function L. *Constants* are parameters that are present in every trace $\tau \in WS$ for the same URL of a request r_j and whose key k and value v never change. An example is the parameter `action=create`, which is in $t1$ of traces τ_1, τ_2, and τ_3 in Example 1. *Don't cares* are parameters that appear in every trace $\tau \in WS$ for the same URL of a request r_j and whose key k remains constant, but whose value v is different in at least one of the requests. One example is `prod=abc`, `prod=def` and `prod=ghi` in $t1$ of Example 1 annotated as `prod=<<DC>>`. An *instance identifier* is a key k whose value v is present in every request r of a trace τ, with different v's in every trace. In Example 1, the parameter `id` is an instance identifier, since it has the value 1 in every request of τ_1, the value 2 in every request of τ_2, and the value 3 in every request of τ_3. Notice that what must remain constant is the value and not the key, so it is possible to have an instance identifier called, e.g., `id` in one request and `iid` in another request. A *user identifier* is a parameter that comes from a response issued by the server, is stored in a cookie, sent in every request of a trace and whose value changes in every trace in WS. In Example 1, only URLs are shown in the traces, but the cookie `sid` is sent with every request, as can be seen towards the end of the example. *Invariants* are values v that remain constant during a trace, change between traces in WS and are not present in every request of a trace (as opposed to instance identifiers). Two examples are the `value` parameter in $t1$ and $t3$ in Example 1 and the `token` in $t4$ and $t5$ of Example 2. Like instance identifiers, invariant *values* should not change, but their *keys* might, so that an invariant can be called, e.g., `price` in one request and `amount` in another. There may be many invariants in a workflow, so they are annotated as `<<I_1>>`, ..., `<<I_n>>` for run-time enforcement.

Step 1 outputs a tuple (PN, L), where PN is a Petri net and L is a labeling function that associates to each transition in the net a URL annotated with the identified data properties. Although (PN, L) is obtained automatically, it can be edited by a user before being sent for monitor synthesis. Control-flow constraints can be changed by graphically adding or removing places or transitions in the Petri net (or tasks and gateways in BPMN), while data properties can be modified by adding or removing annotations on the URLs.

3.2 Step 2 - Monitor synthesis

Step 2 takes as input the (PN, L) from Step 1 and, optionally, augments it with security properties given by the user. As an example, the user can specify authorization constraints $\text{SoD}(tx, ty)$ indicating that tasks tx and ty must be executed by different users. The user must also indicate whether the monitor should enforce an authorization policy to be specified later.

Security properties specification. All behaviors of the web application that satisfy the specified security properties are represented by the executions of a symbolic transition system $S = (V, Tr)$, where V is a set of state variables and Tr is a set of transitions. In general, each workflow task corresponds to one transition. Each transition has a condition and an update part. The conditions specify the constraints that must be satisfied for a task to be executed (e.g., control-flow, data-flow and authorization) and are expressed based on the variables in V, therefore encoding the security properties. The update represents the effect of executing the task (changing the values of the variables in V). See [2] for more details on the variables and transitions in S.

Monitor synthesis. S is fed to a symbolic model checker, which computes a reachability graph RG representing all possible executions of the workflow by a set of symbolic users. A procedure to compute this graph, based on backward reachability, is described in [2]. RG is a directed graph whose edges are labeled by task-user pairs in which users are symbolically represented by variables and whose nodes are labeled by a symbolic representation (namely, a formula of first-order logic) of the set of states from which it is possible to reach a state in which the workflow successfully terminates. A Datalog [4] program M is automatically derived from RG by generating a clause of the form $can\_do(u, t) \leftarrow \beta_n$ for each node n in the graph (β_n is the formula labeling n). M is then translated to SQL [16]. The SQL program is capable of answering—after possibly being instantiated with a concrete authorization policy—user requests to execute tasks in a workflow in such a way that the authorization and execution constraints are not violated, the authorization policy is respected and termination of the workflow is guaranteed, thus enforcing the specified security properties and solving the run-time WSP.

Step 2 outputs a tuple (M, L), where M is the monitor generated from RG and L is the labeling function, which now maps from transitions in S to annotated HTTP requests.

3.3 Step 3 - Run-time monitoring

Step 3 takes as input (M, L) and, if previously specified, an authorization policy TA used to populate a database queried by M, resulting in a concrete monitor.

A reverse proxy intercepts all incoming requests to the application and decides, for each request, whether it is part of a workflow or not. To do so, it tries to match the URL and parameters in the request to annotated URLs and parameters stored in L, taking into account the constant, ignored and don't care values. If there is no match, the proxy forwards the request to the application, as it is not part of any workflow. If there is a match, the proxy associates the request to a task t of a workflow $W(T, U)$ and checks the annotated URL for `<<IID>>` and `<<UID>>` values, extracting the instance i and the user u. The user identifier is a cookie value that must be mapped to a user name in the policy. This is done by capturing login actions, storing the cookies issued to each user, and later retrieving the user names based on the cookie.

To enforce data invariants, when the proxy receives a request for the first URL containing the annotation `inv=<<I_i>>`, it stores the value of the parameter `inv` as v_i. When any subsequent task containing `<<I_i>>` is accessed, the value of the incoming annotated parameter `inc` is compared to the stored value ($v_i = $ `inc`). In these requests, the monitor query $can\_do(u, t) \leftarrow \beta$ is dynamically conjoined with the data invariant condition, becoming $can_do(u, t) \leftarrow \beta \land v_i = $ `inc`. Finally, the proxy issues a request $can\_do(u, t)$ to the monitor of instance i of W and acts based on its response by either forwarding the request or dropping it.

4. EVALUATION

AEGIS was implemented in Python 2.7. We capture execution traces using ZAP, extract data properties from them, aggregate them into an XES log file and use ProM [17] to mine the Petri net. Monitor synthesis is implemented as in [2]. We instantiate mitmproxy[6] with the generated monitor script that intercepts requests and responses, performs URL matching, queries a MySQL database—which stores

---

[6]https://mitmproxy.org/

the authorization policies—by using the synthesized queries, and either forwards or drops the request. The proxy also supports HTTPS connections.

4.1 Experimental setup

We tested AEGIS on the ten open-source applications shown in Table 1, synthesizing monitors in the configurations $\langle \mathcal{P}, \mathcal{C}, \mathcal{I} \rangle$ and $\langle \mathcal{I} \rangle$. #1-4 are ERP platforms, #5-6 are e-health applications and #7-10 are e-commerce applications. Column *Application* contains the name of each application; *Language* shows the language in which it was developed; *Params* describes the predominant method used for parameter passing (although an application can use several methods) and *Downloads* reports the number of downloads (#1-6) or public installations (#7-10).

The different languages show the versatility of the black-box approach, which has to be tailored to support each parameter passing method. The number of downloads and installations is a measure of the popularity of the applications and comes from official repositories (#2, 3, 5, and 6) data in the web page of the project (#1 and 4), or related work [12] (#7-10). The number of actual deployments for #1-6 is not available as they are usually internal to an organization and not indexed by search engines.

We pre-configured the applications using demo data and captured four execution traces for each workflow and two login traces for each application. To compare AEGIS in different ERP applications, we used workflows offered by all of them: *Purchase order* (PO), *Sales order* (SO), *Purchase invoice* (PI), and *Sales invoice* (SI). They are slightly different in each application, varying from 4 to 6 tasks, usually with a gateway defining 2 to 3 alternative execution branches. Figure 4 shows at the top the patient visit workflow mined from OpenEMR (where the lines labeled by = are BoD constraints) and at the bottom the lab analysis workflow mined from BikaLIMS. In these 6 applications, we added the authorization constraints and specified policies with 10 users assigned to each task, generating $\langle \mathcal{P}, \mathcal{C}, \mathcal{I} \rangle$ monitors.

The workflows for e-commerce applications are similar to the one shown in Figure 3. For these applications, we use the $\langle \mathcal{I} \rangle$ configuration, thus neither constraints nor authorization policies were defined. Applications 7 and 8 have a vulnerability allowing the replay of tokens (CVE-2012-4934). Applications 9 and 10 allow an attacker to tamper with a parameter that indicates who should receive the payment for a transaction (CVE-2012-2991).

All applications were deployed as Docker containers and the tests as Selenium scripts, which allows us to automatically test the applications with and without monitoring.

Table 1: Applications used in the experiments

#	Application	Language	Params	Downloads
1	Odoo	Python	JSON	2M
2	Dolibarr	PHP	GET	850k
3	WebERP	PHP	GET	617k
4	ERPNext	Python	JSON	25k
5	OpenEMR	PHP	GET	382k
6	BikaLIMS	Python	REST	111k
7	OpenCart 1.5.3.1	PHP	GET	9M
8	TomatoCart 1.1.7	PHP	GET	119k
9	osCommerce 2.3.1	PHP	GET	80k
10	AbanteCart 1.0.4	PHP	GET	21k

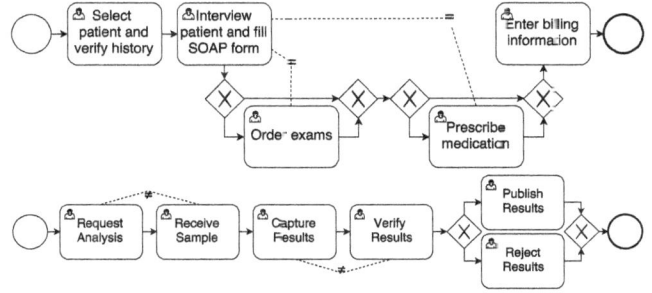

Figure 4: Workflows from OpenEMR (top) and BikaLIMS (bottom)

The experiments ran on a laptop with a 1.3GHz dual-core processor and 8GB of RAM.

4.2 Results

The enforcement of security properties and mitigation of vulnerabilities was successful in all applications; this was confirmed by manual inspection. In applications 1-6, we tried the attacks described in Section 3 (workflow bypass, workflow violations, and authorization violations). The monitor was able to block situations such as the same user executing an entire workflow (SoD violation), and users trying to access tasks that were not assigned to them. In applications 7-10, we tried to exploit the vulnerabilities described above. In applications 7-8, the attacks were unsuccessful because **token** was detected as an invariant and automatically enforced. In applications 9-10, the **PayeeId** parameter was detected as a constant, since every trace in the input was related to the same shop (constants are not enforced, only used to match URLs). We then edited the inferred model by annotating **PayeeId** with **<<I>>**, so that requests with any value of **PayeeId** are controlled by the monitor, and used invariant enforcement with a constant, instead of with the first received value, to check that in every request containing **PayeeId**, its value is equal to the one obtained in the traces.

Table 2 shows the performance of model inference, monitor synthesis, and run-time enforcement. Column *App.* shows the application under test (and the specific workflow tested for ERP applications); *Synth.* shows the time to infer a model from the captured traces and synthesize a monitor for each workflow. *Orig.* reports the time between receiving a request and sending a response with no monitor; *Query* reports the time for the monitor to answer a query (ignoring the time to invoke the script, translate an incoming request to a monitor query, forward the request, etc); *Aegis* reports the time of a response with the monitor script (the time taken by the application, plus translation time, plus querying); and *Overh.* shows the overhead incurred by the use of the monitor (the difference between *Aegis* and *Orig.*). The time in column *Query* varies with the size of a workflow and the number of users and constraints, as reported in [2].

The overhead varied from 8ms to 84ms, with a median of 13.5ms, out of which less than 10ms in most cases is spent in querying the monitor. The variability is due to the complexity of the workflows and the time to translate a request. For instance, Odoo and ERPNext have a large overhead because of the time to process JSON requests. Monitor synthesis is computationally much more expensive, but it is run only once for each workflow and has been shown to be scalable [2].

Table 2: Monitoring overhead

App.	Synth.	Orig.	Query	Aegis	Overh.
Odoo PO	21.3 s	112 ms	6 ms	132 ms	20 ms
Odoo SO	22.4 s	170 ms	7 ms	213 ms	43 ms
Odoo PI	14.3 s	174 ms	7 ms	213 ms	39 ms
Odoo SI	17.9 s	104 ms	7 ms	116 ms	12 ms
Dolibarr PO	14.2 s	93 ms	5 ms	103 ms	10 ms
Dolibarr SO	14.3 s	92 ms	4 ms	104 ms	12 ms
Dolibarr PI	13.2 s	89 ms	5 ms	97 ms	8 ms
Dolibarr SI	14.7 s	90 ms	5 ms	105 ms	15 ms
WebERP PO	20 s	51 ms	6 ms	59 ms	8 ms
WebERP SO	21.1 s	50 ms	5 ms	57 ms	7 ms
WebERP PI	18.3 s	30 ms	6 ms	37 ms	7 ms
WebERP SI	19.5 s	32 ms	4 ms	39 ms	7 ms
ERPNext PO	13.3 s	222 ms	7 ms	251 ms	29 ms
ERPNext SO	12.9 s	327 ms	14 ms	411 ms	84 ms
ERPNext PI	15.9 s	263 ms	10 ms	327 ms	64 ms
ERPNext SI	13.7 s	272 ms	13 ms	318 ms	46 ms
OpenEMR	19.1 s	95 ms	7 ms	112 ms	17 ms
BikaLIMS	31.2 s	306 ms	7 ms	326 ms	20 ms
OpenCart	19.1 s	65 ms	6 ms	77 ms	12 ms
TomatoCart	15.8 s	63 ms	4 ms	71 ms	8 ms
osCommerce	22.2 s	79 ms	7 ms	95 ms	16 ms
AbanteCart	19.8 s	117 ms	8 ms	127 ms	10 ms

5. CONCLUSION

We have described and evaluated Aegis, a tool to enforce authorization policies and constraints, control- and data-flow integrity, and ensure the satisfiability of web applications. Our experiments show the practical viability of our approach in enforcing the desired properties and mitigating related vulnerabilities with a small performance overhead.

Related work. Many works studied authorization, control- and data-flow integrity (separately) in web applications, and mitigation of related vulnerabilities, e.g., [1, 5, 3]. These approaches are white-box, whereas Aegis is black-box. Web application workflow models have been used to find vulnerabilities by identifying behavioral patterns from execution traces [12], but Aegis is focused on enforcement, so the techniques are complementary. Identification of data properties has been used in [20, 12, 14] with different goals. The enforcement of authorization constraints for collaborative web applications was studied in [8, 7], but there was no discussion about workflow satisfiability, and the evaluation was limited to prototypes. The closest related works are BLOCK [9] and InteGuard [20]. Both use a reverse proxy, construct policies using invariants from network traces, and rely on manual identification of critical requests. InteGuard is tailored for multi-party application integration, where most tasks are not performed by humans and workflows must be executed from beginning to end in one shot. Neither tool enforces authorization policies nor constraints.

Future work. We intend to test Aegis in more real-world applications and to explore monitor inlining by embedding synthesized monitors into the applications.

6. REFERENCES

[1] D. Balzarotti, M. Cova, V. Felmetsger, and G. Vigna. Multi-module vulnerability analysis of web-based applications. In *Proc. of CCS*, 2007.

[2] C. Bertolissi, D. R. dos Santos, and S. Ranise. Automated synthesis of run-time monitors to enforce authorization policies in business processes. In *Proc. of ASIACCS*, 2015.

[3] B. Braun, P. Gemein, H.P. Reiser, and J. Posegga. Control-flow integrity in web applications. In *Proc. of ESSoS*, 2013.

[4] S. Ceri, G. Gottlob, and L. Tanca. What You Always Wanted to Know About Datalog (And Never Dared to Ask). *TKDE*, 1(1):146–166, 1989.

[5] M. Cova, D. Balzarotti, V. Felmetsger, and G. Vigna. Swaddler: An approach for the anomaly-based detection of state violations in web applications. In *Proc. of RAID*, 2007.

[6] A. Doupé, L. Cavedon, C. Kruegel, and G. Vigna. Enemy of the state: A state-aware black-box web vulnerability scanner. In *Proc. of USENIX Sec.*, 2012.

[7] P. Gaubatz, W. Hummer, U. Zdun, and M. Strembeck. Enforcing entailment constraints in offline editing scenarios for real-time collaborative web documents. In *Proc. of SAC*, 2014.

[8] P. Gaubatz and U. Zdun. Supporting entailment constraints in the context of collaborative web applications. In *Proc. of SAC*, 2013.

[9] X. Li and Y. Xue. Block: a black-box approach for detection of state violation attacks towards web applications. In *Proc. of ACSAC*, 2011.

[10] X. Li, Y. Xue, and B. Malin. Detecting anomalous user behaviors in workflow-driven web applications. In *Proc. of SRDS*, 2012.

[11] T. Murata. Petri nets: properties, analysis and applications. *Proc. of the IEEE*, 77(4):541–580, 1989.

[12] G. Pellegrino and D. Balzarotti. Toward black-box detection of logic flaws in web applications. In *Proc. of NDSS*, 2014.

[13] M. Schur, A. Roth, and A. Zeller. Mining workflow models from web applications. *TSE*, 41(12):1184–1201, 2015.

[14] A. Sudhodanan, A. Armando, L. Compagna, and R. Carbone. Attack patterns for black-box security testing of multi-party web applications. In *Proc. of NDSS*, 2016.

[15] F. Sun, L. Xu, and Z. Su. Static detection of access control vulnerabilities in web applications. In *Proc. of USENIX Sec.*, 2011.

[16] G. Terracina, N. Leone, V. Lio, and C. Panetta. Experimenting with recursive queries in database and logic programming systems. *Theory Pract. Log. Program.*, 8(2):129–165, 2008.

[17] W.M.P. van der Aalst. *Process Mining*. Springer, 2011.

[18] Q. Wang and N. Li. Satisfiability and resiliency in workflow authorization systems. *TISSEC*, 13(4):40:1–40:35, 2010.

[19] M. Weske. *Business Process Management*. Springer, 2007.

[20] L. Xing, Y. Chen, X. Wang, and S. Chen. Integuard: Toward automatic protection of third-party web service integrations. In *Proc. of NDSS*, 2013.

Discovering Browser Extensions via Web Accessible Resources

Alexander Sjösten
Chalmers University of
Technology
Gothenburg, Sweden
sjosten@chalmers.se

Steven Van Acker
Chalmers University of
Technology
Gothenburg, Sweden
acker@chalmers.se

Andrei Sabelfeld
Chalmers University of
Technology
Gothenburg, Sweden
andrei@chalmers.se

ABSTRACT

Browser extensions provide a powerful platform to enrich browsing experience. At the same time, they raise important security questions. From the point of view of a website, some browser extensions are invasive, removing intended features and adding unintended ones, e.g. extensions that hijack Facebook likes. Conversely, from the point of view of extensions, some websites are invasive, e.g. websites that bypass ad blockers. Motivated by security goals at clash, this paper explores browser extension discovery, through a non-behavioral technique, based on detecting extensions' web accessible resources. We report on an empirical study with free Chrome and Firefox extensions, being able to detect over 50% of the top 1,000 free Chrome extensions, including popular security- and privacy-critical extensions such as Ad-Block, LastPass, Avast Online Security, and Ghostery. We also conduct an empirical study of non-behavioral extension detection on the Alexa top 100,000 websites. We present the dual measures of making extension detection easier in the interest of websites and making extension detection more difficult in the interest of extensions. Finally, we discuss a browser architecture that allows a user to take control in arbitrating the conflicting security goals.

Keywords

Web security; Browser extensions; Large-scale study

1. INTRODUCTION

Browser extensions provide a powerful platform to enrich browsing experience. The Chrome web store currently contains around 43,000 free extensions, with many of these extensions, such as AdBlock, Adobe Acrobat, and Skype having more than 10,000,000 users.

From the security point of view, browser extensions are deployed as a "man in the browser" [27], implying that extensions have privileges to arbitrarily alter the behavior of webpages. Naturally, the power of browser extensions creates tension between the security goals of the webpages and those of the extensions themselves. Let us consider some representative scenarios to illustrate the challenges in balancing these goals.

CODASPY'17, March 22-24, 2017, Scottsdale, AZ, USA
© 2017 ACM. ISBN 978-1-4503-4523-1/17/03. . . $15.00
DOI: http://dx.doi.org/10.1145/3029806.3029820

The first and second scenarios present an exclusive point of view of websites, concerned with malicious extensions. The third scenario presents an exclusive view of extensions, concerned with malicious websites. The fourth scenario illustrates legitimate synergies between websites and extensions. Finally, the fifth scenario illustrates the security goals of websites and extensions at outright clash.

Bank scenario Bank webpages manipulate sensitive information whose unauthorized access may lead to financial losses. It is desirable to detect potentially insecure and vulnerable extensions and prevent extensions from injecting third-party scripts into the bank's webpages. The latter technique is in fact a common practice for many extensions [28, 31]. This scenario motivates the goal of discovering browser extensions, as the knowledge of what extensions run on the webpage can be used for tuning the defense.

Facebook scenario With over a billion daily users [15], Facebook is a popular target for attacks. Since the Facebook application itself is relatively well protected from attacks like cross-site scripting, attackers look for attacks elsewhere. A prevalent threat to user integrity and confidentiality is the use of browser extensions to inject scripts into the Facebook application to gain full access to the user's account [12]. Jagpal et al. [31] identify Facebook as the number one target for malicious extensions, reporting on the proliferation of attacks such as fake content (ad or otherwise) injection and information stealing.

This scenario motivates the need for recognizing browser extensions by webpages. Having an extension detection technique available, the webpage can adapt its behavior to the extensions installed. Research by Facebook's anti-abuse team confirms that this is a realistic scenario [12].

LastPass scenario LastPass [34] is a password manager that permits users to only remember one master password while automatically generating, storing, and filling in passwords for the individual services. The LastPass Chrome extension has currently over 4,000,000 users. Being a sensitive extension, LastPass has been subject to attacks. For example, LostPass [35] is a "pixel-perfect phishing" attack that exploits the fact that LastPass displays its notification in the browser viewport. LostPass fakes a message of an expired session and redirects users to a fake login page where it harvests the master password. (LastPass subsequently responded by interface measures and asking for email confirmation for all logins from new IPs [33].)

This scenario motivates the need to protect sensitive extensions. Being able to detect LastPass is a trigger for phishing attacks via a malicious webpage, as in the case of Lost-Pass. It is in the interest of LastPass to stay undetected. Similar scenarios arise with extensions such as Avast Online Security and Ghostery, popular security- and privacy-critical extensions that can be targeted by malicious websites.

Google Cast scenario Google Cast [26] is a popular extension to play content on a Chromecast device from Chrome. Upon detecting the Google Cast extension, websites like Twitch.tv adjust their functionality and offer richer features.

This scenario highlights the benefit of browser extension detection, as motivated by enriching functionality rather than by security considerations.

AdBlock scenario With over 40,000,000 users, AdBlock is currently the most popular Chrome extension [10]. It is in the very nature of ad blocking to modify webpages, looking for ads and blocking them. These goals are clearly at odds with the webpages' goals. Consequently, some webpages try to detect ad blockers.

This scenario motivates both the need for extension detection from the point of view of webpages and the need for evading discovery from the ad blockers' point of view. As we detail in Section 2, the state of the art for this scenario is much of a cat-and-mouse game.

Security goals at clash The above scenarios demonstrate that the different stakeholders (websites vs. browser extensions) have different interests, resulting in the clash of the respective security goals. Motivated by these security goals, this paper focuses on discovering browser extensions and pursues the following research questions: (i) How to discover browser extensions from within a webpage, i.e, without modifying the browser? and (ii) How can extensions evade detection?

We emphasize that this paper does not assume the interest of webpages over the interest of extensions or vice versa. Instead, we recognize that these different interests are legitimate, even if conflicting. We seek to better understand these interests, conceptually and empirically, and suggest steps to improve the state of the art on both sides.

Non-behavioral extension discovery We refer as *behavioral* to extension discovery techniques that require analyzing the behavior of browser extensions. Behavioral detection is sometimes desirable, when a particular behavior needs to be detected, regardless of what extension triggers it. On the other hand, *non-behavioral* discovery detects extensions without having to analyze their behavior. Non-behavioral detection is attractive when it can be done with low efforts. This motivates our focus on non-behavioral techniques.

In similar vein, when we consider measures against extension discovery, our goal is to stop non-behavioral detection and force attackers to do behavioral analysis of extensions.

Discovery via web accessible resources We explore a non-behavioral technique for discovering extensions, based on so called *web accessible resources* and implement it for detecting Chrome and Firefox extensions. Web accessible resources are the resources accessible in the context of a webpage. These resources enable interaction of extensions with the user via the underlying webpages.

While there are other, more elaborate, ways to set up this kind of interaction without web accessible resources (see Sections 3.2 and 6.2), web accessible resources provide a straightforward mechanism of direct access via URIs. Indeed, as we will see later, web accessible resources are used by many popular extensions.

Our detection is precise, in the sense of no false positives, and robust, as long as extensions require web accessible resources. While behavioral techniques may mistakenly detect an extension based on a monitored behavior, our technique is based on detecting resources that are bound to unique extension ids, implying that we never report an extension that is not present.

Contributions To the best of our knowledge, this work is the first comprehensive effort on non-behavioral extension detection, putting the spotlight on a largely unexplored area and systematically studying the technique and its applicability at large scale. To this end, the paper offers the following contributions:

Precise non-behavioral extension discovery We investigate a non-behavioral extension detection technique, based on web accessible resources (Section 3). Based on unique extension ids, our detection is precise, in the sense of no false positives, and robust, as long as extensions require web accessible resources.

Empirical studies of Chrome and Firefox extensions We report on a empirical study with Chrome's free extensions where we detect over 50% of the top 1,000 free Chrome extensions, including popular security- and privacy-critical extensions such as AdBlock, Last-Pass, Avast Online Security, and Ghostery, and 28% of the Chrome extensions in the study overall (Section 4).

We report on a similar study with Firefox's free extensions (Section 4). Due to Firefox's lax architecture, extensions are not prevented from direct modifications to the UI of the browser. This explains the lesser need for web accessible resources in Firefox extensions and, therefore, lower discovery rates.

Demo webpage for Chrome and Firefox We provide a demo webpage [55] to demonstrate discovery of Chrome and Firefox extensions in practice. This proof-of-concept webpage lists detected extensions once a user visits the page with Chrome or Firefox. This page serves as a starting point, providing a core that can be further developed either as a standalone service or a library for inclusion into other webpages. In fact, our code is already used by INRIA's Browser Extension Experiment [30].

Empirical studies of the Alexa top 100,000 websites We conduct an empirical study of non-behavioral extension discovery on the Alexa top 100,000 websites. Our findings suggest that the technique is not widely known, although we do discover several websites that try to find extensions for types that include fun, productivity, news, weather, search tools, developer tools, accessibility, and shopping (Section 5).

Measures We discuss two types of measures that correspond to the interests of webpages and extensions, respectively. For webpages, we discuss a solution based on extension whitelisting. For extensions, we have recommendations to restrict APIs related to web accessible resources and webpage whitelisting (Section 6). We also discuss behavioral techniques and argue that to be effective, they need to be extension-specific.

2. STATE-OF-THE-ART ARMS RACE

The state of the art is best illustrated with the arms race between ad blockers and ad blocker detectors, with its rival spirit captured by the (blatantly explicit) naming of the respective libraries.

Whenever an extension manipulates the webpage's DOM, it can be discovered using behavioral analysis. For instance, a webpage can discover an ad blocker when the latter removes an ad from the webpage. Since ad blockers act as

```
<script src="showads.js">
<script>
  if(window.canRunAds === undefined)
  {
    // Ad blocking detected
  }
</script>
```

(a) HTML part of fake ad

```
var canRunAds = true;
```

(b) showads.js (fake ad)

Figure 1: Ad-blocking behavioral detection

AdBlock	Remove ads
FAB	Injects bait for AdBlock and analyzes behavior
FFAB	Exploits global property in window object set by FAB
FFFAB	Detects if FFAB has done anything, reverts the changes

Table 1: Ad blocking arms race

good examples of security goals at clash, the rest of this section will focus on the arms race between webpages and ad blockers. Table 1 summarizes the steps in this arms race.

A straightforward approach to check for ad blockers is to create a fake ad which sets a global variable and then check for that specific variable. Figure 1 displays a current solution [29] which works in AdBlock, AdBlock Plus and Ad-Block Pro for Chrome, as well as AdBlock Plus for Firefox, where the default behavior is to block the execution of the file showads.js.

Such a useful behavioral technique is often prepackaged as a JavaScript library marketed for detecting ad blockers, called "anti ad blockers". One such example is F***AdBlock (*FAB*) [11], which helps the users do behavioral analysis during a user-specified time interval. If a certain (user defined) amount of negative results in a row occurs, no ad-blocking tools are deemed to be running. This means the check can be run multiple times, making it harder for ad blockers to hide their presence by delaying their interaction

Just as there are tools designed to help detect ad blockers, there are also tools that detect anti ad blockers. The library F***F***AdBlock (*FFAB*) [37] is an anti anti ad blocker created as a response to the anti ad blocker FAB. FFAB redefines some JavaScript function objects used during FAB's execution, overriding FAB's ad blocker detection mechanism and claims no ad blockers are detected.

But just as FAB is sensitive to behavioral analysis, so is FFAB. In turn, F***F***F***AdBlock (*FFFAB*) [13], is a response to FFAB. FFAB itself is not careful enough when overriding FAB's code, which gives FFFAB an opportunity to detect when FAB's code has been tampered with. When FFFAB detects this manipulation, it restores the original FAB functionality.

Detection of extensions by webpages is possible if the extension somehow modifies the DOM. In addition, behavioral detection is usually cross-browser, as the same behavior will take place no matter which browser is used.

If webpages are forced into behavioral extension detection, they cannot easily determine which extension is causing the behavior, and the extension detection loses precision. If they instead find extensions using unique ids, the extension name for Firefox extensions or a 32-character textual

token for Chrome extensions, the extension can be uniquely determined and the detection is exact.

As this arms race indicates, behavioral extension detection is both error-prone because it is imprecise, and costly because it requires time and effort to keep up with the latest evasion techniques. These reasons motivate the need for a more robust and cheaper technique, bringing us to the study of non-behavioral extension detection in the following sections.

3. FINDING EXTENSIONS VIA WEB ACCESSIBLE RESOURCES

This section provides background on how browser extensions work in Chrome and Firefox, the role of web accessible resources, how they can be used for finding extensions and the attacker models considered in this work.

3.1 Extensions

An *extension* is a program, typically written in a combination of JavaScript, HTML and CSS to extend the browser functionality. Extensions are not to be confused with browser *plugins*, such as Flash and Java, that are compiled and loadable modules that may live outside the browsers' process space. Extensions may alter the content of a webpage (e.g. ad blockers) or add features such as executing personal scripts (e.g. Greasemonkey). Browser extensions are built using architectures defined by the browser vendors. Mozilla is currently working on *WebExtensions* [48], a new API which will have a similar structure as the Chrome extension API.

Chrome extensions Chrome extensions can consist of three different parts [25]: (i) a background page, which is an invisible page containing the main logic of the extension; (ii) UI pages, ordinary HTML pages that display the extension's UI ("browser actions" [19] and "page actions" [20]); and (iii) a content script, JavaScript which executes in the context of the webpage. The content script makes the interaction with the webpage and runs in an isolated world [21]. It has access to some Chrome APIs and can communicate with the background page using message passing [24].

Each Chrome extension must have a manifest file, **manifest.json**, which contains important information about the extension [23]. For this work, the only interesting section in the manifest file is *web_accessible_resources*, which defines which resources are accessible in the context of a webpage [22]. The content of the *web_accessible_resources* section is paths to files. They can be URLs or a path to files relative to the package root and can contain wildcards.

Firefox extensions Firefox extensions written using *WebExtensions* will have the same structure as Chrome extensions. This is because Chrome extensions should be easy to port to Firefox [46], as well as having a more unified cross-browser architecture.

For the rest of this section, we will focus on XUL/XPCOM extensions. As this is how most Firefox extensions currently are written, we will refer to them as "Firefox extensions". These extensions also uses manifest files. The extensions automatically read the file **chrome.manifest** in the extension's root [40, 43]. Differently from Chrome, manifest files in Firefox are not mandatory and one manifest file can refer to other manifest files in sub folders.

Similarly to Chrome, a content script can inject and alter content on the webpage and communicate with the background pages using message passing [42, 41]. In the file chrome.manifest, a flag contentaccessible, which when set to **yes**, makes the specified content web accessible [40].

Differently from Chrome and WebExtensions, Firefox extensions have powerful features such as overlay, to describe extra content to the UI [49] and override, to override a chrome file provided by the application [40].

3.2 Web accessible resources

Both Chrome and Firefox require that extension resources that are referenced in a regular webpage, are flagged as web accessible in the manifest files. In Chrome and WebExtensions this is done with the key *"web_accessible_resources"* [22, 47] and in Firefox extensions with *"contentaccessible=yes"* [40].

If a Chrome content script injects resources into a webpage, the resource must be flagged as web accessible. This makes the resource available using the following schema: chrome-extension://<extensionid>/<pathToFile>, where <extensionid> is a unique identifier for each extension and <pathToFile> is the same as the relative URL from the package root [25].

Similarly for Firefox, if resources from the extension are to be referenced by an untrusted part using <img> or <script> tags, the corresponding registered content package must be flagged with contentaccessible=yes. Doing this would allow for the webpage to load resources from the extension, e.g. images to an <img> tag [40]. The content can then be accessed using the chrome://packagename/content/ schema [40], where the packagename should be unique for all extensions. For WebExtensions, the content can be accessed with moz-extension://<extensionid>/<pathToFile> [47].

Examples of web accessible resources in practice To illustrate web accessible resources and how they differ in Firefox and Chrome, consider two real-world examples: AdBlock and LastPass.

AdBlock for Chrome displays an icon in the browser toolbar which seemingly triggers a popup. This popup is actually an HTML page which loads JavaScript code to interact with the user. Both the HTML and JavaScript files are web accessible resources and must be listed as such [22].

When logging in to a new website with a password, LastPass for Chrome will prompt the user whether this password should be stored. This prompt is actually an "overlay" injected and rendered into the viewport of the visited webpage. The overlay is an HTML resource provided by the extension and marked as web accessible. LastPass for Firefox uses a slightly different approach because Firefox extensions have the ability to modify the browser chrome through *XML User Interface Language (XUL)*. Because this XUL file is only part of the browser chrome it does not need to be accessible from the visited webpage. Therefore, it does not need to be marked as a web accessible resource.

Benefits with web accessible resources While web accessible resources are a convenience, it is possible to do without them. Resources can be represented as strings using data URIs [36], which can be added to the created DOM element before injecting it to the webpage. It is also possible to store the resources on an external server and fetch them from there. However, both of these approaches have disadvantages. Encoding and injecting resources as strings can be difficult to maintain, and storing resources on an external server has potential privacy and security issues.

By using web accessible resources, the resources are stored within the extension. This make them easier to maintain and access with extension APIs.

Finding extensions via web accessible resources Because web accessible resources can be accessed in the context of a given webpage, they can be abused to detect the presence of browser extensions to which the resources belong. As mentioned above, LastPass for Chrome has the overlay file overlay.html marked as web accessible, making it possible to make a request for the file using e.g. XMLHttpRequest. If the resource is present, the request will receive a positive answer, indicating that the extension is installed.

In Firefox, the extension Firebug has contentaccessible=yes set. Similarly to LastPass in Chrome, this makes Firebug detectable without behavior analysis, as the resource can be loaded to a script tag, using onsuccess and onerror to check if the extension is present or not.

Note that thanks to the uniqueness of the extension ids, we obtain a detection technique without false positives. While there is no guarantee that the behavioral techniques precisely detect a given extension, we never report an extension that is not present. Compared to behavioral techniques that may have both false positives and negatives, finding extensions via web accessible resources may have false negatives but no false positives.

3.3 Two attacker models

Recall that we are interested in two perspectives on extension detection: that of a webpage with the goal to enable extension detection (as in the Bank and Facebook scenarios) and that of an extension with the goal to remain hidden (as in the LastPass scenario). Consequently, this yields two attacker models. The first attacker model corresponds to a malicious extension that has been installed on a user's browser, e.g., to leak bank data or hijack likes. The challenge is to detect such extensions. The second attacker model corresponds to a malicious webpage that tries to thwart the functionality of a legitimate extension, e.g., by blocking ads or phishing. The challenge here is to prevent detection of such extensions. In this paper, we address both perspectives, even if their goals are by nature conflicting.

4. EMPIRICAL STUDY OF CHROME AND FIREFOX EXTENSIONS

This section reports on an empirical study to analyze how susceptible free extensions are to be found via web accessible resources.

The study was performed by downloading all free extensions from Chrome web store [18] and Mozilla's add-on store [44], extracting and analyzing their manifest files. The extensions were downloaded in September 2016.

4.1 Chrome

As mentioned in Section 3.1, *web_accessible_resources* in the manifest file can be used to determine extension detection via web accessible resources. If the manifest file does not contain the section *web_accessible_resources*, the extension cannot be detected using this technique. If the only accessible resources of an extension are URLs, we deem the extension non-detectable without behavioral analysis.

A total of 43,429 extensions were downloaded. However, the total amount of extensions where the user statistics were found by the scraper was 43,197 ($\approx$99.5% of all downloaded extensions). The reason for this drop is that some extensions

Category	Chrome	Firefox
Empty accessible resources	148	–
Only URLs	54	–
No manifest file	–	7,396
Detectable	12,154	1,003
No accessible resources	31,073	6,497
Total amount of extensions	43,429	14,896

Table 2: Chrome and Firefox extension results

were removed from the Chrome web store before the scraper had the time to retrieve the user statistics, whereas some extensions (like Google Cast) did not display user statistics.
Results Table 2 displays the results of testing all downloaded Chrome extensions for *web_accessible_resources*. The parsing of the manifest files yielded parse errors for 36 extensions, for which we manually edited the manifest files to remove the errors.

We note that 148 extensions have *web_accessible_resources* set to an empty array in the manifest file, which implies that these extensions have no web accessible resources. Similarly, the 54 extensions which only have URLs as web accessible resources cannot be found with our technique as they do not have resources that should run in the context of the website stored locally in the extension. The "No accessible resources" in Table 2 are all the extensions where the *web_accessible_resources* field was missing in the manifest file, including 146 extensions which had only non-existing resources listed.

In total, 12,154 extensions out of 43,429 could be found using non-behavioral extension detection, which corresponds to ≈28%. Figure 2 shows the amount of detectable extensions sorted by popularity, based on the reported number of users in the Google Chrome web store. For this, we only use the set of extensions for which we could find user statistics, yielding 12,112 extensions detectable out of 43,197. We divide the sorted extensions in groups of 1000, which we call "intervals". We find 70% of the top 10, 62% of the top 100 and 52.7% of the top 1000 extensions with a non-behavioral technique. These extensions include popular security- and privacy-critical extensions such as AdBlock, LastPass, Avast Online Security, Ghostery and Disconnect. The graph also shows a descending trend, indicating that more popular extensions have on average more *web_accessible_resources*.

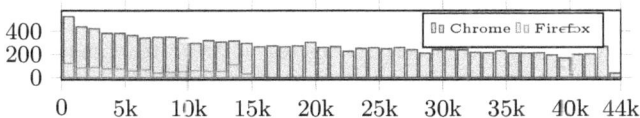

Figure 2: Amount of discoverable browser extensions (y-axis, not stacked) based on extensions' popularity rank (x-axis)

4.2 Firefox

As mentioned in Section 3.1, manifest files for Firefox extensions can be located in several different sub folders of an extension. The manifest files in the sub folders are referenced from `chrome.manifest` in the root directory. For this study, all manifest files were analyzed, including the manifest files in the sub folders.

The `contentaccessible` flag indicates web accessible resources, but we found that a webpage cannot perform a normal `XMLHttpRequest` in order to retrieve the resource. However, it is possible to create a `script` tag with the corresponding `script.src` attribute set to the resource in order

to retrieve it. By attaching `onload` and `onerror` event handlers to this `script` element, it is possible to learn whether the resource could be retrieved. In addition, because the absence of a resource is gracefully handled with the `onerror` handler, no error is reported and this method in Firefox is more discrete than the method used with Chrome.

The amount of Firefox extensions was 17,375. However, some extensions were duplicated in the list on Mozilla's add-on page based on the extension name and the extension id. The scraper found a total of 14,925 unique extensions, but was redirected to a dead link for 29 extensions, yielding the total number of analyzed extensions to 14,896.

Results The results of the study can be seen in Table 2. 7,396 did not have a `chrome.manifest` file in the extension's root directory and 6,381 extensions did not have the flag `contentaccessible` in the `chrome.manifest` file in the root directory. 116 out of the 1,119 extensions who had set `contentaccessible` linked it to non-existing files. We also detected a total of 775 extensions who use `WebExtensions`. Out of those 775 extensions, 11 also defined `chrome.manifest`. 221 had `web_accessible_resources` set, indicating ≈ 28,5% of those extensions should be detectable. Unfortunately, *WebExtensions* extension ids are not stored publicly. One could, in theory, manually install all those extensions and see if they have e.g. an options page [45], which when browsed to would give the extension id. Due to this, we do not consider WebExtensions detectable in this experiment.

1,003 out of 14,896 can be found with web accessible resources, which corresponds to 6.73%. The trend for the detectable extensions can be seen in Figure 2. The interval with the most extensions that are detectable was the top 1000 extensions with 121 detectable extensions (i.e. 12.1%). These extensions include Firebug, Easy Screenshot and Web of Trust. However, no ad blockers nor the popular script blocker Ghostery can be found in Firefox without behavioral analysis. As explained in Section 3.2, Firefox extensions have the ability to directly add to the UI using XUL, so that they do not require web accessible resources like Chrome extensions. Therefore, Firefox extensions need less web accessible resources.

4.3 Comparison of results

One major difference between Chrome and Firefox is how `XMLHttpRequest` is handled. In Firefox, it is not allowed to access `chrome://` with `XMLHttpRequest`, whereas it is possible to access `moz-extension://` in Firefox and `chrome-extension://` in Chrome. The use of web accessible resources, and with that the percentage of detectable extensions, is higher for Chrome. As a Chrome extension cannot make much modifications to the UI of the browser compared to Firefox, there is a greater need for using web accessible resources in Chrome. Similarities could be found in the trends of accessible resources, where both browsers had the largest interval of detectable extensions in the top 1000 extensions, but Chrome had a more clear decrease over the following intervals compared to Firefox.

5. BROWSER EXTENSION DETECTION IN THE ALEXA TOP 100,000

We conducted an empirical study of non-behavioral extension detection on the Alexa top 100,000 websites. Our findings suggest that the technique is not widely known, although we do discover several websites that try to find extensions for types that include fun, productivity, news, weather, search tools, developer tools, accessibility and shopping.

This empirical study has been omitted from this version of our work due to space limitations, but is available in the full version [55].

6. MEASURES

Section 6.1 suggests measures in favor of website developers, while Section 6.2 suggests how extensions can prevent being found by webpages. Finally, Section 6.3 concludes with a discussion of how to resolve security goal clashes. The full version [55] elaborates on further details.

6.1 Measures for webpages: whitelisting extensions

To help webpages guarantee a clean web environment for their content, they can be allowed to specify a whitelist of allowed extensions. Such a measure can be implemented as a policy specified by the webpage and enforced by the browser.

For a web application handling sensitive information, an environment known-to-be free from malware would help secure the user's sensitive data. Such a whitelist can, of course, also be used to block any extensions, e.g. an ad blocker, as well.

We envision the webpage suggests the whitelist. One possibility in this design space is to leave the final decision up to the user, endorsing and/or overriding the whitelist, if desirable. We detail this possibility in Section 6.3.

6.2 Measures for extensions

We discuss some measures to reduce the risk for extensions to be detected using non-behavioral analysis.

Prevent direct access to extension resources from webpage Instead of a direct access from webpages to an extension's resources, webpages would need to go through the extension via a message passing API. This would not prevent detection entirely, but it would allow for an extension to be part of the detection process.

No accessible resources One can avoid web accessible resources by hosting the resources on an external server or use data URIs (see Section 3.2).

Using an external server, with or without the browser's caching mechanism, does not fully prevent detectability via a timing attack. Remotely hosted resources also introduce privacy concerns, as all requests can be monitored by an external party.

Data URIs will remove dependencies on web accessible resources, but a disadvantage is that hard-coded data URIs can be difficult to maintain.

Track script provenance One could potentially track who injected a script and only allow access to a given set of principals. Tracking information flow can, however, make the system slower, but it would allow for web accessible resources to be used by scripts on the webpage that originates from the extension, but not by the actual webpage.

Extension ids In order to avoid detection, an extension developer could change the extension id by resubmitting the same extension. This by itself would be of limited effect since the entire userbase needs to be rebuilt for the extension with the updated id.

As an extension has other means to fetch its resources than via web accessible resources, one can allow the extension to generate a random token and pass it along to the webpage. A webpage which possesses this token can use it to gain access to the extension's resources.

Whitelisting webpages Instead of being active on all webpages a browser visits, extensions could be activated on a case-by-case basis. If an extension is not active on a webpage, and its resources not available to this webpage, then it can not be detected through the presence of web accessible resources. This can be implemented through a user-modifiable whitelist in the browser.

6.3 User to resolve conflicting security goals

Because of the conflicting security goals, it is important to strike a balance of the interests of the different parties by combining webpage measures with extension measures. For example, allowing webpages to whitelist extensions which can be active in their domain, whereas allowing extensions to whitelist webpages which are allowed to communicate with the extensions would help both webpages and extensions reach their goals.

But who should resolve the conflicting security goals? We resort to the "users > developers > browser" principle, as common in the web community folklore. This principle gives users precedence over developers and browsers in the web setting. Driven by this principle, we designate the user as an arbiter to endorse and/or overwrite whitelists provided by webpages and extensions, respectively.

7. RELATED WORK

Non-behavioral extension detection has so far received only scarce attention, primarily in the form of scattered blog posts [6, 3, 2, 4, 1, 5], some referring to outdated browser features and some only traceable in Internet archives [6, 3].

To the best of our knowledge, we are the first to systematically study non-behavioral extension discovery at large in both Chrome and Firefox's extension web stores, as well as the Alexa top 100,000 webpages.

There is a large body of work on detection of maliciously behaving browser extensions. The state of the art is well summarized by Jagpal et al. [31]. The rest of this section focuses on detecting extensions and fingerprinting browsers.

7.1 Detecting extensions

Prior work in detecting extensions has focused on behavioral techniques. For instance, Nikiforakis et al. [52] analyze eleven popular browser extensions that hide the real user agent string from visited websites in order to obfuscate a browser's fingerprint, but observe that the these extensions neglect to remove the same information from the JavaScript environment, making the extension detectable by a visited website through its behavior. This detection mechanism is fragile since, as explained in Section 2, extensions may modify their behavior in order to avoid detection, forcing websites to alter their detection method, triggering an arms race. Using another approach, Thomas et al. [56] detect the in-flight alteration of a webpage, by comparing the DOM of the rendered webpage against the expected DOM. This catch-all method detects all DOM modifying extensions as well as proxies and compromised browsers. Such an approach is more robust, since it will detect all extensions that modify the DOM even when they attempt to evade detection. However, since it does not focus on an extension's specific behavior, it is less precise. Non-behavioral extension detection on the other hand, like the technique presented in this paper, uses simple and cheap checks to determine the presence of a specific extension, without false positives. In addition, an extension can not evade detection by altering its behavior. Instead, the only way for an extension to avoid detection is by removing its web accessible resources, which is not always practical as explained in Section 6.2.

Non-behavioral extension discovery via web accessible resources has only received scarce attention in the form of scattered observations, primarily in blog posts [6, 3, 2, 4, 1, 5], some referring to outdated browser features and some only traceable in Internet archives [6, 3].

We go beyond these observations by systematically studying the entire class of extension discovery via web accessible resources, performing an empirical study with discoverability of all free extensions of the two major browsers, preforming a large scale study of discovery by the top 100,000 Alexa webpages, and proposing measures.

7.2 Fingerprinting browsers

There has been much work on browser fingerprinting. IN-RIA's Browser Extension Experiment [30] is based on our technique and code to enhance browser fingerprinting by detecting extensions. We overview the work on fingerprinting below, noting that the rest of the approaches are less related because they do not address extension detection.

Panopticlick [54] uses such browsers properties as screen resolution, user agent string, timezone, system fonts, and browser plugins to uniquely identify browsers. Browsers can also be fingerprinted through browser quirks [7], canvas fingerprinting [39, 8], dimensions of rendered font glyphs [16], browser histories [53], ECMAScript compliance [50], performance of the JavaScript engine and whitelisted domains in the NoScript extension [38], and more [52, 58].

Nikiforakis et al [52] detect font probing and flash-based proxy evasion as fingerprinting mechanisms provided by three commercial fingerprinting companies, and find 40 websites in the Alexa top 10,000 make use of them. Acar et al. build FPDetective [9] and find 404 websites in the Alexa top million that use JavaScript-based font probing, as well as 145 websites in the Alexa top 10,000 that use Flash-based font probing to fingerprint visitors. Acar et al. [8] study the Alexa top 100,000 and find that canvas fingerprinting is the most commonly used fingerprinting technique, with 5% of the studied websites using it.

Defending against fingerprinting is difficult, if ever possible. There appears to be no one-size-fits-all solution. Several strategies have been suggested. One crude way to address the problem is by simply blocking certain forms of third-party content, such as JavaScript or Flash known to contain fingerprinting code [8, 14, 52, 53, 58]. Similarly crude would be to disable certain functionality in the browser, such as the ability to query pixel-values from a canvas [39].

Instead of blocking third-party content or functionality, a browser could ask for user permission whenever a fingerprintable characteristic of the browser is queried, e.g. reading those pixel-values from a canvas [8, 39, 58].

Yet another approach adds (smart) noise to fingerprintable browser characteristics, thereby randomizing the fingerprint [8, 39, 14, 16, 17, 32, 51, 57, 58]. The reverse approach is to decrease the randomness of the reported browser characteristics by standardizing the set of possible values for fingerprintable resources, such as the list of system fonts, so that all browsers report the same values [16, 39, 52, 58].

Conceding that fingerprinting cannot be stopped, recent work has investigated preventing the exfiltration of the fingerprint itself by monitoring network traffic [57, 16, 50], or even by rewriting a detected fingerprint through a network proxy [59].

8. CONCLUSION

To the best of our knowledge, we have presented the first comprehensive study of non-behavioral browser extension discovery. We have systematically studied the technique and its applicability at large scale. At the core of our technique is detection of web accessible resources that are associated with extensions via unique extension ids. This yields an effective detection technique with no false positives, which we have instantiated for both Chrome and Firefox. We report on an empirical study with free Chrome and Firefox extensions, detecting over 50% of the top 1,000 free Chrome extensions (including such sensitive extensions as AdBlock and LastPass) and over 28% of the Chrome extensions in the study overall. We have conducted an empirical study of non-behavioral extension detection on the Alexa top 100,000 websites. This study confirms that detecting extensions via web accessible resources is not widely known. Nevertheless, we identify websites that perform extension detection for types of extensions that include fun, productivity, news, weather, search tools, developer tools, accessibility, and shopping. We have presented measures for and against browser extension discovery, catering to the needs of website owners and extension developers, respectively. Finally, we have discussed a browser architecture that allows a user to take control in arbitrating the conflicting security goals.

Our code for discovering browser extensions is already used by INRIA's Browser Extension Experiment [30].

Future work focuses on the measures outlined in Section 6. In particular, our short-term goal is to study whether disallowing GET requests from webpages to extension schemas (Firefox disallows `XMLHttpRequest` apart from for WebExtensions, but not GET from HTML elements such as `script` and `img`, whereas Chrome allows all three) will result in breaking functionality of common extensions. Such a study may provide useful input for the future handling of extensions in Chrome and Firefox. We are also experimenting with a prototype based on Chromium to support fine-grained whitelisting policies that give the user the power to temporarily enable and disable extensions depending on what webpages are being visited.

Acknowledgments Thanks are due to Ioannis Papagiannis for the inspirations and helpful feedback. This work was partly funded by Andrei Sabelfeld's Google Faculty Research Award, Facebook Research and Academic Relations Program Gift, the European Community under the ProSecuToR project, and the Swedish research agency VR.

9. REFERENCES

[1] Detecting Chrome Extensions in 2013. http://gcattani.github.io/201303/detecting-chrome-extensions-in-2013/.
[2] Detecting Firefox Extensions Without Javascript. http://kuza55.blogspot.co.uk/2007/10/detecting-firefox-extension-without.html.
[3] Detecting FireFox Extentions. http://ha.ckers.org/blog/20060823/detecting-firefox-extentions/
[4] Sparse Bruteforce Addon Detection. http://www.skeletonscribe.net/2011/07/sparse-bruteforce-addon-scanner.html.
[5] The Evolution of Chrome Extensions Detection. http://blog.beefproject.com/2013/04/the-evolution-of-chrome-extensions.html.

[6] Yet Another Way to Detect Internet Explorer. http://ha.ckers.org/blog/20060821/yet-another-way-to-detect-internet-explorer/.

[7] E. Abgrall, Y. Traon, M. Monperrus, S. Gombault, M. Heiderich, and A. Ribault. XSS-FP: Browser fingerprinting using HTML parser quirks. Technical report, 2012. arXiv:1211.4812 [cs].

[8] G. Acar, C. Eubank, S. Englehardt, M. Juarez, A. Narayanan, and C. Diaz. The web never forgets: Persistent tracking mechanisms in the wild. In *CCS*, 2014.

[9] G. Acar, M. Juarez, N. Nikiforakis, C. Diaz, S. Gürses, F. Piessens, and B. Preneel. FPDetective: Dusting the web for fingerprinters. In *CCS*, 2013.

[10] AdBlock. https://chrome.google.com/webstore/detail/adblock/gighmmpiobklfepjocnamgkkbiglidom.

[11] V. Allaire. FuckAdBlock. https://github.com/sitexw/FuckAdBlock.

[12] Q. Cao, X. Yang, J. Yu, and C. Palow. Uncovering large groups of active malicious accounts in online social networks. In *CCS*, 2014.

[13] clsr. FuckFuckFuckAdBlock. https://gist.github.com/clsr/3f5ca796463a0e6fc8af.

[14] A. FaizKhademi, M. Zulkernine, and K. Weldemariam. FPGuard: Detection and prevention of browser fingerprinting. In *Data and Applications Security and Privacy*, 2015.

[15] http://newsroom.fb.com/company-info/#statistics.

[16] D. Fifield and S. Egelman. Fingerprinting web users through font metrics. In *Financial Cryptography and Data Security*, 2015.

[17] U. Fiore, A. Castiglione, A. De Santis, and F. Palmieri. Countering browser fingerprinting techniques: Constructing a fake profile with google chrome. In *NBiS*, 2014.

[18] Google. Chrome web store. https://chrome.google.com/webstore/category/extensions?hl=en-GB&_feature=free.

[19] Google. chrome.browserAction. https://developer.chrome.com/extensions/browserAction.

[20] Google. chrome.pageAction. https://developer.chrome.com/extensions/pageAction.

[21] Google. Content Scripts. https://developer.chrome.com/extensions/content_scripts.

[22] Google. Manifest - Web Accessible Resources. https://developer.chrome.com/extensions/manifest/web_accessible_resources.

[23] Google. Manifest File Format. https://developer.chrome.com/extensions/manifest.

[24] Google. Message Passing. https://developer.chrome.com/extensions/messaging.

[25] Google. Overview. https://developer.chrome.com/extensions/overview.

[26] Google Cast. https://chrome.google.com/webstore/detail/google-cast/boadgeojelhgndaghljhdicfkmllpafd.

[27] P. Gühring. Concepts against man-in-the-browser attacks. http://www.cacert.at/svn/sourcerer/CAcert/SecureClient.pdf, 2006.

[28] D. Hausknecht, J. Magazinius, and A. Sabelfeld. May I? - Content Security Policy Endorsement for Browser Extensions. In *DIMVA*, 2015.

[29] How to detect Adblock on my website? http://stackoverflow.com/questions/4869154/how-to-detect-adblock-on-my-website.

[30] INRIA. Browser Extension Experiment. https://extensions.inrialpes.fr.

[31] N. Jagpal, E. Dingle, J. Gravel, P. Mavrommatis, N. Provos, M. A. Rajab, and K. Thomas. Trends and lessons from three years fighting malicious extensions. In *USENIX Sec.*, 2015.

[32] P. Laperdrix, W. Rudametkin, and B. Baudry. Mitigating browser fingerprint tracking: Multi-level reconfiguration and diversification. In *SEAMS*, 2015.

[33] I read that LastPass is vulnerable to phishing attacks - should I be concerned? https://lastpass.com/support.php?cmd=showfaq&id=10072.

[34] LastPass. https://lastpass.com/.

[35] LostPass. https://www.seancassidy.me/lostpass.html.

[36] L. Masinter. The "data" URL scheme. http://tools.ietf.org/html/rfc2397.

[37] Mechazawa. FuckFuckAdBlock. https://github.com/Mechazawa/FuckAdBlock.

[38] K. Mowery, D. Bogenreif, S. Yilek, and H. Shacham. Fingerprinting information in JavaScript implementations. In *W2SP*, 2011.

[39] K. Mowery and H. Shacham. Pixel perfect: Fingerprinting canvas in HTML5. In *W2SP*, 2012.

[40] Mozilla. Chrome registration. https://developer.mozilla.org/en-US/docs/Chrome_Registration.

[41] Mozilla. Communicating using "port". https://developer.mozilla.org/en-US/Add-ons/SDK/Guides/Content_Scripts/using_port.

[42] Mozilla. Communicating using "postmessage". https://developer.mozilla.org/en-US/Add-ons/SDK/Guides/Content_Scripts/using_postMessage.

[43] Mozilla. Manifest Files. https://developer.mozilla.org/en-US/docs/Mozilla/Tech/XUL/Tutorial/Manifest_Files.

[44] Mozilla. Most Popular Extensions. https://addons.mozilla.org/en-US/firefox/extensions/?sort=users.

[45] Mozilla. options_ui. https://developer.mozilla.org/en-US/Add-ons/WebExtensions/manifest.json/options_ui.

[46] Mozilla. Porting a Google Chrome extension. https://developer.mozilla.org/en-US/Add-ons/WebExtensions/Porting_a_Google_Chrome_extension.

[47] Mozilla. web_accessible_resources. https://developer.mozilla.org/en-US/Add-ons/WebExtensions/manifest.json/web_accessible_resources.

[48] Mozilla. WebExtensions. https://developer.mozilla.org/en-US/Add-ons/WebExtensions.

[49] Mozilla. XUL Overlays. https://developer.mozilla.org/en-US/docs/Mozilla/Tech/XUL/Overlays.

[50] M. Mulazzani, P. Reschl, M. Huber, M. Leithner, S. Schrittwieser, E. Weippl, and F. Wien. Fast and reliable browser identification with JavaScript engine fingerprinting. In *W2SP*, 2013.

[51] N. Nikiforakis, W. Joosen, and B. Livshits. PriVaricator: Deceiving fingerprinters with little white lies. In *WWW*, 2015.

[52] N. Nikiforakis, A. Kapravelos, W. Joosen, C. Kruegel, F. Piessens, and G. Vigna. Cookieless monster: Exploring the ecosystem of web-based device fingerprinting. In *S&P*, 2013.

[53] L. Olejnik, C. Castelluccia, and A. Janc. Why johnny can't browse in peace: On the uniqueness of web browsing history patterns. In *HotPETs*, 2012.

[54] Panopticlick. https://panopticlick.eff.org/.

[55] A. Sjösten, S. Van Acker, and A. Sabelfeld. Discovering Browser Extensions via Web Accessible Resources. Full version and code. http://www.cse.chalmers.se/research/group/security/extensions.

[56] K. Thomas, E. Bursztein, C. Grier, G. Ho, N. Jagpal, A. Kapravelos, D. McCoy, A. Nappa, V. Paxson, P. Pearce, N. Provos, and M. A. Rajab. Ad injection at scale: Assessing deceptive advertisement modifications. In *S&P*, 2015.

[57] C. F. Torres, H. Jonker, and S. Mauw. FP-block: Usable web privacy by controlling browser fingerprinting. In *ESORICS*, 2015.

[58] R. Upathilake, Y. Li, and A. Matrawy. A classification of web browser fingerprinting techniques. In *NTMS*, 2015.

[59] S. Yokoyama and R. Uda. A proposal of preventive measure of pursuit using a browser fingerprint. In *IMCOM*, 2015.

Graph Automorphism-Based, Semantics-Preserving Security for the Resource Description Framework (RDF)

Zhiyuan Lin

Mahesh Tripunitara

ECE, University of Waterloo, Canada
{z72lin,tripunit}@uwaterloo.ca

ABSTRACT

We address security in the context of the Resource Description Framework (RDF), a graph-like data model for the web. One of RDF's compelling features is a precise, model-theoretic semantics. We first propose a threat model, and under it, observe that the technical challenge is really in hiding information that may be revealed by the structure of an RDF graph. We choose two quantitative, unconditional notions for securing graph-structure from the literature that address the threat model, and adapt them for RDF. We then consider the problem of devising algorithms for achieving a certain level of security while preserving the semantics of the input RDF graph. We observe that there are operations we can perform on an RDF graph that both provide such security and preserve semantics. We observe, further, that there is a natural way to quantify information-loss under these operations, and that there appears to be a natural trade-off between security and information-quality. We study this trade-off and establish fundamental results. We show that the RDF graphs that result from applying the operations induce a lattice that leads to a natural quantification of information-quality. We show also that achieving a certain level of security while retaining a certain level of information-quality is **NP**-complete under polynomial-time Turing reductions. Finally, towards an empirical assessment, we discuss our design and implementation of a reduction to CNF-SAT, and empirical results for two classes of RDF graphs. In summary, our work makes fundamental and practical contributions to semantics-preserving security for RDF.

1. INTRODUCTION

The Resource Description Framework (RDF) is a graph-based data model designed for the web. It is standardized by the World Wide Web Consortium (W3C) [19], and has seen adoption in practice. For example, it is the data model that is used by StarDog [14], the Apache Jena Triple Database [16], DBPedia [3] and GovTrack [7].

CODASPY'17, March 22 - 24, 2017, Scottsdale, AZ, USA

© 2017 Copyright held by the owner/author(s). Publication rights licensed to ACM.
ISBN 978-1-4503-4523-1/17/03. . . $15.00

DOI: http://dx.doi.org/10.1145/3029806.3029827

As with any database, security is an important consideration in the context of RDF data. What we mean by "security" is that we do not want entities to have access to, or even infer, with high probability, information to which they are not authorized. Such unauthorized entities certainly include those that are to have no access to a database. But it could also include those that have some, but not unqualified access. For example, Alice may be authorized to discover the population of a locality, but not the identities of individuals that reside in it. Such a requirement, in conjunction with the fact that Alice may have access to complementary data from outside the database that helps her compromise security (e.g., identify individuals), makes the task of achieving security, or even characterizing a precise notion of "secure," a technical challenge. Indeed, such attacks have been demonstrated in practice [21], albeit not for RDF data.

Of course, it is easy to provide security if that is the only consideration: we simply release no information. But that is usually considered impractical. Thus, the technical challenge is to provide security while preserving the quality of information that is made available. In this context, characterizing information-quality can be a technical challenge.

Furthermore, a compelling feature of RDF is that it comes with a precise semantics [12]. Therefore, in the context of RDF, it is desirable to preserve the semantics of the original data in responses to queries, while providing security. That is, the preservation of semantics is an important aspect of preserving information-quality while providing security.

Contributions We unify all of the above themes in this work. We start by observing that RDF data can be meaningfully perceived and encoded as a kind of graph, which we call an RDF graph. We then observe that hiding labels on nodes and edges is a basic way to provide security. For example, the blatantly identifying information, "Alice," is removed from a node, and this provides some security from identification to the individual whose name is Alice.

However, the structure of the graph can leak information, particularly in conjunction with complementary information to which an attacker may have access, that is extraneous to the RDF data that we seek to secure. We may not even know exactly what such extraneous information is. Consequently, we enunciate a threat model that captures this rather general scenario (see Section 2). Based on the threat model, we argue for particular, quantitative, unconditional notions of security from prior work that are based on graph-automorphism (see Section 3). We adapt this notion to RDF (see Section 4).

```
@prefix    people: <http://www.people.com/>
people:amy    people:gender    female
people:amy    people:age    22
_:b    people:gender    female
_:b    people:age    30
```

Figure 1: An RDF graph shown as a set of triples.

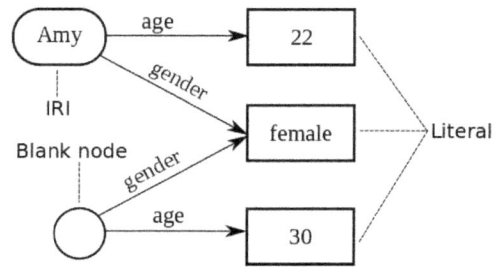

Figure 2: Visualization of Figure 1 as a graph.

We then address the issue of meaningfully characterizing information-quality. As we discuss above, there are two aspects to this. (1) How do we meaningfully characterize information-quality? And, (2) how do we reconcile semantics, which is an appealing feature of RDF? We first address (2), by studying operations that can be applied to an RDF graph G to produce another graph H such that H has the same semantics as G. We then observe that a subset of the operations, each of which corresponds to the removal of some information, can increase security (see Section 4). For that subset of operations, we establish that we induce a lattice of RDF graphs, with the original graph at the top and the empty graph at the bottom. Each edge in the lattice corresponds to an instance of an operation on the graph.

Thus, the number of edges we need to traverse in the lattice, starting at the original RDF graph at the top, to reach an element in the lattice that is an RDF graph that provides the desired level of security, is a natural way to quantify the degradation of information, and therefore information-quality, relative to the original RDF graph (see Section 4).

We then address the problem of devising an algorithm for providing a particular level of security for an RDF graph, while incurring only a certain level of degradation in information-quality. We show that this problem is **NP**-complete, where the **NP**-hardness is under polynomial-time Turing reductions [10] (see Section 4).

With the intent of carrying out an empirical assessment, we reduce the problem efficiently to boolean satisfiability in conjunctive normal form (CNF-SAT) (see Section 4). We have implemented the reduction. We present and analyze empirical results from our implementation together with a constraint solver for two classes of RDF graphs. For example, we look at the manner in which level of security that can be achieved varies with the level of information-degradation we are willing to incur (see Section 5).

As such, our contributions are to both foundations and practice in securing RDF.

Layout   Apart from the sections we mention above, We provide necessary background, and present our threat model in the next section. We discuss related work in Section 6. We conclude with Section 7, which discusses also future work.

2. BACKGROUND AND THREAT MODEL

We begin with a background on RDF that suffices for our work. We discuss also semantics. We then present our threat model.

RDF is "a framework for expressing information about resources. Resources can be anything, including documents,

people, physical objects, and abstract concepts." [19] Such information is expressed as a set of triples, each of the form $\langle subject, predicate, object \rangle$. Figure 1 is an example of such a set. An example of a triple in the set in the figure is $\langle amy, age, 22 \rangle$. We discuss other artifacts that appear in the example below. Such a set of triples can be encoded and visualized as a kind of graph. Thus, we call such a set of triples an RDF graph, and define it as follows.

DEFINITION 1.   *(RDF Graph) An RDF Graph G is a set of triples of the form $\langle subject, predicate, object \rangle$. Each of subject, predicate and object is of a certain type: subject, predicate are* Internationalized Resource Identifier (IRI) *or* blank symbol, *and object is an* IRI, literal *or* blank symbol.

An *IRI* is a generalization of Universal Resource Identifier (URI) that allows more Unicode characters. It is used in RDF as a globally unique identifier for an entity. It explicitly specifies which entity the vertex represents. In other words every appearance of the same IRI represents the same entity even in different RDF graphs. A *blank symbol* serves the same function as an IRI, except that it is anonymous, i.e. does not reveal what entity it represents. A *Literal* in RDF is similar to that in programming languages. They are syntactic representations of boolean, character, string, or numeric values. Each $\langle subject, predicate, object \rangle$ can be seen as a pair of labelled vertices, the *subject* and *object*, connected by a labelled, directed edge, the *predicate*.

In Figure 1, *people:amy* is a shorthand for *http://www.people.com/amy*, which is an IRI. Every appearance of the same IRI, even in another RDF graph, denotes the same entity. Similarly *people:gender* and *people:age* are IRIs. _:b denotes a blank symbol, with a random identifier b that has no explicit meaning. Different blank nodes may have different identifiers associated with them. A graph-like visualization of Figure 1 is Figure 2.

In the RDF standard [12], a predicate of a triple can be an IRI only. However, ter Horst [27] introduced a notion of a *Generalized RDF Graph* which allows blank symbols to be used as the predicate in a triple. In this work, we adopt the generalized notion of RDF graph. Our work is applicable to the more restricted notion as well.

Semantics   An appealing feature of RDF is that it has a precise and meaningful semantics [12, 27]. RDF semantics is model-theoretic. We explain model-theoretic semantics, as it pertains to RDF, via a simple example. Consider the assertion, "Bob is a musician and a parent." An aspect of the assertion is whether it is true. Another is other assertions we can draw from it, e.g., "Bob is a parent." RDF semantics

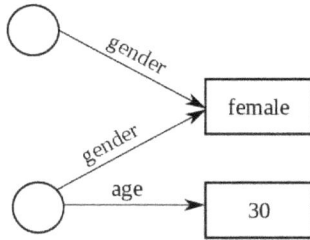

Figure 3: A graph entailed by the graph in Figure 2.

```
SELECT ?x ?y{
    WHERE ?x age ?y .
    FILTER (?y < 25)
}
```

Figure 4: Example SPARQL query for the graph shown in Figure 2. The answer to the query is, "Amy 22"

addresses these two aspects. In RDF semantics, the former is provided by an *interpretation*, and the latter by *entailment*.

An RDF interpretation maps RDF terms such as IRIs to elements of a universe. It also maps triples and RDF graphs to truth-values, which denote whether the statements represented by the triples (or the graph that contains the triples) are true in the real world. When an RDF graph G is true under the interpretation I, we say that I *satisfies* G. We refer the reader to [12, 27] for more details. In our example, for a particular person to whom we refer as "Bob," and particular interpretations of "musician" and "parent," our assertion may be true. For other interpretations, it may be false.

RDF entailment decides whether truth-value is preserved between different graphs. An RDF graph G is said to *entail* an RDF graph H if every interpretation that satisfies G also satisfies H. In other words, the truth of G under *any* interpretation is preserved in H. In this case we write $G \models H$. Entailment helps connect model-theoretic semantics to real-world applications. If A entails B and we assert that A is true in the real world, then we know that B is also true. We can think of the information in B as being contained in A. For example, our assertion, "Bob is a musician and a parent," entails the assertion, "Bob is a parent."

As we discuss further in Section 4, entailment allows us to secure an RDF graph while retaining its semantics. Think of graph G as the original graph and H as the secured version. If G entails H, then H has the same RDF semantics as G. H might not contain as much information as G, but all the information in H is semantically consistent with the information in G.

The *interpolation lemma* [12] allows us to implement this idea syntactically. To explain the interpolation lemma we first define the notion of *instance*: A graph G is an *instance* of another graph H if there exists a partial mapping, h, from the set of blank vertices in H to a set of IRIs, literals, and blank vertices such that G can be obtained from H by replacing every blank vertex b in the domain of h with $h(b)$. The interpolation lemma then simply states that an RDF graph G entails another RDF graph H if and only if a subset of G is an *instance* of H.

The interpolation lemma translates the semantic definition of entailment into simple syntactic requirements. We present an example here, and discuss the specific operations we consider in Section 4. The graph in Figure 3 is entailed by the graph in Figure 2. An operation that results in a new graph that is entailed by this original graph is blanking. We could, for example, blank the vertex labeled "Amy." Thus, the new graph still has a vertex that represents a per-

son, and in that manner, preserves semantics. Similarly, we can delete Amy's age from the graph and still preserve the graph's semantics. Therefore the graph in Figure 2 entails the graph in Figure 3.

SPARQL The de facto standard query language for RDF is SPARQL[22]. In any endeavor to secure an RDF graph, it is important to consider the language via which queries are issued. Indeed, as we discuss in more detail in Section 6, some prior work proposes rewriting of SPARQL queries as a security-mechanism. In Figure 4 we show an example query in SPARQL, and the result of that query when it is issued against the RDF graph in Figure 2. The meaning of the query is: return all x and y such that "x age y" is a triple, and y is less than 25.

For the somewhat strong threat model we adopt below, and the corresponding security property we adopt in the next section, the specifics of SPARQL are rendered irrelevant, except for a particular aspect of semantic entailment. In RDF semantics as specified by Hayes and McBride [12] and ter Horst [27], two blank vertices with distinct identifiers are not assumed to be necessarily distinct. In queries in SPARQL, however, two blank vertices with distinct identifiers represent distinct entities. Arenas et al. [2] give a simple example of two RDF graphs and a SPARQL query, such that under the RDF semantics of [12, 27], we expect the response to the query to be the same for both graphs, but under SPARQL semantics, the responses are different.

In this work we follow the SPARQL semantics, as we expect, as is the case in practice, that SPARQL is the query language via which a user extracts information about an RDF graph. This choice affects the definition of an instance: two blank nodes with distinct identifiers cannot be replaced with the same vertex in a partial mapping from H, to an instance, a subset of G.

Threat model Our threat model is as follows. The "good guy" has an RDF graph G and a subset, A, of vertices in G that he would like to protect. Recall, from our discussions on RDF above, that vertices in an RDF graph are subjects and objects. Thus, protecting the subset of vertices A corresponds to disallowing an adversary from targeting any of those subjects and objects in an attack. This in turn can be achieved by maintaining the anonymity of those vertices.

Let G' be the secure version of G that is released publicly. We model the attacker's prior knowledge with another RDF graph H, which we assume is a subgraph of G. Our threat is: the attacker seeks to deanonymize any of the vertices A in G using the information in G' and H. That is, we deem an

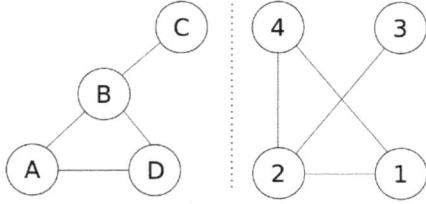

Figure 5: Graph Isomorphism and Automorphism. The graph to the left is non-trivially automorphic, and is isomorphic to the graph to the right.

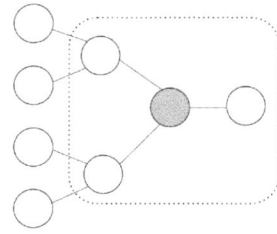

Figure 6: *k-neighbourhood-isomorphism*. The shaded vertex is 3-neighbourhood-isomorphic for a distance-1 neighbourhood. Its distance-1 neighbourhood is shown by the dotted box. The two vertices to its immediate left have isomorphic distance-1 neighbourhoods.

attacker to have succeeded if she is able to correctly identify, within a certain probability, that a vertex in G' is a vertex in H. The probability is a quantification of the desired security. Note that some or all the vertices in A may appear in G' and/or H. We assume also that the attacker has unbounded computational power.

For example, suppose $H \subset G$, the prior knowledge of the attacker, is the graph in Figure 2. And G', the graph that is released publicly, is the graph in Figure 3. We want the anonymity of the node Amy, that appears in G (and H) to be preserved. That is, $A \ni$ Amy. The probability we desire is some value < 1. Then, the attacker succeeds because she is able to identify, with probability 1, that the node with no label, that does not have an edge labelled 'age,' is Amy.

Of course, G may have other nodes that have been removed to result in G', the graph in Figure 3. In our discussion of this example, we bias in favor of the attacker, that one of the unlabelled nodes to the left in Figure 3 is indeed Amy. In any case, if we remove the edge labelled 'age' from the graph in Figure 3, then the attacker succeeds with probability at most $\frac{1}{2}$.

Our threat model may seem *too* strong. Not only do we not bound an attacker with regards to computational power, but also allow H to be any subgraph of G. This models our uncertainly as to the attacker's extraneous or prior knowledge of G. Of course, to allow $H = G$ is meaningless, because then, the attacker has no need to deanonymize any node in G'. However, it is possible that any strict subgraph of G may be the attacker's prior knowledge.

3. ISOMORPHISM-BASED SECURITY

Given the threat model in the previous section, we now discuss notions of "secure" for graphs, that we then adapt to RDF graphs. An initial mechanism for security is to simply blank vertices and edges in an RDF graph. For example, as we do to the node "Amy" in the graph in Figure 2 so that that node is a blank in Figure 3. Indeed, we expect that we must do this, at the minimum, for every vertex in the set A of vertices we seek to protect.

However, this may not suffice. For example, suppose the attacker's extra knowledge, H, a subgraph of the graph in Figure 2, is the two subjects with their corresponding ages. Then given the graph from Figure 3, the attacker is able to identify that Amy is the blank node that does not have an edge to the age "30." Thus, the structure of G' reveals information. This is the technical challenge we address in

this section, and that is the focus of our work. Specifically, we consider three notions from the literature that appear to address exactly the threat model we consider, but for traditional graphs. We then identify relationships between them, which leads us to choose two of the three notions. We adapt these two notions to RDF in the next section.

Common to the notions that we consider, is that they are based on *graph isomorphism* (Iso). Two graphs $G = \langle V_g, E_g \rangle$ and $H = \langle V_h, E_h \rangle$ are said to be *isomorphic* when there exists an invertible mapping $m \colon V_g \to V_h$ such that $\langle u, v \rangle \in E_g$ if and only if $\langle m(u), m(v) \rangle \in E_h$. (Our notation is customary: V_g and V_h are the sets of vertices of G and H respectively, and E_g and E_h are their sets of edges.) Such a mapping is called an isomorphism. A graph is said to be (non-trivially) *automorphic* if it is isomorphic to itself via a mapping that is not the identity. Such a mapping is called an automorphism. For example, in Figure 5, the graph to the left is non-trivially automorphic. An isomorphism is one in which we map A and D to one another, and B and C to themselves. Also, the graph to the left is isomorphic to the graph to the right. An isomorphism is: $A \to 1, \ldots, D \to 4$.

Isomorphism-based security provides anonymity by creating groups of indistinguishable vertices, i.e. for every vertex v there are several other ones that are indistinguishable from v. This lowers the probability that v is correctly re-identified from 1 unconditionally, because the attacker would have to make a blind guess from amongst the group of indistinguishable vertices.

We focus only on isomorphism-based security notions because they comprehensively secure all aspects of the graph structure, compared to other notions such as k-degree-anonymity [17], which only consider the degrees of vertices. We introduce these isomorphism-based security notions below, starting with *k-neighbourhood-isomorphism* [31].

DEFINITION 2. *(k-neighbourhood-isomorphism* [31]) *Given a graph $G = (V, E)$ and integer k, we say a vertex $u \in V$ is k-neighbourhood-isomorphic if there exist at least $k - 1$ other vertices $v_1, \ldots, v_{k-1} \in G$ such that $neighbour(v_1), \ldots, neighbour(v_{k-1})$ and $neighbour(u)$ are isomorphic, where $neighbour(v)$ is the distance 1 neighbourhood of v, i.e. the subgraph of G induced by the set of vertices within distance 1 to v. The graph G is k-neighbourhood-isomorphic if every vertex in G is k-neighbourhood-isomorphic.*

Although the above notion is defined over distance-1 neighbourhood, it can be naturally extended to consider neighbourhood of arbitrary distance d. The work of Zhou and Pei [31] is focused on distance-1 neighbourhood only, therefore we do the same. What we call *k-neighbourhood-isomorphism* is called *k-anonymity* in their work. We adopt our nomenclature to more clearly identify the notion, and because the *k-anonymity* is used extensively in the altogether different context of relational data.

A problem with *k-neighbourhood-isomorphism* is that it considers only limited neighbourhoods. See Figure 6 for example. The shaded vertex is 3-neighbourhood-isomorphic: the two vertices immediately to its left have distance-1 neighbourhoods that are isomorphic to the shaded vertex s. However if we consider the distance-2 neighbourhoods of vertices, the shaded vertex becomes unique. The two other security notions we consider below, *k-symmetry* [29] and *k-automorphism* [32], do not share the same problem because they are defined over the entire graph, and not on limited neighbourhoods.

DEFINITION 3. *(k-automorphism [32]): Given $\langle G, k \rangle$ where G is a graph and k an integer, a graph G is k-automorphic if and only if there exist $k-1$ different automorphisms $f_1, ..., f_{k-1}$ for G such that the following two properties are satisfied by all $v \in G$: (a) $f_i(v) \neq f_j(v)$ for all distinct pairs i, j and, (b) $f_i(v) \neq v$ for all i.*

DEFINITION 4. *(k-symmetry [29]) Given $\langle G, k \rangle$ where G is a graph and k an integer, G is k-symmetric if and only if for each vertex v_i in G there exist $k-1$ different automorphisms $f_{i,1}, ..., f_{i,k-1}$ such that (a) $f_{i,m}(v_i) \neq f_{i,n}(v_i)$ if $m \neq n$, and (b) $f_{i,j}(v_i) \neq v_i$.*

Some clarification of the terms is needed when referring to *k-automorphism*. The *k-automorphism* notion, to our knowledge, was first proposed by Zou et al. [32]. In that work, after proposing a notion of security that they call *k-automorphism*, they attach to it an additional condition that they call the "different match principle." Their work deals exclusively with *k-automorphism* with the different match principle. The property of *k-symmetry* is from the work of Wu et al. [29]. That work simply drops the qualification "with the different match principle" in referring to the work of Zou et al. [32]. We adopt the approach of Wu et al. [29], and simply call the property *k-automorphism*, without qualification.

Both *k-symmetry* and *k-automorphism* are based on the notion of automorphism, and their difference is somewhat nuanced. In the former, it suffices that for each vertex, k different automorphisms exist. Thus, the k automorphisms may be different for each vertex. In *k-automorphism*, on the other hand, the same set of k automorphisms must apply to all vertices. Certainly, if a graph is *k-automorphic*, it is *k-symmetric*. Wu et al. [29] articulate the question as to whether the converse is true, and leave it open. Addressing that question is beyond the scope of our work.

The fact that *k-automorphism* implies *k-symmetry* is interesting from a security perspective: we only have to enforce *k-automorphism* to achieve both. Moreover, we can also show that *k-symmetry* implies *k-neighbourhood-isomorphism*. If a graph $G = (V, E)$ is k-symmetric, then for each $v \in V$ there are at least $k-1$ other automorphisms $f_1, f_2, ..., f_{k-1}$ from G to itself such

that $f_m(v_i) \neq v_i$ and $f_m(v_i) \neq f_n(v_i)$ when $m \neq n$. In other words, there will be at least $k-1$ vertices $f_1(v_i), ..., f_{k-1}(v_i)$ which have neighbourhoods that are isomorphic to $v_i's$, so v_i is *k-neighbourhood-isomorphic*. Therefore G is also *k-neighbourhood-ismorphic*.

The observations above connect the three security notions that we have discussed: *k-automorphism* implies *k-symmetry* and *k-symmetry* implies *k-neighbourhood-isomorphism*. Therefore if we ensure a graph is *k-automorphic*, we know that it is *k-symmetric* and *k-neighbourhood-isomorphic*. This means that *k-automorphism* gives us a strong guarantee. We consider both *k-automorphism* and *k-symmetry* for RDF graphs in the next section.

4. SECURING RDF

We now adapt the notions of *k-automorphism* and *k-symmetry* to RDF graphs. As we discuss in Sections 1 2, our intent is to secure RDF graphs in a manner that preserves semantics.

Two issues need to be addressed in adapting *k-automorphism* and *k-symmetry* from Section 3 to RDF. One is that RDF is more general than the kinds of graph for which the two notions have been considered in the literature. Therefore, we need to generalize those notions to suit RDF. We do so in Section 4.1

A second issue regards information-quality. Our objective is to achieve a desired level of security with as little loss of information as possible. We achieve this goal in two ways. One is that in the process of generating the secure version, G', from G, we make creative use of RDF semantics to maintain the consistency of G' and G. The other is that we provide a quantitative measure of the cost of achieving this semantically consistent security, and require that this cost is minimized.

4.1 Adaptation to RDF Graphs

In this section we define the *k-symmetry* and *k-automorphism* for RDF. The original definition *k-symmetry* and *k-automorphism* are not applicable directly to RDF because they are defined on unlabelled, undirected graphs. RDF on the other hand, can be thought of as having explicit labels on both edges and vertices, except for blank vertices and edges. These labels can contain sensitive or identifying information. Therefore a notion of security for RDF must take these labels into consideration. The definition of an RDF graph has been discussed in Section 1. We show below how we redefine automorphism in this context.

We define the following notations to be used in definitions. Given a graph G, let $subj(G)$ be the set of all subjects, $pred(G)$ the set of all predicates, and $obj(G)$ the set of all objects. We define the *terms* of G to be $T(G) = subj(G) \cup pred(G) \cup obj(G)$. Let B be the set of blank vertices in G; then $B \subseteq T(G)$.

DEFINITION 5. *(Automorphism for RDF) An automorphism on an RDF graph is defined as a bijection $f: T(G) \longrightarrow T(G)$, which has the following properties:*

1. *Given $v \in T(G)$, $f(v) = v$ if $v \notin B$; $f(v) \in B$ if $v \in B$; and*

2. *a triple $(a, b, c) \in G$ iff $(f(a), f(b), f(c)) \in G$.*

341

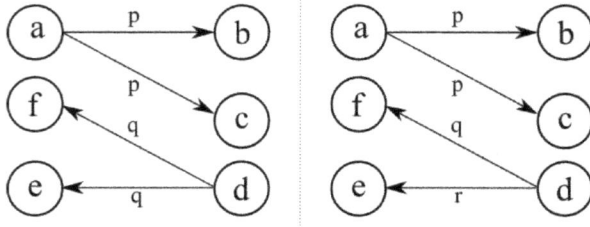

Figure 7: RDF automorphism

Definition 5 is different from the traditional definition of automorphism from Section 3. It recognizes that a non-blank vertex is globally unique, and explicitly identified by its label. Such a vertex under an automorphism cannot be mapped to any other vertex than itself. Blank vertices on the other hand do not have explicit identities. Therefore they can be mapped to other blank vertices.

Moreover, the automorphism applies to the IRIs and blank symbols no matter that they serve as vertices or edges in a graph. IRIs and blank symbols can serve as predicates in triples, in which case they act like edges in a graph. Different appearances of the same IRI as predicates are just instances of the same relationship, therefore an IRI edge can only be mapped to an edge under the same IRI. Different appearances of the same blank symbols as predicates also denote the same relationship, except in this case that the exact identity of the relationship is unspecified. Automorphism for edges can be seen as from edge type to edge type. If we map blank edge type a to blank edge type b, we must map every edge under the type a to an edge under type b. For example, in Figure 7 assuming all vertices and edges are blank, there is an automorphism that maps the vertex a to the vertex d in the left graph, because the blank relationship p can be mapped to q. Such an automorphism however does not exist in the right graph in Figure 7 because the relationship p cannot be mapped to both q and r at the same time. This notion of automorphism is consistent with the RDF semantics we discuss in Section 4.2.

With the notion of automorphism settled, we now define k-symmetry and k-automorphism for RDF.

DEFINITION 6. (k-symmetry for RDF) Given an RDF graph G, let the anonymization set A be a set of vertices $A \subseteq subj(G) \cup obj(G)$. G is k-symmetric with respect to A if:

1. every vertex in A is blank; and

2. for each vertex $v \in A$, there exist k automorphisms $f_1, \ldots, f_k$ such that $f_m(v) \neq f_n(v)$ when $m \neq n$.

DEFINITION 7. (k-automorphism for RDF) Given an RDF graph G, let the anonymization set A be a set of vertices $A \subseteq subj(G) \cup obj(G)$. G is k-automorphic with respect to A if:

1. every vertex in A is blank; and

2. There exist k automorphisms $f_1, \ldots, f_k$ such that $f_m(v) \neq f_n(v)$ for all $v \in A$ when $m \neq n$.

4.2 RDF Semantics and Security

Given the adaptations, in the above section, of the notions of security we consider for RDF, we consider to the issue of semantics. Specifically, we seek to achieve a level of security, e.g., 4-automorphism, while preserving the semantics of the original graph. A consequence of this requirement is that it limits the mechanisms we are allowed to use to achieve security.

The notion of a blank symbol, to which we refer in the definition of RDF graph is an important one in this context, as it represents an anonymous subject, predicate or object. We propose the use of the following two operations to secure an RDF Graph:

1. Removing RDF triples; and,

2. Replacing an IRI vertex or a Literal vertex with a blank vertex.

We point out, with regards to Operation (1) above, that a vertex in an RDF graph can exist only as part of a triple. For example, if there are no edges to an object, a vertex that corresponds to that object is no longer in the RDF graph.

These are of course not the only operations available. Some other works we discussion in Section 6 employs other techniques such as adding vertices and edges. The reason we choose these two operations only is to preserve RDF semantics. The proof of the following theorem is straightforward.

THEOREM 1. Given an RDF graph G, and another RDF graph H obtained from G by application of some sequence of the above two operations. Then $G \vDash H$.

Cost of Security Entailment ensures that the information of the RDF graph is semantically preserved. But it does not measure how much information there is in the secured graph relative to the original. For example, the empty graph is entailed by every RDF graph, but there is zero information-quality in publishing it. In the following, we provide a quantitative measure of information based on entailment.

In the following lemma, we assert that entailment induces a lattice on the graphs that result from all possible sequences of applications of the above two operations on the original graph. At the top of the lattice is the original graph, and at the bottom, is the empty graph. An intermediate entry in the lattice is entailed by its ancestors in the lattice, and an entry's descendants are entailed by this entry and thus all of its ancestors.

LEMMA 1. The entailment relationship $\vDash$ is a partial order over the set of all possible anonymizations of G.

PROOF. Let P be the set of all possible anonymizations of G. Note that P contains G itself and the empty graph. We prove that the entailment relationship $\vDash$ is reflexive, transitive, and anti-symmetric.

Reflexivity: An RDF graph always entails itself.

Transitivity: If $G \vDash H, H \vDash I$, then by interpolation lemma a subset of G is an instance of H, also a subset of H is an instance of I. That means a subset of G is an instance of I. Therefore $G \vDash I$.

Antisymmetry: Given two RDF graphs G and H, If $G \vDash H$ and $H \vDash G$, then G and H are instance of each other. For

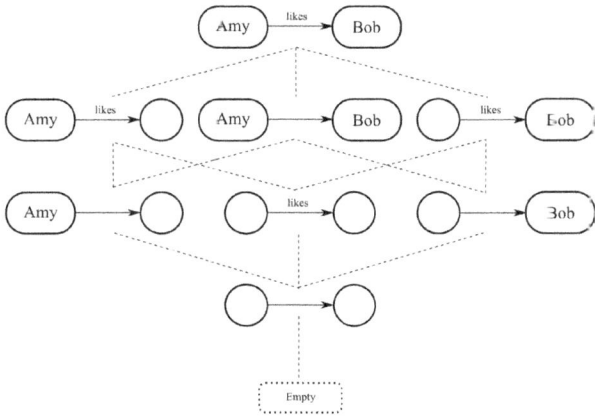

Figure 8: Lattice induced by entailment for one triple.

blank vertices, let h be the partial function used to derive instance relationship. We define $f : T(G) \to T(H)$ where $f(v) = h(v)$ for $v \in domain(h)$, and $f(v) = v$ otherwise. The function f is a bijection because h is an injection and $h(b) \in T(G)$, as discussed in Section 4.2. Therefore the relationship $\vDash$ is antisymmetric. $\square$

It should be noted that the above result is based on the SPARQL notion of entailment. It is unclear whether this result applies to the original RDF simple entailment. As we discuss in Section 2, we adopt the SPARQL notion of entailment for this work. Figure 8 shows a lattice induced from a single triple.

The lattice provides a quantitative approach to measuring the cost of achieving security, which in turn corresponds to (degradation in) information-quality: we simply count the distance from original graph (the top of lattice) to the graph in the lattice that we choose as our secure graph. The longer this distance, the more information we lose, and the higher the cost to achieve security is.

Note that the relationship is not necessarily monotonic. That is, more degradation in information-quality does not necessarily mean we get more security. An easy way to intuit this is to observe in Figure 8, that none of the nodes in the lattice except the bottom one, "Empty," provides any security for Amy or Bob. Indeed, security can even decrease as we descend a lattice. A comprehensive discussion of this non-monotonicity is beyond the scope of this work.

Securing an RDF graph   Now that we have notions of "secure," and a measure of information loss, we address the problem of devising an algorithm that transforms an RDF graph G into another graph G' such that G' preserves the semantics of G but also has a desired level of security. We define the decision problem in the form of a language below.

MINIMAL-k-AUTOMORPHISM $= \{\langle G, k, r, A\rangle$ where G is an RDF graph, $A \subseteq subj(G) \cup obj(G)$, and k, r are integers : there exists an RDF graph G' such that G' is k-automorphic with respect to A and G' is reachable from G in no more than r steps in the lattice induced by entailment.$\}$

It is easy to intuit an upper-bound hardness for MINIMAL-k-AUTOMORPHISM: it lies in **NP**. To intuit a lower-bound hardness of the above problem, we first define k-AUTOMORPHISM for k-automorphism of traditional graphs, that we introduce in Section 3. k-AUTOMORPHISM $= \{\langle G, k\rangle$

where G is a graph and k is an integer, such that G is k-automorphic$\}$. That is, k-AUTOMORPHISM is the problem of determining, given $\langle G, k\rangle$, whether G is k-automorphic.

LEMMA 2. k-AUTOMORPHISM   is   **NP**-hard   under polynomial-time Turing reductions.

The proof for the above lemma is that for the special case that $k = 2$, k-AUTOMORPHISM corresponds exactly to a fixed-point free automorphism, which is known to be **NP**-hard under polynomial-time Turing reductions [18]. We omit the details here.

We now return to MINIMAL-k-AUTOMORPHISM, which we pose above for RDF graphs. We assert, via the following theorem that it, too, is **NP**-hard under polynomial-time Turing reductions. The proof relies on a reduction from k-AUTOMORPHISM.

THEOREM 2. MINIMAL-k-AUTOMORPHISM is **NP**-hard under polynomial-time Turing reductions.

PROOF. We can reduce from the k-AUTOMORPHISM problem defined above. Given $\langle G, k\rangle$ as the input for k-AUTOMORPHISM, we construct an RDF graph G' from G. For every vertex in G, we create a blank vertex in G'. We use only one blank edge type in G' for all the edges we create and for every edge in G, we create two edges in G' that points to opposite directions. Let set A include all the vertices from G'. We then solve MINIMAL-k-AUTOMORPHISM for the input $\langle G', k, 0, A\rangle$. It is easy to see that $\langle G', k, 0, A\rangle \in$ MINIMAL-k-AUTOMORPHISM if and only if $\langle G, k\rangle \in k$-AUTOMORPHISM. $\square$

We can also define a problem MINIMAL-k-SYMMETRY based on k-SYMMETRY. A similar reduction as above establishes that MINIMAL-k-SYMMETRY is **ISO**-hard. **ISO** is Graph Isomorphism: the problem of determining, given two graphs, whether they are isomorphic to one another [8]. **ISO** is thought to be a strict superset of **P**, and a strict subset of **NP**. We omit further details here on account of space.

CNF-SAT Encoding   Given the above complexity results, there is no known algorithm for solving these problems efficiently. Therefore we provide reductions from MINIMAL-k-SYMMETRY and MINIMAL-k-AUTOMORPHISM to CNF-SAT, with the intent of using a SAT solver in practice. We now discuss our reduction from MINIMAL-k-SYMMETRY to CNF-SAT.

Input: $\langle G, k, r, A\rangle$ where G is an RDF graph, k, r are integers, $k < |subj(G) \cup pred(G)|$, $A \subseteq subj(G) \cup obj(G)$.

Additional notations:
We define the following notations to be used in the encoding.

- $V = T(G)$. Let $n = |T(G)|$. $V = [1, n]$.

- V comprises two partitions: B (blank symbols) and $\overline{B}$. Assume $B = [1, b], \overline{B} = [b + 1, n]$.

- Let $f_{i,j} : V \longrightarrow V$ be an automorphism. We define a mapping $g_{i,j} : G' \longrightarrow G'$ for each $f_{i,j}$ such that for triples $t_1, t_2 \in G'$ such that $t_1 = (s_1, p_1, o_1), t_2 = (s_2, p_2, o_2)$,

  $$g_{i,j}(t_1) = t_2 \iff f(s_1) = s_2 \land f(p_1) = p_2 \land f(o_1) = o_2.$$

Boolean variables:

We create the following boolean variables in our CNF-SAT encoding.

1. $\forall v \in V$, a variable x_v such that $x_v = 1$ iff v is blank(ed).

2. $\forall t \in G$, a variable y_t such that $y_t = 1$ iff t is deleted.

3. $\forall v \in V$, a variable z_v such that $z_v = 1$ iff all tuples in which v appears are deleted.

4. $\forall \alpha, \beta \in V, \gamma \in A, \forall \delta \in [1, k]$, a variable $f_{\alpha,\beta,\gamma,\delta}$ such that $f_{\alpha,\beta,\gamma,\delta} = 1$ iff $f_{\gamma,\delta}(\alpha) = \beta$.

5. $\forall \alpha, \beta, \in V, \gamma \in A, \forall \delta \in [1, k]$, an intermediate variable $b_{\alpha,\beta,\gamma,\delta} \iff f_{\alpha,\beta,\gamma,\delta} \wedge x_\beta \wedge \neg z_\beta$.

6. $\forall t_1, t_2 \in G, \forall \gamma \in A, \forall \delta \in [1, k]$, a variable $g_{t_1,t_2,\gamma,\delta}$ such that $g_{t_1,t_2,\gamma,\delta} = 1$ iff $g_{\gamma,\delta}(t_1) = t_2$.

7. $\forall t_1, t_2 \in G, \forall \gamma \in A, \forall \delta \in [1, k]$, an intermediate variable $h_{t_1,t_2,\gamma,\delta} \iff g_{t_1,t_2,\gamma,\delta} \wedge \neg y_{t_1}$.

Clauses, i.e., constraints:

Below we list the CNF-SAT clauses that we generate from the input. For the sake of brevity and clarity we write logical implications of the form $a \implies b$ where necessary. Clauses of these types are transformed to $\neg a \wedge b$ in the actual implementation.

1. $\forall v \in B$, a clause: x_v.

   This encodes vertices already known to be blank.

2. $\forall t = \langle s, p, o \rangle \in G$: $y_t \implies x_s \wedge x_p \wedge x_o$.

   In the lattice, deletion of a triple occurs only after all vertices in the triple are blank(ed).

3. $\forall v \in V$, let $T_v = \{t : t = \langle s, p, o \rangle \in G \wedge (v = s \vee v = p \vee v = o)\}$. $\forall v$, a clause: $y_{t_{v_1}} \wedge \ldots \wedge y_{t_{v_{|T_v|}}} \iff z_v$.

   Vertex considered deleted if and only if every triple in which it appears is deleted.

4. clauses that correspond to: $x_{b+1} + \ldots x_n + y_{t_1} + \ldots + y_{t_{|T|}} \leq r$.
   Number of triples from G that are deleted + Number of vertices that are originally not blank being blanked $\leq r$.

5. $\forall i \in V, \forall \gamma, \delta$: $\neg x_i \wedge \neg z_i \implies f_{i,i,\gamma,\delta}$.

   Vertex not blank and not deleted only if it is mapped to itself.

6. $\forall i \in V, \forall \gamma, \delta$: $x_i \wedge \neg z_i \implies (f_{i,1,\gamma,\delta} \wedge x_1 \wedge \neg z_1) \vee \ldots \vee (f_{i,n,\gamma,\delta} \wedge x_n \wedge \neg z_n)$.

   Vertex is blank and not deleted only if it is mapped to at least one blank vertex that has not been deleted.

   - This is transformed to
     $x_i \wedge \neg z_i \implies b_{i,1,\gamma,\delta} \vee \ldots \vee b_{i,n,\gamma,\delta}$, and
     $b_{\alpha,\beta,\gamma,\delta} \iff f_{\alpha,\beta,\gamma,\delta} \wedge x_\beta \wedge \neg z_\beta$

7. $\forall i, j, p \in V, i \neq j, \gamma \in A, \delta \in [1, k]$, $\neg f_{i,p,\gamma,\delta} \vee \neg f_{j,p,\gamma,\delta}$.

   Two vertices cannot both be mapped to the same vertex.

8. $\forall t_1 = (s_1, p_1, o_1), t_2 = (s_2, p_2, o_2) \in G, \forall \gamma \in A, \delta \in [1, k]$,

   - $\neg y_{t_1} \wedge \neg y_{t_2} \wedge g_{t_1,t_2,\gamma,\delta} \implies f_{s_1,s_2,\gamma,\delta} \wedge f_{p_1,p_2,\gamma,\delta} \wedge f_{o_1,o_2,\gamma,\delta}$
   - $\neg y_{t_1} \wedge \neg y_{t_2} \wedge f_{s_1,s_2,\gamma,\delta} \wedge f_{p_1,p_2,\gamma,\delta} \wedge f_{o_1,o_2,\gamma,\delta} \implies g_{t_1,t_2,\gamma,\delta}$

   We perceive triples as edges in automorphism. This constraint encodes the definition of function $g_{\gamma,\delta}$.

9. $\forall t \in G, \forall \gamma \in A, \delta \in [1, k]$,
   $\neg y_t \implies (g_{t,t_1,\gamma,\delta} \wedge \neg y_{t_1}) \vee \ldots \vee (g_{t,t_{|G|},\gamma,\delta} \wedge \neg y_{t_{|G|}})$.

   - This is transformed to
     $\neg y_t \implies h_{t,t_1,\gamma,\delta} \wedge \ldots h_{t,t_{|G|},\gamma,\delta}$, and
     $h_{t,t_i,\gamma,\delta} \iff g_{t,t_i,\gamma,\delta} \wedge \neg y_{t_i}$.

10. $\forall t, t_1, t_2 \in G$ such that $t_1 \neq t_2$, $\forall \gamma \in A, \delta \in [1, k]$,
    $\neg g_{t,t_1,\gamma,\delta} \vee \neg g_{t,t2,\gamma,\delta}$

    The three constraints above ensures that natural constraint of the automorphism: there is a one-to-one mapping between the triples that are not deleted.

11. $\forall i \in A, \forall j \in V, \forall$ distinct δ, ψ: $\neg z_i \implies \neg d_{i,j,i,\delta} \vee \neg d_{i,j,i,\psi}$.

    The "k" different mappings in k-SYMMETRY, defined only for vertices that have not been deleted.

A similar reduction can be constructed from MINIMAL-k-AUTOMORPHISM to CNF-SAT. The only change is that where a variable $f_{\alpha,\beta,\gamma,\delta}$ is used, we use $f_{\alpha,\beta,\delta}$ to encode only k automorphisms in total, instead of k automorphisms for each $v \in A$.

Efficiency Our reduction runs in time polynomial in the size of its input. However, its output size, as suggested by our subscripts for the boolean variables above, is quartic, i.e., degree 4, in the size of the input. Certainly, a more efficient reduction may exist. An investigation is beyond the scope of this work.

5. EMPIRICAL RESULTS

We have conducted a limited empirical assessment of *k-symmetry* and *k-automorphism* on RDF with the encoding provided in Section 4. Our intent with the empirical assessment is to investigate the relationship between security and information-quality (or cost of achieving security) under realistic graphs of two different classes. More specifically we would like to understand, in practice, how the various parameters such as the input graph G, the level of security k, the anonymization set A and the minimum cost r interact.

For instance, given G and A, it seems reasonable to expect that the minimum cost r required grows with k, but how fast does it grow? Is it harder to anonymize a larger graph? These are some of the questions we investigate in this section. We intentionally keep our RDF graph inputs small so it is easier to intuit relationships between the parameters.

It should be noted that although we have investigated both *k-symmetry* and *k-automorphism*, these two notions exhibit the same behaviour during our experiments. In other words, achieving these two security notions for the same k

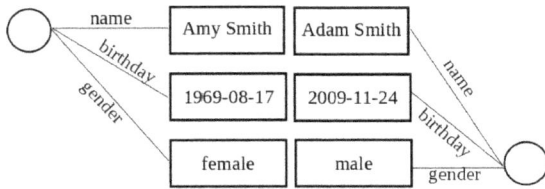

Figure 9: Attribute graph.

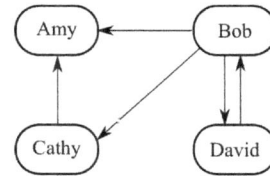

Figure 10: Network graph

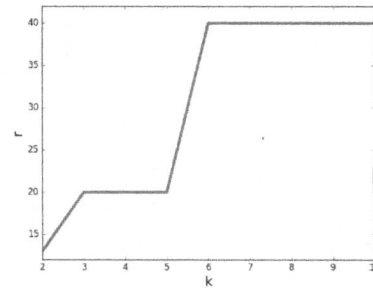

Figure 11: Relationship between k and r for attribute graphs

has the same cost for all the inputs that were tested. Therefore we do not differentiate them in the rest of this section, and just refer to them as *k-security*.

We conduct our empirical assessment over two classes of graphs. One, which we call *network* graphs, are based on examples used in social network anonymization such as [31]. The other, which we call *attribute* graphs are information of US senators retrieved from [7]. The attribute graphs are real life examples of RDF data published online. It also closely resembles other online RDF data sources such as DBpedia in structure. Figure 9 is an example of attribute graphs, and Figure 10 of network graphs. In Figure 10 an edge denotes the *knows* relationship.

The reason we have chosen these two types of graphs for experiments is that they highlight two typical, yet distinct kinds of data that are encoded as RDF graphs. The *network* graphs highlights the relationship between vertices. All the vertices in a *network* graph represent the same type of entities (people in this example) and the graph describes relationship between the entities. The *attribute* graphs, on the other hand, describes attributes of entities. Some of the vertices in the graphs represent people while others represent attributes of these people such as name, gender, and birthday. The *attribute* graph does not contain relationship between entities of the same type. These two characteristics can be mixed of course in one graph. However in practical RDF graphs they are often separated, and from a theoretical standpoint it would be interesting to investigate how their differences would affect security.

Note that our intent is not to assess the performance of our reduction from the previous section. In keeping with this mindset, and to more easily understand how different parameters are related, we keep our inputs small: graphs of at most 25 vertices.

As shown in Figure 9, the attribute graphs have a lot of small components of similar structures. In fact our empirical result shows that this property of the attribute graphs makes it easier to achieve higher-level of security. As we can see from Figure 11, for the input attribute graph, achieving 3-security and 5-security has the same cost. In other words, when 3-security is achieved, 4-security and 5-security is also achieved. This is not a coincidence, but a result of the structure of the attribute graph.

The network graph, in contrast, does not possess this property. As is shown in Figure 12, the cost r increases steadily with the security parameter k. In this case, the cost only stops increasing after the entire graph is removed, in which case it can be seen as infinitely secure. This suggests that achieving the same level of security in an attribute graph is easier than in a network graph of similar size. The structural randomness of the network graph makes it harder to secure.

We also looked at the relationship between the size of the graph and the cost of security. Figure 15 and Figure 14 shows that when the network graphs becomes bigger (with more vertices and proportionally more edges), even if the number of vertices to be secured remains the same, it becomes more costly to achieve a certain level of security. Figure 15 shows the case where we fix the number of vertices to be anonymized and the security parameter k, and investigate the size of the graph (characterized by $|V|$) and the minimum cost r required to achieve k-security. The result shows that the cost r increases as the input graph becomes larger. Figure 14 supports the above observation from another perspective: when r and the number of vertices to be secured are fixed, the smaller a graph is, the easier it is to achieve a high level of security.

Similarly, the set A of vertices to be secured affects the cost of security positively. Figure 13 and Figure 16 together show the intuitive result that for the same graph, achieving a higher-level of security becomes more difficult when more vertices are added to A. Related to the this observation, Figure 17 demonstrates that to achieve the same level of security with the same cost, as the graph becomes larger, the set A needs to be smaller. We can see that at first the size of A is equal to the size of V because the fixed cost r is sufficient to reach k-security for all vertices in V. However as the size of graph grows, k-security can only be reached with cost r for a smaller set A.

6. RELATED WORK

There are several pieces of prior work on RDF security. Most such work [1, 9, 23] studies RDF from the perspective of database access control. Abel et al. [1] for example designed a system that enforces complex security policies by means of re-writing queries. Other works adopt a similar framework, and only propose different policy language

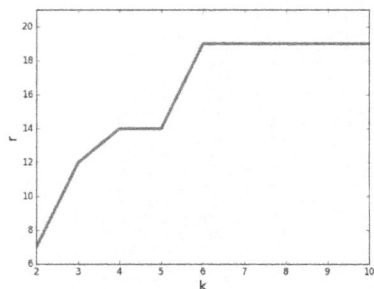

Figure 12: Relationship between k and r for network graphs

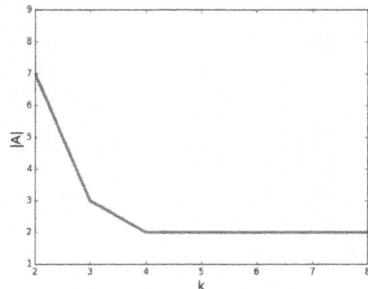

Figure 13: Relationship between k and $|A|$ for network graphs

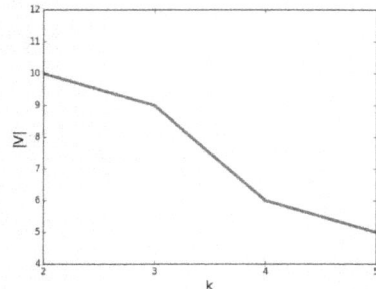

Figure 14: Relationship between k and $|V|$ for network graphs

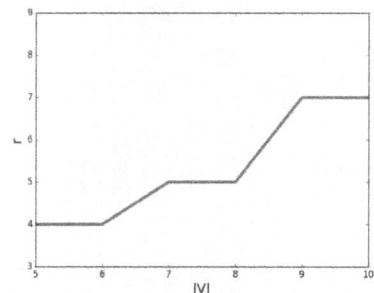

Figure 15: Relationship between $|V|$ and r for network graphs

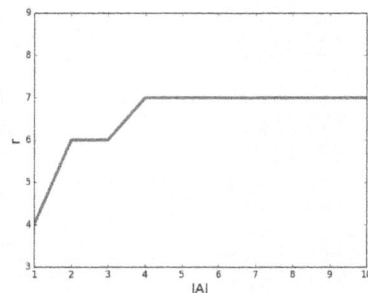

Figure 16: Relationship between $|A|$ and r for network graphs

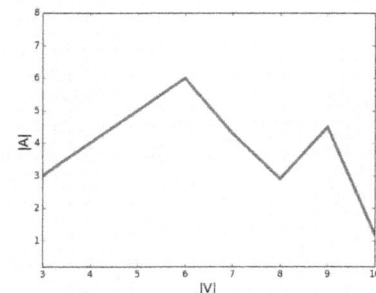

Figure 17: Relationship between $|V|$ and $|A|$ for network graphs

and enforcement mechanisms. A more recent piece of work on RDF access control by Rachapalli et al. [23] proposed three operations for sanitizing vertices, edges and paths in an RDF graph. Their work complements that of Bishop et al. [5], which discusses RDF sanitization and anonymization at a high level.

Some studies [24, 15, 4, 20, 25] deal with the case where RDF data is combined with inference rules to generate more triples. Jain and Farkas [15] for example attach security labels to each triple in RDF and compute labels automatically for inferred triples.

An issue with such work in access control is that they fail to provide a clear notion of security. We believe a clear notion of security is necessary in order to evaluate the proposed techniques: if an operation is designed to achieve security, it should be clear what security guarantee it provides.

Indeed, if we look at the work of Rachapalli et al. [23] in greater detail, the system can be compromised by issuing multiple queries and combining the results. At a high level, that work proposes "sanitizing" the graph that is the result of a query. Suppose we have the following RDF graph, which comprises two triples only.

> Student_1 lives_in House_1
>
> Student_2 lives_in House_2

Suppose that the policy states that the House data should be sanitized. An attacker first issues the following query, q_1, that selects everything.

> SELECT ?a ?b ?c
> WHERE {?a ?b ?c}

We expect that the response for q_1 is:

> Student_1 lives_in XXX
>
> Student_2 lives_in YYY

An attacker can then issue the following query, q_2. The intent of the "MINUS" part of the query is so all triples except those with House_1 as object are to be selected. It is possible to carry out this attack without using "MINUS."

> SELECT ?a ?b ?c
> WHERE {?a ?b ?c
>   MINUS {sameTerm(?c, House_1)}}

We expect that the response to query q_2 is:

> Student_2 lives in YYY

The attacker now immediately infers that Student_1 lives in House_1.

Another important aspect of our work study regards information-quality, which has also been largely ignored in prior work. We base this part of our work on existing work on RDF semantics and more specifically RDF entailment [12, 27, 2]. RDF entailment is originally a notion used to ensure the consistency between an inferred RDF graph and the original graph. In this work we use entailment creatively to ensure that the sanitized graph is consistent with the original with regards to semantics.

Separate from work in RDF security, many security notions have been proposed for traditional graphs under different attack models over the years. Most of these notions were defined in the context of social networks, as it is a prominent use case for graphs. Their results however do apply to graphs in other contexts. The notions are mostly inspired by *k-anonymity* [26], that was defined for relational data. The definitions and techniques however differ in the context of graphs.

Liu and Terzi [17], for example, have proposed *k-degree-anonymity* in order to to prevent degree attacks. They assume that the attacker has prior knowledge of the degrees of some vertices in the graph. Addition and deletion of edges are used in this case to achieve security.

Hay et al. [11] have considered the *vertex refinement attack*, which is a generalization of the degree attack. That work proposes an anonymization approach utilizing random sampling, which retains integrity of summary data of the graph. Thompson and Yao [28] also define security against the degree attack, but in their work the attacker is assumed to know about the degrees of all neighbours within distance i of some vertices. Zheleva and Getoor [30], on the other hand, have considered security for social graphs whose edges are labelled but nodes are not. They used edge anonymization to prevent sensitive relationships from being revealed.

As Narayanan and Shmatikov [21] have demonstrated, it is possible to conduct re-identification attack to a graph with only structural information. Thereafter, more recent notions consider attacks on structural information.

Zhou and Pei [31] have defined the neighbourhood attack in which the adversary tries to re-identify vertices in a graph with prior knowledge of their complete neighbourhood structure. They propose a notion of *k-anonymity* by means of isomorphic neighbourhoods. The technique used to achieve security is inserting edges.

A more recent study by Wu et al. [29] proposes *k-symmetry*, which promises security against all structural attacks. The security notion proposed by [29] is very similar to that in [32], which is termed *k-automorphism*. These two notions are both based on the graph isomorphism problem, and the similarity was acknowledged by the authors. However the relationship between these two notions is unclear.

Imeson et al. [13] studies graph security in the context of integrated circuits. Their security notion is based on the problem of subgraph isomorphism. There, the attacker is explicitly provided two graph inputs, as opposed to only one (the secure graph) as is the case with us. In our work, the attacker's second input graph is some a priori knowledge that the attacker has. As we allow this second graph to be any subgraph of the original graph, it is as though the attacker chooses, and is not given, the second graph.

Other works such as Blocki et al. [6] study graph security from the perspective of differential privacy. Such pieces of work focus on providing summary statistics of the graph instead of the graph itself. The isomorphism-based security notions we discuss in this work focus on securing structural information and do not guarantee differential privacy.

7. CONCLUSION

In this work we make contributions to both theory and practice in the context of securing RDF. We observe that RDF data can be meaningfully encoded as a kind of graph that we call an RDF graph. We enunciate a rather strong threat model, and consider three notions for quantitative, unconditional, isomorphism-based approaches for graph-security from the literature. We pick the strongest two, and

adapt those for RDF. Then, we show that under SPARQL semantics, entailment induces a lattice among RDF graphs under two operations that provide security, while preserving semantics.

The lattice naturally provides us a notion of information-quality, and equivalently, the cost of achieving security. We then consider the problem of computing a secure graph G' from a given RDF graph G such that G' yields some threshold k of security, and does not exceed some threshold r of cost. We show that the problem is **NP**-complete. We then discuss our design and implementation of a reduction to CNF-SAT. We have implemented our reduction and present empirical results for two classes of RDF graphs.

There is considerable scope for future work. One is to establish clear relationships between the various notions for graph-security in traditional graphs related, for example, to their relative strength, and computational complexity. A second topic for future work is consideration of large, realistic RDF databases, and attempting to sanitize them. A third topic is making the reduction to CNF-SAT more efficient so it is practical in realistic settings.

Acknowledgements

We thank the reviewers for their thoughful and constructive reviews. The first author was supported by a scholarship funded by the Natural Sciences and Engineering Research Council of Canada (NSERC).

8. REFERENCES

[1] F. Abel, J. L. De Coi, N. Henze, A. W. Koesling, D. Krause, and D. Olmedilla. Enabling advanced and context-dependent access control in rdf stores. In *The Semantic Web*, pages 1–14. Springer, 2007.

[2] M. Arenas, M. Consens, and A. Mallea. Revisiting blank nodes in rdf to avoid the semantic mismatch with sparql. In *RDF Next Steps Workshop*, pages 26–27, 2010.

[3] S. Auer, C. Bizer, G. Kobilarov, J. Lehmann, R. Cyganiak, and Z. Ives. Dbpedia: A nucleus for a web of open data. In *The semantic web*, pages 722–735. Springer, 2007.

[4] J. Bao, G. Slutzki, and V. Honavar. Privacy-preserving reasoning on the semanticweb. In *Web Intelligence, IEEE/WIC/ACM International Conference on*, pages 791–797. IEEE, 2007.

[5] M. Bishop, J. Cummins, S. Peisert, A. Singh, B. Bhumiratana, D. Agarwal, D. Frincke, and M. Hogarth. Relationships and data sanitization: a study in scarlet. In *Proceedings of the 2010 workshop on New security paradigms*, pages 151–164. ACM, 2010.

[6] J. Blocki, A. Blum, A. Datta, and O. Sheffet. Differentially private data analysis of social networks via restricted sensitivity. In *Proceedings of the 4th conference on Innovations in Theoretical Computer Science*, pages 87–96. ACM, 2013.

[7] L. Civic Impulse. Govtrack. https://www.govtrack.us/. Accessed: 2016-07-01.

[8] T. H. Cormen, C. Stein, R. L. Rivest, and C. E. Leiserson. *Introduction to Algorithms*. McGraw-Hill Higher Education, 2nd edition, 2001.

[9] G. Flouris, I. Fundulaki, M. Michou, and G. Antoniou. Controlling access to rdf graphs. In *Future Internet Symposium*, pages 107–117. Springer, 2010.

[10] O. Goldreich. *Computational Complexity: A Conceptual Perspective*. Cambridge University Press, 2008.

[11] M. Hay, G. Miklau, D. Jensen, D. Towsley, and P. Weis. Resisting structural re-identification in anonymized social networks. *Proceedings of the VLDB Endowment*, 1(1):102–114, 2008.

[12] P. Hayes and B. McBride. Rdf semantics, 2014.

[13] F. Imeson, A. Emtenan, S. Garg, and M. V. Tripunitara. Securing computer hardware using 3d integrated circuit (ic) technology and split manufacturing for obfuscation. In *USENIX Security*, volume 13, 2013.

[14] C. Inc. Stardog: Enterprise data unification with smart graphs. http://stardog.com/. Accessed: 2016-07-01.

[15] A. Jain and C. Farkas. Secure resource description framework: an access control model. In *Proceedings of the eleventh ACM symposium on Access control models and technologies*, pages 121–129. ACM, 2006.

[16] A. Jena. Apache jena. *jena. apache. org [Online]. Available: http://jena. apache. org [Accessed: Mar. 20, 2014]*, 2013.

[17] K. Liu and E. Terzi. Towards identity anonymization on graphs. In *Proceedings of the 2008 ACM SIGMOD international conference on Management of data*, pages 93–106. ACM, 2008.

[18] A. Lubiw. Some np-complete problems similar to graph isomorphism. *SIAM Journal on Computing*, 10(1):11–21, 1981.

[19] F. Manola, E. Miller, and B. McBride. Rdf 1.1 Primer, 2014. Available from https://www.w3.org/TR/2014/NOTE-rdf11-primer-20140225/

[20] A. Mileo, N. Lopes, and S. Kirrane. A logic programming approach for access control over rdf. In *International Conference on Logic Programming (ICLP), Technical Communications*. International Conference on Logic Programming (ICLP), 2012.

[21] A. Narayanan and V. Shmatikov. De-anonymizing social networks. In *Security and Privacy, 2009 30th IEEE Symposium on*, pages 173–187. IEEE, 2009.

[22] E. Prud Hommeaux, A. Seaborne, et al. Sparql query language for rdf. *W3C recommendation*, 15, 2008.

[23] J. Rachapalli, V. Khadilkar, M. Kantarcioglu, and B. Thuraisingham. Towards fine grained rdf access control. In *Proceedings of the 19th ACM symposium on Access control models and technologies*, pages 165–176. ACM, 2014.

[24] P. Reddivari, T. Finin, and A. Joshi. Policy-based access control for an rdf store. In *Proceedings of the Policy Management for the Web workshop*, volume 120, pages 78–83, 2005.

[25] T. Sayah, E. Coquery, R. Thion, and M.-S. Hacid. Inference leakage detection for authorization policies over rdf data. In *IFIP Annual Conference on Data and Applications Security and Privacy*, pages 346–361. Springer, 2015.

[26] L. Sweeney. k-anonymity: A model for protecting privacy. *International Journal of Uncertainty, Fuzziness and Knowledge-Based Systems*, 10(05):557–570, 2002.

[27] H. J. ter Horst. Completeness, decidability and complexity of entailment for rdf schema and a semantic extension involving the owl vocabulary. *Web Semantics: Science, Services and Agents on the World Wide Web*, 3(2):79–115, 2005.

[28] B. Thompson and D. Yao. The union-split algorithm and cluster-based anonymization of social networks. In *Proceedings of the 4th International Symposium on Information, Computer, and Communications Security*, pages 218–227. ACM, 2009.

[29] W. Wu, Y. Xiao, W. Wang, Z. He, and Z. Wang. K-symmetry model for identity anonymization in social networks. In *Proceedings of the 13th international conference on extending database technology*, pages 111–122. ACM, 2010.

[30] E. Zheleva and L. Getoor. Preserving the privacy of sensitive relationships in graph data. In *Privacy, security, and trust in KDD*, pages 153–171. Springer, 2008.

[31] B. Zhou and J. Pei. Preserving privacy in social networks against neighborhood attacks. In *Data Engineering, 2008. ICDE 2008. IEEE 24th International Conference on*, pages 506–515. IEEE, 2008.

[32] L. Zou, L. Chen, and M. T. Özsu. K-automorphism: A general framework for privacy preserving network publication. *Proceedings of the VLDB Endowment*, 2(1):946–957, 2009.

Secure Free-Floating Car Sharing for Offline Cars

Alexandra Dmitrienko
Institute of Information Security
ETH Zurich, Switzerland
alexandra.dmitrienko@inf.ethz.ch

Christian Plappert
Fraunhofer SIT
Darmstadt, Germany
christian.plappert@sit.fraunhofer.de

ABSTRACT

In this paper, we present a new access control system for free-floating car sharing, which achieves a number of appealing features not available in the state-of-the-art solutions. First of all, it does not require online connection for cars, and, therefore, allows car sharing providers to expand their services to areas without reliable network coverage (e.g., with blind spots). Second, the solution is compatible to RFID cards – the most commonly deployed authentication tokens in car sharing, and can be deployed on standard mobile platforms with various hardware features. Third, it is fully compatible with off-the-shelf cars and does not require any intrusive modifications to car's internals.

These new properties can be achieved due to a novel system design which deploys two-factor authentication and combines an RFID card (the real one or emulated in software) with a "soft" authentication token stored on a mobile platform. Such a combination increases security of the solution, preserves backward compatibility to RFID technology and enables great flexibility in protection of authentication secrets on the mobile platform. To demonstrate such a flexibility, we present a platform security concept which can be instantiated in various deployment options and provides the means to achieve best possible security given available hardware

We implemented our solution on Android and instantiated the platform security concept in three different deployment options. We evaluate security of our solution and report performance measurements.

Keywords

Car Sharing; Access Control; DESFire EV1; BLE; NFC

1. INTRODUCTION

Within the last decade, the worldwide market for car sharing has grown exponentially [1, 2] and the rapid development of car sharing solutions is drastically changing the transportation landscape, especially in metropolitan areas [3]. Car sharing membership has grown from 2012 to 2014 by

CODASPY'17, March 22 - 24, 2017, Scottsdale, AZ, USA

© 2017 Copyright held by the owner/author(s). Publication rights licensed to ACM.
ISBN 978-1-4503-4523-1/17/03... $15.00

DOI: http://dx.doi.org/10.1145/3029806.3029807

170% to 4.8 million, with an increasing tendency for 2016 [4]. Car sharing solutions are well accepted by customers due to their inherent benefits: They offer users anytime access to a pool of vehicles for short-term use and enable mobility without the costs of a private car. Although the concept of individual ownership of vehicles is not going to vanish completely, it is increasingly replaced by the car sharing's on-demand mobility approach [5].

In general, car sharing is utilized with either a station-based or a free-floating business concept. While the more traditional station-based car sharing relies on fixed stations where a car needs to be returned after the booking period to the same parking lot where it was taken from, the more flexible and faster growing free-floating model [6] allows the user to pick up and leave cars anywhere in a vendor-defined area. On the downside, however, the free-floating model requires online connection for cars and is limited to locations with reliable network coverage.

With the by now omnipresent smartphones that come with an already built-in variety of communication interfaces like NFC, Bluetooth, GSM and GPS, car sharing solutions became even more convenient for the end user. By utilizing mobile services, users can conveniently search their surroundings for bookable cars and even use their smartphone app as a car key to open booked cars (e.g., *Car2Go* car sharing solution [7]).

However, current car sharing systems suffer from various shortcomings. In particular, the more convenient free-floating car sharing requires online communication with cars during the car opening process. On the other hand, network coverage and quality of data services significantly vary in different locations, and even fully covered urban areas are known to have blind spots with poor signal reception [8]. Hence, for the sake of interoperability and reliability car sharing providers often opt for station-based usage model which is less attractive to end users. Furthermore, car sharing solutions utilizing smartphone apps to download and store electronic car keys impose additional security risks to their customers: Attackers may try to intercept electronic car keys on transit, while they are transferred from the car sharing provider to the users, or when they are stored on users' smartphones. Attackers may also attempt to hijack user accounts to be able to book cars on behalf of legitimate users. Security incidents of that kind already affected Uber [9], a car ride sharing service with more than 8 million of users around the world, – many users reported they were charged for rides they have never taken [10, 11]. Further, compromised Uber accounts were proposed for sale on dark web markets [12] for as little as $1, which indicates that the attack is rolled out on a large scale. Similar attacks are very likely to affect car sharing services, as long as service providers do not address new security threats.

The state-of-the-art approach to harden mobile platform security is to leverage isolated (secure) environments, where apps can execute security sensitive operations (e.g., encryption, signing, etc.) in sub-routines referred to as trusted applications, applets or trustlets. Such environments can be established on top of mobile secure hardware, such as processor-based security extensions [13, 14] (also referred as Trusted Execution Environments, TEEs) and dedicated secure co-processors [15] (also known as Secure Elements, SEs). However, despite the fact that mobile secure hardware is widely deployed today [16], their secure environments are controlled by various stakeholders and normally cannot be used by third party apps. While generally paid access to secure hardware is possible, the process to obtain it is cumbersome [17]. Hence, one has to consider scalable approaches to platform security which can utilize such secure hardware if accessible, while being able to provide secure alternatives otherwise.

In this paper, we aim to tackle shortcomings of state-of-the-art car sharing solutions and propose a new car sharing system which provides a unique combination of properties. It (i) supports for offline cars and, hence, can be used in locations with less reliable network connection and even without it (e.g., in underground garages). Furthermore, it (ii) accurately addresses new security threats and, at the same time, (iii) it can be used with various off-the-shelf mobile platforms with no extra requirements to hardware and installed software. Additionally, (iv) our solution provides interoperability to standards commonly used in car sharing solutions today, and can even be used with off-the-shelf cars without any intrusive modifications. In particular, we make the following contributions:

- We analyze functional and security requirements for offline car sharing systems (Section 2) and design the first smartphone-based car sharing solution for offline cars (Section 3). Our solution leverages two-factor authentication of users and separate delivery of both authenticators to clients and their isolated handling on client platforms in order to harden security against new attack vectors. It provides great flexibility in integration with mobile platforms and backward compatibility to RFID cards – the most commonly deployed authentication tokens in car sharing. Furthermore, it enables range of alternatives for protection of user authenticators on client side, which allows a car sharing provider to select the best option depending on capabilities of user's hardware and achieve the best security possible per user. We provide security analysis of our solution (Section 4).

- We implemented a proof-of-concept prototype for Android smartphones and demonstrated its flexibility by showing several alternatives for protection of user authenticators ranging from the Secure Element (SE) provider hosted on a Mifare DesFire EV1 contactless card to Mifare DesFire EV1 card emulated on top of mobile secure hardware or entirely in software when hosted by user's (trusted) smartwatch (Section 5). For system evaluation we augmented private cars with the

prototyped car lock using a *car key proxy* approach which does not require any intrusive modifications to cars. Our evaluation includes performance measurements of user authentication for various instantiations of SE provider.

To summarize, our solution is the first to provide such a set of properties which improves state of the art for free floating car sharing systems with respect to security and supported functionality.

2. SYSTEM MODEL AND REQUIREMENTS

In this section we provide a high-level overview of our solution, define our system model and adversarial capabilities and analyze security and functional requirements.

2.1 High-level Overview

The core design feature of our solution is a two-factor authentication in order to get access to the cars where the authentication factors are downloaded and handled separately. In a nutshell, the user needs to present two authenticators to the car lock in order to successfully pass authentication. The first authentication factor is created during the user registration process, while the second one is downloaded during car booking. Since both authenticators are obtained in separate sessions, it is more challenging for the adversary to compromise both of them. Further, our solution also handles both authenticators on client side in isolation from each other, which even further increases the burden for the attacker, and, at the same time, enables flexibility for the defender in arranging their protection.

While two-factor authentication is widely used today, e.g., in online banking and for login verification by Internet service providers, to the best of our knowledge it is not used in car sharing applications. Moreover, our scheme is distinguishable from other two-factor authentication schemes, as it combines contactless Radio-frequency Identification (RFID) cards, which are a de-facto standard for access control and widely used in car sharing applications, with "soft" cryptographic tokens – the approach which enables a flexible integration with mobile platforms. Moreover, our solution extends the state-of-the-art in the field of access control solutions for car sharing systems by providing appealing features which are not available in alternative solutions, such as offline user authentication, compatibility with legacy cars and various deployment options.

2.2 System Model

Our system model is depicted in Figure 1 and involves the following entities: the Car Sharing Provider (CSP) C, a car to be shared equipped with the Lock L, and a User U. For simplicity reasons and without loss of generality, we consider a single user and a single car in our system model, which can be easily scaled to a pool of cars and many users.

Each U possesses a client platform consisting of two execution environments, the mobile host H and a Secure Element Provider (SEP) S, which are isolated from each other. Typically a SEP cannot communicate with other entities directly, but such a communication is mediated by the host H which is used as a proxy. However, depending on the deployment option, SEP may or may not have a dedicated user interface.

C is a car sharing provider which defines access rules to cars, i.e., specifies which U is allowed to access which L.

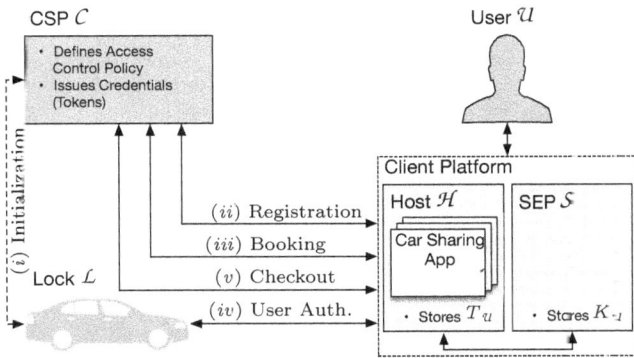

Figure 1 – System Model

$\mathcal{L}$ is either a regular car key lock interfaced with car internals or instantiated using a car key proxy approach as we describe in details in Section 5.1. $\mathcal{L}$ requires access to location and timing information, which is provided either by car's GPS sensor and timer in former case or is available on the car lock itself when latter approach is used.

Authentication factors. The two authentication factors are the user specific key K_u created during user registration and the car access token T_u which is downloaded during the car booking process. On the client side the token T_u resides within the host environment $\mathcal{H}$, while the user-specific key K_u is hosted by $\mathcal{S}$.

2.3 Adversary Model and Assumptions

We define three distinct adversary classes which will be used in Section 4 to elucidate the security of our solution in various deployment options.

Class 1 Adversary. Our first class adversary has full control over the communication between the $\mathcal{H}$, $\mathcal{C}$, $\mathcal{S}$ and $\mathcal{L}$. This means that it can eavesdrop, modify, insert, delete, relay and re-route the protocol messages. However, it cannot compromise the communication channel between $\mathcal{U}$ and $\mathcal{H}$, $\mathcal{H}$ and $\mathcal{S}$, and any of the communication end-points.

Class 2 Adversary. Our second class adversary has all the possibilities of the first class adversary and, additionally, it can compromise user's host $\mathcal{H}$ and gain access to all information stored on it, e.g., credentials, at any time but during user registration process. Further, the communication channel between $\mathcal{H}$ and $\mathcal{S}$ can also be compromised.

Class 3 Adversary. Our third class adversary is similar to the second class, with the only difference that it can compromise $\mathcal{H}$ at any time including user registration.

We exclude relay attacks [18] on the communication between a mobile device of the user and the car lock which are not specific to our car sharing system, but due to the local communication interfaces we rely upon (Near Field Communication (NFC) and Bluetooth Low Energy (BLE)). These attacks can be mitigated by distance bounding techniques [19, 20], which can be easily incorporated into our scheme once they are available on off-the-shelf mobile platforms. Moreover, contactless RFID cards, the most commonly deployed authentication tokens in car sharing, are also susceptible to such relay attacks [21]. We also do not consider denial of service (DoS) attacks, which prevent users from accessing the service. An attacker with full control over communication channels can always disrupt communication and prevent token download, while compromised host can always prevent a car sharing app from launching or delete stored information

including downloaded tokens. These attacks are not specific to our car sharing system, as they can be launched against any mobile application. Furthermore they do not provide any monetary benefits to adversaries and, hence, unlikely to be applied.

2.4 Security Requirements

Our main security objective is to prevent unauthorized access of users to the car sharing service. In particular, only a user $\mathcal{U}$ which possesses both a user key K_u and the car access token T_u should be granted access to the respective lock $\mathcal{L}$. To achieve this objective, a number of security requirements should be fulfilled which we detail in the following.

SR1: Well-established Crypto. Our first security requirement is to rely on open and well-established crypto primitives and algorithms for user authentication, since closed and proprietary systems that are not available for evaluation to a broad security community are more likely to suffer from vulnerabilities. For instance, the common practice to use proprietary protocols in immobilizer systems has lead to their successful exploitations [22, 23, 24, 25], which strongly speaks against the "security by obscurity" approach.

SR2: Confidential Credentials. Our second security requirement is to ensure the confidentiality of authentication credentials (such as cryptographic keys and passwords), and even from users themselves. Otherwise the adversary can use phishing attacks to trick users to reveal their passwords, and later on use them for impersonation. Attacks of that kind are accountable for large scale hijacking and abuse of user accounts of the car ride sharing service Uber [10, 11].

SR3: Isolation. Third, we require isolation between trusted and untrusted components on the mobile platform and that only trusted components can access credentials in clear text. Otherwise, an attacker may deploy mobile malware which can infiltrate credentials from the mobile platform. For instance, mobile banking Trojans like ZeuS/ZitMo [26] use this approach to intercept verification codes sent by banks to the users' mobile phones.

SR4: Strong Credentials. Fourth, we require authentication credentials to be randomly chosen, uniformly distributed and have sufficient length. If not fulfilled, the attacker may have significant chances to succeed in dictionary attacks against user passwords and/or even brute-force cryptographic keys. For instance, in 1998 a 321-bit RSA key used by debit/credit cards of the French bank was factored by an individual [27].

SR5: SEP invocation authorization. Fifth, we require user authorization for every invocation of code executed within SEP $\mathcal{S}$. If security sensitive code executed within SEP is not authorized by the user, it could be triggered by malware rather than by the legitimate car sharing app which can then trigger user authentication on behalf of the user and succeed in user impersonation without actually learning authentication credentials. Such attacks were shown in the past [28] on payment applications such as Google Wallet.

2.5 Functional Requirements

Apart from the security requirements discussed above, we define the following functional requirements.

FR1: Offline Authentication. State-of-the-art car sharing solutions rely on connected cars, which limits their operational area to locations with reliable network connection. To overcome this limitation, we require an offline authentication of users during car (un)locking which enables car sharing services to expand to areas with less reliable or even without any network connection.

FR2: Compatibility. Compatibility significantly increases chances for a successful deployment, as it enables recycling of existing hardware, infrastructure and technologies and, hence, results in reduced time and costs of development and deployment. Our compatibility requirements include: (i) interoperability with contactless RFID cards – the most common authentication token in car sharing solutions, and (ii) the ability to utilize various off-the-shelf mobile platforms with no extra requirements to hardware or system software.

FR3: Flexible Deployment. Our last functional requirement concerns various deployment options, which should achieve the best possible level of security for available user's hardware and preferable usability properties. When available, the car sharing provider may provide different deployment options to different customers, depending on the underlying hardware of their mobile platforms.

Overall, to the best of our knowledge, no other car sharing solution can fulfill similar requirements.

3. SYSTEM DESIGN

In this section we elaborate on system design by providing protocol specification and describing our design choices and deployment alternatives for the platform security concept.

3.1 Protocol Specification

The parties which we specified in our system model (cf. Section 2.2) interact in the following use cases (cf. Figure 1): (i) system initialization, (ii) user registration, (iii) car booking, (iv) user authentication, and (v) user checkout. Below we provide protocol specifications for each use case.

3.1.1 System Initialization

During initialization the car sharing provider initializes the car locks with cryptographic material and registers all the cars in its database. In particular, C initializes each car lock L with a unique car identifier ID_L and two cryptographic keys K^L_{Auth} and K^L_{Enc} over a confidential and authenticated out-of-band channel. For instance, this step can be performed by programming the car lock via local programming interfaces before the lock is installed into the car. The triple $\{ID_L, K^L_{Auth}, K^L_{Enc}\}$ is also stored by C in its local database.

Furthermore, C initializes each S by creating a smartcard application AID with two empty data files FID_U and FID_L, which will be later on used to store the user's identifier and car's location, respectively. Access to the application is protected by an application master key K_M while administrative access to the smartcard which protects against unauthorized operations, e.g., formatting the card and creating/deleting applications, is protected by a smartcard master key. The smartcard master key is kept secret by C and never shared with third parties.

3.1.2 Registration

Before using the car sharing service, U needs to create a user account and associate it with his or her client platform. This is done during user registration which is intended to establish the user-specific key K_U shared between C and S on the client side.

The user registration procedure consists of two phases. In the first phase, out-of-band communication is used to exchange data between U and C. In particular, U submits his or her personal data (such as user name, e-mail address, post address, etc.), identifies payment method and submits the scanned copy of the driving license to the car sharing provider. In return, he or she receives either the pre-programmed smartcard initialized with the user-specific key K_U, or one time password OTP_U which will be later on used to provision K_U into SEP remotely. We do not specify any particular way to establish such an out-of-band channel since similar registration procedures are commonly utilized by mobile applications and well-established techniques exist. For instance, user-specific information can be submitted from U's PC to C over a web form, a pre-initialized smartcard can be picked up in the office of a car sharing provider or sent per post[1], while the one-time password can be delivered via one time accessible link sent by email.

The second phase of *registration* (cf. Figure 2) is only necessary if the customer has received the one time password OTP_U in the first phase. It is initiated by U who sends his credentials *creds* consisting of the user name ID_U and OTP_U, to the mobile host H (step 1), which, in turn, stores ID_U for future use and forwards *creds* over the established Transport Layer Security (TLS) channel to the car sharing provider C (steps 2-3). Upon receive, C verifies *creds* and, if correct, it generates the user-specific key K_U and reconfigures U's SEP to use K_U as an application master key for the AID application. In particular, C first sends a `select_app(AID)` command (step 4) and then authenticates with the application master key K_M (step 5). Afterwards, it selects the file with FID_U (step 6) and writes the identifier ID_U into it (step 7). Finally, it sends a command to change the application master key to K_U (step 8).

Note that the communication between C and S is always mediated by H, which is omitted in Figure 2 and in other protocol figures for brevity. Further, depending on the deployment options which we discuss in Section 3.2, steps 1-3 of the protocol may involve SEP S instead the host H[2]. Moreover, a successful authentication of an entity to SEP implies that all the subsequent communication is protected with a freshly generated session key, which is not explicitly shown to simplify protocol figures. For instance, in Figure 2 steps 6-8 are performed in a channel secured by the session key derived from the authentication in step 5. Finally, all communication between H and C is performed via the TLS channel established at the beginning of the protocol run.

3.1.3 Car Booking

After registration users are allowed to book cars for a self-defined period of time. Booking is done by using the *car booking protocol* depicted in Figure 3, within which U retrieves the car access token T_U and stores it on H.

The protocol is initiated by U, who indicates to H that he or she would like to perform car booking (step 1). In turn, H establishes a TLS session to C and sends user identifier ID_U (steps 2-3) to C. Next, C authenticates the client by ensuring his or her SEP S has the knowledge of K_U: First, it selects the car sharing application AID (step 4), then authenticates with the key K_U (step 5), then selects the file FID_U (step 6) and makes sure it can read the user identifier ID'_U from it

---

[1]This is a state-of-the art approach to deliver access cards used in car sharing today

[2]In particular, in a deployment option where SEP S features its own user interface

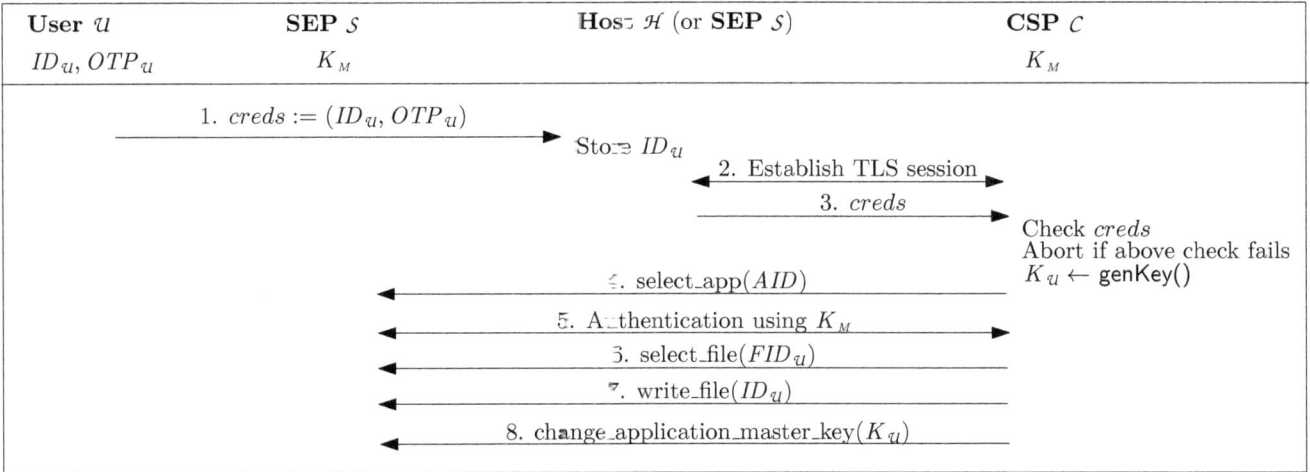

Figure 2 – Registration Protocol (second phase)

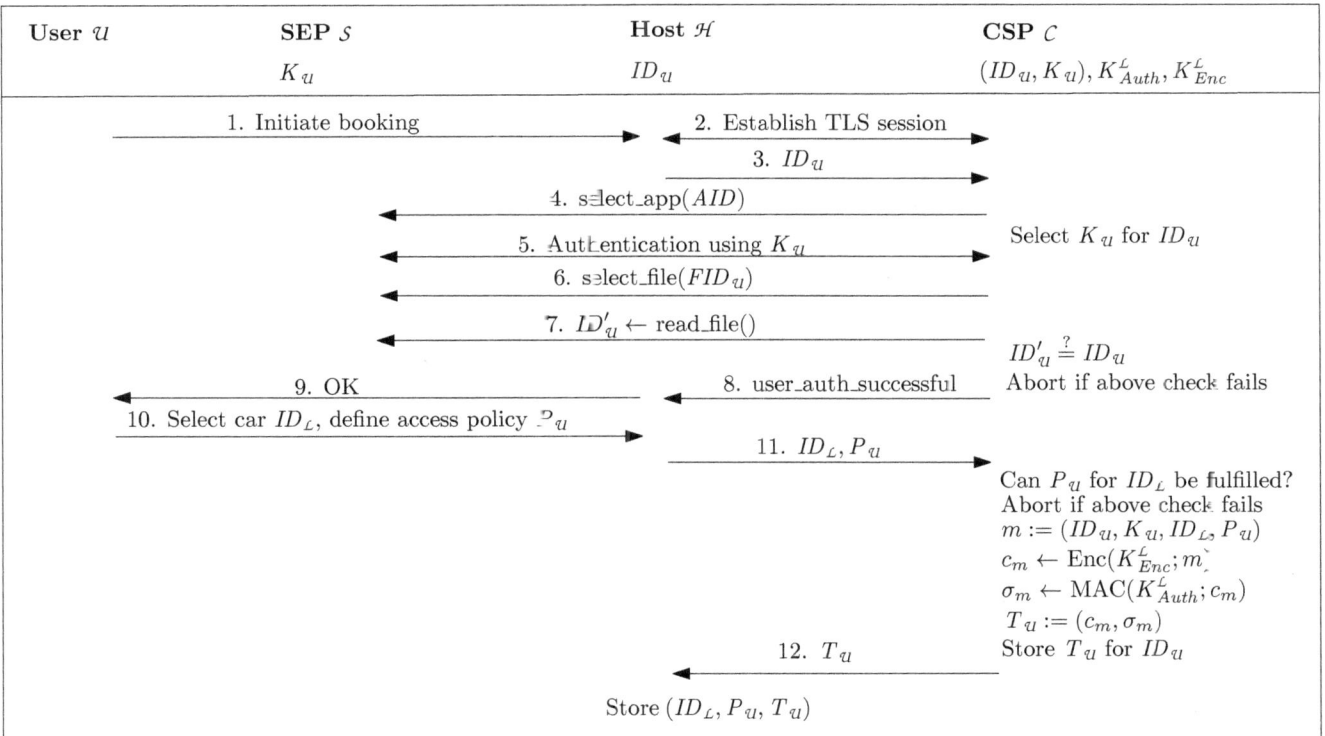

Figure 3 – Car Booking Protocol

(step 7). After a successful validation that the received ID_u from step 3 and the obtained ID'_u from step 7 are equal, u is notified of the successful user authentication (step 8-9). Once authenticated, u can book the car as follows: He selects the car with the identifier ID_L in the mobile app and specifies the desired access policy P_u[3], which are then forwarded by H to C (steps 10-11). After C has verified that the desired access policy can be fulfilled for the respective car, it generates a message m which includes the user identifier ID_u, the user-specific key K_u, the car identifier ID_L, and the access policy P_u. The message m is then encrypted with the encryption

key K_{Enc}^L and its signature σ_m is calculated using the key K_{Auth}^L and Message Authentication Code (MAC) algorithm. The resulting access token T_u consisting of the cipher c_m and the signature σ_m is sent to H (step 12), which stores it along with the car identifier ID_L and the policy P_u.

3.1.4 User Authentication

User authentication is required in order to unlock the car and lock it again after usage. With the *user authentication protocol* u can proof to L that he or she is in the possession of both authenticators, T_u and K_u. Furthermore, L writes the car's location on u's SEP S and the timestamp so that they can be reported to C later on.

The protocol for *user authentication* is depicted in Figure 4.

---

[3]Typically access policy includes validity period of booking, but generally may include more sophisticated statements, e.g., maximum distance, location area, etc.

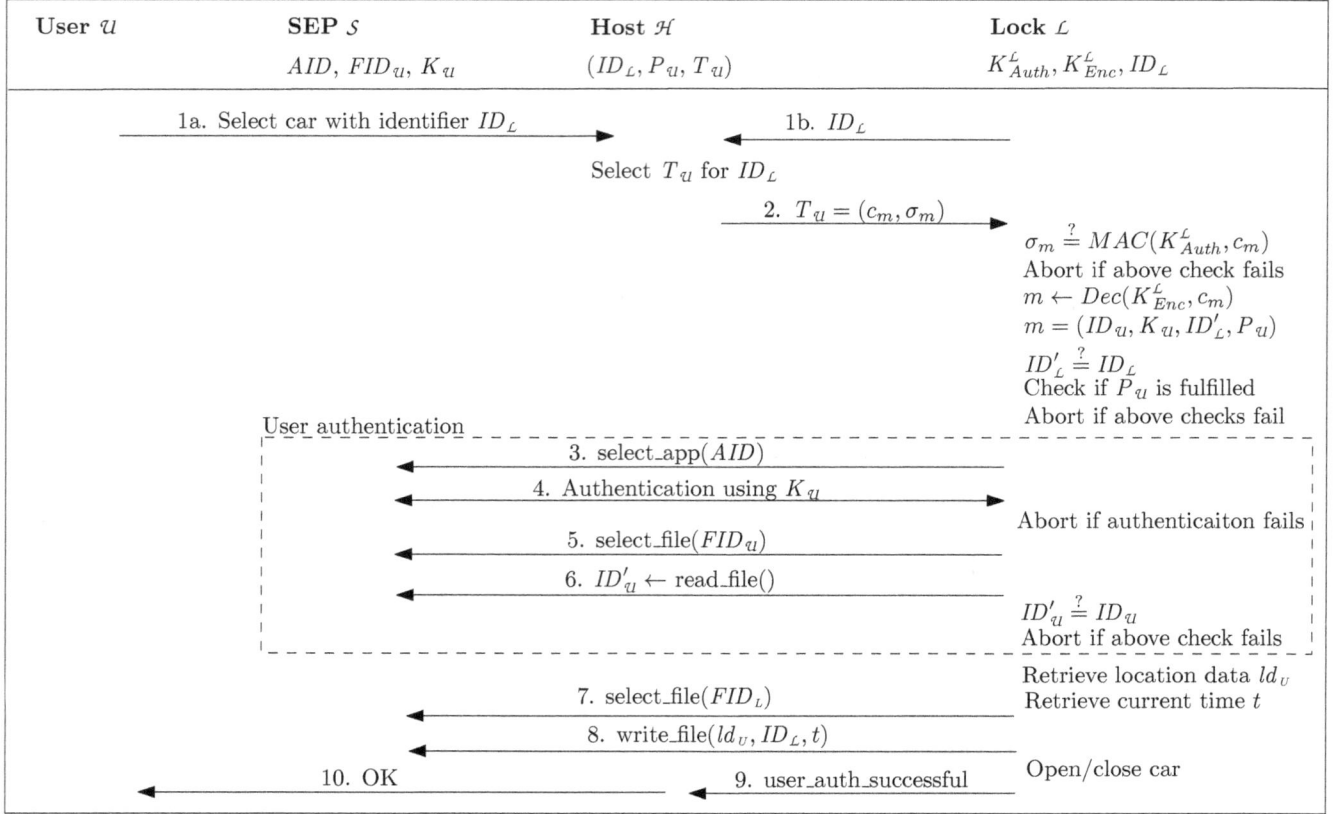

User $\mathcal{U}$	SEP $\mathcal{S}$	Host $\mathcal{H}$	Lock $\mathcal{L}$
	$AID, FID_{\mathcal{U}}, K_{\mathcal{U}}$	$(ID_L, P_{\mathcal{U}}, T_{\mathcal{U}})$	$K^L_{Auth}, K^L_{Enc}, ID_L$

1a. Select car with identifier $ID_L \longrightarrow$ $\longleftarrow$ 1b. ID_L

Select $T_{\mathcal{U}}$ for ID_L

2. $T_{\mathcal{U}} = (c_m, \sigma_m) \longrightarrow$

$\sigma_m \overset{?}{=} MAC(K^L_{Auth}, c_m)$
Abort if above check fails
$m \leftarrow Dec(K^L_{Enc}, c_m)$
$m = (ID_{\mathcal{U}}, K_{\mathcal{U}}, ID'_L, P_{\mathcal{U}})$
$ID'_L \overset{?}{=} ID_L$
Check if $P_{\mathcal{U}}$ is fulfilled
Abort if above checks fail

User authentication

3. select_app(AID)

4. Authentication using $K_{\mathcal{U}}$

Abort if authenticaiton fails

5. select_file($FID_{\mathcal{U}}$)

6. $ID'_{\mathcal{U}} \leftarrow$ read_file()

$ID'_{\mathcal{U}} \overset{?}{=} ID_{\mathcal{U}}$
Abort if above check fails

Retrieve location data ld_U
Retrieve current time t

7. select_file(FID_L)

8. write_file(ld_U, ID_L, t)

Open/close car

10. OK   9. user_auth_successful

Figure 4 – User Authentication Protocol

Depending on the underlying communication technology used for the communication between $\mathcal{L}$ and $\mathcal{H}$, it may have an active or a passive character. In particular, if BLE is used, the protocol is initiated by $\mathcal{U}$ who presses the respective button in the application, while the host infers identifier ID_L of the car to be booked based on $\mathcal{U}$'s input (step 1a). In case of NFC, however, the authentication is initiated by $\mathcal{L}$ which sends its identifier ID_L to the host as soon as the user taps car's NFC reader with the smartphone (step 1b).

Starting from step 2, protocols for NFC and BLE versions are identical: $\mathcal{H}$ fetches the corresponding access token $T_{\mathcal{U}} = (c_m, \sigma_m)$ from its memory and sends it to $\mathcal{L}$ (step 2). Upon receive, the token is verified by $\mathcal{L}$ as follows: First, a MAC is calculated over c_m using the key K^L_{Auth} and the result is compared with σ_m from the token. If verification succeeds, the cipher c_m is decrypted using K^L_{Enc} key. Furthermore, the lock checks if its identifier ID_L matches with the identifier ID'_L contained within the token and if the policy conditions $P_{\mathcal{U}}$ are satisfied. If all the checks pass, the lock initiates authentication with $\mathcal{U}$'s SEP $\mathcal{S}$ to ensure the possession of $K_{\mathcal{U}}$. In particular, $\mathcal{L}$ sends select_app request to $\mathcal{S}$ in order to select the car sharing application AID (step 3), then runs authentication protocol with the key $K_{\mathcal{U}}$ (step 4), selects file $FID_{\mathcal{U}}$ and reads user identifier $ID'_{\mathcal{U}}$ from it (steps 5-6). $ID'_{\mathcal{U}}$ read from the file is then compared with $ID_{\mathcal{U}}$ from the token, and if identical, the authentication is successful. Thereby $\mathcal{L}$ retrieves location information ld_L from $\mathcal{L}$'s GPS and writes it along with ID_L and the current time t into the file FID_L of $\mathcal{S}$ (steps 7-8). Finally, the car opens (resp. closes) and the authentication status is sent to $\mathcal{H}$ (step 9) and a feedback is provided to $\mathcal{U}$ (step 10).

3.1.5 Checkout

With the *checkout protocol* depicted in Figure 5 $\mathcal{U}$ finalizes sharing the car. Thereby, $\mathcal{C}$ retrieves the last location of the car from the user's platform, then updates the car list with the new location information and makes the respective car available again to other customers.

$\mathcal{U}$ initiates the checkout procedure by triggering $\mathcal{H}$ to send the user identifier $ID_{\mathcal{U}}$ and car identifier ID_L to $\mathcal{C}$ over the established TLS session (steps 1-3). In turn, $\mathcal{C}$ authenticates the user (step 4) by executing steps similar to steps 3-6 of the *user authentication* protocol. If successful, $\mathcal{C}$ selects the file FID_L on SEP (step 5) and retrieves location data ld_L of the car, its identifier ID'_L and the timestamp t via read_file operation (step 6). After ensuring that the car identifier retrieved from the file matches the one received from $\mathcal{H}$ at step 3, $\mathcal{C}$ stores location ld_L and time t for the respective car and deletes the token $T_{\mathcal{U}}$. $\mathcal{H}$ is then notified about the successful checkout (step 7), deletes also $T_{\mathcal{U}}$ and provides feedback to $\mathcal{U}$ (step 8).

Note that if the user has no online connection at the moment he stopped using the service, he can lock the car in offline mode by executing user authentiation protocol and run the checkout protocol later on whenever the online connection becomes available.

3.2 Design Choices and Deployment Options

Our platform security concept relies on two isolated environments on the client side, host $\mathcal{H}$ and SEP $\mathcal{S}$, which handle two authentication factors of the user in separation.

Design Choices To achieve greater interoperability across

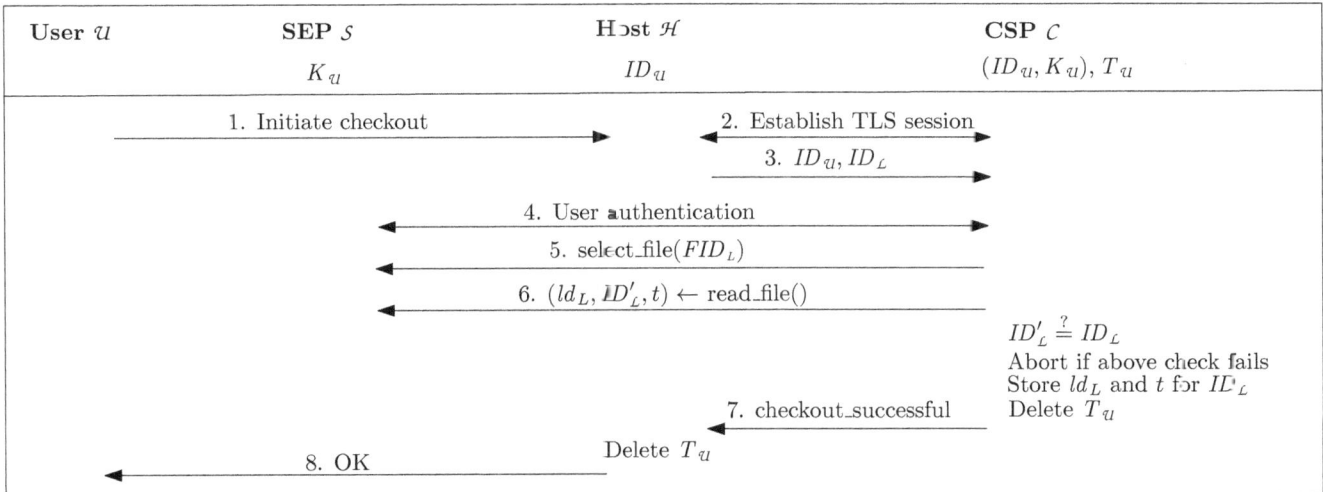

Figure 5 – Checkout Protocol

various mobile platforms, we opted to instantiate SEP $\mathcal{S}$ using the Java card environment, which is a well-standardized execution environment and therefore is widely supported on mobile platforms. This choice enables various deployment options ranging from embedded and removable secure elements (such as UICC-based and ASSD cards [15, 29]) to Java cards emulated in software. Furthermore, software-emulated Java cards can be deployed either on a mobile platform or even provided by external parties, e.g., by user-controlled wearable devices or cloud-based SE providers [30]. Moreover, Java cards can emulate cryptographic RFID cards (such as Mifare and Legic cards) by executing corresponding applets, which allows us to achieve compatibility to contactless RFID cards – the most commonly used authentication token in car sharing solutions, and to enable an additional deployment option based on a contactless smartcard.

Deployment Options Taken into account our security and functional requirements (cf. Section 2), we opt for the following three deployment options: (i) based on a Secure Element, (ii) a contactless smartcard, and (iii) emulated on user's smartwatch. All these options provide strong isolation between SEP $\mathcal{S}$ and host $\mathcal{H}$ and do not require online connection for their communication (and, hence, can achieve offline user authentication). These options can be supported by the car sharing provider simultaneously and be selected on per-user basis depending on capabilities of customer's hardware.

4. SECURITY ANALYSIS

In this section we provide informal security analysis of our solution by showing how the security requirements specified in Section 2.4 are fulfilled. The summary of our analysis is provided in Table 1 which indicates tolerance of various deployment options (cf. Section 3.2) to different adversary classes (cf. Section 2.3).

Well-established crypto. Our protocols rely only on well-established crypto primitives and algorithms. In particular, we use TLS in order to authenticate $\mathcal{C}$ to $\mathcal{H}$ and to protect their subsequent communication. TLS is widely used to secure client-server applications in the web and its security properties are widely studied and well understood. Further, communication with SEP $\mathcal{S}$ relies on standards ISO/IEC

Table 1 – Summary of the Security Analysis

Adversary Classes	Class 1	Class 2	Class 3
Secure Element	+	-	-
Contactless SmartCard	+	+	-
Smartwatch	+	+	+

7816-4/7816-8 developed for contactless identification cards. Moreover, software tokens generated by $\mathcal{C}$ are encrypted using Advanced Encryption Standard (AES), and authenticated using SHA-256 algorithm (cf. Section 5.2). These algorithms and standards represent the state of the art, and even if recognized as vulnerable in the future, they can easily be replaced with more secure versions.

Confidential credentials. Our system relies on the following credentials : (i) master key K_M and (ii) one-time password (OTP) used during user registration, (iii) user key K_u utilized to authenticate the user to CSP $\mathcal{C}$ during car booking, and to SEP $\mathcal{S}$ during checkout and authentication protocols[4], (iv) credentials K_{Enc}^L and K_{Auth}^L leveraged to encrypt and authenticate the token T_u during car booking and to decrypt and verify it during user authentication protocol.

Confidentiality of the master key K_M is ensured by keeping it secret from untrusted parties – it is only available to the SEP $\mathcal{S}$ and CSP $\mathcal{C}$. Similarly, confidentiality of keys K_{Enc}^L and K_{Auth}^L are ensured by making them available only to $\mathcal{C}$ and $\mathcal{L}$, which are trusted. The user key K_u is available to CSP $\mathcal{C}$ and to SEP $\mathcal{S}$ on client side – the end points which cannot be compromised in any of the adversary models. Further, K_u is always protected on transit, i.e., when transferred from $\mathcal{C}$ to SEP $\mathcal{S}$ during user registration, it is protected by the session key established after successful authentication of $\mathcal{C}$ with the master key K_M. Further, it is delivered from $\mathcal{C}$ to $\mathcal{L}$ in the encrypted and authenticated token. Whenever used for user authentication (in booking, checkout and authentication

---
[4]While our adversary model assumes that the car lock is trusted, one could consider approach to increase resilience to car lock compromise by using two distinct keys, e.g., K_u^1 and K_u^2, for authentication to CSP $\mathcal{C}$ and SEP $\mathcal{S}$, respectively.

protocols), it is utilized in a challenge-response manner and, unlike passwords, never leaves the platform.

The way to ensure confidentiality of OTP_u differs in different deployment options. For the deployment options 1 and 2, where SEP S is hosted either by the secure element or by the external contactless smartcard, the OTP_u is given to the host via the user interface (UI) provided by the operating system. Hence, this approach is secure against adversaries of classes 1 and 2, where the adversary is not allowed to compromise the host during user registration. For the third deployment option, where SEP SE is instantiated using user's smartwatch, OTP_u is provided to the (trusted) SEP S directly through the user interface available on the smartwatch instead of giving it to the host H, which makes this deployment option secure against adversaries of classes 1-3.

To resist password-related attacks, such as social engineering and phishing, our solution relies on authentication keys unknown to users, with the only exception of OTP which is used during registration process. To protect the OTP from uncareful users, we represent it in the form of the QR-code so that it is never shown to users in clear text.

Isolation. The approach to establish isolation between SEP S and the host H varies depending on the deployment approach. Specifically, our deployment option 1 (based on the secure element) provides hardware-based isolation, while deployment options 2 and 3 (a smart card and a smartwatch) provide isolation via physical separation. All these options are secure against attacks of all adversary classes.

Strong credentials. Our solution relies on strong cryptographic secrets which are randomly chosen, uniformly distributed and have sufficient length. In particular, we use AES-128 for symmetric and RSA-2048 for asymmetric operations (cf. Section 5 for more details). For OTP used in the user registration, we use a randomly generated 128 bit string. The string is encoded in a QR code which is to be scanned with the smartphone's (smartwatch's) camera during user registration.

Authorized SEP invocation. Generally, SEP invocation authorization requires secure user interface (UI) to indicate user's intention to invoke protected credentials. Because secure elements do not feature their own UI, in our first deployment option (using secure element) SEP invocation is authorized using UI provided by the operating system. Hence, this deployment option can only tolerate class 1 adversary, which assumes that the attacker cannot compromise the mobile host H at any time. In the second deployment option using a contactless card, the user needs to put a smartcard in proximity to the smartphone's NFC reader in order to enable communication between the host H and the SEP S. Hence, we use physical proximity of the card to the reader as indication that invocation is user-authorized. This approach is secure against adversary classes 1-3, as none of the adversaries can enforce proximity of the card to the NFC reader on behalf of the user.

In the third deployment option using a smartwatch, SEP invocation is confirmed using its own UI. Because such an authorization is provided directly to SEP, it is protected against adversaries of all classes.

To summarize, the first deployment option using secure element is secure against class 1 adversary, the second one based on contactless smartcard can tolerate 2nd adversarial class, while the third one utilizing a smartwatch can resist all three adversary classes.

5. PROTOTYPING AND EVALUATION

In this section, we briefly describe our car sharing prototype including hardware and software components and report performance evaluation results.

5.1 Prototype Hardware

For prototyping the mobile host we used Android smartphones Samsung S4 (GT-I9505) and Google Nexus 5 (LG D821) running Android 5.0 and 5.1 (Lollipop), respectively. For the first SE provider deployment option we equipped the S4 with an Giesecke & Devrient Mobile Security Card (MSC) [31] which acts as Secure Element and runs a DESFire applet. For the second deployment option using a contactless smartcard we utilized a Mifare DESFire EV1 smartcard. The third deployment alternative was instantiated using a Samsung Galaxy Gear SM-V700 smartwatch running Android 4.2 as an external SE provider.

The CSP C was hosted by a 64 bit Ubuntu Trusty Tahr (14.04.3 LTS) server running on a quadcore processor (Intel Xeon @ 3.5 GHz) with 16 GB of RAM.

To build a car lock prototype, we opted for a car key proxy approach which enabled compatibility with off-the-shelf cars. In particular, our car lock L is realized as telematics box with the car key fob inside[5], which offers a communication interface with the host H. L is locked inside the car and communicates wirelessly with the smartphone. Once the authentication is successful, L activates the servo motor to push the buttons on the key fob, which results in car opening.

We built the telematics box using Lego Midstorms NXT 2.0, which holds inside the following hardware components: (i) an Arduino Mega Board [33] with either an BLE or NFC shield [34, 35] attached, (ii) a TowerPro MG995 servo [36], (iii) power supply in form of a 9-volt battery for the board and a 6 V-battery (4 AA batteries) for the servo and (iv) the respective car's key. We made the corresponding wiring diagram, step-by-step building instructions for the Lego frame and the photo of the resulting prototype available in [37].

We used two private cars, BMW 118i and BMW X4 xDrive30d, to perform evaluation of our prototype. Both cars feature Go button which can be used to start ignition without using the actual key. This feature requires the car key fob to be inside the vehicle – the requirement which is fulfilled in our case, as the car key is locked inside the telematics box placed inside the car.

5.2 Prototype Software

As summarized in Table 2, our prototype software consists of four modules and includes 21296 LOC in total excluding comments, blank lines and code from the external libraries.

Primitives and Parameter Sizes. The MAC scheme (for token authentication) is implemented based on SHA-256 with a digest size of 256 bits. For the symmetric encryption scheme AES in Cipher Block Chaining (CBC) mode with random padding is used with a key length of 128 Bit. Also the one-time password used in the user registration is a 128 bit

---

[5]Note that many deployed car sharing solutions already lock car keys inside the vehicle (typically in a safe [32] which can be unlocked with the smartcard). All the associated risks are covered by insurances.

Table 2 – Software Modules.

Module	Language	Dependencies	LOC
App	Android	JCAndroid [38], GMaps [39], ZXing [40]	5966
CSP	Java, PHP, CSS	BCC API [41], MySQL Connector [42], ZXing [40], MyEdit [43], JSCal [44]	7501
Lock	C/C++	AVR Crypto Lib [45], Servo Lib [46], NFC Lib [47], BLE Lib [48]	4212
DESFire Applet	Java	DESFire Applet Base [49]	3617
Total LOC			**21296**

BCC: Bouncy Castle Crypto, GMaps: Google Maps

string. To realize communication with the SEP we followed DesFire EV1 standard [50] using AES encryption and CMAC for message authentication.

Host $\mathcal{H}$. Depending on the deployment of SEP, the smartphone should run at least Android 4.3 (alias Jelly Bean) with API level 18 to support the BLE service [51] for the "external emulation" deployment option or at least Android 4.4 (alias KitKat) with API level 19 to support the Host APDU Service [52] necessary for the "contactless smartcard" deployment variant.

The car sharing app is implemented as an Android applicationwhereas the core functionality that drives the respective protocols is implemented as a Software Development Kit (SDK). For the car search we used the Google Maps API [39] as an external map provider to display both the user's and respective cars' positions on a map screen.

Furthermore, to decode the OTP from the QR code during user registration we used the third party library ZXing [40].

Secure Element Provider $\mathcal{S}$. In order to achieve a general compatibility with the commonly deployed DESFire EV1 standard throughout our deployment options, we enhanced a third party implementation of DESFire applet [49] to support crypto primitives like AES and CMAC. The DESFire EV1 applet is then either hosted by the G&D MSC which is inserted into the smartphone for the first deployment option or hosted by the Android-based Java card emulator JCAndroid [38] running on the smartwatch for the third deployment option. Communication with the MSC is done via SEEK for Android's MSC SmartcardService [53] which includes an MSC interface to access the G&D card over special reads and writes to the file system – the approach which requires neither root privileges nor changes to system software.

Since communication with $\mathcal{S}$ is compliant with the DESFire EV1 standard, we could easily adapt our system to support the second deployment option which uses a real DESFire EV1 card as SE provider.

In all deployment approaches we wrapped DESFire's native commands [50] in ISO/IEC 7816 Application Protocol Data Unit (APDU) commands and transmitted them to the DESFire application where they are then further processed.

Car Sharing Provider $\mathcal{C}$. The CSP server is implemented in Java and uses the *Bouncy Castle Crypto API (v1 46)* [41] for cryptographic operations, e.g., encryption, decryption

or signing, as well as to establish the TLS communication with $\mathcal{H}$. Moreover, we used a Java-based *MySQL Connector (v5.1.18)* [42] to connect to the MySQL database (v5.5.46) running on the same platform and again the ZXing [40] library to encode the OTP to a QR code during user registration.

$\mathcal{C}$ further provides an administrative interface for the car sharing provider for displaying and managing the pool of cars and their status which uses the MyEdit [43] and JSCal [44] libraries to conveniently edit MySQL tables and utilize calender functionality.

Lock $\mathcal{L}$. Car lock software is implemented as an Arduino C/C++ application which depends on the *AVR Crypto Library* [45] and the libraries [47, 48] for NFC and BLE shield, respectively. Additionally, the servo shield library [46] is used to control the servo. For the local communication between the car lock and client's host both, BLE and NFC are supported. While BLE is more convenient for the user since he or she can open the car over a distance, NFC is provided for backwards compatibility to solely smartcard-based systems.

5.3 Performance Evaluation

We measured the time required to complete user authentication towards the car in each deployment variant. Measurements were taken 100 times and average values as well as standard deviation are reported.

The overall measurement path is divided into five intervals, where (i) Host2SE interval covers communication between the car sharing app running on the Host $\mathcal{H}$ and the SEP $\mathcal{S}$, (ii) Host2Lock interval corresponds to the communication between $\mathcal{H}$ and the Lock $\mathcal{L}$, and (iii) Lock2Car interval includes the time needed by the servo motor to press the respective key button on the car key fob and, additionally the actual wireless communication between car key and respective car. We depict these intervals in Figure 6.

There are two more intervals which are omitted in the figure for brevity: (iv) the accumulated time of computations taken on each platform and (v) the accumulated discovery time necessary to establish a (BLE or NFC) connection between $\mathcal{H}$ and $\mathcal{L}$, and $\mathcal{H}$ and $\mathcal{S}$, respectively. Thereby, computations are already included into measurements (i) (resp. (ii)) and thus are not additionally added up into the overall authentication time. The results are summarized in Table 3.

Intervals (iii) and (v) unfortunately cannot be influenced by our implementation. While (v) is induced by BLE/NFC discovery performed during connection establishment between smartphone and Lock $\mathcal{L}$, (iii) results from the Lock2Car communication, which is due to our key proxy approach and includes the whole time of the key-to-car authentication. In total, intervals (iii) and (v) sum up into a fixed time ranging from 1.01 to 1.57 s, depending on the deployment option.

The time intervals which can be influenced by our implementation are (i), (ii) and (iv), which contribute 1.87

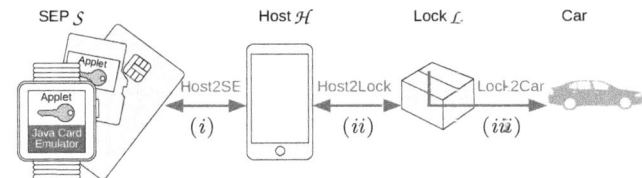

Figure 6 – Measurement Intervals.

to 3.82 s into a measurement path. This time can be improved through further optimizations and by other factors, e.g., through using newer hardware which could improve computation time.

To summarize, the overall authentication time ranges from 2.88 over 4.22 to 5.39 s depending on the deployment option. The longer intervals introduced by the ASSD and Smartwatch deployment option are induced almost entirely by the Host2SE communication and are caused by the limited capabilities of the respective hardware the SE is hosted on and/or the overhead introduced by the SEEK service. Besides hard- and software optimizations, the time required for user authentication can be further improved through integration of the car lock into the car and thus removing the interval (iii) from the measurement path.

Table 3 – User Authentication Performance

Values are given in seconds and show both average as well as standard deviation. Fixed time cannot be influenced by our implementation, while improvable time can be further optimized.

	ASSD Card	Smartcard	Smartwatch
(i) Host2SE	2,15 (±0,10)	0,13 (±0,01)	1,51 (±1,55)
(ii) Host2Lock	1,67 (±0,24)	1,74 (±0,08)	1,69 (±0,37)
(iii) Lock2Car	1,00	1,00	1,00
(iv) Computations	0,26 (±0,23)	0,13 (±0,04)	0,19 (±0,35)
(v) Discovery	0,57 (±0,01)	0,01 (±0,01)	0,02 (±0,02)
Fixed	1,57	1,01	1,02
Improvable	3,82	1,87	3,20
Total	5,39	2,88	4,22

6. RELATED WORK

The main body of the related work in the domain of car sharing is concentrated on such topics as process optimization, car relocation strategies and innovative competitive solutions, but typically does not cover security aspects of car sharing access control systems. For instance, Zhu et al. [54] propose a novel optimization approach to determine the depot location in station-based car sharing systems. Furthermore, in the context of the free-floating model, Formentin et al. [55] address the problem of future bookings by predicting the distance of the nearest available vehicle at a given future instant. Moreover, relocation strategies and algorithms in the free-floating business model are addressed in [56] and [57] that try to distribute cars in the business area according of the predicted booking demand. Finally, Shao et al. [58] present a dynamic car sharing system, that solves traffic congestion by reducing empty seats traveling. Thereby, the participants' smartphones continuously share driver's traveling information with a central server that analyzes and dynamically matches users with similar traveling needs.

The closest to our work is a car sharing solution [59] where the vehicle is equipped with an telematics box that is wired to the car's network and communicates on the one hand with the smartphone via short range wireless communication interfaces (NFC, Bluetooth) and on the other hand with a backend system via the Internet connection which opens the car. However, this solution is different from ours in that it requires Internet connection for cars and needs car modifications in order to attach the telematics box to the car's network.

In the industry sector, NFC-based immobilizer systems supporting car sharing were proposed independently by the automotive component suppliers Valeo [60] and Continen-

tal [61]. They rely on UICC-based SEs of local network operators for the protection of electronic car keys. In contrast, we aimed to avoid stakeholder-owned solutions, as those can only be used by customers of respective network operators. Furthermore, there are no details available in public domain on design and provided features, hence it is not possible to directly compare them with our solution regarding functionality and security. A virtual key service based on the Keyzee App [62] is powered by a Joint Venture of D'Ieteren and Continental, and is already in use by a car-sharing fleet in Monaco [63]. Similar to our telematics box, the Keyzee app works with an in the car integrated BLE box that connects with the smartphone in order to open or close the car [62]. However, in contrast to our solution this box intrusively interferes with the car's bus system [64] and thus invalidates the manufacturer's guarantees.

Related to our work are also smartphone-based access control solutions which were not initially developed for car sharing, but might be adapted to the new use case. With this respect, Arnosti et al. [65] introduced an access control solution which utilizes a microSD-based SE to store security-sensitive information on an NFC-enabled smartphone. However, it relies on an online connection to a central server and is only applicable to smartphones that have the corresponding hardware features (microSD slot). Further, Dmitrienko et al. [66] presented a generic access control system that enables the secure storage of access credentials for different resources on a smartphone. The system's generic approach makes it both applicable for digital and physical resources, like electronic resources or doors. If applied in a car sharing scenario, this solution would provide offline authentication, similar to ours. However, the solution relies on proprietary protocols which are not compatible to smartcards and does not provide various deployment options. Moreover, Abu-Saymeh et al. [67] proposed a framework that quantifies security of the mobile device based on user activities and behavior to secure NFC transactions. According to the identified security level, different authentication methods can be enforced by the system. In their work, authors took significantly different approach to address threats specific to mobile platforms and opted to detect suspicious activity rather than deploy a security architecture for protection of authentication secrets.

7. CONCLUSION

In this work, we propose a car sharing system for free-floating cars that overcomes shortcomings of current state-of-the-art solutions. It supports such new features as (i) offline authentication of users, (ii) compatibility to RFID cards – the commonly used authentication tokens in car sharing, and (iii) compatibility with legacy cars. Moreover, we present (iv) a mobile platform security concept for protection of electronic car keys on user's platforms which provides a flexibility to leverage various types of underlying hardware on client platforms and achieve best possible security given available hardware.

To summarize, our solution combines modern technologies in an intelligent way and, as a result, achieves new attractive features not available in state-of-the-art solutions which increase flexibility and security while preserving backward compatibility.

References

[1] Scott Le Vine, Alireza Zolfaghari, and John Polak. *Carsharing: Evolution, Challenges and Opportunities*. http://www.acea.be/publications/article/sag-report-22-carsharing-evolution-challenges-and-opportunities. 2014.

[2] Metro Vancouver. *The Metro Vancouver car share study – Technical report*. http://www.metrovancouver.org/services/regional-planning/PlanningPublications/MetroVancouverCarShareStudyTechnicalReport.pdf. 2014.

[3] Elliot Martin and Susan Shaheen. *The impact of carsharing on household vehicle ownership*. http://www.uctc.net/access/38/access38_carsharing_ownership.pdf. 2011.

[4] Susan Shaheen and Adam Cohen. *Innovative mobility carsharing outlook*. http://innovativemobility.org/wp-content/uploads/2016/02/Innovative-Mobility-Industry-Outlook_World-2016-Final.pdf. 2016.

[5] Shannon Bouton et al. *Urban mobility at a tipping point*. http://www.mckinsey.com/insights/sustainability/urban_mobility_at_a_tipping_point. 2015.

[6] bcs - Bundesverband CarSharing e.V. *Auf dem Weg zu einer neuen Mobilitätskultur - mehr als eine Million CarSharing-Nutzer*. http://carsharing.de/sites/default/files/uploads/ueber_den_bcs/pdf/bcs_jahresbericht_2014_final.pdf. 2014.

[7] car2go Deutschland GmbH. *How does it work?* https://www.car2go.com/en/berlin/how-does-car2go-work/. 2016.

[8] Which? The consumer interests company. *Mobile phone coverage map*. http://www.which.co.uk/reviews/mobile-phone-providers/article/mobile-phone-coverage-map.

[9] *Uber: Sign up to drive or tap and ride*. https://www.uber.com/.

[10] Alison Griswold. *Looks like Uber got hacked*. http://www.slate.com/blogs/moneybox/2015/02/27/uber_hack_50_000_drivers_may_be_affected_in_2014_security_breach.html. 2015.

[11] Joseph Cox. *Uber users say they're being charged for trips they didn't take*. http://motherboard.vice.com/read/uber-users-say-theyre-being-charged-for-trips-they-didnt-take 2015.

[12] Joseph Cox. *Stolen Uber customer accounts are for sale on the dark web for $1*. Motherboard. 2015.

[13] Tiago Alves and Don Felton. "TrustZone: Integrated hardware and software security". In: *Information Quarterly* (2004).

[14] Jerome Azema and Gilles Fayad. *M-Shield Mobile security technology: Making wireless secure*. http://focus.ti.com/pdfs/wtbu/ti_mshield_whitepaper.pdf. 2008.

[15] Certgate. *Certgate products. cgCard*. http://www.certgate.com/wp-content/uploads/2012/09/20131113_cgCard_Datasheet_EN.pdf. 2012.

[16] Jan-Erik Ekberg, Kari Kostiainen, and N Asokan. "The untapped potential of trusted execution environments on mobile devices". In: *IEEE Security & Privacy* (2014).

[17] Alexandra Dmitrienko et al. "Market-driven code provisioning to mobile secure hardware". In: *Financial Cryptography and Data Security*. 2015.

[18] Yvo Desmedt, Claude Goutier, and Samy Bengio. "Special uses and abuses of the Fiat-Shamir passport protocol". In: *Advances in Cryptology - CRYPTO. Annual International Cryptology Conference*. 1987.

[19] Nils Ole Tippenhauer and Srdjan Čapkun. "ID-based secure distance bounding and localization". In: *European Conference on Research in Computer Security*. 2009.

[20] Aanjhan Ranganathan, Boris Danev, and Srdjan Capkun. "Proximity verification for contactless access control and authentication systems". In: *Annual Computer Security Applications Conference*. 2015.

[21] G. P. Hancke. "Practical attacks on proximity identification systems". In: *IEEE Symposium on Security and Privacy*. 2006.

[22] Sebastiaan Indesteege et al. "A practical attack on KeeLoq". In: *Advances in Cryptology - EUROCRYPT. International Conference on the Theory and Applications of Cryptographic Techniques*. 2008.

[23] Markus Kasper et al. "Breaking KeeLoq in a flash: on extracting keys at lightning speed". In: *2nd International Conference on Cryptology in Africa (AFRICA-CRYPT'09)*. 2009.

[24] Aurélien Francillon, Boris Danev, and Srdjan Čapkun. "Relay attacks on passive keyless entry and start systems in modern cars". In: *Network and Distributed System Security Symposium (NDSS)*. 2011.

[25] Roel Verdult, Flavio Garcia, and Josep Balasch. "Gone in 360 seconds: Hijacking with Hitag2". In: *21st USENIX Security Symposium*. 2012.

[26] Virus News. *Teamwork: How the ZitMo Trojan bypasses online banking security*. http://www.kaspersky.com/about/news/virus/2011/Teamwork_How_the_ZitMo_Trojan_Bypasses_Online_Banking_Security. 2011.

[27] Cedric Ingrand. *French credit card hacker convicted*. http://www.theregister.co.uk/2000/02/26/french_credit_card_hacker_convicted/.

[28] M. Roland, J. Langer, and J. Scharinger. "Applying relay attacks to Google Wallet". In: *International Workshop on Near Field Communication (NFC)*. 2013.

[29] Press Release, Giesecke & Devrient. *G&D makes mobile terminal devices even more secure with new version of smart card in microSD format*. https://www.gi-de.com/en/about_g_d/press/press_releases/G&D-Makes-Mobile-Terminal-Devices-Secure-with-New-MicroSD-Card-g3592.jsp. 2010.

[30] Ramya Jayaram Masti, Claudio Marforio, and Srdjan Capkun. "An architecture for concurrent execution of secure environments in clouds". In: *ACM Cloud Computing Security Workshop*. 2013.

[31] Giesecke & Devrient Secure Flash Solutions. *The Mobile Security Card SE 1.0 offers increased security.* http://www.gd-sfs.com/the-mobile-security-card/mobile-security-card-se-1-0/.

[32] DB AG. *So einfach ist Flinkster.* https://www.flinkster.de/index.php?id=450&&f=3. 2016.

[33] Arduino MEGA 2560. *A microcontroller board based on the ATmega2560.* https://www.arduino.cc/en/Main/ArduinoBoardMega2560.

[34] BLE Shield. *A Bluetooth Low Energy extension for Arduino.* http://redbearlab.com/bleshield/.

[35] NFC Shield. *A NFC extension for Arduino.* http://www.seeedstudio.com/wiki/NFC_Shield_V2.0.

[36] ServoDatabase.com. *TowerPro MG995 servo.* http://www.servodatabase.com/servo/towerpro/mg995.

[37] crjp. *Car2X lock prototype.* https://github.com/crjp/car2x-lock-prototype. 2016.

[38] Technische Universität Darmstadt. *JCAndroid.* http://jcandroid.org/.

[39] Google Inc. *Google Maps Android API.* https://developers.google.com/maps/documentation/android-api/?hl=de.

[40] CZXing. *ZXing project.* https://github.com/zxing.

[41] Legion of the Bouncy Castle Inc. *The legion of the Bouncy Castle.* https://www.bouncycastle.org/index.html.

[42] Oracle Corporation. *MySQL connectors.* https://dev.mysql.com/downloads/connector/.

[43] Platon Group and Contributors. *Instant MySQL table editor and PHP code generator.* http://www.phpmyedit.org.

[44] Mihai Bazon. *DHTML calendar JSCal.* http://dynarch.com/mishoo/calendar.epl.

[45] Daniel Otte. *AVR-Crypto-Lib.* http://www.das-labor.org/wiki/AVR-Crypto-Lib/en.

[46] Michael Margolis. *Servo library for Arduino.* https://github.com/arduino/Arduino/tree/master/libraries/Servo.

[47] Adafruit Industries & Seeed Studio. *Adafruit-PN532.* https://github.com/adafruit/Adafruit-PN532/.

[48] RedBearLab. *RBL BLEShield.* https://github.com/RedBearLab/BLEShield/tree/master/Arduino/libraries/RBL_BLEShield.

[49] Jorge Prado Casanovas and Gauthier Vandamme. *Java Card Desfire emulation.* https://code.google.com/p/java-card-desfire-emulation/.

[50] NXP Semiconductors. *NXP.* Tech. rep. 2015.

[51] Google Inc. *BluetoothGattService.* http://developer.android.com/reference/android/bluetooth/BluetoothGattService.html.

[52] Google Inc. *Host APDU service.* http://developer.android.com/reference/android/nfc/cardemulation/HostApduService.html.

[53] Giesecke & Devrient GmbH. *Secure Element Evaluation Kit for the Android platform.* http://seek-for-android.github.io/.

[54] X. Zhu et al. "Optimization approach to depot location in car sharing systems with big data". In: *IEEE International Congress on Big Data.* 2015.

[55] S. Formentin, A.G. Bianchessi, and S.M. Savaresi. "On the prediction of future vehicle locations in free-floating car sharing systems". In: *Intelligent Vehicles Symposium (IV), 2015 IEEE.* 2015.

[56] Patrick Briest and Christoph Raupach. "The car sharing problem". In: *Annual ACM Symposium on Parallelism in Algorithms and Architectures.* 2011.

[57] S. Weikl and K. Bogenberger. "Relocation strategies and algorithms for free-floating car sharing systems". In: *2012 15th International IEEE Conference on Intelligent Transportation Systems.* 2012.

[58] Jianhua Shao and Chris Greenhalgh. "DC2S: a dynamic car sharing system". In: *ACM SIGSPATIAL International Workshop on Location Based Social Networks.* 2010.

[59] G. Alli et al. "Green Move: Towards next generation sustainable smartphone-based vehicle sharing". In: *Sustainable Internet and ICT for Sustainability (SustainIT), 2012.* 2012.

[60] NFC World. *Orange and Valeo demonstrate NFC car key concept.* http://www.nfcworld.com/2010/10/07/34592/orange-and-valeo-demonstrate-nfc-car-key-concept/. 2010.

[61] Telecom. *Deutsche Telekom and automotive supplier Continental demonstrated car keys.* http://www.telekom.com/innovation/connectedcar/81840. 2011.

[62] Keyzee. *Carsharing - Keyzee in a few words.* http://sandbox.keyzee.eu/en/autopartage/. 2012.

[63] Continental. *Virtual key service for car-sharing companies: D'Ieteren and Continental form joint venture.* http://www.continental-corporation.com/www/pressportal_com_en/themes/press_releases/3_automotive_group/interior/press_releases/pr_2015_03_12_jointventure_en.html.

[64] OTA Keys. *OTA keys. Easy to use, easy to install!* https://www.youtube.com/watch?v=9Iv9VFyErb0. 2015.

[65] Christof Arnosti, Dominik Gruntz, and Marco Hauri. "Secure physical access with NFC-enabled smartphones". In: *International Conference on Advances in Mobile Computing and Multimedia.* 2015.

[66] Alexandra Dmitrienko et al. "SmartTokens: Delegable Access Control with NFC-Enabled Smartphones". In: *International Conference on Trust and Trustworthy Computing.* 2012.

[67] D. Abu-Saymeh, D. e. D. I. Abou-Tair, and A. Zmily. "An application security framework for Near Field Communication". In: *IEEE International Conference on Trust, Security and Privacy in Computing and Communications.* 2013.

Identifying HTTPS-Protected Netflix Videos in Real-Time

Andrew Reed, Michael Kranch

Dept. of Electrical Engineering and Computer Science
United States Military Academy at West Point
West Point, New York, USA
{andrew.reed, michael.kranch}@usma.edu

ABSTRACT

After more than a year of research and development, Netflix recently upgraded their infrastructure to provide HTTPS encryption of video streams in order to protect the privacy of their viewers. Despite this upgrade, we demonstrate that it is possible to accurately identify Netflix videos from passive traffic capture in real-time with very limited hardware requirements. Specifically, we developed a system that can report the Netflix video being delivered by a TCP connection using only the information provided by TCP/IP headers.

To support our analysis, we created a fingerprint database comprised of 42,027 Netflix videos. Given this collection of fingerprints, we show that our system can differentiate between videos with greater than 99.99% accuracy. Moreover, when tested against 200 random 20-minute video streams, our system identified 99.5% of the videos with the majority of the identifications occurring less than two and a half minutes into the video stream.

Keywords

privacy; traffic analysis; dynamic adaptive streaming over HTTP; Netflix

1. INTRODUCTION

As the leading provider of streaming video content in a growing industry, Netflix accounts for more than a third of all traffic in North America [11]. In an effort to improve privacy for their viewers, Netflix recently upgraded their Open Connect infrastructure to provide HTTPS encryption of video content in addition to their ongoing use of HTTPS to protect login and billing information [9]. This new use of HTTPS prevents eavesdroppers from conducting deep packet inspection (DPI), i.e. inspecting HTTP headers and payload data, in order to determine the video that is being streamed. While an improvement, there is a previously disclosed traffic analysis attack that does not rely on DPI to identify the traffic's video content [10].

Since the addition of HTTPS adds a negligible amount of overhead to each video segment, we demonstrate that the aforementioned traffic analysis attack also works against HTTPS-

protected Netflix videos. We then improve upon the previous work by fully automating the fingerprint creation process, thereby enabling us to create an extensive collection of Netflix fingerprints which we then use to conduct a robust assessment of the attack. Finally, we developed a network appliance that can, in real-time, identify HTTPS-protected Netflix videos using IP and TCP headers obtained from passive capture of network traffic.

Our primary contributions are:

- A dataset that contains the fingerprints for 42,027 Netflix videos.

- An automated crawler that creates Netflix video fingerprints.

- A method to identify Netflix videos in real-time that does not rely on application-layer information.

We have made our code available at [4]. The rest of our paper is organized as follows. In Section 2, we describe the previous work that we leverage in our paper. In Section 3, we detail our method for obtaining Netflix fingerprints, and we explain our video identification pipeline in Section 4. Section 5 describes our testing and results. Related work is reviewed in Section 6 and suggestions for future work are outlined in Section 7.

2. BACKGROUND

Our paper builds upon the work conducted by Reed and Klimkowski in [10] concerning Netflix's vulnerability to traffic analysis. We also leverage two tools, adudump [14] and OpenWPM [3], in order to enhance our methods for traffic capture and fingerprint creation. We describe these in detail below.

2.1 DASH and VBR Information Leakage

For browser-based streaming, Netflix first encodes their videos as variable bitrate (VBR) MPEG4 and then streams them using Dynamic Adaptive Streaming over HTTP (DASH) via Microsoft Silverlight [6]. In [10], Reed and Klimkowski show that this combination of DASH and VBR can produce sequences of video segment sizes (i.e. fingerprints) that are unique for each video. They also show that this uniqueness is especially true for Netflix, as Netflix allows for a higher degree of bitrate variation when encoding content compared to other streaming services.

Furthermore, [10] demonstrates that these fingerprints can be created for each encoding of a video by parsing the metadata contained at the beginning of each MPEG4 video file. Within each encoding's metadata is a data structure, referred to as the segment index box (sidx), which lists the sizes for each video segment in the file [5] Since Silverlight needs this information to generate its HTTPS GET requests, the metadata portion of each MPEG4 is requested at the start of the stream. Thus, a researcher

CODASPY'17, March 22-24, 2017, Scottsdale, AZ, USA

ACM 978-1-4503-4523-1/17/03

DOI: http://dx.doi.org/10.1145/3029806.3029821

can build the fingerprints for a video by capturing the metadata transmitted during the first few seconds of a stream; it is not necessary to watch the entire video.

Reed and Klimkowski then outline an identification algorithm for Netflix videos from wireless traffic captures. This identification is done using a six-dimensional kd-tree [1] that stores every two-minute sliding window of each Netflix fingerprint. The six dimensions summarize the overall "size" and "shape" of each window in a way that supports range searches when attempting to identify a portion of a wireless capture. Each range search of the kd-tree produces a shortlist of candidate fingerprint windows that are then checked against the wireless capture using Pearson's product-moment correlation coefficient (r) to determine if a candidate matches the capture.

Although our paper is focused on the wired capture of traffic, Netflix's use of HTTPS presents challenges that are similar to those posed by WPA2-encrypted wireless traffic: (i) application layer data cannot be extracted and (ii) HTTP headers and TLS add overhead to each stream. As shown in Figure 1, however, this additional overhead is quite small and has an almost imperceptible effect on the overall fingerprint. Thus, we harness both the kd-tree and the fingerprint creation technique from [10].

2.2 adudump

adudump[1], presented in [14], is a command line program that uses TCP sequence and acknowledgement numbers to infer the sizes of the application data units (ADUs) transferred over each TCP connection. For example, the 171st video segment of *Home* (3830 kbps encoding) is 2,812,073 bytes. Thus, if a web browser were to send a GET request for this particular segment, adudump would report that the Netflix server responded with a 2,817,667-byte ADU. The additional bytes reported by adudump can be attributed to a 519-byte HTTP header and 5,075 bytes of TLS overhead. Had this same HTTPS response been captured by a program such as tcpdump, then the resultant capture would instead contain the 1,930 individual packets sent by the Netflix server to the browser.

When adudump is run on either a live network interface or a passive network tap, it will log the ADUs for each TCP connection in real-time and print them to stdout. Table 1 shows adudump's output when tracing a sample Netflix video stream. Notice that the direction alternates with every ADU and that all of the outbound ADUs, i.e. the HTTP GETs, are 755-756 bytes, whereas the inbound ADUs, i.e. the video segments, are of varying sizes. This behavior is a direct result of Netflix's use of DASH with VBR.

Since adudump is able to discern between the successive video segments of an HTTPS-protected Netflix stream and report their individual sizes in real-time, we leverage it to provide the input to our identification algorithm. Using adudump as input allows us to conduct kd-tree range searches in Section 4.3 that are tighter than those used in [10].

2.3 OpenWPM

Open Web-Privacy-Measurement (OpenWPM) is a framework for conducting large scale, repeatable web measurement studies [3]. At its core, OpenWPM is simply a Firefox browser that is automated using the Selenium automated browser [13]. For example, OpenWPM takes a list of URLs as input and will visit

---

[1] For access to adudump, please contact Dr. Jeff Terrell at info@altometrics.com.

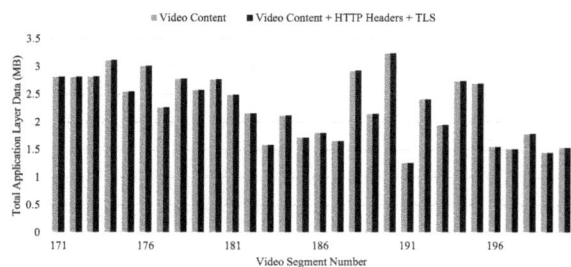

Figure 1: Netflix video overhead due to HTTP headers and TLS (*Home*, 3830 kbps encoding).

Table 1: adudump trace of *Home* (3830 kbps encoding). These are segments 171-180 from Figure 1.

Timestamp	Local PC	Dir.	Netflix Server	Size (B)
1471357732.77583	134.240.17.111.31177	>	198.45.63.167.443	756
1471357736.70148	134.240.17.111.31177	<	198.45.63.167.443	2817667
1471357736.77902	134.240.17.111.31177	>	198.45.63.167.443	756
1471357740.89304	134.240.17.111.31177	<	198.45.63.167.443	2816159
1471357740.97057	134.240.17.111.31177	>	198.45.63.167.443	756
1471357744.45695	134.240.17.111.31177	<	198.45.63.167.443	2822089
1471357744.53453	134.240.17.111.31177	>	198.45.63.167.443	756
1471357748.76052	134.240.17.111.31177	<	198.45.63.167.443	3117490
1471357748.83926	134.240.17.111.31177	>	198.45.63.167.443	756
1471357752.72718	134.240.17.111.31177	<	198.45.63.167.443	2548098
1471357752.80466	134.240.17.111.31177	>	198.45.63.167.443	756
1471357756.87447	134.240.17.111.31177	<	198.45.63.167.443	3014236
1471357756.95195	134.240.17.111.31177	>	198.45.63.167.443	756
1471357760.48768	134.240.17.111.31177	<	198.45.63.167.443	2263764
1471357760.56593	134.240.17.111.31177	>	198.45.63.167.443	756
1471357764.73616	134.240.17.111.31177	<	198.45.63.167.443	2782180
1471357764.81363	134.240.17.111.31177	>	198.45.63.167.443	755
1471357768.73659	134.240.17.111.31177	<	198.45.63.167.443	2577683
1471357768.81421	134.240.17.111.31177	>	198.45.63.167.443	756
1471357772.97218	134.240.17.111.31177	<	198.45.63.167.443	2770492

those sites one at a time until complete. OpenWPM also features several hooks for data collection including an in-band man-in-the-middle proxy [7]. When connecting to a site, the Firefox browser forwards all traffic directly through this proxy. This traffic includes HTTPS which is initially encrypted using the proxy's digital certificate. The proxy then makes an outbound connection to the destination server on behalf of the initial Firefox request. The end state is that all traffic, even encrypted traffic, can be recorded as unencrypted data by the proxy.

3. ACQUIRING FINGERPRINTS

In order to identify an unknown video's traffic in real-time, we first need a database of fingerprints of known video traffic to compare against our captured traffic. This database collection requires three steps: (i) identify a unique URL for every Netflix video, (ii) watch each video to generate the set of unique fingerprints, and (iii) organize these fingerprints in a searchable database.

3.1 Initial Crawl to Gather Video URLs

In order to generate these fingerprints, we first mapped every available video on Netflix. We took advantage of Netflix's search feature to do this mapping by conducting iterative search queries to enumerate all of Netflix's videos. This enumeration was done by visiting https://www.netflix.com/search/<value> where <value> was 'a', then 'b', etc. and then parsing the returned HTML into a list of videos with matching URLs. We also searched for videos by category using the list provided at [8].

These categories can be accessed by browsing to https://www.netflix.com/browse/genre/<id> where <id> is the category number (e.g. 6548 for Comedies, 4814 for Miniseries, and 75405 for Zombie Horror Movies).

Note that these initial URLs could be either (i) a direct link to a movie or (ii) a link to a TV show's episode list. Thus, it is necessary to then visit each scraped URL to determine if it is either a movie or an episode list. If it is the latter, then we send a series of JSON requests to Netflix to enumerate every episode's URL by season. In total, we scraped 42,169 unique video URLs using these two techniques in our two months of Netflix crawling.

3.2 Automated Viewing to Acquire Metadata

In order to record the fingerprints for each video, we made several modifications to the provided OpenWPM platform. This platform traditionally takes a list of URLs as input and then automates browsing to these URLs one at a time in succession as soon as the previous site is loaded. The term loaded includes all of the static and dynamic (JavaScript created) HTML objects in the Document Object Model (DOM) standard [2]. In Netflix's case, this loading meant that OpenWPM would download the DOM, consisting primarily of the background image and the Silverlight plugin but it would not wait for the video to play. As such, we modified OpenWPM to incorporate a delay in order to allow Silverlight time to request the metadata for a video's various encodings before moving on to the next URL.

We also added a module within the proxy to identify the sidx from the requested video's metadata, parse the sidx into fingerprints, and then save the resultant fingerprints into our database. Placing this module within the proxy allowed us to minimize the storage requirement of the database. In general, the proxy would save 7-10 different fingerprints for the various encoding rates within the first 20 seconds of each video stream (acquiring the high definition streams within the first 20 seconds is dependent upon network conditions). Using OpenWPM across four Macbook Pros, we were able to crawl all forty-two thousand URLs within four days.

3.3 Video Database Statistics

Table 2 lists various statistics for the fingerprints in our collection. In total, we collected 330,364 fingerprints from 42,027 videos (average of 7.86 fingerprints per video) which we store in a 1.37 GB text file. As shown, 92% of Netflix's catalog is comprised of television shows. Additionally, Figure 2 shows the breakdown of our database by bitrate. As mentioned in [10], Netflix has historically encoded their browser-based videos at 235, 375, 560, 750, 1050, 1750, 2350, and 3000 kbps, which correspond to the peaks in Figure 2. The emergence of bitrates that fall outside these historic ranges can likely be attributed to the fact that Netflix has recently made improvements in their encoding efficiency [11].

4. VIDEO IDENTIFICATION PIPELINE
4.1 Capturing and Filtering Traffic

Our pipeline begins with adudump, which is run on either a live network interface, a passive network tap (e.g. Endace DAG card), or a pcap file. As adudump logs ADUs, we use a filter to ignore all ADUs except those that are sent from a server on port 443. Additionally, we ignore ADUs that are smaller than 200,000 bytes, as these *could* be audio segments (audio segments are sometimes requested via the same TCP connection used for video segments).

Table 2: Database statistics.

Total Videos			Average Length (h:mm:ss)		
All	Movies	Shows	All	Movies	Shows
42,027	3,247	38,780	0:38:54	1:33:30	0:24:17

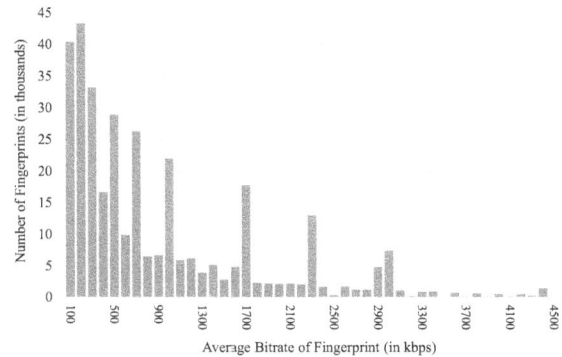

Figure 2: Number of fingerprints by average bitrate. The results are shown in 100 kbps bins. There are 146 fingerprints that exceed 4600 kbps that are not depicted.

4.2 Tracking TCP Connections

We track the following data for each HTTPS TCP connection:

- Timestamp of the first ADU
- Timestamp of the most recent ADU
- A deque containing the sizes of the 30 most recently logged ADUs
- A Boolean to track whether the HTTPS TCP connection has been identified as a Netflix video (initial value: False)
- The title of the video being streamed (initial value: blank)

Once a TCP connection's deque reaches 30 ADUs, and upon the receipt of each new ADU thereafter, we send the deque to the kd-tree for identification.

4.3 kd-Tree Search

Similar to [10], we create a 6D key for each 30-ADU window and conduct a range search of the kd-tree to retrieve a shortlist of potential matches. The ranges for each search are as follows:

- **1st Dimension Min** $= \frac{Total\ Received}{1.0019} - (30 * 525\ bytes)$
- **1st Dimension Max** $= \frac{Total\ Received}{1.0017} - (30 * 515\ bytes)$
- **2nd through 6th Dimension Min**: -0.0001
- **2nd through 6th Dimension Max**: +0.0001

Our 1st dimension ranges are based on these two observations of Netflix traffic:

- HTTP headers add ~520 bytes to each video segment.
- TLS overhead adds ~0.18% to the combined video content plus HTTP headers.

Our ranges for the 2nd through 6th dimensions are based on our observation that the additional overhead from HTTP headers and TLS has a minimal effect on the distribution of data throughout a given 30-ADU window. For instance, the data distributions for the two series shown in Figure 1 differ by no more than ±0.000013.

Once the range search returns a shortlist of candidates, we iterate through the shortlist and calculate Pearson's product-moment correlation coefficient (r) between each candidate and the 30-ADU window. If a candidate results in an $r \geq 0.9999$, then we report the candidate as a match and cease iterating through the shortlist.

Overall, our search of the kd-tree incorporates two changes to Reed and Klimkowski's algorithm. First, since adudump is able to delineate the data belonging to adjacent video segments, it is no longer necessary to identify and discard outliers, as done in the original algorithm's Stage 2. Second, we eliminated Stage 3 as it is now possible to identify a given Netflix stream from a single matching window (see Section 5.2).

4.4 Reporting Videos

If a match is found for a given 30-ADU window, then the *entire* HTTPS TCP connection is marked as "identified" and the video title is saved. It is possible to classify an entire TCP connection in this manner since it will not be reused for consecutive videos (e.g. if a Netflix account is configured to play the next episode automatically). Thus, it is no longer necessary to conduct queries for a TCP connection once it has been identified. That being said, one can determine if and when the Netflix player switches between quality levels by continuing to send updated deques to the kd-tree and logging the bitrate of each matched window. In Section 5.3.3, we refer to these as the *efficient mode* and the *exhaustive mode*, respectively.

Once a TCP connection has been inactive for a period of time (we use a 2-minute period), we delete its data from the list of tracked connections. As the connection is being deleted, we check to see if it has been flagged as a Netflix video. If it has, then we report the TCP connection's 4-tuple, the timestamps of the first and last ADUs, and the video title.

5. EVALUATION

We implemented our algorithm using a client-server architecture.

- **Server**: The server, which we implemented in Java, is tasked with performing the identification steps outlined in Section 4.3.

- **Client**: The client runs as a Linux command pipeline consisting of adudump and two Python scripts: (i) a script to filter the output from adudump and (ii) a script to perform the tasks outlined in Sections 4.2 and 4.4.

5.1 Server Specifications

Table 3 lists the hardware and software that we used for the server. Given our configuration, the server requires 15 minutes to load the kd-tree with all of the Netflix video fingerprints. Once loaded, the database contains 184,248,110 individual windows.

5.2 Assessing Video Uniqueness

In order to assess the uniqueness of the Netflix fingerprints, we conducted the same search described in Section 4.3 for each window in the database and tallied the number of matches returned for each. As shown in Figure 3, 184,246,173 windows return a single result, i.e. more than 99.9989% of all windows are unique.

Interestingly, 126 windows do not even return themselves. Upon further inspection, we found that these windows stem from two movies, *2001: A Space Odyssey* and *The Gospel Road: A Story of Jesus*, both of which have lengthy periods where the screen is completely dark, thereby resulting in "flat" windows that consist of 30 identically-sized segments. Since Pearson's r cannot be

Table 3: Identification Server Specifications.

Operating System	Linux Mint 17.3 MATE
Processors	2x Quad-Core Intel Xeon 2.0 GHz
Memory	32 GB
Manufacture Date	November 2007
Java Version	1.8
Java Heap Allocation	30 GB

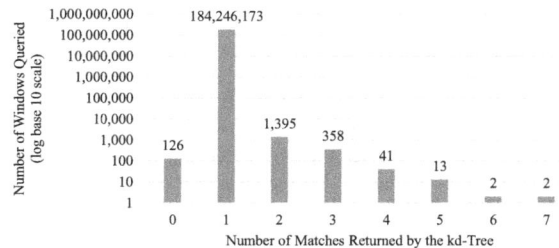

Figure 3: Number of matches returned by the kd-Tree when conducting a search for each window.

computed for a single point, these flat windows cannot be correlated.

Thus, there remains 1,811 windows that return erroneous results, ranging from 1 to 6 mistaken matches. More specifically, these 1,811 windows produce 1,154 unique *pairings* where two windows cannot be distinguished by our algorithm. Of these pairings, 1,053 consist of two windows that are actually the same timeframe of the same video, but from different bitrates. From the remaining 101 pairings (Appendix A), 73 stem from identical footage that exists in multiple videos (e.g. the end credits of *Masha and the Bear* episodes). Only 28 pairings, comprised of 25 distinct windows, represent confusion between unrelated footage. These windows are problematic because, although they primarily consist of complete darkness, they contain enough variation to support the calculation of Pearson's r (i.e. they do not result in a single point, as do the "flat" windows mentioned previously).

In sum, of 184,248,110 total windows:

- 184,246,173 (99.9989%) windows are unique

- 1,786 (0.00097%) windows have the potential to match either (i) the same window from another bitrate or (ii) the same footage in a related video

- 126 (0.000068%) windows are unsearchable due to complete darkness

- 25 (0.000014%) windows have the potential to match an unrelated window due to mostly dark scenes

5.3 Full System Assessment

5.3.1 Experimental Design

For the full system assessment, we first produced a list of 100 randomly-selected Netflix videos that was then given to OpenWPM/Firefox running on two Macbook Pros. Both Macbooks streamed the entire list, with each video being "watched" for 20 minutes before switching to the next video. We chose this duration based on our finding from Table 2 that the vast majority of Netflix content consists of television shows. Considering that (i) television shows that air in 30-minute time slots typically contain 22-24 minutes of video, and that (ii) the Netflix player will skip a show's introduction if an account is set to "auto-play" the next episode, a duration of 20 minutes per video approximates the amount of traffic generated by a viewer watching a half-hour show.

As the videos were being streamed, we used adudump to capture all network traffic traversing the Internet-facing link shared by the two Macbooks. Once complete, we then used our program to process the adudump capture. As mentioned in Section 4.4, our program displays the (i) video title, (ii) start time, and (iii) end time for each *TCP connection* that produces at least one window that matches a fingerprint. For testing purposes, we also configured our program to display the time at which the first window was identified for a given TCP connection[2].

5.3.2 Results

Our full results are listed in Appendix B. When referencing individual video results, the letter indicates which laptop (A or B) generated the stream and the number indicates which video (1-100) was "watched." To summarize our results:

- Our program identified 199 of 200 video streams (99.5%).

- Video B57 generated two, back-to-back TCP connections. Since these connections were separated by only eight seconds, we combined them as a single report. The remaining 198 identifications consisted of a single TCP connection.

- As shown in Figure 4, 51% of the videos were identified before 2:30 had elapsed.

- On average, initial identifications occurred at 3:55, with the earliest occurring at 2:00 and the latest occurring at 12:04.

- Excluding video B85, our program identified an average of 19:19 of each video, with a minimum of 14:39 and a maximum of 20:00 (i.e. the full video).

- Our program identified the full video in 124 instances (62%).

- Across a total of 240,000 seconds' worth of "viewing activity," our program identified 230,698 seconds (96.12%).

Tests such as B63 highlight the effectiveness of our technique. In B63, our program was not able to identify the video until 12:04 into the stream. Despite B63's late identification, our program was still able to identify the full 20-minute timeframe since the underlying TCP connection lasted for the entire duration of the stream.

5.3.3 System Capacity

In addition to assessing our program's accuracy, we also tested our system to estimate the maximum number of concurrent Netflix streams that it can support in real-time. This assessment was done for both modes of operation: *exhaustive* and *efficient*. As mentioned in Section 4.4, in *exhaustive mode* our program will continue to send windows to the kd-tree even after a TCP connection has been identified, as opposed to *efficient mode* which does not send windows for identified TCP connections.

---

[2] In order for our program to successfully identify a video, the Netflix stream must stabilize at a quality level for 30 consecutive video segments. If bandwidth conditions are unstable at the beginning of a stream, then our program will not be able to make an early identification.

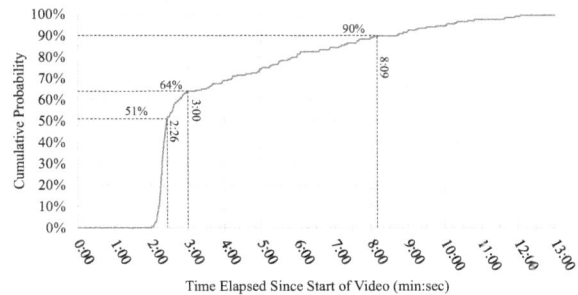

Figure 4: Cumulative probability of identifying a video before a specified amount of time has elapsed.

To begin, we ran our program's *exhaustive mode* 500 times using the adudump capture from Section 5.3.1 and averaged its execution time, yielding an average of 6.56 seconds per iteration. Given this capture, *exhaustive mode* conducted 57,679 window searches per iteration. Thus, our system identified 8,792 windows per second. Furthermore, since a Netflix stream will only generate a new window search every four seconds (i.e. once per video segment received), we estimate that *exhaustive mode* is capable of supporting approximately 35,000 concurrent Netflix streams on our system.

We then ran the same test for *efficient mode*, arriving at an average of 2.48 seconds per iteration, with 12,121 window searches per iteration, i.e. 2.65 times faster than *exhaustive mode* with 21% the number of window searches being conducted. This reduction in the number of windows searches stems from the fact that the Netflix videos in our capture are first identified at 3:55 into the video (on average), which is 19.6% into the 20 minute stream. Overall, we estimate that *efficient mode* is capable of supporting over 92,000 concurrent Netflix streams under similar network conditions. In scenarios where the available bandwidth is constantly fluctuating, Netflix streams might have difficulty finding a stable quality level, thereby reducing *efficient mode's* ability to identify a video early in the stream. Conversely, well-provisioned networks might allow for earlier identifications, thereby increasing *efficient mode's* performance.

6. RELATED WORK

In [16], Zhang et al. provide an overview of the state-of-the-art in traffic classification and state that modern approaches generally rely on (i) machine learning to (ii) identify the applications that are present on a network. Our work differs from these techniques as we neither employ machine learning nor attempt to identify a broad set of network applications. Instead, we focus on identifying the *content* delivered by a *single service*.

Thus, our work is most similar to techniques that exploit the potential for VBR encoding to leak the contents of a particular flow, despite the use of encryption. For instance, earlier work in our domain by Saponas et al. [12] demonstrated that Slingbox video streams could be identified using throughput analysis and a Discrete Fourier Transform-based attack. In another display of VBR data leakage, White et al. [15] demonstrated an attack that reconstructs the transcript of an encrypted VoIP call from its packet sizes.

7. CONCLUSION AND FUTURE WORK

In this paper, we have shown that Netflix's recent upgrade to HTTPS does little to protect the privacy of their users against a passive traffic analysis attack, as we were able to identify 99.5%

of the videos in our tests. Additionally, we presented an automated method to amass Netflix video fingerprints and we conducted a thorough analysis of our database to assess the uniqueness of each fingerprint. We were able to implement our identification pipeline as a program that runs in real-time on limited hardware.

Our work reiterates warnings from previous researchers that VBR encoding can leak details about the underlying content, thereby undermining efforts to protect privacy with encryption. This vulnerability is magnified for DASH streams, as the sequential HTTP GETs generated by DASH correspond to video segment data that can be found in an MPEG4's metadata. As streaming video continues to grow, we believe that streaming services and network researchers should work to solve the privacy issues inherent to DASH and VBR encoding.

To that end, we believe that Netflix could defend against passive traffic analysis by ensuring that the byte-range portion of the HTTP GETs sent by the browser do not perfectly align with individual video segment boundaries. For instance, the browser could average the size of several consecutive segments and send HTTP GETs for this average size. As an alternative approach, the browser could randomly combine consecutive segments and send HTTP GETs for the combined video data. Designing obfuscation techniques for VBR DASH streams that do not degrade video quality remains a potential area for future research.

8. REFERENCES

[1] J. L. Bentley. Multidimensional Binary Search Trees Used for Associative Searching. In *Communications of the ACM*, September 1975.

[2] DOM Standard, https://dom.spec.whatwg.org/.

[3] S. Englehardt and A. Narayanan. Online Tracking: A 1-Million-Site Measurement and Analysis. In *ACM Conference on Computer and Communications Security*, 2016.

[4] GitHub Repository, https://github.com/andrewreed.

[5] ISO/IEC 14496-12:2012, http://standards.iso.org/ittf/ PubliclyAvailableStandards/c061988_ISO_IEC_14496-12_2012.zip.

[6] Microsoft Silverlight, https://www.microsoft.com/silverlight.

[7] mitmproxy, https://mitmproxy.org.

[8] Netflix has tons of hidden categories — here's how to see them, http://mashable.com/2016/01/11/netflix-search-codes.

[9] The Netflix Tech Blog: Protecting Netflix Viewing Privacy at Scale, http://techblog.netflix.com/2016/08/protecting-netflix-viewing-privacy-at.html.

[10] A. Reed and B. Klimkowski. Leaky Streams: Identifying Variable Bitrate DASH Videos Streamed over Encrypted 802.11n Connections. In *IEEE Consumer Communications and Networking Conference*, 2016.

[11] Sandvine Report: Netflix's Encoding Optimizations Result In North American Traffic Share Decline, https://www.sandvine.com/pr/2016/6/22/sandvine-report-netflix-encoding-optimizations-result-in-north-american-traffic-share-decline.html.

[12] T. S. Saponas, J. Lester, C. Hartung, S. Agarwal, and T. Kohno. Devices that Tell on You: Privacy Trends in Consumer Ubiquitous Computing. In *USENIX Security Symposium*, 2007.

[13] Selenium, http://www.seleniumhq.org.

[14] J. Terrell, K. Jeffay, F. D. Smith, J. Gogan, and J. Keller. Passive, Streaming Inference of TCP Connection Structure for Network Server Management. In *IEEE International Traffic Monitoring and Analysis Workshop*, 2009.

[15] A. White, A. Matthews, K. Snow, and F. Monrose. Phonotactic Reconstruction of Encrypted VoIP Conversations: Hookt on fon-iks. In *IEEE Symposium on Security and Privacy*, 2011.

[16] J. Zhang, X. Chen, Y. Xiang, W. Zhou, and J. Wu. Robust Network Traffic Classification. In *IEEE/ACM Transactions on Networking*, August 2015.

APPENDIX

A. Incorrect Pairings.

Shaded pairings denote identical footage.

Video 1			Video 2			
Title	Average Bitrate (kbps)	Starting Segment	Title	Average Bitrate (kbps)	Starting Segment	Reason for Confusion
2001: A Space Odyssey	119	1	The Gospel Road: A Story of Jesus	235	1216	Video 1 begins with several minutes of darkness / Video 2 ends with several minutes of darkness
2001: A Space Odyssey	119	1	The Gospel Road: A Story of Jesus	371	1216	Video 1 begins with several minutes of darkness / Video 2 ends with several minutes of darkness
2001: A Space Odyssey	119	1316	The Agony and the Ecstasy	235	916	Both videos have an intermission consisting of darkness
2001: A Space Odyssey	119	1316	The Agony and the Ecstasy	371	916	Both videos have an intermission consisting of darkness
2001: A Space Odyssey	119	2188	The Agony and the Ecstasy	235	2053	Both videos end with several minutes of darkness
2001: A Space Odyssey	119	2188	The Agony and the Ecstasy	371	2053	Both videos end with several minutes of darkness
2001: A Space Odyssey	119	2189	The Agony and the Ecstasy	235	2054	Both videos end with several minutes of darkness
2001: A Space Odyssey	119	2189	The Agony and the Ecstasy	371	2054	Both videos end with several minutes of darkness
2001: A Space Odyssey	119	2190	The Agony and the Ecstasy	235	2055	Both videos end with several minutes of darkness
2001: A Space Odyssey	119	2190	The Agony and the Ecstasy	371	2055	Both videos end with several minutes of darkness
2001: A Space Odyssey	165	1	The Gospel Road: A Story of Jesus	235	1216	Video 1 begins with several minutes of darkness / Video 2 ends with several minutes of darkness
2001: A Space Odyssey	165	1	The Gospel Road: A Story of Jesus	371	1216	Video 1 begins with several minutes of darkness / Video 2 ends with several minutes of darkness
2001: A Space Odyssey	165	1	The Gospel Road: A Story of Jesus	551	1216	Video 1 begins with several minutes of darkness / Video 2 ends with several minutes of darkness
2001: A Space Odyssey	165	1	The Gospel Road: A Story of Jesus	736	1216	Video 1 begins with several minutes of darkness / Video 2 ends with several minutes of darkness
2001: A Space Odyssey	240	1	The Gospel Road: A Story of Jesus	371	1216	Video 1 begins with several minutes of darkness / Video 2 ends with several minutes of darkness
2001: A Space Odyssey	240	1	The Gospel Road: A Story of Jesus	551	1216	Video 1 begins with several minutes of darkness / Video 2 ends with several minutes of darkness
2001: A Space Odyssey	240	1	The Gospel Road: A Story of Jesus	736	1216	Video 1 begins with several minutes of darkness / Video 2 ends with several minutes of darkness
2001: A Space Odyssey	240	1316	The Agony and the Ecstasy	551	916	Both videos have an intermission consisting of darkness
2001: A Space Odyssey	240	1316	The Agony and the Ecstasy	736	916	Both videos have an intermission consisting of darkness
2001: A Space Odyssey	380	1	The Gospel Road: A Story of Jesus	1029	1216	Video 1 begins with several minutes of darkness / Video 2 ends with several minutes of darkness
2001: A Space Odyssey	380	1	The Gospel Road: A Story of Jesus	1710	1216	Video 1 begins with several minutes of darkness / Video 2 ends with several minutes of darkness
2001: A Space Odyssey	380	1316	The Agony and the Ecstasy	1028	916	Both videos have an intermission consisting of darkness
2001: A Space Odyssey	530	1	The Gospel Road: A Story of Jesus	1029	1216	Video 1 begins with several minutes of darkness / Video 2 ends with several minutes of darkness
2001: A Space Odyssey	530	1	The Gospel Road: A Story of Jesus	1710	1216	Video 1 begins with several minutes of darkness / Video 2 ends with several minutes of darkness
2001: A Space Odyssey	530	1316	The Agony and the Ecstasy	1028	916	Both videos have an intermission consisting of darkness
2001: A Space Odyssey	856	1	The Gospel Road: A Story of Jesus	1029	1216	Video 1 begins with several minutes of darkness / Video 2 ends with several minutes of darkness
2001: A Space Odyssey	856	1	The Gospel Road: A Story of Jesus	1710	1216	Video 1 begins with several minutes of darkness / Video 2 ends with several minutes of darkness
2001: A Space Odyssey	856	1316	The Agony and the Ecstasy	1028	916	Both videos have an intermission consisting of darkness
Las mágicas historias de Plim Plim/Season 1 : Episode 1	1726	360	The Magical Tales of Plim Plim/Season 1 : Episode 1	1726	360	Both videos contain identical footage (Spanish vs. English dialogue)
Masha and the Bear/Season 1 : Episode 1	1576	312	Masha and the Bear/Season 1 : Episode 2	1634	302	Identical end credits
Masha and the Bear/Season 1 : Episode 1	1576	316	Masha and the Bear/Season 1 : Episode 5	1335	309	Identical end credits
Masha and the Bear/Season 1 : Episode 1	1576	317	Masha and the Bear/Season 1 : Episode 5	1335	310	Identical end credits
Masha and the Bear/Season 1 : Episode 1	1576	318	Masha and the Bear/Season 1 : Episode 2	1634	308	Identical end credits
Masha and the Bear/Season 1 : Episode 1	1576	324	Masha and the Bear/Season 1 : Episode 2	1634	314	Identical end credits
Masha and the Bear/Season 1 : Episode 1	1576	326	Masha and the Bear/Season 1 : Episode 5	1335	319	Identical end credits
Masha and the Bear/Season 1 : Episode 1	2140	317	Masha and the Bear/Season 1 : Episode 5	2082	310	Identical end credits
Masha and the Bear/Season 1 : Episode 2	1634	304	Masha and the Bear/Season 1 : Episode 5	1335	307	Identical end credits
Masha and the Bear/Season 1 : Episode 2	306	302	Masha and the Bear/Season 1 : Episode 5	303	305	Identical end credits
Masha and the Bear/Season 1 : Episode 2	306	303	Masha and the Bear/Season 1 : Episode 5	303	306	Identical end credits
Masha and the Bear/Season 1 : Episode 2	306	304	Masha and the Bear/Season 1 : Episode 5	303	307	Identical end credits
Masha and the Bear/Season 1 : Episode 2	306	305	Masha and the Bear/Season 1 : Episode 5	303	308	Identical end credits
Masha and the Bear/Season 1 : Episode 2	306	306	Masha and the Bear/Season 1 : Episode 5	303	309	Identical end credits
Masha and the Bear/Season 1 : Episode 2	306	307	Masha and the Bear/Season 1 : Episode 5	303	310	Identical end credits
Masha and the Bear/Season 1 : Episode 2	306	308	Masha and the Bear/Season 1 : Episode 5	303	311	Identical end credits
Masha and the Bear/Season 1 : Episode 2	306	309	Masha and the Bear/Season 1 : Episode 5	303	312	Identical end credits
Masha and the Bear/Season 1 : Episode 2	306	310	Masha and the Bear/Season 1 : Episode 5	303	313	Identical end credits
Masha and the Bear/Season 1 : Episode 2	306	311	Masha and the Bear/Season 1 : Episode 5	303	314	Identical end credits
Masha and the Bear/Season 1 : Episode 2	306	312	Masha and the Bear/Season 1 : Episode 5	303	315	Identical end credits
Masha and the Bear/Season 1 : Episode 2	306	313	Masha and the Bear/Season 1 : Episode 5	303	316	Identical end credits
Masha and the Bear/Season 1 : Episode 2	306	314	Masha and the Bear/Season 1 : Episode 5	303	317	Identical end credits
Masha and the Bear/Season 1 : Episode 2	306	315	Masha and the Bear/Season 1 : Episode 5	303	318	Identical end credits
Masha and the Bear/Season 1 : Episode 2	306	316	Masha and the Bear/Season 1 : Episode 5	303	319	Identical end credits
Masha and the Bear/Season 1 : Episode 2	306	317	Masha and the Bear/Season 1 : Episode 5	303	320	Identical end credits
Masha and the Bear/Season 1 : Episode 3	3098	317	Masha and the Bear/Season 1 : Episode 5	2854	317	Identical end credits
Masha and the Bear/Season 1 : Episode 3	3098	318	Masha and the Bear/Season 1 : Episode 5	2854	318	Identical end credits
Masha and the Bear/Season 1 : Episode 4	357	307	Masha and the Bear/Season 1 : Episode 6	357	309	Identical end credits
Masha and the Bear/Season 1 : Episode 4	357	310	Masha and the Bear/Season 1 : Episode 9	356	312	Identical end credits
Masha and the Bear/Season 1 : Episode 4	573	314	Masha and the Bear/Season 1 : Episode 6	574	316	Identical end credits
Masha and the Bear/Season 1 : Episode 4	573	317	Masha and the Bear/Season 1 : Episode 6	574	319	Identical end credits
Masha and the Bear/Season 1 : Episode 6	1319	306	Masha and the Bear/Season 1 : Episode 9	1191	306	Identical end credits
Masha and the Bear/Season 1 : Episode 6	1319	307	Masha and the Bear/Season 1 : Episode 9	1191	307	Identical end credits
Masha and the Bear/Season 1 : Episode 6	1319	308	Masha and the Bear/Season 1 : Episode 9	1191	308	Identical end credits
Masha and the Bear/Season 1 : Episode 6	1319	309	Masha and the Bear/Season 1 : Episode 9	1191	309	Identical end credits
Masha and the Bear/Season 1 : Episode 6	1319	312	Masha and the Bear/Season 1 : Episode 9	1191	312	Identical end credits
Masha and the Bear/Season 1 : Episode 6	1319	313	Masha and the Bear/Season 1 : Episode 9	1191	313	Identical end credits
Masha and the Bear/Season 1 : Episode 6	1319	314	Masha and the Bear/Season 1 : Episode 9	1191	314	Identical end credits
Masha and the Bear/Season 1 : Episode 6	1319	315	Masha and the Bear/Season 1 : Episode 9	1191	315	Identical end credits
Masha and the Bear/Season 1 : Episode 6	1865	308	Masha and the Bear/Season 1 : Episode 7	1862	307	Identical end credits
Masha and the Bear/Season 1 : Episode 6	1865	309	Masha and the Bear/Season 1 : Episode 7	1862	308	Identical end credits
Masha and the Bear/Season 1 : Episode 6	2686	307	Masha and the Bear/Season 1 : Episode 9	2660	307	Identical end credits
Masha and the Bear/Season 1 : Episode 6	2686	308	Masha and the Bear/Season 1 : Episode 9	2660	308	Identical end credits
Masha and the Bear/Season 1 : Episode 6	2686	309	Masha and the Bear/Season 1 : Episode 9	2660	309	Identical end credits
Masha and the Bear/Season 1 : Episode 6	2686	313	Masha and the Bear/Season 1 : Episode 9	2660	313	Identical end credits
Masha and the Bear/Season 1 : Episode 6	2686	314	Masha and the Bear/Season 1 : Episode 9	2660	314	Identical end credits
Masha and the Bear/Season 1 : Episode 6	2686	315	Masha and the Bear/Season 1 : Episode 9	2660	315	Identical end credits
Masha and the Bear/Season 1 : Episode 6	2686	319	Masha and the Bear/Season 1 : Episode 9	2660	319	Identical end credits
Masha and the Bear/Season 1 : Episode 6	2686	320	Masha and the Bear/Season 1 : Episode 9	2660	320	Identical end credits
Masha and the Bear/Season 1 : Episode 6	3886	304	Masha and the Bear/Season 1 : Episode 9	3846	304	Identical end credits
Masha and the Bear/Season 1 : Episode 6	3886	305	Masha and the Bear/Season 1 : Episode 9	3846	305	Identical end credits
Masha and the Bear/Season 1 : Episode 6	3886	306	Masha and the Bear/Season 1 : Episode 9	3846	306	Identical end credits
Masha and the Bear/Season 1 : Episode 6	3886	307	Masha and the Bear/Season 1 : Episode 9	3846	307	Identical end credits
Masha and the Bear/Season 1 : Episode 6	3886	308	Masha and the Bear/Season 1 : Episode 9	3846	308	Identical end credits
Masha and the Bear/Season 1 : Episode 6	3886	309	Masha and the Bear/Season 1 : Episode 9	3846	309	Identical end credits
Masha and the Bear/Season 1 : Episode 6	3886	310	Masha and the Bear/Season 1 : Episode 9	3846	310	Identical end credits
Masha and the Bear/Season 1 : Episode 6	3886	311	Masha and the Bear/Season 1 : Episode 9	3846	311	Identical end credits
Masha and the Bear/Season 1 : Episode 6	3886	312	Masha and the Bear/Season 1 : Episode 9	3846	312	Identical end credits
Masha and the Bear/Season 1 : Episode 6	3886	313	Masha and the Bear/Season 1 : Episode 9	3846	313	Identical end credits
Masha and the Bear/Season 1 : Episode 6	3886	314	Masha and the Bear/Season 1 : Episode 9	3846	314	Identical end credits
Masha and the Bear/Season 1 : Episode 6	3886	315	Masha and the Bear/Season 1 : Episode 9	3846	315	Identical end credits
Masha and the Bear/Season 1 : Episode 6	3886	316	Masha and the Bear/Season 1 : Episode 9	3846	316	Identical end credits
Masha and the Bear/Season 1 : Episode 6	3886	317	Masha and the Bear/Season 1 : Episode 9	3846	317	Identical end credits
Masha and the Bear/Season 1 : Episode 6	3886	318	Masha and the Bear/Season 1 : Episode 9	3846	318	Identical end credits
Masha and the Bear/Season 1 : Episode 6	3886	319	Masha and the Bear/Season 1 : Episode 9	3846	319	Identical end credits
Masha and the Bear/Season 1 : Episode 6	3886	320	Masha and the Bear/Season 1 : Episode 9	3846	320	Identical end credits
Masha and the Bear/Season 1 : Episode 7	1197	302	Masha and the Bear/Season 1 : Episode 8	1093	304	Identical end credits
The Gospel of John: King James Version	1052	670	The Gospel of John: Reina-Valera 1960	1052	670	Both videos contain identical footage (English vs. Spanish dialogue)
The Gospel of John: King James Version	1749	1796	The Gospel of John: Reina-Valera 1960	1749	1796	Both videos contain identical footage (English vs. Spanish dialogue)
The Gospel of John: King James Version	1749	1970	The Gospel of John: Reina-Valera 1960	1749	1970	Both videos contain identical footage (English vs. Spanish dialogue)
The Gospel of John: King James Version	2348	797	The Gospel of John: Reina-Valera 1960	2348	797	Both videos contain identical footage (English vs. Spanish dialogue)
The Gospel of John: King James Version	380	1353	The Gospel of John: Reina-Valera 1960	380	1353	Both videos contain identical footage (English vs. Spanish dialogue)
The Gospel of John: King James Version	564	1927	The Gospel of John: Reina-Valera 1960	564	1927	Both videos contain identical footage (English vs. Spanish dialogue)

B. Full System Assessment Results.

#	Video	Laptop A		Laptop B	
		1st Detection	Total Detected	1st Detection	Total Detected
1	A Different World/Season 5 : Episode 5	2:22	18:19	2:11	18:24
2	American Dad!/Season 9 : Episode 9	6:35	18:28	2:13	18:26
3	An Idiot Abroad/Season 1 : Episode 1	2:21	20:00	2:13	20:00
4	Angel/Season 2 : Episode 21	2:18	20:00	2:13	20:00
5	Anthony Bourdain: Parts Unknown/Season 2 : Episode 4	2:51	20:00	2:33	20:00
6	Archer/Season 3 : Episode 8	2:37	17:30	4:34	17:19
7	Army Wives/Season 7 : Episode 12	2:23	20:00	2:15	20:00
8	Arrested Development/Season 1 : Episode 16	2:35	18:07	4:11	19:08
9	Arrow/Season 2 : Episode 10	2:57	20:00	2:11	20:00
10	Beauty & the Beast/Season 1 : Episode 21	3:39	20:00	2:11	20:00
11	Black Butler/Season 1 : Episode 25	2:19	20:00	2:11	20:00
12	Bones/Season 5 : Episode 17	2:45	20:00	2:14	20:00
13	Broadchurch/Season 2 : Episode 3	2:19	20:00	2:15	20:00
14	Buffy the Vampire Slayer/Season 4 : Episode 3	2:17	20:00	2:14	20:00
15	Californication/Season 2 : Episode 2	5:28	20:00	2:23	20:00
16	Casper's Scare School/Season 1 : Episode 9	2:17	20:00	2:21	19:13
17	Cheers/Season 7 : Episode 9	5:13	20:00	7:10	20:00
18	Chuck/Season 2 : Episode 7	2:46	19:58	2:14	20:00
19	Chuggington/Season 3 : Episode 1	2:17	15:54	2:05	15:52
20	Courage the Cowardly Dog/Season 4 : Episode 11	2:13	18:38	2:09	18:45
21	Criminal Minds/Season 3 : Episode 8	2:31	20:00	9:30	20:00
22	Criminal Minds/Season 5 : Episode 3	2:16	20:00	4:20	20:00
23	Cupcake Wars Collection/Collection 2 : Episode 14	2:30	20:00	2:29	20:00
24	Digimon: Digital Monsters/Season 2 : Episode 20	2:53	17:54	2:58	17:53
25	Diners, Drive-Ins and Dives Collection/Collection 2 : Episode 5	2:17	17:08	3:34	17:12
26	Dinotopia: The Mini-Series/Season 1 : Episode 3	2:21	20:00	2:09	20:00
27	Doc Martin/Season 1 : Episode 1	2:52	20:00	2:19	20:00
28	Drop Dead Diva/Season 5 : Episode 7	2:16	20:00	8:08	20:00
29	Ella the Elephant/Season 1 : Episode 9	3:12	19:37	2:20	19:48
30	Food Network Star/Season 10 : Episode 7	2:35	20:00	9:00	20:00
31	Fringe/Season 3 : Episode 19	6:03	20:00	5:32	20:00
32	From Dusk Till Dawn: The Series/Season 2 : Episode 8	2:15	20:00	7:40	20:00
33	Good Luck Charlie/Season 1 : Episode 1	2:21	18:54	2:10	19:03
34	Goosebumps/Season 2 : Episode 7	2:21	18:06	2:34	18:07
35	Grounded for Life/Season 2 : Episode 13	2:41	18:10	6:04	14:39
36	Hawaii Five-0/Season 1 : Episode 11	3:22	20:00	2:18	20:00
37	Hell on Wheels/Season 4 : Episode 3	2:19	20:00	5:15	20:00
38	Heroes/Season 4 : Episode 2	4:53	20:00	4:57	20:00
39	House of Cards/Season 2 : Episode 8	10:48	20:00	2:18	20:00
40	House, M.D./Season 1 : Episode 8	2:14	20:00	6:51	20:00
41	House, M.D./Season 3 : Episode 5	2:15	20:00	10:20	20:00
42	How I Met Your Mother/Season 6 : Episode 18	4:13	18:10	2:08	18:12
43	Johnny Test/Season 6 : Episode 18	2:17	17:58	2:17	17:59
44	LEGO: Legends of Chima/Season 1 : Episode 14	3:57	19:01	7:07	17:58
45	La Familia P. Luche/Season 1 : Episode 37	2:12	19:12	2:00	19:16
46	Lie to Me/Season 2 : Episode 1	4:06	20:00	2:20	20:00
47	Liv and Maddie/Season 2 : Episode 21	2:23	19:36	2:23	19:44
48	Lo que la vida me robó/Season 1 : Episode 73	2:25	20:00	2:22	20:00
49	Madam Secretary/Season 1 : Episode 10	2:11	20:00	2:17	20:00
50	Malcolm in the Middle/Season 5 : Episode 18	2:25	17:57	10:16	18:04
51	Malcolm in the Middle/Season 6 : Episode 4	2:15	18:20	2:15	19:27
52	Marvel's Agents of S.H.I.E.L.D./Season 1 : Episode 20	3:36	20:00	10:01	20:00
53	Masha's Tales/Season 1 : Episode 1	5:27	18:35	2:42	18:33
54	Mighty Morphin Power Rangers/Season 3 : Episode 22	2:20	16:05	2:48	16:08
55	Miss XV/Season 1 : Episode 5	11:39	20:00	9:46	20:00
56	My Name Is Earl/Season 1 : Episode 22	3:30	17:17	2:26	18:18
57	My Name Is Earl/Season 2 : Episode 8	7:39	20:00	9:17	20:00
58	NCIS/Season 1 : Episode 2	2:36	20:00	2:22	20:00
59	NCIS/Season 4 : Episode 12	3:41	20:00	8:59	20:00
60	New Girl/Season 4 : Episode 19	5:47	17:59	2:14	18:03
61	Nurse Jackie/Season 1 : Episode 5	2:24	20:00	11:55	20:00
62	One Tree Hill/Season 3 : Episode 9	5:43	20:00	9:13	20:00
63	One Tree Hill/Season 4 : Episode 11	5:29	20:00	12:04	20:00
64	Power Rangers Jungle Fury/Season 1 : Episode 26	2:20	18:40	5:58	18:37
65	Power Rangers in Space/Season 1 : Episode 5	2:18	16:18	4:44	16:16
66	Prison Break/Season 1 : Episode 15	2:20	20:00	10:37	20:00
67	Rebelde/Season 1 : Episode 10	3:56	20:00	2:15	20:00
68	Rebelde/Season 1 : Episode 312	4:13	20:00	2:18	20:00
69	Rebelde/Season 1 : Episode 380	2:16	20:00	2:15	20:00
70	Rosario + Vampire/Season 2 : Episode 12	2:19	20:00	2:15	20:00
71	Rosario Tijeras/Season 1 : Episode 22	2:20	20:00	2:24	20:00
72	Scrubs/Season 2 : Episode 19	2:03	16:55	2:03	17:59
73	Some Assembly Required/Season 1 : Episode 23	8:52	19:08	11:37	19:12
74	Some Assembly Required/Season 1 : Episode 7	4:57	19:09	2:25	19:14
75	Some Assembly Required/Season 1 : Episode 9	2:36	19:09	8:45	19:18
76	Sons of Anarchy/Season 2 : Episode 2	2:14	20:00	5:49	20:00
77	Star Trek/Season 1 : Episode 24	2:13	20:00	7:58	20:00
78	Star Trek: Enterprise/Season 4 : Episode 10	2:38	20:00	7:16	20:00
79	Stuck in Love	2:16	20:00	2:15	20:00
80	Supernatural/Season 6 : Episode 6	2:09	20:00	2:50	20:00
81	Sword Art Online II/Season 1 : Episode 6	6:52	20:00	2:26	20:00
82	Teresa/Season 1 : Episode 42	7:20	20:00	4:57	20:00
83	That '70s Show/Season 1 : Episode 8	2:24	19:24	2:23	18:27
84	The Blacklist/Season 1 : Episode 6	2:19	20:00	10:03	20:00
85	The Boondocks/Season 2 : Episode 3	8:03	15:03	not detected	20:00
86	The Carrie Diaries/Season 1 : Episode 9	2:36	20:00	2:19	20:00
87	The Day My Butt Went Psycho!/Season 1 : Episode 9	2:09	18:37	2:17	18:28
88	The IT Crowd/Season 3 : Episode 6	3:55	19:29	5:59	19:36
89	The L Word/Season 4 : Episode 10	6:34	20:00	5:59	20:00
90	The Vampire Diaries/Season 1 : Episode 5	2:14	20:00	7:36	20:00
91	The X-Files/Season 1 : Episode 22	2:30	20:00	7:35	20:00
92	The X-Files/Season 3 : Episode 12	5:18	20:00	8:43	20:00
93	Total Drama/Season 1 : Episode 27	2:13	20:00	2:07	20:00
94	Trailer Park Boys/Season 5 : Episode 2	2:13	19:14	2:09	19:05
95	Transformers: Rescue Bots/Season 2 : Episode 20	2:12	18:08	2:11	18:00
96	Tree Fu Tom/Season 2 : Episode 11	2:21	17:09	2:24	17:07
97	Trotro/Season 1 : Episode 10	2:17	17:28	2:04	17:24
98	Victoria/Season 1 : Episode 165	5:01	20:00	2:09	20:00
99	White Collar/Season 5 : Episode 4	2:15	20:00	2:19	20:00
100	Xena: Warrior Princess/Season 2 : Episode 10	2:22	20:00	2:17	20:00

Author Index